IRISH FAMINE IMMIGRANTS in the STATE OF VERMONT

GRAVESTONE INSCRIPTIONS

Compiled by
Ronald Chase Murphy
and
Janice Church Murphy

CLEARFIELD

Printed for
Clearfield Company, Inc. by
Genealogical Publishing Co., Inc.
Baltimore, Maryland
2000

International Standard Book Number: 0-8063-4967-0

Made in the United States of America

PREFACE

1. The Immigrants

Over the past twenty years or so, my spouse and I have traveled the width and breadth of the State of Vermont to collect gravestone inscriptions of the Famine Irish immigrants. At the outset, the cemeteries we visited were primarily Roman Catholic, and to locate them we utilized an 1899 History of the Catholic Church in New England by using the section that outlined the rise of the church in Vermont. There was a brief sketch of each parish, and we began by visiting those communities.

We soon found that some village burial grounds were also productive when there was no Catholic yard in the town. In some communities, a section of the cemetery had been reserved for the Catholic population, probably consecrated by the Catholic Bishop of the Diocese of Boston or his duly authorized representative. Others were simply buried alongside the non-Catholic citizens of the community.

We also discovered that many Irish were resident in the State of Vermont long before the famine. Thomas Maginnis, of Irish descent and an Episcopalian, wrote in his 1913 work, *The Irish Contribution To America's Independence:* "Among the Colonial settlers in the region now called Vermont were families with the following distinctively Irish names: BURKE, BARRETT, KENNEDY, MCCOY, HOGAN, DUNN, LARKIN, MCCONNELL, MOORE, GARVEY, GOFF, CAREY, MCCARRA, DUANE."

The first census of Vermont in the year 1790 shows many recognizable Irish surnames as heads of households. Those prefixed with "Mc" totalled 122. There were three O'Brians, several Collins and Condons, many Barretts and Burkes, plus Caragan, Carey, Carley, Coffin, Conroy, Crowley, Cunningham, Donnihue, Dononghue, Donaghy, Donaly, Doran, Downing, Doyle, Fenton, Fin, Garey, Gleason, Hacket, Hamilton, Harradan, Harrington, Healy, Kelley, Kelly, Kelsey, Kenedy, Larkin, Law, Leonard, Lyon, Maddon, Malone, Moore, More, Patterson, Riley, Stacy, Whaland, and many others. Wherever found, we duly recorded those who appeared to have Irish surnames.

Found in this collection are a few nondenominational burial grounds, an occasional Episcopal yard, and some inscriptions from towns along the Vermont-Canadian border. The thrust of the effort, however, is from Catholic burial yards throughout Vermont, with village grounds being accessed where there was no Catholic cemetery of record.

We also found evidence of mixed marriages where an Irish immigrant female married a native who was probably of a non-Catholic background. We found the same held true for the male immigrant. True love knows no bounds, and, as a college professor of mine once remarked, "they married a girl from the neighborhood."

Of course, this is an oversimplification of the impact that the Irish Catholic had on the White, Anglo-Saxon Protestant majority of Vermont. Since the Protestant Reformation of the English Church, a long simmering mistrust of Rome and those who were "Papist" in religious orientation had been brewing. It was no surprise that the immigrants met opposition as they attempted assimilation.

Prejudice was alive and well in 1846, for in their cultural baggage the Catholic Irish brought with them customs and traditions that were as foreign to the Vermonter as Vermonters' customs were to the native American Indian who laid claim to this territory 10,000 years before the white man came to settle.

In 1963, John Fitzgerald Kennedy wrote of the Know-Nothings, a political party formed in 1845. Also known as the Nativist Party, Kennedy remarked that "the Irish are perhaps the only people in our history with the distinction of having a political party formed against them." The Nativist platform consisted of three planks: (1) vote only for native Americans; (2)require a long period of probation before naturalization; and (3) oppose the Catholic church.

The immigrants arrived poor and destitute; a majority of them were unskilled laborers who could neither read nor write, an apparent result of being victimized by an English feudal system that had oppressed and suppressed the Irish race for centuries.

Dwelling in the midst of a people who did not relish their presence, immigrants were forced to continue a clannish existence, to cling together for support in their occupations, leisure time, and religious and political activities.

In 1846, when famine struck Ireland, there was a relatively small Irish population in Vermont. The sudden influx of strangers just off the "coffin" ships pouring out of Boston and New York or migrating south from Canada began to be seen on the highways and byways of the State.

This influx struck a note of concern for the native. Fortunately, the timing of two events smoothed the way, and the immigrants were welcomed for their brawn as Vermont was just embarking on railroad construction and expansion. As one local newspaper remarked "they are just the type of person that we need to build the lines of our railroads."

By 1850 three lines totaling 279 miles of track had been completed. By 1860 trackage had doubled to 556 miles on nine separate and distinct roads. Branch lines were constructed to reach isolated villages, and track was laid from Eastern to Western Vermont, over and through the Green Mountain range that serves as the backbone of the State.

In 1850, the population of Vermont was 314,120, including 15,377 souls who claimed Irish birth. The Irish figure dropped to 13,480 in 1860, then recovered a bit to 14,080 in 1870, dropped again in 1880 to 11,657. At the turn of the century, 7,453 citizens of Irish nativity were resident in the State.

Railroading was not the only avenue for immigrants seeking employment. The slate mines of southwestern Vermont, centered in Fairhaven, plus the marble quarries of East Dorset, Rutland, and Sutherland Falls (later named Proctor after a benevolent Governor of the State) provided employment during and after the railroad boom.

Agriculture also played an important part in the resettling of the immigrants in an area of occupation that they totally understood. My own immigrant ancestor arrived in mid June of 1850 and within a year had leased a small farm. In 1854, he had purchased acreage in the next town and proceeded to build up a small farm that stayed in the family for 75 years.

After the Civil War, railroad construction was still underway, but the appeal of laboring on the line of a railroad was overshadowed by the prospect of a better life. The Midwest beckoned to the laborer to follow the sun. Many immigrants, and their first-generation American sons and daughters, moved on to greener pastures; they headed west as their Yankee contemporaries had chosen to do earlier in the century.

Those who remained in Vermont found employment in populating the railroad shops, manning the freight and passenger lines, and performing track maintenance and repair. Others reverted to farming, some entered the mercantile world as shopkeepers and grocers, while still others were assimilated into the local employment base as firemen, policemen, publicans, domestics, and laborers. Many others found employment in light manufacturing, operating looms in the woolen mills, or working in the marble yards and lumber businesses in the Chittenden County Villages of Winooski Falls and Burlington. By 1870 the first generation of the immigrants had settled into the regimen of American life. Their place in the community was beginning to solidify. Churches and schools were built, and an amalgamation of old country and new world customs began to dominate their lives.

The immigrants, and their sons and daughters, formed Fenian Brotherhood Cells in most of the counties of the State, supported the Irish anti-English cause in the old country, participated in the Fenian invasions of Canada in 1866 and 1870, held socials, and sent money to Ireland to help in the crusade during the Irish "land wars" of the 1880s. They realized they had a problem with intemperate behavior and formed Temperance Societies, while they organized Irish Benevolent and religious societies to help each other.

As time passed, the attitude of some of the citizenry began to soften. After a quarter century of the Irish presence, village and state level politicians began to realize that the Irish were here to stay and were a voting block to be reckoned with.

There were 14,080 persons with Irish nativity in the 1870 Decennial Census of Vermont. It was reported that 47,155 people of foreign birth resided in Vermont with the Irish representing 29.9% of the total. At that time, there were 83,615 residents of the State having "one or both parents foreign." By applying the 29.9% to that figure, a rough estimate can be arrived at that would indicate 25,000 of the 83,615 had one or more Irish born parents. Adding the 14,080 with Irish nativity to their estimated 25,000 offspring would indicate that the native Irish and Irish-American population of Vermont in 1870 was somewhere in the vicinity of 39,000, or about 12% of the population of the State of Vermont. (Tables X, XVIII, Compendium of 9th Census.)

The Irish segment of the population soon came to be seen as a valuable asset, and politicians began to court the Irish vote. The immigrants and their families were beginning to take their place in society. Still, they stayed together; as late as 1900, Catholic Irish men were still marrying Catholic Irish women.

2. Data Collection

The Irish Famine spanned the years of 1846-1851. In setting parameters for the recording of data, we first agreed that the year of birth had to be 1855 or earlier to cover the children born to the famine immigrants. We did make exceptions to that rule. For instance, some latitude was allowed and often included those born in 1856 to 1859 or so. If an entire family was listed and if the dates of birth of the children began in 1855 or earlier and moved forward, we listed the entire group.

If Irish birth was indicated in the inscription, we recorded the data, regardless of the year of birth.

If the birth was in the British Isles, other than Ireland, we also recorded the data if the place of birth was indicated. Scottish and English inscriptions will be found, although they are few in number.

Many inscriptions, including places of origin, were engraved phonetically. We suspect that the children, or those responsible for providing information to the engraver, had heard the name of the town, townland, or parish mentioned but had never seen it in print. So, the name was recorded as it was heard. For instance, an Arlington, Vermont, memorial recorded the origins of one as "Born In Graugvalla, Parish of Raughmic, County Waterford" and the spouse was recorded as having been born in Schaunicle, Parish of Raughmic, also in County Waterford. Cross checking in the referenced publications, it became apparent that the two were born in Graigavalla and Shanakill, which are both in the Parish of Rathgormuck, County Waterford. In another instance, the Town Of Dromin was recorded as Thaunodromin, and Knocknagoshel was written as "Knuckle-no-gasul." This entry also referred to the town of "Muig-on-ear," which we never resolved.

Some towns and parishes listed defy interpretation but were dutifully recorded as engraved to allow the reader to attempt identification.

The use of the phrase "the Parish of" has in some cases proven to be the civil parish, a Catholic parish, and sometimes, the name of the town wherein lay the church attended by the immigrant prior to their departure for America.

In the INSCRIPTION column (in order to clarify parishes, towns and townlands), we have indicated in parentheses after the incorrect spelling our interpretation of the correct name as found in the aforementioned references. For example:

INSCRIPTION: "Born At Balisteen (Ballysteen), Limerick County, Ireland. Died At Burlington, Vt."

The recording of names also fell victim to phonetic interpretation. Diverse spellings were found for a given family within a burial plot or in various locations in the cemetery. They are recorded as found, so do not be a purist in accepting your ancestor's family name as having had a single spelling.

In recording, we have listed the maiden name where it is inscribed and have placed underscores where it is not known. Therefore, in the case of an inscription where the maiden name is known, it would appear as so:

John FINNERTY
Mary BYRNE Finnerty

If the maiden name was not indicated, it is recorded as:

John FINNERTY

Mary _____ FINNERTY

Do not discard our recording of the inscription,

Matthew O'BRIEN
Mary _____ O'BRIEN

by thinking, "of course, that is her married name." Her surname may well have been O'BRIEN. Marriages in the Catholic church were allowed via dispensation of the Bishop of the Diocese. Second cousins to the third degree were allowed to marry. (Second cousins to the third degree indicated that their grandparents were siblings). It is entirely possible for an O'BRIEN to marry an O'BRIEN under these circumstances.

We have identified those who participated in the American Civil War if their markers contain that information. When found, the tombstone usually identifies the company, regiment, state, and occasionally, the rank held. We have used GAR (Grand Army Of The Republic) as a key identifier. Using that information, you can write to the National Archives to determine the current method for requesting a copy of a veterans record. The correct address:

National Archives Trust Fund (NNMS)
8th & Pennsylvania Avenue, NW
Washington, DC 20408

The form utilized for this request allows retrieval of Pension Applications, which sometimes hold valuable genealogical information, Bounty-Land Warrant Applications, and an extract of your ancestor's Military Record. The cost is not great but you will probably have to write for the form prior to making application for information.

Where a GAR marker was found at the grave site but no inscription was made indicating the military unit, we attempted to resolve by locating the veteran in "Revised Roster of Vermont Volunteers And Lists Of Vermonters Who Served In The Army And The Navy Of The United States During The War Of The Rebellion, 1861-1866.". This long-winded title is a source of information that could be valuable in your research if your ancestor served from the State of Vermont. If an entry was found in the referenced volume that matched the name and community of the individual, we annotated the INSCRIPTION column as follows:

"(GAR - Try Co. E., 6th Vt Vol Inf)"

Abbreviations have been utilized to save space or verify that some information is not present on the tombstone. NOI means "No Other Information" and indicates there is nothing else engraved on the stone. It is also used to indicate that a marker for an indicated spouse is not present. For instance, a marker entry reading "Mary SMITH, wife of William O'BRIEN", followed by a comment in the INSCRIPTION block

(NOI William O'Brien)

indicates that no marker was found in this plot for said William. This does not preclude his being found elsewhere in the cemetery, especially in the case of an early death of the spouse.

Note that any comment in the INSCRIPTION block enclosed with parenthesis is a comment by the researcher and is not inscribed on the marker.

In some instances we have used "Dau" or "D/O" for "Daughter Of" instead of spelling out the complete word. We have used "Ire." for Ireland to save line space. We have used "S/O" in the same fashion to save space while indicating that the entry is actually "Son Of". We have often used "Co." as an abbreviation for "County" for the same reason.

We attempted to define the condition of the markers. "Deteriorated" or "worn" used in any description means that we have had difficulty in reading what was engraved. Here is an important point. We could have misread, misinterpreted, or missed some of the information on the more distressed markers and apologize for that. What has been transcribed is our best take on what was seen. A personal visit and a gravestone rubbing might produce the result you are seeking.

If you find an entry that you wish to pursue, you may write to:

State Of Vermont
General Services Center
Reference/Research
Drawer 33
Montpelier, Vermont, 05633-7601

Phone (802) 828-3286
(802) 828-3701
FAX (802) 828-3710

You may submit a written request for a birth, death, marriage, or divorce record. A phone call may be accepted as well. There is a standard form for requesting a search. If you wish, you can also write to the Town or Village Clerk where the event took place. Be sure to include a self-addressed stamped envelope (SASE) when you go this route. There will always be a fee.

It is possible that you may find some assistance by contacting the curator of the Diocesan Archives for the Catholic Diocese of Burlington. I am not certain if the curator has a research staff to respond to genealogical inquiries. In the past I have visited the office and have found them to be cooperative in attempting to resolve an inquiry. I had to make an appointment. You may contact them at:

Catholic Diocese of Burlington
Curator, Diocesan Archives
350 North Avenue
Burlington, Vermont 05401
(802) 658-6110

In some instances, we listed the death of a child that may have exceeded the 1855 birth year cutoff when the parents are listed on the child's marker but the parents' tombstones are not to be found. Listing a marker that states "John, son of Thomas and Margaret MURPHY" shows that the parents were here at the time of the child's death but may have moved on to another place of residence. In such cases we have listed not only the child but have indexed the parents in an effort to assist family researchers who are attempting to track ancestral migratory paths.

Many famine immigrants who had typically large families remained to spend their days in Vermont. Their children and grandchildren, however, moved on to the great eastern cities while others populated the Midwestern and far western territories during the latter part of the 19th century. We have a small genealogical research business, and it has been our experience that nearly all of the requests received requesting that a search be conducted are from midwestern, southwestern, and west coast addresses.

3. The Cemetery Inscription Report Page

A typical report page heading lists the Vermont village or town where the cemetery is located. In the columnar section of the page, the NAME field lists names copied from the markers; POB indicates the Irish County of Origin if so stated on the gravestone; DOB lists the date of birth or the age at death followed by the DOD field which indicates the date of death. Each cemetery has been assigned a three-digit control number that can be found in the "Key To Cemeteries" section. The control number has the columnar heading of CEM.

The column headed SPOUSE/INDEX indicates that the column can be used for index generation or for making the connection with husband and wife where the inscription claims "His Wife," "Her Husband," "Wife Of," "Husband Of," etc. For instance, an entry that reads:

NAME	SPOUSE/INDEX
Thomas F. O'BRIEN --------------------	MCLAUGHLIN, Mary J.
Mary J. MCLAUGHLIN O'Brien-----------	O'BRIEN, Thomas F.

signals that they were each other's spouse.

Entries that indicate two or more people are buried in the same plot, such as:

NAME	SPOUSE/INDEX
Thomas F. O'BRIEN -------------------	O'BRIEN, Thomas F.
Mary J. MCLAUGHLIN ------------------	MCLAUGHLIN, Mary J.

reflects that no spousal connection is apparent or INDICATED and the column is being used as the source for creation of an index entry.

Use of this column to identify an index entry is also true where individual entries are made in the same plot but no relationship is apparent. For example:

NAME		SPOUSE/INDEX
Susan Ann MURPHY	-------------------	MURPHY, Susan Ann
Mary J. FINNERTY	-------------------	FINNERTY, Mary J.

4. Research Tools

When the place of origin was included in the inscription (i.e. the parish or town) the place name was recorded and cross checked in the *General Alphabetical Index To The Townlands And Towns, Parishes and Baronies of Ireland.* We also used *A Topographical Dictionary Of Ireland"* and a more recent *Ordnance Survey Road Atlas of Ireland* to assist in locating place names.

Brian Mitchell's *A Guide to Irish Parish Registers* and *Guide to Irish Churches And Graveyards* were most helpful in reconciling Civil and Religious Parishes.

To reconcile Irish surnames, we used *The Surnames of Ireland* by Edward MacLysaght.

To verify the Vermont Unit assigned to during the American Civil War (1861-1865) we used a *Revised Roster of Vermont Volunteers And Lists Of Vermonters Who Served In The Army And The Navy Of The United States During The War Of The Rebellion, 1861-1866.*

U. S. Census data for immigrants and railroads were extracted from a *Compendium Of The Ninth Census of The United States, 1870* and *Vermont Heads Of Families At The First Census, 1790.*

The presence of Colonial citizens with Irish surnames was found in *The Irish Contribution To America's Independence* by Thomas Hobbs Maginnis.

We found the basis for sketches of Catholicism in the towns and villages researched in the five volumes of Abby Maria Hemenways's *Vermont Historical Gazetteer,* published from 1867 to 1891.

For the sketches, we also used a *History Of The Catholic Church in the New England States,* the Vermont section identified as The Diocese of Burlington, compiled in the late 1890's by Right Reverend John. S. Michaud, D.D., Bishop of the Diocese, and published in 1899.

In the latter stages of our research we used *Burial Grounds Of Vermont,* Edited by Arthur L. & Frances P. Hyde, published by Vermont Old Cemeteries Association (VOCA), 1991, to locate cemeteries with Irish burials that might not have been listed in other sources.

Finally, our intent in compiling this data has always been to add one more source for the amateur genealogist to check in tracing their immigrant ancestor through the State of Vermont back to their Irish origins. It is by no means a complete survey of the burial grounds of the State of Vermont, and an argument can be made to pursue the study of all cemeteries in the state. Such work would make this collection a complete study, but I fear that we have spent more time on this earth than we will spend in the future, so embarking on a long-term project is probably unlikely.

We hope that this collection will serve the purpose that we sought. It was not intended to be a history of the Irish Immigrant in Vermont, but some historical data and statistics have been included to place in context why some immigrants chose to begin their American journey in the Green Mountain State.

Ronald and Janice Murphy
July 4th, 1998
St. Albans, Vermont

PARISH SKETCHES

In much of our research regarding parish sketches, we have relied upon Reverend Zadock Thompson, *The History Of Vermont(HV)*, Part the Second; Right Reverend John S. Michaud, *A History of the Catholic Church In the New England States(HCCNE):* Volume 2; and Abby Maria Hemenway, *Vermont Historical Gazetteer(VHG)*, Volumes 1-5.

A look at the state of Catholicism in Vermont on the eve of the Irish migration to America at the time of the Great Famine of 1846-1851.

"Vermont could count but a few scattered Catholics within her borders until the arrival of the first Catholic Missionary, the Reverence Jeremiah O'Callaghan, in the year 1830. So great and rapid has been the tide of immigration since that period from Ireland and from the Canada's, that numerous congregations have already sprung up in several places, and although two additional missionaries, the Reverend John B. Daly and the Reverend William Ivers, are now employed in the state, they are hardly adequate to the wants of the population.

The largest congregation in the State has grown up in Burlington where the first catholic church was erected in 1833. Destroyed by fire in 1838, a second church was constructed on a new site and was consecrated by the Right Reverend Benedict Fenwick, Bishop of the Diocese (of Boston) in October of 1841.

The funds for its erection were contributed by the congregation, aided by the liberal donations of the native Americans and by collections obtained in the neighboring cities. The free principle is here observed in the full sense of the word; respect of persons and the worldly terms thine and mine being excluded. The seats being common to all, the first comers select such as they choose.

The clergyman, having no salary or stipend, depends solely on the free will offerings made in the church three times a year -- at Christmas, Easter and Summer, when four or five persons only offer $2 each, 60 or 70, $1 each, 15 fifty cents each, and the great body of the congregation give nothing excepting a few cents they may deposit in the collection box. To this may be added casual donations at marriages and christenings, which are optional to the donors." [1] Reverend Zadock Thompson, *History of Vermont, Part Second*, (Burlington, Vermont, Published by Reverend Zadock Thompson,1853), 203

ALBURG - St. Amadeus Church

Founded in 1886.

Alburg is located in the Town of Alburg, Grand Isle County, and is adjacent to Lake Champlain.

Early Irish Settlers in Alburg: Unknown

Notable Features:

"Alburg is on the Central Vermont Railroad, the northwestern town of Vermont".[2] Right Reverend Stephen A. Michaud, *A History of the Catholic Church in the New England States, Volume 2,* (Boston: Hurd and Everts Company, 1899), 586.

Alburg was populated early in the nineteenth century by French Canadian immigrants. In 1998 it is still the ethnic base of the parish. There were Irish immigrants resident in the community at mid-century. The church was constructed in 1876. There is a Catholic cemetery.

Church Benefactors:

DEUEL, Pardon - Deeded land for chapel in 1858
DEUEL, Nancy
REDDY, Bartly - Deeded land for church, house, school - 1876

ARLINGTON - St. Columban's Church

Founded in 1890.

Arlington, in Bennington County, is one of the oldest towns in the State. It is mentioned in Revolutionary times." [3]

Early Irish Settlers in Arlington: CULLINAN, CANFIELD

Notable Features:

"With the advent of the railroad, Catholics also arrived and settled in this place. In 1874 Reverend Gaffney began the erection of a new church in Arlington. In a visit to Ireland, he had secured a stone from the ruins of Mucross Abbey (Co. Kerry). This was blessed and used as the corner-stone of the new church of St. Columban. It was dedicated in 1875. There are about seventy Catholic families in Arlington-most of them farmers (1899)." [4]

There were "25 or 30 families of Roman Catholics, numbering about 130 persons (1860)". [5]

BAKERSFIELD - St. George's Church

"Bakersfield, In Franklin County, is a mission formerly belonging to Fairfield and now (1899) attached to Highgate." [6]

Early Irish Settlers In Bakersfield: Unknown

Notable Features:

"Reverend George Napoleon Caissy said the first Mass in Bakersfield June 27, 1867. The Church, which was formerly the Town academy, was purchased by deed of February 20, 1872, and the cemetery on September 15, 1869. The occupation of the people is exclusively farming." [7]

"The congregation is composed of about 50 families; 20 Irish and 30 Canadian, and is, upon the whole, quite flourishing." [8]

BARRE - St. Monica's Church

Founded in 1892.

Barre is the headquarters of the granite business in the State of Vermont." [9] Barre is located in the Town of Barre, Washington County.

Early Irish Settlers In Barre:

CONWAY, John; WILLIAMS, Thomas; HERLIHY, Michael; KEOGH, William; MCLAUGHLIN, Bernard

Notable Features:

"The first Mass was celebrated on November 13, 1881, in the old town hall, Main Street. The cornerstone was laid October 2, 1887. At the laying of the cornerstone, the Reverend P. J. Barrett said that, 'among other things, a Barre man, when asked for the loan of a few settees for Catholic service, refused, with the remark that if Catholics came to Barre they would come alone and barefooted. Father Barrett said he did not think they were alone that day, and did not see any barefooted.'" [10]

"Perhaps there is no place in the State of Vermont in which the population has increased so rapidly as in Barre. This remark may apply to the Catholic population also. In the spring of 1882, Father Duglue took the census and found 31 families--about two-thirds Irish and one-third French Canadians. In 1898, a census showed 175 families of Irish extraction, 65 of French Canadians and 100 of Italian families. The parochial records begin with the year 1892. The land for a cemetery was purchased of L. J. Bolster in September, 1894 by D. M. Miles, Michael Garvey, and others representing the congregation." [11]

"Politically, the Catholics of Barre do not carry any exclusive badge. Socially and intellectually, they are the equals of any class in the city". [12]

Church Benefactors: MILES, D. M.; GARVEY, Michael & others.

BARTON - St. Paul's Church

Founded in 1893.

Barton is a town in Orleans County.

Early Irish Settlers In Barton:

KEATING, John; QUINN, Patrick

Notable Features:

"The first Mass in this vicinity was said in the home of Mr. Paquette of West Glover--in 1859. At this time there were five Catholic families -- four French Canadian and one Irish. From that time till the purchase of the meeting house, Mass was usually said in Patrick QUINN's house. The church was formerly a Congregational Meeting house. In order to improve the railway facilities of Barton the business men of Barton and the B. & M. R.R. (Boston and Maine Railroad) bought the church lot by deed of October 11, 1892. The company built a passenger depot on the site. The church was moved to grounds secured by deed of August 29,1892." [13]

"Besides the church, the Catholics have a parochial residence, a hall and a cemetery. (In 1899) There are in Barton about 400 souls, principally of Canadian parentage. The principal business of the town is farming and lumbering." [14]

BELLOWS FALLS - St. Charles' Church

Founded in 1871.

Bellows Falls is located in the Town of Rockingham, Windham County and is on the banks of the Connecticut River.

The First Irish Catholic Settler in Bellows Falls:

COBERTY, John - "His descendants are here still, but no longer kneel before the same altar as their progenitor." [15]

Notable Features:

"Bellows Falls is the junction of several railroads. The construction of these very railroads was the inducement which led Catholics to come and settle here in the year 1848. Towards the end of 1848 Father DALY celebrated the first Mass in a railroad shanty, and afterwards, visited this section once every three months until 1853." [16]

"The Catholic population of Bellows Falls (1899) is about 900 souls. There are 170 Irish and Irish-American families and 30 French-Canadian families. In 1882 few of the Catholics owned their own houses. They lived in tenement houses. Within the last ten years many of them have become property owners. The people are principally employees in the mills or on the railroads. They are a good and generous class of people, and very much attached to their church." [17]

There are two Catholic burial grounds in Bellows Falls. The older of the two is located in the village. The newer, on land purchased in 1894, is located about a mile from town.

BENNINGTON - St. Francis DeSales Church

Founded in 1854.

Bennington is located in the Town of Bennington, Bennington County.

Early Irish Settlers In Bennington:

TRENOR, Thomas in 1798, LYNCH, Patrick in 1803, LYNCH, Anne Charlotte

Notable Features:

"Bennington is a town famous in revolutionary history. Although the Battle of Bennington was not fought within its limits, yet all its preparations and its plan were made there by General John Stark and his officers.

The first Catholic was Thomas Trenor in 1798. The famous railroad magnate, Trenor Park was named after him. A Patrick Lynch came in 1803. His daughter, Ann Charlotte Lynch, who holds an enviable place in American literature, states in her letter to Mr. Froude that she had been baptized in the Catholic Church. The town records show many other Catholic names as holding property in the beginning of this (19th) century.

There were many Catholics in Bennington by the early 'thirties' (1830's). We find the Reverend Father Shanahan came here from Troy (NY) from 1830 to 1834 to minister to the Catholics. The first Mass was probably offered up in 1830. (In 1899) St. Francis de Sales congregation has 275 families or about 1375 souls, all Irish or of Irish descent." [18]
"On the eastern slope, and overlooking the larger village of Bennington, is the Roman Catholic Church of stone, St. Francis De Sales, with adjoining lands upon which are a fine residence for the parish priest and Catholic school and convent." [19]

"The congregation, which embraces the towns of Shaftsbury, Bennington and Pownal, numbers about 175 (in 1859)." [20]

There are two Catholic cemeteries in Bennington, one on the old church grounds, the second diagonally across the highway from the old church. Irish Catholics can also be found in Bennington Park Village Cemetery, south of the village. In 1998, the original St. Frances DeSales Church houses the Bennington Museum. A modern church was completed in 1899.

BLOOMFIELD--St. Stanislaus Church (Mission Of Island Pond)

Bloomfield is located in the Town of Bloomfield, Essex County.

Early Irish Settlers in Bloomfield: Unknown

Notable Features:

"This mission is situated fifteen miles from Island Pond on the Grand Trunk Railroad and the shores of the Connecticut River. The Catholics of North Stratford, NH attended church in Bloomfield and altogether there were about eighty Catholic families and many single men who worked in the saw-mills and wood camps. Eight years ago (circa 1891) a priest of the Diocese of Manchester (NH) took charge of North Stratford. This reduced the number of Catholic families attending Bloomfield church to twenty-five". [21] There is a Catholic cemetery in Bloomfield.

BRANDON - St. Mary's Church

Founded in 1867.

Brandon is in the Town Of Brandon, Rutland County.

Early Irish settlers in Brandon: Unknown

Notable Features:

"At the northern extremity of Rutland County lies the town of Brandon. The establishment of a blast furnace and foundry and the discovery of kaolin, drew many laborers and mechanics to the town. Catholics began to settle in Brandon in the thirties (1830s). They came from Ireland and Canada. The congregation was small and scattered (in 1852). There were about 75 families living in Brandon Village, Forestdale, at the old Brandon quarry and a few in Goshen. There was no rich man and scarcely a land owner amongst the Catholics.

The Reverend John DALY said Mass in various towns and villages as he had no fixed residence. and generally followed the lines of railroads which were then being built through southern and middle Vermont." [22]

"The Catholic congregation of Brandon numbers 225 families(1870)." [23]
There is a Catholic cemetery in Brandon, "purchased by deed of May 8, 1876". [24]

BRATTLEBORO - St. Michael's Church

Founded in 1855.

Brattleboro is located in the Town of Brattleboro, Windham County.

Early Irish Settlers In Brattleboro:

CLANCY - 1843

First Baptism: MORAN, Thomas son of MORAN, Garret and CAVANAUGH, Mary on 11-4-1855

First Marriage: SHEADY, John and CUNNINGHAM, Catherine on 11-4-1856

First Death: GARVEY in 1848 or 1849

Notable Features:

"Vermont historians claim that Brattleboro is the oldest town in the State. It is certain that it is the first place settled by colonists from Massachusetts and Connecticut. Although many distinctively Irish and Catholic names appear among the first settlers of Brattleboro and other Windham County towns as early as 1726-'60, there is nothing to show that they were Catholics.

The building of what was then called the Vermont and Massachusetts Railroad, 1847-'48, brought a number of Catholic men and some families to town, many of whom remained and made Brattleboro their permanent abode. They and their descendants form the greater and substantial part of the Catholic congregation today (1899). They are all Irish, and most of them of Irish birth." [25]

"Meetings were held for several years in a building on Elliot street. In 1863-64 they constructed a good, substantial brick church on Walnut Street. Judging from the large number of persons going to and from this new house, the church is in a flourishing condition.

The number of Catholic families in this town must have been about fifty when the diocese of Burlington was separated from that of Boston (1844). There are 135 families in their congregation and the numbers of pupils taught by the Sisters in 1877 was 125." [26]

"During a very successful. mission held in 1898, 704 persons received communion. The congregation is, and has always been, an English speaking congregation. There are, at present, eight or ten French families. The Catholics of Brattleboro are nearly all property holders--are in rather comfortable circumstances, and intellectually are on par with their neighbors. In politics, the Catholics here are in heart and sympathy, democrats; and hence have no political standing or hope of reward, except the conscious pride of remaining true to political principles under all circumstances." [27]

There is a Catholic cemetery in Brattleboro that dates to 1866.

Church Benefactors:

Mrs. CORCORAN left a bequest of $600 by will. DRISCOLL, Catherine left $1700.

BRISTOL / STARKSBORO - Church of St. Ambrose

Founded in 1893.

Bristol and Starksboro are located in Addison County. Bristol is a market town and Starksboro is in an agricultural region.

Early Irish Settlers in Starksboro and Bristol:

HANNON, Thomas; CASEY, Thomas; HANNON, Francis

First Catholic Child Born in Starksboro: HANNAN, Thomas

First Baptism In Starksboro: CASEY, Honora

First Marriage In Starksboro: MAHER, John and GOLDEN, Bridget

First Baptism In Bristol: HICKEY, Anna

First Marriage In Bristol: DWYER, Albert and MCCLEAN, Celia

[28] (For statistics in foregoing.)

Notable Features:

"The nucleus of the Bristol congregation was formed in the town of Starksboro. Thomas HANNON, now living at the age of eighty five, settled in Starksboro in 1848. Shortly after him came Thomas CASEY, Francis HARMAN (probably Hannon) and their families. The first Mass was celebrated in Starksboro by Rev. Thomas Riordan of Burlington in the year 1854. There were present at this first Mass about a half dozen families and all Irish. When the church was built (in Bristol) in 1877 there were about 500 Catholics, about equally divided between Irish and Canadians. At the present time (1899) there are about 600 Catholics.

Thomas HANNAN was the first Catholic child born in Starksboro in 1851. It is worthy of record that Thomas Hannan was baptized in Burlington by Father O'Callaghan. His mother walked with him from Starksboro to Burlington, and carried him in her arms, a distance of 23 miles.

As in most of our Vermont towns, the Catholics of Bristol hold a respectable place in the community. The Catholics of Bristol are nearly all farmers and belong to the Democratic fold." [29]

There is a cemetery belonging to this congregation. The land purchased in 1897 and blessed on July 17, 1898. There is also a much older Catholic burial ground in the town of Starksboro, although the date of consecration is unknown, it would be circa 1850.

BURLINGTON - Cathedral Of The Immaculate Conception

Founded in 1830.

Burlington is located in the Town of Burlington, Chittenden County, on the shores of Lake Champlain.

Early Irish Settlers in Burlington:

MCWILLIAMS, MCKENNA, SORRIGAN, RHONES, KILLENS, SARSFIELD, ROGAN

Notable Features:

"Colonel Archibald Hyde, a convert to Catholicism in about the year 1835, donated five acres of land on which was erected a church edifice in the northeast part of the village. (Note: rather, the ground now occupied by the cemetery, we are later informed.) The first chapel, St. Mary's, was indeed built there but later having been destroyed by fire, the additional site of the present church was purchased by the Catholic party and the lot given by Mr. Hyde appropriated for a burial yard." [30]

"The Cathedral parish (formerly St. Mary's) is the oldest in the State. Father Jeremiah O'CALLAGHAN came here in July 1830. Here he made his headquarters. He built the first Catholic church in Burlington. It was burned on May 2, 1838. Its destruction was considered the work of incendiaries. At that time opposition to the Catholic church was bitter." [31]

Benefactors to the Church:

Colonel Archibald Hyde

CAMBRIDGE - St. Mary's

Cambridge is in Lamoille County.

Early Irish Settlers of Cambridge: Unknown

Notable Features:

There was no Catholic Church or Cemetery in Cambridge in 1899. In 1998 St. Mary's Church serves the Catholic Congregation. There is no Catholic cemetery.

"there are some 35 Catholic families in this town, some of which attend church at Underhill Centre. The Rev. P. Savoie, of Bakersfield, has service in the Village every two months. (in 1870)" [32]

CASTLETON - St. John The Baptist Church

Founded in 1899.

Castleton is located in The Town of Castleton, Rutland County.

Early Irish Settlers in Castleton:

MCKEAN, James; HOEY, Frank; HUNT, Owen (1830), BRENNAN, Geoffrey (1830), HUNT, Margaret (1832), HUNT, Hannah (1832), MUMFORD, James (1833); DUNAHUE, Alexander, CARRIGAN, Patrick

Notable Features:

"Alexander DUNAHUE, whose parents came originally from Ireland, and died in Castleton, was a peddler, and acquired considerable property. He married in Fair Haven, sometime prior to 1804, Miss Rebecca Norton, youngest daughter of Josiah Norton, Esquire, and resided on the plain a little eastward from Hydeville where he died August 19, 1814, aged 43 years. He was an eccentric person and requested that he might be buried under an appletree, nigh his house, so that his ghost might appear to Mr. Loveland's boys who had troubled him by stealing his apples." [33]

"As early as 1825 we find that some Catholics made their homes in this town. The first arrivals were James MCKEAN and Frank HOEY. In 1830 Owen HUNT and Geoffrey BRENNAN settled here. In March of the next year a son, James BRENNAN, was born to Geoffrey BRENNAN and his wife. The child named James was baptized by a Father Walsh, a missionary priest. James MCKEAN was the godfather; a godmother was dispensed with as there was no other Catholic woman in the place.

In 1832 there arrived Margaret and Hannah HUNT, daughters of Owen Hunt. A few years later the former (Margaret Hunt) married Patrick CARRIGAN. James MUMFORD and his wife came here in 1833. These two families have left numerous descendants who are well and favorably known in many parts of Rutland County.

In 1832 Father O'Callaghan of blessed memory began to visit Castleton three or four times a year. He celebrated Mass in the house of James McKean. The latter's wife, who had been a Protestant, was converted to Catholicism and all her children were baptized. In 1834 and '35 quite a large number of Irish Catholics, mostly relatives of James MCKEAN, left Ireland came to America and settled in Castleton.

In 1837 a numerous family named DERWIN arrived from Dublin, Ireland and made its home here. The mother and one of the daughters were highly educated and did much good among the Catholics by teaching the children their Catechism and preparing them for reception of the Sacraments." [34]

"About 40 families scattered through some of the adjoining towns, with some servants, constitute the congregation. There are, however, many Catholics in other parts of the town, but they form parts of other Congregations. Many are found in Hydeville and the west shore of Castleton Pond to West Castleton." [35]

Benefactors to the Church:

"James McKean, Frank Hoey, Geoffrey Brennan and others, purchased a Wagon and Paint Shop from Elial Bond, and conveyed the deed for land and building to Bishop Fenwick,of Boston,by deed dated September 7, 1835." [36]

CHARLOTTE - Our Lady Of Mount Carmel Church

Charlotte is located in The Town of Charlotte, Chittenden County

Early Irish Settlers in Charlotte:

KEHOE; QUINLAN, John; MCDONALD, QUINLAN, Michael

Notable Features:

"There was for many years a large Society of Friends in the town of Starksboro. In the winter of 1858 and '59, they sold the (meeting) house and it was taken down and the materials carried to Charlotte to be remodeled for a Roman Catholic Church." [37]

"Soon after it (the church) was moved onto a lot at Baptist Corners. The lot was purchased, along with the "Sanford Place" in 1858 or '59, where Mass was said once a month. The church was dedicated in 1864. On the first of November, 1859, a part of the lot was consecrated for a burying ground. The number of communicants (in 1860) who worship at this place is about 500." [38]

"The population of Charlotte at the time of formation of the parish was about 80 families, half of which were Irish and half Canadian. Now in 1898 there are 32 Irish and 66 Canadian families. The Catholics of this mission have a cemetery (circa 1859). Additional land was purchased by Father Campeau from John Quinlan by deed of February 3, 1886." [39]

Benefactors to the Church:

"QUINLAN, John: Was always a generous supporter. He was a prominent citizen of the town, held many civil offices and was representative at Montpelier during one term. RAFFERTY, Peter: Of Montreal, has also been a liberal contributor to the support and welfare of the church." [40]

DANBY - Church Of The Holy Trinity (Mission)

Danby is located in the Town Of Danby, Rutland County.

Early Irish Settlers In Danby: Unknown.

Notable Features:

"The first missionary who paid regular visits to the Catholics who lived about this place was Rev. J. Daly. Since 1854 they have been attended at different intervals by East Rutland, Bennington or East Dorset. East Dorset has now (1872) charge of the mission. Last year they purchased the building which had been built and was once used for a Bank. It having been tastefully repaired, is now used by them as a church." [41]

"Danby is attended from East Dorset. When this mission was established (1872), there were about thirty Catholic families; now (1899) there are 18." [42] There is no Catholic Burial Ground in Danby. The Catholics of Danby are interred at East Dorset, Vermont.

EAST ALBANY - St. John Of The Cross Church

East Albany is in Orleans County.

Early Irish Settlers In East Albany:

RIORDAN, William; GALLAGHER, Edward; GLEASON, Patrick; KEOGH, William; MCLAUGHLIN, Bernard; CROWLEY

Notable Features:

This church was constructed in 1874, the lot being secured in 1859. "There are about 200 souls (in 1898), most all of Irish parentage, and farmers. Father O'CALLAGHAN visited in the "forties" and said Mass in a house owned by a Mr. CROWLEY near the present church. There is a Catholic cemetery near the church, bought September 6, 1861. East Albany was a mission attended from St. Johnsbury, Newport and from time to time visited by a priest from Stanstead Plains, Canada. It is now served by Rev. Joseph Turcot of Barton." [43]

EAST DORSET - St. Jerome's Church

Founded 1868

East Dorset is located in the Town of Dorset, Bennington County

Early Irish Settlers in East Dorset:

MCGUIGAN, Michael; SWEENY, MCDEAVITT, MCBRIDE

Notable Features:

"The first Catholic settlers in East Dorset were Irish. They worked on the construction of the railroad, and afterwards in the marble quarries. The first Mass was celebrated by Father Daly on East Dorset Hill, in the house of Michael MCGUIGAN in 1838. At this time there were about 30 Catholics in Dorset. They were all Irish.

When Dorset was formed into a parish (1868) with Father Gaffney as pastor, there were about 850 Catholics, nearly all Irish, with a sprinkling of French. Now (1899), however, there are only about 250 souls. This marked reduction in number is owing to the fact that the marble works and quarries which gave the principal employment to the people have been closed up during the last twelve years. The people had to seek employment elsewhere. Those remaining find employment in one quarry, and some are farmers. The bulk of the small congregation is Irish.

The Catholics are in general quite intelligent and religious, and keep up the good old customs of religion and hospitality practiced by their forefathers.

There are two Catholic cemeteries--one purchased in the time of Father Cloarec (1860-61), and the new one purchased by Father Gaffney (Circa 1874)". [44]

"There is also a Catholic Church, organized in 1856, in East Dorset. They have a house of worship and are reported by their priest to number 500 members, 250 adults, 150 of which are residents of Dorset. The remaining adults reside in Danby and Manchester, and the remaining members that make up the 500 are baptized children, which are in the Catholic community, recognized as members." [45]

ELY MINES - St. Lawrence's Church

Located in the Town of Vershire, Orange County.

Early Irish Settlers in Ely Mines: Unknown

Notable Features:

"Ely Mines, now called Copperfield, is a mining village in the town of Vershire. It was once a prosperous place. It contains a rich vein of copper. Several Catholic families settled here. It was visited by Bishop DeGoesbriand in 1873 and a church was built in Ely (Mines) in 1880. The church was soon paid for; the mining company was doing a prosperous business, and money was plenty and the Catholics generous.

There are some missions in the eastern part of the State in which Mass is said in private houses or school rooms at fixed times. They are Groton Pond, South Ryegate, Westmore and Burke Hollow." [46]

There is a Catholic cemetery in Ely Mines (South Vershire), long since abandoned and in disrepair.

The parish history submitted to Bishop Michaud failed to mention a significant event that occurred in this village. In 1883 a serious labor-management dispute placed the town in jeopardy for a short period. Output from the mines had diminished. The miners had not been paid nearly $25,000 in back wages as the owners' operating funds had been depleted. Walter Hill Crockett wrote in his 1921 History of Vermont, "In July of 1883, about 300 men, primarily miners, seized the mine, looted the company store, secured arms, seized one hundred and fifty kegs of powder, entered and searched several houses and threatened to blow up bridges and destroy the village of Vershire (Ely Mines), and West Fairlee, unless the money due them was paid by four o'clock the following afternoon."

The State Militia was called out, arriving in the early morning hours of July 7th and rousted the miners from their beds, arrested and placed them under guard. The Governor of the State interceded, and after negotiation with mine owners, arranged to have them pay what they could. Those that were arrested were released after an investigation by the State's Attorney. Many of the miners never submitted a claim against the owners and soon after left the area. Crockett commented, "apparently the miners had been badly treated, some of their families were in destitute circumstances." [47]

Benefactors To the Church:

FOLEY, Cornelius; PIERCE, Frank, Mr. & Mrs. of South Fairlee, BRENNAN, John of FAIRLEE

ENOSBURGH FALLS - St. John The Baptist Church

Founded in 1874.

Located in The Town of Enosburgh, Franklin County, near the Canadian Line.

First Irish Settlers in Enosburgh.

SHANNON, Matthew; GARANT, M.; COLLINS, Patrick

Notable Features:
"Father O'Callaghan's zeal discovered the few Catholics living here. He came and said Mass for them in 1848 in the old schoolhouse. From this year the Catholics were visited by priests occasionally, or attended Mass in Fairfield or Canada.

In 1865 Father Caissy, of Fairfield, built here a church. At this time there were about two hundred Catholics of both nationalities--Irish and French. (In 1899) the number of Catholics belonging to Enosburgh parish has grown to 600." [48]

There is a Catholic cemetery dated circa 1897. There is also an older cemetery on the church grounds which dates to 1864.

"This place has a comfortable church edifice (1870), is partially furnished, with but a trifling debt upon it, a good cemetery, and a well organized congregation. A portion of the Catholics from Berkshire, Franklin, Montgomery and Sheldon, who have no place of worship in their respective towns, attend church at Enosburgh Falls. They are quite numerous in these places and when it is announced that Mass will be celebrated in either of them, on a week day or festival, there is always sure to be a large congregation in attendance." [49]

"They were attended from Fairfield once a month until the month of June, 1868, when having had the benefit of a mission during which over 300 persons approached the Sacraments of Penance and of Holy Eucharist, and more than 80 persons were confirmed, they began to be attended twice a month. In October of 1868 Enosburgh and Bakersfield were formed into a parish." [50]

ESSEX JUNCTION - Holy Family Church

Founded in 1893.

Located in The Village Of Essex Junction, Chittenden County

First Irish Settlers in Essex Junction: Unknown

Notable Features:

"Mass was first said and little mission preached by Reverend Peter Savoie about the year 1874. On July 7, 1884, a lot was secured for a future church. Let it be remarked, by the way, that Essex formerly belonged to the jurisdiction of Winooski Parish (St. Francis Xavier). At the organization of the parish there were about 110 Catholic families. With the exception of fifteen Irish families, the rest are Canadians. The present (1899) population numbers about 700 souls, Irish and Canadians. The Catholics own a cemetery, situated in the suburbs of the village of Essex Junction." [51]

FAIRFAX - St. Magdalen's Church (Mission) (St. Lukes 1997)

St. Luke's Founded in 1943. St. Magadalen was a mission from 1868.

Fairfax is located in The Town of Fairfax, Franklin County. This parish served Fairfax and nearby Binghamville and Fletcher.

First Irish Settlers in Fairfax: Unknown

Notable Features:

"This mission was established (1876) for the benefit of the farmers of Fairfax and Fletcher. In the beginning it was attended by the pastor of Milton but now (1899) the Reverend D. J. O'Sullivan, of St. Albans, says Mass there on Sundays once or twice a month. There are probably twenty five families who belong to this church."[52]

There is a Catholic Cemetery in Fairfax.

FAIRFIELD - St. Patrick's Church

Founded in 1858.

"Fairfield, in Franklin County, is one of the oldest Catholic settlements and parishes in Vermont."[53]

Early Irish Settlers in Fairfield:

RYAN, Thomas; DENIVER, Patrick; KIRK, Peter, KIRK, Lawrence; MCENANY Brothers, KING, Patrick; CARROLL, James; MILES, Terence; CONNELLY, Peter; CONNELLY, Michael

Notable Features:

"The first Catholic settler in this place was Thomas RYAN who came here from Kilkenny, Ireland, in 1812. Soon after he married Catherine BELFORT of Mississiquoi Bay. Of this union were born six children.

The first Mass in Fairfield was said in 1830 by Father O'Callaghan in the house of Thomas Ryan. He was the only Catholic who owned a farm then.

The first priest who attended Fairfield was Father Migneault of Chambly in Quebec, who came here on sick calls. Chambly is about 50 miles distant. Patrick DENIVER's sister was dangerously ill and a man was sent on foot to Chambly. For some reason, Father Migneault was delayed. The woman was expected to die every day, but, at last, the priest arrived and gave her the last sacraments. She died within twenty-four hours.

At about this time, Mrs. Patrick DENIVER gave birth to twins. Some time after their birth she and her sister took the babes in their arms and, in spite of the distance, walked to Chambly to have them baptized."[54]

The first church was built circa 1847. The number of Catholics at the formation of the parish was about 50 Irish families. In 1868, Rev. McCauley intended to give the church a thorough renovation but it was in such poor condition that plans were changed and construction of a new building was proposed. The attempt was combated by many in the congregation, especially by those who had perpetual leases of pews. The bishop appeared personally in Fairfield and advised the parishioners of their responsibility to patience and obedience and construction of the new church proceeded.[55]

"The number of people present at the first Mass was 15. Now (1899) there are one hundred and fifty families, three fourths Irish and the balance Canadians."[56]

"Many families who formerly attended church at Fairfield, now go to Bakersfield, and the numbers of this congregation (Fairfield) have been considerably diminished by the organization of that new parish. It now contains about 115 families--most of them Irish Catholics."[57]

Benefactors to the Church:

Hubbard BARLOW - Donated land for the first church, 1847, and a cemetery circa 1844.

FAIRHAVEN - Our Lady Of Seven Dolors

Founded in 1866.

Fairhaven, in Rutland County, is the headquarters of the slate industry in Vermont.

Early Irish Settlers in Fairhaven: Unknown

Notable Features:

"The first Mass in Fairhaven was said by Father O'Callaghan in the summer of 1836. In 1855 - March 9 -- Father Druon bought a lot on which he built a brick church." [58] Fairhaven was attended by Irish and French Canadian parishioners until 1870 when a church edifice was constructed for the French speaking Catholic population.

"(In 1870) the present edifice is much too small for the congregation which occupies it." [59]

FAIRHAVEN - Church Of St. Louis

Fairhaven is located in Rutland County,

Notable Features:

"The French congregation in Fairhaven was organized in 1869. A lot was bought May 23, 1870, and the Church of St. Louis was built by Father Gagnier in the same year. At the time of the formation of the parish there were about 30 or 40 Canadian families. The population has not very materially increased since. There are today (1899) about 200 souls." [60]

FRANKLIN - Church Of All Saints (St. Mary's)

Located in Franklin Village, Franklin County, the most northerly town in the county, it borders on the Province of Quebec. In 1998 Franklin is a mission parish.

Early Irish Settlers in Franklin: Unknown

Notable Features:

"In 1874 the (Rev. Peter Savoie) built a small frame church, which was blessed by Bishop DeGoesbriand in 1874. There are here forty Catholic families (1899). All the people follow agricultural pursuits. The Catholic population is made up of French Canadians and a few Irish families. Franklin was attended for some time by Father Savoie. After his departure in 1875, the congregation was looked after and attended by the priest of St. Armand, P.Q. (Province of Quebec)." [61]

GEORGIA - Ascension

Georgia is located in Franklin County and is bordered by Lake Champlain and the Chittenden County line.

"The Catholics of Georgia attend church at St. Albans, Fairfax and Milton. They have no church edifice." [62]

In 1998 the mission of Georgia has attained the status of a parish. There is a Catholic church but no Catholic burial ground in Georgia.

GRAND ISLE - St. Joseph (Mission)

There was no Catholic Church or cemetery here in 1899. There is a Catholic mission in 1998.

Grand Isle is located in Grand Isle County in the Champlain Islands

GRANITEVILLE - St. Sylvester's Church

Founded in 1899.

Graniteville is located in The Town of Barre, Washington County.

Early Irish Settlers in Graniteville: Unknown

Notable Features:

"There is a church called St. Sylvester's. This was built in 1895. Mass was first said there in 1892. Graniteville, in the town of Barre, is attached to Northfield and is attended every alternate Sunday. There is a population of 400 souls (in 1899). It is growing steadily, owing to the increase in the granite business." [63]

HIGHGATE CENTER - St. Louis' Church

Founded in 1886.

Located in The Town of Highgate, Village Of Highgate Center, Franklin County. It borders on the Province of Quebec.

Early Irish Settlers in Highgate:

SLOAN, William; O'HEIR, Thomas; O'HEIR, Daniel; SHERIDAN, James; STEELE, John; SLOAN, Bernard; GILLAN, Thomas; HANNA, John; CUNNINGHAM, John, MURPHY, Hugh; CHRISTIE, Adam; CHRISTIE, Alexander

Notable Features:

"Catholics began to settle in Highgate at a very early period. The first Mass was said by Rev. Jeremiah O'Callaghan in 1831 in the home of Thomas O'Heir. All the Catholics were present. Their number at that time was about thirty, Irish and French. The present church (1899) was purchased from the Congregationalists in 1849, and moved to the place on which it now stands. Adam Christie, father of Archbishop Christie, of Oregon, and Thomas O'Heir had charge of the work.

William SLOAN came to reside here as far back as 1824; Thomas O'HEIR in 1825, John CUNNINGHAM and Hugh MURPHY about 1826, Daniel O'HEIR, James SHERIDAN and John STEELE in 1829. In the following years, Bernard SLOAN, Thomas GILLAN and John HANNA made their homes in Highgate.

The Catholic population of Highgate comprises sixty four families (1899), Irish and French. The people for the most part gain their livelihood from farming." [64]

Many of the early Irish settlers in Highgate emigrated from County Down and were of the general vicinity of Kilkeel. [65]

"As was the case at St. Patrick's, in Fairfield, the system adopted in 1849 for the renting of the pews in perpetuity, affording the pew holders a legal right to their sittings, has produced much annoyance and legal entanglements. Shortly after the arrival of Bishop DeGoes-briand in Vermont, a serious trouble in regard to the holding of pews happened in Highgate. A law suit followed. A jury trial was had. As was to be expected at that period of religious prejudice, the verdict was against the Bishop. The church was placed under interdict. However, after a time due submission was made to Catholic authority, and peace reigned along the banks of the Missisquoi." [66]

"Besides the church property itself, the Catholics of Highgate own a rectory and a cemetery. The latter was bought from S. S. Keyes and deeded to Bishop Fitzpatrick of Boston January 25, 1853. The church and cemetery are contiguous to each other." [67]

Church Benefactors:

Mrs. DOOLANG and Alexander CHRISTIE. The latter donated the main altar.

HYDE PARK - St. Theresa's Church

Founded in 1888.

The Village Of Hyde Park is located in Lamoille County and is the shire town.

Early Irish Settlers in Hyde Park:

MANNING, FINNEGAN, STEWART, KELLY

Notable Features:

"The first Mass in this district was said by Rev. P. Savoie in Johnson about 1865. (Johnson is a neighboring village). The church was built by the same priest in Hyde Park in 1872. It was not completed entirely until many years after (1898). The pastor visits the towns of Hardwick and Woodbury in order to bring the comforts of religion to the men working at the granite quarries and sheds.

The Catholic population (1899) is made up of thirty families--eighteen Irish and twelve Canadian The Catholics of Hyde Park district are mostly farmers--good, honest people--the only drawback being that there are not more of them.

There is in Hyde Park a priest's house and also a cemetery. The latter was purchased about 1866." [68]

ISLE LAMOTTE St. Joseph's Church

The Village of Isle LaMotte, Grand Isle County, is located in the Lake Champlain Islands, on an island of the same name. The island is seven miles long and two miles broad and is reached by a man-made causeway.

Early Irish Settlers in Isle La Motte: Unknown

Notable Features:

St. Joseph's church was built in 1871 and Mass was held there later in the same year. "They (Catholics) are principally quarrymen working for a Mr. Fisk who owns the Isle La Motte Limestone Quarries. Right here it is appropriate to introduce the Shrine of St. Anne, distant about two miles from the church. It is the site of Saint Anne's Shrine and promises to become a great source of devotion to the Catholics on either shore of Lake Champlain." [69]

In ethnicity, this is a French Canadian congregation. There is a Catholic burial ground in Isle LaMotte.

ISLAND POND - St. James The Greater

Founded in 1871.

Located in the Village of Island Pond, Town of Brighton, Essex County. It is on the line of the Grand Trunk Railroad, and midway between Montreal and Portland (Maine).

Early Irish Settlers in Island Pond

TRACY, Peter; TRACY, Michael; HALLORAN, John; FLAHERTY, Anthony

Notable Features:

"The building of the Atlantic and St. Lawrence railroad (now the Grand Trunk) in 1853 opened up the State and brought Catholic settlers into Brighton. Many of them are still residents of Island Pond. Many more Catholics arrived between 1856 and 1860. Island Pond had become an important railroad station, a port of entry, the location of a United States Customs House, several lumber mills had been opened, and many lumbering camps had also been started. At the time of the first Mass (1853) there were about a dozen families and many single men who worked on the railroad and in the mills and lumber camps.

In 1861 and 1862 the disappearance of the forests and consequent closing of the mills and camps obliged the employees to either settle in the Village of Island Pond or migrate to the west.

When the parish first formed there were thirty families, Irish and French. Today (1899) there are about 700 souls." [70]

"The (Catholic) Society has exerted a wholesome influence on the congregation by having suppressed, in some measure, intemperance as well as noise and disturbance on the Sabbath. The people contribute liberally to the different objects of the church and society as well as all other objects of charity which are very numerous. Situated as they are upon the great thoroughfare, the Grand Trunk Railway, and there cannot be found a town in the State of equal size where a larger sum can be raised in a short time for benevolent purposes than this." [71]

JOHNSON - St. John The Apostle (Mission)

Johnson is located in Lamoille County.

"This is a mission parish with no Catholic church (in 1860). Johnson has some forty Catholic families which are visited at regular intervals by the priest residing at Bakersfield." [72]

There is a Catholic burial ground in Johnson.

LEICESTER JUNCTION - St. Agnes (Mission of Brandon)

Leicester Junction is a small village in the town of Leicester, Addison County and is the junction of the Addison Railroad and the Rutland and Burlington Railroad.

Early Irish Settlers in Leicester:

WILSON, Peter; WELSH, Henry; MARKANE, John; GRANT, Denis

Notable Features:

"The first Mass was said here by Rev. George N. Caissy of Brandon. The Mass was celebrated in the school house in 1869. The Catholic population of Leicester includes twenty-two families (1899). Their contributions to the building of the church (1883) were very generous. They were also aided by the people of Brandon, Proctor and Rutland." [73]

There is no Catholic cemetery in Leicester Junction.

Church Benefactors:

H. WELSH donated the church lot.

LOWELL - St. Ignatius Church

Lowell is located in Orleans County. Farming is it's exclusive business.

Early Irish Settlers in Lowell:

TRULAND, James; MCGRORTY, Francis; MURRAY, John; MCCAFFREY, M.; GRILLIS, Thomas; MURPHY, Frank; MCCALLISTER, James

Notable Features:

This village was originally known as Kellyvale, the name being that of an earlier proprietor of the town.

"People from Ireland and Canada brought Catholicity into this locality in the thirties. That Apostle of Vermont, Father O'Callaghan, was the first priest to visit Lowell. He said Mass in the house of Francis McGirty (probably McGrorty), on West Hill, about the year 1843.

At this time religious prejudice was rife among Protestants against Catholicity. A priest was considered an emissary of the devil and Mass as idolatry. It is related that when the first Mass was announced, a certain man name Harding, posted himself at the door and tried to stop people from attending the Holy Sacrifice. This man afterwards became ashamed of his conduct and made an apology to the Catholics. There were eight Irish and one Canadian Catholic present at the first Mass.

When the church was built (circa 1867) there were about 40 families, half of which were Canadians. Now (1899) there are 100 families, nearly all French Canadians. Besides the church there is a priest's house and a cemetery. The cemetery was purchased November 8, 1867, by James Truland, with consent of Father Caissy, then pastor." [74]

"A very neat church edifice has been erected this year, 1869, by the Catholics of this town. One of the Priests of Hamsted, (P.Q.) says Mass here once a month on a Sunday. There may be some seventy Catholic families attending the church at Lowell." [75]

The foregoing account, written by Bishop DeGoesbriand, brought a comment from Lowell Town Clerk, Don Curtis, that "not more than half of the number (70) reside in town. I should think, the rest represent towns around." The editor clarified explaining that the Bishop was correct in that he had indicated the number attending Mass in Lowell and did not intend to imply that they were all residents of the village. [76]

LUDLOW - Church of The Annunciation

Founded in 1885.

Ludlow is in Windsor County and is midway between Rutland and Bellows Falls.

Early Irish Settlers of Ludlow and Proctorsville:

REED, SHEA, DALY, KEATING, John; LEONARD, SHERLOCK; MALONEY, Michael; CONNOR, Peter

Notable Features:

"The Honorable Redfield Proctor (U. S. Senator) writes from Washington, D.C. on March 6, 1899 that 'he often heard his mother speak of Bishop Cheverus, who probably stopped in their house, now in the village of Proctorsville, about the year 1820.-- There was but one Catholic family there and one for whom my mother had great respect. The man's name was SHERLOCK. He had many daughters, one of whom became a nun. The Irish were scarce there in those days.'

The first Catholics came to this town with the advent of the railroad in 1847. In 1848 Father Daly began to visit Ludlow and Proctorsville. In the latter place he said Mass in the houses of Michael MALONEY and Peter CONNOR. The few Catholics who were in Ludlow at this time were wont to go to Mass at Proctorsville.

When Mass was first said in Ludlow, the number of Catholics was very small. The building of a woolen mill brought several families to the village. Rev. DALY occasionally said Mass in Ludlow in a shanty near the railroad.

In 1876 when Father McLaughlin began the construction of the church, he found about sixty families, nearly all Irish; the others were French Canadians. Since 1855 the Catholic population has so increased that today there are about 100 Catholic families attending Ludlow church." [77]

There is no Catholic cemetery in Ludlow (nor in Proctorsville and Cavendish) but there is an ancient and substantial part of the Ludlow village cemetery that is dedicated to Catholic burials. Catholic burials will also be found in the village burial grounds in Cavendish and Proctorsville. The two parishes of Ludlow and Proctorsville were closely related being about three miles apart.

LYNDONVILLE - Church Of St. Elizabeth

Founded in 1891.

Lyndonville is a village in Caledonia County.

Early Irish Settlers in Lyndonville: Unknown

Notable Features:

"In the year 1854 Bishop DeGoesbriand said the first Mass in Lyndonville --several Protestants assisted at the services. There were about thirty Catholics present. All these came from the Province of Quebec. Thirty three years ago (circa 1866) the Passumpsic Railroad shops (now the Boston & Maine) were removed to Lyndonville. Several Catholic families came at the same time.

When the parish was formed there were about 60 Catholics. Now (1899) there are about 300, mostly French-Canadians. The people are an industrious, frugal and intelligent class. Many of the men are skilled mechanics in the railroad shops here--some conductors, engineers and trusted employees of the railroad company." [78]

There is a Catholic cemetery in Lyndonville, dating to the spring of 1892.

Church Benefactors:

KEENEY, James; MCPARLIN, William J. were among those contributing materially to the welfare and success of the church.

MANCHESTER - Church Of St. Paul

Founded in 1896.

Manchester is a village in Bennington County, a few miles short of being half way between Bennington and Rutland.

Early Irish Settlers of Manchester:

WOODS, John; SHEEHAN, John; HANLEY, James; HOWLEY, Barney; RYAN, Timothy; COFFEY, Daniel; MCCARTHY, Martin

Notable Features:

"As far as can be ascertained, Father Daly was the first priest to offer up the Holy Sacrifice of the Mass in Manchester. From information obtained there were about 24 families here at the time of the first Mass. They were chiefly Irish. In the early days of this mission the few Catholics here were attracted by work in Clark's Tannery. They were accustomed to hear Mass and receive the sacraments in East Dorset, which was the center for all Catholics between Rutland and Bennington.

When the parish was formed (1896) there were about 250 Catholics in Manchester. There is the same number still here. The majority are Irish. Most of the Catholics are farmers and servants in the famous Equinox House. There is no Catholic cemetery in Manchester. Most of the parishioners own lots in the East Dorset and Arlington cemeteries." [79]

Church Benefactors:

RAMSEY, Mrs. Allen, New York, CONNELL, E. T. of New York, ORVIS, Franklyn H., MARTIN, A. E. & Wife of Manchester, KELLEY, Margaret; DWYER, Margaret, Mrs.

MIDDLEBURY - Church Of The Assumption (St. Mary's)

Founded in 1855.

Middlebury is a village in Addison County.

Early Irish Settlers of Middlebury:

O'FLANAGAN, Timothy

Notable Features:

"The first missionary priest was the Rev. James MacQuade who visited in 1822. He left in 1823 and Middlebury had no priest until 1830 when the Rev. Jeremiah O'Callaghan became missionary for all of Vermont. (In 1859) the number of hearers is about 400 and the number of communicants, 300. By Timothy O'Flanagan". [80]

In 1838 Father Daly was headquartered in Middlebury and Castleton. In Middlebury he purchased a lot and finished construction of the first church in 1840. "We find in the Burlington records that Rev. J. O'Callaghan married a couple here on July 26, 1830, and probably said Mass. There are in Middlebury and the surrounding area, 260 Catholic Families (1899). Most of them are farmers, some work in the marble mills. All of them are of Irish or French Canadian descent." [81]

There are two Catholic burial grounds in the village. The first is in a section of the village burial ground that was set aside as consecrated ground for the early Catholic population. Between the years 1881-1886 a larger burial ground was purchased. It is located immediately adjacent to the village burial ground. (1997)

MIDDLETOWN SPRINGS - St. Anne's

There was no Catholic Church or cemetery here in 1899. There is a Catholic church in 1998. This parish was formed in 1963.

Middletown Springs is in Rutland County.

MILTON - St. Ann's Church

Founded in 1859.

Milton, in Chittenden County, is situated on the banks of the Lamoille River.

Early Irish Settlers of Milton:

MCMULLIN, Francis; MILES, James; PLUNKETT, Patrick; BURNS, Thomas; GRIBBONS, John; CONLIN, Patrick

Notable Features:

"Milton possesses an unusually fine water power. This convenience naturally drew settlers to the vicinity and it early became known as Milton Falls. Sixty years ago (circa 1840) some Catholics were found among the inhabitants. Tradition from those days states that there were about fifty catholic families (1845), mostly French Canadians. On February 10, 1859, the Bishop bought the lot and built the first church. The Catholic population when the parish was formed (1859), was about 250 souls. Now (1899) there are twenty Irish and 60 Canadian families that frequent the church.

The present Catholic cemetery of Milton was bought by Father Landry and blessed by the Bishop during the pastorate of Father Cardinal (1875-1878)." [82]

"The number of Catholic families in Milton and neighborhood is about the same as at Richmond (70). Their church, which is yet in an unfinished state, was built in 1859 and is now (1860) attended once a month, on Sunday, from St. Albans." [83]

"In 1859, Mr. Joseph Clark granted the use of the town hall for a mission. At the end of the mission, the Rt. Rev Bishop of Burlington proposed to build a church, towards which object Mr. Clark also contributed very liberally. The church was finished in 1863. The Catholic population of Milton are composed of French Canadians and Irish and number about 100 families (circa 1875)".[84]

Church Benefactors:

Joseph Clark who contributed to the construction of the Catholic church was a principal owner of the Vermont and Canada Railroad headquartered in St. Albans.

MONTGOMERY CENTER - Church Of St. Isadore The Laborer

Founded in 1890.

Montgomery Center is located in Franklin County.

Early Irish Settlers In Montgomery Center: Unknown

Notable Features:

"The first Mass was said in a log cabin owned by George Cochesne. It was situated on the top of the mountain. The celebrant of the Mass was Rev. Father Lyonnet, of Swanton, and the year, 1855. About fifteen Catholics, all French Canadians, attended. this first Mass. Reverend Father Mathieu built the church in 1882.

There were about 30 Catholics, mostly all Canadians, when the parish was organized (1890). The present (1899) population is 400. Of these, there are only four Irish families. The majority of Catholics are Republicans. A great many of them are farmers and the others work in the mills.

A cemetery was purchased by Rev. L. Clermont on June 27, 1891 and blessed by Rt. Rev. J. S. Michaud." [85]

MONTPELIER - St. Augustine's Church

Founded in 1850.

Montpelier is the capitol of the State and is located in Washington County and is on the line of the Vermont Central Railroad.

Early Irish Settlers of Montpelier:

MURPHY, John; ROURKE, Hugh; BROPHY, Patrick; MALONEY, Michael

Notable Features

"Montpelier is the capital of the State and lays claim to the first Catholic owning land in the State; for a man with the Catholic name of John KELLY claimed the ownership of 5,000 acres of land in 1767. It is not entirely certain that he lived here. In the "thirties" these are the names of Catholic residents who are still remembered; John MURPHY, Hugh ROURKE, Patrick BROPHY, Michael MALONEY.

The first Mass was probably said by Father O'Callaghan in 1830. The Holy Sacrifice of the Mass was offered up in this locality for the first time in the house of John Murphy. There were probably not over 200 (if that many) Catholics here at that time and they were mostly Irish and French Canadians.

When St. Augustine's parish was formed there were about 800 Irish and French Catholics. Now (1899) there are about 2,000, principally Irish, Irish-American and French Canadian. Since the opening of the granite industry in this vicinity, the former are the majority.

Most of the Catholics of Montpelier are of the Democratic faith and for some years have had representatives in the city government. Intellectually, they are on an equality with their fellow citizens and a few of them are prominent businessmen". [86]

"The congregation is the largest in town, being gathered from Montpelier and neighboring towns (circa 1881)." [87]

"The Catholic cemetery of St. Augustine's, which is a little above Main street, in the Clay Hill district, the land which was bought of Thomas Reed and Charles Clark, December 1857, was not deeded or enclosed and blessed by the Bishop until 1860". [88]

Benefactors to the Church:

T. W. WOOD, President of The Academy of Design of America

MORETOWN - St. Patrick's Church

Moretown is a mission of Waterbury and is located in Washington County.

Early Irish Settlers In Moretown:

MURRAY, Daniel; HOGAN, John; CALVY, Patrick; FARRAL, Patrick; DIVINE, Daniel

Notable Features

"The first church was built by Father Druon in 1857 in the center of the cemetery which was purchased by deed of March 15, 1841. The second was constructed by Father Galligan in Moretown Hollow in 1882, on lands bought from Francis HASSETT, by deed of May 8, 1882". [89]

The Catholic population of Moretown was primarily Irish and its chief occupation was that of agriculture although the line of the Vermont Central railway passed through the village of Waterbury, 8 to 10 miles distant.

"Those of this faith (Catholic) are almost entirely Irish. They purchased lands on what is called South Hill. Most of them commenced with very limited means, but by industry have generally prospered, and will now average with others of the town in wealth. There is one school district almost all Irish pupils.

There are now 90 who have grand lists and probably 75 voters, Among the prominent men of the present (1879) are MURRAY, Andrew; HASSETT, Daniel; LYNCH, Patrick; MCCARTY, Thomas; MCCARTY, Charles; and the three KERIN brothers. Moretown is now a central point for the Catholic population of South Duxbury, Fayston, Waitsfield and Warren.

The land for building a church on, and also for a burial ground, was given to the Catholic society by Col. Miller of Montpelier, in 1841. In 1858 the Society built their present church building on South hill, which is a little more than a mile from the village, nearly East." [90]

Church Benefactors:

"The lot on which the church stands was donated in 1855 by LEE, Frank; LEE, Peter; and MILLER, J." [91]

MOUNT HOLLY - Church Of Our Mother Of Mercy (Mission)

This parish in 1998 is known as Our Lady of Mercy.

Mt. Holly is located in Rutland County.

Early Irish Settlers of Mt. Holly:

SMITH, Patrick; DUFFEY, Darby; NOON, Michael; COLLINS, KENNEDY, KELLY, Patrick

Notable Features

"Mt. Holly is almost exclusively a farming town. It is situated on top of the Green Mountains--and even here among the hills of Vermont there are found sons and daughters of Ireland still retaining the faith and the customs of their native land. The Church is located on the highest part of the range. It was built by Father BOYLAN of Rutland in the year 1875. In 1885 Ludlow and Mt. Holly were made into a parish by the Bishop, and Rev. Patrick J. Houlihan became the first pastor. About six years ago (1893) Mt. Holly was assigned to the care of Dr. Glynn of East Dorset.

The Catholic population of Mt.Holly has much decreased. In 1887 a census taken by Father McLaughlin discovered about 60 Catholic families." [92]

Church Benefactors:

The house of the widow SMITH afforded generous hospitality to the priests who attended this mission.

NEWPORT - Star Of The Sea

Founded in 1873.

Newport in Orleans County is located on the shores of Lake Memphramagog.

Early Irish Settlers of Newport:

HOOLIGAN, P.; MITCHELL, John; DUNN, Thomas; and the Messrs. POWERS and O'ROURK

Notable Features

"The town being on the borders of the Province of Quebec, Canadians come to labor and settle here. Some Irish also arrived here from Ireland through Canada. The first Mass in Newport was said in 1840, at Indian Point, by a priest from Canada whose name is forgotten. At the first Mass at Indian Point there were present about 30 Catholics, 25 French and 5 or 6 Irish.

When the parish was established in (1877) there were about 90 families, 70 Canadians and about 20 Irish, scattered in the towns of Newport, Derby, Salem and Coventry. In 1898, there were about 1250 souls in Newport and its missions.

The church was blessed by Father Michaud on August 22nd, 1877. On January 12, 1875, Father Michaud purchased land for a cemetery". [93]

NORTH BENNINGTON - St. John The Baptist Church. (Mission)

Founded in 1885.

North Bennington is located in Bennington County and is in close proximity to Shaftsbury.

Early Irish Settlers of North Bennington And Shaftsbury:

COXSON; EDWIN; COATES; MURRAY, Thomas; BOWEN, Jeremiah; ROBINSON, Thomas; HORTON, James; MADDEN, Thomas; MEAGHER, William; MCCARTHY, Daniel

Notable Features:

"The first Catholic settlers of the mission of North Bennington and Shaftsbury were the families by names of Coxson, Edwin and Coates.

Among those who settled in this part of Bennington and Shaftsbury about the years 1848 and 1849 were Thomas Murray, Jeremiah Bowen, Thomas Robinson, James Horton, Thomas Madden, Michael Madden, William Meacher, Daniel McCarthy.

Rt. Rev. Louis DeGoesbriand said the first Mass for the North Bennington people in 1854 in Daniel MCCARTHY's house, there being present about one hundred. Henceforth Mass was said monthly and alternately in Thomas MADDEN's or in Daniel MCCARTHY's house, and occasionally in the school house of the village when allowed to be said.

The Reverend Father Ryan, seeing the number of Catholics, (there were 120 families), bought on November 1, 1871, the old Universalist Church, added to it thirty feet and the building was fitted for divine service. (In 1898) the population of St. John the Baptist's church, which comprises the Catholics of North Bennington and of Shaftsbury, is now of eighty English-speaking families and two French-speaking families." [94]

NORTHFIELD - Church of St.John The Evangelist

Founded in 1865.

Northfield is located in Washington County, a few miles from Montpelier.

Early Irish Settlers in Northfield:

REYNOLDS, James; MCCARTHY, John; SULLIVAN, John; KELLY, William. Kelly was the last one living in 1899).

Notable Features:

"The first Mass was said by Father O'Callaghan in one of the shanties along the line of the Central Vermont Railroad in 1846. The railroad was then being built from Essex to White River Junction. After this, Mass was celebrated in the old Methodist Hall at Northfield Center. There were about ten or fifteen Irish families in Northfield at the time of the first Mass. There were also a few Canadian families. In 1856 the first church was built by Rev. Z. Druon.

At the present time (1899) there are about ninety English speaking families and about thirty French speaking families in Northfield. Most of the Catholics occupy a creditable position in the community. Their avocations are principally those of farming, railroading and stone cutting. The old church lot and cemetery deed is dated June 1,1854. The records of this church do not antedate the year 1870." [95]

"The church numbers from 600 to 700 communicants (circa 1877)". [96]

Church Benefactors:

Governor Paine donated the land for the Catholic Cemetery in Northfield.

NORTH HERO - Church of St.Benedict Joseph Labre

North Hero is located on the shores of Lake Champlain and is on the island of the same name in Grand Isle County.

Early Irish Settlers of North Hero: Unknown

Notable Features

"September 5, 1887, a lot and house were purchased by the Catholics on the shores of Lake Champlain. A small church was built and dedicated to God under the invocation of a saint of modern times, a hero of Christian charity, Benedict Joseph Labre, on October 19th, 1889. North Hero has a steamboat landing and considerable traffic is carried on here during the navigation season. It is the shire town. There are twenty five catholic families resident here." [97]

Church Benefactors:

Rt. Rev Amadeus Rappe, the first Bishop of Cleveland. Retired to St. Albans,he used his own money for the building of churches and schools.

NORTON MILLS (Now Norton-1997) - Church of St. Bernard

Founded in 1887.

Norton (Mills) is in Essex County and borders on the Province of Quebec.

Early Irish Settlers in Norton Mills:

CONWAY, John

Notable Features

"The people attended services in the parish church on the Canada side before the Bishop erected their territory into a parish. The first Mass was said by Rev. J. Pouliot in a private house in 1886. The number of Catholics at the time of the first Mass was about 400 communicants--300 Canadians and 100 Irish. The number of Catholics has not materially changed since the organization of the parish.

The ground for a cemetery was given by A. M. STETSON in 1887 and it was blessed in 1888." [98]

Church Benefactors:

A. M. STETSON, donated land on which the church is built and land for a cemetery. Mr. STETSON, John BOUTIN, Jacob GRENIER, Oliver BENSON and John CONWAY assisted in building the church. [99]

ORWELL - St. Paul's Church

Founded in 1886.

Orwell, in Addison County, is a farming town situated near the shores of Lake Champlain.

Early Irish Settlers in Orwell:

FANNING, William; KANE, John; CUMMINGS, Michael; CRANE, Michael; CHAMBERLAIN, Thomas.

Notable Features

Canadians who came to work along the lake began to settle here in the forties (1840's). Some Irish also found their way to the fertile lands of Orwell. The good Father Migneault, of Chambly (Quebec), said the first Mass here in a private house in 1840. The church was blessed on May 19th, 1867. At the time of celebration of the first Mass in Orwell there were 30 Catholic families. There are now (1899) 60 families, Irish and French. The only occupation is farming. The Catholics are a hard working, reputable, religious class of people." [100]
"A Catholic church has lately been erected by one of the wealthiest citizens (of Orwell) who has two daughters, members of that church." [101]

PITTSFORD - Church of St. Alphonsus

Founded in 1892.

Pittsford is a farming town in Rutland County.

Early Irish Settlers in Pittsford:

LOUTH, Edward; DUFFY, John, MCCONNELL, Felix; BURNS; LOUTH, James, CARRIGAN, James; HARRINGTON, Timothy

Notable Features

"Pittsford is a farming town in Rutland County. At an early period, however, of the present century (19th) there was a blast furnace in the town. This drew several mechanics and laborers; among them were some Irish Catholics. In 1826, Edward LOUTH and John DUFFY came here to work in the foundry. Here they found two other Irish Catholics, Felix MCCONNELL and a tailor named BURNS. In 1828 these were joined by James LOUTH, whose son and daughter still reside here. In 1829 the little band of Catholics was increased by the arrival of James CARRIGAN and family, whose posterity is now quite numerous in Pittsford and Rutland. In 1830 Timothy HARRINGTON and family joined the little Catholic colony.

In 1830 a Father BURNS made a trip through this part of the State. He baptized four children for Felix MCCONNELL. About three months after Pittsford was visited by Father Fitton, a young priest sent by Bishop Fenwick to look after the spiritual welfare of the Catholics in Vermont.

This priest said the first Mass in Pittsford in the house of James LOUTH at "the furnace". From here Father FITTON drove the next day to Wallingford where he said Mass again in the house of Mr. SHERLOCK, the only Catholic resident in Wallingford at the time.

The above named five families, and the tailor Burns, were the only Catholics to be present at the first Mass, in all about twelve or fourteen persons, and all from Ireland.

At the time of formation of the parish (1866) there were about 200 souls, now (1899) there are about 500, two-thirds of whom are of Irish origin, the balance is made up of French Canadians." [102]

"Pittsford Catholics have also a neat church edifice in the town, built in 1858; and their meetings are quite well attended, though held only about once in two weeks." [103]

"The Catholic Church of Pittsford is made up chiefly of Irish farmers. They number about 100 families and are regularly attended from Brandon. The Catholic Church of Pittsford, which is a substantial brick building, was erected through the care of Rev. Charles Boylan in the year 1859. The congregation also has a grave yard which has not been consecrated." [104]

"The Catholics have a cemetery which was laid out in 1867, the site of which is beautiful, but the grounds have been but little improved." [105]

POULTNEY - St. Raphael's Church

Founded in 1884.

Poultney, in Rutland County, lies on the western border of the State.

Early Irish Settlers in Poultney:

NOLAN, James; MCLAUGHLIN, Terence; MURPHY, Owen; COLLINS, Daniel; HOLLAND, John; HOLLAND, Peter; FLOOD, John; BRENNAN, Daniel

Notable Features

"People began to settle the town before the Revolutionary war. We do not, however, find the names of any Catholics among the first inhabitants. Not until the introduction of railroads in this part of the State, do we discern any Catholics in Poultney.

We have no information of the visit of any priest to Poultney previous to 1846. In this year, that apostle of southern Vermont, the Rev. John B. DALY said Mass in a shanty on the railroad. Subsequently he officiated in the old stone building situated on the hill on the road towards East Poultney. There were about thirty persons present at the celebration of the first Mass." [106]

"At the time of formation of the parish (1884) there were forty Irish families, about 200 individuals. Now (1899) there are about 65 families --about 300 individuals. The occupation of the people is that of farming and of work in the slate quarries. They are an intelligent, hospitable and orderly class of people." [107]

"Poultney has (1867) a Roman Catholic Congregation of 50 families. The church, which is a brick edifice, was commenced in 1864 and completed in 1865." [108]

There is a Catholic Cemetery in Poultney.

PROCTOR - Church Of St. Dominic

Founded in 1893.

Proctor, formerly call Sutherland Falls, is a marble town located in Rutland County.

Early Irish Settlers of Proctor:

O'ROURKE, James; CASEY, James; LEONARD, Thomas; NULTEY, Patrick; RODDY, James; MCGARRY, Bernard; MCLAUGHLIN, John

Notable Features

"Proctor, formerly called Sutherland Falls, is a marble town, for here are some of the quarries, the mills and the offices of the great Vermont Marble Company. The firstCatholics came here to labor in the quarries and mills.

Father Daly, the apostle of southern Vermont was the first priest to visit this place. In June, 1844, he said Mass in the house of a certain John McLaughlin. When a Catholic church was built in West Rutland the Catholics of Proctor were wont to travel over the hills to attend Mass and receive the sacraments there.

We have no data about the number of Catholics when Father Daly said the first Mass. When, however, Father O'Reilly began to attend this place (1872) there were about 40 families, Irish and French about equally divided.

In the year 1879 Proctor was transferred to the jurisdiction of Father MCLAUGHLIN of Brandon. This priest took a census of the Catholic population and found in Proctor, at the Double Road Crossing, about 70 families. In 1893, when Father LONG took charge of the parish he found about 115 Catholic families in Proctor, Irish and French-Canadians about equally divided. There are also 15 Italian families.

There is in Proctor a fine Catholic Cemetery, the land was donated by deed of November 5, 1881, by Senator Proctor to the congregation.

The congregation of Proctor is made up of mechanics and working men and their families. Their only business is quarrying, sawing and dressing marble. They are different in politics as they are in nationality and they are as various in their opinions on national questions as the variegated marble they work." [109]

Church Benefactors:

U. S. Senator Proctor, President of the Vermont Marble Company, and Former Governor of Vermont, gave land by deed dated July 28, 1879, for the church, marble for the foundation and $100 in money. Senator proctor also donated land for the Catholic cemetery in November, 1881.

PROCTORSVILLE - Holy Name Of Mary (Mission)

There was no Catholic Church or cemetery here in 1899. There is a Catholic mission in 1998. See Ludlow.

Proctorsville is in Windsor County.

RANDOLPH - Church Of Sts. Donatian And Rogatian

Founded in 1903.

Randolph is located in Orange County. It is a mission belonging to Windsor.

Early Irish Settlers of Randolph:

MAGINNIS, Peter

Notable Features

"A few families were found here shortly after the introduction of the (Vermont Central) railroad. On March 23, 1863, Father Druon, of Montpelier bought the lot and said the first Mass in the house of Peter MAGINNIS. In the same year Father Druon built the present church." [110]

"There are about 40 families which worship in the Catholic Church edifice of this town. They have Mass once each month-Sunday and are attended by Rev. P. Clavier of Northfield. The church building had been erected by the Very Rev. Z. Druon." [111]

READSBORO - Church Of St. Joachim

Founded in 1895.

Readsboro is a town of Bennington County, on the Massachusetts line. Early Irish Settlers of Readsboro: Unknown

Notable Features

"The mills of the place attracted mechanics and laborers. The first Mass was celebrated by Rev. Father Leduc, a priest from North Adams (Massachusetts), in the house of Edward Goullette. In 1886, the time of the first Mass, there were about one hundred Catholics--Canadians and Italian. At the time of the formation of the parish (1891), there were about 225 Catholics. The number has increased very little since; there are now perhaps 275, Canadians and Italians. Most of the Catholics of Readsboro work in the pulp mills and chair factory. They do not meddle much in politics." [112]

Church Benefactors:

Mr. Romage, a non-catholic, contributed very generously to the building of the church.

RICHFORD - Church Of All Saint's

Richford is a town of Franklin County on the Canadian Border.

Founded in 1899.

Early Irish Settlers of Richford: Unknown

Notable Features

"Richford, up to May, 1899, was a mission attended from Enosburg. The first Mass was celebrated here by Father Lyonnet in 1849. In 1873 Father Mailhiot, of Sutton, Canada, built a small church. The number of Catholics was then 120, comprising both Irish and French. There are now (1899) about 400 Catholics in this place. The Catholics here have a cemetery. It was blessed by Bishop DeGoesbriand in 1891." [113]

"This place is visited by missionary priests from Canada (1869)." [114]

RICHMOND - Our Lady Of The Rosary

Founded in 1865.

Richmond is a town in Chittenden County and is on the line of the Vermont Central Railroad.

Early Irish Settlers of Richmond:

KEEFE, Charles; HANLEY, Patrick

Notable Features

"Richmond is one of the oldest parishes in Vermont; small, indeed, in numbers, but made up of substantial sturdy farmers. In 1848 the first Mass was said in the house of Charles KEEFE by Father O'Callaghan, of Burlington. There were about twelve persons present at this Mass. This comprised all the then known Catholics in this vicinity. They were all Irish. The number of Catholics increased rapidly in ten years. A church was built under the direction of the good Bishop in 1858.

The Catholic population has not varied materially since the formation of the parish. There are sixty-five Irish and American and thirty-five Canadian families, or about 450 souls (in 1899). The Catholics of Richmond are mostly farmers and compare most favorably with the rest of the population. They are generally of the Democratic faith in politics; but what is better still, they are a quiet, orderly, moral and generous class of people." [115]

There is a Catholic cemetery, consecrated in 1868.

RUTLAND - ST. Peter's Church

Founded in 1855.

Rutland is located in Rutland County.

Early Irish Settlers of Rutland:

KELLY, GLEASON, BUTLER, LYSTON, MCMAHON, CLIFFORD, FITZGERALD, BROHON

Notable Features

"The City of Rutland is second in population in the State of Vermont. It is the shire city of Rutland County, and is the center of the most populous and of the most flourishing portion of the state. It has two Catholic churches, one for the French-Canadians and one for the English speaking part of the community.

St. Peter's congregation of Rutland is one of the oldest, most numerous and most substantial in the State. It would be difficult to ascertain who were the first Catholic settlers of this town. There are non-Catholic families bearing the distinctively Celtic and Catholic names of Kelly, Gleason, Butler, etc, whose ancestors came here more than a hundred years ago and were probably Catholic.

Among those who brought the faith here, and whose descendants still retain it, were the Lystons, McMahons, Cliffords, Fitzgeralds, Kellys, Brohons, etc. The two first named coming here in the early (eighteen) thirties; the others with the tide of emigration from Ireland which commenced and continued from 1847.

Father O'Callaghan was the first priest who visited Rutland. He came here in 1830 and said the first Mass in a private house for at that time it could not have been deemed necessary, if possible to hire a hall for such a purpose. In this year, 1830, there were not more than five or six Catholic families, or about 25 to 30 souls in this place.

Rev. Zephyrin Druon was appointed January 10, 1855, the first resident pastor of Rutland. He began the building of a church. It was completed in 1855. The first parochial school was opened in a house on West street with one teacher and about fifty pupils. This was in 1857.

The new cemetery, called Calvary, was purchased by Father Gaffney on July 16, 1887. It is beautifully located and within 5 minutes walk of the church.

Rutland has increased in population and prosperity amazingly during the past twenty years. Catholics have multiplied and they hold today a most creditable place in the community. Socially they compare favorably with other Catholic communities of the same number in New England, being composed of doctors, lawyers, mechanics, merchants, etc." [116]

"Those participating in a parade in Rutland, circa 1870: in the Hibernian Literary Society, KINGSLEY, Dennis; LYSTON, Edward; marshal." [117]

Church Benefactors:

"Many, indeed, of the parishioners have been liberal in their contributions; several have even made sacrifices for the welfare of religion in Rutland. No one, however, was as generous and self-sacrificing as the late Pastor, Father (Charles) Boylan. Every dollar he could possibly spare was used for church, school or convent. He thought of himself last." [118]

RUTLAND - Sacred Heart of Mary

Founded in 1869.

Rutland is in Rutland County.

Early Irish Settlers of Rutland: (See sketch of St. Peter's Church)

Notable Features

Rutland is on the line of the Rutland Railroad. It is a center of the marble industry of the State of Vermont.

"The Congregation of the Sacred Heart of Jesus is composed of French Canadians. It was organized in 1869. In this same year a church was built. In 1890 there were 500 communicants. The failure of the marble companies and the consolidation of some of the others, together with hard times, caused this congregation to lose many of its members. At this writing (1899) there are not more than 200 communicants. A second church was built in 1893. There is a cemetery belonging to this congregation. The land for this was purchased in 1889." [119]

SHELBURNE - Church Of St. Catherine

Founded in 1906.

Shelburne, is located in Chittenden County.

Early Irish Settlers of Shelburne:

O'GRADY, BURKE, GALLAGHER, MCGRATH

Notable Features

"Shelburne, a town of Chittenden County, was formerly part of the parish of Burlington. In 1884 Dr. William Seward Webb built a large and magnificent summer residence in Shelburne. For the accommodation of his Catholic help, he ordered the building of a Catholic chapel on his own grounds. The first Mass in the new church was said by Rev. P.A. Campeau, on December 19, 1895.

The Catholic population of Shelburne is 295 souls (1899). There are sixty families in this mission. There is a Catholic Cemetery, the land was purchased at the same time as the lot for the church." [120]

SHELDON SPRINGS - St. Anthony

Founded in 1906.

There was no Catholic church or cemetery in Sheldon Spring's in 1899. There is a Catholic church and cemetery in 1998.

Sheldon Springs is in Franklin County.

SHOREHAM - Church Of St. Genevieve

Shoreham, located in Addison County, is situated on the shore of Lake Champlain.

Early Irish Settlers of Shoreham: Unknown

Notable Features

"About the year 1856 a building was purchased by the Catholics and converted into a church. During more than twenty five years, Shoreham and Orwell have been united under the control of the same pastors. There are in Shoreham about 115 Catholic families and their number is increasing and would to God that their piety may increase with their population. French Canadians predominate in the Catholic population. Farming is about the only occupation.

Shoreham has a fine Catholic cemetery. The land was purchased by Rev. P.P. Barrett, by deed of June 20, 1883. Previous to this year, Catholics buried their dead in Orwell (VT) or Ticonderoga (NY)." [121]

SOUTH BURLINGTON - St. John Vianney

There was no Catholic church or cemetery in South Burlington in 1899. There is a Catholic church and cemetery in 1998. This parish was formed in 1940.

South Burlington is in Chittenden County.

SOUTH HERO - St. Rose of Lima (Keeler's Bay)

Founded in 1895.

South Hero, located in Grand Isle County, is the southernmost of the Champlain Islands. It is located on the line of the Rutland and Canada railroad.

Early Irish Settlers of South Hero: Unknown

Notable Features

"Keeler's Bay is on the Island of South Hero, in Grand Isle County. In March, 1854, a house and lot were bought by the Catholics and deeded to the Bishop July 8, 1858. This house was converted into a church. It lasted until 1898 when it was consumed by fire. At the present writing a new church is nearly completed and is already used for divine worship. There are at present (1899) about 130 families. When the parish was formed nearly fifty years ago, there were only twenty five families. It is an entirely farming district and the land very productive, especially abounding in fruit.

This place is assuming new importance, by the Rutland and Canada R.R. going through the islands." [122]

SOUTH ROYALTON - St. Matthew (Mission)

There was no Catholic church or cemetery in South Royalton in 1899. There is a Catholic mission in 1998.

South Royalton is in Windsor County.

SPRINGFIELD - Church Of The Maternity Of The Blessed Virgin Mary

Founded in 1900.

Springfield is located in Windsor County.

Early Irish Settlers of Springfield: SEXTON, Thomas

Notable Features

"The first Mass was said in Springfield in 1856 by Rev. Charles O'Reilly who thereafter visited the place from time to time. He used to say Mass in private houses, principally in that of Thomas Sexton. In this latter year (1871) Father Gendreau took charge. During the following year he purchased and remodeled the building which is still used as a church." [123]

There is a Catholic cemetery. Prior to this some Catholics of Springfield were buried in St. Catherine's Cemetery, Charlestown, NH.

ST. ALBANS - Church of the Immaculate Conception (St. Mary's)

Founded in 1847.

St. Albans is located in Franklin County. It is a shire town and the headquarters of the Central Vermont Railroad.

Early Irish Settlers of St. Albans:

KANE, Charles; KELLEY, Barney B.; RYAN, Daniel

Notable Features

"As early as 1825 there were no Roman Catholics in St. Albans with the exception of a few scattered descendants of French Catholics who were visited at intervals by French priests from Canada. When Reverend Jeremiah O'Callaghan came as missionary to Vermont in 1830 he found a few families of Irish and Canadian Catholics in St. Albans and vicinity.

Rev. William Ivers undertook the charge, sometime in 1841. At this period the numbers of those professing this faith had increased to such an extent, through immigration from Ireland and Canada, that the congregation assembling at St. Albans, and gathered partly from the neighboring towns, amounted to 1000.

In 1872 the parish had grown to such proportions that the French Canadian segment of the congregation was separated with the construction of a second Catholic structure, the Church Of The Holy Guardian Angels.

The population of St. Mary's Parish (1899) comprises 350 families and 150 single persons. They are a very intelligent, prosperous class of people. In their ranks are doctors, lawyers, merchants in every line of business. Several of them have occupied and now fill offices of trust and honor in the city and town.

In the early days of Catholicity in St. Albans, a piece of land was secured by the Catholics for burying their dead. The deed is dated July 17, 1845. This little city of the dead became replete with bodies. The present cemetery, Holy Cross, was opened by two deeds, one dated July 8, 1873 the other March 31, 1887." [124]

Church Benefactors:

G.G. Smith & Family; Hon. L. B. Hunt; B. H. Smalley, Esq.; Laura P. Smalley; Mrs. Cynthia Penniman; all converts to Catholicism as did Mr. William H. Hoyt, an Episcopal Priest who became a Catholic Priest.

ST. ALBANS - Church Of The Holy Guardian Angels

Founded in 1872.

St. Albans is located in Franklin County. It is a shire town and the headquarters of the Central Vermont Railroad.

Early Irish Settlers of St. Albans: (See Church Of The Immaculate Conception)

Notable Features

"From an early day, Canadians began to settle along the banks of St. Albans Bay. Until 1872, the Canadians and English speaking Catholics formed one congregation. They had helped to build and contributed to the support of St. Mary's Church (Church of the Immaculate Conception). The transfer of the railroad shops (from Northfield, Vermont just after the Civil War) and the establishment of the headquarters of the C. Vt. R.R. (Central Vermont Railroad) at St. Albans aided very materially to the increase in population and prosperity of the village.

In 1872 there were about 300 Canadian families in St. Albans and vicinity. The Bishop determined to establish a separate parish for the Canadians of St. Albans. On February 16, 1872, a suitable lot for a new church was secured at the corner of Lake and Elm Streets. The basement was completed and roofed. Mass was said for the first time at midnight, Christmas 1872.

There were about 3000 at the time of the formation of the parish, and the number has remained about the same ever since. Calvary cemetery was purchased, laid out and blessed in 1894." [125]

ST. ALBANS BAY - Our Lady Of The Lake

Founded in 1904.

There was no Catholic church or cemetery at St. Albans Bay in 1899. The parish was formed in 1904. This church was dismantled in the 1990's and the rectory sold as a private residence. Parishioners were transferred to St. Mary's and Holy Angel's parishes in the City of St. Albans. The deceased of this parish are interred in Mt. Calvary or Holy Cross cemeteries in St. Albans City and St. Albans Town.

St. Albans Bay is in St. Albans Town, Franklin County.

ST. JOHNSBURY - Church Of Our Lady Of Victories (St. John's)

Founded in 1858.

St. Johnsbury is located in Caledonia County in the northeastern part of the State. It is a shire town.

Early Irish Settlers of St. Johnsbury:

LONERGAN, Peter; BRAY, Michael; DONEGAN, Owen

Notable Features

"We find no traces of any Catholics living in St. Johnsbury previous to 1831. In this year the records of the town and parish show names that savor of Catholicity such as Joseph Lemaire, Narcisse Moreau, Ignace Trahan, Benjamin Blondin, Peter Lonergan, Michael Bray, Joseph Trudel, etc.

The first priests to visit St. Johnsbury were Father O'Callaghan from Burlington, Father Drolet from Montpelier and Father Harper from Canada. They said Mass in the houses of the Catholics, principally in those of Joseph Lemaire, Joseph Trudel and Owen Donagan.

During several years the Catholics were subject to many annoyances and persecutions from religious fanatics called Know-Nothings. These made St. Johnsbury a hotbed of religious and national bigotry and intolerance. To the honor of the Fairbanks family, let it be remarked that they refrained from any participation in this ignoble and unAmerican persecution of their Catholic fellow citizens. The Know-Nothings have gone to their graves, unwept, unhonored and unsung. The Catholics still survive and their church steeple surmounted by a cross looms high above everything in the shire town of Caledonia County.

There is no record of the number of Catholics when the first Mass was said nor even when the parish was formed. During the first year, however, of the pastorate (1858) of the first resident priest there were thirty seven baptisms of French Canadians and twenty-seven of Irish children.

At present (1898) there are two Catholic parishes in St. Johnsbury (see St. Aloysius). The French Canadian counts 410 families and the English speaking parish about 70 families.

The Catholics of St. Johnsbury are found in both political camps, Democratic and Republican. They are a quiet and law observing people.

The Catholics own a large cemetery situated in the suburbs of the city. The land was purchased in June 1876." [126]

Church Benefactors:

ROACH, P.A.; RYAN, John; FITZGERALD, Patrick; were generous in the construction of the church in 1887-1889.

ST. JOHNSBURY - St. Aloysius' Church

Founded in 1896.

St. Johnsbury is located in Caledonia County in the northeast part of the State. It is a shire community.

Notable Features

"Up to 1896 there was only one Catholic Congregation in St. Johnsbury. On August 1st of this year the Bishop decided that the English speaking Catholics should form a separate congregation. There were 75 families whose mother language was English." [127]

STARKSBORO - See Sketch of Church of St. Ambrose, Bristol

SWANTON - Church Of The Nativity Of The Blessed Virgin Mary

Founded in 1854.

Swanton is a Town in Franklin County located on the shores of Lake Champlain and near the U.S. and Canadian boundary.

Early Irish Settlers of Swanton:

MCNALLY, James

Notable Features:

"Swanton, in Franklin County, is a town in which tradition says that the Holy Sacrifice of the Mass was offered up and Catholicity known at a very early period. It is related that the Jesuits established a mission and built a chapel on the banks of the Missisquoi, on the spot where Swanton now stands. This chapel was in existence in 1775.

In the early 'thirties' a few Catholic families had settled in Swanton. About 1831 Father O'Callaghan visited this place and said Mass and administered the sacraments. In 1842 the first Catholic church was built on land donated by James McNally.

When the first Mass was said there were about 40 families. At the time of organization of the parish (1854) there were about 100 families, Irish and French. Since that time the Catholic population has very materially increased. There are now (1899) 330 families, nearly all claiming Canada as their birth place or the home of their ancestors. A few are of the Irish persuasion.

The Catholics have a very fine cemetery which was blessed in 1892 by Bishop DeGoesbriand." [128]

Church Benefactors:

MCNALLY, James. Donated land for first church erected in 1842.

TROY - Sacred Heart of Jesus

Founded in 1931.

There was no Catholic Church Or Cemetery here in 1899. In 1998 the Catholic Congregation of Troy is served by Sacred Heart Of Jesus church.

Troy is located in Orleans County and is in close proximity to the Canadian border.

Early Irish Settlers of Troy: Unknown

Notable Features:

"There are also some families of Irish and French Canadians who have settled among us, who are Roman Catholics. They have but rarely any religious services, but reject all union or connection with other sects or forms of worship." [129]

UNDERHILL - St. Thomas' Parish

Founded in 1872.

Underhill is located in Chittenden County and rests in the western foothills of Mount Mansfield, the peak with the highest elevation in the State of Vermont

Early Irish Settlers of Underhill:

BARRETT, Patrick; MCKENNA; SHANLEY; DUFFEY; MCELROY; MCCOY; FLYNN; BREEN; FLANNERY, M.; DORAN, Patrick; COLE, Patrick

Notable Features:

"Underhill can boast of being one of the oldest Catholic settlements in Vermont. There were Catholics here before there were any priests stationed in the State. It is related that on one occasion a certain Mr. Barrett drove all the way to St. Johns, P.Q., to get a child baptized.

Soon after his arrival in Vermont, Father O'Callaghan in 1830 said the first Mass probably in the house of Patrick Barrett. Bishop DeGoesbriand visited the place on November 15, 1853, less than a week after his arrival in Burlington. He found then around the center sixty-three families. There were about seventy families in this locality when the first Mass was said. They were all of Irish descent. A few lived in Jericho and Essex who attended Mass in Burlington, and up to about 1870, most of them belonged to St. Joseph's in Burlington or to St. Francis', Winooski.

People in those times were not provided with teams. They came to Mass on foot or in ox-teams. The first Mass by the Bishop was said in some private house. On March 19, 1854, Mass was said in the Old Green Mountain Academy. A committee was appointed to select a lot for a church, July 2. The Academy was refused to the Catholics for the purpose of religious services. The Bishop said Mass just inside the door of M. Flannery's house. People assisted at Mass on the lawn, in the shade of the trees.

At the present time (1899) there are about 190 families, about 160 of these are of Irish descent, the remainder--about 30--are of Canadian descent.

The people of this parish are mostly farmers. They are well-to-do, intelligent and well-educated. And, many of them in Underhill, as well as in the other towns of Jericho, Bolton, Cambridge and Essex, have been selected to fill the highest offices within the gift of the people.

There are three Catholic cemeteries in Underhill. The Pleasant Valley Cemetery donated by Patrick DORAN; the Irish Settlement Cemetery, purchased by Rev. Jeremiah O'Callaghan from Patrick COLE; the cemetery at Underhill Center, purchased in 1873 by Father Savoie for $600." [130]

VERGENNES - Church Of St. Peter

Founded in 1881.

Vergennes is located in Addison County.

Early Irish Settlers of Vergennes:

MILLER, John; NASH, Patrick

Notable Features:

"Vergennes, in Addison County, is the oldest and smallest city in New England. It derives its name from the Duke of Vergennes, who was prime minister of France during the American Revolutionary War. In the beginning of this century (19th) it became the home of several emigrants from Canada. Among them were Branchard, Michael Fremere, Joseph Mailloux, John Ambleau. Two Catholic settlers were of a different nationality, as their names prove--John Miller and Patrick Nash.

Tradition tells that a priest from Montreal said Mass here in 1816 or 1818. It is certain, however, that in 1833 Father Petithomme celebrated Mass in the house of John Freniere. Apart from the facts already mentioned, we think it proper to refer to the first visit made by Bishop Fenwick, of Boston, to Vergennes. We quote the following extract from his diary (1842)-----'the Catholics assemble to the number of about seventy or eighty. I addressed them first in English and then in French as many of them were of that nation, principally emigrants from Canada.'

The first land was bought on April 3, 1854. The church lot was secured by deed, November 8, 1855. The first church which is an elegant Gothic structure in brick was begun by Father Cunningham in 1871. The first Mass was said therein in 1874.

When the parish of Vergennes was formed (1874) there were 350 or 400 souls. They were nearly all Canadians. In 1898 there were 850 souls. There were 14 Irish families. The rest are all Canadians or the children of Canadian parents.

There is a Catholic cemetery in Vergennes. The land was bought by Father Picart in 1862." [131]

WALLINGFORD - St. Patrick's Church

Founded in 1910. Church was dedicated in 1866.

Wallingford is in Rutland County.

Early Irish Settlers of Wallingford: Unknown

Notable Features:

"Wallingford is attached to East Dorset as a mission. Father Boylan, of Rutland, built here a pretty and substantial church. A lot was secured by deed of October 3, 1864--the church was dedicated by Bishop DeGoesbriand August 29, 1866.

The Catholics of Wallingford have a cemetery of their own. The land was bought by Father Gaffney by deed of August 2, 1873. The population of this mission when the church was built was 160 families, now (1899) there are 30." [132]

"The Catholics who live in or about Wallingford are few in number, viz.: between 30 and 40 families. They however, deserve as much credit as any congregation in the State, on account of their extraordinary liberality in contributing toward the erection of their church. This building is made of stone, quarried near the village, and is one of the finest in the State for its size. It was built from drawings made by P. C. Kelley, the architect of the Church of West Rutland, St. Albans, East Rutland and the Cathedral of Burlington. The Catholics of Wallingford owe it to the energy of Reverend Charles Boylan that they possess such a fine building. It was blest on the 2d of September. 1866, under the title of St. Patrick." [133]

WATERBURY - Church Of St. Andrew

Founded in 1869.

Waterbury is located in Washington County and is most picturesquely situated in the Winooski Valley.

Early Irish Settlers of Waterbury:

O'CONNOR; BRYAN, Patrick; RYAN, James; KELTY; KING; SPELLICY; MANNING; LINEHAN; CLARKE; and in the neighboring town of Stowe, MCMAHON; LINEHAN; O'CONNOR (may have been CONNOR, Michael or O'CONNER, Michael) [134]

Notable Features:

"Patrick Bryan was an early Irish settler of Waterbury. His son wrote 'My father was born in London and learned his trade there. His parents were Irish, as his name indicates. He came from London to Quebec, and from there directly to Waterbury about 1814 or '15. His family were 6 sons and two daughters." [135]

"The building of the Vermont Central Railroad drew Catholic laborers to this vicinity and many of them made their homes in Waterbury. As usual, Father O'Callaghan was he first priest to visit Waterbury. In which year he said the first Mass is not recorded. Most probably it was about the year '47, the time of the building of the railroad. At this period there were about fifteen Irish families.

In 1857 Waterbury became a mission of Montpelier. Father Druon, then its pastor, built a small church on the hill north of the depot. In 1869, Rev. John Galligan was appointed first resident pastor of Waterbury. By deed of March 11, 1876, Father Galligan purchased a church on Main street from the Advent Society. He had it remodeled into a Catholic place of worship.

The records of this church do not date back beyond 1894. They were most probably lost or burned in the fire of the first church in Northfield (at a time when Waterbury was a mission of that church)." [136]

There is a Catholic cemetery in Waterbury.

WELLS RIVER - Our Lady Of Lourdes Chapel (Now St. Eugene's mission)

Wells River is a village in Orange County.

Early Irish Settlers of Wells River:

SULLIVAN, Jeremiah; DALTON, James; MARKHAM, James; O'NEILL, Mrs.

Notable Features:

"There is here a chapel dedicated to Our Lady Of Lourdes. The building was bought on August 2, 1877, by Father (now Bishop) Michaud, while he was pastor of Newport. It was formerly a school house. The first to say Mass here was Father Daly during the building of the railway.

The Catholic population is about 60 souls (1899). The first to say Mass here was Father Daly during the building of the railroad (1840's). Jeremiah Sullivan, James Dalton, James Markham and Mrs. O'Neill are the pillars of Catholicity in this little mission." [137]

There is no Catholic cemetery in Wells River.

WEST CASTLETON - St. Joseph's Church

West Castleton is a village in Rutland County.

Early Irish Settlers of West Castleton:

Notable Features:

"St. Joseph's Church, which is attended from St. Louis Church, Fair-haven, was built in the summer of 1879 by Rev. P. J. O'Carroll. The land for the church was donated by John Winters, May 13, 1879--the first Mass was celebrated there on November 1, 1879.

The number of Catholics cannot be easily ascertained, being a moving population. When the church was built there was quite a number of Catholics. In 1898 there were about 140 souls, all English speaking people." [138]

There is no Catholic cemetery in West Castleton.

Church Benefactors:

WINTERS, John. Donated land for first church in 1879.

WEST RUTLAND - St. Bridget's Church

Founded in 1857.

West Rutland is located in Rutland County.

Early Irish Settlers of West Rutland: Unknown

Notable Features:

"West Rutland is a village in Rutland County and is the marble town of the State for it was in this place where the first marble quarries were opened and the very finest of marble extracted.

Rev. Francis Picart, a French priest, was the first resident pastor of West Rutland. He came here in 1857--we have no certain date about the celebration of the first Mass. We can suppose, however, that Father O'Callaghan visited West Rutland as soon as there were Catholics here.

Father Daly certainly visited this place, said Mass and administered the sacraments. This fact we learn from individuals whom he baptized and from people who gave him hospitality. The church was dedicated on November 11, 1861.

We have no date regarding the number of Catholics in West Rutland when the first Mass was celebrated. The Catholic population in 1899 is 1500 souls, Irish and Poles. The district schools here are under the control of the Catholics, who outnumber the other denominations. This affords a very easy and pleasant solution of the school question.

This congregation owns a cemetery, the land for which was purchased by Father Lynch, by deed of December 7, 1864." [139]

Those participating in a parade in Rutland, circa 1870: St. Patrick's Benevolent Literary Society of West Rutland, MONAGHAN, Robert; DUFFY, M; MEAGHER, M.; Marshalls. [140]

WEST RUTLAND - Church Of Sacred Heart Of Jesus

West Rutland is located in Rutland County

Early Irish Settlers of West Rutland: Unknown

See sketch of St. Bridget's Church, West Rutland.

Notable Features:

"The congregation of the Sacred Heart of Jesus is composed of French Canadians. It was organized by Father Gagnier in 1869. In this same year the church was built. From 1869 until 1890 the congregation steadily increased. In this latter year, there were 500 communicants. The failure, however, of some of the marble companies, and the consolidation of some of the others, together with hard times, caused this congregation to lose many of its members. At the present writing (1899) there are not more than 200 communicants.

A new church, a frame building, was erected by Rev. J. M. Gelot in 1882. There is a cemetery belonging to the congregation. The land for this was purchased in 1889." [141]

WHITE RIVER JUNCTION - Church Of St. Anthony

Founded in 1869.

White River Junction is in the town of Hartford, Windsor County.

Early Irish Settlers of White River Junction:

MACK; KELLY; FLOOD; GINTY, John; O'NEILL; GLEASON, Thomas Sr.

Notable Features:

"White River Junction is in the town of Hartford, Windsor County. It is the junction of five railroads. It is truly a railroad village. As usual, with the railroads came the sturdy sons of labor who are the mainstay of the church wherever they are found. The names of the first families that located here indicate their origin: The Macks, the Kellys, the Floods, the Gintys, the O'Neills, the Gleasons, etc.

When the first Mass was said in White River Junction neither history nor tradition gives any evidence. History, however, does say that Rev. Hilary Tucker of Boston visited this neighborhood in 1847. He came to Lebanon, New Hampshire, which is four miles from the Junction, attended a sick call, remained three days, and during this time said Mass, heard confession and gave communion to 130 laborers. It is more than probable that the Catholics living at the Junction attended divine service on this occasion.

The number of Catholics at the time of the celebration of the first Mass (circa 1853) was about fifty, of which forty were Irish and ten French. Now (1899) there are 150 Catholic families.

A cemetery (on Nutt Street) was purchased in 1868 and blessed by Bishop DeGoesbriand. (There is also a second cemetery, Mt. Olivet, purchased at a later date.)

Of the Catholics there it may be said: In business their standing is solid and honorable, and in society an orderly and well educated class of people." [142]

WINDSOR - Church Of St. Francis D'Assisium

Founded in 1886.

Windsor is located in Windsor County.

Early Irish Settlers of Windsor:

BURKE; COLLIGAN, Patrick; BRADY, Thomas, MCHUGH, Felix; MCCARTHY, Michael

Notable Features:

"Windsor is a village in Windsor County. It is located on the Connecticut River between Bellows Falls and White River Junction and is one of the earliest towns of the State. The construction of the railroad as usual brought a contingent of Catholics to Windsor. These men were present at the first Mass celebrated by Father Daly in 1847 or '48 in Patrick Colligan's shanty. Father Daly came thereafter twice a year, holding services on his second visit in Mr. McHugh's shanty which stood near the site of the present railroad station. On his next visit he said Mass in Andrew Brady's shanty, the railroad laborers attending against the wishes of their boss.

On July 25, 1881, Father O'Sullivan bought the lot and began construction of the present handsome edifice.

When Windsor was made a parish (1886) there were about forty families, Irish and French. Now (1899) there are about fifty - not a very material increase. There is a Catholic cemetery here, bought by deed of July 21, 1876." [143]

Church Benefactors:

"The church possesses a very fine bell, the gift of the eminent lawyer, William M. Evarts, who was Secretary of State under President Hayes and Senator from New York. His summer house is in Windsor." [144]

WINOOSKI - St. Stephen's

Founded in 1882.

Winooski is located in the Town of Colchester, Chittenden County.

Early Irish Settlers of Winooski:

MCGUIRE, Daniel; FITZPATRICK, William; FITZPATRICK, Martin COURTNEY, John; CASHON, Anthony; MCEVOY, Henry; MCDONALD, John; MCEVOY, William; HOGAN, Patrick

Notable Features:

"At the end of the last century, Winooski became well known on account of its mills. English speaking Catholics did not come until a later period. English speaking Catholics used to go to Mass at St. Mary's Church in Burlington, only two miles distant. This mutual meeting for worship continued until 1871. In this year, Very Rev Father Lynch, V.G.(Vicar General), of Burlington, resolved to build a church for the English speaking Catholics of Winooski.

The number of families when the parish was organized (1871) was about 100. At present (1899) there are about 80 families of Irish extraction and about 8 families of Germans and Poles and a few French. The people of St. Stephen's congregation bury their dead in St. Joseph's Cemetery, Burlington.

In politics most of the Irish cast their votes for the Democracy. The Catholics here hold a high position in social and intellectual life and their business standing is excellent." [145]

WINOOSKI- St. Francis Xavier's Church

Founded in 1868.

Winooski is located in the town of Colchester, Chittenden County.

Early Irish Settlers of Winooski:

See Sketch of St. Stephen's Church.

Notable Features:

"Previous to 1868, the French-speaking Catholics of Winooski attended old St. Joseph's church in Burlington. Their numbers had increased sufficiently to guarantee the organization of a separate congregation. On the fourth Sunday of Lent--which was March 22, 1868--the first Mass was said in Concert Hall, Winooski Block--there were at that time 174 families in Winooski, all Canadians.

At the time of organization of this parish there were about 1700 Catholics, exclusively Canadians. The Bishop wished that this should be a French speaking congregation -- that only those who understood and spoke French could be admitted--no matter of what color or nationality. At the present writing, 1899, the congregation has increased to 2500 souls, all French-Canadians.

This congregation also has a separate cemetery. The land was purchased at the same time as the land for the church and is quite near the church and was blessed by Bishop DeGoesbriand in November, 1870.

The Canadians are very numerous in Winooski, and when united can control the political situation. They occupy an enviable social, political, intellectual standing. They take a great deal of interest in politics; several among them have represented their town in the legislature. Many of them are property holders and the retail trade of the place is almost entirely in their hands." [146]

Church Benefactors:

"The man who most materially helped the pastor in his undertakings was certainly Francis LeClair. He invariably stood by the priest with encouragement and money. In fact, were it not for his generous and material assistance, it is doubtful if the buildings owned by the Catholics of St. Francis Xavier could have been brought to such a a speedy and happy completion." [147]

WOODSTOCK - Our Lady Of The Snows

Founded in 1868.

Woodstock is a village in Windsor County.

Early Irish Settlers of Woodstock

RILEY; HAGGERTY

Notable Features:

"Nearly all the Catholics of Woodstock are Canadians-- a few Irish settled in Woodstock, among whom may be mentioned Messrs. Riley and Haggerty. Father Drolet of Montpelier was the first priest to visit Woodstock. He said Mass there in 1849, in Union Hall. About 200 people attended, most of them Canadians, the others being Irish and Belgian. In the fall of 1894, Father Toupin was appointed resident pastor in Woodstock. He immediately undertook the building of the present church. It was completed during the fall of the following year.

The Catholic population has not varied much since the formation of the parish. (In 1899) there are about 42 families, most of them Canadian. There are five missions attached to Woodstock Parish; Quechee, Barnard, Bethel, South Royalton and Randolph." [148]

Church Benefactors:

The Billings Estate; Captain Elton Smith, F.P. Billings, James Leonard and Louis Bourdon.

FOOTNOTES

[1] Reverend Zadock Thompson, *History of Vermont, Part Second* (Burlington, Vermont: Reverend Zadock Thompson, 1853), 203.

[2] Very Reverend William Byrne, Right Reverend Stephen S. Michaud, *A History of the Catholic Church in the New England States, Volume 2* (Boston: Hurd and Everts Company, 1899), 586.

[3] HCCNE, 2:528.

[4] HCCNE, 2:528.

[5] Abby Maria Hemenway, Vermont Historical Gazetteer, Volume I (Burlington, Vermont: Abby Maria Hemenway, 1867), 132.

[6] HCCNE, 2:519.

[7] HCCNE, 2:519.

[8] VHG, 2:383.

[9] HCCNE, 2:556.

[10] HCCNE, 2:556.

[11] HCCNE, 2:556.

[12] HCCNE, 2:556.

[13] HCCNE, 2:493.

[14] HCCNE, 2:493.

[15] HCCNE, 2:494.

[16] HCCNE, 2:494.

[17] HCCNE, 2:496.

[18] HCCNE, 2:496.

[19] VHG, 5:50.

[20] VHG, 1:163.

[21] HCCNE, 2:522.

[22] HCCNE, 2:498.

[23] VHG, 3:479.

[24] HCCNE, 2:500.

[25] HCCNE, 2:490.

[26] VHG, 5:33.

[27] HCCNE, 2:493.

[28] HCCNE, 2:502.

[29] HCCNE, 2:502.

[30] VHG, 1:551.

[31] HCCNE, 2:471.

[32] VHG, 2:796.

[33] VHG, 3:744.

[34] HCCNE, 2:507.

[35] VHG, 3:539.

[36] HCCNE, 2:507. The building was then converted to a church.

[37] VHG, 1:103.

[38] VHG, 1:744.

[39] HCCNE, 2:509.

[40] HCCNE, 2:509.

[41] VHG, 3:670.

[42] HCCNE, 2:511.

[43] HCCNE, 2:494.

[44] HCCNE, 2:510.

[45] VHG, 1:191. This account by Dorset resident minister, Rev. P.S.

Pratt, circa 1860.

[46] HCCNE, 2:525.

[47] Walter Hill Crockett, History of Vermont, Volume IV (New York: The Century History Company, Inc., 1921), 131.

[48] HCCNE, 2:512.

[49] VHG, 2:383.

[50] VHG, 2:148.

[51] HCCNE, 2:513.

[52] HCCNE, 2:587. In 1998 this parish is named St. Luke's.

[53] HCCNE, 2:514.

[54] HCCNE, 2:515.

[55] HCCNE, 2:515.

[56] HCCNE, 2:516.

[57] VHG, 2:384.

[58] HCCNE, 2:518.

[59] VHG, 3:720. While this sketch is limited in the information that it furnishes, Fair Haven had a substantial Irish population who came to work in the slate quarries. Evidence of this is a large Catholic cemetery (about 3200 graves) where both Irish and French Canadians are interred.

[60] HCCNE, 2:517.

[61] HCCNE, 2:519.

[62] VHG, 2:384.

[63] HCCNE, 2:537.

[64] HCCNE, 2:518.

[65] Ronald C. Murphy, *Preliminary Research in the U.S.A.: Naturalization Records* (Ulster Genealogical & Historical Guild, Newsletter, Volume 1, Number 8, 1982); 240.

[66] HCCNE, 2:518. For more on the clash between Bishop DeGoesbriand and the parishioners of Highgate see Ronald C. Murphy and Jeffrey Potash, *The Highgate Affair* (Vermont History Magazine, Volume 52, Number 1, Winter 1984); 33.

[67] HCCNE, 2:519.

[68] HCCNE, 2:520.

[69] HCCNE, 2:575.

[70] HCCNE, 2:520.

[71] VHG, 1:954.

[72] VHG, 2:800.

[73] HCCNE, 2:502.

[74] HCCNE, 2:522.

[75] VHG, 3:272.

[76] VHG, 3:272.

[77] HCCNE, 2:526. In 1997 correspondence with the Pastor of The Church of the Annunciation, Ludlow, information was provided indicating the Village of Cavendish also had Irish immigrant residents who attended Mass in Proctorsville and Ludlow.

[78] HCCNE, 2:526.

[79] HCCNE, 2:527. Manchester was on the line of the Rutland and Burlington Railroad, a source of employment for many of the early Irish settlers.

[80] VHG, 1:58.

[81] HCCNE, 2:529. Middlebury was also on the line of the Rutland and Burlington Railroad.

[82] HCCNE, 2:530.

[83] VHG, 1:551.

[84] VHG, 1:542. Joseph Clark, a benefactor of the church, was a founder and partner of the Vermont and Canada Railroad.

[85] HCCNE, 2:531.

[86] HCCNE, 2:532.

[87] VHG, 4:289.

[88] VHG, 4:424.

[89] HCCNE, 2:567.

[90] VHG, 1:542. Moretown is a mountain village and in 1998 is a summer and winter tourist resort.

[91] VHG, 4:602.

[92] HCCNE, 2:511.

[93] HCCNE, 2:533.

[94] HCCNE, 2:534.

[95] HCCNE, 2:536. There is also a second and more modern Catholic cemetery in Northfield located on Vermont Route 12 at the northern limits of the village.

[96] HCCNE, 2:538.

[97] HCCNE, 2:536. Those in residence in 1899 were primarily of French Canadian origins.

[98] HCCNE, 2:537.

[99] HCCNE, 2:537.

[100] HCCNE, 2,538.

[101] VHG, 1:74. The corner stone was laid in 1858, but the church was not completed until 1867. The name of the wealthy citizen was not revealed.

[102] HCCNE, 2:539.

[103] VHG, 3:947.

[104] VHG, 3:965.

[105] VHG, 3:951.

[106] HCCNE, 2:541.

[107] HCCNE, 2:542.

[108] VHG, 2:997.

[109] HCCNE, 2:542.

[110] HCCNE, 2:571.

[111] VHG, 2:1005.

[112] HCCNE, 2:543. Readsboro was not visited. In 1899 there was no Catholic cemetery here, and there is none in 1998. In 1899 Readsboro parish consisted of French Canadian and Italian Immigrants.

[113] HCCNE, 2:513.

[114] VHG, 2:384. The Catholics of Richford were generally employed in agriculture.

[115] HCCNE, 2:544.

[116] HCCNE, 2:547. There is also an older cemetery adjacent to Calvary, but the year of consecration is unknown.

[117] VHG, 2:1029.

[118] HCCNE, 2:548.

[119] HCCNE, 2:545.

[120] HCCNE, 2:549.

[121] HCCNE, 2:550.

[122] HCCNE, 2:558.

[123] HCCNE, 2:527.

[124] HCCNE, 2:551. An older Catholic cemetery is located at the rear of Greenwood Cemetery , a village burial ground located on South Main

inscription section was obtained from the few remaining stones and a card file located in the St. Albans Free Library.

[125] HCCNE, 2:555. Very few, if any, English-speaking Catholics became parishioners of Holy Angels, and the Irish population in this parish was limited. The record of those interred in the French cemetery, Mount Calvary, reflects but a few with Irish surnames.

[126] HCCNE, 2:559.

[127] HCCNE, 2:557. As this parish was but three years of age at the time (1899) of this sketch, no statistical information was furnished, nor were names of parishioners mentioned. The two parishes united in 1966 as a result of a fire. For purposes of this collection, the Church of Our Lady of Victories, later known as Notre Dame, should serve as the focal point for the presence of early Irish Catholics in St. Johnsbury, though the parish was predominately French-Canadian. The merger of these congregations resulted in the renaming of Notre Dame and St. Aloysius to St. John's Church.

[128] HCCNE, 2:562.

[129] VHG, 3:331.

[130] HCCNE, 2:563.

[131] HCCNE, 2:565.

[132] HCCNE, 2:511.

[133] VHG, 3:1182.

[134] VHG, 4:868.

[135] VHG, 4:915.

[136] HCCNE, 2:566.

[137] HCCNE, 2:525.

[138] HCCNE, 2:517.

[139] HCCNE, 2:567.

[140] VHG, 3:1029.

[141] HCCNE, 2:546.

[142] HCCNE, 2:568.

[143] HCCNE, 2:570.

[144] HCCNE, 2:571.

[145] HCCNE, 2:573. There is also a small cemetery in Winooski where some English-speaking parishioners are interred. It is located just off Route 15, east of the Village.

[146] HCCNE, 2:571.

[147] HCCNE, 2:572.

[148] HCCNE, 2:574. This parish does not have a Catholic cemetery, but there is a section of Riverside Cemetery on River Street, Route 4, west of the village, dedicated to Catholic burials.

St. Amadeus Cemetery, Alburg, Vermont. Just west of intersection of Route 78 and U. S. Route 2.

NAME	POB	DOB/AGE	DOD	CEM	SPOUSE/INDEX	INSCRIPTION
Patrick O'CONNOR	Co. Kerry	68 Years	12-31-1886	001	O'CONNOR, Patrick	Born In Cahareleaheon(Caherle-
				001		heen), Co. Kerry, Ireland
				001		
Hugh CALLAGHAN		77 Years	03-22-1905	001	MURPHY, Annie	
Annie MURPHY Callaghan		74 Years	09-06-1906	001	CALLAGHAN, Hugh	
Roseannie CALLAGHAN		54 Years	09-15-1906	001	CALLAGHAN, Roseannie	
James CALLAGHAN		1861	1935	001	CALLAGHAN, James	
				001		
Note: This is primarily a burial ground for French-Canadian				001		
immigrants, being in close proximity to the Canadian border				001		

St. Columban Cemetery, Arlington, VT. South of village on U.S. Route 7

NAME	POB	DOB/AGE	DOD	CEM	SPOUSE/INDEX	INSCRIPTION
Lewis WARD	Co.Roscommon	06-10-1836	05-06-1884	002	WARD, Lewis	Native of Parish St.Johns,Co.
				002		Roscommon, Ireland
				002		
Ann A. BRESNEHAN		27Y 2M 26D	11-10-1882	002	BRESNEHAN, Ann A.	(NOI John Bresnehan)
				002	BRESNEHAN, John	
Michael MORRISEY		1841	1921	002	HOGAN, Maria	
Maria HOGAN Morrissey		1845	1922	002	MORRISEY, Michael	
				002		
Philip E. CULLINAN		1853	1904	002	HAYS, Mary A.	
Mary HAYS Cullinan		1852	1918	002	CULLINAN, Philip E.	
				002		
Edmond CULLINAN	Co.Waterford	06-15-1826	03-10-1887	002	MORRISSEY, Ellen	BornIn Graugvalla(Graigavalla)
				002		Parish ofRaughmic(Rathgormuck)
				002		Co. Waterford, Ireland
Ellen MORRISSEY Cullinan	Co. Waterford	01-25-1832		002	CULLINAN, Edmond	Born In Shaunicle (Shanakill),
				002		Parish Of Raughmic (Rathgor-
				002		muck), Co. Waterford, Ire.
				002		
Catherin HAMILTON		1810	1880	002	HAMILTON, Catherine	
Bridget HOGAN		1812	1868	002	HOGAN, Bridget	
Jeremiah HOGAN		1815	1906	002	HOGAN, Jeremiah	
T. BROTHERS		1837	1915	002	BROTHERS, T.	

Name	Origin	Born	Died	Plot	Index name	Notes
				002		
Margaret MORRISSEY Walsh		01-10-1831	09-13-1885	002	MORRISSEY, Margaret	(NOI John W. Walsh)
				002	WALSH, John W.	
				002		
Frank EDGERTON		08-28-1851	07-28-1912	002	MORRISSEY, Mary A.	
Mary E. MORRISSEY Edgerton		12-24-1853	10-06-1883	002	EDGERTON, Frank	
				002		
William MORRISSEY	Co. Waterford	41 Years	03-14-1868	002	MORRISSEY, Ellen	A Native Of Co. Waterford
				002	HAYE, Margaret	
Ellen _____ MORRISSEY				002	MORRISSEY, William	(Cannot read inscription)
Margaret HAYE Morrissey	Co. Waterford	45 Years	09-12-1873	002	MORRISSEY, William	(Cannot read inscription)
				002		
James THOMPSON		1854	1932	002	CULLINAN, Margaret	
Margaret CULLINAN Thompson		1851	1906	002	THOMPSON, James	
				002		
Patrick SHEVLEN		1858	1915	002	ROWEN, Sophia	
Sophia ROWEN Shevlen		1865	1928	002	SHEVLEN, Patrick	
				002		
Edward KENNNEDY		1842	1912	002	KENNEDY, Edward	
				002		
Michael HIGGINS	Co. Waterford	11-26-1826	01-05-1877	002	CULLINAN, Mary	Born In Waterford County, Ire.
				002		Died In Arlington
Mary CULLINAN Higgins	Co. Waterford	04-23-1831	12-18-1889	002	HIGGINS, Michael	Born In Waterford County, Ire.
				002		Died At Arlington
				002		
Thomas MANN Sr.		1854	1940	002	MANN, Ellen	
Ellen _____ MANN		1857	1945	002	MANN, Thomas Sr.	
				002		
James MANN		1848	1880	002	MORRISSEY, Margaret	
Margaret MORRISSEY Mann		1850	1948	002	MANN, James	
				002		
Margaret QUINN		102 Years	02-15-1879	002	QUINN, Margaret	(NOI-Same plot as Pendergast)
James PENDERGAST	Co. Queens	52 Years	05-10-1868	002	PENDERGAST, James	Born In Queens County,
Ireland.				002		
				002	PENDERGAST, Ann	(NOI Spouse Ann)
Mary PENDERGAST		19Y 2M	12-01-1877	002	PENDERGAST, Mary	Dau of James & Ann Pendergast
				002		
John MORRISSEY		1849	1929	002	MANN, Sarah	
Sarah MANN Morrissey		1849	1944	002	MORRISSEY, John	
				002		
Thomas REID		1848	1911	002	DUNN, Mary	
Mary DUNN Reid		1854	1912	002	REID, Thomas	
				002		
William MURPHY	Co. Cork	1811	1851	002	MURPHY, Julie	Native of Co. Cork. Died at
				002		Bennington, VT

Julie _____ MURPHY	Co. Cork	39 Years	1858	002	MURPHY, WIlliam	Native of Co. Cork. Died at
				002	MURPHY, Rev William	Rutland, VT. (Stone) Erected
				002		by Rev. William Murphy IMO
				002		His Dear Parents
				002		
Bridget DELANEY Canfield		60 Years	01-13-1904	002	CANFIELD, Edward	(NOI Edward Canfield)
				002	DELANEY, Bridget	
				002		
Patrick K. WARD	Co. Roscommon	09-17-1830	01-28-1902	002	MULLEN, Bridget	Native of Co. Roscommon, Ire
Bridget MULLEN Ward	Co. Roscommon	10-19-1839	08-10-1881	002	WARD, Patrick K.	Native of Co. Roscommon, Ire
Mary WARD		07-32-1853	08-10-1881	002	WARD, Mary	Dau of Patrick & Bridget Ward
Margaret E. WARD		1858	1884	002	WARD, Margaret E.	Dau of Patrick & Bridget Ward
				002		
Ellen M. _____ WILSON		03-27-1849	11-06-1896	002	WILSON, H.S.	(NOI H.S. Wilson)
Thomas CULLINAN	Co. Waterford	1820	189	002	WILSON, Ellen M.	
Thomas CULLINAN	Co. Waterford	1820	1898	002	CULLINAN, Mary	Born In Waterford, Ireland
Mary _____ CULLINAN	Co. Waterford	1822	1900	002	CULLINAN, Thomas	Born In Waterford, Ireland
				002		
Philip CULLINAN		1816	1882	002	WHALEN, Margaret	
Margaret WHALEN Cullinan		1820	1902	002	CULLINAN, Philip	
				002		
Philip C. CULLINAN		1850	1921	002	MANN, Bridget A.	
Bridget MANN Cullinan		1851	1934	002	CULLINAN, Philip C.	
				002		
Michael KILLION		1852	1925	002	COLTON, Mary	
Mary COLTON Killion		1854	1930	002	KILLION, Michael	
				002		
John HEMINER		79 Years	05-12-1899	002	HEMINER, Gertrude	
Gertrude _____ HEMINER		72 Years	09-11-1896	002	HEMINER, John	
				002		
William J. BYRNE	Co. Wexford	06-29-1852	04-29-1928	002	WELCH, Ellen J.	
				002	FRAWLEY, Mary	
Ellen J. WELCH Byrne		10-24-1857	04-24-1896	002	BYRNE, William J.	(First Wife)
Mary FRAWLEY Byrne		03-25-1852	12-22-1939	002	BYRNE, William J.	(Second Wife)
				002		
Patrick CULLINAN	Co. Waterford	1850	1921	002	CULLINAN, Julia	Born In Raighgormuck(Rathgor-
				002		muck), Co. Waterford, Ireland
Julia _____ CULLINAN	Co. Kerry	1851	1934	002	CULLINAN, Patrick	Born In Co. Kerry, Ireland
				002		
Thomas CULLINAN	Co. Waterford	05-12-1842	05-24-1913	002	NASH, Bridget	Born In Parish of Raigormic,
				002		(Rathgormuck)Co. Waterford,Ire
Bridget NASH Cullinan	Co. Wexford	12-22-1846	05-31-1926	002	CULLINAN, Thomas	Born In The Parish Killamm
				002		(Killann), Co. Wexford, Ire.
Thomas CULLINAN		1872	1946	002	HAND, Catherine	
Catherine HAND Cullinan	Co. Monahan	06-25-1869	02-25-1909	002	CULLINAN, Thomas	Born In Co. Monahan, Ireland

				002		
Edward CAMPBELL		1836	1918	002	CONLIN, Susan	Corporal, Co. A. NY Vols (GAR)
				002		
Susan CONLIN Campbell		1845	1910	002	CAMPBELL, Edward	
				002		
John CONDON		1834	1899	002	CONDON, Mary	
Mary _____ CONDON			1935	002	CONDON, John	
				002		
James E. CANFIELD		1841	1916	002	CULLINAN, Johanna	
Johanna CULLINAN Canfield		1845	1913	002	CULLINAN, James E.	
				002		
Michael WALLACE		1828		002	KEARWIN, Mary	
Mary KEARWIN		1861	1901	002	WALLACE, Michael	
				002		
John GILFETHER		01-06-1833	02-13-1917	002	GILFETHER, Catherine	
Catherine _____ GILFETHER		04-05-1835	04-14-1914	002	GILFETHER, John	
				002		
Michael MORRISSEY	Co. Waterford	09-25-1835	09-05-1905	002	KIERCE, Susan	Born In Co. Waterford,Ireland
Susan KIERCE Morrissey	Co. Clare	08-29-1835	02-07-1894	002	MORRISSEY, Michael	Born In Co. Clare, Ireland
				002		
Patrick CURRAN		1824	1902	002	CURRAN, Ann M.	
Ann M. CURRAN		1829	1915	002	CURRAN, Patrick	
Bridget TIVANAN Curry		1796	1880	002	CURRY, William	(NOI William Curry)
				002	TIVANAN, Bridget	
				002		
Patrick SUMMERS		03-16-1835	12-05-1884	002	SUMMERS, Catharine	
Catharine _____ SUMMERS		77 Years	07-21-1905	002	SUMMERS, Patrick	
				002		
John MORRISSEY	Co. Waterford	77 Years	12-14-1890	002	MORRISSEY, Anne S.	(Both) Born in Grangvalla
Anne S. _____ MORRISSEY	Co. Waterford	80 Years	10-24-1887	002	MORRISSEY, John	(Graigavalla),Parish of Raugh-
				002		nic (Rathgormuck), Co. Water-
				002		ford, Ireland
				002		
William WALSH		1832	1913	002	KELLEY, Katharine	
Katharine KELLEY Walsh		1850	1920	002	WALSH, William	
				002		
James WALSH		03-07-1822		002	WALSH, Bridget	
Bridget _____ WALSH		10-22-1829	07-05-1900	002	WALSH, James	
				002		
John J. COUGHLIN		1848	1916	002	GREGG, Delia M.	
Delia M. GREGG Coughlin		1858	1935	002	COUGHLIN, John J.	
				002		
Hugh KENNA		45 Years	02-01-1874	002	KENNA, Hugh	

Thomas DUNN		57 Years	03-02-1874	002	DUNN, Margaret	
Margaret _____ DUNN		80 Years	02-07-1907	002	DUNN, Thomas	
				002		
Richard DELANEY		1837	1927	002	JACKSON, Julia	
Julia JACKSON Delaney		1839	1910	002	DELANEY, Richard	
				002		
Patrick MORRISSEY		03-18-1827	11-28-1888	002	MORRISSEY, Margaret	
Margaret _____ MORRISSEY		05-02-1827		002	MORRISSEY, Patrick	
				002		
Patrick KEOUGH	Co. Kings	04-20-1820	1900	002	MURRY, Anna Stachia	Born in Tullamore, Kings Co, Ireland
				002		
Anna Stachia MURRY Keough	Co. Waterford	03-20-1828	05-30-1890	002	KEOUGH, Patrick	Born In Tramore, Co.Waterford Ireland
				002		
				002		
Alexander WALSH		1846	1917	002	HAYDEN, Katherine	
Katherine HAYDEN Walsh		1845	1917	002	WALSH, Alexander	
				002		
John TYNAN	Co. Carlow	05-04-1831	12-15-1896	002	DUNN, Rose Anna	Born in Co. Carlow, Ireland
Rose Anna DUNN Tynan	Co. Kings	08-12-1830	01-10-1906	002	TYNAN, John	Born In Kings Co., Ireland
				002		
Patrick CULLINAN		1850	1915	002	HANLEY, Margaret	
Margaret HANLEY Cullinan		1868	1926	002	CULLINAN, Patrick	
				002		
James HANLEY				002	HANLEY, Mary	(NOI James Hanley)
Mary _____ HANLEY		65 Years	05-29-1888	002	HANLEY, James	

St. Monica's Cemetery, Beckley Street, Barre, Vermont

NAME	POB	DOB/AGE	DOD	CEM	SPOUSE	INSCRIPTION
Michael MARRION		1843	1904	004	MARRION, Michael	Co. A. 93rd NY Inf (GAR)
				004		
Martin RILEY		1852	1923	004	MCMAHON, Jane	
				004	BROWN, Mary Ann	
Jane MCMAHON Riley		1856	1896	004	RILEY, Martin	
Mary Ann BROWN Riley		1854	1942	004	RILEY, Martin	
				004		
Margaret MURPHY		05-01-1831	03-05-1894	004	MURPHY, Margaret	
				004		
Michael GARVEY		06-20-1847	07-02-1908	004	_____, Mary	
Mary _____ GARVEY		02-23-1847	11-09-1919	004	GARVEY, Michael	

Name	Birthplace	Born	Died	Code	Spouse	Notes
Hugh GARVEY		1844	1904	004	_____, Annie	
Annie _____ GARVEY		1850	1931	004	GARVEY, Hugh	
				004		
Timothy W. MOYNIHAN		1854	1904	004	MOYNIHAN, Timothy W.	
				004		
James MCGUE		1845	1905	004	MCGOVERN, Anna E.	
Anna E. MCGOVERN McGue		1858	1918	004	MCGUE, James	
				004		
James O'CONNER		40 Years	02-06-1899	004	O'CONNER, James	
				004		
Edward GORMAN		1837	1914	004	FLOOD, Elizabeth	Cos. F,K. 10th & 15th Vt Rgts
Elizabeth FLOOD Gorman		1838	1918	004	GOREMAN, Edward	(GAR)
				004		
F. L. DOYLE		1856	1904	004	DOYLE, F. L.	
				004		
Robert SHANNON		73 Years	08-09-1903	004	SHANNON, Robert	(GAR)Try Co. H,14th RGT, VtVol
				004		
James A. MCKANE		1838	1909	004	_____, Mary	
Mary A. _____ MCKANE		1841	1917	004	MCKANE, James	
				004		
James KELLEY		12-26-1817	03-02-1898	004	_____, Maria H.	
Maria H. _____ KELLEY		04-10-1828	01-22-1899	004	KELLEY, James	
				004		
Patrick MANNING		1845	1909	004	MANNING, Patrick	
				004		
Nancy MOONEY		1842	1917	004	MOONEY, Nancy	
				004		
Peter C. OWENS		1849	1928	004	MILES, Mary J.	
Mary J. MILES Owens		1850	1918	004	OWENS, Peter C.	
				004		
Willis J. HENRY		01-14-1859	06-21-1927	004	KELLEY, Mary J.	
Mary J. KELLEY Henry		12-12-1853	04-12-1923	004	HENRY, Willis J.	
				004		
Patrick HEALY	Co. Tipperary	1830	1918	004	HEALY, Patrick	Born At Tipperary, Ireland
				004		
Patrick CLARK		09-06-1834	05-19-1915	004	_____, Sarah	
Sarah _____ CLARK		11-01-1838	04-16-1907	004	CLARK, Patrick	
				004		
John KINGSTON	Ireland	1822	1900	004	_____, Mary	Native Of Ireland
Mary _____ KINGSTON	Ireland	1826	1898	004	KINGSTON, John	Native Of Ireland
				004		
Nelson HAMEL		02-15-1839	02-16-1923	004	TIERNEY, Mary	
Mary TIERNEY Hamel		05-02-1842	02-07-1907	004	HAMEL, Nelson	
				004		
Sandy COOK		05-07-1840	05-07-1894	004	_____, Elvira	(GAR)Try Co. C.,4th Rgt, VtVol

NAME	POB	DOB/AGE	DOD	CEM	SPOUSE/INDEX	INSCRIPTION
Elvira _____ COOK		1846	1919	004	COOK, Sandy	
				004		
Thomas HOUGHTON		1839	1916	004	MONAGHAN, Margaret	
Margaret MONAGHAN Houghton		1845	1929	004	HOUGHTON, Thomas	
				004		
William SHERIDAN		05-23-1837	07-22-1907	004	KEENAN, Mary	
Mary KEENAN Sheridan		05-09-1836	07-08-1916	004	SHERIDAN, William	

St. Paul's Cemetery, Barton, Vermont. Just off the end of High Street

NAME	POB	DOB/AGE	DOD	CEM	SPOUSE/INDEX	INSCRIPTION
Henry F. CLIFFORD		65 Years	02-18-1903	005	CLIFFORD, Martha S.	
Martha S. _____ CLIFFORD		79 Years	09-24-1919	005	CLIFFORD, Henry F.	
				005		
James CASSIDY		10-13-1845	01-22-1911	005	KEATING, Mary	
Mary KEATING Cassidy		05-01-1853	06-29-1945	005	CASSIDY, James	
				005		
Mitchell LEONARD		10-30-1855	02-19-1927	005	LEONARD, Mitchell	
				005		
E. C. WILKIE		1857	1938	005	GAREY, Joanna H.	
Joanna H. GAREY Wilkie		1857	1951	005	WILKIE, E. C.	
				005		
John KERR		1828	1903	005	SCARRY, Mary	
Mary SCARRY Kerr		1834	1920	005	KERR, John	
				005		
Michael J. RYAN		1857	1939	005	RYAN, Jennie A.	(Span Am War)Co. L. 1st VT Inf
Jennie A. _____ RYAN		1875	1904	005	RYAN, Michael J.	
				005		
Thomas CAHILL		64Y4M18D	09-26-1909	005	RICE, Margaret	
Margaret RICE Cahill		1854	1930	005	CAHILL, Thomas	

NOTE: This is primarily a French Canadian Burial Ground

St.George Cemetery - Bakersfield, Vt (Off Vt Highway 108 in Center of Village)

NAME	POB	DOB/AGE	DOD	CEM	SPOUSE/INDEX	INSCRIPTION
George A. MCNANEY		1850	1907	006	ROARK, Mary	
Mary ROARK McNaney		1852	1923	006	MCNANEY, George A.	

Margaret ____ MCNANEY	74 Years	09-03-1899	006	MCNANEY, Barney	(NOI Barney McNaney)
			006	____, Margaret	
Anna MCNANEY	51 Years	06-12-1896	006	MCNANEY, Anna	
Mary MCNANEY	2Y 9M	11-10-1856	006	MCNANEY, Mary	Children of Barney & Margaret
Ellen MCNANEY	9 Months	11-11-1856	006	MCNANEY, Ellen	McNaney
Lizzie MCNANEY	22 Years	04-23-1889	006	MCNANEY, Lizzie	" " " " "
Barney MCNANEY	26 Years	11-09-1884	006	MCNANEY, Barney	" " " " "
			006		
William H. COOK	07-10-1854	06-23-1925	006	MCGINN, Mary E.	
Mary E. MCGINN Cook			006	COOK, William H.	
			006		
Peter COOK	63 Years	04-19-1833	006	____, Ann C.	
Ann C. ____ COOK	64Y 9M 5D	02-22-1880	006	COOK, Peter	
Julia A. COOK	26Y 5M 18D	04-21-1874	006	COOK, Julia A.	Children of Peter & Ann Cook
Michael P. COOK	20Y 13D	10-10-1877	006	COOK, Michael P.	" " " " " "
			006		
William MORAN	78 Years	07-05-1879	006	____, Nancy	
			006	MORAN, William	(NOI Nancy Moran)
James MORAN	31 Years	05-19-1871	006	MORAN, James	Son Of William & Nancy Moran
			006		
Patrick LAW	10-01-1850	11-28-1924	006	LAW, Patrick	
			006		
William CASEY	1842	1929	006	CASEY, William	(On Erickson Family Stone)
			006		
A. B. ROONEY	03-19-1854	03-31-1922	006	BENNETT, Rossie D.	
Rossie D. BENNETT Rooney	03-08-1863	11-04-1952	006	ROONEY, A. B.	
			006		
Delia A. MCNANY Gray	34Y 13D	03-21-1891	006	GRAY, John	(NOI John Gray)
			006	MCNANY, Delia A.	
			006		
Michael CAREY	1853	1931	006	LAW, Mary A.	
Mary A. LAW Carey	1854	1912	006	CAREY, Michael	
			006		
Francis RAVEY	1825	1899	006	ROONEY, Ann	
Ann ROONEY Ravey	67 Years	04-22-1898	006	RAVEY, Francis	
			006		
James MCENANEY	1838	1923	006	MCENANEY, James	(GAR)Try Co. G. 13th Rgt,Vt
			006		Vol
Edward NULTY	70 Years	11-21-1877	006	CAFFREY, Rose	
Rose CAFFREY Nulty	1815	1896	006	NULTY, Edward	
Terrence NULTY	38Y1M18D	10-25-1878	006	NULTY, Terrence	Died In Boston
Kattie NULTY	26Y 10M	04-04-1881	006	NULTY, Kattie	Died In Bakersfield
Edward NULTY	23Y	05-06-1874	006	NULTY, Edward	
Elizabeth NULTY	1848	1922	006	NULTY, Elizabeth	

Rose NULTY	1854	1928	006	NULTY, Rose	
Thomas NULTY	1853	1934	006	NULTY, Thomas	
			006		
John KEAHOE	62 Years	09-17-1884	006	KEAHOE, John	
			006		
James O'NEILL	56 Years	08-08-1871	006	______, Mary	
Mary ______ O'NEILL	84 Years	08-09-1902	006	O'NEILL, James	
Ann O'NEILL	06-15-1848	05-02-1911	006	O'NEILL, Ann	
			006		
Hugh MAGINN	1814	1890	006	_____, Catharine	
Catharine ____ MAGINN	1822	1894	006	MAGINN, Hugh	
Annie CONNOR	1862	1893	006	CONNOR, Annie	
			006		
Mary Ann O'BRIEN Conley		05-09-1904	006	CONLEY, Patrick	(NOI Patrick Conley)
			006	O'BRIEN, Mary Ann	
James MCELROY	1824	1890	006	MCCOY, Mary A.	
Mary A. MCCOY McElroy	1835	1889	006	MCELROY, James	
			006		
John KENNEDY	06-22-1830	05-13-1903	006	_____, Bridget	
Bridget ___ KENNEDY	1821	1911	006	KENNEDY, John	
			006		
Edward BRADY	1848	1906	006	MCGINN, Alice	
Alice MCGINN Brady	1855	1907	006	BRADY, Edward	
			006		
Lawrence KENNEDY	10-30-1852	10-05-1933	006	MCGINN, Ann	
Ann MCGINN Kennedy	02-16-1850	06-09-1935	006	KENNEDY, Lawrence	
			006		
Bernard MORAN	1859	1918	006	FOOTE, Geneva C.	
Geneva C. FOOTE Moran	1854	1918	006	MORAN, Bernard	
			006		
Jas MCNANY	--	--	006	MCNANY, Jas	(GAR) Co. I, 10 Vt Inf (NOI)
			006		
William M. SINNOT	1850	1910	006	SINNOTT, William M	
			006		
Mary E. SINNOTT	1830	1906	006	SINNOTT, Mary E.	Dau of Moses & Ellinor Roach
			006		Sinnott
Agness SINNOTT Keahoe	1850	1909	006	KEAHOE, Thomas	Dau of Moses & Ellinor Roach
			006	SINNOTT, Agness	Sinnott (NOI Thomas Keahoe)
			006		
Caleb SHELLEY	01-10-1819	06-17-1904	006	LAWRENCE, Mary	
Mary LAWRENCE Shelley	08-15-1825	10-20-1898	006	SHELLEY, Caleb	
			006		
Henry C. LEACH	05-27-1850	03-01-1924	006	SHELLEY, Mary	
Mary SHELLEY Lawrence	01-24-1852	06-03-1919	006	LEACH, Henry C.	

William HOWRIGAN	62 Years	05-15-1878	006	____, Mary	
Mary ____ HOWRIGAN	72 Years	01-18-1892	006	HOWRIGAN, William	
			006		
Moses SINNOT	49 Years	08-07-1854	006	ROACH, Ellenor	
Ellenor ROACH Sinnot	78 Years	11-02-1884	006	SINNOT, Moses	
John E. SINNOTT	81 Years	04-13-1918	006	____, Sarah	
			006	____, Margaret	
Sarah ____ SINNOTT	28 Years	07-17-1886	006	SINNOTT, John E.	
Margaret ____ SINNOTT	23 Years	03-14-1874	006	SINNOTT, John E.	
Jane SINNOTT Rhodes	40 Years	03-17-1874	006	SINNOTT, Jane	Dau's Of Moses & Ellenor
			006		Sinnott (NOI Mr. Rhodes)
Ellenor SINNOTT Duffy	25 Years	12-10-1864	006	SINNOTT, Ellenor	Dau's Of Moses & Ellenor
			006		Sinnott (NOI Mr. Duffy)
			006		
John MCMAHON	07-07-1841	04-03-1911	006	MCMAHON, John	(GAR) Co. G, 13th Vt. Vols
			006		
Thomas MCMAHON	1844	1924	006	MCNANEY, Catherine	
Catherine MCNANEY McMahon	1849	1924	006	MCMAHON, Thomas	
			006		
Hugh MCMAHON	62Y 3M	11-14-1874	006	OWENS, Ann	
Ann OWENS McMahon	85Y 2M	10-19-1883	006	MCMAHON, Hugh	
			006		
John TAGUE	1844	1915	006	MCMAHAN, Bridget	(GAR) Co. G, 13th Vt. Vols
Bridget MCMAHAN Tague	1840	1881	006	TAGUE, John	
			006		
Owen CAMPBELL	67 Years	11-01-1883	006	MELAUEN, Mary	
Mary MELAUEN Campbell	54 Years	04-14-1876	006	CAMPBELL, Owen	(Surname possibly Melaven)
			006		
William MORAN	04-30-1836	12-20-1927	006	MCGETTRICK, Catherine	
Catherine MCGETTRICK Moran	57Y 6M	06-30-1890	006	MORAN, William	
			006		
T.D. RILEY	67 Years	07-13-1888	006	RILEY, T.D.	
			006		
John MCENANY	77 Years	04-05-1895	006	MCENANY, John	
			006		
James HALLINAN	37 Years	06-22-1891	006	MORAN, Ellen A.	
Ellen A. MORAN Hallinan	56 Years	11-23-1905	006	HALLINAN, James	
			006		
James BRADY	87 Years	11-13-1885	006	CAFFARY, Bridget	
Bridget CAFFARY Brady	82 Years	08-02-1892	006	BRADY, James	(Surname possibly Caffrey)
Rose BRADY	43Y8M25D	01-26-1877	006	BRADY, Rose	
			006		
Patrick BRADY	1840	1928	006	SINNOTT, Christina	
Christina SINNOTT Brady	1845	1928	006	BRADY, Patrick	
Eleanor BRADY	--	--	006	BRADY, Eleanor	

NAME	POB	DOB/AGE	DOD	CEM	SPOUSE/INDEX	INSCRIPTION
Agnes BRADY		--	--	006	BRADY, Agnes	
James BRADY		--	--	006	BRADY, James	
Rolland BRADY		--	--	006	BRADY, Rolland	
				006		
Patrick SLOAN		1855	1938	006	MORAN, Phoebe E.	
Phoebe E. MORAN Sloan		1846	1915	006	SLOAN, Patrick	
				006		
Hannah ____ MCGOOKIN		62 Years	05-16-1885	006	MCGOOKIN, Rodney	(NOI Rodney McGookin)
				006	_____, Hannah	
				006		
Barney MCGOOKIN		28 Years	09-04-1862	006	_____, Catherine	(GAR) Co E. 8th Rgt Vt Vols
				006		(Listed as Henry McGookin In
				006		Roster of Vermont Volunteers,
				006		1861-1866-Killed in Action)
Catherine ___ MCGOOKIN		1825	1907	006	MCGOOKIN, Barney	
				006		
Austin MCGRAIL		1854	1935	006	WALKER, Esther	
Esther WALKER McGrail		1856	1937	006	MCGRAIL, Austin	
				006		
Mary CRONAN Beattey		35 Years	12-23-1886	006	BEATTEY, Arthur W.	(NOI Arthur W. Beattey)
				006	CRONAN, Mary	
				006		
James B. LAW		08-01-1843	01-03-1908	006	MURPHY, Elizabeth T.	
Elizabeth T. MURPHY LAW		07-16-1847	03-31-1906	006	LAW, James B.	
				006		
Thomas MORRIS		1817	1906	006	BURKE, Mary	
Mary BURKE Morris		1827	1881	006	MORRIS, Thomas	
				006		
James BOYLAN		1841	1913	006	BOYLAN, James	(GAR) Priv Co. K 6th Vt Vols
				006		Corp Co. K 26th Mass
				006		
Peter GRANGE		86 Years	08-03-1891	006	GRANGE, Peter	
				006		
John BRADY		1832	1888	006	____, Mary	
Mary ___ BRADY		1838	1918	006	BRADY, John	

Restland Cemetery, Bellows Falls, Vermont. On Old Terrace Street. Take left from Vermont Route 5 on VT 121.Top of Hill on Right

NAME	POB	DOB/AGE	DOD	CEM	SPOUSE/INDEX	INSCRIPTION
Michael O'CONNELL		03-12-1847	08-11-1899	007	O'CONNELL, Mary	
Mary E. _____ O'CONNELL		01-12-1844	04-08-1897	007	O'CONNELL, Michael	

Thomas DRISCOLL	Co. Kerry	44 Years	09-24-1886	007	DRISCOLL, Thomas	Native of County Kerry,Parish
				007		Of Abeydorney (Abbeydorney)
				007		
Patrick HARTY		1846	1924	007	MCNAMARA, Bridget	
Bridget MCNAMARA Harty		1842	1912	007	HARTY, Patrick	
				007		
Mary KEANE Marlborough		1842	1912	007	MARLBOROUGH Patrick	(NOI Patrick Marlborough)
				007	KEANE, Mary	
Margaret _____ MALBORO		38 Years	05-10-1874	007	MALBORO, Thomas	(NOI Thomas Malboro. Stone is
				007	MALBORO, Margaret	eroded)
				007		
Mary _____ DRISCOLL			11-22-1886	007	DRISCOLL, Francis	(NOI Francis Driscoll. No DOB
				007	DRISCOLL, Mary	for Mary)
				007		
Daniel HIGGINS		1826	1897	007	O'LEARY, Mary	
Mary O'LEARY Higgins		1823	1913	007	HIGGINS, Daniel	
Joanna M. HIGGINS		24 Years	06-05-1876	007	HIGGINS, Joanna	
Mary E. HIGGINS Ford		20 Years	03-20-1876	007	HIGGINS, Mary E.	(NOI William Ford-Age at death
				007	FORD, William	hard to read-appears to be 20)
Thomas HIGGINS		28 Years	03-10-1886	007	HIGGINS, Thomas	
Katherine HIGGINS		01-03-1849	05-07-1901	007	HIGGINS, Katherine	
Ellen HIGGINS		10-12-1850	12-25-1900	007	HIGGINS, Ellen	
				007		
Thomas LONERGAN		74 Years	03-24-1906	007	LONERGAN, Ellen	
Ellen _____ LONERGAN		41 Years	10-20-1874	007	LONERGAN, Thomas	
				007		
Margaret MCMAHON	Co. Clare	60 Years	11-19-1874	007	MCMAHON, Margaret	Native of Parish of Lahinch,
				007		County Clare, Ireland
				007		
John O'CONNELL		80 Years	08-05-1893	007	O'CONNELL, Catherine	
Catherine _____ O'CONNELL				007	O'CONNELL, John	(Stone badly worn-cannot read)
				007		
Thomas KINIRY		59 Years	03-26-1896	007	CALLAHAN, Bridget	
Bridget CALLAHAN Kiniry		43 Years	03-17-1884	007	KINIRY, Thomas	
				007		
John MCNAMARA			06-06-1892	007	BURKE, Julia	
Julia BURKE McNamara			11-06-1893	007	MCNAMARA, John	
James MCNAMARA		05-08-1858	11-03-1890	007	MCNAMARA, James	
Morris MCNAMARA		01-02-1861	11-27-1883	007	MCNAMARA, Morris	
Michael MCNAMARA		04-14-1867	12-17-1887	007	MCNAMARA, Michael	
				007		
Edward J. HOWARD		08-18-1847	03-20-1913	007	HOWARD, Edward J.	(NOI Spouse Maria S. Cray)
				007	CRAY, Maria S.	

Name		Born	Died		Index	Notes
Eugene E. CRAY		1855	1932	007	CREHAN, Margaret W.	
Margaret W. CREHAN Cray		1855	1929	007	CRAY, Eugene E.	
Annie CREHAN		1853	1886	007	CREHAN, Annie	
				007		
Edward HOGAN		07-15-1826	09-08-1912	007	O'HARE, Bridget	
Bridget O'HARE Hogan		06-20-1825	08-21-1896	007	HOGAN, Edward	
Catherine M. HOGAN		11-22-1851	09-23-1910	007	HOGAN, Catherine M.	
Hugh HOGAN		06-04-1870	10-10-1910	007	HOGAN, Hugh	
				007		
Michael KELLY		1858	1932	007	GORDON, Honora	
Honora GORDON Kelly		1859	1926	007	KELLY, Michael	
				007		
Bridget _____ NEILAN			1883	007	NEILAN, Michael	(Stone virtually unreadable.
				007	NEILAN, Bridget	NOI Michael Neilan)
				007		
Ennis LANE		45 Years	01-13-1888	007	SULLIVAN, Hanora	
Hanora SULLIVAN Lane		72 Years	05-06-1913	007	LANE, Ennis	
				007		
James SLATTERY		1835	1884	007	HOWARD, Ellen	
Ellen HOWARD Slattery		1835	1853	007	SLATTERY, James	
				007		
John POWERS		36 Years	07-04-1870	007	NORMOYLE, Honore	
Honore NORMYLE Powers			09-26-1910	007	POWERS, John	(NOI DOB Honore Normoyle)
				007		
Joseph MCGREEN		1857	1924	007	SAVAGE, Nora	
Nora SAVAGE McGreen		1866	1929	007	MCGREEN, Joseph	
				007		
Thomas LYNCH		76 Years	07-11-1916	007	HOLLAND, Abigail	
Abigail HOLLAND Lynch	Co. Cork	76 Years	07-20-1899	007	LYNCH, Thomas	Born In Dromdaleague, County
				007		Cork, Ireland
				007		
John BRENNAN		1847	1914	007	BRENNAN, Catherine	
Catherine _____ BRENNAN		1848	1916	007	BRENNAN, John	
				007		
Mary GRIFFIN		89 Years	07-17-1884	007	GRIFFIN, Mary	
				007		
Thomas MARLBOROUGH		1844	1919	007	CONDON, Eliza C.	
Eliza C. CONDON Marlborough		1852	1923	007	MARLBOROUGH, Thomas	
				007		
William CONDON		42 Years	11-12-1882	007	CONDON, William	
				007		
John H. MORIARTY		74 Years	10-12-1892	007	O'CONNOR, Johanna	
Johanna O'CONNOR Moriarty		71 Years	05-11-1885	007	MORIARTY, John H.	
Patrick O. DOOLITTLE		32Y 6M	1900	007	DOOLITTLE, Patrick	
Winston P. MORIARTY		36Y 9M	07-31-1887	007	MORIARTY, Winston P.	

John E. CRAY		1857	1917	007	SLATTERY, Mary V.	
Mary V. SLATTERY Cray		1855	1926	007	CRAY, John E.	
P. J. CRAY		1815	1882	007	CRAY, P. J.	His Father
				007		
Ellen CRAY	Co. Kerry		09-06-__	007	CRAY, Ellen	(Impossible to read. County
				007		Kerry and YY/MM of death only)
				007		
Catharine WOLFE		1843	1915	007	WOLFE, Catharine	
				007		
James SULLIVAN		1830	1925	007	O'BRIEN, Ellen	
Ellen O'BRIEN Sullivan		1846	1925	007	SULLIVAN, James	
				007		
John BROWN		1822	1897	007	SULLIVAN, Hanora	
Hanora SULLIVAN Brown		1821	1906	007	BROWN, John	
				007		
John FINNIGAN		37 Years	05-17-1870	007	FINNIGAN, John	(Difficult to read.Age @ death
				007		could be 37, 87 or 97)
				007		
Patrick BOWEN		70 Years	05-07-1882	007	HAGERTY, Ellen	
Ellen HAGERTY Bowen		48 Years	07-29-1875	007	BOWEN, Patrick	
Ellen R. KINIRY		1851	1921	007	KINIRY, Ellen R.	
				007		
John O'CONNELL				007	WELSH, Catherine	(NOI DOB or DOD this family)
Catherine WELSH O'Connell				007	O'CONNELL, John	
Annie O'CONNELL				007	O'CONNELL, Annie	Daughter
Ellen O'CONNEL Cadigan				007	O'CONNELL, Ellen	(NOI Mr. Cadigan)
				007		
Dennis FLAVIN		1840	1903	007	NEILAN, Catherine	
Catherine NEILAN Flavin		1839	1928	007	FLAVIN, Dennis	
Michael NEILAN		1800	1871	007	NEILAN, Michael	
Marty BOOTH		1842	1876	007	BOOTH, Mary	
				007		
Garratt PIERCE		12-24-1841	03-03-1918	007	BRADY, Ellen	
Ellen BRADY Pierce		04-23-1851	04-08-1918	007	PIERCE, Garratt	
				007		
John BROSNAHAN	Co. Kerry	56 Years	10-30-1878	007	LAWLOR, Ellen	Native of Parish of _____, Co.
Ellen Lawlor BROSNAHAN		78 Years	12-07-1908	007	BROSNAHAN, John	Kerry, Ireland.(Cannot read.
Thomas P. BROSNAHAN		04-10-1857	10-15-1927	007	BROSNAHAN, Thomas P.	Possibly Currans or Town of
Nellie M. BROSNAHAN		16Y 8M	12-29-1881	007	BROSNAHAN, Nellie M.	Gullane)
				007		
Jeremiah KEEFE		79 Years	05-03-1886	007	DRISLANE, Mary	
Mary DRISLANE Keefe		89 Years	02-21-1908	007	KEEFE, Jeremiah	
				007		
Mary GRIFFIN		75 Years	12-13-1912	007	GRIFFIN, Mary	

Alice MCCARTHY		68 Years	08-05-1860	007	MCCARTHY, Alice	
				007		
John KING		1847	1909	007	KING, Johanna	
Johanna _____ KING		26Y 5M	09-15-1881	007	KING, John	
				007		
Patrick SHAUGHNESSY		03-15-1835	10-26-1912	007	KING, Margaret	
Margaret KING Shaughnessy		04-10-1850	05-23-1927	007	SHAUGHNESSY, Patrick	
				007		
Michael O'HALLORAN		60 Years	08-07-1890	007	KEEFE, Nora	
Nora KEEFE O'Halloran		08-09-1837	08-29-1918	007	O'HALLORAN, Michael	
Mary BROWN Keefe		53 Years	04-12-1871	007	KEEFE, Cornelius	(NOI Cornelius Keefe)
				007	BROWN, Mary	
				007		
Michael FINN	Co. Cork	56 Years		007	LEARY, Katherine	Born In County Cork, Parish Of
Katherine LEARY Finn	Co. Cork	46 Years		007	FINN, Michael	Bandon (NOI DOD on both)
William FINN		1851	1921	007	FINN, William	
John FINN		1857	1931	007	FINN, John	Erected by John Finn
				007		
Thomas HALLAHAN		1824	04-13-1887	007	CONNELLY, Johanna	
Johanna CONNELLY Hallahan		60 Years	04-07-1896	007	HALLAHAN, Thomas	
Michael HALLAHAN	Co. Cork	1788	05-12-1873	007	HALLAHAN, Michael	Born In Youghal, Co. Cork, Ire
				007		
John SAVAGE			04-04-__	007	SAVAGE, John	(Stone Deteriorated -
				007		unreadable)
David SAVAGE		08-20-1849	10-20-1937	007	KEEFE, Ellen	
Ellen KEEFE Savage		05-08-1849	11-01-1929	007	SAVAGE, David	
				007		
James DUNN		82 Years	12-03-1903	007	DUNN, James	
				007		
Rosanna SMITH Dunn		87 Years	06-17-1905	007	SMITH, Rosanna	(NOI Daniel Dunn)
Lizzie DUNN		19Y 5M	05-29-1874	007	DUNN, Lizzie	Dau Of Rosanna & Daniel Dunn
				007		
Johanne _____ HART	Co. Cork	57 Years	02-18-1865	007	HART, Johanne	Co. Cork, Parish (unreadable)
				007	HART, Daniel	(NOI Daniel Hart)
				007		
Richard WOLFE	Co. Limerick	46 Years	06-01-1870	007	WOLFE, Mary C.	Native of Athea, Co. Limerick
Mary C. WOLFE		1829	1920	007	WOLFE, Richard	Ireland
				007		
Bartholomew REDY		65 Years	09-16-1876	007	SULLIVAN, Catherine	
Catherine SULLIVAN Redy		33 Years	04-24-1863	007	REDY, Bartholomew	
James S. RADY		48 Years	07-19-1906	007	RADY, James S.	
				007		
Margaret REDY		23 Years	07-29-1874	007	REDY, Margaret	D/O Bartholomew and Catherine
				007		Redy

Johanna MURPHY Sullivan	Co. Limerick	85 Years	06-23-1876	007	SULLIVAN, Timothy	Native of Co. Limerick, Ire.
				007		
				007	MURPHY, Johanna	(NOI Timothy Sullivan
				007		
Owen KEEFE		38 Years	07-23-1862	007	TROY, Jane	
Jane TROY Keefe		05-01-1823	04-01-1917	007	KEEFE, Owen	
				007		
Eugene E. FLAVIN		1855	1930	007	SULLIVAN, Julia M.	
Julia M. SULLIVAN Flavin		1854	1947	007	FLAVIN, Eugene E.	
Thomas FLAVIN		1853	1927	007	FLAVIN, Thomas	
				007		
Michael O'CONNOR		12-25-1833	06-25-1906	007	O'CONNOR, Michael	
				007		
James HYDE	Co. Cork			007	HYDE, James	Born In Parish Youghal, County
				007	HYDE, Thomas	Cork, Ireland. SOn Of Thomas &
				007	HYDE, Ellen	Ellen Hyde (NOI DOB-DOD James)
				007		
Patrick M. SULLIVAN		51 Years	02-01-1890	007	SULLIVAN, Margaret	(NOI Spouse Margaret)
				007	SULLIVAN, Patrick M.	
				007		
Thomas MCDONALD		79 Years	06-26-1896	007	BYRNE, Jane	
Jane BYRNE McDonald		84 Years	05-24-1905	007	MCDONALD, Thomas	
William MCDONALD		1859	1918	007	MCDONALD, William	
				007		
				007		
Michael SULLIVAN		19 Years	02-12-1862	007	SULLIVAN, Michael	(Cannot read age at death.
				007		Could be other than 19)
Catherine SULLIVAN		15 Years	09-03-1859	007	SULLIVAN, Catherine	D/o Michael & Margaret
				007		Sullivan
				007	SULLIVAN, Margaret	
				007		
James DRISLAWN		76Y 7M	01-17-1902	007	COLLINS, Mary	
Mary COLLINS Drislawn		62 Years	09-07-1895	007	DRISLAWN, James	
				007		
James DIGGINS		73 Years	01-27-1896	007	DIGGINS, Honora	
Honora ______ DIGGINS		76 Years	12-31-1904	007	DIGGINS, James	
Nora E. DIGGINS		09-13-1854	02-13-1895	007	DIGGINS, Nora E.	Their Children
James J. DIGGINS		09-12-1858	08-12-1882	007	DIGGINS, James	Their Children
				007		
Dan HICKEY		14Y10M6D	08-02-1869	007	HICKEY, Dan	S/O Michael & Margaret Hickey
				007	HICKEY, Michael	
				007	HICKEY, Margaret	
John SHEEHAN				007	SHEEHAN, John	(Stone broken, missing. NOI)
				007		
Mary BROSNAHAN Tyter			1863	007	BROSNASHAN, Mary	(DOB unreadable. NOI William)

Name	Birthplace	Birth/Age	Death	Code	Index Name	Notes
				007	TYTER, William	
				007		
Patrick CASEY			03-06-1892	007	CASEY, Patrick	(DOB unreadable)
				007		
Abby SULLIVAN Tyter		31 Years	05-14-1862	007	SULLIVAN, Abby	(NOI Michael Tyter)
				007	TYTER, Michael	
				007		
Johanna _____ TYTER		31 Years	12-03-1873	007	TYTER, Johanna	(YOD C/B 1878.NOI David Tyter)
				007	TYTER, David	
				007		
Cornelius DONOVAN		1805	1879	007	REARDON, Johanna	
Johanna REARDON Donovan		1809	1860	007	DONOVAN, Cornelius	
Mary A. DONOVAN		1842	1928	007	DONOVAN, Mary A.	
				007		
John RYAN		45 Years	03-27-1866	007	HAYES, Ellen	
Ellen HAYES Ryan		65 Years	03-03-1884	007	RYAN, John	
				007		
Winifred HAYES		74Y7M15D		007	HAYES, Winifred	Mother of Michael Hayes.(NOI DOD)
				007		
Michael HAYES		48 Years	05-08-1875	007	HAYES, Michael	
				007		
John DONOVAN		33 Years	10-31-1867	007	KING, Johanna	
Johanna KING Donovan				007	DONOVAN, John	(NOI DOD-DOD Johanna Kine)
Dennis DONOVAN		27 Years	09-27-1842	007	DONOVAN, Dennis	
				007		
William MELANEY		17 Years	11-20-1864	007	MELANEY, William	
				007		
Timothy CLIFFORD	Co. Kerry	55 Years	09-28-1853	007	CLIFFORD, Timothy	Parish Of Castleisland, County Kerry, Ireland
				007		
Edward FRAWLEY		60 Years		007	FRAWLEY, Edward	(NOI DOD)
				007		
Catherine GRIFFIN Driscoll		35 Years	07-08-1856	007	DRISCOLL, Morris	(NOI Morris Driscoll)
				007	GRIFFIN, Catherine	
				007		
Patrick DRISLANE		1832	1906	007	O'CONNOR, Margaret	
Margaret O'CONNOR Drislane		1836	1909	007	DRISLANE, Patrick	
				007		
Kate SULLIVAN		35 Years	08-27-1898	007	SULLIVAN, Kate	(Does not say if any of these were husband and wife)
Cornelius SULLIVAN		60 Years	06-22-1894	007	SULLIVAN, Cornelius	
Mrs. Hannah SULLIVAN		03-10-1841	02-19-1921	007	SULLIVAN, Hannah	
				007		
Patrick TEHAN		08-01-1856	12-06-1923	007	TEHAN, Elizabeth	
Elizabeth TEHAN		03-17-1859	05-20-1948	007	TEHAN, Patrick	
				007		
John MCCARTHY		1822	1872	007	KEATING, Eliza	

Eliza KEATING McCarthy		1822	1906	007	MCCARTHY, John	
Daniel MCCARTHY		1858	1901	007	MCCARTHY, Daniel	
Patrick MCCARTHY		1854	1904	007	MCCARTHY, Patrick	
Michael MCCARTHY		1833	1858	007	MCCARTHY, Michael	
				007		
Bridget HAYES Flannery	Co. Clare	75 Years	05-21-1883	007	FLANNERY, Daniel	Native Of Ardulagh (Ardnagla),
				007	HAYES, Bridget	Co. Clare, Ireland (NOI Daniel
				007		Flannery)
Thomas O'BRIEN		1830	1914	007	AHERN, Mary	
Mary AHERN O'Brien		1832	1913	007	O'BRIEN, Thomas	
Dr. James E. O'BRIEN		1871	1926	007	O'BRIEN, James E.	
William A. O'BRIEN		1860	1928	007	O'BRIEN, William A.	
Catherine E. O'BRIEN		1858	1934	007	O'BRIEN, Catherine E.	
				007		
Mary MCKOUGH				007		(Old stone. Part Missing. NOI)
				007		
Thomas MCGREEN		08-01-1823	01-14-1846	007	MCGREEN, Alice	
Alice _____ MCGREEN		06-07-1825	09-03-1892	007	MCGREEN, Thomas	
				007		
Patrick FRAWLEY		37 Years	03-__-1857	007	FRAWLEY, Patrick	(Month of death could be May)
				007		
Peter MCGREGOR		53 Years	07-13-1849	007	MCGREGOR, Peter	Native of Perthshire, Scotland
				007		Died At Bellows Falls
				007		
Ellen TYTER Casey		43 Years	10-30-1857	007	CASEY, Patrick	(NOI Patrick Casey. Possibly
				007	TYTER, Ellen	(Patrick Casey W/D 3-6-1892)
Mary ASH Casey		63 Years	11-06-1886	007	CASEY, Patrick	
				007	ASH, Mary	
				007		
Johanna SULLIVAN		1833	1912	007	SULLIVAN, Johanna	
				007		
Thomas GOLDEN		72 Years	08-11-1903	007	GOLDEN, Mary	
Mary _____ GOLDEN		76 Years	11-23-1908	007	GOLDEN, Thomas	
				007		
Jeremiah KEEFE		1857	1927	007	O'CONNELL, Jane	
Jane O'CONNELL Keefe		1865	1928	007	KEEFE, Jeremiah	
				007		
John N. KEEFE		1847	1916	007	KEEFE, Mary	
				007	MURPHY, Katherine	
Mary _____ KEEFE		46Y 5M	12-02-1886	007	KEEFE, John N.	
Katherine MURPHY Keefe		1850	1922	007	KEEFE, John N.	
				007		
Edward BARRETT		1857	1925	007	HOGAN, Sarah F.	
Sarah HOGAN Barrett		1859	1937	007	BARRETT, Edward	
				007		

Name	Birthplace	Born/Age	Died	Ref	Related	Notes
William FLAVIN		1821	1906	007	SULLIVAN, Winifred	
Winifred SULLIVAN Flavin		1826	1903	007	FLAVIN, William	
				007		
James FLAVIN		90 Years	06-29-1887	007	FLAVIN, James	
				007		
John S. CRAY		40 Years	11-14-1888	007	FINN, Julia	
Julia FINN Cray		40 Years	09-22-1888	007	CRAY, John S.	
				007		
Ellen MALONEY Tyter	Co. Kerry	75 Years	12-07-1886	007	TYTER, David	Born In Parish of Lixnaw, Co.
				007	MALONEY, Ellen	Of Kerry, Ire. (NOI David)
				007		
James W. FLAVIN		1857	1925	007	FLAVIN, Margaret E.	
Margaret E. _____ FLAVIN		1856	1947	007	FLAVIN, James W.	
				007		
William STARK		50 Years	12-17-1876	007	STARK, Mary	(NOI Mary Stark)
Ellen STARK		13 Years	05-	007	STARK, William	
Ellen STARK		13 Years	05-25-1877	007	STARK, Ellen	D/O William and Mary Stark
				007		
Emily MURPHY		4 Years		007	MURPHY, Emily	Children of Mr. & Mrs. Patrick
John C. MURPHY		3 Months		007	MURPHY, John C.	Murphy
				007	MURPHY, Patrick	
				007		
Cornelius DOYLE		1857	1917	007	DOYLE, Catherine	
Catherine _____ DOYLE		1857	1931	007	DOYLE, Cornelius	
				007		
Mary Agnes KEANE Marlboro		35 Years	09-03-1891	007	MARLBORO, James	(NOI James Marlboro)
				007	KEANE, Mary Agnes	
				007		
Patrick HACKETT		47 Years	07-14-1891	007	HACKETT, Bridget	
Bridget _____ HACKETT		49 Years	04-01-1895	007	HACKETT, Patrick	
				007		
John J. PIERCE		46 Years	08-03-1899	007	BRENNAN, Margaret	
Margaret BRENNAN Pierce		43 Years	07-03-1902	007	PIERCE, John J.	
				007		
Owen SULLIVAN		1836	1914	007	SULLIVAN, Mary	
Mary _____ SULLIVAN		1841	1923	007	SULLIVAN, Owen	
				007		
Michael O'BRIEN		88 Years	01-29-1888	007	SHEEHAN, Margaret	
Margaret SHEEHAN O'Brien		59 Years	11-30-1913	007	O'BRIEN, Michael	
				007		
Michael O'CONNOR		1821	03-20-1886	007	BROWN, Bridget	
Bridget BROWN O'Connor		1828	06-16-1898	007	O'CONNOR, Michael	
James O'CONNOR		09-29-1858	03-20-1891	007	O'CONNOR, James	
				007		
Thomas GRIFFIN		1841	1927	007	HARTY, Bridget	

Bridget HARTY Griffin		1846	1918	007	GRIFFIN, Thomas	
				007		
John SHERIDAN		68 Years	04-11-1912	007	DANIELS, Delia M.	
Delia M. DANIELS Sheridan			11-20-1927	007	SHERIDAN, John	(NOI DOB Delia M. Daniels)
				007		
John W. BRODERICK		10-15-1847	04-25-1907	007	HOLDEN, Ellen	
Ellen HOLDEN Broderick		12-25-1844	12-27-1894	007	BRODERICK, John W.	
				007		
John MANSFIELD				007	MANSFIELD, John	(GAR)Co. M., 1st VT Cav
				007		
John HOWARD	Co. Kerry	24 Years	11-07-1885	007	HOWARD, John	Native of Tralee,Co. Kerry,Ire
				007		
Bridget BROWN	Co. Mayo	87 Years	03-12-1883	007	BROWN, Bridget	N/O The Parish of Brusoole
				007		(Burrishoole), CO. Mayo, Ire
				007		
Bartholomew COLLINS		74 Years	12-04-1903	007	MORRIS, Sarah	
Sarah MORRIS Collins		84 Years	09-12-1931	007	COLLINS, Bartholomew	
				007		
Bridget O'CONNOR		87 Years	06-16-1884	007	O'CONNOR, Bridget	(NOI Mr. O'Connor)
John O'CONNOR		50 Years	06-06-1887	007	O'CONNOR, John	Son Of Mrs. O'Connor
Mary O'CONNOR		75 Years	11-22-1897	007	O'CONNOR, Mary	
				007		
Johanna SCANLON	Co. Kerry	29 Years	07-13-1884	007	SCANLON, Johanna	N/O Tralee, Co. Kerry, Ire.
				007		
Robert HOWARD		1858		007	SCANLON, Mary	(NOI DOD Mary & Robert Howard)
Mary SCANLON Howard		1860		007	HOWARD, Robert	
				007		
Michael LAWLOR		72 Years	03-04-1885	007	LAWLOR, Michael	
David P. SCANLAN		78Y 6M	09-16-1903	007	LAWLOR, Joanna	
Joanna LAWLOR Scanlan		76Y 4M	03-12-1909	007	SCANLAN, David P.	
				007		
Edward D. MURPHY	Co. Cork	40 Years	10-23-1885	007	MURPHY, Edward D.	N/O Youghal, Co. Cork, Ireland
				007		He Is Not Dead The Child Of My
				007		Affection But Gone Unto That
				007		School Where He No LongerNeeds
				007		My Poor Protection And Christ
				007		Himself Doth Rise.
Patrick HUBBARD	Co. Cork	86 Years	03-03-1895	007	MURPHY, Margaret	N/O Youghal, Co. Cork, Ireland
Margaret MURPHY Hubbard	Co. Cork	02-14-1814	03-03-1895	007	HUBBARD, Patrick	N/O Youghal, Co. Cork, Ireland
				007		
Bartholomew SULLIVAN	Co. Kerry	76 Years	10-26-1886	007	SULLIVAN, Ellen	Born In Co. Kerry, Ireland
Ellen _____ SULLIVAN	Co. Limerick	64 Years	04-28-1886	007	SULLIVAN, Bartholomew	Born In Co. Limerick, Ireland
John SULLIVAN		1855	1949	007	SULLIVAN, Mary	
Mary _____ SULLIVAN		1865	1936	007	SULLIVAN, John	
				007		

Name	Origin	Birth	Death	Code	Relation	Notes
Eugene CRAY	Co. Kerry	05-12-1820	08-26-1905	007	BROSNAHAN, Johanna	Natives Of Tralee, Co. Kerry,
				007		Ireland
Johanna BROSNAHAN Cray	Co. Kerry	06-19-1823	03-09-1906	007	CRAY, Eugene	Natives Of Tralee, Co. Kerry,
				007		Ireland
				007		
Dennis E. CRAY		04-21-1857	10-16-1943	007	EAGAN, Annie M.	
Annie M. EAGAN Cray		03-08-1856	03-01-1903	007	CRAY, Dennis E.	
				007		
Eugene E. CRAY		1855	1932	007	GREHAN, Margaret W.	
Margaret W. GREHAN Cray		1855	1929	007	CRAY, Eugene E.	
				007		
William COUGHLIN		1840	1918	007	COLLINS, Ellen	
Ellen COLLINS Coughlin		1839	1931	007	COUGHLIN, William	
				007		
Michael MORIERTY				007	QUALTERS, Catherine	
Catherine QUALTERS Morierty		70 Years	02-13-1922	007	MORIERTY, Michael	
				007		
John HASSETT		38 Years	08-24-1892	007	HASSETT, John	
				007		
James B. LEE		1853	1919	007	LEE, James B.	
				007		
Jane _____ BILLING		55 Years	06-22-1874	007	BILLING, Henry	(NOI Henry Billing)
				007	BILLING, Jane	
				007		
Elizabeth _____ DONEGAN		68 Years		007	DONEGAN, Thomas	(Thomas Donegan stone is face
				007	DONEGAN, Elizabeth	down. Could not turn it over)
				007		No DOD on EDlizabeth. Stone is
				007		worn)
				007		
Michael M. BEASLEY	Co. Kerry	1836	01-10-1888	007	KEEFE, Nora	Born Ballyrehan, Co. Kerry,Ire
Nora KEEFE Beasley	Co. Kerry	55 Years	12-27-1901	007	BEASLEY, Michael M.	Born In Co. Kerry, Ireland
				007		
Daniel B. RELIHAN		41 Years	04-03-1899	007	KEEFE, Hannah M.	
Hannah M. KEEFE Relihan		72 Years	02-19-1922	007	RELIHAN, Daniel B.	
				007		
James HAYES				007	DALE, Mary A.	(NOI DOB-DOD on James Hayes)
Mary A. DALE Hayes		12-23-1855	01-09-1909	007	HAYES, James	
				007		
James FITZGERALD		35 Years	04-15-1882	007	KELLY, Mary	
Mary KELLY Fitzgerald		32 Years	08-28-1874	007	FITZGERALD, James	
				007		
James TROY		29 Years	07-14-1876	007	TROY, James	
				007		
Thomas LYNCH		66 Years	08-19-1896	007	O'CONNOR, Ann	
		79 Years	11-	007	FRANCIS, Kate	

Ann O'CONNOR Lynch		79 Years	11-26-1908	007	LYNCH, Thomas	
Kate FRANCIS Lynch		22Y 10M	08-03-1880	007	LYNCH, Thomas	
David LYNCH		63 Years	11-13-1917	007	LYNCH, David	
Joanna LYNCH Walsh		29 Years	07-15-1893	007	WALSH, William	(NOI William Walsh)
				007	LYNCH, Joanna	
				007		
Thomas GAFFNEY		80 Years	04-14-1903	007	LEAHY, Ellen	
Ellen LEAHY Gaffney	Co. Limerick	44 Years	04-10-1877	007	GAFFNEY, Thomas	Born At Craloloc (Crataloe),
				007		Co. Limerick, Ireland
William O'BRIEN		1844	1905	007	O'BRIEN, Bridget	
Bridget _____ O'BRIEN		1847	1914	007	O'BRIEN, William	
				007		
Ellen MURPHY Mullen		1821	1879	007	MULLEN, John	(NOI John Mullen)
				007	MURPHY, Ellen	
				007		
Bridget MEEHEN Hogan			12-19-1874	007	HOGAN, John	(NOI John Hogan. This stone is
				007	MEEHEN, Bridget	buried at base. COuld not read
				007		age at death)
				007		
John RILEY		1824	1886	007	COLLINS, Margaret	
Margaret COLLINS Riley		1837	1915	007	RILEY, John	
				007		
Michael COSTIN		1857	1935	007	HARTY, Margaret	
Margaret HARTY Costin		1858	1913	007	COSTIN, Michael	
				007		
Daniel O'BRIEN		1824	1910	007	RYAN, Catherine	
				007	HAYES, Margaret	
Catherine RYAN O'Brien		1830	1878	007	O'BRIEN, Daniel	
Margaret HAYES O'Brien		1837	1910	007	O'BRIEN, Daniel	
				007		
Cornelius HARTY		1802	1877	007	HARTY, Margaret	
Margaret _____ HARTY		1828	1910	007	HARTY, Cornelius	
Cornelius HARTY Jr.		1835	1870	007	HARTY, Cornelius Jr.	
				007		
Patrick MCCAULIFF	Co. Cork	44 Years	07-31-1877	007	MCAULIFF, Patrick	Native Of Parish Of Youghal
				007		Co. Cork, Ireland
				007		
Johannah GALLARAN Kiniry			08-31-1867	007	KINIRY, John	(NOI John Kiniry)
				007	GALLARAN, Johannah	
				007		
Ellen MANYE		32 Years	04-03-1870	007	MANYE, Ellen	Native of Parish ______, Co.
				007		Cork, Ireland. (Could not read
				007		Parish)
Fanny _____ MCCARTHY		77Y 6M	07-12-1875	007	MCCARTHY, James	(NOI James McCarthy)
				007	MCCARTHY, Fanny	

				007		
Thomas SHAUGHNESSY		79 Years	05-25-1923	007	AHEARN, Catherine	
Catherine AHEARN Shaughnessy		78 Years	10-24-1918	007	SHAUGHNESSY, Thomas	
				007		
John MCMAHAN	Co. Clare	08-27-1823	11-11-1868	007	MCMAHAN, Mary Ellen	Born Co. Clare, Ireland
Mary Ellen _____ MCMAHAN		27 Years	03-01-1868	007	MCMAHAN, John	
Daniel MCMAHON		21 Years	02-08-1881	007	MCMAHON, Daniel	S/O John & Mary Ellen McMahon
John MCMAHON		36 Years	01-30-1901	007	MCMAHON, John	
				007		
Catherine _____ DELANEY		61 Years	11-30-1868	007	DELANEY, William	(NOI WIlliam Delaney)
				007	DELANEY, Catherine	
				007		
Dennis DELANEY				007	BOWEN, Catherine	(GAR) Co. F., 4th VT Inf
Catherine BOWEN Delaney				007	DELANEY, Dennis	(NOI DOB-DOD on both)
				007		
Patrick LONERGAN	Co. Tipperary	51Y M D	09-03-1853	007	DWYER, Mary	Tipperary, Ireland
Maty DWYER Lonergan		36 Years	1846	007	LONERGAN, Patrick	(Old stone, weatherworn. Could
				007		not read day/month of death
				007		for Patrick and not sure 1841
				007		is year of death for Mary)
				007		
Edward MORAN		05-06-1839	05-18-1920	007	DELANEY, Kate	
Kate DELANEY Moran		03-27-1843	07-15-1896	007	MORAN, Edward	
				007		
Andrew J. MCCARTHY		1841	1921	007	KINIRY, Nancy	
Nancy KINIRY McCarthy		1840	1914	007	MCCARTHY, Andrew J.	
				007		
William KINIRY		78 Years	05-28-1876	007	DRISCOL, M_____	(This stone is mended where
M_____ DRISCOL Kiniry		66 Years	05-18-1868	007	KINIRY, William	info on spouse is engraved.
				007		DOD and age at death may be
				007		innacurate)
Bartholomew KINIRY		02-01-1832	02-14-1907	007	KINIRY, Ellen	
Ellen _____ KINIRY		04-24-1837	11-30-1921	007	KINIRY, Bartholomew	
				007		
Nora KINIRY Walsh		09-02-1858	03-12-1937	007	WALSH, Thomas	(NOI Thomas Walsh)
				007	KINIRY, Nora	
				007		
A. P. WHITNEY		53 Years	04-04-1873	007	WHITNEY, A.P.	
Mary O'CONOL Whitney		48 Years	09-03-1883	007	O'CONOL, Mary	
				007		
Catherine NELON King		47 Years	08-22-1867	007	KING, Patrick	(NOI Patrick King)
				007	NELON, Catherine	
				007		
William KING		47 Years	08-22-1867	007	KING, Anna M.	
Anna M. _____ KING		1862	1899	007	KING, William	

				007		
Timothy BYRNS	Co. Kerry		03-__-1867	007	BYRNS, Timothy	Native of ________, Co. Kerry,
				007		Ire. (Parish is engraved but
				007		cannot read. In bad state of
				007		deterioration)
				007		
James BROWN		03-17-1830	05-09-1910	007	BROWN, James	
				007		
Julia BROWN Keefe		75 Years	06-25-1894	007	KEEFE, Patrick	Born In Ireland. (NOI Patrick
				007	BROWN, Julia	Keefe)
Julia A. KEEFE		78 Years	05-23-1941	007	KEEFE, Patrick	Born In Ireland
				007		
Thomas HOWARD		15 Years	03-01-1870	007	HOWARD, Thomas	
				007		
Ellen O'DONNELL Howard	Co. Kerry	42 Years	04-12-1873	007	HOWARD, Edward	Native of Co. Kerry, Ireland
				007	O'DONNELL, Ellen	(NOI Edward Howard)
				007		
James MCCARTHY		17 Years	07-27-1869	007	MCCARTHY, James	
				007		
Timothy O'LEARY		78Y3M10D	04-06-1879	007	O'LEARY, Annie N.	
Annie N. _____ O'Leary			09-04-1877	007	O'LEARY, Timothy	(Could not read age at death)
				007		
Thomas O'CONNOR		1835	1876	007	HOWARD, Annie	
Annie HOWARD O'Connor		1840	1902	007	O'CONNOR, Thomas	
				007		
Dennis BROSNAHAN		1822	1879	007	HOWARD, Mary	
Mary HOWARD Brosnahan		1832	1917	007	BROSNAHAN, Dennis	
				007		
M. WOLFE		1820	1864	007	WOLFE, Catherine	
Catherine _____ WOLFE		1834	1880	007	WOLFE, M.	
Richard WOLFE		1856	1877	007	WOLFE, Richard	
				007		
Patrick WOLFE		1857	1920	007	COLLINS, Mary	
Mary COLLINS Wolfe		1864	1940	007	WOLFE, Patrick	
				007		
John T. WOODS		06-06-1842	10-25-1904	007	DALEY, Bridget E.	
Bridget E. DALEY Woods		06-10-1842	05-25-1909	007	WOODS, John T.	
				007		
Edward GORMAN		1850	1920	007	HANNON, Mary	
Mary HANNON Gorman		1865	1932	007	GORMAN, Edward	
Mary CONDON			1920	007	CONDON, Mary	(Date of birth not given)
				007		
James M. RILEY		1854	1919	007	RILEY, James M.	
				007		
Daniel KINIRY		49 Years	03-21-1880	007	KINIRY, Mary	

Name	Age/Birth	Death	Code	Index	Notes
Mary _____ KINIRY	47 Years	11-05-1881	007	KINIRY, Daniel	
			007		
Johanna BOYLE Pierce			007	BOYLE, Johanna	(In state of total deteriora-
			007		tion. Copied as much as could
			007		be interpreted)
			007		
Daniel MCAULIFFE	1845	1900	007	MCAULIFFE, Daniel	
			007		
Patrick MEEHAN	81Y8M1D	11-22-1885	007	LEONARD, Betsey	
Betsey LEONARD Meehan	83 Years	05-09-1893	007	MEHAN, Patrick	
Margaret MEEHAN	68 Years	11-29-1901	007	MEEHAN, Margaret	
			007		
Lizzie MEHAN	18 Years	08-02-1862	007	MEHAN, Lizzie	D/O Patrick & Elizabeth Mehan
			007		
Jane MEEHAN McNamara	78 Years	10-18-1888	007	MCNAMARA, William	D/O Patrick & Elizabeth Mehan
			007		(Year of death fuzzy-could be
			007		1868. NOI William McNamara)
			007		
Simon O'CONNOR	42 Years	09-22-1862	007	O'CONNOR, Simon	
			007		
John HOLLOREN	65 Years	01-11-1904	007	HOLLOREN, Hanora	
Hanora _____ HOLLOREN	65 Years	05-02-1897	007	HOLLOREN, John	
			007		
Patrick CRAY	1849	1925	007	PIERCE, Bridget F.	
Bridget F. PIERCE Cray	1856	1915	007	CRAY, Patrick	
			007		
Michael STACK	67 Years	07-02-1891	007	RIORDIAN, Ellen	
Ellen RIORDIAN Stack	75 Years	06-09-1906	007	STACK, Michael	
			007		
James DORNEY	53 Years	11-28-1891	007	FARRELL, Mary	
Mary FARRELL Dorney	64 Years	01-04-1892	007	DORNEY, James	
			007		
Morris DORNEY	27 Years	08-28-1881	007	DORNEY, Morris	
James DORNEY Jr.	38 Years	01-18-1895	007	DORNEY, James Jr.	
			007		
			007		
			007		
John T. KEEFE	1856	1929	007	FLAVIN, Katherine	
Katherine FLAVIN Keefe	1855		007	KEEFE, John T.	(NOI DOD Katherine Flavin)
			007		
James FLAVIN			007	STACK, Mary	(Very old stone. Everything
			007		unreadable but name)
Mary STACK Flavin	95 Years	03-02-1921	007	FLAVIN, James	
			007		
William FLAVIN	25 Years	01-14-1885	007	RADY, Johanna	

NAME	POB	DOB/AGE	DOD	CEM	SPOUSE/INDEX	INSCRIPTION
Johanna RADY Flavin		52 Years	12-18-1903	007	FLAVIN, William	
				007		
James WALSH	Co. Cork	85 Years	09-17-1873	007	WALSH, James	A Native Of Parish Desert, Co. Cork, Ireland
				007		
				007		
James BRENNAN		64 Years	05-25-1881	007	BRENNAN, Catharine	
Catharine _____ BRENNAN			12-25-1883	007	BRENNAN, James	(Age at death not given)
James BRENNAN		5 Years	1856	007	BRENNAN, James	(Ages at death for children were difficult to read. Might be innacurate but were single digit entries)
Jeremiah BRENNAN		7 Years	1860	007	BRENNAN, Jeremiah	
Mary BRENNAN		1 Years	1857	007	BRENNAN, Mary	
Kate BRENNAN		2 Years	1857	007	BRENNAN, Kate	
				007		
James O'BRIEN		65 Years	08-05-1880	007	O'BRIEN, Catharine	
Catharine _____ O'BRIEN		50 Years	12-04-1864	007	O'BRIEN, James	
				007		
Catharine _____ O'BRIEN		77 Years	08-20-1866	007	O'BRIEN, Thomas	(NOI Thomas O'Brien)
				007	O'BRIEN, Catharine	
				007		
John O'BRIEN		37 Years	08-05-1855	007	O'BRIEN, John	
				007		
Patrick KING		1827	1878	007	KING, Mary	(Possibly this is second wife of Patrick if first wife was Catherine Nelon - This grave not in close proximity to Catherine Nelon)
Mary A. _____ KING		1858	1938	007	KING, Patrick	
				007		
				007		
				007		

St. Charles Cemetery, Bellows Falls, Vermont - South End of Village Off Route 5. Dead End Road Near Bellows Falls Union HS

NAME	POB	DOB/AGE	DOD	CEM	SPOUSE/INDEX	INSCRIPTION
Jeremiah HOGAN		1851	1929	008	CRAY, Mary	
Mary CRAY Hogan		1854	1919	008	HOGAN, Jeremiah	
				008		
Edward HOWARD		1830	1919	008	O'NEILL, Catherine	
Catherine O'NEILL Howard		1854	1926	008	HOWARD, Edward	
				008		
Michael J. O'CONNOR				008	CRAY, Hannah	(No Dates Given. Inscriptions read Father and Mother)
Hannah CRAY O'Connor				008	O'CONNOR, Michael J.	
				008		
Daniel W. RILEY		1855	1932	008	RYAN, Ellen A.	
Ellen A. RYAN Riley		1857	1929	008	RILEY, Daniel W.	
				008		
Edward M. BARRY		1859	1941	008	BOWLER, Ellen	

Ellen BOWLER Barry	1857	1940	008	BARRY, Edward M.	
			008		
James HACKETT	75 Years		008	MURPHEY, Ellen	(No DOD but Childrens Birth
Ellen MURPHEY Hackett	70 Years		008	HACKETT, James	years begin circa 1866)
			008		
Annie _____ WELCH	1850	1903	008	WELCH, Levi	(NOI Levi Welch)
			008	WELCH, Annie	
FICKETT/FLYNN			008	FICKETT/FLYNN	(Burial of Mary A. 1855-1919
			008		But do not know if Fickett or
			008		Flynn.)
			008		
Mary C. CRAY	70 Years	06-14-1900	008	CRAY, Mary C.	(On Usher stone. Ushers are
			008	USHER	children age 5 months and 10
			008		years buried 1898, 1906)
			008		
Thomas SWEENEY	75 Years	12-05-1903	008	GROGEN, Hanora	
Hanora GROGEN Sweeney	82 Years	11-12-1914	008	SWEENEY, Thomas	
			008		
John H. CLARY	51 Years	06-26-1905	008	CLARY, John H.	Of Cadyville, New York
			008		
Amelia HEWITT	1818	1897	008	HEWITT, Amelia	
Catherine D. HEWITT	1844	1916	008	HEWITT, Catherine D.	
Henry B. HEWITT	1852	1937	008	HEWITT, Henry B.	
			008		
Bryan J. O'CONNOR	1856	1940	008	O'CONNOR, Delia	
Delia _____ O'CONNOR	1860	1923	008	O'CONNOR, Bryan J.	
			008		
John J. DRISLANE	12-18-1856	03-18-1937	008	DRISCOLL, Bridget Agnes	
Bridget Agnes DRISCOLL Drislane	02-01-1862	05-23-1898	008	DRISLANE, John J.	
			008		
Dennis D. DRISLANE	11-11-1830	06-06-1918	008	ROCHE, Johanna	
Johanna ROCHE Drislane	01-06-1835	06-19-1897	008	DRISLANE, Dennis D.	
Ellen ROCHE	1850	1940	008	ROCHE, Ellen	
			008		
Michael DIGGINS	63 Years	09-20-1902	008	HACKETT, Maria	
Maria HACKETT Diggins	77 Years	07-27-1925	008	DIGGINS, Michael	
			008		
Thomas HACKETT	79 Years	06-21-1887	008	CONDON, Ellen	
Ellen CONDON Hackett	74 Years	08-22-1891	008	HACKETT, Thomas	
			008		
Mary _____ DOUGLASS	02-06-1854	10-20-1902	008	DOUGLASS, Alonzo	(NOI Alonzo Douglass)
			008	DOUGLASS, Mary	
			008		
Edward FITZSIMMONS	10-17-1834	08-13-1908	008	BARNES, Esther	
Esther BARNES Fitzsimmons	08-11-1836	06-04-1905	008	FITZSIMMONS, Edward	

Name	Origin	Birth	Death	Code	Spouse/Index	Notes
				008		
Edward TYRRELL		1842	1926	008	BROWN, Eliza	
Eliza BROWN Tyrrell		1844	1901	008	TYRRELL, Edward	
				008		
Owen L. MURPHY		1830	1908	008	MURPHY, Owen L.	
				008		
James H. MCDONALD		1855	1931	008	MURPHY, Mary A.	
Mary A. MURPHY McDonald		1857	1934	008	MCDONALD, James H.	
				008		
John J. MURPHY		1855	1927	008	MURPHY, John J.	
				008		
Patrick J. MURPHY		1856	1939	008	MURPHY, Patrick J.	
				008		
Jeremiah SHEA		1855	1930	008	HOLLAND, Catherine	
Catherine HOLLAND Shea		1855	1937	008	SHEA, Jeremiah	
				008		
Mary QUINN		61 Years	01-04-1910	008	QUINN, Mary	
				008		
Anthony STEBBINS		1847	1926	008	TUCKER, Tressa	
Tressa TUCKER Stebbins		59Y5M7D	08-22-1909	008	STEBBINS, Anthony	
				008		
John OAKS		1838	1910	008	BROWN, Nora	
Nora BROWN Oaks		1837	1919	008	OAKS, John	
				008		
John F. ROCHE		1848	1913	008	ROCHE, Anna M.	
Anna M. _____ ROCHE		1859	1924	008	ROCHE, John F.	
				008		
John LAWLOR		1835	1914	008	HULIHAN, Catherine	
Catherine HULIHAN Lawlor		1842	1922	008	LAWLOR, John	
				008		
Thomas MITCHELL		1834	1915	008	COSTELLO, Mary	
Mary COSTELLO Hayes		1851	1912	008	MITCHELL, Thomas	
				008		
John BOWE	Co. Kilkenny	36Y 8M	09-16-1893	008	SHERIDAN, Jane M.	A Native of Parish _____,
				008		Co. Kilkenny, Ireland. (Stone
				008		iw weatherworn)
Jane M. SHERIDAN Bowe		08-07-1858	02-01-1929	008	BOWE, John	
				008		
William BOWE		1861	1939	008	SHERIDAN, Anne	Born In Ireland
Anne SHERIDAN Bowe		1863	1920	008	BOWE, William	Born In Ireland
				008		
William T. HOGAN		1854	1911	008	HOGAN, Mary A.	
Mary A. _____ HOGAN		1857	1923	008	HOGAN, William T.	
				008		
Johannah O'CONNOR		1827	1917	008	O'CONNOR, Johannah	Mother Of Timothy O'Connor.

				008		(NOI Timothy or Mr. O'Connor)
				008		
Anne G. SHERIDAN		1833	1917	008	SHERIDAN, Ann G.	
				008		
Johanna COSTELLO Lynch		1847	1916	008	COSTELLO, Johanna	(NOI John Lynch)
				008	LYNCH, John	
				008		
Daniel J. BROSNAHAN		1855	1927	008	DRISCOLL, Hannah	
Hannah DRISCOLL Brosnahan		1855	1914	008	BROSNAHAN, Daniel J.	
				008		
Bartholemaw SUPPLE		03-15-1850	07-27-1912	008	PIERCE, Mary T.	
Mary T. PIERCE Supple		02-10-1847	10-10-1924	008	SUPPLE, Bartholemaw	
				008		
Barbara DOOLITTLE		05-14-1840	05-23-1902	008	DOOLITTLE, Barbara	
Frank H. MORIARTY		1852	1922	008	LEARY, Johanna E.	(Frank Moriarty and Johanna
Johanna E. LEARY Moriarty		1867	1947	008	MORIARTY, Frank H.	Leary are on Doolittle stone)
				008		
John MCAULIFFE		1842	1904	008	SUPPLE, Mary	
Mary SUPPLE McAuliffe		1844	1919	008	MCAULIFFE, John	
				008		
James MCGOWAN		04-04-1829	09-23-1901	008	KEEFE, Ellen	
Ellen KEEFE McGowan		03-17-1840	04-23-1920	008	MCGOWAN, James	
				008		
Ellen COSTINE Long		47 Years	05-13-1902	008	COSTINE, Ellen	(NOI John Long)
				008	LONG, John	
Daniel FORD	Co. Kerry	01-01-1850	03-14-1905	008	FORD, Daniel	Born Parish Killarney (County
				008		Kerry). Died at Bellows Falls.
				008		We Have Loved Him In Life. Let
				008		Us Not Forget Him In Death.
John BOYLE		74 Years	01-11-1919	008	MORRISSEY, Mary	
Mary MORRISSEY Boyle		80 Years	08-09-1928	008	BOYLE, John	
				008		
Valentine GRAY		1849	1944	008	GRAY, Sarah J.	
Sarah J. _____ GRAY		1854	1930	008	GRAY, Valentine	
				008		
John W. WELCH		1858	1925	008	WELCH, Mary	
Mary _____ WELCH		1855	1943	008	WELCH, John W.	
				008		
John LEENE		1858	1941	008	FINN, Mary	
Mary FINN Leene		1856	1940	008	LEENE, John	
				008		
James C. BRYAN		1833	1911	008	CROWLEY, Eliza	
Eliza CROWLEY Bryan		1841	1883	008	BRYAN, James C.	
				008		
John WALKER		1855	1943	008	WALKER, Ellen	

Ellen _____ WALKER		1851	1930	008	WALKER, John	
				008		
Bernard REYNOLDS		1865	1918	008	REYNOLDS, Bernard	(Does not say if Catherine and
Catherine REYNOLDS		1854	1935	008	REYNOLDS, Catherine	Bernard Reynolds were mates)
				008		
Patrick B. LEEN		1860	1939	008	CRAY, Mary	
Mary CRAY Leen		1845	1929	008	LEEN, Patrick	
				008		
John O'DONNELL		1857	1931	008	O'DONNELL, Catherine	
Catherine _____ O'DONNELL		1860	1942	008	O'DONNELL, John	
				008		
Alfred SMITH		1846	1922	008	NADON, Marguerite	
Marguerite NADON Smith		1849	1928	008	SMITH, Alfred	
				008		
Michael J. WALSH		1866	1928	008	WALSH, Michael J.	(Does not say if Michael Walsh
Mary DRISCOLL		1855	1928	008	DRISCOLL, Mary	and Mary Driscoll were mates)
				008		
John H. CRAY		1847	1934	008	CRAY, Margaret D.	
Margaret D. _____ CRAY		1852	1924	008	CRAY, John H.	

Village Cemetery, Belvidere, Vermont. In center Of Village

NAME	**POB**	**DOB/AGE**	**DOD**	**CEM**	**SPOUSE/INDEX**	**INSCRIPTION**
William WETHERUP	Co. Antrim	70Y07M13D	10-21-1881	105	_____, Nancy	Native Of Carrickfergus, Ire.
				105		Lies Beneath Conquered By The
				105		Hand Of Death
Nancy _____ WETHERUP		80Y 7M	10-24-1874	105	WETHERUP, Hugh	
				105		
John B. MCCUIN		11-15-1827	03-27-1895	105	BUTLER, Ann	
Ann BUTLER McCuin		1829	1907	105	MCCUIN, John B.	
				105		
William LACKEY		70 Years	02-11-1894	105	CAMPBELL, Anna	
Anna CAMPBELL Lackey		57 Years	02-25-1893	105	LACKEY, William	
				105		
Michael L. MCGINNIS		1845	1891	105	MCGINNIS, Michael L.	
				105		
Russel B. DOWNEY		06-22-1814	08-29-1859	105	CASEY, Eliza	
Eliza CASEY Downey		09-12-1817	04-29-1872	105	DOWNEY, Russel B.	
				105		
Dennis BARRY		78 Years	01-08-1892	105	ELDRED, Lois	
Lois ELDRED Barry		1846	1912	105	BARRY, Dennis	

St. Francis de Sales (New burying ground), Bennington, Vt. Main Street, on grounds of Historical Museum

NAME	POB	DOB/AGE	DOD	CEM	SPOUSE/INDEX	INSCRIPTION
Hugh LEE	Co. Longford	46 Years	03-25-1864	009	LEE, Hugh	Born In Longford Co.,Ireland
				009		
Ellen SCANLON McGuire	Co. Longford	74 Years	02-28-1877	009	MCGUIRE, Michael	Native of Soran, Co. Longford,
				009	SCANLON, Ellen	Ireland (NOI Michael McGuire)
				009		
John CONE	Co. Meath	76 Years	02-27-1908	009	GIBNEY, Bridget	Born in Co. "Mead" (Meath),Ire
Bridget GIBNEY Cone	Co. Meath	62 Years	01-05-1896	009	LEE, Hugh	Born In Co. "Mead" (Meath),Ire
				009		
Christopher FLOOD	Co. Meath	73 Years	03-12-1877	009	MELADY, Bridget	Native of Co. Meath, Ireland
Bridget MELADY Flood		78 Years	06-20-1864	009	FLOOD, Christopher	
				009		
Edward GRACE	Co. Wexford	63 Years	04-11-1865	009	_____, Catharine	A Native of Co. Wexford, Ire.
Catharine _____ GRACE	Co. Wexford	65 Years	02-17-1869	009	GRACE, Edward	Native of Co. Wexford, Ireland
Edward GRACE			05-06-1864	009	GRACE, Edward	Died at Culpepper, VA. (GAR)
				009		
Jerry SULLIVAN	Co. Cork	64 Years	07-03-1867	009	SULLIVAN, Jerry	Native of Co. Cork, Ireland
				009		
James MURPHY	Co. Carlow	1822	01-07-1868	009	_____, Catharine	Born In The County Carlow,
				009		Ireland. Died in Connecticut
John LEE	Co. Waterford	54 Years	04-13-1870	009	CASEY, Ann	A Native of Co. Waterford, Ire
Ann CASEY Lee		65 Years	11-25-1912	009	LEE, John	
				009		
Michael CRAVEN				009	_____, Mary	(Deteriorated and unreadable)
				009		
Mary _____ CRAVEN		35 Years	06-15-1872	009	CRAVEN, Michael	Born In Ireland
				009		
Patrick CRAVEN	Co. Roscommon	65 Years	04-17-1872	009	CRAVEN, Patrick	Born In Co. Roscommon, Ireland
				009		
Edward MURRY	Co. Leitrim	29 Years	05-15-1872	009	MURRY, Edward	A Native Of The County Leitrim
				009		Ireland. Son of John & Bridget
				009		Murry.
				009		
John HURLEY	Co. Waterford	80 Years	03-03-1902	009	HURLEY, John	A Native Of The Co. Waterford,
				009		Ireland
				009		
James MCGUIRE	Co. Longford	52 Years	07-11-1861	009	MCGUIRE, James	A Native Of Soran, Parish Of
				009		Killoe, Co. Longford, Irelandd
				009		
John ROURKE	Co. Carlow	62 Years	08-01-1861	009	_____, Mary	Native of the Co. Carlow, Ire.
Mary _____ ROURKE	Co. Waterford	69 Years	09-23-1875	009	ROURKE, John	A Native Of The Co. Waterford,

Name	County	Born/Age	Died	Code	Relatives	Notes
				009		Ireland
Margaret HOGAN Guiltinane	Co. Limerick	60 Years	08-07-1888	009	GUILTINANE, Daniel HOGAN, Margaret	A Native Of Kildimo, County Limerick, Ireland (NOI Daniel Guiltinane)
Catherine CAVENDER Coy	Co. Carlow	40 Years	12-12-1861	009	COY, Thomas CAVENDER, Catherine CAVENDER, Garret	Born In Co. Carlow, Ireland. Daughter Of Garret & Elizabeth Cavender. (NOI Thomas Coy)
John HULIHAN Mary LEONARD Hulihan	Co. Limerick	65 Years 70 Years	08-07-1888 08-25-1899	009	LEONARD, Mary HULIHAN, John	A Native of Co. Limerick, Ire.
Patrick MCGUIRE Ann _____ MCGUIRE	Co. Longford	03-17-1835 12-14-1835		009	_____, Ann MCGUIRE, Patrick	N/O Soran, Co. Longford, Ire
Matthew LEONARD Mary GRIFFIN Leonard	Co. Carlow	11-11-1828 07-17-1830	12-04-1875 06-06-1902	009	GRIFFIN, Mary LEONARD, Matthew	Born In Co. Carlow, Ireland
Michael WELCH	Co. Kilkenny	40 Years	08-17-1878	009	GRIFFIN, Bridget	Native of Co. Kilkenny, Ire.
Bridget GRIFFIN Welch	Co. Carlow	79 Years	05-25-1907	009	WELCH, Michael	Native of Co. Carlow, Ireland
James HOGAN	Co. Limerick	84 Years	01-25-1884	009	HOGAN, James	Native of Parish Kildimo, Co. Limerick, Ireland
Ellen _____ COLLINS	Co. Cork	85 Years	1867	009	COLLINS, Patrick _____, Ellen	A Native Of The Co. Of Cork, Ireland. (Stone damaged. NOI Patrick Collins)
Dennis MCCARTHY	Co. Cork	1825	1910	009	DONOVAN, Ellen	Native of Drimoleague,Co. Cork Ireland
Ellen DONOVAN McCarthy	Co. Cork	1804	1873	009	MCCARTHY, Dennis	Native of Drimoleague,Co. Cork Ireland (According to Brian Mitchell, A Guide To Irish Parish Regis- ters-Drimoleague is a Catholic Parish aka the Civil Parish of Dromdaleague)
Ellen TOBIN Casey	Co. Tipperary	65 Years	08-28-1861	009	CASEY, Thomas TOBIN, Ellen	Born In Parish of "Mallinchor" Co. Tipperary, Ireland. (Stone badly deteriorated - possibly Mullinahone)
Patrick SCULLY	Co. Galway	37 Years	04-25-1859	009	KINNEY, Mary	A Native of Co. Galway, Ire,

Name	Place	Born/Age	Died		Relative	Notes
Mary KINNEY Scully		1824	1892	009	SCULLY, Patrick	
				009		
Martin SCULLY	Co. Galway	40 Years	03-25-1857	009	SCULLY, Martin	A Native of Co. Galway, Ire.
				009		
Julia _____ O'DONNELL	Co. Cork		09-20-1855	009	O'DONNELL, James	A Native of Ireland, Parish Of
				009	_____, Julia	Charliville (No such Parish,
				009		probably Charleville Town).
				009		(NOI James O'Donnell. Her age
				009		at death was 30 or 80 years.
				009		Badly deteriorated).
				009		
Margaret DUONEY Loynes	Co. Waterford	48 Years	11-02-1854	009	LOYNES, Edmond	Native of "Kilros___" Parish
				009	DUONEY, Margaret	Co. Waterford (Could be Kilro-
				009		santy - badly deteriorated)
				009		(NOI Edmond Loynes)
				009		
John MULQUEEN		1845	1906	009	PURCELL, Ann	
Ann PURCELL Mulqueen		1841	1899	009	MULQUEEN, John	
				009		
James GRACE		1840	1898	009	_____, Margaret	
Margaret _____ GRACE		1846	1879	009	GRACE, James	
				009		
Mathew MAHER		1830	1878	009	_____, Elizabeth	
Elizabeth _____ MAHER		1838	1897	009	MAHER, Mathew	
				009		
Thomas POWERS		1842	1895	009	CUNNINGHAM, Katherine	
Katherine CUNNINGHAM Powers		1843	1903	009	POWERS, Thomas	
				009		
Mary HURLEY				009	HURLEY, Mary	
				009		
Thomas MCMAHON		39 Years	02-25-1873	009	BRODERICK, Ellen	
Ellen BRODERICK McMahon		60 Years	03-27-1898	009	MCMAHON, Thomas	
				009		
James MCGUIRE		1829	1892	009	DAVIS, Sarah	
Sarah DAVIS McGuire		1836	1871	009	MCGUIRE, James	
				009		
John WOODS		70 Years	09-26-187_	009	WOODS, John	
				009		
Frank DYER		1852		009	_____, Margaret	
Margaret _____ DYER		1850	1908	009	DYER, Frank	
				009		
Bridget _____ROACH		72 Years	08-19-1856	009	ROACH, John	(NOI John Roach)
				009	_____, Bridget	
				009		
Catherine DONNELLY Muldoon		46 Years	08-04-1858	009	MULDOON, Patrick	(NOI Patrick Muldoon)

			009	DONNELLY, Catherine	
			009		
Thomas MADDEN	80 Years	05-23-1909	009	LEE, Roseanna	
Roseanna LEE Madden	67 Years	01-31-1896	009	MADDEN, Thomas	
			009		
Mary GARTLAND	83 Years	12-07-1889	009	GARTLAND, Mary	
			009		
Nicholas GARTLAND	50 Years	02-18-1856	009	_____, Hanora	
Hanora _____ GARTLAND	63 Years	01-16-1869	009	GARTLAND, Nicholas	
			009		
Edward GUNSHANNON	53 Years	02-16-1883	009	GAVIN, Ann	
Ann GAVIN Gunshannon	38 Years	01-19-1875	009	GUNSHANNON, Edward	
			009		
Joseph LEVINE	01-10-1846	03-17-1920	009	_____, Bridget	
Bridget _____ LEVINE	03-15-1851	03-26-1922	009	LEVINE, Joseph	
			009		
Bryan MCGINNIS	1828	1903	009	DONNOVAN, Catherine	
Catherine DONNOVAN McGinnis	1834	1903	009	MCGINNIS, Bryan	
			009		
Michael MURPHY	1834	1882	009	MULDOON, Mary	
Mary MULDOON Murphy	1820	1899	009	MURPHY, Michael	
			009		
Thomas LEONARD	58 Years	12-04-1862	009	_____, Bridget	
Bridget _____ LEONARD	45 Years	05-01-1869	009	LEONARD, Thomas	
			009		
Martin CASEDY	58 Years	10-21-1874	009	_____, Mary	(NOI Mary _____)
			009	CASEDY, Martin	
			009		
John MCKEON	1818	1880	009	MCGUIRE, Mary	
Mary MCGUIRE McKeon	1822	1882	009	MCKEON, John	
John P. McKeon	1845	1879	009	MCKEON, John P.	
Elizabeth McKeon	1854	1882	009	MCKEON, Elizabeth	
			009		
Ellen BRADY	1841	1859	009	BRADY, Ellen	
			009		
John CONE	75 Years	01-06-1860	009	CONE, John	
			009		
Julia _____ DONOVAN	1798	1870	009	_____, Julia	(NOI Mr. Donovan)
Richard DONOVAN	1834	1863	009	DONOVAN, Richard	
Thomas DONOVAN	1815	1893	009	DONOVAN, Thomas	
Julia DONOVAN O'Brien	1822	1858	009	DONOVAN, Julia	(NOI Mr. O'Brien)
			009		
			009		
Julia SULLIVAN Foran	1847	1908	009		(NOI Mr. Foran)
			009	SULLIVAN, Julia	

Bridget LYNCH Sullivan	1851	1881	009		(NOI Mr. Sullivan)
			009	LYNCH, Bridget	
Margaret SULLIVAN	19 Years	08-23-1857	009	SULLIVAN, Margaret	Dau of J. & C.
Patrick NASH	45 Years	10-05-1866	009	_____, Johanna	
Johannah _____ NASH	52 Years	03-13-1866	009	NASH, Patrick	
			009		
John TARRILL	60 Years	12-25-1861	009	TARRILL, John	
			009		
Lawrence P. TRACY	70 Years	09-10-1874	009	_____, Mary A.	
Mary A. _____ TRACY	65 Years	06-15-1891	009	TRACY, Lawrence P.	
			009		
Bryan CRAHAN	45 Years	08-30-1867	009	_____, Bridget	
Bridget _____ CRAHAN	33 Years	05-01-1868	009	CRAHAN, Bryan	
			009		
John MCMAHON	1830	1897	009	FLEMING, Ellen	
Ellen FLEMING McMahon	1839	1901	009	MCMAHON, John	
			009		
William O'DONNELL	1843	1878	009	GREGORY, Elizabeth	
Elizabeth GREGORY O'Donnell	1845	1880	009	O'DONNELL, William	
			009		
Patrick BAKER	1830	1869	009	SWEENEY, Mary	
Mary SWEENEY Baker	1834	1926	009	BAKER, Patrick	
			009		
John N. MORRISSEY	12-27-1825	10-23-1889	009	_____, Ellen	
Ellen _____ MORRISSEY	08-15-1833	04-09-1895	009	MORRISSEY, John N.	
			009		
Frank C. SULLIVAN	1837	1925	009	LYONS, Julia A.	
Julia A. LYONS Sullivan	1839	1919	009	SULLIVAN, Frank C.	
			009		
William O'DONNELL	1828	1906	009	BOWEN, Johanna	
Johanna BOWEN O'Donnell	1839	1911	009	O'DONNELL, William	
			009		
Thomas LYONS	1842	1914	009	GREGORY, Ellen	
Ellen GREGORY Lyons	1843	1922	009	LYONS, Thomas	
			009		
Patrick TRACEY	60 Years	08-28-1870	009	MORRISSEY, Hannora	
Hannora MORRISSEY Tracey	1828	1909	009	TRACEY, Patrick	
			009		
Michael GRENNAN	1831	1907	009	_____, Jane	
Jane _____ GRENNAN	1836	1891	009	GRENNAN, Michael	
			009		
John J. DOWD	1835	1899	009	MURRAY, Bridget	
Bridget MURRAY Dowd	1838	1916	009	DOWD, John J.	
			009		
Patrick CONE	03-16-1829	01-02-1915	009	BRODERICK, Abigail	

Abigail BRODERICK Cone	02-22-1830	04-23-1903	009	CONE, Patrick	
			009		
Timothy HANRAHAN	70 Years	04-22-1891	009	HARROW, Bridget	
Bridget HARROW Hanrahan	80 Years	12-26-1901	009	HANRAHAN, Timothy	
			009		
Patrick O'DAY	70 Years		009	_____, Annie	
Annie _____ O'DAY	52 Years	06-39-1892	009	O'DAY, Patrick	
			009		
John O'MARA	1855	1914	009	POWERS, Mary	
Mary POWERS O'Mara	1859	1923	009	O'MARA, John	
			009		
Edward MURRAY	78 Years	02-06-1889	009	_____, Ann	
Ann _____ MURRAY	69 Years	09-17-1899	009	MURRAY, Edward	
			009		
Martin CONE	58 Years	06-10-1895	009	_____, Delia	
Delia _____ CONE	68 Years	02-14-1901	009	CONE, Martin	
			009		
James DOYLE	66 Years	07-01-1892	009	DOYLE, James	
			009		
Michael MCKEON	1849	1911	009	MATTISON, Eva	
Eva MATTISON McKeon	1855	1909	009	MCKEON, Michael	
			009		
Roseay CULLION	77 Years	02-26-1875	009	CULLION, Roseay	Erected By Her Sons Daniel & Thomas
			009	CULLION, Thomas	
			009		
John FLYNN	60 Years	04-__-1872	009	O'BRIEN, Mary	
Mary O'BRIEN Flynn	70 Years	08-__-1890	009	FLYNN, John	
			009		
Sarah SILK	43 Years	03-14-186_	009	SILK, Sarah	Sister of James (Silk)
			009	SILK, James	
			009		
Michael CRONIN	09-29-1831	06-03-1901	009	CASEY, Mary	
Mary CASEY Cronin	01-01-1834	12-21-1890	009	CRONIN, Michael	
			009		
James KENNEDY		12-19-1867	009	KENNEDY, James	To The Memory of James Kennedy and John Lynch. Killed at the ore bed 12-19-1867. RIP
John LYNCH		12-19-1867	009	LYNCH, John	
			009		
			009		
Lawrence RILEY	1829	1893	009	_____, Fannie	
			009	_____, Catherine	
Fannie _____ RILEY	1833	1870	009	RILEY, Lawrence	
Catherine _____ RILEY	1844	1904	009	RILEY, Lawrence	
			009		
Edward GREEN	1836	1916	009	BURNS, Mary	
Mary BURNS Green	1843	1910	009	GREEN, Edward	

			009		
Patrick MCGURN	56 Years	01-20-1882	009	MCGURN, Patrick	
			009		
John LEE	1838	1909	009	DONOVAN, Bridget	
Bridget DONOVAN Lee	1836	1889	009	LEE, John	
			009		
Margaret MAHAN Doyle	78 Years	05-09-1905	009	DOYLE, Lawrence	(NOI Lawrence Doyle)
			009	MAHAN, Margaret	
			009		
Nancy M. _____ CARL	48Y3M15D	07-15-1888	009	CARL, E.D.	(NOI E.D. Carl)
			009	_____, Nancy M.	
			009		
Daniel CULLION	02-25-1820	03-26-1899	009	WOODS, Mary	
Mary WOODS Cullion		05-26-1906	009	CULLION, Daniel	
			009		
John MADDEN	1802	1868	009	HAYES, Mary	
Mary HAYES Madden	1821	1896	009	MADDEN, John	
			009		
Margaret LUNDERGAN	57 Years	05-10-1893	009	LUNDERGAN, William	(NOI William)
			009	_____, Margaret	
			009		
John CRAHAN	59 Years	01-22-1886	009	ROBINSON, Catherine	
Catherine ROBINSON Crahan	68 Years	10-08-1904	009	CRAHAN, John	
			009		
William WOOD	65 Years	06-12-1877	009	_____, Betsey	
Betsey _____ WOOD	73 Years	12-13-1885	009	WOOD, William	
			009		
Thomas D. RYAN	03-06-1830	03-18-1904	009	RYAN, Thomas D.	
			009		
James LEAHY	1825	1898	009	STUART, Mary	
Mary STUART Leahy	1828	1901	009	LEAHY, James	
			009		
Johannah _____ O'DONNELL	72 Years	02-28-1879	009	O'DONNELL, John	(NOI John O'Donnell)
			009	_____, Johannah	
			009		
John MCDERMOTT	1845	1889	009	WHITNEY, Mary Ann	
Mary Ann WHITNEY O'Donnell	1850	1923	009	MCDERMOTT, John	
			009		
John CRAVEN	1848	1937	009	_____, Catherine S.	
Catherine S. _____ CRAVEN	1849	1873	009	CRAVEN, John	
			009		
Jeremiah BOWEN	70 Years	01-05-1884	009	_____, Margaret	
Margaret _____ BOWEN	81Y 10M	09-16-1898	009	BOWEN, Jeremiah	
Johanna BOWEN	90 Years	11-11-1873	009		
			009		

Thomas O'CONNELL	1821	1899	009	HENNESSEY, Mary	
Mary HENNESSY O'Connell	1826	1900	009	O'CONNELL, Thomas	(Stone badly deteriorated. Surname of Mary appears to be Hennessey)
			009		
			009		
John SCULLY	1823	1868	009	SCULLY, John	
			009		
Patrick SCULLY	1822	1859	009	KINNEY, Mary	
Mary KINNEY Scully	1824	1892	009	SCULLY, Patrick	
			009		
Philip CASEY	63 Years	02-13-1894	009	GREGORY, Catherine	
Catherine GREGORY Casey	68 Years	02-11-1915	009	CASEY, Philip	
			009		
Emmett B. DALEY	1855	1917	009	HORSFORD, Harriet	
Harriet HORSFORD Daley	1852	1922	009	DALEY, Emmett B.	
			009		
Thomas KINNEY	84 Years	02-13-1914	009	SCULLY, Ellen	
Ellen SCULLY Kinney	76 Years	07-21-1907	009	KINNEY, Thomas	
Malachi SCULLY	90 Years	10-23-1873	009	SCULLY, Malachi	
			009		
Michael HALLORAN	42 Years	10-15-1870	009	MADDEN, Mary	
Mary MADDEN Halloran	80 Years	07-20-1905	009	HALLORAN, Michael	
			009		
Daniel MCCARTHY			009	BOWEN, Ellen	Daniel McCarthy, his wife, Ellen Bowen and family (NOI)
Ellen BOWEN McCarthy			009	MCCARTHY, Daniel	
			009		
James HENNESSEY	1843	1872	009	TYRELL, Margaret	
Margaret TYRELL Hennessey	1845	1918	009	HENNESSEY, James	
			009		
John WALSH	69 Years	06-08-1891	009	_____, Elizabeth	
Elizabeth _____ WALSH		05-09-1917	009	WALSH, John	
			009		
Honora MCCARTHY	1790	1905	009	MCCARTHY, Honora	(Inscription very sharp. Makes her 115 at death if true)
			009		
			009		
Dennis MCCARTHY	1825	1910	009	DONOVAN, Ellen	
Ellen DONOVAN McCarthy	1834	1873	009	MCCARTHY, Dennis	
			009		
James CONE	1851	1923	009	O'MARA, Ellen	
Ellen O'MARA Cone	1846	1914	009	CONE, James	
			009		
Bridget _____ SUMMERS	52 Years	02-15-1873	009	SUMMERS, William	(NOI William Summers)
			009	_____, Bridget	
			009		
Michael O'GRADY	68 Years	02-26-1895	009	_____, Bridget	
Bridget _____ O'GRADY	56 Years	12-12-1887	009	O'GRADY, Michael	

				009		
Edward W. LONERGAN		1853	1929	009	_____, Margaret G.	
Margaret G. _____ LONERGAN		1856	1895	009	LONERGAN, Edward W.	
				009		
W. W. LONERGAN		1830	1873	009	LONERGAN, W. W.	
				009		
John LONERGAN		1822	1895	009	_____, Johanna	
Johanna _____ LONERGAN		1825	1872	009	LONERGAN, John	
				009		
Bernard DOLAN		1827	1893	009	TOOLE, Elizabeth	
Elizabeth TOOLE Dolan		1827	1905	009	DOLAN, Bernard	
Joseph DOLAN		1854	1872	009	DOLAN, Joseph	
Mary DOLAN		1856	1872	009	DOLAN, Mary	
Catherine DOLAN		1862	1936	009	DOLAN, Catherine	
William DOLAN		1831	1903	009	DOLAN, William	(Prob. surname Dolan. Marker says only "William")
				009		
Patrick GRIFFIN		1841	1911	009	MCGRATH, Ann	
Ann MCGRATH Griffin		1833	1908	009	GRIFFIN, Patrick	
				009		
William MCCARTHY		1840	1925	009	O'MARA, Mary	
Mary O'MARA McCarthy		1837	1906	009	MCCARTHY, William	
				009		
John RYAN		1843	1871	009	RYAN, John	
				009		
Bridget LYNCH		1848	1932	009	LYNCH, Bridget	
				009		
Bridget MCCAFFREY		1831	1870	009	MCCAFFREY, Bridget	
				009		
Mary B. SULLIVAN		1852	1918	009	SULLIVAN, Mary B.	
				009		
William CORCORAN		90 Years	04-13-1888	009	KINNALEY, Norah	
Norah KINNALEY Corcoran		70 Years	03-13-1891	009	CORCORAN, William	
				009		
Mary CORCORAN		1837	1910	009	CORCORAN, Mary	
				009		
Bridget LYONS		52 Years	12-25-1869	009	LYONS, Bridget	

St. Francis de Sales (old burying ground), Bennington, Vt. Main Street, Opposite Historical Museum and Next to Monument School

NAME	**POB**	**DOB/AGE**	**DOD**	**CEM**	**SPOUSE/INDEX**	**INSCRIPTION**
Hanora WELCH Kiersey		1855	1933	010	KIERSEY, Mr.	(NOI Mr. Kiersey)
				010	WELCH, Hanora	

Name	Birthplace	Born/Age	Died	Code	Index	Notes
				010		
Martin GRAVIN		73 Years	11-27-1897	010	_____, Bridget	(NOI Bridget)
				010	GRAVIN, Martin	
				010		
Hanora PURCELL		1817	1899	010	PURCELL, Hanora	
Ellen PURCELL		1857	1943	010	PURCELL, Ellen	
				010		
Mathew CORBITT		49 Years	10-27-1879	010	CORBITT, Mathew	
				010		
William CRONIN		81 Years	07-08-1885	010	_____, Mary	
Mary _____ CRONIN		71 Years	03-08-1877	010	CRONIN, William	
William F. CRONIN		1841	1911	010	_____, B.	(NOI Spouse B.)
				010	CRONIN, William F.	
Mary ANDERSON		1847	1910	010	ANDERSON, Mary	
Frances ANDERSON			1911	010	ANDERSON, Frances	(Deteriorated- Cannot read age at death)
				010		
				010		
Katie MCGRAW		23Y 4M	08-19-1876	010	MCGRAW, Katie	Dau of Micheal & _____ McGraw
				010		
Michael WHELAN			06-19-1876	010	WHELAN, Michael	Son of Patrick & Mary Whelan
Dennis WHELAN			1876	010	WHELAN, Dennis	Son of Patrick & Mary Whelan
				010		
Patrick BARRY		1829	1905	010	MOORE, Ellen	
Ellen MOORE Barry		1840	1882	010	BARRY, Patrick	
Margaret _____		1803	1878	010	_____, Margaret	
				010		
Michael DUGGAN	Co. Tipperary	25 Years	03-21-1878	010	DUGGAN, Michael	Co. Tipperary, Ire. Erected By His Cousins
				010		
				010		
Richard BURKE		08-01-1832	08-22-1885	010	BURKE, Richard	
				010		
Patrick RYAN		63 Years	06-17-1897	010	_____, Mary	(GAR Try Co B, 2nd Rgt or Co.I
				010		
Mary _____ RYAN		40 Years	08-02-1881	010	RYAN, Patrick	3rd Rgt, VtVols)
				010		
Mary Ann MACKSEY Dunn		1847	1885	010	DUNN, Edward	(NOI Edward Dunn)
				010	MACKSEY, Mary Ann	
				010		
Thomas HURLEY		86 Years	12-19-1896	010	HURLEY, Thomas	(GAR) Co. C. 169th NY Reg
				010		
Michael HURLEY		63 Years	02-15-1891	010	HURLEY, Michael	(GAR) Co. A. 8th VT Reg
				010		
Patrick HOGAN		1843	1903	010	O'DEA, Ellen	
Ellen O'DEA Hogan		1850	1936	010	HOGAN, Patrick	
				010		

Name	Birth/Age	Death	Code	Relation	Notes
Patrick O'DORTHY	56 Years	05-22-1864	010	_____, Ellen	(C/B Patrick O'DOHERTY but clearly reads O'DORTHY)
			010		
Ellen _____ O'DORTHY	55 Years	02-24-1881	010	O'DORTHY, Patrick	
Anna J. _____ HEALY	01-24-1857	10-03-1884	010	HEALY, Dennis	(NOI Dennis Healy)
			010		
Patrick LYNCH	1816	1886	010	MCGUIRE, Bridget	
Bridget MCGUIRE Lynch	1840	1914	010	LYNCH, Patrick	
			010		
Michael T. MURPHY	34 Years	05-21-1880	010	ROURKE, Ellen	
Ellen ROURKE Murphy	02-27-1847	12-26-1930	010	MURPHY, Michael T.	
			010		
Patrick CONNERS	48 Years	03-28-1866	010	_____, Bridget	
Bridget _____ CONNERS	65 Years	02-05-1885	010	CONNERS, Patrick	
Johanna CONNERS	29 Years	09-02-1881	010	CONNERS, Johanna	
Thomas CONNERS	17 Years	07-15-1880	010	CONNERS, Thomas	
Michael CONNERS	20 Years	01-12-1880	010	CONNERS, Michael	
James CONNERS	21 Years	08-04-1886	010	CONNERS, James	
			010		
Timothy COFFEY	70 Years	02-27-1889	010	_____, Mary	
Mary _____ COFFEY	56 Years	02-16-1879	010	COFFEY, Timothy	
			010		
Patrick J. CASEY	06-1839	07-1885	010	CASEY, Patrick J.	
Michael CASEY	11-18-1810	11-18-1875	010	_____, Bridget	
Bridget _____ CASEY	04-11-1808	04-03-1890	010	CASEY, Michael	
Francis CASEY	12-18-1846	03-28-1874	010	CASEY, Francis	
Dennie CASEY	11-01-1847	02-02-1890	010	CASEY, Dennie	
Catherine CASEY	04-28-1849	08-02-1860	010	CASEY, Catherine	
Bridget CASEY	12-16-1840	01-24-1842	010	CASEY, Bridget	
Mary CASEY	04-16-1841	06-16-1872	010	CASEY, Mary	
Catherine CASEY	06-18-1866	02-26-1868	010	CASEY, Catherine	
Hanora CASEY	10-26-1867	02-27-1868	010	CASEY, Hanora	
Mary CASEY	02-1868	03-1868	010	CASEY, Mary	
Thomas CASEY	07-1870	06-03-1872	010	CASEY, Thomas	
			010		
Daniel CASEY	1845	1917	010	PURCELL, Mary	
Mary PURCELL Casey	1844	1888	010	CASEY, Daniel	(YOD C/B 1883 - deterioration)
			010		
Mary _____ LYNCH	51 Years	09-07-1879	010	LYNCH, William	(NOI William Lynch)
			010	_____, Mary	
			010		
John FITZSIMMONS	1852	1929	010	MCGINNIS, Mary	
Mary MCGINNIS FITSIMMONS	1865	1941	010	FITZSIMMONS, John	
Thomas FITZSIMMONS	52 Years	09-25-1878	010	FITZSIMMONS, Thomas	
			010		
Margaret MCGEE	81 Years	07-19-1887	010	MCGEE, Margaret	

Name	Age/Birth	Death	Section	Index Name	Notes
			010		
Michael MURPHY	1831	1907	010	FLOOD, Mary	
Mary FLOOD Murphy	1831	1888	010	MURPHY, Michael	
			010		
ary Ann AGAN	18Y 4M	12-11-1880	010	AGAN, Mary Ann	D/O Dennis AGAN and Mary Agan
			010		
Timothy EVANS	9 Years	01-28-1881	010	EVANS, Timothy	S/O John EVANS and Ellen Evans
William EVANS	1Y 7M	09-19-1874	010	EVANS, William	S/O John EVANS and Ellen Evans
Thomas EVANS	1 Month	06-03-1868	010	EVANS, Thomas	S/O John EVANS and Ellen Evans
			010		
TIMMONS Family			010	TIMMONS, Family	(Cross & Anchor inscribed. US. Veterans Flag. NOI)
Marty TIMMONS			010	TIMMONS, Marty	
John TIMMONS			010	TIMMONS, John	
			010		
William NUGENT	64 Years	04-01-1881	010	NUGENT, William	
			010		
William J. COX	38 Years	06-24-1896	010	COX, William J.	
Julia O'BRIEN	103 Years	02-14-1880	010	O'BRIEN, Julia	
			010		
Michael RYAN	43 Years	05-22-1881	010	COSTELLO, Catharine	
Catharine COSTELLO Ryan	1837	1917	010	RYAN, Michael	
			010		
Annie HILL	1826	1898	010	HILL, Annie	
			010		
Mary HEALY	1793	1881	010	HEALY, Mary	
			010		
Patrick CALLAHAN	57 Years	09-06-1884	010	_____, Mary	
Mary _____ CALLAHAN	43 Years	03-10-1883	010	CALLAHAN, Patrick	
			010		
Michael WELCH	1840	1920	010	KELLEY, Catherine	
Catherine KELLEY Welch	1841	1918	010	WELCH, Michael	
			010		
			010		
Thomas TOOMEY	06-14-1824	02-08-1903	010	MURPHY, Margaret T.	
Margaret T. MURPHY Toomey	04-10-1833	08-17-1897	010	TOOMEY, Thomas	
			010		
Sarah _____ COYLE	36 Years	12-31-1884	010	COYLE, Martin	(NOI Martin Coyle)
			010	_____, Sarah	
			010		
William CASEY	46 Years	08-16-1908	010	BURKE, Anna	
Anna BURKE Casey	60 Years	03-25-1918	010	CASEY, William	
Patrick CASEY	70 Years	01-22-1877	010	RYAN, Mary	
			010	BOLLARD, Mary	
Mary RYAN CASEY	80 Years	03-08-1896	010	CASEY, Patrick	
Mary BOLLARD Casey	57 Years	01-14-1897	010	CASEY, Patrick	

			010		
Thomas CARRIGAN	1827	1902	010	_____, Hanora	
Hanora _____ CARRIGAN	1827	1897	010	CARRIGAN, Thomas	
			010		
Mary COONEY	1847	1906	010	COONEY, Mary	
			010		
James GUNSHANNON	60 Years	12-02-1895	010	GUNSHANNON, James	
			010		
Michael MULLIGAN	80 Years	03-29-1912	010	BOWEN, Mary	
Mary BOWEN Mulligan	66 Years	07-17-1885	010	MULLIGAN, Michael	
			010		
Mary A. MULLIGAN	1859	1909	010	MULLIGAN, Mary A.	
			010		
Thomas TRACEY		12-15-1896	010	LYONS, Bridget	(NOI DOB)
Bridget LYONS Tracey		03-12-1915	010	TRACEY, Thomas	(NOI DOB)
Dennis TRACEY		09-15-1883	010	TRACEY, Dennis	(NOI DOB)
Alice TRACEY		10-03-1902	010	TRACEY, Alice	(NOI DOB)
			010		
Patrick DAVOCK	1830	1903	010	SHERLOCK, Mary	
Mary SHERLOCK Davock	1831	1906	010	DAVOCK, Patrick	
			010		
John L. GARRY	59 Years	03-18-1902	010	GARRY, John L.	(GAR) Co. D.28th Mass Inf
			010		
MANGAN Family			010	MANGAN, Family	
Andrew MANGAN			010	MANGAN, Andrew	(NOI)
Harold MANGAN			010	MANGAN, Harold	(NOI)
Mary MANGAN			010	MANGAN, Mary	(NOI)
Paul MANGAN			010	MANGAN, Paul	(NOI)
Katherine MANGAN			010	MANGAN, Katherine	(NOI)
			010		
Mortimer CULLITON	1848	1907	010	O'DONNELL, Margaret	
			010	O'CONNELL, Anastasia	
Margaret O'DONNELL Culliton	1847	1894	010	CULLITON, Mortimer	
Anastasia O'CONNELL Culliton	1857	1929	010	CULLITON, Mortimer	
			010		
Francis STOWE			010	STOWE, Francis	(GAR) Co. K. 16th ___ Inf
			010		(Possibly NH or NY. Not in
			010		16th Vermont)
			010		
Matthew COONEY	87 Years	02-26-1890	010	____, Sarah	
Sarah _____ COONEY	90 Years	09-06-1899	010	COONEY, Matthew	
			010		
John LYONS	01-07-1845	09-29-1892	010	KEEGAN, Catherine	A True Friend, Kind Father And
			010		Loving Husband
Catherine KEEGAN Lyons	03-02-1849	11-29-1918	010	LYONS, John	

Name	Place	Born/Age	Died	Code	Index Name	Notes
				010		
Martin MURRAY		10-25-1831	10-09-1918	010	ROBINSON, Mary Ann	
Mary Ann ROBINSON Murray		08-12-1840	07-18-1919	010	MURRAY, Martin	
				010		
				010		
Michael GUNSHANNON	Co. Longford	1825	1882	010	CAMPBELL, Elizabeth	Natives of Co. Longford, Ire.
Elizabeth CAMPBELL	Co. Longford	1821	1903	010	GUNSHANNON, Michael	Natives of Co. Longford, Ire.
Elizabeth A. GUNSHANNON	Co. Longford	1856	1909	010	GUNSHANNON, Elizabeth	Natives of Co. Longford, Ire.
James H. GUNSHANNON	Co. Longford	1858	1903	010	GUNSHANNON, James H.	Natives of Co. Longford, Ire.
Edward J. GUNSHANNON		1864	1916	010	GUNSHANNON, Edward J.	
Bridget E. GUNSHANNON		1868	1935	010	GUNSHANNON, Bridget E.	
Thomas F. GUNSHANNON		1860	1931	010	GUNSHANNON, Thomas F.	
				010		
Michael MCGUIRE			12-27-1887	010	MCGUIRE, Michael	(NOI DOB)
				010		
James POWERS		83 Years	09-1890	010	_____, Hanora	
Hanora _____ POWERS		85 Years	10-1883	010	POWERS, James	
				010		
Michael LEONARD		1831	1903	010	DOWLING, Mary	
Mary DOWLING Leonard		1830	1893	010	LEONARD, Michael	
				010		
Patrick GIBNEY		47 Years	08-19-1884	010	CONE, Mary	
Mary CONE Gibney		60 Years	03-08-1908	010	GIBNEY, Patrick	
				010		
Thomas CONE		86 Years	01-09-1892	010	RYAN, Ellen	
Ellen RYAN Cone	Co. Galway	82 Years	08-09-1889	010	CONE, Thomas	Born In County Galway, Ireland
				010		
James RILEY		85 Years	04-09-1906	010	_____, Bridget	For 57 Years The Faithful Gardener at Hall Farm
				010		
Bridget _____ RILEY	Co. Tipperary	56 Years	10-08-1884	010	RILEY, James	A Native Of Co. Tipperary, Ire
				010		
Mrs. Margaret KANE		1842	1911	010	KANE, Mrs. Margaret	
				010		
John MULLIGAN		1850	1914	010	LAPIERRE, Azilda	
Azilda LAPIERRE Mulligan		1855	1919	010	MULLIGAN, John	
				010		
Bridget MCGROATY Smith		1840	1906	010	SMITH, John	(On CROWLEY stone but no entries for Crowleys or John Smith)
				010		
				010		
				010		
Johanna O'DAY			01-18-1918	010	O'DAY, Johanna	(NOI DOB)
Bridget SHEEHY			12-14-1885	010	SHEEHY, Bridget	(NOI DOB)
				010		
Mary MCCARTHY		88 Years	02-09-1902	010	MCCARTHY, Mary	RIP
				010		

Name	Origin	Born	Died	Code	Index	Notes
Patrick BRANN		72 Years	11-07-1888	010	MADDEN, Mary	
Mary MADDEN Brann		66 Years	06-20-1886	010	BRANN, Patrick	
Thomas BRANN		09-12-1852	01-10-1885	010	BRANN, Thomas	Sons Of P & M Brann
John BRANN		04-24-1859	01-28-1886	010	BRANN, John	Sons Of P & M Brann
				010		
John MADDEN		79 Years	10-17-1891	010	MADDEN, John	
				010		
Patrick KELLY		1834	1904	010	____, Hanora	
Hanora ____ KELLY		1838	1906	010	KELLY, Patrick	
				010		
John BIRMINGHAM		11-25-1838	10-17-1895	010	SMITH, Anna M.	
Anna M. SMITH Birmingham		07-14-1857	01-26-1893	010	BIRMINGHAM, John	
				010		
Mary DOYLE	Co. Carlow	55 Years	08-08-1887	010	DOYLE, Mary	Born In Ballyknock, Co. Carlow Parish of Glynn, Ire. (Could not find civil or religious Parish of Glynn. Ballyknock is in St. Mullins Parish)
				010		
				010		
				010		
				010		
Mary DOYLE		1833	1890	010	DOYLE, Mary	
				010		
				010		
Matthew P. ENRIGHT		1857	1906	010	CUMMINGS, Eliza A.	
Eliza A. CUMMINGS Enright		1861		010	ENRIGHT, Matthew P.	
				010		
Michael O'NIEL		67 Years	11-10-1894	010	O'NIEL, Michael	(GAR) Co. A. 13th VT Rgt.(This was Vermonts "Irish" Regiment. Surname is actually O'NEIL. Home listed as Burlington, VT)
				010		
				010		
				010		
				010		
Patrick NASH		1829	1910	010	GRIFFIN, Margaret	
Margaret GRIFFIN Nash		1831	1887	010	NASH, Patrick	
				010		
Francis GUILTINAN		1839	1909	010	____, Bridget	
Bridget ____ GUILTINAN		1839	1914	010	GUILTINAN, Francis	
				010		
Timothy KIRBY			1903	010	____, Jane	(NOI DOB)
Jane ____ KIRBY			1906	010	KIRBY, Timothy	(NOI DOB)
				010		
Perry MURPHY		1810	1876	010	NOLAN, Mary	
Mary NOLAN Murphy		1825	1888	010	MURPHY, Perry	
Annie MURPHY		1851	1872	010	MURPHY, Annie	
Mary MURPHY		1853	1870	010	MURPHY, Mary	
Thomas MURPHY		1860	1933	010	MURPHY, Thomas	
				010		
Mary ____ GUILTINANE		50 Years	01-09-1888	010	GUILTINANE, Patrick	(NOI Patrick Guiltinane)

				010	_____, Mary	
				010		
Michael MCNAMARA		1842	1902	010	_____, Bridget	
Bridget _____ MCNAMARA		1838	1915	010	MCNAMARA, Michael	
				010		
Richard POWERS		55 Years	02-02-1897	010	_____, Ellen	May His Soul Rest In Peace.
				010	POWERS, Richard	This Stone Erected By His Wife
				010		Ellen Powers.(NOI Ellen)
				010		
Rev. John C. O'DWYER		01-25-1839	12-03-1883	010	O'DWYER, Rev. John C.	May His Soul Rest In Peace.
				010		
Patrick HOGAN		90 Years	10-08-1889	010	_____, Winnifred	
Winnifred _____ HOGAN		87 Years	03-26-1890	010	HOGAN, Patrick	
				010		
Dennis HOGAN		26 Years	07-20-1869	010	HOGAN, Dennis	
				010		
Margaret _____		85 Years	09-26-1926	010	_____, Margaret	(No Surname listed. Does not
				010		say if spouse of Dennis Hogan)
				010		
James SILK		1820	1894	010	_____, Mary	
Mary _____ SILK		1825	1903	010	SILK, James	
Mary SILK		1849	1932	010	SILK, Mary	
James SILK		1855	1936	010	SILK, James	
Margaret SILK		1861	1942	010	SILK, Margaret	
				010		
Michael HOWE	Co. Galway	51 Years	04-21-1889	010	CASSIDY, Sabina	A Native Of The County of
				010		Galway, Ireland
Sabina CASSIDY Howe			03-10-1905	010	HOWE, Michael	
				010		
Julia CONE Craven		1851	1889	010	CRAVEN, John	(NOI John Craven)
				010	CONE, Julia	
				010		
Michael HOGAN				010	O'DAY, Bridget	(NOI DOB-DOD)
Bridget O'DAY Hogan				010	HOGAN, Michael	(NOI DOB-DOD)
				010		
GLEESON _____				010	_____, GLEESON	(Stone face down.Can not read)
				010		
Timothy COLLINS		1829	1907	010	_____, Ellen	
Ellen _____ COLLINS		1827	1902	010	COLLINS, Timothy	
				010		
Michael MALONEY		74 Years	02-14-1901	010	KING, Mary	
Mary KING Maloney		34 Years	04-11-1866	010	MALONEY, Michael	
				010		
Margaret GIBNEY Harris		1846	1924	010	HARRIS, Edward	(NOI Edward Harris)
				010	GIBNEY, Margaret	

Name	Origin	Born	Died	Code	Index Name	Notes
				010		
Ann _____ PENDERGAST	Co. Kings	67 Years	08-26-1889	010	PENDERGAST, James	A Native Of Kings County, Ire.
				010	_____, Ann	(NOI James Pendergast)
				010		
Edward MAGEE		03-17-1833	04-10-1907	010	COFFEY, Ellenor	
Ellenor COFFEY Magee		03-15-1826	11-18-1890	010	MAGEE, Edward	
				010		
Thomas GABBETT		49 Years	01-01-1890	010	GABBETT, Thomas	
				010		
Cornelius MCCARTHY		1849	1929	010	_____, Mary	
Mary _____ MCCARTHY		1839	1919	010	MCCARTHY, Cornelius	
				010		
Michael MARTIN		74 Years	08-05-1911	010	MARTIN, Michael	(GAR) Co. A 4th VT Regt
				010		
Michael J. COSTELLO		1832	1891	010	GREGORY, Sarah	
Sarah GREGORY Costello		1832	1919	010	COSTELLO, Michael J.	
				010		
James QUINN		1819	1900	010	MCGRATH, Mary	
Mary MCGRATH Quinn		1818	1898	010	QUINN, James	
				010		
Margaret STUART			1900	010	STUART, Margaret	(NOI DOB)
Mary E. LEAHY			1911	010	LEAHY, Mary E.	(NOI DOB)
Johanna SCULLY			1900	010	SCULLY, Johanna	(NOI DOB)
				010		
Philip B. DONNELLY		1855	1891	010	DONNELLY, Philip B.	
				010		
John GRIFFIN		1836	1897	010	LEONARD, Mary	
Mary LEONARD Griffin		1825	1893	010	GRIFFIN, John	
				010		
Edmund SKEHAN		1842	1893	010	_____, Margaret	(Stone badly deteriorated)
Margaret _____ SKEHAN		1862	1895	010	SKEHAN, Edmund	
				010		
John WARD		1856	1923	010	_____, Mary	
Mary _____ WARD		1854	1906	010	WARD, John	
Catherine WARD		1809	1892	010	WARD, Catherine	
Mary FLYNN Ward		1852	1930	010	FLYNN, Mary	
				010		
Michael DOYLE		1833	1909	010	DOYLE, Michael	
				010		
Bridget NORMILE		02-01-1832	07-08-1900	010	NORMILE, Bridget	Mother (NOI Father)
				010		
Patrick HURLEY		06-15-1847	09-30-1903	010	HURLEY, Patrick	(GAR) 2nd Vt Battery (Light Artillery)
				010		
				010		
Edward POWERS		1833	1910	010	_____, Margaret	

Margaret _____ POWERS		1843	1916	010	POWERS, Edward	
				010		
Charles MCGUIRE		04-22-1837	10-19-1909	010	MULLIGAN, Bridget	
Bridget MULLIGAN McGuire		05-04-1834	08-02-1893	010	MCGUIRE, Charles	
				010		
Michael LONERGAN		1855	1906	010	PETERS, Mary	
Mary PETERS Lonergan		1857	1930	010	LONERGAN, Michael	
Catherine PETERS		1835	1895	010	PETERS, Catherine	
				010		
John KEENAN		1830	1901	010	MCCAFFREY, Catherine	
Catherine MCCAFFREY Keenan		1842	1906	010	KEENAN, John	

Park Lawn Cemetery, Bennington, Vt.   U.S. Route 7 South of Village

NAME	POB	DOB/AGE	DOD	CEM	SPOUSE/INDEX	INSCRIPTION
John NEHER		1841	1931	011	OTT, Kathrine	
Kathrine OTT Neher		1848	1917	011	NEHER, John	
				011		
John E. HACKETT		1854	1928	011	WARD, Ellen M.	
Ellen M. WARD Hackett		1854	19--	011	HACKETT, John E.	
				011		
Thomas ROBINSON		12-27-1798	3-7-1893	011	FLOOD, Mary	
Mary FLOOD Robinson		12-20-1812	4-12-1887	011	ROBINSON, Thomas	
				011		
George H. ROBINSON		5-30-1850	10-20-1942	011	O'CONNELL, Mary	
Mary O'CONNELL Robinson		3-25-1856	2-15-1922	011	ROBINSON, George H.	
				011		
Maria MADDEN		11-20-1852	4-23-1889	011	ROBINSON, Thomas	
				011		
William F. SLATTERY		1845	1915	011	FLOOD, Bridget	
Bridget FLOOD Slattery		1847	1889	011	SLATTERY, William F.	
				011		
Edward J. MURPHY		1824	1910	011	ROSE, Harriet	
Harriet ROSE Murphy		1832	1909	011	MURPHY, Edward J.	
				011		
John M. HEALY		79 Years	4-6-1918	011	ERWIN, Mary	
				011	BRENNAN, Mary	Of Dennis Healy.(NOI Dennis)
Mary ERWIN Healy		79 Years	1-27-1915	011	HEALY, John M.	
Mary BRENNAN Healy		88 Years	1-16-1881	011	HEALY, Dennis	Our Mother, Mary Brennan, Wife Of Dennis Healy.(NOI Dennis)
				011		
James RYAN		1854	1923	011	DREW, Catherine	

NAME	POB	DOB/AGE	DOD	CEM	SPOUSE/INDEX	INSCRIPTION
Catherine DREW Ryan		1847	1915	011	RYAN, James	
				011		
Michael P. HOGAN		1854	1948	011	HINES, Catherine	
Catherine HINES Hogan		1851	1916	011	HOGAN, Michael P.	
				011		
Truman J. MALLORY		1851	1940	011	NILES, Eva M.	
Eva M. NILES		1859	1914	011	MALLORY, Truman J.	
				011		
John P. MURPHY		1857	1916	011	_____, Mary A.	
Mary A. _____ MURPHY		1861	1933	011	MURPHY, John P.	
				011		
Joseph T. LEONARD		1846	1920	011	SAUSVILLE, Julie	
Julie SAUSVILLE Leonard		1850	1936	011	LEONARD, Joseph T.	
				011		
Ellen KEEFE		1842	1910	011	KEEFE, Ellen	
				011		
Honora CUMMINGS		1830	1911	011	CUMMINGS, Honora	
				011		
Mary CUMMINGS		1854	1927	011	CUMMINGS, Mary	
				011		
Michael MAHER		1854	1913	011	MAHER, Michael	
				011		
John HACKETT		1832	1923	011	O'BRYAN, Cathrine	
Cathrine O'BRYAN Hackett		1834	1911	011	HACKETT, John	
				011		
John HURLEY		1818	1884	011	_____, Julia S.	
Julia S. HURLEY		1820	1886	011	HURLEY, John	
John HURLEY, Jr.		1850	1884	011	HURLEY, John Jr.	
				011		
Richard COOK		1835	1916	011	_____, Sarah A.	
Sarah A. COOK		1846	1933	011	COOK, Richard	
				011		
Edward WINSLOW		1844	1916	011	CRAVEN, Mary	
Mary CRAVEN Winslow		1846	1937	011	WINSLOW, Edward	

St. Stanislaus Cemetery, Bloomfield, Vermont. Left side of Highway 105 about one mile west of village.

NAME	POB	DOB/AGE	DOD	CEM	SPOUSE/INDEX	INSCRIPTION
George BOYNE		48 Years	01-09-1914	012	_____, Kathleen M.	
Kathleen M. _____ BOYNE		62 Years	12-14-1936	012	BOYNE, George	
				012		

Patrick MCGINTY	73 Years	04-29-1885	012	GALLAGHAR, Sarah	
Sarah GALLAGHAR McGinty	84 Years	06-04-1892	012	MCGINTY, Patrick	
			012		
Lewis CONN	67 Years	07-17-1889	012	_____, Mary	(AKA Louis)
Mary _____ CONN	75 Years	04-13-1903	012	CONN, Lewis	
			012		
Michael CONN	36 Years	1893	012	CONN, Michael	
			012		
John CONNOLLY	07-13-1853	10-23-1947	012	_____, Bridget Ann	
Bridget Ann _____ CONNOLLY	12-22-1855	04-23-1929	012	CONNOLLY, John	
			012		
William ROACH	1838	1906	012	_____, Ellen R.	
Ellen R. _____ ROACH	1844	1928	012	ROACH, William	
			012		
John GARDNER			012	GARDNER, John	(NOI)
			012		
Ann KELLY Nelson		1885	012	NELSON, Mr.	(NOI Mr. Nelson)
			012	KELLY, Ann	
			012		
William CORCORAN	21Y5M10D	10-13-1886	012	CORCORAN, William	
			012		
Matilda _____ SHERMAN	49 Years	05-09-1899	012	SHERMAN, Peter	(NOI Peter Sherman)
			012	_____, Matilda	
			012		
Dennis SMITH	42 Years	12-17-1883	012	_____, Rose	
Rose _____ SMITH	61 Years	05-27-1909	012	SMITH, Dennis	
			012		
Peter LARKIN	40Y 3D	12-13-1896	012	LARKIN, Peter	
Rosa LARKIN Davidson	02-18-1862	05-14-1937	012	DAVIDSON, Mr.	(NOI Mr. Davidson)
			012	LARKIN, Rosa	
			012		
James O'DOWD	1853	1924	012	BURNS, Susan	
Susan BURNS O'Dowd	1859	1932	012	O'DOWD, James	
			012		
James O'DOWD	77 Years	04-16-1895	012	_____, Rosie	
Rosie _____ O'Dowd	72 Years	07-29-1889	012	O'DOWD, James	
			012		
Although outside of our search parameters, in this cemetery were			012		
these families:			012		
O'MARA			012	O'MARA	
BELKNAP			012	BELKNAP	
SAUNDERS			012	SAUNDERS	
DALEY			012	DALEY	
SCOTT			012	SCOTT	

St. Mary's Cemetery   Brandon, Vt.   Route 73 off Marble Street

NAME	POB	DOB/AGE	DOD	CEM	SPOUSE/INDEX	INSCRIPTION
John REYNOLDS		78 Years	07-15-1891	013	REYNOLDS, Ellen	
Ellen ____ REYNOLDS		71 Years	11-04-1881	013	REYNOLDS, John	
Patrick REYNOLDS		48 Years	03-04-1892	013	REYNOLDS, Patrick	
John REYNOLDS		1859	1923	013	REYNOLDS, John	
Anna REYNOLDS		1855	1946	013	REYNOLDS, Anna	
				013		
Patrick O'HEARN		1827	1883	013	CULLEN, Ellen	
Ellen CULLEN O'Hearn		1830	1890	013	O'HEARN, Patrick	
Morris O'HEARN		1856	1875	013	O'HEARN, Morris	
Michael O'HEARN		1859	1881	013	O'HEARN, Michael	
Nellie O'HEARN		1862	1868	013	O'HEARN, Nellie	
John O'HEARN		1863	1864	013	O'HEARN, John	
Katie O'HEARN		1868	1875	013	O'HEARN, Katie	
Edmund J. O'HEARN		1865	1915	013	O'HEARN, Edmund J.	
Margaret O'HEARN		1860	1937	013	O'HEARN, Margaret	
				013		
Ellen CASEY			08-17-1882	013	CASEY, Ellen	
				013		
Patrick MCGARRY		82 Years	01-23-1900	013	MCGARRY, Margaret	
Margaret _____ MCGARRY		77 Years	08-31-1892	013	MCGARRY, Patrick	
				013		
Patrick BARRETT		27 Years	02-17-1871	013	BARRETT, Patrick	Son of John & Johanna Barrett
				013	BARRETT, John	(NOI John & Johanna Barrett)
				013	BARRETT, Johanna	
				013		
James JOHNSON		48 Years	08-14-1882	013	JOHNSON, James	
				013		
Catherine DIFFLEY McCall	Co. Longford	79 Years	11-13-1892	013	DIFFLEY, Catherine	D/O of Hugh-Catherine DIFFLEY
				013	MCCALL, Mr.	(NOI Spouse Mr. McCall)
				013		
James MCDONOUGH		21 Years	11-15-1874	013	MCDONOUGH, James	
				013		
Patrick MCDONOUGH		18 Years	06-29-1867	013	MCDONOUGH, Patrick	
				013		
John COLLINS		72 Years	02-21-1886	013	MURPHY, Mary	
Mary MURPHY Collins		96 Years	11-12-1915	013	COLLINS, John	
Cornelius COLLINS		1854	1910	013	RILEY, Katherine	
Katherine RILEY Collins		1850	1932	013	COLLINS, Cornelius	
				013		
John WONDER		84 Years	01-12-1908	013	WONDER, John	(Prob. Wunder. See next entry)

Name	Birthplace	Born	Died	Code	Index	Notes
				013		
Joseph WUNDER		69Y 5M	09-09-1885	013	WUNDER, Caroline	
Caroline _____ WUNDER		74Y 7M	01-31-1889	013	WUNDER, Joseph	
				013		
Edward KANALEY		1828	1910	013	MEEHAN, Margaret	
Margaret MEEHAN Kanaley		1837	1918	013	KANALEY, Edward	
				013		
Edward GRANT		03-14-1810	08-23-1894	013	GRANT, Hannah	
Hannah ____ GRANT	Co. Antrim	70 Years	11-04-1881	013	GRANT, Edward	Born In Co. Antrim, Ireland Died at E. Middlebury, VT
				013		
Henry GRANT		01-25-1844	01-06-1908	013	GRANT, Mary Ellen	
Mary Ellen ____ GRANT		08-20-1867	04-15-1959	013	GRANT, Henry F.	
				013		
John BYRNES		1832	1913	013	GIBNEY, Ann	
Ann GIBNEY Byrnes		1834	1888	013	BYRNES, John	
				013		
Peter DOLAN		08-01-1823	11-08-1891	013	DOLAN, Mary	
Mary _____ DOLAN		05-04-1837	09-16-1906	013	DOLAN, Peter	
				013		
Dennis SCANLAN		1833	1889	013	TULLY, Catherine	
Catherine TULLY Scanlan		1829	1909	013	SCANLAN, Dennis	
Thomas SCANLAN		1856	1905	013	SCANLAN, Thomas	
				013		
James O'HARE		84 Years	04-08-1900	013	O'HARE, Ann	
Ann _____ O'HARE		60 Years	09-28-1890	013	O'HARE, James	
Bridget O'CONNELL		1828	1903	013	O'CONNELL, Bridget	
Elenor WHITTEMOR		1857	1927	013	WHITTEMOR, Elenor	
Bessie O'HARE		1858	19__	013	O'HARE, Bessie	
				013		
Thomas DEVER		1857	1925	013	DEVER, Elizabeth	
Elizabeth ____ DEVER		1854	1937	013	DEVER, Thomas	
				013		
John POWERS		1828	1898	013	CULLINAN, Bridget	
Bridget CULLINAN Powers		1850	1910	013	POWERS, John	
				013		
Patrick CONRY		63 Years	12-18-1893	013	GRIFFIN, Catherine	
Catherine GRIFFIN Conry		62 Years	07-27-1917	013	CONRY, Patrick	
				013		
Richard LYONS		1845	1931	013	O'NEIL, Mary	
Mary O'NEIL Lyons		1846	1921	013	LYONS, Richard	
				013		
Henry J. LESSOR		10-17-1841	08-21-1920	013	PRESTON, Elizabeth	
Elizabeth PRESTON Lessor		03-18-1846	02-01-1915	013	LESSOR, Henry J.	
				013		
John W. BURKE		05-05-1850	02-21-1888	013	BURKE, John W.	

			013		
George RUTLEDGE	03-18-1828	05-28-1891	013	RUTLEDGE, Delia N.	
Delia N. ____ RUTLEDGE	71 Years	07-27-1905	013	RUTLEDGE, George	
			013		
Patrick MURPHY	74 Years	12-06-1891	013	GLYNN, Mary	
Mary GLYNN Murphy	82 Years	03-14-1907	013	MURPHY, Patrick	
Annie MURPHY	35 Years	08-27-1889	013	MURPHY, Annie	
			013		
Michael LYONS	78 Years	04-02-1892	013	LYONS, Michael	
Sarah LYONS	33 Years	10-14-1894	013	LYONS, Sarah	
Mary LYONS		05-22-1914	013	LYONS, Mary	
			013		
Patrick WHALEN	58 Years	12-21-1890	013	CRONIN, Honora	Pvt, Co.H. 5th Vt. Vols
Honora CRONIN Whalen	1839	1902	013	WHALEN, Patrick	
			013		
Catherine TENNIEN	79 Years	11-17-1910	013	TENNIEN, Catherine	
William TENNIEN	29 Years	02-29-1892	013	TENNIEN, William	
James TENNIEN	78 Years	07-25-1932	013	TENNIEN, James	
			013		
Edward SULLIVAN	1852	1928	013	PURCELL, Mary J.	
Mary J. PURCELL Sullivan	1858	1943	013	SULLIVAN, Edward	
			013		
James SULLIVAN	80 Years	01-28-1892	013	SULLIVAN, Ellen	
Ellen _____ SULLIVAN	82 Years	02-20-1905	013	SULLIVAN, James	
James SULLIVAN	75 Years	02-10-1934	013	SULLIVAN, Mary	(NOI DOB-SOS Mary Sullivan)
Mary A. _____ SULLIVAN			013	SULLIVAN, James	
			013		
Patrick MULCAHY	89 Years	10-08-1898	013	MULCAHEY, Ellen B.	
Ellen B. _____ MULCAHY	90 Years	02-27-1905	013	MULCAHEY, Patrick	
			013		
Bridget H. MULCAHY	38 Years	03-27-1893	013	MULCAHEY, Bridget	Dau of P. & E. MULCAHY
			013		
Bartholomew LANDERS	1854	1929	013	LANDERS, Bartholomew	
			013		
John LANDERS	77 Years	12-15-1892	013	LANDERS, John	
			013		
James FOLEY	11-02-1850	03-25-1917	013	FOLEY, Lucy E.	
Lucy E. _____ FOLEY	06-11-1860	09-26-1941	013	FOLEY, James	
			013		
Timothy LYNCH	04-28-1853	11-27-1896	013	REYNOLDS, Bridget A.	
Bridget A. REYNOLDS Lynch		10-26-1925	013	LYNCH, Timothy	
			013		
Peter PHILLIPS	1853	1913	013	PHILLIPS, Peter	
			013		
Ed RAFFERTY	73 Years	12-28-1894	013	RAFFERTY, Ed	

			013		
Patrick J. MULCAHY	1852	1938	013	MCGUIRE, Elizabeth	
Elizabeth MCGUIRE Mulcahy	1851	1921	013	MULCAHY, Patrick J.	
			013		
Elizabeth RAFFERTY	76 Years	02-03-1903	013	RAFFERTY, Elizabeth	
			013		
John T. WELCH	12-25-1840	11-15-1915	013	MCGUIRE, Mary A.	
Mary A. MCGUIRE Welch	46 Years	08-19-1894	013	WELCH, John T.	
			013		
Michael NORTON	60 Years	04-13-1870	013	NORTON, Ann	
Ann ______ NORTON	79 Years	02-17-1894	013	NORTON, Michael	
Peter NORTON	77 Years	01-02-1920	013	NORTON, Peter	
Bernard NORTON	82 Years	02-25-1923	013	NORTON, Bernard	
Patrick NORTON	67 Years	02-19-1925	013	NORTON, Patrick	
Mary D. NORTON	16 Years	12-12-1860	013	NORTON, Mary D.	
Julia NORTON	41 Years	03-07-1898	013	NORTON, Julia	
Michael NORTON	50 Years	11-20-1901	013	NORTON, Michael	
Elizabeth NORTON	75 Years	02-21-1925	013	NORTON, Elizabeth	
Rose NORTON	78 Years	06-07-1925	013	NORTON, Rose	
Margaret NORTON	77 Years	12-22-1933	013	NORTON, Margaret	
			013		
Peter WILSON	1829	1915	013	ANGLIM, Mary	
Mary ANGLIM Wilson	65 Years	12-21-1893	013	WILSON, Peter	
Timothy WILSON	44Y 6M	03-14-1900	013	READY, Elizabeth	
Elizabeth READY Wilson	1860	1919	013	WILSON, Timothy	
Thomas WILSON	1859	1919	013	WILSON, Thomas	
M. Agnes WILSON	1862	1864	013	WILSON, M. Agnes	
Martin WILSON	1866	1932	013	WILSON, Martin	
Anne E. WILSON	1868	1929	013	WILSON, Anne E.	
M. Ellen WILSON	1874	1932	013	WILSON, M. Ellen	
James WILSON	1857	1901	013	WILSON, James	
			013		
Mrs. Patrick TULLY	76 Years	03-26-1908	013	TULLY, Patrick	(NOI Patrick TULLY)
			013		
Mary J. MILES	1831	1901	013	MILES, Mary J.	
			013		
James J. CONDON	05-06-1853	02-27-1924	013	MCDONOUGH, Catherine E.	
Catherine MCDONOUGH Condon	02-13-1853	05-04-1917	013	CONDON, James J.	
Eliza BARRY	03-14-1825	02-15-1900	013	BARRY, Eliza	
			013		
Thomas CLACK	1852	1916	013	MURPHY, Ellen	
Ellen MURPHY Clack	1859	1935	013	CLACK, Thomas	
			013		
James O'BRIEN	1854		013	SULLIVAN, Mary	
Mary SULLIVAN O'Brien	1857	1927	013	O'BRIEN, James	

Name	Origin	Born / Age	Died	Code	Index	Notes
Anna B. SULLIVAN		1860	1932	013	SULLIVAN, Anna B.	
				013		
Mike NORTON		56 Years	06-15-1882	013	NORTON, Susan	
Susan _____ NORTON		55 Years	01-25-1885	013	NORTON, Mike	
				013		
Henry WELCH		93 Years	01-19-1907	013	WELCH, Ellen	
Ellen _____ WELCH		72 Years	03-27-1899	013	WELCH, Henry	
Nancy WELCH		83 Years	03-09-1930	013	WELCH, Nancy	Dau of Henry & Ellen WELCH
				013		
Michael CASMAN		83 Years	10-04-1885	013	CASEY, Honora	In Loving Memory
Honora CASEY Casman		76 Years	07-23-1884	013	CASMAN, Michael	
				013		
Michael DIXON	Co. Monaghan	72 Years	01-28-1886	013	DIXON, Catherine	A Native Of Ireland, County Monaghan.
Catherine _____ DIXON		74 Years	02-19-1892	013	DIXON, Michael	
Elizabeth DIXON		44 Years	01-24-1902	013	DIXON, Elizabeth	
William DIXON		49 Years	08-17-1904	013	DIXON, Phillip	
Phillip DIXON		15 Years	03-01-1863	013	DIXON, William	
Alice DIXON		1 Year	03-01-1863	013	DIXON, Alice	
Michael DIXON		30 Years	12-25-1872	013	DIXON, Michael	
Thomas DIXON		32 Years	06-02-1877	013	DIXON, Thomas	
				013		
John W. POWERS		1846	1922	013	MARKHAM, Anna E.	
Anna E. MARKHAM Powers		1852	1949	013	POWERS, John W.	
				013		
James MULLALY		1854	1929	013	MARKHAM, Mary J.	
Mary J. MARKHAM Mullaly		1859	1949	013	MULLALY, James	
				013		
John GREEN		1849	1928	013	GREEN, Helen	
Helen______ GREEN		1858	1920	013	GREEN, John	
				013		
John DONNELLY		1856	1925	013	LYNCH, Mary	
Mary LYNCH Donnelly		1860	1919	013	DONNELLY, John	
				013		
Jerry WHITE		1856	1921	013	HART, Rose	
Rose HART White		1869	1938	013	WHITE, Jerry	
				013		
William F. WALSH		1857	1936	013	MCGARRY, Mary	
Mary MCGARRY Walsh		1857	1932	013	WALSH, William F.	
				013		
Fred MCINTYRE		1847	1931	013	ST. GEORGE, Rose A.	(Gar)-Co.B. 7th Rgt VT Vol Inf
Rose A. ST. GEORGE McIntyre		1857	1932	013	MCINTYRE, Fred	
				013		
Charles CRAM		08-21-1817	09-01-1863	013	CRAM, Mary C.	
Mary C. _____ CRAM		12-25-1814	02-07-1892	013	CRAM, Charles	
Ellen A. CRAM		08-09-1849	06-03-1866	013	CRAM, Ellen A.	

Name	Born	Died	Code	Index	Notes
Mary H. CRAM	09-22-1845	10-15-1868	013	CRAM, Mary H.	
Henry D. CRAM	07-04-1853	06-25-1897	013	CRAM, Henry D.	
Elizabeth E. CRAM	12-25-1842	05-28-1902	013	CRAM, Elizabeth E.	
John C. CRAM	08-12-1851	05-14-1907	013	CRAM, Katherine S.	
Katherine S. _____ CRAM	06-21-1852	12-23-1931	013	CRAM, John C.	
			013		
Edmund LUNDRIGAN	1843	1912	013	LUNDRIGAN, Hanna	
Hanna _____ LUNDRIGAN	1850	1937	013	LUNDRIGAN, Edmund	
			013		
Peter NICKLAW	09-11-1842	02-19-1909	013	NICKLAW, Mary	
Mary _____ NICKLAW	01-26-1843	06-29-1929	013	NICKLAW, Peter	
			013		
Edward BIRD	10-14-1829	02-23-1908	013	BIRD, Mary E.	
Mary E. _____BIRD	11-01-1827		013	BIRD, Edward	
			013		
Michael O'NEIL		11-29-1919	013	O'NEIL, Margaret	
Margaret _____ O'NEIL	51 Years	02-14-1905	013	O'NEIL, Michael	
			013		
John HOGAN	68 Years	04-28-1890	013	HOGAN, Ann	(GAR) Co. H, 5th Rgt, Vt Vols
Ann _____ HOGAN	68 Years	09-09-1892	013	HOGAN, John	
			013		
Patrick TENNIEN	03-17-1792	06-14-1882	013	TENNIEN, Catherine	
Catherine _____ TENNIEN	60 Years	06-25-1871	013	TENNIEN, Patrick	
			013		
Patrick DONNELLY	1845	1924	013	TENNIEN, Rose	
Rose TENNIEN Donnelly	04-1_-1848	04-17-1880	013	DONNELLY, Patrick	
			013		
Michael CADRAIN	1837	1916	013	CADRAIN, Michael	
			013		
John PALL	1822	02-13-1893	013	PALL, John	
			013		
Patrick TULLY	1825	1901	013	TULLY, Mary	
Mary _____ TULLY	1834	1867	013	TULLY, Patrick	
Catherine TULLY	1859	1862	013	TULLY, Catherine	
			013		
Michael MCGARRY	72 Years	04-24-1879	013	MCGARRY, Michael	
			013		
Eugene RIORDAN	01-29-1857	06-29-1916	013	MCGARRY, Eliza	
Eliza MCGARRY Riordan	06-11-1861	04-20-1891	013	RIORDAN, Eugene	
			013		
Mary MOORE	78 Years	10-29-1883	013	MOORE, Mary	(On O'BRIEN Stone.No O'BRIENs)
			013		
Catie O'BRIEN	3 Years	09-07-1878	013	O'BRIEN, Catie	Dau of Thomas & Ellen O'BRIEN)
			013	O'BRIEN, Ellen	
			013	O'BRIEN, Thomas	

				013		
Morgan O'BRIEN		1841	1914	013	O'BRIEN, Mary	
Mary A. _____ O'BRIEN		1843	1927	013	O'BRIEN, Morgan	
				013		
Patrick MULQUEEN		52 Years	12-26-1867	013	MULQUEEN, Nora	
Nora _____ MULQUEEN		54 Years	06-08-1871	013	MULQUEEN, Patrick	
				013		
David WELCH		1844	1917	013	WELCH, Mary	
Mary _____ WELCH		30 Years	11-17-1879	013	WELCH, David	
				013		
Bernard MCGARRY		73 Years	01-30-1887	013	MCGARRY, Mary	
Mary _____ MCGARRY		68 Years	03-11-1887	013	MCGARRY, Bernard	
				013		
James NUGENT	Co. Longford	84Y 6M	06-30-1878	013	NUGENT, James	A Native of Longford, Ireland
				013		
Thomas TULLEY		44 Years	08-04-1876	013	TULLEY, Thomas	
				013		
William DIXON		43Y 5M	10-03-1879	013	CLINES, Margaret	
Margaret CLINES Dixon		79 Years	03-08-1901	013	DIXON, William	
				013		
Thomas MOHAN		08-01-1853	02-19-1885	013	MOHAN, Thomas	
				013		
Eliza L. MARTIN		62 Years	04-13-1885	013	MARTIN, ELiza L.	
				013		
Joseph COLE		77Y 9M	07-18-1888	013	COLE, Sophia	
Sophia _____ COLE		70Y 8M	03-11-1889	013	COLE, Joseph	
				013		
Thomas POWERS		76 Years	04-23-1895	013	MULQUEEN, Margaret	
Margaret MULQUEEN Powers		75 Years	04-29-1889	013	POWERS, Thomas	
				013		
John BLAKE		1834	1893	013	WALSH, Ann	
Ann WALSH Blake		1837	1922	013	BLAKE, John	
				013		
Peter DOLAN		1814	1890	013	DOLAN, Peter	
Kate DOLAN		1839	1918	013	DOLAN, Kate	(Does not say spouse of Peter)
				013		
Patrick HALLINAN			11_---1888	013	HALLINAN, Hannah	
Hannah _____ HALLINAN			08---_1876	013	HALLINAN, Patrick	
John MARKHAM		1829	1889	013	GRANT, Martha	
Martha GRANT Markham		1830	1922	013	MARKHAM, John	
Edward MARKHAM		1854	1878	013	MARKHAM, Edward	Son of John & Martha MARKHAM
Bridget MARKHAM		1865	1935	013	MARKHAM, Bridget	Dau of John & Martha MARKHAM
				013		
John GRANT		61 Years	11-16-1876	013	GRANT, John	
Martha GRANT		1852	1925	013	GRANT, Martha	

John GRANT Jr.		1856	1929	013	GRANT, John Jr.	
Ellen GRANT		1860	1935	013	GRANT, Ellen	Buried in Schenectady, NY
				013		
James FOLEY		68 Years	01-25-1885	013	FOLEY, Nellie	
Nellie _____ FOLEY		56 Years	06-12-1876	013	FOLEY, James	
				013		
John O'NEIL		1846	1933	013	DIXON, Ellen	
Ellen DIXON O'Neil		1842	1915	013	O'NEIL, John	
				013		
Patrick CLINES		1807	1893	013	CARNEY, Bridget	
Bridget CARNEY Clines		1817	1887	013	CLINES, Patrick	
James CLINES		1844	1865	013	CLINES, James	S/O Patrick & Bridget CLINES
				013		
Patrick CULLINAN		83 Years	10-16-1893	013	CULLINAN, Margaret	
Margaret _____ CULLINAN		92 Years	08-01-1911	013	CULLINAN, Patrick	
				013		
Patrick J. MULLEN		1810	1887	013	MULLEN, Mary	
Mary _____ MULLEN		1821	1896	013	MULLEN, Patrick J.	

Maple Street Catholic Cemetery, Brandon, Vermont

NAME	POB	DOB/AGE	DOD	CEM	SPOUSE/INDEX	INSCRIPTION
James MCCAVET		03Y10M	07-15-1872	121	MCCAVET, James	Son Of John & Ellen McCavet
				121	MCCAVET, John	(NOI John & Ellen McCavet)
				121	MCCAVET, Ellen	
				121		
Bridget MOORE		21Y05M	12-25-1871	121	MOORE, Bridget	D/O Stephen & Catherine Moore
				121	MOORE, Stephan	(NOI Stephen-Catherine Moore)
				121	MOORE, Catherine	
				121		
Ellen _____ VAUGHAN		47 Years	01-19-1876	121	VAUGHAN, Martin	Wife of Martin Vaughan (NOI)
				121	_____, Ellen	
				121		
Mary SCANLEN		02Y06M	02-25-1874	121	SCANLEN, Mary	Children of Thomas and Ellen
Bridget SCANLEN		01Y06M	12-22-1875	121	SCANLEN, Bridget	Scanlen
				121	SCANLEN, Thomas	(NOI Thomas & Elen Scanlen)
				121	SCANLEN, Ellen	
				121		
Mary BLAKE		6 Years	08-12-1866	121	BLAKE, Mary	D/O John & Ann Blake
				121	BLAKE, John	(NOI John & Ann Blake)
				121	BLAKE, Ann	

Name	Birthplace	Age	Date	No.	Surname, Given	Notes
Julia WHALLEN		_ Years	06-21-1868	121	WHALLEN, Julia WHALLEN, Michael WHALLEN, Kate	D/O Michael & Kate Whallen (Age at death is obscured) (NOI Michael & Kate Whallen)
William SULLIVAN		22 Years	08-05-1865	121	SULLIVAN, William	S/O J & E Sullivan (NOI J. E. Sullivan)
Mary HAGERTY Tully		33 Years	07-07-1864	121	HEGARTY, Mary TULLY, Patrick	Daughter of Dennis & Mary Hegarty.Wife of Patrick Tully. (NOI Patrick Tully)
Catharine TULLY		3 Years	07-06-1862	121	TULLY, Catharine	D/o Patrick & Mary Tully
Corp'l Jno DUNN				121	DUNN, Jno	Co. I 10th VT Inf. (NOI DOB, DOD. Resided in St. Albans at Enlistment) (GAR)
Richard WHALAN		02M14D	08-17-1864	121	WHALAN, Richard	S/O P & H Whalan. (NOI P & H)
Edorza MCINTYRE		03 Years	12-22-1862	121	MCINTYRE, Edorza MCINTYRE, Henry MCINTYRE, Matilda	D/O Henry & Matilda McIntyre (NOI Henry & Matilda McIntyre)
Edw'd KELLEY				121	KELLEY, Edw'd	Co. E 12th VT Inf. (NOI DOB, DOD. Enlisted at Goshen, Vt. Died of Dis. 3-17-1863)(GAR)
Charles STEWART	Co. Mayo	32 Years	02-07-1855	121	STEWART, Charles	Of Keloyne, County of Mayo. (This stone deteriorated. POB and age at death both hard to to read. Keloyne not in reference. Possibly Killeen.)
Michael LYNCH Ellen _____ LYNCH		70 Years 53 Years	06-14-1874 09-19-1875	121	_____, Ellen LYNCH, Michael	
Jeremiah SULLIVAN		48 Years	05-27-1863	121	SULLIVAN, Jeremiah	
Mary HALLENAN		55 Years	05-20-1871	121	HALLENAN, Mary	
Michael REYNOLDS				121	REYNOLDS, Michael	Co. E 7th VT Inf. (NOI DOB-DOD Enlisted at Brandon, Vermont. Died of Dis. 10-26-1865-GAR)

NAME	POB	DOB/AGE	DOD	CEM	SPOUSE/INDEX	INSCRIPTION
				121		
Ellen FOY		19 Years	10-19-1865	121	FOY, Ellen	Daus Of Thomas & Bridget Foy.
Catherine FOY			11-13-1861	121	FOY, Catherine	(NOI Age at death-Catherine)
				121	FOY, Thomas	NOI Thomas & Bridget Foy)
				121	FOY, Bridget	
				121		
Hugh CUNNINGHAM		33 Years	11-30-1858	121	_____, Ellen	(NOI Spouse Ellen)
				121	CUNNINGHAM, Hugh	
Catherine CUNNINGHAM		01Y11M	07-28-1858	121	CUNNINGHAM, Catherine	D/O Hugh & Ellen Cunningham

St. Michaels Cemetery - Brattleboro, VT (Oak Grove Avenue, Off Canal Street)

NAME	POB	DOB/AGE	DOD	CEM	SPOUSE/INDEX	INSCRIPTION
Patrick LYNCH	Co. Clare	1826	1874	014	GRIFFIN, Mary	Native(s) Of County Clare
Mary GRIFFIN Lynch	Co. Clare	1848	1914	014	LYNCH, Patrick	Native(s) Of County Clare
				014		
Mary TOMEY O'Connor	Co. Kerry	42 Years	10-13-1875	014	O'CONNOR, Thomas	Native Of Tralee, Co. Kerry
Anna Stacey LEE O'CONNOR		45 Years	03-24-1896	014	O'CONNOR, Thomas	(2nd Wife of Thomas O'Connor)
				014	TOMEY, Mary	(NOI Thomas O'Connor)
				014	LEE, Anna Stacey	
				014		
Dennis LINEHAN		71 Years	12-11-1876	014	_____, Johana	
Johana ____ LINEHAN	Co. Cork	52 Years	02-01-1866	014	LINEHAN, Dennis	Native Of County Cork, Ireland
				014		
Thomas HANLON		77 Years	08-24 1904	014	LINEHAN, Catherine	
Catherine LINEHAN Hanlon	Co. Wicklow	35 Years	10-08-1876	014	HANLON, Thomas	Native of County Wicklow
Martin MARTIN	Co. Limerick	11-12-1792	04-08-1890	014	_____, Catherine	Age 97 Years, 4 Mos, 21 Days
				014		Born in Parish Galbally, Co.
				014		Limerick, Ireland
Catherine ____ MARTIN		85 Years	01-22-1895	014	MARTIN, Martin	
				014		
James AUSTIN	Co. Kerry	76 Years	02-07-1860	014	_____, Margaret	A Native of "Bracklown"
				014		(Brackloon), Co. Kerry, Ire.
Margaret AUSTIN		72 Years	05-05-1872	014	AUSTIN, James	
Bridget AUSTIN Brosnan	Co. Kerry	05-00-1837	04-09-1894	014	BROSNAN, John	Born In County Kerry, Ireland
				014	AUSTIN, Bridget	(NOI John Brosnan)
				014		
Honora AUSTIN Long		73 Years	12-06-1913	014	LONG, James	(NOI James Long)
				014	AUSTIN, Honora	
				014		
James AUSTIN		02-15-1842	11-02-1929	014	KENNEDY, Mary	Son Of James & Margaret Austin

Name	Origin	Age/Born	Died	Ref	Spouse	Notes
Mary KENNEDY Austin		01-05-1856	02-03-1934	014	AUSTIN, James	
				014		
Thomas HICKEY	Co. Limerick	29 Years	11-09-1865	014	____, Mary	Native(s) of County Limerick
Mary ____ HICKEY	Co. Limerick	67 Years	03-10-1877	014	HICKEY, Thomas	Native(s) of County Limerick
				014		
John LILLIS	Co. Limerick	25 Years	09-01-1864	014	LILLIS, John	Native Of County Limerick
Patrick LILLIS	Co. Limerick	72 Years	03-25-1904	014	COLLINS, Ellen	Native Of County Limerick
Ellen COLLINS Lillis	Co. Limerick	65 Years	12-02-1895	014	LILLIS, Patrick	Native Of County Louth
Mary MORTAL Lillis	Co. Limerick	77 Years	09-07-1883	014	LILLIS, James	Native Of County Limerick (NOI
				014	MORTAL, Mary	James Lillis)
				014		
Michael TWOMEY	Co. Cork	58 Years	04-09-1870	014	DUNN, Mary	Parish of(Stone deteriorated),
		58 Years	04-	014		Co. Cork, Ireland
Mary DUNN Twomey		55 Years	08-00-1868	014	TWOMEY, Michael	Native Of County Limerick
				014		
Patrick CUNNINGHAM		60 Years		014	____, Bridget	
Bridget ____ CUNNINGHAM	Co. Cork	59 Years	06-30-1882	014	CUNNINGHAM, Patrick	Native Of Co. Cork, Ireland
				014		
Patrick AUSTIN Sr.		45 Years	1875	014	CONNELL, Mary	
Mary CONNELL Austin		75 Years	06-30-1891	014	AUSTIN, Patrick Sr.	
Patrick AUSTIN Jr.	Nova Scotia	58 Years	05-03-1915	014	AUSTIN, Patrick Jr.	Son Of Patrick & Mary Connell
				014		Austin. Born In Grand Lake,
				014		Nova Scotia
				014		
John AUSTIN	Co. Kerry	76 Years	07-06-1903	014	BOWLER, Margaret	Born In Co. Kerry, Ireland
Margaret BOWLER Austin		65 Years	02-25-1894	014	AUSTIN, John	
				014		
John SULLIVAN	Co. Kerry	05-17-186_	08-28-188_	014	SULLIVAN, John	A Native of "Kinnard" (Kinard)
				014		Co. Kerry, Ireland
				014		
Matthew SULLIVAN	Co. Kerry	08-12-1864	08-08-189_	014	SULLIVAN, Matthew	A Native of "Kinnard" (Kinard
				014		Co. Kerry, Ireland
				014		
Mary A. SULLIVAN Brosnahan		05-30-1852	08-02-1932	014	BROSNAHAN, Daniel W.	(NOI Daniel Brosnahan)
				014	SULLIVAN, Mary A.	
				014		
Francis O'HAGAN	Co. Louth	76 Years	07-01-1913	014	MARTIN, Catherine	Born In Carlingford, County
				014		Louth, Ire. (GAR) Member of
				014		Co. I, 8th Rgt, VT Volunteers
Catherine MARTIN O'Hagan	Co. Limerick	82 Years	12-28-1917	014	O'HAGAN, Francis	A Native of County Limerick
				014		
Arthur MCNAMARA	Co. Cork	67 Years	07-03-1885	014	CARROLL, Mary	A Native of County Cork, Ire.
Mary CARROLL McNamara	Co. Cork	70 Years	03-18-1910	014	MCNAMARA, Arthur	A Native of County Cork, Ire.
				014		
Catherine DOYLE	Co. Kerry	65 Years	09-17-1918	014	DOYLE, Catherine	Born In County Kerry, Ireland

				014		
Ellen GRIFFIN	Co. Kerry	29 Years	01-26-1913	014	GRIFFIN, Ellen	A Native of "Kinnard" (Kinard)
				014		County Kerry, Ireland
Thomas GRIFFIN		1877	1914	014	GRIFFIN, Thomas	(All on same stone as Ellen.
Mary A. GRIFFIN		1870	1935	014	GRIFFIN, Mary A.	Probably Siblings)
James A. GRIFFIN		1867	1937	014	GRIFFIN, James A.	
				014		
Jerry RILEY		1834	1908	014	MCCAULIFFE, Norah	Born In New Market, Ireland
				014	RILEY, Jerry	(Could be Co. Clare, Cork or
				014		Kilkenny)(NOI Norah
				014		McCauliffe)
				014		
Patrick BAKER	Co. Kerry	75 Years	03-26-1900	014	O'DONNELL, Catherine	Born In County Kerry, Ireland
Catherine O'DONNELL Baker	Co. Kerry	86 Years	03-09-1909	014	BAKER, Patrick	Born In Dingle, Co. Kerry, Ire
				014		
Michael BAKER	Co. Kerry	55 Years	03-26-1900	014	CONNOR, Hannah	Native(s) Of Co. Kerry, Ire.
Hannah CONNOR Baker	Co. Kerry	75 Years	03-09-1909	014	BAKER, Michael	Native(s) Of Co. Kerry, Ire.
				014		
Timothy MORAN	Co. Kerry	78 Years	01-16-1899	014	BROSNAN, Mary	Native Of Dingle, Co. Kerry,
				014		Ireland
Mary BROSNAN Moran	Co. Kerry	77 Years	05-26-1904	014	MORAN, Timothy	Native Of Dingle, Co. Kerry, r
				014		Ireland
James DUCEY	Co. Waterford	06-22-1822	06-01-1897	014	DONAHUE, Ellen	Born In Co. Waterford, Ireland
Ellen DONAHUE Ducey	Co. Waterford	03-12-1810	07-16-1898	014	DUCEY, James	Born In Co. Waterford, Ireland
				014		
Daniel LONG	Co. Kerry	03-17-1824	04-14-1900	014	DOYLE, Bridget	Native(s) Of Co. Kerry, Ire.
Bridget DOYLE Long	Co. Kerry	05-12-1830	07-19-1914	014	LONG, Daniel	Native(s) Of Co. Kerry, Ire.
				014		
Daniel MCCAUGHERN	Co. Derry	57 Years	04-27-1873	014	DIMOND, Nancy	Born In Castledawson, County
				014		Derry. Ireland
Nancy DIMOND McCaughern	Co. Derry	05-12-1830	07-19-1914	014	MCCAUGHERN, Daniel	Born In Londonderry, Ireland
Robert MCCAUGHERN	Co. Derry	18 Years	08-26-1873	014	MCCAUGHERN, Robert	Born In Castledawson, County
				014		Derry. Ireland
				014		
John KAINE	Co. Clare	80 Years	11-28-1902	014	BURNS, Ellen	Born In "Bally Malone" (Bally-
				014		malone), Co. Clare, Ireland
Ellen BURNS Kaine	Co. Limerick	85 Years	08-27-1902	014	KAINE, John	Born At "New Castle" (New-
				014		castle), Co. Limerick, Ireland
Mary BURNS	Co. Limerick	65 Years	05-18-1885	014	BURNS, Mary	Born At "New Castle" (New-
				014		castle), Co. Limerick, Ireland
				014		
James O'NEIL	Co. Clare		03-23-1885	014	BAKER, Catherine	Born In Co. Clare, Ireland
Catherine BAKER O'Neil			12-24-1897	014	O'NEIL, James	
				014		
Patrick DOWD	Co. Kerry	61 Years	12-04-1888	014	FLANNAGAN, Mary	Born In Co. Kerry, Ire. Died

Name	County	Age	Date	Code	Relation	Notes
				014		at New Haven, Connecticut
Mary FLANNAGAN Dowd	Co. Clare	70 Years	08-17-1897	014	DOWD, Patrick	Born In Co. Clare, Ire. Died
				014		at New York.
				014		
William MORAN	Co. Kerry	80 Years	03-24-1898	014	BROSNAN, Nora	Native of Dingle, Co. Kerry,Ir
Nora BROSNAN Moran		90 Years	07-14-1920	014	MORAN, William	
				014		
Mary O'CONNOR Moynihan	Co. Kerry		09-05-1876	014	MOYNIHAN, Humphrey	A Native of Co. Kerry, Ireland
				014	O'CONNOR, Mary	(NOI Humphrey Moynihan)
				014		
Honora MOYNIHAN Cummings		75 Years	10-22-1898	014	CUMMINGS, Thomas	
				014		
				014		
Timothy MOYNIHAN	Co. Kerry	66 Years	01-30-1877	014	____, Margaret	Native of County Kerry
Margaret ____ MOYNIHAN	Co. Cork	70 Years	09-13-1895	014	MOYNIHAN, Timothy	A Native Of County Cork
Humphrey MOYNIHAN		11-28-1854	11-13-1894	014	MOYNIHAN, Humphrey	
Mary T. MOYNIHAN		01-17-1866	08-03-1886	014	MOYNIHAN, Mary T.	
				014		
Cornelius CONNELL	Co. Cork	35 Years	10-18-1882	014	CONNELL, Cornelius	A Native Of County Cork, Ire
				014		
John MCCARTY		6 Years	02-11-1868	014	MCCARTY, John	Son Of Bartholomew & Catherine
				014	MCCARTY, Bartholomew	McCarty, Natives of Co. Kerry,
				014		Ire. (NOI Bartholomew and
				014		Catherine McCarty)
				014		
Michael LILLIS	Co. Limerick	80 Years	08-01-1909	014	FLANNAGAN, Bridget	Born At Limerick, Ireland
Bridget FLANNAGAN Lillis	Co. Clare	63 Years	02-24-1896	014	LILLIS, Michael	Born At Kilnamona, County
				014		Clare, Ireland
				014		
Thomas O'CONNOR	Co. Kerry	45 Years	07-13-1876	014	HENCHIE, Margaret	Born In Co. Kerry, Ireland
Margaret HENCHIE O'Connor		70 Years	07-06-1885	014	O'CONNOR, Thomas	
				014		
Jeremiah O'RILEY	Co. Cork	78 Years	03-24-1882	014	O'KEEFE, Catherine	Native(s) Of County Cork, Ire
Catherine O'KEEFE O'Riley	Co. Cork	75 Years	07-30-1882	014	O'RILEY, Jeremiah	Native(s) Of County Cork, Ire
Jeremiah O'RILEY		32 Years	04-29-1876	014	O'RILEY, Jeremiah	Children Of Jeremiah and
Andrew O'RILEY		29 Years	02-25-1867	014	O'RILEY, Andrew	Catherine O'Riley
Daniel O'RILEY		17 Years	03-06-1868	014	O'RILEY, Daniel	" " " " "
				014		
Bartholomew O'RILEY		73 Years	05-28-1906	014	_______, Julia	(Same Stone as Jeremiah &
				014		Catherine O'Riley)
Julia _____ O'RILEY		64 Years	07-03-1907	014	O'RILEY, Bartholomew	
				014		
Michael LILLIS	Co. Limerick	80 Years	06-27-1897	014	____, Mary A.	Native of County Limerick
Mary A. ____ LILLIS	Co. Meath	51 Years	02-06-1882	014	LILLIS, Michael	Native of County Meath, Ire
				014		

Name	County	Age/Born	Died	No.	Spouse	Notes
Honora BAKER	Co. Kerry	24 Years	11-23-1860	014	BAKER, Honora	Native(s) Of Dingle, Co. Kerry
Margaret BAKER	Co. Kerry	78 Years	09-08-1879	014	BAKER, Margaret	Native(s) Of Dingle, Co. Kerry
Mary BAKER	Co. Kerry	42 Years	07-15-1878	014	BAKER, Mary	Native(s) Of Dingle, Co. Kerry
				014		(All Three On Same Stone)
				014		
John GRIFFIN	Co. Kerry	55 Years	05-05-1863	014	MOYNIHAN, Mary	Native of County Kerry, Ire
Mary MOYNIHAN Griffin	Co. Kerry	69 Years	02-29-1888	014	GRIFFIN, John	Native of County Kerry, Ire
				014		
Hannah LILLIS Chandler	Co. Limerick	1845	12-03-1904	014	CHANDLER, George	Born In Limerick, Ireland.(NOI
				014	LILLIS, Hannah	George Chandler)
				014		
Thomas MANNING	Co. Kerry	48 Years	02-20-1871	014	____, Mary	Native(s) Of County Kerry, Ire
Mary ____ MANNING	Co. Kerry	56 Years	12-31-1879	014	MANNING, Thomas	Native(s) Of County Kerry, Ire
				014		
John EAGAN	Co. Limerick	78 Years	1864	014	LILLIS, Mary	Native(s) Of Co. Limerick, Ire
Mary LILLIS Eagan	Co. Limerick	65 Years	07-03-1874	014	EAGAN, John	Native(s) Of Co. Limerick, Ire
				014		
Jeremiah SHEEHAN	Co. Cork	55 Years	1864	014	_____, Katherine	Native(s) Of "Bally Mantle"
				014		(Ballymartle, Co. Of Cork, Ire
				014		(1864 as DOD may be incorrect
				014		Could be 1860. Stone is badly
				014		deteriorated.)
				014		
Michael BROSNAHAN	Co. Kerry	06-12-1815	05-28-1893	014	DINEEN, Julia	Native Of Tralee, Co. Kerry,Ir
Julia DINEEN Brosnahan		02-03-1824	03-10-1903	014	BROSNAHAN, Michael	
				014		
				014		
				014		
Katherine ____ SHEEHAN	Co. Cork	80 Years	07-03-1874	014	SHEEHAN, Jeremiah	Native(s) Of "Bally Mantle"
				014		(Ballymartle), Co. Of Cork,Ire
				014		
William MAHONEY	Co. Cork	68 Years	12-28-1872	014	_____, Katherine	Native(s) Of "Bally Mantle"
				014		(Ballymartle), Co. Of Cork,Ire
Katherine ____ MAHONEY	Co. Cork	63 Years	02-06-1875	014	MAHONEY, William	Native(s) Of "Bally Mantle"
				014		(Ballymartle), Co. Of Cork,Ire
				014		(Same stone as Jeremiah and
				014		Katherine Sheehan)
				014		
Patrick DOYLE		45 Years	05-17-1875	014	_____, Ellen	A Native Of Ireland
Ellen ____ DOYLE		57 Years	04-22-1884	014	DOYLE, Patrick	Widow Of Patrick Doyle. Died
				014		At Keene, New Hampshire. A
				014		Native Of Ireland
				014		
William AHERN	Co. Limerick	51 Years	07-17-1870	014	_____, Johanna	Native(s) Of Newcastle, County
				014		Limerick, Ireland

Johanna ____ AHERN	Co. Limerick	62 Years	11-05-1888	014	AHERN, William	Native(s) Of Newcastle, County
				014		Limerick, Ireland
				014		
Bridget ____ SULLIVAN	Co. Kerry	64 Years	04-17-1887	014	SULLIVAN, James	Widow of James Sullivan. A
				014		Native of Parish ____ (Stone
				014		
Margaret DONAHUE Stewart		35Y 6M	10-13-1876	014	STEWART, Abram	(See Abram Stewart W/D
				014		1-26-96)
				014		
John CORKERY		77 Years	06-08-1892	014	_____, Nora	
Nora ____ CORKERY		60 Years	04-01-1884	014	CORKERY, John	
Ellen CORKERY Keppel		27Y 2M	07-22-1883	014	KEPPEL, Daniel D.	(NOI Daniel Keppel)
				014	CORKERY, Ellen	
Jane CORKERY		1Y 8M	1861	014	CORKERY, Jane	
Martha CORKERY		2Y 1D	1855	014	CORKERY, Martha	
Michael CORKERY		1847	1907	014	_____, Mary	
Mary ____ CORKERY		1853	1929	014	CORKERY, Michael	
Thomas HANNON		1852	1912	014	HANNON, Thomas	
				014		
Catharine MOYNIHAN		59 Years	09-17-1886	014	MOYNIHAN, Catharine	
John BAKER		4 Years	10-09-1888	014	BAKER, John	
				014		
Thomas RYAN		1843	1922	014	_____, Mary	
Mary ____ RYAN		1849	1937	014	RYAN, Thomas	
				014		
James FLANNIGAN		67 Years	11-17-1868	014	FLANNIGAN, James	Father
				014		
Jno CLARK				014	FITZGIBBONS, Johanna	(GAR) 13th Ohio Cav, Co. F.
				014		(NOI Jno Clark)
Johanna FITZGIBBONS Clark		65 Years	09-13-1889	014	CLARK, Jno	
				014		
John O'CONNOR		86Y9M18D	04-04-1936	014	HEFFRON, Mary	
Mary HEFFRON O'Connor		75Y6M6D	05-07-1931	014	O'CONNOR, John	
				014		
Margaret ____ FOLEY		49 Years	06-15-1885	014	FOLEY, Thomas	(NOI Thomas Foley)
				014	_____, Margaret	
Mary D. FOLEY		24Y 3M	12-25-1884	014	FOLEY, Mary D.	
Annie FOLEY		10Y 3M	02-26-1883	014	FOLEY, Annie	
Nellie FOLEY		15Y 10M	03-09-1883	014	FOLEY, Nellie	
Mary ____ HIGGINS				014	HIGGINS, Patrick	(NOI DOD, DOB, Patrick Higgins
				014	_____, Mary	and Mary)
				014		
John MOOR		28 Years	11-30-1880	014	MOOR, John	
				014		
Ellen L. ____ WOOD			09-20-1882	014	WOOD, Simeon	(Stone damaged. Date of Death

Name	Born/Age	Died	Code	Index Name	Remarks
			014		Not Present)
			014		
Ellen GIBNEY	1847	1923	014	GIBNEY, Ellen	
			014		
Nellie HORAN	15Y 8M	06-15-1871	014	HORAN, Nellie	Dau Of Edward & Bridget Horan
			014	HORAN, Edward	
			014		
Lawrence SHEEHAN	1824	1909	014	FITZGERALD, Ellen	
Ellen FITZGERALD Sheehan	1829	1919	014	SHEEHAN, Lawrence	
			014		
Elizabeth C. FLYNN	49Y 6M	05-22-1883	014	FLYNN, Elizabeth C.	
			014		
John KELLY	29 Years	09-08-1875	014	_____, Mary E.	Erected By His Wife In Memory of John Kelly
			014		
Mary E. ____ KELLY	44 Years	05-30-1892	014	KELLY, John	
Thomas F. KELLY			014	KELLY, Thomas F.	Infant Son(s) of J & M Kelly
John KELLY			014	KELLY, John	Infant Son(s) of J & M Kelly
			014		
Michael SHEA	1836	1898	014	HIGGINS, Christina	
Christina HIGGINS Shea	1837	1892	014	SHEA, Michael	
			014		
Charles E. SMITH	01-11-1850	10-23-1886	014	_____, Ellen	
Ellen ____ SMITH	26Y10M6D	11-26-1880	014	SMITH, Charles E.	
			014		
Robert HEFFRON	68 Years	08-05-1885	014	_____, Bridget	
Bridget ____ HEFFRON	1828	1908	014	HEFFRON, Robert	
			014		
Eugene FERRITER	69 Years	01-22-1899	014	O'CONNOR, Mary	
Mary O'CONNOR Ferriter	45 Years	09-04-1882	014	FERRITER, Eugene	
			014		
John GUIHEEN	1842	1932	014	FITZGERALD, Mary	
Mary FITZGERALD Guiheen	1844	1918	014	GUIHEEN, John	
			014		
Mary FLANAGAN Dowd			014	FLANAGAN, Mary	(NOI This Person or Mr. Dowd)
Thomas DOWD	13 Years	08-31-1870	014	DOWD, Thomas	
Mary A. DOWD	76 Years	02-05-1942	014	DOWD, Mary A.	
Katherine A. DOWD	67 Years	08-18-1921	014	DOWD, Katherine A.	Died At New York
John C. DOWD	61 Years	08-04-1916	014	DOWD, John C.	Died At New York
James H. DOWD	70 Years	12-10-1934	014	DOWD, James H.	Died At New York
			014		
John BAKER	1831	1913	014	O'CONNOR, Catherine	
Catherine O'CONNOR Baker	1829	1918	014	BAKER, John	
Joanna DULAN Baker	1799	1869	014	BAKER, Richard	(NOI Richard Baker)
			014	DULAN, Joana	
			014		

Cornelius CROWLEY	65 Years	02-14-1887	014	_____, Catherine	
Catherine ____ CROWLEY	83 Years	02-30-1900	014	CROWLEY, Cornelius	
Patrick MURPHY	35 Years	01-29-1885	014	MURPHY, Patrick	
Catherine CROWLEY Rochford	40 Years	11-05-1898	014	CROWLEY, Catherine	Dau Of C. Crowley. (NOI Mr.
			014	CROWLEY, Catherine	Rochford)
Micah CROWLEY	8Y 9M	03-12-1871	014	CROWLEY, Micah	Son(s) Of C. Crowley
John D. CROWLEY	10M	05-05-1855	014	CROWLEY, John D.	Son(s) Of C. Crowley
			014		
James GRIFFIN	45 Years	JUNE 1901	014	GRIFFIN, James	
			014		
Mrs. Nora TOUHILL	50 Years	04-30-1910	014	_____, Nora	(NOI Mr. Touhill)
			014		
Patrick CALLAHAN			014	_____, Katherine	(NOI DOD/DOB for Patrick)
			014	_____, Anne	
Katherine _____ CALLAHAN	1855	1880	014	CALLAHAN, Patrick	(NOI Patrick Callahan)
Anne ____ CALLAHAN			014	CALLAHAN, Patrick	(NOI DOB/DOD For Anne)
			014		
Peter MATT	07-11-1850	07-04-1926	014	HEBERT, Celesta	
Celesta HEBERT Matt	05-11-1860	02-26-1924	014	MATT, Peter	
			014		
Mrs Katherine WALTON Murphy	50 Years	09-09-1895	014	WALTON, Katherine	(NOI Mr. Murphy)
			014		
Patrick GREGG	58 Years	11-20-1900	014	LILLIS, Catharine	
Catharine LILLIS Gregg	59 Years	11-12-1900	014	GREGG, Patrick	
			014		
Thomas MULLIN	74Y9M26D	11-11-1892	014	MAGNER, Ellen	
Ellen MAGNER Mullin	74Y1M3D	03-04-1906	014	MULLIN, Thomas	
			014		
John O'CONNELL	1848	1917	014	PROUTY, Ella J.	
Ella J. PROUTY O'Connell	1851	1911	014	O'CONNELL, John	
			014		
Daniel MANNING	48 Years	01-05-1884	014	HIGGINS, Ellen	
Ellen HIGGINS Manning	71 Years	10-30-1908	014	MANNING, Daniel	
			014		
William KIDNEY	85 Years	02-02-1885	014	KIDNEY, William	
Margaret J. ___ GRIFFIN	31 Years	04-08-1892	014	GRIFFIN, James F.	(NOI James Griffin)
			014	_____, Margaret J.	
			014		
Michael BAKER	86 Years	01-07-1912	014	GRIFFIN, Johanna	
Johanna GRIFFIN Baker	65 Years	08-11-1890	014	BAKER, Michael	
			014		
John H. MAGUIRE	1849	1883	014	GRIFFIN, Abbie	
Abbie GRIFFIN Maguire	1856	1925	014	MAGUIRE, John H.	
			014		
Mary BOWLER Lahy	25 Years	07-10-1873	014	LAHY, John	(NOI John Lahy)

				014	BOWLER, Mary	
				014		
Bridget KENDY Doyle	Co. Kerry	83 Years	05-06-1872	014	DOYLE, John	Native of County Kerry, Ire.
				014		(NOI John Doyle)
				014		
William H. WHELAN		1850	1888	014	GIBNEY, Jennie	
Jennie GIBNEY Whelan		1859	1925	014	WHELAN, William H.	
				014		
Luke FERRITER		1844	1930	014	FENTON, Eliza Ann	Sergt, Co. A, 3rd Vt Inf, 1861
				014		1865 (GAR)
Eliza Ann FENTON Ferriter		1843	1927	014	FERRITER, Luke	
				014		
Margaret SULLIVAN		75 Years	06-08-1889	014	SULLIVAN, Margaret	
Mary MCCOWLIFF		21 Years	12-26-1885	014	MCCOWLIFF, Mary	
				014		
Thomas MANNING		68 Years	04-25-1888	014	O'CONNER, Bridget	
Bridget O'CONNER Manning		70 Years	02-09-1896	014	MANNING, Thomas	
				014		
John L. HERNEY		20Y5M5D	02-03-1875	014	HERNEY, John L.	Son Of James & Mary Herney
				014	HERNEY, James	
Katie SULLIVAN Brosnahan		19 Years	02-22-1864	014	BROSNAHAN, Patrick	(NOI Patrick Brosnahan)
				014	SULLIVAN, Katie	
				014		
Bridget ____ HANIFAN		27 Years	06-06-1869	014	HANIFAN, Thomas	(NOI Thomas Hanifan)
				014	_____, Bridget	
				014		
Nancy ____ KENNEDY	Co. Kerry	59 Years	03-21-1879	014	KENNEDY, Barney	Native Of Co. Kerry, Ireland
				014	_____, Nancy	(NOI Barney Kennedy)
				014		
Thomas MANNING		56 Years	03-13-1866	014	_____, Ellen	
Ellen ____ MANNING		79 Years	03-24-1885	014	MANNING, Thomas	
John MANNING		18 Years	02-02-1862	014	MANNING, John	
James MANNING		12 Years	03-16-1864	014	MANNING, James	
Dennis MANNING		30 Years	08-24-1882	014	MANNING, Dennis	
				014		
Daniel KAVANAUGH		1836	1911	014	O'CONNOR, Bridget	
Bridget O'CONNOR Kavanaugh		1846	1918	014	KAVANAUGH, Daniel	
				014		
Patrick MORAN		1840	1919	014	SULLIVAN, Betsey	
Betsey SULLIVAN Moran		1832	1912	014	MORAN, Patrick	
				014		
John FLOOD		63 Years	02-02-1875	014	_____, Mary A.	
Mary A. ____ FLOOD		70 Years	02-13-1897	014	FLOOD, John	
				014		
MADDEN Memorial				014	MADDEN, Memorial	

Name	Age/Birth	Death		Index Name	Notes
Martin MADDEN			014	CLAFFERY, Margaret	Sacred To The Memory of Martin
Margaret CLAFFERY Madden			014	MADDEN, Martin	Madden, His Wife Margaret
Mary MADDEN			014	MADDEN, Mary	Claffery And Their Children
Margaret MADDEN			014	MADDEN, Margaret	Mary, Margaret and John. May
John MADDEN			014	MADDEN, John	Their Souls Rest In Peace.
			014		(No Birth Or Death Dates)
			014		
Daniel MAHONEY	50 Years	08-15-1872	014	____, Catharine	
Catharine ____ MAHONEY	56 Years	02-08-1883	014	MAHONEY, Daniel	
			014		
Thomas CUMMINGS	41 Years	11-08-1871	014	CUMMINGS, Thomas	
Ann CUMMINGS	67 Years	10-14-1878	014	CUMMINGS, Ann	
			014		
William CUMMINGS		05-06-1905	014	CUMMINGS, William	(DOD Not Indicated)
			014		
John LYNCH	1847	1934	014	CURRAN, Margaret	
Margaret CURRAN Lynch	1836	1906	014	LYNCH, John	
			014		
Mary DONOVEN	20 Years	05-18-1866	014	DONOVEN, Mary	
			014		
Margaret HALLAREN	57 Years	02-25-1865	014	HALLAREN, Margaret	
			014		
Joseph FENTON	90 Years	01-19-1901	014	FITZGERALD, Elaine	
Elaine FITZGERALD Fenton	71 Years	06-23-1893	014	FENTON, Joseph	
			014		
Michael KELLY			014	KELLY, Michael	(GAR) Co. E 1st VT H Art
			014		
William KELLEY	35 Years	03-18-1891	014	KELLEY, William	
			014		
Catherine ____ KENNEDY	1844	1877	014	KENNEDY, William	(NOI William Kennedy)
			014	____, Catherine	
Jane KENNEDY	1870	1873	014	KENNEDY, Jane	Children Of William and
Daniel KENNEDY	1873	1874	014	KENNEDY, Daniel	Catherine Kennedy)
			014		
Dennis COLLINS	69 Years	01-29-1885	014	____, Catherine	(NOI Catherine Collins)
Katie COLLINS	23Y9M6D	07-22-1876	014	COLLINS, Katie	Children Of Dennis and
Hannah COLLINS	29Y6M4D	04-10-1881	014	COLLINS, Hannah	Catherine Collins)
Tommy COLLINS	13Y8M6D	05-31-1888	014	COLLINS, Tommy	
Dennie COLLINS	18Y11M21D	10-01-1880	014	COLLINS, Dennie	
			014		
Daniel L. DUGGAN	1856	1936	014	____, Sarah	
Sarah ____ DUGGAN	1847	1931	014	DUGGAN, Daniel L.	
			014		
Katy CONNOR Greaney	45 Years	08-08-1879	014	GREANEY, Jeremiah	Native of Ballyboher,Co. Kerry
			014	CONNOR, Katy	Ireland (No Ballyboher listed

Name	Age / Born	Died	Code	Index Name	Notes
			014		for Co. Kerry. One listed in
			014		Co. Wexford--There is a Bally-
			014		bowler in Co. Kerry and Parish
			014		Ballinvoher, also Kerry) (NOI
			014		Jeremiah Greaney)
			014		
			014		
Johanna GREANEY	22Y 6M	02-02-1873	014	GREANEY, Johanna	
			014		
			014		
Margaret DUNLEVY	60 Years	09-16-1884	014	DUNLEVY, Margaret	
			014		
Mary FITZGERALD	52 Years	02-20-1894	014	FITZGERALD, Mary	
			014		
Barney BRESLIN			014	HURD, Ellen	(GAR) Co. A, 13th VT Inf
Barney BRESLIN			014	BRESLIN, Barney	(NOI DOB/DOD)
Ellen HURD Breslin	30 Years	02-05-1877	014	BRESLIN, Barney	
			014		
James MACK	1853	1932	014	BAKER, Nora	
Nora BAKER Mack	1855	1914	014	MACK, James	
			014		
McMenimen MEMORIAL			014	MCMENIMEN, Memorial	
Father (MCMENIMEN)	1835	1907	014	MCMENIMEN, Father	(NOI Re: Names for Father and
Mother (MCMENIMEN)	1836	1881	014	MADDEN, Martin	Mother)
Henry C. MCMENIMEN	1855	1877	014	MCMENIMEN, Henry C.	
Catharine COLDEN	1864	1865	014	COLDEN, Catharine	
Mary (MCMENIMEN)	1869	1870	014	MCMENIMEN, Mary	
Catharine (MCMENIMEN)	1863	1924	014	MCMENIMEN, Catharine	
Catherine WALSH Leahy	1845	1925	014	LEAHY, David	(NOI David Leahy)
			014	WALSH, Catherine	
			014		
Patrick LEAHY	45 Years	03-01-1878	014	O'CONNOR, Catherine	
Catherine O'CONNOR LEAHY	32 Years	04-23-1874	014	LEAHY, Patrick	
			014		
Patrick DUFFY	02-18-1806	03-12-1878	014	____, Susan	
Susan ____ DUFFY	08-15-1817	11-28-1873	014	DUFFY, Patrick	
Sarah DUFFY	05-09-1857	06-02-1890	014	DUFFY, Sarah	
Thomas DUFFY	12-23-1838	06-20-1872	014	DUFFY, Thomas	
Rose DUFFY	02-26-1851	03-05-1917	014	DUFFY, Rose	
Catherine DUFFY	11-14-1840	09-02-1908	014	DUFFY, Catherine	
Mary DUFFY	09-15-1864	08-25-1865	014	DUFFY, Mary	
Frank DUFFY	12-23-1868	11-09-1873	014	DUFFY, Frank	
			014		
James FERRITER	78 Years	07-08-1895	014	MANNING, Ellen	
Ellen MANNING Ferriter	42 Years	09-27-1872	014	FERRITER, James	

John FERRITER		20 Years	01-16-1873	014	FERRITER, John	
Maurice FERRITER		68 Years	12-15-1915	014	FERRITER, Maurice	
Patrick FERRITER		35 Years	10-03-1902	014	FERRITER, Patrick	
Bridget FERRITER		51 Years	07-12-1924	014	FERRITER, Bridget	
				014		
				014		
James SULLIVAN	Co. Kerry	49 Years	04-03-1877	014	_____, Ellen	(NOI Ellen)
				014	SULLIVAN, James	
Michael SULLIVAN		3Y 3M	07-02-1865	014	SULLIVAN, Michael	
John SULLIVAN	Co. Kerry	10Y 3M	03-11-1866	014	SULLIVAN, John	Born In Dingle, Co. Kerry, Ire
				014		Son Of James & Ellen Sullivan
James HANNON		1840	1917	014	_____, Bridget	
Bridget _____ HANNON		1840	1873	014	HANNON, James	
Walter HANNON		1863	1864	014	HANNON, Walter	
Henry HANNON		1869	1922	014	HANNON, Henry	
Rose SULLIVAN		1871	1894	014	SULLIVAN, Rose	
				014		
James DEMPSEY		1835	1883	014	_____, Margaret	
Margaret _____ DEMPSEY		1839	1887	014	DEMPSEY, James	
				014		
Thomas J. SULLIVAN		21Y 10M	04-23-1878	014	SULLIVAN, Thomas J.	
Katie SULLIVAN		18Y 3M	09-07-1878	014	SULLIVAN, Katie	
Patrick SULLIVAN		1Y 11D	MAY 1866	014	SULLIVAN, Patrick	
Katie SULLIVAN				014	SULLIVAN, Katie	(NOI On Second Katie)
Thomas SULLIVAN				014	SULLIVAN, Thomas	(NOI On Second Thomas)
				014		
Johanna _____ CROWNINGSHIELD		60 Years	08-12-1891	014	CROWNINGSHIELD, Asa	(NOI Asa Crowningshield)
				014	_____, Johanna	
				014		
Ellen MORIARITY		50 Years	07-28-1862	014	MORIARITY, Ellen	
				014		
Johanna FITZGERALD Moriarity		55 Years	02-20-1875	014	MORIARITY, Edmund	(NOI Edmund Moriarity)
				014	FITZGERALD, Johanna	
				014		
Michael HIGGINS		63 Years	03-28-1894	014	GRIFFIN, Mary	
Mary GRIFFIN Higgins		74 Years	07-28-1906	014	HIGGINS, Michael	
Patrick HIGGINS		32 Years	01-11-1900	014	HIGGINS, Patrick	
Mary HIGGINS		60 Years	01-26-1915	014	HIGGINS, Mary	
Abbie HIGGINS		72 Years	06-12-1929	014	HIGGINS, Abbie	
				014		
Johanna BROSNAHAN		78 Years	11-02-1919	014	BROSNAHAN, Johanna	
				014		
Johanna _____ BROSNAHAN		23 Years	08-12-1874	014	BROSNAHAN, Patrick	(NOI Patrick Brosnahan)
				014	_____, Johanna	
				014		

Name	Age/Born	Died		Relation	Notes
Mary LONG Flahive	46 Years	09-11-1865	014	FLAHIVE, John	(NOI John Flahive)
			014	LONG, Mary	
			014		
Patrick DOOLING	54 Years	06-16-1880	014	_____, Abbie	
Abbie ____ DOOLING	67 Years	05-05-1896	014	DOOLING, Patrick	
			014		
Michael DUNDON	55 Years	05-21-1903	014	FLEMING, Hannah	
Hannah FLEMING Dundon	87 Years	01-02-1934	014	DUNDON, Michael	
			014		
Eugene O'DONNELL	40 Years	03-22-1883	014	DOUDE, Catharine	
Catharine DOUDE O'Donnell	59 Years	02-18-1900	014	O'DONNELL, Eugene	
Catharine DOUDE	65 Years	06-15-1864	014	DOUDE, Catharine	
			014		
John DOYLE	18 Years	10-12-1868	014	DOYLE, John	
Kate CARMODY Doyle	1817	1900	014	CARMODY, Kate	
Mary DEVINE Landerfin	1837	1920	014	LANDERFIN, Mary	
			014		
Daniel FITZGERALD	1816	1866	014	MAGNER, Honora	
Honora MAGNER Fitzgerald	1827	1866	014	FITZGERALD, Daniel	
James FITZGERALD	1854	1889	014	FITZGERALD, James	
Johanna FITZGERALD	1861	1873	014	FITZGERALD, Johanna	
			014		
Mrs. James MAGNER	1798	1885	014	MAGNER, James	(NOI James Magner nor Maiden name of Mrs. James Magner)
			014		
James MAGNER Jr.	1836	1869	014	MAGNER, James Jr.	
Honora MAGNER	1867	1867	014	MAGNER, Honora	
William MAGNER	1870	1891	014	MAGNER, William	
			014		
Maurice BROWN	32 Years	08-10-1855	014	_____, Hanora	
Hanora ____ BROWN	76 Years	03-03-1899	014	BROWN, Maurice	
			014		
Julia ____ BROWN	35 Years	06-13-1888	014	BROWN, Thomas	(NOI Thomas Brown)
			014	_____, Julia	
			014		
Timothy C. SHEA	03-25-1832	02-28-1905	014	KELLY, Bridget	
			014	CARROLL, Margaret	
			014		
Bridget KELLY Brown	08-12-1838	06-09-1870	014	SHEA, Timothy C.	
Margaret CARROLL Brown	02-12-1845	03-06-1905	014	SHEA, Timothy C.	
			014		
Maurice AUSTIN	76 Years	02-08-1901	014	CURRAN, Bridget	
Bridget CURRAN Austin	76 Years	07-14-1905	014	AUSTIN, Maurice	
			014		
Abram F. STEWART	55 Years	01-26-1896	014	LONG, Mary A.	(See Margaret Donahue Stewart who died 10-18-1876)
			014		

Mary A. LONG Stewart	97Y4M9D	02-06-1938	014	STEWART, Abram F.	
			014		
Ellen ____ HOGAN	49 Years	08-25-1900	014	HOGAN, David	(NOI David Hogan)
			014	_____, Ellen	
			014		
John LONG	60 Years	10-19-186	014	_____, Catherine	A Native Of Ireland
Catherine ____ LONG	87 Years	03-12-1897	014	LONG, John	
			014		
Dennis GRADY	55 Years	01-22-1879	014	AUSTIN, Catherine	
			014	FITZGERALD, Catherine	
Catherine AUSTIN Grady	36 Years	11-10-1867	014	GRADY, Dennis	
Catherine FITZGERALD Grady	70 Years	01-21-1892	014	GRADY, Dennis	
			014		
James GRADY	1855	1935	014	DONNELLY, Eliza	
Eliza DONNELLY Grady	1854	1947	014	GRADY, James	
			014		
Maurice BOWLER	68 Years	03-31-1897	014	AUSTIN, Mary	
Mary AUSTIN Bowler	39 Years	07-13-1871	014	BOWLER, Maurice	
			014		
Edmund CAREY	02-01-1833	08-26-1904	014	FLAVIN, Mary	
Mary FLAVIN Carey	04-23-1836	08-13-1871	014	CAREY, Edmund	
			014		
William AHERN	51 Years	07-17-1870	014	_____, Johanna	
Johanna ____ AHERN	62 Years	11-05-1888	014	AHERN, William	
Daniel AHERN	29Y 4M	12-28-1887	014	AHERN, Daniel	
Catherine LAWRENCE	27Y 3M	10-19-1879	014	LAWRENCE, Catherine	
Mary AHERN	37 Years	12-08-1886	014	AHERN, Mary	
			014		
Ellen Elizabeth MARTIN Ferriter	31 Years	11-03-1871	014	FERRITER, Luke	Beloved Wife Of Luke Ferriter.
			014	MARTIN, Ellen Elizabeth	(See Luke Ferriter W/D 1930)
			014		
Eugene FERRITER	78 Years	11-05-1928	014	HAGGERTY, Mary	
Mary HAGGERTY Ferriter	68 Years	03-08-1920	014	FERRITER, Eugene	
			014		
Baxter HOWARD	1841	1877	014	WELSH, Bridget	
Bridget WELSH Howard	1838	1923	014	HOWARD, Baxter	
			014		
Michael HOPKINS	06-10-1847	10-17-1904	014	MANNING, Annie	
Annie MANNING Hopkins	05-05-1856	10-08-1918	014	HOPKINS, Michael	
			014		
Michael GRIFFIN	1834	1899	014	O'NEIL, Mary	
Mary O'NEIL Griffin	1838	1911	014	GRIFFIN, Michael	
Michael GRIFFIN	1858	1870	014	GRIFFIN, Michael	
Abbie GRIFFIN	1865	1928	014	GRIFFIN, Abbie	
Annie GRIFFIN	1873	1888	014	GRIFFIN, Annie	

Mary GRIFFIN		1860	1935	014	GRIFFIN, Mary	
John GRIFFIN		1868	1943	014	GRIFFIN, John	
				014		
John DEVINE		1834	1910	014	DOOLING, Catherine	(GAR) Co. C, 10 Ohio
Catherine DOOLING Devine			05-02-1917	014	DEVINE, John	
Mary DEVINE		1877	1937	014	DEVINE, Mary	
				014		
John T. KAINE		1858	1951	014	MORAN, Bridget	
Bridget MORAN Kaine		71 Years	11-02-1925	014	KAINE, John T.	
				014		
Thomas JUDGE		87 Years	04-28-1898	014	MCCORMACK, Hanora	
Hanora MCCORMACK Judge		56 Years	01-22-1894	014	JUDGE, Thomas	
				014		
Martin F. DUNN		06-21-1863	12-15-1925	014	BAKER, Mary Celia	
Mary Celia BAKER Dunn		03-09-1859	10-18-1897	014	DUNN, Martin F.	
				014		
Catherine Agnes RALEIGH		06-20-1866	09-08-1889	014	RALEIGH, Catherine Agnes	
Bridget T. RALEIGH		03- -1854	06-07-1931	014	RALEIGH, Bridget T.	
Mary RALEIGH Barry		06-10-1858	04-03-1905	014	BARRY, John	(NOI John Barry)
				014	RALEIGH, Mary	
Patrick RALEIGH		76 Years	01-29-1893	014	FRAWLEY, Catherine	
Catherine FRAWLEY Raleigh		70 Years	02-17-1903	014	RALEIGH, Patrick	
Peter C. BRENNAN		42Y 4M	03-31-1901	014	BRENNAN, Peter C.	
				014		
Thomas A. MURPHY		1851	1918	014	SULLIVAN, Ellen	
Ellen SULLIVAN Murphy		1850	1942	014	MURPHY, Thomas A.	
Frederick MURPHY		11 Months		014	MURPHY, Frederick	Son (NOI)
				014		
Bridget CONNOLLY	Co. Clare	05-24-1838	11-05-1908	014	CONNOLLY, Bridget	
				014		
John B. DUNLEVY		1847	1910	014	HURLEY, Sarah J.	
Sarah J. HURLEY Dunlevy		1854	1942	014	DUNLEVY, John B.	
				014		
Ellen MURNANE		1817	1913	014	MURNANE, Ellen	
				014		
Mary O'DONNELL Toomey		1841	1908	014	TOOMEY, John	(NOI John Toomey)
				014		
Mary SHEA Whealon		08-20-1831	07-19-1906	014	WHEALON, John	(NOI John Whealon)
				014		
Cornelius FITZGERALD		1852	1927	014	HENNESSEY, Ella M.	
Ella M. HENNESSEY Fitzgerald		1857	1950	014	FITZGERALD, Cornelius	
				014		
Francis HICKEY		53 Years	11-19-1881	014	REDDIN, Anne	(Erected by) Anne Hickey In
				014		Memory Of Her Husband
Anne REDDIN Hickey		87Y 6M	05-06-1923	014	HICKEY, Francis	

Name	Place	Born/Age	Died	Lot	Index	Notes
				014		
Catherine MCCARTY Moore		72Y 5M	08-29-1890	014	MOORE, James	(NOI James Moore)
				014	MCCARTY, Catherine	
				014		
Patrick GRADY		1821	1892	014	MCSWEENEY, Abbie	
Abbie MCSWEENEY Grady		1838	1926	014	GRADY, Patrick	
Abbie GRADY		1868	1921	014	GRADY, Abbie	
Katherine GRADY		1879	1897	014	GRADY, Katherine	
Norah GRADY		1875	1938	014	GRADY, Norah	
James GRADY		1869	1900	014	GRADY, James	
Elizabeth GRADY		1866	1948	014	GRADY, Elizabeth	
Helena GRADY		1883	1902	014	GRADY, Helena	
Hannah GRADY		1864	1943	014	GRADY, Hannah	
John T. GRADY		1870	1950	014	MORAN, Mary	
Mary MORAN Grady	Co. Cork	1869	1949	014	GRADY, John T.	Born In Mallow, Co. Cork
				014		
Hugh FOLEY		12-24-1831	01-27-1894	014	HEFFRON, Catherine	AE 63
Catherine HEFFRON Foley		11-17-1829	09-27-1897	014	FOLEY, Hugh	AE 68
				014		
James H. HACKETT		25Y 11M	06-05-1890	014	HACKETT, James H.	
				014		
William REDDIN		1844	1901	014	O'HARA, Mary	
Mary O'HARA Reddin		1856	1922	014	REDDIN, William	
Mathew M. REDDIN		1878	1936	014	REDDIN, Mathew M.	
				014		
John MURPHY		40Y 8M	03-30-1888	014	_____, Johanna	
Johanna ____ MURPHY		85Y 2M	09-18-1935	014	MURPHY, John	
Margaret E. MURPHY		1873	1949	014	MURPHY, Margaret E.	
Josephine E. MURPHY		1876	1956	014	MURPHY, Josephine E.	
Katherine A. MURPHY		1881	1939	014	MURPHY, Katherine A.	
				014		
Patrick MURPHY		62 Years	10-04-1889	014	DWYER, Catherine	
Catherine DWYER Murphy			09- -1896	014	MURPHY, Patrick	
				014		
Lawrence HEAPHY		03-12-1835	04-18-1910	014	FLEMING, Catherine	
Catherine FLEMING Heaphy		06-24-1840	08-24-1895	014	HEAPHY, Lawrence	
				014		
James MACK Sr.		85 Years	06-17-1892	014	WELCH, Ellen	
Ellen WELCH Mack		98 Years	11-16-1901	014	MACK, James Sr.	
				014		
Patrick Joseph FENTON		1841	1916	014	HART, Sarah Frances	(GAR) Conn. Vols (NOI)
Sarah Frances HART Fenton		1848	1898	014	FENTON, Patrick Joseph	
				014		
David CAREY		1850	1932	014	BREEN, Katherine G.	
				014	BUTLER, Nanno	

Katherine G. BREEN Carey	1855	1893	014	CAREY, David	
Nanno BUTLER Carey	1850	1926	014	CAREY, David	
			014		
John O'BRIEN	66Y1M4D	01-24-1900	014	CANTLOW, Ellen	
Ellen CANTLOW O'Brien	73Y3M2D	12-31-1909	014	O'BRIEN, John	
			014		
Daniel M. BROSNAHAN	1846	1926	014	REDDIN, Mary	
			014	TUBBERT, Mary	
Mary REDDIN Brosnahan	1861	1893	014	BROSNAHAN, Daniel M.	
Mary TIBBERT Brosnahan	1863	1924	014	BROSNAHAN, Daniel M.	
			014		
Patrick GRIFFIN	75 Years	12-27-1900	014	HARTLEY, Mary	
Mary HARTLEY Griffin	70 Years	08-25-1894	014	GRIFFIN, Patrick	
			014		
Joseph C. PERRY	59 Years	08-02-1897	014	____, Annie M.	
Annie M. ___ PERRY	75 Years	10-23-1910	014	PERRY, Joseph	
			014		
John BREEN	88 Years	06-21-1896	014	MOYNIHAN, Ellen	
Ellen MOYNIHAN Breen	75 Years	08-20-1897	014	BREEN, John	
			014		
James H. CAUFIELD	50 Years	10-01-1895	014	FENTON, Eliza T.	
Eliza T. FENTON Caufield	1842	04-07-1923	014	CAUFIELD, James H.	Born In Ireland
			014		
James CASSIDY	1828	1924	014	____, Mary	
Mary ____ CASSIDY	1829	1904	014	CASSIDY, James	
Charles CASSIDY	1872	1914	014	CASSIDY, Charles	
Michael FITZGIBBONS	1871	1900	014	FITZGIBBONS, Michael	
			014		
James CLURE	12-23-1850	12-17-1897	014	MARONEY, Bridget A.	
Bridget A. MARONEY Clure	05-14-1855	09-20-1940	014	CLURE, James	
Elizabeth DONAHUE	51 Years	06-02-1897	014	DONAHUE, Elizabeth	
			014		
Martin DUNN	1837	1913	014	CASS, Anastasia	
Anastasia CASS Dunn	1841	1921	014	DUNN, Martin	
William DUNN	1875	1896	014	DUNN, William	
Nicholas DUNN	1880	1933	014	DUNN, Nicholas	
			014		
Margaret CORDON	06-24-1824	06-04-1900	014	CORDON, Margaret	
			014		
Patrick MANNING	1858	1926	014	KENNEDY, Mary	
			014	CURRY, Honora	
Mary KENNEDY Manning	1853	1898	014	MANNING, Patrick	
Honora CURRY Manning	1874	1949	014	MANNING, Patrick	
			014		
Maurice KENNEDY	86 Years	08-15-1897	014	KENNEDY, Maurice	

Name	Place	Born	Died	Code	Index	Note
John KENNEDY		37 Years	01-20-1899	014		
				014		
Charles BEAN Sr.		1847	1901	014	____, Mary Jane	
Mary Jane ____ BEAN		1852	1937	014	BEAN, Charles Sr.	
Charles J. BEAN		1871	1901	014	BEAN, Charles J.	
Florence BEAN		1887	1888	014	BEAN, Florence	
Ella L. BEAN		1885	1960	014	BEAN, Ella L.	
				014		
Thomas COLEMAN		1853	1887	014	CAUFIELD, Catherine	
Catherine CAUFIELD Coleman		1851	1916	014	COLEMAN, Thomas	
Annie COLEMAN		1877	1900	014	COLEMAN, Annie	
Frederick COLEMAN		1883	1911	014	COLEMAN, Frederick	
				014		
Bartholomew REDDING		1845	1918	014	MACK, Ellen M.	
Ellen M. MACK Redding		1850	1932	014	REDDING, Bartholomew	
				014		
Owen FOLEY		60 Years	03-02-1901	014	MURRAY, Mary	
Mary MURRAY Foley		70 Years	03-25-1915	014	FOLEY, Owen	
				014		
Patrick CONNARN		1850	1916	014	GREANEY, Bridget	
Bridget GREANEY Connarn		1854	1923	014	CONNARN, Patrick	
				014		
Lawrence STAMPS		85 Years	06-04-1933	014	____, Margaret	
Margaret ____ STAMPS		85Y5M7D	01-22-1914	014	STAMPS, Lawrence	
George Emery WHITNEY		12-04-1857	12-30-1909	014	____, Mary	
Mary ____ WHITNEY		1865	1945	014	WHITNEY, George Emery	
				014		
Daniel MORIARITY	Co. Kerry	1832	1903	014	MORIARITY, Daniel	Born In County Kerry, Ireland
				014		
John A. FENTON		1856	1940	014	DOOLING, Nellie	
Nellie DOOLING Fenton		1859	1943	014	FENTON, John A.	
				014		
Frank G. ADAM		10-26-1856	01-27-1915	014	HERBERT, Mary E.	
Mary E. HERBERT Adam		40Y6M28D	04-23-1904	014	ADAM, Frank G.	
				014		
Daniel F.D. SULLIVAN		1849	1921	014	____, Mary J.	
Mary J. ____ SULLIVAN		1871	1949	014	SULLIVAN, Daniel F.D.	
Joseph SULLIVAN		1904	1904	014	SULLIVAN, Joseph	
				014		
Thomas J. SEARS		10-31-1858	11-03-1950	014	STEWART, Margaret H.	
Margaret H. STEWART Sears		09-02-1858	01-25-1917	014	SEARS, Thomas J.	
				014		
Rev. P. CUNNINGHAM		1839	1904	014	CUNNINGHAM, Rev. P.	
				014		
Michael J. MOYAN		1851	1921	014	KENNEDY, Johanna C.	

Johanna C. KENNEDY Moyan	1856	1931	014	MOYAN, Michael J.	
			014		
Patrick RYAN	1829	1907	014	HEAPHY, Bridged	
Bridged HEAPHY Ryan	1829	1912	014	RYAN, Patrick	
			014		
Walter M. MURPHY	68 Years		014	TULLY, Mary	
Mary Tully MURPHY			014	MURPHY, Walter M.	
Mary S. MURPHY	1Y 16D		014	MURPHY, Mary S.	
			014		
Michael W. MANNING	08-08-1851	12-16-1902	014	DOYLE, Nora C.	
Nora C. DOYLE Manning	04-13-1864	02-05-1916	014	MANNING, Michael W.	
			014		
Jerry LEAHY	72 Years	03-22-1925	014	LEAHY, Jerry	Born In Ireland
			014		
William MARTIN	1839	1924	014	____, Mary	
Mary ____ MARTIN	1841	1923	014	MARTIN, William	
			014		
John TOOMEY	1846	1903	014	MARTIN, Mary A.	
Mary A. MARTIN Toomey	1846	1916	014	TOOMEY, John	
			014		
Patrick KANE	1848	1924	014	____, Anna	
Anna ____ KANE	1845	1928	014	KANE, Patrick	
			014		
John AHER	09-25-1825	06-29-1897	014	STACK, Margaret	
Margaret STACK Aher	09-04-1843	12-01-1901	014	AHER, John	
Thomas J. AHER	01-01-1874	03-06-1936	014	AHER, Thomas J.	
Nellie E. AHER	01-03-1884	01-25-1955	014	AHER, Nellie E.	
			014		
Thomas J. WALSH	11-20-1868	12-25-1943	014	MURPHY, Mary	
Mary MURPHY Walsh	06-15-1858	10-28-1938	014	WALSH, Thomas J.	
			014		
Daniel V. MANNING	1854	1929	014	COLEBROOK, Martha V.	
Martha J. COLEBROOK Manning	1863	1933	014	MANNING, Daniel V.	
			014		
Patrick J. FENTON	06-10-1846	02-20-1931	014	____, Mary E.	
Mary E. ____ FENTON	03-04-1847	11-14-1940	014	FENTON, Patrick J.	
			014		
Patrick CUMMINGS	1850	1902	014	WELSH, Bridget	
Bridget WELSH Cummings	1855	1926	014	CUMMINGS, Patrick	
			014		
Edward P. MCGARRIGLE	10-29-1850	01-07-1934	014	____, Eugenia	
Eugenia ____ MCGARRIGLE	08-07-1868	10-04-1951	014	MCGARRIGLE, Edward	
			014		
John J. ECKELS Sr.	1855	1926	014	MAGEE, Katherine	
Katherine MAGEE ECKELS	1854	1943	014	ECKELS, John J. Sr.	

Name	Born	Died	Plot	Index name	Notes
			014		
John MACK	1840	1911	014	CRONIN, Ellen	
Ellen CRONIN Mack	1844	1925	014	MACK, John	
			014		
Thomas FLOOD	09-16-1850	05-27-1911	014	FLOOD, Thomas	U.S. Navy 1862-1865
Elizabeth T. FLOOD	1865	1926	014	FLOOD, Elizabeth T.	
John S. FLOOD	1853	1936	014	FLOOD, John S.	
			014		
John D. SULLIVAN		02-11-1920	014	SULLIVAN, John D.	In Memory of John D. Sullivan
			014		(NOI DOB or Age At Death)
Daniel SULLIVAN	1873	1940	014	SULLIVAN, Daniel	
			014		
Thomas HANNON	1850	1926	014	HANNON, Thomas	
Henry HANNON		1881	014	HANNON, Henry	
Isabell HANNON	1858		014	HANNON, Isabell	
Edward HANNON	1855		014	HANNON, Edward	
			014		
Thomas MULLIN	1855	1924	014	O'BRIEN, Mary	
Mary O'BRIEN Mullin	1858	1945	014	MULLIN, Thomas	
Dr. James SULLIVAN	1884	1971	014	SULLIVAN, Dr. James	
Helen M. SULLIVAN	1886	1975	014	SULLIVAN, Helen M.	
Elizabeth M. SULLIVAN	1889	1971	014	SULLIVAN, Elizabeth M.	
			014		
John C. MURPHY	1867	1940	014	LEACH, Mable J.	
Mable J. LEACH Murphy	1875	1924	014	MURPHY, John C.	
			014		
Daniel E. CROWLEY	1848	1923	014	____, Margaret	
Margaret ____ CROWLEY	1860	1951	014	CROWLEY, Daniel E.	
			014		
Annie ____ CALLAHAN	1850	1930	014	CALLAHAN, Patrick	(NOI Patrick Callahan)
			014	_____, Annie	
			014		
Johanna MURPHY Colebrook	1856	1919	014	COLEBROOK, Barney	(NOI Barney Colebrook)
			014	MURPHY, Johanna	
Thomas MURPHY	1862	1919	014	MURPHY, Thomas	
Martin T. MURPHY	1863	1935	014	MURPHY, Martin T.	
			014		
John GALVIN	1854	1911	014	FLANNERY, Mary Jane	
Mary Jane FLANNERY Galvin	1856	1914	014	GALVIN, John	
			014		
Patrick CLURE	03-25-1848	11-05-1931	014	MURPHY, Catherine	
Catherine MURPHY Clure	08-10-1851	07-30-1913	014	CLURE, Patrick	
George W. SHERMAN	09-18-1862	02-09-1949	014	CLURE, Catherine A.	
Catherine A. CLURE Sherman	05-05-1878	12-17-1962	014	SHERMAN, George W.	
			014		

William G. SHIPPEE	1850	1954	014	JOHNSON, Ella Jane	
Ella Jane JOHNSON Shippee	1879	1920	014	SHIPPEE, William G.	
			014		
William MCCONNELL	10-31-1849	01-07-1928	014	MCCONNELL, William	
			014		
Patrick FLEMING	1848	1923	014	EARLY, Catherine	
Catherine EARLY Fleming	1860	1942	014	FLEMING, Patrick	
			014		
Michael SEARS	1825	1901	014	FITZGERALD, Catherine	
Catherine FITZGERALD Sears	1824	1895	014	SEARS, Michael	
			014		
Mary WELCH Fleming	95 Years	02-07-1881	014	FLEMING, Patrick	(NOI Patrick Fleming)
			014	WELCH, Mary	
			014		
Michael DEVINE	1833	1914	014	MORAN, Elizabeth	
Elizabeth MORAN Devine	1834	1916	014	DEVINE, Michael	
Catherine DEVINE	1865	1865	014	DEVINE, Catherine	
W. R. DEVINE	1887	1937	014	DEVINE, W. R.	
			014		
Cornelius SULLIVAN	51 Years	06-16-1877	014	_____, Catharine	
Catharine ____ SULLIVAN	67 Years	09-05-1894	014	SULLIVAN, Cornelius	
James C. SULLIVAN	01-11-1866	12-03-1927	014	SULLIVAN, James C.	
Agnes SULLIVAN			014	SULLIVAN, Agnes	(No DOB/DOD--Agnes Sullivan)
Elizabeth MULONEY	1858	1941	014	MULONEY, Elizabeth	
			014		
Martin AUSTIN	04-09-1838	07-25-1905	014	BROSNAHAN, Elizabeth	
Elizabeth BROSNAHAN Austin	01-06-1839	11-15-1933	014	AUSTIN, Martin	
			014		
Cornelius BROSNAHAN	73 Years	11-10-1877	014	_____, Catherine	
Catherine ____ BROSNAHAN	72 Years	03-12-1888	014	BROSNAHAN, Cornelius	
			014		
James Francis BOWLER	85 Years	11-12-1921	014	FITZGERALD, Ellen J.	
Ellen J. FITZGERALD Bowler	68 Years	03-23-1906	014	BOWLER, James Francis	
Katherine FITZGERALD	69 Years	02-18-1872	014	FITZGERALD, Katherine	
Edward BOWLER	18 Years	02-12-1882	014	BOWLER, Edward	
			014		
Thomas FENTON	52 Years	11-20-1904	014	DOOLIN, Katie A.	
Katie A. DOOLIN Fenton	31 Years	01-28-1887	014	FENTON, Thomas	
Mary FERRITER Fenton	78 Years	12-20-1891	014	FENTON, Andrew	(NOI Andrew Fenton)
			014	FERRITER, Mary	
			014		
Cornelius SULLIVAN	59 Years	05-12-1905	014	SULLIVAN, Cornelius	
Mathias SULLIVAN	1840	1907	014	BROSNAHAN, Mary	
Mary BROSNAHAN Sullivan	1849	1917	014	SULLIVAN, Mathias	
			014		

NAME	POB	DOB/AGE	DOD	CEM	SPOUSE/INDEX	INSCRIPTION
Mary HERLEY		60 Years	05-04-1881	014	HERLEY, Mary	
John F. HERLEY		63 Years	12-18-1913	014	GALVIN, Mary A.	
Mary A. GALVIN Herley		74 Years	12-17-1926	014	HERLEY, John F.	
				014		
Maurice O'CONNOR		1822	1898	014	MARTIN, Catherine	
Catherine MARTIN O'Connor		1822	1886	014	O'CONNOR, Maurice	
Edmund O'CONNOR		1850	1870	014	O'CONNOR, Edmund	
Mary C. O'CONNOR		1856	1937	014	O'CONNOR, Mary C.	
				014		
Job LONG		1838	1919	014	HANNIFAN, Mary	(GAR) Co. D. 11 MASS Vols
Mary HANNIFIN Long				014	LONG, Job	
				014		
Thomas LYNCH			1917	014	_____, Bridget	
Bridget F. _____ LYNCH		1841	1900	014	LYNCH, Thomas	
				014		
John MARTIN				014	_____, Elizabeth	
Elizabeth _____ MARTIN				014	MARTIN, John	
Alice MARTIN		186		014	MARTIN, Alice	
Elizabeth MARTIN		1868		014	MARTIN, Elizabeth	
William E. MARTIN		186		014	MARTIN, William E.	
				014		
James ROCHFORD				014	O'CONNOR, Mary	
Mary O'CONNOR Rochford				014	ROCHFORD, James	
				014		
John J. BLAKE		06-24-1858	08-20-1928	014	WHITE, Agnes A.	
Agnes A. WHITE Blake		12-25-1863	08-05-1923	014	BLAKE, John J.	

St. Ambrose Cemetery, off Bristol-New Haven Road, Bristol, Vt

NAME	POB	DOB/AGE	DOD	CEM	SPOUSE/INDEX	INSCRIPTION
John H. HANLIN		72 Years	08-29-1919	015	SLATTERY, Mary A.	
Mary A. SLATTERY Hanlin		73Y 11M	06-02-1922	015	HANLIN, John H.	
				015		
Frank BLANCHARD		08-16-1857	04-16-1907	015	MURPHEY, Hannah	
Hannah MURPHEY Blanchard		05-14-1866	07-12-1950	015	BLANCHARD, Frank	
				015		
James MCGARL		91 Years	12-29-1921	015	COUNERTY, Hannah	(Surname may be McCarl-see daughter)
				015		
Hannah COUNERTY McGarl		63 Years	04-17-1899	015	MCGARL, James	
Rose Ann MCGARL		33 Years	10-08-1897	015	MCGARL, Rose Ann	
Edward T. MCGARL		05-10-1866	01-29-1939	015	MCGARL, Edward T.	
George B. COLLAMER		07-11-1864	02-27-1906	015	MCCARL, Margaret	

Name	Place	Birth/Age	Death	Code	Related	Note
Margaret MCCARL Coleman		10-16-1862	08-28-1957	015	COLLAMER, George B.	
				015		
Hubert T. CASEY		1854	1927	015	_____, Ellen D.	
Ellen D. _____ CASEY		1865	1958	015	CASEY, Hubert T.	
				015		
James WARD		80 Years	02-25-1914	015	COUGHLIN, Alice L.	
Alice L. COUGHLIN Ward		77 Years	10-11-1914	015	WARD, James	
Cornelius COUGHLIN		71 Years	12-05-1905	015	COUGHLIN, Cornelius	
				015		
Patrick GILL		1826	1908	015	AMORE, Hanor(a)	
Hanor AMORE Gill		1828	1901	015	GILL, Patrick	
Joseph ASH		1862	1938	015	GILL, Katherine M.	
Katherine M. GILL Ash		1867	1952	015	ASH, Joseph	
				015		
Thomas BUTLER		42 Years	01-02-1883	015	MITCHELL, Ellen	
Ellen MITCHELL Butler		73 Years	02-03-1916	015	BUTLER, Thomas	
				015		
Thomas GILL		1856	1880	015	_____, Mary	
Mary _____ GILL		1861	1914	015	GILL, Thomas	
				015		
James W. CASEY		1868	1932	015		
John SADLIER		67 Years	08-02-1879	015	DAVERN, Mary	
Mary DAVERN Sadlier		88 Years	02-12-1894	015	SADLIER, John	
Michael CASEY	Co. Clare	81 Years	08-16-1912	015	SADLIER, Alice	Native of Co. Clare, Ireland
Alice SADLIER Casey	Co. Tipperary	89Y 5M	02-16-1927	015	CASEY, Michael	Native of Co.Tipperary,Ireland
				015		
Nicholas GRAVELLE		77 Years	02-17-1901	015	DWIRE, Margaret	
Margaret DWIRE Gravelle		97 Years	07-24-1910	015	GRAVELLE, Nicholas	
				015		
William RYAN			06-12-1916	015	RYAN, William	
				015		
Finora J. DALTON		1858	1945	015	DALTON, Finora J.	
				015		
Alice CAFFREY Taylor		1859	1906	015	CAFFREY, Alice	(NOI Mr. Taylor)
				015		
Patrick O'NEILL		1821	1907	015	NOWLAND, Bridget G.	
Bridget G. NOWLAND O'Neill		1831	1875	015	O'NEILL, Patrick	
Mary A. O'NEILL		1857	1903	015	O'NEILL, Mary A.	
Edward P. O'NEILL		1854	1915	015	O'NEILL, Edward P.	
John O'NEILL		1866	1928	015	O'NEILL, John	
Francis O'NEILL		1864	1931	015	O'NEILL, Francis	
Helen O'NEILL		1863	1932	015	O'NEILL, Helen	
Dr. William O'NEILL		1867	1933	015	O'NEILL, Dr. William	
Margaret C. O'NEILL		1861	1936	015	O'NEILL, Margaret C.	
				015		

Nancy COONERTY Coughlin		38 Years	02-15-1860	015	COUGHLIN, John	(NOI John Coughlin)
				015	COONERTY, Nancy	
				015		
Patrick CASEY	Co. Galway	68 Years	03-29-1893	015	_____, Catherine	Native of Co. Galway, Ireland
Catherine _____ CASEY	Co. Donegal	54 Years	09-25-1891	015	CASEY, Patrick	Native of Donegal, Ireland
Mary CASEY		51 Years	03-02-1915	015	CASEY, Mary	
Dennis CASEY		Infant	02-17-1868	015	CASEY, Dennis	
Ambrose J. CASEY			10-03-1867	015	CASEY, Ambrose J.	
Thomas C. CASEY		22 Years	04-16-1881	015	CASEY, Thomas C.	
				015		
James H. CASEY		51 Years	05-25-1927	015	COUGHLIN, Nellie	
Nellie COUGHLIN Casey		42 Years	03-12-1902	015	CASEY, James H.	
				015		
Thomas CASEY		12-26-1827	09-06-1916	015	_____, Bridget	
Bridget _____ CASEY		52 Years	02-15-1876	015	CASEY, Thomas	
Mary _____ CASEY		46YyM26D	02-06-1899	015	CASEY, Thomas	
Katherine C. CASEY		09-08-1860	11-21-1955	015	CASEY, Katherine C.	
Alice CASEY		1888	1960	015	CASEY, Alice	
				015		
John P. CASEY	Co. Clare	61 Years	08-07-1889	015	_____, Bridget	A Native Of Co. Clare, Ireland
Catherine CARROLL Casey		88 Years	09-27-1916	015	CASEY, John P.	
Alice E. CASEY		56 Years	11-06-1914	015		
Catherine CASEY O'Connor		09-17-1865	03-26-1950	015	CASEY, Catherine	(NOI Mr. O'Connor)
				015		
John GARLAND		04-22-1820	73 Years	015	_____, Margaret	
Margaret _____ GARLAND		07-02-1822	87 Years	015	GARLAND, John	
				015		
Daniel HAYES		42 Years	07-15-1868	015	DOLAN, Mary	
Mary DOLAN Hayes		70 Years	04-29-1901	015	HAYES, Daniel	
Daniel Hayes Jr		68 Years	04-17-1929	015	CROWLEY, Bridget	
Bridget CROWLEY Hayes		87 Years	11-13-1946	015	HAYES, Daniel Jr.	
				015		
Edmond HANNAN		1857	1944	015	GEARY, Mary	
Mary GEARY Hannan		1875	1931	015	HANNAN, Edmond	
				015		
Michael BUTLER		74 Years	09-17-1897	015	_____, Bridget	
Bridget _____ BUTLER		89 Years	05-06-1917	015	BUTLER, Michael	
				015		
John W. HANNAN		62 Years	10-27-1916	015	CASEY, Annora	
Annora CASEY Hannan		82 Years	03-23-1940	015	HANNAN, John W.	
				015		
James MINAHAN		84 Years	03-24-1905	015	BUTLER, Bridget	
Bridget BUTLER Minahan		69 Years	01-02-1898	015	MINAHAN, James	
				015		
Andrew J. DILLON		80 Years	11-04-1918	015	SHANAHAN, Ann G.	

Name	Born/Age	Died		Related	Notes
Ann G. SHANAHAN Dillon	64 Years	07-28-1911	015	DILLON, Andrew J.	
Eliza GRIFFIN Shanahan	72 Years	10-17-1885	015	SHANAHAN, John	(NOI John Shanahan)
			015	GRIFFIN, Eliza	
			015		
Michael HOGAN	1792	1883	015	MCNAMARA, Johanna	
Johanna MCNAMARA Hogan	1804	1882	015	HOGAN, Michael	
Elizabeth HOGAN	1835	1905	015	HOGAN, Elizabeth	
Edmond HANNON	1818	1898	015	HOGAN, Margaret	
Margaret HOGAN Hannon	1828	1901	015	HANNAN, Edmond	
John CROWLEY	1850	1927	015	HANNON, Joanna	
Joanna HANNON Crowley	1852	1920	015	CROWLEY, John	
Elizabeth J. HANNON	1858	1932	015	HANNON, Elizabeth J.	
Julia H. MCCOY	1861	1947	015	MCCOY, Julia H.	
Edmond HANNON	1864	1930	015	HANNON, Edmond	
			015		
William H. LIDDY	1851	1936	015	_____, Mary Anne	
Mary Anne _____ LIDDY	1849	1934	015	LIDDY, William	
			015		
Bernard MCCLEAN	58 Years	10-31-1892	015	MCCLEAN, Bernard	
			015		
Own (Owen) MCCLEAN	66 Years	02-24-187_	015	MCCLEAN, Own	
			015		
Patrick COUNERTY	63 Years	01-17-1906	015	NICHOLS, Mary	Co. G. 14th Rgt Vt Vols (GAR)
Mary NICHOLS Counerty	1851	1935	015	COUNERTY, Patrick	
			015		
James P. MURPHY	1862		015	HANNAN, Margaret	
Margaret HANNAN Murphy	1861	1923	015	MURPHY, James P.	
			015		
Michael HANNON	57 Years	05-21-1885	015	GARNNER, Ellen	
Ellen GARNNER Hannon	86 Years	01-06-1915	015	HANNON, Michael	
Mary FREEMAN	1849	1942	015	FREEMAN, Mary	
			015		
Michael HANNON	1858	1924	015	BUTLER, Hannie	
Hannie BUTLER Hannon	1863	1943	015	HANNON, Michael	
			015		
Gerritt D. CROWLEY	1852	1920	015	_____, Flora E.	
Flora E. _____ CROWLEY	1868	1932	015	CROWLEY, Gerritt D.	
			015		
Irvin J. MURRAY	1847	1930	015	WELCH, Katherine	
Katherine WELCH Murray	1850	1923	015	MURRAY, Irvin J.	
			015		
James H. GILL	73 Years	03-10-1928	015	HANNON, Mary E.	
Mary E. HANNON Gill	52 Years	05-13-1913	015	GILL, James H.	
			015		
Richard COURSEY	1826	1908	015	MALANA, Catherine	(Both Coursey and DeCoursey

Name	Place	Born/Age	Died	Code	Index Name	Notes
				015		families in this burialground)
Catherine MALANA Coursey		1832	1915	015	COURSEY, Richard	
				015		
Richard DECOURSEY				015	MULLINGS, Mary A.	
Mary A. MULLINGS DeCoursey		41 Years	03-27-1915	015	DECOURSEY, Richard	
				015		
Michael CROWLEY	Co. Clare	69 Years	12-18-1884	015	FITZGERALD, Margaret	A Native of Quin,Co. Clare,Ire
Margaret FITZGERALD Crowley	Co. Limerick	72 Years	06-19-1904	015	CROWLEY, Michael	A Native of "Hoherloud", Co.
				015		Limerick,Ire.(Not In Index)
Hannie CROWLEY		5 Years	08-10-1869	015	CROWLEY, Hannie	
Mikie CROWLEY		1 Year	03-16-1863	015	CROWLEY, Mikie	
Michael E. CROWLEY		64 Years	03-12-1931	015	DECOURSEY, Margaret E.	
Margaret DECOURSEY Crowley		51Y 7M	12-10-1915	015	CROWLEY, Michael E.	
				015		
John BURKE		57 Years	02-11-1882	015	_____, Katherine	
Katherine _____ BURKE		92 Years	09-12-1923	015	BURKE, John	
				015		
Joseph B. RIVERS		04-27-1837	07-24-1901	015	MCPHELIN, Margaret	
Margaret MCPHELIN Rivers		DEC 1825	MAR 1915	015	RIVERS, Joseph B.	
Mary E. RIVERS Murphy		06-11-1861	05-19-1902	015	MURPHY, Thomas	(NOI Thomas Murphy)
				015	RIVERS, Mary E.	
				015		
George MOTT		1852	1915	015	MULLEN, Bridget	
Bridget MULLEN Mott		1855	1913	015	MOTT, George	
				015		
John WELCH		1846	1890	015	LEONARD, Johanna	
Johanna LEONARD Welch		1846	1929	015	WELCH, John	
				015		
William HINES		1833	1910	015	FITZGERALD, Hannah	
Hannah FITZGERALD Hines		1832	1914	015	HINES, William	
				015		
Owen J. MCSHANE		1853	1933	015	_____, Anna	
Anna _____ MCSHANE		1856	1925	015	MCSHANE, Owen	
				015		
Charles MACK		1847	1929	015	BEANE, Anna	
Anna BEANE Mack		1855	1940	015	MACK, Charles	
				015		
Thomas O'CONNOR		1852	1885	015	LEONARD, Ellen	
Ellen LEONARD O'Connor		1854	1940	015	O'CONNOR, Thomas	
				015		
Michael MEEHAN		1858	1919	015	BUTLER, Mary	
Mary BUTLER Meehan		1860	1940	015	MEEHAN, Michael	
				015		
Kevin P. HEFFERNAN	Co. Limerick	1902	1959	015	LAFAYETTE, Zita M.	
Zita M. LAFAYETTE Heffernan		1898	1974	015	HEFFERNAN, Kevin P.	

Immaculate Conception Cemetery, Corner of Hyde St. and Archibald St., Burlington, Vermont

NAME	POB	DOB/AGE	DOD	CEM	SPOUSE/INDEX	INSCRIPTION
Edward W. MCKNIGHT		1855	1910	016	MCNALLY, Bridget E.	
Bridget E. MCNALLY McKnight		1857	1896	016	MCKNIGHT, Edward W.	
				016		
M. COLLINS		1852	1923	016	COLLINS, M.	
				016		
Michael MALLOY		1847	1894	016	RAFFERTY, Catherine	
Catherine RAFFERTY Malloy		1851	1925	016	MALLOY, Michael	
				016		
Edward SHANLEY		1846	1904	016	SHANLEY, Edward	
				016		
Norah KANE			05-04-1901	016	KANE, Nora	
				016		
Daniel COGGINS		66 Years	01-23-1897	016	COGGINS, Daniel	
				016		
William D. HOGAN		05-06-1842	05-03-1896	016	BOYLE, Susan M.	
Susan M. BOYLE Hogan		05-02-1846	04-13-1905	016	HOGAN, William D.	
				016		
James SHANLEY		1847	1896	016	GALLAGHER, Frances	
Frances GALLAGHER Shanley		1852	1920	016	SHANLEY, James	
				016		
Dennis WELCH		1834	1904	016	GEARY, Hannah	
Hannah GEARY Welch		1840	1916	016	WELCH, Dennis	
W.H.KELLEY			JAN 1920	016	BALDWIN, Margaret	
				016	_____, Agnes B.	
Margaret BALDWIN Kelley			01-04-1900	016	KELLEY, W. H.	
Agnes B. _____ KELLEY			01-03-1926	016	KELLEY, W. H.	
				016		
Thomas B. COFFEY		1840	1919	016	SHEEHAN, Bridget	
Bridget SHEEHAN Coffey		1838	1912	016	COFFEY, Thomas B.	
Anna B. COFFEY				016	COFFEY, Anna B.	(NOI)
Henry J. COFFEY				016	COFFEY, Henry J.	(NOI)
Jennie M. COFFEY				016	COFFEY, Jennie M.	(NOI)
				016		
John SHEA		1847	1904	016	WALSH, Mary	
Mary WALSH Shea		1862	1932	016	SHEA, John	
Charles WALSH		1834	1897	016	RYDER, Cecily	
Cecily RYDER Walsh		1840	1901	016	WALSH, Charles	
				016		
James E. LEONARD		1856	1907	016	MATTIMORE, Ellen	
Ellen MATTIMORE Leonard		1852	1925	016	LEONARD, James E.	

Name	Born	Died	Plot	Spouse	Notes
			016		
William EARLEY	1820	1899	016	EARLEY, William	
			016		
Michael EARLEY	1824	1895	016	EARLEY, Michael	
			016		
Daniel CAMPBELL	1824	1900	016	LEWIS, Mary	
Mary LEWIS Campbell	1841	1925	016	CAMPBELL, Daniel	
			016		
Next Plot-individual stones			016		
Father	1834	1902	016		
Mother	1838	1909	016		
Catherine CAMPBELL	1851	1936	016	CAMPBELL, Catherine	
Katie			016		
			016		
William E. HAYES	1852	1939	016	_____, Elizabeth L.	
Elizabeth L. _____ HAYES	1853	1937	016	HAYES, William E.	
			016		
Edward NOONAN	1855	1900	016	CASEY, Anna	
Anna CASEY Noonan	1865	1934	016	NOONAN, Edward	
			016		
Margaret HALLORAN Kennedy	58 Years	01-20-1900	016	HALLORAN, Margaret	Rest In Peace.(NOI Mr. Kennedy
			016		
Patrick HALLORAN	48 Years	11-04-1893	016	HALLORAN, Patrick	
			016		
John L. MURPHY	1861	1940	016	MCGRATH, Bridget	
Bridget MCGRATH Murphy	1861	1942	016	MURPHY, John L.	
			016		
Edward MCAVOY	1837	1921	016	_____, Mary	
Mary _____ MCAVOY			016	MCAVOY, Edward	(Birth & Death dates are below ground and could not read)
			016		
			016		
Michael PURCELL	87 Years	08-11-1903	016	TUNNEY, Ann	
Ann TUNNEY Purcell	72 Years	06-18-1898	016	PURCELL, Michael	
			016		
Ellen MCMANUS	1857	1932	016	MCMANUS, Ellen	
			016		
Michael CORCORAN	1844	1914	016	GALLAGHER, Lucy	
Lucy GALLAGHER Corcoran	1852	1929	016	CORCORAN, Michael	
			016		
Josephine GLEASON	1839	1929	016	GLEASON, Josephine	
			016		
Thomas FITZSIMMONS	1846	1932	016	HOGAN, Maria	
Maria HOGAN Fitzsimmons	07-08-1851	11-14-1894	016	FITZSIMMONS, Thomas	
			016		
William MCGRATH	1864	1937	016	MURPHY, Mary E.	

Mary E. MURPHY McGrath		1864	1941	016	MCGRATH, William	
				016		
John R. REDMOND		1837	1906	016	KENNEDY, Alice E.	
Alice E. KENNEDY Redmond		1835	1904	016	REDMOND, John R.	
				016		
Thomas H. MCAVOY		1840	1893	016	FINNESSY, Margaret	
Margaret FINNESSY McAvoy		1850	1934	016	MCAVOY, Thomas H.	
				016		
Mary MOYNIHAN Smith		1854	1917	016	SMITH, Daniel	(NOI Daniel Smith)
				016		
James BARRY		1818	1902	016	DOWNS, Catherine	
Catherine DOWNS Barry	Co. Clare	69 Years	12-27-1894	016	BARRY, James	Born In Newgrove,County Clare, Ireland. (Newgrove AKA Ballyslattery)
				016		
				016		
M. J. BARRY		1855	1926	016	BURKE, Mary J.	
Mary J. BURKE Barry		1868	1937	016	BARRY, M.J.	
				016		
Michael MCGETTRICK		1850	1902	016	_____, Johanna	
Johanna _____ MCGETTRICK		1861	1951	016	MCGETTRICK, Michael	
				016		
Michael STOKES		34Y 6M	07-21-1893	016	DONAHOE, Margaret	
Margaret DONAHOE Stokes				016	STOKES, Michael	(NOI Margaret Donahoe)
				016		
Patrick RYAN	Co. Tipperary	75 Years	05-03-1907	016	HEALY, Catherine	Born In Co. Tipperary, Ireland
Catherine HEALY Ryan		1848	1917	016	RYAN, Patrick	
				016		
Martin CARROLL	Co. Tipperary	33Y01M02D	07-22-1893	016	CARROLL, Martin	Born In Co. Tipperary, Ireland Killed At Proctor, Vermont
				016		
				016		
Michael GILL		1843	1916	016	LAVELLE, Mary	
Mary LAVELLE Gill		1848	1924	016	GILL, Michael	
				016		
Patrick MCMAHON		1822	1878	016	DOHERTY, Catherine	
Catherine DOHERTY McMahon		1828	1902	016	MCMAHON, Patrick	
Their Children				016		
Cornelius L. MCMAHON		1853	1924	016	MCMAHON, Cornelius L.	
Joanna E. MCMAHON		1863	1945	016	MCMAHON, Joanna E.	
Patrick W. MCMAHON				016	MCMAHON, Patrick	
Mary A. MCMAHON				016	MCMAHON, Mary A.	
Henry C. MCMAHON		1860	1920	016	MCMAHON, Henry C.	
Michael D. MCMAHON		1858	1935	016	MCMAHON, Michael D.	
Margaret A. MCMAHON		1866	1944	016	MCMAHON, Margaret A.	
				016		
Michael D. MCMAHON		1858	1935	016	LONERGAN, Mary	
Mary LONERGAN McMahon		1865	1941	016	MCMAHON, Michael D.	

Name	Born	Died	Code	Index	Notes
			016		
Patrick E. MCSWEENEY	1862	1938	016	MCMAHON, Margaret A.	Doctor, MS, MD, FACS
Margaret MCMAHON McSweeney	1866	1944	016	MCSWEENEY, Patrick E.	
			016		
Orlo LUCE	1859	1937	016	MCMAHON, Joanna	
Joanna MCMAHON Luce	1863	1945	016	LUCE, Orlo	
			016		
BARRY Family (No Dates)			016	BARRY, Memorial	
Mother			016		
Father			016		
William BARRY			016	BARRY, William	
Rose BARRY			016	BARRY, Rose	
Mary E. PHELAN			016	PHELAN, Mary E.	
Margaret BARRY			016	BARRY, Margaret	
Mary BARRY			016	BARRY, Mary	
Michael BARRY			016	BARRY, Michael	
			016		
Patrick J. HURSON	1839	1915	016	DONAHUE, Ellen	
Ellen DONAHUE Hurson	1853	1916	016	HURSON, Patrick J.	
			016		
Rose FARRELL	1855	1939	016	FARRELL, Rose	Mother
			016		
Michael DOHERTY	08-01-1837	06-06-1906	016	DOHERTY, Michael	(Does not indicate if husband
Elizabeth DOHERTY	12-13-1840	07-21-1893	016	DOHERTY, Elizabeth	& wife but on same stone)
			016		
Edward MEEHAN	88 Years	06-27-1903	016	MEEHAN, Edward	
			016		
John DONLIN	1818	1904	016	MCSHERRY, Mary	
Mary MCSHERRY Donlin	1825	1907	016	DONLIN, John	
Patrick J. DONLIN	1857	1930	016	MINAHAN, Katherine M.	
Katherine M. MINAHAN Donlin	1863	1907	016	DONLIN, Patrick J.	
			016		
Thomas COOK	50 Years	04-21-1892	016	DOYLE, Margaret	
Margaret DOYLE Cook	51 Years	05-27-1892	016	COOK, Thomas	
			016		
Michael E. MOORE	08-27-1855	07-18-1893	016	LYNCH, Ellen	
Ellen LYNCH Moore	1853	1899	016	MOORE, Michael E.	
John MOORE	10-25-1857	05-03-1892	016	MOORE, John	
Patrick J. LYNCH	1865	1916	016	MOORE, Mary	
Mary MOORE Lynch	1863	1917	016	LYNCH, Patrick J.	
			016		
Thomas L. DUNN			016	_____, Catherine A.	(Top half of this stone is
Catherine A. _____ DUNN			016	DUNN, Thomas L.	missing. No dates given)
Cora L. DUNN			016	DUNN, Cora L.	
Mary A. DUNN			016	DUNN, Mary A.	

Name	Born	Died		Index	Notes
			016		
Charles BLACK	1831	1894	016	MORRISON, Ellen	
Ellen MORRISON Black	1839	1922	016	BLACK, Charles	
			016		
John H. BYRNES	1856	1946	016	MADIGAN, Mary	
Mary MADIGAN Byrnes	1857	1946	016	BYRNES, John H.	
James MADIGAN	1815	1895	016	KENNEDY, Katherine	
Katherine KENNEDY Madigan	1827	1924	016	MADIGAN, James	
			016		
			016	O'NEIL, James	(YOB Could Be 1806)
			016		
Patrick O'NEIL	03-17-1814	01-16-1894	016	O'NEIL, Patrick	
			016		
Thomas MURPHY	1831	1926	016	_____, Eliza	
			016	MONAHAN, Catherine	
Eliza _____ MURPHY	50 Years	03-06-1893	016	MURPHY, Thomas	Born In Whitehall, NY
Catherine MONAHAN Murphy	1849	1924	016	MURPHY, Thomas	
Helen MURPHY Lynch	1889	1916	016	MURPHY, Helen	(NOI Mr. Lynch)
			016		
Dennis M. MURPHY	43 Years	05-23-1893	016	_____, Anna M.	
Anna M. _____ MURPHY	1853	1933	016	MURPHY, Dennis M.	
			016		
John FITZGERALD	1848	1883	016	MCRAVY, Jennie	
Jennie MCRAVY Fitzgerald	1847	1907	016	FITZGERALD, John	
			016		
Mary A. HALLIHAN	1853	1933	016	HALLIHAN, Mary A.	
			016		
John BYRNES	1802	1877	016	BYRNES, John	(Does not say if John-Bridget
Bridget BYRNES	1819	1894	016	BYRNES, Bridget	were husband and wife)
Elizabeth BYRNES	1858	1888	016	BYRNES, Elizabeth	
Julia BYRNES	1853	1925	016	BYRNES, Julia	
			016		
Anna MCGETTRICK	1851	1920	016	MCGETTRICK, Anna	
			016		
FULTON Family			016		(No dates indicated)
Father			016		
Mother			016		
Elvie FULTON	1859	1915	016	FULTON, Elvie	
E. J. F.			016		
			016		
Michael B. CORLEY	1822	1910	016	CLARK, Ann	
Ann CLARK Corley	1830	1875	016	CORLEY, Michael B.	
			016		
John J. COONERTY	08-01-1833	08-31-1907	016	CORLEY, Catherine M.	
Catherine CORLEY Coonerty	12-20-1836	04-04-1900	016	COONERTY, John J.	

				016		
J. W. DALEY		1852	1932	016	REDDINGTON, Mary	
Mary REDDINGTON Daley		1852	1913	016	DALEY, J. W.	
				016		
John E. LAVELL		1858	1926	016	LAVELL, John E.	Born Jericho, VT 1858, Died
				016		Burlington, VT, 1926
Miles CUNNINGHAM		1855	1938	016	LAVELL, Ellen	
Ellen LAVELL Cunningham		1868	1936	016	CUNNINGHAM, Miles	
John LAVELL	Co. Mayo	1821	1890	016	DOLAN, Ann	Born In Newport,Ireland. (New-
				016		port in Co. Mayo & Tipperary.
				016		Probably Co. Mayo as wife born
				016		Westport which is in Co. Mayo)
				016		Died at Burlington, VT
Ann DOLAN Lavell	Co. Mayo	1833	1907	016	LAVELL, John	Westport (Co. Mayo) Ireland
				016		Died At Burlington, VT.
Peter J. LAVELL		1856	1909	016		Born Jericho, VT 1856, Died
				016		Richmond, VT, 1909
				016		
John MCCARTY		1845	1896	016	HEALY, Ellen	
Ellen HEALY McCarty		1848	1924	016	MCCARTY, John	
				016		
James HALLARON		47 Years	01-16-1899	016	_____, Mary	
Mary _____ HALLARON		43 Years	10-09-1892	016	HALLARON, James	
				016		
John O'HALLORAN		85 Years	01-18-1899	016	HENNESY, Hanora	
Hanora HENNESY O'Halloran		80 Years	11-18-1896	016	O'HALLORAN, John	
				016		
Peter E. MARENGO		1854	1923	016	FOLEY, Katherine	
Katherine FOLEY Marengo		1857	1937	016	MARENGO, Peter E.	
				016		
John COLLINS		1837	1906	016	BRADY, Mary	
Mary BRADY Collins		1832	1917	016	COLLINS, John	
Mary TOOMEY Collins		1801	1887	016	TOOMEY, Mary	(NOI Mr. Collins)
				016		
Thomas HENNESY	Co. Carlow	67Y 5M	05-30-1879	016	_____, Bridget	Born In Co. Carlow, Ireland
Bridget _____ HENNESY		74 Years	01-28-1901	016	HENNESY, Thomas	
				016		
James H. MCKENNA		08-27-1838	08-17-1902	016	HALLIHAN, Eliza	PVT, Co. I, 1st Rgt,Vt Vol Cav
Eliza HALLIHAN McKenna		12-22-1845	01-01-1922	016	MCKENNA, James H.	
				016		
William T. HANLON		1859	1929	016	CURRIN, Mary	
Mary CURRIN Hanlon		1859	1894	016	HANLON, William T.	
				016		
Owen COSTELLO		1832	1912	016	BURNS, Kate	
Kate BURNS Costello		1846	1924	016	COSTELLO, Owen	

				016		
Jane DORMAN		72 Years	03-25-1879	016	DORMAN, Jane	(Stone badly deteriorated)
				016		
William POWERS		1842	1910	016	_____, Harriet	
Harriet _____ POWERS		1849	1899	016	POWERS, William	
				016		
Robert C. CROKER		04-08-1850	11-02-1894	016	CURTIS, Ida Margaret	
Ida Margaret CURTIS Croker		08-07-1858	06-16-1895	016	CROKER, Robert C.	
				016		
Matthew COLLINS		1845	1913	016	TOBIN, Ann	
				016	_____, Catherine	
Ann TOBIN Collins		1844	1880	016	COLLINS, Matthew	
Catherine _____ COLLINS		1840	1900	016	COLLINS, Matthew	
				016		
Bridget POTTER Henebery	Co. Limerick	34 Years	10-06-1874	016	HENEBERY, James	Born In The Parish of Adare,
				016	POTTER, Bridget	Co. Limerick, Ireland. Died at
				016		Winooski, Vermont (NOI James
				016		Henebery)
				016		
David BURKE	Co. Cork	05-14-1809	03-10-1879	016	FLYNN, Mary	Born In Mallow, County Cork,
				016		Ireland.Died in Middlebury, VT
Mary FLYNN Burke	Co. Cork	1816	10-18-1898	016	BURKE, David	Born In Mallow,Parish of Burn-
				016		fort, Co. Cork, Ireland. Died
				016		In Middlebury, Vermont. (No
				016		Parish of Burnfort--there is
				016		a Town of Burnfort, Parish of
				016		Mourneabbey)
Mary BURKE		46 Years	07-12-1901	016	BURKE, Mary	Daughter
John B. BURKE		12-21-1849	09-07-1874	016	BURKE, John B.	Son
Annie C. BURKE			07-09-1885	016	BURKE, Annie C.	Sister Mary LORETT (NOI DOB)
				016	LORETT, Sister Mary	
				016		
Michael KILLIN		1828	1878	016	_____, Eliza	
Eliza _____ KILLIN		1827	1904	016	KILLIN, Michael	
				016		
Levi PROCTOR		1848	1887	016	WELCH, Mary	
Mary WELCH Proctor		1847	1925	016	PROCTOR, Levi	
James STAFFORD		1801	1874	016	STAFFORD, James	
				016		
W. P. QUINN		1855	1945	016	HAYES, Bid	(Bid is dimunitive of Bridget)
Bid HAYES Quinn		1858	1933	016	QUINN, W. P.	
James QUINN		1841	1886	016	HAYES, Winifred	
Winifred HAYES Quinn		1842	1922	016	QUINN, James	
Annie QUINN		1805	1880	016	QUINN, Annie	
Rose QUINN		1845	1883	016	QUINN, Rose	

				016		
Patrick MADIGAN		01-12-1847	01-16-1886	016	CRIMMINS, Julia	
Julia CRIMMINS Madigan		10-03-1856	11-05-1884	016	MADIGAN, Patrick	
John MADIGAN		52 Years	08-13-1896	016	BAKER, Bridget	
Bridget BAKER Madigan			03-12-1916	016	MADIGAN, John	
				016		
Patrick COSGROVE		1822	1901	016	_____, Susan	
Susan _____ COSGROVE		1831	1887	016	COSGROVE, Patrick	
Their Children				016		
Mary Ann COSGROVE		1852	1935	016	COSGROVE, Mary Ann	
Andrew COSGROVE		1853	1875	016	COSGROVE, Andrew	
Maggie COSGROVE		1859	1883	016	COSGROVE, Maggie	
Elizabeth COSGROVE		1862	1939	016	COSGROVE, Elizabeth	
John COSGROVE		1865	1900	016	COSGROVE, John	
Patrick J. COSGROVE		1868	1945	016	COSGROVE, Patrick J.	
				016		
Elijah J. CUSHMAN		49 Years	07-01-1884	016	_____, Katie M.	
Katie M. _____ CUSHMAN				016	CUSHMAN, Elijah J.	(Possibly Cosgrove. Same plot)
				016		
Andrew STONE		1839	1878	016	HARRIS, Margaret	
Margaret HARRIS Stone		1836	1916	016	STONE, Andrew	
				016		
Robert ARNOLD		1833	1912	016	SALTUS, Susan Zoe	
Susan Zoe SALTUS Arnold		1835	1907	016	ARNOLD, Robert	
Mary ARNOLD		9 Months	1853	016	ARNOLD, Mary	
George W. ARNOLD		1858	1879	016	ARNOLD, George W.	
				016		
James W. RILEY		1843	1914	016	RILEY, James W.	
				016		
Henry ARNOLD		1842	1911	016	MCCULLAUGH, Ann	
Ann MCCULLAUGH Arnold		1842	1917	016	ARNOLD, Henry	
				016		
Patrick ROURKE		74 Years	03-17-1901	016	MCGARL, Ellen	
Ellen MCGARL Rourke		83 Years	05-27-1913	016	ROURKE, Patrick	
				016		
Patrick CONNELL	Co. Clare	67 Years	04-11-1880	016	_____, Hanorah	Born In Co. Clare, Ireland.
				016		Died at Winooski, Vermont.
				016		(Stone deteriorated-could not
				016		read info on spouse Hanorah)
Hanorah _____ CONNELL				016	CONNELL, Patrick	
				016		
James MADIGAN		1839	1922	016	MCELROY, Bridget	
Bridget MCELROY Madigan		1838	1923	016	MADIGAN, James	
				016		
Joseph ARNOLD		1837	1918	016	CUMMINGS, Mary Salome	

Name	Born	Died	Code	Related	Notes
Mary Salome CUMMINGS Arnold	1843	1914	016	ARNOLD, Joseph	
			016		
Maurice WALSH	35 Years	05-21-1880	016	WALSH, Maurice	Died In The Community Of The
			016		Church And Strengthened By Her
			016		Sacraments. In Your Charity
			016		Pray For The Repose Of MySoul.
			016		
Elizabeth RILEY Lacy	56 Years	08-22-1889	016	LACY, Patrick H.	Died At Burlington, Vt. (NOI
			016	RILEY, Elizabeth	Patrick H. Lacy)
William MANGAN	1826	1896	016	GANEY, Mary	
Mary GANEY Mangan	1835	1897	016	MANGAN, William	
			016		
Terrance MCHUGH	1815	1889	016	MCCAFFREY, Sarah	
Sarah MCCAFFREY McHugh	1825	1888	016	MCHUGH, Terrance	
Sarah A. MCHUGH	1859	1882	016	MCHUGH, Sarah A.	
William H. MCHUGH	1866	1889	016	MCHUGH, William H.	
Mary MCHUGH			016	MCHUGH, Mary	(NOI DOB, DOD of Mary McHugh)
James MCHUGH			016	MCHUGH, James	(NOI DOB, DOD of James McHugh)
			016		
William NEWTON	1854		016	LYNCH, Ellen	
His Wives			016	BURNS, Rosa	
Ellen LYNCH Newton	1851	1900	016	NEWTON, William	
Rosa BURNS Newton	1856	1880	016	NEWTON, William	
			016		
Honora MULLINS	1847	1916	016	MULLINS, Honora	(Does not say if Dennis &
Dennis MULLINS	1850	1875	016	MULLINS, Dennis	Honora were husband and wife)
Patrick A. RITCHIE	1841	1909	016	MULLINS, Catharine	
Catherine MULLINS Ritchie	1841	1912	016	RITCHIE, Patrick A.	
Catherine HENNESEY Mullins	1815	1882	016	MULLINS, John	(NOI John Mullins)
			016		
Thomas MANN	1838	1920	016	_____, Margaret	
Margaret _____ MANN	1836	1908	016	MANN, Thomas	
			016		
Dennis MULQUEEN	54 Years	11-21-1882	016	FARRELL, Bridget	
Bridget FARRELL Mulqueen	69 Years	05-23-1903	016	MULQUEEN, Dennis	
Ellen MULQUEEN	22 Years	02-18-1880	016	MULQUEEN, Ellen	
John MULQUEEN	37 Years	09-14-1892	016	MULQUEEN, John	
			016		
Thomas CORRIGAN	1859	1909	016	FARRELL, Eliza J.	
Eliza J. FARRELL Corrigan	1860	1912	016	CORRIGAN, Thomas	
			016		
Ellen HARRAN Shanley	1848	1880	016	SHANLEY, William	(NOI William Shanley)
			016		
Bartholomew MCGETTRICK	1845	1926	016	HALEY, Catherine	
Catherine HALEY McGettrick	1845	1919	016	MCGETTRICK, Bartholomew	

				016		
Bridget CLOREN Hassett		62 Years	05-05-1903	016	HASSETT, Patrick	(NOI Patrick Hassett)
				016	CLORIN, Bridget	
Martin C. CLORIN		1807	1892	016	HYNES, Ann	
Ann HYNES Clorin		1817	1898	016	CLORIN, Martin C.	
Julia FORAN		75 Years		016	FORAN, Julia	(NOI DOB/DOD of Julia Foran)
Dennis FORAN		1843	1912	016	CLORIN, Mary	
Mary CLORIN Foran		1843	1928	016	FORAN, Dennis	
				016		
Charles RITCHIE		1840	1930	016	MCCULLAUGH, Mary	
Mary MCCULLAUGH Ritchie		1844	1922	016	RITCHIE, Charles	
				016		
Thomas O'DONNELL		1819	1875	016	CASEY, Catherine	
Catherine CASEY O'Donnell		1833	1901	016	O'DONNELL, Thomas	
				016		
Milo C. GRATON		1850	1912	016	SHEEHY, Deborah H.	
Deborah H. SHEEHY Graton		1845	1911	016	GRATON, Milo C.	
				016		
William WATSON		1840	1912	016	WATSON, William	(GAR) Co. F, 6TH Rgt, VT Vols
				016		
John J. MOONEY		1856	1928	016	_____, Mary Ann	
Mary Ann _____ MOONEY		1863	1929	016	MOONEY, John J.	
				016		
Thomas COX		35 Years	01-14-1890	016	COX, Thomas	
				016		
Catherine RYAN		75 Years	01-11-1890	016	RYAN, Catherine	A Native Of Ireland
				016		
Mrs. B. A. WHITE		65 Years	07-12-1908	016	WHITE, Mrs. B.A.	(NOI Mr. White)
W. H. WHITE		21 Years	06-15-1889	016	WHITE, W. H.	
Hannah BRESNEHEN		08-15-1845	10-01-1913	016	BRESNEHAN, Hannah	
				016		
Edward DWYER		1834	1919	016	BOYLE, Mary Ann	
Mary Ann BOYLE Dwyer		51 Years	03-10-1893	016	DWYER, Edward	
				016		
John Edward HOGAN		1853	1914	016	MEEHAN, Elizabeth	
				016	RUSH, Mary	
Elizabeth MEEHAN Hogan		03-22-1857	12-25-1889	016	HOGAN, John Edward	
Mary RUSH Hogan		04-15-1868	03-15-1954	016	HOGAN, John Edward	
				016		
James GROGAN	Co. Clare	60 Years	03-27-1889	016	_____, Margaret	Born In Co. Clare, Ireland
				016		Died at Burlington, Vermont
Margaret _____ GROGAN			10-09-1894	016	GROGAN, James	Died at Burlington, Vermont
Lawrence Edward GROGAN		26Y07M07D	06-25-1884	016	GROGAN, Lawrence E.	Born At Williston, Vermont
				016		Died At Burlington, Vermont
William GROGAN		31 Years	01-02-1886	016	GROGAN, William	Died At Burlington, Vermont

Name	County	Born	Died	Code	Index name	Notes
Ellen GROGAN		1868	1929	016	GROGAN, Ellen	(Does not say if spouse)
				016		
John CROKER		82 Years	05-01-1890	016	POWERS, Mary	
Mary POWERS Croker		75 Years	04-22-1903	016	CROKER, John	
Catherine ADAMS		77 Years	09-12-1881	016	ADAMS, Catherine	(Does not indicated if spouse)
Mary J. CROKER		65 Years	12-09-1915	016	CROKER, Mary J.	
Edward CROKER		04-22-1857	01-29-1909	016	HARRAN, Elizabeth	
Elizabeth HARRAN Croker		09-14-1860	12-06-1911	016	CROKER, Edward	
Thomas J. CROKER		1842	1868	016	CROKER, Thomas J.	Son Of John & Mary Croker. PVT
				016		Co. G, 14 U.S.Inf. Oct 14 1861
				016		Wounded 6-27-1862 at Gaines
				016		Mills, VA. Discharged 4-2-1863
				016		
Robert GREEN		1838	1923	016	REAGAN, Johannah	
Johannah REAGAN Green		1847	1921	016	GREEN, Robert	
David REAGAN		65 Years	09-01-1904	016	REAGAN, David	
Bartholomew REAGAN		78 Years	11-24-1889	016	COTTER, Mary	Born In Ireland
Mary COTTER Reagan		74 Years	02-11-1887	016	REAGAN, Bartholomew	Born In Ireland
				016		
Thomas RYAN		46 Years	08-26-1878	016	_____, Jane	
Jane _____ RYAN		61 Years	05-22-1898	016	RYAN, Thomas	
				016		
Michael MCKENZIE		1780	1882	016	LAVELLE, Mary	
Mary LAVELLE McKenzie		1794	1884	016	MCKENZIE, Michael	
Austin MCKENZIE		1842	1912	016	HART, Kate	Co. M. 1st Rgt Vt Cav (GAR)
Kate HART McKenzie		1847	1931	016	MCKENZIE, Austin	
Lizzie MCKENZIE		1847	1876	016	MCKENZIE, Lizzie	
				016		
Catherine CANNON	Co. Mayo	1798	1876	016	CANNON, Catherine	Born In Westport (Co. Mayo),
				016		Ireland.Died at Burlington, VT
Mary O'REAGAN		1854	1927	016	O'REAGAN, Mary	(Same Stone--Catherine Cannon
				016		
John GLEASON		1849	1913	016	CANNON, Sarah	Born South Burlington, Vermont
				016		Died Burlington, Vermont
Sarah CANNON Gleason	Co. Mayo	1839	1912	016	GLEASON, John	Born In Westport (Co. Mayo),
				016		Ireland. Died Burlington, VT
				016		
Patrick WELCH	Co. Limerick	1845	1914	016	FORAN, Catherine	Born In Askeaton,Co. Limerick,
				016		Ireland
Catherine FORAN Welch	Co. Kerry	1851	1930	016	WELCH, Patrick	Born In Ballyheige, Co. Kerry
				016		Ireland
Mary WELCH		1806	1881	016	WELCH, Mary	Born In Ireland
				016		
John O'NEIL		1846	1928	016	CROWLEY, Margaret	
Margaret CROWLEY O'Neil		1850	1925	016	O'NEIL, John	

Peter O'NEIL		1808	1884	016	_____, Dinah	
Dinah _____ O'NEIL		1812	1897	016	O'NEIL, Peter	
				016		
Patrick DOLAN		81 Years	07-22-1886	016	DOLAN, Patrick	
				016		
James KENNEDY		1850	1918	016	_____, Bridget	
Bridget _____ KENNEDY		1854	1921	016	KENNEDY, James	
				016		
Honora DOYLE Marinan	Co. Clare	35 Years	12-03-1878	016	MARINAN, Con	Craugh_____, Co. Clare, Ire
				016	DOYLE, Honora	(Badly eroded-NOI Looks like)
				016		(Craughahoulth--no such town
				016		or parish. NOI Con Marinan)
				016		
Thomas P. DALEY		1855	1920	016	CAULEY, Margaret	
Margaret CAULEY Daley		27 Years	08-24-1890	016	DALEY, Thomas P.	
Martin CAULEY		63 Years	07-21-1893	016	MCGETTRICK, Bridget	
Bridget MCGETTRICK Cauley		59 Years	01-08-1897	016	CAULEY, Martin	
				016		
James RILEY		1851	1918	016	_____, Johanna	
Johanna _____ RILEY		1856	1933	016	RILEY, James	
				016		
Johanna F. MCMAHON Sullivan		06-13-1851	09-21-1883	016	SULLIVAN, Thomas F.	(NOI Thomas F. Sullivan)
Thomas F. MCMAHON		03-14-1853	09-19-1874	016	MCMAHON, Thomas F.	
Michael MCMAHON		72 Years	06-10-1896	016	_____, Mary	
Mary _____ MCMAHON		74 Years	06-17-1894	016	MCMAHON, Michael	
				016		
James B. HARVEY		32Y 5M	10-28-1872	016	HARVEY, James B.	
				016		
William POWDERLY		52 Years	07-06-1896	016	POWDERLY, William	
				016		
Patrick MCGRATH		1834	1914	016	READY, Margaret	
Margaret READY McGrath		05-10-1845	08-17-1877	016	MCGRATH, Patrick	
				016		
William FITZGERALD		1843	1898	016	_____, Mary E.	
Mary E. _____ FITZGERALD		1845	1918	016	FITZGERALD, William	
				016		
Harry O'NEILL		1842	1913	016	O'REILLY, Mary A.	
Mary A. O'REILLY O'Neill			1884	016	O'NEILL, Harry	
				016		
Michael SULLIVAN		38 Years	07-31-1875	016	SULLIVAN, Michael	(Badly deteriorated)
				016		
John GORMAN		1830	1898	016	LANG, Winifred	
Winifred LANG Gorman		1834	1907	016	GORMAN, John	
				016		
Patrick HOGAN		1848	1916	016	_____, Margaret	

Margaret _____ HOGAN	1846	1935	016	HOGAN, Patrick	
			016		
John BURNS	67 Years	03-19-1874	016	_____, Catherine	
Catherine _____ BURNS	82 Years	02-18-1901	016	BURNS, John	
Patrick BURNS		04-30-1874	016	BURNS, Patrick	Son (Balance of stone buried)
			016		
John NOLAN	1838	1905	016	POWERS, Catherine	
Catherine POWERS Nolan			016	NOLAN, John	(No DOB/DOD on Catherine)
			016		
Michael DULLAHAN	1849	1922	016	DWYER, Ellen	
Ellen DWYER Dullahan	1850	1901	016	DULLAHAN, Michael	
			016		
Thomas DWYER	1818	1878	016	CASEY, Mary	
Mary CASEY Dwyer	1819	1893	016	DWYER, Thomas	
Michael DWYER	1856	1888	016	DWYER, Michael	
			016		
Matthew GANEY	90 Years	05-25-1879	016	RING, Margaret	
Margaret RING Ganey	82 Years	10-22-1883	016	GANEY, Matthew	
Matthew GANEY 2nd	1843	1917	016	GANEY, Matthew 2D	
John GANEY	1839	1884	016	DUFFY, Bridget C.	
Bridget C. DUFFY Ganey	1840	1927	016	GANEY, John	
			016		
James MORRISON			016	MORRISON, James	(GAR) Co. D. 13th Vt Inf.(No DOB/DOD)
			016		
			016		
John MORRISON		11-29-1894	016	MORRISON, John	(Spouse indicated but cannot read stone. No DOB indicated)
			016		
			016		
Simon MURPHY	82 Years	04-03-1885	016	_____, Margaret	
Margaret _____ MURPHY	85 Years	11-06-1898	016	MURPHY, Simon	
			016		
Edmond O'NEIL	62 Years	12-09-1901	016	HURLEY, Bridget	(GAR) Co. G. 2nd Rgt Vt Vol
			016	BAKER, Mary	In Memory Of My Wife And Baby
			016		
Bridget HURLEY O'Neil	28 Years	08-20-1869	016	O'NEIL, Edmond	
Infant O'NEIL		08-20-1869	016	O'NEIL, Infant	
Mary BAKER O'Neil	85 Years	09-25-1927	016	O'NEIL, Edmond	
			016		
Joseph BROCKNEY	76 Years	04-06-1920	016	_____, Florence	(GAR) Co. G. 96th Rgt NY Vol
Florence _____ BROCKNEY	73 Years	09-16-1924	016	BROCKNEY, Joseph	
			016		
Michael COURTNEY	1835	1917	016	_____, Margaret	
Margaret _____ COURTNEY	1840	1894	016	COURTNEY, Michael	
Johanna DONAHUE	1806	1870	016	DONAHUE, Johanna	
			016		

Name	Born	Died		Spouse	Notes
John FARRELL			016	HURLEY, Bridget	(GAR) Co. G. 2nd Rgt Vt Inf
			016	FARRELL, John	(No DOB/DOD Bridget Hurley)
			016		
Catherine BURNS	1826	1900	016	BURNS, Catherine	
			016		
John C. FARRELL	1842	1906	016	_____, Margaret	
Margaret M. _____ FARRELL	1849	1902	016	FARRELL, John C.	
			016		
Jane NEWMAN Manning	39 Years	01-30-1870	016	MANNING, Michael	(NOI Michael Manning)
			016		
Patrick LAVELLE	1840	1909	016	WARD, Ellen	
Ellen WARD Lavelle	1838	1907	016	LAVELLE, Patrick	
			016		
Alexander COURTNEY	1836	1869	016	COURTNEY, Alexander	
			016		
Ella _____ CORCORAN	1854	1913	016	CORCORAN, Edward	(NOI Edward Corcoran)
			016		
Martin H. CORLEY	1855	1934	016	CATHWRIGHT, Susan N.	
Susan N. CATHWRIGHT Corley	1859	1917	016	CORLEY, Martin H.	
			016		
Joseph BIRKE	1839	1913	016	_____, Matilda	
Matilda _____ BIRKE	1839		016	BIRKE, Joseph	(No DOD indicated)
			016		
Catherine D. MCCLELLAN	1855	1948	016	MCCLELLAN, Catherine D.	
			016		
Jeremiah O'SULLIVAN	1835	1919	016	_____, Sarah A.	
Sarah A. _____ O'SULLIVAN	1838	1913	016	O'SULLIVAN, Jeremiah	
			016		
Michael CUSIC		04-25-1869	016	CUSIC, Michael	(Bottom of stone buried)
Mary CUSIC	72 Years	03-17-1896	016	CUSIC, Mary	(Does not indicate if spouse of Michael Cusic)
			016		
			016		
Patrick COYLE	1810	1870	016	NEWMAN, Mary	
Mary NEWMAN Coyle	1815	1869	016	COYLE, Patrick	
Thomas COYLE	1853	1891	016	COYLE, Thomas	
Mary COYLE	1828	1903	016	COYLE, Mary	
			016		
William HARDACRE	62 Years	01-15-1901	016	O'SULLIVAN, Catherine	
Catherine O'SULLIVAN Hardacre	1841	1915	016	HARDACRE, William	
			016		
John SHEEHY	84 Years	12-08-1897	016	SHEEHY, John	A Native Of Ireland. (Age at death could be 34 Years. Stone is badly deteriorated)
			016		
			016		
			016		
Cornelius GREANEY	1803	1888	016	_____, Elizabeth	

Name	Born / Age	Died		Relation	Notes
Elizabeth _____ GREANEY	1836	1919	016	GREANEY, Cornelius	
Maurice GREANEY	1857	1868	016	GREANEY, Maurice	(Does not say if Maurice & Hanora are husband and wife)
Hanora COLLINS	1853	1873	016	COLLINS, Hanora	
			016		
Edward H. TWOHEY	1845	1910	016	MCMAHON, Mary	
Mary MCMAHON Twohey	1847	1929	016	TWOHEY, Edward H.	
			016		
Thomas SLAMON	62 Years	02-13-1894	016	REDMON, Bridget	
			016	CORLEY, Mary	
Bridget REDMON Slamon	23 Years	03-26-1869	016	SLAMON, Thomas	
Mary CORLEY Slamon	57 Years	03-27-1889	016	SLAMON, Thomas	
			016		
Alexander MORRISON	1856	1919	016	COSGROVE, Sarah	
Sarah COSGROVE Morrison	1855	1953	016	MORRISON, Alexander	
			016		
Michael GARVEY	1828	1872	016	GARVEY, Michael	
			016		
Daniel SULLIVAN	1837	1902	016	_____, Johanna	
Johanna _____ SULLIVAN	1844	1905	016	SULLIVAN, Daniel	
			016		
Richard O'NEIL	38 Years	11-26-1875	016	O'NEIL, Richard	(GAR) PVT Co. K 6 Rgt Vt Vol
			016		
Catherine _____ SHEAHAN	67 Years	08-17-1873	016	SHEAHAN, William	(NOI William Sheahan-stone is deteriorated. YOD in question)
			016	_____, Catherine	
			016		
Patrick MURPHY	12 Years	02-01-1887	016	MURPHY, Patrick	
Elizabeth FINNESSY Murphy	87 Years	07-20-1920	016	MURPHY, Patrick	(NOI Patrick Murphy)
			016	FINNEY, Elizabeth	
			016		
James TIERNEY	1852	1924	016	LAVALLEY, Matilda	
Matilda LAVALLEY Tierney	1861	1938	016	TIERNEY, James	
			016		
Francis H. MCCALE	1856	1918	016	MCGUIRE, Jennie A.	
Jennie A. MCGUIRE McCale	1869		016	MCCALE, Francis H.	(No DOD)
			016		
Mary V. _____ STONE			016	STONE, Charles	(Most of stone below ground--and unreadable)
			016		
			016		
William FRANCIS	68 Years	12-16-1911	016	FRANCIS, William	
			016		
John DOYLE	46 Years	08-27-1886	016	DOYLE, John	Erected By His Wife. (She is not indicated)
			016		
James B. KELLEY	1858	1908	016	_____, Ellen	
Ellen _____ KELLEY	1860	1938	016	KELLEY, James B.	

			016		
John MCCAFFREY	1859	1928	016	MCGRATH, Ellen	
Ellen MCGRATH McCaffrey	1854	1907	016	MCCAFFREY, John	
			016		
Catharine MCDONAL Dupaw	12-11-1847	05-22-1882	016	DUPAW, G. H.	(NOI G. H. Dupaw)
			016		
John HICKEY	50 Years	12-17-1870	016	_____, Mary	
Mary _____ HICKEY	40 Years	06-01-1868	016	HICKEY, John	
			016		
Patrick COLLINS	1804	1903	016	KENNEDY, Catherine	
Catherine KENNEDY Collins	1843	1918	016	COLLINS, Patrick	
			016		
Michael HICKEY	47 Years	11-03-1867	016	HICKEY, Michael	(Stone buried. Indicates Irish
			016		POB but cannot read)
William WHEELER	1810	1880	016	MCCAFFREY, Susan	
Susan MCCAFFREY Wheeler	1830	1897	016	WHEELER, William	
Mary A. WHEELER	1850	1874	016	WHEELER, Mary A.	
James M. WHEELER	1852	1891	016	WHEELER, James M.	
Catherine WHEELER	1808	1897	016	WHEELER, Catherine	
			016		
P. Christopher GORDON	56 Years	03-22-1888	016	_____, Anna	
Anna _____ GORDON	40Y 6M	05-24-1886	016	GORDON, P. Christopher	
			016		
Edward E. SNOW	1840	1908	016	_____, Ellen	(GAR) Wagoner, Co. H, 2 VT
			016	FINNISEY, Mary	Vol Inf
Ellen _____ SNOW	1844	1911	016	SNOW, Edward E.	
Mary FINNISEY Snow	47Y 9M	03-13-1889	016	SNOW, Edward E.	
			016		
Jennie F. MCKENNA McLane	39 Years	11-28-1885	016	MCLANE, Henry W.	(NOI Henry McLane)
			016		
Reverend Patrick MCKENNA	03-02-1850	02-25-1926	016	MCKENNA, Rev. Patrick	Late Pastor of St. Monica's
			016		Church, Barre, Vt. Ordained
			016		12-17-1881
			016		
Reverend Maurice MCKENNA	07-31-1866	07-14-1945	016	MCKENNA, Rev. Maurice	Late Pastor of Holy Angels
			016		Church, Chicago, Illinois.
			016		Ordained 03-05-1898
			016		
Frank BROWN	1856	1932	016	_____, Lillian M.	
Lillian M. _____ BROWN	1867	1943	016	BROWN, Frank	
			016		
John F. KELLY	1850	1920	016	KELLY, John F.	
			016		
Jeremiah CROWLEY	1822	1889	016	CORLEY, Ann	
Ann CORLEY Crowley	1832	1923	016	CROWLEY, Jeremiah	

Catherine CORLEY		1846	1926	016	CORLEY, Catherine	
				016		
Thomas COURTNEY		15 Years	01-30-1867	016	COURTNEY, Thomas	
				016		
Frank MORAN		1859	1944	016	STAPLETON, Bridget	
Bridget STAPLETON Moran		1853	1924	016	MORAN, Frank	
				016		
Peter BUTLER		52 Years	01-01-1882	016	BUTLER, Peter	
				016		
Thomas MCCARTY		1805	1887	016	_____, Margaret	
Margaret _____ MCCARTY		1804	1879	016	MCCARTY, Thomas	
Thomas MCCARTY JR		1842	1901	016	MCCARTY, Thomas JR	
Nora MCCARTY		1868	1915	016	MCCARTY, Nora	
Mary MCCARTY		1864	1921	016	MCCARTY, Mary	
Elizabeth MCCARTY		1850	1923	016	MCCARTY, Elizabeth	
				016		
Nicholas SMITH		1833	1903	016	RYAN, Johanna	
Johannna RYAN Smith		1840	1882	016	SMITH, Nicholas	
				016		
Francis Ryan LEE		43 Years	06-11-1867	016	LEE, Francis Ryan	
				016		
Jno NOONAN				016	NOONAN, Jno	(GAR) Sergt, Co. G, 14 U.S.Inf (No DOB/DOD indicated)
				016		
				016		
John BURKE		1852	1892	016	MCGRATH, Catherine	
Catherine MCGRATH Burke		1850	1922	016	BURKE, John	
Bridget BURKE		1828	1980	016	BURKE, Bridget	
				016		
Bridget CALDWELL	Co. Meath	62 Years	04-09-1867	016	CALDWELL, Bridget	Born In Kells, County Meath, Ireland.Erectd By Her Daughter Mrs. Mary MULLIGAN
				016	MULLIGAN, Mrs. Mary	
				016		
Michael BRIDGEMAN		1814	1886	016	MCGLYNN, Bridget	
Bridget MCGLYNN Bridgeman		1822	1892	016	BRIDGEMAN, Michael	
Michael BRIDGEMAN		1856	1866	016	BRIDGEMAN, Michael	
Johanna BRIDGEMAN		1848	1866	016	BRIDGEMAN, Johanna	
Thomas BRIDGEMAN		1847	1867	016	BRIDGEMAN, Thomas	
Edward J. BRIDGEMAN		1845	1868	016	BRIDGEMAN, Edward J.	
Mary BRIDGEMAN		1854	1930	016	BRIDGMAN, Mary	
				016		
Mary A. WELCH		20 Years	09-04-1874	016	WELCH, Mary A.	Born In Richmond, Vermont
				016		
Annie B. WELCH			11-__-1874	016	WELCH, Annie B.	Born In Richmond, Vermont Died in Bolton, Vermont (NOI)
				016		
				016		
Daniel SULLIVAN			03-17-1879	016	_____, Mary	(NOI)

Name	Born/Age	Died	No.	Spouse/Index	Note
Mary _____ SULLIVAN		12-20-1883	016	SULLIVAN, Daniel	(NOI)
			016		
Michael H. SULLIVAN	1836	1907	016	O'SULLIVAN, Honora	
Honora O'SULLIVAN Sullivan	1851	1924	016	SULLIVAN, Michael H.	
			016		
Patrick H. CORLEY	1841	1923	016	BRIDGEMAN, Helen M.	
Helen M. BRIDGEMAN Corley	1844	1915	016	CORLEY, Patrick H.	
Bartholomew CORLEY	1784	1866	016	_____, Bridget	
Bridget _____ CORLEY	1802	1875	016	CORLEY, Bartholomew	
			016		
David MCAULIFFE	1833	1886	016	POWERS, Ellen	
Ellen POWERS McAuliffe	1841	1904	016	MCAULIFFE, David	
Mary MCAULIFFE	1860	1866	016	MCAUILIFFE, Mary	
James MCAULIFFE	1867	1868	016	MCAULIFFE, James	
Martha MCAULIFFE	1865	1868	016	MCAULIFFE, Martha	
Robert MCAULIFFE	1869	1870	016	MCAULIFFE, Robert	
Anna MCAULIFFE	1857	1929	016	MCAULIFFE, Anna	
William H. MCAULIFFE	1858	1937	016	MCAULIFFE, William H.	
Henry J. MCAULIFFE	1880	1942	016	MCAULIFFE, Henry J.	
			016		
John O'MARA	1837	1903	016	_____, Mary	
Mary _____ O'MARA	1838	1903	016	O'MARA, John	
Margaret O'MARA	1869	19__	016	O'MARA, Margaret	
Lawrence O'MARA			016	O'MARA, Thomas	(NOI)
Thomas O'MARA			016	O'MARA, Lawrence	(NOI)
Anna O'MARA			016	O'MARA, Anna	(NOI)
			016		
Margaret MCGILLAGH		03-26-1911	016	MCGILLAGH, Margaret	(NOI)
			016		
Dennis GREANEY	62 Years	05-24-1880	016	DEADY, Mary	
Mary DEADY Greaney	75 Years	01-16-1911	016	GREANEY, Dennis	
			016		
Jeremiah DEADY	1847	1913	016	O'BRINE, Ellen	
Ellen O'BRINE Deady	1847	1916	016	DEADY, Jeremiah	
			016		
John DADY	69 Years	04-12-1890	016	_____, Johannah	
Johannah _____ DADY	71 Years	02-22-1889	016	DADY, John	
Michael DADY	29 Years	11-29-1880	016	DADY, Michael	
John DADY	43 Years	11-10-1899	016	DADY, John	
Katherine C. DEADY			016	DEADY, Katherine C.	(NOI)
Catherine DADY	18 Years	08-25-1862	016	DADY, Catherine	
Mary Frances DADY	15Y 4M	06-04-1875	016	DADY, Mary Frances	
			016		
Denis BROWN SR	75 Years	06-__-1868	016	BROWN, Dennis Sr.	
James M. BROWN	36 Years	10-03-1904	016	BROWN, James M.	

Name	Born	Died		Index	Note
Denis BROWN JR	1840	1914	016	_____, Margaret	
Margaret _____ BROWN	56 Years	05-12-1893	016	BROWN, Denis Jr.	
			016		
John ARNOLD	07-10-1808	12-26-1881	016	CUMMINS, Adeline	
Adeline CUMMINS Arnold	10-15-1809	04-12-1888	016	ARNOLD, John	
Felecia ARNOLD	02-22-1792	05-03-1861	016	ARNOLD, Felecia	Mother of John Arnold
			016		
Charles CUSHMAN	06-10-1816	07-07-1885	016	CUSHMAN, Charles	
			016		
James GRIBBIN	1833	1903	016	MCLANE, Nancy	
Nancy MCLANE Gribbin	1831	1908	016	GRIBBIN, James	
			016		
Lawrence NAVEL	88 Years	02-22-1885	016	_____, Bridget	
Bridget _____ NAVEL	79Y 6M	12-08-1892	016	NAVEL, Lawrence	
			016		
Maurice SULLIVAN	1815	1907	016	JOHNSON, Mary	
Mary JOHNSON Sullivan	1829	1898	016	SULLIVAN, Maurice	
James SULLIVAN	1867	1870	016	SULLIVAN, James	
John SULLIVAN	1850	1885	016	SULLIVAN, John	
Daniel SULLIVAN	1860	1910	016	SULLIVAN, Daniel	
			016		
Bryan READY	76 Years	12-27-1891	016	EARLEY, Bridget	
Bridget EARLY Ready	73 Years	07-14-1891	016	READY, Bryan	
Mary EARLY	92 Years	1878	016	EARLEY, Mary	
Anne READY	4 Years	03-05-1851	016	READY, Ann	
Mary READY	18 Years	06-16-1863	016	READY, Mary	
Elizabeth READY	7 Years	06-24-1863	016	READY, Elizabeth	
			016		
James TAYLOR	1825	1909	016	SULLIVAN, Catherine	
Catherine SULLIVAN Taylor	1834	1901	016	TAYLOR, James	
			016		
John O'MALLEY		1916	016	DURKIN, Bridget	(NOI)
Bridget DURKIN O'Malley		1908	016	O'MALLEY, John	(NOI)
			016		
Mary HART			016	HART, Mary	(Stone is buried)
			016		
John MCELROY	1854	1904	016	MCKENZIE, Mary	
Mary MCKENZIE McElroy	1865	1948	016	MCELROY, John	
			016		
Peter L. CROSS	1847	1926	016	MCHUGH, Catherine	
Catherine MCHUGH Cross	1848	1923	016	CROSS, Peter L.	
			016		
Jane FAGAN	1828	1912	016	FAGAN, Jane	Faithful Unto Death
			016		
Grace CHELSEA	1850	1916	016	CHELSEA, Mary	

				016		
Edward DOHENY		35 Years	04-11-1866	016	DOHENY, Edward	
				016		
John FAGAN		62 Years	04-20-1849	016	BANNON, Rose	
Rose BANNON Fagan		81 Years	08-23-1877	016	FAGAN, John	
Michael FAGAN		17 Years	08-28-1847	016	FAGAN, Michael	
Rose MCNANNY		25 Years	12-20-1842	016	MCNANNY, Rose	(Stone deteriorated)
				016		
Stephen MICHAUD		1811	1847	016	ROGAN, Catherine	Parents--Bishop of Providence
Catherine ROGAN Michaud		1811	1904	016	MICHAUD, Stephen	RI, Rt Rev John S. Michaud,DD
				016		(Later Bishop of Diocese of
				016		Burlington, VT)
				016		
Patrick COUGHLIN		69 Years	09-25-1891	016	CULLEN, Joanna	
Joanna CULLEN Coughlin		69 Years	11-15-1908	016	COUGHLIN, Patrick	
				016		
Mrs. Alice O'CALLAGHAN	Co. Kilkenny			016	O'CALLAGHAN, Mrs. Alice	Born In Co. Kilkenny, Ireland
				016		(Reset of stone is missing)
Thomas KENNEDY		1794	1840	016	_____, Martha	
Martha _____ KENNEDY		1795	1882	016	KENNEDY, Thomas	
Sarah A. KENNEDY		1823	1902	016	KENNEDY, Sarah A.	
				016		
Matthew TEAGUE		42 Years	02-04-1847	016	MCCARTHY, Hanna	
Hanna MCCARTHY Teague		36 Years	08-20-1847	016	TEAGUE, Matthew	
				016		
Maria _____ CARNEY		32 Years	05-21-1842	016	CARNEY, John	This Stone Is Erected By John
				016	_____, Maria	Carney In Memory Of Maria
				016		Carney,His Loving & Affection-
				016		ate Wife Whose Remains Are
				016		Here Interred & Who Died In
				016		Middlebury, Vt.
				016		
Ellen _____ O'CONNOR		36 Years	02-28-1844	016	O'CONNOR, Terrence	Sacred To The Memory Of Ellen
				016	_____, Ellen	O'Connor Of Burlington-Erected
				016		By Her Husband Terrance
				016		O'Connor
				016		
Margrett _____ MCDONNELL		21 Years	01-18-1842	016	MCDONNELL, James	Died At Middlebury (VT) (NOI
				016	_____, Margrett	James McDonnell)
Mary MCDONNELL		8 Months	09-13-1842	016	MCDONELL, Mary	D/O of James & Margrett McDon-
				016		nell.Died At Middlebury,VT
				016		
Lucy MCDONOUGH		08-28-1854	02-21-1941	016	MCDONOUGH, Lucy	
				016		
George F. COLLISON		1843	1932	016	MULLINS, Mary A.	

Mary A. MULLINS Collison		1848	1916	016	COLLISON, George F.	
				016		
John O'BRINE		68 Years	07-21-1857	016	_____, Mary	
Mary _____ O'BRINE		47 Years	02-25-1846	016	O'BRINE, John	
				016		
Garrett MURRAY		68 Years	03-13-1893	016	_____, Mary	
Mary _____ MURRAY		62 Years	11-03-1886	016	MURRAY, Garrett	
				016		
John DONNELLY		1843	1911	016	HOGAN, Anna	
Anna HOGAN Donnelly		1850	1908	016	DONNELLY, John	
				016		
Peter E. DURHAM		1852	1924	016	DURHAM, Peter E.	
				016		
John S. O'BRIEN		1852	1935	016	BROWN, Mary E.	
Mary E. BROWN O'Brien		1862	1921	016	O'BRIEN, John S.	
William O'BRIEN		1804	1879	016	O'BRIEN, William	
				016		
Martin DALEY		08-15-1820	01-21-1893	016	GALLAGHER, Sarah	
Sarah GALLAGHER Daley		06-03-1826	10-06-1914	016	DALEY, Martin	
Hugh GALLAGHER		1791	1854	016	O'NEILL, Sarah	
Sarah O'NEILL Gallagher		1803	1847	016	GALLAGHER, Hugh	
Sarah DALEY		07-06-1849	09-19-1854	016	DALEY, Sarah	
Mary DALEY		11-05-1853	09-15-1854	016	DALEY, Mary	
				016		
Thomas SEXTON	Co. Clare	65 Years	12-06-1880	016	_____, Mary	Born In County Clare, Ireland.
				016		Died In Burlington, Vermont
				016		Erected By His Son Timothy
Mary _____ SEXTON		1808	1894	016	SEXTON, Thomas	
				016		
Thomas HASTINGS	Co. Clare	65 Years	07-28-1881	016	_____, Bridget	Born In Co. Clare, Ireland
				016		Erected by John HASTINGS.
Bridget _____ HASTINGS	Co. Clare	35 Years	09-28-1876	016	HASTINGS, Thomas	Born In Co. Clare, Ireland
				016		Died In Burlington (VT)
				016		
John FITZGERALD		1849	1933	016	COFFEY, Kate	
Kate COFFEY Fitzgerald		1854	1916	016	FITZGERALD, John	
				016		
Georgianna PAINE		58 Years	02-03-1872	016	PAINE, Georgianna	Mother. (NOI Mr. Paine)
				016		
Capt. William NEWTON		1829	1907	016	_____, Rose	
Rose _____ NEWTON		1839		016	NEWTON, William	
Jennie NEWTON		1859	1892	016	NEWTON, Jennie	Daughter
				016		
John E. SHERIDAN		1849	1926	016	_____, Mary A.	
Mary A. _____ SHERIDAN		1856	1900	016	SHERIDAN, John E.	

Name	Place	Birth	Death	Code	Index	Notes
				016		
Owen E. RYAN		1854	1881	016	KELLEY, Mary A.	
Mary A. KELLEY Ryan		1854	1886	016	RYAN, Owen E.	
				016		
Phillip MCCAFFREY			08-19-1882	016	BAIRD, Susan	
Susan BAIRD McCaffrey			12-29-1908	016	MCCAFFREY, Phillip	
				016		
J. Adam SMITH		1844	1908	016	SMITH, J. Adam	PVT Co. G, 5th U.S. Art
				016		
Margaret ____ MCDONALD			07-01-1862	016	MCDONALD, Alexander	(Rest of stone buried - NOI Alexander McDonald)
				016		
John CASHON	Co. Clare	75 Years	10-18-1902	016	GRIFFIN, Mary	Born In Killaloe,Clare County, Ireland
				016		
Mary GRIFFIN Cashon		03-22-1839	01-21-1913	016	CASHON, John	
Margaret CASHEN		50 Years	11-13-1889	016	CASHEN, Margaret	
Dennis CASHEN		45 Years	11-25-1884	016	CASHEN, Dennis	
Mary CASHEN		65 Years	12-18-1888	016	CASHEN, Mary	
Anthony CASHEN		12-26-1780	03-02-1877	016	COONEY, Catherine	
Catherine COONEY Cashen		06-24-1798	04-15-1862	016	CASHEN, Anthony	
				016		
Patrick BRYAN		51 Years	12-11-1847	016	BRYAN, Patrick	Of Waterbury (VT)
Sarah S. _____ BRYAN			07-02-1873	016	_____, Sarah S.	(Stone partially buried)
				016		
Patrick LYNCH				016	LYNCH, Patrick	(GAR) Co. F, 5th VT Inf (NOI DOB/DOD)
				016		
				016		
Michael CARROLL		1849	1921	016	O'DONNELL, Jennie F.	
Jennie F. O'DONNELL Carroll		1854	1917	016	CARROLL, Michael	
				016		
Philip HAMMEN				016	HAMMEN, Philip	(GAR) Co. C, 2nd VT Inf (NOI DOB/DOD)
				016		
				016		
Patrick MCVEY		64Y 8M	08-15-1840	016	MCVEY, Patrick	
				016		
Thomas ARBUCKLE		1837	1908	016	_____, Cecelia Louisa	(NOI Cecelia)
				016	ARBUCKLE, Thomas	
				016		
Mary W. _____ GRIFFIN		40 Years	01-18-1880	016	GRIFFIN, Mary W.	Mother Of John & M Griffin (NOI Mr. Griffin)
				016		
				016		
Patrick DUNN		84 Years	02-07-1878	016	FEIGHELLE, Mary	
Mary FEIGHELLE Dunn		40 Years	12-06-1844	016	DUNN, Patrick	(Deteriorated stone.Doubt that Feighelle is correct spelling)
				016		
William DUNN		1841	1902	016	MOREN, Bridget	
Bridget MOREN Dunn		36 Years	12-22-1878	016	DUNN, William	

Name	Place	Born/Age	Died	Code	Index Name	Notes
				016		
Margaret DEGNAN Moren		52 Years	05-16-1862	016	DEGNAN, Margaret	Mother of Bridget Moren
				016		
Alice MORAN Hart		52 Years	10-22-1844	016	HART, James	(NOI James Hart. Stone buried)
				016	MORAN, Alice	
				016		
John R. MAHER				016	MAHER, John R.	(Stone buried) In Loving Memory
				016		
Joseph CRONAN		18Y 6M	10-22-1862	016	CRONAN, Joseph	Son Of J & M Cronan
				016		
James RUSSELL		1833	1907	016	_____, Mary A.	
Mary A. _____ RUSSELL		1834	1917	016	RUSSELL, James	
Edmond RUSSELL		1799	1865	016	_____, Margaret	
Margaret _____ RUSSELL		1799	1883	016	RUSSELL, Edmond	
				016		
Thomas RUSSELL		21 Years	05-22-1863	016	_____, Margaret	Killed In Battle At Vicksburg
Margaret _____ RUSSELL		1845	1864	016	RUSSELL, Thomas	
				016		
Mary _____ CRONAN		65 Years	07-14-1843	016	CRONAN, Mary A.	May The Lord Have Mercy On The
				016		Soul Of Mary Cronan Who Depar-
John CRONAN		4 Years	06-07-1840	016	CRONAN, John	ted This Life--Also, John
				016		Cronan Who Departed This Life-
				016		
John MCCARTHY			06-30-1843	016	MCCARTHY, John	Son Of Patrick & Catherine
				016	MCCARTHY, Patrick	McCarthy, Natives of Cashel,
				016		Ireland. (Probably Co. Cork-
				016		but there are at least 20
				016		counties with a Cashel.
				016		
Mathew HANNEN				016	HANNEN, Mathew	In Memory Of My Father and
Julia _____ HANNEN				016	_____, Julia	Mother (NOI)
				016		
Bridget _____ LADAM			08-21-95	016	LADAM, Alford	(NOI Alford Ladam)
				016		
Theresa FARRELL Spillane	Co. Longford	1855	1936	016	SPILLANE, Patrick	Born In Longford, Ireland
				016	FARRELL, Theresa	(NOI Patrick Spillane)
				016		
Mary A. FARRELL	Co. Longford	1883	1952	016	FARRELL, Mary A.	Born In Longford, Ireland
				016		
Edward LYNCH		1821	1886	016	_____, Catherine	
Catherine _____ LYNCH		1826	1888	016	LYNCH, Edward	
Bridget LYNCH		1857	1883	016	LYNCH, Bridget	
Michael LYNCH		1861	1931	016	LYNCH, Michael	
				016		
John FOLEY		60 Years	12-19-1910	016	BROWN, Nora	

Nora BROWN Foley		1854	1930	016	FOLEY, John	
				016		
William READY		50 Years	08-23-1883	016	FARRELL, Margaret	
Margaret FARRELL Ready		1834	1913	016	READY, William	
				016		
Mary O'GRADY	Co. Fermanagh	72 Years	11-11-1878	016	O'GRADY, Mary	Who Died In Burlington, Vt.
				016		She Was Born In Enniskillen,
				016		Co. Fermanagh, Ireland
				016		
James BEATTY	Co. Dublin	68 Years	06-28-1891	016	BEATTY, James	Born In The City Of Dublin,
				016		Ireland
				016		
Patrick FLYNN	Co. Waterford	51 Years	04-11-1863	016	FLYNN, Patrick	A Native of Garry Duff (Garry-
				016		duff), Co. Waterford, Ireland
				016		
John COTTER	Co. Cork	44 Years	08-13-1862	016	COTTER, John	A Native of Co. Cork, Parish
				016		of Watergrasshill, Ireland.
				016		(No such parish, but probably
				016		Watergrasshill Town)
				016		
James GOEG		1815	1891	016	REAGAN, Hanora	
Hanora REAGAN Goeg		1827	1864	016	COEG, James	
				016		
John RYAN	Co. Waterford		01-16-1846	016	RYAN, John	A Native of Cuille Mile, Co.
				016		Waterford, Ireland. (No such
				016		town. Could not find in ref)
				016		
James WHALEN		1802	1866	016	HENNESSEY, Bridget	
Bridget HENNESSEY Whalen		1818	1896	016	WHALEN, James	
				016		
James MCBRINE	Co. Fermanagh	03-24-1771	10-22-1850	016	MCBRINE, James	A Native Of The County Of
				016		Fermanagh, Ireland. Died In
				016		Richmond, Vermont
				016		
Francis KELLEY		50 Years	05-08-1868	016	_____, Mary	Sacred To The Memory Of My
Mrs Mary _____ KELLEY		50 Years	04-16-1880	016	KELLEY, Francis	Father--My Mother
				016		
Thomas FLINN		1841	1922	016	FLINN, Thomas	(GAR) Corp, Co. F., 4th Vt Vol
				016		Inf
				016		
Patrick CONWAY	Co. Tyrone	34 Years	03-09-1873	016	MCKEOUGH, Bridget	Died in London,England. A
				016		Native Of Co. Tyrone, Ireland
Bridget MCKEOUGH Conway		73 Years	09-18-1910	016	CONWAY, Patrick	Dau of F & C McKeough
				016		
Col. A. W. HYDE		1786	1847	016	HYDE, Col. A. W.	In Memory Of Col. A. W. Hyde,

				016		1786-1847,Who Gave To The Cath
				016		olics of Burlington in 1830,
				016		The Land For This Cemetery.
				016		This Monument Donated By
				016		Thomas A., John B. & James E.
				016		Cosgrove
				016		
Mary _____ EUSTACE		27 Years	10-08-____	016	EUSTACE, Thomas	(Deteriorated.Probably 1840's.
				016	_____, Mary	NOI Thomas Eustace)
Mary _____ DONAHOE		30 Years	04-22-18__	016	DONAHOE, Denis	(Deteriorated.Probably 1840's.
				016	_____, Mary	NOI Denis Donahoe)
				016		
John SULLIVAN		27 Years	02-03-1842	016	SULLIVAN, John	
				016		
Alvah BUNNELL		17 Years	04-16-1851	016	BUNNELL, Alvah	
				016		
Catherine BONNELL	Co. Tipperary			016	BONNELL, Catherine	Born In The Co. Tipperary, Ire
				016		(NOI DOB/DOD.Deteriorated. Old
				016		stone. Probably 1840's)
				016		
Margaret FINN			04-23-1928	016	FINN, Margaret	Died @ St. Joseph's Orphanage.
				016		She Lived For God And The
				016		Poor.
				016		
James CASEY		1818	1907	016	_____, Bridget	(GAR)Pvt Co. D, 8th Vt Vol Inf
Bridget _____ CASEY		1834	1915	016	CASEY, James	
				016		
Thomas RYAN		01-26-1858	05-19-1931	016	PURCELL, Susan	
Susan PURCELL Ryan		09-29-1861	03-09-1925	016	RYAN, Thomas	
				016		
Mathew MCGETTRICK		62Y 7M	11-06-1872	016	MCGETTRICK, Mathew	
Dr. Patrick MCMAHON		1854	1911	016	SHANLEY, Catherine	
Catherine SHANLEY McMahon		1856	1922	016	MCMAHON, Patrick	
				016		
Michael F. KELLY		1835	1912	016	QUINN, Ann	
Ann QUINN Kelly		1839	1907	016	KELLY, Michael F.	
				016		
Anna _____ O'GRADY				016	O'GRADY, James	Anna, Wife and Infant Daughter
Infant O'GRADY				016	_____, Anna	of James O'Grady. (NOI James)
				016	O'GRADY, Infant	
				016		
Capt John O'GRADY Jr.		34 Years	07-10-1860	016	O'GRADY, Capt. John Jr	My Husband. (NOI spouse)
				016		
Francis LOGAN		85 Years	01-28-1877	016	LOGAN, Francis	
				016		

Silas HINKLEY		48 Years	12-15-1859	016	_____, Mary A.	(NOI Spouse)
				016	HINKLEY, Silas	
				016		
Mary A. HINKLEY		5Y 6M	02-10-1858	016	HINKLEY, Mary A.	Dau Of Silas & Mary A. Hinkley
				016		
Maria HOGAN Corley		1826	1904	016	CORLEY, M. B.	(NOI M. B. Corley)
				016		
Thomas PASHBY		1844	1908	016	PASHBY, Thomas	(GAR) Co. D., 61st NY Vol
				016		
Nicholas KILLEN		66 Years	08-15-1857	016	LOGAN, Catherine	
Catherine LOGAN Killen		70 Years	12-13-1859	016	KILLEN, Nicholas	Erected 1861 By Her Affection-
				016		ate Brother, Francis LOGAN
				016		
William H. O'GRADY		05-18-1824	08-24-1858	016	O'GRADY, William H.	
				016		
Margaret MORAN O'Grady	Co. Queens	05-25-1795	10-18-1856	016	O'GRADY, John	In Memory Of Margaret Moran,
				016	MORAN, Margaret	Wife Of John O'GRADY, Born At
				016		Borris-In-Ossory, Queens Co.,
				016		(Leix), Ireland. Died at Shel-
				016		burne, VT (NOI John O'Grady)
				016		
John KANE		9M 2D	08-20-1835	016	KANE, John	Son Of Denis & Mary Kane
				016	KANE, Denis	
				016		
Michael J. MURPHY		33 Years	11-24-1873	016	_____, Elizabeth	(GAR) Co. M, 1st Rgt, VT Cav
				016		Born At Burlington, Vermont
Elizabeth _____ MURPHY		65 Years	0-4-12-1909	016	MURPHY, Michael J.	
				016		
William MURPHY		65 Years	06-24-1867	016	MURPHY, William	
				016		
Cornelius WHALEN		1826	1913	016	O'NEIL, Margaret	
Margaret O'NEIL Whalen		1829	1913	016	WHALEN, Cornelius	
				016		
Thomas BUTLER	Co. Kilkenny	02-02-1838	08-19-1876	016	BUTLER, Thomas	Born In Parish of "Wark Gay"
	Co. Kerry			016		(Hard to read. Could be Wind
				016		Gap, Co. Kilkenny, Ire(Stone
				016		badly eroded. Co. F. 6th Rgt
				016		(GAR)
				016		
John KELLEY		1840	1917	016	KELLEY, John	(GAR) Co. F, 6th VT Inf
				016		
Patrick MALONEY				016	KELLEY, Ellen	(NOI DOB/DOD)
Ellen KELLEY Maloney				016	MALONEY, Patrick	(NOI DOB/DOD)
				016		
Lawrence KELLEY			03-31-1867	016	KELLEY, Lawrence	(Rest of stone is missing)

			016		
John MYERS	56 Years	08-22-1868	016	O'NEIL, Ellen	
			016	TAGUE, Ann	
Ellen O'NEIL Myers	27 Years	07-11-1839	016	MYERS, John	
Ann TAGUE Myers	47 Years	01-22-1853	016	MYERS, John	
Dr. John T. MYERS	27 Years	10-28-1867	016	MYERS, Dr. John T.	Children of John & Ann Myers
Ellen MYERS	7 Days	11-12-1843	016	MYERS, Ellen	Children of John & Ann Myers
William MYERS	8 Months	07-13-1839	016	MYERS, William	(Probably son of John & Ellen)
			016		
James LANG	1817	1902	016	CASSIDY, Mary	
Mary CASSIDY Lang	72 Years	11-03-1894	016	LANG, James	
James LANG	1854	1924	016	LANG, James	
Patrick Henry LANG	1852	1923	016	LANG, Patrick Henry	
Mary LANG	5 Years	08-15-1854	016	LANG, Mary	
Catherine LANG	24 Years	04-02-1876	016	LANG, Catherine	
B. B. LANG	1848	1908	016	Lang, B. B.	
			016		
Mary MCGAUGHAN	1852	1917	016	MCGAUGHAN, Mary	Mother (NOI)
			016		
Michael COOK	1845		016	FLYNN, Catherine	
Catherine FLYNN Cook	1852	1916	016	COOK, Michael	
Father	1810	1855	016		
Mother	1822	1897	016		
William COOK	1851	1905	016	COOK, William	
			016		
Michael LONERGAN	24 Years	05-15-1865	016	MCMAHON, Sarah	
Sarah MCMAHON Lonergan	37 Years	02-27-1881	016	LONERGAN, Michael	
Sarah MCMAHON	85 Years	04-05-1895	016		
			016		
John MCDONNELL	56 Years	03-__-____	016	_____, Catherine	(Stone damaged. NOI spouse)
			016	MCDONNELL, John	
			016		
Murt FARRELL			016	_____, Catherine	(No dates are indicated)
Catherine _____ FARRELL			016	FARRELL, Murt	(No dates are indicated)
			016		
Christopher FARRELL		08-18-____	016	FARRELL, Christopher	Died At Winooski Falls, VT (Stone damaged-missing-circa 1850)
			016		
			016		
			016		
Catherine LONERGAN			016	LONERGAN, Catherine	Dau Of Thomas & Mary LONERGAN (NOI)
			016		
Bridget LONERGAN			016	LONERGAN, Bridget	Dau Of Thomas & Mary LONERGAN (NOI)
			016		
			016		
John LONERGAN	04-07-1838	08-06-1902	016	_____, Mary	In Memory Of John Lonergan, A

Name	Origin	Born/Age	Died	Code	Index Name	Notes
				016	LONERGAN, John	Native of Ireland Who, Having
				016		Made The United States His
				016		Adopted Country, Defended It
				016		In The Civil War And At The
				016		Battle Of Gettysburg With Dis-
				016		tinction as Capt. Co. A, 13th
				016		Vt Regiment And Was Awarded A
				016		Medal Of Honor By Congress.
				016		He Was Twice Named Deputy Col-
				016		lector Of Customs. Born On
				016		April 7, 1838, He Died August
				016		6, 1902, Believing In Future
				016		Life And In The Destiny Of
				016		This Dear Land-RIP (NOI Spouse
				016		Mary)
				016		
Martin GLEESON	Co. Clare	1820	1904	016	GLEESON, Martin	Native Of County Clare,Ire.
				016		Erected By His Son Patrick
				016		
Jeremiah LEE		1849	1899	016	MCNIFF, Catherine	
Catherine MCNIFF Lee		1844	1906	016	LEE, Jeremiah	
				016		
Judath _____ QUINLEN		37 Yers	03-14-1853	016	QUINLEN, M.	(NOI M. Quinlen)
				016	_____, Judath	
				016		
James LEE		1812	1895	016	_____, Honora	
Honora _____ LEE		1824	1898	016	LEE, James	
Edward M. LEE		09-23-1853	11-12-1879	016	LEE, Edward M.	Born At Burlington, Vermont.
				016		Died At Aspinwall, Age 26.
Hanora LEE		07-26-1851	10-31-1852	016	LEE, Hanora	
Katie LEE		10-06-1861	04-14-1862	016	LEE, Katie	
Maggie LEE		01-13-1857	09-10-1861	016	LEE, Maggie	
Mary A. LEE		11-23-1862	08-10-1863	016	LEE, Mary A.	
James LEE		03-18-1866	01-08-1868	016	LEE, James	
				016		
John O'REILLY				016	O'REILLY, John	Native Of ____. (Half of stone
				016		is missing. Circa 1850's)
				016		
Ellen CROTTY	Co. Limerick	60 Years	04-19-1879	016	CROTTY, Ellen	IMO Of Ellen Crotty, Wife
				016		of (unreadable), Native of The
				016		Parish Of (unreadable), County
				016		of Limerick, Ireland. (This
				016		stone severely deteriorated)
Hugh DORMAN	Co. Down	57 Years	07-13-1855	016	_____, Alice	Born At Drumbeau (Drumbo), Co.
				016	DORMAN, Hugh	Down, Ireland. Erected By His

				016		Wife, Alice. (NOI Alice)
				016		
Francis MCKEOUGH	Co. Tyrone	68 Years	04-30-1884	016	TEAGUE, Catherine	Born In Co. Tyrone, Ireland
Catherine TEAGUE McKeough		80 Years	09-04-1891	016	MCKEOUGH, Francis	
				016		
Thomas REDINGTON		76 Years	06-26-1882	016	_____, Margaret	
Margaret _____ REDDINGTON		33 Years	04-19-1862	016	REDINGTON, Thomas	
				016		
Michael NICHOLS		18 Years	09-27-1869	016	NICHOLS, Michael	Erected By Michael & Catherine Nichols In Memory Of Their Beloved Son.
				016		
				016		
Mary Ann NICHOLS		17Y 7M	02-19-1875	016	NICHOLS, Mary Ann	
Catherine _____ NICHOLS		50 Years	10-29-1876	016	_____, Catherine	(NOI Michael Nichols)
				016	NICHOLS, Michael	
Patrick O'BRIEN				016	O'BRIEN, Patrick	His Wife And Family (NOI)
				016		
Moses LEARY		1830	1910	016	CASSIDY, Catherine	
Catherine CASSIDY Leary		1836	1921	016	LEARY, Moses	
				016		
Thomas FEIGHONEY				016	_____, Ann	(Two stones - damaged and
Ann _____ FEIGHONEY				016	FEIGHONEY, Thomas	deteriorated. Circa 1850. NOI)
				016		
Barnard MCCULLAUGH		78 Years	03-16-1879	016	MCGUCKIEN, Mary	
Mary MCGUCKIEN McCullaugh		66 Years	05-25-1877	016	MCCULLAUGH, Barnard	(Surname possibly MCGOOKIN)
				016		
Thomas CROSBY	Co. Wexford	05-20-1806	01-09-1883	016	POWERS, Anna Statia	Born In Co. Wexford, Ireland
Anna Statia POWERS Crosby		04-15-1822	03-07-1895	016	CROSBY, Thomas	
				016		
Bridget A. CROSBY		05-20-1853	04-17-1881	016	CROSBY, Bridget A.	(Does not indicate if these
James D. CROSBY		04-14-1847	10-25-1857	016	CROSBY, James D.	are husband and wife)
				016		
Sylvester BARRON		20Y 4M	03-19-1878	016	BARRON, Sylvester	Son Of John & Mary BARRON
				016		
John NOONAN		62 Years	07-01-1889	016	MCKENZIE, Mary	
Mary MCKENZIE Noonan		1827	1915	016	NOONAN, John	
				016		
Daniel R. BRACKEN		1838	1912	016	DOWNS, Sabina E.	
Sabina E. DOWNS Bracken		1836	1908	016	BRACKEN, Daniel R.	
				016		
Patrick MORAN		1817	1848	016	DEGNAN, Bridget	
Bridget DEGNAN Moran		1823	1898	016	MORAN, Patrick	
Maria MORAN		1846	1911	016	MORAN, Maria	Dau Of Patrick & Bridget MORAN
				016		
Filicite _____ CROOKER		40 Years	01-16-1850	016	CROOKER, Amasa	(NOI Amasa Crooker)
				016		

Name	Origin	Born/Age	Died	Code	Index	Notes
John MULLINS				016	MULLINS, John	(GAR) Co. B. 17 VT INF (NOI)
				016		
Hiram J. WOOD		56 Years	06-21-1878	016	WOOD, Hiram J.	(GAR) Pvt Co. H 17 VT Vols
				016		
Patrick MCWILLIAMS		77 Years	01-31-1872	016	_____, Mary	
Mary _____ MCWILLIAMS		73 Years	12-06-1882	016	MCWILLIAMS, Patrick	
Andrew MCWILLIAMS		20 Years	01-16-1848	016	MCWILLIAMS, Andrew	
Joseph MCWILLIAMS				016	MCWILLIAMS, Joseph	(NOI)
John E. MCWILLIAMS				016	MCWILLIAMS, John E.	(NOI)
Margaret MCWILLIAMS		11 Months		016	MCWILLIAMS, Margaret	(NOI)
				016		
Patrick CANNON		73 Years	09-15-1890	016	_____, Catherine	
Catherine _____ CANNON		67 Years	04-03-1884	016	CANNON, Patrick	
Mary CANNON		2 Years	1850	016	CANNON, Mary	
				016		
Mary KENNEDY Mooney		1832	1919	016	MOONEY, John	(NOI John Mooney)
				016		
Hugh MCWILLIAMS		33 Years	01-18-1870	016	_____, Minnie	
Minnie _____ MCWILLIAMS		73 Years	12-06-1882	016	MCWILLIAMS, Hugh	(Bottom of stone buried)
				016		
Alfred RICKEY		1849	1920	016	MARTIN, Catherine	(GAR) Co. B, 115th Rgt NY Inf
Catherine MARTIN Rickey		1850	1938	016	RICKEY, Alfred	
				016		
Francis RHONE	Co. Tyrone	01-20-1802	09-04-1880	016	GARY, Elizabeth	A Native Of County Tyrone, Ire
Elizabeth GARY Rhone	Co. Down	01-23-1804	02-04-1875	016	RHONE, Francis	A Native Of The Co. Down,Ire
John RHONE		08-03-1833	07-26-1834	016	RHONE, John	
William H. RHONE		09-26-1845	07-03-1848	016	RHONE, William H.	
Francis Patrick RHONE		05-25-1835	01-28-1876	016	RHONE, Francis Patrick	
Mary RHONE		43 Years	09-19-1904	016	RHONE, Mary	
James E. RHONE		39 Years	11-__-1881	016	RHONE, James E.	
				016		
Mathew MCWILLIAMS		44 Years	02-24-1847	016	MCWILLIAMS, Mathew	
				016		
Bridget CUSICK		1842	1917	016	CUSICK, Bridget	(This stone is deteriorated.
Martin KEEFE		24 Years	1847 (?)	016	KEEFE, Martin	Not sure of dates-interpreted)
Elizabeth KEEFE		71 Years	06-21-1879	016	KEEFE, Elizabeth	(She died in Winooski, Vt)
				016		
Owen DOLAN		1831	1910	016	SMULLIN, Mary	
Mary SMULLIN Dolan		1825	1916	016	DOLAN, Owen	
				016		
John KENNEDY		1820	1893	016	HOGAN, Mary	
				016	SULLIVAN, Margaret	
Mary HOGAN Kennedy		1832	1860	016	KENNEDY, John	
Margaret SULLIVAN Kennedy		1835	1906	016	KENNEDY, John	
				016		

Elizabeth LARKIN		07-17-1866	016	LARKIN, Elizabeth	(Stone is partially buried)
			016		
John O'CONNER	1807	1880	016	O'BRIAN, Ellen	
Ellen O'BRIAN O'Conner	1827	1895	016	O'CONNER, John	
			016		
Luke B. BOLGER	1855	1922	016	LEARY, Catherine	
Catherine LEARY Bolger	1861	1911	016	BOLGER, Luke B.	
			016		
Catherine _____ MCGUYRE	80 Years	05-10-1889	016	MCGUYRE, Daniel	(NOI Daniel McGuyre)
James MCGUYRE	15 Years	02-20-1855	016	MCGUYRE, James	
Bridget MCGUYRE	20 Years	12-11-1856	016	MCGUYRE, Bridget	
John MCGUYRE			016	MCGUYRE, John	Son
Catharine MCGUYRE			016	MCGUYRE, Catharine	Daughter
			016		
John MCGOUGH	1838	1915	016	LARKIN, Mary	
Mary LARKIN McGough	1840	1922	016	MCGOUGH, John	
			016		
Elisabeth POWERS	22 Years	03-11-1870	016	POWERS, Elisabeth	
Thomas POWERS	21 Years	04-27-1873	016	_____, Bridget G.	
Bridget G. _____ POWERS	37 Years	10-09-1866	016	POWERS, Thomas	
John CROSBY	28 Years	04-28-1859	016	POWERS, John	
Mary POWERS	60 Years	04-17-1875	016	POWERS, Mary	
John POWERS	65 Years	10-06-1866	016	POWERS, John	
Kittie POWERS	33 Years	10-06-1888	016	POWERS, Kittie	
			016		
Matthew DUFFY	1804	1860	016	RILEY, Mary	
Mary RILEY Duffy	1811	1863	016	DUFFY, Matthew	
Julia D. STACY	1835	1857	016	STACY, Julia D.	
Catherine DUFFY	1833	1887	016	DUFFY, Catherine	
Anna DUFFY	1849	1904	016	DUFFY, Anna	
Elizabeth FALLON	1845	1910	016	FALLON, Elizabeth	
			016		
Edward NASH	18 Years	05-__-1858	016	NASH, Edward	
			016		
Bernard COONEY	1807	1872	016	_____, Cecelia	
Cecelia _____ COONEY	1812	1857	016	COONEY, Bernard	
Thomas COONEY	1840	1922	016	COONEY, Thomas	Son
			016		
Martin MCDONNELL	59 Years	02-10-1862	016	_____, Bridget	(Deteriorated.Not sure of 1862
Bridget _____ MCDONNELL			016	MCDONNELL, Martin	
William MCDONNELL	28 Years	03-15-____	016	MCDONNELL, William	
Mary A. MCDONNELL	22 Years	02-10-1857	016	MCDONNELL, Mary Ann	
Michael MCDONNELL	20 Years	12-18-1858	016	MCDONNELL, Michael	
Bridget MCDONNELL	17 Years	07-17-1858	016	MCDONNELL, Bridget	
Peter MCDONNELL	22 Years	04-16-1862	016	MCDONNELL, Peter	

				016		
Owen GOLDEN	Co. Sligo	77 Years	06-23-1873	016	DENEEN, Lillian	Co. Sligo
Lillian DENEEN Golden				016	GOLDEN, Owen	(NOI)
				016		
William JOHNSON		1855	1927	016	SULLIVAN, Mary E.	
Mary E. SULLIVAN Johnson		1858	1921	016	JOHNSON, William	
				016		
Margaret CASEY		56 Years	03-10-1853	016	CASEY, Margaret	Dau--Martin & Elizabeth CASEY
				016		
James CASEY		09-12-1825	08-12-1899	016	KINSELLA, Ann	
Ann KINSELLA Casey		06-22-1838	11-22-1900	016	CASEY, James	
Thomas CASEY		1857	1859	016	CASEY, Thomas	
Margaret CASEY		1858	1860	016	CASEY, Margaret	
Martin CASEY		1860	1862	016	CASEY, Martin	
James CASEY		1862	1864	016	CASEY, James	
Robert CASEY		1864	1866	016	CASEY, Robert	
Enos CASEY		1866	1868	016	CASEY, Enos	
John CASEY		1871	1878	016	CASEY, John	
Elizabeth M. CASEY		1868	1880	016	CASEY, Elizabeth M.	
Margaret KINSELLA		1850	1896	016	KINSELLA, Margaret	
				016		
Michael CANN (CANA?)			__-__-1850	016	CANN, Michael	A Native Of The Parish Of
				016		Portro__(Possibly Portroe
				016		Town), Co. Tipperary, Ire (NOI
				016		Deteriorated)
				016		
Thomas H. MURPHY		1859	1917	016	_____, Mary A.	
Mary A. _____ MURPHY		1864	1921	016	MURPHY, Thomas H.	
				016		
Suzanna O'NEILL		1840	1912	016	O'NEILL, Suzanna	(Possibly husband and wife.
William O'NEILL		1844	1924	016	O'NEILL, Michael	Does not say so)
				016		
C. MAHONEY		1850		016	_____, Joanna	(NOI DOD)
Joanna _____ MAHONEY		1853		016	MAHONEY, C.	(NOI DOD)
				016		
Michael MCEVOY		58 Years	10-30-1876	016	MCEVOY, Michael	
				016		
William B. MCCARTY		01-05-1858	03-31-1914	016	DONLIN, Jane A.	
Jane A. DONLIN McCarty		01-05-1859		016	MCCARTY, William	(NOI DOD)
				016		
Johanna ENRIGHT		20 Years	07-11-1849	016	ENRIGHT, Johanna	
				016		
Patrick CONLON		1818	1893	016	O'MEARA, Mary	
Mary O'MEARA Conlon		1825	1909	016	CONLON, Patrick	
Bridget CONLON		1827	1894	016	CONLON, Bridget	

Name	Born	Died	Code	Related	Notes
			016		
Charles C. FINNIGAN	1841	1907	016	_____, Maria J.	
Maria J. _____ FINNIGAN	1849	1907	016	FINNIGAN, Charles C.	
			016		
Johanna CONNERS		06-03-1855	016	CONNERS, Johanna	Dau Of Batt & Margaret Conners
			016	CONNERS, Batt	(Cannot read - weathered)
			016		
Mary A. _____ CLARK	24 Years	08_--_1872	016	CLARK, John	(NOI John Clark)
			016	_____, Mary	
			016		
Elizabeth B. SMITH	1837	1915	016	SMITH, Elizabeth B.	(Possibly husband and wife.
Henry C. RYAN	1853	1915	016	RYAN, Henry C.	Does not say so)
			016		
John J. BARRY	1855	1924	016	GARVEY, Mary	
Mary GARVEY Barry	1859	1928	016	BARRY, John J.	
John BARRY	1810	1894	016	DOWNS, Hanora	
Hanora DOWNS Barry	1820	1893	016	BARRY, John	
			016		
John W. LOUTHER	1857	1935	016	MCCARTHY, Ellen A.	
Ellen A. MCCARTHY Louther	1857	1928	016	LOUTHER, John W.	
			016		
Malachi SHANLEY	1848	1913	016	CROSS, Elizabeth	
Elizabeth CROSS Shanley	1847	1915	016	SHANLEY, Malachi	
			016		
Bridget MCCALE Leary	1842	1900	016	LEARY, Henry	(NOI Henry Leary)
			016		
R. F. LEE	02-10-1854		016	_____, Nellie	(NOI DOD)
Nellie _____ LEE	07-11-1858	09-29-1873	016	LEE, R. F.	
P. LEE	01-15-1831	02-01-1916	016	_____, Ellen	
Ellen _____ LEE	06-10-1830	10-17-1882	016	LEE, P.	
Richard LEE	06-11-1799	07-07-1875	016	_____, Margaret	
Margaret _____ LEE	11-24-1791	11-24-1881	016	LEE, Richard	
			016		
James COLLINS		04-30-1906	016	FITZGERALD, Kathrine	(NOI DOB)
Kathrine FITZGERALD Collins		09-05-1903	016	COLLINS, James	(NOI DOB)
			016		
Thomas LARNER	1857	1930	016	BURKE, Kate	
Kate BURKE Larner	1855	1904	016	LARNER, Thomas	
			016		
Daniel O'BRIEN	1857	1930	016	KEEFE, Bridget	
Bridget KEEFE O'Brien	1855	1904	016	O'BRIEN, Daniel	
			016		
Joseph DUNPHY	44 Years	03-20-1872	016	_____, Susie	By His Wife Susie. (NOI Susie)
			016		
Philip WARD	1841	1913	016	WARD, Philip	(GAR) Co. H. 2nd Vt Vol Inf

				016		
Michael FARRELL	Co. Kings	1809	1849	016	MANYING, Maria	Born In Kings (Offaly) County,
				016		Ire.Died at Williston, Vermont
Maria MANYING Farrell	Co. Kings	1810	1860	016	FARRELL, Michael	Born In Kings (Offaly) County,
				016		Ire.Died in Burlington,Vermont
Mary Ann FARRELL	Co. Kings	1844	1912	016	FARRELL, Mary Ann	Born In Kings (Offaly) County,
				016		Ire. Died at Burlington, VT
Marcella FARRELL		1848	1918	016	FARRELL, Marcella	Born In Hemmingford (Quebec)
				016		Canada. Died Burlington, Vt.
				016		(Same stone-- Michael Farrell)
				016		
John O'BRINE		34 Years	11-17-1849	016	O'BRINE, John	
				016		
Bridget _____ WARD		39 Years	02-18-1850	016	WARD, Barney	(NOI Barney Ward)
				016		
James DOLAN		1826	1896	016	MURRAY, Mary	
Mary MURRAY Dolan		1829	1907	016	DOLAN, James	
Charles L. DOLAN		1847	19__	016	DOLAN, Charles L.	(NOI DOD)
Katherine L. DOLAN		1856	19__	016	DOLAN, Katherine L.	(NOI DOD)
Philip F. DOLAN		1862	1890	016	DOLAN, Philip F.	
Mary DOLAN French		1863	19__	016	DOLAN, Mary	(NOI Mr. French - DOD)
Elizabeth DOLAN		1864	1865	016	DOLAN, Elizabeth	
Jennie DOLAN		1866	1873	016	DOLAN, Jennie	
				016		
Mary A. _____ O'BRIEN		1833	1862	016	O'BRIEN, Mary A.	Erected by Edward E. O'Brien
Her Children				016		In Memory Of His Loving Mother
Edward E. O'BRIEN				016	O'BRIEN, Edward E.	(NOI Spouse)
Amelia O'BRIEN				016	O'BRIEN, Amelia	
				016		
James FLYNN		1845	1913	016	_____, Elizabeth	Co. H. 9th Rgt Vt Vols (GAR)
Elizabeth _____ FLYNN		1853	1931	016	FLYNN, James	
				016		
Robert POWERS		73 Years	12-25-1848	016	POWERS, Robert	(Does not state if husband and
Ellenor POWERS		72 Years	03-22-1846	016	POWERS, Ellenor	wife)
				016		
Mary RUSSELL Powers		35 Years	03-07-1857	016	POWERS, Robert	(Same plot as above)
				016	RUSSELL, Mary	
				016		
John CROWLEY		1815	1892	016	MULCAHY, Mary	
Mary MULCAHY Crowley		1818	1907	016	CROWLEY, John	
Jeremiah CROWLEY		1848	1859	016	CROWLEY, Jeremiah	
Cornelius CROWLEY		1848	1870	016	CROWLEY, Cornelius	
Timothy CROWLEY		1846	1902	016	CROWLEY, Timothy	
Thomas CROWLEY		1863	1882	016	CROWLEY, Thomas	
Michael CROWLEY		1858	1920	016	CROWLEY, Michael	

			016		
Mary MCCARROLL	18 Years	01-28-1867	016	MCCARROLL, Mary	(Not sure of age at death Weathered. Could be 68)
			016		
			016		
James HALINAN	74 Years	01-08-1910	016	HALINAN, James	
			016		
Ann MURDOCK	1843	1922	016	MURDOCK, Ann	
			016		
Mary BOYCE	33 Years	12-06-1853	016	BOYCE, Mary	
			016		
Julia MCDANE	5Y 4M	09-20-1855	016	MCDANE, Julia	Dau Of J & M.A. McDane
			016		
Patrick CARTY	75Y 8M	12-04-1887	016	CARTY, Patrick	
John CARTY	14Y 1M	05-26-1854	016	CARTY, Alice	Son Of Patrick Carty
Alice CARTY	8Y 5M	09-27-1860	016	CARTY, John	
James CARTY	77 Years	02-09-1859	016	_____, Elizabeth	
Elizabeth _____ CARTY	77 Years	10-01-1857	016	CARTY, James	
Maria CARTY	14 Years	06-04-1850	016	CARTY, Maria	
			016		
James BURKE	03-20-1822	05-24-1909	016	_____, Ann	
Ann _____ BURKE	12-22-1820	09-25-1902	016	BURKE, James	
			016		
Nancy READY	27 Years	03-12-1872	016	READY, Nancy	
			016		
Bridget KELLEY Sheridan	1853	1931	016	KELLEY, Bridget	(NOI A Mr. Sheridan)
			016		
Bridget COLLINS Connor	1832	1907	016	CONNOR, John	(NOI John Connor)
			016	COLLINS, Bridget	
			016		
Winefred SHERIDAN	60 Years	12-10-1875	016	SHERIDAN, Winefred	
			016		
Mary _____ SHANAHAN	86 Years	08-09-1906	016	SHANAHAN, James	(NOI James Shanahan)
			016		
John CORVIN	1843	1923	016	HARRINGTON, Bridget	
Bridget HARRINGTON Corvin	1843	1932	016	CORVIN, John	
			016		
Jane BURKE O'Brien	1856	1937	016	BURKE, Jane	(NOI Mr. O'Brien)
			016		
Edward R. LYNCH	1853	1933	016	SPLAIN, Catherine	
Catherine SPLAIN Lynch	1863	1935	016	LYNCH, Edward R.	
			016		
Patrick SHEEHAN	60 Years	03-15-1883	016	_____, Hanora	
Hanora _____ SHEEHAN	64Y 2M	06-28-1887	016	SHEEHAN, Patrick	
Bridget SHEEHAN	1854	1918	016	SHEEHAN, Bridget	
William F. SHEEHAN	1859	1893	016	SHEEHAN, William F.	

Maria SHEEHAN	4Y 2M	04-27-1854	016	SHEEHAN, Maria	
			016		
Patrick H. COFFEE	1856	1925	016	_____, Elizabeth J.	
Elizabeth J. _____ COFFEE	1862	1930	016	COFFEE, Patrick H.	
			016		
Bridget _____ DENNING	38 Years	02-08-1876	016	DENNING, James	(NOI James Denning)
			016		
Patrick MADDEN	74 Years	08-25-1883	016	_____, Helen	
Helen _____ MADDEN	70 Years	02-28-1879	016	MADDEN, Patrick	
Mary MADDEN	32Y 2M	10-28-1877	016	MADDEN, Mary	
Julia C. MADDEN	19 Years	07-01-1870	016	MADDEN, Julia C.	
John MADDEN	21 Years	07-29-1864	016	MADDEN, John	
			016		
William O'BRIEN	1840	1904	016	_____, Ellen	
Ellen _____ O'BRIEN	1839	1909	016	O'BRIEN, William	
Children			016		
Albert J. O'BRIEN	10 Months		016	O'BRIEN, Albert J.	
Eddie O'BRIEN	1 Day		016	O'BRIEN, Eddie	
Katie O'BRIEN	2 Days		016	O'BRIEN, Katie	
John W. O'BRIEN	1865	1924	016	O'BRIEN, John W.	
			016		
Patrick H. MURPHY	1861	1904	016	_____, Mary A.	
Mary A. _____ MURPHY	1861	1899	016	MURPHY, Patrick H.	
			016		
Patrick MURPHY	1833	1898	016	HOGAN, Ann	
Ann HOGAN Murphy	1837	1910	016	MURPHY, Patrick	
			016		
Barney GRAHAM	99 Years	10-02-1901	016	BLACK, Rosanna	
Rosanna BLACK Graham	12-10-1832	03-27-1896	016	GRAHAM, Barney	
			016		
Thomas E. LYNCH	61 Years	12-14-1912	016	BEAUREGARD, Josephine	
Josephine BEAUREGARD Lynch	67 Years	12-20-1929	016	LYNCH, Thomas E.	
			016		
Anthony DONNELLY	11-28-1844		016	KANE, Ellen	(NOI DOD)
Ellen KANE Donnelly	05-20-1848		016	DONNELLY, Anthony	(NOI DOD)
			016		
Bridget GILLIGAN	57 Years	06-10-1893	016	GILLIGAN, Bridget	
			016		
Patrick C. READY	38 Years	01-08-1907	016	READY, Patrick C.	
			016		
John J. SULLIVAN	42Y 6M	04-27-1893	016	RYAN, Nora J.	
Nora J. RYAN Sullivan	76 Years	10-16-1924	016	SULLIVAN, John J.	
			016		
John HANLON	1855	1917	016	_____, Sarah E.	
Sarah E. _____ HANLON	1858	1926	016	HANLON, John	

Name	Origin	Born/Age	Died	Code	Index	Notes
				016		
Thomas J. MURPHY		1873	1939	016	HODGES, Julia	
Julia HODGES Murphy		1869	1952	016	MURPHY, Thomas J.	
Mary HODGES		1866	1940	016	HODGES, Mary	
James MURPHY		1870	1934	016	MURPHY, James	
				016		
Moses MURPHY		83 Years	01-15-1884	016	_____, Catherine	
Catherine _____ MURPHY		70 Years	12-03-1870	016	MURPHY, Moses	
Edward MURPHY		36 Years	10-22-1874	016	MURPHY, Edward	
Catherine MURPHY		38 Years	03-07-1885	016	MURPHY, Catherine	
				016		
Michael GRYNING		85 Years	11-21-1880	016	_____, Nancy	
Nancy _____ GRYNING		67 Years	07-04-1876	016	GRYNING, Michael	
Edward GRYNING		23 Years	12-18-1872	016	GRYNING, Edward	
				016		
Martin D. HANLEY		1839	1899	016	GORMLEY, Margaret	
Margaret GORMLEY Hanley		1840	1898	016	HANLEY, Martin D.	(Surname possibly GEORMLEY)
				016		
Edward HANLEY		67 Years	02-05-1871	016	KENIAN, Catherine	
Catherine KENIAN Hanley		67 Years	05-28-1878	016	HANLEY, Edward	(Surname possibly Keenan)
				016		
William J. CANNING		1858	1914	016	ROCHE, Julia E.	
Julia E. ROCHE Canning		1853	1909	016	CANNING, William J.	
				016		
Patrick EGAN				016	NEVILLE, Joanna E.	(NOI DOB/DOD)
Joanna E. NEVILLE Egan		1855	1917	016	EGAN, Patrick	
				016		
Thomas W. O'SULLIVAN		68 Years	01-12-1911	016	FEENEY, Esther	
Esther FEENEY O'Sullivan		1862	1950	016	O'SULLIVAN, Thomas W.	
				016		
Patrick FARRELL		92 Years	01-16-1865	016	FARRELL, Patrick	
				016		
Patrick JOYCE	Co. Mayo	42 Years	03-25-1877	016	JOYCE, Patrick	Native Of (Parish of) "Claire" Island (Clare Island), County Mayo, Ireland
				016		
				016		
				016		
Patrick MCGUIRE		58 Years	02-26-1895	016	MCGUIRE, Patrick	
				016		
Elizabeth KIRBEE Donnelly		55 Years	05-15-1904	016	DONNELLY, Patrick	(NOI Patrick Donnelly)
				016	KIRBEE, Elizabeth	
				016		
Elizabeth MCWILLIAMS Kirby		11-16-1830	06-19-1877	016	KIRBY, Andrew	(NOI Andrew KIRBY)
				016	MCWILLIAMS, Elizabeth	
Agnes J. KIRBY		06-24-1856	01-31-1892	016	KIRBY, Agnes J.	
Johnnie KIRBY		04-23-1853	06-14-1865	016	KIRBY, Johnnie	

				016		
Thomas BAKER		1844	1922	016	CASEY, Ann	(GAR) Co.B 17th Rgt VT Vol Inf
Ann CASEY Baker		1844	1922	016	BAKER, Thomas	
				016		
Mary KENNEDY Farrell	Co. Tipperary	01-06-1841	01-15-1910	016	FARRELL, James	Born In Co. Tipperary, Ire
				016		(NOI James Farrell)
				016		
William HANLEY		95 Years	10-17-1897	016	HANLEY, William	
Nathan HANLEY		26 Years	06-26-1865	016	HANLEY, Nathan	
				016		
John CASEY		65 Years	04-17-1907	016	O'DONNELL, Mary P.	Erected to The Memory Of John
				016		Casey And His Children By His
				016		Wife
Mary P. O'DONNELL Casey		1843	1912	016	CASEY, John	
				016		
Hannah KENNEDY Sager		1836	1913	016	KENNEDY, Hannah	(NOI Mr. Snager)
				016		
Catherine KNIRK Kennedy	Co. Limerick	02-19-1803	02-24-1864	016	KENNEDY, Cornelius	Born At Balisteen (Ballysteen)
				016	KNIRK, Catherine	Limerick County, Ireland. Died
				016		at Burlington, Vermont.Erected
				016		by her children.(NOI Cornelius
				016		Kennedy)
				016		
Thomas F. BARRETT		66 Years	11-14-1913	016	BARRETT, Thomas F.	
				016		
John SPENCER		1834	1910	016	MCDONALD, Mary	
Mary MCDONALD Spencer		1826	1911	016	SPENCER, John	
Mary SPENCER		1858	1871	016	SPENCER, Mary	Daughter
				016		
Edward MELLEDY		84 Years	03-22-187_	016	_____, Elizabeth	(NOI spouse Elizabeth)
				016	MELLEDY, Edward	
				016		
Lawrence KELLEY				016	KELLEY, Lawrence	(GAR)Co. D 3rd (or 8th) Vt Inf
				016		(NOI DOB/DOD)
				016		
David KEEF				016	KEEF, David	(Badly deteriorated-can't read
Charles KEEF				016	KEEF, Charles	(Badly deteriorated-can't read
				016		
Abby _____ FLANAGAN		37 Years	06-15-1871	016	FLANAGAN, F. B.	(NOI F. B. FLANAGAN)
				016		
Almon J. CLARK		1853	1932	016	KENNEDY, Anne T.	
Anne T. KENNEDY Clark		58 Years	02-07-1903	016	CLARK, Almon J.	
				016		
John KENNA		24 Years	08-14-187_	016	_____, Ellen	
Ellen _____ KENNA		37 Years	09-28-1872	016	KENNA, John	

Name	Place	Age/Born	Died	Code	Index	Notes
				016		
Edmund FITZGERALD		82 Years	12-26-1896	016	MANGIN, Catherine	
Catherine MANGIN Fitzgerald		67 Years	10-07-1887	016	FITZGERALD, Edmund	
Edward FITZGERALD		21 Years	03-27-1872	016	FITZGERALD, Edward	Son Of E. & C. Fitzgerald
Maggie FITZGERALD		19 Years	09-09-1871	016	FITZGERALD, Maggie	Dau Of E. & C. Fitzgerald
				016		
James FITZGERALD		1855	1922	016	WING, Anne	
Anne WING Fitzgerald		1856	1943	016	FITZGERALD, James	
James FITZGERALD		1821	1871	016	MEAD, Catherine	
Catherine MEAD Fitzgerald		1819	1899	016	FITZGERALD, James	
Their Children				016		
Thomas FITZGERALD		1840	1898	016	FITZGERALD, Thomas	
Mary FITZGERALD		1843	1916	016	FITZGERALD, Mary	
				016		
John P. DELANEY		1840	1914	016	_____, Ellen	
Ellen _____ DELANEY		1842	1909	016	DELANEY, John P.	
				016		
Bridget _____ RYAN		53 Years	10-16-1873	016	RYAN, Philip	(NOI Philip RYAN)
				016	_____, Bridget	
Bridget M. RYAN		18Y 7M	08-08-1865	016	RYAN, Bridget	Dau Of P & B Ryan
				016		
Maurice FLYNN				016	COLLINS, Bridget	(Inscription reads) Maurice
				016		Flynn, His Wife, Bridget Col-
				016		lins & Children. (NOI DOB/DOD)
Bridget COLLINS Flynn				016	FLYNN, Maurice	
				016		
George SHIRLEY				016	WALL, Bridget	(NOI DOB/DOD)
Bridget WALL Shirley				016	SHIRLEY, George	(NOI DOB/DOD)
				016		
Ann MURPHY	Co. Cork	74 Years	09-19-1887	016	MURPHY, Ann	Born In Co. Cork, Ireland
				016		
Simon CUNNINGHAM		31 Years	08-01-1883	016	_____, Nellie	
Nellie _____ CUNNINGHAM		18Y 7M	08-08-1865	016	CUNNINGHAM, Simon	
				016		
Patrick O'DONOGHUE			JUN - 1883	016	CASEY, Margaret	
Margaret CASEY O'Donoghue			DEC - 1900	016	O'DONOGHUE, Patrick	
Rev. Thomas O'DONOGHUE		JAN - 1858	MAY - 1914	016	O'DONOGHUE, Rev Thomas	Ordained DEC - 1887
				016		
Mary HABERLAND		93 Years	05-27-1892	016	HABERLAND, Mary	
Catherine KENNEDY		68 Years	02-02-1902	016	KENNEDY, Catherine	
Michael DELAHUNTY		67 Years	02-02-1914	016	KENNEDY, Mary A.	
Mary A. KENNEDY Delahunty		67 Years	12-18-1922	016	DELAHUNTY, Michael	
				016		
Jeremiah O'BRIEN		78 Years		016	DEADY, Bridget M.	(Possible DOB 8-6-1823)
Bridget M. DEADY O'Brien		76 Years	05-27-1898	016	O'BRIEN, Jeremiah	

Name	Place	Born	Died	Code	Index	Notes
				016		
Patrick H. BURNS		JUL 1857	07-17-1906	016	_____, Mary Jane	
Mary Jane _____ BURNS			08-22-1891	016	BURNS, Patrick	(NOI DOB)
				016		
Elizabeth MCCONVILLE		1845	1910	016	MCCONVILLE, Elizabeth	
Sarah MCCONVILLE		1843	1890	016	MCCONVILLE, Sarah	
Mary CARAHER				016	CARAHER, Mary	(NOI DOB/DOD)
				016		
Michael GLEASON		1849	1927	016	POPE, Mary	
Mary POPE Gleason		1856	1920	016	GLEASON, Michael	
				016		
James KIRBY		1834	1917	016	KIRBY, James	
				016		
William J. MURPHY		08-16-1864	08-31-1909	016	KENNEDY, Nora W.	
Nora W. KENNEDY Murphy		08-18-1867	05-04-1942	016	MURPHY, William J.	
				016		
James GRIFFIN		1809	1893	016	ROONEY, Hanora	
Hanora ROONEY Griffin		1813	1871	016	GRIFFIN, James	
John GRIFFIN		50 Years	03-25-1899	016	GRIFFIN, John	
Ann GRIFFIN				016	GRIFFIN, Ann	(NOI DOB/DOD)
				016		
Thomas MEAGHER	Co. Tipperary	75 Years	04-05-1884	016	_____, Mary	A Native of Co. Tipperary, Ire
Mary _____ MEAGHER		75 Years	06-23-1907	016	MEAGHER, Thomas	
Philip MEAGHER		32 Years	01-16-1882	016	MEAGHER, Philip	Died At Portland, Oregon
Thomas MEAGHER Jr.		24 Years	06-11-1879	016	MEAGHER, Thomas Jr.	Died At Chicago, Illinois
John MEAGHER		23 Years	10-27-1880	016	MEAGHER, John	Died At Janesville, Minnesota
Edward F. MURRAY		1868	1947	016	MEAGHER, Catherine	
Catherine MEAGHER Murray		1871	1965	016	MURRAY, Edward F.	Wife Of Edward F. Murray, MD.
Martin MEAGHER		82 Years	11-07-1933	016	MEAGHER, Martin	
				016		(NOI Edward F. Murray)
Alexander POWERS		11-19-1858	12-06-1902	016	CUMMINS, Margaret	
Margaret CUMMINS Powers		1860	1938	016	POWERS, Alexander	
				016		
William COFFEY		1815	1872	016	HAYES, Hanorah	
Hanorah HAYES Coffey		1810	1895	016	COFFEY, William	
				016		
John COSTELLO		1833	1903	016	HAYES, Ann	
Ann HAYES Costello		1841	1920	016	COSTELLO, John	
				016		
John CROTTY		19Y 3M	04-03-1873	016	CROTTY, John	Son Of James & Bridget Crotty
				016		(Could be Grotty-stone worn)
James REDMOND		1800	1873	016	CAVANAUGH, Mary	
Mary CAVANAUGH Redmond		1811	1873	016	REDMOND, James	
Ann CAVANAUGH Whalon		1833	1917	016	CAVANAUGH, Ann	Daughter. (NOI Mr. WHALON)
				016		

Patrick MCKENZIE		1840	1903	016	HIGGINS, Rose A.	
Rose A. HIGGINS McKezsie		1856	1936	016	MCKENZIE, Patrick J.	
				016		
James HENRY		65 Years	01-07-1873	016	RYAN, Catherine	
Catherine RYAN Henry		64 Years	10-08-1884	016	HENRY, James	
				016		
Edward MCGRATH			06-09-1864	016	MCGRATH, Edward	Son Of Owen & Bridget McGrath
				016		(NOI DOB)
				016		
Bridget _____ MCGRATH		60 Years	10-31-1872	016	MCGRATH, Owen	(NOI Owen McGrath)
				016	_____, Bridget	
				016		
Stephen COLLINS	Co. Limerick	1837	1926	016	_____, Catherine	Born In Newtown, Limerick
				016		Ireland
Catherine _____ COLLINS		1838	1924	016	COLLINS, Stephen	Born In Newton, Limerick
				016		Ireland
				016		
Joanna BRESNEHAN			1913	016	BRESNEHAN, Joana	(NOI DOB)
				016		
Patrick BARRON		58 Years	07-12-1877	016	SLATTERY, Julia	
Julia SLATTERY Barron		66 Years	01-13-1892	016	BARRON, Patrick	
				016		
James O'DONNELL		81 Years	03-27-1925	016	KENNELLY, Hannah	
Hannah KENNELLY O'Donnell		66 Years	10-02-1905	016	O'DONNELL, James	
				016		
John READY		1841	1909	016	MELODY, Jane	
Jane MELODY Ready		1847	1904	016	READY, John	
				016		
David HOGAN		1854	1923	016	FITZGERALD, Bridget	
Bridget FITZGERALD Hogan		1846	1928	016	HOGAN, David	
				016		
John B. MARTIN		1854	1925	016	LEMAIRE, Ellen M.	(Possibly this couple are
Ellen B. LEMAIRE Martin		1854	1932	016	MARTIN, John B.	Franco-American)
				016		
Albert E. REYNOLDS		1849	1925	016	SHERIDAN, Martha A.	
Martha A. SHERIDAN Reynolds		1852	1921	016	REYNOLDS, Albert E.	
				016		
James BARRETT		1834		016	CAVANAUGH, Mary	(NOI DOD)
Mary CAVANAUGH Barrett		1832	1905	016	BARRETT, James	
				016		
Thomas PAINE		59 Years	11-29-1885	016	PAINE, Thomas	
				016		
James MCCABE				016	MCCABE, James	(Very Old Stone-no inscription
				016		
Dennis NOONAN		1805	1885	016	DONOVAN, Mary	

Mary DONOVAN Noonan		1825	1895	016	NOONAN, Dennis	
				016		
Ellen Garvey KELLEY			03-22-1903	016	KELLEY, John O.	(NOI John O. Kelley. NOI DOB)
Sarah J. KELLEY		03-17-1854	03-28-1889	016	KELLEY, Sarah J.	
Charles E. KELLEY		06-29-1870	12-20-1887	016	KELLEY, Charles E.	
George KELLEY			03-26-1903	016	KELLEY, George	(NOI DOB)
John KELLEY			05-02-1904	016	KELLEY, John	(NOI DOB)
				016		
Bridget _____ MCGRATH		76 Years	02-26-1884	016	MCGRATH, Robert	(NOI Robert McGrath)
				016	_____, Bridget	
Bridget MCGRATH		18Y 5M	05-08-1862	016	MCGRATH, Bridget	Dau Of R & B McGrath
				016		
Ellen HURSON	Co. Tyrone		1884	016	HURSON, Ellen	Born In Co. Tyrone, Ireland
				016		
Anne HURSON	Co. Tyrone		1906	016	HURSON, Anne	Born In Co. Tyrone, Ireland
				016		
Mary Jane HURSON	Co. Tyrone		1943	016	HURSON, Mary Jane	Born In Co. Tyrone, Ireland
				016		
Alice HURSON	Co. Tyrone		1949	016	HURSON, Alice	Born In Co. Tyrone, Ireland
				016		
John HURSON	Co. Tyrone	06-07-1805	08-21-1869	016	HURSON, John	Born In Co. Tyrone, Ireland
				016		
Frank HURSON	Co. Tyrone	06-15-1869	04-11-1890	016	HURSON, Frank	Born In Co. Tyrone, Ireland
				016		
James GALLAGHER		31Y 6M	07-07-1889	016	GALLAGHER, James	Erected By Richard Gallagher
				016	GALLAGHER, Richard	In Memory Of His Son
				016		
Edward GORMAN		1833	1905	016	LAMBERT, Katherine	
Katherine LAMBERT Gorman		1840	1912	016	GORMAN, Edward	
				016		
Capt. J. Henry KIRBY		1826	1890	016	THOMPSON, Elizabeth	
Elizabeth THOMPSON Kirby		1832	1901	016	KIRBY, J. Henry	
				016		
William H. BABCOCK		1855	1928	016	O'DONNELL, Laura A.	
Laura A. O'DONNELL Babcock		1852	1939	016	BABCOCK, William H.	
				016		
Thomas BUCKLEY				016	O'CONNOR, Anna	Thomas Buckley & His Wife Anna
Anna O'CONNOR Buckley				016	BUCKLEY, Thomas	O'Connor. (NOI DOB/DOD)
				016		
Francis CANNING		84 Years	05-05-1891	016	SULLIVAN, Judith	
Judith SULLIVAN Canning		1852	11-24-1896	016	CANNING, Francis	
Edward J. CANNING		19 Years	11-28-1871	016	CANNING, Edward J.	Died In Beverley, Mass.
				016		
John J. KENNEDY		1832	1916	016	_____, Mary	
Mary _____ KENNEDY		1836	1902	016	KENNEDY, John J.	

Name	Origin	Age/Born	Died	Code	Related	Notes
Helen KENNEDY			03-15-1958	016	KENNEDY, Helen	(NOI DOB)
Michael E. KENNEDY		1867	1889	016	KENNEDY, Michael E.	
John J. KENNEDY		1870	1932	016	KENNEDY, John J.	
Cornelius E. KENNEDY			01-11-1939	016	KENNEDY, Cornelius E.	(NOI DOB)
				016		
James P. STAPLETON		1849	1931	016	MCNAMARA, Catherine	
Catherine NCNAMARA Stapleton		1853	1922	016	STAPLETON, James P.	
				016		
James HALPIN		28 Years	02-17-1887	016	HALPIN, James	Son Of Andrew & Catherine
				016	HALPIN, Andrew	Halpin
				016		
Daniel O'LEARY	Co. Cork	90 Years	09-01-1897	016	BUCKLEY, Margaret	Born In Co. Cork, Ireland
				016		Died In Winooski, Vermont
Margaret BUCKLEY O'Leary	Co. Cork	78 Years	10-03-1891	016	O'LEARY, Daniel	Born In Co. Cork Ireland
				016		Died In Winooski, Vermont
Nora O'LEARY		34 Years	08-22-1886	016	O'LEARY, Nora	Died In Winooski, Vermont
				016		
Daniel CONNOLLY		1848	1926	016	HOULIHAN, Hanora	
Hanora HOULIHAN Connolly		1842	1911	016	CONNOLLY, Daniel	
				016		
Julia BURNS Collier		69 Years	08-05-1895	016	COLLIER, James	(NOI James COLLIER)
				016		
Mary _____ MCGOWAN		25Y 8M	07-02-1878	016	MCGOWAN, P. J.	(NOI P. J. McGowan)
				016	_____, Mary	
				016		
Catherine _____ KELLY		35 Years	11-08-1868	016	KELLY, James	(NOI James Kelly)
				016	_____, Catherine	
				016		
John J. KELLY		06-02-1848	05-02-1896	016	HIGGINS, Sarah A.	
Sarah A. HIGGINS Kelly		1844	1919	016	KELLY, John J.	
Bridget KELLY		14Y 6M	03-27-1863	016	KELLY, Bridget	Daughter
				016		
Patrick KELLY	Co. Limerick	72 Years	06-25-1870	016	KELLY, Patrick	Native of Co.Limerick, Ireland
				016		(First Initial of Spouse is J)
				016		
Zeb MITCHELL		35 Years	04-25-1874	016	MITCHELL, Zeb	(GAR) Co. C 12th Regt Vt Vols
				016		
Patrick HOGAN		1848	1916	016	_____, Margaret	
Margaret _____ HOGAN		1846	1935	016	HOGAN, Patrick	
				016		
John MORRISON			11-07-1894	016	MORRISON, John	(Spouse indicated-unreadable)
				016		
James MORRISON				016	MORRISON, James	(GAR) Co. D 13th Vt Inf
				016		(NOI DOB-DOD)
				016		

Name	Birthplace	Born/Age	Died	Code	Spouse	Notes
John BURNS		67 Years	03-19-1874	016	_____, Catherine	
Catherine _____ BURNS		82 Years	02-18-1901	016	BURNS, John	
				016		
Harry O'NEILL		1842	1914	016	O'REILLY, Mary A.	
Mary A. O'REILLY O'Neill			1884	016	O'NEILL, Harry	(NOI DOB)
				016		
James A. RILEY		1851	1913	016	_____, Johanna	
Johanna _____ RILEY		1856	1933	016	RILEY, James A.	
				016		
Michael MCMAHON		72 Years	06-10-1896	016	_____, Mary	
Mary _____ MCMAHON		74 Years	06-17-1894	016	MCMAHON, Michael	
Thomas F. MCMAHON		03-14-1853	07-09-18	016	SULLIVAN, Joanna F.	Son Of M & M McMahon
Joanna F. SULLIVAN McMahon		06-13-1851	09-21-1888	016	MCMAHON, Thomas F.	
				016		
Patrick MCGRATH		1834	1914	016	READY, Margaret	
Margaret READY McGrath		05-10-1845	08-17-1877	016	MCGRATH, Patrick	
				016		
Mary Ann SPENCE		1846	1929	016	SPENCE, Mary Ann	
				016		
Thomas MONAHAN		1846	1917	016	DORAN, Catherine	
Catherine DORAN Monahan		1848	1918	016	MONAHAN, Thomas	
				016		
James E. CROWLEY		1848	1908	016	_____, Bridget	
Bridget _____ CROWLEY		1853	1935	016	CROWLEY, James E.	
				016		
Philip NASH		1811	1886	016	_____, Johanna	
Johanna _____ NASH		1831	1903	016	NASH, Philip	
				016		
Stephen CONNERS	Co. Clare	82 Years	12-30-1887	016	_____, Mary	Born In Co. Clare, Ireland
Mary _____ CONNERS			10-03-1875	016	CONNERS, Stephen	
				016		
Patrick MULQUEENE	Co. Clare	03-14-1823	08-19-1878	016	POWERS, Catharine	Sacred To The Memory of
				016		Patrick Mulqueene. Died at
				016		Burlington Co.
Catherine POWERS Mulqueene	Co. Wexford	55 Years	07-03-1879	016	MULQUEENE, Patrick	Born In Co. Wexford, Ireland.
				016		Died In Burlington, (VT)
				016		(Stone badly eroded)
				016		
Daniel FINNISSY		1856	1901	016	DORAN, Mary	
Mary DORAN Finnissy		1857	1922	016	FINNISSY, Daniel	
				016		
Elmira _____ SULLIVAN		55 Years	08-27-1899	016	SULLIVAN, Cornelius	(NOI Cornelius Sullivan)
				016		
John SHEERAN		1841	1923	016	FINNEY, Ellen	
Ellen FINNEY Sheeran		1837	1921	016	SHEERAN, John	

Name	Born/Age	Died	Code	Index	Notes
			016		
James MCKANNA	1856	1890	016	HYLAND, Elizabeth	
Elizabeth HYLAND McKanna	1856	1933	016	MCKANNA, James	
			016		
Michael BURKE		08-21-1889	016	_____, Mary	(NOI DOB)
Mary _____ BURKE		03-07-1905	016	BURKE, Michael	(NOI DOB)
			016		
John J. KENNEDY	1837	1916	016	_____, Mary	
Mary _____ KENNEDY	1936	1902	016	KENNEDY, John J.	
			016		
Austin GILL	70 Years	06-10-1908	016	_____, Bridget	
Bridget _____ GILL	44 Years	07-31-1899	016	GILL, Austin	
			016		
Mary CUSICK	15Y 8M	02-26-1870	016	CUSICK, Mary	Dau Of Patrick & Mary Cusick
			016		
John P. KANE	1850	1937	016	KANE, John P.	
			016		
Patrick RUSSELL	75 Years	07-24-1868	016	_____, Catherine M.	
Catharine M. _____ RUSSELL	71 Years	04-07-1864	016	RUSSELL, Patrick	
			016		
James CALLAHAN	1824	1894	016	COLLINS, Bridget	
Bridget COLLINS Calahan	1829	1920	016	CALLAHAN, James	
James CALLAHAN	1862	1898	016	CALLAHAN, James	
William CALLAHAN	1870	1908	016	CALLAHAN, William	
Michael CALLAHAN	1860	1916	016	CALLAHAN, Michael	
Edward CALLAHAN	1854	1928	016	CALLAHAN, Edward	
Margaret CALLAHAN	1867	1929	016	CALLAHAN, Margaret	
Mary CALLAHAN	1856	1930	016	CALLAHAN, Mary	
			016		
Patrick CRONIN	1842	1913	016	CRONIN, Patrick	Born In Ireland. Co. M 1st Reg
			016		Of Frontier Cavalry (i.e. Home
			016		Guard protecting U.S. Canadian
			016		Border from incursions by Con-
			016		federate Raiders.British North
			016		American-Canadians were sympa-
			016		thetic to the Southern cause)
			016		
Patrick SHANLEY	55 Years	05-27-1872	016	SHANLEY, Patrick	(NOI Mrs. Shanley)
Lawrence SHANLEY	14 Years	11-20-1868	016	SHANLEY, Lawrence	
Michael SHANLEY	11Y 7M	05-28-1864	016	SHANLEY, Michael	
			016		
Philip DOWER	73 Years	05-10-1900	016	_____, Hanora	
Hanora _____ DOWER	76 Years	03-05-1902	016	DOWER, Philip	
Margaret DOWER	1Y 6M	04-23-1859	016	DOWER, Margaret	
Mary DOWER	2Y 5M	02-20-1864	016	DOWER, Mary	

Name	Origin	Born/Age	Died	Code	Index name	Notes
				016		
Daniel HENLEY		22 Years	05-15-1864	016	HENLEY, Daniel	(Probably surname Hanley)
				016		
Bridget HANLEY		74 Years	06-04-1872	016	HANLEY, Bridget	
				016		
John QUINN		03-20-1826	10-27-1886	016	_____, Mary A.	
Mary A. _____ QUINN		07-12-1837	01-04-1890	016	QUINN, John	
Mary A. QUINN		06-27-1859	01-21-1878	016	QUINN, Mary A.	
Ellen A. QUINN		07-21-1863	07-27-1864	016	QUINN, Ellen A.	
Helen J. QUINN		07-16-1868	08-16-1869	016	QUINN, Helen J.	
				016		
James BOLGER		1825	1891	016	_____, Margaret	
Margaret _____ BOLGER		1830	1877	016	BOLGER, James	
James F. BOLGER		1863	1905	016	_____, Maria C.	
Maria C. _____ BOLGER		1860	1925	016	BOLGER, John	
John BOLGER		1851	1865	016	BOLGER, James F.	
Margaret BOLGER		1855	1864	016	BOLGER, Mary	
Mary A. BOLGER		1866	1880	016	BOLGER, Margaret	
Thomas BOLGER		1868	1918	016	BOLGER, Thomas	
				016		
John RYAN		1830	1901	016	KENNA, Sarah	
Sarah KENNA Ryan		1838	1912	016	RYAN, John	
Julia RYAN		1859	1865	016	RYAN, Julia	
John RYAN		1867	1911	016	RYAN, John	
Michael RYAN		1873	1874	016	RYAN, Michael	
Julia A. RYAN		1875	1899	016	RYAN, Ulia A.	
				016		
Ann CONWAY	Co. Clare	40 Years	02-07-1865	016	CONWAY, Ann	Native Of Bridgetown, County Clare, Ireland
				016		
				016		
Thomas H. COSTELLO		1818	1907	016	_____, Catharine M.	
Catharine M. _____ COSTELLO		1823	1906	016	COSTELLO, Thomas H.	
Ellen COSTELLO		1852	1927	016	COSTELLO, Ellen	
John COSTELLO		1864	1943	016	COSTELLO, John	
George COSTELLO		1859	1928	016	COSTELLO, George	
Margaret COSTELLO		1850	1864	016	COSTELLO, Margaret	
Mary COSTELLO		1854	1879	016	COSTELLO, Mary	
James COSTELLO		1856	1864	016	COSTELLO, James	
Charles KREWET		1876	1961	016	_____, Delia	
Delia _____ KREWET		1876	1953	016	KREWET, Charles	
Kathleen BOYCE Dower		1883	1914	016	DOWER, F. P.	(NOI F.P. Dower)
				016	BOYCE, Kathleen	
				016		
Rosamond GALLAGHER		06-15-1830	11-20-1907	016	GALLAGHER, Rosamond	
				016		

James BURKE		3 Years	02-17-1864	016	BURKE, James	
John BURKE		10 Years	04-21-1873	016	BURKE, John	
Mary COLLINS		60 Years	02-11-1875	016	COLLINS, Mary	
Daniel BURKE		1863	1904	016	____, Margaret	
Margaret ____ BURKE		1863	1904	016	BURKE, Daniel	
John BURKE		24 Years	03-04-1882	016	BURKE, John	
				016		
Thomas O'NEILL	Co. Clare	1820	08-23-1899	016	____, Bridget	Born In County Clare, Ireland.
				016	O'NEILL, Thomas	(NOI Bridget)
J. H. O'NEILL		26 Years	06-02-1880	016	O'NEILL, J. H.	Son Of Thomas &Bridget O'Neill
Patrick O'NEILL		5Y 2M	02-16-1864	016	O'NEILL, Patrick	
Katie O'NEILL		10 Years	06-12-1866	016	O'NEILL, Katie	
Patrick O'NEILL		2 Years	09-19-1871	016	O'NEILL, Patrick	
Nellie O'NEILL		7 Years	06-17-1876	016	O'NEILL, Nellie	
				016		
Bridget ENGLISH Moore		1826	1879	016	ENGLISH, Bridget	(NOI Spouse)
Michael MOORE		1830	1900	016	____, Margaret	
Margaret ____ MOORE		1827	1862	016	MOORE, Michael	
Ellen MOORE Dooley		1852	1873	016	MOORE, Ellen	(NOI Mr. Dooley)
James MOORE		1853	1873	016	MOORE, James	
Joseph MOORE		1861	1885	016	MOORE, Joseph	
Mary E. ENGLISH		1846	1928	016	ENGLISH, Mary E.	
John CORRIGAN		1851	1930	016	ENGLISH, Annie	
Annie ENGLISH Corrigan		1853	1934	016	CORRIGAN, John	
				016		
Michael BURKE		1825	1899	016	CAVANAUGH, Anna	
Anna CAVANAUGH Burke		1827	1886	016	BURKE, Michael	
Jane BURKE		1854	1864	016	BURKE, Jane	
Ann BURKE		1851	1864	016	BURKE, Ann	
Mary BURKE		1856	1935	016	BURKE, Mary	
Ellen BURKE		1860	1943	016	BURKE, Ellen	
				016		
Michael CASEY		75 Years	06-11-1879	016	CONNORS, Hannora	Formerly Of South Burlington
Hannora CONNORS Casey		76 Years	02-02-1896	016	CASEY, Michael	
				016		
Maggie CASEY		10 Years	09-20-1863	016	CASEY, Maggie	Dau Of Michael & Hannora Casey
Mary CASEY				016	CASEY, Mary	(NOI DOB-DOD)
				016		
James HAYES		12-13-1854	09-05-1863	016	HAYES, James	
Jennie HAYES		10-12-1869	11-04-1871	016	HAYES, Jennie	
Patrick HAYES		1828	1906	016	____, Katherine	
Katherine ____ HAYES		69 Years	07-07-1890	016	HAYES, Patrick	
Nellie L. HAYES		10-19-1867	12-22-1890	016	HAYES, Nellie L.	
Mary A. HAYES		04-__-1865	02-04-1887	016	HAYES, Mary A.	(Day of Birth is 09 or 03)
				016		

Name	Born	Died	Code	Spouse/Relation	Notes
Patrick FITZSIMMONS	1845	1918	016	BARRY, Bridget	
Bridget BARRY Fitzsimmons	1852	1895	016	FITZSIMMONS, Patrick	
John M. FITZSIMMONS	1879	1947	016	SULLIVAN, Mary	
Mary SULLIVAN Fitzsimmons	1871	1932	016	FITZSIMMONS, John M.	
Mary STAY	1857	1921	016	STAY, Mary	
			016		
Thomas MOORE	1839	1916	016	DOWER, Ellen	
Ellen DOWER Moore	1850	1920	016	MOORE, Thomas	
			016		
James H. FARRELL	1838	1913	016	DUFFEY, Mary	
Mary DUFFEY Farrell	1857	1928	016	FARRELL, James H.	
			016		
James O'NEILL	1844	1922	016	CASEY, Mary A.	
Mary A. CASEY O'Neill	1861	1943	016	O'NEILL, James	
			016		
John NASH	93 Years	02-12-1911	016	_____, Jane	
Jane _____ NASH	53 Years	07-24-1886	016	NASH, John	
Mary J. NASH		08-22-1863	016	NASH, Mary J.	(NOI DOB)
Patrick NASH		05-__-1867	016	NASH, Patrick	(NOI DOB or Day of Death)
James NASH		08-__-1868	016	NASH, James	(NOI DOB or Day of Death)
Martin NASH		10-__-1869	016	NASH, Martin	(NOI DOB or Day of Death)
Richard NASH		02-__-1870	016	NASH, Richard	(NOI DOB or Day of Death)
Mary NASH		07-__-1869	016	NASH, Mary	(NOI DOB or Day of Death)
James NASH		02-07-1870	016	NASH, James	(NOI DOB)
Patrick NASH		02-01-1876	016	NASH, Patrick	(NOI DOB)
			016		
Patrick SHEEHAN	1836	1921	016	_____, Bridget	
Bridget _____ SHEEHAN	1847	1907	016	SHEEHAN, Patrick	
			016		
Patrick DILLON	1824	1884	016	BOYLAN, Mary	
Mary BOYLAN Dillon	1846	1924	016	DILLON, Patrick	
			016		
James GALVIN	1833	1917	016	SPLAIN, Bridget	
Bridget SPLAIN Galvin	1839	1918	016	GALVIN, James	
			016		
William H. HOYT JR	04-10-1851	02-14-1914	016	HOYT, William H. Jr.	
Jennie F. HOYT	03-26-1841	12-15-1913	016	HOYT, Jennie F.	
			016		
Nathaniel Amory TUCKER	08-12-1811	02-25-1873	016	DEMING, Maria	Brevet LtCol, USA. Born In Milton, VT. Died At Burlington, VT.
			016		
			016		
Maria DEMING Tucker	03-10-1817	07-20-1904	016	TUCKER, Nathaniel Amory	
			016		
Fanny FOLLETT Deming	06-19-1788	03-14-1878	016	DEMING, Eleazer	Born In Bennington. Died at Burlington (VT).(NOI Eleazer
			016	FOLLETT, Fanny	

Name	Birth	Death	Code	Relation	Notes
			016		Deming)
George Aloysuis HOYT	12-14-1852	03-14-1871	016	HOYT, George Aloysuis	Son Of William Henry and Anne Deming Hoyt
Rev. William H. HOYT	01-08-1813	12-11-1883	016	DEMING, Anne	Born Sandwich, NH. Died at New York City. Received into Catholic Church In 1846. Ordained (to Catholic Priest-hood) 05-26-1877. (He was an Episcopal Minister in Saint Albans, VT. Converted 1846. Became Priest after death of wife. Not Irish but a friend of the immigrant)
Anne DEMING Hoyt	07-21-1819	01-16-1875	016	HOYT, Rev. William H.	Born Burlington, VT. Died at New York City.
Julia SCAMMON Hoyt	01-10-1850	09-14-1899	016	HOYT, Francis SCAMMON, Julia	Dau Of E. Parker and Margaret Stebbins Scammon (NOI Francis Hoyt)
Charles Albert HOYT	07-29-1839	04-18-1903	016	SHERMAN, Julia	Born Burlington, VT. Died at Pasadena, CA
Julia SHERMAN Hoyt	03-31-1834	10-29-1905	016	HOYT, Charles Albert	Born At Sandwich, NH. Died at Brooklyn, NY. Wife of Charles A. Hoyt and Daughter Of Enoch & Julia Hoit Sherman
Martin CLARK		06-25-1899	016	CORLEY, Bridget	(NOI DOB)
Bridget CORLEY Clark		09-17-1920	016	CLARK, Martin	(NOI DOB)
Thomas CUSHING	07-09-1832	06-21-1912	016	CORCORAN, Margaret	
Margaret CORCORAN Cushing	11-12-1853	01-06-1903	016	CUSHING, Thomas	
Richard CUSHING	05-10-1834	08-14-1896	016	SHEA, Johanna	
Johanna SHEA Cushing	1841	1923	016	CUSHING, Richard	
Edward SHERIDAN	50 Years	10-22-1903	016	SPLAIN, Ellen	
Ellen SPLAIN Sheridan	51 Years	07-24-1907	016	SHERIDAN, Edward	
James HENNIGAN	62 Years	07-22-1890	016	_____, Bridget	
Bridget _____ HENNIGAN	84 Years	01-10-1903	016	HENNIGAN, James	
Mary HENNIGAN	28 Years	10-29-1885	016	HENNIGAN, Mary	

Name	Origin	Born/Age	Died	Code	Index	Notes
Bridget HENNIGAN		1859	1938	016	HENNIGAN, Bridget	
Thomas HENNIGAN		33 Years	01-18-1894	016	BEIRNE, Margaret T.	
Margaret T. BEIRNE Hennigan		76 Years	04-24-1936	016	HENNIGAN, Thomas	
				016		
Patrick FILBON		85 Years	12-12-1896	016	GILL, Mary	
Mary GILL Filbon		83 Years	09-18-1910	016	FILBON, Patrick	
				016		
Mary FILBON Farrell		02-06-1853	03-01-1882	016	FARRELL, Philip	Born In Burlington (VT). (NOI
				016		Philip Farrell)
				016		
James D. MCCARTHY		1851	1926	016	_____, Anna B.	
Anna B. _____ MCCARTHY		1853	1932	016	MCCARTHY, James D.	
				016		
James Edmund BURKE		1849	1943	016	O'ROURKE, Sarah	
Sarah O'ROURKE Burke		1849	1926	016	BURKE, James Edmund	
				016		
Patrick MCGRATH		1827	1900	016	GARVEY, Margaret	
Margaret GARVEY McGrath		1828	1895	016	MCGRATH, Patrick	
				016		
Jeremiah NOONAN		62Y06M03D	06-09-1901	016	CLAREY, Margaret	
Margaret CLAREY Noonan		1847	1932	016	NOONAN, Jeremiah	
				016		
Patrick CLARK	Co. Longford	03-14-1827	12-24-1918	016	BARRY, Margaret	Born In Co. Longford, Ireland
Margaret BARRY	Co. Cork	50 Years	06-27-1890	016	CLARK, Patrick	Native of Fermoy, Co. Cork,
				016		Ireland.
Mary Ann CLARK		9Y 10M	08-27-1861	016	CLARK, Mary Ann	
Patrick William CLARK		1Y 21M	08-21-1863	016	CLARK, Patrick William	
James Richard CLARK		10-31-1856	03-17-1886	016	CLARK, James Richard	
Charles Henry CLARK		03-01-1853	02-23-1925	016	CLARK, Charles Henry	
				016		
Michael SHAHEN		1815	1900	016	BARRY, Bridget	
Bridget BARRT Shahen		1813	1887	016	SHAHEN, Michael	
Harry LEONARD		1862	1929	016	SHAHEN, Bridget	
Bridget SHAHEN Leonard		1858	1940	016	LEONARD, Harry	
				016		
Joseph AHEARN		60 Years	05-01-1880	016	MURPHY, Mary	
Mary MURPHY Ahearn		75 Years	11-15-1890	016	AHEARN, Joseph	
John AHEARN		6 Years	09-22-1863	016	AHEARN, John	
				016		
Bernard GALLAGHER		1812	1897	016	MCDONOUGH, Anna	
Anna MCDONOUGH Gallagher		1816	1899	016	GALLAGHER, Bernard	
Elizabeth GALLAGHER		1857	1861	016	GALLAGHER, Elizabeth	
Mary GALLAGHER		1847	1897	016	GALLAGHER, Mary	
				016		
Patrick HOGAN		76 Years	08-03-1875	016	DWYER, Mary	(Also a Catherine on stone -

				016		deteriorated - can not read)
Mary DWYER Hogan		80 Years	03-20-1897	016	HOGAN, Patrick	
Bridget HOGAN		76 Years	03-04-1895	016	HOGAN, Bridget	
				016		
Patrick GILLULEY		36 Years	10-15-1879	016	GILLULEY, Patrick	
				016		
DELANEY-CLARK				016		
Thomas Alban DELANEY		1862	1928	016	CLARK, Mary	
Mary CLARK Delaney		1863	1935	016	DELANEY, Thomas Alban	
Honora _____ CLARK		27 Years	03-22-1862	016	CLARK, Michael	
Daniel CLARK		6 Months	01-04-1862	016	CLARK, Daniel	
Michael CLARK		60 Years	01-04-1892	016	_____, Honora	
Alice GORMLEY Clark		70 Years	09-26-1903	016	CLARK, Michael	
Annie CLARK		14 Days	04-07-1867	016	CLARK, Annie	
Nellie CLARK		4 Years	03-21-1876	016	CLARK, Nellie	
				016		
Kate READY		1849	1932	016	READY, Kate	
				016		
Bridget READY				016	READY, Bridget	Dau Of Patrick & Hanora Ready.
				016		(Very old stone. Can not read)
				016		
John FINNESSEY		65 Years	06-02-1911	016	FINNESSEY, John	Son Of John Finnessey
				016		
Michael FINNESSEY		53 Years	09-16-1895	016	FINNESSEY, Michael	Son Of John Finnessey
				016		
Catherine _____ WALKER		24 Years	03-15-1861	016	WALKER, Henry	(NOI Henry Walker-stone
				016	_____, Catherine	damaged)
				016		
Mary O'LEARY Noonan	Co. Wexford	03-10-1833	04-16-1878	016	NOONAN, J.	Born In Co. Wexford, Ireland
				016	O'LEARY, Mary	(NOI J. Noonan)
				016		
Martin O'HALLORAN	Co. Clare	1838	04-08-1915	016	O'HALLORAN Mrs. Martin	Born In County Clare, Ireland
				016		(On Heimonicker stone)
				016		
Mrs. Martin O'HALLORAN	Co. Limerick	70 Years	07-14-1905	016	O'HALLORAN, Martin	Born In Newtown, Limerick
				016		Ireland
				016		
Michael COLLINS	Co. Limerick	86 Years	07-15-1886	016	_____, Johannah	Native of Newtown,Co. Limerick
				016		(YOD could be 1860-stone worn)
Johannah _____ COLLINS		80 Years	09-23-1880	016	COLLINS, Michael	(Age at death could be 80)
				016		
Michael COLLINS	Co. Limerick	1844	04-12-1915	016	BYRNES, Catherine	Native of Co.Limerick, Ireland
Catherine BYRNES	Co. Limerick	93 Years	05-03-1945	016	COLLINS, Michael	Native of Co.Limerick, Ireland
				016		
				016		

Name	Place	Birth/Age	Death	Code	Spouse/Relation	Notes
Thomas E. DOOLEY		1847	1928	016	PICKETT, Anna M.	
Anna M. PICKETT Dooley				016	DOOLEY, Thomas E.	(NOI DOB/DOD Anna M. Pickett)
				016		
John W. HENRY		33 Years	01-02-1883	016	_____, Annie	(NOI Annie)
				016		
John MCHUGO		06-20-1824	02-27-1887	016	WARD, Winnifred	Born In Ireland
Winnifred WARD McHugo		1825	1911	016	MCHUGO, John	
Margaret MCHUGO		1851	1919	016	MCHUGO, Margaret	
Thomas MCHUGO		1856	1893	016	MCHUGO, Thomas	
Bridget MCHUGO		1866	1895	016	MCHUGO, Bridget	
Ellen A. MCHUGO		1864	1953	016	MCHUGO, Ellen A.	
				016		
Rev. John C. MCLAUGHLIN		1845	1928	016	MCLAUGHLIN, Rev. John	
James MCLAUGHLIN		1805	1871	016	_____, Ann	
Ann _____ MCLAUGHLLIN		1813	1865	016	MCLAUGHLIN, James	
Mary A. MCLAUGHLIN			1899	016	MCLAUGHLIN, Mary A.	(NOI DOB)
James MCLAUGHLIN JR		1843	1865	016	MCLAUGHLIN, James Jr.	
Margaret MCLAUGHLIN			1906	016	MCLAUGHLIN, Margaret	(NOI DOB)
				016		
Patrick J. MAXWELL			12-26-1872	016	MAXWELL, Patrick J.	(NOI DOB)
				016		
John FROSE	Co. Clare	53 Years	08-04-1871	016	FROSE, John	Native of Co. Clare, Ireland
				016		
Mary KING	Co. Mayo	18 Years	10-24-1861	016	KING, Mary	Turanion (Tiraninny),Co. Mayo, Ireland. Dau of Joseph King. (As close as I can get with a possible town name)
				016		
				016		
				016		
				016		
Robert J. BROWN		1841	1917	016	_____, Catherine D.	
Catherine D. _____ BROWN		1854	1922	016	BROWN, Robert J.	
				016		
Garrett M. COSGRIFF		1851	1922	016	COYNE, Margaret M.	
				016	_____, Winifred A.	
Margaret M. COYNE Cosgriff		1870	1929	016	COSGRIFF, Garrett M.	
Winifred A. _____ COSGRIFF		38Y 1M	08-06-18__	016	COSGRIFF, Garrett M.	(Cannot read year of death)
				016		
Jeremiah O'BRIEN		1820	1910	016	_____, Catherine	
Catherine _____ O'BRIEN		74 Years	11-25-1887	016	O'BRIEN, Jeremiah	
Jeremiah O'BRIEN		33 Years	10-19-1890	016	O'BRIEN, Jeremiah	
				016		
Michael MULQUEEN			09-26-1876	016	MCAVOY, Ann	(NOI DOB)
Ann MCAVOY Mulqueen			08-11-1905	016	MULQUEEN, Michael	(NOI DOB)
				016		
Edward JOHNSON		1781	1860	016	MCKENNA, Susan	
Susan MCKENNA Johnson		1783	1867	016	JOHNSON, Edward	

Thomas JOHNSON	1827	1908	016	JOHNSON, Thomas	(GAR)Pvt Co F. 13th Vt Vol Inf
			016		
Michael DONAHUE	61 Years	12-01-1865	016	BOYLE, Mary	
Mary BOYLE Donahue	57 Years	01-06-1861	016	DONAHUE, Michael	
			016		
Francis MCKANNA	1833	1878	016	_____, Catherine	
Catherine _____ MCKANNA	1825	1908	016	MCKANNA, Francis	
			016		
Bridget MILLEN McWilliam		12-29-1894	016	MCWILLIAM, Michael	Wife Of The Late Michael McWilliam. (NOI DOB)
			016		
			016		
Thomas LEONARD		04-19-1873	016	_____, Bridget	
Bridget _____ LEONARD	24Y 6M	10-18-1873	016	LEONARD, Thomas	
			016		
Thomas CUMMINGS	1814	1886	016	POWERS, Catherine	
Catherine POWERS Cummings	1816	1904	016	CUMMINGS, Thomas	
Anna CUMMINGS	1858	1860	016	CUMMINGS, Anna	
Johanna E. CUMMINGS	1850	1896	016	CUMMINGS, Johanna E.	
			016		
Mary GRACE Cain	70 Years	10-01-1862	016	GRACE, Mary	(NOI Mr. Cain)
			016		
James CAIN	45 Years	NOV 1870	016	MARONEY, Fanny	
Fanny MARONEY Cain	1830	1900	016	CAIN, James	
			016		
CANNON/SHERIDAN			016		
James J. CANNON	1855	1926	016	SHERIDAN, Mary	
Mary SHERIDAN Cannon	1855	1930	016	CANNON, James J.	
			016		
John SHERIDAN	1851	1937	016	SHERIDAN, John	
			016		
Patrick SHERIDAN	75 Years	09-13-1896	016	_____, Catherine	
Catherine _____ SHERIDAN	68 Years	04-08-1882	016	SHERIDAN, Patrick	
			016		
John H. BAIRD	1852	1886	016	BAIRD, John H.	
			016		
Daniel MCAVOY	1818	1901	016	_____, Bridget	
Bridget _____ MCAVOY	1817	1886	016	MCAVOY, Daniel	
John E. MCAVOY	1851	1887	016	MCAVOY, John E.	(Does not indicate relationship between John & Bridget)
Bridget MCAVOY	1862	1888	016	MCAVOY, Bridget	
			016		
Patrick D. MILLS	1861	1932	016	HAYES, Elizabeth	
Elizabeth HAYES Mills	1856	1929	016	MILLS, Patrick D.	
			016		
Thomas SKAHEN	26 Years	09-01-1885	016	SKAHEN, Thomas	Died In Winooski (VT)
Nora SKAHEN		04-19-1885	016	SKAHEN, Nora	Died In WInooski (VT)

Lilie SKAHEN			07-01-1884	016	SKAHEN, Lilie	
				016		
Patrick SPILLANE		38 Years	03-06-1896	016	SPILLANE, Patrick	The Beloved Son Of John D. &
				016		Honora Spillane. Died In
				016		Winooski (VT)
				016		
John D. SPILLANE	Co. Kerry	82 Years	09-13-1888	016	SULLIVAN, Honora	Born In the Parish of Tahala,
				016		Co. Kerry, Ireland (No such
				016		Parish. Probably Tahilla Town
				016		in Parish Kilcrohane) Died In
				016		Winooski (VT)
Honora SULLIVAN Spillane	Co. Kerry	69 Years	10-22-1888	016	SPILLANE, John D.	Born In The Parish Of Tahala,
				016		Co. Kerry, Ireland (No such
				016		Parish. Probably Tahilla Town
				016		in Parish Kilcrohane)(Erected
				016		By Their Son Patrick) Died In
				016		Winooski (VT)
				016		
Ellen SPILLANE Mahoney		37 Years	12-09-1893	016	SPILLANE, Ellen	Daughter Of John D. & Honora
				016		Spillane.Died in Winooski (VT)
				016		(NOI Mr. Mahoney)
				016		
Patrick GLEASON		03-17-1816	07-28-1898	016	KENNEDY, Bridget	
Bridget KENNEDY Gleason		02-02-1823	04-12-1899	016	GLEASON, Patrick	
				016		
Patrick DOWNS		1837	1916	016	BROWN, Bridget	
Bridget BROWN Downs		1846	1915	016	DOWNS, Patrick	
				016		
Bryan FOLEY		76 Years	12-17-1900	016	FLANNELLY, Ann	
Ann FLANNELLY Foley		39 Years	07-03-1860	016	FOLEY, Bryan	
				016		
Patrick DONLAN		1829	1881	016	KANE, Mary Ann	
Mary Ann KANE Donlan		1833	1906	016	DONLAN, Patrick	
				016		
Edward P. MCELLIGOTT				016	SMITH, Mary E.	(NOI DOB/DOD)
Mary E. SMITH McElligott				016	MCELLIGOTT, Edward P.	(NOI DOB/DOD)
Bessie M. MCELLIGOTT				016	MCELLIGOTT, Bessie M.	(NOI DOB/DOD)
Leo E. MCELLIGOTT				016	MCELLIGOTT, Leo E.	(NOI DOB/DOD)
Peter SMITH				016	FARMER, Catherine	(NOI DOB/DOD)
Catherine FARMER Smith				016	SMITH, Peter	(NOI DOB/DOD)
William SMITH				016	SMITH, William	(NOI DOB/DOD)
John SMITH				016	SMITH, John	(NOI DOB/DOD)
Anna M. SMITH				016	SMITH, Anna M.	(NOI DOB/DOD)
				016		
John O'DONNELL		42 Years	01-25-1859	016	_____, Margaret	

Name	Origin	Birth/Age	Death	Code	Spouse	Notes
Margaret _____ O'DONNELL		46 Years	05-26-1864	016	O'DONNELL, John	
				016		
Daniel WALL		01-05-1839	02-14-1907	016	MITTEN, Margaret	
Margaret MITTEN Wall			1872	016	WALL, Daniel	(NOI DOB)
				016		
Mary CROWE		24 Years	1859	016	CROWE, Mary	
Bridget CROWE		90 Years	05-17-1906	016	CROWE, Bridget	
				016		
James FALLON		98 Years	05-30-1897	016	NUGENT, Sarah	
				016	FITZGERALD, Katie	
Sarah NUGENT Fallon		34 Years	02-11-1838	016	FALLON, James	
Katie FITZGERALD Fallon		86 Years	01-11-1883	016	FALLON, James	
				016		
Michael MCKENZIE		70 Years	06-19-1917	016	LANG, Bridget Mary	(GAR) Sgt Co. F 6th Regt VT Inf
				016		
Bridget Mary LANG McKenzie		10-13-1848	08-04-1903	016	MCKENZIE, Michael	Born In Burlington (VT)
				016		
Thomas HENRY	Co. Sligo	64 Years	08-15-1887	016	GILLULEY, Sarah	Born In Co. Sligo, Ireland
Sarah GILLULEY Henry	Co. Roscommon	72 Years	05-17-1901	016	HENRY, Thomas	Born In Co. Roscommon, Ireland
				016		
Michael O'KEEFE		34 Years	08-04-1882	016	FLOOD, Mary	
Mary FLOOD O'Keefe		26 Years	10-12-1882	016	O'KEEFE, Michael	
				016		
Charles S. GREEN		1852	1888	016	MCGREEVY, Jane A.	
Jane A. MCGREEVY		1852	1932	016	GREEN, Charles S.	
Margaret C. MCGREEVY		1830	1915	016	MCGREEVY, Margaret C.	
				016		
Thomas LEONARD		1830	1902	016	BARRETT, Catherine	
Catherine BARRETT Leonard		1840	1921	016	LEONARD, Thomas	
				016		
Katie MCFARLAND Flynn		27 Years	11-03-1877	016	FLYNN, David O.	
				016		
Michael FLYNN	Co. Cork	74 Years	02-24-1892	016	_____, Ellen	Native of Co. Cork, Ireland
Ellen _____ FLYNN		83 Years	06-25-1904	016	FLYNN, Michael	
				016		
Catherine _____ FLYNN	Co. Cork	73 Years	05-03-1859	016	FLYNN, David	A Native of Co. Cork, Ireland (NOI David Flynn)
				016		
				016		
John BOYLE		74 Years	02-24-1892	016	BOYLE, John	
Katherine J. BOYLE		1868	1929	016	BOYLE, Katherine J.	
Helen E. BOYLE		1874	1935	016	BOYLE, Helen E.	
Anthony BOYLE		1834	1958	016	BOYLE, Anthony	
				016		
Kittie M. BOYLE Foster		07-17-1862	08-24-1891	016	FOSTER, H. S.	(NOI H. S. Foster)
				016		

Name	Origin	Born/Age	Died	Code	Relation	Notes
James H. MURRAY		1823	1892	016	CORLEY, Mary	
Mary CORLEY Murray		1824	1906	016	MURRAY, James H.	
Mary J. MURRAY		1858	1889	016	MURRAY, Mary J.	
				016		
William DENNING		1837	1901	016	ELLIOTT, Caroline	
Caroline ELLIOTT Denning		1837	1906	016	DENNING, William	
				016		
Robert MCLAUGHLIN		75 Years	10-11-1907	016	MCDURMOND, Jane	
Jane MCDURMOND McLaughlin		52 Years	09-12-1890	016	MCLAUGHLIN, Robert	
				016		
Maria HOGAN Corley		1826	1904	016	CORLEY, M. B.	(NOI M.B. Corley)
				016		
Thomas PASHBY		1844	1908	016	PASHBY, Thomas	(GAR) Co. D. 61st N.Y. Vol
				016		
Margaret _____ BURKE	Co. Clare	80 Years	02-15-1877	016	BURKE, William	Born In Co. Clare, Ireland. (NOI William Burke) (Age at death reads "about 80 Years")
				016		
				016		
				016		
Patrick MCGREEVY		03-25-1851	07-02-1923	016	BURKE, Margaret E.	Born In Beekmantown, NY,. Died in Winooski (VT)
				016		
Margaret E. BURKE McGreevy	Co. Mayo	03-12-1849	07-21-1883	016	BURKE, William	Born In Co. Mayo, Ire. Died in Winooski (VT)
				016		
				016		
Mary _____ SOURDIFF		60 Years	10-24-1911	016	SOURDIFF, Peter	(NOI Peter Sourdiff)
				016		
Daniel SHEEHAN		1814	1898	016	_____, Joanna	
Joanna _____ SHEEHAN		1816	1901	016	SHEEHAN, Daniel	
				016		
Patrick HENLEY		85 Years	11-20-1909	016	_____, Bridget	
Bridget _____ HENLEY		77 Years	01-12-1903	016	HENLEY, Patrick	
Patrick HENLEY JR		10-02-1857	05-31-1894	016	HENLEY, Patrick Jr.	
Thomas HENLEY		77 Years	03-22-1894	016	HENLEY, Thomas	About 77 Years
Bridget HENLEY		1854	1898	016	HENLEY, Bridget	
John HENLEY		1878	1880	016	HENLEY, John	
				016		
Thomas ROACH		58 Years	08-14-1871	016	_____, Bridget	(NOI Bridget)
				016	ROACH, Thomas	
John ROACH		6 Years	08-21-1858	016	ROACH, John	Son Of Thomas & Bridget Roach
William ROACH			01-11-1898	016	_____, Anna	(NOI Anna A.)
				016	ROACH, William	
Anna A. ROACH		6 Years	08-21-1858	016	ROACH, Anna A.	Dau Of William & Anna Roach
				016		
Maurice BYRNES		1818	1892	016	DILLON, Ellen	
				016	FOX, Margaret	
Ellen DILLON Byrnes		1826	1861	016	BYRNES, Maurice	

Margaret FOX Byrnes	1829	1910	016	BYRNES, Maurice	
Edward BYRNES	1854	1864	016	BYRNES, Edward	His Son
			016		
Patrick CONNORS	26 Years	08-15-1853	016	CONNORS, Patrick	
			016		
Ann CONNORS	83 Years	03-29-1900	016	CONNORS, Ann	
			016		
Edward RUSH	1823	1886	016	BARRETT, Joanna	
Joanna BARRETT Rush	1835	1921	016	RUSH, Edward	
Edward J. RUSH	1856	1862	016	RUSH, Edward J.	
George L. RUSH	1858	1861	016	RUSH, George L.	
			016		
Richard D. TURNER	1845	1919	016	_____, Elizabeth	
Elizabeth _____ TURNER	1845	1927	016	TURNER, Richard D.	
Mary J. BUTLER	1828	1892	016	BUTLER, Mary J.	
			016		
Patrick FARRELL	1842	1920	016	CONNELL, Mary	
Mary CONNELL Farrell	1842	1905	016	FARRELL, Patrick	
			016		
Michael CURTIS	1852	1928	016	_____, Anna W.	
Anna W. _____ CURTIS	1859	1936	016	CURTIS, Michael	
			016		
James MCKENZIE	1834	1912	016	_____, Ellen	
Ellen _____ MCKENZIE	1848	1924	016	MCKENZIE, James	
			016		
Horace BABCOCK	88 Years	12-04-1908	016	_____, Mary	
Mary _____ BABCOCK	76 Years	11-15-1897	016	BABCOCK, Horace	
			016		
Richard BURKE	1843	1927	016	O'NEIL, Anna C.	
Anna C. O'NEIL Burke	1849	1935	016	BURKE, Richard	
			016		
J. H. MCCAFFREY	1857	1929	016	MCDONALD, Emma	
Emma MCDONALD McCaffrey			016	MCCAFFREY, J. H.	(NOI Emma McDonald McCaffrey)
			016		
Michael O'BRIEN	1854	1930	016	POWERS, Sarah	
Sarah POWERS O'Brien	1860	1913	016	O'BRIEN, Michael	
			016		
Simon BULLOCK	03-16-1843	10-10-1931	016	_____, Sarah	
Sarah _____ BULLOCK	05-11-1845	10-10-1898	016	BULLOCK, Simon	
			016		
Nellie A. RENIHAN		05-28-1935	016	RENIHAN, Nellie A.	(NOI DOB)
Lauretta R. RENIHAN		05-18-1947	016	RENIHAN, Lauretta R.	(NOI DOB)
			016		
John S. MURPHY	68 Years	09-04-1903	016	_____, Ann R.	
Ann R. _____ MURPHY		1916	016	MURPHY, John S.	(NOI DOB)

Name	Place	Born	Died	Code	Index	Notes
				016		
Michael ENRIGHT		1858	1930	016	HYLAND, Anna	
Anna HYLAND Enright		1858	1937	016	ENRIGHT, Michael	
				016		
Edward NASH	Co. Limerick	48 Years	05-27-1858	016	NASH, Edward	Born At _______ Co. Limerick, Ireland. (Stone is damaged)
				016		
David E. FLYNN		1849	1927	016	BREWIN, Ellen	
Ellen BREWIN Flynn		1855	1914	016	FLYNN, David E.	
				016		
Melvin J. EARLEY		1849	1927	016	O'HARA, Catherine J.	
Catherine J. O'HARA Earley		1855	1914	016	EARLEY, Melvin J.	
				016		
Lucilla Frances O'SULLIVAN			05-23-1934	016	SWEENEY, Walter D.	(NOI Walter D. Sweeney)
				016		
Joseph SULLIVAN		83 Years	03-09-1924	016	_____, Ann J.	
Ann J. _____ SULLIVAN		65 Years	01-01-1911	016	SULLIVAN, Joseph	
				016		
Margaret BANAGAN		1843	1915	016	BANAGAN, Margaret	
				016		
Patrick CASSIDY		1821	1904	016	MCDONOUGH, Lucy	
Lucy MCDONOUGH Cassidy		1825	1860	016	CASSIDY, Patrick	
Luke CASSIDY		1858	1903	016	CASSIDY, Luke	
Annie CASSIDY		1868	1882	016	CASSIDY, Annie	
				016		
John CLARK		06-24-1821	10-06-1899	016	MCDONOUGH, Bridget	
Bridget MCDONOUGH Clark		09-20-1832	10-23-1878	016	CLARK, John	
Mary Jane CLARK		03-09-1856	10-23-1900	016	CLARK, Mary Jane	
Anne CLARK Bullard		1854	1924	016	CLARK, Anne	(NOI Mr. Bullard)
				016		
Joseph LAUZON		1830	1909	016	CAVANAUGH, Ann	
Ann CAVANAUGH Lauzon		1842	1914	016	LAUZON, Joseph	
				016		
Walter HOY		90 Years	10-12-1931	016	_____, Elizabeth M.	
Elizabeth M. _____ HOY		64 Years	12-22-1900	016	HOY, Walter	
				016		
Hugh J. WHYTE		1819	1883	016	WOOD, Mary Anne	
Mary Anne WOOD Whyte		1823	1905	016	WHYTE, Hugh J.	
Catherine M. WHYTE		1857	1923	016	WHYTE, Catherine M.	
Maria WHYTE		1862	1932	016	WHYTE, Maria	
R. Amanda WHYTE		1866	1931	016	WHYTE, R. Amanda	
				016		
Frank WARD		66 Years	11-22-1909	016	_____, Mary E.	(GAR) Co. H 2nd Reg VT Vols (GAR stone says 1846-1909)
				016		
Mary E. _____ WARD		1845	1917	016	WARD, Frank	
				016		

John BRESNEHAN		1849	1884	016	KIERNAN, Ellen	
Ellen KIERNAN Bresnehan		1853	1910	016	BRESNEHAN, John	
				016		
Mary MOYLAN	Co. Tipperary		03-02-1911	016	MOYLAN, Mary	(NOI DOB)Born In Co. Tipperary
John MOYLAN			12-16-1919	016	MOYLAN, Margaret	(NOI DOB)
Margaret MOYLAN			10-03-1908	016	MOYLAN, John	(NOI DOB)
				016		
Edward HYNES		1854	1922	016	CROWLEY, Julia C.	
Julia C. CROWLEY Hynes		1854	1939	016	HYNES, Edward	
				016		
George H. BABCOCK		1851	1902	016	BREWIN, Anna	
Anna BREWIN Babcock		1857	1929	016	BABCOCK, George H.	
				016		
Thomas WALSH		1831	1901	016	DOWNEY, Margaret	
Margaret DOWNEY Walsh		1837	1910	016	WALSH, Thomas	
Bridget WALSH Bullock			08-05-1894	016	BULLOCK, Simon	(No Simon Bullock this plot.
				016		See preceding entry)
Thomas WALSH			1868	016	WALSH, Thomas	Infant
James WALSH		18 Years	01-31-1898	016	WALSH, James	
Bridget DOWNEY		33 Years	10-14-1868	016	DOWNEY, Bridget	
				016		
Patrick P. KENNEDY		53 Years	06-16-1900	016	KENNEDY, Patrick P.	
				016		
John MURRIN		1831	1912	016	MCGINLEY, Mary	
Mary MCGINLEY Murrin		1838	1921	016	MURRIN, John	
				016		
Margaret MCGINLEY		1846	1917	016	MCGINLEY, Margaret	
				016		
Patrick HYLAND		1807	1873	016	QUINN, Hannah	
Hannah QUINN Hyland		1820	1915	016	HYLAND, Patrick	
Mary HYLAND		1848	1918	016	HYLAND, Mary	
Michael HYLAND		1852	1928	016	HYLAND, Michael	
Margaret HYLAND		1841	1929	016	HYLAND, Margaret	
				016		
William W. WHEELER		1856	1918	016	_____, Julia A.	
Julia A. _____ WHEELER		1857	1899	016	WHEELER, William W.	
				016		
James E. MILES		1848	1919	016	ROONEY, Elizabeth	
Elizabeth ROONEY Miles		1849	1908	016	MILES, James E.	
				016		
John LAVELLE		42 Years	03-13-1893	016	MURPHY, Mary Ann	
Mary Ann MURPHY Lavelle		85 Years	01-24-1943	016	LAVELLE, John	
Jane MURPHY		1863	1949	016	MURPHY, Jane	Sister
				016		
Thomas F. AHEARN		1852	1915	016	BURKE, Bridget	

Name	Born	Died		Spouse / Index	Notes
Bridget BURKE Ahearn	18__	1899	016	AHEARN, Thomas F.	
			016		
John KELLEY	1836	1905	016	KENNEDY, Catharine	
Catharine KENNEDY Kelley	1846	1919	016	KELLEY, John	
Helen F. KENNEDY Bears	1859	1898	016	BEARS, A. P.	Beloved Sister(NOI A.P. Bears)
			016		
Patrick DWYER	07-28-1838	02-01-1896	016	MCSWEENEY, Margaret	
Margaret MCSWEENEY Dwyer	99 Years	03-08-1937	016	DWYER, Patrick	
			016		
Nelson BACON	1830	1899	016	LANGAN, Catherine A.	
Catherine A. LANGAN Bacon	1832	1900	016	BACON, Nelson	
			016		
John J. MCLAUGHLIN	1855	1933	016	PAYNE, Anna	
Anna PAYNE McLaughlin	1854		016	MCLAUGHLIN, John J.	(NOI DOD)
			016		
Julia A. SEXTON Delaney	1854	1900	016	DELANEY, G. M.	(NOI G. M. Delaney)
			016		
Susan MULHERON Donahue	1852	1915	016	MULHERON, Susan	(NOI Mr. Donahue)
Mary MATTIMORE	1810	1900	016	MATTIMORE, Mary	
Eliza A. MATTIMORE	1842	1910	016	MATTIMORE, Eliza A.	
Thomas F. MULHERON	1852	1929	016	MATTIMORE, Sarah M.	
Sarah M. MATTIMORE Mulheron	1854	1926	016	MULHERON, Thomas F.	
			016		
John O'SULLIVAN	1826	1898	016	MCAVOY, Margaret	
Margaret MCAVOY O'Sullivan	1833	1894	016	O'SULLIVAN, John	
Rev. William Joseph O'SULLIVAN	1855	1915	016	O'SULLIVAN, Rev William	Ordained 1880
Rev. Daniel Joseph O'SULLIVAN	1853	1918	016	O'SULLIVAN, Rev Daniel	Ordained 1876
			016		
Albert J. GRAHAM	1839	1899	016	READY, Ellen	CPL, Co. E. 12th Regt USA
Ellen READY Graham	1839	1909	016	GRAHAM, Albert J.	
			016		
John F. BARABY	10-10-1839	08-21-1903	016	CUMMINGS, Margaret	
Margaret CUMMINGS Baraby	05-17-1849	01-09-1913	016	BARABY, John F.	
			016		
John MULQUEEN	1857	1932	016	DONAHUE, Mary E.	
Mary E. DONAHUE Mulqueen	1857	1908	016	MULQUEEN, John	
			016		
Moses L. SANBORN	1853	1911	016	LACEY, Catherine	
Catherine LACEY Sanborn	1863	1949	016	SANBORN, Moses L.	
			016		
James MCCAFFREY	1834	1898	016	CAVANAGH, Katherine	
Katherine CAVANAGH McCaffrey	1843	1929	016	MCCAFFREY, James	
			016		
Alexander MCDOWELL	05-01-1840		016	MACKEY, Anna	(NOI DOD)
Anna MACKEY McDowell	01-02-1837	11-26-1920	016	MCDOWELL, Alexander	

Name	Birth	Death	Code	Spouse/Relation	Notes
			016		
Michael KELLY	1786	1861	016	WALSH, Mary	
Mary WALSH Kelly	1800	1849	016	KELLY, Michael	
John E. KELLY	1825	1893	016	HARTT, Margaret	
Margaret HARTT Kelly	1834	1893	016	KELLY, John E.	
			016		
Peter DEVEREAUX	11-02-1852	12-02-1903	016	DEVEREAUX, Peter	
			016		
John H. BLACK	1849	1912	016	HOGAN, Hannah	
Hannah HOGAN Black	1847	1917	016	BLACK, John H.	
			016		
John ENRIGHT	12-25-1820	11-12-1896	016	ORMOND, Johanna	
Johanna ORMOND Enright	10-16-1832	03-26-1904	016	ENRIGHT, John	
			016		
Patrick ENRIGHT	1855	1919	016	_____, Mary E.	
Mary E. _____ ENRIGHT	1859	1929	016	ENRIGHT, Patrick	
			016		
John COSGRIFF	03-14-1824	01-27-1896	016	BARRY, Ellen	
Ellen BARRY Cosgriff	06-23-1824	05-21-1897	016	COSGRIFF, John	
Julia COSGRIFF	11-30-1850	04-06-1862	016	COSGRIFF, Julia	
Hannah COSGRIFF	12-23-1857	09-04-1878	016	COSGRIFF, Hannah	
John B. COSGRIFF	09-17-1860	06-15-1918	016	STEWART, Bessie	
Bessie STEWART Cosgriff	01-08-1877	03-16-1950	016	COSGRIFF, John B.	
			016		
Patrick E. SHEEHAN	1858	1923	016	HUGHES, Ida L.	
Ida L. HUGHES Sheehan	1865	1926	016	SHEEHAN, Patrick E.	
			016		
James BAIRD	1856	1856	016	BAIRD, James	
			016		
Daniel CLARK	1838	1884	016	SULLIVAN, Rebecca	
Rebecca SULLIVAN Clark	1840	1878	016	CLARK, Daniel	
John CLARK	1843	1909	016	SHEEHAN, Katherine	
Katherine SHEEHAN Clark	1848	1935	016	CLARK, John	
Elizabeth D. CLARK	1867	1957	016	CLARK, Elizabeth D.	
			016		
William MURPHY	02-03-1855	09-10-1902	016	FINNEGAN, Alice E.	
Alice E. FINNEGAN Murphy	10-30-1856	10-07-1919	016	MURPHY, William	
			016		
Stephen LOVEJOY	07-04-1840	10-13-1910	016	LOVEJOY, Stephen	(GAR) Co. D. 1st Reg Vt Vol
			016		
Anthony MCGALE	1835	1912	016	MOFFETT, Bridget	
Bridget MOFFETT McGale	1835	1900	016	MCGALE, Anthony	
			016		
Thomas NASH		1933	016	BRADSHAW, Mary A.	(NOI DOB)
			016	BRADSHAW, Ella	

Mary A. BRADSHAW Nash		1909	016	NASH, Thomas	(NOI DOB)
Ella BRADSHAW		1925	016	NASH, Thomas	(NOI DOB)
			016		
Richard RYAN	04-15-1834	08-14-1907	016	RYAN, Richard	(GAR) Co. C. 16th Regt NY Vols
			016		
John BREEN	1844	1901	016	DONAHUE, Ann	
Ann DONAHUE Breen	1839	1921	016	BREEN, John	
			016		
James FREEMAN			016	MURRAY, Maria	Erected by Daughter Mary A.
			016		Freeman. (NOI DOB/DOD)
Maria MURRAY Freeman			016	FREEMAN, James	(NOI DOB/DOD)
Margaret FREEMAN			016	FREEMAN, Margaret	(NOI DOB/DOD)
Ann MURRAY			016	MURRAY, Ann	(NOI DOB/DOD)
			016		
Mary A. GOEG Dutton	43 Years	01-17-1899	016	DUTTON, Herbert	(NOI Herbert Dutton)
			016	GOEG, Mary A.	
Jeremiah GOEG	78 Years	08-07-1901	016	MELLENDY, Mary	
Mary MELLENDY Goeg	77 Years	12-25-1902	016	GOEG, Jeremiah	
			016		
Oscar H. PINNEY	09-18-1852	04-02-1911	016	_____, Mary E.	
Mary E. _____ PINNEY	1854	1941	016	PINNEY, Oscar H.	
			016		
William CONNORS	2Y 10M	06-14-1851	016	CONNORS, William	Son Of _____ & Mary CONNORS
			016		
James GOEG	97 Years	09-08-1859	016	GOEG, James	
			016		
James WILLIAMS	20 Years	05-30-1852	016	WILLIAMS, James	
			016		
Samuel WILLIAMS	45 Years	03-19-1856	016	WILLIAMS, Samuel	
			016		
James D. FOLEY	37 Years	04-17-1878	016	_____, Elizabeth B.	
Elizabeth B. _____ FOLEY	26 Years	12-12-1886	016	FOLEY, James D.	
			016		
Ellen SHERIDAN	12Y 6M	06-11-1853	016	SHERIDAN, Ellen	D/O Patrick & Ellen Sheridan
			016		
Mary A. _____ MCGETTRICK	27 Years	12-22-1881	016	MCGETTRICK, Michael	Wife of Michael McGettrick
			016	_____, Mary A.	(NOI Michael McGettrick)
			016		
Ann O'BRYAN Foley	71 Years	03-16-1903	016	FOLEY, Patrick	Wife of Patrick Foley
			016		(NOI Patrick Foley)
Margaret E. COURTNEY Haley			016	HALEY, John	(NOI DOB/DOD or John Haley)
			016		
William RYAN	68 Years	07-13-1856	016	_____, Mary	
Mary _____ RYAN	60 Years	01-05-1878	016	RYAN, William	
Mathew RYAN	43 Years	03-18-1885	016	RYAN, Mathew	

Thomas RYAN		18 Years	09-15-1867	016	RYAN, Thomas	
James RYAN		16 Years	09-23-1869	016	RYAN, James	
				016		
Michael KELLY	Co. Limerick	11-29-1815	01-12-1886	016	_____, Catherine	Born In Co. Limerick, Ireland
Catherine _____ KELLY	Co. Limerick	12-23-1819	03-28-1896	016	KELLY, Michael	Born In Co. Limerick, Ireland
Maggie E. KELLY		5Y 9M	05-15-1866	016	KELLY, Maggie E.	
Bridget KELLY		2Y 3M	09-20-1856	016	KELLY, Bridget	
David C. KELLY		6M 19D	07-29-1856	016	KELLY, David C.	
				016		
Bridget COSTELLO		1 Year	01-27-1858	016	COSTELLO, Bridget	Daughter Of Martin & Bridget
				016		Costello
				016		
William DWYER	Co. Wicklow	67 Years	02-03-1853	016	_____, Ellen	Resident of the City of Dublin
				016		And Born In Co. Wicklow, Ire.
Ellen _____ DWYER		50 Years	08-12-1870	016	DWYER, William	
				016		
Louis J. MCMAHON		1853	1921	016	GARDNER, Emma C.	
Emma C. GARDNER McMahon		1855	1923	016	MCMAHON, Louis J.	
				016		
Thomas J. TULLEY		1849	1905	016	CORBETT, Ellen	
Ellen CORBETT Tulley		1862	1950	016	TULLEY, Thomas J.	
Mary CORBETT		1858	1951	016	CORBETT, Mary	
				016		
Honora KELLY McEvoy		49 Years	02-21-1852	016	MCEVOY, Henry	
				016		
Emma DOWD		24 Years	06-03-1874	016	DOWD, Emma	
				016		
Patrick DOWD		57 Years	06-07-1882	016	CLARK, Ellen	
Ellen CLARK Dowd		30 Years	11-08-185_	016	DOWD, Patrick	(Stone is deteriorated)
John H. DOWD		30 Years	08-21-1892	016	DOWD, John H.	
Patrick F. DOWD		24 Years	10-17-1893	016	DOWD, Patrick F.	
				016		
Thomas FITZGERALD		1842	1917	016	_____, Elizabeth	
Elizabeth _____ FITZGERALD		1863	1931	016	FITZGERALD, Thomas	
				016		
Mary PORTER		1816	1892	016	PORTER, Mary	
				016		
Betsey PORTER				016	PORTER, Betsey	Dau Of Thomas N. & Mary Porter
				016		(NOI DOB/DOD)
				016		
John HARNEY	Co. Clare	66 Years	09-09-1851	016	HARNEY, John	Native of Parish of "Kilmuh"
				016		Co. Clare, Ireland (No such
				016		Parish. Possibly Kilmurry or
				016		Killimer.)(NOI Margaret)
Mary HARNEY		20 Years	04-20-1852	016	HARNEY, Mary	Dau Of John & Margaret Harney

Catharine HARNEY		20 Years	03-13-1859	016	HARNEY, Catherine	Dau Of J & M Harney
				016		
James MULCAHY		08-07-1810	09-21-1881	016	_____, Margaret	
Margaret _____ MULCAHEY		SEP 1814	SEP 1902	016	MULCAHY, James	
Jennie MULCAHY Harvey		01-18-1849	09-10-1872	016	HARVEY, James	(NOI James Harvey)
				016	MULCAHY, Jennie	
Clara HARVEY		01-10-1872	08-15-1873	016	HARVEY, Clara	
				016		
Nancy BARNEY Ryan		40 Years	11-16-1855	016	RYAN, John	(NOI John Ryan)
				016		
Elizabeth B. _____ BREEN		49 Years	05-13-1875	016	BREEN, Patrick	And His Seven Children (NOI
				016		Patrick BREEN)
				016		
Timothy ATKINSON	Co. Westmeath	73 Years	02-17-1854	016	ATKINSON, Timothy	Native of The Parish of Bally
				016		more, Co. Westmeath, Ireland
				016		
John HANLEY		82 Years	09-02-1877	016	_____, Margaret	
Margaret _____ HANLEY		81 Years	01-07-1878	016	HANLEY, John	
				016		
John D. NASH		10-18-1859	07-16-1919	016	NASH, John D.	
				016		
Austin LAVELLE		1812	1884	016	COGGINS, Bridget	
Bridget COGGINS Lavelle		1810	1898	016	LAVELLE, Austin	
				016		
John SHEEHY				016	MELLEDY, Ann	And His Son, John. Erected by
				016		His Wife. (NOI DOB/DOD for
				016		John Sheehy and his son John)
Ann MELLEDY Sheehy		70 Years	10-17-1898	016	SHEEHY, John	
				016		
James CONNOR		1856	1936	016	COURSEY, Josie	
Josie COURSEY Connor		1859	1936	016	CONNOR, James	
				016		
Bridget O'BYRNE Splain		1850	1924	016	SPLAIN, Daniel	(NOI Daniel Splain)
				016		
John FORD			08-20-1837	016	FORD, John	(NOI DOB)
				016		
John KEELEY	Co. Tipperary			016	KEELEY, John	Native of Co. Tipperary, Ire
				016		S/O Michael & Elizabeth Keeley
				016		
James F. WHALEN		1857	1924	016	BURKE, Ellen	
Ellen BURKE Whalen		1858	1927	016	WHALEN, James F.	
				016		
Jane BUTLER				016	BUTLER, Jane	IMO Jane Butler. (Very
				016		old stone. NOI DOB/DOD)
				016		

John A. DIXON		79 Years	11-04-1898	016	DIXON, John	(Relationships not indicated)
Ann DIXON		68 Years	02-15-1937	016	DIXON, Ann	
Margaret DIXON		85 Years		016	DIXON, Margaret	(NOI DOD)
				016		
Margaret DIXON	Co. Limerick	80 Years		016	DIXON, Margaret	Died In Burlington, Vermont
Dorothy DIXON	Co. Limerick	68 Years	05-03-1885	016	DIXON, Dorothy	Natives of Co. Limerick, Ire.
				016		Daughter Of Margaret Dixon
Richard DIXON	Co. Limerick	38 Years		016	DIXON, Richard	Natives of Co. Limerick, Ire.
				016		Son Of Margaret Dixon.
John DIXON	Co. Limerick	38 Years	11-04-1898	016	DIXON, John	Natives of Co. Limerick, Ire.
				016		
Ann MCGREEVY		1831	1901	016	MCGREEVY, Ann	
				016		
Mary RILEY McClane			08-09-1885	016	MCCLANE, Joseph	(NOI DOB, Joseph McClane)
				016	RILEY, Mary	
				016		
Charles S. MURRAY		07-26-1848	03-20-1892	016	MURRAY, Charles S.	Born In Ireland
				016		
Thomas B. MURRAY		01-14-1858	01-08-1889	016	MURRAY, Thomas B.	Born In Burlington, VT
				016		
John J. CROWLEY		1853	1933	016	CONNERS, Elizabeth	
Elizabeth CONNERS Crowley		1856	1918	016	CROWLEY, John J.	
				016		
John DONOVAN		74 Years	02-07-1881	016	DOLAN, Ann	
Ann DOLAN Donovan		35 Years	08-25-1851	016	DONOVAN, John	
Catherine DONOVAN		10 Years	10-15-1853	016	DONOVAN, Catherine	Daughter
				016		
William CASSIDY		1837	1914	016	FARRELL, Mary	
Mary FARRELL Cassidy		1848	1929	016	CASSIDY, William	
				016		
John RYAN		28 Years	06-15-1851	016	DOLAN, Ann	(Broken stone next "Margaret")
				016		
John J. FLAHERTY	Co. Limerick		1893	016	FITZGERALD, Ellen	Born In Co. Limerick, Ireland
Ellen FITZGERALD Flaherty			1897	016	FLAHERTY, John J.	
				016		
Elizabeth AHEARN			01-29-1877	016	AHEARN, Elizabeth	(NOI DOB)
				016		
Mary Ann FARRELL				016	FARRELL, Mary Ann	(NOI DOB/DOD)
				016		
Ann CANNON	Co. Mayo	1846	1907	016	CANNON, Ann	Native of Westport, County
				016		Mayo, Ireland
				016		
Mary CANNON	Co. Mayo	1852	1908	016	CANNON, Mary	Native of Westport, County
				016		Mayo, Ireland
				016		

Name	County	Age/Birth	Death		Relation	Notes
Mary POWERS Neenan	Co. Wexford	70 Years	05-23-1893	016	NEENAN, Edward	Born In Co. Wexford, Ireland
				016		
Daniel CONNER	Co. Kerry	22 Years	08-__-1849	016	CONNOR, Daniel	Native of Muig-on-Ear, Parish
				016		of "Knuckle-no-Gasul", (Knock-
				016		nagoshel) (Co. Kerry), Ireland
				016		(Could not find town in index)
				016		
Bernard GUNNING	Co. Longford	81 Years	05-20-1906	016	FARRELL, Maria	Native of Co.Longford, Ireland
Maria FARRELL Gunning	Co. Longford	35 Years	10-14-1888	016	GUNNING, Bernard	Native of Co.Longford, Ireland
				016		
John MCGREEVY	Co. Roscommon	61 Years	03-05-1877	016	HENRY, Thomas	Born In _______ Co. Roscommon
				016		Ireland. (Stone is damaged)
				016		Died In Winooski, Vermont
				016		
Mary SULLIVAN	Co. Tipperary	45 Years	05-01-1870	016	SULLIVAN, Mary	Native Of Ireland, County
				016		Tipperary
Daniel SULLIVAN		23 Years	09-17-1877	016	SULLIVAN, Daniel	Son Of Mary Sullivan
				016		
John FROST	Co. Clare	53 Years	08-04-1871	016	FROST, John	Native Of County Clare,Ireland
				016		

Following are in Adjunct Burial Ground - On Riverside Avenue, Burlington, VT, But In Same Burial Ground

Name	County	Age/Birth	Death		Relation	Notes
Hugh DALEY		1856	1934	016	_____, Margaret G.	
Margaret G. _____ DALEY		1856	19__	016	DALEY, Hugh	
				016		
Elizabeth BRADY Shannon		04-25-1836	03-19-1910	016	SHANNON, Matthew	(NOI Matthew Shannon)
				016	BRADY, Margaret	
				016		
Mary MCGEE		70 Years	07-09-1911	016		
				016		
Catherine O'BRIEN Speirman		65 Years	02-20-1913	016	SPIERMAN, Robert	(NOI Robaert Speirman)
				016	O'BRIEN, Catherine	
				016		
Dennis CROWLEY		1864	1939	016	COLLINS, Julia	
Julia COLLINS Crowley	Co. Limerick	1875	1930	016	CROWLEY, Dennis	Born In Limerick, Ireland
				016		
Daniel J. O'BRIEN		1855	1929	016	BRADLEY, Hannah	
Hannah BRADLEY O'Brien		1857	1938	016	O'BRIEN, Daniel J.	
				016		
Peter LYNCH		02-02-1859	09-29-1927	016	CALLAHAN, Bridget A.	
Bridget A. CALLAHAN Lynch		1861	1934	016	LYNCH, Peter	

Mt. Calvary Cemetery, Burlington, VT Archibald Street. (This is predominantly a Franco-American Burial Ground)

NAME	POB	DOB/AGE	DOD	CEM	SPOUSE/INDEX	INSCRIPTION
Joseph BURKE		1853	1901	017	LAPIERRE, Josephine	
Josephine LAPIERRE Burke		1854		017	BURKE, Joseph	
				017		
Mary SMITH		09-14-1851	01-23-1896	017	SMITH, Mary	
				017		
Henry LEONARD		1844	1908	017	_____, Adell	
Adell _____ LEONARD		1853	1920	017	LEONARD, Henry	His Beloved Wife
				017		
Gabriel WARD		70 Years	10-29-1898	017	WARD, Gabriel	
				017		
John RILEY		58 Years	12-10-1914	017	STONE, Lucy	
Lucy STONE Riley		56 Years	01-13-1913	017	RILEY, John	
				017		
Frank P. RIVERS		1847	1934	017	MCGOVERN, Catherine	
Catherine MCGOVERN Rivers		1850	1922	017	RIVERS, Frank P.	
				017		
(The following are Sisters of a Religious Order)				017		
				017		
Jane CONNOLLY		1845	1899	017	CONNOLLY, Jane	
Mary HOAR		1853	1901	017	HOAR, Mary	
Catherine GERAGHTY		1850	1945	017	GERAGHTY, Catherine	
Ellen B. CORLEY		1860	1916	017	CORLEY, Ellen B.	
Genevieve P. ALEN		1825	1907	017	ALEN, Genevieve	
Honora EAGEN		1846	1911	017	EGAN, Honora	
Elizabeth JOYCE		1854	1932	017	JOYCE, Elizabeth	
Ellen MOORE		1857	1939	017	MOORE, Ellen	
Elizabeth CAMIS		1850	1925	017	CAMIS, Elizabeth	
Ann ROCHE		1878	1927	017	ROCHE, Ann	
Mary MULQUEEN		1858	1921	017	MULQUEEN, Mary	
Mary LACEY		1847	1921	017	LACEY, Mary	
Ann O'REILLY		1837	1922	017	O'REILLY, Ann	
				017		
Peter J. BUTLER		1858	1928	017	BUTLER, Peter J.	
				017		
Edward BARTEMY		1836	1912	017	MILES, Caroline	
Caroline MILES Bartemy		1840	19__	017	BARTEMY, Edward	
				017		
Francis S. MURRAY		28 Years		017	KIRBY, Ellen	
Ellen KIRBY Murray		05-30-1847	01-21-1885	017	MURRAY, Francis S.	
				017		

Peter B. CROSS		1843	1914	017	FITZGERALD, Margaret	
Margaret FITZGERALD Cross		1848	1906	017	CROSS, Peter B.	
				017		
Lewis JORDAN		1838	1910	017	LEPP, Mary E.	
Mary E. LEPP Jordan		1847	1938	017	JORDAN, Lewis	
				017		
F. PLOOF		1858	1938	017	BRESNEHAN, K.	
K. BRESNEHAN Ploof		1853	1929	017	PLOOF, F.	
				017		
Victoria RILEY Guyette		44 Years	08-11-1894	017	GUYETTE, Thomas	(NOI Thomas Guyette)
				017	RILEY, Victoria	
				017		
Minnie MURPHY				017	MURPHY, Minnie	(No Inscription - old stone)
				017		
John W. GATES		11-02-1807	09-16-1888	017	GATES, John W.	
				017		
Henry L. MINER		1823	1910	017	GATES, Matilda	Co. C. 10th Reg Vt Vols(GAR)
Matilda GATES Miner		1845	1923	017	MINER, Henry L.	
				017		
Adaline BURKE		1836	1900	017	BURKE, Adaline	

Hillside Cemetery, Castleton, Vermont. West of VIllage, Right Off Route 4A Onto Cemetery Lane

NAME	POB	DOB/AGE	DOD	CEM	SPOUSE/INDEX	INSCRIPTION
Daniel GEARY			05-12-1878	108	GEARY, Daniel	(Stone is broken. Unreadable)
				108	GEARY, Eliza	(NOI Eliza Geary)
				108		
George HUNTER		1825	1885	108	HUNTER, George	
				108		
Mary WILLIAMS Hughes		50 Years	05-12-1879	108	WILLIAMS, Mary	(NOI Owen Hughes)
				108	HUGHES, Owen D.	
				108		
Joseph COLLINS		1851	1932	108	RUSSELL, Louise M.	
Louise M. RUSSELL Collins		1852	1928	108	COLLINS, Joseph	
				108		
Maryett KELLEY Griswold		23Y 12D	12-15-1849	108	KELLEY, Maryett	D/O of D. & C. Kelley. (NOI Philip Griswold)
				108	GRISWOLD, Philip	
				108		
Catherine MURRAY		90 Years	01-27-1919	108	MURRAY, Catherine	
				108		
Francis HOY		76 Years	11-01-1844	108	FOY, Mary	

Mary _____ HOY	83 Years	12-23-1851	108	FOY, Francis	
			108		
Edmund W. GRIFFITH	1845	1916	108	_____, Mary C.	
Mary C. _____ GRIFFITH	1865	1939	108	GRIFFITH, Edmund W.	
			108		
William DEMPSEY	1856	1941	108	_____, Annie	
Annie _____ DEMPSEY	1861	1943	108	DEMPSEY, William	
			108		
Michael HYNES	10-08-1836	07-14-1893	108	_____, Mary G.	(GAR) Co. B, 2nd Rgt, Vt Vols
Mary G. _____ HYNES	04-02-1843	03-28-1897	108	HYNES, Michael	Age 54 Years
			108		
Patrick MCCARTHY	1849	1937	108	MCCARTHY Patrick	
Mary MCGINLEY McCarthy	1848	1917	108	MCGINLY, Mary	
			108		
Owen R. PRITCHARD	04-24-1849	07-17-1914	108	PRITCHARD, Owen R.	
			108		
James BRENNAN	03-19-1831	07-27-1913	108	BROUGH, Catherine	
Catherine BROUGH Brennan	05-02-1834	07-03-1896	108	BRENNAN, James	
			108		
Catherine MCKEOUGH	1841	1916	108	MCKEOUGH, Catherine	
			108		
Mathew MCGINNIS	12-18-1823	04-27-1901	108	MCGINNIS, Mathew	
			108		
William H. WALSH	56Y10M7D	03-07-1913	108	MCGINNIS, Mary J.	
Mary J. MCGINNIS Walsh	1859	1931	108	WALSH, William H.	
Patrick T. SAMMON	1855	1928	108	WALCH, Mary	
Mary WALSH Sammon	1854	1931	108	SAMMON, Patrick T.	
Michael RYAN	75 Years	10-11-1880	108	HICKEY, Katherine	
Katherine HICKEY	84 Years	01-18-1902	108	RYAN, Michael	
John RYAN	06-03-1849	08-11-1906	108	RYAN, John	
Richard RYAN	1859	1914	108	MEIGHER, Josephine	
Josephine MEIGHER Ryan	1865	1949	108	RYAN, Richard	
Cornelius RYAN	1853	1920	108	RYAN, Cornelius	
			108		
Edward J. MCCANN	1856	1932	108	MCCANN, Mary	
Mary _____ MCCANN	1857	1925	108	MCCANN, Edward J.	
			108		
John BROUGH	1841	1912	108	CARMODY, Susanna	
Susanna CARMODY Brough	1849	1942	108	BROUGH, John	
			108		
Jeremiah GRADY	1830	1895	108	GRADY, Susan	
Susan _____ GRADY	1837	1897	108	GRADY, Jeremiah	
			108		
Rollin GLEASON	11-27-1826	06-06-1909	108	GREGORY, Caroline	
Caroline GREGORY Gleason	05-02-1834	10-02-1896	108	GLEASON, Rollin	

Name	Birth/Age	Death	Plot	Index	Notes
			108		
Joseph A. CLIFFORD	1839	1887	108	MCCOY, Caroline A.	
Caroline A. MCCOY Clifford	1839	1909	108	CLIFFORD, Joseph A.	
			108		
James MCMULLEN	09-25-1804	05-02-1896	108	_____, Mary Jane	
Mary Jane _____ MCMULLEN	07-31-1814	03-27-1861	108	MCMULLEN, James	
James W. COMSTOCK	1846	1928	108	MCMULLEN, Mary Jane	
Mary Jane MCMULLEN Comstock	1836	1906	108	COMSTOCK, James W.	
Mary D. MCMULLEN	01-01-1843	04-02-1894	108	MCMULLEN, Mary D.	
James H. MCMULLEN	1836	1918	108	MCMULLEN, James H.	
			108		
Thomas HACKETT	1817	1910	108	FOLEY, Mary	
Mary FOLEY Hackett	1828	1878	108	HACKETT, Thomas	
William HACKETT	25 Years	01-31-1892	108	HACKETT, William	
James HACKETT	33 Years	02-06-1893	108	HACKETT, James	
Matilda HACKETT	1856	1932	108	HACKETT, Matilda	
Susan HACKETT	1854	1934	108	HACKETT, Susan	
Mary HACKETT	1864	1942	108	HACKETT, Mary	
Mathias HACKETT	43 Years	02-08-1890	108	HACKETT, Mathias	
Margaret HACKETT	7 Years	03-16-1865	108	HACKETT, Margaret	
Julia _____ CALLAHAN			108	CALLAHAN, Julia	(In Thomas Hackett plot. NOI
			108	CALLAHAN, Dennis	DOB/DOD or Dennis Callahan)
			108		
William B. MCGRORTY		09-09-1905	108	MCGRORTY, William B.	In Memory Of Capt. William B.
			108		McGrorty, USA, Who DIed in St.
			108		Paul, Minn. (NOI DOB. In same.
			108		plot: Geraldine D: 10-26-1916)
			108		
Bryan MCKEAN	77 Years	10-03-1872	108	WHITE, Mary	
Mary WHITE McKean	78 Years	12-23-1881	108	MCKEAN, Bryan	
Mary MCKEAN	17 Years	09-28-1840	108	MCKEAN, Mary	
Margaret MCKEAN	33 Years	03-15-1864	108	MCKEAN, Margaret	
			108		
P. C. MOONEY	65 Years	10-08-1879	108	_____, Lorinda W.	
Lorinda W. _____ MOONEY	56Y 9M	05-12-1879	108	MOONEY, P.C.	
			108		
William BRADY	55 Years	09-28-1861	108	_____, Ruth E.	
Ruth E. _____ BRADY	71 Years	01-08-1871	108	BRADY, William	
			108		
Jeremiah ARMSTRONG	81 Years	03-14-1842	108	_____, Anna	
Anna _____ ARMSTRONG	84 Years	09-27-1843	108	ARMSTRONG, Jeremiah	
Dudley ARMSTRONG	17 Years	08-16-1804	108	ARMSTRONG, Dudley	
John D. ARMSTRONG	44 Years	06-12-1843	108	ARMSTRONG John D.	
Levi ARMSTRONG	37 Years	06-09-1832	108	ARMSTRONG, Levi	
			108		

Thomas F. MCDOWELL		1829	1904	108	ROSS, Caroline S.	
Caroline S. ROSS McDowell		1839	1915	108	MCDOWELL, Thomas F.	
Thomasena MCDOWELL		1859	1860	108	MCDOWELL, Thomasena	
William S. MCDOWELL		1856	1860	108	MCDOWELL, William S.	
Charles H. MCDOWELL		1874	1939	108	MCDOWELL, Charles H.	

Village Cemetery, High Street, Cavendish, VT

NAME	**POB**	**DOB/AGE**	**DOD**	**CEM**	**SPOUSE/INDEX**	**INSCRIPTION**
William CONNALLY		63Y 2M	05-20-1883	109	_____, Mary	
Mary _____ CONNALLY		65 Years	10-28-1886	109	CONNALLY, William	
				109		
Margaret NEVILLE McNamara		52 Years	03-02-1872	109	MCNAMARA, Patrick	(NOI Patrick McNamara)
				109	NEVILLE, Margaret	
				109		
Michael S. QUIRK		60 Years	03-24-1875	109	QUIRK, Michael S.	
				109		
Kate _____ HARNETT		19Y7M5D	02-22-1873	109	HARNETT, Daniel	(NOI Daniel Harnett)
				109	_____, Kate	
				109		
Dennis HURLEY		53 Years	01-23-1905	109	HURLEY, Dennis	
				109		
John SHEEHAN	Co. Kerry	65Y 6M	01-07-1893	109	CUNNINGHAM, Ellen	Native of Co. Kerry, Ireland
Ellen CUNNINGHAM Sheehan		96 Years	03-27-1926	109	SHEEHAN, John	
				109		
Charles E. GILCHRIST		05-09-1855	03-12-1917	109	_____, Elizabeth C.	
Elizabeth C. _____ GILCHRIST		03-30-1855	12-08-1931	109	GILCHRIST, Charles E.	
				109		
Thomas H. HADLEY		12-10-1858	09-10-1910	109	_____, Maria S.	Born In Birmingham, England
				109		Died In Cavendish, Vermont
Maria S. _____ HADLEY		08-28-1856	11-29-1936	109	HADLEY, Thomas H.	Born In Capetown, South Africa
				109		Died In Providence, RI
				109		
James J. MCMAHON		1851	1922	109	HALEN, Emily A.	
Emily A. HALEN McMahon		1848	1929	109	MCMAHON, James J.	
				109		
Patrick WALSH		1836	1911	109	BOYLE, Julia	
Julia BOYLE Walsh		1836	1912	109	WALSH, Patrick	
				109		
Patrick GLEASON		53 Years	02-16-1890	109	_____, Catherine	
Catherine _____ GLEASON		69 Years	07-09-1909	109	GLEASON, Patrick	

NAME	POB	DOB/AGE	DOD	CEM	SPOUSE/INDEX	INSCRIPTION
William WALLIS		02-05-1820	08-21-1886	109	_____, Elizabeth	
Elizabeth _____ WALLIS		12-08-1826	08-19-1892	109	WALLIS, William	
				109		
James WALLIS		04-04-1822	01-17-1902	109	CROSS, Esther	
				109	LYONS, Ellen	
Esther CROSS Wallis		03-30-1823	03-30-1855	109	WALLIS, James	
Ellen LYONS Wallis		11-12-1832	09-24-1894	109	WALLIS, James	
				109		
George J. WALLIS		11-28-1844	04-15-1865	109	WALLIS, George J.	(GAR)Co. G. 7th VT Vols
				109		
Alexander MACOY		11-08-1816	04-08-1849	109	FARR, Mary R.	
Mary R. FARR Macoy		10-18-1816	08-22-1897	109	MACOY, Alexander	
				109		
Ellen E. CARY		23 Years	05-25-1868	109	CARY, Ellen E.	Drowned Near Spring Mill
				109		
James WARD		58 Years	06-14-1854	109	WARD, James	
				109		
John James WHITEHEAD		29 Years	05-02-1854	109	WHITEHEAD, John James	Late of Rochbale, Lancashire, England
				109		
				109		
Roger MCNAMARA		21 Years	04-15-1859	109	MCNAMARA, Roger	
				109		
Mary MCNAMARA		1Y 4D	05-03-1859	109	MCNAMARA, Mary	D/O Patrick MCNAMARA& Margaret
				109		
Peter O'CONNOR		47Y9M16D	06-29-1863	109	_____, Julia	Erected By Julia O'Connor
Julia _____ O'CONNOR		53y4M10D	09-05-1863	109	O'CONNOR, Peter	
Peter O'CONNOR		18Y5M	10-29-1862	109	O'CONNOR, Peter	

Our Lady Of Mt. Carmel Cemetery, Spear St. Extension, Charlotte, VT

NAME	POB	DOB/AGE	DOD	CEM	SPOUSE/INDEX	INSCRIPTION
Patrick J. BURGIN		59 Years	11-12-1873	019	CARNEY, Mary	
Mary CARNEY Burgin		88 Years	11-13-1901	019	BURGIN, Patrick J.	
Grace BURKE BURGIN		84 Years	10-23-1877	019	BURGIN, Joseph	(NOI Joseph Burgin)
				019	BURKE, Grace	
Michael BURGIN		8Y 4M	02-15-1857	019	BURGIN, Michael	Son of Patrick & Mary Burgin
				019		
John STAPLETON		73 Years	07-17-1909	019	RAFTERY, Mary	
Mary RAFTERY Stapleton		70 Years	03-08-1913	019	STAPLETON, John	
				019		
Thomas FALLON		62 Years	04-18-1886	019	_____, Catharine	
Catharine _____ FALLON		50 Years	03-19-1870	019	FALLON, Thomas	

Thomas FALLON Jr.	19Y 4M	09-07-1873	019	FALLON, Thomas Jr.	Son of Thomas/Catharine Fallon
			019		
Michael KEHOE	31 Years	03-29-1863	019	KEHOE, Michael	
Joseph KEHOE	20 Years	03-18-1864	019	KEHOE, Joseph	
Patrick KEHOE	76 Years	09-11-1873	019	_____, Bridget	
Bridget _____ KEHOE	82 Years	05-16-1880	019	KEHOE, Patrick	
John KEHOE	39 Years	12-11-1873	019	KEHOE, John	
			019		
Ann _____ MOONEY	63Y 8M	05-08-1874	019	MOONEY, John	(NOI John Mooney)
			019	_____, Ann	
			019		
James MOONEY	1831	1908	019	_____, Ellen	
Ellen _____ MOONEY	54 Years	05-30-1890	019	MOONEY, James	
Mary MOONEY	1861	1905	019	MOONEY, Mary	
			019		
Timothy STEBBINS	12-18-1825	07-14-1913	019	_____, Rachel	
Rachel _____ STEBBINS	03-15-1834	03-07-1924	019	STEBBINS, Timothy	
			019		
Ellen _____ GAFFNEY	86 Years	08-31-1872	019	GAFFNEY, John	(NOI John Gaffney)
			019	_____, Ellen	
			019		
Catharine _____ O'DWIRE		09-06-1873	019	O'DWIRE, John	(NOI John O'Dwire.Stone worn)
			019	_____, Catherine	
			019		
			019	LARKIN, Margaret	(NOI DOB/DOD)
Owen COGAN			019	COGAN, Owen	(NOI DOB/DOD)
Margaret LARKIN Cogan					
Patrick F. COGAN	11Y 5M	02-19-1874	019	COGAN, Patrick F.	
Thomas COGAN	6 Years	04-15-1863	019	COGAN, Thomas	
Mary A. COGAN	4Y 6M	04-10-1863	019	COGAN, Mary A.	
Minnie COGAN	6Y 4M	02-23-1874	019	COGAN, Minnie	
Katie COGAN	2 Das	10-02-1865	019	COGAN, Katie	
			019		
Joseph CARPENTER	1778	1876	019	RUSSELL, Emily	
Emily RUSSELL Carpenter	1817	1879	019	CARPENTER, Joseph	
			019		
Matilda RUSSELL Thomas	56 Years	01-05-1886	019	THOMAS, John	(NOI John Thomas)
			019	RUSSELL, Matilda	
			019		
Michael NAYLON	76 Years	05-13-1887	019	_____, Margaret	
Margaret _____ NAYLON	69 Years	07-22-1889	019	NAYLON, Michael	
Ellen NAYLON	23 Years	03-27-1877	019		
			019		
Emma _____ MCGOWAN		__-19-1884	019	MCGOWAN, George	(NOI George McGowan.Stone worn
			019	_____, Emma	

Name	Age/Birth	Death	Plot	Index	Notes
Michael GAFFANY	56 Years	04-09-1881	019	ROYSTAN, Mary J.	
Margaret _____ GAFFANY	1828	1908	019	DONLON, Martin F.	
			019		
John LEHNEN			019	HALLEY, Ellen	
Ellen HALLEY	42 Years	05-26-1902	019	LEHNEN, John	
			019		
Austin SHELDON	96 Years	12-01-1898	019	_____, Martha	
Martha _____ SHELDON			019	SHELDON, Austin	
			019		
Dennis MCDONALD	1823	1902	019	HEIRER, Eliza	
Eliza HEIRER McDonald	1822	1903	019	MCDONALD, Dennis	
			019		
M. T. FLEMING	1814	1900	019	FARREL, Mary	
Mary FARREL Fleming	1826	1906	019	FLEMING, M. T.	
Mary FLEMING	1854	1911	019	FLEMING, Mary	
Kate FLEMING	1856	1921	019	FLEMING, Kate	
John FLEMING	1845	1930	019	FLEMING, John	
			019		
Michael FLEMING	09-20-1814	03-27-1900	019	FLEMING, Michael	(Same plot as above. Probably Michael and M.T. Fleming are same person)
			019		
			019		
			019		
Catherine MOONEY	1858	1929	019		
			019		
Mary LAVEY SEARS	86 Years	05-11-1897	019	SEARS, Edward	(NOI Edward Sears)
			019	LAVEY, Mary	
			019		
Patrick MURRAY	69 Years	02-10-1873	019	MURRAY, Patrick	(NOI Spouse)
Maria MURRAY	22 Years	09-16-1866	019	MURRAY, Maria	
William O. MURRAY	26 Years	02-21-1874	019	MURRAY, William O.	
			019		
Catherine DWYER Mills	40 Years	12-12-1872	019	MILLS, Francois	(NOI Francois Mills)
			019	DWYER, Catherine	
			019		
Patrick MCENTEE	64 Years	09-07-1868	019	KENNEY, Ann	
Ann KENNEY McEntee	74 Years	09-21-1892	019	MCENTEE, Patrick	
			019		
James TERRY	70 Years	03-25-1881	019	TERRY, James	
			019		
Joseph CURAVOO	77 Years	04-06-1905	019	MAHONEY, Margaret	
Margaret MAHONEY Curavoo	74 Years	07-04-1904	019	CURAVOO, Joseph	
			019		
David SEARS	76 Years	08-01-1871	019	_____, Mary S.	
Mary S. _____ SEARS	97 Years	11-20-1893	019	SEARS, David	

Michael O'BRIEN		76 Years	03-07-1892	019	_____, Julia	
Julia _____ O'BRIEN		71 Years	04-30-1892	019	O'BRIEN, Michael	
Mary O'BRIEN		2 Mos	10- -1878	019	O'BRIEN, Mary	
Ellen O'BRIEN		44 Years	02-17-1891	019	O'BRIEN, Ellen	
Mary O'BRIEN		19 Years	08-14-1876	019	O'BRIEN, Mary	
				019		
William D. KELLEY		48 Years	04-14-1875	019	GAFFANY, Ellen	
Ellen GAFFANY Kelley		1830	1904	019	KELLEY, William D.	
				019		
Michael BRADLEY		1826	1908	019	_____, Ellen	
Ellen _____ BRADLEY		75 Years	04-04-1899	019	BRADLEY, Michael	
John BRADLEY		1862	1926	019	BRADLY, John	
Martin FLANLY		87 Years	09-12-1868	019	FLANLY, Martin	
				019		
Dominic HART		84 Years	06-18-1888	019	HART, Dominic	
				019		
James MCDONOUGH		1828	1916	019	_____, Bridget	
Bridget _____ MCDONOUGH		1830	1910	019	MCDONOUGH, James	
Mother --		1786	1850	019		
Fanny (MCDONOUGH?)		1818	1906	019	_____, Fanny	
Rose (MCDONOUGH?)		1810	1890	019	_____, Rose	
				019		
Catharine MONAHAN Cassidy	Co. Fermanagh	90 Years	08-14-1880	019	CASSIDY, John	Born in Parish Of Magheracul-
				019	MONAHAN, Catherine	money, Co. Fermanagh, Ireland
				019		(NOI John Cassidy)
				019		
Mary CASSIDY	Co. Fermanagh	60 Years	03-07-1873	019	CASSIDY, Mary	Dau of John & Catherine
				019		Cassidy. Born in Parish Of
				019		Magheraculmoney,Co. Fermanagh,
				019		Ireland
				019		
Catherine HALLERAN Condon		44 Years	03-15-1868	019	CONDON, James	(NOI James Condon)
				019	HALLERAN, Catherine	
				019		
Patrick CONDON		20 Years	04-03-1881	019	CONDON, Patrick	S/O James & Catherine Condon
				019		
John HART		1852	1941	019	_____, Elen J.	
Elen J. _____ HART		30 Years	09-20-1888	019	HART, John	
				019		
Peter STACY		1826	1909	019	DOYLE, Bridget	
Bridget DOYLE Stacy		1843	1905	019	STACY, Peter	
Laurence RAFTERY	Co. Galway	71 Years	05-13-1883	019	RAFTERY, Laurence	Native of Co. Galway, Ireland
Patrick Thomas RAFTERY		02-04-1841	04-27-1917	019	BURGEN, Ellen	(Also on stone - Prevost and
Ellen BURGEN Raftery		07-04-1851	07-24-1921	019	RAFTERY, Patrick Thomas	Michaud)

NAME	POB	DOB/AGE	DOD	CEM	SPOUSE/INDEX	INSCRIPTION
Peter LARMY		77 Years	11-14-1914	019	_____, Louisa	(Surname possibly Laramee)
Louisa _____ LARMY		88 Years	01-05-1931	019	LARMY, Peter	
				019		
Joseph QUINLAN		1861	1937	019	MURPHY, Anna	
Anna MURPHY Quinlan		1870	1958	019	QUINLAN, Joseph	
Ellen M. QUINLAN		1868	1960	019	QUINLAN, Ellen M.	
Michael QUINLAN		1840	1920	019	QUINLAN, Michael	
William QUINLAN		1844	1905	019	QUINLAN, William	
Dennis QUINLAN		1857	1859	019	QUINLAN, Dennis	
John QUINLAN		06-24-1813	09-06-1__2	019	HARVEY, Margaret	(DOD illegible-deteriorated)
Margaret HARVEY Quinlan		1834	1919	019	QUINLAN, John	
Mary A. QUINLAN		1859	1916	019	QUINLAN, Mary A.	
				019		
Ellen HARNEY		11-01-1825	04-04-1901	019	HARNEY, Ellen	Dau of John & Margaret Harney
				019	HARNEY, John	
				019		
Eli AMOUR		1845	1911	019	MYERS, Margaret	
Margaret MYERS Amour		1850	1934	019	AMOUR, Eli	
				019		
Lucy _____ LARMAY		38 Years	11-15-1875	019	LARMAY, George	(NOI George Larmay (Laramee?)
				019	_____, Lucy	
				019		
Alice QUINLAN		16Y 3D	04-25-1875	019	QUINLAN, Alice	Dau of William & E. Quinlan
Katy QUINLAN		3Y 1M	09-11-1865	019	QUINLAN, Katy	Dau of William & E. Quinlan
James HEATH		27Y 17D	07-03-1864	019	HEATH, James	S/O Samuel Heath(NOI Samuel)
				019	HEATH, Samuel	

St. John Of The Cross, E. Albany, VT Creek Road, 1-1/2 Miles South Of The Church

NAME	POB	DOB/AGE	DOD	CEM	SPOUSE/INDEX	INSCRIPTION
Timothy CROWLEY		75 Years	10-26-1873	021	MCCUE, Bridget	
Bridget MCCUE Crowley		53 Years	02-28-1873	021	CROWLEY, Timothy	
				021		
Mary A. MARLOW Crowley		26Y2M14D	07-26-1878	021	CROWLEY, Thomas	(NOI Thomas Crowley)
				021	MARLOW, Mary E.	
				021		
John BRODERICK		1789	1869	021	BRODERICK, John	
				021		
Michael BRODERICK		93 Years	03-30-1869	021	BRODERICK, Michael	
				021		
Ellen _____ KELLEY		73 Years	08-24-1870	021	KELLEY, Lawrence	(NOI Lawrence Kelley)
				021	_____, Ellen	

			021		
Rose SHATNEY Laclair	38 Years	03-26-1877	021	LACLAIR, Charles	(NOI Charles LaClair)
			021	SHATNEY, Rose	
			021		
Mary _____ MURDOCK	34 Years	1864	021	MURDOCK, David	(NOI David Murdock)
			021	_____, Mary	
			021		
John MCGUYRE	40 Years	01-01-1881	021	MCGUYRE, John	(Probably McGuire)
			021		
Mathew MAGUIRE	19 Years	09-30-1864	021	MAGUIRE, Mathew	S/O Peter and Johana Maguire
			021		
Mathew MAGUIRE	77 Years	03-27-1877	021	MAGUIRE, Mathew	
			021	MAGUIRE, Peter	
			021		
Jacob O. DOUGLAS	05-17-1828	10-19-1909	021	GARROW, Elizabeth	
Elizabeth GARROW Douglas	05-16-1842	05-13-1917	021	DOUGLAS, Jacob O.	
			021		
John THY	70 Years	10-03-1888	021	_____, Bridget	(NOI Bridget)
			021	THY, John	
			021		
Martin GLEESON	10-10-1820		021	WATERS, Mary	(NOI Mary Waters)
			021	GLEESON, Martin	
			021		
E. P. RICHARDSON	1820	1932	021	MCCUE, Mary	
Mary MCCUE Richardson	1833	1899	021	RICHARDSON, E. P.	
			021		
James RYAN	1830	1877	021	WATERS, Kate	
Kate WATERS Ryan	1838	1889	021	RYAN, James	
			021		
Michael GLEESON	01-03-1846	01-15-1863	021	GLEESON, Michael	
Martin GLEESON	05-13-1855	05-13-1862	021	GLEESON, Martin	
John GLEESON	06-25-1853	10-05-1864	021	GLEESON, John	
			021		
William HOGAN	55 Years	08-02-1875	021	HOGAN, William	
			021		
Annie B. MCCUE	36 Years	03-12-1882	021	MCCUE, Annie B.	Erected By Her Brother, Peter
			021	MCCUE, Peter	McCue. Formerly of Ireland.
			021		McCue. Formerly of Ireland.
Bridget _____ MCCUE	95 Years	12-22-1889	021	MCCUE, Michael	(NOI Michael McCue)
			021	_____, Bridget	
			021		
Patrick ROWEN	1846	1906	021	BURKE, Ellen	
Ellen BURKE Rowen	1860	1905	021	ROWEN, Patrick	
			021		

Name	Origin	Born/Age	Died	Code	Relation	Notes
Dominic F. DENNISON		1847	1935	021	MULLANEY, Bridget	
Bridget MULLANEY Dennison		1852	1930	021	DENNISON, Dominic F.	
				021		
Mary CAROL McLaughlin		79Y9M14D	10-09-1900	021	MCLAUGHLIN, William	(NOI William McLaughlin - her surname probably Carroll)
				021	CAROL, Mary	
				021		
Patrick QUINN		61 Years	05-02-1886	021	CULLINAN, Mary	
Mary CULLINAN Quinn		80 Years	03-17-1899	021	QUINN, Patrick	
Bridget HEHIR		88 Years		021	HEHIR, Bridget	(Surname appears to be Hehir but stone is worn.Same plot as Patrick & Mary Quinn)
				021		
				021		
				021		
Patrick TUNNEY		72 Years	04-04-1865	021	_____, Bridget	
Bridget _____ TUNNEY		88 Years	02-01-1885	021	TUNNEY, Patrick	
John TUNNEY		66 Years	05-12-1893	021	MURPHY, Ellen	
Ellen MURPHY Tunney		82 Years	02-20-1913	021	TUNNEY, John	
				021		
Katie MURPHY		24 Years	12-18-1879	021	MURPHY, Katie	
John MURPHY		35 Years	07-20-1880	021	MURPHY, John	
				021		
William J. MCCAFFREY		11-09-1849		021	RYAN, Ellen	
Ellen RYAN McCaffrey		03-15-1853	03-29-1898	021	MCCAFFREY, William J.	
				021		
John KILGALLEN		1835	1901	021	JOHNSON, Mary	
Mary JOHNSON Kilgallen		1838	1929	021	KILGALLEN, John	
				021		
Patrick KILGALLEN		76 Years	09-21-1900	021	KILGALLEN, Patrick	Born In Ireland
				021		
Patrick KILGALLEN		1861	1938	021	RYAN, Mary	
Mary RYAN Kilgallen		1859	1946	021	KILGALLEN, Patrick	
				021		
John MULLANEY		1847	1923	021	_____, Louisa	
Louisa _____ MULLANEY		1870	1957	021	MULLANEY, John	
				021		
Patrick A. RYAN	Co. Mayo	01-28-1869	09-20-1894	021	RYAN, Patrick A.	Born In Middletown, Co. Mayo, Ireland
				021		
				021		
John HUGHES		1845	1933	021	GLYNN, Catherine	
				021	BROWN, Kate	
Catherine GLYNN Hughes		1844	1878	021	HUGHES, John	
Kate BROWN Hughes		1847	1928	021	HUGHES, John	
				021		
Patrick GLYNN		75Y 6M	02-09-1874	021	_____, Catherine	
Catherine _____ GLYNN		82 Years	02-15-1886	021	GLYNN, Patrick	
Maria A. GLYNN		1836	1857	021	GLYNN, Maria A.	

				021		
Thomas P. JOHNSON		52 Years	09-25-1892	021	GALLAGHER, Kate	
Kate GALLAGHER Johnson		49Y 6D	11-06-1894	021	JOHNSON, Thomas P.	
Cathrine GALLAGHER Hennesy	Co. Cork	1818	03-05-1894	021	HENNESY, John	Born 1818 in Glanworth, Co.
				021	GALLAGHER, Cathrine	Cork, Ireland. (NOI John
				021		Hennesy)
				021		
Tom ROUEN		1855	1899	021	ROUEN, Tom	
John ROUEN		1867	1900	021	ROUEN, John	
Edward ROUEN		27Y 10M	05-01-1884	021	ROUEN, Edward	
Michael ROUEN		61 Years	01-27-1895	021	RILEY, Bridget	
Bridget RILEY Rouen		1829	1897	021	ROUEN, Michael	
				021		
Edmond GALLAGHER	Co. Cork	1818	1904	021	KILGALLEN, Ann	Born In County Cork, Ireland
Ann KILLGALLEN Gallagher	Co. Mayo	1821	01-03-1877	021	GALLAGHER, Edmond	Born In Mayo County, Ireland
				021		
Thomas CLARK		59 Years	01-23-1868	021	CLARK, Thomas	
				021		
Winniford _____ RUIN		43 Years	08-16-1877	021	RUIN, Patrick	(NOI Patrick Ruin - surname
				021	_____, Winniford	is possibly ROUEN)
				021		
John WATERS		1807	1889	021	MCCARTY, Ellen	
Ellen MCCARTY Waters		09-29-1826	05-19-1891	021	WATERS, John	
				021		
				021		
William REILLY		1815	1906	021	CORLY, Margaret	
				021		
				021	KILGALAN, Bridget	
Margaret CORLY Reilly		1825	1861	021	REILLY, William	
Bridget KILGALAN Reilly		1830	1902	021	REILLY, William	
				021		
Andrew MCCAFFREY		16Y 5M	04-08-1870	021	MCCAFFREY, Andrew	
				021		
Patrick MCCAFFREY		03-17-1823	04-22-1901	021	CASSIDY, Mary	
Mary CASSIDY McCaffrey		05-05-1824	03-02-1898	021	MCCAFFREY, Patrick	
				021		
Thomas MCCAFFREY		46 Years	12-20-1903	021	MCCAFFREY, Thomas	
				021		
Mary A. MCCAFFREY		01-17-1855	07-07-1936	021	MCCAFFREY, Mary A.	
				021		
Robert STEWART		61 Years	06-01-1874	021	CLARK, Mary	
Mary CLARK Stewart		1815	01-23-1892	021	STEWART, Robert	
				021		
Owen MARLOW		1823	1894	021	FARRELL, Bridget	
Bridget FARRELL Marlow		1819		021	MARLOW, Owen	

Nellie A. MARLOW	1857	1937	021	MARLOW, Nellie A.	
Mary A. MARLOW	1853	1879	021	MARLOW, Mary A.	
			021		
Michael J. CORLEY	1833	1909	021	GLYNN, Ann	Born In Ireland
Ann GLYNN CORLEY	1838	1920	021	CORLEY, Michael J.	Born In Ireland
			021		
Thomas KILGARLAN			021	BARNICLE, Catherine	(No DOB/DOD Thomas Kilgarlan)
Catherine BARNICLE Kilgarlan	71 Years	10-03-1887	021	KILGARLAN, Thomas	
Winneford KILGALLEN	28 Years	10-19-1871	021	KILGALLEN, Winneford	
			021		
John KILGARLAN	1815	1898	021	COMER, Mary	
Mary COMER Kilgarlan	1820		021	KILGARLAN, John	
			021		
Patrick FLANAGAN	50 Years	08-25-1873	021	MARTIN, Julia	
Julia MARTIN Flanagan	74Y 11M	12-08-1896	021	FLANAGAN, Patrick	
Mary Ann FLANAGAN	15Y 6M	11-01-1869	021	FLANAGAN, Mary Ann	D/O Patrick & Julia Flanagan
			021		
William ANSBRO	1844	1921	021	_____, Mary	
Mary _____ ANSBRO	1857	1919	021	ANSBRO, William	
			021		
Catherine _____ BURKE	10-21-1825	06-15-1909	021	BURKE, Walter	(NOI Walter Burke)
			021	_____, Catherine	
			021		
John SINON	69 Years	05-04-1903	021	SINON, John	
			021		
Timothy HUGHES	1855	1892	021	CLARK, Esther	
Esther CLARK Hughes	1861	1917	021	HUGHES, Timothy	
			021		
Julia A. BURKE Sinon	36Y7M18D	04-02-1895	021	SINON, J.V. Jr.	(NOI J.V. Sinon unless this is same person as John Sinon)
			021	BURKE, Julia A.	
			021		
Richard W. ROWEN	05-06-1860	06-20-1935	021	SINON, Mary	
Mary SINON ROWEN	55Y1M19D	04-19-1920	021	ROWEN, Richard W.	
			021		
(Mr.) GALLAGHER	11-19-1857	03-08-1921	021	RENFREW, Clara	(Stone says only Father and Mother but main headstone is dedicated to Clara RENFREW)
Clara RENFREW Gallagher	06-05-1861	02-21-1909	021	GALLAGHER, Mr.	
			021		
			021		
Edward M. GALLAGHER	09-25-1855	02-25-1928	021	WATERS, Kate	
Kate WATERS Gallagher	09-20-1857	05-05-1939	021	GALLAGHER, Edward	
			021		
Thomas F. BOWEN	1809	1893	021	BRODERICK, Bridget	
Bridget BRODERICK Bowen	1820	1903	021	BOWEN, Thomas	
Maria M. BOWEN	1850	1909	021	BOWEN, Maria M.	
Anthony F. BOWEN	1860	1938	021	BOWEN, Anthony F.	

NAME	POB	DOB/AGE	DOD	CEM	SPOUSE/INDEX	INSCRIPTION
Lawrence P. BOWEN		1859	1940	021	BOWEN, Lawrence P.	
				021		
Ann POWERS McCue			11-05-1887	021	MCCUE, James	(NOI James McCue)
				021	POWERS, Ann	
				021		
Thomas DURKIN		33Y 1M	12-31-1886	021	DURKIN, Thomas	
				021		
Martin DURKIN		11-07-1847	05-14-1926	021	RICHARDSON, Julia	
Julia RICHARDSON Durkin		04-11-1857	03-21-1911	021	DURKIN, Martin	
				021		
Peter HORAN		52 Years	08-20-1870	021	HORAN, Peter	
				021		
Nancy HOGAN Ryan		42 Years	08-15-1870	021	RYAN, James	(NOI James Ryan)
				021	HOGAN, Nancy	
				021		
Julia _____ HOGAN	Co. Galway	82 Years	05-10-1884	021	HOGAN, John	Died In Albany (VT). A Native of Co. Galway, Ireland. (NOI John Hogan)
				021	_____, Julia	
				021		
				021		
Thomas FLEMINGS		63 Years	01-16-1868	021	FLEMINGS, Thomas	
				021		
Thomas F. BOWEN		1852	1910	021	BOWEN, Thomas F.	
				021		
Michael MURPHY				021	MURPHY, Michael	(Marker reads: Michael Murphy and Family - Son Willie Died 08-25-1868)
Willie MURPHY			08-25-1868	021	MURPHY, Willie	
				021		
				021		
Peter GLYNN		58 Years	06-15-1893	021	GALLAGHER, Hanora	(NOI Hanora Gallagher)
				021	GLYNN, Peter	
				021		
John KEATING		86 Years	11-23-1918	021	CONNOR, Kate	
Kate CONNOR Keating		47 Years	06-11-1882	021	KEATING, John	

Congregational Church Cemetery, East Berkshire, VT

NAME	POB	DOB/AGE	DOD	CEM	SPOUSE/INDEX	INSCRIPTION
Orland MCCARTY		47Y2M17D	03-18-1882	003	MCCARTY, Orland	
				003		
Hannah E. MCCARTY		01-31-1826	01-23-1906	003	MCCARTY, Hannah E.	
				003		
John MCCARTY		10-31-1796	02-22-1874	003	COBURN, Sally	
Sally COBURN McCarty		12-11-1799	02-25-1892	003	MCCARTY, John	

				003		
Norman MCCARTY		1832	1916	003	MCCALLISTER, Jane	
Jane MCCALLISTER McCarty		1840	1928	003	MCCARTY, Norman	

St. Jerome Cemetery, E. Dorset, VT. Take Morse Road off Route 7, two miles to Squirrel Hill Road. Cemetery on Left

NAME	POB	DOB/AGE	DOD	CEM	SPOUSE/INDEX	INSCRIPTION
Thomas CARLON	Co. Roscommon	32 Years	08-01-1868	022	CARLON, Thomas	Native of Parish Kilmore, Co. Roscommon, Ireland
				022		
				022		
Bridget _____ YOUNG		28 Years	11-05-1870	022	YOUNG, Edward	(NOI Edward Young)
				022	_____, Bridget	
				022		
Rose Anna MCLAUGHLIN		01-13-1858	01-23-1869	022	MCLAUGHLIN, Rose Anna	
Thomas MCLAUGHLIN		09-22-1862	12-22-1867	022	MCLAUGHLIN, Thomas	
William MCLAUGHLIN		11-28-1866	12-23-1867	022	MCLAUGHLIN, Willliam	
Andrew MCLAUGHLIN		12-15-1864	12-20-1867	022	MCLAUGHLIN, Andrew	
				022		
Susan MCPHILIMY		3 Years	03-22-1868	022	MCPHILIMY, Susan	Dau of John & Ann McPhilimy
				022	MCPHILIMY, John	
				022		
Peter MCGARRY		20 Years	11-16-1867	022	MCGARRY, Peter	
				022		
John BRESNEHAN		54 Years	04-08-1871	022	BRESNEHAN, John	
				022		
Mary Jane MCDEVIT		6M 20D	08-02-1875	022	MCDEVIT, Mary Jane	Dau of J. & E. McDevit
				022		
Margaret MCDEVIT		1 Month	01-14-1874	022	MCDEVIT, Margaret	Dau of J. & E. McDevit
				022		
Michael MCGUIGAN	Co. Derry	77 Years	10-23-1891	022	DAILY, Margaret	Native Of Dery County (County Derry), Ireland
				022		
Margaret DAILY McGuigan	Co. Kings	55 Years	06-24-1871	022	MCGUIGAN, Michael	Native of Kings County, Ire.
				022		
James MCGUIGAN		11-05-1848	11-05-1899	022	MCGUIGAN, James	Son of Margaret & Michael McGuigan
				022		
				022		
Lawrence MOLLOY		3Y 7D	07-17-1872	022	MOLLOY, Lawrence	Son of Patrick & Eliza Molloy
				022		
Mary E. MOLLOY		10Y 8M 5D	07-16-1872	022	MOLLOY, Mary E.	Son of Patrick & Eliza Molloy
				022	MOLLOY, Patrick	
				022		

Name	Origin	Age / Birth	Death		Relations	Notes
Lawrence MOLLOY	Co. Kildare	82 Years	01-01-1871	022	_____, Margaret	Native Of Kildare County, Ire.
Margaret _____ MOLLOY		96 Years	09-28-1886	022	MOLLOY, Lawrence	
				022		
Daniel SHERIDAN		04-29-1871	09-17-1872	022	SHERIDAN, Daniel	Son of Thomas & Mary Sheridan
				022	SHERIDAN, Thomas	
				022		
Sarah Jane SHERIDAN		03-25-1867	09-10-1867	022	SHERIDAN, Sarah Jane	Dau of Thomas & Mary Sheridan
				022		
Annie MALLOY		03Y 01M	02-26-1867	022	MALLOY, Annie	Dau of Edward & Mary Malloy
				022	MALLOY, Edward	
				022		
Ann KEARIGAN Hanly	Co. Roscommon	34 Years	10-25-1866	022	HANLY, John	Native Of Parish of Kilglass,
				022	KEARIGAN, Ann	Co. Roscommon, Ireland. (NOI
				022		John Hanly)
				022		
John DOLAN		59 Years	07-06-1866	022	DOLAN, John	
				022		
Hannah REAGAN		01Y05M20D	08-30-1866	022	REAGAN, Hannah	Dau of 'Daniel' & Ellen Reagan
				022	REAGAN, Daniel	
				022		
Owen SWEENEY	Co. Cork	66 Years	10-06-1878	022	CONNOLLY, Catherine	Native Of Lick, Parish of
				022		Creagh, Co. Cork, Ireland.
				022		(Could not find 'Lick'. It is
				022		possibly Licknavar which is in
				022		Parish Creagh)
				022		
Catherine CONNOLLY Sweeney	Co. Cork	69 Years	11-08-1874	022	SWEENEY, Owen	Native Of Lick, Parish of
				022		Creagh, Co. Cork, Ireland.
				022		(See note on spouse - Owen
				022		Sweeney)
				022		
Catherine SWEENEY		21Y05M05D	01-31-1867	022	SWEENEY, Catherine	Daughter. A Native of Dorset,
				022		Vermont. Erected by Jeremiah
				022		Sweeney.
				022		
Jeremiah SWEENEY	Co. Cork	67 Years	07-22-1880	022	SWEENEY, Jeremiah	Native of County Cork, Ireland
				022		
John HOURAGAN	Co. Cork	88Y 6M	10-15-1877	022	HOURAGAN, John	Native of Coole Mane (Cool
				022		main) Parish of Kil Britten
				022		(Kilbrittain, Co. Cork, Ire.
				022		
John O'HEARNE	Co. Waterford	68 Years	09-09-1884	022	_____, Margaret	Native Of Co. Waterford, Ire.
Margaret _____ O'HEARNE			09-25-1901	022	O'HEARNE, John	(NOI DOB)
				022		
John O'HERON		17Y 5MO	10-26-1873	022	O'HERON, John	Son of John & Margaret O'Heron

				022		(Probably O'HEARNE)
				022		
John DACY		09Y02M12D	04-23-1865	022	DACY, John	S/O Timothy & Catherine Dacy
				022	DACY, Timothy	
				022		
John MALONEY		09Y02M12D	04-23-1865	022	MALONEY, John	Son of James & Mary Maloney
				022	MALONEY, James	
				022		
Sarah CARNEY Sherlock		38 Years	12-22-1869	022	SHERLOCK, Michael	(NOI Michael Sherlock)
				022	CARNEY, Sarah	
				022		
Ann CUNNINGHAM Carroll	Co. Roscommon	38 Years	05-08-1874	022	CARROLL, John	Native Of Parish of Kilglass,
				022	CUNNINGHAM, Ann	Co. Roscommon, Ireland. (NOI
				022		John Carroll)
				022		
Sarah CUNNINGHAM Condon	Co. Roscommon	40 Years	12-01-1867	022	CONDON, George	Native Of Parish of Kilglass,
				022	CUNNINGHAM, Sarah	Co. Roscommon, Ireland. (NOI
				022		George Condon)
				022		
Bridget _____ CARLON	Co. Roscommon	28 Years	04-06-1862	022	CARLON, Patrick	Native Of Parish of Kilglass,
				022	_____, Bridget	Co. Roscommon, Ireland. (NOI
				022		Patrick Carlon)
				022		
Thomas MCLAUGHLIN	Co. Kings	1818	1887	022	MCLAUGHLIN, Thomas	Native Of Kings Co., Ireland
				022		
Mathew MCLAUGHLIN		05Y 01M	06-13-1860	022	MCLAUGHLIN, Mathew	Son Of Kerin & Catharine
				022	MCLAUGHLIN, Kerin	McLaughlin
				022		McLaughlin
Bernard MCLAUGHLIN		06Y 08M	04-11-1860	022	MCLAUGHLIN, Bernard	Son Of Kerin & Catharine
				022		McLaughlin
				022		
Robert DUNN		01Y08M24D	10-07-1860	022	DUNN, Robert	Son Of John & Honnora Dunn
				022	DUNN, John	
				022		
Michael SLATTERY	Co. Tipperary	28 Years	08-21-1860	022	SLATTERY, Michael	Born In Tiperary, Ireland (Co.
				022		Tipperary)
				022		
Edward BOWERS		87 Years	10-27-1879	022	_____, Catherine	
Catharine _____ BOWERS	Co. Kilkenny	64 Years	09-28-1860	022	BOWERS, Edward	Native of Gragarina, Parish Of
				022		Moinroin, Co. Kilkenny. No
				022		such place as Gragarina. Could
				022		be Graiguenamanagh. No parish
				022		Moinroin. Could be Mooncoin.
				022		
Mary SULLIVAN		28Y 09M	__-25-1870	022	SULLIVAN, Mary	(This stone reads 'Born in the

NAME	POB	DOB/AGE	DOD	CEM	SPOUSE/INDEX	INSCRIPTION
				022		Parish of Ballydonahue, Co.
				022		K_____. Ireland. There is a
				022		town of Ballydonohoe in Co.
				022		Kerry. This stone badly worn)
				022		
Erril CARNEY	Co. Kings	70 Years	10-06-1877	022	_____, Sarah	Native of Kings Co., Ireland
Sarah _____ CARNEY		94 Years	12-01-1895	022	CARNEY, Erril	
				022		
Baby PRENDERGAST		--	02-13-1870	022	PRENDERGAST, Baby	Infant Son Of P. F. & M.A.
				022		Prendergast
				022		
Bridget _____ KELLY	Co. Limerick	65 Years	03-15-1872	022	KELLY, Patrick	Of The Parish of Adare, County
				022	_____, Bridget	Limerick, Ireland (NOI Patrick
				022		Kelly)
				022		
John KELLY	Co. Limerick	26 Years	08-22-1863	022	KELLY, John	Of The Parish of Adare, County
				022		Limerick, Ireland
				022		
Frankie STONE		13 Months	07-26-1862	022	STONE, Frankie	Son Of David & Mary Stone
				022	STONE, David	
				022		
Richard MCNAMARA		55 Years	01-18-1881	022	_____, Mary Ann	
Mary Ann _____ MCNAMARA		42 Years	02-08-1879	022	MCNAMARA, Richard	
David MCNAMARA		19 Years	09-01-1887	022	MCNAMARA, David	Son Of William & Mary McNamara
John MCNAMARA		03-29-1867	09-30-1890	022	MCNAMARA, John	
Richard MCNAMARA		07-03-1869	11-28-1890	022	MCNAMARA, Richard	
				022		
Richard HANLAN				022	HANLAN, Richard	(GAR) Co. I, 14th Vt Inf.
				022		(NOI DOB-DOD)
				022		
Thomas CARLON	Co. Roscommon	60 Years	12-25-1866	022	FLYNN, Mary	Native Of Co. Roscommon, Ire.
Mary FLYNN Carlon	Co. Kings	77 Years	11-06-1909	022	CARLON, Thomas	A Native of Kings Co., Ireland
				022		
William MCNAMARA		10 Years??	04-11-1864	022	MCNAMARA, William	
				022		
Francis TULLY		11Y02M02D	04-14-1869	022	TULLY, Francis	Son Of William & Ann TULLY
Ellen TULLY		10Y04M03D	03-27-1873	022	TULLY, Ellen	Dau Of William & Ann TULLY
				022	TULLY, William	

St. Jerome Cemetery, E. Dorset, VT. Just of Route 7 on Church Grounds

NAME	POB	DOB/AGE	DOD	CEM	SPOUSE/INDEX	INSCRIPTION
Michael MYLOTT		1835	1911	102	_____, Margaret Anna	

Name	Origin	Born	Died		Relation	Notes
Margaret Anna _____ MYLOTT		1834	1911	102	MYLOTT, Michael	
				102		
John BYRNE		34 Years	05-09-1891	102	BYRNE, John	
				102		
Patrick GAHERTY		1831	1910	102	GAHERTY, Patrick	(GAR) Co. A. 13th Rgt (Vt) Inf
				102		
James CONNOR		1818	1916	102	GRADY, Margaret	
Margaret GRADY Connor		1831	1907	102	CONNOR, James	
				102		
Thomas MCLAUGHLIN	Co. Kings	1818	1887	102	RIGNEY, Margaret	Natives of Kings Co.,Ireland
Margaret RIGNEY McLaughlin	Co. Kings	1828	1906	102	MCLAUGHLIN, Thomas	Natives of Kings Co.,Ireland
				102		
James G. FAHY		1845	1925	102	HOULIHAN, Mary	
Mary HOULIHAN Fahy		1855	1923	102	FAHY, James G.	
				102		
Thomas MCGRATH		57 Years	03-04-1886	102	MCGRATH, Thomas	
				102		
Edward DIFFLEY		45 Years	09-04-1893	102	DIFFLEY, Edward	
				102		
Patrick BURKE			06-01-1890	102	BURKE, Patrick	
				102		
John MAGUIRE		06-24-1806	11-27-1888	102	HENEY, Mary Teresa	
Mary Teresa HENEY Maguire		12-12-1818	02-28-1865	102	MAGUIRE, John	
				102		
Patrick MCDONALD		1848	1932	102	_____, Catherine	
Catherine _____ MCDONALD		1859	1887	102	MCDONALD, Patrick	
				102		
James MALONEY		78 Years	06-01-1890	102	ROURKE, Mary	
Mary ROURKE Maloney		68 Years	05-14-1888	102	MALONEY, James	
				102		
Mary MCGUIGEN	Co. Leitrim	01-01-1807		102	MCGUIGEN, Mary	Born In The Co. Leitrim, Ire.
				102		
James BOWERS		79 Years	06-04-1909	102	_____, Eliza	
Eliza _____ BOWERS		59 Years	03-07-1881	102	BOWERS, James	
				102		
James MCCURDY		78 Years	06-08-1896	102	GREEN, Jane	
Jane GREEN McCurdy		63 Years	05-08-1891	102	MCCURDY, James	
				102		
Thomas REVI		69 Years	06-16-1913	102	GRANT, Katherine	(Surname probably RAVEY)
Katherine GRANT Revi		37 Years	06-04-1881	102	REVI, Thomas	
				102		
Johannah LEAHY			06-13-1886	102	LEAHY, Johannah	Died At Manchester, VT
				102		
Matthew MCDEVITT		1825	1902	102	STUART, Margaret	
				102	PERKINSON, Mary	

Margaret STUART McDevitt		1824	1861	102	MCDEVITT, Matthew	
Mary PERKINSON McDevitt		1822	1907	102	MCDEVITT, Matthew	
James CARNEY		1853	1881	102	CARNEY, James	
				102		
James PURCELL	Co. Tipperary	59 Years	10-18-1880	102	PURCELL, Mrs. James	Native of Co. Tipperary, Ire.
Mrs. James PURCELL		56 Years	06-11-1884	102	PURCELL, James	
				102		
Patrick PURCELL		1855	1934	102	FOLEY, Mary	
Mary FOLEY Purcell		1856	1936	102	PURCELL, Patrick	
				102		
Patrick DONOVAN	Co. Waterford	67 Years	04-10-1866	102	_____, Bridget	A Native of Dremana (Dromana),
				102		Parish of Aglish, Waterford
				102		County, Ireland
Bridget _____ DONOVAN		95 Years	02-04-1898	102	DONOVAN, Patrick	
				102		
Mary DONOVAN Kearns		32 Years	06-13-1873	102	KEARNS, John	(NOI John Kearns)
				102	DONOVAN, Mary	
				102		
Lawrence O'BRIEN	Co. Meath	86 Years	10-08-1881	102	O'BRIEN, Lawrence	Born In County Meath, Ireland.
				102	O'BRIEN, Catherine	Erected by Catherine & Bridget
				102	O'BRIEN, Bridget	O'Brien(NOI Catherine/Bridget)
				102		
Dennis MCKEEGAN		04-09-1843	09-26-1884	102	FLYNN, Catherine	
Catherine FLYNN McKeegan		11-26-1850	08-29-1926	102	MCKEEGAN, Dennis	
				102		
James HORAN		1846	1922	102	CONDON, Marie C.	
Marie CONDON Horan		1847		102	HORAN, James	
				102		
Charles BOWEN		24Y1M28D	10-11-1875	102	BOWEN, Charles	Son Of John & Anna Bowen
				102		
Ann MURRY Stuart	Co. Roscommon	91Y1M29D	05-03-1881	102	STUART, Francis	In Memory Of--Born In The
				102	MURRY, Ann	Parish of Killmore (Kilmore),
				102		Co. Roscommon, Ireland. (NOI
				102		Francis Stuart)
				102		
John S. STUART	Co. Roscommon	82 Years	02-21-1891	102	FOX, Ellen	Born In The Parish of Killmore
				102		(Kilmore), Co. Roscommon, Ire
Ellen FOX Stuart	Co. Roscommon			102	STUART, John S.	Born In The Parish of Killmore
				102		(Kilmore), Co. Roscommon, Ire
				102		(No DOB/DOD Ellen Fox)
				102		
Erril P. CARNEY		30 Years	11-01-1873	102	CARNEY, Erril P.	
				102		
Mary HORAN	Co. Tipperary	07-04-1815	03-21-1890	102	HORAN, Mary	Born In The County of
				102		Tipperary, Ireland

				102		
Thomas HILL		77 Years	04-17-1908	102	_____, Bridget	
Bridget _____ HILL		38 Years	09-13-1876	102	HILL, Thomas	
				102		
James LEE		10-25-1821	09-16-1894	102	LOWLOR, Mary A.	
Mary LOWLOR Lee		59 Years	09-03-1882	102	LEE, James	
				102		
William MOORE		36 Years	07-11-1876	102	MOORE, William	
Cathrin MOORE Battis		44 Years	11-06-1880	102	BATTIS, Curtis	(NOI Curtis Battis)
				102	MOORE, Cathrin	
John MOORE		12-25-1799	02-12-1890	102	_____, Julia A.	(Marker does not indicate if
Julia A. _____ MOORE		12-25-1801	08-16-1892	102	MOORE, John	John & Julia Moore are husband
				102		and wife.)
				102		
Patrick KELLEY	Co. Roscommon	03-17-1806	03-23-1876	102	CLINE, Elizabeth	Born In The Parish Killglass
				102		(Kilglass),Co. Roscommon, Ire.
Elizabeth CLINE Kelley	Co. Roscommon	07-08-1810	02-02-1878	102	KELLEY, Patrick	Born In The Parish Killglass
				102		(Kilglass),Co. Roscommon, Ire.
				102		
Thomas KELLEY		42 Years	03-31-1882	102	_____, Mary	
Mary _____ KELLEY		55 Years	02-17-1926	102	KELLEY, Thomas	
				102		
John MCDEVITT	Co. Tyrone	05-12-1826	11-21-1889	102	MCPHILMNY, Rebecca	Born In The Parish of Ardstra,
				102		(Ardstraw),Co. Tyrone, Ireland
Rebecca MCPHILMNY McDevitt	Co. Tyrone	1841	01-06-1879	102	MCDEVITT, John	Born In The Parish of Ardstra,
				102		(Ardstraw),Co. Tyrone, Ireland
				102		Died In Dorset, Vermont,Age 37
				102		Years. (Surname probably is
				102		McPhilomy)
				102		
John MCPHILOMY	Co. Tyrone	46 Years	05-01-1879	102	MCDEVITT, Ann	Born In Lislean (Lisleen), Co.
				102		Tyrone, reland. (Lisleen is in
				102		the Parish of Ardstraw)
Ann MCDEVITT McPhilomy	Co. Tyrone	1913	01-06-1879	102	MCPHILOMY, John	Born In Lislean (Lisleen), Co.
				102		Tyrone, Ireland.(Lisleen is in
				102		the Parish of Ardstraw)
				102		Died In Dorset, Vermont,Age 37
				102		
Patrick PHALEN		56 Years	09-13-1893	102	BOWEN, Annie	
Annie BOWEN Phalen		54 Years	11-14-1893	102	PHALEN, Patrick	
				102		
Jeremiah GRADY		75 Years	11-11-1897	102	O'BRIEN, Mary	
Mary O'BRIEN Grady		72 Years	07-30-1903	102	GRADY, Jeremiah	
				102		
Daniel COFFEY	Co. Cork		04-12-1906	102	O'BRIEN, Catharine	Born In Desert Parish, Cork

Name	Place	Birth/Age	Death	Ref.	Relation	Remarks
				102		County, Ireland
Catharine O'BRIEN Coffey	Co. Westmeath		01-29-1891	102	COFFEY, Daniel	Born In Delvin Parish, Westmeath County, Ireland.
Edward HAYES		1822	1862	102	CONDON, Eliza	
Eliza CONDON Hayes		1821	1902	102	HAYES, Edward	
John HAYES		1853	1877	102	HAYES, John	
Edward HAYES		1856	1927	102	HAYES, Edward	
William KELLEY	Co. Kilkenny	68 Years	04-04-1879	102	KELLEY, William	Born In Parish of Ballyhale, Kilkeney (Kilkenny) County, Ireland. (No such Parish. Probably Ballyhale Town)
Thomas TOUHY	Co. Limerick	07-10-1847	06-14-1877	102	TOUHY, Thomas	Born In The Parish of Croagh, Co. Limerick, Ireland
Bridget _____ HOCTOR		46 Years	10-05-1878	102	HOCTOR, Michael _____, Bridget	(NOI Michael Hoctor)
John TOUHY	Co. Limerick	06-20-1812	11-06-1887	102	TOUHY, John	Born In The Parish of Croagh, Co. Limerick, Ireland
Michael COLLINS	Co. Kilkenny	24Y 6M	08-11-1869	102	COLLINS, Michael	Here Rest The Remains of Michael Collins, A Native Of The Parish of Graigue, Co. Kilkenny, Ireland. (No such Catholic Parish as Graigue. Could be Town of Graigue or Parish of Graiguenamanagh. See other Collins family members)
Edward COLLINS		32 Years	04-26-1878	102	COLLINS, Edward	(Same stone as Michael Collins
Maurice COLLINS	Co. Kilkenny	03-22-1834	06-04-1908	102	POTTER, Mary	Native of Graigue, County Kilkenny, Ireland
Mary POTTER Collins		02-11-1848		102	COLLINS, Maurice	Born In Dorset, Vermont
John COLLINS	Co. Kilkenny	05-12-1846	03-15-1904	102	_____, Bridget	Natives of Graigue, County Kilkenny, Ireland
Bridget _____ COLLINS	Co. Kilkenny	09-10-1857	08-01-1891	102	COLLINS, John	Natives of Graigue, County Kilkenny, Ireland
David STONE		11-14-1829	03-05-1896	102	RITCHIE, Mary	
Mary RITCHIE Stone		02-29-1839	06-10-1901	102	STONE, David	

Name	Origin	Born	Died	Section	Relation	Notes
William WHALON		56 Years	04-10-1871	102	_____, Bridget	
Bridget _____ WHALON		90 Years	04-28-1900	102	WHALON, William	
				102		
John DUNN		08-10-1817	01-28-1907	102	PURTELL, Honora	
Honora PURTELL Dunn		06-19-1818	08-29-1891	102	DUNN, John	(Surname probably Purcell)
				102		
Patrick DUNN		03-17-1836	1912	102	CUNNINGHAM, Margaret	
Margaret CUNNINGHAM Dunn		04-23-1842	04-14-1900	102	DUNN, Patrick	
				102		
John GREEN		1820	1902	102	_____, Mary	
Mary _____ GREEN		1826	1901	102	GREEN, John	
Mary L. _____ VETAL		1842	1887	102	VETAL, Frank	
Frank VETAL		1882	1901	102	VETAL, Frank	
				102		
Thomas SULLIVAN		1856	1905	102	REAGAN, Ellen	
Ellen REAGAN Sullivan		1853	1933	102	SULLIVAN, Thomas	
				102		
Andrew MCDONALD	Co. Roscommon	1861	1941	102	DIFFLEY, Bridget	Born In Co. Roscommon, Ireland
Bridget DIFFLEY McDonald	Co. Roscommon	1865	1932	102	MCDONALD, Andrew	Born In Co. Roscommon, Ireland
John MCDONALD	Co. Roscommon	1863	1888	102	MCDONALD, Andrew	Born In Co. Roscommon, Ireland (Same stone as Andrew McDonald inscription of "Brother".)
				102		
				102		
				102		
Philip GALLAGHER		1848	1927	102	MCNAMARA, Julia	
Julia MCNAMARA Gallagher		1861	1911	102	GALLAGHER, Philip	
				102		
Jeremiah REAGAN	Co. Cork	03-03-1826	07-12-1889	102	COFFEY, Ellen	Born In The Parish of Kilmacabee (Kilmacabea),Co. Cork, Ire
				102		
Ellen COFFEY Reagan	Co. Cork	03-22-1835	01-06-1920	102	REAGAN, Jeremiah	Born In The Parish of Desertserjes (Desertserges), County Cork, Ireland
				102		
				102		
				102		
John CARROLL		11-01-1831	05-24-1898	102	CASEY, Mary	A Native of Ireland
Mary CASEY Carroll		01-01-1832	07-01-1887	102	CARROLL, John	A Native of Ireland
				102		
William MCBRIDE		1847	1913	102	_____, Mary	
Mary _____ MCBRIDE		1852	1926	102	MCBRIDE, William	
				102		
Michael CUNNINGHAM		1858	1917	102	CUNNINGHAM, Michael	
				102		
Dennis RILEY		1852	1915	102	STONE, Mary	
Mary STONE Riley		1864	1938	102	RILEY, Dennis	
				102		
John LEARY		1853	1909	102	LEARY, John	
				102		

Edward MOLLOY		1824	1915	102	_____, Mary	
Mary _____ MOLLOY		1826	1915	102	MOLLOY, Edward	
				102		
Michael CUNNINGHAM		1835	1915	102	IGOE, Bridget	
Bridget IGOE Cunningham		1837	1912	102	CUNNINGHAM, Michael	
				102		
Edward HUGHES		1845	1917	102	SWEENEY, Mary	
Mary SWEENEY Hughes		1848	192_	102	HUGHES, Edward	
John SWEENEY		1850	1917	102	SWEENEY, John	
				102		
Martin MCLAUGHLIN		1832	1918	102	TULLY, Ann	
Ann TULLY McLaughlin		1833	1927	102	MCLAUGHLIN, Martin	
				102		
William Charles WHALON		1853	1936	102	WHALON, William Charles	
				102		
John Bartholomew KIRK		1847	1916	102	BURNS, Ellen	
Ellen BURNS Kirk		1851	1937	102	KIRK, John Bartholomew	
				102		
Daniel LEARY		84 Years	07-19-1906	102	BROWN, Ellen	
Ellen BROWN Leary		03-15-1826	10-30-1915	102	LEARY, Daniel	
				102		
James MCBRIDE		1818	1906	102	MCDEVITT, Mary	
Mary MCDEVITT McBride		1827	1911	102	MCBRIDE, James	
				102		
Barney GARVEY		1824	1889	102	_____, Ann	
Ann _____ GARVEY		37 Years	11-07-1867	102	GARVEY, Barney	
				102		
William COREY		1844	1944	102	YOUNG, Mary A.	
Mary A. YOUNG Corey		1852	1933	102	COREY, William	
				102		
James QUIGLEY	Co. Armagh	1834	1907	102	MCGEE, Rose	Natives of Co. Armagh, Ireland
Rose MCGEE Quigley	Co. Armagh	1832	1904	102	QUIGLEY, James	Natives of Co. Armagh, Ireland
				102		
Patrick CALLINAN	Co. Limerick	03-17-1844	04-21-1906	102	ROGERS, Margaret	Native of County Limerick
Margaret ROGERS Callinan	Co. Cavan	1847	01-06-1921	102	CALLINAN, Patrick	Native of County Cavan
Patrick ROGERS	Co. Cavan	60 Years	12-21-1901	102	ROGERS, Patrick	Born In Coote Hill, County Cavan, Ireland
				102		
				102		
John MCDEVITT		1833	1913	102	_____, Jane	
Jane _____ MCDEVITT		1826	1901	102	MCDEVITT, John	
				102		
ernard HANLEY		12-25-1816	09-27-1891	102	HANLEY, Bernard	
				102		
Michael CUNNINGHAM	Co. Roscommon	1833	01-05-1891	102	MYLOTT, Mary	Born In Boyle, Co. Roscommon, Ireland
				102		

Name	Birthplace	Born	Died	Page	Spouse	Notes
Mary MYLOTT Cunningham		09-15-1844	12-02-1926	102	CUNNINGHAM, Michael	
				102		
James HOULIHAN	Co. Clare	05-10-1810	08-27-1897	102	TOUHEY, Mary	Born In The Parish of Kildy-
				102		sart, Co. Clare, Ireland
Mary TOUHEY Houlihan	Co. Clare	05-10-1810	08-27-1897	102	HOULIHAN, James	Born In Low Island, Parish of
				102		Kildysart, Co. Clare, Ireland.
				102		(Cannot find "Low Island" in
				102		Co. Clare but found in Co.
				102		Mayo & Co. Cork)
				102		
John CORNELL		09-__-1848	04-__-1899	102	GARVEY, Sarah	(GAR) Co. M., 10th NY Cavalry
Sarah GARVEY Cornell		1854	1930	102	CORNELL, John	
				102		
James GODEY		06-12-1844	03-15-1904	102	KELLEY, Nancy	
Nancy KELLEY Godey		04-15-1851	08-21-1889	102	GODEY, James	
				102		
William GODEY		76 Years	1892	102	PURCELL, Margaret	
Margaret GODEY Purcell		72 Years	1892	102	GODEY, William	
				102		
Michael SHERLOCK		1838	18__	102	PHALEN, Sarah	
Sarah PHALEN Sherlock		1849	1932	102	SHERLOCK, Michael	
				102		
Patrick AGAN	Co. Roscommon	90 Years	05-24-1895	102	HANLEY, Sarah	Born In County Roscommon, Ire.
Sarah HANLEY Agan		72 Years	03-13-1891	102	AGAN, Patrick	
John JOYCE		76 Years	01-20-1901	102	HANLEY, Mary	
Mary HANLEY Joyce		72 Years	02-17-1899	102	JOYCE, John	
				102		
Owen BRADY		1831	1892	102	_____, Margaret	
Margaret _____ BRADY		1835	1911	102	BRADY, Owen	
				102		
Daniel O'SULLIVAN		41 Years	03-07-1873	102	PICKETT, Margaret	
Margaret PICKETT O'Sullivan		87 Years	11-16-1907	102	O'SULLIVAN, Daniel	
				102		
John KELLEHER		1831	1901	102	COSGROVE, Rose	
Rose COSGROVE Kelleher		1839	1915	102	KELLEHER, John	
John J. COSGROVE		1837	1893	102	COSGROVE, John J.	
				102		
James KELLY		01-26-1826	10-11-1889	102	_____, Margaret	
Margaret _____ KELLY		02-10-1845	12-22-1910	102	KELLY, James	
				102		
Luke O'CONNOR		1824	1896	102	_____, Mary	
Mary _____ O'CONNOR		1826	1904	102	O'CONNOR, Luke	
				102		
John HORAN		1847	1902	102	_____, Bridget	
Bridget _____ HORAN		1853	1906	102	HORAN, John	

Name	Place	Born	Died		Relatives	Notes
				102		
Patrick MOORE		60 Years	05-13-1896	102	HOWARD, Margaret	
Margaret HOWARD Moore		88 Years	03-18-1924	102	MOORE, Patrick	
				102		
John FLYNN		1827	1896	102	SCANLEN, Ellen	
Ellen SCANLEN Flynn		1820	1898	102	FLYNN, John	
				102		
Thomas SHERIDAN		12-16-1838	05-30-1911	102	HAYES, Mary	
Mary HAYES Sheridan		03-25-1841	08-13-1905	102	SHERIDAN, Thomas	
				102		
John QUILTER	Co. Kerry	05-17-1820	02-10-1898	102	TOOHEY, Mary	Born In Ballingtoher (Ballintogher), Parish of Ballingara, Co. Kerry, Ireland (No such Parish.)
				102		
				102		
				102		
Mary TOOHEY Quilter	Co. Galway	01-18-1836	03-23-1921	102	QUILTER, John	Born In Parish of Gourteln, Co. Galway, Ireland. (No such Parish - possibly town of Gorteen or Gortaleam) Mayo & Co. Cork)
				102		
				102		
				102		
				102		
				102		
Michael CANARY		1817	1895	102	_____, Bridget	(Surname is possibly Keniry)
Bridget _____ Canary		1831	1867	102	CANARY, Michael	
				102		
John KEATING	Co. Queens	08-05-1829	01-18-1892	102	SHERIDAN, Maria	Born In Queens (Leix) Co, Ire.
Maria SHERIDAN Keating	Co. Roscommon	03-18-1844	05-13-1900	102	KEATING, John	Born In Co. Roscommon, Ireland
				102		
Daniel SHERIDAN		1795	1888	102	CLINE, Ann	
Ann CLINE Sheridan		1810	1892	102	SHERIDAN, Daniel	
James SHERIDAN		1836	1890	102	SHERIDAN, James	
Martin SHERIDAN		1835	1916	102	KELLY, Ann	
Ann KELLY Sheridan		1843	1905	102	SHERIDAN, Martin	
				102		
James LAWLER		1838	1915	102	CASSIDY, Cathrine	
Cathrine CASSIDY Lawler		1850	1920	102	LAWLER, James	
John LAWLER		52 Years	07-28-1886	102	LAWLER, John	
				102		
Owen MCNABOE		1823	1896	102	KELLY, Mary	
Mary KELLY McNaboe		1837	1903	102	MCNABOE, Owen	
				102		
Patrick BURNS		01-16-1816	07-23-1897	102	_____, Mary	
Mary _____ BURNS		1799	1899	102	BURNS, Patrick	
				102		
Maria _____ CARNEY		68 Years	08-23-1886	102	CARNEY, Patrick	(NOI Patrick Carney)
				102	_____, Maria	
				102		

Patrick LOVETT		03-12-1829		102	LOVETT, Patrick	
				102		
Kerin MCLAUGHLIN		1821	1899	102	CARNEY, Catherine	
Catherine CARNEY McLaughlin		1824	1899	102	MCLAUGHLIN, Kerin	
				102		
Owen HANLON		1846	1915	102	MCBRIDE, Ellen	
Ellen MCBRIDE Hanlon		1844	19__	102	HANLON, Owen	
				102		
Patrick NAVIN		1840	1911	102	CURLANE, Annie	
Annie CURLANE Navin		1843	1894	102	NAVIN, Patrick	
				102		
Thomas BURNS		1825	1905	102	COLEMAN, Anna	
Anna COLEMAN Burns		1831	1891	102	BURNS, Thomas	
				102		
Daniel DALEY		71 Years	01-18-1903	102	MCDEVITT, Susan	
Susan MCDEVITT Daley		1840	1920	102	DALEY, Daniel	
				102		
John O'GRADY		79 Years	05-13-1898	102	_____, Catherine	
Catherine _____ O'GRADY		67 Years	07-26-1895	102	O'GRADY, John	
				102		
Martin FOLEY		1816	1898	102	KENIRY, Catherine	
Catherine KENIRY Foley		1815	1892	102	FOLEY, Martin	
				102		
James FLYNN		01-10-1824	03-28-1897	102	SHEA, Catherine	
Catherine SHEA Flynn		04-16-1826	05-20-1911	102	FLYNN, James	
				102		
Joseph MCBRIDE		05-12-1844	05-03-1892	102	MCBRIDE, Joseph	
				102		
Jeremiah MCDONNELL	Co. Cork	49 Years	07-31-1890	102	HORAN, Ellen	Native of Parish of Cree, (Creagh), Co. Cork, Ireland
				102		
Ellen HORAN McDonnell	Co. Tipperary	04-15-1845		102	MCDONNELL, Jeremiah	Born In Co. Tipperary, Ireland
				102		
Cornelius MCCAULEY		45Y 2M	07-03-1873	102	MCBRIDE, Mary Ann	
Mary Ann MCBRIDE McCauley		41Y3M6D	04-26-1885	102	MCCAULEY, Cornelius	
				102		
Thomas DALTON		03-07-1827	07-25-1896	102	FANNIN, Ellen	
Ellen FANNIN Dalton		05-23-1829	05-26-1909	102	DALTON, Thomas	
James DALTON		06-26-1859	04-22-1884	102	DALTON, James	
				102		
Michael MCBRIDE		1839	1904	102	_____, Jane	
Jane _____ MCBRIDE		32 Years	12-05-1870	102	MCBRIDE, Michael	
Catherine AGAN McBride		1817	1900	102	AGAN, Catherine	
				102		
John WELCH		60 Years	12-14-1882	102	_____, Hannah	
Hannah _____ WELCH		68 Years	11-14-1900	102	WELCH, John	

				102		
George CONDON		1831	1893	102	_____, Bridget	
Bridget _____ CONDON		1833	1893	102	CONDON, George	
				102		
William SENNETT		1845	1921	102	MALONE, Catherine	(NOI Catherine Malone)
				102	SENNETT, William	
				102		
William HANLEY		76 Years	10-09-1893	102	_____, Hannora	(Age at death could be 78 Yrs)
Hannora _____ HANLEY		67 Years	10-31-1882	102	HANLEY, William	
				102		
James TUOHY		73 Years	06-06-1888	102	MURPHY, Mary	
Mary MURPHY Tuohy		06-01-1838	01-20-1919	102	TUOHY, James	
				102		
Robert GORMLEY		1840	1920	102	MCDEVITT, Margaret	
Margaret MCDEVITT Gormley		41 Years	05-04-1895	102	GORMLEY, Robert	
				102		
Timothy HOCTOR		12-07-1807	06-11-1890	102	BAKER, Harriet	
Harriet BAKER Hoctor		05-10-1810	01-30-1882	102	HOCTOR, Timothy	
				102		
James M. MCDEVITT		1838	1886	102	_____, Anne	
Anne _____ MCDEVITT		1843	1923	102	MCDEVITT, James M.	
				102		
John BOWEN		1841	1892	102	BURNS, Ellen	(GAR) Co. K., 14th Reg, Vt Inf
Ellen BURNS Bowen		1841	1932	102	BOWEN, John	
				102		
John MCDEVITT		1849	1919	102	MCGUIGEN, Ellen	
Ellen MCGUIGEN McDevitt		1846	1927	102	MCDEVITT, John	
				102		
John C. CONDON		1856	1932	102	HALEY, Kate E.	
Kate HALEY Condon		1869	1937	102	CONDON, John C.	

St. Lawrence Mission Cemetery, Ely Mines (Vershire), Vt

These are all of the stones in this lonely, isolated cemetery. It is located near South Vershire, Vermont. Vershire has been known as Copperfield and Ely Mines and mined copper in the late 1800's.

NAME	POB	DOB/AGE	DOD	CEM	SPOUSE/INDEX	INSCRIPTION
John DOYLE		1845	1930	023	DOYLE, Catherine	
Catherine _____ DOYLE		1855	1930	023	DOYLE, John	
Mary E. DOYLE		19 Years	01-26-1890	023	DOYLE, Mary E.	Dau Of John & Kate Doyle
				023		
William TEAGUE		1861	19__	023	KENNEDY, Catherine	

Catherine KENNEDY Teague		1845	1919	023	TEAGUE, William	
				023		
Isabella M. FOLEY		3Y 8M	02-03-1884	023	FOLEY, Isabella M	Dau Of Cornelius & Eliza M.
				023	FOLEY, Eliza M.	Foley (NOI Parents)
				023	FOLEY, Cornelius	
				023		
Mary E. MURPHY		09-03-1879	10-07-1891	023	MURPHY, Mary E.	Dau Of M & C Murphy (NOI)
				023	MURPHY, M.	
				023	MURPHY, C.	
				023		
Bridget _____ WELSH		41 Years	05-17-1880	023	_____, Bridget	(NOI Richard Welsh)
				023	WELSH, Richard	
				023		
KENNEDY				023		(Stone toppled. Cannot read)
				023		
John S. WALSH	Co. Tipperary	17Y10M15D	06-01-1881	023	WALSH, John S.	Son Of Thomas & Mary Walsh
				023	WALSH, Thomas	Native of Cloghan (Clogher),
				023	WALSH, Mary	Co. Tipperary, Ire. Erected
				023		His Father, Thomas Walsh

St. John The Baptist - Enosburg Falls (Old Cemetery - On Missisquoi Street, Enosburg Village)

NAME	POB	DOB/AGE	DOD	CEM	SPOUSE/INDEX	INSCRIPTION
Matthew SHANNON		1822	1884	024	HARVEY, Catherine	
Catherine HARVEY Shannon		1838	1875	024	SHANNON, Matthew	
				024		
James SPEARS		76 Years	09-12-1878	024	SLONE, Mary	
Mary SLONE Spears		92 Years	02-05-1896	024	SPEARS, James	(Surname Probably Sloan)
				024		
Jeremiah ENRIGHT		68 Years	10-29-1881	024	ENRIGHT, Jeremiah	
		1852	1872	024		Son Of Jeremiah & Mary Enright
				024		(Name of son is missing)
Kattie MURPHY Benoit		---	12-17-1879	024	BENOIT, Joseph	(NOI Joseph Benoit--This stone
				024	MURPHY, Kattie	in poor condition.)
				024		
Francis RANDALL		72Y 1M 13D	10-12-1890	024	GABAREE, Eliza	(GAR) Co. K. 6th Vt Vols
Eliza GABERIE Randall		66 Years	06-12-1889	024	RANDALL, Francis	(Surname probably Gaboury)
				024		
Susan ERWIN		06-25-1814	08-29-1892	024	ERWIN, Susan	
				024		
Christopher LAFLEY		68 Years	11-05-1886	024	LONGEY, Margaret	
Margaret LONGEY Lafley		41 Years	05-14-1874	024	LAFLEY, Christopher	

				024		
Catharine HOUSTON		42 Years	03-17-1875	024	HOUSTON, Catharine	
				024		
Susan ____ HOUSTON		65 Years	05-14-1881	024	HOUSTON, Patrick	(NOI Patrick Houston)
				024	_____, Susan	
				024		
Michael LADEN		61 Years	10-02-1879	024	LAVERY, Lucy	
Lucy Lavery LADEN		41 Years	12-10-1891	024	LADEN, Michael	
				024		
Roger COLLINS		80 Years	04-14-1895	024	HOWIE, Margaret J.	
Margaret J. HOWIE		65Y 11M	05-10-1888	024	COLLINS, Roger	
				024		
Bridget SLOAN Trainer		87 Years	05-18-1893	024	TRAINER, Owen	(NOI Owen Trainer)
				024	SLOAN, Bridget	
Catharine WOODS		76 Years	06-06-1894	024	WOODS, Catharine	
				024		
John COLLINS		08-10-1845		024	MILES, Sarah J.	
Sarah J. MILES Collins		09-19-1853	05-28-1889	024	COLLINS, John	
				024		
Peter HART		65 Years	05-14-1881	024	HART, Peter	
				024		
Sarah J. SLAMMON		36Y11M30D	01-25-1880	024	SLAMMON, Sarah J.	(Stone reads "wife of" but section with spouses name is missing. Death year might be 1890. Difficult to read.
				024		
				024		
				024		

St.John The Baptist - Enosburg Falls (New Cemetery - Cross River on Vt Highway 108, left after bridge, 2 miles)

NAME	POB	DOB/AGE	DOD	CEM	SPOUSE/INDEX	INSCRIPTION
-						
Barney SPEARS		1835	1913	025	HOUSTON, Mary	
Mary HOUSTON Spears		1835	1905	025	SPEARS, Barney	
				025		
George HOUSTON		1852	1939	025	WOODS, Mary A.	
Mary A. WOODS Houston		1857	1926	025	HOUSTON,George	
				025		
John O'BRIEN		1837	1923	025	_____, Catherine	
Catherine ____ O'BRIEN		1841	1904	025	O'BRIEN, John	
				025		
James HOUSTON		1854	1931	025	HOUSTON, James	
				025		
John KING		1845	1926	025	HOUSTON, Anna	(GAR)Co F. 9th Regt Vt Vol Inf

Anna HOUSTON King		1849	1930	025	KING, John	(Surname probably Gaboury)
				025		
John COLLINS		1840	1929	025	BRANNAN, Mary J.	
Mary J. BRANNAN Collins		1856	1929	025	COLLINS, John	
				025		
George ERWIN		1850	1926	025	COUTURE, Mary	
Mary COUTURE Erwin		1857	1935	025	ERWIN, George	
				025		
Mitchell MCDERMOTT		1833	1932	025	_____, Adeline	
Adeline ____ MCDERMOTT		1849	1933	025	MCDERMOTT, Mitchell	
				025		
Mary Ann DOWNS Mullen		79 Years	11-16-1898	025	MULLEN, Bartholomew	(NOI Bartholomew Mullen)
				025	DOWNS, Mary Ann	
				025		
Eliza A. MULLEN		53Y 10M	01-18-1902	025	MULLEN, Eliza A.	
				025		
Michael MURPHY		1857	1922	025	MULLEN, Mary Ann	
Mary Ann MULLEN Murphy		1856	1920	025	MURPHY, Michael	
				025		
P.H. COLLINS		1853	1920	025	WOODS, Rosa	
Rosa WOODS Collins		1860	1901	025	COLLINS, P.H.	
				025		
Andrew WOODS		07-12-1830	04-29-1911	025	SPEARS, Ann	
Ann SPEARS Woods		05-15-1831	09-12-1913	025	WOODS, Andrew	
				025		
Nancy COLLINS Woods		1844	1900	025	SHERIDAN, Thomas	(NOI Thomas Sheridan)
				025	COLLINS, Nancy	(NOI Mr. Woods)
				025		
David LAWRENCE		93Y 8M	06-20-1903	025	LAWRENCE, David	
				025		
Michael J. LADEN		1849	1918	025	LADEN, Michael J.	
				025		
Joseph H. BEAULAC		1852	1924	025	RODDY, Mary E.	
Mary E. RODDY Beaulac		1850	1932	025	BEAULAC, Joseph H.	

Holy Family Cemetery, Essex Junction, VT U.S. Route 2A At Edge of Village

NAME	POB	DOB/AGE	DOD	CEM	SPOUSE/INDEX	INSCRIPTION
John HOWRIGAN		1843	1914	026	WESTON, Lucy	
Lucy WESTON Howrigan		1851	1927	026	HOWRIGAN, John	
				026		
William O'BRINE		1852	1918	026	_____, Ann	

Name	Birth	Death	No.	Cross-reference
Ann _____ O'BRINE	1845		026	O'BRINE, William
			026	
Edward NOLAN	1854	1932	026	ST. PIERRE, Amelia
Amelia ST. PIERRE Nolan	1862	1937	026	NOLAN, Edward
			026	
Henry BROTHERS	1837	1926	026	MILLER, Mary
Mary MILLER Brothers	1847	1926	026	BROTHERS, Henry
			026	
James GLYNN	80 Years	11-24-1897	026	_____, Catherine
Catherine _____ GLYNN	75 Years	02-23-1896	026	GLYNN, James
			026	
Michael R. KEARNEY	1856	1938	026	_____, Lillian
Lillian _____ KEARNEY	1875	1958	026	KEARNEY, Michael R.
			026	
John EARLEY	1831	1907	026	MCLANE, Sarah
Sarah McLANE Earley	1833	1913	026	EARLEY, John
			026	
John THOMAS	1841	1925	026	BIXBY, Martha
			026	BURNELL, Juilian
Martha BIXBY Thomas	1857	1909	026	THOMAS, John
Juilian BURNELL Thomas	1840	1922	026	THOMAS, John
			026	
John KANE	90 Years	04-22-1906	026	KANE, John
			026	
John FORVELL	1855		026	ALLEN, Terrier
Terrier ALLEN Forvell	1861	1909	026	FORVELL, John
			026	
John DONAHUE	1839	1915	026	MCCARTY, Ellen
			026	CAREY, Abbie D.
Ellen MCCARTY Donahue	1845	1914	026	DONAHUE, John
Abbie D. CAREY Donahue	1866	1956	026	DONAHUE, John
			026	
Roger HARTY	1835	1931	026	CONNOR, Anne
Anne CONNOR Harty	1841	1904	026	HARTY, Roger
			026	
John HANLEY	1830	1902	026	DOON, Mary
Mary DOON Hanley	1838	1909	026	HANLEY, John
			026	
Thomas B. HANLEY	1838	1905	026	DUFFEY, Kate
Kate DUFFEY Hanley	1842	1931	026	HANLEY, Thomas B.
			026	
			026	

St. Patrick's Cemetery, Fairfield Center, VT.   West of St. Patrick's Church (Within View)

NAME	POB	DOB/AGE	DOD	CEM	SPOUSE/INDEX	INSCRIPTION
Edward H. WALLACE	Co. Kilkenny	63 Years	06-19-1900	027	CASSIN, Mary	Born In Kilkenny, Ireland
Mary CASSIN Wallace		1851	1935	027	WALLACE, Edward H.	
				027		
John WALLACE	Co. Kilkenny	78 Years	01-22-1875	027	MORRISSEY, Margaret	Born In Kilkenny, Ireland
Margaret MORRISSEY Wallace	Co. Kilkenny	1795	03-12-1884	027	WALLACE, John	Born In Kilkenny, Ireland
				027		
Thomas EDWARDS	Co. Clare	56 Years	07-18-1857	027	LAWLER, Joanna	Born In Co. Clare, Ireland
Joanna LAWLER Edwards		67 Years	05-08-1876	027	EDWARDS, Thomas	
				027		
Kate TOWLE	Co. Armagh	80 Years	05-14-1910	027	TOWLE, Kate	Born In Co. Armagh, Ireland
				027		
Francis RYAN	Co. Kilkenny	68 Years	09-19-1868	027	_____, Margaret	A Native Of Kilkenny, Ireland
Margaret _____ RYAN		78 Years	05-20-1883	027	RYAN, Francis	
				027		
Peter CONLEY	Co. Monaghan	75 Years	09-30-1883	027	BRADY, Nancy	Born In County Monohan
Nancy BRADY Conley		80 Years	12-09-1887	027	CONLEY, Peter	
				027		
Timothy COLLINS	Co. Sligo	77 Years	08-08-1877	027	COLLINS, Timothy	A Native of the City of Sligo, Ireland
				027		
Patrick COLLINS	Co. Sligo	104 Years	01-27-1852	027	KILLY, Nancy	A Native of the City of Sligo, Ireland
				027		
Nancy KILLY Collins	Co. Sligo	101 Years	12-23-1867	027	COLLINS, Patrick	A Native of the City of Sligo, Ireland
				027		
				027		
John MCGEE	Co. Louth	19Y 3M	01-06-1874	027	MCGEE, John	A Native of Haggardstown, Co. Louth, Ireland
				027		
				027		
Patrick FLOOD	Co. Queens	67 Years	09-15-1871	027	_____, Ann	A Native of the Parish of Castlebrack,Queens Co. (Leix), Ireland
				027		
				027		
Ann _____ FLOOD	Co. Queens	88 Years	02-11-1888	027	FLOOD, Patrick	Born In Queens Co. (Leix), Ireland. Stone Erected By John Mackin.
				027		
				027		
				027		
M. O. DONOGHUE	Co. Limerick	73 Years	04-23-1898	027	TIERNEY, Ellen	Of Pallaskenry, County of Limerick, Ireland
				027		
Ellen TIERNEY Donoghue		49 Years	09-30-1889	027	DONOGHUE, M. O.	
				027		
Edward SLOAN		87 Years	03-26-1897	027	O'HEAR, Sarah	
Sarah O'HEAR Sloan		88 Years	01-28-1912	027	SLOAN, Edward	

				027		
John O'BRIEN		42 Years	09-01-1874	027	O'BRIEN, John	Civil War Soldier
				027		
Owen COLLEN		75 Years	08-12-1889	027	MCCANA, Nancy	
Nancy MCCANA Collen		02-02-1824	01-31-1901	027	COLLEN, Owen	
				027		
John H. RILEY		1852	1900	027	_____, Hattie	
Hattie _____ RILEY		1865	1934	027	RILEY, John H.	
				027		
Daniel RILEY		06-07-1822	02-28-1902	027	STEELE, Catherine	
Catherine STEELE Riley		05-04-1835	12-05-1893	027	RILEY, Daniel	
				027		
Hugh MCNICHOLS		62Y 10M	01-03-1864	027	_____, Mary	
Mary _____ MCNICHOLS		71Y 9M	02-20-1880	027	MCNICHOLS, Hugh	
				027		
James H. BRENNAN		1856	1929	027	HOWRIGAN, Alice S.	
Alice S. HOWRIGAN Brennan		1860	1928	027	BRENNAN, James H.	
				027		
Rosa ROONEY Ryan		02-04-1838	10-07-1867	027	RYAN, William	(NOI William Ryan)
				027	ROONEY, Rose	
				027		
James ROONEY		12-12-1795	12-03-1882	027	ROONEY, James	
				027		
Bridget KING Rooney		04-07-1847	11-15-1873	027	ROONEY, John	(NOI John Rooney)
				027	KING, Bridget	
				027		
James BRANNAN		84 Years	11-19-1861	027	_____, Jane	(NOI Jane. Stone damaged)
				027	BRANNAN, James	
				027		
William MEEHAN		08-10-1820	02-01-1898	027	FITZGERALD, Anne	
Anne FITZGERALD Meehan		11-15-1822	07-17-1903	027	MEEHAN, William	
				027		
Thomas ROONEY		1840	1894	027	KING, Ellen	
Ellen KING Rooney		1845	1884	027	ROONEY, Thomas	
				027		
James H. BRENNAN		1816	1884	027	_____, Kittie	
Kittie _____ BRENNEN		1820	1862	027	BRENNAN, James	
Catie BRENNAN		1850	1870	027	BRENNAN, Catie	
				027		
John ROWLEY	Co. Leitrim	70 Years	06-03-1871	027	ROWLEY, John	Born Ireland, County Leitrim
				027	_____, Elizabeth	(NOI Elizabeth Rowley)
Hanora ROWLEY		29Y 11M	10-16-1860	027	ROWLEY, Hanora	Dau of John & Elizabeth Rowley
				027		
Julia MALONE Hoyt		68 Years	09-12-1876	027	HOYT, William	(NOI William Hoyt)
				027	MALONE, Julia	

			027		
Bridget _____ CLAREY	51 Years	10-20-1878	027	CLAREY, John	(NOI John Clarey)
			027	_____, Bridget	
			027		
James T. ROONEY	28Y 9M	02-08-1881	027	ROONEY, James T.	
			027		
James ROONEY	05-01-1814	04-05-1890	027	BREEN, Mary	
Mary BREEN Rooney	08-25-1823	04-10-1907	027	ROONEY, James	
			027		
William HOWRIGAN	11-10-1850	12-09-1904	027	BRENNAN, Mary	
Mary BRENNAN Howrigan	07-23-1858	06-16-1913	027	HOWRIGAN, William	
			027		
Abbie MADDEN Daniels	1852	1889	027	DANIELS, Charles	(NOI Charles Daniels)
			027	MADDEN, Abbie	
			027		
James FEE	83 Years	04-14-1897	027	MCGINN, Katherine	
Katherine MCGINN Fee	1822	1919	027	FEE, James	
James MCGINN	1832	1916	027	MCGINN, James	
			027		
Patrick TRAINER	1794	1875	027	_____, Margaret	
Margaret _____ TRAINER	1810	1880	027	TRAINER, Patrick	
Owen TRAINER	1832	1870	027	TRAINER, Owen	
			027		
David FITZGERALD	1847	1930	027	CARNEY, Annie E.	
Annie E. CARNEY Fitzgerald	36Y 6M	02-19-1891	027	FITZGERALD, David	
			027		
Patrick SHANNON	84 Years	08-19-1877	027	FINNERTY, Bridget	
Bridget FINNERTY Shannon	56 Years	12-19-1852	027	SHANNON, Patrick	
			027		
Mary A. MOORE Fox	27 Years	07-04-1888	027	FOX, Leslie A.	(NOI Leslie A. Fox)
			027	MOORE, Mary A.	
			027		
Thomas MOORE	67 Years	02-04-1891	027	WRIGHT, Johanna E.	
			027	_____, Ellen	
Johanna E. WRIGHT Moore	1828	1908	027	MOORE, Thomas	
Ellen _____ MOORE	33 Years	11-20-1854	027	MOORE, Thomas	
			027		
Thomas HALE	65 Years	02-06-1864	027	BURNS, Ann	
Ann BURNS Hale	80 Years	10-22-1891	027	HALE, Thomas	
			027		
Patrick BURNS	62 Years	06-30-1864	027	HALE, Mary	
Mary HALE Burns	48 Years	12-24-1859	027	BURNS, Patrick	
			027		
William DOWNEY	64 Years	01-18-1852	027	DOWNEY, William	
			027		

Richard G. BOOZAN	35 Years	01-21-1887	027	BOOZAN, Richard C.	
			027		
Richard BOOZAN	84 Years	12-13-1903	027	GEDNY, Margaret	
Margaret GEDNY Boozan	37 Years	05-02-1866	027	BOOZAN, Richard	
			027		
Patrick FAILEY	1838	1915	027	OWEN, Elizabeth	
			027	_____, Margaret	
Elizabeth OWEN Failey	54 Years	02-12-1898	027	FAILEY, Patrick	
Margaret _____ FAILEY	29 Years	01-11-1863	027	FAILEY, Patrick	
			027		
Patrick KELLEY	73Y 9M	11-05-1875	027	_____, Margaret	
Margaret _____ KELLEY	72Y 3M	11-15-1884	027	KELLEY, Patrick	
Bridget KELLEY	13Y 10M	04-30-1862	027	KELLEY, Bridget	Dau of P & M Kelley (Bridget Kelley & Martin Tobin on same marker)
Martin TOBIN	41 Years	09-24-1894	027	TOBIN, Martin	
			027		
			027		
Peter COLLEN	70 Years	01-08-1892	027	_____, Lizzie	
Lizzie _____ COLLEN	40 Years	08-06-1862	027	COLLEN, Peter	
Ann COLLEN	61 Years	09-07-1895	027	COLLEN, Ann	
Mary C. COLLEN McDonald	38 Years	08-07-1906	027	COLLEN, Mary C.	(NOI Mr. McDonald)
			027		
Ann _____ O'NEILL	65 Years	05-22-1861	027	O'NEILL, Terrance	(NOI Terrance O'Neill)
			027	_____, Ann	
			027		
John THOMAS	63 Years	07-12-1859	027	_____, Mary	
Mary _____ THOMAS	62 Years	02-29-1859	027	THOMAS, John	
			027		
James RYAN	93 Years	02-12-1894	027	BRANNAN, Bridget	
Bridget BRANNAN Ryan	68 Years	04-15-1886	027	RYAN, James	
Mary RYAN	15 Years	02-03-1859	027	RYAN, Mary	
Ann RYAN	7 Years	02-03-1859	027	RYAN, Ann	
Jane RYAN	5 Years	02-03-1859	027	RYAN, Jane	
Catherine RYAN		02-06-1859	027	RYAN, Catherine	
			027		
Margaret T. OWENS Shannon	43Y7M24D	04-22-1889	027	SHANNON, James T.	(NOI James T. Shannon)
			027	OWENS, Margaret T.	
			027		
Patrick MCENANY	63 Years	03-21-1897	027	O'BRIEN, Alice	
			027	_____, Mary	
Alice O'BRIEN McEnany	48 Years	09-04-1884	027	MCENANY, Patrick	
Mary _____ MCENANY	37Y 6M	06-01-1866	027	MCENANY, Patrick	
			027		
Thomas MORAN	22Y 8M	11-29-1864	027	MORAN, Thomas	
			027		
Lawrence FLYNN	80 Years	11-28-1880	027	FLYNN, Lawrence	(Flynn family stones all in

Mary FLYNN	03-21-1848	05-31-1909	027	FLYNN, Mary	poor shape and difficult to
Jane FLYNN			027	FLYNN, Jane	read. Stones for Jane and
Thomas FLYNN	52 Years	07-20-1861	027	FLYNN, Thomas	Catherine are damaged)
Catherine FLYNN			027	FLYNN, Catherine	
			027		
Thomas BURNS	76 Years	03-28-1902	027	BURNS, Thomas	
			027		
Michael MCQUEENEY	1820	1876	027	_____, Catherine	
Catherine _____ MCQUEENEY	1820	1886	027	MCQUEENEY, Michael	
			027		
Enos MCKENNA			027	_____, Nancy	(Stone deteriorated - hard to
Nancy _____ MCKENNA	21 Years	05-22-18_7	027	MCKENNA, Enos	read)
			027		
Michael CONLEY	80 Years	05-16-1885	027	MCKENNA, Mary	
Mary MCKENNA Conley	84 Years	07-05-1897	027	CONLEY, Michael	
			027		
John MCKENNA	85 Years	07-23-1849	027	MCKENNA, John	
Francis MCKENNA	31 Years	03-11-1851	027	MCKENNA, Francis	
			027		
Margaret MOHAN			027	MOHAN, Margaret	(Deteriorated. Stone is old)
			027		
Moses SINNOTT	49 Years	08-07-1854	027	SINNOTT, Moses	
			027		
Ellen F. DUFFEY	25 Years	12-10-1864	027	DUFFY, Ellen F.	
			027		
James CORBLESS	69 Years	08-25-1861	027	CORBLESS, James	
			027		
Catherine _____ WATERS	64 Years	12-24-1864	027	WATERS, Thomas	(NOI Thomas Waters. From per-
			027	CORBLESS, Catherine	sonal research, found this per
			027		sons surname to be Corbless)
			027		
Nicholas CORBLESS	90 Years	12-09-1882	027	_____, Margaret	
Margaret _____ CORBLESS	73Y 7M	01-22-1876	027	CORBLESS, Nicholas	
			027		
Garrett BARRY	84Y 8M	12-07-1873	027	BARRY, Garrett	
			027		
Patrick C. BARRY	1828	1912	027	HANLEY, Mary	
Mary HANLEY Barry	1831	1904	027	BARRY, Patrick C.	
			027		
Patrick GILOUAGLY	49Y 6M	12-15-1869	027	_____, Mary	
Mary _____ GILOUAGLY	38Y3M26D	08-26-1857	027	GILOUAGLY, Patrick	
			027		
Patrick DUFFY (?)	50 Years	05-06-1869	027	KENNEDY, Margaret	(Top half of stone missing.
			027		Not sure if Patrick Duffy but
			027		stone immediately adjacent to

Name	Born / Age	Died	Code	Index	Notes
			027		Margaret Kennedy)
Margaret KENNEDY Duffy	65 Years	03-21-1866	027	DUFFY, Patrick	
			027		
Bernard MCGINN	1817	1865	027	HALEGAN, Mary	
Mary HALEGAN McGinn	1821	1881	027	MCGINN, Bernard	
Patrick MCGINN	1854	1888	027	MCGINN, Patrick	Son of B & M McGinn
			027		
Bernard O'NEIL	84 Years	07-05-1876	027	HARRISON, Rose	
Rose HARRISION O'Neil	72 Years	05-03-1875	027	O'NEIL, Bernard	
			027		
Michael SOWERS	50 Years	01-13-1882	027	FLOOD, Ann	
Ann FLOOD Sowers	75 Years	01-30-1908	027	SOWERS, Michael	
			027		
John O'NEILL	1831	1895	027	CARRIGAN, Ann	
Ann CARRIGAN O'Neill	1837	1901	027	O'NEILL, John	
			027		
James HURLEY	02-02-1859	03-31-1898	027	CORCORAN, Hannah	
Hannah CORCORAN Hurley	04-02-1860	03-26-1942	027	HURLEY, James	
			027		
James W. CARROLL	42Y 3M	05-19-1873	027	_____, Mary E.	
Mary E. _____ CARROLL	32Y 10M	04-24-1867	027	CARROLL, James W.	
James CARROLL	86 Years	06-05-1883	027	WARD, Bridget	
Bridget WARD Carroll	87Y7M18D	09-18-18	027	CARROLL, James	
Margaret W. CARROLL	02-22-1838	11-05-1927	027	CARROLL, Margaret W.	
Caroline J. CARROLL	04-03-1851	02-13-1925	027	CARROLL, Caroline J.	
			027		
Thomas MCGINN	78 Years	01-08-1860	027	MCENANY, Bridget	
Bridget MCENANY McGinn	98 Years	04-13-1889	027	MCGINN, Thomas	
			027		
Peter MARRION	65 Years	03-29-1865	027	_____, Bridget	
Bridget _____ MARRION	85 Years	10-20-1900	027	MARRION, Peter	
			027		
Sarah CALLAN	24 Years	05-11-1874	027	CALLAN, Sarah	Dau Of Patrick & Elizabeth Callan
			027		
			027		
Timothy CORCORAN	1829	1916	027	BARRY, Mary	
Mary BARRY Corcoran	1823	1887	027	CORCORAN, Timothy	
			027		
John BARRY	1835	1916	027	HANRAHAN, Catherine	
Catherine HANRAHAN Barry	1833	1873	027	BARRY, John	
			027		
Mary GARTLAND	1847	1912	027	GARTLAND, Mary	
			027		
Daniel CARNEY	1831	1891	027	RILEY, Catherine	
Catherine RILEY Carney	1815	1904	027	CARNEY, Daniel	

Name	Age/Born	Died	Code	Index Name	Notes
James CARNEY	1854	1898	027	CARNEY, James	
John CARNEY	1849	1872	027	CARNEY, John	
William CARNEY	1845	1874	027	CARNEY, William	
Daniel CARNEY Jr.	1850	1874	027	RILEY, Rose Ann	
Rose Ann RILEY Carney	24 Years	02-15-1874	027	CARNEY, Daniel Jr.	
			027		
Patrick MCMAHAN	85 Years	07-31-1879	027	MCMAHAN, Patrick	
			027		
Peter O'HEAR	101 Years	07-31-1879	027	MCMAHAN, Alice	
Alice MCMAHAN O'Hear	75 Years	01-15-1883	027	O'HEAR, Peter	
			027		
Stephen HALLINAN	53Y 6M	06-13-1873	027	MELLEN, Ann	
Ann MELLEN Hallinan	40 Years	03-02-1867	027	HALLINAN, Stephen	
			027		
Lawrence KIRK	70 Years	10-17-1869	027	SHARKEY, Mary	
Mary SHARKEY Kirk	68 Years	08-01-1879	027	KIRK, Lawrence	
			027		
Maryann _____ LEACH	32 Years	06-24-1871	027	LEACH, Benjamin	(NOI Benjamin Leach)
			027	_____, Maryann	
			027		
Rev. Thomas RIORDAN	29 Years	10-04-1861	027	RIORDAN, Rev. Thomas	(Pastor of St. Patricks Church until his death).
			027		
			027		
Rosa TEAGUE	22Y 9M	01-23-1865	027	TEAGUE, Rosa	
			027		
Bridget O'REILLY	3Y5M4D	08-29-1862	027	O'REILLY, Bridget	Dau Of Thomas & ELiza O'Reilly
			027		
John H. DENIVER	46 Years	11-04-1867	027	_____, Mary A.	
Mary A. _____ DENIVER	41Y 21D	05-10-1870	027	DENIVER, John H.	
			027		
William RYAN		1860	027	RYAN, William	(Stone damaged. Part missing)
			027		
Jerome NEVINS	03-11-1832	12-17-1901	027	_____, Mary	
Mary _____ NEVINS	02-09-1832	09-24-1899	027	NEVINS, Jerome	His Beloved Wife
			027		
Catherine _____ NAVINS	42Y4M12D	09-12-1864	027	NAVINS, James	(NOI James Navins)
			027		
Edward D. NEVINS		1865	027	_____, Margaret	(Stone deteriorated. Cannot read)
Margaret _____ NEVINS	64 Years	03-07-1873	027	NEVINS, Edward D.	
Bridget NEVINS		01-10-1842	027	NEVINS, Bridget	Dau Of E. & M. Nevins
			027		
John NEVINS	20Y11M18D	06-07-1848	027	NEVINS, John	
			027		
John LAW	18Y8M4D	08-22-1864	027	LAW, John	Son Of John & Mary Law. (GAR) Co. G., 4th Rgt, Vt Vols.
			027		

			027		Wounded at North Ann River,
			027		Virginia 5-23-1864.
			027		
Bartholomew TWIGGS	30 Years	12-20-1870	027	TWIGGS, Bartholomew	(Does not say if husband and
			027		wife)
Hannah TWIGG	30 Years	02-15-1865	027	TWIGG, Hannah	
			027		
Ellen _____ DRISCOLL	42 Years	12-24-1864	027	DRISCOLL, Timothy	(NOI Timothy Driscoll)
			027		
Mary CONNELL Fitzgerald	69 Years	08-23-1902	027	FITZGERALD, John	(NOI John Fitzgerald)
			027		
Mary FITZGERALD	31 Years	04-01-1895	027	FITZGERALD, Mary	Dau Of John & Mary Fitzgerald
			027		
James R. FITZGERALD	27Y 10M	04-06-1899	027	FITZGERALD, James R.	S/O Patrick& Hannah Fitzgerald
			027		
Michael CLARK	1798	1886	027	MCENEANY, Bridget	
Bridget MCENEANY Clark	1813	1883	027	CLARK, Michael	
Nicholas CLARK	1837	1902	027	CLARK, Nicholas	
John A. CLARK	1857	1953	027	MOORE, Joan E.	
Joan E. MOORE	1858	1902	027	CLARK, John A.	
			027		
Darby COX	98 Years	06-12-1885	027	COX, Darby	
			027		
Michael GARVEY	65 Years	12-02-1884	027	MCGINN, Mary	
Mary MCGINN Garvey	54 Years	01-27-1890	027	GARVEY, Michael	
			027		
Cathrine MEIGHAN Cluskey	62 Years	05-04-1869	027	CLUSKEY, William	(NOI William Cluskey)
			027		
Henry BEAULAC	64 Years	02-10-1894	027	O'NEIL, Mary	
Mary O'NEIL Beaulac	74 Years	10-06-1906	027	BEAULAC, Henry	
			027		
Sarah HALE	1847	1925	027	HALE, Sarah	
			027		
Bartholomew HALE	1839	1918	027	HALE, Bartholomew	
			027		
Mary CARROLL	49 Years	04-12-1883	027	CARROLL, Mary	(Stone deteriorated/damaged
			027		Year of death could be 1863)
			027		
William GILWEE	57 Years	02-05-1879	027	_____, Ann	(NOI Ann)
			027	GILWEE, William	
			027		
George BOYLAN	40 Years	01-14-1884	027	BOYLAN, George	
			027		
Peter BOYLAN			027	_____, Catherine	(Half of stone missing. No
			027		dates legible)

Catherine _____ BOYLAN	72 Years	04-15-1875	027	BOYLAN, Peter	
			027		
Daniel MCAULIFFE	1834	1886	027	_____, Julia F.	
Julia F. _____ MCAULIFFE	1842	1915	027	MCAULIFFE, Daniel	
Their Children			027		
Lucy MCAULIFFE			027	MCAULIFFE, Lucy	(NOI on children Lucy, Linus
Linus MCAULIFFE			027	MCAULIFFE, Linus	Mary and Michael McAuliffe)
Mary MCAULIFFE			027	MCAULIFFE, Mary	
Michael MCAULIFFE			027	MCAULIFFE, Michael	
			027		
Bridget SLOAN Moran	23Y1M13D	03-13-1876	027	MORAN, Thomas	(NOI Thomas Moran)
			027	SLOAN, Bridget	
			027		
Bridget _____ MELLEN	75 Years	02-26-1866	027	MELLEN, John	(NOI John Mellen)
			027	_____, Bridget	
			027		
Bernard DONNELLY	62 Years	10-29-1873	027	DONNELLY, Bernard	
			027		
Mary A. MACKIN Martin	52 Years	07-07-1887	027	MARTIN, Edgar S.	(NOI Edgar S. Martin)
			027	MACKIN, Mary A.	
			027		
Catharine _____ FAILEY	06-15-1841	10-07-1903	027	FAILEY, Lawrence Jr.	(NOI Lawrence Failey Jr)
			027	_____, Catherine	
			027		
Lawrence FAILEY Sr.	81 Years	11-10-1881	027	_____, Catharine	
Catharine _____ FAILEY	77 Years	06-14-1881	027	FAILEY, Lawrence Sr.	
Francis FAILEY	25 Years	1864	027	FAILEY, Francis	(GAR) Died at Newbern,NC, 1864
			027		Defending His Country's Flag.
			027		A Good And Faithful Soldier.
			027		(Not in reference)
Mary A. FAILEY	35 Years	02-07-1881	027	FAILEY, Mary A.	
			027		
Joanna FITZGERALD	1817	1905	027	FITZGERALD, Joanna	
			027		
Michael FITZGERALD	1808	1892	027	BARREY, Hannah	
Hannah BARREY Fitzgerald	1831	1891	027	FITZGERALD, Michael	
Emma FITZGERALD	1869	1918	027	FITZGERALD, Emma	
John FITZGERALD	1858	1923	027	FITZGERALD, John	
Mary FITZGERALD	1851	1925	027	FITZGERALD, Mary	
John FITZGERALD	1852	1859	027	FITZGERALD, John	
James FITZGERALD	1855	1859	027	FITZGERALD, James	
Hannah FITZGERALD	1856	1859	027	FITZGERALD, Hannah	
Michael FITZGERALD	1857	1859	027	FITZGERALD, Michael	
			027		
Peter KELLEY	80 Years	12-10-1917	027	KELLEY, Peter	

			027		
Ellen DALY Kelley	31Y 4M	04-10-1868	027	KELLEY, Michael	(NOI Michael Kelley)
			027	DALY, Ellen	
			027		
Andrew KELLEY	08-15-1827	09-27-1914	027	_____, Julia	
Julia _____ KELLEY	58 Years	06-02-1889	027	KELLEY, Andrew	
			027		
Terrence RODDY	24 Years	08-15-1862	027	RODDY, Terrence	
Owen RODDY	3 Years	04-17-1853	027	RODDY, Owen	S/O Michael & Catharine RODDY
			027		
Michael RODDY	24 Years	04-16-1869	027	RODDY, Michael	
			027		
Michael RODDY	80 Years	09-05-1884	027	_____, Catharine	(GAR) Co. A, 17th Vt Inf
Catharine _____ RODDY	77 Years	05-03-1888	027	RODDY, Michael	
			027		
Margaret BRENNAN	1853	1925	027	BRENNAN, Margaret	
			027		
James BRENNAN	82 Years	02-03-1896	027	CARROLL, Rose	
Rose CARROLL Brennan	46 Years	04-19-1869	027	BRENNAN, James	
			027		
Rodney MCGOOKIN	45 Years	04-09-1866	027	MCGOOKIN, Rodney	
			027		
Francis RYAN	53 Years	09-03-1897	027	BRENNAN, Ellen	
Ellen BRENNAN Ryan	1861	1939	027	RYAN, Francis	
			027		
Ann KIRK Jr.	11 Days	06-19-1832	027	KIRK, Ann Jr.	Dau Of Lawrence & Mary Kirk
			027		
Ann KIRK Sr.	96 Years	08-04-1844	027	KIRK, Ann Sr.	
			027		
Michael CAMPBELL	74 Years	07-13-1905	027	TWIGG, Mary	
Mary TWIGG Campbell	55 Years	04-15-1895	027	CAMPBELL, Michael	
			027		
Margaret CAMPBELL	1840	1918	027	CAMPBELL, Margaret	
			027		
Thomas CAMPBELL	82 Years	09-09-1878	027	CAMPBELL, Thomas	
			027		
Bridget _____ MCENANY	57 Years	02-02-1852	027	MCENANY, Patrick	(NOI Patrick McEnany)
			027		
Michael MARRON	1818	1879	027	KEENAN, Bridget	
Bridget KEENAN Marron	1823	1861	027	MARRON, Michael	
			027		
Nancy _____ DONLEY	60 Years	11-18-1845	027	DONLEY, Arthur	(NOI Arthur Donley)
			027		
Terence TEAGUE	68Y 6M	10-09-1865	027	_____, Hannah	
Hannah _____ TEAGUE	35 Years	09-14-1845	027	TEAGUE, Terence	

			027		
Barney MCNANY	62 Years	07-28-1887	027	MCNANY, Barney	(GAR) 7th Rgt, VtVols (Surname
			027		probably McEnany)
			027		
James FITZGERALD	22 Years	03-01-1857	027	FITZGERALD, James	
			027		
Patrick EDWARDS	23 Years	06-24-1864	027	EDWARDS, Patrick	(GAR)15 NY Indp Battery.Killed
			027		At The Battle Of Petersburgh.
			027		Buried On The Field.
			027		
Margaret EDWARDS	29 Years	02-02-1870	027	EDWARDS, Margaret	D/O of Thomas & Joanna Edwards
Joanna EDWARDS	21 Years	11-12-1869	027	EDWARDS, Joanna	D/O of Thomas & Joanna Edwards
Nancy EDWARDS	6 Years	07-09-1854	027	EDWARDS, Nancy	D/O of Thomas & Joanna Edwards
			027		(NOI Thomas EDWARDS & Joanna)
			027		
Thomas MOLONY	81 Years	12-06-1853	027	_____, Catharine	
Catharine _____ MOLONY	74 Years	12-19-1865	027	MOLONY, Thomas	
			027		
Patrick MINER	90 Years	10-23-1881	027	MINER, Patrick	
			027		
Matthew MCENANY	70 Years	08-29-1874	027	_____, Ann	
Ann _____ MCENANY	66 Years	06-26-1868	027	MCENANY, Matthew	
			027		
Hugh MCENANY	59Y 5M	09-10-1859	027	_____, Mary	
Mary _____ MCENANY	75 Years	05-09-1874	027	MCENANY, Hugh	
			027		
Joseph W. WALLACE	1839	1918	027	O'KEEFE, Margaret	
Margaret O'KEEFE Wallace	1863	1911	027	WALLACE, Joseph W.	
			027		
Peter OWENS	56 Years	01-28-1867	027	_____, Ann	
Ann _____ OWENS	72 Years	08-18-1888	027	OWENS, Peter	
James OWENS	32 Years	12-24-1880	027	OWENS, James	
			027		
Peter MORAN	1797	1879	027	DORAN, Ann	
Ann DORAN Moran	1827	1869	027	MORAN, Peter	
Mary MORAN McKee	1850	1936	027	MORAN, Mary	(NOI McKee)
Elizabeth H. MORAN	1862	1926	027	MORAN, Elizabeth H.	
			027		
Bridget _____ OWENS	50Y3M7D	03-17-1898	027	OWENS, Thomas	(NOI Thomas Owens)
			027		
Edward KIRLEY	74 Years	10-09-1876	027	_____, Bridget	
Bridget _____ KIRLEY	84 Years	10-18-1886	027	KIRLEY, Edward	
Elizabeth A. KIRLEY	01-13-1846	01-11-1874	027	KIRLEY, Elizabeth A.	
Margaret KIRLEY	1839	1927	027	KIRLEY, Margaret	
			027		

Mathew M. NOWLAND	61 Years	02-24-1894	027	KING, Ann	
Ann KING Nowland	82 Years	03-21-1919	027	NOWLAND, Mathew M.	
			027		
Patrick KING	74 Years	10-27-1870	027	DOOLEY, Ellen	
Ellen DOOLEY King	74 Years	03-27-1885	027	KING, Patrick	
			027		
Patrick TEAGUE	44 Years	06-10-1859	027	MCENANEY, Bridget	
Bridget MCENANEY Teague	68Y 6M	04-11-1890	027	TEAGUE, Patrick	
			027		
Edward NOWLAND	11-07-1842	11-19-1905	027	BRANON, Mary	
Mary BRANON Teague	01-26-1861		027	NOWLAND, Edward	
			027		
John DUFFY	75 Years	11-22-1895	027	WESTON, Mary	(These two are probably man &
Mary WESTON	71 Years	05-17-1884	027	DUFFY, John	wife, but does not say so. In-
			027		terred next to each other)
			027		
Frances MCMAHON	32 Years	03-26-1844	027	MCMAHON, Frances	
			027		
Patrick HOUSTON Sr.	03-17-1784	05-17-1876	027	____, Sally	Aged 92 Years
Sally ____ HOUSTON		11-01-1846	027	HOUSTON, Patrick Jr.	
Sarah HOUSTON	1844	1857	027	HOUSTON, Sarah	Dau Of P & S Houston
George HOUSTON	3 Years	01-13-1844	027	HOUSTON, George	Son Of Patrick & Ann Houston
			027		
R. H. SHARKEY	1844	1911	027	____, Mary	
Mary ____ SHARKEY	1847	1935	027	SHARKEY, R. H.	
			027		
Joseph K. WALLACE	1838	1908	027	WALLACE, Joseph K.	
			027		
John SHARKEY	1795	1876	027	____, Ann	
Ann ____ SHARKEY	1805	1887	027	SHARKEY, John	
Bridget SHARKEY	1829	1863	027	SHARKEY, Bridget	
			027		
James MACKIN	64 Years	01-01-1865	027	____, Ann	Erected By His Son Charles
Ann ____ MACKIN	52 Years	11-28-1858	027	MACKIN, James	
			027		
Patrick HOWRIGAN	87 Years	07-05-1852	027	HOWRIGAN, Patrick	
			027		
Patrick HOWRIGAN	88 Years	11-15-1891	027	MCCARTY, Catherine	
Catherine MCCARTY Howrigan	65Y 4M	09-28-1880	027	HOWRIGAN, Patrick	
			027		
Hannah DONLEY Noland	32Y6M7D	08-06-1880	027	NOLAND, E. N.	(NOI E.N. Noland)
Mary A. NOLAND	1828	1913	027	NOLAND, Mary A.	
John NOLAND	78 Years	10-22-1871	027	KIRLAN, Bridget	
Bridget KIRLAN Noland			027	NOLAND, John	(Stone is broken. DOD/DOD on
			027		Bridget Kirlan is missing)

Name	Age/Born	Died	Code	Relation	Notes
			027		
Rose _____ DUFFY	84 Years	01-27-1868	027	DUFFY, James	(NOI James Duffy)
			027		
Patrick DUFFY	74 Years	01-01-1865	027	_____, Bridget	
Bridget _____ DUFFY	38 Years	11-28-1858	027	DUFFY, Patrick	
			027		
Catherine DUFFY	1829	1903	027	DUFFY, Catherine	
			027		
Lawrence MCGUE	68 Years	07-29-1897	027	TYNAN, Mary	
Mary TYNAN McGue	1833	1918	027	MCGUE, Lawrence	
			027		
Patrick TIERNEY	70 Years	12-29-1867	027	_____, Mary	
Mary _____ TIERNEY	67 Years	01-28-1871	027	TIERNEY, Patrick	
			027		
John TIERNEY	06-08-1832	06-13-1896	027	HOWRIGAN, Margaret	(GAR) Co. E., 12th Rgt,Vt Vols
Margaret HOWRIGAN Tierney	03-15-1837	05-18-1929	027	TIERNEY, John	
			027		
William RYAN	32Y 11M	01-14-1874	027	RYAN, William	
			027		
Catherine RYAN	1848	1910	027	RYAN, Catherine	Dau of Frances & Margaret Ryan
Margaret RYAN	1835	03-04-1919	027	RYAN, Margaret	Dau of Frances & Margaret Ryan
Thomas D. RYAN	22Y 6M	05-07-1856	027	RYAN, Thomas D.	
Mary Ann RYAN	18Y 11M	05-01-1857	027	RYAN, Mary Ann	
			027		
Lawrence BOYLAN	63 Years	03-23-1881	027	BOYLAN, Lawrence	
			027		
James RILEY	45 Years	12-04-1860	027	RILEY, James	
			027		
John BROGAN	55 Years	06-09-1863	027	BROGAN, John	
			027		
James ROGERS	29 Years	09-27-1866	027	ROGERS, James	Son Of P & C Rogers
Patrick ROGERS	69 Years	06-23-1875	027	MULHERON, Catharine	
Catharine MULHERON Rogers			027	ROGERS, James	(Most of this stone missing so no DOB/DOD)
			027		
James W. KELLY		10-09-1864	027	KELLY, James W.	Son Of Andrew & Julia Kelly
			027		
James BRYAN	56Y 16D	02-16-1882	027	BRYAN, James	
			027		
Thomas Reed RYAN	1790	1864	027	BELFORD, Catherine	
Catherine BELFORD Ryan	1800	1852	027	RYAN, Thomas Reed	
William M. RYAN	24Y1M6D	12-13-1854	027	RYAN, William M.	Son Of Thomas & Catherine Ryan
			027		
John FITZGERALD	1848	1913	027	GILWEE, Mary	
Mary GILWEE Fitzgerald	1855	1930	027	FITZGERALD, John	
			027		

Barnard ROONEY	63 Years	06-16-1884	027	ROONEY, Barnard	
			027		
John ROONEY	56 Years	11-16-1845	027	ROONEY, John	
			027		
Bridget _____ FOSTER	30 Years	12-12-1863	027	FOSTER, D. H.	(NOI D.H. Foster)
			027	_____, Bridget	
			027		
Mary WARD Gartland	25 Years	02-04-1852	027	GARTLAND, Patrick	(NOI Patrick Gartland)
			027	WARD, Mary	
			027		
James J. WARD	47Y 6M	10-14-1867	027	GILWEE, Mary	
Peter WARD	77 Years	01-24-1867	027	_____, Catharine	
Catharine _____ WARD			027	WARD, Peter	(Stone broken. Dates missing)
			027		
Patrick CONLEY	24 Years	06-10-1865	027	CONLEY, Patrick	
			027		
Catherine CONLEY Furey	27 Years	09-19-1870	027	FUREY, MAJ. W. A.	(NOI MAJ. W. A. Furey)
			027	CONLEY, Catherine	
			027		
Peter CONLEY	22 Years	06-01-1877	027	CONLEY, Peter	
Nancy CONLEY	19 Years	10-17-1879	027	CONLEY, Nancy	
			027		
Edmund NEVINS	1805	1876	027	_____, Mary	
Mary _____ NEVINS	1800	1883	027	NEVINS, Edmund	
Patrick NEVINS	1841	1909	027	HOWRIGAN, Ellen	
Ellen HOWRIGAN Nevins	1855	1931	027	NEVINS, Patrick	
Mary Ann NEVINS	1849	1881	027	NEVINS, Mary Ann	
			027		
Timothy SHANNASEY	34 Years	04-08-1873	027	COSGROVE, Sarah	
Sarah COSGROVE Shannasey	04-05-1839	05-28-1917	027	SHANNASEY, Timothy	
			027		
Michael MCGETTRICK	05-14-1806	05-08-1863	027	MCGETTRICK, Michael	
			027		
Richard CONNOR	1840	1923	027	GILL, Margaret	
Margaret GILL Connor	1848	1882	027	CONNOR, Richard	
			027		
Patrick MCENANEY	1833	1905	027	MILES, Julia	
Julia MILES McEnaney	1837	1915	027	MCENANEY, Patrick	
			027		
John PLUM	45 Years	01-23-1883	027	PLUM, John	
			027		
Michael GREEN	48Y 6M	09-08-1888	027	MURPHY, Ann	(GAR) Co. E., 1st Rgt, Vt Vols
Ann MURPHY Green	48Y 10M	06-18-1892	027	GREEN, Michael	
			027		
Mary A. MALONEY McAuliff	47 Years	07-22-1896	027	MCAULIFF, Michael Jr.	(NOI Michael McAuliff Jr)

Ellen O'REILLEY McAuliff	24 Years	07-26-1894	027	MCAULIFF, Michael Jr.	(NOI Michael McAuliff Jr)
			027	MALONEY, Mary A.	
			027	O'REILLEY, Ellen	
			027		
Charles MCQUEENEY	1846	1879	027	MCQUEENEY, Charles	
			027		
James RILEY	1828	1906	027	KILLEN, Sarah	
Sarah KILLEN Riley	1839	1908	027	RILEY, James	
			027		
Thomas FITZGERALD	1855	1910	027	CARNEY, Katherine	
Katherine CARNEY Fitzgerald	1860	1933	027	FITZGERALD, Thomas	
			027		
Ann _____ ROONEY	67 Years	11-15-1872	027	ROONEY, Barney	(NOI Barney Rooney)
Peter BRANNAN	87 Years	10-19-1873	027	_____, Margaret	
Margaret _____ BRANNAN	70 Years	05-17-1872	027	BRANNAN, Peter	
			027		
Elizabeth MCMAHON O'Connell	54 Years	12-20-1846	027	O'CONNELL, John	(NOI John O'Connell)
			027		
Thomas ENRIGHT	22 Years	05-08-1863	027	_____, Kate	(GAR) Co. E, 12th Rgt, Vt Vols
Kate _____ ENRIGHT	55 Years	11-23-1893	027	ENRIGHT, Thomas	
			027		
John FAILY	95 Years	05-12-1867	027	FAILY, John	
			027		
John MACKIN	1833	1916	027	FLOOD, Bridget	
Bridget FLOOD Mackin	1832	1916	027	MACKIN, John	
			027		
John FITZGERALD	76 Years	09-04-1883	027	GENOUGH, Mary	
Mary GENOUGH	65 Years	03-29-1879	027	FITZGERALD, John	
			027		
James HOWRIGAN	1843	1910	027	COLLINS, Mary	
Mary COLLINS Howrigan	1847	1944	027	HOWRIGAN, James	
			027		
Frank MCGETTRICK	04-04-1836	06-30-1888	027	MCGETTRICK, Frank	
			027		
Mary Ann DENNIS	45 Years	12-15-1887	027	DENNIS, Mary Ann	
			027		
Martin MOLONEY	57 Years	09-17-1876	027	MOLONEY, Martin	
			027		
Mathew TEAGUE	1835	1916	027	_____, Bridget	(GAR-Try Co. F,7th Rgt,VtVols)
Bridget _____ TEAGUE	1845	1926	027	TEAGUE, Mathew	
James TEAGUE	1843	1925	027	TEAGUE, James	
			027		
Thomas RYAN	1846	1916	027	RYAN, Thomas	
J. D. RYAN	1859	1939	027	RYAN, J. D.	
Margaret S. RYAN	1863	1950	027	RYAN, Margaret S.	

			027		
	1831	1922	027	O'BRIEN, Eliza	
Barney MCENANY	1834	1921	027	MCENANY, Barney	
Eliza O'BRIEN McEnany			027		
	03-04-1835	11-22-1911	027	KING, Margaret	
Thomas KIRLEY	1839	1916	027	KIRLEY, Thomas	
Margaret KING Kirley			027		
			027	SLOAN, Nancy	(NOI Michael Fitzgerald)
Michael F. FITZGERALD	67 Years	03-07-1914	027	FITZGERALD, Michael F.	
Nancy SLOAN Fitzgerald			027		
	1842	1933	027	MCENANEY, Mary J.	
James MCMAHON	1840	1926	027	MCMAHON, James	
Mary J. MCENANEY McMahon			027		
	1842	1933	027	BRENNAN, Rose	
William ROONEY	1854	1939	027	ROONEY, William	
Rose BRENNAN Rooney			027		
			027	SMITH, George T.	(NOI George T. Smith)
Elizabeth SLOAN Smith	1854	1925	027	SLOAN, Elizabeth	
			027		
	1843	1916	027	MCDONALD, Mary	
Edgar J. WRY	1840	1922	027	WRY, Edgar J.	
Mary MCDONALD Wry			027		
Nancy ROONEY	10-30-1844	06-30-1922	027	ROONEY, Nancy	
			027		
	1831	1912	027	LEONARD, Katherine	
Patrick MACKIN	1833	1910	027	MACKIN, Patrick	
Katherine LEONARD Mackin			027		
	1846	1912	027	FLYNN, Ellen	
Patrick SLOAN	1842	1910	027	SLOAN, Patrick	
Ellen FLYNN Sloan			027		
	03-12-1854	10-03-1919	027	FANTON, Lucy R.	
Bernard T. RODDY	10-20-1857	12-20-1949	027	RODDY, Bernard T.	
Lucy R. FANTON Roddy			027		
	1825	1900	027	MCDONALD, Mary	
John MILES	1827	1906	027	MILES, John	
Mary MCDONALD Miles			027		
Terrence MILES	1825	1900	027	MALONE, Mary	
			027	_____, Catherine	
Catherine _____ MILES	61 Years	07-10-1874	027	MILES, Terrence	
Mary MALONE Miles	1827	1906	027	MILES, Terrence	Son Of Terry & Mary Miles
James MILES	13Y 5M	04-30-1841	027	MILES, James	(NOI DOB/DOD Mary Miles
Mary MILES			027	MILES, Mary	Dau Of T & C Miles
Bridget MILES	4 Years	11-26-1859	027	MILES, Bridget	(NOI Thomas Ryan)
Margaret MILES Ryan	41Y 6M	09-15-1874	027	RYAN, Thomas	
			027	MILES, Margaret	

NAME	POB	DOB/AGE	DOD	CEM	SPOUSE/INDEX	INSCRIPTION
				027		
Mary CORBLIS Branan		54 Years	02-22-1850	027	BRANAN, John	(NOI John Branan)
				027	CORBLIS, Mary	
				027		
Peter COX		44 Years	04-07-1850	027	FLANAGAN, Mary	
Mary FLANAGAN Cox		65 Years	03-01-1880	027	COX, Peter	
				027		
Edward COX		74 Years	03-24-1920	027	COX, Edward	
				027		
Thomas COX		99 Years	05-20-1906	027	MCLAUGHLIN, Mary	
Mary MCLAUGHLIN Cox		78 Years	01-17-1881	027	COX, Thomas	
				027		
Edward OWENS		6 Years	04-03-1853	027	OWENS, Edward	Children of Peter & Ann Owens
Sarah J. OWENS		2 Years	08-14-1854	027	OWENS, Sarah J.	Children of Peter & Ann Owens
				027		
John MALONEY		1799	1853	027	_____, Mary	
Mary _____ MALONEY		1811	1887	027	MALONEY, John	
Thomas MALONEY		1843	1904	027	MALONEY, Thomas	
				027		
Hugh GARTLIN		22 Years	03-06-1869	027	KERLEY, Mary	
Mary KERLEY Gartlin		61 Years	12-25-1876	027	GARTLIN, Hugh	
				027		
Patrick BRANNAN		1817	1901	027	ENGLISH, Mary	
Mary ENGLISH Brannan		1825	1885	027	BRANNAN, Patrick	
J. B. BRANNAN		1846	1902	027	BRANNAN, J. B.	
Kate ENGLISH		1832	1897	027	ENGLISH, Kate	
				027		
Patrick MALONEY		1833	1853	027	MALONEY, Patrick	
William MALONEY		1837	1861	027	MALONEY, William	
Richard MALONEY		1840	1905	027	MALONEY, Richard	(Did not say if Ellen Rooney
Ellen M. ROONEY		1849	1897	027	ROONEY, Ellen M.	was spouse of Richard Maloney)
				027		
Hugh CAREY		72 Years	04-01-1886	027	STEWART, Mary	
Mary STEWART Carey		65 Years	01-13-1883	027	CAREY, Hugh	

Barlow Cemetery, Fairfield, Vt. Adjacent to St. Patricks Cemetery, West of St. Patrick's Church

NAME	POB	DOB/AGE	DOD	CEM	SPOUSE/INDEX	INSCRIPTION
William TODD	Co. Armagh	1759	05-10-1830	028	TODD, William	In Memory of William Todd,
				028		Born 1759 in Roughan, Armagh
				028		County. Emigrated to America
				028		in 1818.

Sanderson Corners, Fairfax, Vermont - on Fletcher-Binghamville Road

NAME	POB	DOB/AGE	DOD	CEM	SPOUSE/INDEX	INSCRIPTION
George CORRIGAN		1850	1917	030	MINOR, Sarah J.	
Sarah J. MINOR Corrigan		1863	1921	030	CORRIGAN, George	
				030		
Charles THOMAS		1855	1934	030	DRISCOLL, Nellie	
				030	DRISCOLL, Sarah J.	
Nellie DRISCOLL Thomas		1861	1882	030	THOMAS, Charles	
Sarah DRISCOLL Thomas		1856	1925	030	THOMAS, Charles	
				030		
Patrick DRISCOLL		1820	1912	030	RYAN, Mary	(GAR) Co. K., 11th VT Vols
				030		Native Of Ireland
Mary RYAN Driscoll		1838	1907	030	DRISCOLL, Patrick	
				030		
John DRISCOLL		1856	1910	030	DRISCOLL, John	
				030		
James E. CORRIGAN		1839	1901	030	CORRIGAN, Sarah J.	
Sarah J. _____ CORRIGAN		1838	1909	030	CORRIGAN, James E.	
				030		
Thomas G. RYAN		1841	1925	030	SPAULDING, Annette M.	
Annette M. SPAULDING Ryan		1849	1894	030	RYAN, Thomas G.	
				030		
William John MORRISON		1850	1916	030	DRISCOLL, Mary J.	
Mary J. DRISCOLL Morrison		1851	1927	030	MORRISON, William John	
				030		
Ella DRISCOLL Clarey		1850	1933	030	DRISCOLL, Ella	(NOI Mr. Clarey)
				030		
John B. MOSSEY		1841	1904	030	MAHON, Jennie	(U.S. Flag - no other marker)
Jennie MAHON Mossey		1845	1913	030	MOSSEY, John B.	
				030		
E. L. JAMIESON Corrigan		42Y10M14D	12-24-1892	030	JAMIESON, E. L.	(NOI R. R. Corrigan)
				030	CORRIGAN, R. R.	
				030		
Joseph MCNEIL		1844	1910	030	RANSOM, Emma	
Emma RANSOM McNeil		1857	1922	030	MCNEIL, Joseph	
				030		
John DOLAN		1846	1916	030	TABOR, Jennie A.	(U.S. Flag - no other marker)
Jennie A. TABOR Dolan		1858	1906	030	DOLAN, John	
				030		
Robert MCNEIL		1810	1887	030	MCNEIL, Mary	(U.S. Flag - no other marker)
Mary _____ MCNEIL		1806	1893	030	MCNEIL, Robert	
John MCNEIL		1832	1905	030	MCNEIL, John	

NAME	POB	DOB/AGE	DOD	CEM	SPOUSE/INDEX	INSCRIPTION
Jane MCNEIL			01-22-1915	030	MCNEIL, Jane	(NOI DOB)
Reuben MCNEIL		1849	1870	030	MCNEIL, Reuben	
William MCNEIL		1846	1875	030	MCNEIL, William	
				030		
William H. DRISCOLL				030	SPAULDING, Matilda J.	(GAR) Co. H. 7th Rgt VT Vols
				030	FOSTER, Addie M.	
Matilda J. SPAULDING Driscoll				030	DRISCOLL, William H.	
Addie M. FOSTER Driscoll				030	DRISCOLL, William H.	
				030		
William A. MARTIN		12-02-1842	03-04-1894	030	FLYNN, Ella	
Ella FLYNN Martin		1852	1925	030	MARTIN, William A.	
				030		
Peter R. CURLEY		02-02-1844	03-02-1900	030	KING, Armina A.	
Armina A. KING Curley		09-13-1844	01-18-1929	030	CURLEY, Peter A.	
				030		
Edgar T. BURNS		1839	1918	030	SMITH, Elizabeth	(GAR) Co. F. 7th VT Vols
Elizabeth SMITH Burns		1832	1909	030	BURNS, Edgar T.	
				030		
L. A. DUNN, DD		1814	1888	030	DUNN, Lucy A. T.	Pastor,Baptist Church, Fairfax 1842-1871. Pres. Iowa Central Union 1871-1888
				030		
				030		
Lucy A. T. _____ DUNN		1811	1853	030	DUNN, L. A.	
Arvilla H. DUNN		1824	1904	030	DUNN, Arvilla H.	
John N. DUNN		1855	1928	030	DUNN, John N.	
Idalette DUNN		1856	1907	030	DUNN, Idalette	
Mary A. DUNN		1863	1880	030	DUNN, Mary A.	
Cornelia A. DUNN		1844	1910	030	DUNN, Cornelia A.	
George A. DUNN				030	DUNN, George A.	Killed At Appomattox, Virginia 1st VT Cav (GAR) - 4-8-1865)
				030		
Albert T. DUNN		1850	1903	030	DUNN, Albert T.	
Lucy A. DUNN		1852	1922	030	DUNN, Lucy A.	

St. Mary's Cemetery, Northern End Of Village on Route 22A, Fairhaven, Vermont

NAME	POB	DOB/AGE	DOD	CEM	SPOUSE/INDEX	INSCRIPTION
Michael KELLY		75 Years	06-15-1889	032	_____, Catherine	
Catherine _____ KELLY		72 Years	04-30-1890	032	KELLY, Michael	
				032		
Edward RYAN		06-11-1834	10-20-1902	032	STAPLETON, Mary	(GAR Marker-Not in reference)
Mary STAPLETON Ryan		07-03-1842	01-11-1906	032	RYAN, Edward	
				032		
Michael REAL	Co. Limerick	55 Years	03-27-1883	032	FOGERTY, Mary	Native of Parish _______, Co

				032		Limerick, Ireland
Mary FOGERTY Real		54 Years	01-24-1887	032	REAL, Michael	
				032		
Hugh YOUNG		1848	1889	032	_____, Mary	
Mary _____ YOUNG		1854	1890	032	YOUNG, Hugh	
				032		
John D. MAHAR		1846	1903	032	RYAN, Anna	
Anna RYAN Mahar		1849	1931	032	MAHAR, John D.	
				032		
Dennis FOGARTY		49 Years	08-05-1879	032	FOGARTY, Dennis	
				032		
Miles MCDONOUGH		1810	1899	032	CAIN, Bridget	
Bridget CAIN McDonough		1822	1918	032	MCDONOUGH, Miles	
				032		
Michael MCDONOUGH		76 Years	06-28-1903	032	LORICAN, Mary	
Mary LORICAN McDonough		54 Years	03-28-1889	032	MCDONOUGH, Michael	
				032		
Mary _____ MCCARTY	Co. Kilkenn	30 Years	12-27-1864	032	MCCARTY, John	Parish of Wingap (No such
				032		Parish--Probably Windgap Town)
				032		Co. Kilkenny, Ire. (NOI John
				032		McCarty)
				032		
Hanah SHEA Reynolds	Co. Cork	26 Years	01-28-1853	032	REYNOLDS, James	Native of Parish of Kilgar-
				032		riff, Co. Cork, Ireland
				032	SHEA, Hanah	(NOI James Reynolds) Native
				032		of Co. Cork, Ireland
				032		
Catherine KELLEY Pendergast		40 Years	07-00-1862	032	PENDERGAST, Patrick	(NOI Patrick Pendergast)
				032	KELLEY, Catherine	
				032		
Thomas CAIN		1825	1884	032	CAVANAUGH, Mary	
Mary CAVANAUGH Cain		1832	1885	032	CAIN, Thomas	
John CAIN		3 Years		032	CAIN, John	
Mary CAIN		2 Years		032	CAIN, Mary	
				032		
Mary PRESTON Crawley		31Y 20D	10-20-1863	032	CRAWLEY, Michael	(NOI Michael Crawley)
				032	PRESTON, Mary	
Louis PRESTON		33Y08M14D	10-31-1862	032	PRESTON, Louis	
				032		
Richard DELEHANTY	Co. Kilkenny	66 Years	12-19-1872	032	_____, Mary M.	Natives of "Balyha____", Co.
				032		Kilkenny, Ireland
Mary M. _____ DELEHANTY	Co. Kilkenny	55 Years	04-10-1862	032	DELEHANTY, Richard	Natives of "Balyha____", Co.
				032		Kilkenny, Ireland
				032		
Margaret HOGAN Roach		24 Years	07-17-1870	032	ROACH, John	(NOI John ROACH)

				032	HOGAN, Margaret	
Katie O'CONNELL		17 Years	01-05-1896	032	O'CONNELL, Katie	
				032	HOGAN, Margaret	
				032	O'CONNELL, Katie	
				032		
Patrick J. KELLY		03-17-1814	09-30-1877	032	MCCARTHY, Sarah	(GAR-Try 1st Vt Cav Rgt,Co. I)
Sarah MCCARTHY Kelly		01-01-1826	04-15-1907	032	KELLY, Patrick J.	
Sarah Alia KELLY		06-01-1859	03-20-1907	032	KELLY, Sarah Alia	
Margaret J. KELLY		08-29-1856	04-05-1919	032	KELLY, Margaret J.	
				032		
Lawrence HALLORAN		36 Years	12-17-1863	032	HALLORAN, Lawrence	(Age at death c/b 38 Years)
				032		
James HUGHES		80 Years	07-30-1902	032	_____, Bridget	
Bridget _____ HUGHES		57 Years	09-06-1891	032	HUGHES, James	
				032		
Patrick SLOAN		03-16-1827	11-21-1907	032	QUINN, Ellen	
Ellen QUINN Sloan		10-31-1837	10-15-1914	032	SLOAN, Patrick	
				032		
Henry DUCEY		1836	1912	032	_____, Ann	
Ann _____ DUCEY		1843	1915	032	DUCEY, Henry	
				032		
John HICKEY		1837	1904	032	_____, Ann	
Mary _____ HICKEY		1849	1926	032	HICKEY, John	
Margaret _____ HICKEY		1839	1867	032	HICKEY, John	
Patrick HICKEY		1835	1857	032	HICKEY, Patrick	
Lawrence HICKEY		1841	1867	032	HICKEY, Lawrence	
Thomas HICKEY		1846	1895	032	HICKEY, Thomas	
Martin HICKEY		1852	1874	032	HICKEY, Martin	
				032		
Patrick BURKE		57 Years	02-09-1882	032	_____, Mary	
Mary _____ BURKE		78 Years		032	BURKE, Patrick	
				032		
Jeremiah DUNLEA		1851	1873	032	DUNLEA, Jeremiah	
				032		
Elizabeth COFFEE Bradey	Co. Kings	45 Years	08-29-1863	032	BRADEY, Terrance	Kings Co., Ire. (NOI Terrance
				032	COFFEE, Elizabeth	Bradey - Now Co. Offaly)
				032		
William BOLTON		70 Years	12-19-1866	032	_____, Jane	
Jane _____ BOLTON		74 Years	04-10-1874	032	BOLTON, William	
Joseph BOLTON		24 Years	06-__-1864	032	BOLTON, Joseph	
				032		
Thomas HOPKINS		42 Years	12-20-1848	032	_____, Anne	
Anne _____ HOPKINS		62 Years	01-22-1870	032	HOPKINS, Thomas	
				032		
John POWERS			11-04-1878	032	BOYLE, Julia	

Julia BOYLE Powers			01-19-1879	032	POWERS, John	
				032		
Dennis STARR	Co. Tipperary	1837	1907	032	MALONEY, Margaret	Natives of Co. Tipperary, Ire.
Margaret MALONEY Starr	Co. Tipperary	1843	1914	032	STARR, Dennis	Natives of Co. Tipperary, Ire.
Dennis STARR Jr.		1861	1900	032	STARR, Dennis Jr.	
John STARR		10 Days	07-15-1867	032	STARR, John	
Nora STARR		1796	1871	032	STARR, Nora	
				032		
John ROCHE		76 Years	10-15-1889	032	ROCHE, John	
				032		
James CARMODY	Co. Limerick	1824	12-31-1892	032	_____, Margaret	Born In Co. Limerick, Ireland
				032	_____, Bridget	
Margaret _____ CARMODY	Co. Limerick	01-06-1833	06-20-1890	032	CARMODY, James	Born In Co. Limerick, Ireland
Bridget _____ CARMODY		01-06-1833	06-20-1890	032	CARMODY, James	
Johanna CARMODY		32 Years	06-16-1898	032	CARMODY, Johanna	(D/O James & Margaret Carmody)
James P. CARMODY			10-22-1940	032	CARMODY, James P.	(S/O James & Margaret Carmody)
Margaret CARMODY		07-05-1851	12-09-1873	032	CARMODY, Margaret	D/O James & Bridget Carmody
Bridget CARMODY				032	CARMODY, Bridget	D/O James & Bridget Carmody
				032		
William FOLEY			02-08-1863	032	FOLEY, William	
				032		
Jane LEONARD		65 Years	04-03-1872	032	LEONARD, Jane	
Johannah LEONARD		86 Years	05-29-1888	032	LEONARD, Johannah	
				032		
John GRADY		1823	1906	032	HANON, Mary	
Mary HANON Grady		1821	1909	032	GRADY, John	
				032		
Michael EDWARD		77 Years	04-01-1889	032	_____, Eliza	
Eliza _____ EDWARD		51 Years	02-06-1878?	032	EDWARD, Michael	
				032		
Michael FOLEY		40 Years	01-09-1863	032	KENNEDY, Mary	
Mary KENNEDY Foley		80 Years	02-05-1906	032	FOLEY, Michael	
				032		
Margaret _____ MANE		27 Years	05-04-1874	032	MANE, John Jr.	(NOI John Mane Jr.)
				032	_____, Margaret	
				032		
Mrs. Lawrence HANLEY		1843	1911	032	HANLEY, Lawrence	(NOI Lawrence Hanley)
				032		
Patrick MAYHAN		03-07-1817	09-04-1880	032	_____, Julia	
Julia _____ MAYHAN		10-08-1819	11-19-1878	032	MAYHAN, Patrick	
				032		
Mary _____ CONWAY		45 Years	01-11-1873	032	CONWAY, Daniel	(NOI Daniel Conway)
				032	_____, Mary	
				032		
John CAIN		75 Years	03-28-1904	032	RYAN, Sarah	

Sarah RYAN Cain		80 Years	03-18-1909	032	CAIN, John	
Hannah CAIN		03-26-1855	10-02-1908	032	CAIN, Hannah	
				032		
Patrick DUNN				032	_____, Bridget	(No DOB/DOD on Patrick DUNN)
Bridget _____ DUNN		53 Years	06-02-1882	032	DUNN, Patrick	
Mary DUNN		11Y 9M	07-19-1861	032	DUNN, Mary	
Bridget DUNN		06-29-1861	08-06-1862	032	DUNN, Bridget	
				032		
Catherine CAFFRY Dupont		32 Years	04-18-1863	032	DUPONT, Isaac	(NOI Isaac Dupont)
				032	CAFFRY, Catherine	
				032		
Patrick STARR		1811	1893	032	RYAN, Julia	
Julia RYAN Starr		1816	1888	032	STARR, Patrick	
Julia STARR		1855	1861	032	STARR, Julia	
Michael STARR		1859	1861	032	STARR, Michael	
Julia STARR		1862	1870	032	STARR, Julia	
William P. STARR		1853	1937	032	STEELE, Delia	
Delia STEELE Starr		1866	1931	032	STARR, William P.	
				032		
Bridget _____ HOLLERAN		76 Years	06-09-1877	032	HOLLERAN, Michael	(NOI Michael Holleran)
				032	_____, Bridget	
Thomas E. LADEN		52 Years	12-23-1885	032	HOLLERAN, Margaret	
Margaret HOLLERAN Laden		61 Years	07-11-1895	032	LADEN, Thomas	
				032		
Edward SHEEHAN				032	SHEEHAN, Edward	Family Of Edward Sheehan (NOI)
				032		
Matthew HOLLORAN		58 Years	10-09-1872	032	_____, Bridget	
Bridget _____ HOLLORAN		75 Years	04-12-1893	032	HOLLORAN, Matthew	
				032		
James CREADY		66 Years	03-17-1858	032	CREADY, James	
				032		
Bridget _____ HOLRON			05-11-1854	032	HOLRON, Matthew	(NOI Matthew Holron)
				032		
Patrick HOLRON	Co. Tipperary	03-__-1826	07-28-1899	032	MCCREARY, Kate	Parish of Ballina, County
				032		Tipperary, Ire. (No such
				032		parish-probably Ballina town).
Kate MCCREARY Holron	Co. Roscommon		10-31-1894	032	HOLRON, Patrick	Parish of "Crisnah", Co. Ros-
				032		common(No such town or parish)
				032		
Patrick H. GREEN		1837	1911	032	MURPHY, Bridget	
Bridget MURPHY Green		1835	1911	032	GREEN, Patrick H.	
				032		
Thomas LARKIN	Co. Longford	47 Years	10-11-1872	032	LARKIN, Thomas	Native of Parish Kinagry, Co.
				032		of Longford, Ireland (No such
				032		parish, town or townland)

Michael MEAGHER		1849	1918	032	RYAN, Jane	
Jane RYAN Meagher		1853	1932	032	MEAGHER, Michael	
				032		
John MALEY	Co. Clare	75 Years	04-05-1895?	032	O'HALLERIN, Ellen	Born In "Ballyvirgil" (Bally-
				032		vergin), Co. Clare, Ireland
Ellen O'HALLERIN Maley	Co. Clare	66 Years	01-02-1892	032	MALEY, John	Born in "Ballyvirgil" (Bally-
				032		vergin) Co. Clare, Ireland
				032		
John HOGAN				032	CARROLL, Sarah	(No DOB/DOD on John Hogan)
Sarah CARROLL Hogan		70 Years	04-16-1902	032	HOGAN, John	
				032		
Daniel SULLIVAN		58 Years	06-10-1868	032	_____, Elizabeth	
Elizabeth _____ SULLIVAN		59 Years	09-08-1894	032	SULLIVAN, Daniel	
Timothy SULLIVAN		33 Years	11-29-1884	032	SULLIVAN, Timothy	
				032		
Johnf HAYES		06-29-1818	01-31-1899	032	WHITE, Sarah	
Sarah WHITE Hayes		1821	1908	032	HAYES, John	
Johnie HAYES		33 Years	09-27-1894	032	HAYES, Johnie	
				032		
Nicholas P. HATCH		06-29-1820	08-28-1884	032	BRADLEY, Alice	
Alice BRADLEY Hatch		54 Years	04-08-1872	032	HATCH, Nicholas P.	
				032		
James KENNEDY				032	KENNEDY, James	Native of the Parish Of Castle
				032		Connell. (Probably Town of
				032		Castleconnel,Co. Limerick, Ire
				032		Erected By Christopher Kennedy
				032		In Honor Of His Son. (Part of
				032		this stone missing.No DOB-DOD)
				032		
Dennis MEERS			04-11-1871	032	_____, Anne	
Anne _____ MEERS		85 Years	05-12-1905	032	MEERS, Dennis	
				032		
Thomas NOLAN		28 Years	02-29-1908	032	NOLAN, Thomas	
Martin NOLAN		64 Years	06-02-1893	032	NOLAN, Martin	
Mary NOLAN		74 Years	06-24-1911	032	NOLAN, Mary	
				032		
John O'BRIEN		60 Years	04-11-1871	032	_____, Bridget	(NOI Bridget O'Brien)
				032	O'BRIEN, John	
Jerry O'BRIEN		19 Years	12-29-1889	032	O'BRIEN, Jerry	S/O John & Bridget O'Brien
				032		
Patrick WHITE		1812	1872	032	FERGUSON, Annie	
Annie FERGUSON White		1817	1904	032	WHITE, Patrick	
Katherine WHITE		1848	1910	032	WHITE, Katherine	Daughter
				032		
John O'CONNELL		21 Years	11-12-1871	032	O'CONNELL, John	

				032		
Bridget _____ BOYLE		92 Years	12-29-1893	032	BOYLE, Michael	(NOI Michael Boyle)
				032	_____, Bridget	
William KELLEY		67 Years	03-06-1907	032	KELLEY, William	(Spouse died 8-6-1920. NOI)
				032		
				032		
Martin O'BRIEN		63 Years	05-02-1872	032	O'BRIEN, Martin	
				032		
Margaret DOOLEY		78 Years	08-29-1876	032	DOOLEY, Margaret	
Patrick BRENNAN		22 Years	04-30-1878	032	BRENNAN, Patrick	
				032		
Katherine O'BRIEN Dolan		1855	1919	032	DOLAN, George T.	(NOI George T. Dolan)
				032	O'BRIEN, Katherine	
				032		
Daniel CROWLEY	Co. Cork	67 Years	05-21-1880	032	DRISCOLL, Ellen	Native of the Parish of Skull,
				032		Co. Cork, Ireland
Ellen DRISCOLL CROWLEY	Co. Cork	65 Years	04-28-1886	032	CROWLEY, Daniel	Native of Skull,Co. Cork, Ire.
				032		
Patrick MCNAMARA				032	MCNAMARA, Patrick	(NOI)
Hanora MCNAMARA				032	MCNAMARA, Hanora	(NOI)
				032		
Catherine BURKE Corbett		55 Years	08-27-1883	032	CORBETT, James	(NOI James Corbett)
				032	BURKE, Catherine	
Maggie CORBETT		20 Years	01-11-1885	032	CORBETT, Maggie	
Thomas CORBETT		17 Years	01-26-1885	032	CORBETT, Thomas	
Michael CORBETT		21 Years	10-05-1872	032	CORBETT, Michael	
Julia CORBETT		19 Years	10-22-1872	032	CORBETT, Julia	
				032		
				032		
John SMALL	Co. Down	47 Years	02-13-1874	032	SMALL, John	Native of The Parish of Morn,
				032		Co. Down, Ireland. There is no
				032		parish of Morn--was a Roman
				032		Catholic parish of Mourne
				032		Lower which, with the Parish
				032		of Kilkeel were both in the
				032		Civil Parish of Kilkeel)
MORGAN FAMILY				032	MORGAN, Family	
Father		1848	1908	032	MORGAN, Father	(GAR Marker)
Mother		1844	1916	032	MORGAN, Mother	
				032		
Sarah _____ RYAN		62 Years	04-08-1874	032	RYAN, Daniel	(NOI Daniel Ryan)
				032	_____, Sarah	
				032		
Rodger CORBETT		42 Years	11-25-1883	032	O'BRIEN, Margaret	
Margaret O'BRIEN Corbett		38 Years	11-28-1887	032	CORBETT, Rodger	(YOD could be 1897)

				032		
Catherine BRADLEY		70 Years	12-16-1872	032	BRADLEY, Catherine	
				032		
Thomas HART				032	DORSEY, Mary	
Mary DORSEY Hart		1816	1881	032	HART, Thomas	
Margaret HART		1853	1916	032	HART, Margaret	Daughter
				032		
Thomas FOX		83 Years	01-26-1894	032	CRONAN, Juliana	
Juliana CRONAN Fox	Co. Clare	56 Years	04-13-1873	032	FOX, Thomas	Native Miltown (Milltown), Co.
				032		Clare, Ireland
Elizabeth FOX Boyle		50 Years	12-28-1885	032	BOYLE, Martin	(NOI Martin Boyle)
				032	FOX, Elizabeth	
John O. FOX		1841	1899	032	_____, Bridget	
Bridget _____ FOX		1840	1920	032	FOX, John O.	
				032		
William MCLAUGHLIN		11-__-1814	01-28-1894	032	_____, Bridget	
Bridget _____ MCLAUGHLIN		75 Years	01-12-1876	032	MCLAUGHLIN, William	
				032		
John O'DEA		71 Years	06-10-1894	032	_____, Joan	
Joan _____ O'DEA		48 Years	01-20-1878	032	O'DEA, John	
				032		
Thomas PINDERS		67 Years	04-13-1914	032	O'CONNELL, Catherine	
Catherine O'CONNELL Pinders		44 Years	11-20-1891	032	PINDERS, Thomas	
				032		
James DOOLAN	Co. Waterford	65 Years	02-20-1894	032	RYAN, Mary	Native of Co. Waterford,Ire.
Mary RYAN Doolan	Co. Limerick	40 Years	06-07-1877	032	DOOLAN, James	Native of Co. Limerick, Ire.
				032		
John BUNNIE		06-20-1832	12-25-1896	032	SHEA, Ellen	
Ellen SHEA Bunnie		1833	1915	032	BUNNIE, John	
				032		
Patrick MCGRATH		1842	1901	032	MAHAR, Mary	
Mary MAHAR McGrath		1843	1923	032	MCGRATH, Patrick	
				032		
James O'CONNOR		76 Years	07-03-1899	032	_____, Hannorah	
Hannorah _____ O'CONNOR		83 Years	01-21-1904	032	O'CONNOR, James	
				032		
William P. CROWLEY		26 Years	03-06-1890	032	CROWLEY, William P.	
Mother		1839	1895	032	CROWLEY, Mother	
Father		1832	1877	032	CROWLEY, Father	
				032		
Sarah _____ DICKLOW		62 Years	07-05-1878	032	DICKLOW, Joseph	(NOI Joseph Dicklow)
				032	_____, Sarah	
				032		
Margaret _____ O'BRIEN		69 Years	10-30-1877	032	O'BRIEN, William	(NOI William O'BRIEN)
				032	_____, Margaret	

				032		
James QUIGLEY		12-17-1856	07-24-1873	032	QUIGLEY, James	
				032		
John E. BALDWIN		05-01-1847		032	QUIGLEY, Julia	
Julia QUIGLEY Baldwin		05-10-1847	10-19-1902	032	BALDWIN, John E.	
				032		
Michael COFFEY				032	KEOUGH, Margaret	
Margaret KEOUGH Coffey	Co. Tipperary	55 Years	04-13-1865	032	COFFEY, Michael	Born In _______, County
				032		Tipperary, Ireland
				032		
John REGAN		1847	1895	032	RYAN, Catherine	
Catherine RYAN Regan		1856	1937	032	REGAN, John	
				032		
John REGAN		62 Years	01-20-1891	032	_____, Hannah	
Hannah _____ REGAN		80 Years	04-30-1910	032	REGAN, John	
				032		
Frank TIE		58 Years	02-09-1915	032	_____, Parmilie	(Surname possibly TIGHE)
Parmilie _____ TIE		31 Years	04-17-1889	032	TIE, Frank	
				032		
John LEWIS		1851	1912	032	MCINERNEY, Margaret	
Margaret MCINERNEY Lewis		1847	1902	032	LEWIS, John	
				032		
Michael LEWIS		1851	1924	032	FOLEY, Bridget	
Bridget FOLEY Lewis		1853	1897	032	LEWIS, Michael	
				032		
Patrick FOLEY		1853	1903	032	CORBETT, Nora	
Nora CORBETT Foley		1855	1922	032	FOLEY, Patrick	
				032		
Jeremiah DURICK		48 Years	05-31-1884	032	LEWIS, Bridget	
Bridget LEWIS Durick		1845	1917	032	DURICK, Jeremiah	
				032		
Mary _____ HUGHES	Co. Waterford	59 Years*	05-12-1881	032	HUGHES, John	(NOI John Hughes. Age at death
				032	_____, Mary	could be "69" Years Born in)
				032		Co. Waterford, Ireland.
				032		
Philip LEAHY		1837	1902	032	_____, Catherine	
Catherine _____ LEAHY		1849	1926	032	LEAHY, Philip	
				032		
Michael HAYES	Co. Clare	1808	02-15-1885	032	_____, Margaret	Born In County Clare, Ireland
Margaret _____ HAYES	Co. Tipperary	1824	12-10-1893	032	HAYES, Michael	Born In Co. Tipperary, Ireland
				032		
Jeremiah CROWLEY		1859	1906	032	RYAN, Bridget	
Bridget RYAN Crowley		1860	1938	032	CROWLEY, Jeremiah	
				032		
Joseph DAGENAIS		1850	1929	032	CROWLEY, Rosalie	

Rosalie CROWLEY Dagenais		1857	1939	032	DAGENAIS, Joseph	
Father		1816	1904	032		
Mother		1828	1887	032		
				032		
Michael T. BURKE		1857	1929	032	_____, Mary E.	
Mary E. _____ BURKE		1862	1928	032	BURKE, Michael T.	
				032		
Philip WELCOME		07-22-1821	11-22-1901	032	_____, Rose	
Rose _____ WELCOME		10-27-1835	05-29-1916	032	WELCOME, Philip	
				032		
Kate _____ BURKE			__-25-1856	032	BURKE, William	(NOI William Burke)
				032	_____, Kate	
				032		
James KICHLAM		58 Years	06-15-1905	032	_____, Margaret	
Margaret _____ KICHLAM		39 Years	03-14-1886	032	KICHLAM, James	
				032		
Michael MEAGHER		84 Years	09-22-1893	032	HARNEY, Bridget	(GAR Marker-not in reference)
Bridget HARNEY Meagher		98 Years	12-17-1910	032	MEAGHER, Michael	
				032		
Patrick EGAN		12-23-1840	09-11-1894	032	HINES, Mary	
Mary HINES Egan		08-15-1846	05-19-1919	032	EGAN, Patrick	
				032		
Maurice O'DONNELL		1844	1888	032	BURKE, Margaret	
Margaret BURKE O'Donnell		1847	1924	032	O'DONNELL, Maurice	
				032		
Daniel O'NEILL		10-26-1866	09-26-1902	032	O'NEILL, Daniel	Born In County Cork, Ireland.
Michael O'NEILL	Co. Cork	07-07-1840	05-18-1912	032	SHERIDAN, Margaret	(GAR) Co. K, 2nd NY Cavalry
				032		Native of Co. Tipperary,Parish
Margaret SHERIDAN O'Neill	Co. Tipperary	12-26-1839	05-31-1895	032	O'NEILL, Michael	of Castletown (No such parish.
				032		Could be Parish Castletownarra
				032		or Town of Castletown)
				032		
Timothy MCLOUGHLIN			04-20-1911	032	_____, Anna	
Anna _____ MCLOUGHLIN		43 Years	03-28-1885	032	MCLOUGHLIN, Timothy	
				032		
John BURNS		1836	1868	032	_____, Hannah	
Hannah _____ BURNS		1838	1886	032	BURNS, John	
				032		
John DORSEY		75 Years	02-17-1885	032	DORSEY, John	(YOD appears to be 1885)
				032		
Richard MURPHY		1857	1907	032	GETTINGS, Sarah	
Sarah GETTINGS Murphy		1856	1919	032	MURPHY, Richard	
John GETTINGS		1858	1893	032	GETTINGS, John	
				032		
Matthew CROWLEY		1851	1919	032	MCCORMICK, Margaret	

Name	Origin	Born/Age	Died	Code	Index	Notes
Margaret MCCORMICK Crowley		22Y 6M	03-16-1861	032	CROWLEY, Matthew	
				032		
Patrick RADIGAN		1815	1899	032	DUNN, Elizabeth	
Elizabeth DUNN Radigan		1827	1897	032	RADIGAN, Patrick	
Margaret RADIGAN		1807	1887	032	RADIGAN, Margaret	
Michael RADIGAN		1856	1920	032	RADIGAN, Michael	
Bridget RADIGAN		1857	1923	032	RADIGAN, Bridget	
Mary E. RADIGAN		1861	1924	032	RADIGAN, Mary E.	
Thomas R. RADIGAN		1867	1928	032	RADIGAN, Thomas R.	
Anne T. RADIGAN		1876	1966	032	RADIGAN, Anne T.	
				032		
John MURPHY		1894		032	CUMMINGS, Mary	
Mary CUMMINGS Murphy		1930		032	MURPHY, John	
				032		
John GRADY		75 Years	11-07-1895	032	MAHAR, Bridget	
Bridget MAHAR Grady		52 Years	06-09-1896	032	GRADY, John	
				032		
				032		
William BRENNAN Sr.		1780?	1848	032	BRENNAN, William Sr.	
William BRENNAN		1820	1900	032	GEELAN, Bridget	
Bridget GEELAN BRENNAN		1831	1902	032	BRENNAN, William	
Cathrine BRENNAN		1874	1966	032	BRENNAN, Cathrine	
Daniel G. BRENNAN		1868	1950	032	_____, Elizabeth H.	
Elizabeth H. _____ BRENNAN		1866	1904	032	BRENNAN, Daniel G.	
Annie BRENNAN		1855	1929	032	BRENNAN, Annie	
Edward BRENNAN		1872	1895	032	BRENNAN, Edward	
William BRENNAN Jr.		1866	1928	032	BRENNAN, William Jr.	
				032		
Patrick WALLACE		12-04-1847	01-26-1927	032	_____, Anastasia	
Anastasia _____ WALLACE		12-24-1849	03-25-1923	032	WALLACE, Patrick	
				032		
Daniel DELOHERY	Co. Cork	36 Years	02-19-1864	032	DELOHERY, Daniel	A Native of County Cork, Ire. (GAR) Co. K., 2nd NY Cavalry
				032		
				032		
James FOX		01-15-1821	10-12-1899	032	MOLONEY, Margaret	
Margaret MOLONEY Fox		12-24-1825	10-22-1896	032	FOX, James	
				032		
James KEEVLAN		79 Years	11-16-1913	032	MCCANN, Mary	
Mary MCCANN Keevlan		53 Years	11-13-1898	032	KEEVLAN, James	
				032		
Michael HEFFERN		76 Years	12-29-1915	032	_____, Ann	
Ann _____ HEFFERN		62 Years	02-14-1906	032	HEFFERN, Michael	
Father		1835	1918	032	HEFFERN, Father	
Mother		1820	1910	032	HEFFERN, Mother	
Ella HEFFERN		1858	1934	032	HEFFERN, Ella	

Name	Born	Died	Code	Index	Notes
			032		
Terrance SLOAN	1840	1922	032	O'ROURKE, Mary	
Mary O'ROURKE Sloan	1843	1931	032	SLOAN, Terrance	
			032		
Edward MURPHY	1885	1960	032	FOSTER, Florence	
Florence FOSTER Murphy	1878	1927	032	MURPHY, Edward	
			032		
Mary L. DUFFANY	1822	1919	032	DUFFANY, Mary L.	
John L. DUFFANY	1854	1895	032	DUFFANY, John L.	
			032		
Owen DORAN	1846	1924	032	_____, Catherine	
Catherine _____ DORAN	1844	1933	032	DORAN, Owen	
			032		
Ellen BOLGER Conway	1854	1925	032	BOLGER, Ellen	(NOI Mr. Conway)
			032		
John O'BRIEN	1867	1929	032	MURPHY, Catherine	
Catherine MURPHY O'Brien	1869	1927	032	O'BRIEN, John	
			032		
Thomas HOGAN	1844	1930	032	GRACE, Mary	
Mary GRACE Hogan	1845	1930	032	HOGAN, Thomas	
			032		
Dennis TOWERS	1849		032	O'BRIEN, Bridget	
Bridget O'BRIEN Towers	1869	1925	032	TOWERS, Dennis	
			032		
John W. COFFEY	1853	1930	032	DURIVAGE, Selina	
Selina DURIVAGE Coffey	1858	1936	032	COFFEY, John W.	
			032		
Thomas CARTY	1820	1902	032	CULKINS, Mary	
Mary CULKINS Carty	1826	1905	032	CARTY, Thomas	
			032		
Rev. Thomas Raymond CARTY		03-06-1927	032	CARTY, Rev. Thomas R.	Native of Fair Haven. Ordained in Paris 6-29-1888
			032		
			032		
Joel S. CARTY	1854	1935	032	CARTY, Joel S.	
			032		
Michael BLAKE	01-05-1867	01-06-1905	032	O'SHEA, Catherine	
Catherine O'SHEA Blake	09-28-1845	02-15-1915	032	BLAKE, Michael	Inscription reads: "His Wife, Catherine O'Shea Cagney" ??
			032		
			032		
James FOLEY	1858	1907	032	_____, Katherine	
Katherine _____ FOLEY	1863	1943	032	FOLEY, James	
			032		
Patrick QUINN	1851	1915	032	FINNEGAN, Anastasia	
Anastasia FINNEGAN Quinn	1851	1887	032	QUINN, Patrick	(YOB could be 1861)
			032		

Thomas J. MURPHY		1867	1938	032	BARRON, Margaret	
Margaret BARRON Murphy		1868	1946	032	MURPHY, Thomas J.	
Rev. Jeremiah J. O'BRIEN	Co. Tipperary	05-15-1885	03-05-1960	032	O'BRIEN, Rev. Jeremiah	Born In Newport,Co. Tipperary, Ireland
				032		
				032		
Daniel O'DAY		1850	1932	032	O'DAY, Daniel	
				032		
Daniel F. CARMODY		1857	1941	032	BARRETT, Mary	
Mary BARRETT Carmody		1861	1934	032	CARMODY, Daniel F.	
Rev. Patrick Joseph BARRETT		1857	1933	032	BARRETT, Rev. Patrick J.	
				032		
Michael J. CARMODY		1849	1929	032	MAHAR, Julia	
Julia MAHAR Carmody		1853	1941	032	CARMODY, Michael J.	
				032		
George T. MURPHY		1887	1934	032	_____, Helen M.	
Helen M. _____ MURPHY		1885	1946	032	MURPHY, George T.	
				032		
Timothy J. MURPHY		1864	1921	032	BREARTON, Elizabeth	
Elizabeth BREARTON Murphy		1867	1942	032	MURPHY, Timothy J.	
Rev. Edward Patrick MURPHY		1898	1936	032	MURPHY, Rev. Edward P.	
Henry F. MURPHY		1899	1965	032	MURPHY, Henry F.	
Marguerite MURPHY		1902		032	MURPHY, Marguerite	
Julia M. MURPHY		1896	1975	032	MURPHY, Julia M.	
				032		
Michael O'DAY		1854	1920	032	CUMMINGS, Margaret	
Margaret CUMMINGS O'Day		1855	1932	032	O'DAY, Michael	
				032		
Mitchell CLINE		1834	1916	032	DUCLOS, Mary	
Mary DUCLOS Cline		1851	1922	032	CLINE, Mitchell	
				032		
Thomas R. MAYHAR		1843	1916	032	RYAN, Mary	
Mary RYAN Mayhar		1841	1916	032	MAYHAR, Thomas R.	
				032		
Rev. Henry LANE	Co. Cork	10-03-1846	04-15-1907	032	LANE, Rev. Henry	Born In County Cork, Ireland
				032		
Philip QUIGLEY		1842	1912	032	QUIGLEY, Philip	
				032		
Timothy CALEY		1840	1888	032	HAYNES, Jane	
Jane HAYNES Caley		1842	1910	032	CALEY, Timothy	
				032		
Patrick MAHAR		60 Years	03-23-1917	032	MAHAR, Patrick	
				032		
John DELEHANTY		1851	1916	032	_____, Hannah M.	
Hannah M. _____ DELEHANTY		1868	1958	032	DELEHANTY, John	
				032		

Patrick MALONE		1832	1909	032	KENNEDY, Mary	
Mary KENNEDY Malone		1833	1903	032	MALONE, Patrick	
				032		
Bridget CARROLL Starr		1834	1918	032	STARR, Michael	(NOI Michael Starr)
				032	CARROLL, Bridget	
				032		
Martin H. DOOLEY		1852	1913	032	SLOAN, Elizabeth	
Elizabeth SLOAN Dooley		1855	1928	032	DOOLEY, Martin H.	
				032		
James T. HAYES		1857		032	MINOGUE, Mary	
Mary MINOGUE Hayes		1856	1915	032	HAYES, James T.	
				032		
Charles K. WILLIAMS		1855	1923	032	_____, Mary A.	
Mary A. _____ WILLIAMS		1855	1917	032	WILLIAMS, Charles K.	
				032		
James DELEHANTY		11-24-1844	08-16-1917	032	_____, Mary	
Mary _____ DELEHANTY		05-23-1847	07-29-1888	032	DELEHANTY, James	
				032		
Charles Michael COFFEE		08-06-1851	01-19-1915	032	O'BRIEN, Mary J.	
Mary J. O'BRIEN Coffee		06-02-1859	1936	032	COFFEE, Charles Michael	
				032		
Edward LEONARD		1844	1917	032	HARRIS, Bridget	
Bridget HARRIS Leonard		1856	1928	032	LEONARD, Edward	
				032		
Michael KENNEDY		08-18-1849	03-13-1911	032	TREAHEY, Mary	
Mary TREAHEY Kennedy		05-25-1851	01-20-1924	032	KENNEDY, Michael	
Rev. Msgr John M. KENNEDY		11-09-1881	05-15-1874	032	KENNEDY, Rev Msgr John	Ordained 12-24-1909
Mary E. KENNEDY		05-24-1874	12-23-1956	032	KENNEDY, Mary E.	
				032		
John MALONE		1838	1919	032	BARRETT, Margaret	
Margaret BARRETT Malone		1836	1926	032	MALONE, John	
				032		
Mr. George SWEENEY		1838	1913	032	_____, Sarah	
Mrs. Sarah _____ SWEENEY		1842	1911	032	SWEENEY, George	
				032		
John LEONARD	Co. Cork	1842	1912	032	DWYER, Bridget	Native of Co. Cork, Ireland
				032	LEONARD, Owen	Son of Owen Leonard and Ellen O'Connell
				032		
Bridget DWYER Leonard		1844	1924	032	LEONARD, John	
				032		
Mary BOLAND Treahey		69 Years	04-26-1888	032	TREAHEY, John	(NOI John Treahey)
				032	BOLAND, Mary	
				032		
James TREAHEY		1847	1900	032	TREAHEY, James	
				032		

Name	Place	Age/Born	Died	Code	Index	Notes
Hannah TREAHEY		34 Years	09-12-1887	032	TREAHEY, Hannah	Dau of John & Mary Treahey
				032		
John HUMPHREYS		1844	1916	032	BRENNAN, Ann	(GAR) Co. F., 14th VT Vols
Ann BRENNAN Humphreys		1846	1913	032	HUMPHREYS, John	
				032		
Thomas J. DOWNES		07-10-1817	08-10-1885	032	_____, Catherine	
Catherine _____ DOWNES		04-03-1829	03-24-1901	032	DOWNES, Thomas J.	
Mary L. DOWNES O'Keefe		20 Years	02-15-1871	032	O'KEEFE, Frank	(NOI Frank O'KEEFE)
				032	DOWNES, Mary L.	
Katie DOWNES McCarty		04-30-1864	04-03-1892	032	MCCARTY, E.S.	(NOI E.S. McCarty)
				032	DOWNS, Katie	
John E. DOWNES		01-06-1856	11-21-1886	032	DOWNES, John E.	
Thomas B. DOWNES		06-20-1857	04-19-1885	032	DOWNES, Thomas B.	
				032		
Patrick MCGRATH		89 Years	01-12-1887	032	_____, Mary	
Mary _____ MCGRATH		88 Years	11-18-1893	032	MCGRATH, Patrick	
Mary MCGRATH		36 Years	07-08-1890	032	MCGRATH, Mary	
				032		
James HUMPHREYS		87 Years	01-15-1895	032	_____, Ellen	
Ellen _____ HUMPHREYS		72 Years	03-14-1890	032	HUMPHREYS, James	
Mary HUMPHREYS Carroll		26 Years	02-03-1879	032	CARROLL, Patrick	(NOI Patrick Carroll)
				032	HUMPHREYS, Mary	
				032		
John DONNELLY	Co. Cavan	44 Years	03-25-1851	032	_____, Roseanna	A Native of The Parish of Drum
				032		(No such Parish.Could be Drung
				032		Drumgoon, Drumlane, Drumlumman
				032		Drumreilly. (NOI Roseanna)
				032		
Peter DONNELLY		22 Years	1864	032	DONNELLY, Peter	Son of John& Roseanna Donnelly
				032		He Was Killed At Petersburg,
				032		Virginia
Edward BURNS		76 Years	04-24-1904	032	BURNS, Edward	
Mrs. Rosa BURNS		69 Years	04-05-1879	032	BURNS, Mrs. Rosa	
				032		
Dennis HOGAN		1849	1913	032	DOLAN, Jane	
Jane DOLAN Hogan		1849	1926	032	HOGAN, Dennis	
				032		
Thomas KEEVLAN		1832	1906	032	CARVEY, Mary	
Mary CARVEY Keevlan		1831	1926	032	KEEVLAN, Thomas	
				032		
Richard CARRICK		89 Years	09-08-1909	032	COMER, Maria	
Maria COMER Carrick		85 Years	03-06-1899	032	CARRICK, Richard	
John CARRICK		13 Years	04-02-1867	032	CARRICK, John	
Richard C. CARRICK		1858	1930	032	CARRICK, Richard C.	
				032		

Name	Origin	Age/Born	Died	No.	Index	Notes
Michael MCGAGUE		72 Years	10-01-1904	032	AGAN, Mary	
Mary AGAN McGague		58 Years	04-19-1885	032	MCGAGUE, Michael	
Patrick AGAN	Co. Kilkenny	83 Years	10-18-1876	032	AGAN, Patrick	Native of Parish Windgap, Co.
				032		Kilkenny, Ireland
Ellen AGAN		36 Years	04-28-1865	032	AGAN, Ellen	
				032		
William S. WARNER		42 Years	05-19-1888	032	WARNER, William S.	
				032		
Bridget _____ DUFFEY		55 Years	11-10-1875	032	DUFFEY, Thomas	(NOI Thomas Duffey)
				032	_____, Bridget	
				032		
John MCINERNY		57 Years	07-12-1865	032	_____, Mary Ann	(NOI Mary Ann)
				032	MCINERNY, John	
				032		
John MCINERNY		8Y 5M	06-21-1861	032	MCINERNY, John	
				032		
John M. RYAN		06-24-1832	01-20-1913	032	BOLAND, Elizabeth	
Elizabeth BOLAND Ryan		80 Years	04-08-1911	032	RYAN, John M.	
Catherine RYAN		17 Years	09-10-1872	032	RYAN, Catherine	
Hannah RYAN		30 Years	03-14-1898	032	RYAN, Hannah	
Margaret RYAN		45 Years	09-12-1898	032	RYAN, Margaret	
Ellen RYAN		36 Years	11-18-1899	032	RYAN, Ellen	
Patrick BOLAND	Co. Limerick	50 Years	03-04-1861	032	BOLAND, Patrick	Born In The Parish of Roberts-
Bridget RYAN		18Y 9M 8D	05-18-1882	032	RYAN, Bridget	town, Co. Limerick, Ireland
Margaret RYAN Quillinan		79 Years	03-11-1877	032	QUILLINAN, Charles	(NOI Charles Quillinan)
				032	RYAN, Margaret	
Mary J. RYAN Keenan		40 Years	10-15-1897	032	KEENAN, Michael B.	(NOI Michael B. Keenan)
				032	RYAN, Mary J.	
				032		
John S. MAHAR	Co. Tipperary	03-23-1815	04-23-1893	032	MINOGUE, Julia	Native Of Co. Tipperary, Ire.
Julia MINOGUE Mahar		11-09-1825	03-27-1898	032	MAHAR, John S.	
Dennis MAHAR		12-09-1857	08-25-1881	032	MAHAR, Dennis	
William MAHAR		12-15-1855	12-25-1855	032	MAHAR, William	
John MAHAR		12-15-1855	12-15-1855	032	MAHAR, John	
Michael MAHAR		08-08-1848	09-05-1849	032	MAHAR, Michael	
Thomas MAHAR		03-31-1858	04-01-1858	032	MAHAR, Thomas	
Patrick MAHAR		03-09-1869	03-09-1869	032	MAHAR, Patrick	
				032		
Michael MCNAMARA		41 Years	02-07-1863	032	MCNAMARA, Michael	
				032		
William MCNAMARA		1857	1914	032	MCNAMARA, William	My Beloved Brother. May His
				032		Soul Rest In Peace
				032		
William MCNAMARA		03-23-1837	11-23-1891	032	CAMPBELL, Eliza	
Eliza CAMPBELL McNamara		06-14-1839	12-29-1897	032	MCNAMARA, William	

				032		
Cornelius LANIGAN		71 Years	03-08-1894	032	KEESHAN, Sarah	
Sarah KEESHAN Lanigan		77 Years	01-26-1908	032	LANIGAN, Cornelius	
				032		
Dennis HOGAN	Co. Tipperary	52 Years	01-14-1867	032	_____, Bridget	Natives of Parish _____,
				032		Co. Tipperary, Ireland
				032		(Stone down - deteriorated)
Bridget _____ HOGAN	Co. Tipperary	45 Years	01-06-1867	032	HOGAN, Dennis	Natives of Parish _____,
				032		Co. Tipperary, Ireland
				032		(Stone down - deteriorated)
				032		
				032		
Patrick GARVIN		38 Years	12-25-1872	032	GARVIN, Patrick	
				032		
Mary _____ DONOVAN		65 Years	09-24-1885	032	DONOVAN, Dan	(NOI Dan Donovan)
				032	_____, Mary	
Patrick DONOVAN		3 Years	07-03-1864	032	DONOVAN, Patrick	
Catherine D. HURLEY		14 Years	08-27-1865	032	HURLEY, Catherine D.	
James HURLEY		47 Years	04-07-1882	032	HURLEY, James	
				032		
Cornelius HAYES	Co. Tipperary	12-25-1824	12-04-1885	032	TOOHEY, Mary	Born In The Parish Of Bally
				032		William, Co. Tipperary, Ire.
				032		(No such Parish. Probably
				032		Town of Ballywilliam).
Mary TOOHEY Hayes		1828	1903	032	HAYES, Cornelius	
Patrick HAYES		07-04-1861	06-04-1865	032	HAYES, Patrick	Son Of Cornelius & Mary Hayes
Bridget GORMAN		01-11-1805	01-11-1878	032	GORMAN, Bridget	
				032		
Thomas MAHAR		68 Years	02-01-1893	032	_____, Julia	
Julia _____ MAHAR		37 Years	04-30-1863	032	MAHAR, Thomas	
Michael MAHAR		27Y 25D	04-25-1881	032	MAHAR, Michael	
John MAHAR		24Y 9M	05-01-1893	032	MAHAR, John	
				032		
John RYAN		75 Years	11-17-1881	032	TORPHEY, Mary	
Mary TORPHEY Ryan		72 Years	04-23-1884	032	RYAN, John	
Patrick RYAN		21 Years	03-20-1862	032	RYAN, Patrick	
Lawrence Francis RYAN		06-14-1848	08-12-1898	032	RYAN, Lawrence Francis	
Michael RYAN		54 Years	01-23-1887	032	RYAN, Michael	
Winnie RYAN		9 Months		032	RYAN, Winnie	"Little Winnie"
George RYAN				032	RYAN, George	Infant Children
Tommy RYAN				032	RYAN, Tommy	Infant Children
				032		
John WINTERS		66 Years	06-13-1880	032	_____, Mary	
Mary _____ WINTERS		46 Years	10-02-1872	032	WINTERS, John	
				032		

Name	Origin	Age/Born	Died	Plot	Index	Notes
Patrick COTTER		72 Years	03-05-1890	032	_____, Margaret	
Margaret _____ COTTER		79 Years	08-01-1901	032	COTTER, Patrick	
				032		
John FLOOD		76 Years	12-28-1885	032	BURKE, Ann	
Ann BURKE Flood	Co. Tipperary	68 Years	12-28-1883	032	FLOOD, John	Native Of The Parish Of Upper-church, Co. Tipperary, Ireland
				032		
William HYNES		28 Years	12-16-1879	032	HYNES, William	
				032		
Dennis LEONARD		25 Years	12-01-1867	032	LEONARD, Dennis	
				032		
Laurence KINSELLA		1829	1907	032	BURKE, Ellen	
Ellen BURKE Kinsella		1834	1906	032	KINSELLA, Laurence	
				032		
Mary CLIFFORD Sullivan		47 Years	09-29-1876	032	SULLIVAN, Lot	(NOI Lot Sullivan)
				032	CLIFFORD, Mary	
				032		
Mary CARNEY		10 Years	01-16-1866	032	CARNEY, Mary	
Catherine CARNEY		1837	11-24-1907	032	CARNEY, Catherine	
				032		
Thomas TRAYNOR		1831	1905	032	_____, Catherine M.	
Catherine M. _____ TRAYNOR		1842	1910	032	TRAYNOR, Thomas	
James TRAYNOR		1864	1865	032	TRAYNOR, James	
Thomas TRAYNOR		1879	1889	032	TRAYNOR, Thomas	
Ann MULLEN		1844	1866	032	MULLEN, Ann	
Mary MULLEN		1846		032	MULLEN, Mary	
				032		
Dennis QUINN		1869	1920	032	TRAYNOR, Elizabeth	
Elizabeth TRAYNOR Quinn		1869	1935	032	QUINN, Dennis	
Jane MCMAHON		71 Years	07-27-1903	032	MCMAHON, Jane	
Thomas QUINN		85 Years	12-29-1909	032	QUINN, Thomas	
Mary J. QUINN		1872	1917	032	QUINN, Mary J.	
				032		
Sarah M. DOYLE Brough		24 Years	01-26-1877	032	BROUGH, John	Dau of John & Margaret Doyle
				032	DOYLE, M.	
				032		
John DOYLE	Co. Wicklow	41 Years	04-28-1869	032	_____, Margaret	A Native of the Co.Wicklow,Ire
Margaret _____ DOYLE		69 Years	08-01-1888	032	DOYLE, John	
				032		
Michael MINOGUE	Co. Tipperary	22 Years	07-25-1865	032	MINOGUE, Michael	Native of The Parish of Castle town (No such parish. Could be Parish Castletownarra or Town of Castletown). Erected by His Sister Hannora. (In this plot
				032		
				032		
				032		
				032		

Name	Origin	Born/Age	Died	Code	Index	Notes
				032		individual stones Mother,
				032		Father, Bridget, Michael, Mary
				032		- NOI)
				032		
Mathew DOOLEY		1814	1868	032	_____, Mary	
Mary _____ DOOLEY		1818	1901	032	DOOLEY, Mathew	
Mathew DOOLEY JR		1859	1879	032	DOOLEY, Mathew Jr.	
				032		
Geoffrey BRENNAN	Co. Queens	52 Years	12-04-1847	032	THOMPSON, Mary	Native of Queens County, Ire.
				032		Died in Castleton, VT. (Queens
				032		County is now County Leix)
Mary THOMPSON Brennan	Co. Kings	75 Years	02-18-1868	032	BRENNAN, Geoffrey	Native Kings County, Ireland.
				032		Died in Castleton, VT. (Kings
				032		County is now County Offaly)
				032		
William O'BRIEN		75 Years	10-03-1887	032	_____, Bridget	
Bridget _____ O'BRIEN		64 Years	08-11-1890	032	O'BRIEN, William	
Catherine O'BRIEN		1857	1928	032	O'BRIEN, Catherine	
				032		
John J. COLLINS		30 Years	03-21-1874	032	COLLINS, John J.	
				032		
James KEENAN		1831	1907	032	BURKE, Elenor A.	
Elenor A. BURKE Keenan		1835	1905	032	KEENAN, James	
Isabella KEENAN		11-11-1854	10-01-1872	032	KEENAN, Isabella	
Margaret KEENAN		11-01-1856	07-05-1861	032	KEENAN, Margaret	
Mary Ellen KEENAN		03-04-1862	08-12-1863	032	KEENAN, Mary Ellen	
Francis KEENAN		01-13-1872	01-10-1889	032	KEENAN, Francis	
James KEENAN JR		05-27-1864	02-11-1900	032	KEENAN, James Jr.	
				032		
Patrick MINOGUE		44 Years	02-16-1869	032	_____, Julia	Son Of J(ames) & Norah Minogue
Julia _____ MINOGUE		50 Years	03-10-1882	032	MINOGUE, Patrick	
Mary MINOGUE		2M 15D	08-15-1854	032	MINOGUE, Mary	Dau Of Patrick & Julia Minogue
John MINOGUE		01-11-1859	11-16-1880	032	MINOGUE, John	Son Of Patrick & Julia Minogue
James MINOGUE		77Y 7M	09-29-1868	032	MINOGUE, James	
James MINOGUE		34 Years	08-12-1862	032	MINOGUE, James	Son Of J(ames) & Norah Minogue
Annie MINOGUE		38 Years	08-20-1897	032	MINOGUE, Annie	
				032		
Thomas DOWNS		20 Years	09-05-1865	032	DOWNS, Thomas	S/O Edward & Margaret Downs.
				032	DOWNS, Edward	Killed.(Could be GAR, Co I,
				032		9th Rgt, Buried at Cypress
				032		Hill, NY)
				032		
Michael KEENAN		74 Years	03-24-1903	032	DALY, Margaret	
Margaret DALY Keenan		78 Years	12-31-1876	032	KEENAN, Michael	
Mary A. KEENAN		13 Years	08-09-1868	032	KEENAN, Mary A.	

Name	County	Age/Born	Died	Code	Spouse/Related	Notes
John P. KEENAN		36 Years	10-24-1900	032	KEENAN, John P.	
Margaret KENNEDY Keenan		1836	1911	032	KENNEDY, Margaret	
				032		
Laurance MCKENNA	Co. Meath	15 Years	03-20-1866	032	MCKENNA, Laurance	Born In Parish Waters Town,
				032		Co. "Maith" (Meath), Ireland.
				032		(No such Parish. Could be Town
				032		of Waterstown, Co.Westmeath or
				032		Walterstown, Co. Meath - There
				032		is a Parish Batterstown in
				032		Co. Meath. Marker is badly
				032		deteriorated).
				032		
John HAWES		78 Years	10-29-1887	032	LEONARD, Bridget	
Bridget LEONARD Hawes		90 Years	04-15-1924	032	HAWES, John	
				032		
Stephen WALSH		63 Years	02-17-1868	032	WALSH, Stephen	(Stone badly deteriorated)
				032		
John DUGGAN		1833	1914	032	KANE, Bridget	
Bridget KANE Duggan		1833	1869	032	DUGGAN, John	
				032		
Mary _____ KANE		42 Years	04-01-1860	032	KANE, John	(NOI John Kane)
				032	_____, Mary	
Michael KANE		22 Years	10-31-187_	032	~~KANE~~, Michael	Son Of John & Mary Kane
				032		
John CANNEY	Co. Clare	70 Years	10-13-1893	032	O'MARA, Catharine	Born In Co. Clare, Ireland
Catharine O'MARA Canney	Co. Waterford	38 Years	02-20-1875	032	CANNEY, John	Native Of Carrigibeg (Carrick-
				032		beg), Co. Waterford, Ireland
				032		
Michael BURNS		1828	1912	032	SLOAN, Ellen	"Their Three Children" (NOI)
				032	MCDONALD, Ellen	
Ellen SLOAN Burns		1828	1865	032	BURNS, Michael	
Ellen MCDONALD Burns		1841	1921	032	BURNS, Michael	
				032		
Ellen SLOAN Burns		37 Years	12-24-1865	032	BURNS, Michael	(Original marker-same person)
				032		
Mary _____ MURTHUR		55 Years	07-25-1865	032	MURTHUR, John	
				032		
Martin GIBBONS		22 Years	12-31-1877	032	GIBBONS, Martin	
				032		
James GIBBONS	Co. Tipperary	50 Years	10-29-1861	032	_____, Mary	A Native Of The County of
				032		Tipperary, Ireland. Erected
				032		By His Wife Mary Gibbons.
Mary _____ GIBBONS		45 Years	10-03-1870	032	GIBBONS, James	
				032		
				032		

Mary BRENNAN		17Y 4M	09-20-1860	032	BRENNAN, Mary	Dau Of John & Mary Brennan
				032	BRENNAN, John	
				032		
Mary _____ WINTER		37 Years	01-19-1858	032	WINTER, Bartholomew	(NOI Bartholomew Winter. This
				032	_____, Mary	marker is down and ½ buried)
				032		
John RAFFORTY		22 Years	08-02-1862	032	RAFFORTY, John	S/O John & Catharine Rafforty
				032		
Dennis HOGAN		87 Years	07-27-1869	032	_____, Johanna	
Johannah _____ HOGAN		77 Years	08-07-1863	032	HOGAN, Dennis	
Daniel HOGAN		78 Years	01-15-1891	032	HOGAN, Daniel	
John HOGAN		72 Years	01-20-1894	032	HOGAN, John	
Johannah HOGAN		60 Years	01-17-1894	032	HOGAN, Johannah	
				032		
Mary HOGAN Maher		33 Years	01-09-1865	032	MAHER, Joseph	(NOI Joseph Maher)
				032	HOGAN, Mary	
				032		
Patrick DELEHANTY		07-12-1809	08-30-1888	032	_____, Mary	
Mary _____ DELEHANTY		05-24-1814	01-24-1864	032	DELEHANTY, Patrick	
Rev. Patrick DELEHANTY		08-15-1852	05-06-1888	032	DELEHANTY, Rev. Patrick	
				032		
Thomas BURKE		62 Years	08-03-1877	032	_____, Frances	
Frances _____ BURKE		65 Years	08-11-1874	032	BURKE, Thomas	(Stone says prename "Francis")
Bridget BURKE		21 Years	01-11-1855	032	BURKE, Bridget	
Michael BURKE		40 Years	07-d1-1881	032	BURKE, Michael	
				032		
James O'BRIEN		98 Years	03-29-1872	032	_____, Ellen	
Ellen _____ O'BRIEN			05-16-1865	032	O'BRIEN, James	
				032		
John O'GRADY		34 Years	12-18-1871	032	O'GRADY, John	
				032		
Nancy HAUGH		19 Years	02-23-1865	032	HAUGH, Nancy	Daus Of James & Bridget Haugh
Ellen HAUGH		15 Years	02-26-1858	032	HAUGH, Ellen	Daus Of James & Bridget Haugh
Mary HAUGH		21 Years	04-25-1861	032	HAUGH, Mary	Daus Of James & Bridget Haugh
				032		(NOI James & Bridget Haugh.)
				032		
John BOLGER		1848	1917	032	BOLGER, John	(Surname possibly Bulger)
				032		
Thomas BOLGER	Co. Kilkenny	66 Years	01-01-1866	032	HENNESSY, Mary	Born In Dunmore, Co. Kilkenny,
				032		Ireland. Died at Fairhaven,VT
				032		(Two markers for this person)
				032		
Mary HENNESSY Bolger	Co. Kilkenny	1816	10-30-1889	032	BOLGER, Thomas	Born In Windgap, Co. Kilkenny,
				032		Ireland. Died at Fairhaven,VT
				032		

Edward RYAN	Co. Tipperary	51 Years	03-05-1880	032	_____, Mary	Native of Co. Tipperary, Ire.
Mary _____ RYAN		65 Years	01-20-1889	032	RYAN, Edward	
				032		
Richard CONNOLLY		52 Years	07-26-1869	032	CONNOLLY, Richard	
John RYAN		35 Years	08-23-1867	032	RYAN, John	
Patrick CONNOLLY		42 Years	09-26-1868	032	CONNOLLY, Patrick	
				032		
Patrick BREE	Co. Sligo	86 Years	03-05-1894	032	_____, Catherine	Natives of Parish of Ballina-
				032		
				032		(Ballynakill), Co. Sligo, Ire.
Catherine _____ BREE	Co. Sligo	63 Years	07-28-1886	032	BREE, Patrick	Natives of Parish of Ballina-
				032		kil (Ballynakill), Co. Sligo,
				032		Ire.
				032		
Patrick CASSIDY		31 Years?	11-18-1879	032	CASSIDY, Patrick	
				032		
James MCGUINESS		02-13-1846	02-21-1897	032	_____, Margaret	(GAR Try Co. A,6th RGT VtVols)
Margaret _____ MCGUINESS		12-28-1845	08-18-1920	032	MCGUINESS, James	
				032		
Timothy FINNIGAN	Co. Cork	61 Years	10-25-1877	032	FINNIGAN, Timothy	A Native Of Co. Cork, Ireland
				032		
John FINNIGAN		46 Years	02-09-1869	032	FINNIGAN, John	
				032		
Kate MCDONOUGH O'Dell		01-20-1834	01-20-1903	032	O'DELL, Albert	(NOI Albert O'Dell)
				032	MCDONOUGH, Kate	
				032		
John KELLEY		66 Years	10-23-1888	032	_____, Margaret	
Margaret _____ KELLEY		65 Years	03-01-1894	032	KELLEY, John	
Mary KELLEY		44 Years	08-13-1867	032	KELLEY, Mary	
Edward KELLEY		45 Years	11-07-1900	032	KELLEY, Edward	
				032		
Patrick MAHONEY	Co. Limerick	1840	1908	032	KELLEY, Mary	Natives of Co. Limerick, Ire.
Mary KELLEY Mahoney	Co. Limerick	1840	1911	032	MAHONEY, Patrick	Natives of Co. Limerick, Ire.
Michael MAHONEY		1842	1871	032	MAHONEY, Michael	
				032		
John CUMMINGS		78Y 4M	04-04-1886	032	HUGHES, Mary	
Mary HUGHES Cummings		1810	1906	032	CUMMINGS, John	
William CUMMINGS		14 Years	03-27-1867	032	CUMMINGS, William	Son Of John & Mary Cummings
James CUMMINGS		05-22-1840	12-18-1924	032	CUMMINGS, James	(GAR) Co. M., 4th U.S. Cav
				032		
James LAWLER		27Y 8M	10-08-1870	032	DUPONT, Catharine	Son Of Christopher & Catharine Lawler
				032		
Catharine DUPONT Lawler		1834	1896	032	LAWLER, James	
				032	LAWLER, Christopher	
				032		

Name	Origin	Born/Age	Died	Code	Index	Remarks
Timothy CLIFFORD		55 Years	03-11-1871	032	_____, Abigail	
Abigail _____ CLIFFORD		1826	1894	032	CLIFFORD, Timothy	
				032		
Michael O'CONNELL		1815	1891	032	LYONS, Abigail	
Abigail LYONS O'Connell		1818	1871	032	O'CONNELL, Michael	
				032		
John GORMAN	Co. Limerick	1836	1916	032	KELLY, Hanora	Natives of Co. Limerick, Ire.
Hanora KELLY Gorman	Co. Limerick	1839	1879	032	GORMAN, John	Natives of Co. Limerick, Ire.
				032		
John BUNNEY		27 Years	12-12-1891	032	BUNNEY, John	
				032		
Michael KENNY	Co. Clare		02-28-1875	032	KENNY, Michael	Native of Co. Clare, Ireland. (Stone damaged-part missing)
				032		
				032		
Patrick H. HUMPHREY		68 Years	10-14-1905	032	HUMPHREY, Patrick H.	(GAR) Co. F, 14th Vt Vol
				032		
Richard MURPHY				032	MURPHY, Richard	
Ellen BUNNEY Murphy				032	BUNNEY, Ellen	
Elizabeth MURPHY				032	MURPHY, Elizabeth	
Ellen MURPHY				032	MURPHY, Ellen	
Margaret MURPHY				032	MURPHY, Margaret	
				032		
James BUNNEY		1837	1913	032	COYNE, Anna	
Anna COYNE Bunney		1841	1914	032	BUNNEY, James	
Thomas COYNE		1813	1897	032	COYNE, Thomas	
				032		
Martin WIGINS		48 Years	03-14-1854	032	WIGINS, Martin	
				032		
Thomas MCGUIRE		1837	1913	032	MCGLOUGHLYN, Mary Jane	
Mary J. MCGLOUGHLYN McGuire		1847	1899	032	MCGUIRE, Thomas	
John C. MCGUIRE		1866	1904	032	MCGUIRE, John C.	
Joseph MCGUIRE		1871	1872	032	MCGUIRE, Joseph	
David J. RUTLEDGE		1857	1928	032	MCGUIRE, Mary Elizabeth	
Mary E. MCGUIRE Rutledge		1863	1918	032	RUTLEDGE, David J.	
				032		
Thomas QUINN		31 Years	05-26-1878	032	_____, Bridget	
Bridget _____ QUINN		46Y 11M	09-09-1892	032	QUINN, Thomas	
				032		
John GLEASON		63 Years	06-24-1882	032	KELLY, Johanna	
Johanna KELLY Gleason		46 Years	03-13-1872	032	GLEASON, John	
Richard KELLY			03- -1926	032	KELLY, Richard	
Mary A. KELLY			12-18-1933	032	KELLY, Mary A.	
				032		
Jeremiah MULVEY		1846	1918	032	HANLEY, Bridget	
Bridget HANLEY Mulvey		1846	1917	032	MULVEY, Jeremiah	

Name	Origin	Birth/Age	Death	Ref	Relation	Notes
William WILLIAMS	Co. Kings	70 Years	09-20-1872	032	WILLIAMS, William	A Native of Kings Co., Ireland (Now Co. Offaly)
				032		
				032		
John COLLINS		46 Years	04-10-1872	032	_____, Mary	
Mary _____ COLLINS		50 Years	05-09-1875	032	COLLINS, John	
				032		
Hugh BURNS		1832	1901	032	BURNS, Hugh	
				032		
Robert HANLEY	Co. Limerick	64 Years	02-11-1873	032	O'DONNELL, Bridget	A Native Of Parish of White Forge, Co. Limerick, Ire. (GAR) (Could not find town;townland parish in references.Could not find Civil war org in ref.)
				032		
				032		
				032		
				032		
Bridget O'DONNELL Hanley		84 Years	04-02-1897	032	HANLEY, Robert	
				032		
Patrick DOWNEY		1806	1881	032	_____, Ann	
Ann _____ DOWNEY		1817	1872	032	DOWNEY, Patrick	
				032		
Patrick MURTHUR		67 Years	01-15-1907	032	_____, Margaret	
Margaret _____ MURTHUR		53 Years	03-09-1889	032	MURTHUR, Patrick	
				032		
Edward BOLGER		33 Years	12-03-1875	032	BOLGER, Edward	
				032		
Martin TOOHEY		60 Years	12-12-1894	032	_____, Catharine	
Catharine _____ TOOHEY		73 Years	12-20-1908	032	TOOHEY, Martin	
				032		
John PENDORS		25 Years	05-03-1876	032	PENDORS, John	
				032		
Richard BUTLER		75 Years	12-03-1876	032	_____, Anna E.	
Anna E. _____ BUTLER		1854	1923	032	BUTLER, Richard	
Richard BUTLER		06-25-1854	11-04-1901	032	BUTLER, Richard	
				032		
Patrick C. BURKE		1836	1873	032	_____, Annie	
Annie _____ BURKE		1846	1903	032	BURKE, Patrick C.	
				032		
John FOLEY		1831	1897	032	SHEEHAN, Margaret	
Margaret SHEEHAN Foley		1839	1891	032	FOLEY, John	
				032		
John CAMPBELL		1842	1894	032	TREAHEY, Eliza	
Eliza TREAHEY Campbell		1856	1896	032	CAMPBELL, John	
				032		
Michael BRENNAN		02-10-1846	05-01-1909	032	MAHAR, Mary	
Mary MAHAR Brennan		09-07-1850	06-03-1909	032	BRENNAN, Michael	
				032		
William CALLAHAN				032	CALLAHAN, William	

Name	Born/Age	Died	Code	Spouse/Index	Note
Mary _____ CALLAHAN			032	_____, Mary	
Elizabeth CALLAHAN			032	CALLAHAN, Elizabeth	
Charles CALLAHAN			032	CALLAHAN, Charles	
Edward CALLAHAN			032	CALLAHAN, Edward	
Ellen CALLAHAN			032	CALLAHAN, Ellen	
			032		
Owen MURPHY	06-12-1804	07-04-1885	032	_____, Bridget	
Bridget _____ MURPHY	03-24-1816	05-20-1880	032	MURPHY, Owen	
Mary MURPHY	01-20-1858	02-11-1875	032	MURPHY, Mary	
Philip MURPHY	09-01-1857	05-18-1926	032	MURPHY, Philip	
			032		
Mary A. COTTER	09-25-1854	08-06-1913	032	COTTER, Mary A.	
			032		
Dudley COSTELLO	69 Years	04-28-1877	032	_____, Mary	
Mary _____ COSTELLO	95 Years	12-26-1900	032	COSTELLO, Dudley	
			032		
Richard CONWAY	68 Years	11-09-1908	032	BULGER, Catherine	
Catherine BULGER Conway	38 Years	05-03-1885	032	CONWAY, Richard	
			032		
John POCKETT	1832	1903	032	_____, Elizabeth	
Elizabeth _____ POCKETT	1837	1875	032	POCKETT, John	
			032		
Dennis HENNESY	52 Years	10-15-1879	032	HENNESY, Dennis	
			032		
Mary Ann _____ DEMPSEY	38 Years	12-05-1876	032	DEMPSEY, John	(NOI John Dempsey)
			032	_____, Mary Ann	
			032		
Julia _____ MCGRATH	64 Years	08-13-1878	032	MCGRATH, Philip	(NOI Philip McGrath)
			032	_____, Julia	
			032		
Mathew BUCKLEY	1822		032	KILEY, Mary	
Mary KILEY Buckley	1826	1904	032	BUCKLEY, Mathew	
Michael BURNS	78 Years	07-10-1889	032	_____, Bridget	
Bridget _____ BURNS	62 Years	03-25-1879	032	BURNS, Michael	
			032		
Patrick H. KEENAN	1853	1913	032	FLANAGAN, Mary	
Mary FLANAGAN Keenan	1858	1939	032	KEENAN, Patrick H.	
			032		
James A. CAMPBELL	08-17-1852	04-28-1892	032	CAMPBELL, James A.	
			032		
James CAMPBELL	72 Years	12-09-1872	032	HORAN, Elizabeth	
Elizabeth HORAN Campbell	70 Years	11-28-1882	032	CAMPBELL, James	
			032		
Thomas CAMPBELL	88 Years	08-14-1884	032	CAMPBELL, Thomas	
			032		

Name	County	Age	Date	Code	Index	Notes
Mary CAMPBELL		71 Years	05-12-1908	032	CAMPBELL, Mary	
				032		
William GLEASON		1845	1887	032	FOGARTY, Ellen	
Ellen FOGARTY Gleason		1847	1880	032	GLEASON, William	
				032		
Mrs. Bridget _____ CULKINS	Co. Sligo		02-05-1875	032	_____, Bridget	Native Of The County Sligo, Ire
				032		(NOI Mr. Culkins)
Hannah CULKINS			10-12-1900	032	CULKINS, Hannah	
Lovina CULKINS			05-12-1907	032	CULKINS, Lovina	
Sophia CULKINS			09-14-1885	032	CULKINS, Sophia	
				032		
John BOYLE		1840	1919	032	O'BRINE, Catherine	
Catherine O'BRINE Doyle		1840	1934	032	BOYLE, John	
				032		
Margaret ____ CARRIGAN		61 Years	08-28-1875	032	CARRIGAN, T.	(NOI T. Carrigan)
				032	_____, Margaret	
				032		
Winnifred _____ MCKAY		65 Years	11-22-1877	032	MCKAY, Daniel	(NOI Daniel McKay)
				032	_____, Winifred	
				032		
Dennis MCNAMARA	Co. Clare	70 Years	04-28-1896	032	MCMAHON, Catherine	Native of Killaloe, Co. Clare,
				032		Ireland
Catherine MCMAHON McNamara	Co. Clare	66 Years	10-03-1893	032	MCNAMARA, Dennis	Native of Craigbrien (Crag-
				032		brien), Co. Clare, Ireland
				032		
Elizabeth _____ NICHOLSON		31 Years	03-04-1874	032	NICHOLSON, M.	(NOI M. Nicholson)
				032	_____, Elizabeth	
				032		
Thomas MCNAMARA		62 Years	02-07-1879	032	MCNAMARA, Thomas	
				032		
Catherine NOONAN Grace	Co. Limerick	68 Years	12-16-1878	032	GRACE, Thomas	Native of Cloverfield, Parish
				032		Kilteely, Co. Limerick, Ire.
Patrick KETT	Co. Limerick	70 Years	08-11-1891	032	HILLIARD, Mary	A Native of Co. Limerick, Ire.
Mary HILLIARD Kett	Co. Limerick	68 Years	12-17-1879	032	KETT, Patrick	A Native of Co. Limerick, Ire.
				032		
Patrick MINOGUE	Co. Tipperary	35 Years	01-18-1858	032	_____, Winefred	Native of Parish (cannot read)
				032		Co. Tipperary, Ireland
Winefred _____ MINOGUE		55 Years	04-16-1878	032	MINOGUE, Patrick	
				032		
Bridget _____ BROWN		72 Years	10-02-1903	032	BROWN, John J.	(NOI John J. Brown)
				032	_____, Bridget	
				032		
Ann _____ MCMAHON	Co. Clare	60 Years	08-10-1876	032	MCMAHON, Michael	Native of Glen_______, (Glen-
				032		inagh) Co. Clare, Ireland.
				032		(NOI Michael McMahon - stone

Name	Origin	Born/Age	Died	Code	Related	Notes
				032		deteriorated)
				032		
John HAUGH		04-01-1835	08-28-1892	032	MCMAHON, Catherine	
Catherine MCMAHON Haugh		12-22-1843	11-26-1900	032	HAUGH, John	
Ann MCMAHON		1819	1876	032	MCMAHON, Ann	Mother (Possible spouse of Michael McMahon)
				032		
				032		
John BURNS Jr.		25Y3M13D	03-02-1881	032	BURNS, John Jr.	
				032		
Mary Ann BURNS		20Y3M23D	10-04-1877	032	BURNS, Mary Ann	
				032		
Michael FITZGERALD	Co. Limerick	58 Years	02-21-1882	032	DOYLE, Catherine	Native of Co. Limerick, Ire.
Catherine DOYLE Fitzgerald	Co. Limerick	52 Years	03-12-1880	032	FITZGERALD, Michael	Native of Co. Limerick, Ire.
				032		
Ann _____ LEAMY	Co. Tipperary	75 Years	01-19-1884	032	LEAMY, Michael	Wife Of Michael Leamy Who Is Buried In Ballynahinch, Tipperary, Ireland
				032		
				032		
Patrick LEAMY		55 Years	10-02-1893	032	FITZGERALD, Mary	
Mary FITZGERALD Leamy		05-26-1860	08-18-1923	032	LEAMY, Patrick	
				032		
Dennis O'CONNELL		76 Years	12-20-1893	032	_____, Hannorah	
Hannorah _____ O'CONNELL		65 Years	10-02-1883	032	O'CONNELL, Dennis	
Bridget O'CONNELL		35 Years	01-25-1888	032	O'CONNELL, Bridget	
				032		
Sarah HAYS Coffee	Co. Tipperary	04-26-1825	04-16-1880	032	COFFEE, Thomas	Parish of Balla_____, County Tipperary, Ireland (NOI Thomas Coffee) (Could not read)
				032	HAYS, Sarah	
				032		
				032		
Catherine GEELEN Igo	Co. Roscommon	58 Years	05-04-1880	032	IGO, Michael	Native of Parish of Killglass, Co. Roscommon, Ireland. (NOI Michael Igo)
				032	GEELEN, Catherine	
				032		
				032		
Patrick CAIN		63 Years	04-07-1880	032	_____, Johannah	
Johannah _____ CAIN		62 Years	07-06-1880	032	CAIN, Patrick	
				032		
Bridget _____ HOGAN		33 Years	07-14-1881	032	HOGAN, Thomas	(NOI Thomas Hogan)
				032	_____, Bridget	
				032		
Patrick ROCHE		1837	1909	032	_____, Ellen	
Ellen _____ ROCHE		48 Years	05-16-1894	032	ROCHE, Patrick	Beloved Wife Of Patrick Roche
				032		
Catharine BRAY Clark		75 Years	06-09-1882	032	CLARK, Andrew	(NOI Andrew Clark)
				032	BRAY, Catharine	
				032		
Michael HICKEY		1810	1887	032	HICKEY, Michael	

				032		
Mary _____ DONAHUE		24Y 6M	10-01-1885	032	DONAHUE, Charles	(NOI Charles Donahue)
				032	_____, Mary	
				032		
John CARROLL		82 Years	08-22-1883	032	CASEY, Alice	
Alice CASEY Carroll		76 Years	09-10-1896	032	CARROLL, John	
William CARROLL		1857	1904	032	CARROLL, William	
				032		
William BURKE	Co. Cork	61 Years	10-13-1882	032	WALSH, Mary	A Native of Co. Cork, Ireland
Mary WALSH Burke	Co. Cork	72 Years	03-12-1896	032	BURKE, William	A Native of Town Of Donerale
				032		(Doneraile), Co. Cork, Ireland
Edmund BURKE		1830	1913	032	BURKE, Edmund	
Maria BURKE Ryan		02-04-1845	08-07-1933	032	RYAN, John P.	(NOI John P. RYAN)
				032	BURKE, Maria	
John E. BURKE		05-27-1854	10-30-1909	032	BURKE, John E.	
Charles E. BURKE		34Y 13D	02-17-1897	032	BURKE, Charles E.	
				032		
Thomas DOLAN		56 Years	02-13-1883	032	BELLEW, Elizabeth	
Elizabeth BELLEW Dolan		73 Years	01-27-1907	032	DOLAN, Thomas	
John DOLAN		56 Years	10-17-1917	032	CRAGIN, Catherine	
Catherine CRAGIN Dolan		80 Years	12-25-1938	032	DOLAN, John	
				032		
				032	_____, Mary	(NOI Mary Kinsella)
Patrick KINSELLA		28 Years	02-14-1871	032	KINSELLA, Patrick	
				032		
Joseph RYAN		04-01-1828	12-10-1910	032	O'NEIL, Mary	(GAR-Could not find in ref.)
Nancy O'BRIEN Ryan	Co. Tipperary	62 Years	09-01-1886	032	RYAN, Joseph	Native of The Parish of Castle
				032		town (No such parish. Could be
				032		Parish Castletownarra or Town
				032		of Castletown), Co. Tipperary
Mary O'NEIL Ryan		05-02-1837	12-09-1910	032	RYAN, Joseph	
James F. RYAN		1862	1917	032	RYAN, James F.	
				032		
Bridget BELLEW Smith			09-02-1921	032	SMITH, Patrick	(NOI Patrick Smith)
Mary F. DOLAN		26 Years	02-10-1889	032	DOLAN, Mary F.	
George T. DOLAN				032	DOLAN, George T.	
				032		
Patrick BYRNE		73 Years	06-14-1894	032	_____, Maria	
Maria _____ BYRNE		83 Years	06-09-1905	032	BYRNE, Patrick	
				032		
Patrick REGAN		1818	1891	032	ROONEY, Mary	
Mary ROONEY Regan		1818	1886	032	REGAN, Patrick	
Winifred REGAN		1850	1911	032	REGAN, Winifred	
				032		
Mary BARRETT Walsh		11-10-1844	12-16-1874	032	WALSH, William	(NOI William Walsh)

Name	Note	Birth/Age	Death	Code	Index Name	Remarks
				032	BARRETT, Mary	
				032		
Terrence O'CONNOR		52 Years	09-05-1887	032	HALLSEY, Hannorah	
Hannorah HALLSEY O'Connor		1843	1925	032	O'CONNOR, Terrence	
				032		
Ann CONWAY Duggan		53 Years	06-17-1887	032	DUGGAN, John	(NOI John DUGGAN)
				032	CONWAY, Ann	
				032		
Patrick GRACE		44 Years	06-22-1886	032	_____, Bridget	
Bridget _____ GRACE		56 Years	04-21-1902	032	GRACE, Patrick	
				032		
James FITZPATRICK		56 Years	12-11-1886	032	REGAN, Bridget	
Bridget REGAN Fitzpatrick		70 Years	12-22-1914	032	FITZPATRICK, James	
				032		
William DENNIN		03-17-1859	12-06-1899	032	HAYS, Margaret	Killed In The Slate Quarries
Margaret HAYS Dennin		11-17-1860	12-13-1926	032	DENNIN, William	Born In Ireland
				032		
William SHELLEY		1853	1907	032	DOWNS, Anna	
Anna DOWNS Shelley		1855	1928	032	SHELLEY, William	
				032		
Michael MINOGUE		1842	1889	032	QUIGLEY, Bridget	
Bridget QUIGLEY Minogue		1841	1934	032	MINOGUE, Michael	
				032		
James HINCHEY	Co. Clare		12-13-1886	032	_____, Hannah	Born In County Clare, Ireland
Hannah _____ HINCHEY		1812	1901	032	HINCHEY, James	
				032		
Patrick KEENAN		1820	1891	032	QUIGLEY, Mary	
Mary QUIGLEY Keenan		1820	1931	032	KEENAN, Patrick	
				032		
John WHITE		70 Years	04-30-1886	032	_____, Catherine	
Catherine _____ WHITE		70 Years	02-15-1893	032	WHITE, John	
				032		
John STEVENSON		07-01-1841	01-09-1917	032	SHAY, Abigail E.	
Abigail E. SHAY Stevenson		07-05-1845	05-22-1892	032	STEVENSON, John	
				032		
Alexander WALSH		84 Years	08-27-1904	032	_____, Clarissa M.	
Clarissa M. _____ WALSH		69 Years	01-06-1883	032	WALSH, Alexander	
				032		
Thomas E. WALSH		1853	1925	032	MCDONOUGH, Catherine J.	
Catherine J MCDONOUGH Walsh		1854	1933	032	WALSH, Thomas E.	
				032		
David H. KENT		1849	1919	032	_____, Mary Ellen	
Mary Ellen _____ KENT		38Y9M12D	10-12-1889	032	KENT, David H.	
				032		
Thomas MURPHY			10-06-1892	032	BUTLER, Julia	

Name	Origin	Born	Died	Code	Related	Notes
Julia BUTLER Murphy			05-08-1889	032	MURPHY, Thomas	
				032		
Mary RYAN Roach		48 Years	02-02-1890	032	ROACH, John	(NOI John Roach)
				032	RYAN, Mary	
				032		
Mathias DELEHANTY		05-12-1842	07-10-1899	032	_____, Bridget	
Bridget _____ DELEHANTY		08-10-1852	10-09-1901	032	DELEHANTY, Mathias	
				032		
Patrick MCDERMOTT		58 Years	08-22-1880	032	_____, Bridget	
Bridget _____ MCDERMOTT		70 Years	10-02-1912	032	MCDERMOTT, Patrick	
				032		
James DOOLEY		59 Years	09-27-1900	032	_____, Sarah	
Sarah _____ DOOLEY		44 Years	11-18-1893	032	DOOLEY, James	
				032		
Paul DICKLOW		04-25-1848	10-14-1907	032	CRAWLEY, Mary	
Mary CRAWLEY Dicklow		04-23-1853	11-01-1928	032	DICKLOW, Paul	
				032		
Jermiah MALONE		1846	1934	032	RYAN, Catherine	
Catherine RYAN Malone		1846	1915	032	MALONE, Jermiah	
				032		
Penelope MALONE		1843	1903	032	MALONE, Penelope	
				032		
Henry HYNES		1852	1910	032	KINSELLA, Anna	
Anna KINSELLA Hynes		1855	1993	032	HYNES, Henry	
				032		
Thomas GLEASON Sr.			10-20-1900	032	_____, Bridget	
Bridget _____ GLEASON			06-03-1901	032	GLEASON, Thomas Sr.	
				032		
Alexander SWEENEY		64 Years	07-31-1891	032	_____, Mary J.	
Mary J. _____ SWEENEY		65 Years	09-21-1898	032	SWEENEY, Alexander	
				032		
John BARRY	Co. Cork	1818	1900	032	DOOLEY, Mary	Born In Co. Cork, Ireland
Mary DOOLEY Barry	Co. Limerick	1836	1908	032	BARRY, John	Native of Co. Limerick, Ire.
				032		
William PURCELL		1814	1902	032	_____, Alice	
Alice _____ PURCELL		1830	1900	032	PURCELL, William	
				032		
John CALLAGHAN		1851	1913	032	_____, Elizabeth M.	
Elizabeth M. _____ CALLAGHAN		1866	1937	032	CALLAGHAN, John	
				032		
James MURPHY		03-31-1864	03-01-1900	032	MCDERMOTT, Mary	
Mary MCDERMOTT Murphy		1866	1940	032	MURPHY, James	
				032		
Thomas CARROLL		1839	1916	032	QUINN, Ann	
Ann QUINN Carroll		1842	1903	032	CARROLL, Thomas	

Name	Birth	Death	No.	Index
			032	
Patrick CROWLEY	1830	1911	032	WHITE, Mary
Mary WHITE Crowley	1834	1906	032	CROWLEY, Patrick
			032	
Timothy STARR	1849	1904	032	GREGORY, Josephine
Josephine GREGORY Starr	1854	1911	032	STARR, Timothy
			032	
John HOGAN	1816	1902	032	WHITE, Mary
Mary WHITE Hogan	1816	1909	032	HOGAN, John
			032	
Daniel RYAN	1855	1904	032	HOGAN, Bridget
Bridget HOGAN Ryan	1859	1916	032	RYAN, Daniel
			032	
Henry C. MOORE	1850	1901	032	SAMMON, Ellen
Ellen SAMMON Moore	1855	1929	032	MOORE, Henry C.
			032	
Owen HAYES	1832	1901	032	MINOGUE, Ellen
Ellen MINOGUE Hayes	1837	1929	032	HAYES, Owen
			032	
Richard SHANAHAN	1844	1922	032	KELLY, Mary
Mary KELLY Shanahan	1856	1901	032	SHANAHAN, Richard
			032	
John DURICK	1835	1906	032	COPPS, Helen
Helen COPPS Durick	1833	1901	032	DURICK, John
			032	
Daniel CAIN	1856	1930	032	MURPHY, Mary
Mary MURPHY Cain	1861	1919	032	CAIN, Daniel
			032	
John H. FOY	1851	1902	032	MCDONOUGH, Margaret D.
Margaret D. MCDONOUGH Foy	1852	1913	032	FOY, John H.
			032	
Thomas HICKEY	1832	1913	032	MURPHY, Eliza
Eliza MURPHY Hickey	1843	1903	032	HICKEY, Thomas
			032	
Edward DELEHANTY	1849	1906	032	_____, Bridget
Bridget _____ DELEHANTY	1858	1934	032	DELEHANTY, Edward
			032	
Patrick H. DOWNES	1847	1902	032	_____, Bridget
Bridget _____ DOWNES	1851	1912	032	DOWNES, Patrick H.
			032	
Bridget MCDONOUGH	75 Years	05-19-1903	032	MCDONOUGH, Bridget
			032	
Michael HANLEY	03-17-1845	02-12-1913	032	WALSH, Ruth
Ruth WALSH Hanley	12-03-1854	09-22-1914	032	HANLEY, Michael
			032	

Name	Born	Died	Code	Index
Robert HANLEY	1850	1903	032	_____, Julia
Julia _____ HANLEY	1857	1920	032	HANLEY, Robert
			032	
Thomas SULLIVAN	12-22-1844	03-26-1908	032	HOLLERAN, Margaret
Margaret HOLLERAN Sullivan	03-28-1855	11-15-1902	032	SULLIVAN, Thomas
			032	
Michael TOOHEY		09-18-1940	032	_____, Mary A.
Mary A. _____ TOOHEY	50 Years	09-14-1903	032	TOOHEY, Michael
			032	
John MURPHY	1855	1907	032	O'BRIEN, Nellie
Nellie O'BRIEN Murphy	1858	1922	032	MURPHY, John
			032	
John C. EATON	1847		032	_____, Catharine C.
Catharine C. _____ EATON	1846	1905	032	EATON, John C.
			032	
Matthew HOLLERAN	64 Years	03-03-1888	032	_____, Margaret
Margaret _____ HOLLERAN	74 Years	08-05-1905	032	HOLLERAN, Matthew
Michael O'BRIEN	30 Years	04-01-1859	032	O'BRIEN, Michael
			032	
James CALL	1843	1894	032	CARRIGAN, Jane
Jane CARRIGAN Call	1849	1941	032	CALL, James
			032	
Patrick HARRIS	79 Years	09-06-1903	032	GRADY, Hannorah
Hannorah GRADY Harris	74 Years	03-20-1896	032	HARRIS, Patrick
			032	
John GRACE	1848	1926	032	_____, Julia
Julia _____ GRACE	1853	1910	032	GRACE, John
			032	
Richard HANRAHAN	1828	1907	032	RONAN, Catharine
Catharine RONAN Hanrahan	1833	1908	032	HANRAHAN, Richard
			032	
Richard LAVERY	1840	1911	032	O'BRIEN, Sara A.
Sara A. O'BRIEN Lavery	1850	1932	032	LAVERY, Richard
			032	
Thomas BOWES	1854	1914	032	RYAN, Jane
Jane RYAN BOWES	1853	1925	032	BOWES, Thomas
			032	
John RYAN	06-24-1842	01-24-1910	032	RYAN, John
			032	
George B. BROWN	1854	1932	032	BROWN, George B.

Village Burial Ground - Franklin, VT (Adjacent to St. Mary's Cemetery)

NAME	POB	DOB/AGE	DOD	CEM	SPOUSE/INDEX	INSCRIPTION
Robert MCCOONS		22 Years	07-11-1871	033		
				033		
William J. RILEY		06-09-1823	03-09-1899	033	DUNTON, Cleora P.	
Cleora P. DUNTON Riley		08-16-1829	05-23-1901	033	RILEY, WIlliam J.	
				033		
O. H. RILEY, MD		08-02-1853	05-22-1893	033	RILEY, O. H., MD	

St. Mary's Cemetery - Franklin, VT (Adjacent to Village Burial Ground)

NAME	POB	DOB/AGE	DOD	CEM	SPOUSE/INDEX	INSCRIPTION
Patrick KENNEDY		03-24-1847	11-02-1919	034	ROONEY, Nancy	
Nancy ROONEY Kennedy		10-02-1840	06-03-1916	034	KENNEDY, Patrick	
				034		
Charles MULLEN		03-23-1836	01-19-1904	034	ROONEY, Rose	
Rose ROONEY Mullen		12-10-1844	04-07-1917	034	MULLEN, Charles	

St. Sylvester, Quarry Hill Road, Graniteville, Vermont

NAME	POB	DOB/AGE	DOD	CEM	SPOUSE/INDEX	INSCRIPTION
Michael GRAHAM		1844	1917	035	GRAHAM, Michael	GAR 1861-1865-Try Co. A, 17th Rgt, VtVols
				035		
Patrick KEOUGH		1831	1919	035	KEOUGH, Patrick	Erected by A.O.H. Div. No 3
				035		
James BOYCE		1855	1935	035	O'CONNOR, Susan B.	
Susan B. O'CONNOR		1859	1933	035	BOYCE, James	
				035		
Thomas W. ROARK		1849	1922	035	ROARK, Thomas W.	
Mary A. _____ (Roark?)		1861	1928	035	_____, Mary A.	(Did not say if spouse of Thomas Roark)
				035		
				035		
Owen MCCUE		1856	1925	035	_____, Mary	
Mary _____ McCue		1862	1942	035	MCCUE, Owen	
				035		
John O. BOYCE		11-16-1851	10-08-1926	035	_____, Jennie C.	

NAME	POB	DOB/AGE	DOD	CEM	SPOUSE/INDEX	INSCRIPTION
Jennie C. _____ BOYCE		07-19-1855	05-16-1936	035	BOYCE, John O.	
				035		
Felix MCWHIRK		1866	1929	035	MCWHIRK, Felix	(Relationship not shown b/w Felix & Samuel McWhirk & Mary Spence- all same plot)
Mary SPENCE		1855	1922	035	SPENCE, Mary	
Samuel MCWHIRK		1857	1930	035	MCWHIRK, Samuel	
				035		
John MURPHY		1848	1921	035	WALSH, Ellen	
Ellen WALSH Murphy		1852	1948	035	MURPHY, John	
				035		
Anthony DONAHUE		1834	1916	035	SHERIDAN, Ellen Lee	
Ellen Lee SHERIDAN Donahue		1839	1918	035	DONAHUE, Anthony	
				035		
Patrick HALLIGAN		1860	1931	035	HALLIGAN, Patrick	(NOI relationship Patrick/Anna
Anna HALLIGAN		1859	1946	035	HALLIGAN, Anna	
				035		
James DONAHUE		1848	1918	035	DONAHUE, James	
				035		
Catherine O'CONNOR Staples		72 Years	05-05-1921	035	O'CONNOR, Catherine	(NOI Mr. Staples)

St. Norbert's Cemetery, Hardwick, Vermont. One-half mile from Hardwick Main Street, Route 15.

This cemetery was not dedicated until late in the nineteenth century. Those interred are primarily French-Canadian in origins.

NAME	POB	DOB/AGE	DOD	CEM	SPOUSE/INDEX	INSCRIPTION
James SINON		01-29-1851	10-28-1940	126	_____, Mary Ann	
Mary Ann _____ SINON		01-14-1854	05-20-1928	126	SINON, James	
				126		
Michael CASHMAN		1832	1932	126	CASHMAN, Michael	
				126		
John SHEEHAN		1838	1884	126	GALLAGHER, Nora M.	
Nora M. GALLAGHER Sheehan		1850	1930	126	SHEEHAN, John	
				126		
Martin J. JOHNSON		1848	1938	126	GALLAGHER, Mary J.	
Mary J. GALLAGHER Johnson		1851	1923	126	JOHNSON, Martin J.	
				126		
Margaret MALONEY Johnson		1856	1939	126	JOHNSON, George	(NOI George Johnson)
				126	MALONEY, Margaret	

St. Louis Cemetery, Highgate Center, Vt. On Route 78, Just West of The Village

NAME	POB	DOB/AGE	DOD	CEM	SPOUSE/INDEX	INSCRIPTION
Henry H. HALE		1847	1916	036	MALONEY, Anna L.	
Anna L. MALONEY Hale		1868	1915	036	HALE, Henry H.	
				036		
James A. LANE		1833	1910	036	BEAULAC, Margaret M.	
Margaret M. BEAULAC Lane		1845	____	036	LANE, James A.	
				036		
Charles H. KEENAN		61 Years	06-12-1913	036	KEENAN, Charles H.	
				036		
Eliza HYDE Keenan		1821	1915	036	KEENAN, Eliza HYDE	
				036		
OTIS OHEERE				036	OHEERE/OTIS	
Michael		1846	1936	036	______, Ellen	(Not sure of who belongs to OTIS and who are O'HEERE'S-Try the Federal Census for 1860)
Ellen		1848	1934	036	______, Michael	
Daniel		1853	1934	036	______, Elizabeth	
Elizabeth		1843	1918	036	______, Daniel	
Emma		1881	1908	036	______, Emma	
				036		
John MANAHAN		1852	1910	036	BRENMER, Edna	
Edna BRENMER Manahan		1871	1908	036	MANAHAN, John	
				036		
Charles O'KANE		03-24-1845	04-05-1923	036	MCCARTY, Mary	
Mary MCCARTY O'Kane		02-14-1852	09-07-1925	036	O'KANE, Charles	
				036		
James SPEARS		1856	1914	036	MCGUE, Rosa	
Rosa MCGUE Spears		1860	1954	036	SPEARS, James	
Agnes M. SPEARS		1888	1905	036	SPEARS, Agnes M.	
				036		
Edward E. SLOAN		1852	1917	036	HANNA, Mary E.	
Mary E. HANNA Sloan		1859	____	036	SLOAN, Edward E.	
				036		
Thomas O'HEERE		1822	1915	036	HANNA, Bridget	
Bridget HANNA O'Heere		1823	1884	036	O'HEERE, Thomas	
John O'HEERE		1853	1921	036	O'HEERE, John	
Mary O'HEERE				036	O'HEERE, Mary	
Elizabeth O'HEERE				036	O'HEERE, Elizabeth	
James O'HEERE				036	O'HEERE, James	
				036		
Margaret ____ DILLON		73 Years	03-06-1877	036	DILLON, John	A Native Of Knocklong, Co. Limerick, Ire
				036		
Alice DILLON		54 Years	06-18-1892	036	DILLON, Alice	Dau of John & Mary Dillon

			036		
Bridget MCQUILLIAN	78 Years	06-11-1890	036	MCQUILLIAN, Bridget	
			036		
Daniel O'HEAR	1809	1861	036	_____, Nancy	
Nancy ____ O'HEAR	1812	1879	036	O'HEAR, Daniel	
			036		
Ann MALONEY	4 Years	06-02-1850	036	MALONEY, Ann	Dau Of Daniel & Mary Maloney
			036		
Daniel MALONEY	76Y1M11DA	07-05-____	036	MALONEY, Daniel	
			036		
Dennis SLOAN	58 Years	04-04-1900	036	SLOAN, Dennis	(GAR) Co. B, 3rd Reg, Vt Vols
			036		
John SPEARS	87Y 6M	11-24-1919	036	O'HEAR, Ellen	
Ellen O'HEAR Spears	69Y 9M	09-08-1899	036	SPEARS, John	
			036		
William COOK	1830	1903	036	RAYMOND, Virginia	
Virginia RAYMOND Cook	1846	1934	036	COOK, William	
			036		
Richard SLOAN	77 Years	06-16-1889	036	MALOY, Mary	
Mary MALOY Sloan	77 Years	01-16-1889	036	SLOAN, Richard	
			036		
James HANNA	68Y5M20D	06-20-1892	036	MCMAHON, Margaret	
Margaret MCMAHON Hanna	58Y10M21D	04-13-1894	036	HANNA, James	
			036		
Michael MCMAHON	100Y10M8D	08-06-1893	036	HANNA, Nancy	
Nancy HANNA McMahon	74 Years	05-30-1862	036	MCMAHON, Michael	
			036		
Mary ___ DEAVER	45 Years	12-25-1849	036	DEAVER, Neil	(NOI Neil Deaver)
			036	_____, Mary	
			036		
John DOLTON	60 Years	01-13-1850	036	DOLTON, John	
			036		
Emily M. ____ COOK	47Y 7M	03-05-1884	036	_____, Emily	
			036		
Jerry GOODHEART	60 Years	11-27-1850	036	GOODHEART, Jerry	
			036		
Andrew HANNA	1832	1899	036	MURPHY, Mary	
Mary MURPHY Hanna	1821	1902	036	HANNA, Andrew	
			036		
John MINOR	82Y 2M	05-30-1872	036	____, Mary L.	
Mary L. ___ MINOR	67Y 6M	03-24-1857	036	MINOR, John	
			036		
Samuel COOK	52 Years	05-01-1853	036	____, Jane	
Jane ___ COOK	89 Years	10-05-1892	036	COOK, Samuel	
			036		

Mary DWYER Hanna	38 Years	09-13 1883	036	HANNA, James	(NOI James Hanna)
			036	DWYER, Mary	
			036		
Catharine CAIN Bolac	64 Years	11-27-1884	036	BOLAC, Paul	(NOI Paul Bolac - correct
			036	CAIN, Catherine	spelling may be Beaulac)
			036		
Nicholas HANNA	1789	1883	036	HANNA, Nicholas	
James HANNA	1830	1900	036	HANNA, James	
John HANNA	1832	1901	036	HANNA, John	
			036		
John STEEL	94Y 4M	10-21-1882	036	____, Elizabeth	
Elizabeth ____ STEEL	80 Years	03-11-1876	036	STEEL, John	
			036		
William GARLAND	85Y 1M	11-04-1886	036	_____, Mary	(NOI Mary. See next entry for
			036	GARLAND, William	source of spouses nanme)
			036		
Alfred GARLAND			036	GARLAND, Alfred	Son Of William & Mary Garland
			036		(NOI On This stone)
			036		
John A. MCGOWEN	1848	1919	036	MCGOWEN, John A.	
			036		
Thomas MCGOWEN	1853	1930	036	MCGOWEN, Thomas	
			036		
Libbie CALLAN McGowen	39Y 6M	03-05-1886	036	MCGOWEN, Thomas	(NOI Thomas - possibly spouse
			036	CALLAN, Libbie	of Thomas in prior entry -same
			036		Plot)
			036		
Bridget _____ MCGOWEN	80 Years	11-17-1898	036		Mother
			036		
Patrick SHERIDAN	30 Years	07-25-1865	036	HOYT, Mary	
Mary HOYT Sheridan	47 Years	01-02-1891	036	SHERIDAN, Patrick	
			036		
James ROGERS	1832	1910	036	CALLAHAN, Mary	
Mary CALLAHAN Rogers	1839	1884	036	ROGERS, James	
			036		
Thomas CALAHAN	1836	1907	036	______, Sophia	
Sophia ____ CALAHAN	1835	1897	036	CALAHAN, Thomas	
			036		
Bridget HANNA O'Heere	62Y 7M	11-21-1884	036	O'HEERE, T.	(See Thomas O'HEERE,1822-1915)
			036	HANNA, Bridget	
			036		
Neal WOODS	60 Years	02-17-1866	036	WOODS, Neal	

Highgate Center Cemetery, Highgate Center, Vt. On Route 78, Just West of The Village

NAME	POB	DOB/AGE	DOD	CEM	SPOUSE/INDEX	INSCRIPTION
Ann MCCARTY McLeod		56 Years	07-29-1902	103	MCLEOD, Peter	(NOI Peter McLeod)
				103	MCCARTY, Ann	
				103		
Aaron P. BURDICK		1842	1916	103	KEENAN, Sarah Ann	Co. I,6th RGT, Vt Vol Inf(GAR)
Sarah Ann KEENAN Burdick		1853	1934	103	BURDICK, Aaron P.	
				103		
John BUTLER		70Y 6M	04-28-1874	103	MCFEETERS, Mary	
Mary MCFEETERS Butler		85Y03M05D	09-24-1896	103	BUTLER, John	
Anna J. BUTLER		19Y10M04D	06-08-1868	103	BUTLER, Anna J.	
Ann Jane BUTLER		9Y 2M	09-05-1847	103	BUTLER, Ann Jane	
John BUTLER Jr.		46Y11M06D	01-10-1884	103	BUTLER, John Jr.	
Elizabeth BUTLER		07-14-1840	03-01-1906	103	BUTLER, Elizabeth	
				103		
Hannah E. MCGOWAN Mather		45Y06M26D	07-06-1873	103	MATHER, Atla E.	(NOI Atla E. Mather)
				103	MCGOWAN, Hannah E.	
				103		
William ROBINSON		08-07-1818	09-23-1864	103	MCKENNEY, Melinda	
Melinda MCKENNEY Robinson		04-15-1820	04-20-1887	103	ROBINSON, William	
Arthur W. ROBINSON		04-21-1844	01-31-1863	103	ROBINSON, Arthur W.	
				103		
Thomas HAGEN		64 Years	07-03-1870	103	_____, Margaret	
				103	_____, Mary Melissa	
Margaret _____ HAGEN		38 Years	05-28-1850	103	HAGEN, Thomas	
Mary Melissa _____ HAGEN		08-15-1821	02-18-1902	103	HAGEN, Thomas	
Thomas HAGEN			1856	103	HAGEN, Thomas	Son of Thomas & (cannot read)
				103		
Timothy MCCARTY		12-25-1850	06-11-1934	103	_____, D.	(NOI Spouse D)
				103	MCCARTY, Timothy	
				103		
James CRAIG		12-23-1886	11-04-1901	103	CRAIG, James	Born In Ireland
				103		
William MCKINEY		69 Years	10-18-1869	103	_____, Hanna	
Hannah _____ MCKINEY		55 Years	07-12-1865	103	MCKINEY, William	
Emiley MCKINEY		5 Years	10-08-1845	103	MCKINEY, Emiley	Daughter
Caroline MCKINEY		31 Years	05-02-1867	103	MCKINEY, Caroline	Daughter
				103		
George FINLEY		51 Years	07-25-1897	103	FINLEY, George	Co. I, 56th MASS Regt (GAR)
				103		
Mary A. MCALLISTER Mason		39Y 8M	12-23-1878	103	MASON, G.C.	D/O J.C. MCALLISTER. (NOI G.C. Mason)
				103	MCALLISTER, Mary A.	

				103		
James H. ROACH		06-20-1840	10-22-1870	103	ROACH, James H.	Born At Dewainsburge,NY. Died
				103		At Highgate, Vt
				103		
Henry STINEHOUR		80 Years	04-16-1867	103	CORIGAN, Margaret	
Margaret CORIGAN Stinehour		55 Years	12-20-1873	103	STINEHOUR, Henry	
				103		
Ransom D. MCCLURE		1842	1912	103	AUSTIN, Jane E.	
				103	MCKINNEY, Addie	
Jane E. AUSTIN McClure		1846	1884	103	MCCLURE, Ransom D.	
Addie MCKINNEY McClure		1848	1929	103	MCCLURE, Ransom D.	
				103		
Hellen MCCUMMINS Russell		42 Years	11-14-1883	103	RUSSELL, A.B.	(NOI A.B.Russell)
				103	MCCUMMINS, Hellen	
				103		
Richard MOORE		1818	1899	103	MOORE, Richard	
				103		
Francis FRIOT		10-05-1837	10-23-1922	103	MCCUMMINGS, Mary	
Mary MCCUMMINGS Friot		08-25-1851	07-27-1911	103	FRIOT, Francis	
				103		
Eldad B. STEARNS		75Y 4M	01-25-1888	103	MEGEE, Dolly	
Dolly A. MEGEE Stearns		1818	1893	103	STEARNS, Eldad B.	
				103		
Ebenezer B. SPOONER		1839	1914	103	MCKINNEY, Martha	
Martha MCKINNEY Spooner		1845	1892	103	SPOONER, Ebenezer B.	
				103		
Sanford U. CARMAN		02-07-1828	05-10-1907	103	MAGOWEN, Susan D.	
Susan D. MAGOWAN Carman		07-04-1835	09-15-1916	103	CARMAN, Sanford U.	
				103		
John MCCLURE		04-22-1838	10-26-1909	103	STEWART, Mary	
Mary STEWART McClure		1872	1930	103	MCCLURE, John	
				103		
William MCCARTHY		1855	1928	103	MCCARTHY, William	
				103		
Charles W. BUTLER		06-15-1850	01-04-1923	103	JOHNSON, Mary J.	
Mary J. JOHNSON Butler		05-20-1856	12-03-1934	103	BUTLER, Charles W.	

Episcopal Cemetery, Highgate Falls, VT . On Route 207, South of Highgate Center

NAME	POB	DOB/AGE	DOD	CEM	SPOUSE/INDEX	INSCRIPTION
Charles MAKENNEY		04-14-1829	04-04-1863	118	MAKENNEY, Charles	
				118		

Walter MAKINEY	25 Years	12-17-1853	118	MAKINEY, Walter	
			118		
William CONNER	60 Years	07-26-1837	118	CONNER, Elizabeth	
Elizabeth _____ CONNER	87Y2M18D	10-03-1872	118	CONNER, William	
			118		
Thomas CONNER	67Y3M15D	11-15-1873	118	CONNER, Thomas	
			118		
Thomas MCDONOUGH	65 Years	02-18-1854	118	MCDONOUGH, Thomas	
			118		
George C. CUSSON	74Y2M18D	05-05-1882	118	CORNERS, Ann	
Ann CORNERS Cusson	67Y1M4D	02-22-1885	118	CUSSON, George C.	(Surname probably CONNERS)
			118		
Jay W. DURKEE	1852	1921	118	HANNA, Mary E.	
Mary E. HANNA Durkee	1857	1939	118	DURKEE, Jay W.	
			118		
Samuel MCKENNY	8 Months	02-__-1835	118	MCKENNY, Samuel	(S/O James MCKENNY & Nancy)
			118		
Julius MCKENNY	13 Months	09-07-1839	118	MCKENNY, Julius	(S/O James MCKENNY & Nancy)
			118		
David HUNTER	82 Years	12-29-1898	118	HUNTER, David	(GAR)Co. K. 7th VT Vols.Pixley
			118		Post No. 102
			118		
Owen E. SHERIDAN	1823	1904	118	SHERIDAN, Owen E.	
			118		
Thomas CAIN	10-07-1818	04-20-1890	118	BUTLER, Mary	
Mary BUTLER Cain	11-04-1827	06-05-1902	118	CAIN, Thomas	
Elizabeth C. CAIN	1Y2M16D	06-12-1851	118	CAIN, ELizabeth C.	
			118		
John HARVEY	09-02-1848		118	HARVEY, Nancy	(Unsure if 9-2-1848 DOB/DOD)
Nancy _____ HARVEY	09-20-1828	05-20-1909	118	HARVEY, John	
			118		
Charles BUTLER	93 Years	01-13-1881	118	ANDERSON, Ann	
Ann ANDERSON Butler	59 Years	12-02-1874	118	BUTLER, Charles	
Alice A. MEAD Butler	20Y 6M	06-02-1876	118	BUTLER, C.W.	(NOI C.W.Butler-same plot as
			118		(Charles Butler)
			118		
Thomas COWLEY	78 Years	04-24-1867	118	COWLEY, Margaret	
Margaret _____ COWLEY	58 Years	02-15-1874	118	COWLEY, Thomas	
Thomas COWLEY JR.		07-04-1853	118	COWLEY, Thomas Jr.	(Age/DOB at Death Obscured)
			118		
W. P. WELCH	1850	1915	118	WELCH, W. P.	
			118		
Margaret _____ HARRINGTON	50Y7M28D	01-02-1872	118	HARRINGTON, James	(GAR marker but NOI and no
			118	HARRINGTON, Margaret	stone for James Harrington)
			118		Try 2nd Baty Lt Artly, VtVols

NAME	POB	DOB/AGE	DOD	CEM	SPOUSE/INDEX	INSCRIPTION
Ralph M. DEAL		1847	1932	118	BRENNAN, Maria L.	
Maria L. BRENNAN Deal		06-23-1853	01-08-1903	118	DEAL, Ralph M.	

St. Teresa, Hyde Park, Vermont

NAME	POB	DOB/AGE	DOD	CEM	SPOUSE/INDEX	INSCRIPTION
John W. STEWART		1850	1929	037	_____, Ellen A.	
Ellen A. _____ STEWART		39Y 9M	12-15-1891	037	STEWART, John W.	
				037		
John STEWART		1823	1891	037	_____, Mary	
Mary _____ STEWART		1827	1913	037	STEWART, John	
				037		
Terrance O'HARE				037	O'HARE, Terrance	
				037		
Hugh SAVAGE		1857	1943	037	_____, Annie	
Annie _____ SAVAGE		1856	1902	037	SAVAGE, Hugh	
				037		
Michael MANNING		1841	1919	037	_____, Ellen D.	SGT, Co. D, 5th Vt Vols (GAR)
Ellen D. _____ MANNING		1844	1929	037	MANNING, Michael	
				037		
Patrick KELLEY		1830	1900	037	KIRK, Rosa	
Rosa KIRK Kelley		1838	1917	037	KELLEY, Patrick	
Mary KELLEY		1860	1863	037	KELLEY, Mary	
Elizabeth C. KELLEY		1862		037	KELLEY, Elizabeth C.	(NOI Date of death)
James P. KELLEY		1863		037	KELLEY, James P.	(NOI Date of death)
Two Infant Children				037	KELLEY, Infant	Two Infant Children
				037		
John MALONEY		1831	1907	037	NOLAND, Sarah	
Sarah NOLAND Maloney		1842	1905	037	MALONEY, John	
				037		
Mary Ann COX HAYFORD		1843	1912	037	HAYFORD, Jacob	(NOI Jacob Hayford)
				037	COX, Mary Ann	
				037		
George WARDLEIGH		1852	1926	037	_____, Margaret	
Margaret _____ WARDLEIGH			1930	037	WARDLEIGH, George	
				037		
John P. CLEARY		10-20-1854	12-23-1916	037	CLEARY, John P.	
				037		
Catherine MINER		1842	1920	037	MINER, Catherine	
				037		
James RODDY		1844	1927	037	_____, Maria	
Maria _____ RODDY		1846	1918	037	RODDY, James	

			037		
Peter AGIN	62 Years	04-09-1900	037	AGIN, Peter	(GAR) Member Of Co. E, 7th
			037		Vt. Vols. He Has Answered His
			037		Last Roll Call
			037		
Terrance FINNEGAN	1829	1915	037	_____, Mary Ann	
Mary Ann _____ FINNEGAN	1839	1920	037	FINNEGAN, Terrance	
			037		
Patrick WAUGH	1848	1920	037	SHERLOCK, Ann M.	
			037		
Patrick GILLEN	1821	1906	037	_____, Margaret A.	
Margaret A. _____ GILLEN	1827	1894	037	GILLEN, Patrick	
			037		
Margaret _____ FINNEGAN	57 Years	10-21-1888	037	FINNEGAN, Peter	(NOI Peter Finnegan. Age at
			037	_____, Margaret	death possibly 87 Yrs)
			037		
Charles A. FINNEGAN	1850	1889	037	TOWNE, Mary Hunt	
Mary HUNT Towne	1844	1931	037	FINNEGAN, Charles A.	
			037		
Gavin TYNDALL	1857	1933	037	SAVAGE, Alice	
Alice SAVAGE Tyndall	1857	1923	037	TYNDALL, Gavin	
			037		
Bernard G. ROONEY	1844	1916	037	KIRK, Anne	
Anne KIRK Rooney	1849	1920	037	ROONEY, Bernard	
			037		
John PERRY	1838	1916	037	BREO, Mary L.	
Mary L. BREO Perry	1843	1910	037	PERRY, John	
			037		
Margaret H. COX	1843	1926	037	COX, Margaret H.	
Jennie COX	1838	1931	037	COX, Jennie	
Agnes B. COX Corbett	1849	1934	037	CORBETT, Edmond	(NOI Edmond Corbett)
			037	COX, Agnes B.	
			037		
John TYNDALL	1848	1938	037	SAVAGE, Mary A.	
Mary A. SAVAGE Tyndall	1852	1910	037	TYNDALL, John	
			037		
James ROCK	1840	1931	037	VALLEY, Margaret	
Margaret VALLEY Rock	1845	1923	037	ROCK, James	

St. Joseph's Cemetery, Isle LaMotte, Vermont. Located Behind St. Joseph's Catholic Church In Village

NAME	POB	DOB/AGE	DOD	CEM	SPOUSE/INDEX	INSCRIPTION
Florence E. HOLCOMBE Callaghan		02-15-1852	08-31-1891	038	CALLAGHAN, James	(NOI James Callaghan)
				038	HOLCOMBE, Florence E.	
				038		
Thomas FORD		1822	1892	038	MURRAY, Mary A.	
Mary A. MURRAY Ford		1822	1883	038	FORD, Thomas	
John FORD		1857	1889	038	FORD, John	
Jennie FORD		1868	1890	038	FORD, Jennie	
Edward FORD		1861	1894	038	FORD, Edward	
Sarah BRIGGS		1863	1918	038	BRIGGS, Sarah	
Margaret FORD		1855	1922	038	FORD, Margaret	
				038		
Francis EARLEY		67 Years	07-02-1888	038	MCTAGUE, Ann	May His Soul Rest In Peace
Ann MCTAGUE Earley		80 Years	10-01-1897	038	EARLEY, Francis	May Her Soul Rest In Peace
				038		
BOWMAN/EARLEY				038		
Catherine EARLEY Bowman				038	BOWMAN, Mr.	(NOI DOB-DOD - Mr. Bowman)
				038	EARLEY, Catherine	
Esther Mina EARLEY				038	EARLEY, Esther Mina	(NOI DOB-DOD)
				038		
Note: This is primarily a burial ground for French-Canadian				038		
immigrants being in close proximity to the Canadian border.				038		

North or Methodist Cemetery, Isle LaMotte, VT. Near crossroads in center of Village.

NAME	POB	DOB/AGE	DOD	CEM	SPOUSE/INDEX	INSCRIPTION
John P. KELLY		19Y11M20D	06-28-1862	039	KELLY, John P.	Son Of John and Florence Kelly
				039		
James DOOLIN	Co. Tipperary	80Y 5M	09-04-1901	039	KELLEY, Mary L.	Born In Clahean (Clogheen),Co.
				039	_____, Johannah	Tipperary, Ireland
Johannah _____ Doolin		32 Years	07-19-1862	039	DOOLIN, James	
Mary L. KELLEY Doolin		1836	1905	039	DOOLIN, James	
				039		
Martha A. DOOLIN Parker		12-04-1855	07-09-1906	039	PARKER, Albert	(NOI Albert Parker)
				039	DOOLIN, Martha A.	
				039		

Amasa H. DOLAN		03-10-1849	05-17-1920	039	NUMMY, Sarah A.	(NOI Sarah Nummy)
				039	DOLAN, Amasa H.	
				039		
Agnes E. BAKER Doolin		36 Years	03-20-1888	039	DOOLIN, Amasa H.	Died In Southbridge, Ma.
				039	BAKER, Agnes E.	

St. James The Greater Parish Cemetery, Pleasant Street, Island Pond, Vermont

NAME	POB	DOB/AGE	DOD	CEM	SPOUSE/INDEX	INSCRIPTION
Martin LEE		11-15-1839	02-10-1903	040	_____, Mary	
Mary _____ LEE		06-15-1848	08-02-1926	040	LEE, Martin	
				040		
Eli GILBERT		12-16-1844	10-03-1913	040	CUSHING, Mary S.	(GAR) Co. G, 17th Reg VT Vols
Mary S. CUSHING Gilbert		06-25-1855	08-07-1922	040	GILBERT, Eli	
				040		
Willie E. BROWN		35Y 5M	07-12-1893	040	BROWN, Willie E.	Beloved Son Of John & Bridget Brown
				040		
Thomas A. BROWN		34 Years	09-27-1894	040	BROWN, Thomas A.	
				040		
Anna BOYCE Osborne		07-22-1833	02-01-1912	040	OSBORNE, John	(NOI John Osborne)
				040	BOYCE, Anna	
				040		
Patrick CURRAN		1818	1905	040	BARRETT, Julia	(GAR Flag-Not in reference)
Julia BARRETT Curran		1830	1908	040	CURRAN, Patrick	
				040		
Mary _____ DONLAN		67 Years	10-10-1876	040	DONLAN, Peter	(NOI Peter Donlan)
				040	_____, Mary	
				040		
Mary Ann QUINE Moffatt		32 Years	04-30-1875	040	MOFFATT, Joseph	(NOI Joseph Moffatt - Possibly Joseph Moffett who married Mary Ann McElroy and buried elsewhere in this cemetery)
				040	QUINE, Mary Ann	
				040		
				040		
				040		
John M. WOODS		24Y11M21D	04-02-1871	040	WOODS, John M.	
				040		
John LORANCE		25 Years	05-15-1879	040	LORANCE, John	
				040		
Rosilla B. SCOTT		44 Years	08-24-1882	040	SCOTT, Rosilla B.	
				040		
Thomas GRIFFIN		56 Years	02-12-1873	040	GRIFFIN, Thomas	
				040		
Mary _____ DOWLING		67 Years	10-10-1876	040	DOWLING, Peter	(NOI Peter Dowling)

Name	Place	Born	Died	Code	Index	Notes
				040	_____, Mary	
				040		
John MURPHY		43Y8M27D	05-12-1883	040	MCFARLIN, Sarah	
Sarah MCFARLIN Murphy		1839	1918	040	MURPHY, John	
				040		
John RICE		05-30-1830	06-05-1903	040	O'BRINE, Mary	
Mary O'BRINE Rice		11-01-1835	10-17-1878	040	RICE, John	
				040		
Thomas FOLEY		21Y 6M	06-09-1873	040	FOLEY, Thomas	
				040		
Stephen MARONEY		12-26-1837	06-21-1921	040	_____, Johanna	
Johanna _____ MARONEY		12-25-1837	07-07-1899	040	MARONEY, Stephen	
				040		
Joseph MOFFETT		1842	1913	040	MCELROY, Mary Ann	
Mary Ann MCELROY Moffett		1838	1900	040	MOFFETT, Joseph	
				040		
Flavia LETTER		11-10-1839	06-06-1892	040	FINNEGAN, Bridget	
Bridget FINNEGAN Letter		01-06-1831	04-19-1916	040	LETTER, Flavia	
				040		
Timothy CARROLL		1844	1893	040	ELLIS, Mary A.	
Mary A. ELLIS Carroll		1842	1921	040	CARROLL, Timothy	
				040		
Edward MCFARLIN		01-17-1837	04-04-1888	040	_____, Ellen L.	
Ellin L. _____ MCFARLIN		12-09-1845	12-08-1920	040	MCFARLIN, Edward	
				040		
Jeremiah G. STEADY		06-15-1826	05-17-1911	040	CORIVEAU, Hannah	
Hannah CORIVEAU Steady		08-10-1838	12-27-1916	040	STEADY, Jeremiah G.	
				040		
Leonard STEADY		1853	1925	040	DUNN, Mary	
Mary DUNN Steady		1855	1932	040	STEADY, Leonard	
				040		
Peter KANE		1841	1930	040	_____, Ellen	
Ellen _____ KANE		08-12-1844	05-09-1906	040	KANE, Peter	
				040		
Hugh RICE		03-31-1837	11-25-1899	040	_____, Elizabeth	Born In Halifax, PQ
Elizabeth _____ RICE		05-06-1845	11-20-1918	040	RICE, Hugh	
				040		
Andrew E. LAMB		37 Years	06-09-1894	040	LAMB, Andrew E.	
				040		
Kate CUNNINGHAM	Co. Clare	05-24-1849	12-24-1869	040	CUNNINGHAM, Kate	Dau Of Marcus G. CUNNINGHAM &
				040		Eliza. Born In Co. Clare, Ire.
				040		
Catherine MCGUIRE Chadwick		06-09-1842	10-09-1907	040	CHADWICK, John	(NOI John Chadwick)
				040	MCGUIRE, Catherine	
				040		

Name	Origin	Born/Age	Died	Code	Related	Notes
Edward FINNEGAN		63 Years	09-13-1895	040	CHADWICK, Catherine L.	
Catherine CHADWICK Finnegan		1842	1930	040	FINNEGAN, Edward	
				040		
Marcus HOLLAND		46 Years	08-30-1901	040	HOLLAND, Marcus	Husband
				040		
John HALLORAN	Co. Galway	03-21-1829	06-05-1910	040	TRACY, Delia	Born In Galway, Ireland
Delia TRACY Halloran	Co. Galway	09-24-1840	03-21-1897	040	HALLORAN, John	Born In Galway, Ireland
Julia HANNON Tracy		85 Years	09-13-1895	040	TRACY, M.	Wife Of M. Tracy(NOI M. Tracy)
				040	HANNON, Julia	
				040		
Catherine GRIFFIN Paquette		09-11-1847	12-18-1906	040	PAQUETTE, Frank	(NOI Frank Paquette)
				040	GRIFFIN, Catherine	
				040		
Robert KILPATRICK		42 Years	12-28-1876	040	_____, Helen	
Helen _____ KILPATRICK		77 Years	10-08-1907	040	KILPATRICK, Robert	
John KILPATRICK		22Y 2M	08-20-1877	040	KILPATRICK, John	(Same plot Robert Kilpatrick)
Mary A. KILPATRICK		16 Years	06-08-1877	040	KILPATRICK, Mary A.	(Same plot Robert Kilpatrick)
				040		
James MONAGHAN		1825	1903	040	_____, Margaret J.B.	
Margaret J.B. ____ MONAGHAN		44Y 4D	02-26-1881	040	MONAGHAN, James	
John MONAGHAN		11Y 10M	06-11-1866	040	MONAGHAN, John	(Same plot w James Monaghan)
				040		
Susan M. SHANNON Murphey		28Y 29D	01-23-1879	040	MURPHEY, John	(NOI John Murphey)
				040	SHANNON, Susan M.	
				040		
Rose HEARN Quinn		70 Years	09-24-1884	040	QUINN, John	Erected By Thomas W. RICHFORD
				040	HEARN, Rose	(NOI John Quinn)
				040		
Elizabeth MCGRATH Monaghan		29 Years	10-17-1888	040	MONAGHAN, Patrick L.	(NOI Patrick Monaghan). (Full
				040	MCGRATH, Elizabeth	Name - Elizabeth Maud McGrath)
				040		
William WALKER		1838	1896	040	_____, Anne	
Anne _____ WALKER		1842	1897	040	WALKER, William	
				040		
Catherine NEAGLE Rice		69 Years	09-20-1885	040	RICE, Hugh	(NOI Hugh Rice)
				040	NEAGLE, Catherine	
				040		
William CAHILL		1848	1916	040	RICE, Lizzie	
Lizzie RICE Cahill		30 Years	07-06-1882	040	CAHILL, William	
				040		
				040		
Bernard GUNN		1819	1891	040	KANE, Elizabeth	
Elizabeth KANE Gunn		1820		040	GUNN, Bernard	
				040		
Michael SMITH		07-20-1857	10-02-1900	040	FINNEGAN, Katherine L.	

Name	Place	Born/Age	Died	Code	Index	Notes
Katherine L. FINNEGAN Smith		01-12-1858	04-18-1888	040	SMITH, Michael	
George SMITH		06-10-1822	06-24-1897	040	RYAN, Julia	
Julia RYAN Smith		03-24-1831	05-24-1884	040	SMITH, George	
				040		
Adar LETTERS		61 Years	04-21-1878	040	LETTERS, Adar	Dau of C & M.A. Letters
				040		
Patrick COFFEY		81Y4M16D	02-08-1894	040	GALVIN, Mary	
Mary GALVIN Coffey		78 Years	12-18-1891	040	COFFEY, Patrick	
John COFFEY		39 Years	02-08-1886	040	COFFEY, John	
				040		
Thomas FOLEY		75 Years	12-20-1902	040	TIERNEY, Kate	
Kate TIERNEY Foley		71 Years	12-24-1898	040	FOLEY, Thomas	
Patsey FOLEY		31 Years	03-01-1885	040	FOLEY, Patsey	Son of Thomas & Kate Foley
Sarah FOLEY		52 Years	06-11-1913	040	FOLEY, Sarah	Son of Thomas & Kate Foley
John FOLEY		64 Years	11-20-1919	040	FOLEY, John	Son of Thomas & Kate Foley
Thomas FOLEY		63 Years	02-12-1926	040	FOLEY, Thomas	Son of Thomas & Kate Foley
				040		
Andrew TRACY	Co. Galway	84 Years	02-06-1874	040	TRACY, Andrew	
Catherine TRACY		29Y5M13D	03-19-1883	040	TRACY, Catherine	
Peter TRACY		70Y1M6D	08-05-1890	040	FOLAN, Mary	
Mary FOLAN Tracy		64Y 10M	01-11-1894	040	TRACY, Peter	
Andrew E. TRACY		1852	1926	040	TRACY, Andrew E.	
Thomas C. TRACY		1865	1942	040	TRACY, Thomas C.	
				040		
Patrick FLAHERTY		06-25-1853	08-28-1901	040	COYNE, Ellen	
Ellen COYNE Flaherty		01-31-1846	03-20-1920	040	FLAHERTY, Patrick	
				040		
John LINEHAN		1832	1920	040	ROACHE, Mary Ellen	
Mary Ellen ROACHE Linehan		57 Years	06-15-1889	040	LINEHAN, John	Wife And Mother
				040		
Thomas WHITE		1836	1869	040	SMITH, Mary	
Mary SMITH White		1847	1908	040	WHITE, Thomas	
				040		
James O'KEEFFE		66 Years	08-17-1885	040	ROCHE, Ellen	
Ellen ROCHE O'Keeffe		60 Years	08-25-1885	040	O'KEEFFE, James	
James O'KEEFFE		56 Years	05-01-1915	040	O'KEEFFE, James	
Patrick O'KEEFFE		03-17-1849	----------	040	O'KEEFFE, Patrick	
				040		
Ann _____ MCKINLEY		51Y 3M	07-11-1886	040	MCKINLEY, Moses	(NOI Moses McKinley)
				040	_____, Ann	
				040		
John MOFFETT			06-12-1881	040	MOFFETT, John	(Lower half of stone buried)
				040		
Hugh DONAHUE		57 Years(?)	08-26-1892	040	DONAHUE, Hugh	
				040		

NAME	POB	DOB/AGE	DOD	CEM	SPOUSE/INDEX	INSCRIPTION
Dennis GLEESON		80 Years	08-22-1895	040	LAMB, Margaret	
Margaret LAMB Gleeson		08-20-1830	05-19-1910	040	GLEESON, Dennis	
Edward GLEESON		06-22-1856	09-08-1920	040	GLEESON, Edward	
Dennis C. GLEESON		1872	1940	040	GLEESON, Dennis C.	
Martin J. GLEESON		1868	1951	040	GLEESON, Martin J.	
				040		
William SLOAN		30Y1M1D	01-18-1910	040	SLOAN, William	
				040		
David A. SLOAN		1849	1910	040	NOLAN, Mary	
Mary NOLAN Sloan		1855		040	SLOAN, David A.	
				040		
A. F. ELIE, MD		1859	1928	040	CONWAY, Catherine	
Catherine CONWAY Elie		33 Years	07-17-1898	040	ELIE, A.F., MD.	
				040		
Patrick FOLEY		02-03-1827	07-10-1898	040	FOLEY, Patrick	
Delia B. FOLEY		03-11-1867	05-05-1898	040	FOLEY, Delia B.	Dau Of Patrick Foley
				040		
Hannah _____ FLAHERTY		60 Years	04-01-1891	040	FLAHERTY, Anthony	(NOI Anthony Flaherty)
				040	_____, Hannah	
				040		
Patrick PHENEY		1816	1868	040	_____, Margaret	
Margaret _____ PHENEY		1808	1890	040	PHENEY, Patrick	
John PHENEY		1857	1872	040	PHENEY, John	
				040		
James DUNNE		1845	1924	040	_____, Mary	
Mary _____ DUNNE		1849	1925	040	DUNNE, James	

Lakeview Cemetery, Catholic Section, Pleasant Street, Island Pond, Vermont

NAME	POB	DOB/AGE	DOD	CEM	SPOUSE/INDEX	INSCRIPTION
Joseph WELCH		1846	1935	104	PARE, Marceline	
Marceline PARE Welch		1864	1923	104	WELCH, Joseph	
				104		
Ellen FITZGERALD Wade		04-26-1844	08-13-1911	104	WADE, Elisha	(NOI Elisha Wade)
				104	FITZGERALD, Ellen	
				104		
James M. COOPER		1853	1943	104	_____, ALice M.	
Alice M. _____ COOPER		1861	1931	104	COOPER, James M.	
				104		
James MEEHAN		84Y4M2D	07-02-1913	104	MEEHAN, James	Father
				104		
John H. MURPHY		10-10-1846	03-09-1941	104	SMITH, Mary A.	

Mary A. SMITH Murphy		04-23-1861	11-24-1944	104	MURPHY, John H.	
				104		
George DYER		1852	1917	104	_____, Manda	
Manda _____ DYER		1860	1940	104	DYER, George	
				104		
Henry A. FLINT		70 Years	12-19-1905	104	_____, Sarah A.	(GAR-Not in reference)
Sarah R. _____ FLINT		60Y6M	03-17-1904	104	FLINT, Henry	
				104		
Thomas CAHILL		64Y4M18D	09-26-1909	104	RICE, Margaret	
Margaret RICE Cahill		1854	1930	104	CAHILL, Thomas	

St. John's Cemetery, Johnson, Vermont. Just East of the Village on Route 15

NAME	POB	DOB/AGE	DOD	CEM	SPOUSE/INDEX	INSCRIPTION
Patrick HASSETT		1823		124	_____, Catharine	
Catharine _____ HASSETT		1826	1892	124	HASSETT, Patrick	
				124		
Francis MINOR		89 Years	09-21-1894	124	_____, Margaret	
Margaret _____ MINOR		83 Years	09-22-1892	124	MINOR, Francis	
				124		
James DOUGHERTY		72 Years	10-06-1877	124	COX, Ann	May His Soul Rest In Peace
Ann COX Dougherty		70 Years	12-29-1893	124	DOUGHERTY, James	May Her Soul Rest In Peace
				124		
Alicia A. BUTLER		2 Years	01-12-1864	124	BUTLER, Alicia A.	Dau Of Lewis & Harriett Butler
				124	BUTLER, Lewis	
				124	BUTLER, Harriett	
				124		
John MYERS		65Y1M15D	04-19-1851	124	_____, Mary	
Mary _____ MYERS		62Y2M25D	06-07-1860	124	MYERS, John	

Whiting Hill Cemetery, Johnson, Vt. In center of village.

NAME	POB	DOB/AGE	DOD	CEM	SPOUSE/INDEX	INSCRIPTION
James DOUGHERTY		04-09-1796	06-10-1878	125	HALL, Celia	Twelve Years Pastor Of The
				125		Congregational Church in
				125		Milton & Sixteen Of The
				125		Congregational Church in
				125		Johnson.Born In Park, Ireland.
				125		Died in Johnson".(There are 42

NAME	POB	DOB/AGE	DOD	CEM	SPOUSE/INDEX	INSCRIPTION
				125		towns listed as "Park" in 14 Counties)
Celia HALL Dougherty		06-25-1800	11-15-1836	125	DOUGHERTY, James	Born In South Hero (VT). Died In Milton (VT). Dau Of Alpheus And Mercy Hall.
Sarah Curran DOUGHERTY		08-13-1834	10-03-1861	125	DOUGHERTY, Sarah	Born In Shefford, PQ (Canada) Died In Johnson (VT). Dau Of James And Celia Hall Dougherty
John CRISTY		78 Years	04-09-1867	125	_____, Roxanna B.	
Roxanna B. _____ CRISTY		70 Years	07-22-1866	125	CRISTY, John	
Willard MCLENATHAN		75 Years	07-11-1878	125	MCLENATHAN, Willard	
_____ MCCLENATHAN		2Y6M22D	12-14-1859	125	MCCLENATHAN, Male	Son Of Wm. & L. McClenathan
Willard FERGURSON		43 Years	05-23-1861	125	_____, Minerva	
Minerva _____ FERGURSON		63 Years	04-05-1870	125	FERGURSON, Willard	
Archibald FURGASON		41Y10M10D	07-03-1839	125	_____, Dorothy FURGASON, Archibald	(NOI spouse Dorothy)
Mary T. FURGASON		13Y18D	06-16-1846	125	FURGASON, Mary T.	Dau Of Archibald & Dorothy Furgason
Hartwell F. FURGASON		3Y3M23D	09-20-1830	125	FURGASON, Hartwell F.	
Mary T. FURGASON		13Y18D	06-16-1846	125	FURGASON, Mary T.	Dau Of Archibald & Dorothy Furgason

O'Neill Catholic Cemetery, Lemington, Vermont. Route 102. North of Columbia covered bridge. On the bank of the Connecticut River

NAME	POB	DOB/AGE	DOD	CEM	SPOUSE/INDEX	INSCRIPTION
Richard MORGAN		66 Years	09-28-1852	128	MORGAN, Richard	
Mary A. _____ PARNELL		41 Years	02-26-1882	128	PARNELL, Peter _____, Mary A.	(NOI Peter Parnell)

William H. CLARK	73Y5M9D	12-19-1887	128	_____, Margaret	(GAR Try Co. E., 2nd Rgt)
Margaret _____ CLARK	41 Years	02-26-1882	128	CLARK, William H.	(NOI Peter Parnell)
			128		
Catherine _____ ROONEY	17Y 4M	04-19-1878	128	ROONEY, Barnard	(NOI Barnard Rooney)
			128	_____, Catherine	
			128		
George MCCREA	1805	1880	128	CANNON, Ellen	
Ellen CANNON McCrea	1818	1878	128	MCCREA, George	
			128		
Catherine SWEENEY Patton	67 Years	06-05-1881	128	PATTON, James	(NOI James Patton)
			128	SWEENEY, Catherine	
			128		
Mary F. PATTON O'Mara	31Y 2M	05-17-1883	128	O'MARA, John	(NOI John O'Mara)
			128	PATTON, Mary F.	
			128		
Peter DALEY	72 Years	01-15-1897	128	DONOGHUE, Catherine B.	(Second stone reads 1824-1897)
Catherine B. DONOGHUE Daley	75 Years	11-09-1897	128	DALEY, Peter	(Second stone reads 1822-1897)
			128		
John CANNON	97 Years	01-16-1891	128	CANNON, John	
			128		
Richard DUNN	10 Weeks	03-09-1879	128	DUNN, Richard	S/O Joseph & Martha Dunn.(NOI
			128	DUNN, Joseph	Joseph and Martha Dunn)
			128		
Patrick GLEASON	57Y 8M	08-05-1862	128	_____, Sopharona	
Sopharona C. _____ GLEASON	81Y 11M	06-05-1887	128	GLEASON, Patrick	
Emeline A. GLEASON	18Y 2M	09-15-1863	128		
Ellen M. GLEASON	16Y 4M	06-07-1867	128		
			128		
Michael PARNELL	74 Years	10-04-1865	128	_____, Margaret	
Margaret _____ PARNELL	62Y 2M	07-22-1868	128	PARNELL, Michael	
Lawrence PARNELL	27 Years	01-22-1861	128		
			128		
Mary O'NEILL Dunn	85 Years	09-17-1899	128	DUNN, Patrick	(NOI Patrick Dunn)
			128	O'NEILL, Mary	
			128		
Con O'NEIL	85Y7M15D	11-02-1890	128	O'NEIL, Con	(See Bridget O'Neil Possibly
			128		spouse of Con O'Neil)
			128		
James O'NEILL	17Y10M15D	08-06-1863	128	O'NEILL, James	GAR -(Not in reference.Try New
			128		Hampshire.) Son of Con and
			128		Bridget M. O'Neill.
			128		
Jessie M. SHALLOW	2Y6M10D	08-10-1887	128	SHALLOW, Jessie M.	D/O John & Catherine Shallow
			128		
John O'NEILL	84Y5M2D	11-26-1895	128	_____, Ellen	

Ellen _____ O'NEILL	65 Years	12-29-1900	128	O'NEILL, John	
			128		
Ann O'NEILL McLear	82 Years	04-28-1903	128	MCLEAR, Daniel	(NOI Daniel McLear)
			128	O'NEILL, Ann	
			128		
Susanna O'NEILL Corr	83Y8M3D	05-20-1900	128	CORR, Michael	(NOI Michael Corr)
			128	O'NEILL, Susanna	
			128		
Bridget O'NEIL	62 Years	02-01-1887	128	O'NEIL, Bridget	(See Con O'Neil. Possibly
			128		spouse of Con Bridget O'Neil)
			128		Buried At Blackstone, Mass.
			128		
Patrick SHALLOW	28 Years	05-23-1867	128	SHALLOW, Patrick	
			128		
Mary Ann ____ SHALLOW	18 Years	07-03-1872	128	SHALLOW, John	(NOI John Shallow)
			128	SHALLOW, Mary Ann	
			128		
Jemia. _____ DUNN	57 Years	06-14-1876	128	DUNN, Thomas	(NOI Thomas Dunn)
			128	DUNN, Jemia.	
			128		
Thomas S. ROWE	12-10-1849	03-07-1900	128	ROWE, Thomas S.	
			128		
William ROWE	67 Years	11-28-1867	128	ROWE, William	
			128		
James ROWE	19Y 6M	04-05-1873	128	ROWE, James	S/O Patrick & Joanna Rowe
			128		
Johanner ROWE	3 Years	05-02-1890	128	ROWE, Johanner	
			128		
Patrick E. ROWE	03-17-1815	04-01-1909	128	_____, Joanna	GAR - (Not in reference. Try
			128		New Hampshire/Massachusetts.
Joanna _____ ROWE	65 Years	05-02-1894	128	ROWE, Patrick E.	
			128		
Robert MORRISON	75 Years	12-20-1853	128	_____, Mary	
Mary _____ MORRISON	92 Years	05-10-1873	128	MORRISON, Robert	
			128		
Patrick CLARY Jr.	17Y 1M	08-06-1876	128	CLARY, Patrick Jr.	S/O Patrick & Margaret Clary
			128	CLARY, Patrick	
			128	CLAREY, Margaret	
			128		
John G. GORMAN	1852	1935	128	_____, Susan D.	
Susan D. _____ GORMAN	1852	1927	128	GORMAN, John D.	
			128		
Mary Jane _____ MORRISON	45Y2M12D	05-09-1864	128	MORRISON, William	(NOI WIlliam Morrison)
(See next stone)			128	_____, Mary Jane	
Mary Jane HOLBROOK Morrison	45 Years	05-09-1864	128	MORRISON, William	

NAME	POB	DOB/AGE	DOD	CEM	SPOUSE/INDEX	INSCRIPTION
				128		
John MORRISON		16 Years	07-05-1868	128	MORRISON, John	
				128		
Charles MORRISON		1845	1930	128	MORRISON, Charles	GAR (Not in reference. Try New
				128		Hampshire or Massachusetts)
				128		
Anna M. CASSIDY		6 Months	12-04-1878	128	CASSIDY, Anna M.	D/O F. & C.J. Cassidy
				128		
Infant STAPLETON			10-29-1883	128	STAPLETON, Infant	Infant D/O James & Salome
				128	STAPLETON, James	Stapleton
				128	STAPLETON, Salome	
				128		
Thomas B. STAPLETON			1880	128	STAPLETON, Thomas	S/O James & Salome Stapleton

St. Ignatius Cemetery, Lowell, Vermont   Route 58 on Church grounds (Old Cemetery)

NAME	POB	DOB/AGE	DOD	CEM	SPOUSE/INDEX	INSCRIPTION
Bridget MCGLINN McGourty		69 Years	01-13-1868	042	MCGOURTY, Francis	A Native Of Ireland (NOI
				042	MCGLINN, Bridget	Francis McGourty)
				042		
John MURRAY		48Y 7M	08-25-1876	042	MURRAY, John	A Native Of Ireland
				042		
William MURRAY		56 Years	04-06-1889	042	MURRAY, William	
				042		
Michael DYER		1839	1913	042	KELTY, Ann	
Ann KELTY Dyer		1838	1925	042	DYER, Michael	
				042		
Patrick MURPHY		77 Years	07-09-1897	042	MCGOURTY, Rosa	(Note: No marker found for
				042		Patrick Murphy who was born
				042		in Co. Cavan, 1823, and was
				042		spouse of Margaret McGourty-
				042		both of Lowell, Vt.Per records
				042		of Secy of State of Vt.)
				042		
Rosa MCGOURTY Murphy	Co. Dublin	87 Years	11-08-1914	042	MURPHY, Patrick	Born In Dublin, Ireland
				042		
John MCGLINN		46 Years	12-26-1862	042	MCGLINN, John	A Native Of Ireland
				042		
Frank P. SULLIVAN		1836		042	SULLIVAN, Margaret	
Margaret _____ SULLIVAN		1839	1915	042	SULLIVAN, Frank	
				042		

Timothy BLANCHARD	1838	1918	042	BLANCHARD, Mary	
Mary _____ BLANCHARD	1852	1902	042	BLANCHARD, Timothy	
			042		
James TRULAND	75Y5M5D	10-31-1885	042	TRULAND, James	
			042		
John MCALLISTER	1842	1931	042	KELLY, Rosette	
Rosette KELLY McAllister	58Y 4M	12-05-1905	042	MCCALLISTER, John	
			042		
Mary TRUELAND McAllister	83Y1M20D	07-01-1892	042	MCCALLISTER, James	(NOI James McAllister)
			042	TRUELAND, Mary	
			042		
James MURPHY	1825	1901	042	HOGAN, Mary	
Mary HOGAN Murphy	1835	1910	042	MURPHY, James	
			042		
Mary Ann MCELROY Truland	38Y5M19D	05-07-1888	042	TRULAND, John	(NOI John Truland)
			042	MCELROY, Mary Ann	
			042		
Katie _____ RYAN	75Y 10M	07-26-1875	042	_____, Katie	(NOI D. Ryan)
			042	RYAN, D.	
Edmund FORD	73 Years	07-02-1881	042	FORD, Edmund	
			042		
Felix MARTIN	38 Years	02-15-1898	042	MARTIN, Felix	
			042		
John GILBERT	70 Years	07-06-1894	042	WOODS, Mary	
Mary WOODS Gilbert	73 Years	10-27-1902	042	GILBERT, John	
			042		
Bridget _____ DUTTON	63 Years	06-08-1894	042	DUTTON, Francis	(NOI Francis Dutton)
			042	_____, Bridget	
			042		
John HAMMEL	35Y 7D	03-06-1897	042	HAMMEL, John	
			042		
John B. HAMMEL	49Y 4M	06-30-1883	042	HAMMEL, John B.	
			042		
Mary E. FLEMING	22Y6M16D	12-06-1877	042	FLEMING, Mary E.	Dau Of T & H Fleming
			042		
Patrick KELLEY	50 Years	08-31-1874	042	MULLEN, Ellen	
Ellen MULLEN Kelley	80 Years	05-11-1901	042	KELLEY, Patrick	
			042		
Thomas GILBERT	65 Years	03-16-1897	042	KILLEN, Mary	
Mary KILLEN Gilbert	69 Years	02-18-1901	042	GILBERT, Thomas	
			042		
Jennie MURPHY Chamberlain	27 Years	05-30-1896	042	CHAMBERLAIN, George	(NOI George Chamberlain)
			042	MURPHY, Jennie	
			042		
Henry MURPHY	29Y2M8D	05-24-1887	042	MURPHY, Henry	

				042		
John A. MARTIN		01-06-1848	03-14-1902	042	GREEN, Mary	
Mary GREEN Martin			02-12-1885	042	MARTIN, John A.	
				042		
John R. SULLIVAN		1842	1925	042	MCALLISTER, Nellie	
Nellie MCALLISTER Sullivan		1844	1926	042	SULLIVAN, John R.	
				042		
Peter M. GARDNER		66Y10M10D	11-20-1899	042	GARDNER, Mary	(GAR) 1ST NH Cavalry
Mary _____ GARDNER		87 Years	08-08-1928	042	GARDNER, Peter M.	
				042		
Peter MARTIN		07-15-1820	03-17-1917	042	DUCHARME, Aurilla	
Aurilla DUCHARME Martin		68Y5M22D	04-22-1892	042	MARTIN, Peter	
				042		
Edward MURPHY		67Y 6M	04-10-1883	042	MURPHY, Edward	
Edward F. MURPHY		21Y 6M	12-23-1882	042	MURPHY, Edward F.	
Patrick FINNEGAN				042	FINNEGAN, Patrick	(GAR) Co. H., 9th VT Infantry
John O. SULLIVAN		82 Years	09-12-1885	042	GALLIVAN, Catherine	
Catherine GALLIVAN Sullivan		77 Years	05-17-1883	042	SULLIVAN, John O.	
Mary A. SULLIVAN		46 Years	11-13-1884	042		
John FINNEGAN		90 Years	09-15-1915	042	REILLY, Ann	
Ann REILLY Finnegan		52 Years	08-28-1885	042	FINNEGAN, John	
				042		
Frank MCGORTY		1844	1879	042	MCGORTY, Elizabeth E.	
Elizabeth E. _____ MCGORTY		1844	1916	042	MCGORTY, Frank	
				042		
John MCGLINN		46 Years	12-26-1862	042	KILBRIDE, Ann	
Ann KILBRIDE McGlinn		50 Years	04-20-1868	042	MCGLINN, John	
				042		
John SEYMOUR		01-15-1839	01-26-1920	042	SEYMOUR, John	

St. Ignatius Cemetery, Lowell, Vermont - On Route 100, North of Village (New Cemetery)

NAME	POB	DOB/AGE	DOD	CEM	SPOUSE/INDEX	INSCRIPTION
James A. MCALLISTER		1851	1924	098	GREEN, Delia	
Delia GREEN McAllister		1867	1958	098	MCALLISTER, James A.	
				098		
W. J. MALONEY		09-26-1842	06-10-1917	098	SULLIVAN, Julia C.	
Julia C. SULLIVAN Maloney		10-28-1842	07-19-1919	098	MALONEY, W. J.	
				098		
John BRAHANA		1826	1904	098	KELTY, Bridget	
Bridget KELTY Brahana		1836	1909	098	BRAHANA, John	
				098		

Francis MURPHY		1832	1906	098	MURPHY, Margaret	
Margaret _____ MURPHY		1835	1926	098	MURPHY, Francis	
				098		
Joseph GODDARD		1846	1927	098	HAMILTON, Mary	(GAR) Vol Co. H. 5th Vt Reg
				098		Vol Co. C. 11th Vt Reg
Mary HAMILTON Goddard		1857	1941	098	GODDARD, Joseph	
				098		
Francis T. MURPHY		09-17-1853	07-27-1944	098	HICKEY, Mary J.	
Mary J. HICKEY Murphy		07-24-1851	01-24-1911	098	MURPHY, Francis T.	
				098		
Catharine FINNEGAN McElroy		1823	1858	098	MCELROY, John	
John MCELROY		1822	1913	098	FINNEGAN, Catharine	
William MCELROY		1855	1937	098	MCELROY, William	
Catharine MCELROY		1851	1921	098	MCELROY, Catharine	
				098		
Dennis SHORTSLEEVE		1841	1923	098	GODDARD, Elmira	(GAR) Priv. Co. D. 5th Rgt Vt
Elmira GODDARD Shortsleeve		1841	1924	098	SHORTSLEEVE, Dennis	
				098		
John MARTIN		1842	1923	098	MCGLYNN, Mary Ann	
Mary Ann MCGLYNN Martin		1848	1918	098	MARTIN, John	

Pleasant View Cemetery, Ludlow, VT. On High Street. Opposite Catholic Church

NAME	**POB**	**DOB/AGE**	**DOD**	**CEM**	**SPOUSE/INDEX**	**INSCRIPTION**
Frank SNOW		1848	1934	043	MCMAHON, Lucy	
Lucy MCMAHON Snow		1858	1940	043	SNOW, Frank	
				043		
Ann _____ MALONEY		61Y 3M	08-26-1886	043	MALONEY, Matthew	(NOI Matthew Maloney)
				043	MALONEY, Ann	
				043		
Harry O'TOLE		1828	07-24-1889	043	GLASS, Mary	Born In Dumfrees, Scotland
				043		A Member Of Co. I, 2nd Rgt,
				043		VT Vols (GAR)
Mary GLASS O'Tole		1833	10-09-1908	043	O'TOLE, Harry	Born In Beruichon, Tweed,
				043		Scotland
Michael O'TOLE		1855	1925	043	DUGAN, Rachel	(NOI Rachel Dugan)
				043	O'TOLE, Michael	
				043		
James BARRY		35 Years	04-29-1887	043	CRONAN, Hannah	
Hannah CRONAN Barry		1854	1929	043	BARRY, James	
				043		

Daniel HEHIR	62 Years	06-09-1896	043	HEHIR, Mary	
Mary _____ HEHIR	57 Years	10-27-1890	043	HEHIR, Daniel	
			043		
L. R. HARVEY	1823	1898	043	COLBY, L.E.	
L. E. COLBY Harvey	1825	1904	043	HARVEY, L.R.	
			043		
John AYLWARD	01-05-1805	07-22-1898	043	MURPHY, Julia	
Julia MURPHY Aylward	05-10-1829	06-19-1896	043	AYLWARD, John	
John P. AYLWARD	1850	1910	043	AYLWARD, John P.	
Edward AYLWARD	1854	1932	043	AYLWARD, Edward	
			043		
Michael LANE	1844	1932	043	LANE, Bridget L.	
Bridget L. _____ LANE	1850	1918	043	LANE, Michael	
			043		
Martin M. TARBELL	1841	1893	043	FARWELL, Julia M.	(GAR) Co. D. 7th VT Vet Vol
Julia M. FARWELL Tarbell	1844	1908	043	TARBELL, Martin M.	
David FARWELL	1815	1892	043	LOCKE, Julia B.	
Julia B. LOCKE Farwell	1822	1849	043	FARWELL, David	Buried In Danby, VT
			043		
Michael LUCAS			043	SULLIVAN, Margarette	In Loving Memory (NOI DOB-DOD For Michael Lucas)
			043		
Margarette SULLIVAN Lucas	1811	1901	043	LUCAS, Michael	(Possibly nee Lucas. On same stone is William R. LUCAS, 1878-1918. Co. A. 1st VT Reg-Spanish American War)
			043		
			043		
			043		
Nellie LUCAS	1858	1917	043	LUCAS, Nellie	
Charles August LUCAS	1850	1929	043	DONNELLY, Mary Ann	
Mary Ann DONNELLY Lucas	1854	1894	043	LUCAS, Charles August	
			043		
David FLEMING	67Y4M24D	11-05-1904	043	FLEMING, David	(GAR Marker but inscription reads "U. S. Marine Corps")
			043		
	1858	1917	043		
Patrick PHELAN	01-13-1845	02-04-1904	043	DUNNE, Alice	
Alice DUNNE Phelan	02-18-1853	12-29-1925	043	PHELAN, Patrick	
			043		
Mary _____ KELLEY	46 Years	06-14-1885	043	KELLEY, Martin	(NOI Martin Kelley)
			043		
Michael GILLIGAN	1822	1909	043	COLLOPY, Margaret	Natives Of Ireland
Margaret COLLOPY Gilligan	1821	1907	043	GILLIGAN, Michael	Natives Of Ireland
Timothy F. GILLIGAN	25Y2M6D	10-11-1879	043	GILLIGAN, Timothy F.	S/O Michael& Margaret Gilligan
			043		
John AGAN	1845	1879	043	AGAN, John	(Does not Indicate If Spouse)
Amanda AGAN	1848	1911	043	AGAN, Amanda	(Does Not Indicate If Spouse)
			043		
Daniel HANNON	55 Years	06-28-1869	043	LEATHEDE, Margaret	(Daniel Hannon has a second

			043		stone with same information)
Margaret LEATHEDE Hannon	69 Years	08-21-1883	043	HANNON, Daniel	
			043		
Thomas MCMAHON	84 Years	09-11-1885	043	_____, Bridget	
Bridget _____ MCMAHON	60 Years	03-21-1884	043	MCMAHON, Thomas	
			043		
John RILEY	35 Years	02-08-1884	043	RILEY, John	(Stone is down)
			043		
Alexander SNOW	03-30-1835	05-10-1904	043	_____, Bridget	(GAR - Try Co. G, 7th Rgt, VT
Bridget _____ SNOW	12-24-1835	06-03-1914	043	SNOW, Alexander	Vols. Listed as Alix Snow)
			043		
Joseph DUNN	02-14-1813	03-24-1898	043	_____, Lucinda M.	
Lucinda M. _____ DUNN	11-03-1808	06-22-1881	043	DUNN, Joseph	
			043		
Thomas FRENCH	73Y5M2D	10-14-1888	043	MCCOLLUM, Sarah A.	
Sarah A. MCCOLLUM French	68Y4M9D	04-01-1887	043	FRENCH, Thomas	
			043		
Henry C. DICKERMAN	10-11-1833	08-08-1906	043	DUNN, Martha E.	
Martha E. DUNN Dickerman	10-27-1844	03-30-1926	043	DICKERMAN, Henry C.	
			043		
Timothy KENNEDY	08-07-1827	08-12-1874	043	DUGGAN, Julia	
Julia DUGGAN Kennedy	08-03-1831	12-09-1904	043	KENNEDY, Timothy	
Sarah Ann KENNEDY	02-23-1858	03-16-1864	043	KENNEDY, Sarah Ann	
John KENNEDY	03-19-1856	01-20-1920	043	KENNEDY, John	
Timothy E. KENNEDY	06-12-1866	04-11-1931	043	KENNEDY, Timothy E.	
			043		
John BRINN	84 Years	06-21-1904	043	_____, Sarah R.	
Sarah R. _____ BRINN	86 Years	12-25-1914	043	BRINN, John	
George WHITLOW	90Y1M15D	02-15-1881	043	WHITLOW, George	Father
			043		
Samuel L. PINNEY	73 Years	09-29-1910	043	CROSBY, Jane	(GAR) Co. C 6th Rgt Vt Vols
Jane CROSBY Pinney	71 Years	02-13-1907	043	PINNEY, Samuel L.	
			043		
James P. LYNCH	27Y 17D	09-23-1885	043	LYNCH, James	S/O Patrick & Mary Lynch
Patrick LYNCH	80 Years	05-06-1880	043	LYNCH, Mary	(NOI Mary. Stone next to
			043	LYNCH, Patrick	Patrick Lynch says "Mother")
			043		
Joseph KENWORTHY	49 Years	03-28-1883	043	RILEY, Bridget	
Bridget RILEY Kenworthy	78 Years	06-03-1903	043	KENWORTHY, Joseph	
			043		
Daniel HARTNETT	80 Years	12-26-1915	043	LYNCH, Hannah	
Hannah LYNCH Hartnett	70 Years	12-15-1909	043	HARTNETT, Daniel	
			043		
Thomas W. CONNORS	1855	1885	043	SULLIVAN, Mary	
Mary SULLIVAN Connors	1853	1920	043	CONNORS, Thomas W.	

Name	Born	Died		Spouse/Related	Notes
			043		
Jona GILL Tasker	01-01-1837	12-30-1884	043	GILL, Jona	Born In Leeds, Yorkshire,Engl.
			043	TASKER, Mr.	Died In Ludlow, Vermont
Hannah GILL	07-31-1840	02-17-1890	043	GILL, Hannah	
			043		
Victor BRINN	03-16-1855	03-19-1941	043	____, Sarah E.	
Sarah E. ______ BRINN	24Y 2M	03-31-1884	043	BRINN, Victor	
Amelia BRINN	1855	1930	043		
			043		
Harry M. CLARKE	07-03-1822	02-24-1881	043	CLARKE, Annie	Born In London, England. Died
			043		in Ludlow, Vermont
Annie _____ CLARKE	05-15-1822	11-09-1894	043	CLARKE, Harry M.	Born In England.Died in Ludlow
			043		
CONNOLLY			043	CONNOLLY, Family	
Mother	1853	1922	043		(NOI)
Father	1842	1928	043		
			043		
Miama _____ GAREY	50 Years	03-24-1867	043	GAREY, Stephen	(NOI Stephen Garey)
			043	GAREY, Miama	
			043		
George H. BOWKER	1828	1883	043	TULLY, Maria	
Maria TULLY Bowker	1836	1900	043	BOWKER, George H.	
			043		
Bernard M. LEONARD	1847	1901	043	LEONARD, Bernard	(Does Not Indicate if Husband
Julia LEONARD	1856	1945	043	LEONARD, Julia	and Wife)
Bridget LEONARD	1814	1883	043	LEONARD, Bridget	
Abel MCCOY	1839	1908	043	MCCOY, Abel	(Does Not Indicate if Husband
Sarah MCCOY	1845	1906	043	MCCOY, Sarah	and Wife).Leonard-Vail-Kenney
			043		Memorial
			043		
Michael PURCELL	62 Years	06-03-1884	043	____, Johanna	
Johanna _____ PURCELL	61 Years	10-17-1889	043	PURCELL, Michael	
			043		
Michael SULLIVAN	1829	1911	043	MANNING, Anna	
Anna MANNING Sullivan	1848	1888	043	SULLIVAN, Michael	
			043		
Michael KELLY	1819	1894	043	O'GRADY, Hannah	
Hannah O'GRADY Kelley	1824	1899	043	KELLY, Michael	
			043		
Daniel HAYES	85 Years	01-17-1908	043	DOYLE, Mary	
Mary DOYLE Hayes	1825	1913	043	HAYES, Daniel	
			043		
Henry C. GLEASON	1853	1938	043	HARRIS, Elizabeth	
Elizabeth HARRIS Gleason	1858	1914	043	GLEASON, Henry C.	
			043		

Name	Birthplace	Born/Age	Died	Code	Spouse/Index	Notes
Martin MEEHAN		12-20-1835	01-02-1893	043	MALONEY, Mary	
Mary MALONEY Meehan		1834	1911	043	MEEHAN, Martin	
				043		
Patrick LANE	Co. Limerick	80 Years	09-13-1885	043	DAVENPORT, Martha	Natives Of The Parish Of
				043		Askeaton, Co. Limerick, Ire.
Martha DAVENPORT Lane	Co. Limerick	68 Years	02-18-1892	043	LANE, Patrick	Natives Of The Parish Of
				043		Askeaton, Co. Limerick, Ire.
				043		
Joseph CONNORS		1857	1923	043	BOWKER, Mary Ann	
Mary Ann BOWKER Connors		1855	1934	043	CONNORS, Joseph	
				043		
Bernard MOON		1817	1900	043	MOON, Bernard	
				043		
William GRANT		65 Years	05-16-1871	043	GRANT, Mary	
Mary _____ GRANT		72 Years	11-01-1876	043	GRANT, William	
Bessie GRANT		62 Years	08-14-1902	043	GRANT, Bessie	Sister
William GRANT		69 Years	11-14-1912	043	GRANT, William	Brother
Alice M. LYNCH		25 Years	09-27-1892	043	LYNCH, Alice M.	
				043		
William H. LYNCH		1839	1895	043	LYNCH, Margaret	
Margaret _____ LYNCH		1834	1909	043	LYNCH, William H.	
				043		
James DARCY		1844	1918	043	DUFFICY, Bridget	
Bridget DUFFICY Darcy		1851	1939	043	DARCY, James	
				043		
John MAHON		03-03-1841	04-15-1905	043	HESELTINE, Delania W.	
Delanie HESELTINE Mahon		08-26-1849	05-11-1927	043	MAHON, John	D/O Cephas & Alvira Terrell
				043		Heseltine
				043		
James WARD		01-29-1895	07-12-1872	043	DILWORTH, Ellen	
Ellen DILWORTH Ward		09-29-1818	11-17-1886	043	WARD, James	
Samuel WARD		04-14-1848	02-10-1869	043	WARD, Samuel	
				043		
Joshua S. KELY		21Y 24D	01-24-1854	043	KELY, Joshua S.	
				043		
John Henman SARGENT		51Y11M9D	01-11-1886	043	HANLEY, Ann Eliza	
Ann Eliza HANLEY Sargent		06-26-1840	11-03-1916	043	SARGENT, John Henman	
				043		
Charles H. KNEELAND		1844	1875	043	BOYNTON, Ann Eliza	
Ann Eliza BOYNTON Kneeland		1850	1872	043	KNEELAND, Charles H.	
				043		
Patrick F. CROSBY		1846	1920	043	_____, Catherine E.	
Catherine E. _____ CROSBY		1845	1938	043	CROSBY, Patrick F.	
				043		
John DAILEY		08-20-1838	05-02-1911	043	BOYLE, Mary	(GAR) Co. H 10th Reg VtVol Inf

				043		(This is the largest memorial
Mary BOYLE Dailey		1841	1916	043	DAILEY, John	in the cemetery. A 15'-20'
				043		Celtic Cross)
				043		
Thomas HARTNETT		03-17-1829	08-04-1909	043	DAILEY, Hanora	
Hanora DAILEY Hartnett		85 Years	07-29-1826	043	HARTNETT, Thomas	
				043		
Thomas RILEY		1840	1899	043	RILEY, Susan	(Riley-Wykes Memorial)
Susan _____ RILEY		1842	1924	043	RILEY, Thomas	
				043		
James BOWKER		1858	1916	043	SULLIVAN, Maggie A.	
Maggie A. SULLIVAN Bowker		1857	1946	043	BOWKER, James	
				043		
Bernard F. KEARNEY		1852	1923	043	DOUGHERTY, Ann	
Ann DOUGHERTY Kearney		1854	1931	043	KEARNEY, Bernard F.	
				043		
James MCDERMOTT		1837	1914	043	CROSBY, Mary H.	(GAR) Co. G. 2nd Reg Vt Vols
Mary H. CROSBY McDermott		1850	1914	043	MCDERMOTT, James	
				043		
John LOONEY		59 Years	07-16-1914	043	LOONEY, John	(Does not indicate if husband
Orilla _____ LOONEY		67 Years	03-08-1928	043	LOONEY, Orilla	and wife. Stones side by side)
				043		
William MCCANN		1857	1931	043	SULLIVAN, Hannah	
Hannah SULLIVAN McCann		1860	1952	043	MCCANN, William	
				043		
Maggie TIERNEY				043	TIERNEY, Maggie	Only D/O Barney TIERNEY and
				043	TIERNEY, Barney	Margaret (NOI)
				043	TIERNEY, Margaret	
				043		
Thomas F. MCDONALD		1853	1906	043	MCDONALD, Carrie B.	
Carrie B. _____ MCDONALD		1867	1954	043	MCDONALD, Thomas F.	
				043		
Mary MCCOLLOM		14Y 6M	09-14-1852	043	MCCOLLUM, Mary	D/O John McCollum & Betsey
				043	MCCOLLUM, John	
				043	MCCOLLUM, Betsey	
				043		
Margaret _____ MCCOLLUM		60 Years	02-23-1806	043	MCCOLLUM, Margaret	W/O Thomas MCCOLLUM(NOI
				043		Thomas McCollum)
				043	MCCOLLUM, Thomas	
				043		
Owen DONAHUE		1838	1912	043	LOVEDAY, Margaret	
Margaret LOVEDAY Donahue		1840	1922	043	DONAHUE, Owen	
Ellen DONAHUE		1815	1875	043	DONAHUE, Ellen	
				043		
William MORRISEY	Co. Waterford	1810	07-03-1899	043	MORRISEY, Ellen	A N/O The Town Of Dungarvan

				043		Co. Waterford, Ireland. Died
				043		In Rutland, Vermont
				043		
Ellen _____ MORRISEY	Co. Waterford	45 Years	10-10-1860	043	MORRISEY, William	A N/O The Town Of Dungarvan
				043		Co. Waterford,Ireland. Erected
				043		By William Morrisey IMO His
				043		Beloved Wife
				043		
				043		(Stone is down and broken-NOI)
Thomas LYNCH				043		
		60 Years	09-04-1863	043	_____, Mary	
Patrick SULLIVAN		48 Years	10-08-1863	043	SULLIVAN, Patrick	
Mary _____ SULLIVAN				043		
		56Y 9M	12-11-1892	043	_____, Katharine	
Dennis GEEHAN		67Y 4M	05-26-1902	043	GEEHAN, Dennis	
Katharine _____ GEEHAN				043		
			12-20-1882	043	LYNCH, James	(Stone is down and broken-NOI)
James LYNCH				043		age is obscured.Has GAR Marker
				043		but no entry in reference)
				043		
		21 Years		043	LYNCH, Michael	(Stone worn. DOD obscured) S/O
Michael LYNCH				043	LYNCH, Michael	Michael LYNCH and Mary (NOI)
				043	LYNCH, Mary	
				043		
		1847	1923	043	DAILEY, Bridget	
Patrick NEALON				043	POND, Eva M.	
		1857	1930	043	NEALON, Patrick	
Bridget DAILEY Nealon		41Y9M12D	01-12-1890	043	NEALON, Patrick	
Eva M. POND Nealon		78 Years	12-02-1871	043	LANE, Margaret	
Margaret LANE				043		
Michael NEALON	Co. Limerick	76 Years	11-02-1880	043	LANE, Ann	B/I Limerick Co.,Ireland. Died
				043		In Ludlow, Vermont
		65 Years	02-13-1884	043	NEALON, Michael	
Ann LANE Nealon				043		
		78 Years	11-28-1896	043	_____, Mary	B/I _______ Ireland. Died At
John REED				043		Ludlow, Vermont (This stone
				043		is badly deteriorated)
Mary _____ REED	Co. Cork	67 Years	09-20-1884	043	REED, John	A N/O The Parish of Castle-
				043		Island, Co. Cork,Ireland. Died
				043		at Ludlow, Vermont.(This stone
				043		is badly deteriorated)
		48 Years	01-29-1906	043	REED, John	
John REED		1783	1871	043	BARRY, Katherine	
Katherine BARRY		1848	1932	043	REED, Michael	
Michael REED				043		

John HORAN		01-29-1900	043		(Cannot read age at death)
	48 Years	11-19-1881	043	HORAN, John	(Cannot read name - both badly deteriorated)
			043		
			043		
Katherine BARRY	88 Years	01-23-1871	043	BARRY, Katherine	N/O The Parish Of R____berry County Of Cork, Ire. (Appears to be same person on John REED stone)
			043		
			043		
			043		
			043		
James O'MARA	1813	1893	043	_____, Johanna	
Johanna _____ O'MARA	1821	1904	043	O'MARA, James	
Michael DAILEY	1839	1920	043	_____, Bridget	
Bridget _____ DAILEY	1844	1933	043	DAILEY, Michael	
			043		
John HAYES	78 Years	01-07-1908	043	_____, Bridget	
Bridget _____ HAYES	72 Years	01-02-1844	043	HAYES, John	
Thomas BOYLE	108 Years	11-15-1886	043	BROWN, Margaret	
Margaret BROWN Boyle	76 Years	02-03-1879	043	BOYLE, Thomas	
			043		
Margaret _____ GEEHAN	52 Years	02-14-1903	043	_____, Margaret	(NOI Timothy Geehan)
			043	GEEHAN, Timothy	
			043		
Timothy SULLIVAN	18Y 6M	01-08-1862	043	SULLIVAN, Timothy	(GAR) Member Co. C 6th VT Vols Died Camp Griffin, VA. Son Of Patrick & Margaret Sullivan
			043		
			043		
			043		
Patrick SULLIVAN	83Y 2M	05-18-1897	043	_____, Margaret	
Margaret _____ SULLIVAN	78Y 11M	02-03-1892	043	SULLIVAN, Patrick	
			043		
Michael DORSEY	09-29-1835	05-17-1898	043	_____, Margaret	
Margaret _____ DORSEY	12-15-1833	10-20-1910	043	DORSEY, Michael	
			043		
William H. DAILEY	1844	1929	043	SULLIVAN, Mary	
Mary SULLIVAN Dailey	1854	1908	043	DAILEY, William H.	
Daniel S. DAILEY		02-27-1897	043	DAILEY, Daniel S.	
Timothy DAILEY	1807	06-04-1892	043	DAILEY, Timothy	(NOI DOB)
Joanna BABBETT Dailey	1841	03-05-1893	043	BABBETT, Joanna	
			043		
Michael SHEA	70Y 4M	01-30-1892	043	_____, Mary	
Mary _____ SHEA	85 Years	07-21-1901	043	SHEA, Michael	
John SHEA	04-20-1851	08-01-1911	043	SHEA, John	
Margaret SHEA	05-01-1849	11-08-1936	043	SHEA, Margaret	
Annie SHEA	6Y 5M	05-17-1861	043	SHEA, Annie	
Katie SHEA	19Y 19D	05-19-1866	043	SHEA, Katie	
			043		

Name	Place	Born	Died	Code	Index	Notes
John KEATING		1852	1923	043	CRONAN, Mary	
Mary CRONAN Keating		1853	1940	043	KEATING, John	
				043		
Patrick H. KEATING		1850	1940	043	KEATING, Patrick	(Does not indicate if spouses)
Margaret J. KEATING		1853	1941	043	KEATING, Margaret J.	(Probably)
				043		
O'CONNOR				043	O'CONNOR, Family	
Mother		1832	1903	043		
Father		1821	1903	043		
Sarah O'CONNOR		1864	1936	043		
Lena O'CONNOR		1866	1896	043		
				043		
William QUIRK		68Y 9M	02-19-1898	043	_____, Catharine	
Catharine _____ QUIRK		72Y 5M	10-21-1894	043	QUIRK, William	
				043		
John BARRETT		1836	1925	043	BARRETT, John	
				043		
Mathias BARRETT		1840	1918	043	BARRETT, Mathias	
				043		
James MULLOY	Co. Sligo	1840	1893	043	MCDERMOTT, Margaret	B/I Ballymote, Co. Sligo, Ire.
Margaret MCDERMOTT Mulloy	Co. Sligo	1842	1916	043	MULLOY, James	B/I Ballymote, Co. Sligo, Ire.
				043		
John MCGOWAN				043	MCGOWAN, John	(GAR) Co. C 6th Vt Inf (NOI)
				043		
Mary MCENANY Snow		1845	1925	043	MCENANY, Mary	
				043		
Patrick KIERNAN		1821	1909	043	_____, Julia	
Julia _____ KIERNAN		1818	1896	043	KIERNAN, Patrick	
Lawrence KIERNAN		1850	1914	043	KIERNAN, Lawrence	
				043		
Mathew KIERNAN		1857	1936	043	KIERNAN, Mathew	
Patrick KIERNAN Jr.		1853	1932	043	KIERNAN, Patrick Jr.	
				043		
Melvina _____ HORAN		40 Years	04-10-1896	043	_____, Melvina	(NOI John Horan)
				043	HORAN, John	
				043		
Dennis MCGRATH		60 Years	11-20-1899	043	_____, Mary	
Mary _____ MCGRATH		66Y 2M	10-29-1901	043	MCGRATH, Dennis	
				043		
George H. BOWKER		1856	1900	043	BOWKER, George H.	
				043		
John R. BIXBY		08-11-1845	02-14-1916	043	FLAHERTY, Joanna	
Joanna FLAHERTY Bixby		08-17-1854	09-11-1915	043	BIXBY, John R.	
				043		
John O. ROGERS		1825	1905	043	ROGERS, John O.	

Name	Birth	Death	Code	Spouse/Relation	Note
			043		
Frank W. AGAN	12-18-1869	05-13-1934	043	SAFFORD, Cora Alice	
Cora Alice SAFFORD Agan	01-21-1854	08-15-1899	043	AGAN, Frank W.	
			043		
John RYAN	06-24-1843	01-25-1904	043	RYAN, John	(Does not indicate if spouses)
Katherine RYAN	07-10-1850	06-14-1922	043	RYAN, Katherine	
			043		
Thomas CAVANAUGH	1847	1907	043	CAVANAUGH, Thomas	
			043		
Abbie M. HAMMOND	05-22-1823	02-03-1908	043	HAMMOND, Abbie M.	
			043		
Joseph M. ALLEN	1848	1925	043	DARCY, Cora	
Cora DARCY Allen	1859		043	ALLEN, Joseph M.	
John S. DARCY	1836	1904	043	_____, Ruth C.	
Ruth C. _____ DARCY	1839	1915	043	DARCY, John S.	
			043		
James E. DOYLE	1857	1946	043	_____, Ethel P.	
Ethel P. _____ DOYLE	1876	19	043	DOYLE, James E.	
			043		
John DARCY	1838	1877	043	BOWMAN, Mary A.	
Mary A. BOWMAN Darcy	1846	1911	043	DARCY, John	
			043		
Daniel KEATING	1833	1904	043	GRANT, Bridget	
Bridget GRANT Keating	1834	1913	043	KEATING, Daniel	
			043		
Fred N. COLBY	1851		043	HENRY, Jane E.	
Jane E. HENRY Colby	1842	1919	043	COLBY, Fred N.	
			043		
Merritt A. SAWYER	1852	1926	043	MCWAIN, Jennie R.	
Jennie R. MCWAIN Sawyer	1852	1910	043	SAWYER, Merritt A.	
			043		
T. S. DAILEY	1848	1904	043	GILLIGAN, Elizabeth N.	
Elizabeth N. GILLIGAN Dailey	1857	1936	043	DAILEY, T. S.	
			043		
Charles E. BATES	09-15-1836	06-02-1910	043	HART, Mary	
Mary HART Bates	03-07-1844	09-08-1908	043	BATES, Charles E.	
			043		
Jess M. COLBY	1840	1905	043	CURRAN, Mary C.	
Mary C. CURRAN Colby	1862		043	COLBY, Jess M.	
			043		
John HAYES	78 Years	01-07-1908	043	_____, Bridget	
Bridget _____ HAYES	72 Years	01-02-1884	043	HAYES, John	
			043		
Michael DAILEY	1839	1920	043	_____, Bridget	
Bridget _____ DAILEY	1844	1933	043	DAILEY, Michael	

				043		
Thomas BOYLE		108 Years	11-15-1886	043	BROWN, Margaret	
Margaret BROWN Boyle		76 Years	02-03-1879	043	BOYLE, Thomas	
				043		
John T. BOYLE		1830	1901	043	_____, Katherine	
Katherine _____ BOYLE		1844	1914	043	BOYLE, John T.	
				043		
Maggie _____ SULLIVAN		27 Years	05-29-1878	043	_____, Maggie	Sister (NOI Thomas Sullivan)
				043	SULLIVAN, Thomas	
				043		
Isaiah B. SEARS		42 Years	06-05-1883	043	KEATING, Julia	
Julia KEATING Sears		48 Years	07-27-1895	043	SEARS, Isaiah B	
				043		
John KEATING		61 Years	08-21-1875	043	_____, Margaret	
Margaret _____ KEATING		86 Years	02-24-1896	043	KEATING, John	
				043		
Daniel J. KEATING		1839	1916	043	LEONARD, Bridget	(GAR)Co. H. 10th Reg VT Vols
Bridget LEONARD Keating		1843	1927	043	KEATING, Daniel J.	
				043		
Julia C. MARSH		08-10-1850	07-26-1874	043	MARSH, Julia C.	
				043		
Edward J. FANNING		1834	1928	043	FANNING, Edward J.	
				043		
Alexander MCDONALD		57 Years	03-30-1870	043	KIRWIN, Bridget	
Bridget KIRWIN McDonald		77 Years	10-03-1889	043	MCDONALD, Alexander	

St. Elizabeth's Cemetery, **Lyndonville**, **VT**

NAME	**POB**	**DOB/AGE**	**DOD**	**CEM**	**SPOUSE/INDEX**	**INSCRIPTION**
Margaret _____ CAHILL		1828	1911	044	CAHILL, James	(NOI James Cahill)
				044	_____, Margaret	
				044		
Sarah _____ KENNEDY		1817	1905	044	KENNEDY, Bartholomew	(NOI Bartholomew Kennedy)
				044	_____, Sarah	
				044		
Owen MCFARLAND		1831	1922	044	BRADY, Mary	
Mary BRADY McFarland		1845	1928	044	MCFARLAND, Owen	
Edward MCFARLAND		1877	1937	044	MCFARLAND, Edward	
				044		
Mary HAGAN Branigan		05-__-1837	12-__-1893	044	HAGAN, Mary	(NOI Mr. Branigan)
				044		
Mary NEAGLE McFarlin		69 Years	12-30-1894	044	MCFARLIN, William J.	(NOI William J. McFarlin)

Name	Place	Born/Age	Died	No.	Relation	Note
				044	NEAGLE, Mary	
				044		
John RILEY	Co. Galway	1853	1926	044	ROCH, Mary	
Mary ROCH Riley		1850	1911	044	RILEY, John	
M. John RILEY		1814	1895	044	RILEY, M. John	
Thomas WARD		69 Years	07-10-1909	044	WARD, Thomas	
				044		
Cornelius BUCKLEY		84 Years	10-31-1907	044	CROWLEY, Mary	
Mary CROWLEY Buckley		74 Years	09-26-1907	044	BUCKLEY, Cornelius	
John BUCKLEY		60 Years	1924	044	BUCKLEY, John	
				044		
Frank LONE		02-14-1833	04-14-1907	044	_____, Sarah	
Sarah _____ LONE		1845	1927	044	LONE, Frank	
				044		
Oliver COUNTER		04-20-1844	09-10-1910	044	SHANTY, Kate	
Kate SHANTY Counter		48Y1M10D	06-01-1901	044	COUNTER, Oliver	
				044		
Sarah A. KELLETT Aldrich		57Y 9M	05-16-190_	044	ALDRICH, W. J.	(NOI W. J. Aldrich)
				044	KELLETT, Sarah A.	
				044		
John B. MCLURE		57Y 6M	01-20-1904	044	MCLURE, John B.	
				044		
Kate TURNER		1845	1927	044	TURNER, Kate	
				044		
Nora BECK		1849	1928	044	BECK, Nora	
				044		
Catherine S. COLLINS		1845	1922	044	COLLINS, Catherine S.	
				044		
Edward RICE		04-15-1845	07-20-1916	044	RICE, Edward	
				044		
Joseph WATCHIE		1852	1926	044	CAHILL, Elizabeth	
Elizabeth CAHILL Watchie		1850	1917	044	WATCHIE, Joseph	
				044		
William T. MCFARLAND		1835	1927	044	RICE, Mary	
Mary RICE McFarland		1839	1920	044	MCFARLAND, William T.	
				044		
Benjamin F. SMITH		1839	1922	044	POWER, Mary	
Mary POWER Smith		1852	1939	044	SMITH, Benjamin F.	
				044		
John CLEARY		05-25-1849	02-21-1914	044	MCARTHUR, Louise	
Louise MCARTHUR Cleary		11-08-1863	11-11-1955	044	CLEARY, John	
				044		
James CROFTON		1836	1922	044	_____, Catherine	
Catherine _____ CROFTON		1848	1933	044	CROFTON, James	
				044		

NAME	POB	DOB/AGE	DOD	CEM	SPOUSE/INDEX	INSCRIPTION
				044		
John NORTON		1845	1915	044	NORTON, John	
				044		
James BOWEN		1842	1897	044	BOWEN, James	
				044		
Patrick DONAHUE		1817	02-10-1907	044	_____, Margaret	
Margaret _____ DONAHUE		1833	10-29-1913	044	DONAHUE, Patrick	
				044		
Maria MCFARLIN	Co. Cavan	1817	02-10-1907	044	MCFARLIN, Maria	Born In Co. Cavan, Ireland
				044		
John MCCANN		1855	1908	044	MCCANN, John	(Does not say if husband and
Margaret MCCANN		1853	1933	044	MCCANN, Margaret	wife)
				044		
Thomas AHEARN		12-20-1837	06-06-1920	044	AHEARN, Thomas	(Born In Ireland)
				044		
Margaret TRUDDEN McNulty		1829	1909	044	MCNULTY, John	(NOI John McNulty)
				044	TRUDDEN, Margaret	

St. Mary's Cemetery   Middlebury, VT.   Off Hillcrest Street - West of Village

NAME	POB	DOB/AGE	DOD	CEM	SPOUSE/INDEX	INSCRIPTION
John POWERS		10-09-1828	12-26-1890	046	TINNEY, Catharine	
Catharine TINNEY Powers		02-14-1830	11-12-1896	046	POWERS, John	
				046		
John ROCHFORD		1820	1896	046	KANE, Bridget	
Bridget KANE Rochford		1835	1901	046	ROCHFORD, John	
Patrick J. ROCHFORD		1862	1897	046	ROCHFORD, Patrick J.	
Bridget FARRELL Rochford		1855	1893	046	ROCHFORD, Michael	(NOI Michael Rochford)
				046	FARRELL, Bridget	
Mary ROCHFORD		1891	1892	046	ROCHFORD, Mary	(Dau of Bridget & Michael
				046		Rochford
Martha E. BRIGGS		1855	1900	046	BRIGGS, Martha E.	
				046		
William MCCAULEY		01-15-1830	08-01-1893	046	GARTLAND, Margaret	
Margaret GARTLAND McCauley		05-03-1833	10-27-1895	046	MCCAULEY, William	
				046		
James TIERNEY	Co. Kings	1830	1896	046	FARLEY, Mary	Born In Kings Co. Ireland
Mary FARLEY Tierney	Co. Cavan	1830	1893	046	TIERNEY, James	Born Co. Cavan, Ireland
				046		
Joseph ADAMS		1841	1924	046	_____, Mary	
Mary ____ ADAMS		1843	1922	046	ADAMS, Joseph	
				046		

Name	Born	Died	Code	Index Name	Notes
Francis SHORKEY	1855		046	SHORKEY, Francis	
Selina SHORKEY	1857	1892	046	SHORKEY, Selina	
			046		
GALVIN FAMILY			046	GALVIN, Family	(Large monument - 10 feet - but NOI DOB/DOD)
Mother	1833	1900	046	GALVIN, Mother	
Father	1828	1901	046	GALVIN, Father	
Dennis J. GALVIN	1868	1892	046	GALVIN, Dennis J.	
Ellen GALVIN	1867	1894	046	GALVIN, Ellen	
Mary A. GALVIN	1857	1896	046	GALVIN, Mary A.	
Katherine GALVIN	1874	1897	046	GALVIN, Katherine	
			046		
Charles A. COLLINS	1842	1915	046	DONNELLY, Ellen	(GAR) Co. C, 7th VT Vols
Ellen DONNELLY Collins	1839	1927	046	COLLINS, Charles A.	
			046		
Michael STAPLETON	1823	1895	046	CARROLL, Anna	
Anna CARROLL Stapleton	1822	1888	046	STAPLETON, Michael	
Patrick Henry STAPLETON	1854	1885	046	STAPLETON, Patrick Henry	
James E. STAPLETON	1852	1901	046	STAPLETON, James E.	
Andrew T. STAPLETON	1856	1926	046	STAPLETON, Andrew T.	
			046		
Michael BOYLAN	1817	1892	046	_____, Hannah	
Hannah _____ BOYLAN	1817	1897	046	BOYLAN, Michael	
Michael BOYLAN Jr.	1855	1890	046	_____, Mary A.	
Mary A. _____ BOYLAN	1847	1942	046	BOYLAN, Michael Jr.	
			046		
GRACE FAMILY			046	GRACE, Family	
Mother	1818	1890	046	GRACE, Mother	(NOI Names of Mother,Father)
Father	1806	1850	046	GRACE, Father	
			046		
Jeremiah DOODY	1817	1904	046	_____, Mary	
Mary _____ DOODY	1812	1906	046	DOODY, Jeremiah	
John H. DOODY	1853	1940	046	FOOTE, Lillian V.	
Lillian V. FOOTE Doody	1861	1933	046	DOODY, John H.	
			046		
William ROACH	72 Years	09-22-1877	046	CONNOR, Catherine	
Catherine CONNOR	70 Years	04- -1879	046	ROACH, William	
			046		
John ROACH	93 Years	12-03-1894	046	CONNOR, Margaret	
Margaret CONNOR	86 Years	12-07-1894	046	ROACH, John	
Hannorah ROACH	18 Years	07-07-1855	046	ROACH, Hannorah	(Dau of John & Margaret Roach)
Edward ROACH	28 Years	03-24-1866	046	ROACH, Edward	(Son of John & Margaret Roach)
James ROACH	27 Years	03-17-1873	046	ROACH, James	" " " " " "
John ROACH	32 Years	09- -1872	046	ROACH, John	" " " " " "
Dennis ROACH	13 Years	03-24-1866	046	ROACH, Dennis	" " " " " "
William ROACH	4 Years	09-03-1854	046	ROACH, William	" " " " " "

Name	Place	Age/Birth	Death	Code	Index	Notes
				046		
Thomas SULLIVAN		63 Years	08-02-1903	046	CARNEY, Mary	
Mary CARNEY Sullivan		78 Years	10-19-1918	046	SULLIVAN, Thomas	
Mary E. ______ RYAN		34 Years	02-23-1908	046	RYAN, W.H.	(NOI W. H. Ryan)
				046	______, Mary	
Anna G. SULLIVAN		83 Years	09-01-1959	046	SULLIVAN, Anna G.	
				046		
Bridget MCNULLA		78 Years	04-14-1933	046	MCNULLA, Bridget	
John MCNULLA		21 Years	10-13-1878	046	MCNULLA, John	
Ellen MCNULLA		23 Years	01-15-1879	046	MCNULLA, Ellen	
Mary MCNULLA McLaughlin		39 Years	09-08-1885	046	MCLAUGHLIN, James	(NOI James McLaughlin)
				046	MCNULLA, Mary	
Michael MCNULLA		55 Years	09-11-1867	046	______, Bridget	
Bridget ______ MCNULLA		70 Years	03-02-1895	046	MCNULLA, Michael	
				046		
Ellen GILL McMahon		36 Years	10-28-1899	046	MCMAHON, John	(NOI John McMahon)
				046	GILL, Ellen	
				046		
Peter TULLY	Co. Cavan	80 Years	08-03-1889	046	MCWILLIAMS, Isabelle	Of County Cavan, Ireland
Isabelle MCWILLIAMS Tully		85 Years	01-21-1905	046	TULLY, Peter	
				046		
Patrick MULLIGAN		1829	1912	046	HALEY, Mary L.	(GAR-Try Co.E, 14th Rgt,VtVol)
Mary L. HALEY Mulligan		1840	1914	046	MULLIGAN, Patrick	
Jane MULLIGAN		1831	1911	046	MULLIGAN, Jane	
Catherine J. MULLIGAN		1872	1887	046	MULLIGAN, Catherine J.	
Mary A. MULLIGAN		1868	1951	046	MULLIGAN, Mary A.	
Jerome B. MULLIGAN		1864	1910	046	MULLIGAN, Jerome B.	
John P. MULLIGAN		1877	1907	046	MULLIGAN, John P.	
Anne C. MULLIGAN		1883	1927	046	MULLIGAN, Anne C.	
				046		
Andrew TULLY		68 Years	04-21-1916	046	TULLY, Andrew	
George E. TULLY		1868	1928	046	TULLY, George E.	
Margaret TULLY		1845	1930	046	TULLY, Margaret	
Mary F. TULLY		1857	1937	046	TULLY, Mary F.	
				046		
Timothy SULLIVAN		03-30-1843	04-24-1903	046	______, Mary E.	
Mary E. ______ SULLIVAN		03-14-1851	04-25-1893	046	SULLIVAN, Timothy	
				046		
Daniel SULLIVAN		04-13-1812	12-02-1893	046	TWOMEY, Mary	
Mary TWOMEY Sullivan		03-25-1814	05-17-1893	046	SULLIVAN, Daniel	
Humphrey C. SULLIVAN		1850	1926	046	SULLIVAN, Humphrey C.	
Mary L. SULLIVAN		1857	1928	046	SULLIVAN, Mary L.	
				046		
Thomas MCGUIRE		66Y 12D	06-18-1900	046	______, Kate	
Kate ______ MCGUIRE		45Y 7M 5D	10-23-1885	046	MCGUIRE, Thomas	

Charles MCGUIRE	64 Years	06-10-1928	046	MCGUIRE, Charles	
			046		
James MCANNULLA	88 Years	04-29-1883	046	____, Isabella	
Isabella ____ MCANNULLA	67 Years	12-10-1874	046	MCANNULLA, James	
			046		
James BROWN	95 Years	12-05-1895	046	____, Mary	
Mary ______ BROWN	75 Years	01-26-1877	046	BROWN, James	
William BROWN	47 Years	09-09-1883	046	BROWN, William	
			046		
Michael MACK	03-27-1856	10-12-1915	046	FITTS, Mary	
Mary FITTS Mack	09-03-1858	03-27-1923	046	MACK, Michael	
			046		
MACK			046	MACK	(Memorial Reads MACK-MCNERTNEY FROM IRELAND - PERPETUAL CARE But NOI)
MCNERTNEY			046	MCNERTNEY	
			046		
			046		
Michael MACK	1812	1865	046	NESTER, Bridget Mary	
Bridget Mary NESTER Mack	1816	1897	046	MACK, Michael	
William MACK	1853	1865	046	MACK, William	
Fannie MACK	1866	1885	046	MACK, Fannie	
Katherine MACK Mylott	1862	1938	046	MYLOTT, Bartholomew	(NOI Bartholomew Mylott)
			046	MACK, Katherine	
			046		
Thomas BUCKLEY	1826	1919	046	ROACH, Elizabeth	
Elizabeth ROACH Buckley	1836	1921	046	BUCKLEY, Thomas	
			046		
James ROACH	87 Years	12-28-1896	046	____, Mary	
Mary _____ ROACH	83 Years	05-07-1883	046	ROACH, James	
Thomas ROACH	05- -1831	01-09-1897	046	ROACH, Thomas	
Catharine ROACH	43 Years	09-02-1881	046	ROACH, Catharine	
			046		
Michael HALPIN	1842	1916	046	ROCH, Hannah	
Hannah ROCH Halpin	1842	1923	046	HALPIN, Michael	
			046		
James O'CONNOR	04-04-1829	10-08-1902	046	HALPIN, Mary	
Mary HALPIN O'Connor	01-13-1841	11-22-1909	046	O'CONNOR, James	
			046		
Patrick HALPIN	73 Years	03-28-1918	046	BARRY, Julia	
Julia BARRY Halpin	76 Years	01-08-1936	046	HALPIN, Patrick	(GAR) Co.G, 8th Vt Vols
			046		
Thomas HALPIN	67 Years	01-13-1872	046	MEEHAN, Bridget	
Bridget MEEHAN Halpin	68 Years	12-18-1879	046	HALPIN, Thomas	
			046		
Sarah Jane MCBRIDE Mullen	26Y 2M	11-02-1882	046	MULLEN, James	Daughter of John & Mary A. McBride. NOI James Mullen
			046	MCBRIDE, Sarah Jane	

Name	Birth/Age	Death	Plot	Spouse/Relation	Notes
			046	MCBRIDE, John	
			046		
Daniel D. SULLIVAN	40Y 1M 10D	11-01-1882	046	CASEY, Mary	
Mary CASEY Sullivan	70Y 5M 28D	10-25-1913	046	SULLIVAN, Daniel D.	
			046		
James BARRY	04-15-1826	02-24-1881	046	ROURKE, Mary	
Mary ROURKE Barry	08-15-1822	05-06-1901	046	BARRY, James	
James G. BARRY	03-04-1852	11-23-1909	046	BARRY, James G.	
Ann ROURKE	73 Years	08-11-1909	046	ROURKE, Ann	
Margaret Elizabeth BARRY	5 Weeks	09-19-1847	046	BARRY, Margaret E.	Dau of James & Mary Barry
Infant Son BARRY	3 Days	11-01-1864	046	BARRY, Infant Son	
Infant Son BARRY	3 Days	11-15-1864	046	BARRY, Infant Son	
Mary Ann BARRY	9 Years	12-09-1864	046	BARRY, Mary Ann	
			046		
Jeremiah O'LEARY	1815	1900	046	KEOGH, Mary	
Mary KEOGH O'Leary	1820	1892	046	O'LEARY, Jeremiah	
Mary O'LEARY	10-22-1840	05-06-1863	046	O'LEARY, Mary	
Jeremiah O'LEARY Jr.	12-16-1855	11-29-1873	046	O'LEARY, Jeremiah Jr.	
Catherine O'LEARY	07-16-1860	06-22-1876	046	O'LEARY, Catherine	
Elizabeth O'LEARY	1857		046	O'LEARY, Elizabeth	
			046		
James SULLIVAN	55 Years	01-29-1860	046	______, Mary	(NOI Mary)
			046	SULLIVAN, James	
Dennis SULLIVAN	13 Years	10-09-1860	046	SULLIVAN, Dennis	Son of James & Mary Sullivan
Timothy SULLIVAN			046	SULLIVAN, Timothy	(Stone badly deteriorated)
			046		
Sarah Ellen O'CONNOR	12-20-1855	12-03-1876	046	O'CONNOR, Sarah Ellen	Dau of Christopher & Mary
			046	O'CONNOR, Christopher	O'Connor(NOI Christopher/Mary)
			046		
Patrick CONDON	66 Years	06-09-1910	046	COLLINS, Mary E.	
Mary E. COLLINS Condon	77 Years	01-07-1922	046	CONDON, Patrick	
John CONDON	10 Months	09-14-1870	046	CONDON, John	
Elizabeth CONDON	14 Years	04-21-1887	046	CONDON, Elizabeth	
James E. COLLINS	19 Years	05-14-1870	046	COLLINS, James E.	
Dennis COLLINS	36 Years	11-12-1853	046	HART, Elizabeth	
Elizabeth HART Collins	76 Years	05-11-1885	046	COLLINS, Dennis	
			046		
Thomas BARRY	40 Years	02-12-1852	046	DALY, Mary	
Mary DALY Barry	63 Years	01-06-1883	046	BARRY, Thomas	
William LARNER	1848	1888	046	BARRY, Maria	
Maria BARRY Larner	1851	1887	046	LARNER, William	
Michael LARNER	1879	1933	046	LARNER, Michael	
			046		
John O'CONNOR	40Y 7M 12D	07-28-1881	046	O'CONNOR, John	Our Father
Maranda L. ____ O'CONNOR	10-26-1829	05-02-1893	046	_____, Maranda L.	

Bridget _____ O'CONNOR	75 Years	08-16-1864	046	_____, Bridget	Wife of John O'Connor
			046		
James B. HUGHES	1842	1912	046	MCMAHON, Katherine	
Katherine MCMAHON Hughes	1850	1912	046	HUGHES, James B.	
			046		
James HALEY	1839	1915	046	HALEY, James	
			046		
Jeremiah F. HALEY	29Y 8M	10-18-1873	046	MCMAHON, Mary A.	
Mary A. MCMAHON Haley	91Y 5M	01-13-1934	046	HALEY, Jeremiah F.	
			046		
Thomas BARRY	1826	1863	046	MCMAHON, Mary A.	
Margaret O'ROURKE Barry	1830	1902	046	HALEY, Jeremiah F.	
M. Elizabeth BARRY	1858	1932	046	BARRY, M. Elizabeth	
Julia A. BARRY	1860	1949	046	BARRY, Julia A.	
			046		
Jeremiah HALEY	44 Years	09-07-1845	046	ROURKE, Catherine	
Catherine ROURKE	70 Years	01-22-1889	046	HALEY, Jeremiah	
James ROURKE	65 Years	12-22-1849	046	ROURKE, James	
			046		
Eugene J. ROURKE	59 Years	01-14-1913	046	MADIGAN, Mary J.	
Mary J. MADIGAN	34 Years	05-21-1885	046	ROURKE, Eugene J.	
Owen ROURKE	84 Years	08-28-1905	046	ROURKE, Owen	
			046		
Elizabeth _____ ROURKE	70 Years	12-01-1892	046	_____, Elizabeth	
Mary Ann ROURKE	03-09-1850	03-09-1880	046	ROURKE, Mary Ann	
			046		
James FARRELL	07-25-1831	11-29-1903	046	_____, Honora	
Honora _____ ROURKE	08-21-1828	06-18-1882	046	FARRELL, James	
			046		
James SMITH	1848		046	MACK, Mary	
Mary MACK Smith	1840	1912	046	SMITH, James	
			046		
Mary MITCHENE Burns	74 Years	12-02-1900	046	BURNS, James	(NOI James Burns
			046	MITCHENE, Mary	
			046		
Dennis MCHUGH	1832	1922	046	_____, Elizabeth	
Elizabeth ____ MCHUGH	1847	1912	046	MCHUGH, Dennis	
			046		
Patrick CARROLL	1833	1907	046	BARRY, Julia	
Julia BARRY Carroll	1838	1916	046	CARROLL, Patrick	
			046		
MCHUGH FAMILY			046	MCHUGH, Family	(NOI DOB/DOD)
George MCHUGH			046	MCHUGH, George	
Catherine _____ MCHUGH			046	_____, Catherine_	
			046		

Name	Born / Age	Died	Code	Relative	Notes
Joseph MURRAY	07-13-1840	06-24-1928	046	MURRAY, Delia	
Delia _____ MURRAY	10-20-1844	03-12-1911	046	MURRAY, Joseph	
Peter ADAM	1797	1875	046	ADAM, Ester	
Ester ADAM	1800	1893	046	ADAM, Peter	
			046		
William COOLIHAN	63 Years	04-26-1882	046	_____, Margaret	
Margaret ____ COOLIHAN	64 Years	08-05-1882	046	COOLIHAN, William	
Willie COOLIHAN	21 Years	08-05-1875	046	COOLIHAN, Willie	Son of William & Margaret
Phelps COOLIHAN	1857	1921	046	COOLIHAN, Phelps	Son of William & Margaret
Alice COOLIHAN	1857	1934	046	COOLIHAN, Alice	
			046		
			046		
Thomas GALVIN	1855	1936	046	GALVIN, Thomas	
Henry GALVIN	1855	1932	046	GALVIN, Henry	
			046		
John GALVIN	19 Years	07-06-1863	046	GALVIN, John	Member of Co. K, 1st VT CAV.
			046		Killed Between Hagerstown &
			046		Williamsport, MD. (GAR)
Patrick GALVIN	68 Years	11-06-1916	046	GALVIN, Patrick	
John GALVIN	40 Years	12-12-1854	046	_____, Margaret	
Margaret _____ GALVIN	94 Years	12-16-1906	046	GALVIN, John	
			046		
George J. HODGES	06-01-1846	07-05-1924	046	GRANT, Rachael	
Rachael GRANT Hodges	05-15-1849	08-31-1919	046	HODGES, George J.	
			046		
James SULLIVAN	1815	1894	046	_____, Margaret	A Veteran of Two Wars, 1846 &
Margaret ___ SULLIVAN	53 Years	01-23-1883	046	SULLIVAN, James	1861. 2nd VT Infantry (GAR)
			046		(Mexican War)
			046		
Patrick CONDON	80 Years	12-02-1917	046	HODGES, Elizabeth	
Elizabeth HODGES Condon	74 Years	02-26-1916	046	CONDON, Patrick	
John CONDON	58 Years	02-08-1866	046	BARRY, Ellen	
Ellen BARRY Condon	59 Years	05-28-1878	046	CONDON, John	
Ellen CONDON	32 Years	06-26-1874	046	CONDON, Ellen	
Mary CONDON	21 Years	11-20-1865	046	CONDON, Mary	
Julia CONDON	14 Years	05-06-1865	046	CONDON, Julia	
Kattie CONDON	8 Years	06-02-1865	046	CONDON, Kattie	
			046		
Charles TULLEY	1850	1936	046	KIELY, Anna	
Anna KIELY Tulley	1863	1955	046	TULLEY, Charles	
			046		
John BAXTER	61 Years	06-28-1884	046	____, Mary E.	
Mary E. ____ BAXTER	80 Years	11-08-1886	046	BAXTER, John	
			046		
Nancy Eleanor BROWN	12-25-1830	04-29-1887	046	BROWN, Frank	(NOI Frank Brown)

			046	_____, Nancy	
			046		
Daniel J. O'CONNELL	1858	1921	046	CAREY, Margaret	
Margaret CAREY O'Connell	1861	19__	046	O'CONNELL, Daniel J.	
			046		
James TULLY	1853	1930	046	O'CONNELL, Margaret M.	
Margaret M. O'CONNELL Tully	1861	1940	046	TULLY, James	
			046		
James HALNON	87 Years	04-04-1885	046	HALNON, James	
John HALNON	75 Years	09-02-1907	046	TULLY, Isabelle	
Isabelle TULLY Halnon	85 Years	10-09-1936	046	HALNON, John	
			046		
William HALNON	1841	1926	046	_____, Elizabeth	
Elizabeth ____ HALNON	1850	1933	046	HALNON, William	
			046		
John J. O'CONNELL	1850	1922	046	_____, Nellie	
Nellie ____ O'CONNELL			046	O'CONNELL, John	(NOI Nellie O'Connell)
			046		
James HINCKS	1849	1920	046	SMITH, Mary	
Mary SMITH Hincks	1852	1911	046	HINCKS, James	
Sarah H. MCCORMACK	1881	1983	046	MCCORMACK, Sarah H.	
			046		
Nelson SEYMOUR	1846	1879	046	SEYMOUR, Nelson	
Catherine SEYMORE Kyle	1846	1919	046	SEYMORE, Catherine	(Does not say she is spouse)
			046		
John CAFFREY	75 Years	01-25-1889	046	MCCANN, Bridget	
Bridget MCCANN Caffrey	84 Years	05-29-1907	046	CAFFREY, John	
John T. CAFFREY	17 Years	12-21-1861	046	CAFFREY, John T.	
Wm. CAFFREY	62 Years	07-27-1913	046	CAFFREY, Wm.	
Anne Elizabeth CAFFREY	75 Years	08- -1924	046	CAFFREY, Anne E.	(Does not say if spouse or Sister of Wm. Caffrey)
			046		
Israel SHACKETT	01-12-1840		046	VASSAU, Alicia	
Alicia VASSAU Shackett	05-11-1845	06-17-1903	046	SHACKETT, Israel	
			046		
Patrick J. COSTELLO	66 Years	12-16-1910	046	DALTON, Esther	
Esther DALTON Costello	77 Years	10-11-1960	046	COSTELLO, Patrick J.	
			046		
William L. COSTELLO	20 Years	11-24-1900	046	COSTELLO, William L.	
Edward F. COSTELLO	49 Years	06-11-1921	046	COSTELLO, Edward F.	
Leo T. COSTELLO	51 Years	06-04-1945	046	COSTELLO, Leo T.	
			046		
John FOLEY	03-16-1849	12-29-1905	046	MANOR, Jennie E.	
Jennie E. MANOR Foley	06-10-1861	06-12-1919	046	FOLEY, John	
			046		
Charles E. GEE	09-06-1854	02-12-1895	046	GEE, Charles E.	

				046		
Edward OAKES		27 Years	04-21-1866	046	OAKES, Edward	
				046		
Mary MORONEY			03-24-1872	046	MORONEY, Mary	Dau of Patrick & Elizabeth
				046	MORONEY, Patrick	Moroney (NOI DOB or age)
				046		
Ellen COSGROVE		5 Months	08-03-1837	046	COSGROVE, Ellen	
Mary COSGROVE		04Y 13M	04-13-1843	046	COSGROVE, Mary	
William COSGROVE		06Y 03M	09-18-1843	046	COSGROVE, William	
Patrick COSGROVE		11 Years	04-02-1843	046	COSGROVE, Patrick	
				046		
Michael MEHAN		67 Years	03-07-1847	046	MEHAN, Michael	
				046		
Mary ____ CROKER		19 Years	05-01-1844	046	CROKER, John	(NOI John Croker)
				046	____, Mary	
				046		
Edward MEHAN		03 Years	10-13-1852	046	MEHAN, Edward	Son Of John & Maria Mehan
				046	MEHAN, John	
				046		
Clarinda STORY		09 Months	04-28-1849	046	STORY, Clarinda	Dau of Jerome & Sop___ Story
				046	STORY, Jerome	
				046		
Edward WILKINSON		13 Years	07-06-1841	046	WILKINSON, Edward	Son of George & Eliza Wilkin-
				046	WILKINSON, George	son. Drowned
				046		son. Drowned
John BUCKLEY		63 Years	04-09-1886	046	____, Catherine	
Catherine ____ BUCKLEY				046	BUCKLEY, John	(Cannot read DOB/DOD)
				046		
James GORMAN		65 Years	03-08-1871	046	____, Mary	(NOI Mary)
Eliza Jane GORMAN		15 Years	07-14-1853	046	GORMAN, Eliza Jane	Dau of James & Mary Gorman

Old Catholic Burial Ground, Middlebury, VT. Off Hillcrest Street - West Of Village

NAME	POB	DOB/AGE	DOD	CEM	SPOUSE/INDEX	INSCRIPTION
Charles TURNER		66 Years	1926	047	____, Elizabeth	
Nancy GRANT Turner		55 Years	1933	047	HALNON, William	
				047		
John DORSEY		35 Years	04-03-1843	047	____, Julia	
Julia ____ DORSEY		45 Years	02-06-1850	047	DORSEY, John	
				047		
Martin DORSEY		17 Years	10-11-1848	047	DORSEY, Martin	
				047		

CAMPBELL FAMILY			1850	047	CAMPBELL, Family	Three Infants of J&R Campbell
				047		
James ROACH		16 Years	09-11-1854	047	ROACH, James	Children of William-Catherine
Edward ROACH		16 Years	09-12-1854	047	ROACH, Edward	Roach.(NOI William-Catherine)
Mary ROACH		20 Years	10-11-1861	047	ROACH, Mary	
				047	ROACH, William	
				047		
Patrick DUNIHUE		24 Years	04-04-1862	047	DUNIHUE, Patrick	
				047		
Cornelius FARLEY	Co. Cavan	71 Years	02-07-1868	047	FARLEY, Cornelius	Native of Co. Cavan, Ireland
				047		
Dennis CARMODY	Co. Clare	60 Years	04-15-1869	047	CARMODY, Dennis	Native of Parish Kilmurry-McMahon, Co. Clare, Ireland
				047		
				047		
Thomas O'DONNELL	Co. Clare	45 Years	11-29-1869	047	CARMODY, Ellen	Native of Parish Kilmurry-McMahon, Co. Clare, Ireland
				047		
Ellen CARMODY O'Donnell	Co. Clare	44 Years	02-22-1869	047	O'DONNELL, Thomas	Native of Parish Kilmurry-McMahon, Co. Clare, Ireland
				047		
				047		
				047		
Morris GREGG	Co. Cork	67 Years	11-19-1899	047	GREGG, Morris	A Native Of Blackpool, A Suburb Of Cork Ireland
				047		
MANNY Family Manny This stone is unique in that it contains information on the family of William & Jane Knear MANNY. It is not evident that Wm. & Jane and others came to this country, but some did.				047	MANNY, Family	Suburb Of Cork Ireland
				047		
				047		
				047		
				047		
				047		
				047		
				047		
				047		
William MANNY	Co. Tyrone			047	KNEAR, Jane	Natives of Sesanore, Tille-valley, Tyrone, Ireland.
Jane KNEAR Manny	Co. Tyrone			047	MANNY, William	(Seskinore, Tullyvally)
				047		
MANNY Daughters:				047	MANNY, Daughters	(Seskinore, Tullyvally)
				047		
Jane MANNY McClean	Co. Tyrone			047	MCCLEAN, Jane Manny	Died In Ireland
Mary MANNY Lisco	Co. Tyrone	1793	1873	047	LISCO, George	(NOI George Lisco)
				047	MANNY, Mary	
Isabella MANNY Southwell	Co. Tyrone			047	SOUTHWELL, Robert	(NOI Robert Southwell)
				047	MANNY, Isabella	
Nancy MANNY Beebe	Co. Tyrone			047	BEEBE, Henry	(NOI Henry Beebe)
				047	MANNY, Nancy	
				047		
MANNY Sons:				047		

				047	MANNY, Sons	(Seskinore, Tullyvally)
Daniel MANNY	Co. Tyrone	1785	1865	047	MANNY, Daniel	Died at Vicars, Quebec
William MANNY	Co. Tyrone	1795	1871	047	____, Anne	
Anne ____ MANNY		1816	1859	047	MANNY, William	
Robert MANNY	Co. Tyrone			047	MACNEIL, Mary	Died at Half Day, Illinois
Hugh MANNY	Co. Tyrone	1801	1802	047	MANNY, Hugh	(NOI Mary MacNeil)
Mary MACNEIL Manny				047	MACNEIL, Mary	
Robert K. MANNY		1826	1849	047	MANNY, Robert K.	Children of Hugh and Mary
Elizabeth MANNY		1830	1849	047	MANNY, Elizabeth	McNeil MANNY
Margaret MANNY		1834	1849	047	MANNY, Margaret	
				047		
Julia Joanna LATREMOUILLE	Co. Limerick	05- -1796	07-18-1822	047	LATREMOUILLE, Nicholas	Born in the City of Limerick (NOI Nicholas Latremouille)

Village Burial Ground, Middletown Springs, Vermont

NAME	POB	DOB/AGE	DOD	CEM	SPOUSE/INDEX	INSCRIPTION
William K. NORTON		01-24-1822	05-29-1891	048	CLARK, Helen	
Helen CLARK Norton		1824	1918	048	NORTON, William K.	
William H. NORTON		08-15-1855	07-07-1884	048	NORTON, William H.	
				048		
Edward S. HARRINGTON		1852	1914	048	HARRINGTON, Edward S.	
Julia A. JENNING Harrington		1824	1906	048	JENNING, Julia A.	
				048		
James W. YALE		1832	1912	048	CARRIGAN, Mary A.	
Mary A. CARRIGAN Yale		1840	1920	048	YALE, James W.	
				048		
James MATHEWS		09-25-1850	01-17-1923	048	CAIRNS, Janette	
Janette CAIRNS Mathews		08-27-1852	10-23-1937	048	MATHEWS, James	
				048		
Samuel T. KELLEY		08-31-1847	12-09-1921	048	LOBDELL, Julia A.	
Julia A. LOBDELL Kelley		06-02-1850	06-01-1938	048	KELLEY, Samuel T.	
				048		
Thomas S. MCLOUGHLIN		1847	1930	048	CREDY, Mary	
Julia KILBOURN McLoughlin		1846	1941	048	STONE, Henry	
				048		
William B. O'HARE		05-10-1848	08-10-1910	048	WELLS, Lilian A.	Co. A 6th Rgt Vt Vols (GAR)
Lilian A. WELLS O'Hare		06-18-1866	04-12-1936	048	O'HARE, William B.	
				048		
Thomas MURDOCK		1833	1908	048	MCCLELLAND, Mary	
Mary MCCLELLAND Murdock		1840	1918	048	MURDOCK, Thomas	
				048		

NAME	POB	DOB/AGE	DOD	CEM	SPOUSE/INDEX	INSCRIPTION
John CAIRNS		04-18-1817	11-06-1887	048	_____, Agnes	70 Years 6 Months 18 Days
Agnes _____ CAIRNS		07-20-1824	12-10-1903	048	CAIRNS, John	79 Years 4 Months 20 Days
Anstyss CAIRNS		23Y 1M 12D	02-06-1878	048	CAIRNS, Anstyss	
				048		
Calvin LEONARD		1811	1867	048	CASWELL, Abigail	
Abigail CASWELL Leonard		1817	1899	048	LEONARD, Calvin	
				048		
Emmett LEONARD		1846	1919	048	FARWELL, Alice E.	
Alice E. FARWELL Leonard		1848	1926	048	LEONARD, Emmett	
				048		
A. J. LEONARD		1815	1893	048	MOSLEY, Esther	
Esther MOSLEY Leonard		1819	1874	048	LEONARD, A. J.	
Frances LEONARD		1842	1854	048	LEONARD, Francis	
Nettie LEONARD		1858	1861	048	LEONARD, Nettie	
Allie LEONARD		1863	1875	048	LEONARD, Allie	

St. Ann's Cemetery, Middle Road, Milton, VT

NAME	POB	DOB/AGE	DOD	CEM	SPOUSE/INDEX	INSCRIPTION
Israel ROBERTS		1832	1905	049	NOLAN, Sarah	
Sarah NOLAN Roberts		1836	1905	049	ROBERTS, Israel	
				049		
John MURRAY		1839	1914	049	CATARECT, Helen	
Helen CATARECY Murray		1841	1909	049	MURRAY, John	
				049		
Alexander A. BARRY		1852	1937	049	BRUNELLE, Sophia	
Sophia BRUNELLE Barry		1846	1937	049	BARRY, Alexander A.	
				049		
John MACKEY		1812	1898	049	_____, Clara	
Clara ____ MACKEY		1823	1906	049	MACKEY, John	
				049		
Mike CARROLL			1928	049	CARROLL, Mike	
				049		
James O'NEIL				049	O'NEIL, James	(NOI Dates of Birth and Death)
Annie O'NEIL				049	O'NEIL, Annie	Dau of James O'Neil (NOI)
Patrick O'NEIL				049	O'NEIL, Patrick	Son of James O'Neil (NOI)
				049		
James DUFFY		1829	1915	049	FAY, Ann	
Ann FAY Duffy		1830	1883	049	DUFFY, James	
Michael A. DUFFY		1872	1898	049	DUFFY, Michael A.	Erected IMO Michael A. Duffy,
				049		Born in West Georgia, VT and
				049		disappeared in NY City 1898.

			049		
Rose Ellen DUFFY	1859	1876	049	DUFFY, Rose Ellen	
James C. DUFFY	1860	1908	049	DUFFY, James C.	
Mary Ann DUFFY	1862	1865	049	DUFFY, Mary Ann	
Margaret A. DUFFY	1864	1922	049	DUFFY, Margaret A.	
William J. DUFFY	1868	1886	049	DUFFY, William J.	
Patrick S. Duffy, MD	1870	1943	049	HALE, Katherine	Captain, Medical Corp, WWI
Katherine HALE Duffy	1885	1919	049	DUFFY, Patrick S.	
Rose FAY	1836	1889	049	FAY, Rose	
			049		
Patrick ROWLEY	1836	1918	049	_____, Elizabeth	Erected By Patrick Rowley IMO
			049		Of His Dead
Elizabeth _____ ROWLEY	1838	1923	049	ROWLEY, Patrick	
Teresa ROWLEY			049	ROWLEY, Teresa	(NOI DOB/DOD)
Barrett ROWLEY	1864	1907	049	ROWLEY, Barrett	
Frederick H. BARRETT	1862	1904	049	BARRETT, Frederick H.	
			049		
Owen CONLIN	1832	1905	049	CLINTON, Jane	
Jane CLINTON Conlin	1803	1905	049	CONLIN, Owen	
			049		
Emerson Michael KENNEDY	06-20-1848	02-15-1930	049	FLYNN, Mary	
Mary FLYNN KENNEDY	08-10-1851	05-27-1946	049	KENNEDY, Emerson Michael	
			049		
Harry N. DUTTON		10-30-1941	049	KENNEDY, Cecelia	
Cecelia KENNEDY DUTTON		09-07-1940	049	DUTTON, Harry N.	
			049		
Thomas MCMULLEN	03-__-1862	04-__-1949	049	SHERRY, Margaret	
Margaret SHERRY McMullen	11-__-1859	04-__-1917	049	MCMULLEN, Thomas	
Joseph MCMULLEN	11-__-1853	04-__-1941	049	MCMULLEN, Joseph	
Peter J. SMITH	1857	1942	049	HOWLEY, Jennie	
Jennie HOWLEY Smith	1858	1919	049	SMITH, Peter J.	
Bernard J. SMITH	1890	1916	049	SMITH, Bernard J.	
Frankie J. SMITH	1889	1889	049	SMITH, Frankie J.	
Perley J. SMITH	1891	1891	049	SMITH, Perley J.	
			049		
Ellen _____ O'BRIEN	76 Years	11-04-1881	049	O'BRIEN, Patrick	(NOI Patrick O'Brien)
			049	_____, Ellen	
			049		
Sarah A. GRIBBIN	33 Years	01-26-1872	049	GRIBBIN, Sarah A.	
Catharine DUFFY Galvin	43Y 11M	12-03-1875	049	GALVIN, John	(NOI John Galvin)
			049	DUFFY, Catharine	
			049		
Michael MCGEE	47Y5M19D	11-27-1884	049	MCGEE, Michael	
			049		
Margaret BIRNEY McGee	95th Yr	03-11-1897	049	MCGEE, Tole	(NOI Tole McGee. Adjacent to

Name	Born/Age	Died	Code	Index	Notes
			049	BIRNEY, Margaret	Michael McGee W/D 11-27-1884)
			049		
James LOGUE	75 Years	02-28-1869	049	LOGUE, James	
			049		
Thomas TUNNEY	1800	1883	049	DUNN, Ellen	
Ellen DUNN Tunney	1816	1897	049	TUNNEY, Thomas	
Charles E. TUNNEY	1855	1894	049	TUNNEY, Charles E.	
Lewis J. TUNNEY	08-27-1860		049	MELAVEN, Frances M.	
Frances M. MELAVEN Tunney	04-22-1869	05-10-1893	049	TUNNEY, Lewis J.	
			049		
Daniel O'KANE	1851	1930	049	MCGEE, Margaret	
			049	REAVY, Anna J.	
Margaret MCGEE O'Kane	56Y 7M	10-03-1906	049	O'KANE, Daniel	
Anna J. REAVY O'Kane	1869	1932	049	O'KANE, Daniel	
			049		
Michael MCGEE	1837	1870	049	CONLIN, Catherine	
Catherine CONLIN McGee	1831	1890	049	MCGEE, Michael	
James MCGEE	1868	1911	049	MCGEE, James	
John MCGEE	1861	1926	049	O'CONNOR, Margaret	
Margaret O'CONNOR McGee	1858	1911	049	MCGEE, John	
			049		
Robert NULTY	1836	1913	049	____, Theresa M.	
Theresa M.______ NULTY	59Y 4M	05-30-1899	049	NULTY, Robert	
			049		
Dennis DONAHOE	57TH Yr	03-06-1865	049	DONAHOE, Dennis	
			049		
Joseph DONAHOE	28TH Yr	06-17-1867	049	DONAHOE, Joseph	
			049		
James H. MELAVEN	1832	1917	049	HOWRIGAN, Alice	
Alice HOWRIGAN Melaven	1849	1921	049	MELAVEN, James H.	
Eugene E. MELAVEN	1857	1888	049	MELAVEN, Eugene E.	
			049		
Martin DOUGHERTY	73 Years	04-21-1883	049	____, Catharine	
Catharine ____ DOUGHERTY	43 Years	12-29-1866	049	DOUGHERTY, Martin	
Catharine ____ DOUGHERTY	25 Years	05-07-1842	049	DOUGHERTY, Martin	
Andrew DOUGHERTY	21 Years	11-26-1864	049	DOUGHERTY, Andrew	(GAR) Son of Martin--Catharine
			049		Killed in Danville, VA. Try Co
			049		D., 10th Rgt, VtVols
			049		
			049		
Peter KING	1839	1900	049	EUSTACE, Esther	(GAR) Co. B., 1st VT Cavalry
Esther EUSTACE King	1843	1907	049	KING, Peter	
			049		
Patrick DUFFY	1820	1901	049	MAHONEY, Mary Ann	
Mary Ann MAHONBEY Duffy	1829	1906	049	DUFFY, Patrick	

Name	Place	Age / Born	Died	Code	Index Name	Notes
				049		
John CAIN		70 Years	03-21-1875	049	CAIN, John	
				049		
Peter LANIGAN		28 Years	06-12-1882	049	LANIGAN, Peter	S/O Wm. & H. Lanigan (NOI)
				049	LANIGAN, William	
				049		
James LANIGAN		17Y _M 29D	09-10-1873	049	LANIGAN, James	S/O Wm. & H. Lannigan. (Stone Broken. Deteriorated. NOI)
				049		
				049		
Mary RAFFERTY		75 Years	08-12-1892	049	RAFFERTY, Mary	(Engraved on Back of Stone - "Wm & Mary O'Neill". (NOI)
William O'NEILL				049	O'NEILL, William	
Nary _____ O'NEILL				049	_____, Mary	
				049		
John KAIN		1838		049	PLUNKETT, Ellen	
Ellen PLUNKETT Kain		1840	1912	049	KAIN, John	
Anne KAIN		1873	1874	049	KAIN, Anne	
George H. KAIN		1884	1898	049	KAIN, George H.	
Francis C. KAIN		1889	1896	049	KAIN, Francis C.	
Patrick PLUNKETT		1805	1875	049	KIRK, Mary	
Mary KIRK Plunkett		1804	1877	049	PLUNKETT, Patrick	
Thomas PLUNKETT		1838	1875	049	PLUNKETT, Thomas	
John PLUNKETT		1840	1883	049	PLUNKETT, John	
Bridget PLUNKETT		1836	1904	049	PLUNKETT, Bridget	
James PLUNKETT		1843	1908	049	PLUNKETT, James	
				049		
James MOILES		77Y 2M	06-14-1870	049	MOILES, James	
				049		
Catharine DUNN		29 Years	01-15-1862	049	DUNN, Catharine	Dau Of John & Margarite Dunn.
				049	DUNN, John	
				049		
Patrick BYRNE		60 Years	09-27-1854	049	BYRNE, Patrick	(Stone worn. Age appears to be '60')
				049		
				049		
Patrick BYRNES		37 Years	09-08-1864	049	BYRNES, Patrick	
				049		
Thomas BYRN	Co. Louth	55 Years	05-11-1872	049	BYRN, Thomas	
				049		
				049		(With the exception of a BYRNE
				049		
"BYRNE"				049		
Catherine BYRNE				049	BYRNE, Catherine	there were no surnames listed
James BYRNE				049	BYRNE, James	for this family nor were Dates
Agnes BYRNE				049	BYRNE, Agnes	of birth or death listed)
Baby BYRNE				049	BYRNE, Baby	(NOI)
Patrick BYRNE				049	BYRNE, Patrick	(NOI)

Father BYRNE			049	BYRNE, Father	(NOI)
Mother BYRNE			049	BYRNE, Mother	(NOI)
Charles BYRNE			049	BYRNE, Charles	(NOI)
Jennie BYRNE			049	BYRNE, Jennie	(NOI)
Alice BYRNE			049	BYRNE, Alice	(NOI)
Mary BYRNE			049	BYRNE, Mary	(NOI)
			049		
John CLINTON	1835	1908	049	O'KANE, Eliza	
Eliza O'KANE Clinton	1853	1909	049	CLINTON, John	
Henry CLINTON	1839	1906	049	O'KANE, Bridget	
Bridget O'KANE Clinton	1856	1926	049	CLINTON, Henry	
John CLINTON	1784	1887	049	KERN, Margaret	
Margaret KERN Clinton	1810	1867	049	CLINTON, John	
			049		
Michael DONAHUE	1833	1917	049	MATTAMORE, Ann	
Ann MATTAMORE Donahue	1827	1880	049	DONAHUE, Michael	
James DONAHUE	1856	1913	049	DONAHUE, James	
Josephine E. DONAHUE	1865	1949	049	DONAHUE, Josephine E.	
			049		
James A. DONAHUE	1853	1929	049	NEENAN, Mary A.	
Mary A. NEENAN Donahue	1856	1925	049	DONAHUE, James	
			049		
Francis MCMULLEN	1812	1909	049	HENDERSON, Elizabeth	
Elizabeth HENDERSON McMullen	1823	1898	049	MCMULLEN, Francis	
Sarah MCMULLEN	1864	1866	049	MCMULLEN, Sarah	
James MCMULLEN	1866	1884	049	MCMULLEN, James	
John MCMULLEN	1856	1927	049	MCMULLEN, John	
Alexander MCMULLEN	1862	1923	049	SMITH, Linda S.	
Linda S. SMITH McMullen	1870	1926	049	MCMULLEN, Alexander	
			049		
Mary MOREN Howley	61Y 3M	11-20-1877	049	HOWLEY, James	(NOI James Howley).
			049	MOREN, Mary	
			049		
Patrick MCGRATH	1810	1892	049	TUBERTY, Mary	
Mary TUBERTY McGrath	1819	1899	049	MCGRATH, Patrick	
Michael MCGRATH	1842	1917	049	MCMULLEN, Mary	
Mary MCMULLEN McGrath	1852	1938	049	MCGRATH, Michael	
Bridget MCGRATH	20Y 3M	04-19-1872	049	MCGRATH, Bridget	
Patrick MCGRATH	21Y 7M	08-19-1873	049	MCGRATH, Patrick	
			049		
Francis McMullen, JR	1858	1904	049	MCNALLY, Eliza	
Eliza MCNALLY McMullen	1864	1905	049	MCMULLEN, Francis Jr.	
			049		
John KING	78 Years	05-21-1881	049	KING, John	

St. Isadore's Cemetery - Montgomery Center, Vt (On Vt. Route 242 West, Route 105, 1 mile from Village)

NAME	POB	DOB/AGE	DOD	CEM	SPOUSE/INDEX	INSCRIPTION
Hannora DUGAN Hayes		72Y 10M	12-15-1891	050	HAYES, John	(NOI John Hayes)
				050	DUGAN, Hannora	
				050		
Mary MACKAY Gilmore		1841	1896	050	GILMORE, John A.	(NOI John Gilmore
				050	MACKAY, Mary	
				050		
Harry SMITH	England	12-28-1865	05-01-1923	050	SMITH, Harry	

St. Augustine's Cemetery, Montpelier, VT. Lincoln Avenue at top of Ewing Street

NAME	POB	DOB/AGE	DOD	CEM	SPOUSE/INDEX	INSCRIPTION
Martin FITZGERALD		55 Years	03-28-1865	051	FITZGERALD, Martin	
				051		
Jeremiah MAHONEY		1836	1919	051	FINN, Ellen	
Ellen FINN Mahoney		1843	1901	051	MAHONEY, Jeremiah	
				051		
John MAHONEY		1805	1870	051	MCCARTHY, Julia	
Julia MCCARTHY Mahoney		1807	1874	051	MAHONEY, John	
Their Children				051		
Ellen MAHONEY		1831	1847	051	MAHONEY, Ellen	
Elizabeth MAHONEY		1833	1905	051	MAHONEY, Elizabeth	
Mary MAHONEY		1835	1857	051	MAHONEY, Mary	
Julia MAHONEY		1838	1843	051	MAHONEY, Julia	
John MAHONEY		1840	1843	051	MAHONEY, John	
Julia A. MAHONEY		1844	1861	051	MAHONEY, Julia A.	
Thomas A. MAHONEY		1846	1903	051	MAHONEY, Thomas A.	
				051		
William M. MURPHY		1848		051	SULLIVAN, Bridget	(NOI DOD William Murphy)
Bridget SULLIVAN Murphy		1856	1918	051	MURPHY, William M.	
				051		
Timothy CORCORAN		1855	1934	051	______, Anna	
Anna ______ CORCORAN		1854	1929	051	CORCORAN, Timothy	
				051		
Bernard CARNEY		1854	1919	051	RYAN, Margaret J.	
Margaret J. RYAN Carney		1861	1929	051	CARNEY, Bernard	
				051		

Name	Origin	Born/Age	Died	Code	Index Name	Notes
Ann TIMMONS		1830	1901	051	TIMMONS, Ann	
				051		
David CALLAHAN		32 Years	12-01-1879	051	CALLAHAN, David	Died In Moretown (VT)
David H. CALLAHAN				051	CALLAHAN, David H.	
Josephine J. CALLAHAN				051	CALLAHAN, Josephine J.	
				051		
Patrick CALLAHAN		1843	1929	051	PRICE, Catherine	
Catherine PRICE Callahan		1842	1925	051	CALLAHAN, Patrick	
				051		
John GUARE		1832	1900	051	MCMAHON, Sarah	
Sarah MCMAHON Guare		1844	1926	051	GUARE, John	
				051		
John PORTAL	Co. Clare	87 Years	09-17-1911	051	TIERNEY, Margaret	Natives Of Co. Clare, Ireland
Margaret TIERNEY Portal	Co. Clare	83 Years	07-26-1904	051	PORTAL, John	Natives Of Co. Clare, Ireland
				051		
Eliza PORTALL		9Y 6M	11-20-1862	051	PORTALL, Eliza	Dau Of John & Margaret Portall
				051		
John CARROLL	Co. Kerry	76 Years	08-16-1866	051	TIERNEY, Bridget	Native Of Co. Kerry, Ireland
Bridget TIERNEY Carroll	Co. Clare	63 Years	03-09-1875	051	CARROLL, John	Native Of Co. Clare, Ireland
				051		
William MARSHALL		1822	1864	051	MARSHALL, William	(Does not say if Mary was the
Mary MARSHALL		1839	1911	051	MARSHALL, Mary	spouse of William)
Martin MADDIGAN		56 Years	08-04-1867	051	MADDIGAN, Martin	
				051		
Mary _____ CARROLL		36 Years	05-28-1868	051	CARROLL, Andrew	(NOI Andrew Carroll)
				051	_____, Mary	
				051		
John MOONEY				051	MOONEY, John	(NOI John Mooney)
				051		
Margaret FARRALL McGuffie		23 Years	05-03-1867	051	MCGUFFIE, Christopher	(NOI Christopher McGuffie. A
				051	FARRALL, Margaret	badly deteriorated marker.)
				051		
John MCGUE		71 Years	08-11-1879	051	_____, Catherine	
Catherine _____ MCGUE		49 Years	04-25-1866	051	MCGUE, John	
Thomas MCGUE		33 Years	09-22-1863	051	MCGUE, Thomas	
				051		
Family of John GLEASON				051	GLEASON, Family	
				051		
Patrick GIBBONS		1836	1867	051	_____, Catherine	
Catherine _____ GIBBONS		1833	1906	051	GIBBONS, Patrick	
Gibbons CHILDREN				051	GIBBONS, Children	
Michael GIBBONS				051	GIBBONS, Michael	(NOI DOB-DOD)
David GIBBONS				051	GIBBONS, David	(NOI DOB-DOD)
Katie GIBBONS				051	GIBBONS, Katie	(NOI DOB-DOD)
				051		

Name	Place	Age / Born	Died	Code	Index	Notes
Thomas MORIARTY		68 Years	01-02-1901	051	PRENDIVILLE, Joana	
Joana PRENDIVILLE Moriarity		43 Years	08-05-1883	051	MORIARTY, Thomas	
				051		
John MORIARTY		06-24-1820	02-20-1890	051	LAWLER, Hanora	
Hanora LAWLER Moriarty		01-15-1822	12-31-1888	051	MORIARTY, John	
				051		
Patrick MCMAHON		1828	1917	051	_____, Catherine	
Catherine _____ MCMAHON		1838	1925	051	MCMAHON, Patrick	
Michael MCMAHON		1872	1924	051	MCMAHON, Michael	
Honora MCMAHON		1874	1883	051	MCMAHON, Honora	
James J. MCMAHON		1876	1920	051	MCMAHON, James J.	
John P. MCMAHON		1878	1917	051	MCMAHON, John P.	
Thomas F. MCMAHON		1879	1927	051	MCMAHON, Thomas F.	
				051		
Francis SMITH		1786	1860	051	_____, Marguerite	
Marguerite _____ SMITH		1782	1863	051	SMITH, Francis	
				051		
Alexander CAMPBELL		1839	1905	051	O'CONNOR, Catherine	
Catherine O'CONNOR Campbell		1841	1882	051	CAMPBELL, Alexander	
Infant Child				051	CAMPBELL, Infant	(NOI DOB-DOD)
Alexander CAMPBELL				051	CAMPBELL, Alexander	(NOI DOB-DOD)
Katie CAMPBELL				051	CAMPBELL, Katie	(NOI DOB-DOD)
Frank CAMPBELL				051	CAMPBELL, Frank	(NOI DOB-DOD)
Nora CAMBELL				051	CAMBELL, Nora	(NOI DOB-DOD)
Jennie CAMPBELL		1865	1887	051	CAMPBELL, Jennie	
				051		
Patrick CORRY		84Y 6M	05-01-1886	051	_____, Mary	
Mary _____ CORRY		84Y 5M	03-12-1891	051	CORRY, Patrick	
Bridget CORRY		26 Years	05-04-1865	051	CORRY, Bridget	
				051		
Margaret MCMILLAN		36 Years	05-12-1886	051	MCMILLAN, Margaret	
				051		
Hugh ROAKS		76 Years	01-11-1871	051	SCOTT, Margaret	
Margaret SCOTT Roaks		63 Years	01-09-1859	051	ROAKS, Hugh	
				051		
Frank BUTTERFLY		58 Years	11-04-1903	051	SAVAGE, Hannah	(GAR) Member of 3rd VT Bat
Hannah SAVAGE Butterfly				051	BUTTERFLY, Frank	
				051		
Michael MCMAHON	Co. Clare	30 Years	03-04-1874	051	MCMAHON, Michael	A Native of Cahir Murphy(Caher
				051	MCMAHON, Thomas	murphy), Parish of Kilmihil,
				051		Co. Clare, Ireland. Erected By
				051		His Brother Thomas
				051		
Catherine A. MCMAHON Killeen		27 Years	10-31-1867	051	KILLEEN, Michael	(NOI Michael Killeen)
				051	MCMAHON, Catherine A.	

Name	Origin	Age/Born	Died	Code	Index	Notes
Ellen MCMAHON		23 Years	01-31-1873	051	MCMAHON, Ellen	
				051		
Margaret GANNON		76 Years	02-11-1916	051	GANNON, Margaret	
Thomas GANNON		87 Years	05-19-1879	051	_____, Margaret	
Margaret _____ GANNON		62 Years	06-08-1875	051	GANNON, Thomas	
				051		
Francis BROWN		1834	1897	051	_____, Mary	
Mary _____ BROWN		1827	1907	051	BROWN, Francis	
Francis BROWN Jr.		1858	1911	051	BROWN, Francis Jr.	
				051		
John BURKE		19 Years	11-05-1861	051	BURKE, John	Died At Laurence Junction, VA
				051		(Probably GAR-not in refrnce.)
Walter BURKE		20 Years	03-05-1863	051	BURKE, Walter	Died At Wolf Run Shore, VA.
				051		(GAR-Try Co. H, 13th Rgt,VtVol
				051		
Nellie F. _____ BURKE		24Y 9M	03-27-1876	051	BURKE, James W.	(NOI James W. Burke)
				051	_____, Nellie F.	
				051		
Catherine MAHER Burke	Co. Tipperary	76 Years	01-22-1892	051	BURKE, John	Native Of Co. Tipperary, Ire.
				051	MAHER, Catherine	(NOI John Burke)
				051		
John MCAVOY		1835	1897	051	MCGRATH, Bridget	
Bridget MCGRATH McAvoy		1834	1879	051	MCAVOY, John	
Ann Eliza MCAVOY		1867	1881	051	MCAVOY, Ann Eliza	
Mary MCGRATH Vincent		1829	1881	051	MCGRATH, Mary	
				051		
Edward DELANY	Co. Tyrone	59 Years	08-28-1862	051	_____, Mary	From The County of Tyrone,
				051	DELANEY, Edward	Ireland. (NOI Mary)
				051		
Charles E. DELANY		21 Years	03-04-1871	051	DELANY, Charles E.	Son Of E & M Delany
Rose Ann DELANY		9Y 6M 9D	09-21-1857	051	DELANY, Rose Ann	Dau Of Edward & Mary Delany
				051		
Timothy SULIVAN		61 Years	05-22-1875	051	SULIVAN, Timothy	
				051		
John GLINNEY	Co. Clare	03-04-1839	01-08-1916	051	SEXTON, Elizabeth	Born In County Clare, Ireland
Elizabeth SEXTON Glinney	Co. Clare	08-17-1840	11-05-1906	051	GLINNEY, John	Born In County Clare, Ireland
				051		
Patrick GLINNEY		1831	1911	051	PAINE, Julia	
				051	DOHERTY, Bridget	
Julia PAINE GLINNEY		1827	1877	051	GLINNEY, Patrick	
Bridget DOHERTY Glinney		1841	1912	051	GLINNEY, Patrick	
				051		
Stephen BURGEN		12-26-1836	12-25-1886	051	SEXTON, Hannah	
Hannah SEXTON Burgen		1838	1908	051	BURGEN, Stephen	
				051		

Name	Place	Born/Age	Died	Code	Index	Notes
Frank M. CORRY		1855	1941	051	COTTER, Margaret	
Margaret COTTER Corry		1857	1938	051	CORRY, Frank M.	
				051		
Hannie SULLIVAN				051	SULLIVAN, Hannie	(Stone down-part missing-NOI)
				051		
Richard WELCH		26 Years	07-04-1867	051	WELCH, Richard	
				051		
Catherine GIBBONS		1812	1876	051	GIBBONS, Catherine	(Relationships not shown for
Nora GIBBONS		1852	1908	051	GIBBONS, Nora	this Gibbons-Stone memorial)
John STONE		1838	1896	051	STONE, John	
Ellen STONE		1846	1917	051	STONE, Ellen	
				051		
William GIBBONS		82 Years	12-27-1912	051	GANNON, Mary	
Mary GANNON Gibbons		56 Years	04-15-1895	051	GIBBONS, William	
David GIBBONS		70 Years	06-22-1863	051	RYAN, Margaret	
Margaret RYAN Gibbons		76 Years	06-09-1878	051	GIBBONS, David	
				051		
Catherine HURLEY			10-04-1894	051	HURLEY, Catherine	(NOI DOB)
Patrick COUGHLAN			05-26-1901	051	HURLEY, Mary	(NOI DOB)
Mary HURLEY Coughlan			08-18-1919	051	COUGHLAN, Patrick	(NOI DOB)
				051		
Patrick PENDER		90 Years	09-11-1905	051	_____, Mary	
Mary _____ PENDER		82 Years	02-25-1898	051	PENDER, Patrick	
Bridget _____ MCCUE		35 Years	10-17-1880	051	MCCUE, Michael	(NOI Michael McCue)
				051	_____, Bridget	
				051		
Mary PENDER		39 Years	08-28-1893	051	PENDER, Mary	
Lawrence PENDER		29 Years	03-28-1894	051	PENDER, Patrick	
				051		
John MCNAMARA	Co. Clare		08-14-1899	051	MCNAMARA, John	Of Lissyscasey (Liscasey),
				051		County Clare, Ireland. RIP
				051		(NOI DOB)
				051		
Nancy KERIN Costello		1839	1881	051	COSTELLO, Michael	(NOI Michael Costello)
				051	KERIN, Nancy	
				051		
John CULLEN			10-01-1880	051	_____, Mary	(Stone is damaged. No DOB)
Mary _____ CULLEN		77Y 4M	02-18-1907	051	CULLEN, John	
				051		
Bridget MCNAMARA		1857	1881	051	MCNAMARA, Bridget	
Ellen MCMAHON		1861	1889	051	MCMAHON, Ellen	
				051		
William DWYER		1827	1881	051	DWYER, William	Native Of County Wexford, Ire.
				051		(Does not indicate if husband
Bridget DWYER		1835	1909	051	DWYER, Bridget	& wife)

Nancy DWYER Mitchell		1869	1900	051	MITCHELL, Nancy DWYER	
				051		
Patrick MCMAHON	Co. Clare	57 Years	07-30-1887	051	MCMAHON, Patrick	A Native Of Lissycasey (Lis-
				051		casey, County Clare, Ireland
				051		
Martin O'DAY		54 Years	12-03-1893	051	O'DAY, Martin	
				051		
James C. FINN		11-07-1851	03-01-1941	051	MEE, Elizabeth	
Elizabeth MEE Finn		05-11-1852	04-11-1948	051	FINN, James C.	
				051		
Patrick CONLIN		1817	1893	051	MORAN, Mary	
Mary MORAN Conlin		1837	1922	051	CONLIN, Patrick	
				051		
Thomas J. CONLON		1858	1914	051	MORAN, Catharine	
Catharine MORAN Conlon		1858	1913	051	CONLON, Thomas J.	
				051		
Jeremiah MCCORMACK		1850	1925	051	HURLEY, Ellen	(On Stone of John H. Sweeney)
Ellen HURLEY McCormack		1847	1922	051	MCCORMACK, Jeremiah	
John H. SWEENEY		10-12-1864	04-16-1894	051	SWEENEY, John H.	
				051		
James SPELLICY		32 Years	05-13-1890	051	SPELLICY, James	
John SPELLICY		92 Years	09-15-1886	051	MCMAHON, Bridget	
Bridget MCMAHON Spellicy		68 Years	06-20-1885	051	SPELLICY, John	
Patrick SPELLICY		38 Years	02-20-1892	051	SPELLICY, Patrick	
				051		
Bridget A. GIBBONS Conlin		11-25-1867	01-15-1897	051	CONLIN, Patrick H.	Born In Worcester, VT. (NOI
				051	GIBBONS, Bridget A.	Patrick H. Conlin)
				051		
WILLIAMS Family				051	WILLIAMS, Family	
Mother WILLIAMS		11-06-1853	01-02-1899	051	WILLIAMS, Father	
Mother WILLIAMS		05-18-1845	09-21-1886	051	WILLIAMS, Mother	
				051		
Patrick LYNCH	Co. Leitrim	02-03-1819	10-04-1883	051	CARRIGAN, Mary	Born In Leitrim County, Ire.
				051		Died In Moretown, Vermont
Mary CARRIGAN Lynch	Co. Leitrim	10-06-1827	08-15-1900	051	LYNCH, Patrick	Born In County Leitrim, Ire.
				051		Died In Montpelier, Vermont
				051		
Michael LYNCH	Co. Leitrim	03-16-1826	01-16-1884	051	_____, Jane H.	Born In Leitrim, Ireland
				051		Died In Moretown, Vermont
Jane H. _____ LYNCH		08-15-1837	06-23-1902	051	LYNCH, Michael	
				051		
William CANNING		1840	1901	051	CANNING, William	(Does not state if husband and
Teresa CANNING		1842	1888	051	CANNING, Teresa	wife)
				051		
William HORNBROOKE		1839	1919	051	MCCARRON, Mary	

Mary MCCARRON Hornbrooke	1843	1927	051	HORNBROOKE, William	
			051		
John H. TURNEY	1855	1925	051	PRICE, Maria	
Maria PRICE Turney	1857	1932	051	TURNEY, John H.	
			051		
John MURPHY	1849	1927	051	DONAHUE, Sophia	
Sophia DONAHUE Murphy	1856	1936	051	MURPHY, John	
			051		
William CORRIGAN	1852	1935	051	POTTER, Ellen	
Ellen POTTER Corrigan	1855	1926	051	CORRIGAN, William	
			051		
Thomas E. MCMAHON	1839	1920	051	_____, Mary D.	Father
Mary D. _____ MCMAHON	1850	1928	051	MCMAHON, Thomas E.	Mother
			051		
Joseph F. CARROW	1853	1918	051	SMITH, Julia	
Julia SMITH Carrow	1863	1948	051	CARROW, Joseph F.	
			051		
George FITZGERALD	08-18-1855	10-28-1933	051	_____, Bridget D.	
Bridget D. _____ Fitzgerald	09-25-1853	04-21-1944	051	FITZGERALD, George	
			051		
Michael O'GRADY			051	O'NEIL, Catherine	Erected By Ann O'GRADY In
Catherine O'NEIL O'Grady			051	O'GRADY, Michael	Loving Memory of Her Father
			051	O'GRADY, Ann	And Mother (NOI DOB-DOD
			051		
James RYLE	1841		051	CANNING, Maria	(NOI DOD)
Maria CANNING Ryle	1843		051	RYLE, James	
			051		
Joseph FITZGERALD	1824	1899	051	CULLEN, Elizabeth	
Elizabeth CULLEN Fitzgerald	1831	1907	051	FITZGERALD, Joseph	
Martin M. FITZGERALD	1869	1911	051	FITZGERALD, Martin M.	
Edward J. FITZGERALD	1860	1918	051	FITZGERALD, Edward J.	
William H. FITZGERALD	1861	1930	051	FITZGERALD, William H.	
Bridget M. FITZGERALD	1858	1937	051	FITZGERALD, Bridget M.	
Joseph M. FITZGERALD	1857	1940	051	FITZGERALD, Joseph M.	
Mary A. FITZGERALD	1867	1941	051	FITZGERALD, Mary A.	
			051		
M.J. DOYLE			051	DOYLE, A. E.	(NOI DOB/DOD)
A.E. DOYLE			051	DOYLE, M. J.	(NOI DOB/DOD)
			051		
Michael KELLEHER	1847	1899	051	DUGGAN, Mary	
Mary DUGGAN Kelleher	1850	1928	051	KELLEHER, Michael	
			051		
Timothy J. KELLEHER	1854	1905	051	LIVINGSTON, Charlotte	
Charlotte LIVINGSTON Kelleher	1854	1915	051	KELLEHER, Timothy J.	
			051		

Name	Birth	Death	Code	Spouse	Note
Henry L. E. SMITH	1862	1937	051	HARRIS, Margaret M.	
Margaret M. HARRIS Smith	1855	1917	051	SMITH, Henry L. E.	
			051		
Thomas FARRELL	06-09-1848	06-24-1921	051	LYNCH, Mary	
Mary LYNCH Farrell	1851	1927	051	FARRELL, Thomas	
			051		
William O'NEIL	1825	1900	051	KELTY, M.	
M. KELTY O'Neil	1826		051	O'NEIL, William	
			051		
Martin MEE	1853	1912	051	CANTY, Mary	
Mary CANTY Mee	1863	1916	051	MEE, Martin	
			051		
Martin HORAN	1831	1912	051	MCMAHON, Mary	
Mary MCMAHON Horan	1846	1917	051	HORAN, Martin	
			051		
Patrick GORMAN	1842	1900	051	CORCORAN, Mary	
Mary CORCORAN Gorman	1844	1915	051	GORMAN, Patrick	
			051		
M. J. GIBBONS	1853	1905	051	GIBBONS, M. J.	
			051		
James MACKIN	1853	1945	051	FITZGERALD, Mary	
Mary FITZGERALD Mackin	1853	1920	051	MACKIN, James	
			051		
John MEE	1814	1900	051	HAVEY, Mary	
Mary HAVEY Mee	1816	1902	051	MEE, John	
			051		
John MCMAHON	1849	1920	051	NEENAN, Mary	
Mary NEENAN McMahon	1848	19__	051	MCMAHON, John	(NOI DOD)
John CUNNINGHAM	1859	1917	051	MCMAHON, Margaret	
Margaret MCMAHON Cunningham	1870	19__	051	CUNNINGHAM, John	(NOI DOD)
			051		
Joseph SHOREY	09-26-1824	05-25-1891	051	KING, Mary E.	
Mary E. KING Shorey	05-07-1831	05-02-1905	051	SHOREY, Joseph	
			051		
Martin MARKHAM	11-11-1840	________	051	O'GORMAN, Winnifred	(Cannot read DOD)
Winnifred O'GORMAN Markham	03-13-1839	09-06-1915	051	MARKHAM, Martin	
			051		
John DONAHUE	1853	1903	051	MEE, Ann	
Ann MEE Donahue	1851	1930	051	DONAHUE, John	
			051		
Theodore BROWN	04-25-1827	01-21-1908	051	_____, Sophia	
Sophia _____ BROWN	05-22-1832	09-22-1901	051	BROWN, Theodore	
			051		
Henry WELCH	1830	1905	051	_____, Margaret	
Margaret _____ WELCH	1840	1906	051	WELCH, Henry	

Name	Birth	Death	Code	Index	Notes
			051		
Charles L. ANDREWS	02-10-1847		051	ANDREWS, Charles L.	(Does not state if husband and
Catherine F. ANDREWS	03-14-1850	01-24-1908	051	ANDREWS, Catherine F.	wife - NOI DOD Charles)
			051		
Thomas CANTILLION	1843	1910	051	TEHAN, Mary	
Mary TEHAN Cantillion	1847	1934	051	CANTILLION, Thomas	
			051		
D. T. MCGOVERN	1841	1902	051	BULGER, Elizabeth	
Elizabeth BULGER McGovern	1844	1914	051	MCGOVERN, D. T.	
			051		
Thomas MORAN	1842	1909	051	MORAN, Thomas	
			051		
Bridget NATHAN	1836	1914	051	NATHAN, Bridget	
			051		
Lewis WOOD	1838	1915	051	LEMERY, Josephine	(GAR) 1ST LT NH Vols 1861-1865
Josephine LEMERY Wood	1849	1907	051	WOOD, Lewis	
			051		
Mary A. SHANLEY	1834	1919	051	SHANLEY, Mary A.	
			051		
James SUPPLLE	1837	1914	051	NATHAN, Catherine	
Catherine NATHAN Suppl le	1838	1911	051	SUPPLLE, James	
			051		
Michael M. CORRY	1843	1914	051	CORRY, Michael M.	(GAR Marker-Not in reference)
Mary M. RYAN	1844	1938	051	RYAN, Mary M.	Nee Ryan
Ellen GORMAN	1840	1920	051	GORMAN, Ellen	Nee Corry
			051		
James JONES	1820	1860	051	_____, Bridget	
Bridget _____ JONES	1822	1905	051	JONES, James	
			051		
Henry CREAGAN	70 Years	05-17-1865	051	_____, Margaret	
Margaret _____ CREAGAN	49 Years	04-18-1864	051	CREAGAN, Henry	Wife Of Henry Creagan of Stowe
			051		
Timothy LYNCH		01-03-1853	051	LYNCH, Timothy	Son Of Thomas & Mary Lynch.
			051		(NOI DOB. DOD Year C/B 1858)
			051		
Margaret _____ MEEHAN	35 Years	07-05-1869	051	MEEHAN, Michael	(NOI Michael Meehan. Age at
			051	_____, Margaret	death appears to be "35")
T. CASEY			051	CASEY, T.	(NOI) Inscription reads "T.
			051		Casey, Wife & Family"
			051		
Austin KERIN	1828	1904	051	HASSETT, Ellen	
Ellen HASSETT Kerin	1839	1910	051	KERIN, Austin	
Mortimer KERIN	1860	1886	051	KERIN, Mortimer	
Thomas KERIN	1874	1912	051	KERIN, Thomas	
Nora KERIN	1879	1882	051	KERIN, Nora	

				051		
Catherine _____ QUINN		30 Years	12-10-1861	051	QUINN, Peter	(NOI Peter Quinn)
				051	_____, Catherine	
				051		
Lawrence FITZGERALD		1825	1897	051	_____, Mary	
Mary _____ FITZGERALD		1826	1898	051	FITZGERALD, Lawrence	
				051		
Joseph SLATTERY		1826	1888	051	_____, Ann	
Ann _____ FITZGERALD		1825	1874	051	SLATTERY, Joseph	
Patrick SLATTERY		1846	1900	051	SLATTERY, Patrick	
Anna MOORE		1806	1869	051	MOORE, Anna	
				051		
Humphrey CAMPBELL		1847	1907	051	PREMO, Julia	(GAR) 3RD VT BATT
				051	GARCEAU, Celina	
Julia PREMO Campbell		1846	1880	051	CAMPBELL, Humphrey	
Celina GARCEAU Campbell		1850	1911	051	CAMPBELL, Humphrey	
				051		
Bridget KANE		04-09-1832	08-24-1888	051	KANE, Bridget	
				051		
Daniel MANNING		80 Years	05-04-1902	051	MAHANEY, Honora	
Honora MAHANEY Manning		60 Years	08-17-1884	051	MANNING, Daniel	(Surname C/B MAHONEY)
John MANNING		20 Years	09-11-1867	051	MANNING, John	
Mary MANNING		15 Years	10-07-1867	051	MANNING, Mary	
				051		
Margaret _____ HANRAHAN		30 Years	01-07-1881	051	HANRAHAN, James	(NOI James Hanrahan)
				051	_____, Margaret	
				051		
Annie E. WINTERS ROWELL		1854	1924	051	ROWELL, Charles	(NOI Charles Rowell)
				051	WINTERS, Annie E.	
				051		
Anna BURKE McGaffrey			1880	051	MCGAFFREY, James	(NOI James McGaffrey, DOB)
				051	BURKE, Anna	
				051		
Michael O'GORMAN	Co. Clare	26Y8M26D	12-12-1874	051	O'GORMAN, Michael	A Native Of The Parish Of
				051		Kilmihil Town, Co. Clare, Ire.
Philip PRESTON		05-07-1834	01-06-1904	051	KERWAN, Ann	
Ann KERWAN Preston	Co. Tipperary	08-04-1834	03-26-1878	051	PRESTON, Philip	Born In St. Johnstown, County
				051		Tipperary, Ireland, Age 44.
Richard PRESTON		01-17-1862	02-22-1885	051	PRESTON, Richard	
Ellen M. DEVINE Preston		06-29-1854	06-27-1892	051	PRESTON, J. Phillip	(NOI J. Phillip Preston)
				051	DEVINE, Ellen M.	
				051		
John DEVINE		1826	1911	051	MONAHAN, Bridget	(GAR) 8TH VT CO. G
Bridget MONAHAN Devine		1829	1905	051	DEVINE, John	
				051		

Henry CAMPBELL		1854	1911	051	EMMONS, Mary	
Mary EMMONS Campbell		1861	1883	051	CAMPBELL, Henry	
				051		
Thomas H. CORRY		1840	1925	051	CORRY, Thomas H.	
				051		
John O'GRADY		1826	1909	051	______, Jane	
Jane ______ O'GRADY		1828	1875	051	O'GRADY, John	
				051		
Mary J. DONAHUE		25 Years	01-12-1879	051	DONAHUE, Mary J.	
Thomas DONAHUE		70 Years	05-09-1875	051	______, Margaret	
Margaret ______ DONAHUE		63 Years	01-01-1879	051	DONAHUE, Thomas	
Michael DONAHUE		71 Years	03-06-1917	051	DONAHUE, Michael	
				051		
Mary SUPPLL Morrow		79 Years	05-08-1903	051	MORROW, Patrick	(NOI Patrick Morrow)
				051	SUPPLL, Mary	
				051		
Mary HENNEBERRY		1842	1924	051	HENNEBERRY, Mary	
				051		
John MURPHY			09-08-1883	051	______, Johanna	(NOI DOB - These two are on
Johanna ______ MURPHY		60 Years	04-20-1876	051	MURPHY, John	headstone of Mortimer Downey.
Mortimer DOWNEY				051	DOWNEY, Mortimer	Stone is down/broken. Cannot
				051		read Downey inscription)
Michael MCGARRON		65 Years	08-22-1865	051	MCGARRON, Michael	
				051		
John MAGEE John MAGEE				051		
Catharine ______ MAGEE		02-02-1845	11-06-1926	051	MAGEE, John	
				051		
Michael PRICE		1820	1904	051	KERIN, Honora	
Honora KERIN Prive		1830	1875	051	PRICE, Michael	
				051		
Morty KERIN	Co. Clare	01-06-1796	12-23-1876	051	______, Mary	Natives of Co. Clare, Ireland
Mary ______ KERIN	Co. Clare	09-29-1798	01-24-1879	051	KERIN, Morty	Natives of Co. Clare, Ireland
				051		
Catherine DALY Connor		28 Years	11-16-1866	051	CONNOR, Dennis	(NOI Dennis Connor)
				051	DALY, Catherine	
				051		
Dennis MINEHAN		59 Years	09-07-1898	051	LAHEY, Mary	
Mary LAHEY Minehan		68 Years	06-08-1900	051	MINEHAN, Dennis	
				051		
John SEYMOUR			02-03-1881	051	______, Louisa	(NOI DOB)
Louisa ______ SEYMOUR		76 Years	02-28-1881	051	SEYMOUR, John	
				051		
Louis RODNEY		58 Years	09-04-1888	051	______, Glema A.	
Glema A. ______ RODNEY				051	RODNEY, Louis	(NOI DOB-DOD)
				051		

Name	Origin	Birth/Age	Death	Code	Index	Notes
Peter ROSE		78 Years	12-19-1866	051	_____, Glema A.	
Glema A. _____ ROSE		12-25-1798	07-23-1880	051	ROSE, Peter	
				051		
Maggie A. _____ HARDIGAN		29 Years	04-08-1876	051	HARDIGAN, John	(NOI John Hardigan)
				051		
Robert DEVINE		1832	1914	051	DEVINE, Robert	(GAR) CO. F 2ND VT REG
John DEVINE		1834	1914	051	DEVINE, John	(GAR) CO. H 3RD VT REG
				051		
Timothy QUINN		72 Years	10-04-1900	051	QUINN, Timothy	
				051		
John O'BRIEN		19 Years	06-05-1870	051	O'BRIEN, John	
				051		
Patrick PHILLIPS	Co. Clare	54 Years	09-10-1876	051	PHILLIPS, Patrick	Parish of Kilmurray (Kilmurry)
				051		County Clare, Ireland
				051		
Patrick KANE		03--1824	10--1824	051	_____, Maria	
Maria _____ KANE		09--1831	02--1899	051	KANE, Patrick	
Ann S. KANE		01--1854	05--1925	051	KANE, Ann S.	
				051		
Arthur ALLEN		1823	1896	051	_____, Eliza	
Eliza _____ ALLEN		1826	1875	051	ALLEN, Arthur	
				051		
William J. MCNANNIS		25 Years	05-12-1865	051	_____, Margaret	
Margaret _____ MCNANNIS				051	MCNANNIS, William J.	(Stone deteriorated. Age at
				051		death was 53 or 83 years. Year
				051		of death was 1853 or 1883)
				051		
Mary _____ KELLEY		55 Years	03-20-1884	051	KELLEY, Cornelius	(NOI Cornelius Kelley)
				051	_____, Mary	
				051		
Francis SWEENEY		82 Years	02-17-1911	051	HURLEY, Mary	
Mary HURLEY Sweeney		53 Years	07-31-1885	051	SWEENEY, Francis	
				051		
Daniel E. SWEENEY		09-15-1853	05-05-1910	051	CONNELL, Mary	
Mary CONNELL Sweeney		08-03-1853	06-24-1924	051	SWEENEY, Daniel E.	
Michael MORIARTY		65 Years	08-14-1886	051	REARDON, Margaret	
Margaret REARDON Moriarty		08-03-1853	01-04-1910	051	MORIARTY, Michael	
				051		
Daniel PEMBROKE		1806	1898	051	REARDON, Mary	
Mary REARDON Pembroke		1821	1893	051	PEMBROKE, Daniel	
				051		
Patrick CARROLL		1814	1890	051	CURLEY, Eliza	
Eliza CURLEY Carroll		1817	1885	051	CARROLL, Patrick	
				051		
James L. CUTLER		1851	1867	051	CUTLER, James L.	(Does not state if husband and

Mary L. CUTLER	1858	1947	051	CUTLER, Mary L.	wife)
			051		
Patrick FARRELL	1834	1915	051	HURLEY, Ellen	
Ellen HURLEY Farrell	1843	1889	051	FARRELL, Patrick	
Betsy WHO	1850	1918	051	_____, Betsey	(Does not say if surname is
			051		Farrell or Hurley)
			051		
M.G. HERLIHY	09-28-1857	01-09-1909	051	_____, Mary J.	
Mary J. _____ HERLIHY	1855	1927	051	HERLIHY, M. G.	
			051		
John G. MEE	1841	1893	051	HOGAN, Mary A.	
Mary A. HOGAN Mee	1841	1903	051	MEE, John G.	
			051		
Daniel CROWLEY	1836	1906	051	_____, Mary	
Mary _____ CROWLEY	1837	1911	051	CROWLEY, Daniel	
			051		
John DALY	1849	1903	051	O'NEIL, Margaret	
Margaret O'NEIL Daly	1855	1908	051	DALY, John	
			051		
William H. HEAVEY	04-09-1855	10-13-1945	051	HAYES, Catherine A.	
Catherine A. HAYES Heavey	04-07-1855	10-08-1915	051	HEAVEY, William H.	
			051		
Michael D. HURLEY	07-09-1854	10-21-1894	051	MORIARTY, Katherine	
Katherine MORIARTY Hurley	1854	1914	051	HURLEY, Michael D.	
			051		
Edward A. MCKENNA	1843	1924	051	O'GRADY, Catherine	
			051	O'GRADY, Ann	
Catherine O'GRADY McKenna	1845	1911	051	MCKENNA, Edward A.	
Ann O'GRADY MCKENNA	1843	1915	051	MCKENNA, Edward A.	
			051		
John COGHLAN	1849	1921	051	JARVIS, Harriet	
Harriet JARVIS Coghlan	1855	1908	051	COGHLAN, John	
			051		
John EWING	1822	1899	051	MORRIS, Ann	
Ann MORRIS Ewing	1818	1910	051	EWING, John	
Father EDMOND	1844	1911	051	EDMOND, Father	(Not sure if surname is Ewing)
			051		
James C. SIMMONS	1830	1898	051	FITZGERALD, Catherine	
Catherine FITZGERALD Simmons	1844	1910	051	SIMMONS, James C.	
			051		
John HERBERT	1827	1914	051	SULLIVAN, Ellen	
Ellen SULLIVAN Herbert	1837	1907	051	HERBERT, John	
			051		
Charles P. GILL	1832	1939	051	CALLAHAN, Mary A.	
			051	WHITE, Mary A.	

Name	Birth	Death	Code	Relation	Note
Mary A. CALLAHAN Gill	1871	1895	051	GILL, Charles P.	
Mary A. WHITE Gill	1872	1961	051	GILL, Charles P.	
			051		
S. D. MAHONEY			051	FORAN, Mary	(NOI DOB-DOD)
Mary FORAN Mahoney	1832	1914	051	MAHONEY, S. D.	
Mahoney Children			051	MAHONEY, Children	
Catherine MAHONEY			051	MAHONEY, Catherine	(NOI DOB-DOD)
Mary MAHONEY			051	MAHONEY, Mary	(NOI DOB-DOD)
Sylvester MAHONEY			051	MAHONEY, Sylvester	(NOI DOB-DOD)
			051		
Patrick L. LYONS	10-17-1847	09-10-1911	051	BAXTER, Mary A.	
Mary A. BAXTER Lyons	02-05-1847	08-01-1931	051	LYONS, Patrick L.	
			051		
Patrick ROAKES	1828	1898	051	MCMANNIS, Sarah	
Sarah MCMANNIS Roakes	1836	1916	051	ROAKES, Patrick	
			051		
Joseph M. FITZGERALD	1851	1911	051	GORMAN, Mary E.	
Mary E. GORMAN Fitzgerald	1852	1913	051	FITZGERALD, Joseph M.	
			051		
Martin FITZGERALD	1811	1866	051	BRODERICK, Catherine	
Catherine BRODERICK Fitzgerald	1816	1899	051	FITZGERALD, Martin	
Mary A. FITZGERALD	1852	1937	051	FITZGERALD, Mary A.	
Edward A. FITZGERALD	1858	1939	051	FITZGERALD, Edward A.	
			051		
Luke MEE	1818	1893	051	FALLAN, Winefred	
Winefred FALLAN Mee	1817	1896	051	MEE, Luke	
			051		
John EMMONS	1855	1915	051	MEE, Margaret	
Margaret MEE Emmons	1854	1935	051	EMMONS, John	
			051		
T. H. DEMOREST	1841	1910	051	_____, Mary	
Mary _____ DEMOREST	1852	1923	051	DEMOREST, T. H.	
			051		
Jeremiah HARRIGAN	1836	1902	051	DOHERTY, Ellen	
Ellen DOHERTY Harrigan	1832	1913	051	HARRIGAN, Jeremiah	
			051		
Thomas CORVEN	1848	1907	051	_____, Katherine	
Katherine _____ CORVEN	1857	1952	051	CORVEN, Thomas	
			051		
John CRONIN	75 Years	07-13-1910	051	CRONIN, John	
			051		
Daniel CRONIN	1847	1915	051	CRONIN, Daniel	
			051		
Thomas BURKE	1855	1916	051	MEDLAR, Mary	
Mary MEDLAR Burke	1855	1942	051	BURKE, Thomas	

				051		
Ellen CONLLEY		1845	1920	051	CONLLEY, Ellen	
				051		
Michael O'GRADY		1854	1933	051	_____, Honorah	
Honorah _____ O'GRADY		1857	1952	051	O'GRADY, Michael	
				051		
Patrick O'GRADY		1853	1911	051	O'GRADY, Patrick	
				051		
William PETERSON		1834	1906	051	FERRAN, Bridget E.	(GAR) Co. K 3RD VT REGT
Bridget E. FERRAN Peterson		1836	1912	051	PETERSON, William	
				051		
Patrick MCCARTY		1848	1923	051	O'HAGAN, Jane F.	
Jane F. O'HAGAN McCarty		1860	1916	051	MCCARTY, Patrick	
				051		
William O'DWYER	Co. Waterford	53Y8M20D	01-21-1881	051	O'DWYER, William	A Native Of _____, Co. Waterford, Ire. (Could not read)
				051		

St. Patrick's Cemetery, Moretown, VT   Moretown Common Road, Right on Road 41 (Southhill)

NAME	POB	DOB/AGE	DOD	CEM	SPOUSE/INDEX	INSCRIPTION
Daniel MURPHY		70 Years	10-15-1869	052	_____, Mary	
Mary _____ MURPHY		76 Years	01-09-1885	052	MURPHY, Daniel	
				052		
Joseph WARD		19Y 3M	12-11-1879	052	WARD, Joseph	
				052		
Michael RYLE		85 Years	10-20-1890	052	_____, Mary	
Mary _____ MURPHY		86 Years	12-16-1890	052	RYLE, Michael	
Patrick RYLE		30 Years	11-28-1883	052	RYLE, Patrick	
				052		
John SULLIVAN		92 Years	03-26-1892	052	CAVANAUGH, Ellen	Born In Ireland
Ellen CAVANAUGH Sullivan		70 Years	01-05-1893	052	SULLIVAN, John	Born In Ireland
Thomas SULLIVAN		65 Years	09-18-1905	052	SULLIVAN, Thomas	
				052		
Andrew J. MURRAY		1848	1879	052	MURRAY, Andrew J.	
Thomas A. MURRAY		1852	1874	052	MURRAY, Thomas A.	
				052		
Mary O'CONNOR Riley		34 Years	04-21-1871	052	RILEY, James	Wife of James Riley(NOI James)
				052	O'CONNOR, Mary	
William J. RILEY		2 Years	04-26-1870	052	RILEY, William J.	
Frankie J. RILEY		6 Months	05-14-1870	052	RILEY, Frankie J.	
				052		
Mary FLANAGAN		75 Years	04-06-1875	052	FLANAGAN, Mary	

Name	Origin	Born/Age	Died	Code	Index	Notes
John G. FLANAGAN		1860	1929	052	FLANAGAN, John G.	
William FLANAGAN		73 Years	02-16-1883	052	WHALEN, Julia	
Julia WHALEN Flanagan		67 Years	03-26-1899	052	FLANAGAN, William	
Julia A. FLANAGAN		16 Years	05-10-1885	052	FLANAGAN, Julia A.	
Ellen S. FLANAGAN		20 Years	04-10-1893	052	FLANAGAN, Ellen S.	
				052		
Michael REYNOLDS		1796	1858	052	____, Mary	
Mary ____ REYNOLDS		1804	1873	052	REYNOLDS, Michael	
				052		
Francis LEE		62 Years	11-18-1854	052	LEE, Francis	
				052		
Peter LEE		1806	1890	052	REYNOLDS, Catherine	
Catherine REYNOLDS Lee		1811	1901	052	LEE, Peter	
Michael LEE		1835	1858	052	LEE, Michael	
Thomas LEE		1837	1865	052	LEE, Thomas	
Mary Ann LEE		1840	1860	052	LEE, Mary Ann	
Jane S. LEE		1844	1865	052	LEE, Jane S.	
Peter B. LEE Jr.		1856	1885	052	LEE, Peter B. Jr.	
James B. LEE		1853		052	LEE, James B.	
Catherine A. LEE		1850		052	LEE, Catherine A.	
John F. LEE		1846		052	LEE, John S.	
				052		
Margaret COLEMAN Ryan		70 Years	12-09-1859	052	RYAN, Simon	Wife of Simon Ryan (NOI Simon)
				052	COLEMAN, Margaret	
				052		
Frank KELLEY		33 Years	11-17-1850	052	KELLEY, Frank	
				052		
Thomas FOLEY		80 Years	10-01-1886	052	RYAN, Catherine	
Catharine RYAN Foley		71 Years	02-01-1905	052	FOLEY, Thomas	
				052		
John FLYNN		05-20-1813	01-28-1890	052	MEIGHAN, Sarah	
Sarah MEIGHAN Flynn		05-24-1819	11-09-1886	052	FLYNN, John	
				052		
Malachi KEOUGH		92Y 8M	10-13-1885	052	FLYNN, Bridget	
Bridget FLYNN Keough		91Y 6M	07-06-1897	052	KEOUGH, Malachi	
				052		
James MCCOY		76 Years	02-10-1871	052	____, Ellen	
Ellen ____ MCCOY		78 Years	06-15-1875	052	MCCOY, James	
				052		
Cornelius FINN	Co. Cork	59 Years	11-12-1865	052	REYNOLDS, Mary	Born In Parish Knuckaville
				052		(Knockavilly),Co. of Cork, Ire
Mary REYNOLDS Finn	Co. Leitrim	77 Years	06-07-1897	052	FINN, Cornelius	Born In Drumshambo, Co. of
				052		Leitrim, Ire.
Margaret FINN		1849	1937	052	FINN, Margaret	
Mary FINN		19 Years	02-22-1859	052	FINN, Mary	

Jane FINN		3 Years	12- -1849	052	FINN, Jane	
				052		
Bridget ____ COLLINS	Co. Limerick	56 Years	10-07-1864	052	COLLINS, Cornelius	Born In County of Limerick,
				052	_____, Bridget	Parish of Doone (Doon). (NOI
				052		Cornelius Collins)
				052		
Thomas FLINN	Co. Roscommon	42Y 11M	03-09-1862	052	DONLAN, Mary	Born in Kilmore, Parish of
				052		Tochmaconnel (Taghmaconnell)
				052		Co. Roscommon, Ire (This
				052		stone not in burial plot.
				052		Found in trash pile)
				052		
Mary DONLAN Flinn	Co. Roscommon	88 Years	03-13-1907	052	FLINN, Thomas	Born in Kilmore, Parish of
				052		Tochmaconnel (Taghmaconnell)
				052		Co. Roscommon, Ire
Anna FLINN		1848	1881	052	FLINN, Anna	
Thomas FLINN		1820	1862	052	FLINN, Thomas	
Mary FLINN		1847	1862	052	FLINN, Mary	
Anna B. FLINN		1849	1862	052	FLINN, Anna B.	
Thomas FLINN		1851	1862	052	FLINN, Thomas	
				052		
Julia ____ RYLE		1842	1872	052	RYLE, Jerry	(NOI Jerry Ryle)
				052	_____, Julia	
Mary ____ RYLE		1852	1890	052	RYLE, Jerry	
				052	_____, Mary	
				052		
Richard WELCH	Co. Longford	71 Years	09-06-1858	052	WELCH, Richard	A Native of Longford Co., Ire.
				052		
Francis DONAHUE		79 Years	04-16-1884	052	_____, Catherine	
Catherine ____ DONAHUE		72 Years	01-16-1890	052	DONAHUE, Francis	
James DONAHUE		28 Years	04-20-1885	052	DONAHUE, James	
				052		
Jeremiah CREAN		06-24-1818		052	MORIARTY, Mary	
Mary MORIARTY Crean		03-25-1817	11-30-1884	052	CREAN, Jeremiah	
Ira CREAN		12-10-1850	08-15-1853	052	CREAN, Ira	
				052		
John FARNHAM		65 Years	05-02-1892	052	_____, Pauline	(GAR-Try Co.E, 8th Rgt,VtVols)
Pauline ____ FARNHAM		92 Years	02-08-1916	052	FARNHAM, John	
				052		
Paulina FARNHAM		22 Years	06-25-1880	052	FARNHAM, Paulina	Dau Of John & Polly Farnham
				052		
Mary ____ HAYES		28 Years	01-28-1875	052	HAYES, Patrick	(NOI Patrick Hayes)
				052	_____, Mary	
				052		
William HORNBROOK		1810	1872	052	MCCARTY, Catherine	

Name	Origin	Birth/Age	Death		Spouse/Index	Notes
Catherine MCCARTY Hornbrook		1813	1879	052	HORNBROOK, William	
Daniel HORNBROOK		1840	1860	052	HORNBROOK, Daniel	
Nancy HORNBROOK		1841	1858	052	HORNBROOK, Nancy	
Timothy HORNBROOK		1842	1874	052	HORNBROOK, Timothy	(GAR) Co. D, 2nd VT Vols
Catherine HORNBROOK		1843	1934	052	HORNBROOK, Catherine	
Ellen HORNBROOK		1849	1872	052	HORNBROOK, Ellen	
Henry HORNBROOK		1850	1877	052	HORNBROOK, Henry	
				052		
John HORNBROOK		03-29-1836	05-16-1929	052	_____, Bridget D.	Born In Strafford, VT. Died in Chelsea, Mass.(GAR-Not in ref)
				052		
Bridget D. _____ HORNBROOK		08-11-1848	04-18-1900	052	HORNBROOK, John	Born In Moretown, VT. Died in New York City age 52Y 8M 2D.
				052		
Dennis CORKERY		80 Years	10-29-1885	052	____, Bridget	
Bridget ____ CORKERY		75 Years	03-03-1883	052	CORKERY, Dennis	
				052		
Henry GORMAN		3Y 18D	09-18-1868	052	GORMAN, Henry	
				052		
Daniel TEHEAN	Co. Kerry	67 Years	05-11-1875	052	TEHEAN, Daniel	A Native of Co. Kerry, Ire
				052		
Michael TAYLOR	Co. Clare	47 Years	09-20-1878	052	TAYLOR, Michael	Native of Kilkee, Clare Co Ire
				052		
Daniel MCGIFF	Co. Westmeath	1816	09-09-1874	052	MCGIFF, Daniel	Born in Drumraney, Westmeath County, Ire.
				052		
				052		
Thomas DEVINE	Co. Dublin	50 Years	04-03-1857	052	_____, Mary	A Native of Ballyboughil, Co, Dublin, Ire. Husband of Mary Devine. (NOI Mary Devine. This stone found in trash pile)
				052		
				052		
				052		
				052		
Mary M. ___ DEVINE		29 Years	12-14-1862	052	DEVINE, Thomas	Wife Of Thomas Devine(Probably is spouse of foregoing Thomas Devine. Note age difference. Mother and two children died in a 41 day period)
				052		
				052		
				052		
				052		
Catharine DEVINE		9 Years	11-18-1862	052	DEVINE, Catherine	
Daniel DEVINE		2 Years	12-29-1862	052	DEVINE, Daniel	
				052		
Thomas MCCARTHY	Co. Cork	97 Years	12-23-1885	052	O'DAY, Catharine	Native of Cloyne,Co. Cork, Ire
Catharine O'DAY McCarthy	Co. Cork			052	MCCARTHY, Thomas	Native of Dungourney,Co. Cork, Ire. (No Date of birth/death)
				052		
				052		
James KEELTY	Co. Sligo	74 Years	09-09-1872	052	_____, Mary	Native of Co. Sligo, Ireland
Mary _____ KELTY	Co. Sligo	85 Years	11-24-1891	052	KEELTY, James	Born In Co. Sligo, Ireland
				052		
Thomas J. O'NEIL		11-06-1850	03-17-1870	052	O'NEIL, Thomas J.	

Name	Origin	Age/Born	Died	Code	Index	Notes
Anna M. O'NEIL		11-26-1849	01-11-1862	052	O'NEIL, Anna M.	
				052		
Patsy BURKE		3Y 2M	11-04-1878	052	BURKE, Patsy	Son Of Mike & Mary Burke
				052	BURKE, Mike	
				052		
Thomas RYAN		36 Years	02-09-1871	052	RYAN, Thomas	
				052		
John O'LARA		51 Years	03-05-1862	052	_____, Mary	
Mary ____ O'LARA	Co. Sligo	47 Years	03-11-1861	052	O'LARA, John	
				052		
William E. DOON		8 Months	08-26-1867	052	DOON, William E.	Son Of James & Ellen Doon
				052	DOON, James	
				052		
Daniel COLLINS		1842	1899	052	CORKERY, Catherine	
Catherine CORKERY		1846	1912	052	COLLINS, Daniel	
				052		
Ellen MURPHY Donovan	Co. Wexford	50Y 2M	11-10-1882	052	DONAVON, James	Born In Wexford, Ireland
				052	MURPHY, Ellen	(NOI James Donavon)
				052		
Jane ____ O'NEILL	Co. Dublin	29 Years	07-24-1859	052	O'NEILL, John	Native of Dublin, Ireland.
				052	_____, Jane	(NOI John O'Neill)
				052		
Jane KIRWAN	Co. Dublin	80 Years	03-20-1862	052	KIRWAN, Jane	A Native of Dublin, Ireland.
				052		
Ann HAGAN KENNEDY	Co. Dublin	73 Years	09-15-1891	052	HAGAN, Ann	Born In Dublin, Ireland.(NOI
				052		Mr. Kennedy)
				052		
Mary ____ DONAHUE		77 Years	10-23-1884	052	DONAHUE, James	Wife of James Donahue. (NOI
				052	_____, Mary	James Donahue)
				052		
Hannorah MURPHY		24 Years	03-31-1869	052	MURPHY, Hannorah	Dau of Michael & Mary Murphy
Margaret MURPHY		24 Years	02-20-1875	052	MURPHY, Margaret	Dau of Michael & Mary Murphy
				052	MURPHY, Michael	
				052		
Bridget ____ CASEY		27 Years	05-01-1868	052	CASEY, William	Wife of William Casey. (NOI
				052	_____, Bridget	William Casey)
				052		
Daniel HASSETT		72 Years	04-08-1880	052	____, Fanny	
Fanny ____ HASSETT		60 Years	08-01-1867	052	HASSETT, Daniel	
Joanna HASSETT		34 Years	02-25-1880	052	HASSETT, Joanna	
				052		
Elizabeth DEVINE		26 Years	11-10-1877	052	DEVINE, Elizabeth	Dau of Thomas & Mary Devine
				052		
Patrick MULVANY		62 Years	06-09-1896	052	MULVANY, Patrick	He Was Born In Ireland
				052		

Name	Origin	Age/Born	Died	No.	Index	Notes
Thomas REEVES		50 Years	03-10-1864	052	REEVES, Thomas	
Edward REEVES		12 Years	01-23-1873	052	REEVES, Edward	
				052		
Patrick EAGAN		1811	1853	052	____, Catharine	
Catharine ____ EAGAN		1815	1879	052	EAGAN, Patrick	
John EAGAN		1796	1877	052	EAGAN, John	
Robert EAGAN		1845	1865	052	EAGAN, Robert	Co. B
				052		
Thomas KEELTY	Co. Sligo	73 Years	03-29-1872	052	KEELTY, Thomas	Native of Co. Sligo, Ireland
				052		
Mathew WHALEN		63 Years	02-03-1891	052	KELTY, Nancy Teresa	
Nancy Teresa KELTY Whalen		33 Years	01-27-1863	052	WHALEN, Mathew	
				052		
Bridget Kelty MEANY		32 Years	05-25-1871	052	MEANY, Patrick	(NOI Patrick Meany)
				052	KELTY, Bridget	
Infant MEANY			05-21-1871	052	MEANY, Infant	Infant Son
				052		
Annie DONNELLY Harris		12-25-1847	05-16-1899	052	HARRIS, J.C.	Wife of J.C. Harris. (NOI J.C.
				052	DONNELLY, Annie	Harris)
				052		
James H. DILLON		6 Years	02-11-1865	052	DILLON, James H.	Son of E. & C. Dillon
				052		
Sophia ____ DONNELLY		69 Years	04-23-1879	052	DONNELLY, P.	Wife of P. Donnelly. (NOI
				052	_____, Sophia	P. Donnelly
				052		
James H. DILLON		5 Years	02-11-1864	052	DILLON, James H.	Son of E. & K. Dillon
				052		
Timothy CASEY	Co. Cork	75 Years	01-11-1892	052	EVENS, Ellen	Erected by Timothy Casey & His
				052		Wife, Ellen Eavens, Natives of
				052		Parish of Caugheroug (Caheragh
				052		or Caherlag),County Cork, Ire.
				052		In Memory of of their beloved
				052		Children.
Ellen EVENS Casey	Co. Cork	56 Years	03-25-1877	052	CASEY, Timothy	Beloved Wife of Timothy Casey
				052		(Note on Timothy's stone her
				052		surname is "EAVENS.)
Cornelius CASEY		2 Months	08_ -1849	052	CASEY, Cornelius	
Catherine CASEY		2 Months	12_ -1853	052	CASEY, Catherine	
Hanora CASEY		4Y 8M	09_ -1862	052	CASEY, Hanora	
Timothy CASEY		2Y 4M	09_ -1862	052	CASEY, Timothy	
Julia CASEY		13 Years	03-13-1869	052	CASEY, Julia	
				052		
Thomas CANNING		2 Years	09-12-1853	052	CANNING, Thomas	Erected by Michael Canning &
Eliza CANNING		3 Years	08-15-1849	052	CANNING, Eliza	His Wife Catherine Cahal,
Ellen CANNING		28 Years		052	CANNING, Ellen	Natives of Waterpark,Parish of

Name	Place	Age/Born	Died		Index	Notes
				052	CANNING, Michael	Lismore, County of Cork, Ire.
				052	CAHAL, Catherine	(NOI Michael Canning &
				052		Catherine Cahal)
				052		
Dennis DONOVAN		38 Years	08-01-1883	052	DONOVAN, Dennis	
				052		
Mary A. DONOVAN	Co. Cork	19 Years	07-28-1868	052	DONOVAN, Mary A.	Daughter of James & Annorah
				052	DONOVAN, James	Donovan, Native of the Parish
				052		Kinegh (Kinneigh),Co. Cork,Ire
				052		
Michael MURRAY	England	08-20-1836	12-15-1873	052	MURRAY, Michael	Born at Steely Bridge, England
				052		Died at Fort Rand, DC. (Found
				052		this stone in trash pile)
Patrick MURRAY		01-06-1811	03-28-1887	052	CALLAHAN, Mary	
Mary CALLAHAN Murray		07-06-1811		052	MURRAY, Patrick	(No DOB/DOD on stone)
Michael MURRAY		12-02-1838	12-25-1863	052	MURRAY, Michael	(Possibly same Michael Murray
				052		as foregoing although DOB &
				052		DOD at variance).
Mary MURRAY		11-05-1859	05-20-1866	052	MURRAY, Mary	
James MURRAY		04-25-1841	03-15-1888	052	MURRAY, James	
				052		
Ellen MORRISEE		11 Years	02-13-1864	052	MORRISEE, Ellen	Dau of John & Nancy Morrisee
				052	MORRISEE, John	
				052		
Jeremiah HEALEY	Co. Cork	79 Years	07-24-1883	052	HEALEY, Jeremiah	A Native of Co. Cork, Ireland
				052		
Catharine O'NEIL O'Grady		39 Years	03-25-1855	052	O'GRADY, Michael	(NOI Michael O'Grady)
				052	O'NEIL, Catherine	
				052		
Cornelius MCCARTY		15 Years	11-20-1858	052	MCCARTY, Cornelius	Sons of John--Johannah McCarty
William MCCARTY		9 Years	01-03-1860	052	MCCARTY, William	
				052		
Mary SULLIVAN Collins	Co. Cork	33 Years	05-07-1855	052	COLLINS, Cornelius	A Native of Kielnaclash (Kilna
				052	SULLIVAN, Mary	clasha), Parish of Abbey Strow
				052		ley (Abbeystrowry), County of
				052		Cork, Ire. (NOI Cornelius
				052		Collins)
				052		
Michael FENTON		39 Years	07-27-1857	052	____, Mary	
Mary ____ FENTON		70 Years	09-14-1880	052	FENTON, Michael	
				052		
Eugene MCCARTY				052	____, Margaret	(No dates of birth or death
				052	____, Ellen	indicated for any member of
Margaret ____ MCCARTY				052	MCCARTY, Eugene	this family)
Ellen ____ MCCARTY				052	MCCARTY, Eugene	

Margaret MCCARTY				052	MCCARTY, Margaret	Their Daughters
Kate MCCARTY				052	MCCARTY, Kate	" "
Annie MCCARTY				052	MCCARTY, Annie	" "
Clara MCCARTY				052	MCCARTY, Clara	" "
				052		" "
John F. LEE		11-03-1846	12-27-1916	052	BROWN, Hattie L.	
Hattie L. BROWN Lee		08-21-1851	07-04-1885	052	LEE, John F.	
				052		
Mary WHALEN Murphy		52 Years	11-27-1894	052	MURPHY, Andrew	(NOI Andrew Murphy)
				052	WHALEN, Mary	
				052		
Timothy CASHMAN	Co. Cork	60 Years	11-23-1850	052	____, Mary	He Was A Native Of Co. Cork,
				052		Ire. Erected By His Wife Mary.
Mary ____ CASHMAN	Co. Cork	68 Years	09-12-1869	052	CASHMAN, Timothy	Note: Mary, John & Joanna all
John FLANAGAN	Co. Cork	80 Years	04-11-1880	052	CASHMAN, Joanna	in same plot. Stone reads:
Joanna CASHMAN Flanagan	Co. Cork	83 Years	07-15-1910	052	FLANAGAN, John	Natives of Co. Cork, Ireland
John S. FLANIGAN		42 Years	03-25-1906	052	FLANIGAN, John S.	
				052		
Henry WINTERS		2 Years	09-14-1850	052	WINTERS, Henry	S/O Patrick--Catherine Winters
				052	WINTERS, Patrick	
				052		
Dennis CONNERS		30 Years	05-08-1846	052	O'BRIEN, Catherine	A Native of Ireland
Catherine O'BRIEN Conners		25 Years	03-30-1848	052	CONNERS, Dennis	Daughter of Mannis O'Brien
				052		
Mary O'BRIEN		38 Years	07-31-1855	052	O'BRIEN, Mary	Daughter of Mannis O'Brien
				052	O'BRIEN, Mannis	
				052		
Thomas DALY		15 Years	05-29-1845	052	DALY, Thomas	S/O Patrick & Clementine Daly
				052	DALY, Patrick	
				052		
Timothy MURPHY		1821	1880	052	____, Johanna	
Johanna ____ MURPHY		1829	1911	052	MURPHY, Timothy	
Eliza MURPHY		1843	1927	052	MURPHY, Eliza	
				052		
Joseph MURPHY		1867	1913	052	MURPHY, Joseph	
				052		
Catherine FOREN	Co. Clare	55 Years	06-25-1854	052	FOREN, Catherine	Native of Kilkee, Clare, Ire
				052		Erected by her children
				052		
Mary Ann HOGAN		4Y 11M	10-25-1858	052	HOGAN, Mary Ann	Dau of Dennis & Sarah Hogan
				052	HOGAN, Dennis	Dau of Dennis & Sarah Hogan
				052		
John HOGAN		08-02-1802	12-24-1885	052	COLEMAN, Johanna	
Johannah COLEMAN Hogan		02-04-1808	09-04-1891	052	HOGAN, John	
Stephan HOGAN		12-23-1826	01-15-1894	052	MEE, Mary	

NAME	POB	DOB/AGE	DOD	CEM	SPOUSE/INDEX	INSCRIPTION
Mary MEE HOGAN		11-03-1848	10-04-1866	052	HOGAN, Stephan	
John HOGAN		02-19-1865	12-05-1888	052	HOGAN, John	
Ellen HOGAN		02-03-1848	10-22-1888	052	HOGAN, Ellen	
				052		
Timothy MCGRATH	Co. Tipperary	34 Years	03-26-1850	052	MCGRATH, Timothy	Native of Bird Hill (Birdhill) County Tipperary, Ireland. (Stone found in trash pile)
				052		
				052		

St. Mary's Cemetery, Newport, Vermont. Pleasant Street Extension

NAME	POB	DOB/AGE	DOD	CEM	SPOUSE/INDEX	INSCRIPTION
William PARKER		1781	1838	054		
				054		
Thomas PARKER		1826		054	_____, Mary	
Mary _____ PARKER		1822	1906	054	PARKER, Thomas	
William MCLURE		1832	1854	054	MCLURE, William	
				054		
Thomas NORTON		1848	1926	054	MORIARTY, Margaret	
Margaret MORIARTY Norton		1850	1926	054	NORTON, Thomas	
				054		
Timothy MITCHELL		03-21-1851	04-29-1882	054	_____, Alice	
Alice _____ MITCHELL		12-06-1852	06-30-1878	054	MITCHELL, Timothy	
John MITCHELL		06-20-1824	04-26-1897	054	_____, Nora	
Nora _____ MITCHELL		10-18-1828	11-20-1901	054	MITCHELL, John	
				054		
Mary E. COOLEY LaBonte		08-28-1852	10-24-1902	054	LABONTE, David	(NOI David LaBonte)
				054	COOLEY, Mary E.	
				054		
Peter MORRILL		06-17-1854	09-06-1903	054	MOLINEAUX, Mary	
Mary MOLINEAUX Morrill		09-08-1853	09-16-1912	054	MORRILL, Peter	
				054		
James MCNEIL		1841	1912	054	HALEY, Jane	
Jane HALEY McNeil		1842	1925	054	MCNEIL, James	
				054		
Michael J. MULLAVEY		1834	1897	054	TURCOTT, Aurilla M.	
Aurilla M. TURCOTT Mullavey		1854	1933	054	MULLAVEY, Michael J.	
				054		
Ann DAY		08-__-1841	10-20-1916	054	DAY, Ann	
				054		
John PRANCE		03-25-1841	03-06-1925	054	CUSHING, Emely	
Emely CUSHING Prance		10-24-1844	04-26-1909	054	PRANCE, John	
				054		

Thomas P. DALEY	1854	1922	054	KELLY, Bridget L.	Catholic Order of Foresters
Bridget L. KELLY Daley	1857	1917	054	DALEY, Thomas P.	
			054		
Thomas FLEMING	04-15-1848	11-14-1899	054	FLEMING, Thomas	(GAR) Co. B., 8th Rgt, Vt Vols
			054		
Edward RYAN	1836	1917	054	MCLURE, Mary	
Mary MCLURE Ryan	11-17-1839	02-27-1899	054	RYAN, Edward	
			054		
Catherine NORTON	1828	1899	054	NORTON, Catherine	Mother
			054		
Patrick BUCKLEY	1831	1898	054	O'CONNOR, Ann	
Ann O'CONNOR Buckley	1827	1903	054	BUCKLEY, Patrick	
			054		
John CARNEY	05-07-1827	05-20-1899	054	_____, Catherine	
Catherine _____ CARNEY	07-20-1844		054	CARNEY, John	
			054		
Thomas DUNN	1828		054	SHIPPE, Esther	
Esther SHIPPE Dunn	1835	1899	054	DUNN, Thomas	
			054		
Patrick NORTON	1851	1901	054	_____, Kathrine	
Kathrine _____ NORTON	1862	1895	054	NORTON, Patrick	
			054		
Francis WRIGHT	92Y6M15D	08-11-1897	054	_____, Margaret	
Margaret _____ WRIGHT		02-23-18_7	054	WRIGHT, Francis	(Stone deteriorated. Cannot read DOB and YOD)
			054		
			054		
Edward DONEGAN	10-08-1807	12-03-1882	054	BOWE, Sarah	
Sarah BOWE Donegan	03-31-1812	01-02-1879	054	DONEGAN, Edward	
Patrick BOWE	03-17-1793	09-25-1878	054	BOWE, Patrick	
			054		
Owen DONEGAN	1817	1882	054	PARKER, Margaret	
Margaret PARKER Donegan	1818	1890	054	DONEGAN, Owen	
Lizzie DONEGAN	1846	1931	054	DONEGAN, Lizzie	
Josie S. DONEGAN	1855	1924	054	DONEGAN, Josie S.	
			054		
George W. RANN	07-15-1831	02-01-1896	054	MURPHY, Margaret	
Margaret MURPHY Rann	69 Years	04-02-1902	054	RANN, George W.	
Margaret MURPHY	96 Years	09-14-1885	054	MURPHY, Margaret	
			054		
Edward MURPHY	70 Years	10-31-1893	054	CONNOR, Mary	
Mary CONNOR Murphy			054	MURPHY, Edward	
			054		
Francis G. POWERS	70Y6M17D	11-07-1885	054	_____, Ann	
Ann _____ POWERS	58 Years	10-08-1876	054	POWERS, Francis G.	
Lizzie L. POWERS	20Y5M8D	02-02-1880	054	POWERS, Lizzie L.	

				054		
Charles DERUSHA		06-15-1833	06-02-1880	054	GRIFFIN, Mary	
Mary GRIFFIN Derusha		06-24-1836	06-12-1924	054	DERUSHA, Charles	
				054		
William MITCHELL		05-16-1842	10-23-1915	054	_____, Kate D.	
Kate D. _____ MITCHELL		06-24-1848	07-03-1931	054	MITCHELL, William	
				054		
John CARROLL		04-30-1855	03-07-1914	054	REGAN, Ellen	
Ellen REGAN Carroll		05-08-1863		054	CARROLL, John	

St. **John The Baptist Cemetery, Mechanic Street, North Bennington, Vermont**

NAME	**POB**	**DOB/AGE**	**DOD**	**CEM**	**SPOUSE/INDEX**	**INSCRIPTION**
Mary MURPHY Fleming		1900	1977	055	MURPHY, Mary	
Kenneth J. FLEMING		1901	1983	055	FLEMING, Kenneth J.	
				055		
Daniel COLLINS		1827	1917	055	MCMAHON, Mary	
Mary MCMAHON Collins		1838	1912	055	COLLINS, Daniel	
				055		
Nellie PICKETT Mooney		1859	1919	055	PICKETT, Nellie	(NOI Mr. Mooney)
				055		
William EDGAR		06-29-1846	08-14-1923	055	HARLAN, Bridget	
Bridget HARLAN Edgar		08-27-1846	12-15-1925	055	EDGAR, William	
				055		
Margaret MCMAHON		1815	1895	055	MCMAHON, Margaret	
John MCMAHON		1847	1888	055	MCMAHON, John	
Ann MCMAHON		1848	1925	055	MCMAHON, Ann	
				055		
Michael CORCORAN		09-24-1848	12-19-1918	055	MCGUIRE, Ellen	
Ellen MCGUIRE Corcoran		08-05-1860	03-06-1894	055	CORCORAN, Michael	
John CORCORAN		05-12-1846	01-29-1916	055	CORCORAN, John	
				055		
Patrick BARNES		1854	1935	055	_____, Margaret	
Margaret _____ BARNES		1860	1940	055	BARNES, Patrick	
				055		
Mark MCGOVERN		1850	1921	055	_____, Margaret	
Margaret _____ MCGOVERN		1852	1921	055	MCGOVERN, Mark	
				055		
Thomas POWERS		1831	1909	055	_____, Anastasia	
Anastasia _____ POWERS		1838	1899	055	POWERS, Thomas	
Nora POWERS		1867	1964	055		
Edward L. DAILEY		1870	1913	055	_____, Ellen	

Ellen _____ DAILEY	1869	1937	055	DAILEY, Edward L.	
			055		
John FITZGERALD		04-14-1887	055	FITZGERALD, John	(Does not say if husband--wife
Honora FITZGERALD		02-06-1905	055	FITZGERALD, Honora	NOI DOB / age at death)
			055		
William MEAGHER	1821	1906	055	HENNEBERY, Bridget	
Bridget HENNEBERY Meagher	1830	1892	055	MEAGHER, William	
John Henry MEAGHER	1859	1892	055	MEAGHER, John Henry	
Edward MEAGHER	1868	1894	055	MEAGHER, Edward	
William MEAGHER	1865	1921	055	MEAGHER, William	
Margaret MEAGHER	1865	1939	055	MEAGHER, Margaret	
Patrick MEAGHER	1858	1929	055	MEAGHER, Patrick	
Catherine MEAGHER	1858	1932	055	MEAGHER, Catherine	
Mary MEAGHER	1854	1913	055	MEAGHER, Mary	
James MEAGHER	1873	1926	055	MEAGHER, James	
Richard MEAGHER	1867	1933	055	MEAGHER, Richard	
			055		
Catherine GRIFFIN	11-19-1858	12-01-1934	055	GRIFFIN, Catherine	
			055		
Michael DOWNS	68 Years	03-27-1907	055	DOWNS, Michael	
			055		
Thomas FARRELL	1854	1942	055	_____, Margaret	
Margaret _____ FARRELL	1873	1936	055	FARRELL, Thomas	
			055		
Henry S. SHANAHAN	1840	1907	055	CASSIDY, Bridget	
Bridget CASSIDY Shanahan	1842	1915	055	SHANAHAN, Henry S.	
John H. SHANAHAN	1868	1938	055	SHANAHAN, John H.	
Sabinia SHANAHAN Baldwin	1878	1906	055	BALDWIN, William	(NOI William Baldwin)
			055	SHANAHAN, Sabinia	
			055		
Elizabeth POWERS Cummings	1848	1930	055	CUMMINGS, Hugh	(NOI Hugh Cummings)
			055	POWERS, Elizabeth	
Thomas CUMMINGS	1872	1931	055	CUMMINGS, Thomas	
Hugh CUMMINGS	1877	1954	055	CUMMINGS, Hugh	
			055		
Paul CUNNINGHAM	1834	1904	055	MOONEY, Mary	
Mary MOONEY Cunningham	1856	1931	055	CUNNINGHAM, Paul	
John MOONEY	1821	1886	055	CUNNINGHAM, Ellen	
Ellen CUNNINGHAM Mooney	1829	1893	055	MOONEY, John	
Edward MOONEY	1862	1889	055	MOONEY, Edward	(S/O John & Ellen Mooney)
			055		
Patrick MCCARTHY	1847	1921	055	O'CONNELL, Margaret A.	
Margaret O'CONNELL McCarthy	1852	1925	055	MCCARTHY, Patrick	
			055		
Martin F. CUMMINGS	1852	1909	055	PRICE, Bridget M.	

Name	Born	Died		Spouse/Index	Notes
Bridget M. PRICE Cummings	1860	1921	055	CUMMINGS, Martin F.	
			055		
James HORTON	1845	1914	055	TRACEY, Katherine J.	
Katherine J. TRACEY Horton	1855	1913	055	HORTON, James	
Francis E. HORTON	1860	1907	055	HORTON, Frances E.	
			055		
James LEONARD	1856	1928	055	FITZGERALD, Johannah	
Johannah FITZGERALD Leonard	1858	1908	055	LEONARD, James	
David LEONARD	1835	1922	055	LEONARD, David	
Bridget LEONARD	1897	1971	055	LEONARD, Bridget	
Bridget C. LEONARD	1835	1918	055	LEONARD, Bridget C.	
John LEONARD	1858	1918	055	LEONARD, John	Her Son(Of Bridget C. Leonard)
			055		
James P. MORRISSEY	1840	1917	055	MCGRATH, Bridget	
Bridget MCGRATH Morrissey	1841	1915	055	MORRISSEY, James P.	
			055		
Michael MULCAHEY	1833	1910	055	COLLINS, Nora	
Nora COLLINS Mulcahey	1857	1909	055	MULCAHEY, Michael	
			055		
Michael CRAVEN	1855	1917	055	CONNOLLY, Mary	
Mary CONNOLLY Craven	1855	1936	055	CRAVEN, Michael	
			055		
Timothy MCCARTHY	1849	1917	055	_____, Mary E.	
Mary E. _____ MCCARTHY	1855	1904	055	MCCARTHY, Timothy	
			055		
Edward J. DONNELLY	1849	1927	055	NASH , Mary A.	
Mary A. NASH Donnelly	1863	1927	055	DONNELLY, Edward J.	
			055		
Bartholomew CASEY	1852	1906	055	JONES, Margaret	
Margaret JONES Casey	1858	1932	055	CASEY, Bartholomew	
			055		
James SCAREY	1828	1904	055	HOWE, Julia	
Julia HOWE Scarey	1837	1907	055	SCAREY, James	
			055		
Antone MYERS	05-10-1840	02-05-1931	055	_____, Mary L.	(Probably French-Canadian)
Mary L. _____ MYERS	06-20-1841	03-27-1916	055	MYERS, Antone	
			055		
William H. MURPHY	1847	1929	055	HOREY, Annie	
Annie HOREY Murphy	1848	1926	055	MURPHY, William H.	
			055		
Patrick GRIFFIN	1820	1897	055	CASEY, Bridget	
Bridget CASEY Griffin	1836	1912	055	GRIFFIN, Patrick	
			055		
Michael O'KEEFE	1826	1906	055	_____, Johanna	
Johanna _____ O'KEEFE	1829	1911	055	O'KEEFE, Michael	

NAME	POB	DOB/AGE	DOD	CEM	SPOUSE/INDEX	INSCRIPTION
				055		
John DONLAN		1839	1925	055	DERMODY, Catherine	
Catherine DERMODY Donlan		1847	1912	055	DONLAN, John	
				055		
Joseph M. MURPHY		1872	1946	055	POWERS, Mary E.	
Mary E. POWERS Murphy		1874	1953	055	MURPHY, Joseph M.	
				055		
John POWERS		1848	1916	055	JONES, Mary	
Mary JONES Powers		1850	1921	055	POWERS, John	
				055		
Roscoe R. COLE		12-15-1865	03-02-1941	055	QUINN, Kate C.	
Kate C. QUINN Cole		01-15-1857	09-05-1903	055	COLE, Roscoe R.	
				055		
James HEWSON		1838	1894	055	DORAN, Margaret	
Margaret DORAN Hewson		1839	1921	055	HEWSON, James	
Anna C. HEWSON		1866	1909	055	HEWSON, Anna C.	
George HEWSON		1877	1960	055	HEWSON, George	
William HEWSON		1874	1919	055	HEWSON, William	
Richard HEWSON		1868	1956	055	HEWSON, Richard	
Ellen HEWSON		1865	1929	055	HEWSON, Ellen	
Edward M. HEWSON		1866	1936	055	HEWSON, Edward M.	

Calvary Cemetery - Northfield, VT. (New Cemetery - North of Village on Vermnt Route 12)

NAME	POB	DOB/AGE	DOD	CEM	SPOUSE/INDEX	INSCRIPTION
Stephen BURKE		29 Years	07-19-1857	056	BURKE, Stephen	
				056		
Michael BURKE	Co. Tipperary	12-26-1802	10-31-1866	056	____, Catherine	A Native of Golden, County
				056		Tipperary, Ireland
Catharine ____ BURKE	Co. Cork	06-05-1801	11-08-1871	056	BURKE, Michael	A Native of Watergrass Hill,
				056		Co. Cork, Ireland
				056		
James DOLAN	Co. Cavan	1827	1888	056	CONWELL, Margaret	County "Caven" (Cavan), Ire
Margaret CONWELL Dolan	Co. Donegal	1830	1908	056	BURKE, Michael	(See William Conwell)
William CONWELL	Co. Donegal	1839	1911	056	CONWELL, William	A Native of "Killybeges"
				056		(Killybegs), Co. "Doneygall"
				056		(Donegal), Ireland. 8th Regt,
				056		Indiana Volunteers
				056		
William DALTON		1856	1936	056	____, Margaret	
Margaret ____ DALTON		1856	1932	056	DALTON, William	
				056		

Name	Born	Died	Code	Index	Notes
Hannah DUGGAN	1840	1921	056	DUGGAN, Hannah	
			056		
John THORNE	1857	1946	056	____, Mary	
Mary ____ THORNE	1862	1943	056	THORNE, John	
			056		
James HAYES	03-26-	01-22-1924	056	HAYES, James	(Did not say if James & Julia
Julia HAYES	08-15-1851	07-17-1932	056	HAYES, Julia	were husband and wife)
Bridget TEAHAN	02-15-1843	12-19-1918	056	TEAHAN, Bridget	
Mary HAYES Barton	08-03-1879	04-09-1919	056	HAYES, Mary	(NOI Mr. Barton)
			056		
			056		
Jeremiah MCCARTHY	1858	1945	056	DOLAN, Rose E.	
Rose E. DOLAN McCarthy	1872	1939	056	MCCARTHY, Jeremiah	
William C. MCCARTHY	1898	1952	056	MCCARTHY, William C.	
Felix E. MCCARTHY	1861	1932	056	MCCARTHY, Felix E.	
			056		
John DONNELLY	1830	1901	056	DONNELLY, John	
			056		
Michael BROWN	1855	1909	056	THURN, Ethelonia	
Ethelonia THURN Brown	1848	1925	056	BROWN, Michael	
			056		
Richard KENNEDY	1848	1916	056	FITZGERALD, Mary	
Mary FITZGERALD Kennedy	1861	1904	056	KENNEDY, Richard	
James L. KENNEDY	1877	1905	056	KENNEDY, James L.	
Thomas C. KENNEDY	1878	1944	056	KENNEDY, Thomas C.	
Richard W. KENNEDY	1880		056	KENNEDY, Richard W.	
Clarisa J. KENNEDY	1881	1954	056	KENNEDY, Clarisa J.	
Clara J. KENNEDY	1882	1967	056	KENNEDY, Clara J.	
John P. KENNEDY	1885	1896	056	KENNEDY, John P.	
Frank E.KENNEDY	1887		056	KENNEDY, Frank E.	
			056		
Nicholas FLOOD	05-15-1839	06-25-1919	056	____, Bridget	
Bridget ____ FLOOD	08-15-1835	12-27-1915	056	FLOOD, Nicholas	
			056		
Cornelius L. SPLOYD	1857	1919	056	DONAHUE, Julia L.	
Julia L. DONAHUE Sployd	1857	1947	056	SPLOYD, Cornelius L.	
			056		
John KEOUGH	1829	1920	056	CANNAN, Hanora	
Hanora CANNAN Keough	1836	1910	056	KEOUGH, John	
Margaret CARRIGAN	1837	1925	056	CARRIGAN, Margaret	
			056		
Jeremiah KELLEY	1832	1864	056	DONAHUE, Ann	(GAR) Co. I, 11th Reg, Vt Vols
Ann DONAHUE Kelley	1835	1926	056	KELLEY, Jeremiah	
Elizabeth KELLEY	1855	1894	056	KELLEY, Elizabeth	
John KELLEY	1858	1916	056	KELLEY, John	

Robert W. KELLEY	1861	1925	056	KELLEY, Robert W.	
Johanna KELLEY	1864		056	KELLEY, Johanna	
			056		
Henry HOGAN	1842	1930	056	TEHAN, Mary	
Mary TEHAN Hogan	1841	1914	056	HOGAN, Henry	
William HOGAN	1840	1913	056	HOGAN, William	
			056		
John KINGSTON Sr.	1826	1900	056	KINGSTON, Mary	
Mary KINGSTON Kingston	1826	1898	056	KINGSTON, John Sr.	
John KINGSTON Jr.	1851	1920	056	MCDONOUGH, Mary	
Mary MCDONOUGH Kingston	1859	1922	056	KINGSTON, John Jr.	
			056		
Dennis DONAHUE	1847	1920	056	_____, Mary	
Mary ___ DONAHUE	1857	1938	056	DONAHUE, Dennis	
			056		
David HASSETT	08-28-1836	04-14-1911	056	BURKE, Mary A.	
Mary A. BURKE Hassett	10-13-1836	02-02-1914	056	HASSETT, David	Here in The Peace Of Christ
			056		Rests Mary A. Burke, Wife Of
			056		David Hassett. Born at Willi-
			056		ston, Vermont, Died at North-
			056		field.
			056		
Margaret MULCAHY Holland	1838	1914	056	HOLLAND, Timothy	(NOI Timothy Holland)
			056	MULCAHY, Margaret	
			056		
Michael FLINN	1854	1931	056	_____, Mary	
Mary ___ FLINN	1870	1931	056	FLINN, Michael	
			056		
Dennis DONAHUE	1811	1875	056	LYNCH, Johanna	
Johanna LYNCH Donahue	1808	1903	056	DONAHUE, Dennis	
John DONAHUE	1842	1864	056	DONAHUE, John	
Ellen M. DONAHUE	1845	1926	056	DONAHUE, Ellen M.	
			056		
Katharine DONAHUE Corry	1855	1912	056	DONAHUE, Catherine	Our Mother. (NOI Mr. Corry)
			056		
Jeremiah MCCARTHY	1857	1921	056	O'NEILL, Mary	
Mary O'NEILL McCarthy	1855	1925	056	MCCARTHY, Jeremiah	
Katherine CRIMMINS McCarthy	1832	1913	056	CRIMMINS, Katherine	
			056		
Barbara THURN Grace	02-29-1855	03-02-1914	056	GRACE, Andrew	(NOI Andrew Grace)
			056	THURN, Barbara	
			056		
William KINGSTON	1840	1910	056	KINGSTON, William	
			056		
John BURKE	1820	1863	056	CONNELL, Ellen	

Name	Born	Died		Spouse	Notes
Ellen CONNELL Burke	1819	1904	056	BURKE, John	
			056		
Michael DONELLY	1836	1917	056	MEEHAN, Katherine	
Katherine MEEHAN Donelly	1836	1914	056	DONELLY, Michael	
			056		
James CANNON	1844	1920	056	GLENNON, Catharine	
Catharine GLENNON Cannon	1850	1933	056	CANNON, James	
			056		
Patrick CANNAN	07-19-1834	06-29-1913	056	CRONAN, Winifred	
Winifred CRONAN Cannan	11-27-1841	05-31-1926	056	CANNAN, Patrick	
			056		
Michael O'GRADY	1826	1899	056	HANLON, Mary	
Mary HANLON O'Grady	1834	1916	056	O'GRADY, Michael	
			056		
John KINSLEY	1849	1929	056	_____, Mary A.	(GAR) Co. E, 17th Vt. Vols
Mary A. ___ KINSLEY	1855	1935	056	KINSLEY, John	
			056		
Mathias CANNON	1838	1925	056	CRONIN, Mary	
Mary CRONIN Cannon	1839	1910	056	CANNAN, Mathias	
"Aunt" MARY	1836	1921	056	MARY, "Aunt"	
Michael CANNON	50Y2M3D	07-18-1890	056	GLENNON, Bridget	
Bridget GLENNON Cannon			056	CANNAN, Michael	(No Dates For Bridget Glennon)
			056		
Michael KINSLEY	1842	1932	056	FISCHER, Sarah	(GAR) Co. D, 1st Reg, Vt. Vols
Sarah FISCHER Kinsley	1863	1936	056	KINSLEY, Michael	
			056		
Edward FOLEY	1841	1908	056	RYLE, Margaret	
Margaret RYLE Foley	1841	1926	056	FOLEY, Edward	
			056		
Edward CUSHING	1839	1921	056	_____, Mary	
Mary ____ CUSHING	1849	1927	056	CUSHING, Edward	
			056		
Michael SULLIVAN	1838	1915	056	COLLINS, Nancy	
Nancy COLLINS Sullivan	1845	1936	056	SULLIVAN, Michael	
			056		
Nicholas FLOOD	05-15-1839	06-25-1915	056	_______, Bridget	
Bridget ____ FLOOD	08-18-1835	10-27-1816	056	FLOOD, Nicholas	
			056		
Henry LAFLEY	1853	1905	056	DOLAN, Mary	
Mary DOLAN Lafley	1862	1944	056	LAFLEY, Henry	

Calvary Cemetery - Northfield, VT. (Old Cemetery - On East Street)

NAME	POB	DOB/AGE	DOD	CEM	SPOUSE/INDEX	INSCRIPTION
John MORIARTY		1839	1914	057	DOOLEY, Katharine	
Katharine DOOLEY Moriarty		1848	1914	057	MORIARTY, John	
Jennie M. MORIARTY		1866	1945	057	MORIARTY, Jennie M.	
Harry E. MORIARTY		1878	1927	057	MORIARTY, Harry E.	
				057		
Richard CARRIGAN		1830	1893	057	STACK, Mary	
Mary STACK Carrigan		1848	1905	057	CARRIGAN, Richard	
				057		
T. O'GRADY		72 Years	09-06-1894	057	____, Bridget	
Bridget ____ O'GRADY		73 Years	11-12-1892	057	O'GRADY, T.	
John O'GRADY		1852	1933	057	O'GRADY, John	
Thomas O'GRADY		40 Years	08-02-1907	057	O'GRADY, Thomas	
				057		
Patrick O'GRADY		1827	1920	057	MACKSEY, Ellen	
Ellen MACKSEY O'Grady		1845	1900	057	O'GRADY, Patrick	
Richard O'GRADY				057	O'GRADY, Richard	
Bernard O'GRADY				057	O'GRADY, Bernard	
Patrick O'Grady JR.				057	O'GRADY, Patrick Jr.	
				057		
Thomas DEVINE		50 Years	04-03-1857	057	ELIOT, Mary	
Mary ELIOTT Devine		49 Years	10-21-1866	057	DEVINE, Thomas	
Thomas DEVINE		43 Years	08-16-1890	057	DEVINE, Thomas	
James DEVINE		29 Years	08-17-1886	057	DEVINE, James	
M. DEVINE		51 Years	12-30-1900	057	DEVINE, M.	
Christopher DEVINE		29 Years	12-11-1867	057	DEVINE, Christopher	
Elizabeth DEVINE		26 Years	11-10-1871	057	DEVINE, Elizabeth	
				057		
				057		
Patrick MCNAMARA		03-16-1817	11-27-1908	057	ELLIOT, Alice	
Alice ELLIOT McNamara		11-01-1830	05-24-1901	057	MCNAMARA, Patrick	
Julia MCNAMARA		1853	1872	057	MCNAMARA, Julia	
Alice MCNAMARA		1861	1863	057	MCNAMARA, Alice	
John H. MCNAMARA		09-12-1858	01-06-1929	057	MCNAMARA, John H.	
Alice MCNAMARA		1872	1931	057	MCNAMARA, Alice	
				057		
John LYNCH		05-15-1863	12-26-1888	057	____, Johannah	
Johannah ____ LYNCH		05-02-1861	11-26-1896	057	LYNCH, John	
				057		
John CLEURY	Co. Clare	77 Years	02-06-1889	057	CARROLL, Margaret	Native of Parish of Inisdimon

Name	Origin	Age/Born	Died	No.	Stone	Notes
				057		(Probably Ennistymon (Kilmana-
				057		heen & Clooney) Co. Clare.)
Margaret CARROLL Cleury		83 Years	11-03-1905	057	CLEURY, John	
Johnie CLEURY		33 Years	03-13-1887	057	CLEURY, Johnie	Died At Marshall, Texas
				057		
Bridget HOLLAND Cashen		1851	1889	057	CASHEN, James	(NOI James Cashen)
				057	HOLLAND, Bridget	
Margaret E. CASHEN		1884	1885	057	CASHEN, Margaret E.	
Julia A. CASHEN		1886	1887	057	CASHEN, Julia A.	
Timothy CASHEN		1888	1888	057	CASHEN, Timothy	
				057		
James DOHENY		1828	1917	057	O'CONNOR, Mary	
Mary O'CONNOR Doheny		1849	1912	057	DOHENY, James	
Michael DOHENY		1879	1885	057	DOHENY, Michael	
Edward DOHENY		1873	1916	057	DOHENY, Edward	
Margaret A. DOHENY		1878	1941	057	DOHENY, Margaret A.	
Katherine C. DOHENY		1876	1953	057	DOHENY, Katherine C.	
				057		
Michael SPILLANE		1832	1924	057	HOLLAND, Hanora	
Hanora HOLLAND Spillane		1837	1924	057	SPILLANE, Michael	
				057		
Patrick MCCARTY	Co. Cork	40 Years	09-23-1866	057	MCCARTY, Patrick	Native of Dunmanway, Co. Cork
				057		
Lawrence SPLAINE		1828	1916	057	SPLAINE, Lawrence	
				057		
Ellen B. CONNELL Ryan		11-04-1857	12-10-1888	057	RYAN, Maurice	(NOI Maurice Ryan)
				057	CONNELL, Ellen B.	
				057		
John HARRINGTON		45 Years	08-18-1903	057	_____, Anne	
Anne _____ HARRINGTON			11-27-1927	057	HARRINGTON, John	
Maurice HARRINGTON		78 Years	02-09-1884	057	O'CONNELL, Julia	
Julia O'CONNELL Harrington		80 Years	05-30-1897	057	HARRINGTON, Maurice	
James HARRINGTON		21Y 4M	08-13-1864	057	HARRINGTON, James	Son Of Maurice & Julia
				057		Harrington
				057		
Sarah _____ HANLON				057	HANLON, Michael	(NOI Michael Hanlon & Stone is
				057	_____, Sarah	Broken. Date portion missing)
				057		
Theresa DOUGHERTY			DEC 1855	057	DOUGHERTY, Theresa	Dau of A & Mary Dougherty
				057		(NOI DOB or Parents)
				057		
James TIERNEY		38 Years	05-06-1855	057	TIERNEY, James	
				057		
Maurice CONNELL		70 Years	09-15-1856	057	CONNELL, Maurice	
				057		

Hannora ___ LAWLOR		47Y 11M	01-05-1875	057	LAWLOR, Morris	(NOI Morris Lawlor)
				057	_____, Hannora	
				057		
David RYAN	Co. Cork	38 Years	01-12-1861	057	RYAN, David	(Looks Like Mallow, Co. Cork, but badly deteriorated)
				057		
				057		
Mary CLANCY		50 Years	01-09-1859	057	CLANCY, Mary	Mother
				057		
Thomas ELLIOT		68 Years	08-26-1896	057	DELANY, Mary	
Mary DELANY Elliot		75 Years	11-19-1905	057	ELLIOT, Thomas	
Julia ELLIOT		12-22-1854	03-06-1879	057	ELLIOT, Julia	
Christopher ELLIOT		04-01-1863	04-20-1898	057	ELLIOT, Christopher	
Thomas ELLIOT Jr.		04-23-1868	10-01-1912	057	ELLIOT, Thomas Jr.	
Patrick H. ELLIOT		12-01-1860	04-11-1902	057	_____, Hattie W.	
Hattie W. ____ ELLIOT		01-27-1869	04-07-1953	057	ELLIOT, Patrick H.	
				057		
Cornelius HURLEY		33Y 6M	06-13-1867	057	HURLEY, Cornelius	
James HURLEY		22Y 2M	06-16-1883	057	HURLEY, James	
Cornelius HURLEY		33Y 5M	12-11-1898	057	HURLEY, Cornelius	
John C. HURLEY		09-18-1861	11-22-1909	057	O'DONAHUE, Mary	
Mary O'DONAHUE Hurley		04-11-1863	11-06-1940	057	HURLEY, John C.	
John Gregory HURLEY		1893	1962	057	HURLEY, John Gregory	
Edward Timothy HURLEY		1895	1965	057	HURLEY, Edward Timothy	
Paul O'Donahue HURLEY		1900	1964	057	HURLEY, Paul O'Donahue	
Mary Dorothy HURLEY		1887	1972	057	HURLEY, Mary Dorothy	
James Cornelius HURLEY		1890	1896	057	HURLEY, James Cornelius	
Anna Cornelia HURLEY		1897	1981	057	HURLEY, Anna Cornelia	
				057		
Michail HURLEY		16Y 4M	01-27-1865	057	HURLEY, Michail	Son of John & Mary Hurley
				057		
				057		
				057		
Rodger MOYNAHAN		18 Years	05-08-1880	057	MOYNAHAN, Rodger	Son Of Jerry & Johana Moynahan Killed At Mineville, NY. (NOI Parents)
				057	MOYNAHAN, Jerry	
				057		
				057		
Thomas KINSLEY		82 Years	05-20-1899	057	MALANY, Sarah	
Sarah MALANY Kinsley		78 Years	06-08-1884	057	KINSLEY, Thomas	
				057		
Michael PEMBROKE		01-10-1825	04-07-1880	057	BROWN, Mary	
Margaret BROWN Pembroke		06-06-1829	01-15-1898	057	PEMBROKE, Michael	
Katherine PEMBROKE		08-25-1854	03-16-1938	057	PEMBROKE, Katherine	
Margaret PEMBROKE		07-02-1861	10-21-1939	057	PEMBROKE, Margaret	
Michael PEMBROKE		05-10-1863	01-14-1940	057	PEMBROKE, Michael	
Thomas B. PEMBROKE		04-25-1866	10-27-1931	057	PEMBROKE, Thomas B.	

				057		
Michael LYNCH		1811	1903	057	MCCARTY, Margaret	
Margaret MCCARTY Lynch		1822	1903	057	LYNCH, Michael	
Michael LYNCH		1855	1920	057	LYNCH, Michael	
John LYNCH		05-15-1863	12-26-1888	057	LYNCH, John	
Johanah LYNCH		05-02-1861	11-26-1896	057	LYNCH, Johanah	
				057		
Michael SULLIVAN		1817	1911	057	ERVING, Mary E.	
Mary E. ERVING Sullivan		1853	1889	057	SULLIVAN, Michael	
				057		
John CRIMMINS	Co. Kerry	07-25-1836	03-10-1895	057	____, Catherine H.	Native(s) Of Co. Kerry, Ire.
Catherine H. ___ CRIMMINS	Co. Kerry	11-21-1835	05-24-1908	057	CRIMMINS, John	Native(s) Of Co. Kerry, Ire.
				057		
Augustus SHONTELL		67 Years	01-17-1907	057	COLE, Mary	(GAR) Co. B., 13th Vt
Mary COLE Shontell		49Y3M19D	10-22-1890	057	SHONTELL, Augustus	
				057		
Michael CORCORAN		78 Years	03-17-1902	057	_____, Sarah	
Sarah ____ CORCORAN		60 Years	08-01-1891	057	CORCORAN, Michael	
Cornelius CORCORAN		30 Years	12-28-1890	057	CORCORAN, Cornelius	
Daniel CORCORAN		19 Years	02-25-1887	057	CORCORAN, Daniel	
John LYNCH		02-14-1857	08-08-1924	057	LYNCH, John	
Catherine LYNCH		02-19-1858	02-19-1953	057	LYNCH, Catherine	
				057		
Timothy MALONEY		60 Years	07-31-1870	057	MACK, Hanora	
Hanora MACK Maloney		37Y 8M	08-31-1861	057	MALONEY, Timothy	
Rebecca MALONEY		3 Months	09-21-1861	057	MALONEY, Rebecca	
Timothy MALONEY		1Y 9M	05-16-1856	057	MALONEY, Timothy	
Elizabeth MALONEY		5 Years	08-28-1863	057	MALONEY, Elizabeth	
				057		
John MOLONEY		45 Years	08-31-1865	057	STAR, Sarah	
Sarah STAR Moloney		86 Years	08-23-1912	057	MOLONEY, John	
John MOLONEY		1Y 9M	06-16-1864	057	MOLONEY, John	
				057		
Michael KINSLEY		44 Years	08-05-1870	057	STARR, Ann	
Ann STARR Kinsley		70 Years	10-21-1892	057	KINSLEY, Michael	
Michael KINSLEY		20Y7M8D	01-23-1877	057	KINSLEY, Michael	
Dinnes KINSLEY			05-01-1869	057	KINSLEY, Dinnes	(Cannot read age at death)
				057		
Edward WHITE		10-12-1825	01-07-1908	057	LADUKE, Catherine	
Catherine LADUKE White		06-06-1824	03-13-1895	057	WHITE, Edward	
				057		
James FARRELL		32 Years	11-06-1876	057	_____, Mary	
Mary ____ FARRELL		88 Years	01-22-1932	057	FARRELL, James	
				057		
P. GILBERT		1833	1916	057	______, Ellen	

Name	Origin	Age/Born	Died	Code	Index	Remarks
Ellen ___ GILBERT		1835	1915	057	GILBERT, P.	
				057		
Edward HOLLAND		7 Years	08-02-1859	057	HOLLAND, Edward	Son Of Michael & Ellen Holland
				057	HOLLAND, Michael	
				057		
Michael CASHEN		05-13-1827	11-04-1895	057	CAHILL, Bridget	
Bridget CAHILL Cashen		07-10-1830	06-30-1913	057	CASHEN, Michael	
				057		
				057		
				057		
				057		
Thomas EVERETT	Co. Kilkenny	63 Years	07-25-1864	057	_____, Mary	Native of Co. Kilkenny, Ire.
Mary ____ EVERETT	Co. Kilkenny	58 Years	06-13-1865	057	EVERETT, Thomas	Native of Co. Kilkenny, Ire.
				057		
John MCVAY	Co. Dublin	52Y10M4D	03-24-1886	057	______, Mary	Native of Dublin, Ireland. Co.
				057		(GAR) Co. C. 15th Rgt VT Vols
				057		(NOI Mary)
				057		
Catherine CRONAN	Co. Galway	27 Years	11-27-1862	057	CRONAN, Catherine	Dau of P & C Cronan. Native of
				057		Parish of Athleague, County
				057		Galway, (Stone Deteriorated)
				057		
John MCCARTHY	Co. Cork	33Y11M12D	09-19-1861	057	_____, Hannorah	Native of Parish Kilmichael,
				057		Co. Cork, Ire. Killed at
				057		Montpelier (Vermont).
Hannorah ___ MCCARTHY		84 Years	11-17-1907	057	MCCARTHY, John	
				057		
Rodger DONAHOE	Co. Kerry	53 Years	09-16-1857	057	____, Ellen	Husband of Ellen Donahoe and
				057	DONAHOE, Rodger	Son Of John & Hannora Donahoe.
				057	DONAHOE, John	Native of Co. Kerry, Ireland
				057		(NOI Ellen Donahoe)
				057		
Nancy KINGSTON Collins	Co. Cork	64 Years	08-06-1876	057	COLLINS, Bartholomew	Native of The Parish of Drimo-
				057	KINGSTON, Nancy	league, Co. Cork, Ireland.
				057		(NOI Bartholomew Collins)
				057		
Patrick COLLINS	Co. Cork	28 Years	02-03-1870	057	COLLINS, Patrick	Son Of Bartholomew & Nancy
				057		Collins. Native of Drimoleague
				057		Co. Cork, Ireland
				057		
Patrick O'DAY	Co. Limerick	----	----	057	O'DAY, Patrick	(Did not state relationship of
Bridget O'DAY	Co. Limerick	62 Years	10-26-1888	057	O'DAY, Bridget	Patrick & Bridget O'Day)
Lizzie O'DAY		37 Years	07-20-1897	057	O'DAY, Lizzie	
				057		
Catherine O'BRIEN	Co. Clare	67 Years	02-22-1870	057	O'BRIEN, Catherine	Parish of 'Facle' (Feakle),

				057		Co. Clare, Ireland
Patrick O'BRIEN		22 Years	06-11-1860	057	O'BRIEN, Patrick	(Same Plot as Catherine
				057		O'Brien)
				057		
Edmond STACK	Co. Kerry	65 Years	03-30-1880	057	DALY, Mary	Native of Parish of "Kenmare",
				057		Co. Kerry, Ire (Deteriorated)
				057		
Mary DALY Stack	Co. Kerry	30 Years	12-23-1859	057	STACK, Edmond	And Her Baby Ann. Native of
				057	STACK, Baby Ann	Parish of 'Balycady' (Bally-
				057		kealy, Ballyseedy), Co. Kerry
				057		Ire.(Stone badly deteriorated)
John STACK	Northfield,Vt	21Y 3M 28D	09-26-1874	057	STACK, John	Son Of Edmond & Mary Stack.
				057		Native of Northfield, VT.
				057		
Margaret CARNEY Sexton	Co. Tipperary	46 Years	11-20-1869	057	SEXTON, James	A Native of Co. Tipperary, Par
				057	CARNEY, Margaret	Castletown (Castletownarra),
				057		Castletown, Ire (NOI James
				057		Sexton)
				057		
James RYAN	Co. Waterford	78 Years	01-20-1888	057	LEAHY, Hanora	A Native of Castlemiles, Co.
				057		Waterford, Ire.
Hanora LEAHY Ryan		89 Years	03-10-1907	057	RYAN, James	
Anstais RYAN		8Y1M5D	09-05-1849	057	RYAN, Anstais	
Anstais RYAN		2Y 2M	12-28-1856	057	RYAN, Anstais	
				057		
William KELLY		1822	1900	057	____, Catherine	
Catherine ____ KELLY		1826	1903	057	KELLY, William	
Patrick KELLY		1853	1898	057	KELLY, Patrick	
				057		
Anne KELLY		19Y 8M	12-29-1875	057	KELLY, Anne	Dau Of William & Catherine
				057		Kelly
				057		
Bernard CONNELL		1831	1900	057	KEOUGH, Bridget	
Bridget KEOUGH Connell		1833	1919	057	CONNELL, Bernard	
				057		
William HANAN	Co. Clare	2 Years	05-09-1857	057	HANAN, William	Son(s) Of John & Bridget Hanan
Cornelious HANAN	Co. Clare	3 Years	04-29-1856	057	HANAN, Cornelious	Son(s) Of John & Bridget Hanan
				057	HANAN, John	
				057		
Peter MCGUINNESS		07-07-1818	10-14-1894	057	________, Bridget	
Bridget ___ MCGUINNESS		08-15-1813		057	MCGUINNESS, Peter	
Margaret MCGUINNESS		6M 27D	02-27-1856	057	MCGUINNESS, Peter	
				057		
Father DUPHINEY		71 Years	09-11-1864	057	DUPHINEY, Father	(Possibly Duffany??)
				057		

Bridget ___ SULLIVAN		47 Years	12-30-1880	057	SULLIVAN, Daniel	(NOI Daniel Sullivan)
Ellen SULLIVAN		24 Years	06-24-1877	057	SULLIVAN, Ellen	Dau of Danl & Bridget Sullivan
Nora D. SULLIVAN		12 Years	12-05-1869	057	SULLIVAN, Nora D.	
				057		
Mary HOGAN Hartley		1790	1874	057	HARTLEY, James	(NOI James Hartley)
				057	HOGAN, Mary	
				057		
William HAUGHS		40 Years	09-24-1864	057	HAUGHS, William	
				057		
Lawrence DELANY		50 Years	11-30-1881	057	DELANY, Lawrence	
				057		
Bridget OSBORNE Starr		1831	1865	057	OSBORNE, Bridget	
				057		
Margaret CONWAY Cavanaugh	Co. Limerick	58 Years	06-13-1863	057	CAVANAUGH, Lawrence	Native(s) Of Co. Limerick
				057	CONWAY, Margaret	
Lawrence CONWAY	Co. Limerick	52 Years	10-06-1865	057	CONWAY, Lawrence	Native(s) Of Co. Limerick
				057		Her Brother
Stephen CAVANAUGH	Co. Limerick	23 Years	09-14-1866	057	CAVANAUGH, Stephen	Native(s) Of Co. Limerick
				057		
William MURPHY		45 Years	10-16-1862	057	____, Margaret	
Margaret ___ MURPHY		76 Years	11-17-1905	057	MURPHY, William	
Mary A. MURPHY		41 Years	08-29-1902	057	MURPHY, Mary A.	
Lizzie C. MURPHY Gilligan		50 Years	02-02-1890	057	GILLIGAN, P. C.	(NOI P.C. Gilligan)
Julia MURPHY		11 Years	08-12-1868	057	MURPHY, Julia	
James C. MURPHY		31 Years	07-08-1886	057	MURPHY, James C.	
				057		
Jerry COONAN		23Y 1M	07-02-1866	057	COONAN, Jerry	
				057		
Catherine WATERS		13Y 3D	05-28-1866	057	WATERS, Catherine	Dau Of James--Catherine Waters
				057		
Daniel MURPHY		6Y6M17D	08-12-1868	057	MURPHY, Daniel	Son Of John & Hanora Murphy
				057	MURPHY, John	
				057		
Margaret DAILEY		18 Years	01-01-1871	057	DAILEY, Margaret	Dau of P & E Dailey, And An
				057		Infant
				057		
Patrick O'NEILL	Co. Cork	79 Years	08-14-1887	057	________, Ellen	(Probably Dunmanway, Co. Cork,
				057		But Stone Badly Deteriorated)
Ellen ____ O'NEILL	Co. Cork	56 Years	07-22-1867	057	O'NEILL, Patrick	Native Of Dunmanway, Co. Cork
				057		
Michael MALOY		25 Years	10-13-1871	057	____, Margaret	
Margaret ___ MALOY		85 Years	11-15-1926	057	MALOY, Michael	
				057		
Cornelius HURLEY		1828	1871	057	O'LEARY, Mary L.	
Mary L. O'LEARY Hurley		1816	1913	057	HURLEY, Cornelius	

Name	Origin	Born/Age	Died	Code	Index	Notes
Mary HURLEY		1851	1925	057	HURLEY, Mary	Dau Of Cornelius & Mary Hurley
Michael HURLEY		1793	1883	057	HURLEY, Michael	
				057		
Peter MORRIS		1815	1895	057	MADDIN, Mary J.	
Mary J. MADDIN Morris		1817	1897	057	MORRIS, Peter	
				057		
Joseph DERRY		86 Years	12-31-1888	057	DERRY, Joseph	
				057		
John HALEY		76 Years	07-26-1886	057	HALEY, John	
				057		
Patrick DUGGAN		03-20-1825	05-26-1893	057	GRANDFIELD, Nancy	
Nancy GRANDFIELD Duggan		03-05-1835	06-29-1902	057	DUGGAN, Patrick	
				057		
Richard SULLIVAN		10 Years	04-07-1863	057	SULLIVAN, Richard	Son Of John & Catherine
				057	SULLIVAN, John	Sullivan
				057		
Timothy HARRIGAN		1845	1923	057	DONOVAN, Mary	
Mary DONOVAN Harrigan		1845	1898	057	HARRIGAN, Timothy	
Dennis HARRIGAN		1853	1881	057	HARRIGAN, Dennis	
John HARRIGAN		1849	1867	057	HARRIGAN, John	
Ellen GOGGIN		1831	1907	057	GOGGIN, Ellen	
				057		
William RAYCROFT		63 Years	07-28-1903	057	_____, Eliza A.	(GAR) 6th Vt.Co. I. & K.,
Eliza A. _____ RAYCROFT		29 Years	04-21-1876	057	RAYCROFT, William	1861-1865
				057		
James HAYES		1829		057	KANE, Bridget	
Bridget KANE HAYES		06-01-1830	02-21-1917	057	HAYES, James	
				057		
Richard TYNAN		56 Years	09-13-1866	057	TYNAN, Richard	
				057		
Patrick MARR		72 Years	03-16-1874	057	_____, Ellen	(NOI Ellen Marr)
Jno MARR				057	MARR, Jno	Co. A, 17th US Inf
				057		
John DONAHUE	Co. Cavan	62 Years	09-24-1869	057	DONAHUE, John	
				057		
James GUBBINS	Co. Tipperary	70 Years	04-21-1858	057	GUBBINS, James	Native of Co.Tipperary, Parish
				057		Of _____. (Could be Inch or
				057		Emly - Stone deteriorated)
				057		
Thomas EVERETT	Co. Kilkenny	63 Years	07-25-1864	057	_____, Mary	Native of Co. Kilkenny, Ire.
Mary ____ EVERETT	Co. Kilkenny	58 Years	06-13-1865	057	EVERETT, Thomas	Native of Co. Kilkenny, Ire.
				057		
John MCVAY	Co. Dublin	52Y10M4D	03-24-1886	057	______, Mary	Native of Dublin, Ireland.
				057		(GAR) C, 15th Rgt, Vt Vols.
				057		(NOI Mary)

Name	Origin	Age/Born	Died	Plot	Related	Remarks
				057		
Catherine CRONAN	Co. Galway	27 Years	11-27-1862	057	CRONAN, Catherine	Dau of P & C Cronan. Native of
				057		Parish of ______, Co. Galway.
				057		(Stone deteriorated).
				057		
John HURLEY	Co. Cork	70 Years	08-07-1876	057	O'NEIL, Mary	Born In Carbery (Carbery
				057		Island) Co. Cork, Ireland
Mary O'NEIL Hurley	Co. Cork	82 Years	12-02-1888	057	HURLEY, John	Born In Dunmanway, Co. Cork, Ire
Sarah HURLEY		28Y 3M	09-06-1874	057	HURLEY, Sarah	
James HURLEY		37Y 6M	01-01-1879	057	HURLEY, James	
				057		
John MCCARTHY	Co. Cork	33Y11M12D	09-19-1861	057	_____, Hannorah	Native of Parish Kilmichael,
				057		Co. Cork, Ire. Killed at
				057		Montpelier (Vermont).
				057		
Hannorah ___ MCCARTHY		84 Years	11-17-1907	057	MCCARTHY, John	
				057		
Rodger DONAHOE	Co. Kerry	53 Years	09-16-1857	057	____, Ellen	Husband of Ellen Donahoe and
				057		Son Of John & Hannora Donahoe.
				057	DONAHOE, John	Native of Co. Kerry, Ireland
				057		
John HOLLAND	Co. Cork	54 Years	07-13-1872	057	BOUGHEN, Margaret	Native of Parish of Bandon,
				057		Co. Cork, Ireland
Margaret BOUGHEN Holland	Co. Cork	80 Years	10-24-1898	057	HOLLAND, John	Native of County Cork, Parish
				057		Of Bandon
				057		
Dennis HOLLAND	Co. Cork	80 Years	08-14-1897	057	RAIRDON, Margaret	Native of Parish Kilmichael,
				057	COTTER, Mary	Co. Cork, Ireland
				057	SWEENEY, Margaret	
Margaret RAIRDON Holland	Co. Cork	75 Years	07-10-1864	057	HOLLAND, Dennis	Native of Parish Kilmichael.
				057		Co. Cork, Ireland
Mary COTTER Holland	Co. Cork	30 Years	02-03-1865	057	HOLLAND, Dennis	Native of Parish Kilmichael.
				057		Co. Cork, Ireland
Margaret SWEENEY Holland		1839	1914	057	HOLLAND, Dennis	Wife of Dennis Holland
				057		
John MCCARTY	Co. Cork	66 Years	09-06-1888	057	________, Ellenor	Native of Glynn, Parish of
				057	MCCARTY, John	Dunmanway, Co.Cork, Ire.
				057		(NOI Ellenor - but see next
				057		entry - O'Leary Plot -
				057		perhaps you can sort it out)
John MCCARTY		10-31-1858	10-27-1911	057	MCCARTY, John	Children of John & Ellenor
Ellenor MCCARTY				057	MCCARTY, Ellenor	McCarty
Julia MCCARTY				057	MCCARTY, Julia	
Margaret MCCARTY				057	MCCARTY, Margaret	
Mary MCCARTY		23 Years	04-15-1888	057	MCCARTY, Mary	

Florance MCCARTY		2 Years	07-04-1855	057	MCCARTY, Florance	
Michael MCCARTY		12 Days	12-06-1859	057	MCCARTY, Michael	
Florance MCCARTY		13 Days	08-23-1854	057	MCCARTY, Florance	
				057		
Charles O'LEARY	Co. Cork	62 Years	06-01-1876	057	MCCARTY, Elennor	Native of Co. Cork, Ireland
Elennor MCCARTY O'Leary		81 Years	11-23-1913	057	O'LEARY, Charles	
				057		
Ellen _____ KELLY	Co. Cork	49 Years	01-01-1878	057	KELLY, John	Native of Co. Cork, Parish of Dunmanway. (NOI John Kelly)
				057		
				057		
				057		
James COLLINS	Co. Cork	----	----	057	_____, Mary	Native of Parish Drimoleague, Co. Cork, Ireland
				057		
Mary _____ COLLINS	Co. Cork	34 Years	11-06-1859	057	COLLINS, James	Native of Parish Drimoleague, Co. Cork, Ireland
				057		
				057		
Mathias CANNAN	Co. Roscommon	82 Years	08-19-1878	057	KEOUGH, Bridget	Born In the Parish of ______, Co. Roscommon, Ireland
				057		
Bridget KEOGH Cannan	Co. Roscommon	71 Years	11-16-1868	057	CANNAN, Mathias	A Native of the County of Roscommon, Ireland
				057		
Thomas CANNAN		45Y 11M	08-21-1878	057	_____, Mary K.	
Mary K. ___ CANNAN		81Y 29D	09-13-1912	057	CANNAN, Thomas	
Mary Anna CANNAN		17Y2M14d	11-20-1874	057	CANNAN, Mary Anna	Dau Of Thomas & Mary Cannan
				057		
Patrick MORIARTY	Co. Kerry	98 Years	01-23-1890	057	_____, Nancy	Native(s) Of Co. Kerry, Ire.
Nancy _____ MORIARTY	Co. Kerry	65 Years	12-24-1871	057	MORIARTY, Patrick	Native(s) Of CO. Kerry, Ire.
				057		
Patrick FARRELL	Co. Leitrim	84 Years	01-31-1874	057	FARRELL, Patrick	A Native of Co. Leitrim, Ire
				057		
Michael COLLINS	Co. Cork	63 Years	05-21-1896	057	CUSHING, Mary	A Native of Drimoleague, Co. Cork, Ireland
				057		
Mary CUSHING Collins		62 Years	05-22-1900	057	COLLINS, Michael	
James COLLINS		77 Years	09-05-1907	057	CUSHING, Mary	Brother of Michael Collins
Edmond RYAN	Co. Cork	02-20-1827	12-04-1900	057	LEAHY, Ellen	Native(s) Of Co. Cork, Ire.
Ellen LEAHY Ryan	Co. Cork	03-17-1827	02-12-1916	057	RYAN, Edmond	Native(s) Of Co. Cork, Ire.
				057		
John LEAHY	Co. Cork	98 Years	05-05-1881	057	LEAHY, John	Native Of Kilcummer, Co. Cork, Ireland
				057		
				057		
Edward SWEENEY	Co. Cork	27 Years	12-11-1867	057	_____, Ellen	A Native of Bandon, Co. Cork, Ireland. Erected by His Beloved Wife, Ellen.(NOI Ellen)
				057	SWEENEY, Edward	
				057		
				057		
Thomas RILEY	Co. Longford	75Y5M8D	10-18-1872	057	_____, Ann	A Native of Co. Longford, Ire.
Ann _____ RILEY	Co. Longford	74Y 6M	04-22-1878	057	RILEY, Thomas	A Native of Co. Longford, Ire.

Name	County	Age / Born	Died	Code	Related	Notes
				057		
Ellen EAGAN	Co. Limerick	23Y 7M	10-02-1869	057	EAGAN, Ellen	Daughter Of John & Johanna
				057	EAGAN, John	Eagan. A Native of Glin (Glin
				057		Town), Co. Limerick, Ireland
				057		(NOI John & Johanna Eagan)
				057		
Michael DOYLE	Co. Kilkenny	1816	1864	057	____, Mary	Native of Co. Kilkenny, Ire.
Mary _____ DOYLE		1831	1909	057	DOYLE, Michael	
				057		
Elizabeth SULLIVAN	Co. Limerick	18 Years	08-01-1867	057	SULLIVAN, Elizabeth	Daughter of John Sullivan and
				057	SULLIVAN, John	Catherine Nash.Parents Natives
				057	NASH, Catherine	Of Co. Limerick. (NOI Parents)
				057		
Martin DOOLEY	Co. Kings	25 Years	11-28-1871	057	DOOLEY, Martin	A Native of The Parish Kelley
				057		(Killeigh Town),Co. Kings, Ire
				057		(Now Co. Offaly)
				057		
John KELTY		1804	1880	057	____, Bridget	
Bridget ____ KELTY	Co. Sligo	56 Years	07-25-1872	057	KELTY, John	A Native of The Parish Of_____
				057		Co. Sligo, Ireland
				057		
Francis HUGHES	Co. Galway	73 Years	02-11-1868	057	HUGHES, Francis	In Memory of Francis Hughes, A
				057		Native of Kilkerrin,Co. Galway
				057		Who Departed This Life In
				057		Royalton, Vermont
				057		
Michael FLANNERY	Co. Clare	88 Years	02-01-1890	057	____, Catherine	A Native Of Co. Clare, Ireland
Catherine ____ FLANNERY	Co. Clare	87 Years	12-21-1883	057	FLANNERY, Michael	A Native Of Co. Clare, Ireland
John FLANNERY		62 Years	09-08-1905	057	FLANNERY, John	
James FLANNERY		18 Years	09-28-1865	057	FLANNERY, James	
Timothy FLANNERY		32 Years	02-28-1876	057	FLANNERY, Timothy	
				057		
James AHERN	Co. Cork	60 Years	10-16-1866	057	AHERN, James	Native Of The Parish Of Bally
				057		macoda, (No Such Parish, try
				057		Ballymacoda Town, Parish Of
				057		Kilmacdonogh, Co. Cork)
				057		
				057		
William KILEY	Co. Limerick	58 Years	10-12-1868	057	POWER, Ellen	A Native Of Co. of Limerick,
				057	____, Catherine	Parish of Kilbenny(Kilbeheny),
				057		Ireland. Erected by his wife.
				057		
Ellen POWER Kiley	Co. Limerick	32 Years	01-17-1857	057	KILEY, William	A Native Of County Limerick.
				057		Erected By William Kiley of
				057		the Same County.

				057		
Catherine ____ KILEY	Co. Limerick	56 Years	10-11-1870	057	KILEY, William	A Native Of The Co.Of Limerick
				057		Parish Of Kilbenney(Kilbeheny)
				057		
Michael FITZMORRIS	Co. Kerry	46Y11M12D	03-03-1866	057	_____, Katherine	A Native Of The County Carry
				057		(Kerry), Ireland
Katherine ___ FITZMORRIS		05-03-1835	09-01-1907	057	FITZMORRIS, Michael	
				057		
John MCVAY	Co. Antrim	52Y10M11D	03-24-1886	057	MCVAY, John	A Native Of Antrim County, Ire
				057		(GAR) Co. C. 15th Rgt,Vt. Vols
				057		
Ellen O'NEILL Ahern	Co. Cork	56 Years	07-22-1867	057	AHERN, Patrick	A Native Of Dunmanway,Co. Cork
				057	O'NEILL, Mary	(NOI Patrick Ahern)
				057		
Daniel MCGRATH		1818	1893	057	_______, Mary	
				057		
Mary ____ MCGRATH	Co. Limerick	70 Years	04-08-1894	057	MCGRATH, Daniel	Native of Limerick, Ireland
				057		
Patrick SPILLANE	Co. Cork	76 Years	01-05-1901	057	FINN, Julia	Native of Midleton (Middleton)
				057		Cork, Ireland
Julia FINN Spillane	Co. Cork	88 Years	01-13-1911	057	SPILLANE, Patrick	Native of ______, Cork Ireland
John SPILLANE		42 Years	01-15-1912	057	SPILLANE, John	
Eugene SPILLANE		17 Years	06-12-1872	057	SPILLANE, Eugene	
Catherine SPILLANE		26 Years	11-24-1860	057	SPILLANE, Catherine	
Mary MARSHALL		32 Years	09-17-1861	057	MARSHALL, Mary	
				057		
Hanorah MALONEY Clancy	Co. Clare	1811	1898	057	CLANCY, Thomas	Native(s) Of County Clare, Ire
Thomas CLANCY	Co. Clare	1818	1900	057	MALONEY, Hanorah	Native(s) Of County Clare, Ire
Henry CLANCY		1853	1918	057	____, Elizabeth E.	
Elizabeth E. ___ CLANCY		1861	1939	057	CLANCY, Henry	
				057		
Michael LEE	Co. Kildare	72 Years	01-18-1885	057	____, Margaret	Native Of County Kildare, Ire
Margaret ____ LEE	Co. Clare	75 Years	08-02-1891	057	LEE, Michael	Native of ________, O'Briens-
				057		bridge, Co. Clare, Ireland
				057		
James STACK	Co. Limerick	65 Years	06-30-1879	057	_____, Julia	Native Of County Limerick, Ire
Julia _____ STACK	Co. Tipperary	63 Years	04-28-1885	057	STACK, James	Native of Tipperary, Ireland
Julia STACK		1858	1927	057	STACK, Julia	
Hanorah STACK		37 Years	04-01-1885	057	STACK, Hanorah	
James R. STACK		04-06-1858	11-13-1940	057	STACK, James R.	
John STACK		06-17-1855	08-25-1904	057	_______, Honora	
Honora ____ STACK		05-12-1857	08-28-1911	057	STACK, John	
				057		
Patrick KELLY	Co. Roscommon	67Y11M14D	02-24-1885	057	CANNAN, Margaret	Native Of County Roscommon,Ire
Margaret CANNAN Kelly		66 Years	03-14-1897	057	KELLY, Patrick	

Name	County	Born/Age	Died	Code	Spouse/Relative	Notes
				057		
Robart PAINE	Co. Cork	51 Years	06-22-1880	057	____, Ellen	Native Of County Cork, Ire.
Ellen ____ PAINE		61 Years	02-07-1893	057	PAINE, Robert	
John PAINE		35 Years	06-10-1883	057	PAINE, John	
Hannah ____		75 Years	06-10-1926	057	____, Hannah	
				057		
Michael J. CONWAY	Co. Kerry	1840	1914	057	DONAHUE, Mary Ann	Native Of County Kerry, Ire.
Mary Ann DONAHUE Conway		1845	1930	057	CONWAY, Michael J.	
Hanora CONWAY	Co. Kerry	1820	1898	057	CONWAY, Hanora	Mother of Michael J. Conway
				057		
Timothy GLENNON	Co. Roscommon	82 Years	08-08-1894	057	RYAN, Catherine	Native Of 'Tochma-Connell',
				057		(Taghmaconnell), County
				057		Roscommon, Ireland
Catherine RYAN Glennon	Co. Waterford	74 Years	01-16-1886	057	GLENNON, Timothy	Native of 'Temple-Michael'
				057		(Templemichael), County
				057		Waterford, Ireland
Timothy Glennon JR.		1852	1914	057	GLENNON, Timothy Jr.	
Thomas GLENNON		1849	1931	057	GLENNON, Thomas	
				057		
				057		
David BARRY	Co. Cork	75 Years	03-17-1895	057	MCGRATH, Mary	Native Of County Cork, Ireland
Mary MCGRATH Barry		70 Years	04-08-1894	057	BARRY, David	
Daniel MCGRATH		1818	1893	057	MCGRATH, Daniel	
John MCGRATH		1857	1920	057	____, Mary	
Mary ____ MCGRATH		1856	1935	057	MCGRATH, John	
				057		
John DONAHUE	Co. Kerry	06-24-1809	09-25-1893	057	SHEA, Margaret	Native Of Glenflesk (Found no
				057		town of Glenflesk. There is a
				057		Roman Catholic Parish of this
				057		name in County Kerry.)
				057		
Margaret SHEA Donahue	Co. Kerry			057	DONAHUE, John	Native of Glenflesk, Co. Kerry
Johanna DONAHUE		02-15-1859	02-24-1877	057	DONAHUE, Johanna	(See foregoing)
Jerry DONAHUE		04-09-1849	05-11-1864	057	DONAHUE, Jerry	
Roger DONAHUE		04-15-1847	09-14-1906	057	CAFFERY, Bridget	
Bridget CAFFREY Donahue		10-12-1845	11-14-1905	057	DONAHUE, Roger	
				057		
Jeremiah O'NEILL	Co. Cork	82 Years	11-29-1894	057	LANE, Catharine	Native(s) Of Dunmanway,Co.Cork
Catharine LANE O'Neill	Co. Cork	76 Years	04-21-1900	057	O'NEILL, Jeremiah	Native(s) Of Dunmanway,Co.Cork
				057		
Timothy DONAHUE	Co. Cork	75 Years	08-07-1896	057	DOHERTY, Mary	Native of Parish of 'Glen'
				057		(Found no such parish),
				057		Dunmanway, Co. Cork, Ireland
Mary DOHERTY Don,ahue		59 Years	01-30-1886	057	DONAHUE, Timothy	
				057		

William COTTER	Co. Cork	86 Years	06-16-1913	057	_______, Mary	Native of The Parish of Kil-
				057		michael, Co. Cork, Ireland
Mary _____ COTTER	Co. Clare	78 Years	09-25-1908	057	COTTER, William	Native Of County Clare,Ireland
Ann GUINANE	Co. Clare	75 Years	02-10-1878	057	GUINANE, Ann	Native Of County Clare,Ireland
Kate COTTER Donovan	Co. Cork	56 Years	02-06-1889	057	DONOVAN, Bartholomew	Native Of County Cork, Ireland
John W. COTTER		07-03-1855	11-30-1911	057	COTTER, John W.	
Maggie A. COTTER		09-22-1857		057	COTTER, Maggie A.	
Mary J. COTTER		06-14-1861	01-10-1951	057	COTTER, Mary J.	
Lizzie M. COTTER		02-02-1857	02-25-1939	057	COTTER, Lizzie M.	
				057		
Patrick MCCARTHY	Co. Cork	40 Years	09-23-1866	057	MCCARTHY, Patrick	Native Of Dunmanway, Co. Cork
				057		
Mary _____ DOLAN	Co. Kings	31 Years	12-06-1863	057	DOLAN, M.	Native of Parish Kelley (No
				057		such Parish - Could be
				057		Killeigh Town), Kings Co. Ire
				057		(Now Co. Offaly)
				057		
Bedsey K. ___ DOLAN	Ireland	65 Years	09-10-1867	057	DOLAN, John	Born In Ireland. (NOI John D.)
				057	_____, Bedsey K.	
				057		
Hanora O'GRADY	Co. Limerick	3Y 3M	03-07-1859	057	O'GRADY, Hanora	Dau of Thomas--Bridget O'Grady
				057	O'GRADY, Thomas	A Native of Limerick County,
				057		Ireland
				057		
William MCAULIFFE	Co. Cork	1838	1916	057	SULLIVAN, Bridget	Native Of Co. Cork, Ireland
Bridget SULLIVAN McAuliffe	Co. Kerry	1841	1873	057	MCAULIFFE, William	Native Of Co. Kerry, Ireland
Bridget DOHERTY Sullivan	Co. Kerry	1811	1903	057	SULLIVAN, Michael	Native Of Co. Kerry, Ireland
				057	DOHERTY, Bridget	(Same stone--Bridget Sullivan
				057		McAuliffe-NOI Michael Sullivan
Michael SULLIVAN		1863	1865	057	SULLIVAN, Michael	
Elizabeth SULLIVAN		1862	1881	057	SULLIVAN, Elizabeth	
John SULLIVAN		1865	1891	057	SULLIVAN, John	
Dennis SULLIVAN		1866	1884	057	SULLIVAN, Dennis	
Franciece SULLIVAN		1871	1891	057	SULLIVAN, Franciece	
Bridget SULLIVAN		1867	1921	057	SULLIVAN, Bridget	
				057		
Jeremiah DUGGAN	Co. Kerry	104 Years	11-26-1865	057	DUGGAN, Jeremiah	Native Of Co. Kerry, Ireland
Martin DUGGAN		42 Years	05-20-1858	057	DUGGAN, Martin	(Same plot as Jeremiah Duggan)
				057		
Mary CARY	Co. Tipperary	80 Years	03-20-1892	057	CARY, Mary	Native Of County Tipperary,
				057		Parish Castletown (Castletown-
				057		arra), Ireland
Bridgett CARY	Co. Tipperary	82 Years	02-24-1900	057	CARY, Bridgett	Native Of County Tipperary,
				057		Parish Castletown (Castletown-
				057		arra), Ireland

Name	County	Age	Date	Code	Relation	Remarks
Elizabeth O'NEILL	Co. Kilkenny	18 Years	01-01-1864	057	O'NEILL, Elizabeth	Dau of W. & C. O'Neill. Native of County Kilkenny, Ireland
Catherine ____ FINN	Co. Sligo	50 Years	03-02-1876	057	FINN, David _____, Catherine	Native of the Parish of Kilglass, County Sligo, Ireland (NOI David Finn)
Julia ____ FINN	Co. Cork		01-24-1861	057	FINN, Owen	Native of the Parish of 'Knucksaville' (Knocksaville) Co. Cork, Ire.-(NOI Owen Finn)
Ann _____ WARD	Co. Sligo	28 Years	02-13-1861	057	WARD, Patrick _____, Ann	Native of 'Rahaim'(Rahara, Rahawny), Co. Sligo, Ireland (NOI Patrick Ward)
Patrick HASSETT	Co. Clare	31Y 6M	02-18-1861	057	HASSETT, Patrick	Native of the Parish of 'Burraknock' (Burren Knock), Co. Clare, Ireland (Stone badly deteriorated)
Bridget MORIARTY	Co. Clare	40 Years	12-20-1866	057	MORIARTY, John MORIARITY, Bridget	Native of 'Brarn' (Burren, Burrane), Co. Clare, Ireland (NOI John Moriarty) (Stone badly deteriorated)
Michael FRAWLEY	Co. Limerick	70 Years	NOV 1864	057	_____, Margaret	Native of '_____' County Limerick, Ireland. (Stone badly deteriorated)
Margaret ____ FRAWLEY		65 Years	01-05-1875	057	FRAWLEY, Michael	
Catherine ____ CORBETT	Co. Roscommon	37Y4M17D	03-18-1866	057	CORBETT, Michael _____, Catherine	Native of Co. Roscommon, Ire. A Good Daughter, Faithful Wife And Tender Mother.(NOI Michael Corbett)
Michael HOGAN	Co. Derry	96 Years	01-16-1895	057	DUGGAN, Isabelle	Native of Derry Co., Ireland
Isabelle DUGGEN Hogan	Co. Derry	09-18-1822	06-18-1857	057	HOGAN, Michael	Native of Londonderry, Ireland
Nancy A. HAYES	Co. Cork	40 Years	07-20-1879	057	HAYES, Michael	She Was A Native Of 'Lindisfarne' (could not find), Co. Cork, Ireland
Timothy HOLLAND	Co. Cork	87 Years	07-31-1918	057	______, Mary	A Native of Kilmichael, Co. Cork, Ireland

Mary ____ HOLLAND		39 Years	02-13-1871	057	HOLLAND, Timothy	
				057		
Philip HARTLEY	Co. Kilkenny	57 Years	06-07-1884	057	RYAN, Anastatia	A Native of Flemingstown, Par
				057		of Glenmore. Co. Kilkenny,Ire
				057		
Anastasia RYAN Hartley	Co. Cork	1831	1920	057	HARTLEY, Philip	Native of Youghall, Co. Cork
				057		
Catherine ____ DOLAN	Co. Cavan	35 Years	05-12-1861	057	DOLAN, James	A Native of the County Cavan,
				057		Parish 'Killina' (Killinagh),
				057		Ireland. (NOI James Dolan
Bridget DOLAN			03-15-1852	057	DOLAN, Bridget	Dau of J & C Dolan
				057		
John KERINS	Co. Clare	42 Years	12-20-1859	057	KERINS, John	A Native of County Clare, Ire.

Note: All North Hero and Grand Isle Cemeteries are Grouped Under Cemetery Number 058
There are no Catholic Cemeteries in North Hero, Grand Isle and South Hero, all townships in the Champlain Islands

Jerusalem Cemetery, North Hero, Vermont - on Lakeview Drive

NAME	POB	DOB/AGE	DOD	CEM	SPOUSE/INDEX	INSCRIPTION
David HARVEY		12-26-1801	03-12-1852	058	TRUMAN, Hannah	
				058	DEAVITT, Julia Ann	
Hannah TRUMAN Harvey		03-10-1792	01-30-1890	058	HARVEY, David	
Julia Ann DEAVITT Harvey		25 Years	10-16-1835	058	HARVEY, David	IMO Julia Ann, Wife Of David
				058		Harvey & Only Daughter Of John
				058		and Anna Deavitt
				058		
John W. DURHAM		1855	1929	058	MCBRIDE, Mary	
Mary MCBRIDE Durham		1857	1928	058	DURHAM, John W.	

North End Cemetery, North Hero, Vermont - on North End Road Off Lakeview Drive

NAME	POB	DOB/AGE	DOD	CEM	SPOUSE	INSCRIPTION
Jedson KELLEY		22 Months	05-15-1856	058	KELLEY, Jedson	S/O John & Florence Kelley

NAME	POB	DOB/AGE	DOD	CEM	SPOUSE	INSCRIPTION
				058	KELLEY, John	(NOI John & Florence Kelley)
				058	KELLEY, Florence	
				058		
James B. REAY		04-12-1847	01-30-1920	058	MCBRIDE, Nancy	
Nancy MCBRIDE Reay		43 Years	01-12-1891	058	REAY, James B.	
				058		
James E. MCBRIDE		48Y 6M	10-13-1894	058	BELL, Ada	
Ada BELL McBride		83 Years	12-07-1930	058	MCBRIDE, James E.	
				058		
Samuel KINCAID		86 Years	09-26-1902	058	KINCAID, Samuel	
				058		
				058		
				058		
William R. DONALDSON		1842	1917	058	TOWN, Mary E.	
Mary E. TOWN Donaldson		1844	1906	058	DONALDSON, William	

Hyde Cemetery, North Hero, Vermont - On West Shore Road

NAME	POB	DOB/AGE	DOD	CEM	SPOUSE	INSCRIPTION
James TASSIE		59 Years	04-27-1871	058	FERGUSON, Ann	
Ann FERGUSON Tassie		63 Years	05-28-1875	058	TASSIE, James	
				058		
James TASSIE		1857	1926	058	CUNNINGHAM, Margaret	
Margaret B. CUNNINGHAM Tassie		1864	1915	058	TASSIE, James	
				058		
Amos H. GLADDEN		10-07-1847	11-08-1927	058	PENNIE, Elizabeth A.	
Elizabeth A. PENNIE Gladden		08-30-1848	02-07-1923	058	GLADDEN, Amos A.	
				058		
Robert TASSIE		1841	1919	058	DODDS, Agnes B.	
Agnes B. DODDS Tassie		11-16-1843	05-01-1900	058	TASSIE, Robert	
				058		
James MCBRIDE		62 Years	08-19-1884	058	MCNEIL, Ruth	
Ruth MCNEIL McBride		70 Years	01-21-1895	058	MCBRIDE, James	
Emily MCBRIDE		2 Years	05-10-1852	058	MCBRIDE, Emily	Children Of James Ruth McBride
Malcom MCBRIDE		5Y 6M	05-08-1858	058	MCBRIDE, Malcom	Children Of James Ruth McBride
Emma E. MCBRIDE		3 Years	12-14-1862	058	MCBRIDE, Emma E.	Children Of James Ruth McBride
Ella M. MCBRIDE		5 Years	04-28-1874	058	MCBRIDE, Ella M.	Children Of James Ruth McBride
				058		
James Bird DODDS		22 Years	08-13-1870	058	DODDS, James Bird	
Mary HARRINGTON Dodds		56 Years	04-08-1883	058	DODDS, James	(Does not say if James Bird Dodds & Mary Harrington were husband and wife)
				058		
				058		

Name	Birth/Age	Death	Code	Related	Notes
			058		
John N. PARKER	07-27-1849	10-20-1913	058	MCBRIDE, Alvira	
Alvira MCBRIDE Parker	03-26-1855	04-28-1904	058	PARKER, John N.	
			058		
David DODDS	62 Years	03-01-1890	058	DODDS, Sarah Jane	
Sarah Jane _____ DODDS	39Y 10M	04-03-1881	058	DODDS, David	
			058		
Peter MCCUMMINGS	1815	1873	058	MCCUMMINGS, Elizabeth	
Elizabeth _____ MCCUMMINGS	1822	1882	058	MCCUMMINGS, Peter	
Elijah MCCUMMINS	7 Years	02-13-1856	058	MCCUMMINS, Elijah	
			058		
Harriett LAVIGNE McDonnell	1822	1882	058	MCCUMMINGS, Peter	
			058		
Matthew WATSON	1850	1891	058	ANDERSON, Agnes	
Agnes ANDERSON Watson	1848	1930	058	WATSON, Matthew	
			058		
George TUDHOPE	74 Y 9M	08-21-1902	058	TUDHOPE, Sarah	Born Paisley, Scotland
Sarah _____ TUDHOPE	56 Years	02-08-1881	058	TUDHOPE, George	
			058		
William ANDERSON	31Y 17D	01-30-1850	058	ANDERSON, William	Native Of Scotland. Drowned
			058		
James TUDHOPE	04-12-1834	06-11-1921	058	MONTGOMERY, Mary	Born Paisley, Scotland
Mary MONTGOMERY Tudhope	07-01-1834	10-05-1910	058	TUDHOPE, James	Born Paisley, Scotland
			058		
John TUDHOPE	1861	1941	058	TUDHOPE, John	Born Paisley, Scotland
			058		
John F. TASSIE	28Y 11M	12-07-1866	058	TASSIE, John	
			058		
James DODDS	56Y3M23D	06-28-1876	058	DODDS, James	
			058		
Matthew W. DODDS	1854	1940	058	HUTCHINS, Sarah	
Sarah HUTCHINS Dodds	1857	1937	058	DODDS, Matthew	
			058		
John DODDS	68 Years	01-25-1832	058	DODDS, John	
			058		
John DODDS	01-05-1818	03-01-1893	058	HAZEN, Hulda	Paisley, Scotland
Hulda A. HAZEN Dodds	10-07-1823	02-21-1879	058	DODDS, John	
			058		
James Addison DODDS	06-09-1846	10-27-1912	058	KINGSLEY, Jennie	
Jennie KINGSLEY Dodds	08-21-1859	10-10-1941	058	DODDS, James Addison	
			058		
James DODD	1788	1856	058	DONALD, Agnes	Farmer, near Paisley, Scotland
Agnes DONALD Dodd	1790	1862	058	DODD, James	Native Of Dumbartonshire, Scotland

South Cemetery, North Hero, Vermont - Off Abenaki Road

NAME	POB	DOB/AGE	DOD	CEM	SPOUSE	INSCRIPTION
Jerry FARRELL		81 Years	03-29-1912	058	BELROSE, Joanna	
Joanna BELROSE Farrell		39 Years	02-08-1899	058	FARRELL, Jerry	
				058		
Lucy G. MOONEY		40 Years	07-20-1879	058	MOONEY, Lucy G.	
				058		
Adelade E. HOGAN		1845	1924	058	HOGAN, Adelade	
				058		
Amy COLTON Fitzgerald		86 Years	8-15-1846	058	FITZGERALD, John	Relict Of John Fitzgerald,Died
				058		In The 86th Year of Her Age
				058	COLTON, Amy	(NOI John Fitzgerald)
				058		
John MCMASTER		31 Years	11-05-1811	058	MCMASTER, John	
John K. MCMASTER		3 Years	03-26-1815	058	MCMASTER, John K.	

Grand Isle Station Cemetery, Grand Isle, Vt.

NAME	POB	DOB/AGE	DOD	CEM	SPOUSE	INSCRIPTION
Bridget ELWOOD Kelly		1816	1902	058	ELWOOD, Bridget	
				058		
B. F. MOONEY		79 Years	11-10-1902	058	MOONEY, Mary Ann	
Mary Ann _____ MOONEY		78 Years	02-11-1916	058	MOONEY, B. F.	

Grand Isle Village Cemetery, Grand Isle, Vt. U. S. Route 2, South of Village

NAME	POB	DOB/AGE	DOD	CEM	SPOUSE	INSCRIPTION
Daniel MCDIXON		02-28-1839	08-23-1903	058	ROBINSON, Esther	
Esther ROBINSON McDixon		06-19-1844		058	MCDIXON, Daniel	(NOI DOD)
				058		
DR A.H.W. JACKSON		11-14-1816	04-07-1889	058	MCGOWAN, Maria L.	
Maria L. MCGOWAN Jackson		07-27-1827	07-21-1908	058	JACKSON, A.H.W.	
				058		
Jessie F. MOONEY		5Y 10M	05-18-1863	058	MOONEY, Jessie F.	D/O F.C. & L. Mooney
				058		

NAME	POB	DOB/AGE	DOD	CEM	SPOUSE/INDEX	INSCRIPTION
Isabell GARLAND		78 Years	03-12-1890	058	GARLAND, Isabell	
				058		
James DONOVAN		49 Years	01-13-1899	058	MACOMBER, Sarah A.	
Sarah A. MACOMBER Donovan		69 Years	05-04-1922	058	DONOVAN, James	
				058		
Emaline A. MCGOWAN Hurlbut		68Y 8M	04-22-1881	058	HURLBUT, Hiram	
				058	MCGOWAN, Emaline A.	
				058		
William C. MCGOWAN		1825	1897	058	ROBINSON, Hannah	
Hannah ROBINSON McGowan		44 Years	07-23-1871	058	MCGOWAN, William C.	
				058		
James E. MCGOWAN		11-06-1815	01-05-1901	058	MCGOWAN, Caroline	
Caroline _____ MCGOWAN		1821	1883	058	MCGOWAN, James E.	
				058		
Robert MCGOWAN		79 Years	03-28-1870	058	MCGOWEN, Elizabeth F.	
Elizabeth F. _____ MCGOWAN		1789	1863	058	MCGOWAN, Robert	
Laura MCGOWAN Hale		1829	1876	058	MCGOWAN, Laura	(NOI Mr. Hale)
Eliza MCGOWAN Dixon		1813	1875	058	MCGOWAN, Eliza	(NOI Mr. Dixon)
George MCGOWEN		1818	1871	058	MCGOWEN, George	
Amanda MCGOWEN		1810	1851	058	MCGOWEN, Amanda	

St. Bernard Cemetery, Norton, Vermont. Cemetery opposite church.

NAME	POB	DOB/AGE	DOD	CEM	SPOUSE/INDEX	INSCRIPTION
Lawrence WELCH		03-14-1860	05-09-1929	059	WELCH, Lawrence	

No other burials that fit the criteria for this search.

Old Catholic Cemetery, Norton, Vermont. East side Route 114, 2/10 of a mile south of Church Hill Road, 220 yds up logging road.

NAME	POB	DOB/AGE	DOD	CEM	SPOUSE/INDEX	INSCRIPTION

This cemetery was not dedicated until late in the nineteenth century. Those interred are primarily French-Canadian in origins. I could find only twenty or so standing markers. It is cared for but is apparent that many stones are missing.

NAME	POB	DOB/AGE	DOD	CEM	SPOUSE/INDEX	INSCRIPTION
Mrs. John GRIFFIN		04-16-1815	89 Years	127	GRIFFIN, John	(NOI John Griffin & Mrs. John Griffin)
				127		
				127		
John Joseph SHEA		11-09-1862	01-07-1922	127	SHEA, John Joseph	

St. Paul's Cemetery, 2 Miles On North Orwell Road to Old Village Cemetery, Turn Right. 1.2 miles to Cemetery, Orwell, Vermont

NAME	POB	DOB/AGE	DOD	CEM	SPOUSE/INDEX	INSCRIPTION
Peter MARTIN		01-14-1823	10-30-1903	060	SANTOS, Margaret	
Margaret SANTOS Martin		11-01-1844	04-01-1896	060	MARTIN, Peter	
				060		
Jeremiah QUINN		06-10-1854	10-26-1912	060	CONWAY, Margaret	
Margaret CONWAY Quinn		05-03-1853	04-01-1927	060	QUINN, Jeremiah	
				060		
John P. FITZGERALD		1853	1925	060	DUMAN, Josephine E.	
Josephine DUMAN Fitzgerald		1856		060	FITZGERALD, John P.	
				060		
John E. CONWAY		1855	1936	060	BEAUVAIS, Agnes M.	
Agnes M. BEAUVAIS Conway		1866	1936	060	CONWAY, John E.	
				060		
John PARNELL		1829	1909	060	CONWAY, Honora	
Honora CONWAY Parnell		1841	1913	060	PARNELL, John	
				060		
Henry STONE		01-31-1828	1913	060	CREDY, Mary	
Mary CREDY Stone		1825	1902	060	STONE, Henry	
				060		
William GRONE		71 Years	09-13-1883	060	GRONE, William	
				060		
Alfred BEHAN		05-07-1829	10-01-1906	060	CARBANS, Angeline	
Angeline CARBANS Behan		12-22-1835	09-18-1897	060	BEHAN, Alfred	
				060		
Mary _____ MORRIS		52 Years	12-23-1884	060	MORRIS, E.	(NOI E. Morris)
				060	_____, Mary	
				060		
Patrick MALONE	Co. Queens	1823	12-04-1875	060	MALONE, Patrick	Born In Queens County,Ireland
				060		Died In Shoreham (VT)
				060		
Michael SULLIVAN Sr.		84 Years	01-29-1882	060	CARTY, Hannah	
Hannah CARTY Sullivan		73 Years	04-29-1879	060	SULLIVAN, Michael Sr.	
Michael SULLIVAN		68 Years	02-29-1896	060	SULLIVAN, Michael	
Michael SULLIVAN		32 Years	08-06-1898	060	SULLIVAN, Michael	(Year of death could be 1895)
Annie SULLIVAN		21 Years	04-08-1894	060	SULLIVAN, Annie	
				060		
Patrick BARRON		63 Years	04-07-1901	060	HICKEY, Anna	
Anna HICKEY Barron		70 Years	04-21-1917	060	BARRON, Patrick	
				060		
Michael GARVEY		66 Years	01-24-1877	060	_____, Margaret	Died In Shoreham (VT)
Margaret _____ GARVEY		64 Years	03-22-1877	060	GARVEY, Michael	Died In Shoreham (VT)

Roseanna GARVEY	1840	1920	060	GARVEY, Roseanna	
			060		
Michael CUMMINGS	1810	1882	060	CAIN, Mary	
Mary CAIN Cummings	1815	1883	060	CUMMINGS, Michael	
_____ CUMMINGS	1844	1925	060	NEWAN, Alice	Co. D. 4th Vt Vols (GAR)
Alice NEWAN Cummings	1847	1888	060	CUMMINGS, ______,	
			060		
Mary T. _____ RYAN	31 Years	06-27-1888	060	RYAN, Daniel	(NOI Daniel Ryan)
			060	_____, Mary T.	
			060		
Thomas PURCELL	78 Years	04-05-1875	060	PURCELL, Thomas	
Thomas PURCELL	1826	1912	060	GALLAGHER, Hanora	
Hanora GALLAGHER Purcell	1831	1918	060	PURCELL, Thomas	
			060		
Patrick QUIRK	48 Years	03-21-1872	060	_____, Margaret	
Margaret _____ QUIRK	52 Years	10-20-1877	060	QUIRK, Patrick	
			060		
Thomas K. BURKE	1845	1927	060	BURNS, Rose	
Rose BURNS Burke	1855	1930	060	BURKE, Thomas K.	
Mary BURNS Salter	1859	1910	060	SALTER, Mr.	(NOI Mr. Salter)
			060	BURNS, Mary	
			060		
James W. PURCELL	1857		060	RUGG, Ellen	(NOI DOD)
Ellen RUGG Purcell	1855		060	PURCELL, James W.	(NOI DOD)
			060		
John B. RYAN	1859	1944	060	FORCIER, Loude	
Loude FORCIER Ryan	1847	1921	060	RYAN, John B.	
			060		
William A. CHAMBERLAIN	07-19-1851	03-19-1906	060	CRAWFORD, Kate J.	
Kate CRAWFORD Chamberlain	06-07-1852	12-09-1926	060	CHAMBERLAIN, William A.	
			060		
Michael J. DEWITT	1840	1924	060	LAVERY, Ellen M.	
Ellen M. LAVERY Dewitt	1844	1914	060	DEWITT, Michael J.	
			060		
Patrick SULLIVAN	1848	1918	060	SULLIVAN, Patrick	
			060		
John SULLIVAN	72 Years	03-29-1914	060	LAVERY, Ellen	
Ellen LAVERY Sullivan	64 Years	04-25-1906	060	SULLIVAN, John	
			060		
James M. COBURN	1841	1909	060	MCAULEY, Katherine	Born In Ireland
Katherine MCAULEY Coburn	1845	1916	060	COBURN, James M.	Born In Ireland
			060		
James DEWITT	81 Years	07-27-1894	060	HARTIGAN, Bridget	
Bridget HARTIGAN Dewitt	70 Years	08-07-1903	060	DEWITT, James	
			060		

Name	Origin	Born/Age	Died	Code	Index	Notes
John HAYES		52 Years	02-03-1899	060	QUINN, Mary	(U.S. Flag on Grave-no GAR)
Mary QUINN Hayes		78 Years	08-23-1919	060	HAYES, John	Try Co. C., 11th Rgt, VtVols
				060		
Michael DEWITT		03-13-1816	04-16-1893	060	HEFFERMAN, Bridget	
Bridget HEFFERMAN Dewitt		08-15-1837	09-30-1897	060	DEWITT, Michael	(Surname could be HEFFERNAN)
				060		
Ellen GREEN Welsh		65 Years	05-07-1907	060	WELSH, John	(NOI John Welsh)
				060	GREEN, Ellen	
				060		
John CRONIN		1842	1920	060	SULLIVAN, Margaret	
Margaret SULLIVAN Cronin		1842	1928	060	CRONIN, John	
				060		
William SHANNON		57 Years	08-13-1895	060	SHANNON, William	May His Soul Rest In Peace
				060		
James PURCELL		01-12-1854	09-26-1907	060	_____, Agnes A.	
Agnes A. ____ PURCELL		02-10-1858	03-11-1944	060	PURCELL, James	
				060		
Patrick PURCELL		70 Years	01-02-1893	060	DEWITT, Mary	
Mary DEWITT Purcell			08-07-1904	060	PURCELL, Patrick	
				060		
Jeremiah BURKE		1815	1891	060	KEATING, Nancy	
Nancy KEATING Burke		1821	1905	060	BURKE, Jeremiah	
Mary BURKE		1857	1921	060	BURKE, Mary	
Robert BURKE		1853	1926	060	BURKE, Robert	
				060		
John RYAN		1844	1930	060	GREEN, Catherine	
Catherine GREEN Ryan		1847	1926	060	RYAN, John	
				060		
William RYAN	Co. Limerick	68 Years	03-07-1886	060	_____, Bridget	Native of Parish _____, County
				060		Limerick, Ireland (Cannot read
				060		Parish name)
Bridget _____ RYAN		74 Years	11-21-1894	060	RYAN, William	
				060		
Edmond O'SHEA		1832	1910	060	WALSH, Mary	
Mary WALSH O'Shea		1836	1906	060	O'SHEA, Edmond	
				060		
Frank BEAUVAIS		06-01-1838	03-24-1907	060	_____, Mary J.	
Mary J. _____ BEAUVAIS	Co. Limerick	03-25-1833	09-07-1891	060	BEAUVAIS, Frank	Born In Limerick, Ireland
				060		
Ellen _____ HAMMEL		53 Years	04-26-1892	060	HAMMEL, John	(NOI John Hammel)
				060	_____, Ellen	
				060		
James GRIMES		33 Years	10-28-1866	060	_____, M. A.	
M.A. _____ GRIMES				060	GRIMES, James	(No DOB-DOD for M.A.)
				060		

NAME	POB	DOB/AGE	DOD	CEM	SPOUSE/INDEX	INSCRIPTION
Dennis O'BRIEN		67 Years	09-13-1899	060	FOGARTY, Bridget	
Bridget FOGARTY O'Brien		65 Years	01-21-1899	060	O'BRIEN, Dennis	
				060		
John O'BRIEN		11Y 10M	11-23-1872	060	O'BRIEN, John	Son Of Denis & Bridget O'Brien
				060		
Bridget _____ LAVERY		06-24-1803	03-25-1888	060	LAVERY, Patrick	Born In Ireland. (NOI Patrick Lavery)
				060	_____, Bridget	
				060		
Mathew CONWAY		25 Years	07-21-1876	060	CONWAY, Mathew	
				060		
Maurice SULLIVAN		1810	1888	060	SWEENEY, Katherine	
Katherine SWEENEY Sullivan		1827	1902	060	SULLIVAN, Maurice	
Hannah SULLIVAN		1822	1846	060	SULLIVAN, Hannah	
Margaret E. SULLIVAN		1853	1880	060	SULLIVAN, Margaret E.	
				060		
Ellen _____ SULLIVAN		34 Years	04-05-1874	060	SULLIVAN, Patrick	(NOI Patrick Sullivan)
				060	_____, Ellen	
				060		
Thomas BOURKE		1825	1902	060	LAVERY, Catherine	
Catherine LAVERY Bourke		1820	1900	060	BOURKE, Thomas	

St. Alphonsus Cemetery, U. S. Route 7, Pittsford, Vermont

NAME	POB	DOB/AGE	DOD	CEM	SPOUSE/INDEX	INSCRIPTION
Charles MALONE		76 Years	08-27-1891	061	_____, Bridget	
Bridget _____ MALONE		83 Years	05-13-1904	061	MALONE, Charles	
Charles Malone JR		27 Years	09-27-1880	061	MALONE, Charles Jr.	
Mary MALONE Wetmore		47 Years	12-27-1895	061	MALONE, Mary	(NOI Mr. Wetmore)
R. C. MALONE		03-01-1861	08-17-1904	061	MALONE, R. C.	
				061		
Mathew MCENANY		1848	1891	061	MCENANY, Mathew	
				061		
Edward DOOLIN		45 Years	07-11-1875	061	SHELVEY, Kate	
Kate SHELVEY Doolin		73 Years	04-23-1910	061	DOOLIN, Edward	
				061		
Kate DOOLIN		84 Years	10-01-1905	061	DOOLIN, Kate	
				061		
Patrick DOOLIN		03-17-1812	10-20-1907	061	WHITE, Mary	
				061	ARMSTRONG, Rosa	
Rosa ARMSTRONG Doolin		11-03-1819	01-17-1858	061	DOOLIN, Patrick	
Mary WHITE Doolin		06-01-1823	02-25-1901	061	DOOLIN, Patrick	
				061		

Michael MULLIN		05-03-1842	01-19-1928	061	RILEY, Mary Ann	
Mary Ann RILEY Mullin		03-01-1843	09-19-1923	061	MULLEN, Michael	
Katie MULLIN		03-09-1863	08-03-1891	061	MULLIN, Katie	
Patrick MULLIN		08-28-1859	06-21-1856	061	MULLIN, Patrick	
John H. MULLIN		01-28-1865	09-28-1901	061	MULLIN, John H.	
				061		
Thomas MULLIN		28 Years	10-28-1868	061	MULLIN, Thomas	
				061		
Francis MULLIN		24 Years	02-23-1877	061	MULLIN, Francis	
				061		
Arthur MULLIN	Co. Tyrone	82 Years	08-24-1887	061	MCGEE, Mary	Born In Town Of Killyliss,
				061		Co. Tyrone, Ire.
Mary MCGEE Mullin	Co. Tyrone	72 Years	05-10-1888	061	MULLIN, Arthur	Born In Town Of Eden Crannon
				061		(Edenacrannon) Co. Tyrone, Ire
				061		
Patrick MULLIN		1836	1905	061	MCGUIRK, Margaret	
Margaret MCGUIRK Mullin		1850	1916	061	MULLIN, Patrick	
				061		
John MULLIN		1846	1908	061	TIERNAY, Mary A.	
Mary A. TIERNAY Mullin		1849	1911	061	MULLIN, John	
Arthur Mullin JR		1848	1927	061	MULLIN, Arthur Jr.	
				061		
Thomas Jefferson HENNESSEY		1833	1904	061	EGAN, Catherine	Co C., U.S.A., 10th VT (GAR)
Catherine EGAB Hennessey		1843	1909	061	HENNESSEY, Thomas J.	
				061		
Frank CARRIGAN		1842	1919	061	CARRIGAN, Frank	
Mother CARRIGAN		1847	1935	061	CARRIGAN, Mother	
				061		
Catharine TIMBERS Carrigan		55 Years	10-20-18_9	061	CARRIGAN, John	(NOI John Carrigan. Stone
				061		
				061	TIMBERS, Catherine	deteriorated.DOD hard to read)
				061		
Henry CLARK		33 Years	10-02-1869	061	CLARK, Henry	
				061		
Cornelius MEEHAN		1815	1898	061	_____, Honora	
Honora _____ MEEHAN		55 Years	11-28-1875	061	MEEHAN, Cornelius	
				061		
Michael O'DONNELL	Co. Limerick	76 Years	09-07-1880	061	MEEHAN, Mary	Native of Parish of "Loroga",
				061		(No parish. There is a town of
				061		Lurraga), Co. Limerick, Ire.
				061		
Mary MEEHAN O'Donnell	Co. Limerick	1820	09-19-1911	061	O'DONNELL, Michael	Born In Limerick, Ireland
Ellen O'DONNELL		18 Years	09-08-1873	061	O'DONNELL, Ellen	
Nancy O'DONNELL		29 Years	03-11-1889	061	O'DONNELL, Nancy	
John O'DONNELL		07-18-1865	05-27-1919	061	O'DONNELL, John	

Name	Birth/Age	Death	Code	Related	Notes
			061		
Patrick HIGGINS	1833	1913	061	DOOLIN, Ann	
Ann DOOLIN Higgins	1841	1913	061	HIGGINS, Patrick	
			061		
Patrick CARRIGAN	83 Years	05-05-1853	061	CARRIGAN, Patrick	
Arthur CARRIGAN	54 Years	10-19-1862	061	CARRIGAN, Arthur	
James CARRIGAN	4 Years	01-14-1852	061	CARRIGAN, James	Son Of J.F. & J. Carrigan
Mary J. CARRIGAN	1838	1907	061	CARRIGAN, Mary J.	
Frank CARRIGAN	78 Years	08-12-1888	061	KING, Julia	
Julia KING Carrigan	40 Years	01-01-1852	061	CARRIGAN, Frank	
James KING	42 Years	11-11-1852	061	KING, James	
James F. FALLOON	10Y 6M	11-18-1872	061	FALLOON, James F.	Son Of J. & B. Falloon. (NOI)
			061		
John DUFFY	1831	1901	061	CARRIGAN, Ann E.	
Ann E. CARRIGAN Duffy	1836	1922	061	DUFFY, John	
			061		
			061		
Marcella ____ LOWTH	05-__-1780	06-26-1848	061	LOWTH, James	Here Lies All That Remains Of
			061	_____, Marcella	Marcella, Wife Of James Lowth,
			061		Born In Ireland in May, 1780.
			061		(NOI James Lowth)
			061		
Joseph B. CARRIGAN	1849	1926	061	LOWTH, Marcella	
Marcella LOWTH Carrigan	1850	1931	061	CARRIGAN, Joseph B.	
			061		
James CARRIGAN	55th Yr	08-30-1858	061	CARRIGAN, James	
			061		
Walter RATICAN	77 Years	07-06-1848	061	RATICAN, Walter	
			061		
			061		
John CARRIGAN	1840	1898	061	MCENANY, Rose A.	
			061	MCENANY, Mary A.	
Rose A. MCENANY Carrigan	26Y 4M28D	09-17-1868	061	CARRIGAN, John	
Mary A. MCENANY Carrigan	1842	1928	061	CARRIGAN, John	
			061		
James WHITE	03-06-1820	03-01-1893	061	_____, Mary	
Mary _____ WHITE	05-08-1830	05-15-1893	061	WHITE, James	
			061		
Kate WHITE Mullin	02-19-1858	01-26-1908	061	WHITE, Kate	(NOI Mr. Mullin)
John E. WHITE	04-20-1855	04-30-1858	061	WHITE, John E.	
John M. WHITE	01-18-1862	03-21-1862	061	WHITE, John M.	
Charles H. WHITE	08-07-1867	12-03-1868	061	WHITE, Charles H.	
Anne M. WHITE	03-16-1860	03-26-1862	061	WHITE, Anne M.	
			061		
Mary A. MOONEY Carrigan	11-10-1860	07-17-1907	061	CARRIGAN, George E.	(NOI George Carrigan)

Name	Origin	Born/Age	Died	Code	Related	Notes
				061	MOONEY, Mary A.	
				061		
William MOONEY		05-15-1829	04-13-1882	061	CAVANAUGH, Catherine	
Catherine CAVANAUGH Mooney		12-03-1834	09-30-1868	061	MOONEY, William	
				061		
John MCCAIL		76 Years	04-24-1874	061	_____, Mary	
Mary _____ MCCAIL		68 Years	02-28-1895	061	MCCAIL, John	
Catherine J. MCCAIL		26Y 6M	09-26-1880	061	MCCAIL, Catherine J.	
William B. MCCAIL		28Y 9M	07-16-1893	061	MCCAIL, William B.	
				061		
Thomas TENNIEN		49Y 9M	09-07-1865	061	_____, Catharine	
Catharine _____ TENNIEN		08-02-1827	11-29-1932	061	TENNIEN, Thomas	
				061		
Patrick FOX		77Y 3M	05-14-1875	061	FOX, Patrick	
				061		
Michael PHALEN	Co. Kilkenny	45 Years	03-06-1849	061	_____, Mary	Native of Urlingford, Kilkenny County, Ireland
				061		
Mary _____ PHALEN	Co. Kilkenny	66 Years	04-21-1874	061	PHALEN, Michael	Native Of Urlingford, Kilkenny County, Ireland
				061		
Charles HART		1845	1914	061	_____, Mary A.	
Mary A. _____ HART		1849	1907	061	HART, Charles	
Charles J. HART		12-1845	07-21-1914	061	_____, Mary A.	(GAR) Co. C., 11th VT Inf
				061		
Michael HALPIN		06-1809	03-1865	061	_____, Elizabeth	
Elizabeth _____ HALPIN		08-1816	07-1878	061	HALPIN, Michael	
Michael HALPIN		07-1852	04-1877	061	HALPIN, Michael	
Elizabeth HALPIN Cooley		02-1843	10-1881	061	COOLEY, E. A.	(NOI E. A. Cooley)
				061	HALPIN, Elizabeth	
				061		
Philip HALPIN		05-1838	07-1869	061	HALPIN, Philip	(GAR) Mbr, Co. I, 2nd VT Vols
Mary J. HALPIN		08-1840	04-1875	061	HALPIN, Mary J.	
				061		
Matthew MULLIGAN		1834	1880	061	MCCAWLEY, Mary	Born In Ireland,Died in Pittsford. Age 46 Years
				061		
Mary MCCAWLEY Mulligan	Co. Leitrim	06-24-1840	03-08-1915	061	MULLIGAN, Matthew	Born In Leitrim County, Ire. Married Matt Mulligan 11-24-1861.Married John Hanley 1-24-1886. (NOI John Hanley)
				061	HANLEY, John	
				061		
				061		
				061		
Sophie NOLAN Austin		1821	1867	061	AUSTIN, Daniel	(NOI Daniel Austin)
				061	NOLAN, Sophie	
Sophie AUSTIN		1853	1870	061	AUSTIN, Sophie	
Delina AUSTIN		1856	1874	061	AUSTIN, Delina	
				061		
O. E. CUNNINGHAM		1855	1934	061	CUNNINGHAM, O. E.	

				061		
Patrick OATES		76 Years	11-28-1909	061	MCDONNELL, Mary	Born In Co. Roscommon, Parish
Mary MCDONNELL Oates	Co. Roscommon	52 Years	03-15-1890	061	OATES, Patrick	of Kilglass, Ireland
				061		
				061		
Jane _____ MCKEARIN		60 Years	09-30-1883	061	MCKEARIN, Michael	(NOI Michael McKearin)
				061	_____, Jane	
				061		
Bridget _____ MCENANEY		45 Years	07-11-1868	061	MCENANEY, Thomas	(NOI Thomas McEnaney)
				061	_____, Bridget	
				061		
Lancelot MCKEOUGH		67 Years	04-15-1871	061	_____, Winaford	
Winaford _____ MCKEOUGH		71 Years	07-01-1873	061	MCKEOUGH, Lancelot	
				061		
Richard MOONEY		1857		061	_____, Mary A.	
Mary A. _____ MOONEY		1866	1925	061	MOONEY, Richard	
				061		
Cornelius BRADLEY		1843	1906	061	_____, Mary Jane	
Mary Jane _____ BRADLEY		1845	1915	061	BRADLEY, Cornelius	
				061		
James CUNNINGHAM		62 Years	11-24-1872	061	_____, Elizabeth	
Elizabeth _____ CUNNINGHAM		65 Years	08-05-1875	061	CUNNINGHAM, James	
John CUNNINGHAM		02-13-1853	03-25-1917	061	CUNNINGHAM, John	
				061		
Thomas J. HAGAN		1841	1912	061	HORTON, Mary E.	
Mary E. HORTON Hagan		1843	1904	061	HAGAN, Thomas J.	
				061		
				061		
				061		
John O'BRIEN		1849	1933	061	O'DONNELL, Catherine	
Catherine O'DONNELL O'Brien		1852	1919	061	O'BRIEN, John	
				061		
John KEOGH		1843	1931	061	KEOGH, John	(GAR Marker) Co. C.12th VT Vol
				061		
Adam RADLEY		1845	1901	061	RADLEY, Adam	(GAR) Co. B. 44th Rgt, NY Vols
				061		
Rose MATTHEWS Smith		1849	1942	061	MATTHEWS, Rose	(NOI Mr. Smith)
				061		
James CASEY Sr.			1847	061	_____, Mary	
Mary _____ CASEY		72 Years	09-21-1882	061	CASEY, James Sr.	
James CASEY		45 Years	05-13-1905	061	_____, Margaret	
Margaret _____ CASEY		63 Years	12-25-1913	061	CASEY, James Jr.	
				061		
NAYLON FAMILY				061	NAYLON, Family	
Father NAYLON		1846	1918	061	NAYLON, Father	(GAR Marker)

Name	Origin	Born/Age	Died	Code	Related	Notes
Mother NAYLON		1842	1989	061	NAYLON, Mother	
				061		
Bernard DENNING		1832	1912	061	_____, Jane B.	
Jane B. ____ DENNING		1839	1912	061	DENNING, Bernard	
				061		
Robert ELLIOTT		1827	1895	061	_____, Mary	
Mary _____ ELLIOTT		1835	1911	061	ELLIOTT, Robert	
Thomas ELLIOTT		1857	1881	061	ELLIOTT, Thomas	
James ELLIOTT		1853	1887	061	ELLIOTT, James	
Robert ELLIOTT		1859	1915	061	ELLIOTT, Robert	
Elizabeth ELLIOTT		1869	1920	061	ELLIOTT, Elizabeth	
Mary E. MCDEVITT		1863	1940	061	MCDEVITT, Mary E.	
William A. ROCKWOOD		1853	1935	061	ELLIOTT, Margaret A.	
Margaret E. ELLIOTT Rockwood		1865	1931	061	ROCKWOOD, William A.	
				061		
Lawrence A. CRAHAN				061	WEBB, Anne	
Anne WEBB Crahan				061	CRAHAN, Lawrence W.	
John CRAHAN				061	CRAHAN, John	
William CRAHAN		1861	1923	061	CRAHAN, William	
Mary A. CRAHAN		1879	1979	061	CRAHAN, Mary A.	
				061		
Richard MOONEY	Co. Meath	51 Years	06-30-1879	061	CONLIN, Mary	Born in Watertown, Co. Meath,
				061		Ire (No such town or parish.
				061		There is a "Waterstown" in
				061		County Westmeath and "Warrens-
				061		town" in Meath)Stone inscribed
				061		"Mother" (NOI)
				061		
				061		
Mary CONLIN Mooney		79 Years	08-14-1903	061	MOONEY, Richard	
				061		
Frank MOONEY		35Y 8M	07-10-1898	061	MOONEY, Frank	
				061		
Patrick COONEY				061	COONEY, Patrick	(GAR) Co. A, 7th VT Inf
				061		
Charles REILEY	Co. Meath	38 Years	10-10-1848	061	REILEY, Charles	Born In The Parish Of Navan,
				061		County Meath, Ireland
				061		
Thomas E. DUNOON		02-1845	1922	061	SHANNON, Mary A.	
Mary A. SHANNON Dunoon		1845	1926	061	DUNOON, Thomas E.	
				061		
Patrick MCDEVITT		05-28-1855	10-22-1928	061	MCLAUGHLIN, Sarah	
Sarah MCLAUGHLIN McDevitt		02-01-1858	01-29-1904	061	MCDEVITT, Patrick	
				061		
Daniel ROLLINS		1856	1936	061	_____, Ellen P.	

Name	Origin	Born	Died	Code	Relation	Notes
Ellen P. _____ ROLLINS		1866	1924	061	ROLLINS, Daniel	
				061		
Laurence CRAHAN		1844	1915	061	CUNNINGHAM, Mary	
Mary CUNNINGHAM Crahan		1848	1926	061	CRAHAN, Laurence	
				061		
Michael LYONS		1855	1893	061	RILEY, Julia	
Julia RILEY Lyons		1855	1912	061	LYONS, Michael	
				061		
Martin FITZPATRICK		1818	1909	061	DUFFY, Margaret	
Margaret DUFFY Fitzpatrick		1835	1922	061	FITZPATRICK, Martin	
Katherine A. FITZPATRICK		1858	1937	061	FITZPATRICK, Katherine	
				061		
Martin FITZPATRICK		1853	1931	061	_____, Mary	
Mary _____ FITZPATRICK		1859	1937	061	FITZPATRICK, Martin	
				061		
Daniel Austin JR		02-04-1855	10-02-1895	061	O'DONNELL, Mary	
Mary O'DONNELL Austin		01-27-1854	02-27-1925	061	AUSTIN, Daniel Jr.	
				061		
John MCCORMICK		1838	1907	061	SHELVEY, Margaret	
Margaret SHELVEY McCormick		1840	1924	061	MCCORMICK, John	
				061		
Robert Henry DRAKE		03-08-1847	01-07-1929	061	FITZPATRICK, Mary E.	
Mary E. FITZPATRICK Drake		05-22-1865	08-15-1939	061	DRAKE, Robert Henry	(Middle name is Elizabeth)
				061		
John BALDWIN	Co. Waterford	78 Years	10-07-1893	061	PENDERGAST, Bridget	Born In Co. Waterford, Ireland
Bridget PENDERGAST Baldwin	Co. Kilkenny	88 Years	03-14-1899	061	BALDWIN, John	Born In Co. Kilkenny, Ireland
				061		
John O'NEIL			08-30-1906	061	_____, Ellen	
Ellen _____ O'NEIL	Co. Kilkenny	80 Years	02-27-1886	061	O'NEIL, John	A Native Of Calin (Callan Town), Co. Kilkenny, Ireland
				061		
				061		
Bridget _____ WARD		81 Years	09-13-1899	061	WARD, John W.	(NOI John W. Ward)
				061		
Edward MURPHY		71 Years	11-14-1893	061	MURPHY, Edward	
				061		
James HALPIN		1845	1927	061	O'BRIEN, Mary	
Mary O'BRIEN Halpin		1842	1915	061	HALPIN, James	
				061		
James O'DONNELL		1850	1924	061	ELLIOTT, Kate	
Kate ELLIOTT O'Donnell		1855	1917	061	O'DONNELL, James	
				061		
James E. FLEMMING		1858	1900	061	_____, Julia D.	
Julia D. _____ FLEMMING		1850	1929	061	FLEMMING, James E.	
				061		
John O'BRIEN		06-25-1808	11-18-1892	061	ROACH, Julia	

Name	Origin	Birth	Death	Code	Relation	Notes
Julia ROACH O'Brien		08-15-1815	01-24-1899	061	O'BRIEN, John	
Bridget O'BRIEN Connell		08-08-1847	03-29-1896	061	O'BRIEN, Bridget	Dau Of John & Julia O'Brien.
				061		(NOI Mr. Connell)
				061		
Michael CONNOLLY		1850	1932	061	MULLIN, Anna	
Anna MULLIN Connolly		1844	1938	061	CONNOLLY, Michael	
Mrs. Martin CONNOLLY		1825	1911	061	CONNOLLY, Martin	(NOI Martin Connolly)
Mary CONNOLLY		1860	1899	061	CONNOLLY, Mary	
				061		
Matthew M. FOX		1829	1904	061	ATWOOD, Frances E.	
				061	SHERIDAN, Anora	
Frances E. Atwood FOX		1835	1968	061	FOX, Matthew M.	
Anora SHERIDAN Fox		1843	1930	061	FOX, Matthew M.	
				061		
Thomas MCKEON		1824	1882	061	FITZPATRICK, Ann	
Ann FITZPATRICK McKeon		1824	1910	061	MCKEON, Thomas	
Mary MCKEON		1848	1936	061	MCKEON, Mary	
				061		
Jane CARNEY	Co. Longford	88 Years	10-07-1906	061	CARNEY, Jane	Born Granite (Granard), County
				061		Longford, Ireland. Died at
				061		Salisbury, VT
				061		
Michael DUFFY		09-1801	04-1886	061	MCCOY, Mary	
Mary MCCOY Duffy		10-1802	09-1881	061	DUFFY, Michael	
David DUFFY		08-1847	08-30-1873	061	DUFFY, David	
Mary DUFFY		08-1848	08-31-1913	061	DUFFY, Mary	
				061		
				061		
James DOOLIN		04-03-1839	04-13-1924	061	_____, Margaret	
Margaret ____ DOOLIN		12-08-1840	07-18-1911	061	DOOLIN, James	
				061		
John DUFFY	Co. Meath	72 Years	02-12-1869	061	_____, Mary	A Native Of Ballina, Co. Meath
				061		Ireland, From Which Place He
				061		Emigrated in 1826 (Parish c/b
				061		Killyon. Index also lists
				061		Ballina or Bective as Parish
				061		Balsoon)
Mary _____ DUFFY		73 Years	06-06-1878	061	DUFFY, John	
				061		
John CANDON	Co. Cork	11-18-1836	05-06-1899	061	CANDON, John	Born In County Cork, Ireland
				061		
Patrick CANDON		51 Years	11-18-1875	061	CANDON, Patrick	(Stone badly worn. YOD appears
				061		to be 1875)
				061		
Ann CANDON		03-18-1843	05-19-1932	061	CANDON, Ann	Born In Pittsford, (VT)

				061		
Owen SHALVEY	Co. Meath	06-16-1808	11-23-1849	061	SHALVEY, Owen	IMO Owen Shalvey. Departed
				061		this life Nov 23,1849, Age 41.
				061		Born In Rathkenney (Rathkenny)
				061		Co. Meath Ireland,Jun 16, 1808
				061		
Gilbert SHELVEY		37Y 10M	12-16-1883	061	SHELVEY, Gilbert	
Thomas SHELVEY	Co. Meath	72 Years	06-18-1871	061	_____, Margaret	Born In Rathkenney (Rathkenny)
				061		Co. Meath, Ireland
Margaret _____ SHELVEY		75 Years	10-03-1882	061	SHELVEY, Thomas	
James SHELVEY		26 Years	08-08-1878	061	SHELVEY, James	
				061		
Thomas F. TENNIEN		08-30-1840	10-02-1916	061	TENNIEN, Thomas F.	
				061		
John FLEMING		1826	1902	061	CONNOLLY, Aileen	
Aileen CONNOLLY Fleming		1832	1920	061	FLEMING, John	
Theresa A. FLEMING		1855	1907	061	FLEMING, Theresa A.	
Ellen FLEMING		1857	1919	061	FLEMING, Ellen	
Jennie FLEMING		1861	1913	061	FLEMING, Jennie	
Martin FLEMING		1863	1863	061	FLEMING, Martin	
				061		
Mary FALLOON		1839	1914	061	FALLOON, Mary	
				061		
Daniel REED		82 Years	08-13-1906	061	SULLIVAN, Julia	Born In Ireland
				061		
				061		
				061		
Julia SULLIVAN Reed		69 Years	12-05-1909	061	REED, Daniel	Born In Ireland
				061		
Patrick SHELVEY		47Y1M9D	03-23-1881	061	MURPHY, Mary	
Mary MURPHY Shelvey		40 Years	05-30-1886	061	SHELVEY, Patrick	
				061		
Michael CARRIGAN		1850	1926	061	FLEMING, Maria	
Maria FLEMING Carrigan		1853	1912	061	CARRIGAN, Michael	
				061		
John KEENAN		1837	1906	061	DOWLING, Nancy	
Nancy DOWLING Keenan		1840	1920	061	KEENAN, John	
				061		
Edward HEREY		43 Years	10-16-1843	061	CARRIGAN, Catherine	
Catherine CARRIGAN Herey		74 Years	01-11-1892	061	HEREY, Edward	
				061		
Christopher HEREY				061	HEREY, Christopher	Died At New Orleans,LA, Age 17
				061		(GAR) 2nd NY Vet Cav
				061		
Walter CARRIGAN		1830	1906	061	MCALLISTER, Elizabeth	

Elizabeth MCALLISTER Carrigan		1832	1888	061	CARRIGAN, Walter	
				061		
Michael MCDERMOTT		47 Years	01-16-1883	061	_____, Mary B.	(NOI Spouse, Mary B.)
				061	MCDERMOTT, Michael	
				061		
Mary _____ COFFEY		75 Years	08-18-1875	061	COFFEY, Patrick	(NOI Patrick Coffey)
				061	_____, Mary	
				061		
Frank BAKER		1839	1916	061	_____, Eliza	
Eliza _____ BAKER		1836	1920	061	BAKER, Frank	
				061		
Francis BAKER		86 Years	10-29-1866	061	_____, Eliza	
Eliza _____ BAKER		87 Years	05-18-1887	061	BAKER, Francis	
				061		
Alexander BEAN		1826	1911	061	BEAN, Alexander	Co.A, 12th Rgt & Co. B,7th Rgt
				061		Vt Vols (GAR)
Richard CRAHAN		11-1852	12-18-1923	061	CLARK, Eliza	
Eliza CLARK Crahan			03-24-1916	061	CRAHAN, Richard	
				061		
Martin B. SHERIDAN		1854	1809	061	FALLOON, Catherine A.	
Catherine A. FALLOON Sheridan		1858	1914	061	SHERIDAN, Martin B.	
				061		
Mary A. FALLOON		1839	1914	061	FALLOON, Mary A.	
				061		
George CHRISTMAS Sr.		1847	1922	061	LANDER, Kate	
				061		
				061		
Kate LANDER Christmas		1850	1917	061	CHRISTMAS, George Sr.	
				061		
Jerry RIORDAN		08-07-1828	08-24-1910	061	_____, Mary	
Mary _____ RIORDAN		05-24-1838	05-02-1910	061	RIORDAN, Jerry	
Jeremiah RIORDAN		1850	1892	061	RIORDAN, Jeremiah	
				061		
Daniel HENNESEY	Co. Longford	01-28-1804	08-02-1862	061	HENNESEY, Daniel	Died At Baton Rouge,Louisiana.
				061		Born In Co. Longford, Ireland.
				061		Co. G, 7th Vt Vol Rgt (GAR)
				061		
Charles REILLY	Co. Meath	38 Years	10-10-1848	061	REILLY, Charles	Born In The Parish of Navan,
				061		Co. Meath, Ireland.
				061		
Patrick REILLY		67 Years	04-03-1879	061	REILLY, Patrick	
				061		
James REILLY		56 Years	04-29-1875	061	REILLY, James	Co. H, 1st Vermont Cav. (GAR)

St. Raphael's Cemetery, Poultney, VT

NAME	POB	DOB/AGE	DOD	CEM	SPOUSE/INDEX	INSCRIPTION
James HARNEY		1859	1910	062	BRADY, Bridget	Born In Ireland
Bridget BRADY Harney		73Y 11M	06-02-1922	062	HARNEY, James	Born In Ireland
				062		
Francis H. CASSIDY		1849	1911	062	LEAMY, Mary Ann	
Mary Ann LEAMY Cassidy		1850	1927	062	CASSIDY, Francis H.	
				062		
John BURNS		1828	1914	062	FANNING, Mary	
Mary FANNING Burns		1818	1907	062	BURNS, John	
				062		
John MALONEY		1839	1919	062	LEONARD, Katherine	
Katherine LEONARD Maloney		1831	1914	062	MALONEY, John	
James S. MALONEY		1837	1905	062	MALONEY, James S.	
				062		
Michael MCMORROW		1818	1904	062	MCMORROW, Michael	
				062		
Bridget DALY Dunn		1816	1906	062	DUNN, John	(NOI John Dunn)
				062	DALY, Bridget	
				062		
Jeremiah O'CONNELL	Co. Cork	01-06-1840	09-18-1905	062	_____, Catherine	
				062		
				062		
Catherine _____ O'CONNELL	Co. Clare	06-25-1854	06-14-1889	062	O'CONNNELL, Jeremiah	
				062		
John W. MURPHY		1860	1922	062	MCNAMARA, Kate	
				062	REGAN, Anna	
Kate MCNAMARA Murphy		1858	1905	062	MURPHY, John W.	
Anna REGAN Murphy		1869	1960	062	MURPHY, John W.	
				062		
James B. CARMODY		1858	1918	062	CARVAY, Bridget A.	
Bridget A. CARVAY Carmody		1865	1929	062	CARMODY, James B.	
				062		
John WILLIAMS		07-04-1832	01-09-1915	062	BUSHA, Matilda	
Matilda BUSHA Williams		07-28-1836	05-19-1906	062	WILLIAMS, John	
				062		
Thomas HARNEY		1845	1899	062	MOLONEY, Mary Helen	
Mary Helen MOLONEY Harney		1852	1914	062	HARNEY, Thomas	
				062		
Michael MACK	Co. Clare	1824	1904	062	KENNEDY, Margaret	Natives of County Clare,Ire.
				062		

Margaret KENNEDY Mack	Co. Clare	1840	1908	062	MACK, Michael	Natives of County Clare,Ire.
				062		
				062		
Mary MCNAMARA Maloney	Co. Clare	81 Years	10-02-1899	062	MALONEY, Patrick	Born In "Balaquilen",(Bally-
				062	MCNAMARA, Mary	Quin), Barony of Tulla, Parish
				062		of "Kilfenore" (Kilfenora),Co.
				062		Clare,Ire.(NOI Patrick
				062		Maloney)
Patrick MACK		1832	1895	062	CAIRNS, Bridget Mary	
Bridget Mary CAIRNS Mack		1840	1921	062	MACK, Patrick	
				062		
Joseph WHITE		1845	1925	062	WHITE, Joseph	
				062		
James LARKIN		1822	1888	062	____, Catherine	
Catherine ____ LARKIN		1824	1898	062	LARKIN, James	
Charles LARKIN		1875	1912	062	LARKIN, Charles	
Maria LARKIN		1856	1936	062	LARKIN, Maria	
James LARKIN		1860	1924	062	LARKIN, James	
Frank HOPE		1845	1890	062	HOPE, Frank	
				062		
Bridget CARTLAND McGinn		73 Years	04-07-1892	062	MCGINN, Patrick	(NOI Patrick McGinn)
				062	CARTLAND, Bridget	
				062		
Rose MCGINN		1851	1916	062	MCGINN, Rose	
				062		
Michael MOONEY		59 Years	03-26-1894	062	DUNN, Bridget	
Bridget DUNN Mooney			03-15-1899	062	MOONEY, Michael	
				062		
Keerin F. MOONEY		1841	1904	062	MCGINN, Mary	
Mary MCGINN Mooney		1848	1922	062	MOONEY, Keerin F.	
				062		
J. Bernard POWERS		1866	1946	062	FERRY, Mary	
Mary FERRY Powers		1849	1897	062	POWERS, J. Bernard	
				062		
John T. BROUGH				062	DUNN, Elizabeth T.	(No DOB/DOD on this family of
Elizabeth T. DUNN Brough				062	BROUGH, John T.	Brough and Dunn -- all in same
William DUNN Sr.				062	DELEHANTY, Ann	family plot)
Ann DELEHANTY Dunn				062	DUNN, William Sr.	
Maria DUNN				062	DUNN, Maria	
William H. DUNN Jr.				062	DUNN, William H. Jr.	
Katherine DUNN				062	DUNN, Katherine	
Anna F. DUNN Brough				062	BROUGH, Kenneth J.	(NOI Kenneth J. Brough)
				062	DUNN, Anna F.	
Katherine DUNN				062	DUNN, Katherine	
Martha M. DUNN Marshall		1879	1944	062	MARSHALL, J. H.	(NOI J. H. Marshall)

				062	DUNN, Martha M.	
Patrick DUNN				062	DUNN, Patrick	(NOI DOB/DOD)
John DUNN				062	DUNN, John	(NOI DOB/DOD)
				062		
Owen J. HAYES		1859	1925	062	GARVAY, Mary E.	
Mary E. GARVAY Hayes		12-06-1896	02-10-1896	062	HAYES, Owen J.	Born in West Castleton, VT
				062		
Hanora HOGAN Dundon		1830	1910	062	DUNDON, James	(NOI James Dundon)
				062	HOGAN, Hanora	
				062		
Thomas O'KEEFE		40 Years	03-30-1895	062	DUNDON, Mary	
Mary DUNDON O'Keefe				062	O'KEEFE, Thomas	
				062		
Ann STARR McCarty		1823	1907	062	MCCARTY, P.	(NOI P. McCarty)
				062	STARR, Ann	
				062		
Edward BUTLER	Co. Cork	1802	05-22-1890	062	DRISCOLL, Mary	Born In Dunmanway,Co. Cork,Ire
Mary DRISCOLL Butler		1812	04-15-1890	062	BUTLER, Edward	
Catherine BUTLER		1850	1862	062	BUTLER, Catherine	Dau of E. & M. Butler
John BUTLER		1855	1919	062	BUTLER, John	
Edward BUTLER Jr.		1852	1932	062	HALEY, Anne	
Anne HALEY Butler		1850	1917	062	BUTLER, Edward Jr.	
				062		
				062		
Patrick FLANAGAN		1824	1898	062	NOONE, Mary	Native of Ireland
Mary NOONE Flanagan		1845	1924	062	FLANAGAN, Patrick	
				062		
Peter HOLLAND		1813	1895	062	LANE, Mary	(Holland,Whitty and Bethel all
Mary LANE Holland		1832	1911	062	HOLLAND, Peter	on one large Holland marker).
George H. WHITTY		1851	1927	062	HOLLAND, Margaret	
Margaret HOLLAND Whitty		1853	1930	062	WHITTY, George H.	
Daniel BETHEL		1851	1924	062	HOLLAND, Mary	
Mary HOLLAND Bethel		1856	1941	062	BETHEL, Daniel	
				062		
Patrick SEYMOUR		1849	1938	062	HICKEY, Mary	
Mary HICKEY Seymour		1849	1899	062	SEYMOUR, Patrick	
				062		
Mary Ann CLIFFORD Penders		1857	1933	062	PENDERS, Thomas	(NOI Thomas Penders)
				062	CLIFFORD, Mary Ann	
				062		
Michael RYAN		79 Years	09-01-1896	062	BRADSHAW, Mary	
Mary BRADSHAW Ryan		83 Years	11-25-1902	062	RYAN, Michael	
				062		
John HANNAN		1844	1898	062	RYAN, Hanorah	

Hanorah RYAN Hannan	1849	1903	062	HANNAN, John	
			062		
James HANNAN	1850	1898	062	RYAN, Catherine	
Catherine RYAN Hannan	1861	1917	062	HANNAN, James	
			062		
John MCINERNEY	1843	1932	062	MINOUGE, Julia	
Julia MINOUGE McInerney	1854	1924	062	MCINERNEY, John	
			062		
James BUTLER			062	MORRISEY, Julia	(No DOB/DOD James Butler)
Julia MORRISEY Butler	59 Years	12-17-1905	062	BUTLER, James	
Maggie BUTLER Hayes	99 Years	01-09-1908	062	BUTLER, Maggie	(NOI Mr. Hayes)
			062		
Ann BURKE	70 Years	11-20-1898	062	BURKE, Ann	
			062		
James E. POWERS	1863	1924	062	BURKE, Margaret	
Margaret BURKE Powers	1849	1924	062	POWERS, James E.	
			062		
Patrick E. CARMODY	1855	1935	062	GRIFFITH, Mary E.	
Mary E. GRIFFITH Carmody	1858	1932	062	CARMODY, Patrick E.	
			062		
Bridget GALLAGHER	1856	1946	062	GALLAGHER, Bridget	
			062		
Michael HOLLAND	1850	1924	062	_____, Margaret	
Margaret _____ HOLLAND	1857	1936	062	HOLLAND, Michael	
			062		
James HOGAN	1853	1936	062	DOLAN, Anna	
Anna DOLAN Hogan	1862	1944	062	HOGAN, James	
			062		
John WALLACE	1842	1924	062	O'KEEFE, Mary	
Mary O'KEEFE Wallace	1852	1935	062	WALLACE, John	
Luke O'KEEFE	1857	1923	062	O'KEEFE, Luke	
			062		
William H. BURNS	1855	1934	062	PHALEN, Margaret	
Margaret PHALEN Burns	1864	1951	062	BURNS, William H.	
			062		
Edward COMEY	1851	1923	062	_____, Ellen	
Ellen _____ COMEY	1859	1947	062	COMEY, Edward	
			062		
Edward DRISCOLL	1849		062	CROSS, Mary Ann	(Edward Driscoll and Mary Ann
Mary Ann CROSS Driscoll	1846		062	DRISCOLL, Edward	Cross are on same stone as
John SOUTH	1871	1913	062	SOUTH, John	John South. Second stone, same
Edward DRISCOLL		10-11-1918	062	DRISCOLL, Edward	plot is Edward Driscoll. Prob-
			062		ably same person)
			062		
Richard D. MCGRATH	1845	1911	062	BARRY, Julia	

Julia BARRY McGrath	1852	1911	062	MCGRATH, Richard D.	
			062		
Patrick BRAYTON	1855	1934	062	SCANNEL, Hanorah	
Hanorah SCANNEL Brayton	1860	1911	062	BRAYTON, Patrick	
			062		
Patrick LARKIN	1848	1932	062	_____, Julia	
Julia _____ LARKIN	58 Years	06-25-1908	062	LARKIN, Patrick	
			062		
Edward MCGRATH	1846	1923	062	MCDONALD, Katherine	
Katherine MCDONALD McGrath	1845	1903	062	MCGRATH, Edward	
			062		
William KENNEDY	1837	1908	062	KEEFE, Ellen	
Ellen KEEFE Kennedy	1841	1910	062	KENNEDY, William	
			062		
David QUIRK	1847	1917	062	_____, Catherine	
Catherine _____ QUIRK	1850	1908	062	QUIRK, David	
			062		
John O'KEEFE	1853	1916	062	_____, Margaret	
Margaret _____ O'KEEFE	1863	1931	062	O'KEEFE, John	
			062		
John HOLLAND	1811	1901	062	LANE, Ellen	Natives of Ireland
Ellen LANE Holland	1824	1909	062	HOLLAND, John	Natives of Ireland
			062		
John MCMORROW	1820	1905	062	ROONEY, Margaret	
Margaret ROONEY McMorrow	1828	1910	062	MCMORROW, John	
			062		
Thomas GRIFFITH	1828	1902	062	MELVIN, Mary	
Mary MELVIN Griffith	1825	1906	062	GRIFFITH, Thomas	
Edward GRIFFITH	01-25-1849	12-31-1870	062	GRIFFITH, Edward	
Thomas J. GRIFFITH	05-06-1860	12-07-1886	062	GRIFFITH, Thomas J.	
			062		
John FLOOD	1849	1915	062	_____, Mary A.	
Mary A. _____ FLOOD	1860	1954	062	FLOOD, John	
			062		
Patrick BRENNAN	05-16-1847	10-02-1897	062	MCCARTY, Margaret	
Margaret MCCARTY Brennan	05-27-1857	06-21-1929	062	BRENNAN, Patrick	
			062		
Michael CARVAY	1835	1898	062	MAHAR, Mary	
Mary MAHAR Carvay	1835	1899	062	CARVAY, Michael	
			062		
John CAHILL	1848	1903	062	LYNCH, Eliza	
Eliza LYNCH Cahill	1849	1902	062	CAHILL, John	
			062		
William DUDLEY	75 Years	05-31-1901	062	RILEY, Margaret	
Margaret RILEY Dudley	36 Years	09-24-1865	062	DUDLEY, William	

Name	County	Born/Age	Died	Code	Related	Remarks
				062		
David PARRO		07-24-1831	08-20-1892	062	DALTON, Rosella	
Rosella DALTON Parro		08-30-1835	04-19-1890	062	PARRO, David	
				062		
Michael DYNAN	Co. Limerick	35 Years	04-09-1871	062	LYNCH, Mary	Native of the Co. Limerick,Ire
Mary LYNCH Dynan		86 Years	11-15-1917	062	DYNAN, Michael	
				062		
Edward RIEL		74 Years	05-11-1902	062	LYNCH, Hannora	
Hannora LYNCH Riel	Co. Kerry	53 Years	02-16-1890	062	RIEL, Edward	A Native of Brandon,Co. Kerry,
				062	LYNCH, Jeremiah	Ireland. Dau of Jeremiah and
				062		Mary Lynch. (No such town as
				062		Brandon. Could be Brandonwell)
				062		
John LYNCH Sr.		12-09-1802	02-12-1867	062	BRADSHAW, Ann	
Ann BRADSHAW Lynch		09-11-1805	04-10-1896	062	LYNCH, John Sr.	
Michael LYNCH		1849	1932	062	RYAN, Mary	
Mary RYAN Lynch		1854	1928	062	LYNCH, Michael	
				062		
John GORMAN		62 Years	10-27-1907	062	LYNCH, Johanna	
Johanna LYNCH Gorman		52 Years	11-15-1895	062	GORMAN, John	
				062		
Mathew HOGAN	Co. Tipperary	50 Years	11-30-1890	062	_____, Catherine	Native of _________, Parish of
				062		Youghal (Yougalarra), County
				062		Tipperary,Ireland (Cannot read
				062		town name-stone deteriorated)
Catherine _____ HOGAN		49 Years	09-04-1891	062	HOGAN, Mathew	
				062		
Francis CARRIGAN		1827	1890	062	HARRISON, Margaret	
Margaret HARRISON Carrigan		1830	1902	062	CARRIGAN, Francis	
				062		
William HANLEY	Co. Roscommon	10-10-1839	09-21-1891	062	HANLEY, William	Born In Parish of Kilglass,Co.
				062		Roscommon, Ireland
				062		
William DONAHUE		1840	1924	062	HARRISON, Margaret	
Bridget MOONEY Donahue		36 Years	10-04-1883	062	DONAHUE, William	
Margaret _____ DONAHUE		1845	1923	062	DONAHUE, William	
Miles FOLEY		1855	1920	062	MCCARTY, Hannah	
Hannah MCCARTY Foley				062	FOLEY, Miles	
				062		
Luke QUINN	Co. Wexford	64 Years	09-18-1891	062	_____, Ellen	Native of Parish ________, Co.
				062		Wexford, Ire (Deteriorated)
Ellen _____ QUINN		72 Years	08-09-1893	062	QUINN, Luke	
				062		
Martin DRISCOLL	Co. Clare	52 Years	05-16-1887	062	KIELY, Mary	A Native of Parish of Kilimy
				062		(Killeany,Killeely,Killimer)

			062		Co. Clare, Ireland
			062		
Mary KIELY Driscoll	1852	1933	062	DRISCOLL, Martin	
			062		
Timothy KIELY	1814	1887	062	_____, Margaret	
Margaret _____ KIELY	1828	1889	062	KIELY, Timothy	
Eugene KIELY	1846	1921	062	KIELY, Eugene	
Catherine KIELY	1858	1950	062	KIELY, Catherine	
			062		
William BETHEL	1852	1932	062	POWERS, Mary	
Mary POWERS Bethel	1861	1942	062	BETHEL, William	
			062		
William BETHEL	75 Years	01-21-1900	062	COLLINS, Ellen	
Ellen COLLINS Bethel	73 Years	01-26-1893	062	BETHEL, William	
			062		
Michael COSTELLO	1849	1915	062	BETHEL, Sarah A.	
Sarah A. BETHEL Costello	1849	1910	062	COSTELLO, Michael	
			062		
John REGAN	1824	1907	062	GEELAN, Mary Ann	
			062		
			062		
Mary Ann GEELAN Regan	1826	1912	062	REGAN, John	
			062		
James P. MURPHY	03-29-1856	01-16-1913	062	BETHEL, Ellen	
Ellen BETHEL Murphy	06-02-1854	07-08-1928	062	MURPHY, James P.	
			062		
John T. BETHEL	1850	1932	062	MOONEY, Mary	
Mary MOONEY Bethel	1851	1930	062	BETHEL, John T.	
			062		
John E. POWERS	89 Years	08-01-1917	062	MOONEY, Margaret	
Margaret MOONEY Powers	54 Years	09-30-1896	062	POWERS, John E.	
			062		
Daniel B. BREE	1852	1915	062	BREE, Daniel B.	
Andrew BREE	1859	1926	062	BREE, Andrew	
			062		
John BREE	1844	1895	062	_____, Catherine	
Catherine _____ BREE	1844	1929	062	BREE, John	
			062		
Martin H. BREE	1848	1921	062	BREE, Martin H.	
James BREE	1861	1927	062	BREE, James	
Ethel E. BREE	1874	1906	062	BREE, Ethel E.	
			062		
John DRISCOLL			062	BRENNAN, Jane	(No dates on Driscoll Family)
Jane BRENNAN Driscoll			062	DRISCOLL, John	
James Francis DRISCOLL			062	DRISCOLL, James Francis	

NAME	POB	DOB/AGE	DOD	CEM	SPOUSE/INDEX	INSCRIPTION
William DRISCOLL				062	DRISCOLL, William	
Martin Richard DRISCOLL				062	DRISCOLL, Martin Richard	
Joan DRISCOLL				062	DRISCOLL, Joan	
Mary DRISCOLL				062	DRISCOLL, Mary	
				062		
Martin HAYES	Co. Tipperary	1824	12-10-1898	062	HAYES, Martin	Born in Co. Tipperary, Ire
				062		
Michael HAYES	Co. Clare	06-__-1808	02-15-1885	062	HAYES, Michael	Born in Co. Clare, Ireland
				062		
Mary _____ HUGHES	Co. Down	65 Years	05-19-1881	062	HUGHES, John	Native of Co. Down, Ireland.
				062	_____, Mary	(NOI John Hughes)
				062		
James HARVEY		1859	1910	062	BRADY, Bridget	Born In Ireland
Bridget BRADY Harvey		1863	1951	062	HARVEY, James	Born In Ireland

St. Dominicks Cemetery, Proctor, Vermont. South Street, Route 3, Opposite St. Dominicks Catholic Church

NAME	POB	DOB/AGE	DOD	CEM	SPOUSE/INDEX	INSCRIPTION
John O'CONNELL		46 Years	10-05-1892	063	O'CONNELL, John	
				063		
Patrick E. BRESNEHAN		1849	1934	063	OATES, Ellen	
Ellen OATES Bresnehan		1860	1949	063	BRESNEHAN, Patrick E.	
				063		
John HARTNETT		1854	1934	063	_____, Maria A.	
Maria A. _____ HARTNETT		1859	1920	063	HARTNETT, John	
				063		
James F. CARNEY		1851	1926	063	_____, Margaret	
Margaret _____ CARNEY		1848	1917	063	CARNEY, James F.	
Bernard CARNEY		1841	1917	063	TIERNAN, Katherine	
Katherine TIERNAN Carney		1853	1940	063	CARNEY, Bernard	
				063		
Michael DONNELLY		1853	1916	063	LYNCH, Bridget	
Bridget LYNCH Donnelly		1855	1934	063	DONNELLY, Michael	
				063		
Charles G. PREEDOM		1841	1904	063	PAUL, Elizabeth J.	
Elizabeth J. PAUL Preedom		1849	1910	063	PREEDOM, Charles G.	
				063		
John MCLAUGHLIN		1854	1900	063	TIERNAN, Elizabeth	
Elizabeth TIERNAN McLaughlin		1864	1933	063	MCLAUGHLIN, John	
				063		
Thomas LEONARD		03-20-1820	03-19-1909	063	LEONARD, Thomas	

Name	Age/Born	Died	Cem.	Index	Notes
			063		
John CAIN	77 Years	03-24-1900	063	CONIFF, Rose	
Rose CONIFF Cain	38 Years	01-03-1875	063	CAIN, John	
			063		
William CASEY	1824	1905	063	MANGIN, Ann	
Ann MANGIN Casey	1831	1886	063	CASEY, William	
			063		
Bernard MCGARRY	1850	1912	063	_____, Sophia	
Sophia _____ MCGARRY	1850	1918	063	MCGARRY, Bernard	
			063		
Edward FEAN	66 Years	11-16-1905	063	_____, Ann	
Ann _____ FEAN	45 Years	11-17-1884	063	FEAN, Edward	
			063		
Mary A. FEAN O'Neil	19 Years	10-30-1886	063	O'NEIL, J.	(NOI J. O'Neil.This stone worn
			063		not sure if age at death is 19
			063		
John B. FLANAGAN	1842	1914	063	DWYER, Mary	
Mary DWYER Flanagan	1847	1904	063	FLANAGAN, John B.	
			063		
			063		
James HANEY	1852	1940	063	TREE, Mary A.	
Mary A. TREE Haney	1861	1932	063	HANEY, James	
			063		
Patrick NUTLY	1832	1915	063	CUSACK, Bridget	
Bridget CUSACK Nutly	01-01-1841	02-14-1909	063	NUTLY, Patrick	
			063		
James E. HALEY	1852	1926	063	_____, Catherine E.	
Catherine E. _____ HALEY	1853	1925	063	HALEY, James E.	
			063		
Family of Timothy And Martha Noonan			063	NOONAN, Family	
			063		
Timothy NOONAN			063	_____, Martha	
Martha _____ NOONAN			063	NOONAN, Timothy	
Thomas J. NOONAN			063	NOONAN, Thomas J.	
Patrick W. NOONAN			063	NOONAN, Patrick W.	
Michael R. NOONAN			063	NOONAN, Michael R.	
James P. NOONAN			063	NOONAN, James P.	
Eleanor N. CROWLEY			063	CROWLEY, Eleanor N.	Dau Of Arthur & Ellen CROWLEY
			063	CROWLEY, Arthur	
			063		
James E. HANEY		08-06-1910	063	HANEY, James E.	Connecticut/PVT 1CL 60 Inf DIV
			063		(American Legion Marker. NOI)
			063		
Martin J. SCULLEY	38Y 3M	11-20-1885	063	SCULLEY, Martin J.	
			063		

NAME	POB	DOB/AGE	DOD	CEM	SPOUSE/INDEX	INSCRIPTION
William M. STANLEY		1848	1902	063	LENNON, Bridget	
Bridget LENNON Stanley		1852	1926	063	STANLEY, William M.	
				063		
James CONNOR		82 Years	11-26-1910	063	CONNIFF, Ann	
Ann CONNIFF Connor		63 Years	01-16-1892	063	CONNOR, James	
				063		
Patrick BARRETT		80 Years	04-23-1897	063	BROPHY, Elizabeth	
Elizabeth BROPHY Barrett		75 Years	02-23-1898	063	BARRETT, Patrick	
Bridget BARRETT		34 Years	10-10-1892	063	BARRETT, Bridget	
				063		
Bridget HANLEY			01-25-1914	063	HANLEY, Bridget	(NOI)
				063		
Henry PENDERS		1831	1899	063	HEALEY, Margaret	
Margaret HEALEY Penders		1839	1926	063	PENDERS, Henry	
				063		
James MCKEARIN		03-03-1857	08-13-1904	063	O'NEIL, Mary	
Mary O'NEIL McKearin		11-01-1860	02-04-1934	063	MCKEARIN, James	
				063		
William H. MCKEARIN		42 Years	05-22-1904	063	_____, Anna	
Anna _____ MCKEARIN		50 Years	10-03-1905	063	MCKEARIN, William H.	
				063		
Patrick J. BARRETT		05-14-1852	03-08-1903	063	_____, Margaret K.	
Margaret K. _____ BARRETT		11-26-1860	07-11-1936	063	BARRETT, Patrick J.	
				063		
James MCCOURT		04-17-1850	06-11-1895	063	_____, Elizabeth	
Elizabeth _____ MCCOURT		73 Years	01-16-1925	063	MCCOURT, James	
				063		
James RODDY		1840	1892	063	CURRY, Mary	
Mary CURRY Roddy		1844	1913	063	RODDY, James	
				063		
Winifred BENSON		01-31-1820	02-16-1889	063	BENSON, Winifred	
				063		
John BARRETT		04-26-1851	05-07-1928	063	JERRY, Mary A.	
Mary A. JERRY Barrett		12-28-1859	12-18-1935	063	BARRETT, John	

Riverside Cemetery, Proctor, Vermont. South Street,Route 3, Opposite St. Dominick's Catholic Church

NAME	POB	DOB/AGE	DOD	CEM	SPOUSE/INDEX	INSCRIPTION
Thomas EVANS	Wales	03-19-1859	11-13-1894	107	EVANS, Thomas	Born At Menai Bridge, North Wales
				107		
				107		
Horace S. GIBBS		1849	1948	107	DURKIN, Jennie	

Jennie DURKIN Gibbs		1849	1913	107	GIBBS, Horace S.	
				107		
Martin C. ROHAN		1836	1900	107	_____, Sarah K.	
Sarah K. _____ ROHAN		1847	1899	107	ROHAN, Martin C.	
				107		
George N. KEEFE		1855	1910	107	_____, Hattie A.	
Hattie A. _____ KEEFE		1869	1931	107	KEEFE, George N.	
				107		
William W. CARY		1844	1914	107	SPAFFORD, Harriett	(GAR) Co. F 1ST REG Vt Vols
				107		Co. F 6TH REG Vt Vols
Harriett SPAFFORD Cary		1845	1900	107	CARY, William W.	
				107		
Thomas P. BURNS		1850	1920	107	_____, Octavia	
Octavia _____ BURNS		1849	1931	107	BURNS, Thomas P.	
				107		
Robert MCGREGOR		1842	1905	107	_____, Mary J.	
Mary J. _____ MCGREGOR		1845	1922	107	MCGREGOR, Robert	
				107		
James A. KELL		09-07-1850	05-14-1895	107	_____, Catherine J.	
Catherine J. _____ KELL		01-15-1851	05-06-1910	107	KELL, James A.	

Hillcrest Cemetery, Proctorsville, Vermont. East of Village on Route 103

NAME	POB	DOB/AGE	DOD	CEM	SPOUSE/INDEX	INSCRIPTION
James HALEY		1814	1897	099	SHEEHAN, Hannah	
Hannah SHEEHAN Haley		1822	1897	099	HALEY, James	
				099		
Frank M. DUGAN		1858	1935	099	HALEY, Mary A.	
Mary A. HALEY Dugan		1856	1941	099	DUGAN, Frank M.	
				099		
Martin A. ROSS		78 Years	04-10-1914	099	DUNBAR, Sellinda	
Sellinda DUNBAR Ross		75 Years	10-24-1939	099	ROSS, Martin A.	
				099		
Russell H. FARR		1852	1913	099	MCNULTY, Susie	
Susie MCNULTY Farr		1857	1918	099	FARR, Russell H.	
				099		
Mathew STEWART		1844	1925	099	RILEY, Mary	
Mary RILEY Stewart		1848	1890	099	STEWART, Mathew	
				099		
Levi GASSETT		1797	1869	099	MCNEILL, Hannah	
Hannah MCNEILL Gassett		1796	1887	099	GASSETT, Levi	
				099		

William SHAW	07-31-1831	12-16-1900	099	SHAW, Ann Elizabeth	
Ann Elizabeth _____ SHAW	08-02-1828	05-24-1910	099	SHAW, William	
William SHAW	04-26-1854	09-11-1909	099	SHAW, William	
			099		
Joseph MALONY	01-27-1851	10-30-1910	099	MALONY, Joseph	
			099		
Martha TIERNEY	72 Years	04-03-1920	099	TIERNEY, MARTHA	
			099		
Patrick FAGAN	35 Years	05-31-1878	099	MALONY, Mary	(GAR Marker-No Unit Desig-try Co. E, 2nd U.S. Sharpshooters, Vt Vols)
Mary MALONY Fagan	78 Years	09-29-1921	099	FAGAN, Patrick	
			099		
			099		
Hannah FAGAN Diggins	31Y4M28D	07-17-1872	099	DIGGINS, Michael	(NOI Michael Diggins)
			099	FAGAN, Hannah	
			099		
Thomas FAGAN	88 Years	04-04-1889	099	FAGAN, Alice	
Alice _____ FAGAN	66 Years	12-03-1872	099	FAGAN, Thomas	
			099		
John CARY	89Y8M23D	03-31-1903	099	PARKHURST, Mary	(GAR) Co. K. 15th Rgt. Died at Soldiers Home, Bennington, VT
			099		
Mary PARKHURST Cary	63Y8M25D	06-21-1882	099	CARY, John	
			099		
James MALONY	72 Years	07-19-1886	099	MOYLAN, Mary	
Mary MOYLAN Malony	64 Years	04-14-1887	099	MALONY, James	
Michael MALONY	44 Years	10-27-1898	099	MALONY, Michael	
William MALONY	41Y11M15D	10-04-1907	099	MALONY, William	
Margaret MALONY	60Y1M23D	07-23-1919	099	MALONY, Margaret	
Nellie E. MALONY	56 Years	09-24-1920	099	MALONY, Nellie E.	
			099		
John K. MCDONALD	1853	1914	099	GIBSON, Ida M.	
Ida M. GIBSON McDonald	1865	1958	099	MCDONALD, John K.	
			099		
John W. MCNULTY	1856	1924	099	HICKS, Sylvia	
Sylvia HICKS McNulty	1863	1936	099	MCNULTY, John W.	
			099		
Charles H. COXON	1853	1943	099	COXON, Charles H.	
			099		
Dennis HOLLAND	07-23-1855	07-21-1943	099	WITHERELL, Addie M.	Co. F., 1st U.S. Art, US Army
Addie M. WITHERELL Holland	11-12-1867	10-23-1929	099	HOLLAND, Dennis	
			099		
Alexander STEWART	88 Years	03-17-1892	099	STEWART, Mary	
Mary _____ STEWART	89 Years	06-18-1893	099	STEWART, Alexander	
			099		

St. Donatian and St. Rogatian Cemetery, S. Main to to Maple, Turn Rt on Edgewood, Randolph, Vermont

NAME	POB	DOB/AGE	DOD	CEM	SPOUSE/INDEX	INSCRIPTION
Matthew C. CARNEY		08-03-1854	08-14-1919	064	_____, Nellie W.	
Nellie W. _____ CARNEY		12-10-1859	04-11-1945	064	CARNEY, Matthew C.	
				064		
Patrick WYNN		03-20-1830	04-22-1907	064	EGAN, Mary	
Mary EGAN Wynn		05-15-1839	01-01-1868	064	WYNN, Patrick	
Bridget A. WYNN		11-28-1858	03-17-1875	064	WYNN, Bridget A.	Their Daughter
				064		
Peter M. O'CONNELL		09-29-1827	09-29-1905	064	KIELY, Joanna	
Joanna KIELY O'Connell		02-28-1845	08-11-1914	064	O'CONNELL, Peter M.	
				064		
Thomas CONNOLLY		02-02-1844	09-14-1920	064	BURKE, Honoria	
Honoria BURKE Connolly		12-12-1847	02-14-1920	064	CONNOLLY, Thomas	
				064		
John SHERLOCK		1848	1913	064	_____, Lucy A.	
Lucy A. _____ SHERLOCK		1861	1952	064	SHERLOCK, John	
				064		
Patrick MCGINNESS		1844	1912	064	SHERLOCK, Ann M.	
Ann M. SHERLOCK McGinness		1845	1930	064	MCGINNESS, Patrick	
Mother		1813	1919	064	_____, Mother	(No surname given)
Mary A. _____		1849	1905	064	_____, Mary A.	(No surname given)
Nellie C. _____				064	_____, Nellie C.	(No surname given)
				064		
John BOLIN		1833	1914	064	DRISCOLL, Mary	
Mary DRISCOLL Bolin		1831	1914	064	BOLIN, John	
				064		
James MANNIX		1843	1915	064	TAGGART, Bella	
Bella TAGGART Mannix		1844	1926	064	MANNIX, James	
				064		
John FLEMING		08-01-1833	01-08-1916	064	HICKEY, Mary	
Mary HICKEY Fleming		02-01-1833	01-18-1908	064	FLEMING, John	
				064		
Elmore B. DOYLE		1857	1947	064	FLEMING, Elizabeth G.	
Elizabeth G. FLEMING Doyle		1863	1939	064	DOYLE, Elmore B.	
				064		
William B. MCCORMACK		1840	1912	064	MCCORMACK, William B.	
				064		
Benjamin BEAN		84 Years	08-08-1915	064	BEAN, Benjamin	(GAR -Not in reference.)
				064		
Andrew F. KERVICK		1852	1907	064	WYNN, Nettie	
Nettie WYNN Kervick		18__	1927	064	KERVICK, Andrew F.	

				064		
Patrick P. WYNN		1840	1914	064	_____, Elizabeth M.	
Elizabeth M. _____ Wynn		1842	1921	064	WYNN, Patrick P.	
				064		
Thomas WYNN		1844	1921	064	PRICE, Bridget	
Bridget PRICE Wynn		1857		064	WYNN, Thomas	
				064		
Michael O'CONNOR	Co. Galway	87 Years	05-25-1902	064	_____, Bridget	O Lord Have Mercy On The Souls
				064	O'CONNOR, Michael	of Michael O'Connor, Bridget
				064		and niece Mary. Natives Of The
				064		Parish Of Ballymacward, County
				064		Galway, Ireland
				064		
Mary HAUFLER Carr	Co. Galway	05-05-1847	12-07-1924	064	HAUFLER, Mary	(Possibly this is the niece
				064		Mary considered for mercy)
				064		
James SEXTON		1834	1907	064	CARNEY, Bridget	
Bridget CARNEY Sexton		1838	1916	064	SEXTON, James	
				064		
Bernard GARLAND		67 Years	01-05-1906	064	_____, Ann	(Appears to be 67 Years)
Ann _____ GARLAND		68 Years	07-03-1901	064	GARLAND, Bernard	
				064		
Bridget O'CONNOR		62 Years	07-30-1884	064	O'CONNOR, Bridget	
				064		
William H. SHIRLOCK		1854	1916	064	WYNN, Annie	
Annie WYNN Shirlock		1863	1950	064	SHIRLOCK, William H.	
				064		
Dominick WYNN		95 Years	02-01-1878	064	_____, Margaret	
Margaret _____ WYNN		83 Years	1886	064	WYNN, Dominick	(Stone deteriorated. Best
				064		guess on DOB/DOD)
Domnick WYNN		46 Years	12-28-1881	064	_____, Elizabeth M.	
				064		
Mathew O'BRIEN	Co. Limerick	72 Years	03-25-1878	064	_____, Alice	A Native Of Co. Limerick, Ire.
Alice _____ O'BRIEN		60 Years	04-28-1879	064	O'BRIEN, Mathew	
				064		
Edward ROPPE		1861	1939	064	WYNN, Annie	
Annie WYNN Roppe		1853	1918	064	ROPPE, Edward	
				064		
Thomas O'ROURKE		1840	1913	064	_____, Mary	
Mary _____ O'ROURKE		1833	1922	064	O'ROURKE, Thomas	
				064		
Ellen H. WYNN Goodrich		45Y10M24D	02-24-1895	064	GOODRICH, George R.	(NOI George R. Goodrich)
				064	WYNN, Ellen H.	
				064		
Michael WYNN		69 Years	10-14-1881	064	_____, Mary	

NAME	POB	DOB/AGE	DOD	CEM	SPOUSE/INDEX	INSCRIPTION
Mary _____ WYNN		70 Years	07-08-1878	064	WYNN, Michael	(Cannot read age at death)
Michael WYNN			08-03-1878	064	_____, Bridget	
Bridget _____		30 Years	08-04-1878	064	WYNN, Michael	
				064		
Peter KELEHER		1829	1883	064	SULLIVAN, Mary	
Mary SULLIVAN Keleher		1837	1907	064	KELEHER, Peter	
John KELEHER		1859	1935	064	ARMSTRONG, Mary J.	
Mary J. ARMSTRONG Keleher		1869	1939	064	KELEHER, John	
				064		
Dominick WYNN		71Y 8M	08-21-1886	064	ARMSTRONG, Ann	
Ann ARMSTRONG Wynn		81 Years	05-07-1902	064	WYNN, Dominick	
				064		
				064		
Patrick O'CONNELL		70 Years	09-15-1880	064	GRIFFIN, Ellen	
Ellen GRIFFIN O'Connell		79 Years	03-22-1905	064	O'CONNELL, Patrick	
John O'CONNELL		25 Years	05-28-1885	064	O'DONNELL, John	S/O Patrick & Ellen O'Connell
				064		
Margaret CAIRNS		33 Years	01-26-1887	064	CAIRNS, Margaret	
				064		
Bartholomew FENTON		1843	1923	064	GRIFFIN, Martha	
Martha GRIFFIN Fenton		1851	1880	064	FENTON, Bartholomew	
Martha FENTON Carmody		1868	1914	064	FENTON, Martha	(NOI Carmody)
				064		
James GRIFFIN		76 Years	01-__-1882	064	_____, Sarah	
Sarah _____ GRIFFIN		66 Years	01-23-1873	064	GRIFFIN, James	
				064		
Mary WYNN Crowe		59Y6M15D	12-__-1898	064	CROWE, David	

All Saints Cemetery - Richford, VT (2 miles before village on Vermont Route 105)

NAME	POB	DOB/AGE	DOD	CEM	SPOUSE/INDEX	INSCRIPTION
Charles HANEY		65 Years	09-09-1894	066	GRACE, Mary	(GAR) Co. C. of 5th Vt Vols
Mary GRACE Haney		12-24-1840	08-13-1893	066	HANEY, Charles	
				066		
Peter M. FLANAGAN		07-25-1853	07-16-1909	066	_____, Josephine E.	
Josephine E. ___ FLANAGAN		09-24-1861	12-06-1934	066	FLANAGAN, Peter M.	
				066		
John BARRY		68 Years	11-21-1877	066	BARRY, John	
				066		
John SLOAN		60 Years	07-09-1901	066	MACKREL, Margaret	
Margaret MACKREL Sloan		90 Years	07-19-1929	066	SLOAN, John	

Name	Born	Died	Code	Relation	Notes
			066		
Michael BERRY	1835	1919	066	WALSH, Bridget	
Bridget WALSH Berry	1835	1909	066	BERRY, Michael	
			066		
Jeremiah ENRIGHT	12- -1815	10- -1881	066	SIMM, Mary Ann	
Mary Ann SIMM Enright	09- -1817	03- -1904	066	ENRIGHT, Jeremiah	
			066		
William ENRIGHT	1845	1930	066	HANNA, Eliza	
Eliza HANNA Enright	1859	1921	066	ENRIGHT, William	
			066		
John J. ENRIGHT	1843	1919	066	MATTIMORE, Mary	
Mary MATTIMORE Enright	1837	1917	066	ENRIGHT, John J.	
			066		
Thomas HAUGHEY	03- -1840	01- -1912	066	DEVANEY, Mary	
Mary DEVANEY Haughey	12- -1830	02- -1915	066	HAUGHEY, Thomas	
			066		
Hannibal ENRIGHT	1856	(NOI)	066	MATTIMORE, Bridget A.	
Bridget A. MATTIMORE Enright	1855	1914	066	ENRIGHT, Hannibal	
			066		
Martin F. DONLON	1848	1911	066	ROYSTAN, Mary J.	
Mary J. ROYSTAN Donlon	1852	1915	066	DONLON, Martin F.	
			066		
John RILEY	1837	1925	066	HAUGHIAN, Bridgid L.	
Bridgid L. HAUGHIAN Riley	1847	1927	066	RILEY, John	
			066		
Peter MCGETTRICK	1849	1926	066	ROYSTAN, Mary J.	
Mary MILES McGettrick	1855	1928	066	DONLON, Martin F.	
			066		
Mary BROWN Bashaw Monteith	1854	1920	066	MONTEITH, John	(NOI John Monteith)
			066	BROWN, Mary	
			066		
Daniel E. MURPHY	1866	1949	066	NUTTING, Bertha M.	
Bertha M. NUTTING Murphy	1874	1924	066	MURPHY, Daniel E.	
			066		
Martin MATTIMORE			066	____, Alice	Children of Martin & Alice
Alice ____ MATTIMORE			066	MATTIMORE, Martin	Mattimore - Sarah, John,
Sarah MATTIMORE			066	MATTIMORE, Sarah	Annie, Thomas -(NOI DOB/DOD-
John MATTIMORE			066	MATTIMORE, John	NOI Spouse Alice)
Annie MATTIMORE			066	MATTIMORE, Annie	
Thomas MATTIMORE			066	MATTIMORE, Thomas	

Our Lady Of The Holy Rosary, Richmond, Vt. Left from Rte 2 East onto Baker Street, turn left on Tilden

NAME	POB	DOB/AGE	DOD	CEM	SPOUSE/INDEX	INSCRIPTION
Barney E. KEEFE		1856	1920	067	KEEFE, Barney	
				067		
John COLLINS	Co. Clare	1835	1910	067	CULLIGAN, Mary	Born In County Clare, Ireland
Mary CULLIGAN Collins		1841	1918	067	COLLINS, John	
				067		
John FITZSIMMONS		1857	1928	067	SMITH, Sarah T.	
Sarah T. SMITH Fitzsimmons		1857	1934	067	FITZSIMMONS, John	
				067		
Thomas PHILLIPS		1837	1917	067	CORVIN, Catherine C.	
Catherine C.CORVIN Phillips		1842	1916	067	PHILLIPS, Thomas	
				067		
John J. CANNON		1853	19	067	MARTIN, Jennie	
Jennie MARTIN Cannon		1859	1914	067	CANNON, John J.	
				067		
Thomas B. WHALEN		1855	1929	067	BURKE, Anna	
Anna BURKE Whalen		1860	1933	067	WHALEN, Thomas B.	
				067		
Joanna CASEY		07-12-1845	04-23-1905	067	CASEY, Joanna	
				067		
John E. KENNEDY		1856	1935	067	RUSSELL, Mary A.	
Mary A. RUSSELL Kennedy		1856	1919	067	KENNEDY, John E.	
				067		
Thomas HENLEY		1851	1929	067	EGAN, Ellen	
Ellen EGAN Henley		1856	1933	067	HENLEY, Thomas	
				067		
Charles KEEFE		1850	1911	067	HOWRIGAN, Ellen	
Ellen HOWRIGAN Keefe		1863	1923	067	KEEFE, Charles	
				067		
Joseph W. STRONG		1856	1932	067	SISTERS, Mary A.	
Mary A. SISTERS Strong		1863	1951	067	STRONG, Joseph W.	
				067		
Edward CULLEN		1854	1917	067	RAVEY, Anna	
Anna RAVEY Cullen		1857	1933	067	CULLEN, Edward	
				067		
Thomas MORAN		1843	1925	067	BOYLAN, Catherine	
Catherine BOYLAN Moran		1846	1921	067	MORAN, Thomas	

St. Mary's Cemetery (Old Burial Ground), Richmond, VT 1/2 Mile West From Round Church On Cochran Road

NAME	POB	DOB/AGE	DOD	CEM	SPOUSE/INDEX	INSCRIPTION
Cornelius O'BRIEN			1897	068	WARD, Hannah	
Hannah WARD O'Brien			1902	068	O'BRIEN, Cornelius	
				068		
Cornelius O'BRIEN		1857	1937	068	BENWAY, Julia A.	
Julia A. BENWAY O'Brien		1858	1941	068	O'BRIEN, Cornelius	
				068		
James KEHOE		80 Years	04-09-1872	068	_____, Mary	
Mary _____ KEHOE		75 Years	04-24-1873	068	KEHOE, James	
Bridget KEHOE		62 Years	09-12-1903	068	KEHOE, Bridget	
Lizzie KEHOE		1867	1951	068	KEHOE, Lizzie	
Edward KEHOE		62 Years	04-08-1894	068	KEHOE, Edward	
Margaret KEHOE		75 Years	06-22-1896	068	KEHOE, Margaret	
Miles KEHOE		60 Years	06-09-1886	068	KEHOE, Miles	
Mary KEHOE		1834	1908	068	KEHOE, Mary	
James KEHOE		68 Years	10-15-1904	068	HARRINGTON, Ann	
Ann HARRINGTON Kehoe		73 Years	12-15-1911	068	KEHOE, James	
				068		
Barney CONNOR		1823	1898	068	CONNOR, Barney	
				068		
Daniel P. MCGARGHAN		05-03-1842	05-31-1918	068	_____, Mary	
Mary ____ MCGARGHAN		04-05-1846	09-18-1895	068	MCGARGHAN, Daniel P.	
				068		
Martin PURTEL		1856	1939	068	_____, Bridget	
Bridget ____ PURTEL		1859	1953	068	PURTEL, Martin	
				068		
Michael KEHOE		1823	1899	068	KENNEDY, Mary	
Mary KENNEDY Kehoe		1832	1915	068	KEHOE, Michael	
John E. KEHOE		1857	1873	068	KEHOE, John E.	
				068		
John O'BRIEN		1844	1917	068	_____, Mary A.	
Mary A. ____ O'BRIEN		1832	1915	068	O'BRIEN, John	
				068		
Michael O'BRIEN		05-09-1828	11-10-1896	068	_____, Mary	
Mary _____ O'BRIEN		05-06-1840	11-10-1879	068	O'BRIEN, Michael	
				068		
John CULLIGAN		1854	1944	068	_____, Winifred	
Winifred _____ CULLIGAN		1859	1954	068	CULLIGAN, John	
				068		
Michael MURPHY		09-13-1853	04-05-1936	068	HARRINGTON, Ellen	
Ellen HARRINGTON Murphy		46Y 3M 16D	08-20-1895	068	MURPHY, Michael	

				068		
Thomas J. LYNCH		1850	1935	068	HARRINGTON, Margaret	
Margaret HARRINGTON Lynch		1852	1922	068	LYNCH, Thomas J.	
				068		
Patrick MCDONOUGH		07-10-1832	06-02-1904	068	MCMAHON, Ellen	
Ellen MCMAHON McDonough		05-23-1836	03-02-1916	068	MCDONOUGH, Patrick	
				068		
John O'ROURKE				068	_____, Catherine	GAR Marker (No dates indicated
Catherine _____ O'ROURKE				068	O'ROURKE, John	for any family member)-GAR not
Thomas O'ROURKE				068	O'ROURKE, Thomas	in reference.)
James O'ROURKE				068	O'ROURKE, James	
Richard O'ROURKE				068	O'ROURKE, Richard	
Mary O'ROURKE				068	O'ROURKE, Mary	
				068		
Edward FRANCIS		05-01-1844	06-23-1894	068	KAVANAUGH, Ellen	
Ellen KAVANAUGH Francis		04-08-1843	03-31-1873	068	FRANCIS, Edward	
				068		
James MCCABE		1840	1904	068	CLARK, Catherine	
Catherine CLARK McCabe		1859	1902	068	MCCABE, James	
				068		
John RYAN		1839	1909	068	_____, Lavinia	(No info listed for others)
Lavinia _____ RYAN		1854	1938	068	RYAN, John	
Kate RYAN				068	RYAN, Kate	
Emery STONE				068	STONE, Emery	
Alexander MCCABE				068	MCCABE, Alexander	
Matthew RYAN		54 Years		068	RYAN, Matthew	
				068		
John O'BRIEN		1850	1896	068	HENLEY, Mary	
Mary HENLEY O'Brien		1852	1929	068	O'BRIEN, John	
				068		
William M. POWERS		11-22-1857	09-08-1888	068	POWERS, Anna	(NOI on spouse Anna)
				068	POWERS, William M.	
				068		
Patrick GLEASON		1844	1911	068	HARRINGTON, Kate	
Kate HARRINGTON Gleason		1843	1885	068	GLEASON, Patrick	
				068		
Michael LARNER	Co. Galway		04-13-1890	068	_____, Margaret O.	Native Of Co. Galway, Ireland
Margaret O. _____ LARNER	Co. Limerick		04-19-1894	068	LARNER, Michael	Native of Co. Limerick, Ire.
Mark W. LARNER		01-15-1855	10-21-1886	068		
				068		
Andrew HENLEY		1826	1886	068	RAY, Ellen	(GAR Try Co. A., 1st RGT Cav,
Ellen RAY Henley		1824	1898	068	HENLEY, Andrew	VT. Vols)
Andrew HENLEY		1857	1900	068	HENLEY, Andrew	
				068		
Bryan LOVELL		72 Years	03-14-1879	068	LOVELL, Bryan	

Name	Age/Born	Died	Code	Related	Notes
			068		
Dennis LACEY	77 Years	05-12-1889	068	_____, Catherine	
Catherine _____ LACEY	72 Years	07-04-1883	068	LACEY, Dennis	
Margaret LACEY	02-18-1845	04-11-1904	068	LACEY, Margaret	Dau of Dennis/Catherine LACEY
Ann LACEY Kehoe	68 Years	10-04-1884	068	KEHOE, Michael	(NOI Michael KEHOE)
			068	LACEY, Ann	
			068		
John PHILLIPS	1839	1906	068	_____, Bridgit	
Bridget _____ PHILLIPS	1840	1910	068	PHILLIPS, John	
			068		
John J. MCGOVEN	06-06-1843	04-14-1912	068	DOYLE, Mary C.	(GAR Marker.Stone says MCGOVEN
Mary C. DOYLE McGoven	06-15-1848	04-25-1913	068	MCGOVEN, John J.	Could be MCGOVERN or MCGOWEN)
			068		
Andrew MCGOVERN	41 Years	09-13-1885	068	MCGOVERN, Andrew	
			068		
Patrick MCGOVERN	81 Years	03-17-1926	068	_____, Julia L.	
Julia L. _____ MCGOVERN	1856	1929	068	MCGOVERN, Patrick	
			068		
Michael CASEY	1834	1888	068	_____, Ellen	(GAR-Try Co.F, 6th Rgt,VtVols)
Ellen _____ CASEY	1846	1917	068	CASEY, Michael	
			068		
John WELCH	82 Years	08-29-1890	068	_____, Ellen	
Ellen _____ WELCH	75 Years	11-02-1892	068	WELCH, John	
Thomas M. WELCH	30 Years	12-17-1885	068	WELCH, Thomas M.	
			068		
Mary COFFEE Sexton	59 Years	02-16-1882	068	SEXTON, Lawrence	(NOI Lawrence Sexton)
			068	COFFEE, Mary	
			068		
James MCGARGHAN	79 Years	02-20-1879	068	O'BRINE, Mary	
Mary O'BRINE McGarghan	92 Years	06-15-1894	068	MCGARGHAN, James	
Michael MCGARGHAN	1845	1915	068	MCGARGHAN, Michael	
			068		
Bridget _____ WALKER	36 Years	10-11-1873	068	WALKER, Henry	(NOI Henry Walker)
			068	_____, Bridget	
			068		
John C. BERRY	1849	1934	068	MCGARGHAN, Ellen	
			068	BEACHWELL, Jane	
Ellen MCGARGHAN Berry	1849	1890	068	BERRY, John C.	
Jane BEACHWELL Berry	1853	1939	068	BERRY, John C.	
			068		
John MALONE	50 Years	11-20-1876	068	_____, Catherine	Natives Of Ireland
Catherine _____ MALONE	65 Years	07-06-1887	068	MALONE, John	Natives Of Ireland
			068		
Jeremiah MAHONEY	1824	1887	068	_____, Nancy	
Nancy _____ MAHONEY	1836		068	MAHONEY, Jeremiah	

Name	Origin	Age/Born	Died	Code	Index	Notes
				068		
Thomas HARRINGTON		80 Years	08-24-1894	068	QUILTY, Mary	
Mary QUILTY Harrington		75 Years	10-14-1891	068	HARRINGTON, Thomas	
				068		
Thomas LEONARD		1831	1912	068	HARRINGTON, Mary	
Mary HARRINGTON Leonard		1840	1932	068	LEONARD, Thomas	
				068		
Peter E. BURKE		1837	1897	068	_____, Catherine	
Catherine _____ BURKE		1844	1902	068	BURKE, Peter E.	
				068		
John CLARK	Co. Monaghan	33 Years	07-20-1875	068	CLARK, John	Native of Co. Monaghan, Town-land of Tullynample, Parish of Crin (Currin). Erected by Peter & James CLARK, brothers.
				068	CLARK, Peter	
				068	CLARK, James	
				068		
				068		
				068		
William DAILEY		28 Years	09-11-1873	068	DAILEY, William	
				068		
Daniel KELLEY		70 Years	05-01-1869	068	KELLEY, Daniel	
				068		
James DOWD		1825	1879	068	_____, Bridget	
Bridget _____ DOWD		1829	1907	068	DOWD, James	
Peter DOWD		1861	1925	068	DOWD, Peter	
Margaret DOWD Brennan		1857	1939	068	DOWD, Margaret	(NOI Mr. Brennan)
				068		
Dennis DOWD		54 Years	11-15-1879	068	DOWD, Dennis	
				068		
James TOBIN		72 Years	06-01-1896	068	_____, Mary	
Mary _____ TOBIN		60 Years	09-19-1889	068	TOBIN, James	
				068		
James N. DOWER		87 Years	05-04-1904	068	WELCH, Mary	(GAR Marker - Try Co. C. 9th Rgt, Vt. Vols and Co. A. 9th Rgt)
Mary WELCH Dower		63 Years	05-03-1878	068	DOWER, James N.	
				068		
Martin REEDY		57 Years	10-01-1905	068	REEDY, Martin	
Bridgit REEDY		54 Years	01-01-1908	068	REEDY, Bridgit	
John REEDY		71 Years	02-27-1890	068	_____, Bridgit	
Bridgit _____ REEDY		58 Years	03-07-1884	068	REEDY, John	
Patrick REEDY		19 Years	05-18-1874	068	REEDY, Patrick	Son Of J & B Reedy
				068		
James MCLANE		72 Years	10-04-1870	068	DIXON, Ellen	
Ellen DIXON McLane		76 Years	09-01-1876	068	MCLANE, James	
John MCLANE		34 Years	07-20-1872	068	MCLANE, John	Son Of J & E McLane
				068		
Michael REGAN		1832	1905	068	RYAN, Jane	
Jane RYAN Regan		1824	1902	068	REGAN, Michael	

				068		
James WHALON		63 Years	12-07-1883	068	______, Bridgit	
Bridget ______ WHALON		60 Years	02-14-1878	068	WHALON, James	
				068		
John WINN		97 Years	06-05-1890	068	CLARK, Mary	
Mary CLARK Winn		96 Years	03-28-1903	068	WINN, John	
				068		
Catherine ______ RYAN		29 Years	03-14-1876	068	RYAN, John	(NOI John RYAN)
				068	______, Catherine	
				068		
John FORD		1845	1899	068	STACK, Margaret	
Margaret STACK Ford		1852	1931	068	FORD, John	
Margaret FORD		58 Years	08-04-1870	068	FORD, Margaret	
				068		
David HOWRIGAN		1822	1906(08)	068	WHALEN, Mary	
Mary WHALEN Howrigan		1837	1895	068	HOWRIGAN, David	
				068		
Margaret SHEEDY	Co. Clare	31 Years	04-20-1868	068	SHEEDY, Margaret	Native of Ballymolony, County Clair (Clare),Ireland
				068		
				068		
Margaret O'NEIL		20 Years	03-06-1872	068	O'NEIL, Margaret	Dau of John & Mary O'Neil. Died in Duxbury (VT) At Residence Of Her Parents
				068	O'NEIL, John	
				068	O'NEIL, Mary	
				068		
Timothy O'KEEFE	Co. Cork	47 Years	01-25-1871	068	O'NEIL, Mary	Native of Co. Cork, Ireland
Mary O'NEIL O'Keefe		76 Years	02-21-1902	068	O'KEEFE, Timothy	
John O'KEEFE		19 Years	07-06-1874	068	O'KEEFE, Timothy	
Ellen O'KEEFE		19 Years	09-20-1879	068	O'KEEFE, Ellen	
				068		
Peter CULLIGAN		1829	1894	068	______, Betsey	
Betsey ______ CULLIGAN		1828	1917	068	CULLIGAN, Peter	
				068		
John TOBIN		1838	1922	068	TERRY, Bridget	(GAR) Try Co. F., 6th RGT, VT. Vols)
Bridget TERRY Tobin		1828	1914	068	TOBIN, John	
				068		
Patrick O'BYRNE		1833	1920	068	______, Ellen	
Ellen ______ O'BYRNE		1836	1915	068	O'BYRNE, Patrick	
				068		
James HART		1808	1873	068	MCCABE, Mary	
Mary MCCABE Hart		1810	1889	068	HART, James	
James HART		1848	1933	068	HART, James	
				068		
Charles KEEFE	Co. Fermanagh	03-20-1811	03-09-1873	068	MCBRYNE, Mary	
Mary MCBRYNE Keefe		82 Years	09-06-1896	068	KEEFE, Charles	
				068		

Name	Place	Birth/Age	Death	Code	Index Name	Notes
Ellen MCGRATH		11-11-1873	11-21-1874	068	MCGRATH, Ellen	Children Of W & A McGrath
Infant Daughter			04-23-1875	068		(NOI W & A McGrath)
Eddie MCGRATH		03-24-1876	10-09-1878	068	MCGRATH, Eddie	
				068	MCGRATH, W.	
				068		
Michael DOHERTY		90 Years	10-06-1880	068	CAVIN, Elizabeth Mary	
Elizabeth Mary CAVIN Doherty		77 Years	06-10-1891	068	DOHERTY, Michael	
Mary Agnes DOHERTY			05-01-1878	068	DOHERTY, Mary Agnes	(NOI DOB)
Clara Belle DOHERTY			08-13-1890	068	DOHERTY, Clarabelle	(NOI DOB)
D. J. DOHERTY		1849	1884	068	DOHERTY, D. J.	
Johnny DOHERTY		8 M		068	DOHERTY, Johnny	(NOI DOB-DOD)
				068		
John G. GALLAGAR		81 Years	12-28-1880	068	CAVANAUGH, Elizabeth	
Elizabeth CAVANAUGH Gallagar		78 Years	10-02-1887	068	GALLAGAR, John G.	
				068		
Catherine _____ CAVANAH		88 Years	12-19-1872	068	CAVANAH, Catherine	
				068		
Dennis SHEEHAN		87 Years	04-28-1890	068	_____, Catherine	
Catherine _____ SHEEHAN		80 Years	06-07-1880	068	SHEEHAN, Dennis	
John SHEEHAN		42 Years	03-06-1883	068	SHEEHAN, John	
				068		
Bridget _____ KELLEY		45 Years	06-01-1880	068	KELLEY, Thomas	(NOI Thomas Kelley)
				068	_____, Bridget	
				068		
Peter FLANNERY	Co. Mayo	62 Years	07-22-1896	068	_____, Catherine	Native of Westport, County Mayo
Catherine _____ FLANNERY	Co. Mayo	42 Years	12-19-1879	068	FLANNERY, Peter	County Mayo
Martin SHEEHAN		1854	1916	068	SHEEHAN, Martin	
Peter SHEEHAN		1858	1906	068	SHEEHAN, Peter	
Edward SHEEHAN		1862	1918	068	SHEEHAN, Edward	
Catherine SHEEHAN		1865	1934	068	SHEEHAN, Catherine	
Ellen SHEEHAN		1869	1934	068	SHEEHAN, Ellen	
Bridget SHEEHAN		1859	1936	068	SHEEHAN, Bridget	
				068		
Robert C. BERRY		02-11-1847	08-09-1919	068	PHILLIPS, Mary	
Mary PHILLIPS Berry		08-23-1843	03-30-1903	068	BERRY, Robert C.	
				068		
George BLACKWELL		1807	1879	068	RYAN, Mary	
Mary RYAN Blackwell		1816	1908	068	BLACKWELL, George	
				068		
Thomas RYAN			06-08-1882	068	RYAN, Thomas	Erected by Son John
				068		
Michael TURNEY		65 Years	08-08-1880	068	TURNEY, Michael	
				068		
Peter STRONG		1860	1914	068	STRONG, Peter	
Ellen STRONG		1884	1900	068	STRONG, Ellen	

NAME	POB	DOB/AGE	DOD	CEM	SPOUSE/INDEX	INSCRIPTION
Frances STRONG		100Y 7M 17D	07-29-1888	068	STRONG, Frances	
				068		
Thomas SWEENEY		1832	1904	068	_____, Ann	
Ann _____ SWEENEY		1831	1903	068	SWEENEY, Thomas	
				068		
Ellen DAILEY	Co. Waterford	47 Years	09-12-1870	068	DAILEY, Ellen	Parish of Garinhon (Garran-
				068		baun) Co. Of Waterford, Ire.

St. Josephs Cemetery, Rutland, Vermont. On Stratton Road east of U.S. Route 7

NAME	POB	DOB/AGE	DOD	CEM	SPOUSE/INDEX	INSCRIPTION
				069		
William FOSTER		1847	1922	069	FOSTER, William	
				069		
Henry MCINTYRE		06-20-1804	09-14-1890	069	_____, Nattalee	
Nattalee _____ MCINTYRE		07-01-1816	09-13-1898	069	MCINTYRE, Henry	
				069		
Robert ROSS		1856	1901	069	ROSS, Robert	
				069		
Alfred PHELPS		1851	1923	069	DWIRE, Olive	
Olive DWIRE Phelps		1852	1932	069	PHELPS, Alfred	

Calvary Cemetery, Meadow Street (South of St. Peter's Church) Rutland, VT

NAME	POB	DOB/AGE	DOD	CEM	SPOUSE/INDEX	INSCRIPTION
Michael CROW	Co. Clare	83 Years	05-02-1894	070	HAGERTY, Mary	Native of Carrigh-Rath, (Hard
				070		to read. Possible that "Car-
				070		righ-Rath" is Parish Rath),
				070		County Clare, Ireland
Mary HAGERTY Crow	Co. Donegal	73Y 9MO	09-03-1893	070	CROW, Michael	Native Of Parish Inver,
				070		County Donegal, Ireland
Daniel MCNAMARA	Co. Clare	38 Years	02-25-1882	070	MCNAMARA, Daniel	Born In The Parish Of Killain
				070		(Killeany) (or possibly the
				070		Town of Killeen) Co. Clare
Bryan JUDGE	Co. Roscommon	55 Years	04-10-1898	070	CONLON, Ann E.	Born In Boyle, Co. Roscommon
Ann E. CONLON Judge	Co. Roscommon	52 Years	01-08-1904	070	JUDGE, Bryan	Born In Boyle, Co. Roscommon
				070		
James HINCHEY		1845	1925	070	QUIRK, Hanora	
Hanora QUIRK Hinchey	Co. Kerry	May 1844	08-26-1904	070	HINCHEY, James	Wife Of James Hinchey, Co.
				070		Kerry, Ireland

Name	County	Born/Age	Died	Code	Index	Notes
Sarah HINCHEY Tulley	Co. Clare	1803	June 1895	070	HINCHEY, Sarah	Born In Co. Clare, Ireland (Same stone as James & Hanora Quirk Hinchey-NOI Mr. Tulley)
James MCLAUGHLIN	Co. Roscommon	80 Years	1903	070	WALSH, Bridget	Born County Roscommon, Ire.
Bridget WALSH McLaughlin	Co. Mayo	1836	1913	070	MCLAUGHLIN, James	Born In County Mayo, Ireland
William Henry DENNEHY	Co. Limerick	01-18-1875	01-14-1904	070	DENNEHY, William Henry	A Native Of Rock Hill, County Limerick, Ireland. Erected by his sister Nora M. Dennehy
Reverend Charles O'REILLY	Co. Cavan	12-26-1824	05-16-1910	070	O'REILLY, Rev. Charles	Born In Baharna(Could not find in references) County Cavan, Ireland
Maria LYNCH	Co. Meath	1847	11-07-1928	070	LYNCH, Maria	Born In Athboy, Co. Meath,Ire (Same stone as Rev Charles O'Reilly)
Alice _____ GRIFFIN	Co. Cork	73 Years	07-25-1892	070	GRIFFIN, John _____, Alice	Native of County Cork, Ireland (NOI John Griffin).
Patrick GRIFFIN	Co. Cork	23 Years	06-12-1873	070	GRIFFIN, Patrick	Son Of John & Alice Griffin. Native of Co. Cork, Ireland Erected by Bridget Griffin
Thomas CANNON	Co. Dublin	1826	1904	070	LOVEDAY, Bridget	Native Of Sewards (Swords), Chapel Lizard (Chapelizod), County Dublin, Ireland
Bridget LOVEDAY Cannon		1830	1919	070	CANNON, Thomas	
Patrick DALTON		1836	1912	070	CONINGTON, Bridget	Born In Ireland
Bridget CONINGTON Dalton		49 Years	12-12-1891	070	DALTON, Patrick	Born In Ireland
Stephen CUNNINGHAM	Co. Clare	60 Years	09-14-1893	070	_________, Bridget	Native Of County Clare, Ire
Bridget _____ CUNNINGHAM		No dates	No Dates	070	~~CUNNINGHAM~~, Stephen	Native Of County Clare, Ire
Patrick MCLAUGHLIN	Co. Roscommon	1832	1908	070	_________, Bridget	(Both) Born in Parish of Killglass (Kilglass), Co. Roscommon, Ireland
Bridget _____ MCLAUGHLIN	Co. Roscommon	1834	1909	070	~~MCLAUGHLIN~~, Patrick	
Mary SULLIVAN	Co. Limerick	92 Years	12-23-1884	070	SULLIVAN, Mary	Native Of Co. Limerick, Ire.
Honora MAGNER Hassett	Co. Clare	78 Years	06-02-1876	070	HASSETT, Michael	Wife of Michael Hassett. A Native of Kilkee, Co. Clare,
Patrick MCLAUGHLIN	Co. Leitrim	Mar 1808	10-30-1883	070	O'ROURKE, Bridget	Natives of Drumkeeran, Lietrim County Ireland
Bridget O'ROURKE McLaughlin	Co. Leitrim	Jun 1813	07-12-1878	070	MCLAUGHLIN, Patrick	Natives Of Drumkeeran, Lietrim County, Ireland

Name	County	Born	Died	Code	Relation	Notes
Catherine MCLAUGHLIN Reedy	Co. Leitrim	08-15-1844	03-23-1873	070	REEDY, Maurice	Native Of Drumkeeran,
				070	MCLAUGHLIN, Catherine	Lietrim County Ireland
				070		(NOI Maurice Reedy)
				070		
James HANRAHAN	Co. Limerick	06-11-1820	06-21-1888	070	_____, Ellen	Father of Dr. John Hanrahan
				070		Born In Ballingrane (Ballin-
				070		garrane), Parish of Cappa
				070		(Cappagh), Co. Limerick,Ire
				070		Lietrim County Ireland
Ellen _____ HANRAHAN	Co. Limerick	12-25-1818	No entry	070	HANRAHAN, James	Born In The Parish of Glynn
				070		(Glin), Co. Limerick, Ire.
Dr. John HANRAHAN		06-18-1843	12-26-1920	070	_____, Frances M.	Father of Dr. John Hanrahan
Frances M. _____ HANRAHAN		06-12-1860	03-01-1900	070	HANRAHAN, John, Dr.	
				070		
John CADEN	Co. Mayo	80 Years	04-15-1878	070	_____, Mary	Native of Parish of Cross-
				070		molina, Co. Mayo, Ireland
Mary _____ CADEN	Co. Mayo	73 Years	09-17-1885	070	CADEN, John	
				070		
John CADEN	Co. Mayo	26 Years	09-13-1874	070	CADEN, John	Native of Parish of Cross-
				070		molina, Co. Mayo, Ireland
Thomas CADEN		29 Years	09-27-1881	070	CADEN, Thomas	(Not sure if Bridget and
Bridget CADEN		1853	1924	070	CADEN, Bridget	Thomas are spouse)
John L. HOLMES		1856	1932	070	CADEN, Mary A.	
Mary A. CADEN Holmes		1850	1924	070	HOLMES, John L.	
John CADEN		58 Years	03-24-1899	070	CADEN, John	
				070		
Dennis CAWLEY	Co. Sligo	64 Years	10-10-1879	070	DYER, Mary	Native of Co. Sligo, Ire.
				070		(GAR) Co.F. 13th Regt U.S. Inf
Mary DYER Cawley	Co. Sligo	72 Years	12-28-1889	070	CAWLEY, Dennis	Native of Co. Sligo, Ire.
Mary A. CAWLEY		91 Years	07-10-1947	070	CAWLEY, Mary A.	
				070		
Thomas MADIGAN	Co. Clare	35 Years	12-22-1874	070	MADIGAN, Thomas	Parish of Kilmury, County
				070		Clare, Ireland
James CUSACK	Co. Clare	73 Years	02-15-1890	070	CUSACK, James	Native of Parish Rath, Co
				070		Clare, Ireland
Helen CUSACK	Co. Limerick	No date	No date	070	CUSACK, Helen	Native of Adare, County
				070		Limerick, Ireland (same
				070		stone as James Cusack)
John MANGAN	Co. Clare	63 Years	03-25-1891	070	_____, Catherine	Native Of Parish Kilmurray
				070		(Kilmurry) Co. Clare, Ire.
Catherine _____ MANGAN		08-15-1837	02-24-1903	070	MANGAN, John	
				070		
Bernard MCMURRY	Co. Leitrim	84 Years	11-02-1886	070	MCMURRY, Bernard	Native of Parish Of Killaragy
				070		(Killarga) Co. Leitrim, Ire
Ann MCMURRY		AUG 1840	MAR 1911	070	MCMURRY, Ann	

Thomas KELLEY		34 Years	03-06-1885	070	MANGAN, Annie	
Annie MANGAN Kelley		33 Years	03-07-1887	070	KELLEY, Thomas	
James MCGUIRE	Co. Roscommon	73 Years	06-20-1892	070	MCGUIRE, James	Native of Parish Kilglass, Co.
				070		Roscommon, Ire. Co.F. 6th Vt
Thomas WINTERS	Co. Roscommon	73 Years	09-21-1891	070	_____, Margaret	Native of Aughamore (Aghamore)
				070		Parish of Killoglass(Kilglass)
				070		Co. Roscommon, Ire.
Margaret _____ WINTERS		64 Years	01-20-1893	070	WINTERS, Thomas	
				070		
James FITZGERALD	Co. Kerry	75 Years	10-04-1896	070	_____, Nancy	Born In Tralee, Co Kerry, Ire.
				070		
Nancy _____ FITZGERALD		76 Years	08-02-1907	070	FITZGERALD, James	
				070		
James MORAN	Co. Clare	52 Years	02-19-1867	070	_____, Margaret	Born In Castletown, Co. Clare,
				070		Ireland
Margaret ___ MORAN		73 Years	10-07-1883	070	MORAN, James	
Bridget SLATTERY	Co. Clare		01-08-1903	070	SLATTERY, Bridget	Born Broadford, Co. Clare, Ire
Patrick SLATTERY		1812	1878	070	______, Mary	(Same stone as Bridget. Listed
				070		as 'Father - Patrick)
				070		
Mary _____ SLATTERY		1815	1870	070	SLATTERY, Patrick	(Same stone as Bridget. Listed
				070		as 'Mother - Mary)
				070		
Jane FLYNN	Co. Cork	36 Years	05-20-1872	070	FLYNN, Jane	Native of Parish Bantry,(No
				070		such Parish - probably Bantry
				070		Town), Co. Cork, Ireland
				070		
______ DUFFICY	Co. Roscommon	None	None	070	DUFFICY, ______	Stone Broken. Primary interree
Bridget DUFFICY		1848	1878	070	DUFFICY, Bridget	unknown. Parish unreadable.
Darby DUFFICY			1899	070	DUFFICY, Darby	Co. Roscommon, Ireland
				070		
Margaret CROWE	Co. Clare	44 Years	11-29-1881	070	CROWE, William	Born In The Townland Tully-
				070		crina (Tullycreen) in the
				070		Parish of Kilmurry-McMahon
				070		(Kilmurry),Co. Clare, Ireland
Michael CROWE		1836	1906	070	_____, Margret	
				070	CROWE, Michael	
Thomas SPELLMAN	Co. Cork	61 Years	12-18-1877	070	_____, Mary	Born In Ballymartle,Co. Cork
Mary _____ SPELLMAN		75 Years	05-13-1898	070	SPELLMAN, Thomas	
				070		
Michael MALONEY	Co. Clare	1826	None	070	WORRALL, Elizabeth	Born Clare, Ireland
				070		
Elizabeth WORRALL Maloney	Co. Clare	1840	10-02-1900	070	MALONEY, Michael	Born Clare, Ireland. Died at
				070		Cuttingsville, Vermont
				070		

Patrick CLIFFORD	Co. Tipperary	70 Years	07-23-1853	070	HICKEY, Hannora	Native Of The Parish Of Castletown (Castletownarra & Probably town of Castletown) Co. Tipperary
Hannora HICKEY Clifford	Co. Tipperary	65 Years	08-11-1866	070	CLIFFORD, Patrick	Native Of The Parish Of Castletown (Castletownarra & Probably town of Castletown) Co. Tipperary
Thomas FOLEY	Co. Waterford	12-20-1824	12-03-1899	070	FOLEY, Thomas	Born In Lismore, Waterford Co.
Philip GOOLEY	Co. Tipperary	1839	09-15-1884	070	CLIFFORD, Hannah	Born In Parish of Clohally(No. town or parish by this name)
Hannah CLIFFORD Gooley	Co. Tipperary	1833	12-20-1894	070	GOOLEY, Philip	Born In the Parish of Cashel-town (Castletownarra and pro-bably town of Castletown), Co. Tipperary
John SULLIVAN	Co. Kerry	48Y 8M	10-19-1869	070	SHEEHAN, Ellen	Native Of County Kerry, Ire.
Ellen SHEEHAN Sullivan	Co. Kerry	78 Years	10-11-1901	070	SULLIVAN, John	Born In Lestroytown,(No such or Parish). Co. Kerry, Ireland
John MCMAHON	Co. Dublin	70 Years	11-25-1898	070	CLIFFORD, Ann	Native Of Rowlestown, County Dublin, Ireland
Ann CLIFFORD McMahon	Co. Tipperary	65 Years	01-26-1890	070	MCMAHON, John	Native of Parish of Castletown (Castletownarra-probably Town of Castletown) Co. Tipperary
Patrick BROHAN		1811	1901	070	CANEY, Mary	
Mary CANEY Brohan		1826	1889	070	BROHAN, Patrick	
Bridget BROHAN		1854	1903	070	BROHAN, Bridget	
Honora _____ PILLON		55 Years	07-08-1893	070	PILLON, Michael _____, Honora	(NOI Michael Pillon)
Mary HEALEY		80 Years	09-24-1895	070	HEALEY, Mary	
Patrick CARRIGAN		1827	1895	070	_____, Bridget	
Bridget _____ CARRIGAN		1830	1923	070	CARRIGAN, Patrick	
Dennis KELLIHER		1815	1895	070	HODNETT, Ellen	
Ellen HODNETT Kelliher		1814	1902	070	KELLIHER, Dennis	
James P. CROWLEY		1849	1903	070	CROWLEY, James P.	

Thomas ROONEY	1822	1895	070	MCLAUGHLIN, Ellen	
Ellen MCLAUGHLIN Rooney	1838	1912	070	ROONEY, Thomas	
			070		
John MCCAVET	1837	19000-1862	070	MCDERMOTT, Ellen	
Ellen MCDERMOTT McCavet	1845	1933	070	MCCAVET, John	
			070		
Michael DONOVAN	56 Years	06-25-1903	070	_________, Ann	
Ann _____ DONOVAN	58 Years	01-01-1902	070	DONOVAN, Michael	
			070		
John R. HYNES	68 Years	01-03-1899	070	WALSH, Ellen W.	
Ellen W. WALSH Hynes	58 Years	12-15-1892	070	HYNES, John R.	
Mary A. HYNES Quigley	1856	1926	070	HYNES, Mary A.	(NOI Mr. Quigley)
			070		
John MCLAUGHLIN	1815	1897	070	MCGUIRE, Elizabeth	
Elizabeth MCGUIRE McLaughlin	1815	1900	070	MCLAUGHLIN, John	
John C. MCLAUGHLIN, Jr.	1849	1924	070	MCLAUGHLIN, John C. Jr.	
Patrick MCLAUGHLIN	1853	1928	070	MCLAUGHLIN, Patrick	
Margaret MCLAUGHLIN	1861	1918	070	MCLAUGHLIN, Margaret	
			070		
Martin A. MURPHY	1850	1924	070	MURPHY, Martin A.	
Mary A. MURPHY	1859	1935	070	MURPHY, Mary A.	
			070		
Adelia CUMMINGS	1844	1920	070	CUMMINGS, Adelia	Mother
			070		
Anna MONAHAN Valiquette	1856	1935	070	VALIQUETTE, Edward	
Edward A. VALIQUETTE	1851	1924	070	MONAHAN, Anna	
James DALY	1788	1879	070	DALY, James	
Mary Ann DALY Valiquette	1827	1881	070	VALIQUETTE, Louis	(NOI Louis Valiquette)
			070	DALY, Mary Ann	
			070		
Owen MONAHAN	1848	1925	070	GRAHAM, Julia Ann	
Julia Ann GRAHAM Monahan	1856	1889	070	MONAHAN, Owen	
			070		
John SALMON	38 Years	07-04-1866	070	SALMON, John	
Barbara SALMON Caslin	82 Years	07-25-1915	070	SALMON, Barbara	(NOI Mr. Caslin)
			070		
James CONLIN	1836	1912	070	FELL, Margaret	
Margaret FELL Conlin	1842	1919	070	CONLIN, James	(GAR) Co. B, 7th Rgt Vt
			070		
Thomas DUFFY	1828	1917	070	O'DONNELL, Julia	
Julia O'DONNELL Duffy	1830	1909	070	DUFFY, Thomas	
			070		
Mary A. SAUNDERS	34 Years	07-02-1889	070	COWLEY, William	(NOI William Cowley)
			070	_____, Mary A.	
Katherine E. SAUNDERS	1850	1916	070	SAUNDERS, Katherine E.	

Name	Born	Died	Code	Spouse
Charles W. MCGUIRK	1858	1938	070	SAUNDERS, Nora A.
Nora A. SAUNDERS McGuirk	1857	1923	070	MCGUIRK, Charles W.
			070	
James C. CARBINE	1847	1887	070	WARD, Catherine
Catherine WARD Carbine	1850	1935	070	CARBINE, James C.
			070	
Dr. J. C. KEENAN	1837	1903	070	HUGHES, Mary
Mary HUGHES Keenan	1835	1911	070	KEENAN, J. C.
			070	
Michael CAPELESS	65 Years	04-20-1913	070	GAFFNEY, Katie
Katie GAFFNEY Capeless	41Y 4M	12-11-1888	070	CAPELESS, Michael
			070	
Frank O. HICKEY	1849	1933	070	CAMPBELL, Sarah
Sarah CAMPBELL Hickey	1848	1924	070	HICKEY, Frank O.
			070	
Patrick MANGAN	1834	1879	070	TOOHEY, Ann
Ann TOOHEY Mangan	1843	1907	070	MANGAN, Patrick
Bridget MANGAN	1800	1875	070	MANGAN, Bridget
Thomas TOOHEY	1811	1881	070	TOOHEY, Thomas
Mary TOOHEY	1809	1872	070	TOOHEY, Mary
Ellen TOOHEY	1857	1887	070	TOOHEY, Ellen
			070	
Timothy J. MURPHY	1855	1926	070	O'BRIEN, Mary E.
Mary E. O'BRIEN Murphy	1854	1943	070	MURPHY, Timothy J.
			070	
Hugh DUFFY	1855	1920	070	KEENAN, Anna
Anna KEENAN Duffy	1869	1928	070	DUFFY, Hugh
			070	
E. D. WELCH	1851	1925	070	WELCH, E. D.
Annie WELCH	1857	1958	070	WELCH, Annie
			070	
Michael B. HANEY	1851	1927	070	TOOHEY, Bridget
Bridget TOOHEY Haney	1846	1913	070	HANEY, Michael B.
			070	
John CAPELESS	1830	1911	070	CRONIN, Julia
Julia CRONIN Capeless	1843	1923	070	CAPELESS, John
			070	
John P. CROWLEY	1843	1918	070	CAVANAUGH, Belinda
Bedelia CAVANAUGH Crowley	1844	1893	070	CROWLEY, John P.
			070	
Peter STEBBINS	08-30-1846	08-26-1931	070	LALOR, Emma
Emma LALOR Stebbins	02-06-1863	12-17-1939	070	STEBBINS, Peter
			070	
Edward LALOR	56 Years	09-11-1872	070	O'HALLORAN, Mary
Mary O'HALLORAN Lalor	52 Years	01-28-1880	070	LALOR, Edward

Edward LALOR		1854	1920	070	COFFEY, Mary E.	
Mary E. COFFEY Lalor		1864	1940	070	LALOR, Edward	
				070		
				070		(NOI John O'Laughlin)
John O'LAUGHLIN		1840	1914	070	O'LAUGHLIN, John	His Wives:Johanna O'Brien(NOI)
Florence CROWLEY				070	CROWLEY, Florence	Ann Faraher NOI), Ellen Duffy
				070	O'BRIEN, Johanna	(NOI)
				070	FARAHER, Ann	
				070	DUFFY, Ellen	
				070		
Timothy CROWLEY		1846	1868	070	CROWLEY, Timothy	
				070		
Jno CONNELLY		----	----	070	CONNELLY, Jno	(GAR Co. K. 1st Vt Inf
				070		
John GLEASON		1828	1903	070	_____, Bridget	
Bridget _____ GLEASON		55 Years	11-29-1884	070	GLEASON, John	
Patrick GLEASON		32 Years	12-17-1884	070	GLEASON, Patrick	
John GLEASON		32 Years	03-22-1876	070	GLEASON, John	
				070		
John SULLIVAN		1837	1872	070	SULLIVAN, John	
Mary SULLIVAN		1835	1907	070	SULLIVAN, Mary	
				070		
Bryan MCDONOUGH		1824	1904	070	GILRAIN, Ann	
Ann GILRAIN McDonough		1833	1901	070	MCDONOUGH, Bryan	
				070		
Patrick TOOHEY		75 Years	12-01-1892	070	RYAN, Margaret	
Margaret RYAN Toohey		51 Years	09-23-1877	070	TOOHEY, Patrick	
				070		
John P. COLLINS		1851	1919	070	COLLINS, John P.	
Bridget PURCELL		1863	1904	070	PURCELL, Bridget	
				070		
Jeremiah COLLINS		1814	1870	070	COHALAN, Ellen	
Ellen COHALAN Collins		1822	1892	070	COLLINS, Jeremiah	
				070		
Michael TIERNEY		01-14-1826	12-23-1892	070	WARD, Mary	
Mary WARD Tierney		01-01-1836	04-12-1894	070	TIERNEY, Michael	
				070		
James TOOHEY		62 Years	03-05-1915	070	RYAN, Margaret	
Maria KENNEDY Toohey		66 Years	03-02-1923	070	TOOHEY, Patrick	
				070		
Dennis O'SHEA		84 Years	07-07-1903	070	_____, Mary	A Native Of County Down, Ire.
Mary _____ O'SHEA	Co. Down	54 Years	11-05-1879	070	O'SHEA, Dennis	
				070		
Thomas CUMMINGS		1853	1947	070	WALSH, Mary	
Mary WALSH Cummings		1860	1931	070	CUMMINGS, Thomas	

Name	Birthplace	Born/Age	Died	Code	Index	Notes
				070		
Michael WALSH		55 Years	11-12-1895	070	_____, Mary A.	
Mary A. _____ WALSH		57 Years	02-01-1899	070	WALSH, Michael	
				070		
Jeremiah DUFFICY		08-04-1820	11-13-1905	070	HIGGINS, Mary	
Mary HIGGINS Dufficy		02-02-1813	10-25-1896	070	DUFFICY, Jeremiah	
				070		
Katherine TIGHE	Co. Roscommon	1864	1955	070	TIGHE, Katherine	Born In County Roscommon, Ire.
				070		
John B. MCMAHON		1840	1910	070	MCMAHON, John B.	
Thomas J. DOOLEY		----	1930	070	MCMAHON, Roseanna	
Roseanna MCMAHON Dooley		----	1897	070	DOOLEY, Thomas J.	
				070		
Dennis BRADLEY		59 Years	10-03-1897	070	BRADLEY, Dennis	
				070		
John HEWITT		53 Years	01-20-1891	070	HEWITT, John	
Mary A. STEVENS Hewitt		40YR 7MO	01-08-1887	070	STEVENS, Mary A.	
Ann STEVENS		79 Years	05-07-1893	070	STEVENS, Ann	Mother Of Mary A. Hewitt
				070		
Edward CONNELL		59 Years	11-16-1901	070	BURKE, Mary	
Mary BURKE Connell		64 Years	09-03-1908	070	CONNELL, Edward	
				070		
John GILMAN		1853	1922	070	_____, Margaret	
Margaret _____ GILMAN		1857	1930	070	GILMAN, John	
				070		
Dennis DRISLANE		1832	1892	070	___, Hanora	
Hanora _____ DRISLANE		1832	1922	070	DRISLANE, Dennis	
				070		
Timothy O'LEARY		1847	1922	070	GRADY, Johannah	
Johannah GRADY O'Leary		1860	1911	070	O'LEARY, Timothy	
				070		
Michael FAGAN		64 Years	08-01-1880	070	MCDERMOTT, Margaret	
Margaret MCDERMOTT Fagan		73 Years	08-14-1922	070	FAGAN, Michael	
				070		
Eugene ASHE		1848	1935	070	PUTNAM, Agness	
Agness PUTNAM Ashe		1850	1922	070	ASHE, Eugene	
				070		
Edward QUIRK		07-27-1846	05-02-1910	070	DINN, Ellen M.	(GAR) Co. B. 7th Vt Vols
Ellen M. DINN Quirk		1847	1899	070	QUIRK, Edward	
				070		
Michael GEARITY		70 Years	04-06-1899	070	GILLFEATHER, Mary	
Mary GILLFEATHER Gearity		67 Years	02-27-1888	070	GEARITY, Michael	
				070		
John LLOYD		1822	1907	070	DWYER, Hanora	
Hanora DWYER Lloyd		1826	1906	070	LLOYD, John	

Name	Birth	Death	Code	Related	Note
			070		
Thomas MCGETTRICK	1839	1906	070	_____, Katherine	
Katherine _____ MCGETTRICK	1842	1915	070	MCGETTRICK, Thomas	
			070		
Annie CONROY Wynn	50 Years	10-02-1894	070	WYNN, Thomas	(NOI Thomas Wynn)
			070	CONROY, Annie	
			070		
Patrick DOWLING	1829	1904	070	DOWLING, Patrick	
Mary DOWLING	1834	1911	070	DOWLING, Mary	
			070		
William BURKE	1852	1921	070	_____, Hannah	
Hannah _____ BURKE	1855	1933	070	BURKE, William	
			070		
Patrick MONOHAN Jr.	68 Years	12-21-1914	070	O'LEARY, Margaret	
Margaret O'LEARY Monahan	30 Years	02-21-1881	070	MONOHAN, Patrick Jr.	
Patrick MONAHAN Sr.	84 Years	07-26-1883	070	_____, Margaret	
Margaret _____ MONAHAN	78 Years	02-20-1889	070	MONAHAN, Patrick Sr.	
			070		
Anne CONNELL Moore	66Y 3M	03-13-1921	070	MOORE, Thomas	(NOI Thomas Moore)
			070	CONNELL, Anne	
			070		
Michael WELSH	1834	1905	070	OWENS, Mary	
Mary OWENS Welsh	1836	1904	070	WELSH, Michael	
			070		
John MCGUIRK	1831	1918	070	DOOLEY, Alice	
Alice DOOLEY McGuirk	1834	1926	070	MCGUIRK, John	
			070		
Jane WHITE	1824	1896	070	WHITE, Jane	
			070		
Thomas J. DONOVAN	1855	1889	070	DONOVAN, Thomas J.	
Ellen K. DONOVAN	1859	1922	070	DONOVAN, Ellen K.	
			070		
Mary O'HALLORAN Thompson	3-1826	7-1907	070	THOMPSON, James	(NOI James Thompson)
			070	O'HALLORAN, Mary	
			070		
Catherine THOMPSON Morgan	11-22-1851	02-02-1900	070	MORGAN, Charles	(NOI Charles Morgan)
			070	THOMPSON, Catherine	
			070		
Julia CLANCY Battles	36 Years	08-27-1886	070	BATTLES, Bernard	(NOI Bernard Battles)
			070	CLANCY, Julia	
			070		
John J. FOLEY	11-06-1838	----	070	_____, Annie	(DOD Not Recorded)
Annie _____ FOLEY	06-10-1839	----	070	FOLEY, John J.	(DOD Not Recorded)
			070		
Hugh HILL	1836	1909	070	NUGENT, Sarah	

Name	Birth	Death	Code	Relation	Notes
Sarah NUGENT Hill	1843	1913	070	HILL, Hugh	
			070		
Bernard HIGGINS	1817	1867	070	SULLIVAN, Katherine	
Katherine SULLIVAN Higgins	1829	1904	070	HIGGINS, Bernard	
			070		
Thomas HIGGINS Jr.	56 Years	01-21-1903	070	KELLY, Catherine	
Catherine KELLY Higgins	----	----	070	HIGGINS, Thomas Jr.	(NOI DOB/DOD Catherine Kelly)
Thomas HIGGINS	82 Years	09-16-1882	070	HIGGINS, Thomas	
Anna HIGGINS	27 Years	07-21-1880	070	HIGGINS, Anna	
			070		
Michael DUGAN	08-15-1818	07-29-1899	070	_____, Ann	
Ann _____ DUGAN	63 Years	01-06-1894	070	DUGAN, Michael	
			070		
Mary BARRY	1823	1912	070	BARRY, Mary	
Patrick BRADSHAW	1840	1880	070	_____, Margaret	
Margaret _____ BRADSHAW	1857	1930	070	BRADSHAW, Patrick	
			070		
John TRAVERS	6-1824	----	070	GLEASON, Ellen	(GAR) Co. B. 9th VT Vols (NOI)
Ellen GLEASON Travers	8-1834	----	070	TRAVERS, John	(NOI DOD)
			070		
Patrick CAIN	1845	1927	070	CAIN, Patrick	
Honor CAIN	1824	1884	070	CAIN, Honor	
John BARRETT	1844	1909	070	BARRETT, John	
Bridget CAIN Barrett	1849	1940	070	CAIN, Bridget	
			070		
Edward EUSTACE	1830	1911	070	_____, Mary M.	
Mary M. _____ EUSTACE	1840	1905	070	EUSTACE, Edward	
			070		
Michael FOX	1853	1937	070	KIELEY, Ellen	
Ellen KIELEY Fox	1852	1903	070	FOX, Michael	
			070		
John GLEASON	80 Years	12-09-1909	070	_______, Julia	(GAR) Co. H 14th Rgt 1862.
			070		Died At Bennington, Vt.
Julia _____ GLEASON	67 Years	09-27-1891	070	GLEASON, John	
			070		
Patrick LYNCH	1833	1905	070	LYNCH, Patrick	
Bridget O'BRIEN	1837	1924	070	O'BRIEN, Bridget	
			070		
Michael FARRELL	1832	1876	070	NEARY, Ellen	
Ellen NEARY Farrell	1833	1897	070	FARRELL, Michael	
Mary NEARY	1828	1894	070	NEARY, Mary	
			070		
Nicholas HOWLEY	1822	1903	070	_____, Johanna	
Johanna _____ HOWLEY	1832	1911	070	HOWLEY, Nicholas	
			070		

Name	Born/Age	Died		Cross-reference	Notes
Patrick KELLEY	1839	1894	070	HOWLEY, Cathern	
Cathern HOWLEY Kelley	1854	1893	070	KELLEY, Patrick	
			070		
William HICKEY	1837	1908	070	LUDDY, Ellen	
Ellen LUDDY Hickey	1837	1899	070	HICKEY, William	
			070		
Nicholas CLIFFORD	1842	1899	070	FOLEY, Catherine	
Catherine FOLEY Clifford	1845	1928	070	CLIFFORD, Nicholas	
			070		
James DWYER	63 Years	04-20-1913	070	FEAN, Nora	
Nora FEAN Dwyer	49 Years	03-03-1896	070	DWYER, James	
Charles DWYER	----	08-09-1921	070	FEAN, Johannah	
Johanna FEAN Dwyer	74 Years	06-29-1918	070	DWYER, Charles	
			070		
T.S. SWEENEY	1837	1911	070	_____, Hannah	
Hannah _____ SWEENEY	1842	1890	070	SWEENEY, T. S.	
			070		
John O. SPELLMAN	1854	1927	070	SPELLMAN, John O.	Mayor Of Rutland, Vt. 1900
William P. SPELLMAN	1849	1912	070	SPELLMAN, William P.	
			070		
Daniel MAHONEY	1823	1903	070	_____, Elizabeth	
Elizabeth _____ MAHONEY	1834	1899	070	MAHONEY, Daniel	
			070		
Martin BOLIN	65 Years	06-30-1885	070	___, Margaret Mary	
Margaret Mary _____ BOLIN	75 Years	08-05-1901	070	BOLIN, Martin	
			070		
Dennis SHOULDICE	1851	1910	070	HOGAN, Maria	
Maria HOGAN Shouldice	1862	1927	070	SHOULDICE, Dennis	
Margaret SHOULDICE	1856	1906	070	SHOULDICE, Margaret	
John SHOULDICE	1856	1924	070	HOGAN, Julia	
Julia HOGAN Shouldice	1864	1900	070	SHOULDICE, John	
			070		
Thomas TOOHEY	1842	1928	070	KELLY, Eleanor	
Eleanor KELLY Toohey	1842	1923	070	TOOHEY, Thomas	
			070		
Thomas O'BRIEN	1853	1893	070	TOOHEY, Mary	
Mary TOOHEY O'Brien	34 Years	12-31-1899	070	O'BRIEN, Thomas	
			070		
James JOHNSTON	1836	1936	070	JOHNSTON, James	(GAR) Co. D 7th Vt. Inf
			070		
James PURCELL	1852	1929	070	DUMPHREY, Catherine	
Catherine DUMPHREY Purcell	1855	1906	070	PURCELL, James	
			070		
Patrick TRAYNOR	1818	1906	070	_______, Bridget	
Bridget _____ TRAYNOR	1838	1915	070	TRAYNOR, Patrick	

Name	Birth/Age	Death	Code	Spouse/Relation	Notes
			070		
Joseph DOUGHERTY	----	03-04-1888	070	ROWLAND, Ellen	(NOI DOB)
Ellen ROWLAND Dougherty	----	05-09-1900	070	DOUGHERTY, Joseph	(NOI DOB)
			070		
John MONAHAN	----	1905	070	MCNAMARA, Catherine	(NOI DOB)
Catherine MCNAMARA Monahan	----	1882	070	MONAHAN, John	(NOI DOB)
			070		
Patrick R. LONG	76 Years	08-06-1912	070	DONAHUE, Johannah	
Johannah DONAHUE Long	65 Years	07-08-1914	070	LONG, Patrick R.	
			070		
John BAKER	77 Years	01-29-1908	070	DONAHUE, Johannah	
Ellen FITZGERALD Baker	44 Years	05-01-1870	070	LONG, Patrick R.	
			070		
Thomas MCDERMOTT	1822	1881	070	REYNOLDS, Bridget	
Bridget REYNOLDS McDermott	1831	1884	070	MCDERMOTT, Thomas	
Thomas MCDERMOTT	1854	1914	070	MCDERMOTT, Thomas	
Mary A. MCDERMOTT	1855	1942	070	MCDERMOTT, Mary A.	
			070		
Patrick RILEY	1831	1883	070	MCNIFF, Bridget	
Bridget MCNIFF Riley	1836	1913	070	RILEY, Patrick	
			070		
Catherine MULHARN	1834	1900	070	MULHARN, Catherine	(On Traynor Stone)
			070		
Peter J. MULLEE	1850	1918	070	CAMPBELL, Martha F.	
Martha F. CAMPBELL Mullee	1851	1899	070	MULLEE, Peter J.	
			070		
Edward T. LYSON	1838	1912	070	MCGRATH, Anna	(GAR) Co. K 12th Vt
Anna MCGRATH Lyson	1846	1902	070	LYSON, Edward T.	
			070		
Alexander KEEFE	84 Years	11-11-1909	070	DRISLAINE, Ellen	
Ellen DRISLANE Keefe	76 Years	03-03-1912	070	KEEFE, Alexander	
			070		
Cornelius CORNEIN	1843	1918	070	______, Mary	
Mary ___ CORNEIN	1839	1922	070	CORNEIN, Cornelius	
			070		
Timothy O'LEARY	82 Years	04-19-1908	070	SWEENEY, Margaret	
Margaret SWEENEY O'Leary	63Y 8M	03-04-1891	070	O'LEARY, Timothy	
			070		
James T. RILEY	03-25-1846	----	070	HOLLAND, Mary	(NOI DOD)
Mary HOLLAND Riley	12-03-1855	----	070	RILEY, James T.	(NOI DOD)
			070		
John LYNCH	66 Years	01-08-1893	070	____, Ann	
Ann _____ LYNCH	48 Years	08-30-1883	070	LYNCH, John	
Annie WOOLLEN	71 Years	04-11-1929	070	WOOLLEN, Annie	
			070		

Name	Origin	Born	Died	Code	Adjacent	Notes
Thomas HARTNEY		01-02-1841	03-14-1872	070	HARTNEY, Thomas	
Patrick TYLER		03-16-1836	11-16-1923	070	SULLIVAN, Mary	
Mary SULLIVAN Tyler		02-05-1839	05-22-1912	070	TYLER, Patrick	
Michael FURLONG		02-14-1823	06-20-1890	070	_____, Catherine	
Catherine _____ FURLONG		05-20-1841	04-17-1920	070	FURLONG, Michael	
Ellen _____ SULLIVAN		09-01-1816	06-05-1874	070	SULLIVAN, Michael	(NOI Michael Sullivan)
				070	_____, Ellen	
				070		
Patrick KEEFE		08-01-1842	12-26-1914	070	_____, Johanna	
Johanna _____ KEEFE		03-25-1848	08-02-1900	070	KEEFE, Patrick	
				070		
Thomas F. MORONEY		----	05-05-1927	070	O'DONNELL, Mary	(DOB Not Recorded)
Mary O'DONNELL Moroney		----	12-21-1938	070	MORONEY, Thomas F.	(DOB Not Recorded)
				070		
Thomas DUNN		1835	1890	070	HICKEY, Bridget	
Bridget HICKEY Dunn		1834	1889	070	DUNN, Thomas	
				070		
John CROSBY		1843	1918	070	MORRISSEY, Bridget	(GAR) Co. I 2nd Vt Rgt
Bridget MORRISSEY Crosby		1850	19__	070	CROSBY, John	
				070		
Frank L. CASAVAW		1846	1904	070	MULLEE, Anne	
Anne MULLEE Casavaw		1849	1911	070	CASAVAW, Frank L.	
				070		
Thomas F. MANGAN		1833	1901	070	MURTAUGH, Mary	
Mary MURTAUGH Mangan		1833	1913	070	MANGAN, Thomas F.	
				070		
Jeremiah HEALY		1830	1903	070	_____, Johanna	
Johannah _____ HEALY		1836	1915	070	HEALY, Jeremiah	
				070		
Patrick MCDONOUGH		1824	1904	070	MCDONOUGH, Patrick	
Margaret C. MCDONOUGGH		1829	1885	070	MCDONOUGGH, Margaret C.	
George AVERY		1854	1899	070	AVERY, George	
Mary Ann AVERY		1855	1940	070	AVERY, Mary Ann	
				070		
David M. ROACH		64Y 11M	05-04-1898	070	MURRAY, Margaret	
Margaret MURRAY Roach		63Y 3M	04-08-1897	070	ROACH, David M.	
				070		
Charles H. MCGINNIS		1851	1898	070	_____, Katherine	
Katherine _____ MCGINNIS		1852	1916	070	MCGINNIS, Charles H.	
				070		
William CLIFFORD	Co. Tipperary	1832	1904	070	HOLLERAN, Bridget	(Adjacent to Patrick Clifford N/O Castletown, Co. Tipperary)
				070		
Bridget HOLLERAN Clifford		1840	1906	070	CLIFFORD, William	
				070		
John WINTERS		57 Years	06-23-1882	070	MALONEY, Mary	

Name	Birth/Age	Death	Code	Index	Note
Mary MALONEY Winters	84 Years	07-01-1919	070	WINTERS, John	
Hanora WINTERS	98 Years	07-23-1879	070	WINTERS, John	
			070		
John MATTHEWS	12-08-1856	05-13-1900	070	_____, Anne	
Anne _____ MATTHEWS	03-25-1856	07-31-1899	070	MATTHEWS, John	
			070		
Phillip FITZPATRICK	23 Years	05-08-1871	070	FITZPATRICK, Phillip	
			070		
Timothy O'MARA	1822	1904	070	SULLIVAN, Ellen	
Ellen SULLIVAN O'Mara	63 Years	04-15-1899	070	O'MARA, Timothy	
			070		
Bartholomew C. COSTELLO	08-04-1841	02-01-1907	070	SWEENEY, Ellen	
Ellen SWEENEY Costello	12-18-1846	01-26-1919	070	COSTELLO, Bartholomew	
			070		
William CAGNEY	05-22-1852	06-11-1915	070	FEAN, Margaret	
Margaret FEAN Cagney	04-18-1852	05-31-1902	070	CAGNEY, William	
			070		
Patrick MCGARRY	1840	1900	070	_____, Bridget	
Bridget _____ MCGARRY	1847	1915	070	MCGARRY, Patrick	
			070		
Michael CROWE	1836	1909	070	_____, Margaret	
Margaret _____ CROWE	44 Years	11-29-1881	070	CROWE, Michael	
			070		
John HALPIN	1843	1902	070	DILLON, Margaret	
Margaret DILLON Halpin	1844	1905	070	HALPIN, John	
			070		
John HOWARD	1832	1901	070	PENDERGAST, Margaret	
Margaret PENDERGAST Howard	1835	1910	070	HOWARD, John	
			070		
Daniel J. CONNOR	70 Years	02-06-1901	070	CROWE, Bridget	
Bridget CROWE Connor	85 Years	11-02-1924	070	CONNOR, Daniel J.	
			070		
Patrick MALONEY	90 Years	09-12-1909	070	CAIN, Bridget	
			070	HEHEIR, Catherine	
Bridget CAIN Maloney	32 Years	04-18-1857	070	MALONEY, Patrick	
Catherine HEHEIR Maloney	75 Years	09-13-1903	070	MALONEY, Patrick	
			070		
Margaret HIGGINS Parris	1855	1924	070	PARRIS, John J.	(NOI John J. Parris)
			070	HIGGINS, Margaret	
			070		
John SHANNON	1847	1934	070	GRIFFIN, Hanora	
Hanora GRIFFIN Shannon	1856	1934	070	SHANNON, John	
			070		
Alexander EUSTACE	1855	1930	070	FOLEY, Julia	
Julia FOLEY Eustace	1865	1945	070	EUSTACE, Alexander	

Name	Place	Born / Age	Died	Code	Index Name	Notes
				070		
Thomas MCMAHON	Co. Clare	79Y 5M	05-22-1893	070	_____, Margaret	A Native Of Kings County, Ire
Margaret _____ MCMAHON	Co. Kings	54Y 1M	11-13-1872	070	MCMAHON, Thomas	A Native Of Co. Clare, Ire.
				070		
Dennis LONG		1835	1929	070	WALSH, Mary	
Mary WALSH Long		1846	1924	070	LONG, Dennis	
				070		
John C. BRUTEN		1853	1934	070	LYNCH, Nellie E.	
Nellie E. LYNCH Bruten		1863	1929	070	BRUTEN, John C.	
				070		
Frank DUPUIS		1852	1925	070	LYNCH, Lucy	
Lucy LYNCH Dupuis		1851	1934	070	DUPUIS, Frank	
				070		
Dennis O'SHEA		1848	1929	070	O'ROURKE, Ellen Julia	
Ellen Julia O'ROURKE O'Shea		1859	1926	070	O'SHEA, Dennis	
				070		
Mathew FLYNN		1863	1945	070	MAHER, Mary	
Mary MAHER Flynn		1852	1928	070	FLYNN, Mathew	
				070		
Catherine CANTY		1841	1916	070	CANTY, Catherine	
				070		
William H. SEWARD		1852	1936	070	___, Catherine E.	
Catherine E. _____ SEWARD		1856	1946	070	SEWARD, William H.	
				070		
James WALSH		1848	1923	070	_____, Nellie A.	
Nellie A. _____ WALSH		1854	1929	070	WALSH, James	
				070		
Thomas J. FITZGERALD		1842	1899	070	LYNAUGH, Anna	
Anna LYNAUGH Fitzgerald		1843	1905	070	FITZGERALD, Thomas J.	
				070		
Frank KELLEY		1794	1886	070	WATERS, Mary	
Mary WATERS Kelley		1834	1904	070	KELLEY, Frank	
Mary KELLEY		1851	1933	070	KELLEY, Mary	D/O Frank & Mary Kelley
Michael J. KELLEY		31Y 10M	04-10-1888	070	KELLEY, Michael J.	
Bridget KELLEY		17Y 4M	12-23-1868	070	KELLEY, Bridget	D/O Frank & Mary Kelley
Katie KELLEY		1Y 5M	02-25-1869	070	KELLEY, Katie	D/O Frank & Mary Kelley
				070		
Mary CONNORS		1851	1912	070	CONNORS, Mary	
				070		
John ROURK		1829	1913	070	ROURK, John	
Ann BONFIELD		1839	1911	070	BONFIELD, Ann	
				070		
George DUFFY		1825	1891	070	_____, Mary	
Mary _____ DUFFY		1831	1899	070	DUFFY, George	
				070		

Name	Place	Born/Age	Died	Code	Relation	Notes
Ellen BUTLER Billings		09-10-1838	09-05-1897	070	BILLINGS, J.S.	Our Beloved Mother
				070	BUTLER, Ellen	(NOI J.S. Billings)
				070		
Peter CUMMINGS		1837	1886	070	___, Elizabeth	
Elizabeth _____ CUMMINGS		1840	1907	070	CUMMINGS, Peter	
James MCNAMARA		1814	1868	070	_____, Bridget	
Bridget _____ MCNAMARA		1820	1892	070	MCNAMARA, James	
				070		
Thomas TEELON		1836	1910	070	COOLEY, Bridget	Erected by Thomas Teelon
Bridget COOLEY Teelon		1854	1900	070	TEELON, Thomas	
				070		
Lawrence KINGSLEY		52 Years	05-03-1892	070	_______, Ellen	(GAR) Co. I, 2nd Vt Infantry
Ellen _____ KINGSLEY		80 Years	02-10-1921	070	KINGSLEY, Lawrence	
Dennis KINGSLEY		1828	1909	070	KINGSLEY, Dennis	
				070		
John HEALEY		1811	1888	070	BRUEN, Ann	
Ann BRUEN Healey		1812	1863	070	HEALEY, John	
Thomas HEALEY		1844	1862	070	HEALEY, Thomas	(GAR) Co. , 4th Vt Infantry
Captain John HEALEY		1843	1901	070	HEALEY, John, Capt.	(GAR) Co. F, 1st Vt H.A.
Bridget HEALEY		1828	1916	070	HEALEY, Bridget	
				070		
Thomas HANNON		1849	1913	070	CONROY, Mary A.	
Mary A. CONROY		1850	1893	070	HANNON, Thomas	
				070		
Ann GORDON		57 Years	08-12-1898	070	GORDON, Ann	In Memory Of Mrs. Ann Gordon
				070		
Bridget BURNS McDonough		60 Years	04-22-1893	070	MCDONOUGH, James	(NOI James McDonough)
				070	BURNS, Bridget	
				070		
Edward WALSH	Co. Mayo	88 Years	02-21-1873	070	_____, Ann	A Native Of The Parish of
				070		Crossmolina, Co. Mayo, Ire.
Ann _____ WALSH		82 Years	05-29-1874	070	WALSH, Edward	
				070		
Patrick KINNALLY		63 Years	08-20-1906	070	KINNALLY, Patrick	
Margaret KINNALLY		102 Years	02-18-1893	070	KINNALLY, Margaret	
				070		
James CONLINE		03-17-1848	11-08-1915	070	KELLY, Margaret	
Margaret KELLT Conline		10-25-1862	04-05-1912	070	CONLINE, James	
				070		
Patrick MELDON		39 Years	04-25-1864	070	MELDON, Patrick	
				070		
Thomas PENDERGAST		78 Years	12-26-1901	070	_______, Margaret	
Margaret _____ PENDERGAST		68 Years	06-02-1891	070	PENDERGAST, Thomas	
				070		
Frank CONNIFF		1842	1922	070	_____, Norah	

Norah _____ CONNIFF	1843	1921	070	CONNIFF, Frank	
			070		
Timothy SULLIVAN	63 Years	01-30-1876	070	_____, Catharine	
Catharine _____ SULLIVAN	78 Years	08-03-1898	070	SULLIVAN, Timothy	
			070		
Andrew SIMONDS	60 Years	03-04-1880	070	_____, Catherine	
Catherine _____ SIMONDS	59 Years	12-17-1887	070	SIMONDS, Andrew	
James F. SIMONDS	32 Years	10-27-1885	070	SIMONDS, James F.	
Jennie E. SIMONDS Lalor	34 Years	11-04 1885	070	LALOR, E.G.	(NOI E.G. Lalor)
			070	SIMONDS, Jennie E.	
			070		
Bartholomew CONNOR	62 Tears	02-05-1885	070	CONNOR, Bartholomew	
			070		
Luke KELLEY	1832	1917	070	_____, Anne	
Anne _____ KELLEY	1832	1908	070	KELLEY, Luke	
			070		
Michael WALSH	1849	1905	070	_____, Catherine M.	
Catherine M. WALSH	1849	1939	070	WALSH, Michael	
James E. WALSH	1841	1911	070	WALSH, James E.	(GAR) Co. H 5th Vt Vol Regt
			070		
(Father) ANTHONY	1836	1911	070	ANTHONY, Father	
(Mother) ANTHONY	1845	1923	070	ANTHONY, Mother	
			070		
Timothy STARR	74 Years	05-14-1889	070	RICHARDSON, Annie	
Annie RICHARDSON Starr	82 Years	01-05-1900	070	STARR, Timothy	
Patrick STARR	96 Years	10-02-1880	070	STARR, Patrick	
			070		
Thomas SHELVEY	37 Years	08-04-1887	070	STARR, Mary	
Mary STARR Shelvey	1850	1939	070	SHELVEY, Thomas	
			070		
Daniel J. COCKLIN	1833	1893	070	___, Elizabeth D.	
Elizabeth D. _____ COCKLIN	1832	1918	070	COCKLIN, Daniel J.	
			070		
John W. BRISLIN	1845	1928	070	CONERTON, Catherine	
Catherine CONERTON Brislin	1845	1914	070	BRISLIN, John W.	
			070		
Michael SWEENEY	1845	1907	070	_____, Elizabeth	
Elizabeth _____ SWEENEY	1847	1880	070	SWEENEY, Michael	
			070		
Jeremiah FENTON	1818	1894	070	FITZGERALD, Mary	
Mary FITZGERALD	1824	1884	070	FENTON, Jeremiah	
			070		
John MCNAMARA	11-17-1831	06-19-1883	070	WALSH, Mary	
Mary WALSH McNamara	03-07-1836	07-02-=1883	070	MCNAMARA, John	
E. C. CARRIGAN	1853	1888	070	MCNAMARA, Nellie	

Nellie MCNAMARA Carrigan	1864	1939	070	CARRIGAN, E.C.	
			070		
Honora MCCARTHY Browne	1833	1863	070	BROWNE, Honora McCarthy	
Mary O'SULLIVAN Browne	1800	1865	070	BROWNE, Mary O'Sullivan	
Henry BROWNE	1824	1889	070	BROWNE, Henry	
Mary BROWNE Ryan	1855	1900	070	RYAN, Mary Browne	
Bridget O'SHEA Brown	1839	1916	070	BROWN, Bridget O'Shea	
			070		
Nancy STARR Creed	1852	1924	070	CREED, Nancy Starr	
			070		
Robert T. MCLAUGHLIN	1852	1911	070	MCLAUGHLIN, Robert T.	
			070		
James R. MURRAY	02-18-1849	06-29-1921	070	MCNIFF, Mary	
Mary MCNIFF Murray	06-10-1853	02-07-1935	070	MURRAY, James R.	
			070		
James MCNIFF	87 Years	08-09-1911	070	________, Ellen	
Ellen _____ MCNIFF	65 Years	02-07-1892	070	MCNIFF, James	
			070		
Thomas CANTY	1836	1929	070	KELLY, Bridget	
Bridget KELLY Canty	1836	1914	070	CANTY, Thomas	
			070		
Dominick CORCORAN	1846	1918	070	___, Winifred A.	
Winifred A. _____ CORCORAN	1849	1929	070	CORCORAN, Dominick	
			070		
Thomas HIGGINS	1830	1922	070	SULLIVAN, Mary	
Mary SULLIVAN Higgins	1834	1908	070	HIGGINS, Thomas	
			070		
Michael REEDY	1847	1892	070	BOLAND, Margaret M.	
Margaret M. BOLAND Reedy	1852	1935	070	REEDY, Michael	
			070		
Patrick MCLAUGHLIN	1832	1908	070	______, Bridget	
Bridget _____ MCLAUGHLIN	1834	1909	070	MCLAUGHLIN, Patrick	
			070		
Henry CALLAHAN	07-29-1856	07-06-1891	070	CALLAHAN, Henry	
			070		
Peter DONAHUE	No date	12-15-1919	070	______, Bridget	
Bridget _____ DONAHUE	68 Years	12-11-1912	070	DONAHUE, Peter	
			070		
John REARDON	1827	1905	070	BROWN, Joanna	
Joanna BROWN Reardon	1837	1872	070	REARDON, John	
Honora REARDON	1835	1907	070	REARDON, Honora	Sister of John Reardon
			070		
Kate TRACY	1845	1919	070	TRACY, Kate	
			070		
Patrick BROWN	1821	1903	070	COLLINS, Julia	

Julia COLLINS Brown	1837	1911	070	BROWN, Patrick
			070	
James CORCORAN	40 Years	01-17-1879	070	CORCORAN, James
			070	
Michael FLYNN	02-08-1826	08-20-1888	070	___, Elizabeth
Elizabeth _____ FLYNN	02-02-1832	05-30-1904	070	FLYNN, Michael
			070	
Patrick REEDY	65 Years	04-12-1895	070	___, Catherine
Catherine _____ REEDY	81 Years	09-23-1911	070	REEDY, Patrick
			070	
John CONNORS	56 Years	03-18-1899	070	MAGNER, Ellen
Ellen MAGNER Connors	83 Years	08-09-1913	070	CONNORS, John
			070	
Peter CORCORAN	1833	1924	070	DOYLE, Ellen
Ellen DOYLE Corcoran	1839	1916	070	CORCORAN, Peter
			070	
Patrick MULIHAN	71 Years	01-01-1899	070	_____, Margaret
Margaret _____ MULIHAN	60 Years	02-26-1883	070	MULIHAN, Patrick
			070	
Michael MCLAUGHLIN	1823	1903	070	MCNIFF, Ann
Ann MCNIFF McLaughlin	1840	1905	070	MCLAUGHLIN, Michael
			070	
James SWEENEY	1850	1923	070	SLATTERY, Margaret
Margaret SLATTERY Sweeney	1850	1923	070	SWEENEY, James
			070	
James FLAHERTY	1855	No Date	070	FLAHERTY, James
Mary FLAHERTY	1852	1902	070	FLAHERTY, Mary
Mary FLAHERTY	1830	No Date	070	FLAHERTY, Mary
			070	
Hugh CLINE	No date	11-06-1861	070	BECKETT, Hanorah
Hanorah BECKETT Clinre	No Date	04-09-1895	070	CLINE, Hugh
Annie CLINE	No Date	01-20-1888	070	CLINE, Annie
Thomas CLINE	No Date	09-26-1936	070	CLINE, Thomas
B.M. CLINE	1855	1923	070	CLINE, B.M.
Jennie CLINE	1851	1925	070	CLINE, Jennie
Thomas CLINE	1859	1936	070	CLINE, Thomas
Mary BECKETT	No Date	06-31-1908	070	BECKETT, Mary
Anna BECKETT	No Date	08-17-1908	070	BECKETT, Anna
			070	
Patrick SCANLAN	65 Years	07-11-1880	070	_____, Bridget
Bridget _____ SCANLAN	81 Years	03-13-1901	070	SCANLAN, Patrick
Bernard DEVINE	62 Years	04-27-1901	070	DEVINE, Bernard
John J. SCANLAN	12-25-1858	02-07-1913	070	SCANLAN, John J.
			070	
P. H. FLANNERY	09-11-1838	07-05-1867	070	MCCORMACK, Anne

Name	Born	Died	Ref.	Related	Note
Anne MCCORMACK Flannery	1841	1923	070	FLANNERY, P. H.	
Edw. C. KELLY	03-31-1846	11-24-1891	070	FLANNERY, Katherine M.	
Katherine M. FLANNERY Kelly	05-07-1847	05-20-1903	070	KELLY, Edw. C.	
Patrick FLANNERY	1788	1854	070	_________, Margaret	
Margaret _____ FLANNERY	1800	1884	070	FLANNERY, Patrick	
Cornelius FLANNERY	1832	1855	070	FLANNERY, Cornelius	(Son-Patrick/Margaret Flannery
Anna FLANNERY	1837	1854	070	FLANNERY, Anna	(Dau-Patrick/Margaret Flannery
Timothy FLANNERY	1843	1883	070	FLANNERY, Timothy	(Son-Patrick/Margaret Flannery
			070		
Julia GLEASON	51 Years	02-02-1894	070	GLEASON, Julia	
Sarah _____ HOGAN	66 Years	08-07-1872	070	HOGAN, Patrick	(NOI Patrick Hogan)
			070	_____, Sarah	
Michael HOGAN	1848	1912	070	HOGAN, Michael	
Margaret MAHAR Hogan	1853	1911	070	MAHAR, Margaret	
			070		
Matthew MCGUIRK	71 Years	08-28-1899	070	POWDERLY, Ann	
Ann POWDERLY McGuirk	88 Years	11-25-1922	070	MCGUIRK, Matthew	
			070		
Patrick GILRAIN	1844	1931	070	POWDERLY, Elizabeth	
Elizabeth POWDERLY Gilrain	1842	1929	070	GILRAIN, Patrick	
Mary BURKE McLaughlin	85 Years	11-27-1872	070	MCLAUGHLIN, Michael	(NOI Michael McLaughlin)
			070	BURKE, Mary	
Ellen MCLAUGHLIN Gilrain	75 Years	10-06-1890	070	GILRAIN, Bartholomew	
Bartholomew GILRAIN	80 Years	03-08-1896	070	MCLAUGHLIN, Ellen	
Michael GILRAIN	01-01-1856	02-18-1925	070	HAINES, Catherine	
Catherine HAINES Gilrain	07-17-1858	04-19-1938	070	GILRAIN, Michael	
Patrick MCLAUGHLIN	78 Years	04-01-1886	070	MCLAUGHLIN, Patrick	
			070		
John B. DYER	1853	1935	070	_____, Catherine	
Catherine _____ DYER	1866	1942	070	DYER, John B.	
			070		
Edward MCGINNIS	01-11-1848	08-08-1890	070	MCLAUGHLIN, Barbara A.	
Barbara A. MCLAUGHLIN McGinnis	04-25-1849	11-30-1928	070	MCGINNIS, Edward	
Marya MCGINNIS	1853	1921	070	MCGINNIS, Marya	
			070		
James MURPHY	88 Years	04-12-1912	070	POULE, Julia	
Julia POULE Murphy	76 Years	06-08-1896	070	MURPHY, James	
Peter MURPHY	88 Years	01-10-1890	070	MURPHY, Peter	
J. B. MURPHY	41 Years	10-08-1895	070	MURPHY, J. B.	
			070		
Francis MANGAN	1826	1890	070	_____, Catherine	
Catherine _____ MANGAN	1834	1872	070	MANGAN, Francis	
Mary A. MANGAN	1855	1920	070	MANGAN, Mary A.	
			070		
Patrick RYAN	1824	1899	070	_____, Jane	

Jane _____ RYAN	1827	1893	070	RYAN, Patrick	
Ella M. RYAN	1848	1924	070	RYAN, Ella M.	
Helena E. RYAN	1859	1926	070	RYAN, Helena E.	
			070		
Michael DARBY	1806	1878	070	HENNESSY, Catherine	
Catherine HENNESSY Darby	1823	1891	070	DARBY, Michael	
John J. DARBY	1852	1875	070	DARBY, John J.	
Michael P. DARBY	1859	1879	070	DARBY, Michael P.	
Mary E. DARBY	1849	1886	070	DARBY, Mary E.	
James DARBY	1854	1901	070	DARBY, James	
Johanna DARBY	1856	1923	070	DARBY, Johanna	
Catherine G. DARBY	1864	1933	070	DARBY, Catherine G.	
			070		
Andrew MANGAN	1833	1894	070	EGAN, Bridget	Their children Grace 7 Mos Ambrose 3 Mos, Charles 3 Mos
			070		
Bridget EGAN Mangan	1825	1894	070	MANGAN, Andrew	
Patrick A. MANGAN	1859	1942	070	HIGGINS, Nellie	
Nellie HIGGINS Mangan	1856	1912	070	MANGAN, Patrick A.	
			070		
Patrick MCDONOUGH	1825	1890	070	MCDONOUGH, Mrs. Patrick	
Mrs. Patrick MANGAN	1827	1896	070	MCDONOUGH, Patrick	
Bridget MITCHELL	1834	1899	070	MITCHELL, Bridget	
			070		
James MORAN	52 Years	02-10-1867	070	_____, Margaret	
Margaret _____ MORAN	73 Years	10-17-1888	070	MORAN, James	
			070		
Patrick Whitley	45 Years	05-12-1875	070	_____, Mary	
Mary _____ WHITLEY	45 Years	02-29-1876	070	WHITLEY, Patrick	
			070		
Peter BUTLER	1831	1904	070	MCNAMARA, Mary Ann	
Mary Ann MCNAMARA Butler	1848	1936	070	BUTLER, Peter	
			070		
John SULLIVAN	45 Years	04-28-1894	070	SULLIVAN, John	
			070		
James DALEY	1856	1916	070	_____, Margaret	
Margaret _____ DALEY	1861	1924	070	DALEY, James	
Michael DALEY	1830	1900	070	DALEY, Michael	
Mary A. DALEY	1855	1889	070	DALEY, Mary A.	
John DALEY	1859	1889	070	DALEY, John	
			070		
Honora CROWLEY	1850	1937	070	CROWLEY, Honora	
			070		
Rose KEENAN	88 Years	12-31-1893	070	KEENAN, Rose	
Mary J. KEENAN	39 Years	07-04-1890	070	KEENAN, Mary J.	
			070		

Patrick LOFTUS	41 Years	03-19-1882	070	CADEN, Kate	
Kate CADEN Loftus	1840	09-02-1914	070	LOFTUS, Patrick	
			070		
Annie MCANANEY	09-22-1844	01-04-1887	070	MCANANEY, Annie	
Bridget MCANANEY	10-15-1846	04-10-1904	070	MCANANEY, Bridget	
Catherine MCANANEY Lawler	60 Years	01-15-1892	070	LAWLER, Martin	(NOI Martin Lawler)
			070	MCANANEY, Catherine	
Mary MCANANEY Shorter	56 Years	01-07-1890	070	SHORTER, John	(NOI John Shorter)
			070	MCANANEY, Mary	
			070		
John WELCH	No date	05-12-1926	070	WELCH, John	
Betsey MULLANEY Welch	No date	04-10-1865	070	MULLANEY, Betsey	
			070		
Peter MCMANUS	1837	1919	070	MULLANEY, Margaret	
Margaret MULLANEY McManus	1835	1908	070	MCMANUS, Peter	
Mary MULLANEY McDonough	1827	1910	070	MULLANEY, Mary	(NOI Mr. McDonough)
			070		
Michael DUGAN	No date	01-12-1929	070	MULLANEY, Mary	
Mary MULLANEY Dugan	No date	11-27-1905	070	DUGAN, Michael	
			070		
Michael BRISLIN	1826	02-07-1907	070	DOUGHERTY, Catherine	Co. F. 13th Regt U.S. Inf
Catherine DOUGHERTY	1838	1916	070	BRISLIN, Michael	
			070		
Owen MANGAN	1812	1890	070	MALONEY, Anne	
Anne MALONEY Mangan	1829	1912	070	MANGAN, Owen	
			070		
Patrick STEWART	55 Years	01-31-1884	070	_____, Bridget	
Bridget _____ STEWART	65 Years	07-17-1893	070	STEWART, Patrick	
			070		
Peter FAHY	62 Years	01-17-1885	070	_____, Bridget	
Bridget _____ FAHY	69 Years	03-02-1891	070	FAHY, Peter	
Hanora FAHY	18 Years	05-20-1887	070	FAHY, Hanora	
Winnie FAHY	22 Years	06-21-1877	070	FAHY, Winnie	
			070		
James TYNAN	1807	1872	070	MCCALL, Honour	
Honour MCCALL Tynan	1820	1880	070	TYNAN, James	
Bridget T. MORRIS	1847	1874	070	MORRIS, Bridget T.	
			070		
Henry C. CHENEY	1846	1922	070	TYNAN, Ellen I.	
Ellen I. TYNAN Cheney	1854	1918	070	CHENEY, Henry C.	
			070		
Bernard CARROLL	57 Years	11-10-1889	070	_____, Mary E.	
Mary E. _____ CARROLL	75 Years	11-24-1915	070	CARROLL, Bernard	
			070		
Douglas WILKINS	1830	1889	070	GAVIN, Ann A.	

Ann A. GAVIN Wilkins	1848	1927	070	WILKINS, Douglas	
			070		
John EUSTACE	07-24-1819	10-22-1901	070	BARTLETT, Margaret	
Margaret BARTLETT Eustace	11-25-1825	03-30-1903	070	EUSTACE, John	
			070		
John WILKINSON	1842	1908	070	SHERIDAN, Ann	
Ann SHERIDAN WIlkinson	1847	1889	070	WILKINSON, John	
			070		
John GRIFFIN	1843	1900	070	CAPELESS, Ellen	
Ellen CAPELESS Griffin	1842	1903	070	GRIFFIN, John	
			070		
John K. MCLAUGHLIN	Jun 1824	Oct 1890	070	STEWART, Mary	
Mary STEWART McLaughlin	May 1834	Jun 1910	070	MCLAUGHLIN, John K.	
Barbara A. MCLAUGHLIN	Jan 1795	Aug 1872	070	MCLAUGHLIN, Barbara A.	
Nellie M. MCLAUGHLIN Eustace	Feb 1855	Sep 1881	070	EUSTACE, J. M.	(NOI J.M. Eustace)
			070	MCLAUGHLIN, Nellie M.	
			070		
Timothy COAKLEY	70 Years	No Date	070	HARRINGTON, Catherine	
Catherine HARRINGTON Coakley	78 Years	No Date	070	COAKLEY, Timothy	
Ella COAKLEY	1876	1953	070	COAKLEY, Ella	Buried In Los Angeles, Calif
	1876	1953	070		Calvary Cemetery
			070		
Daniel CATEN	12-06-1829	08-03-1902	070	SULLIVAN, Margaret	
Margaret SULLIVAN Catren	03-17-1831	11-04-1895	070	CATEN, Daniel	
John J. CATEN	12-09-1857	06-27-1901	070	WALSH, Sarah E.	
Sarah E. WALSH	01-06-1861	10-29-1895	070	CATEN, John J.	
			070		
Patrick HOWARD	85 Years	05-09-1924	070	_____, Mary	
Mary _____ HOWARD	79 Years	09-11-1921	070	HOWARD, Patrick	
			070		
Frank CARMODY Sr.	1838	1904	070	_____, Mary	
Mary _____ CARMODY	1834	1915	070	CARMODY, Frank Sr.	
			070		
Owen CARLON	1835	1920	070	MURRAY, Bridget	
Bridget MURRAY Carlow	1850	1903	070	CARLON, Owen	
			070		
Margaret FITZGERALD	1845	1895	070	FITZGERALD, Margaret	
			070		
Owen REARDON	1844	1917	070	REARDON, Mrs. Owen	
Mrs. Owen REARDON	1843	1921	070	REARDON, Owen	
			070		
Daniel O'BRIEN	98 Years	11-09-1905	070	_____, Mary	
Mary _____ O'BRIEN	83 Years	09-29-1903	070	O'BRIEN, Daniel	
			070		
Michael GRIFFIN	69 Years	07-06-1885	070	LYNCH, Mary	

Name		Birth/Age	Death	Code	Index	Notes
Mary LYNCH Griffin		78 Years	08- -1937	070	GRIFFIN, Michael	
Michael H. GRIFFIN		44 Years	05-15-1900	070	GRIFFIN, Michael H.	
				070		
George JOHNSON		1853	1928	070	MCDONOUGH, Winifred	
Winifred MCDONOUGH Johnson		1855	1902	070	JOHNSON, George	
				070		
James BURKE		1816	1894	070	MCCUE, Margaret	
Margaret MCCUE Burke		1832	1908	070	BURKE, James	
				070		
Richard JOHNSON		76 Years	05-21-1885	070	CARROLL, Delia	
Delia CARROLL Johnson		56 Years	03-15-1872	070	JOHNSON, Richard	
Margaret _____ JOHNSON		49 Years	08-22-1890	070	JOHNSON, Edward	(NOI Edward Johnson)
				070	_____, Margaret	
				070		
Thomas KELLEY		1852	1936	070	KELLEY, Thomas	
				070		
Richard LLOYD		02-01-1824	12-15-1909	070	MALONEY, Hanora	
Hanora MALONEY Lloyd		12-24-1831	11-14-1899	070	LLOYD, Richard	
				070		
James MCGINN		1806	1879	070	MCLAUGHLIN, Mary	
Mary MCLAUGHLIN McGinn		1809	1902	070	MCGINN, James	
Michael J. MCGINN		1847	1934	070	FITZGERALD, Katie A.	
Katie A. FITZGERALD McGinn		1850	1902	070	MCGINN, Michael J.	
				070		
James KELLEY		1820	1880	070	KELLEY, James	
Mary KELLEY		1823	1893	070	KELLEY, Mary	
Margaret O'DAY		1786	1891	070	O'DAY, Margaret	
				070		
Micheal DEMPSEY		1816	1896	070	_____, Johanna	
Johanna _____ DEMPSEY		1818	1906	070	DEMPSEY, Michael	
Stephen DEMPSEY		1858	1896	070	DEMPSEY, Stephen	
				070		
Dennis BOWEN		1827	1898	070	_____, Bridget	
Bridget _____ BOWEN		1832	1907	070	BOWEN, Dennis	
Thomas BOWEN		1829	1898	070	BOWEN, Thomas	
				070		
Patrick SHEEHAN		1853	1923	070	_____, Bridget	
Bridget A. _____ SHEEHAN		1853	1938	070	SHEEHAN, Patrick	
				070		
William CRONAN		1838	1910	070	SULLIVAN, Catherine	(GAR) Co. B. 7th Vt Regt
Catherine SULLIVAN Cronan		1840	1912	070	CRONAN, William	
				070		
Mortimer SULLIVAN	Co. Kerry	55 Years	05-10-1873	070	CALLAHAN, Margaret	Native Of County Kerry ,Ire
Margaret CALLAHAN Sullivan	Co. Clare	65 Years	09-16-1890	070	SULLIVAN, Mortimer	Native Of County Clare, Ire
James T. CALLAHAN		50 Years	06-17-1906	070	SULLIVAN, Bridget	

Bridget SULLIVAN Callahan	72 Years	08-19-1930	070	CALLAHAN, James T.
Joseph A. ROUNDS	63 Years	12-05-1917	070	SULLIVAN, Margaret A.
Margaret A. SULLIVAN Rounds	70 Years	No Date	070	ROUNDS, Joseph A.
Arthur A. SULLIVAN	50 Years	05-15-1915	070	SULLIVAN, Arthur A.
			070	
Ellen KEANE McLaughlin	1819	1891	070	MCLAUGHLIN, Ellen Keane
			070	
Patrick TOOMEY	1834	1894	070	O'LEARY, Bridget
Bridget O'LEARY Toomey	1842	1885	070	TOOMEY, Patrick
John O'LEARY	1806	1865	070	O'LEARY, John
			070	
Dennis RYAN	1818	1899	070	MCKENNA, Mary
Mary MCKENNA Ryan	1828	1900	070	RYAN, Dennis
Hanora RYAN	1852	1865	070	RYAN, Hanora
Mary RYAN	1870	1888	070	RYAN, Mary
Agnes RYAN	1866	1894	070	RYAN, Agnes
Dennis M. RYAN	1858	1910	070	RYAN, Dennis M.
John J. RYAN	1854	1917	070	RYAN, John J.
Edward RYAN	1856	1936	070	MURPHY, Bridget
Bridget MURPHY Ryan	1862	1936	070	RYAN, Edward
			070	
Hugh SLOAN	47 Years	07-17-1899	070	CALLAHAN, Rose
Rose CALLAHAN Sloan	54 Years	06-16-1909	070	SLOAN, Hugh
			070	
Robert MAGEEN	1828	1915	070	MAGEEN, Robert
			070	
John CONNOLLY	1812	1854	070	_____, Mary
Mary _____ CONNOLLY	1816	1892	070	CONNOLLY, John
			070	
James BUTLER	1827	1917	070	FARRELL, Catherine
Catherine FARRELL Butler	1834	1917	070	BUTLER, James
Thomas L. BUTLER	1857	1929	070	SALMON, Margaret
Margaret SALMON Butler	1856	1915	070	BUTLER, Thomas L.
			070	
Martin FARRELL	61 Years	09-25-1893	070	_____, Bridget
Bridget _____ FARRELL	71 Years	09-02-1905	070	FARRELL, Martin
			070	
Richard BUTLER	1832	1900	070	HIGGINS, Bridget
Bridget HIGGINS Butler	1837	1930	070	BUTLER, Richard
Margaret L. BUTLER	1866	1899	070	BUTLER, Margaret L.
Mary A. DUNN	1857	1900	070	DUNN, Mary A.
Thomas BUTLER	1806	1884	070	BRENNAN, Mary
Mary BRENNAN Butler	1803	1866	070	BUTLER, Thomas
Mary BILLINGS	1844	1907	070	BILLINGS, Mary
John HIGGINS	1812	1899	070	HIGGINS, John

Name	Origin	Born/Age	Died	Code	Index	Notes
Richard BUTLER		1874	1940	070	BUTLER, Richard	
				070		
Alice MCGUIGAN		1803	1875	070	MCGUIGAN, Alice	
				070		
John MCDERMOTT	Co. Sligo	55 Years	05-08-1889	070	OWENS, Katherine	
Katherine OWENS McDermott		60 Years	01-06-1905	070	MCDERMOTT, John	
				070		
Patrick MAGUIRE		1827	1904	070	KEELEY, Mary E.	
Mary E. KEELEY Maguire		1837	1895	070	MAGUIRE, Patrick	
Kate MAGUIRE		1830	1865	070	MAGUIRE, Kate	
Anne MAGUIRE		1858	1940	070	MAGUIRE, Anne	
				070		
Thomas STEWART		66 Years	03-03-1895	070	BURNS, Mary	(GAR) Privte, Co. E, 77th Regt NY Vols
				070		
Mary BURNS Stewart		60 Years	10-25-1908	070	STEWART, Thomas	
				070		
Thomas COLEMAN		35 Years	01-10-1875	070	COLEMAN, Thomas	
				070		
Frank BISHOP		1850	1934	070	ABARE, Phoebe	
Phoebe ABARE Bishop		1864	1944	070	BISHOP, Frank	
				070		
Catherine GEOGHEGAN		97 Years	04-16-1901	070	GEOGHEGAN, Catherine	
				070		
William CONROY		39 Years	04-22-1895	070	CONROY, William	
Mary CONROY		90 Years	01-28-1903	070	CONROY, Mary	
				070		
James KINGSLEY		1839	1896	070	KINGSLEY, James	
Ellen KINGSLEY		1838	1926	070	KINGSLEY, Ellen	
				070		
Michael KINGSLEY		1826	1858	070	KELLEY, Bridget	
Bridget KELLEY Kingsley		1826	1900	070	KINGSLEY, Thomas	
Bridget R. KINGSLEY		1791	1861	070	KINGSLEY, Bridget R.	
				070		
Edward J. WYNN		08-05-1847	09-24-1889	070	HURLEY, Ellen N.	
Ellen N. HURLEY Wynn		12-25-1848	10-10-1917	070	WYNN, Edward J.	
Bridget WYNN		1843	1920	070	WYNN, Bridget	
Catherine Elizabeth WYNN		05-01-1815	01-27-1890	070	WYNN, Catherine Elizabeth	
Thomas B. WYNN		01-25-1845	03-26-1886	070	WYNN, Thomas B.	
Catherine E. WYNN		10-23-1851	10-11-1885	070	WYNN, Catherine E.	
Anna WYNN		1849	1927	070	WYNN, Anna	
				070		
Patrick DUGAN		03-17-1823	10-11-1895	070	________, Maria	
Maria _____ DUGAN		07-18-1833	03-11-1901	070	DUGAN, Patrick	
				070		
Michael KINSELLA		1826	1893	070	DONOVAN, Mary	

Mary DONOVAN Kinsella	1830	1881	070	KINSELLA, Michael
			070	
John SHERIDAN	1795	1873	070	CAREY, Catherine
Catherine CAREY Sheridan	1820	1900	070	SHERIDAN, John
Margaret SHERIDAN	1855	1869	070	SHERIDAN, Margaret
Timothy SHERIDAN	1846	1870	070	SHERIDAN, Timothy
James E. SHERIDAN	1857	1929	070	HAMMEL, Mary E.
Mary E. HAMMEL Sheridan	1860	1938	070	SHERIDAN, James S.
			070	
John CLIFFORD	85 Years	10-25-1895	070	SHERIDAN, Mary
Mary SHERIDAN Clifford	68 Years	08-23-1899	070	CLIFFORD, John
Bridget M. CLIFFORD	1847	1936	070	CLIFFORD, Bridget
			070	
John D. LYSTON	1844	1920	070	RALEIGH, Mary
Mary RALEIGH Lyston	1849	1905	070	LYSTON, John D.
			070	
Sarah E. FAULKNER	05-16-1852	07-29-1893	070	FAULKNER, Sarah E.
			070	
Daniel MALONEY	1834	1916	070	HEHIR, Margaret
Margaret HEHIR Maloney	1839	1919	070	MALONEY, Daniel
			070	
John DUNN	1853	1922	070	BUTLER, Elizabeth
Elizabeth BUTLER Dunn	1865	1934	070	DUNN, John
			070	
Daniel DUNN	1845	1911	070	DUNN, Daniel
			070	
Martin MCMAHON	1840	1912	070	MCGUIRK, Honora
Honora MCGUIRK McMahon	1827	1886	070	MCMAHON, Martin
			070	
Gilbert MORRIS	74 Years	10-03-1914	070	GALLAGHER, Ann
Ann GALLAGHER Morris	52 Years	12-01-1904	070	MORRIS, Gilbert
			070	
John C. CLARK	1826	1888	070	MCKENNA, Elizabeth
Elizabeth MCKENNA Clark	1841	1910	070	CLARK, John C.
			070	
CALLAHAN FAMILY			070	CALLAHAN, Family
Father (CALLAHAN)	1841	1910	070	CALLAHAN, Father
Mother (CALLAHAN)	1841	1910	070	CALLAHAN, Mother
Stephen CALLAHAN	1864	1880	070	CALLAHAN, Stephen
Thomas CALLAHAN	1852	1881	070	CALLAHAN, Thomas
Margaret CALLAHAN	1859	1926	070	CALLAHAN, Margaret
John J. CALLAHAN	1864	1929	070	CALLAHAN, John J.
Mary E. CALLAHAN	1856	1944	070	CALLAHAN, Mary E.
			070	
Thomas KENNEDY	1839	1913	070	WHITE, Mary

Name	Born	Died		Cross-reference	Notes
Mary WHITE Kennedy	1845	1910	070	KENNEDY, Thomas	
			070		
Dennis J. SULLIVAN	1844	1914	070	LAWLOR, Catherine	(GAR) Co. D. 46 Mass Inf
Catherine LAWLOR Sullivan	1846	1912	070	SULLIVAN, Dennis J.	
			070		
James RICE	62 Years	08-03-1902	070	RICE, James	
			070		
Michael J. HOGAN	12-07-1844	01-08-1902	070	GLEASON, Bridget	
Bridget GLEASON Hogan	02-03-1845	01-27-1910	070	HOGAN, Michael J.	
			070		
Thomas BROWN	1826	1911	070	BROWN, Mrs. Thomas	
Mrs. Abigail CORBETT	1801	1894	070	CORBETT, Mrs. Abigail	
Mrs. Thomas BROWN	1831	1891	070	BROWN, Thomas	
Mrs. Ellen E. MULCAHY	1849	1913	070	MULCAHY, Mrs. Ellen E.	
William A. BROWN	1859	1930	070	BROWN, William A.	
James J. BROWN	1854	1938	070	BROWN, James J.	
Margaret E. BROWN	1844	No date	070	BROWN, Margaret E.	
Michael G. TIERNAN	1856	1928	070	____, Catherine A.	
Catherine A. _____ TIERNAN	1857	1935	070	TIERNAN, Michael	
			070		
William ONEY	1831	1903	070	ONEY, William	(GAR) Co. K. 12th Vt Inf
James CONLIN	1804	1860	070	CONLIN, James	
Alice CONLIN	1792	1878	070	CONLIN, Alice	
Mary CONLIN	1841	1859	070	CONLIN, Mary	
John CONLIN	1833	1907	070	CONLIN, John	
Jennie CONLIN	1847	1915	070	CONLIN, Jennie	
			070		
Philip MURPHY	1822	1907	070	EGAN, Sarah	
Sarah EGAN Murphy	1828	1910	070	MURPHY, Philip	
			070		
William SMITH	10-26-1855	12-05-1928	070	SMITH, William	
Mary H. SMITH	05-01-1833	09-28-1921	070	SMITH, Mary H.	
Patrick SMITH	03-17-1828	02-16-1876	070	SMITH, Patrick	
Mary A. SMITH	05-27-1857	06-02-1940	070	SMITH, Mary A.	
Thomas J. SMITH	11-30-1860	09-21-1888	070	SMITH, Thomas J.	
James P. SMITH	01-14-1859	01-05-1907	070	SMITH, James P.	
			070		
John KENNEDY	1829	1904	070	BAGLEY, Johanna	
Johanna BAGLEY Kennedy	1836	1919	070	KENNEDY, John	
			070		
John STUART	05-16-1834	01-29-1907	070	GILOOLY, Bridget	
Bridget GILOOLY Stuart	07-02-1849	02-23-1942	070	STUART, John	
			070		
Heman JACKSON	1838	1923	070	OWENS, Bridget	(GAR) Co. F. 10th Rgt Vt Vols
Bridget OWENS Jackson	1850	1928	070	JACKSON, Heman	

Name	Birth	Death		Related	Notes
			070		
James SAGE	1825	1911	070	MURRAY, Annabelle	
Annabelle MURRAY Sage	1838	1924	070	SAGE, James	
			070		
Patrick FAGAN	58Years	01-27-1904	070	CONLON, Margaret T.	(GAR) Co. H. 2nd Rgt Minn Vol Inf
			070		
Margaret T. CONLON Fagan	1840	1928	070	FAGAN, Patrick	
			070		
Bridget K. MCDONOUGH	1828	1911	070	MCDONOUGH, Bridget K.	
Patrick A. MCDONOUGH	1859	1932	070	MCDONOUGH, Patrick A.	
James J. MELVIN	1845	1904	070	MELVIN, James J.	
			070		
James MCGUIRK	01-28-1852	12-16-1911	070	MCGUIRK, James	
Katherine A. CORCORAN McGuirk	02-03-1856	09-21-1925	070	CORCORAN, Katherine A.	
			070		
Ellen CARROLL O'Laughlin	66Years	12-07-1910	070	O'LAUGHLIN, Bernard	(NOI Bernard O'Laughlin)
			070	CARROLL, Ellen	
			070		
			070		
Mary A. HANEY	1846		070	HANEY, Mary A.	
Jane D. STEWART	1810	1882	070	STEWART, Jane D.	
			070		
James H. MAGUIRE	1849	1919	070	MOLONEY, Mary J.	
Mary J. MOLONEY Maguire	1849	1921	070	MAGUIRE, James H.	
			070		
Margaret DYER	1845	1918	070	DYER, Margaret	
Patrick DYER	1827	1899	070	DYER, Patrick	
			070		
Cornelius J. COCHLIN	1852	1928	070	MALONE, Catherine	
Catherine MALONE Cochlin	1863	1919	070	COCHLIN, Cornelius J.	
			070		
William TAYLOR	1849	1928	070	FEE, Catherine	
Catherine FEE	1856	1926	070	TAYLOR, William	
			070		
Patrick CROWLEY	1847	1944	070	COPPINGER, Bridget	
Bridget COPPINGER Crowley	1868	1962	070	CROWLEY, Patrick	
			070		
James CONNOLLY	1854	1947	070	CURTIN, Mary	
Mary CURTIN Connolly	1855	1917	070	CONNOLLY, James	
			070		
Michael CAIN	45 Years	05-17-1875	070	CAIN, Michael	
			070		
James W. GREAVES	1844	1931	070	LYNSLEY, Mary A.	Co. I 1st Vt Cav (GAR)
Mary A. LYNSLEY	1859	1917	070	GREAVES, James	
			070		

John MORIARTY	1852	1916	070	BOYLE, Mary	
Mary BOYLE Moriarty	1853	1933	070	MORIARTY, John	
			070		
Daniel HEFFERNAN	1848	1930	070	MCCARTHY, Mary A.	
Mary A. MCCARTHY Heffernan	1854	1928	070	HEFFERNAN, Daniel	
			070		
Joseph B. SQUIER	1850	1945	070	SQUIER, Joseph B.	
			070		
Patrick W. CASEY	1855	1916	070	TENNIEN, Alice A.	
Alice A. TENNIEN Casey	1855	1928	070	CASEY, Patrick W.	
			070		
Patrick HENNESSY	02-12-1838	03-04-1904	070	COYLE, Anna	
Anna COYLE Hennessy	11-25-1842	10-18-1923	070	HENNESSY, Patrick	
			070		
William RYAN	1844	1921	070	QUIRK, Julia A.	
Julia A. QUIRK Ryan	1844	1931	070	RYAN, William	
			070		
William RYAN	70 Years	04-25-1908	070	RYAN, William	
			070		
Michael COLLINS	1853	1908	070	_____, Bridget	
Bridget _____ COLLINS	1852		070	COLLINS, Michael	
			070		
Frank SCANLON	73 Years	03-21-1906	070	SCANLON, Frank	
			070		
Michael P. RYAN	1852	1906	070	KEEFE, Mary A.	
Mary A. KEEFE Ryan	1858	1925	070	RYAN, Michael P.	
			070		
Patrick FARRELL	1834	1905	070	CLINE, Ellen	
Ellen CLINE Farrell	1842	1908	070	FARRELL, Patrick	
			070		
Patrick J. MCLAUGHLIN	1849	1928	070	_____, Jennie E.	
Jennie E. _____ MCLAUGHLIN	1851	1909	070	MCLAUGHLIN, Patrick J.	
			070		
Margaret E. DOUGHERTY	94 Years	08-09-1914	070	DOUGHERTY, Margaret E.	
			070		
Roger REILLY	1845	1915	070	REILLY, Roger	
Ann REILLY	1838	1909	070	REILLY, Ann	
Mary MCGUIRE Reilly	1805	1878	070	REILLY, Peter	(NOI Peter Reilly)
			070	MCGUIRE, Mary	
			070		
John CALLAHAN	1829	1905	070	MACKEY, Elizabeth	
Elizabeth MACKEY Callahan	1832	1911	070	CALLAHAN, John	
			070		
Robert Maher (MOHER)	06-24-1845	01-21-1940	070	WALSH, Mary	
Mary WALSH Maher	01-21-1862	03-14-1905	070	MAHER, Robert	

Name	Birth/Age	Death	Code	Spouse/Index
			070	
Timothy CLARK	1818	1902	070	_____, Margaret
Margaret _____ CLARK	1826	1903	070	CLARK, Timothy
			070	
Margaret B. BURNS	1849	1912	070	BURNS, Margaret B.
Timothy C. HALPIN	1853	1927	070	BARRY, Ellen
Ellen BARRY Halpin	1853	1932	070	HALPIN, Timothy C.
			070	
Timothy GLEASON	1849	1918	070	SHEEDY, Mary
Mary SHEEDY Gleason	1856	1910	070	GLEASON, Timothy
			070	
Daniel DERVIN	1832	1909	070	MCLAUGHLIN, Mary
Mary MCLAUGHLIN Dervin	1840	1912	070	DERVIN, Daniel
			070	
Daniel GEARITY	1841	1921	070	MCLAUGHLIN, Mary
Mary BATTLES Gearity	1847	1904	070	GEARITY, Daniel
			070	
Hugh KELLEY	72 Years	12-03-1901	070	O'DONNELL, Mary
Mary O'DONNELL Kelley	50 Years	12-06-1861	070	KELLEY, Hugh
			070	
Mrs. Mary A. ALLEN	70 Years	08-08-1921	070	ALLEN, Mrs. Mary A.
			070	
Miss Anna K. MURPHY	77 Years	07-16-1922	070	MURPHY, Miss Anna K.
			070	
Mrs. Mary E. BARRY	75 Years	03-08-1927	070	BARRY, Mrs. Mary E.
			070	
Miss Ann DONNELLY	81 Years	07-16-1922	070	DONNELLY, Miss Ann
			070	
Miss Mary HAYDEN	75 Years	03-01-1918	070	HAYDEN, Miss Mary
			070	
Miss Mary WALSH	75 Years	12-03-1917	070	WALSH, Miss Mary
			070	
Miss Elizabeth F. ARMSTRONG	65 Years	01-28-1917	070	ARMSTRONG, Miss Elizabeth F.
			070	
Mary KENNEDY	67 Years	01-05-1913	070	KENNEDY, Mary
			070	
Mrs. Mary BOUDEN	60 Years	04-29-1912	070	BOUDEN, Mrs. Mary
			070	
Miss Catherine RYAN	75 Years	05-03-1911	070	RYAN, Miss Catherine
			070	
Miss Nora O'DAY	81 Years	08-06-1909	070	O'DAY, Miss Nora
			070	
Mrs. Julia A. DEWEY	72 Years	04-27-1907	070	DEWEY, Mrs. Julia A.
			070	
Mrs Ellen COLLISON	82 Years	10-30-1905	070	COLLISON, Mrs Ellen

			070	
Herbert A. SEWELL	1855	1917	070	SIMPSON, Anna M.
Anna M. SIMPSON Sewell	1856	1935	070	SEWELL, Herbert A.
			070	
Reverend T. J. GAFFNEY	1843	1906	070	GAFFNEY, Reverend T. J.
			070	
Michael LEONARD	1842	1888	070	MACDONALD, Ellen
Ellen MACDONALD Leonard	1844	1909	070	LEONARD, Michael
			070	
Daniel CLINE	1849	1934	070	HACKETT, Jennie
Jennie HACKETT Cline	1857	1913	070	CLINE, Daniel
			070	
James P. SULLIVAN	1854	1920	070	_____, Margaret A.
Margaret A. _____ SULLIVAN	1857	1909	070	SULLIVAN, James P.
			070	
Martin J. MILLEE	63 Years	04-15-1913	070	RILEY, Ann M.
Ann M. RILEY Millee	86 Years	10-17-1932	070	MILLEE, Martin J.
			070	
Patrick KELLY	1826	1910	070	_____, Betsey
Betsey _____ KELLY	1831	1925	070	KELLY, Patrick
			070	
George D. PATTERSON Sr.	1846	1935	070	SLATTERY, Annie C.
Annie C. SLATTERY Patterson	1849	1914	070	PATTERSON, George D. Sr.
			070	
Bridget WHITTEN	08-12-1852	07-17-1937	070	WHITTEN, Bridget
			070	
Dennis LYONS	1832	1915	070	BOLAN, Catherine
Catherine BOLAN Lyons	1839	1914	070	LYONS, Dennis
			070	
Thomas MCDONNELL	1842	1910	070	CARROLL, Mary
Mary CARROLL McDonnell	1845	1910	070	MCDONNELL, Thomas
			070	
Robert JOHNSON	47 Years		070	MURPHY, Catherine
Catherine MURPHY Johnson		05-15-1861	070	JOHNSON, Robert
			070	
Timothy HIGGINS	1823	1926	070	_____, Mary
Mary _____ HIGGINS	1841	1916	070	HIGGINS, Timothy
			070	
James O'HEARN	1826	1876	070	BARRY, Mary
Mary BARRY O'Hearn	1827	1889	070	O'HEARN, James
			070	
Edward MCGUE	1838	1913	070	MCCOOL, Bridget
Bridget MCCOOL McGue	1833	1918	070	MCGUE, Edward
			070	
Michael CURRAN		12-05-1915	070	STEPHENSON, Mary

Name	Born	Died	Code	Index	Notes
Mary STEPHENSON Curran	1833	05-13-1941	070	CURRAN, Michael	
			070		
Michael P MCCORMICK	62 Years	03-27-1909	070	MCCORMICK, Michael P.	1st Sgt 11th Infantry USA
			070		Enlisted 1869 Retired 1900
			070		
Mary MURPHY Sammon	65 Years	04-03-1888	070	SAMMON, Timothy	(NOI Timothy Sammon)
			070	MURPHY, Mary	
			070		
Bridget MURPHY Burns		07-27-1914	070	BURNS, Edward	(NOI Edward Burns)
			070	MURPHY, Bridget	
			070		
Patrick CARRIGAN	1836	1868	070	CLANCY, Catherine	
Catherine CLANCY Carrigan	1836	1914	070	CARRIGAN, Patrick	
			070		
Patrick BRISLIN	1820	1868	070	_____, Bridget T.	
Bridget T. _____ BRISLIN	1822	1868	070	BRISLIN, Patrick	
Henry E. BRISLIN	1853	1880	070	BRISLIN, Henry E.	
Margaret _____ BRISLIN	1851	1872	070	_____, Margaret	
			070		
			070		
Mary A. SPELLMAN Novak	1854	1919	070	NOVAK, Albert	(NOI Albert Novak)
			070	SPELLMAN, Mary A.	
Ellen E. MCCARTHY	1837	1913	070	MCCARTHY, Ellen E.	
			070		
James B. TITUS	1846	1916	070	WYNNE, Mary	
Mary WYNNE Titus	1846	1913	070	TITUS, James B.	
			070		
John MYLOTT	1842	1912	070	MAGUIRE, Mary Eveline	
Mary Eveline MAGUIRE Mylott	1846	1913	070	MYLOTT, John	
			070		
James KENNEDY	52 Years	07-19-1887	070	KANE, Bridget	
Bridget KANE Kennedy	34 Years	11-29-1887	070	KENNEDY, James	
			070		
Jeremiah J. MURPHY	1850	1912	070	_____, Margaret S.	
Margaret S. _____ MURPHY	1852	1928	070	MURPHY, Jeremiah J.	
			070		
James E. CREED	1854	1936	070	TIERNAN, Annie	
Annie TIERNAN Creed	1860	1925	070	CREED, James E.	
			070		
Anthony HOGAN	1825	1890	070	FOLEY, Margaret	
Margaret FOLEY Hogan	1833	1871	070	HOGAN, Anthony	
			070		
John O'NEIL	1852	1935	070	CONLINE, Anna M.	
Anna M. CONLINE O'Neil	1852	1913	070	O'NEIL, John	
			070		

NAME	POB	DOB/AGE	DOD	CEM	SPOUSE/INDEX	INSCRIPTION
John FARRELL		48 Years	02-11-1880	070	NAVEN, Annie	
Annie NAVEN Farrell		29Y 14D	05-20-1882	070	FARRELL, John	
				070		
John MCTIERNEY		1854	1918	070	MCTIERNEY, John	
				070		
John FOX		1847	1920	070	CRONIN, Johanna	
Johanna CRONIN Fox		1846	1919	070	FOX, John	
				070		
Annie _____ HENRY		35 Years	06-12-1886	070	HENRY, William P.	(NOI William P. Henry)
				070	_____, Annie	
Patrick KELLEY		23 Years	10-22-1869	070	KELLEY, Patrick	
Timothy KELLEY		49Y 11M	02-04-1859	070	_____, Ann	
Ann _____ KELLEY		49 Years	04-02-1866	070	KELLEY, Timothy	
Charles B. CARLIN		1841		070	KELLEY, Mary A.	(GAR) Co. F. 3rd Vt Regt
Mary A. KELLEY Carlin		1845	1917	070	CARLIN, Charles B.	
				070		

West Street Cemetery (Old Catholic), Rutland, Vermont

NAME	POB	DOB/AGE	DOD	CEM	SPOUSE/INDEX	INSCRIPTION
Bridget DUGAN		70 Years	07-09-1890	123	DUGAN, David	(NOI David Dugan)
				123	DUGAN, Bridget	(NOI John & Ellen McCavet)
				123		
James STEWART		47 Years	02-12-1883	123	STEWART James	(Does not say if Ann Stewart
Ann STEWART		54 Years	11-21-1883	123	STEWART, Ann	was spouse of James Stewart)
				123		
Kate DUFFACY Stewart		61 Years	10-21-1884	123	STEWART, Michael	(NOI Michael Stewart)
				123	DUFFACY, Kate	
				123		
Thomas MCGUINESS	Co. Cavan	26Y02M25D	01-26-1886	123	MCGUINESS, Thomas	A Native Of County Cavan, Ire.
				123		May His Soul Rest In Peace
				123		
P. C. WATERS				123	WATERS, P.C.	(GAR) Co. G. 5th VT Vols.(Name
				123		is Patrick.Enlistd at Rutland)
				123		
Edward CARROLL		11 Years	09-30-1870	123	CARROLL, Edward	
Timothy CARROLL		16 Years	10-19-1870	123	CARROLL, Timothy	
Honor _____ CARROLL		56 Years	06-02-1878	123	CARROLL, Timothy	(NOI Spouse Timothy Carroll)
				123	_____, Honor	
				123		
Thomas F. KENNEDY		27Y01M	08-28-1884	123	KENNEDY, Thomas F.	(NOI Bridget Kennedy)
				123	_____, Bridget	

Name	Origin	Age	Date	No.	Names on stone	Notes
Mamie KENNEDY		2 Months	08-15-1882	123	KENNEDY, Mamie	D/O Thomas & Bridget Kennedy
Michael MALONE	Co. Tipperary	25 Years	10-19-1870	123	MALONE, Michael	A Native Of The Parish Of Castletown, Co. Tipperary, Ire
Bridget _____ BURNS			04-__-__	123	BURNS, James _____, Bridget	(NOI James Burns. Stone is badly worn. Cannot read DOD or age at death)
Jno MCGINNIS				123	MCGINNIS, Jno	(GAR) 9th Vt Inf. (See Co. B & Co. C. as LT. Died of disease on 11-10-1865. Name-John E.)
P. O'RILEY				123	O'RILEY, P.	(GAR) 5th Vt, Co. B. (Did not find in reference)
Margaret AGEN		10 Years	11-03-1857	123	AGEN, Margaret AGEN, Michael AGEN, Mary	D/O Michael & Mary Agen (NOI Michael & Mary Agen)
Annie MCDERMOTT		7 Months	06-01-1877	123	MCDERMOTT, Annie MCDERMOTT, Briny MCDERMOTT, Sarah	D/O Briny & Sarah McDermott (NOI Briny & Sarah McDermott)
Elizabeth COONEY Catherine COONEY		77 Years 09-05-1829	03-30-1884 07-28-1885	123	COONEY, Elizabeth COONEY, Catherine	Born In Cicily (sp)
William BURNS		21 Years	04-05-1880	123	BURNS, William	S/O Edward & Bridget Burns
Bridget CLIFFORD Burns	Co. Tipperary			123	BURNS, Edward CLIFFORD, Bridget	Native Of The Parish Of Castle town, Co. Of Tipperary, Ire. (NOI Edward Burns,her DOB-DOD)
Mary KELLY O'Connor	Co. Clare	66 Years	09-17-1866	123	O'CONNOR, Michael KELLY, Mary	Native Of County Clare, Ire. Erected By John O'Connor. May Her Soul Rest In Peace. (NOI Michael O'Connor)
Jno O'BRIEN				123	O'BRIEN, Jno	(GAR) 2nd Vt Baty (Lt Arty)
Michael SLATTERY		20 Years	08-22-1871	123	SLATTERY, Michael	Son Of Timothy & Mary Slattery Died In Chicago
Timothy SLATTERY Mary GLEASON Slattery	Co. Kings Co. Tipperary	84 Years 56 Years	05-08-1880 03-15-1866	123	GLEASON, Mary SLATTERY, Timothy	Native Of Kings County, Ire. Native Of Co. Tipperary, Ire.

Agnes SLATTERY		83 Years	12-19-1941	123	SLATTERY, Agnes	
				123		
Julia SLATTERY		30 Years	05-13-1875	123	SLATTERY, Julia	D/O Timothy & Mary Slattery
				123		
Matthew SLATTERY		82 Years	02-06-1917	123	SLATTERY, Matthew	(GAR) Co. K. 12th Regt Vt Vols
				123		
Mary SLATTERY		20 Years	09-22-1877	123	SLATTERY, Mary	D/O John & Catherine Slattery
				123		
Timothy SLATTERY		12 Years		123	SLATTERY, Timothy	Sons of Timothy--Mary Slattery
James SLATTERY		5 Years		123	SLATTERY, James	
				123		
Rody-Julia-Kitty-Maggie-Timothy				123		Infant Children of John and
				123		Catherine Slattery
				123		
John R. SLATTERY		49 Years	03-15-1884	123	_____, Catherine	Born In Montreal, Canada
Catherine _____ SLATTERY		82 Years	02-06-1919	123	SLATTERY, John R.	
				123		
Sarah SLATTERY Kirkpatrick		40 Years	09-30-1915	123	KIRKPATRICK, John	
				123	SLATTERY, Sarah	
				123		
Lieut Martin MCMANUS				123	MCMANUS, Martin	Co. C., 5th VT Inf (GAR)
				123		
George O'KEEFE		6Y1M	07-13-1881	123	O'KEEFE, George	Children of James/Rose O'KEEFE
Lizzie O'KEEFE		2Y11M	10-28-1881	123	O'KEEFE, Lizzie	
				123		
Daniel KELLEY		66 Years	04-07-1870	123	_____, Bridget	(YOD Could be 1876)
Bridget _____ KELLEY	Co. Mayo	70 Years	04-08-1871	123	KELLEY, Daniel	A Native Of Co. Mayo. Ireland
				123		May Their Souls Rest In Peace
				123		
Matthew MCGUIRK	Co. Meath	84 Years	07-09-1871	123	REILLEY, Honor	A Native Of Lobinstown, County
				123		Meath, Ireland
Honor REILLEY McGuirk	Co. Meath	89 Years	04-01-1876	123	MCGUIRK, Matthew	A Native Of Mitchelstown, Co.
				123		Meath, Ireland
				123		
Betsey _____ WILSON		56 Years	04-10-1873	123	WILSON, William	(NOI William Wilson)
				123	_____, Betsey	
				123		
Patrick MCGUIRK		47 Years	07-13-1864	123	MCGUIRK, Patrick	Natives of Lobinstown
Jane MCGUIRK			1833	123	MCGUIRK, Jane	Natives of Lobinstown
				123		
Patrick FAGAN		61 Years	10-19-1886	123	FAGAN, Patrick	Born In New Boston, Ireland
				123		(No such town. There is a
				123		Boston in Kildare, Queens,
				123		Tipperary and Clare.)
				123		

Ann TIERNAN		65 Years	01-13-1886	123	TIERNAN, Ann	Mother
				123		
Annie _____ HAYWARD		03-31-1855	01-15-1877	123	HAYWARD, James R.	(NOI James R. Hayward)
				123	_____, Annie	
				123		
Peter FAGAN				123	FAGAN, Peter	(GAR) Co. B. (NOI but try
				123		Co. C. 16th Regt. This stone
				123		deteriorated- wifes name is
L. _____ FAGAN		49 Years	03-30-1876	123		missing.)
Sarah W. FAGAN			1868	123		(Stone deteriorated.)
				123		
Nancy TULLEY		14Y11D	05-01-1864	123	TULLEY, Nancy	D/O J & M Tulley
				123		
Margaret FAGAN		55 Years	06-20-1879	123	FAGAN, Margaret	(Stone is down)
				123		
Thomas CONLINE		68 Years	01-28-1862	123	CUNNINGHAM, Mary	
Mary CUNNINGHAM Conline		54 Years	07-31-1870	123	CONLINE, Thomas	
				123		
Bartholomew COLLINS	Co. Cork	68 Years	08-01-1887	123	GILRAIN, Ann	Native Of County Cork, Ireland
Ann GILRAIN Collins	Co. Leitrim	54 Years	07-31-1870	123	COLLINS, Bartholomew	Native of Parish of Killapiaue (Killargue), Co. Leitrim, Ire.

St. Catherine's Cemetery, Falls Road, Shelburne, VT

NAME	POB	DOB/AGE	DOD	CEM	SPOUSE/INDEX	INSCRIPTION
James SHERIDAN		1810	1882	071	MCDERMOTT, Anna S.	
Anna S. MCDERMOT Sheridan		1816	1892	071	SHERIDAN, James	
William J. SHERIDAN		1856	1923	071	MCGARRY, Helen	
Helen MCGARRY Sheridan		1879	1929	071	SHERIDAN, William J.	
				071		
John W. NOONAN		1856	1925	071	PURCELL, Kate	
Kate PURCELL Noonan		1865	1949	071	NOONAN, John W.	
				071		
Arthur J. AUCLAIR		1860	1940	071	KEELEY, Annie E.	
Annie E. KEELEY Auclair		1857	1935	071	AUCLAIR, Arthur J.	
				071		
Annie L. MCGEE Thorp				071	THORP, Herbert C.	(NOI Herbert C. Thorp)
				071	MCGEE, Annie L.	
				071		
John H. MORRILL		1853	1929	071	MORRILL, Rosana	
Rosana _____ MORRILL		1865	1963	071	MORRILL, John H.	
				071		

Name	Birth	Death	Code	Spouse/Index	Notes
William MCDONALD	1853	1927	071	WALSH, Elizabeth	
Elizabeth WALSH McDonald	1855	1928	071	MCDONALD, William	
			071		
John MCGEE	1840	1913	071	DORR, Katherine	
Katherine DORR McGee	1841	1913	071	MCGEE, John	
			071		
Andrew PURCELL	86 Years	01-20-1892	071	PURCELL, Mary	
Mary _____ PURCELL	73 Years	12-04-1899	071	PURCELL, Andrew	
Anthony J. PURCELL	42 Years	02-07-1904	071	NOONAN, Kate I.	
Kate I. NOONAN Purcell	59 Years	04-22-1926	071	PURCELL, Anthony J.	
			071		
James CASEY	1829	1904	071	BOLAND, Margaret	
Margaret BOLAND Casey	1834	1929	071	CASEY, James	
Mary BOLAND Hoey	1835	1930	071	BOLAND, Mary	(NOI Mr. Hoey)
Elizabeth J. HOEY	1865	1949	071	HOEY, Elizabeth J.	
			071		
John MCKENZIE	1829	1913	071	HART, Bridget	
Bridget HART McKenzie	1840	1915	071	MCKENZIE, John	
			071		
Thomas MOILES	1841	1905	071	MOILES, Thomas	
			071		
John QUINLAN	1853	1914	071	MCDONALD, Mary	
Mary MCDONALD Quinlan	1855	1931	071	QUINLAN, John	
			071		
Thomas COGANS	76 Years	07-16-1906	071	COGANS, Julia	
Julia _____ COGANS	1845	1928	071	COGANS, Thomas	
Mary COGANS	1872	1940	071	COGANS, Mary	
Michael COGANS	1874	1940	071	COGANS, Michael	
Patrick COGANS	1848	1918	071	COGANS, Patrick	
			071		
Kate FINNESSY	72 Years	02-05-1930	071	FINNESSY, Kate	
			071		
Anthony DONNELLY	01-01-1838	01-02-1911	071	MCGRATH, Margaret	Co. A 13th Rgt (Irish) Vt Vols
Margaret MCGRATH Donnelly	01-06-1835	10-08-1897	071	DONNELLY, Anthony	
Ellen DONNELLY	1867	1935	071	DONNELLY, Ellen	
Margaret DONNELLY	1872	1948	071	DONNELLY, Margaret	
			071		
William C. MCGEE	1854	1936	071	CORMAN, Mary A.	
Mary A. CORMAN McGee	1855	1916	071	MCGEE, William C.	
			071		
Cornelius E. CROWLEY	1841	1918	071	DOWER, Margaret A.	
Margaret A. DOWER Crowley	1848	1923	071	CROWLEY, Cornelius E.	
			071		
James MURPHY	1860	1924	071	SMITH, Ellen G.	
Ellen G. SMITH Murphy	1859	1937	071	MURPHY, James	

St. Anthony's Catholic Cemetery, Sheldon Springs, Vermont - Just Off Route 105, Sheldon Springs, Vermont

NAME	POB	DOB/AGE	DOD	CEM	SPOUSE/INDEX	INSCRIPTION

St. Anthony's Church was not organized as a Parish until 1907 and this cemetery was not dedicated until some time after that. Those interred are primarily of French-Canadian ethnicity or do not fit the parameters of this collection. Burial of Catholics took place in the Sheldon Village and Rice Hill (Union) Cemeteries.

NAME	POB	DOB/AGE	DOD	CEM	SPOUSE/INDEX	INSCRIPTION
Daniel DUFFY		1851	1920	114	GERO, Sarah	
Sarah GERO Duffy		1851		114	DUFFY, Daniel	
				114		
				114		

Sheldon Cemetery, Sheldon, Vermont. Prospect Street, off Main Street

NAME	POB	DOB/AGE	DOD	CEM	SPOUSE/INDEX	INSCRIPTION

This Cemetery Divided Into An Old and New Burial Ground - Inscriptions from Mary Sloan Mackin to Louisa P. Magowan Are In The Old Lot With The Balance Being Interred In The Newer Ground

NAME	POB	DOB/AGE	DOD	CEM	SPOUSE/INDEX	INSCRIPTION
				115		
Mary SLOAN Mackin		44 Years	09-09-1896	115	MACKIN, Charles	(NOI Charles Mackin)
				115	SLOAN, Mary	
				115		
Eliza FARRELL		1819	1901	115	FARRELL, Eliza	
William WHITE		85 Years	08-14-1904	115	HUSBAND, Sarah	(GAR) Co. I 10th Rgt VT Vols
Sarah HUSBAND White		65 Years	11-18-1888	115	WHITE, William	
Katie A. WHITE		20 Years	10-13-1873	115	WHITE, Katie A.	
Sarah WHITE		23 Years	04-04-1882	115	WHITE, Sarah	
				115		
Robert HOGAN		79 Years	04-30-1875	115	HOGAN, Mary	
Mary _____ HOGAN		74 Years	03-17-1877	115	HOGAN, Robert	
				115		
Mary J. HOGAN Husband		48 Years	03-08-1887	115	HUSBAND, George	(NOI George Husband)
				115	HOGAN, Mary J.	
				115		
Capt. William H. WRIGHT		1835	1915	115	HOGAN, Sarah	(GAR) Co. C. 5th VT Vol Inf
Sarah HOGAN Wright		1835	1920	115	WRIGHT, William H.	
				115		
Libbie S. WRIGHT Robson		22Y 11M	01-20-1867	115	ROBSON, J. T.	(NOI J.T. Robson) D/O Dorastus WRIGHT and Eliza
				115		
				115	WRIGHT, Libbie S.	

Name	Birth/Age	Death	Ref	Spouse/Related	Notes
James MCNANEY	43 Years	12-14-1865	115	MALONEY, Sarah	(GAR) Co. C. 11th VT Vols
Sarah MALONEY McNaney	71 Years	07-20-1894	115	MCNANEY, James	
Edward MCNANEY	34 Years	04-08-1882	115	MCNANEY, Edward	Sons of James & Sarah MCNANEY
Barnard MCNANEY	22 Years	10-13-1881	115	MCNANEY, Barnard	Sons of James & Sarah MCNANEY
James R. MCNANEY	22 Years	04-15-1887	115	MCNANEY, James R.	Sons of James & Sarah MCNANEY
Unknown (MCNANEY?)	91Y 1M	06-26-1859	115		(In Same Plot as James & Sarah McNaney. Stone is down, name missing)
H. C. BILLADO	1860		115	MCNANEY, J. E.	
J. E. MCNANEY Billado	1850	1921	115	BILLADO, H. C.	
John GANSON	54 Years	12-13-1838	115	GANSON, John	(Does not state if John & Mary Ganson were man & wife)
Mary GANSON	74 Years	10-27-1860	115	GANSON, Mary	
Cyrus MCKENEY	23 Years	06-21-1839	115	MCKENEY, Cyrus	S/O Charles MCKENEY & Melinda
Prusella CHADWICK Moran	37Y 8D	10-21-1880	115	MORAN, William CHADWICK, Prusella	(NOI William Moran)
J. W. SHELDON	03-27-1779	03-07-1866	115	MAGOWAN, Louisa O.	(Full Name was Joshua Willard Sheldon)
Louisa O. MAGOWAN	27 Years	03-26-1853	115	SHELDON, J. W.	
End Of Old Burial Ground			115		
William MCFEETERS	1807	1890	115	TODD, Ann	
Ann TODD McFeeters	1817	1894	115	MCFEETERS, William	
James MCFEETERS	1839	1911	115	MCFEETERS, James	
Samuel MCFEETERS	1841	1862	115	MCFEETERS, Samuel	(GAR) Co. K. 6TH VT Vols
William MCFEETERS	1843	1918	115	MCFEETERS, William	
Charles T. MCFEETERS	1845	1939	115	MCFEETERS, Charles T.	
Joseph MCFEETERS	1848	1930	115	MCFEETERS, Joseph	
Elizabeth MCFEETERS	1850	1926	115	MCFEETERS, Elizabeth	
Susan MCFEETERS	1853	1934	115	MCFEETERS, Susan	
Emmett MCFEETERS	1855	1929	115	MCFEETERS, Emmett	
Ella MCFEETERS	1858	1874	115	MCFEETERS, Ella	
Annie MCFEETERS	1860	1936	115	MCFEETERS, Annie	
James MCFEETERS	1839	1911	115	BRYAN, Catherine	(See William McFeeters Family)
Catherine BRYAN McFeeters	1847	1892	115	MCFEETERS, James	
James MCFEETERS	87Y 10M	02-02-1869	115	MCFEETERS, Ann	(Local History says James McF. came here from Londonderry,Ire

Name	Birth/Age	Death	Page	Relation	Notes
			115		in 1827 w/wife Ann & 4 ch.
			115		Andrew,James,William, Mary)
Ann _____ MCFEETERS	56 Years	06-21-1833	115	MCFEETERS, James	
			115		
Andrew MCFEETERS	73Y5M23D	04-16-1871	115	WALLACE, Ellen	
Ellen WALLACE McFeeters	86 Years	04-13-1903	115	MCFEETERS, Andrew	
			115		
James MCFEETERS	06-04-1814	01-12-1903	115	RILEY, Isabella	
Isabella RILEY McFeeters	08-06-1816	04-21-1893	115	MCFEETERS, James	
Andrew MCFEETERS	1844	1865	115	MCFEETERS, Andrew	(GAR) Co. L. 1st VT Cav
William MCFEETERS	1846	1858	115	MCFEETERS, William	
John A. MCFEETERS	1848		115	MCFEETERS, John	(GAR) Co. K. 6th VT Vols
James MCFEETERS	1851		115	MCFEETERS, James	
Elizabeth MCFEETERS	1841		115	MCFEETERS, Elizabeth	
Valencourt MCFEETERS	1842	1867	115	MCFEETERS, Valencourt	
Benjamin MCFEETERS	1853	1939	115	MCFEETERS, Benjamin	
Ida A. MCFEETERS	1857		115	MCFEETERS, Ida A.	
			115		
William MCFEETERS	1843	1918	115	REGAN, Ella	(See William McFeeters Family)
Ella REGAN McFeeters	1856	1913	115	MCFEETERS, William	
			115		
Robert MCLEOD	1840	1921	115	THOMPSON, Georgie E.	
Georgie E. THOMPSON McLeod	1866	1944	115	MCLEOD, Robert	
			115		
Barney MALONE	1842	1925	115	HUNTER, Flora A.	
Flora A. HUNTER Malone	1843	1911	115	MALONE, Barney	
Margaret MALONE	1837	1920	115	MALONE, Margaret	
			115		
William M. KILLAM	1826	1906	115	MOODY, Sarah E.	
Sarah E. MOODY Killam	1825	1879	115	KILLAM, William M.	
Sarah KILLAM	1851	1873	115	KILLAM, Sarah	
			115		
Charles P. HOGAN	1843	1915	115	MAYNARD, Thirza	(GAR) Co. E. 7th Rgt Vt Vols
Thirza MAYNARD Hogan	1847	1926	115	HOGAN, Charles P.	
			115		
James SMALLEY	84 Years	07-21-1873	115	MACFARLAND, Susan	
Susan MACFARLAND Smalley	75 Years	07-11-1879	115	SMALLEY, James	
			115		
Clayton M. STUFFLEBEAM	1853	1924	115	SHANNON, Florence C.	
Florence C. SHANNON Stufflebeam	1857	1937	115	STUFFLEBEAM, Clayton M.	
			115		
George W. MAYNARD	08-07-1840	02-27-1911	115	MCCONNELL, Susan A.	
Susan A. MCCONNELL Maynard	04-27-1853	11-20-1936	115	MAYNARD, George W.	
			115		
William ERWIN	1809	1881	115	MCMEEKIN, Matty E.	

NAME	POB	DOB/AGE	DOD	CEM	SPOUSE/INDEX	INSCRIPTION
Matty E. MCMEEKIN Erwin		1817	1894	115	ERWIN, William	
William J. ERWIN		13 Years	05-20-1874	115	ERWIN, William	Their Children
James ERWIN		1833	1905	115	ERWIN, James	
David ERWIN		1853	1934	115	ERWIN, David	
Lucy J. ERWIN		1855	1943	115	ERWIN, Lucy J.	
Annie ERWIN		1857		115	ERWIN, Annie	
William J. ERWIN		1861	1874	115	ERWIN, William J.	
				115		
David ERWIN		1853	1934	115	SANBORN, Margaret I.	
Margaret I. SANBORN Erwin		1849	1914	115	ERWIN, David	
				115		
Isaac GIBBS		1842	1911	115	KIRLEY, Catherine	
Catherine KIRLEY Gibbs		1837	1914	115	GIBBS, Isaac	

Sheldon Union Cemetery (Rice Hill) In Northeast Part of Town Just Off Route 78, Sheldon, Vermont

NAME	POB	DOB/AGE	DOD	CEM	SPOUSE/INDEX	INSCRIPTION
Judson D. SMITH		63Y 8M	07-15-1906	116	ERWIN, Mary M.	
Mary M. ERWIN Smith		28Y 7M	03-07-1875	116	SMITH, Judson D.	
				116		
Thomas ERWIN		80 Years	04-24-1886	116	GILBART, Eliza	
Eliza GILBART Erwin		65 Years	06-21-1893	116	ERWIN, Thomas	
				116		
Mary Ann TODD		84 Years	04-28-1866	116	TODD, Mary Ann	
				116		
John ERWIN		86 Years	06-05-1871	116	ERWIN, Jane	
Jane _____ ERWIN		83 Years	07-17-1870	116	ERWIN, John	
				116		
Maria ERWIN Spear		67 Years	11-26-1894	116	SPEAR, Noah	(Noah is buried elsewhere in this burial ground)
				116	ERWIN, Maria	
				116		
James REILEY		64 Years	04-28-1856	116	REILEY, Mary	
Mary _____ REILEY		74Y 9M	08-22-1869	116	REILEY, James	
Mary Ann REILEY		17Y5M4D	02-07-1847	116	REILEY, Mary Ann	D/O James REILEY & Mary
				116		
Malinda RILEY Bradley		58Y8M14D	02-07-1884	116	BRADLEY, C. S.	(NOI C.S. Bradley)
				116	RILEY, Malinda	
				116		
John REGAN		85 Years	09-19-1887	116	REGAN, Margery	
Margery _____ REGAN		81 Years	06-20-1895	116	REGAN, John	
William John REGAN		6 Months	05-13-1851	116	REGAN, William John	Son of John Regan & Margery
				116		

Name	Born/Age	Died	Page	Index Name	Notes
William REGAN	1817	1893	116	ERWIN, Mary Ann	
Mary Ann ERWIN Regan	1824	1881	116	REGAN, William	
			116		
Edwin A. BARNES	38Y 8M	01-02-1875	116	BARNES, Edwin A.	(NOI spouse 'H')
			116		
Jonathan RICE	08-27-1810	03-31-1895	116	RICE, Zoe	
			116	ERWIN, Sarah	
Zoe _____ RICE	08-14-1809	12-17-1851	116	RICE, Jonathan	
Sarah ERWIN Rice	12-14-1818	07-01-1899	116	RICE, Jonathan	
			116		
James MCCLUER	87Y8M21D	03-31-1865	116	MCCLUER, Rebecca	
Rebecca _____ MCCLUER	69 Years	03-27-1850	116	MCCLUER, James	
			116		
William KELLEY	4 Weeks	02-24-1845	116	KELLEY, William	S/O James KELLEY & Matilda
			116	KELLEY, James	
			116	KELLEY, Matilda	
			116		
Nathaniel MCLURE	76 Years	03-28-1893	116	MCLURE, Amaretta	
Amaretta _____ MCLURE	72 Years	07-06-1889	116	MCLURE, Nathaniel	(Nee Mitchell per other source)
			116		
Noah SPEAR	83Y 11M	10-11-1907	116	SPEAR, Noah	
			116		
Mary _____ KENNEDY	60 Years	03-08-1885	116	KENNEDY, Martin	(NOI Martin Kennedy)
			116	KENNEDY, Mary	
			116		
James DOOLIN	02-01-1858	09-20-1914	116	JOHNSON, Dell	
Dell JOHNSON Doolin	10-05-1863	06-25-1919	116	DOOLIN, James	
			116		
Robert A. REGAN	1848	1927	116	SMITH, Abbie F.	
Abbie F. SMITH Regan	1853	1915	116	REGAN, Robert A.	
			116		
William Henry DUNTON	1854	1933	116	MCFEETERS, Ida A.	
Ida A. MCFEETERS Dunton	1857	1934	116	DUNTON, William Henry	
			116		
J. W. ERWIN	1839	1920	116	ERWIN, J. W.	Son Of Ralph ERWIN & Jane
			116		
J. B. ERWIN	1848	1926	116	ERWIN, Eliza Ann	
Eliza Ann _____ ERWIN	01-04-1854	12-19-1912	116	ERWIN, J. B.	
			116		
William J. ERWIN	24Y6M5D	11-21-1858	116	ERWIN, William J.	Son Of Ralph ERWIN & Jane
			116		
Ralph ERWIN	85 Years	05-27-1884	116	RILEY, Jane	
Jane RILEY Erwin	82 Years	04-06-1893	116	ERWIN, Ralph	

Sheldon Poor Farm Cemetery, Sheldon, Vermont. Poor Farm Road

NAME	POB	DOB/AGE	DOD	CEM	SPOUSE/INDEX	INSCRIPTION
Elizabeth O'BRINE		07-15-1808	07-26-1892	129	O'BRINE, Elizabeth	Born In Ireland. Died at Sheldon, Vt.
				129		
				129		
Elizabeth MCGEE		1850	1922	129	MCGEE, Elizabeth	
				129		
Elizabeth HURLEY		1849	1936	129	HURLEY, Elizabeth	
				129		
Thomas LYNCH		1864	1936	129	LYNCH, Thomas	
				129		
M. MCAULIFF		1837	1915	129	MCAULIFF, M.	
John DULLAHAN		1868	1936	129	DULLAHAN, John	
				129		
Catherine KELLEY		1863	1936	129	KELLEY, Catherine	
				129		
James STEWART		1850	1919	129	STEWART, James	
				129		
Joseph DELANEY		1850	1919	129	DELANEY, Joseph	
				129		
Mary HOAGE		1844	1914	129	HOAGE, Mary	
				129		
Terene MCNALLY		1832	1912	129	MCNALLY, Terene	(Probably Terence but clearly reads 'Terene'.)
				129		
				129		
Patrick BRADY			04-20-1912	129	BRADY, Patrick	An American Soldier. (American Flag at grave-NOI age @ death)
				129		
				129		
Stiles MCMULLEN		1797	1904	129	MCMULLEN, Stiles	
				129		
William LEE		1827	1905	129	LEE, William	
				129		
Jane DONOVAN		1849	1905	129	DONOVAN, Jane	
				129		
William H. BROWN		1877	1905	129	BROWN, William H.	
				129		
Sidney SMITH		1820	1908	129	SMITH, Sidney	
				129		
James SULLIVAN		1852	1906	129	SULLIVAN, James	
				129		
Jerry LYONS		1818	1905	129	LYONS, Jerry	
				129		

James KELLEY	1821	1909	129 129	KELLEY, James	
George COLEMAN	1870	1930	129 129	COLEMAN, George	
Edward CLARK	1833	1926	129 129	CLARK, Edward	
James FIELD	1843	1902	129 129	FIELD, James	
John FROST	1877	1927	129 129	FROST, John	
Patrick GARRY	1849	1902	129 129	GARRY, Patrick	
David MURPHY	1861	1901	129 129	MURPHY, David	
Joshua PATRICK	1828	1901	129 129	PATRICK, Joshua	
David MATTHEWS	1867	1927	129 129	MATTHEWS, David	
George MILES	1859	1926	129 129	MILES, George	
John DURACK	1876	1926	129 129	DURACK, John	
Michael HANLEY	1831	1903	129 129	HANLEY, Michael	
Harrison FOX	1831	1901	129 129	FOX, Harrison	
Uriah HAGGANS	1842	1901	129 129	HAGGANS, Uriah	
William HAGGANS	1836	1901	129 129	HAGGANS, William	
Dewey MURPHY		1901	129 129	MURPHY, Dewey	(NOI Age at death or DOB)
Mary MURPHY	1877	1899	129 129	MURPHY, Mary	
Charles GAFENY	1831	1896	129 129	GAFENY, Charles	
Mary Jane REYNOLDS	1850	1895	129 129	REYNOLDS, Mary Jane	
William FARLEY		1891	129 129	FARLEY, William	(NOI Age at death or DOB)
Mary MURPHY		1893	129 129	MURPHY, Mary	(NOI Age at death or DOB)
Fred LOYD	1843	1898	129 129	LOYD, Fred	
Patrick MARIGAN	1824	1898	129	MARIGAN, Patrick	

				129		
Mariah COLLINS		1837	1897	129	COLLINS, Mariah	
				129		
John SWENOR		1815	1890	129	SWENOR, John	
				129		
Henry MCGEE		1830	1892	129	MCGEE, Henry	
				129		
Margaret LYONS		1814	1892	129	LYONS, Margaret	
				129		
William SWANTON			1894	129	SWANTON, William	(NOI Age at death or DOB)
				129		
John MARSHALL		1814	1894	129	MARSHALL, John	
				129		
John COWLEY		1830	1894	129	COWLEY, John	
				129		
Frank COBURN		1869	1946	129	COBURN, Frank	
				129		
William FARNHAM		1824	1894	129	FARNHAM, William	
				129		
William LINCH		1819	1894	129	LINCH, William	
				129		
Martha A. RICHARDSON		1840	1894	129	RICHARDSON, Martha A.	
				129		
Arthur MOFFATT		1866	1950	129	MOFFATT, Arthur	

St. Genevieve Cemetery, Shoreham, Vermont. Just Off Route 22A.

NAME	POB	DOB/AGE	DOD	CEM	SPOUSE/INDEX	INSCRIPTION
Eugene LEONARD	Co. Cork	1845	1921	072	_____, Mary	Born In County Cork
Mary _____ LEONARD	Co. Cork	1849	1931	072	LEONARD, Eugene	Born In County Cork
				072		
Hannah LEONARD	Co. Cork	27 Years	01-10-1869	072	LEONARD, Hannah	Daughter of Owen and Ellen
				072		Leonard. A Native of Co. Cork
				072		
Owen LEONARD	Co. Cork	09-05-1805	08-18-1893	072	O'CONELL, Ellen	Born In County Cork, Ireland
Ellen O'CONNELL Leonard	Co. Cork	10-20-1812	04-27-1889	072	LEONARD, Owen	Born In County Cork, Ireland
				072		
Johannah LEONARD	Co. Cork	1842	1869	072	LEONARD, Johannah	Born In County Cork, Ireland
				072		
Katherine LEONARD Mackin	Co. Cork	1833	1910	072	MACKIN, Mr.	Born In County Cork, Ireland
				072	LEONARD, Katherine	(NOI Mr. Mackin)
				072		

Name	Origin	Born	Died	Plot	Index	Notes
Michael O'KEEFE	Co. Cork	1850	1895	072	O'KEEFE, Michael	Born In County Cork, Ireland
				072		
William SULLIVAN		1845	1921	072	LEONARD, Ellen	
Ellen LEONARD Sullivan		1847	1911	072	SULLIVAN, William	
				072		
Dennis F. MACAULEY		1855	1920	072	CARROLL, Mary Jane	
Mary Jane CARROLL Macauley		1858	1923	072	MACAULEY, Dennis F.	
				072		
Lewis HANFIELD		01-12-1847	07-27-1925	072	BURKE, Mary E.	
Mary E. BURKE Hanfield		01-12-1853	02-22-1893	072	HANFIELD, Lewis	
				072		
Thomas DUDLEY		36 Years	09-11-1893	072	DUDLEY, Thomas	
				072		
Ellen _____ CONDON		87 Years	06-12-1890	072	CONDON, Michael	(NOI Michael Condon)
				072	_____, Ellen	
				072		
Terry CONDON		1791	1888	072	_____, Elizabeth F.	
Elizabeth F. _____ CONDON		1793	1858	072	CONDON, Terry	
Elizabeth CONDON		1838	1893	072	CONDON, Elizabeth	
Mary CONDON Rooney		1833	1909	073	ROONEY, Mr.	(NOI Mr. Rooney)
				072	CONDON, Mary	
				072		
Patrick J. MEEHAN		1849	1918	072	GORMAN, Bridget	
Bridget GORMAN Meehan		1856	1937	072	MEEHAN, Patrick J.	
				072		
Patrick GRIMES	Co. Kings	11-06-1836	08-16-1933	072	SCANLON, Mary	Born In Kings (Offaly) County, Ireland
				072		
Mary SCANLON Grimes	Co. Waterford	08-18-1834	05-26-1898	072	GRIMES, Patrick	Born In Waterford County, Ireland. Died in Shoreham(VT)
				072		
				072		
Thomas CARTY		1846	1916	072	MCCARRAGHER, Mary A.	
Mary A. MCCARRAGHER Carty		1854	1938	072	CARTY, Thomas	
				072		
Simon CARTY		1813	1905	072	CARTY, Simon	
				072		
Michael BURKE		1825	1898	072	WHITE, Bridget	
Bridget WHITE Burke		1825	1898	072	BURKE, Michael	
				072		
Michael ROURKE		34 Years	02-18-1886	072	ROURKE, Michael	(Spouse First Initial "M")
				072		
Catherine CONORS Rourke	Co. Cork	75 Years	11-02-1883	072	ROURKE, Patrick	Born In Parish "Megelia"
				072	CONORS, Catherine	(Mogeely), Co. Cork, Ireland.
				072		(NOI Patrick ROURKE on this
				072		stone but see O'Rourke plot
				072		following)

Name	Born	Died	Code	Index	Notes
			072		
John O'ROURKE	1845	1915	072	CAMPBELL, Catherine	
Catherine CAMPBELL O'Rourke	1855	1936	072	O'ROURKE, John	
Patrick O'ROURKE	1815	1901	072	O'ROURKE, Patrick	
Catherine CONNERS	1808	1883	072	CONNERS, Catherine	
Ellen C. WELSH	1836	1863	072	WELSH, Ellen C.	
Ellen WELCH	1867		072	WELCH, Ellen	
Patrick O'ROURKE	1839	1904	072	O'ROURKE, Patrick	
			072		
Patrick MULLALY	1844	1893	072	_____, Mary J.	
Catherine CAMPBELL O'Rourke	1855	1936	072	MULLALY, Patrick	
			072		
John J. LEONARD	1852	1903	072	BASHAW, Harriett	
Harriett BASHAW Leonard	1861	1936	072	LEONARD, John J.	
			072		
John S. LEONARD	74 Years	06-12-1899	072	_____, Catherine	
Catherine _____ LEONARD	90 Years	06-11-1932	072	LEONARD, John S.	
			072		
James A. LEONARD	27Y 8M	03-07-1881	072	LEONARD, James A.	
			072		
Lewis HAMMOND	1828	1887	072	HARTIGAN, Catherine	
Catherine HARTIGAN Hammond	1827	1906	072	HAMMOND, Lewis	
			072		
John HARTIGAN	59 Years	09-10-1893	072	HARTIGAN, John	
			072		
Michael HARTIGAN	1831	1892	072	HARTIGAN, Michael	(Does not indicate if Michael Hartigan & Mary Ann Hartigan were man and wife)
Mary Ann HARTIGAN	1840	1904	072	HARTIGAN, Mary Ann	
			072		
			072		
Patrick W. HARTIGAN	63 Years	08-04-1893	072	QUIRK, Bridget	
Bridget QUIRK Hartigan			072	HARTIGAN, Patrick	(Possibly QUINN. Deteriorated)
			072		
Maurice SULLIVAN	1824	1910	072	RIVET, Genevieve	
Genevieve RIVET Sullivan	1830	1911	072	SULLIVAN, Maurice	
			072		
J. J. MCGINTY	1849	1910	072	COOK, Ellen	
Ellen COOK McGinty	1850	1919	072	MCGINTY, J. J.	
			072		
Lawrence O'ROURKE	1852	1934	072	MACK, Mary	
Ellen COOK McGinty	1857	1952	072	O'ROURKE, Lawrence	
			072		
John STOKES	1837	1888	072	O'NEIL, Bridget	
Bridget O'NEIL Stokes	1845	1892	072	STOKES, John	

South Hero Village Cemetery, South Hero, Vermont

NAME	POB	DOB/AGE	DOD	CEM	SPOUSE/INDEX	INSCRIPTION
Ann _____ DOUGHERTY		46 Years	12-03-1872	073	DOUGHERTY, Thomas	(NOI Thomas Dougherty)
				073	DOUGHERTY, Ann	
				073		
James DOUGHERTY		1845	1913	073	CLINTON, Margaret	
Margaret CLINTON Dougherty		1845	1910	073	DOUGHERTY, James	
				073		
SGT James CONLIN				073	CONLIN, James	Co. C. 8th VT Inf
James CONLIN		39 Years	07-18-1873	073	CONLIN, Jane	
Jane _____ CONLIN		58 Years	08-27-1904	073	CONLIN, James	
				073		
Eleanor _____ MOONEY		25 Years	01-14-1818	073	MOONEY, S______	IMO, Wife Of S______ Mooney
				073		(NOI S_____ Mooney. Could not
				073		read first name,stone is worn)
				073		
James Franklin MCBRIDE		1849	1915	073	PHELPS, Emma	
Emma PHELPS McBride		1860	1952	073	MCBRIDE, James Franklin	
				073		
Joseph KELLEY		1849	1934	073	KELLY, Joseph	
				073		
Calvin MCBRIDE		56 Years	04-03-1893	073	GORDON, Julia	
Julia GORDON McBride		44 Years	09-03-1883	073	MCBRIDE, Calvin	
				073		
Thomas MCBRIDE		72 Years	04-13-1868	073	BLACK, Susan	
Susan BLACK McBride		73 Years	12-12-1877	073	MCBRIDE, Thomas	
				073		
James BUTLER		19 Years	09-21-1919	073	BUTLER, James	
				073		
Angeline BUTLER		20 Years	10-21-1831	073	BUTLER, Angeline	
				073		
Mary B. KINNEY Mooney		66 Years	04-08-1868	073	MOONEY, Hercules	(NOI Hercules Mooney)
				073	KINNEY, Mary B.	
				073		
Lucy Ann _____ COLEMAN		42Y 6M	10-17-1866	073	COLEMAN, H.H.	(NOI H. H. Coleman)
				073	COLEMAN, Lucy Ann	
				073		
Mary Jane MOONEY		23Y 6M	10-19-1855	073	MOONEY, Mary Jane	D/O H & M.B. Mooney
				073		
Joseph BUTLER		1740	1824	073	BUTLER, Joseph	SGT, Continental Line, Revo-
				073		lutionary War
				073		

NAME	POB	DOB/AGE	DOD	CEM	SPOUSE/INDEX	INSCRIPTION
James MCGRAW		1851	1926	073	MAHONEY, Eliza	
Eliza MAHONEY McGraw		1856	1935	073	MCGRAW, James	

St. Mary's Cemetery, Springfield, VT - On Vermont Route 106, West of Village on N. Springfield Road

NAME	POB	DOB/AGE	DOD	CEM	SPOUSE/INDEX	INSCRIPTION
John BRADY		1830	1910	074	O'ROURKE, Mary	
Mary O'ROURKE Brady		1851	1916	074	BRADY, John	
				074		
John MAHER		1859	1949	074	MOORE, Ellen	
Ellen MOORE Maher		1862	1903	074	MAHER, John	
				074		
Michael J. SMITH		02-08-1853	09-17-1917	074	MCCUE, Jane B.	
Jane B. MCCUE Smith		04-04-1844	02-05-1920	074	SMITH, Michael J.	
				074		
Cornelius CAIN		79Y 6M	12-02-1925	074	MURPHY, Ellen	
Ellen MURPHY Cain		74 Years	03-30-1919	074	CAIN, Cornelius	
				074		
Joseph FERGUSON		03-26-1836	02-26-1913	074	DOUGLAS, Sarah	
Sarah DOUGLAS Ferguson		10-21-1837	01-18-1917	074	FERGUSON, Joseph	
				074		
Thomas CARMODY		1836	1906	074	SPILLANE, Catherine	(GAR) Co. E. 16th Rgt VT Vols
Catherine SPILLANE Carmody		1835	1916	074	CARMODY, Thomas	
James CARMODY		1856	1910	074	CARMODY, James	
Edward CARMODY		1857	1910	074	CARMODY, Edward	
				074		
John WRIGHT		1855	1936	074	FERGUSON, Mary	
Mary FERGUSON Wright		1861	1939	074	WRIGHT, John	
				074		
Daniel F. DONNELLY		1854	1937	074	MAHAR, Mary A.	
Mary A. MAHAR Donnelly		1857	1933	074	DONNELLY, Daniel F.	
				074		
William O'BRIEN		1852	1923	074	CONLIN, Margaret	
Margaret CONLIN O'Brien		1852	1923	074	O'BRIEN, William	
				074		
James BROMLEY		1850	1920	074	DILLON, Matilda	
Matilda DILLON Bromley		1843	1918	074	BROMLEY, James	
				074		
Patrick RILEY		1835	1912	074	MEEHAN, Kate	
Kate MEEHAN Riley		1842	1920	074	RILEY, Patrick	
				074		
Thomas DWYER		73 Years	02-08-1911	074	RILEY, Mary	

NAME	POB	DOB/AGE	DOD	CEM	SPOUSE/INDEX	INSCRIPTION
Mary RILEY Dwyer		72Y 11M	06-17-1913	074	DWYER, Thomas	
				074		
Thomas SEXTON		1839	1910	074	SEXTON, Ann	(GAR) Co. I 3rd Reg. VT Vols
Ann B. _____ SEXTON		1836	1918	074	SEXTON, Thomas	
Michael FARRELL		1852	1924	074	FARRELL, Nellie	
Nellie K. _____ FARRELL		1861	1952	074	FARRELL, Michael	

St. Catherine Cemetery - Charleston, NH (Springfield, Vt Catholics Buried here Prior to late 1900's)

NAME	POB	DOB/AGE	DOD	CEM	SPOUSE/INDEX	INSCRIPTION
Patrick AHERN		1828	1909	901	COFFEY, Mary	
Mary COFFEY Ahern		1838	1925	901	AHERN, Patrick	
				901		
Patrick O'LEARY		1839	1915	901	COFFEY, Elizabeth	
Elizabeth COFFEY O'Leary		1842	1915	901	O'LEARY, Patrick	
				901		
James MULLIGAN		1834	1913	901	_________, Maria	Company D, 7 Rgt, Mass Vol Inf
Maria ________ MULLIGAN		1837	1909	901	MULLIGAN, James	
				901		
Patrick MORONEY	Co. Clare	68 Years	10-18-1886	901	COLLINS, Margaret	Born in Feakle, Co. Clare, Ire
Margaret COLLINS Moroney		56 Years	04-02-1884	901	MORONEY, Patrick	
				901		
Thomas DEVINE		78 Years	05-03-1925	901	MEEHAN, Bridget	
Bridget MEEHAN Devine		74 Years	06-08-1905	901	DEVINE, Thomas	
				901		
Michael CORBITT		1828	1876	901	TORPEY, Margaret	
Margaret TORPEY Corbitt		1830	1903	901	CORBITT, Michael	
Bridget TORPEY		1792	1882	901	TORPEY, Bridget	
				901		
Samuel RICHARDSON		06-11-1839	03-21-1917	901	O'DONNELL, Martha F.	
Martha O'DONNELL Richardson		11-30-1843	08-08-1903	901	RICHARDSON, Samuel	
				901		
Catherine MCCABE		67 Years	12-09-1905	901	MCCABE, Catherine	
				901		
Sylvester JUDD		1842	1924	901	CARROLL, Margaret M.	
Margaret M. CARROLL Judd		1834	1909	901	JUDD, Sylvester	
				901		
Mary RUANE McMahon	Co. Galway	80 Years	10-28-1874	901	MCMAHON, William	Native Of Corrigh Connaught Co Galway. NOI William McMahon
				901	RUANE, Mary	
				901		
Sarah _______ MARONEY		80 Years	05-17-1893	901	MARONEY, Michael	(NOI William Maroney)
				901	_____, Sarah	

Name	Place	Born/Age	Died	Code	Relation	Notes
				901		
Sylvester JUDD		1842	1924	901	CARROLL, Margaret M.	
				901		
Timothy O'LEARY		78Y3M10D	04-06-1879	901	DWYER, Nancy	
Nancy DWYER O'Leary		74Y10M10D	03-27-1901	901	O'LEARY, Timothy	
				901		
Patrick O'CONNOR		86 Years	11-08-1924	901	BUTLER, Mary	
Mary BUTLER O'Connor		43 Years	02-25-1893	901	O'CONNOR, Patrick	
				901		
William DAVIS		1842	1916	901	CUDMORE, Annie	
Annie CUDMORE Davis		1843	1908	901	DAVIS, William	
				901		
Patrick CONDON		08-04-1843	09-13-1896	901	HANNING, Ellen	
Ellen HANNING Condon		05-02-1849	07-03-1897	901	CONDON, Patrick	
				901		
John SULLIVAN		1844	1896	901	O'BRIEN, Ellen M.	
Ellen M. O'BRIEN Sullivan		1855	1940	901	SULLIVAN, John	
				901		
Thomas MARONEY		58 Years	02-08-1895	901	MCMAHON, Catherine	
Catherine MCMAHON Maroney		40 Years	08-01-1884	901	MARONEY, Thomas	
				901		
Margaret _____ O'BRIEN	Co. Cork	70 Years	02-18-1887	901	O'BRIEN, Thomas	Born In County Cork, Ireland
				901	_____, Margaret	(NOI Thomas O'Brien)
				901		
John DONOVAN		45 Years	06-25-1875	901	FEELEY, Mary	
				901		
Mary FEELEY Donovan		1838	1911	901	DONOVAN, John	
				901		
John CONDON		61 Years	04-05-1907	901	______, Catherine	
Catherine ______ CONDON		68 Years	06-21-1914	901	CONDON, John	
				901		
Michael MEANY		72 Years	09-13-1900	901	______, Anastasia	
Anastasia ______ MEANY		40 Years	12-11-1880	901	MEANEY, Michael	
				901		
Mary HANNING Ferguson	Co. Cork	71 Years	01-09-1890	901	FERGUSON, John	Born In County Cork, Ireland
				901	HANNING, Mary	NOI John Ferguson
				901		
Bridget _____ BARTLEY		60 Years	12-05-1892	901	BARTLEY, Owen	(NOI Owen Bartley)
				901	_____, Bridget	
				901		
John DESMOND		79 Years	06-25-1905	901	MAHANEY, Catherine	
Catherine MAHANEY Desmond		60 Years	03-23-1889	901	DESMOND, John	
				901		
Michael GALVIN			04-01-1894	901	MADIGAN, Bridget	
Bridget MADIGAN Galvin			02-06-1910	901	GALVIN, Michael	

			901		
John GALWAY	03-31-1848	03-11-1920	901	CODY, Bridget	
Bridget CODY Galway	01-15-1840	04-15-1898	901	GALWAY, John	
			901		
John LOONEY	77Y10M8D	04-21-1905	901	______, Mary	
Mary ______ LOONEY	52 Years	11-13-1885	901	LOONEY, John	
			901		
Thomas MALONEY	75 Years	09-04-1912	901	HOLLOREN, Nora	
Nora HOLLOREN Maloney	70 Years	01-10-1904	901	MALONEY, Thomas	
			901		
Ellen GRIFFIN	78 Years	01-18-1892	901	GRIFFIN, Ellen	
			901		
Cornelius CALLAHAN	1820	1908	901	______, Bridget	
Bridget ______ CALLAHAN	1825	1912	901	CALLAHAN, Cornelius	
			901		
Jane DUGAN	1832	1918	901	DUGAN, Jane	
			901		
Mary DUGAN Wilmoth	74Y4M	11-23-1894	901	WILMOTH, Daniel	(NOI Daniel Wilmoth)
			901	DUGAN, Mary	
			901		
William CARRIGAN	1826	1896	901	TULLY, Margaret	
Margaret TULLY Carrigan	1837	1920	901	CARRIGAN, William	
			901		
John LYNCH	76 Years	12-16-1915	901	______, Mary	
Mary ______ LYNCH	65 Years	10-07-1903	901	LYNCH, John	
			901		
Margaret A. LYNCH Hanlon	26Y8M12D	06-30-1893	901	HANLON, John	(Probably Native Born (1866)-- Inscription is worth repeating "Amiable, she won all; Intelli gent, she charmed all; fervent she loved all and dead she saddened all.")
			901	LYNCH, Margaret A.	
			901		
			901		
			901		
			901		
Joseph T. DORSEY	78Y5M19D	11-01-1923	901	______, Hannah	
Hannah ____ DORSEY	72Y7M15D	12-09-1925	901	DORSEY, Joseph T.	
			901		
John RYAN	69 Years	05-10-1889	901	LARKIN, Anna	
Anna LARKIN Ryan	68 Years	10-11-1887	901	RYAN, John	
			901		
Mary HARTNETT	90 Years	10-09-1899	901	HARTNETT, Mary	
			901		
Nellie F. HARTNETT Morris	2-26-1859	09-14-1905	901	MORRIS, James	NOI James Morris
			901	HARTNETT, Nellie F.	
			901		
Henry DUGAN	03-19-1829	11-01-1901	901	MORRIS, Bridget	
Bridget MORRIS Dugan	03-09-1829	11-05-1884	901	DUGAN, Henry	

				901		
Patrick MORRIS		70 Years	05-20-1892	901	_____, Ann	
Ann _____ MORRIS		68 Years	08-27-1898	901	MORRIS, Patrick	
				901		
William DILLON		03-05-1834	04-25-1892	901	_____, Ellen	
Ellen _____ DILLON		04-23-1833	03-04-1923	901	DILLON, William	
				901		
Timothy MCMAHAN	Co. Clare	67 Years	08-13-1878	901	_____, Mary	Native Of County Clare, Ire
Mary _____ MCMAHAN	Co. Clare	70 Years	10-08-1883	901	MCMAHAN, Timothy	Born In The County Clare, Ire
				901		
John CARMODY	Ireland	1833	1892	901	CORBETT, Mary	Born In Ireland
				901		(GAR) Co. A., 3rd VT Vol Inf
Mary CORBETT Carmody	Ireland	1830	1922	901	CARMODY, John	Born In Ireland
John CARMODY			10-10-1865	901	CARMODY, John	Son Of John & Mary Carmody of
				901		Springfield, VT
				901		
Edmund BROWN		73 Years	05-02-1928	901	DONOVAN, Julia E.	
Julia E. DONOVAN Brown		48 Years	5-5-1901	901	BROWN, Edmund	
				901		
Bridget REYNOLDS Carroll		8-25-1824	02-15-1898	901	CARROLL, Patrick	NOI Patrick Carroll
				901	REYNOLDS, Bridget	
				901		
John CARLEY		1836	1893	901	_____, Julia	
Julia _____ CARLEY		1850	1923	901	CARLEY, John	
				901		
Daniel FINNIGAN		90 Years	06-18-1888	901	MCNABOE, Elizabeth	
Elizabeth MCNABOE Finnigan		79Y7M29D	06-29-1893	901	FINNIGAN, Daniel	
				901		
James LYONS		75 Years	04-21-1891	901	_____, Catherine	
Catherine _____ LYONS		69 Years	10-20-1902	901	LYONS, James	
				901		
Patrick SHEEDY	Co. Clare	75 Years	11-20-1883	901	CONNOR, Bridget	Natives Of County Clare,Ire.
Bridget CONNOR Sheedy	Co. Clare	49 Years	07-06-1875	901	LYONS, James	Natives Of County Clare,Ire.
				901		
David TYLER		1832	1897	901	MCNAMARA, Bridget	
Bridget MCNAMARA Tyler		1837	1918	901	TYLER, David	
				901		
John DOLAN		94 Years	07-08-1893	901	FORD, Bridget	(NOI Bridget Ford)
				901	DOLAN, John	
				901		
Michael J. HEARNS		1826	1913	901	_____, Winifred D.	
Winifred D. _____ HEARNS		1837	1921	901	HEARNS, Michael J.	
				901		
Richard O'BRIEN		46 Years	01-22-1881	901	_____, Joanna	
Joanna _____ O'BRIEN		54 Years	09-30-1894	901	O'BRIEN, Richard	

NAME	POB	DOB/AGE	DOD	CEM	SPOUSE/INDEX	INSCRIPTION
				901		
John CAHALANE		85 Years	08-16-1916	901	_____, Mary	
Mary _____ CAHALANE		77 Years	05-23-1917	901	CAHALANE, John	
				901		
John FITZGERALD	Co. Kerry	1853	1932	901	_____, Ellen	Born In Tralee, Ireland
Ellen_____ FITZGERALD		1856	1940	901	FITZGERALD, John	
				901		
Thomas FLYNN	Ireland			901	FLYNN, Thomas	
				901		
Bridget _____ SULLIVAN		59Y4M	08-08-1883	901	SULLIVAN, T.O.	(NOI T.O. Sullivan) (GAR)
				901	_____, Bridget	
				901		
John HANNING	Co. Cork	80 Years	09-05-1903	901	CALLAHAN, Ellen	Born In Liscarrol, Co. Cork
Ellen CALLAHAN Hanning	Co. Cork	68 Years	01-14-1895	901	HANNING, John	Born In Liscarrol, Co. Cork

Holy Cross Cemetery, Fairfax Street, St. Albans, Vermont

NAME	POB	DOB/AGE	DOD	CEM	SPOUSE/INDEX	INSCRIPTION
John BROWN		04-10-1835	05-01-1887	075	PRESTON, Bridget	
Bridget PRESTON Brown	Co. Tipperary		07-20-1871	075	BROWN, John	Native of Nenagh, County
				075		Tipperary, Ireland
				075		
James LEAHY	Co. Waterford	30Y 6M	04-27-1876	075	LEAHY, James	Native of Tallou Bridge,
				075		County Waterford, Ireland
				075		
Thomas LEAHY		69Y 6M	05-15-1891	075	FAHY, Allice	
Allice FAHY Leahy			05-09-1885	075	LEAHY, Thomas	
Tommi LEAHY		1Y 7M	12-14-1863	075	LEAHY, Thomas	
				075		
Patrick J. CULLEN	Co. Dublin	27 Years	01-06-1883	075	CULLEN, Patrick J.	Native of Woodside, County
				075		Dublin, Ireland
				075		
Patrick CLARKE	Co. Monaghan	11-01-1808	10-03-1865	075	DUFFEY, Sarah	Native Of Co. Monaghan, Ire.
Sarah DUFFEY Clarke		12-20-1806	09-07-1877	075	CLARKE, Patrick	
				075		
Michael CORBETT		58Y 1M	10-28-1887	075	WELCH, Mary	
				075	SEXTON, Jane	
Mary WELCH Corbett	Co. Tipperary	33 Years	09-21-1878	075	CORBETT, Michael	Native Of Co. Tipperary, Ire.
Jane SEXTON Corbett	Co. Clare	46 Years	05-14-1876	075	CORBETT, Michael	Native Of Co. Clare, Ireland
				075		
Thomas CUNNINGHAM	Co. Armagh	40 Years	08-08-1880	075	CUNNINGHAM, Thomas	Native of Crossmaglen, County
				075		Armagh, Ireland

				075		
Thomas CUNNINGHAM		10-28-1856	09-04-1878	075	CUNNINGHAM, Thomas	Born In Brandon, Vermont.
				075		Erected by his father, Thomas
				075		CUNNINGHAM, a native of Co.
				075		Armagh, Ireland
				075		
Patrick SULLIVAN		60 Years	02-15-1891	075	ROGERS, Margaret	
Margaret ROGERS Sullivan		06-17-1826	05-18-1888	075	SULLIVAN, Patrick	Born In Ireland.Dau of Anthony
				075		& Rosa ROGERS
				075		
Mary HASTINGS McMahon	Co. Clare	57 Years	02-23-1874	075	MCMAHON, Michael	Native of Cannon Island, Co.
				075	HASTINGS, Mary	Clare, Ireland (NOI Michael
				075		MCMAHON)
				075		
John KENNEDY	Co. Tipperary	04-15-1804	02-15-1891	075	O'BRIEN, Mary	A Native of Co. Tipperary, Ire
Mary O'BRIEN Kennedy	Co. Tipperary	11-05-1806	05-14-1889	075	KENNEDY, John	A Native of Co. Tipperary, Ire
James KENNEDY		38Y 8M	01-07-1883	075	KENNEDY, James	Son Of John & Mary KENNEDY
				075		
George JOHNSON	Co. Louth	09-06-1782	01-25-1864	075	JOHNSON, George	Native of Mansfieldtown, Co.
				075		Louth, Ireland. Died at
				075		Georgia, Vermont
				075		
Thomas MURPHY	Co. Kilkenny	75 Years	04-01-1926	075	MURPHY, Thomas	Born In Co. Kilkenny, Ireland
				075		
Mary MCGOUGH Agnew	Co. Monaghan	67 Years	03-23-1874	075	AGNEW, James	A Native of Augill (Could not
				075	MCGOUGH, Mary	find this town in references)
				075		County Monaghan, Ireland
				075		(NOI James AGNEW)
				075		
Patrick BARNES	Co. Limerick		07-03-1876	075	CARROLL, Mary	Both Natives of Co. Limerick,
Mary CARROLL Barnes	Co. Limerick		04-17-1883	075	BARNES, Patrick	Ireland (Erected by their son
				075		Michael)
				075		
Charles MACKIN	Ireland	1832	1926	075	MURPHY, Mary	Ireland
Mary MURPHY Mackin	Co. Louth	40 Years	10-06-1876	075	MACKIN, Charles	Born In Thornfield, Co. Louth,
				075	MURPHY, Peter	Ireland. Dau of Peter & Mary
				075		MURPHY
				075		
Timothy SEXTON	Co. Clare	41 Years	12-05-1887	075	_____, M.J.	Born In Co. Clare, Ireland
				075		(NOI On Spouse "M.J.")
				075		
Thomas DULING		1835	1909	075	_____, Anne M.	
Anne N._____ DULING		1838	1901	075	DULING, Thomas	
				075		
John BRENNAN		73 Years	05-05-1889	075	MURPHY, Margaret	

Name	Age / Born	Died	Plot	Index Name	Notes
Margaret MURPHY Brennan	45 Years	02-27-1877	075	BRENNAN, John	
Anne Jane BRENNAN	27Y 2M	04-07-1879	075	BRENNAN, Anne Jane	Daughter of John and Margaret
			075		BRENNAN
E.H. TWIGG	29 Years	01-06-1879	075	TWIGG, E.H.	(Same Plot as BRENNANs)
			075		
Barney KELLEY	11-20-1847	03-09-1915	075	MCSORLEY, Nancy A.	
Nancy A. MCSORLEY Kelley	31Y 6M 7D	04-21-1879	075	KELLEY, Barney	
			075		
Mary FITZGERALD Greene	1852	1892	075	GREENE, M.D.	(NOI M.D. GREENE)
			075	FITZGERALD, Mary	
Thomas FITZGERALD	29 Years	11-21-1878	075	FITZGERALD, Thomas	
			075		
James KELLEY	74 Years	10-23-1870	075	______, Catharine	
Catharine ______ KELLEY	70 Years	11-08-1878	075	KELLEY, James	(Catharine nee CUNNINGHAM per
James KELLEY	65 Years	04-09-1899	075	KELLEY, James	researcher's family records)
Ann KELLEY	84 Years	08-21-1917	075	KELLEY, Ann	
Elizabeth KELLEY Sands	69 Years	11-12-1911	075	SANDS, Patrick	
Patrick SANDS	55 Years	10-10-1896	075	KELLEY, Elizabeth	
			075		
Michael MOORE	58 Years	08-10-1862	075	IRWIN, Elizabeth	
Elizabeth IRWIN Moore	36 Years	06-13-1848	075	MOORE, Michael	
Elizabeth MOORE	18 Years	05-27-1860	075	MOORE, Elizabeth	
Margaret MOORE	22 Years	07-17-1869	075	MOORE, Margaret	
Ellen MOORE	04-06-1840	11-07-1912	075	MOORE, Ellen	
			075		
William IRWIN	75 Years	11-21-1876	075	IRWIN, William	(Did not indicate if husband
Mary IRWIN	92 Years	06-26-1880	075	IRWIN, Mary	wife but probably is so)
			075		
Thomas J. KEENAN	02-02-1832	11-28-1891	075	MOORE, Mary A.	
Mary A. MOORE Keenan	04-04-1835	01-20-1893	075	KEENAN, Thomas J.	
			075		
John O'NEILL	03-25-1823	03-16-1908	075	______, Elizabeth	
Elizabeth ______ O'NEILL	08-29-1828	08-08-1910	075	O'NEILL, John	
Daniel O'NEILL	81 Years	12-09-1878	075	DUFEY, Sara	
Sara DUFEY O'Neill	51 Years	05-05-1848	075	O'NEILL, Daniel	(NOI Daniel O'NEILL)
			075		(NOI Daniel O'NEILL)
Mary Ann O'NEILL	19Y11M22D	08-26-1851	075	O'NEILL, Mary Ann	
			075		
Catherine O'NEILL	1Y3M22D	01-18-1850	075	O'NEILL, Catherine	Child of John O`NEILL &
			075	MURPHY, Catherine	Catherine MURPHY
			075		
Elizabeth O'NEILL	7Y10M1D	06-10-1864	075	O'NEILL, Elizabeth	Child of John O`Neill &
			075	AIKEN, Sidney	Sidney AIKEN
			075		
William D. O'NEILL	3Y3M26D	06-20-1864	075	O'NEILL, William D.	Child of John O`Neill &

Name	Birth/Age	Death	Code	Index Name	Notes
			075		Sidney AIKEN
			075		
James QUINN	72 Years	04-27-1881	075	QUINN, James	
John QUINN	24 Years	08-07-1859	075	QUINN, John	Son Of James & Sarah QUINN
Daniel QUINN	72 Years	08-21-1875	075	QUINN, Daniel	Son Of James & Sarah QUINN
Charles QUINN	1853	1923	075	WARD, Elizabeth C.	
Elizabeth C. WARD Quinn	1867	----	075	QUINN, Charles	
			075		
Edward MCGEE	1848	1902	075	MURPHY, Alice	
Alice MURPHY McGee	1851	1930	075	MCGEE, Edward	
			075		
Richard F. LEAHY	1856	1929	075	CLARKE, Margaret	
			075	DOYLE, Mary E.	
Margaret CLARKE Leahy	1855	1891	075	LEAHY, Richard F.	
Mary E. DOYLE Leahy	1867	1948	075	LEAHY, Richard F.	
			075		
Harriet ______ COWLEY	44Y7M19D	1-16-1884	075	COWLEY, William	(NOI William COWLEY)
			075	_____, Harriett	
			075		
Anna BURKE	1855	1916	075	BURKE, Anna	
			075		
Robert SMITH	70Y 8M	12-21-1893	075	_____, Ellen	
Ellen _____ SMITH	72Y 9M	11-08-1891	075	SMITH, Robert	
			075		
William J. MCDONNELL	1852	1914	075	GARVEY, Rose	
Rose GARVEY Smith	1856	1899	075	MCDONNELL, William J.	
			075		
Patrick HASSETT	12-15-1856	03-08-1900	075	O'NEILL, Margaret	
Margaret O'NEILL Hassett	10-08-1858	01-04-1935	075	HASSETT, Patrick	
			075		
Peter MCGUE	37 Years	08-27-1880	075	MCGUE, Peter	
			075		
Mrs. Ann MURPHY	6-1823	12-1896	075	MURPHY, Mrs. Ann	Of Worcester, Mass
			075		
Peter MCENANY	58 Years	11-24-1894	075	MCENANY, Peter	
Laura MCENANY	1843	1881	075	MCENANY, Laura	
			075		
Mary A. MANAHAN Dufresne	1846	1928	075	DUFRESNE, Wilfred M.	
Wilfred M. DUFRESNE	1848	1921	075	MANAHAN, Mary A.	
			075		
John T. SMITH	1845	1911	075	SEXTON, Jane	
Jane SEXTON Smith	1847	1924	075	SMITH, John T.	
			075		
Elizabeth KENNEDY O'Laughlin	6-20-1838	02-03-1894	075	O'LAUGHLIN, John	(NOI John O'Laughlin)
			075	KENNEDY, Elizabeth	

Name	Birthplace	Age / Born	Died	Code	Spouse	Notes
				075		
Patrick MULLEN	Ireland	62 Years	1844	075	MCNIECE, Sarah	Died In Ireland
Sarah MCNIECE Mullen		80 Years	11-24-1877	075	MULLEN, Patrick	Died In St.Albans
				075		
Arthur MULLEN		1821	1903	075	DUNLEAVY, Mary	
Mary DUNLEAVY Mullen		1830	----	075	MULLEN, Arthur	
				075		
John F. SULLIVAN		47Y 1M 17D	08-10-1897	075	SULLIVAN, John F.	
				075		
James D. HOGAN	Co. Tyrone	44 Years	03-21-1899	075	MURPHY, Mary A.	(Native of Co. Tyrone, Ireland
				075		per researchers family record)
Mary A. MURPHY Hogan		83 Years	04-16-1937	075	HOGAN, James	Stone reads: Mary Comstock
				075		1854-1937 (2nd marriage)
				075		
Mathew LAWLOR		1837	1906	075	WOODS, Mary	
Mary WOODS Lawlor		1830	1900	075	LAWLOR, Mathew	
Edward FITZGERALD		1822	1850	075	FITZGERALD, Edward	
				075		
Thomas O'CONNELL		1834	1904	075	MULLEN, Theresa	
Theresa MULLEN O'Connell		1834	191_	075	O'CONNELL, Thomas	
				075		
Patrick RAGAN		1835	1907	075	AGNEW, Catharine	
Catharine AGNEW Ragan		36 Years	11-10-1876	075	RAGAN, Patrick	
				075		
John G. DRISCOLL		56 Years	02-27-1880	075	RYAN, Ellen	This Monument Has Been Erected
Ellen RYAN Driscoll		08-01-1831	04-29-1914	075	DRISCOLL, John G.	By Catharine DRISCOLL IMO Her
Catharine DRISCOLL		61 Years	01-09-1872	075	DRISCOLL, Catharine	Her Beloved Brother, William
William DRISCOLL		31 Years	09-09-1864	075	DRISCOLL, William	
				075		
Patrick SULLIVAN		64 Years	05-31-1875	075	----, Ellen	(NOI Ellen)
				075		
William CORBETT	Co. Kilkenny	73 Years	12-09-1868	075	CANFALL, Catharine	Natives Of Co. Kilkenny, Ire
Catharine CANFALL Corbett	Co. Kilkenny	47 Years	12-12-1849	075	CORBETT, William	Natives Of Co. Kilkenny, Ire
				075		
Daniel SULLIVAN		1808	1887	075	_____, Mary	Erec By Mary SULLIVAN WELCHMAN
Mary ____ SULLIVAN		1809	1877	075	SULLIVAN, Daniel	
Hannah SULLIVAN		1845	1869	075	SULLIVAN, Hannah	Dau. Of Daniel & Mary SULLIVAN
				075		
James CONNERS		65 Years	03-01-1872	075	_____, Mary	
Mary ____ CONNERS		78 Years	08-04-1889	075	CONNERS, James	
Catherine CONNERS Sullivan		23 Years	11-28-1862	075	SULLIVAN, Patrick	(NOI Patrick SULLIVAN)
				075	CONNERS, Catherine	
John CONNERS		1847	1912	075	_____, Rose F.	
Rose F. _____ CONNERS		1849	1918	075	CONNERS, John	
Joanna CONNERS		39 Years	09-23-1893	075	CONNERS, Joanna	

			075		
Owen TWIGG	08-15-1812	10-18-1904	075	CROWLEY, Catherine	
Catherine CROWLEY Twigg	06-01-1820	09-21-1884	075	TWIGG, Owen	
			075		
Edward MEHAN	50 Years	05-31-1885	075	_____, E.	
			075		
Bridget MCKENNEY Cunningham	89 Years	04-06-1886	075	CUNNINGHAM, John	(NOI John CUNNINGHAM)
			075	MCKENNEY, Bridget	
Ella CUNNINGHAM	42 Years	01-08-1880	075	CUNNINGHAM, Ella	
			075		
Terence ROGERS	52 Years	03-05-1852	075	SLOAN, Ann	
Ann SLOAN ROGERS	89 Years	05-29-1891	075	ROGERS, Terence	
John S. ROGERS	58 Years	09-15-1904	075	______, Rose S.	
Rose S. ___ ROGERS	68 Years	09-14-1919	075	ROGERS, John S.	
			075		
John NEENAN	75 Years	10-24-1897	075	SEXTON, Catherine	(NOI Catherine SEXTON)
			075	NEENAN, John	
			075		
Philip DELLIGAN	1812	1901	075	GALLAGHER, Fannie	
Fannie GALLAGHER Delligan	1813	1893	075	DELLIGAN, Philip	
			075		
Ann ____ WALL	46 Years	12-27-1880	075	WALL, John	(NOI John WALL)
			075	_____, Ann	
			075		
James HAND	49 Years	05-25-1877	075	HAND, James	
			075		
Bernard MCENANY	42 Years	08-25-1882	075	BOYLAN, Bridget	
Bridget BOYLAN McEnany	28Y 3M	05-03-1881	075	MCENANY, Bernard	
			075		
James SHEEHEY	06-10-1852	09-05-1903	075	DONOVAN, Margaret	
Margaret DONOVAN Sheehey	07-21-1850	05-23-1922	075	SHEEHEY, James	
			075		
Matthew HENNESSY	1817	1871	075	PHELAN, Mary	
Mary PHELAN Hennessy	1819	1912	075	HENNESSY, Matthew	
Mary MULHALL Phelan	1795	1882	075	MULHALL, Mary	
			075		
Walter Henry LYON	1844	1926	075	ST. JOHNS, Julie	
Julie E. St. J. Fairfield	1846	1913	075	LYON, Walter Henry	
Lewis C. FAIRFIELD	1846	1875	075	FAIRFIELD, Lewis C.	
			075		
Patrick O'CONNELL	1838	1904	075	_______, Margaret	
Margaret ___ O'CONNELL	1843	_____	075	O'CONNELL, Patrick	
			075		
Bernard DELLIGAN	1849	1937	075	MCDONALD, Mary Ann	
Mary Ann MCDONALD DELLIGAN	1859	1940	075	DELLIGAN, Bernard	

Name	Born	Died	Code	Index	Notes
			075		
Michael D. POWERS	09-29-1837	03-27-1914	075	MULVANEY, Bridget	
Bridget MULVANEY POWERS	02-11-1836	03-26-1914	075	POWERS, Michael D.	
			075		
Patrick DOOLING	82 Years	09-17-1877	075	SWANTON, Ann	
Ann SWANTON Dooling	92 Years	10-22-1889	075	DOOLING, Patrick	
			075		
Jeremiah SULLIVAN	1825	1879	075	MURPHY, Catherine	
Catherine MURPHY Sullivan	1826	1905	075	SULLIVAN, Jeremiah	
			075		
Thomas M. TIERNEY	06-21-1843	08-14-1890	075	ANDREWS, Mary A.	
Mary A. ANDREWS Tierney	03-28-1853	06-25-1925	075	TIERNEY, Thomas M.	
			075		
Joseph TIERNEY	07-03-1833	01-01-1885	075	TIERNEY, Joseph	
			075		
John ANDREWS	09-11-1816	05-04-1888	075	TIFFANY, Sarah	
Sarah TIFFANY Andrews	07-30-1817	09-04-1893	075	ANDREWS, John	
			075		
Jeremiah FITZGERALD	1802	1896	075	SULLIVAN, Susan	
Susan SULLIVAN Fitzgerald	55 Years	02-18-1874	075	FITZGERALD, Jeremiah	
John J. TANGNEY	25Y 1M	12-25-1870	075	TANGNEY, John J.	
			075		
Bernard FINNEGAN	44 Years	06-29-1862	075	TIERNEY, Mary	(GAR-Co. C, 5th Rgt, VtVols)
Mary TIERNEY Fennegan	57 Years	10-17-1872	075	FINNEGAN, Bernard	
Peter FINNEGAN	1848	1918	075	FINNEGAN, Peter	
Eleanor FINNEGAN	1842	1920	075	FINNEGAN, Eleanor	
M. Anne FINNEGAN	1855	1888	075	FINNEGAN, M. Anne	
Catherine FINNEGAN	1850	1893	075	FINNEGAN, Catherine	
Eliza L. FINNEGAN	1852	1893	075	FINNEGAN, Eliza L.	
James B. FINNEGAN	1846	1922	075	FINNEGAN, James B.	
Annie FAILEY Finnegan	1873	1954	075	FAILEY, Annie	
			075		
Peter CROWLEY	68 Years	12-01-1894	075	HENNESSEY, Catherine	
Catherine HENNESSEY Crowley	70 Years	06-04-1899	075	CROWLEY, Peter	
			075		
John MCPECK	06-15-1852	01-10-1917	075	MCPECK, John	Born In Scotland
			075		
Michael SULLIVAN	1846	1883	075	MCSORLEY, Mary J.	
Mary J. MCSORLEY Sullivan	1850	1909	075	SULLIVAN, Michael	
Mary MCSORLEY	1808	1892	075	MCSORLEY, Mary	
			075		
John DANIELS	71 Years	10-23-1915	075	JONES, Catherine	
Catherine JONES Daniels	41 Years	01-25-1886	075	DANIELS, John	
			075		
Thomas B. KENNEDY	1838	1903	075	HOWRIGAN, Catherine	(GAR) Capt, Co. K,6th Vt. Vols

Name	Born/Age	Died	Code	Index	Notes
Catherine HOWRIGAN Kennedy	1848	1935	075	KENNEDY, Thomas B.	
Thomas KENNEDY	1795	1875	075	CAVENAUGH, Mary	
Mary CAVENAUGH	1805	1906	075	KENNEDY, Thomas	
			075		
Philip GILLIN	67Y6M19D	10-23-1883	075	GILLIN, Philip	
			075		
Mary L. CLEARY	1830	1910	075	CLEARY, Mary L.	
			075		
Thomas FLOOD	36Y2M11D	11-06-1883	075	FLOOD, Thomas	
			075		
Peter KIRK	57 Years	03-21-1884	075	______, Julia	
Julia _____ KIRK	62 Years	10-31-1890	075	KIRK, Peter	
			075		
Michael DRISCOLL	57 Years	03-21-1884	075	MCCARTY, Johanna	
Johanna MCCARTY Driscoll	62 Years	10-31-1890	075	DRISCOLL, Michael	
			075		
Simon MALONEY	03-04-1818	07-11-1882	075	______, Bridget	
Bridget ____ MALONEY	03-02-1827	09-02-1895	075	MALONEY, Simon	
			075		
Edward DOYLE	1841	1890	075	MULLEN, Ann	
Ann MULLEN Doyle	1833	1904	075	DOYLE, Edward	
Celia DOYLE Lawlor	1833	1904	075	DOYLE, Celia	(NOI Mr. LAWLOR)
			075		
Edward KELLEY	1853	1917	075	DANIELS, Mary	
Mary DANIELS	1887	1938	075	KELLEY, Edward	
			075		
William F. HOEY	1848	1904	075	LAFFEY, Mary A.	
Mary A. LAFFEY Hoey	1856	1887	075	HOEY, William F.	
			075		
Andrew DOUGHERTY	63 Years	05-04-1881	075	O'BRINE, Mary	
Mary O'BRINE Dougherty	----	04-15-1900	075	DOUGHERTY, Andrew	(No age or DOB indicated)
			075		
MURPHY (ENDOWED)			075	MURPHY, Endowed	Mother, Father, Mary, John, Helena, Wife Of J.H.STROUBE Jr (No surnames/DOB/DOD indicated on marker)
Mother MURPHY			075		
Father MURPHY			075		
Mary MURPHY			075		
John MURPHY			075		
Helena MURPHY Stroube			075	STROUBE, J. H. Jr.	(NOI J. H. STROUBE Jr.)
			075		
Allice KELLEY Delehanty	36Y 11M 6D	09-06-1873	075	DELEHANTY, Michael	By Her Affectionate Children
			075	KELLEY, Allice	(NOI Michael DELEHANTY)
			075		
Patrick RYAN	02-04-1832	09-30-1915	075	KENNEDY, Ellen	
			075	FLINN, Ellen	
Ellen KENNEDY Ryan	05-18-1834	10-17-1873	075	RYAN, Patrick	

Ellen FLINN Kennedy	04-13-1837	03-19-1917	075	RYAN, Patrick	
			075		
Thomas FLYNN	1845	1911	075	______, Louisa	
Louisa _____ FLYNN	1845	1890	075	FLYNN, Thomas	
			075		
Edward DULLAHAN	42 Years	03-20-1886	075	DULLAHAN, Edward	
			075		
John DULING	30 Years	03-24-1865	075	EUSTACE, Mary	Died In Baltimore, Maryland
			075		(GAR) Co. F, 8 Reg Vt Vols
Mary EUSTACE Duling	83 Years	03-22-1922	075	DULING, John	
Thomas EUSTACE	87 Years	08-09-1886	075	EUSTACE, Thomas	
			075		
Hugh FERRY	02-02-1806	04-05-1880	075	_____, Nancy	(NOI Nancy FERRY)
			075	FERRY, Hugh	
Patrick FARRY	6Y 10M	10-05-1849	075	FARRY, Patrick	Son Of Hugh And Nancy FARRY
			075		
Honora MCCARTHY	77 Years	07-15-1894	075	MCCARTHY, Honora	
			075		
Cornelius DONAHOE	26Y 10M	01-02-1883	075	DONAHOE, Cornelius	Son Of Owen and Mary DONAHOE
			075	DONAHOE, Owen	
			075		
Michael GRIFFIN			075	COLLINS, Annie	(NOI DOB/DOD Michael GRIFFIN)
Annie COLLINS Griffin	48Y 10M	05-13-1899	075	GRIFFIN, Michael	(Same Stone Michael GRIFFIN)
			075		
John BUTLER	88 Years	10-19-1898	075	MCMAHON, Elizabeth	
Elizabeth MCMAHON Butler	55 Years	01-18-1877	075	BUTLER, John	
			075		
Frank X. CLARKE	1839	1886	075	MALONEY, Catherine	
Catherine MALONEY Clarke	1853	1918	075	CLARKE, Frank X.	
Ellen CLARKE Ryan	12-25-1837	03-11-1853	075	RYAN, Ellen	Dau. Of Patrick & Sarah CLARKE
			075		(Possibly Patrick and Sarah
			075		DUFFEY CLARKE in foregoing
			075		text (NOI Mr. RYAN)
			075		
Ellen O'NEIL Carroll	67Y 5M	09-18-1883	075	CARROLL, John	(NOI John CARROLL)
			075	O'NEILL, Ellen	
			075		
Charles O'NEIL	96 Years	10-26-1876	075	KEENAN, Catherine	
Catherine KEENAN O'neil	86 Years	04-05-1880	075	O'NEIL, Charles	
			075		
John FOLLON	76 Years	05-10-1856	075	FOLLON, John	
			075		
Thomas FOLLAN			075	FOLLAN, Thomas	(GAR) Co E. 12th Vt Vols (NOI
			075		DOB/DOD)
Kate FALLON	1859	1942	075	FALLON, Kate	

			075		
John MOLLOY	1821	1848	075	MURREY, Katherine	
Katherine MURREY Molloy	1824	1847	075	MOLLOY, John	
			075		
James MCDONOUGH	74 Years	02-12-1874	075	______, Ann	
Ann ______ MCDONOUGH	90 Years	01-31-1888	075	MCDONOUGH, James	
			075		
Michael MCDONOUGH	39 Years	12-09-1846	075	MCDONOUGH, Michael	
			075		
Rosanna MCDONOUGH	03-09-181_	02-18-1853	075	MCDONOUGH, Rosanna	Daughter Of Michael & Bridget MCDONOUGH
			075	MCDONOUGH, Michael	
			075		
Elizabeth CALLAN Ward	1845	1906	075	WARD, Richard	(NOI Richard WARD)
			075	CALLAN, Elizabeth	
Elizabeth CALLAN Ward	02-21-1846	03-27-1906	075	WARD, Richard	(NOI Richard WARD)(Duplicate)
			075	CALLAN, Elizabeth	
Catharine CALLAN McArty	23Y 4M 21D	11-19-1865	075	MCARTY, D.	(NOI D. McArty)
			075	CALLAN, Catherine	
Michael CALLAN	79Y 7M	12-05-1886	075	CALLAN, Michael	
Mary CALLAN	80 Years	06-16-1902	075	CALLAN, Mary	
Patrick CALLAN	12 Years	08-12-1863	075	CALLAN, Patrick	
Anastasia CALLAN Rooney	39Y 2M 27D	07-07-1887	075	ROONEY, John	(NOI John ROONEY)
			075	CALLAN, Anastasia	
			075		
Catherine O'NEIL	1833	1926	075	O'NEIL, Catherine	
			075		
John MCQUEENEY	1833	1916	075	MCQUEENEY, John	
Ella MCQUEENEY	1863	1925	075	MCQUEENEY, Ella	
			075		
Mary COWLEY	38 Years	08-31-1872	075	COWLEY, John	(NOI John COWLEY)
			075	_____, Mary	
			075		
Moses MOLLOY	1825	1906	075	MCDONOUGH, Mary E.	
Mary E. MCDONOUGH Molloy	1837	1910	075	MOLLOY, Moses	
			075		
John RAGIN	42 Years	05-10-1853	075	RAGIN, John	Erected By His Wife(NOI Wife)
			075		
Cornelius RAGIN	71 Years	07-23-1864	075	RAGIN, Cornelius	
			075		
William SCANLON	1843	1923	075	______, Margaret	
Margaret ___ SCANLON	1851	1934	075	SCANLON, William	
			075		
Mrs. Bridget DOCKRY	69 Years	10-13-1877	075	DOCKRY, Mrs. Bridget	(NOI Mr. DOCKRY)
			075		
John AUSTIN Family			075	AUSTIN, John	(Memorial Only - NOI)

				075		
Dennis FLANAGAN		1829	1890	075	____, Mary	
				075	JOHNSON, Rose	
Mary ____ FLANAGAN		1828	1870	075	FLANAGAN, Dennis	
Rose JOHNSON Flanagan		1831	1911	075	FLANAGAN, Dennis	
Sarah A. FLANAGAN Lord		1858	1890	075	LORD, Dayton E.	(NOI Dayton E. LORD)
				075	FLANAGAN, Sarah A.	
				075		
John SKELLY		71 Years	10-30-1871	075	GRADY, Bridget	
Bridget GRADY Skelly		83 Years	05-15-1902	075	SKELLY, John	
				075		
Mary STEERE		1843	1885	075	STEERE, Mary	
				075		
James CARROLL		1834	1912	075	CARROLL, James	
				075		
Mary DOYLE		1825	1905	075	DOYLE, Mary	
				075		
Maria DISLEY		1840	1912	075	DISLEY, Maria	
				075		
Catharine KELLY Murphy	Co. Armagh	88 Years	10-20-1869	075	MURPHY, Owen	A Native of the Co. Armagh,
				075	KELLY, Catherine	Parish of Mullabane (Forkhill
				075		Parish) Erected By Her Son
				075		Thomas. (NOI Owen Murphy)
				075		
Sarah MURPHY Ragin	Co. Armagh	65Y 10M	03-18-1901	075	RAGIN, Dennis	(NOI Dennis RAGIN)
				075	MURPHY, Sarah	
				075		
Sarah A. MURPHY Murphy		05-04-1853	12-05-1926	075	MURPHY, John H.	(NOI John H. MURPHY but he is
				075	MURPHY, Sarah A.	interred - no marker. Both
				075		were surnamed MURPHY and were
				075		cousins to the 3rd degree per
				075		researcher's family records)
				075		
Mary Ann MURPHY Murphy		25 Years	10-08-1858	075	MURPHY, Thomas	(NOI Thomas MURPHY but he is
				075		interred - no marker-son of
				075		Owen & Catherine KELLY MURPHY)
				075	MURPHY, Mary Ann	(Both were surnamed MURPHY but
				075		found no evidence of blood re-
				075		lationship - She was daughter
				075		of Hugh MURPHY and Catherine
				075		QUINN - researchers family)
				075		
Owen H. MURPHY		1879	1918	075	DECELL, Beaulah	(NOI Beaulah Decell)
				075		
Owen A. MURPHY		05-02-1832	01-11-1881	075	MURPHY, Owen A.	

				075		
Catharine E. MURPHY Curten		05-10-1841	10-18-1865	075	CURTEN, John	(NOI John CURTEN)
				075	MURPHY, Catherine E.	
				075		
Peter H. MURPHY		05-18-1840	04-15-1863	075	MURPHY, Peter H.	
				075		
Catharine QUINN Murphy	Co. Down	12-02-1810	08-15-1884	075	MURPHY, Hugh	(NOI Hugh MURPHY-This Person
				075	QUINN, Catherine	also married to Artubon HOYT
				075		who was buried at Fairfield)
				075		(Hugh Murphy died Fairfield in
				075		1841 & has no memorial)
Bertie D. RICE		1873	1965	075	HOGAN, Sadie L.	
Sadie L. HOGAN Rice		1880	1966	075	RICE, Bertie D.	
				075		
Patrick MCCARTY		82 Years	09-09-1893	075	MCCARTY, Patrick	
Mary Ann MCCARTY		25 Years	02-10-1875	075	MCCARTY, Mary Ann	
Patrick MCCARTY JR.		26 Years	11-13-1879	075	MCCARTY Patrick Jr.	
				075		
James MCEVOY		1845	01-16-1869	075	MCEVOY, James	Son Of John MCEVOY & Ann
				075	MCEVOY, John	LAWLOR. Born in Phillipsburg,
				075	LAWLOR, Ann	PQ (Province of Quebec),
				075		Died at St. Albans, Age 24 Yr
				075		
Julia STAPLETON Lawlor	Co. Tipperary	1797	11-26-1863	075	LAWLOR, John	NOI John LAWLOR)
				075	STAPLETON, Julia	
				075		
William MCEVOY		42 Years	09-30-1904	075	MCEVOY, William	
				075		
Julia LAWLOR		80	09-19-1909	075	LAWLOR, Julia	
				075		
Mary LAWLOR		73	01-11-1896	075	LAWLOR, Mary	
				075		
Ellen LAWLOR		58	02-13-1886	075	LAWLOR, Ellen	
				075		
Ann MCEVOY		82 Years	07-20-1901	075	MCEVOY, Ann	
				075		
John WHITE		77Y 3M	06-01-1877	075	NOLAN, Mary	
Mary NOLAN White		73 Years	07-29-1883	075	WHITE, John	
Maggie WHITE		20Y 3M	01-20-1862	075	WHITE, Maggie	
Bridget WHITE		34Y 5M	07-15-1871	075	WHITE, Bridget	
Thomas WHITE		27Y 5M	01-15-1871	075	WHITE, Thomas	
George WHITE		21Y 6M	06-27-1878	075	WHITE, George	
				075		
Cornelius REGAN JR.		76 Years	03-08-1902	075	MCAULIFFE, Mary A.	(NOI Mary A. MCAULIFFE)
				075	REGAN, Cornelius Jr.	

Michael REGAN	23 Years	10-02-1872	075	REGAN, Michael	
			075		
William CROSS	1840	1921	075	CROSS, William	
			075		
James CAHILL	82 Years	08-19-1859	075	NOLAN, Mary	
Mary _____ CAHILL	90 Years	06-26-1892	075	WHITE, John	
William CAHILL	8Y 3M	12-25-1840	075	CAHILL, William	
			075		
James MCIVER	1836	1907	075	MCIVER, James	
Margaret E. MURPHY McIver	1872	1910	075	MURPHY, Margaret E.	
Mary Elizabeth MCKEVER		01-20-1876	075	MCKEVER, Mary Elizabeth	Dau of James & Ellen McKEVER
Sarah A. MURPHY	1832	1906	075	MURPHY, Sarah A.	
Isabel MCIVER Carroll	1838	1884	075	CARROLL, James	(NOI James CARROLL)
			075	MCIVER, Isabel	
Felix MCIVER	77 Years	11-14-1884	075	_____, Margaret	
Margaret _____ MCIVER	60 Years	12-11-1878	075	MCIVER, Felix	
			075		
Henry WOODS	1849	1895	075	WOODS, Henry	
Henry WOODS	1819	1887	075	_______, Julia	
Julia ____ WOODS	1821	1882	075	WOODS, Henry	
			075		
John MCCARTY		1882	075	CROWLEY, Hannah	
Hannah CROWLEY McCarty		1892	075	MCCARTY, John	
Eliza M MCCARTY	15Y 8M	02-17-1874	075	MCCARTY, Eliza M.	
Ellen MCCARTY McQuestion	1852	1889	075	MCCARTY, Ellen	
			075		
William MULLEN	1841	1885	075	O'NEIL, Anna	
Anna O'NEIL Mullen	1842	1872	075	MULLEN, William	
			075		
ATKINSON Family			075	ATKINSON, Family	
William ATKINSON			075	MURPHY, Mary	(NOI On This Family No Dates
Mary MURPHY Atkinson			075	ATKINSON, William	On Marker)
Michael ATKINSON			075	ATKINSON, Michael	
Thomas ATKINSON			075	ATKINSON, Thomas	
Thomas MULLEN			075	MULLEN, Thomas	
Joseph J. MULLEN			075	MULLEN, Joseph J.	
			075		
Charles BAIRD	09-22-1820	09-09-1900	075	DUYEA, Julia	
Julia DUYEA Baird	10-07-1847	05-19-1913	075	BAIRD, Charles	
			075		
Joseph YOUNG	1844	1911	075	MCCANSE, Mary I.	
Mary I. MCCANSE Young	1846	1928	075	YOUNG, Joseph	
			075		
Jeremiah CRONEN	75 Years	11-08-1870	075	______, Mary	
Mary ____ CRONEN	57 Years	01-05-1856	075	CRONEN, Jeremiah	

Name	Place	Born/Age	Died	Plot	Index	Notes
				075		
Mary ____ CRONNEN			01-06-1853	075	CRONNEN, Mary	This stone in same plot as Jeremiah CRONEN - not sure if two Marys are same person)
				075		
				075		
				075		
Thomas HUDON		46 Years	05-07-1885	075	HUDON, Thomas	Erected By His Friends
				075		
Mary J. ___ BURSEY		84 Years	02-11-1886	075	BURSEY, Henry	(NOI Henry BURSEY)
				075	_____, Mary	
				075		
Patrick CLARY		52Y 8M	11-19-1883	075	CLARY, Patrick	
				075		
William H. MAHONEY		1850	1929	075	MCGEE, Katherine	
Katherine MCGEE Mahoney		1865	1923	075	MAHONEY, William H.	
George D. MAHONEY		1846	1870	075	MAHONEY, George D.	
				075		
Cathrine ____ DOYLE			11-12-1875	075	DOYLE, Joseph	(NOI Joseph DOYLE)
				075	_____, Cathrine	
				075		
Kate HENESY Daly	Co. Limerick	47 Years	03-06-1882	075	DALY, John	Native of Killeely, County Limerick, Ire. (NOI John DALY)
				075	HENESY, Kate	
				075		
Ellen WELCH Donelly				075	DONELLY, Peter	NOI Peter DONELLY - Stone partially missing so no dates. Would be 1870-1890)
				075	WELCH, Ellen	
				075		
				075		
Ellen FINN		63 Years	12-14-1912	075	FINN, Ellen	
				075		
Catharine ____ TURNER		58 Years	08-05-1870	075	TURNER, Peter	(NOI Peter TURNER)
				075	_____, Catharine	
				075		
John DOMEY		04-29-1823	06-22-1873	075	DOMEY, John	
				075		
Rosanna ____ BURNS		52 Years	04-16-18__	075	BURNS, Michael	(NOI Michael BURNS-Stone has been repaired. Cement over year of death)
				075	_____, Rosanna	
				075		
				075		
James MCGETTRICK		1852	1913	075	MCGETTRICK, James	
				075		
Nathan A. BUCK		1840	1913	075	CASEY, Bridget	
Bridget CASEY Buck		1844	1892	075	BUCK, Nathan A.	
				075		
Rosa _____ CALLAN		1838	1910	075	CALLAN, Rosa _____	"Mother"
				075		
John DRISCOLL			1907	075	DRISCOLL, John	

Name	Place	Born/Age	Died	Code	Index	Notes
Timothy DRISCOLL		97 Years	04-13-1901	075	DRUM, Bridget	
Bridget DRUM Driscoll		82 Years	04-07-1899	075	DRISCOLL, Timothy	
				075		
Michael C. POWERS		1829	1916	075	FLYNN, Ellen	
Ellen FLYNN Powers		1831	1914	075	POWERS, Michael C.	
Mary DUNN		1850	1928	075	DUNN, Mary	
				075		
Denis DINEEN	Co. Cork	1878	1915	075	DINEEN, Denis	Born Hedgefield, Co. Cork
				075		
John SWEENEY		82 Years	03-04-1889	075	SWEENEY, John	
				075		
Mary CONNERS McGarey		1826	1913	075	CONNERS, Mary	
				075		
Patrick H. MALLOY		1845	1912	075	______, Mary J.	
Mary J. _____ MALLOY		1853	1901	075	MALLOY, Patrick H.	
Mary M. MALLOY		1890	1911	075	MALLOY, Mary	
				075		
Matilda MCDERMOTT Alexander		60 Years	03-07-1904	075	ALEXANDER, Arthur	(NOI Arthur ALEXANDER)
				075	MCDERMOTT, Matilda	
				075		
Ann QUINN Holmes		81 Years	10-11-1895	075	HOLMES, H.	(NOI H. HOLMES)
				075	QUINN, Ann	
				075		
Thomas COLEMAN		1861	1938	075	DOON, Mary	
Mary DOON Coleman		1857	1951	075	COLEMAN, Thomas	
Thomas COLEMAN		1888	1889	075	COLEMAN, Thomas	
Margaret M. COLEMAN		1890	1982	075	COLEMAN, Margaret M.	
Mary E. COLEMAN		1892	1898	075	COLEMAN, Mary E.	
Annie COLEMAN		1894	1990	075	COLEMAN, Annie	
				075		
Alexander MCCONNELL		1856	1926	075	BUTLER, Rosa A.	
Rosa A. BUTLER McConnell		1859	1925	075	MCCONNELL, Alexander	
				075		
Julia M. _____ YOUNG		1835	1900	075	YOUNG, H.	(NOI H. YOUNG)
				075	_____, Julia	
(Mrs) Mary Y. MCCARTHY		1853	1903	075	MCCARTHY, Mrs. Mary Y.	(NOI Mr. MCCARTHY)
				075		
Thomas SEERY		1843	1917	075	GRIFFIN, Ellen	
Ellen GRIFFIN Seery		1845	1919	075	SEERY, Thomas	
Patrick H. SEERY		1879	1899	075	SEERY, Patrick H.	
Catherine D. SEERY		11-24-1875	04-19-1896	075	SEERY, Catherine D.	
				075		
John HURLEY		05-06-1857	03-11-1924	075	_____, Margaret	
Margaret ___ HURLEY		12-25-1866	07-17-1926	075	HURLEY, John	
Mary Catherine HURLEY		02-13-1894	02-17-1894	075	HURLEY, Mary Catherine	Dau of John & Margaret HURLEY

Name	Origin	Born/Age	Died	No.	Index	Notes
				075		
Margaret DACEY Hurley	Co. Cork	74 Years	03-11-1894	075	HURLEY, Patrick	(NOI Patrick HURLEY)
				075	DACEY, Margaret	
				075		
C. E. HURLEY		1849	1911	075	HURLEY, C. E.	
				075		
Joseph WILLETT		1839	1897	075	MCCARTY, Mary	
Mary MCCARTY Willett		1845	1913	075	WILLETT, Joseph	
				075		
Margaret O'BRIEN Andrews		12-15-1846	11-01-1918	075	O'BRIEN, Margaret	(NOI Mr. ANDREWS)
				075		
Julia O'BRIEN Powers		12-10-1821	05-23-1901	075	O'BRIEN, Julia	(NOI Mr. POWERS)
				075		
Jerry C. MCCARTHY		1856	1935	075	BARRY, Julia A.	
Julia A. BARRY McCarthy		1868	1940	075	MCCARTHY, Jerry	
Nealy MCCARTHY		1Y 5M	03-25-1864	075	MCCARTHY, Nealy	
Rosa MCCARTHY		9Y 10M	08-22-1875	075	MCCARTHY, Rosa	
				075		
Cornelius MCCARTHY		82 Years	12-25-1914	075	DORAN, Ann	
Ann DORAN MCCARTHY		66Y10M13D	11-08-1896	075	MCCARTHY, Cornelius	
				075		
Patrick SCANLON		87 Years	10-25-1896	075	DRUM, Mary	
Mary DRUM Scanlon		32 Years	06-04-1853	075	SCANLON, Patrick	
				075		
James SCANLON		66 Years	02-13-1916	075	WARD, Mary	
Mary WARD Scanlon		62 Years	11-15-1915	075	SCANLON, James	
				075		
Michael RYAN		64 Years	10-18-1894	075	O'BRIEN, Mary	To The Memory Of Michael RYAN,
Mary O'BRIEN Ryan		1836	1909	075	RYAN, Michael	This Monument is Erected By
				075		His Loving Wife. May His Soul
				075		Rest In Peace. Amen.
				075		
Julia OWENS McKenney		75 Years	04-15-1891	075	MCKENNEY, Enos	(NOI Enos MCKENNEY)
				075	OWENS, Julia	
Patrick MCKENNEY		42 Years	03-12-1894	075	MCKENNEY, Patrick	
Mary A. MCKENNEY		1860	1914	075	MCKENNEY, Mary A.	
Bridget L. MCKENNEY		1858		075	MCKENNEY, Bridget L.	
				075		
James CAMPBELL		1835		075	MAGNER, Ellen	
Ellen MAGNER Campbell		1841	1915	075	CAMPBELL, James	
				075		
James STEWART		1820	1903	075	O'ROARK, Mary D.	
Mary D. O'ROARK Stewart		1826	1895	075	STEWART, James	
				075		
Henry WALKER		1831	1881	075	O'NEIL, Mary	

Mary O'NEIL Walker	1847	1934	075	WALKER, Henry	
			075		
Edward BRENNAN	1821	1895	075	BAGLEY, Catherine	
Catherine BAGLEY Brennan	1819	1890	075	BRENNAN, Edward	
Anna T. BRENNAN	1858	1931	075	BRENNAN, Anna T.	
Nellie BRENNAN	1862	1945	075	BRENNAN, Nellie	
Rose BRENNAN Abell	1856	1933	075	BRENNAN, Rose	(NOI Mr. ABELL)
Maggie BRENNAN	1861	1898	075	BRENNAN, Maggie	
			075		
J. J. TURNER	43Y 2M	02-04-1890	075	LAPAN, Mary	
Mary LAPAN Turner	75 Years	04-17-1910	075	TURNER, J. J.	
			075		
Mary GROGAN	1805	1896	075	GROGAN, Mary	
			075		
Eliza LAWLOR Taylor	77 Years	09-29-1908	075	LAWLOR, Eliza	
			075		
Peter LITTLE	1846	1932	075	MILES, Mary Ann	
Mary Ann MILES Little	1852	1923	075	LITTLE, Peter	
Peter LITTLE SR.	1850	1890	075	LITTLE, Peter Sr.	
			075		
Michael MCGRATH	08-12-1850	04-25-1889	075	BURKE, Ellen	
Ellen BURKE McGrath	02-20-1856	11-23-1911	075	MCGRATH, Michael	
			075		
Edward RYAN	64 Years	11-16-1888	075	MURPHY, Ann	
Ann MURPHY Ryan	62 Years	02-04-1887	075	RYAN, Edward	
			075		
Charles H. DALY	34Y4M15D	05-07-1889	075	DALY, Charles H.	
			075		
Patrick BURNS	38Y 4M	07-14-1890	075	BRENNAN, Anna	
Anna BRENNAN Burns	72 Years	01-31-1928	075	BURNS, Patrick	
			075		
Nicholas STEWART	1855	1926	075	COLLINS, Mary E.	
Mary E. COLLINS Stewart	1859	1955	075	STEWART, Nicholas	
			075		
Thomas SULLIVAN	56 Years	01-21-1897	075	SULLIVAN, Thomas	
			075		
James J. CARNEY	58Y 3M	12-09-1887	075	MCDONOUGH, Rose	
Rose MCDONOUGH Carney	11-17-1832	11-30-1907	075	CARNEY, James J.	
			075		
Dennis MYNIHAN	1845	1890	075	BUTLER, Jane	(This info was on a MCCONNELL
Jane BUTLER Mynihan	1845	1885	075	MYNIHAN, Dennis	marker. NOI on McConnells
			075		Could be MOYNIHAN, MANAHAN)
Daniel F. SULLIVAN	1852	1939	075	MCCARTHY, Mary Ann	
Mary Ann MCCARTHY Sullivan	1854	1900	075	SULLIVAN, Daniel F.	
			075		

Margaret O'DAY	57 Years	03-06-1916	075	O'DAY, Margaret	
			075		
John SHEEHAN	1830	1906	075	DONOVAN, Mary A.	
Mary A. DONOVAN Sheehan	1838	1906	075	SHEEHAN, John	
			075		
John CARROLL	1826	1896	075	CASEY, Johannah	
Johannah CASEY Carroll	1833	1921	075	CARROLL, John	
Maurice P. CARROLL	1854	1886	075	CARROLL, Maurice P.	
Daniel F. CARROLL	1858	1888	075	CARROLL, Daniel F.	
Edward CARROLL	1859	1900	075	CARROLL, Edward	
Timothy E. CARROLL	1863	1893	075	CARROLL, Timothy E.	
John W. CARROLL	1856	1898	075	________, Jane	
Jane ______ CARROLL	1857	1894	075	CARROLL, John W.	
Hannah CARROLL	1871	1878	075	CARROLL, Hannah	
			075		
John REAGAN	1851	1921	075	KELLY, Elizabeth	
Elizabeth KELLY	1856	1894	075	REAGAN, John	
			075		
Thomas CARROLL	08-28-1815		075	MOSS, Mary	
Mary Moss CARROLL	74 Years	09-26-1891	075	CARROLL, Thomas	
			075		
James KEENAN	1837	1910	075	SMITH, Mary	
Mary SMITH Keenan	05-00-1839	02-04-1906	075	KEENAN, James	
			075		
John MURPHY	54 Years	01-18-1886	075	________, Bridget	
Bridget ______ MURPHY	1829	1914	075	MURPHY, John	
Katie MURPHY	7 Years	04-11-1872	075	MURPHY, Katie	
Sarah MURPHY	11 Months	11-21-1867	075	MURPHY, Sarah	
Eliza MURPHY	2 Years	09-18-1872	075	MURPHY, Eliza	
			075		
Peter H. KEENAN	1828	1906	075	CASEY, Mary Ann	
Mary Ann CASEY Keenan	1833	1903	075	KEENAN, Peter	
			075		
Michael MCCARTY	1836	1908	075	MCCARTY, Michael	(GAR) Co. A., 8th VT Vol
			075		
Michael C. FINN	1855	1937	075	FINN, Michael C.	(Does not indicate if Michael and Margaret were husband and wife)
Margaret E. FINN	1864	1902	075	FINN, Margaret E.	
			075		
			075		
Martin DOYLE	1823	1901	075	MCBRIDE, Rose	
Rose MCBRIDE Doyle	1825	1892	075	DOYLE, Martin	
			075		
Edward KINGSLEY	1850	1931	075	DUFFY, Rose	
			075	DUFFY, Mary	
Rose A. DUFFY Kingsley	1858	1891	075	KINGSLEY, Edward	

Name	Birth	Death	Code	Index	Notes
Mary E. DUFFY Kinglsey	1857	1921	075	KINGSLEY, Edward	
			075		
A. J. SHERLOCK	06-08-1831	03-30-1888	075	SHERLOCK, A. J.	"Dear Husband And Father"
			075		
Michael ROACH	1820	1905	075	HENNESSY, Mary	
Mary HENNESSY Roach	1837	1910	075	ROACH, Michael	
			075		
Thomas O'HEARE	76 Years	07-26-1903	075	FEE, Mary	
Mary FEE O'Heare	71 Years	05-11-1904	075	O'HEARE, Thomas	
James O'HEARE	1854	1923	075	O'HEARE, James	
John B. O'HEARE	1860	1923	075	O'HEARE, John B.	
Patrick O'HEARE	1868	1937	075	O'HEARE, Patrick	
			075		
MCGRATH FAMILY			075	MCGRATH, Family	
Father MCGRATH	1841	1915	075	MCGRATH, Father	
Mother MCGRATH	1842	1919	075	MCGRATH, Mother	
			075		
John SWEENEY	1856	1903	075	PRESTON, Julia	
Julia PRESTON Sweeney	1858	1928	075	SWEENEY, John	
			075		
James H. ROONEY	1836	1917	075	CALLAN, Mary	
Mary CALLAN Rooney	1850	1921	075	ROONEY, James H.	
			075		
James Knox Polk DULING	09-04-1844	10-05-1904	075	DULING, James Knox Polk	
			075		
Thomas CAHILL	03-31-1820	09-21-1897	075	______, Eliza	
Eliza ____ CAHILL	10-28-1828	04-02-1903	075	CAHILL, Thomas	
James H. CAHILL	07-22-1852		075	WEBLEY, Lillian O.	
Lillian O. WEBLEY Cahill	08-06-1883	09-29-1913	075	CAHILL, James H.	
			075		
James M. FRAWLEY	55 Years	04-13-1903	075	FRAWLEY, James M.	(GAR) Co. D., 5th VT Inf
			075		
Michael F. SULLIVAN	1854	1933	075	MCENANY, Agnes C.	
Agnes C. MCENANY Sullivan	1863	1937	075	SULLIVAN, Michael F.	
			075		
Laurence HANLEY	1821	1897	075	______, Ellen	
Ellen ____ HANLEY	1831	1903	075	HANLEY, Laurence	
			075		
Thomas PRIOR	1836	1908	075	DAGNAN, Elizabeth	
Elizabeth DAGNAN Prior	1838	1913	075	PRIOR, Thomas	
			075		
Patrick REAGAN	1832	1895	075	______, Ellen	
Ellen ____ REAGAN	1834	1921	075	REAGAN, Patrick	
			075		
Owen MARRON	75 Years	10-10-1928	075	WHITE, Elizabeth	

Name	Birth	Death	Code	Index Name	Notes
Elizabeth WHITE Marron	41 Years	03-27-1895	075	MARRON, Owen	
			075		
Catherine ____ JENNINGS	1823	1899	075	JENNINGS, James	(NOI James JENNINGS)
			075	_____, Catherine	
			075		
James BURNS	1836	1910	075	MCMAHON, Elizabeth	
Elizabeth MCMAHON Burns	1838	1892	075	BURNS, James	
			075		
John BUTLER	1845	1925	075	ANDREWS, Sarah A.	
Sarah A. ANDREWS Butler	1850	1923	075	BUTLER, John	
			075		
Thomas MILES	1831	1908	075	________, Hannah	
Hannah _____ MILES	1833	1904	075	MILES, Thomas	
			075		
Michael BARNES	1852	1920	075	________, Nellie	
Nellie _____ BARNES	1861	1951	075	BARNES, Michael	
			075		
Thomas O'NEIL	06-25-1848	11-25-1910	075	FOLEY, Mary	
Mary FOLEY O'Neil	04-06-1834	05-05-1934	075	O'NEIL, Thomas	
			075		
Rosana A. ROGERS	04-25-1842	11-14-1906	075	ROGERS, Rosana A.	(Children of Anthony & Mary B. ROGERS)
Jane ROGERS	05-24-1844	06-12-1905	075	ROGERS, Jane	
Catherine ROGERS McKenzie	07-12-1834	04-22-1906	075	MCKENZIE, Horace	(NOI Horace MCKENZIE)
			075	ROGERS, Catherine	
John P. ROGERS	03-24-1840	03-08-1905	075	ROGERS, John P.	
			075		
Mary PAYANT	1842	1925	075	PAYANT, Mary	
			075		
Mary J. WHYTE Butler	01-14-1853	05-06-1906	075	BUTLER, Bernard	(NOI Bernard BUTLER)
			075	WHYTE, Mary J.	
			075		
Daniel DALY	03-17-1855	02-02-1915	075	SHERLOCK, Esther Ellen	
Esther Ellen SHERLOCK Daly	04-11-1852	10-29-1907	075	DALY, Daniel	
			075		
Robert M. WHELAN	09-14-1848	04-27-1935	075	GIBBONS, B. Ellen	
B. Ellen GIBBONS Whelan	08-10-1850	08-24-1937	075	WHELAN, Robert M.	
			075		
John C. DALEY	1830	1907	075	____, Catharine H.	
Catharine H. ____ DALEY	1831	1914	075	DALEY, John C.	
			075		
Nellie SHACKETT	1855	1906	075	SHACKETT, Nellie	
			075		
Mary CAREY McGettrick	1855	1924	075	MCGETTRICK, Michael	(NOI Michael MCGETTRICK)
			075	CAREY, Mary	
			075		

Name	Born	Died	Code	Index	Notes
John LANE	1818	1905	075	FOLEY, Margaret	
Margaret FOLEY Lane	1827	1915	075	LANE, John	
			075		
William MULCAHEY	1840	1915	075	DONOVAN, Cathrine	
Cathrine DONOVAN Mulcahey	1844	1906	075	MULCAHEY, William	
Mary A. MURPHY	1876	1933	075	MURPHY, Mary A.	
			075		
John SULLIVAN	1820	1894	075	HURLEY, Elizabeth	
Elizabeth HURLEY Sullivan	1828	1901	075	SULLIVAN, John	
Rev. Daniel SULLIVAN	1854	1924	075	SULLIVAN, Rev. Daniel	Ordained 1897.
			075		
Michael J. POWERS	73 Years	10-24-1920	075	POWERS, Michael J.	(Did not say if Michael-Nancy were husband and wife. Same stone but back to back.)
Nancy POWERS	63 Years	10-16-1902	075	POWERS, Nancy	
			075		
Timothy MANAHAN	1820	1895	075	KILEY, Bridget	
Bridget KILEY Manahan	1823	1911	075	MANAHAN, Timothy	
Daniel MANAHAN	1845	1896	075	MANAHAN, Daniel	(GAR) Enlisted in Co. K, 13th Rgt.Reenlisted Co. M, Frontier Cavalry, 26th NY Regt
			075		
			075		
			075		
John MANAHAN	06-16-1852	05-01-1910	075	MANAHAN, John	(GAR) Enlisted in Co. K, 13th VT Rgt
			075		
			075		
Patrick FLYNN	1841	1927	075	KENNEDY, Charlotte	
Charlotte KENNEDY Flynn	1846	1934	075	FLYNN, Patrick	
			075		
Patrick GARTLAND	1823	1900	075	BRENNAN, Mary	
Mary BRENNAN Gartland	1831	1912	075	GARTLAND, Patrick	
			075		
Henry COLEMAN	01-16-1850	07-01-1913	075	_____, Hannah	
Hannah ____ COLEMAN	1850	1925	075	COLEMAN, Henry	
			075		
Daniel SULLIVAN	12-25-1841	08-14-1903	075	WELCH, Nora	
Nora WELCH Sullivan	11-24-1842	06-20-1910	075	SULLIVAN, Daniel	
			075		
James S. POWERS	1841	1903	075	______, Anna B.	
Anna B. ___ POWERS	1859	1935	075	POWERS, James S.	
			075		
Catharine FORD McNally	1830	1923	075	MCNALLY, John	(NOI John MCNALLY)
			075	FORD, Catharine	
			075		
P. J. DOUGHERTY	1849	1884	075	CLARK, Katherine J.	
Katherine J. CLARK Dougherty	1847	1914	075	DOUGHERTY, P. J.	
			075		
John BRENNAN	1856	1925	075	BRENNAN, John	

Owen MCGINN	1858	1926	075	_____, Rhoda	
Rhoda _____ MCGINN	1860	1945	075	MCGINN, Owen	
			075		
Stephen CARROLL	1857	1929	075	SMITH, Mary	
Mary SMITH Carroll	1858	1942	075	CARROLL, Stephen	
			075		
James S. EATON	1856	1931	075	DWYER, Mary	
Mary DWYER Eaton	1866	1945	075	EATON, James S.	
			075		
Ann J. TURNER	1849	1938	075	TURNER, Ann J.	
			075		
Julia ROONEY	1854	1946	075	ROONEY, Julia	
			075		
Thomas R. MCCARTHY	1857	1924	075	DELLIGAN, Bridget	
Bridget DELLIGAN McCarthy	1859	1935	075	MCCARTHY, Thomas R.	
			075		
Sarah M. RONAN	1837	1926	075	RONAN, Sarah M.	
			075		
Henry A. BABCOCK	1854	1931	075	MURPHY, Mary J.	
Mary J. MURPHY Babcock	1856	1919	075	BABCOCK, Henry A.	
			075		
Bridget S. DRISCOLL	06-09-1846	03-20-1926	075	DRISCOLL, Bridget S.	
			075		
Thomas MCENANY	08-15-1826	12-12-1887	075	HAND, Rose	
Rose HAND McEnany	04-11-1837	01-26-1916	075	MCENANY, Thomas	
			075		
James H. WARD	1855	1926	075	WHYTE, Elizabeth C.	
Elizabeth C. WHYTE Ward	1859	1934	075	WARD, James H.	
			075		
James M. MURPHY	1874	1935	075	MURPHY, James M.	
			075		
Thomas H. MILES	1855	1930	075	DWYER, Margaret J.	
Margaret J. DWYER Miles	1861	1939	075	MILES, Thomas H.	
			075		
Frank J. MURPHY	1875	1968	075	MOODY, Lolita J.	
Lolita J. MOODY Murphy	1885	1933	075	MURPHY, Frank J.	
			075		
Henry MCDERMOTT	1819	1912	075	RICHARDS, Margaret	
Margaret RICHARDS McDermott	1827	1910	075	MCDERMOTT, Henry	
James MCDERMOTT	1852	1936	075	MCDERMOTT, James	
			075		
Michael MAGIFF	1852	1935	075	MANN, Frances	
Frances MANN Magiff	1851	1931	075	MAGIFF, Michael	
			075		
Daniel MAGIFF	1817	1874	075	_____, Ellen	Buried In Moretown,VT Did not

find a marker in Moretown)

Name	Born	Died	Code	Index
			075	
Ellen _____ MAGIFF	1821	1908	075	MAGIFF, Daniel
			075	
Ellen L. EUSTICE	02-15-1835	11-05-1910	075	EUSTICE, Ellen L.
			075	
John WHITE	1844	1911	075	FARRELL, Ellen
Ellen FARRELL White	1846	1924	075	WHITE, John
			075	
John RYAN	06-17-1836	04-05-1908	075	_____, Elizabeth M.
Elizabeth M. _____ RYAN	10-29-1842	05-05-1909	075	RYAN, John
			075	
Michael CLANCY	1836	1908	075	DUNN, Mary
Mary DUNN Clancy	1839	1924	075	CLANCY, Michael
			075	
John LONG	1850	1915	075	_____, Mary
Mary _____ LONG	1847	1918	075	LONG, John
			075	
William SHERIDAN	1842	1923	075	NEVINS, Johanna
Johanna NEVINS Sheridan	1839	1908	075	SHERIDAN, William
			075	
James S. FINN	1849	1918	075	_____, Margaret
Margaret _____ FINN	1854	1923	075	FINN, James S.
			075	
Patrick WARD	1831	1911	075	STEELE, Elizabeth
Elizabeth STEELE Ward	1831	1914	075	WARD, Patrick
			075	
Daniel CORCORAN	1852	1922	075	CORCORAN, Daniel
			075	
Edward MAUN	1829	1911	075	TOBIN, Joanna
Joanna TOBIN Maun	1829	1912	075	MAUN, Edward
John E. MAUN	1855	1924	075	MAUN, John E.
Ellen S. MAUN	1859	1945	075	MAUN, Ellen S.
Anna G. MAUN	1858	1928	075	MAUN, Anna G.
			075	
Joseph J. LANGTON	1846	1922	075	_____, Mary
Mary _____ LANGTON	1846	1925	075	LANGTON, Joseph J.
			075	
Francis MCGETTRICK	1836	1888	075	BRADY, Bridget
			075	BRADY, Nellie A.
Bridget BRADY McGettrick	1853	1928	075	MCGETTRICK, Francis
Nellie A. BRADY McGettrick	1855	1927	075	MCGETTRICK, Francis
			075	
John H. MULLEN	10-18-1864	01-30-1913	075	GILLIN, Sarah A.
Sarah A. GILLIN Mullen	03-01-1856	03-03-1936	075	MULLEN, John H.
			075	

Peter MCGINN	05-27-1850	09-22-1912	075	MCGINN, Peter	
Ann MCGINN	06-04-1848	10-05-1912	075	MCGINN, Ann	
James A. MCGINN	06-04-1847	11-08-1931	075	O'HEAR, Katherine	
Katherine O'HEAR McGinn	04-12-1854	11-03-1917	075	MCGINN, James A.	
Sylvester MCGINN	04-12-1857	11-21-1916	075	RITCHIE, Lillian	
Lillian RITCHIE McGinn	09-12-1873	07-09-1957	075	MCGINN, Sylvester	
			075		
Charles E. SULLIVAN	1854	1918	075	SULLIVAN, Charles E.	
Margaret G. SULLIVAN	1864	1943	075	SULLIVAN, Margaret G.	
			075		
Edna J. LARKIN Hazzard	02-29-1857	12-06-1914	075	HAZZARD, Philander	(NOI Philander Hazzard)
			075	LARKIN, Edna J.	
			075		
Thomas RITCHIE	1838	1924	075	BURNS, Mary	
Mary BURNS Ritchie	1838	1917	075	RITCHIE, Thomas	
			075		
Felix MCGETTRICK	1847	1919	075	MORRIS, Elizabeth	(GAR) Co. F., 2nd Reg, U.S. Sharpshooters
			075		
Elizabeth MORRIS McGettrick	1851	1915	075	MCGETTRICK, Felix	
			075		
John GRACE	1829	1875	075	KELLY, Mary	
Mary KELLY Grace	1833	1912	075	GRACE, John	
			075		
William POWERS	1852	1935	075	WARD, Bridget	
Bridget WARD Powers	1857	1940	075	POWERS, William	
			075		
Henry MULDOON	1851	1917	075	_____, Mary Ann	
Mary ANN _____ MULDOON	1863	1954	075	MULDOON, Henry	
			075		
Nathen L. WALKER	06-03-1849	11-13-1917	075	SCANLON, Mary	
Mary SCANLON Walker	06-04-1853	10-17-1930	075	WALKER, Nathen L.	
			075		
John BRENNAN	1847	1926	075	MCGOOKIN, Margaret	
Margaret MCGOOKIN Brennan	1854	1926	075	BRENNAN, John	
			075		
Henry C. ROLLO	01-04-1848	09-20-1913	075	MILES, Jane	
Jane MILES Rollo	04-13-1844	06-09-1916	075	ROLLO, Henry C.	
			075		
Daniel MINER			075	_____, Elizabeth	
Elizabeth _____ MINER	1844	1925	075	MINER, Daniel	

Greenwood Cemetery, St. Albans, Vermont (Village Burial Ground), Opposite 165 South Main Street

NAME	POB	DOB/AGE	DOD	CEM	SPOUSE/INDEX	INSCRIPTION
John B. MCCARROLL		1831	1874	076	MCCARROLL, John B.	(Stone emblazoned with "IHS")
				076		
Mother _____ MCCARROLL		1799	1887	076	MCCARROLL, Father	
				076		
Father _____ MCCARROLL		1793	1862	076	MCCARROLL, Mother	
				076		
Thomas MCCARROLL		1827	1890	076	MCCARROLL, Thomas	
				076		
Henry L. PATTERSON		32Y5M4D	10-22-1864	076	PATTERSON, Henry L.	(GAR) Co. B, 1ST VT CAV. Died in Washington, DC
				076		
				076		
Oscar M. PATTERSON		1840	1888	076	MOONEY, Harriett S.	
Harriet S. MOONEY Patterson		1844	1931	076	PATTERSON, Oscar M.	
				076		
Thomas THORNE		1836	1890	076	MORRIS, Ellen	
Ellen MORRIS Thorne		1833	1910	076	THORNE, Thomas	
				076		
Francis E. MCFARLAND		04-19-1807	05-22-1899	076	CLARK, Betsey Almira	
Betsey Almira CLARK McFarland		64 Years	05-12-1878	076	MCFARLAND, Francis E.	Dau Of David & Anna Clark and Wife of Francis McFarland
				076		
				076		
Archibald MCLANE	Co. Tyrone	23Y 9M	07-24-1864	076	MCLANE, Archibald	A Native of Keenaghan, Tyrone County, Ireland. Not Dead But Liveth
				076		
				076		
				076		
Eliza MCCHESNEY Green		75Y 5D	01-03-1883	076	GREEN, Henry	(NOI Henry Green)
				076	MCCHESNEY, Eliza	
				076		
Thomas MOONEY		56 Years	02-01-1812	076	MOONEY, Thomas	(NOI Henry Green)
				076		
Daniel RYAN		54 Years	02-08-1810	076	RYAN, Daniel	Sacred To Memory Of
				076		
William N. RYAN		25 Years	04-25-1826	076	RYAN, William N.	Sacred To Memory Of
				076		
Julia TOOHEY		3Y 4M	02-11-1874	076	TOOHEY, Julia	Dau Of John & Mary TOOHEY
				076	TOOHEY, John	
				076	TOOHEY, Mary	
Hugh MOONEY		59 Years	1831	076	_____, Hannah	Born In The Townland Of _____ Ireland.
				076		
Hannah _____ MOONEY		64 Years	09-27-1849	076	MOONEY, Hugh	

			076		
Hugh MOONEY	24Y 4M	01-27-1848	076	MOONEY, Hugh	
			076		
Sarah _____ MOONEY	16 Years	1833	076	_____, Sarah	
			076		
Peter B. BROUGH	1805	1895	076	WATTS, Jane E.	
Jane E. WATTS Brough	1816	1902	076	BROUGH, Peter B.	
			076		
Robert MCALLISTER	60 Years	03-23-1870	076	HALE, Mary	
Mary HALE McAllister	63 Years	12-02-1883	076	MCALLISTER, Robert	
			076		
John PALMER	86 Years	07-09-1889	076	NIXON, Ellen	
Ellen NIXON Palmer		12-05-1895	076	PALMER, John	
			076		
Hamilton John PALMER	51Y7M5D	10-11-1892	076	DAVIS, Hannah	
Hannah DAVIS Palmer	07-18-1846	02-16-1922	076	PALMER, Hamilton John	
			076		
John ANDERSON	09-11-1808	01-15-1896	076	_____, Maria	Born Dundee, Scotland
Maria _____ ANDERSON	63Y10M24D	12-15-1878	076	ANDERSON, John	
			076		
Mary DEARDEN	81 Years	03-01-1877	076	DEARDEN, Mary	(This stone is deteriorated.
			076		The Year of death appears to
			076		be 1877)
			076		
William FINLAY	1881	1909	076	FINLAY, William	Glasgow, Scotland. Man to Man
			076		The Warld O'er Shall Brothers
			076		Be
			076		
Isaac J. CROWLEY	10-03-1830	10-12-1903	076	CRONKRITE, Clara J.	
Clara L. CRONKRITE Crowley	1852	1934	076	CROWLEY, Isaac J.	
			076		
George MCGOWAN	1828	1912	076	_____, Mary A.	
Mary A. _____ MCGOWAN	1835	1914	076	MCGOWAN, George	
			076		
William W. MCARTHUR	10-14-1848	06-07-1897	076	WILKINS, Evangeline	
Evangeline WILKINS McArthur	03-08-1854	10-05-1915	076	MCARTHUR, William W.	
			076		
George A. SWEENY	04-25-1853	11-02-1892	076	WHEELER, Helen	
Lelen WHEELER Sweeny	1852	1905	076	SWEENY, George A.	
			076		
Joseph D. SWEENY	15Y5M8D	04-08-1863	076	SWEENY, Joseph D.	
			076		
William H. SWEENY	20Y 3M	05-26-1861	076	SWEENY, William H.	
			076		
Hamilton F. SWEENY		10-11-1865	076	SWEENY, Hamilton F.	

Name	Birthplace	Born	Died	Code	Index	Notes
				076		
Patrick A. SWEENY	Co. Dublin	05-__-1809	10-__-1887	076	PALMER, Isabella	A Native Of The Cty Of Dublin,
				076		Ireland. Could be County or
				076		City. Probably County.)
Isabella PALMER Sweeny	Co. Sligo	05-__-1816	08-28-1888	076	SWEENY, Patrick A.	A Native Of The Cty of Sligo
				076		Ireland (Same observation as
				076		above on use of Cty)
				076		
James CURRY		04-30-1843	02-27-1920	076	O'DELL, Almira	
Almira O'DELL Curry		12-23-1843	07-01-1906	076	CURRY, James	
				076		
Mary DOYLE Andress		1855	1919	076	ANDRESS, J. D.	Wife Of J. D. Andress(NOI J.D.
				076	DOYLE, Mary	Andress)
				076		
Margery RYAN		24 Years	07-3-1879	076	RYAN, Margery	Dau Of A. & G.F. Ryan
				076		
J. W. REARDON		1852	1938	076	_____, Agnes	
Agnes _____ REARDON		1868	1953	076	REARDON, J. W.	
				076		
William MCCARTY		05-22-1837	03-08-1901	076	MANLEY, Mary L.	
Mary L. MANLEY McCarty		09-01-1837	07-02-1920	076	MCCARTY, William	
				076		
Peter WILLET		10-01-1845	12-14-1895	076	O'MEARA, Delia	
Delia O'MEARA Willet				076	WILLET, Peter	(NOI DOB-DOD Delia O'Meara)
				076		
George CASSIDY		1852	1928	076	_____, Sarah J.	
Sarah J. _____ CASSIDY		1853	1886	076	CASSIDY, George	
				076		
Dennis GILMORE		10-18-1823	07-27-1909	076	_____, Nancy A.	
Nancy A. _____ GILMORE		02-20-1829	07-08-1902	076	GILMORE, Dennis	
				076		
W. D. MACCALLUM		1854	1906	076	_____, Eliza G.	
Eliza G. _____ MACCALLUM		1845	1948	076	MACCALLUM, W. D.	
				076		
Marshall H. DOWNEY		1843	1916	076	ASHLEY, Hattie M.	(GAR) Co. F. 10th VT
Hattie M. ASHLEY Downey		1848	1914	076	DOWNEY, Marshall H.	
				076		
Patrick MOONEY		11-28-1812	09-08-1892	076	BREAKEY, Catherine W.E.	
Catherine BREAKEY Mooney		01-08-1818	09-26-1879	076	MOONEY, Patrick	
William H. MOONEY		1849	1930	076	BATES, Belle	
Belle BATES Mooney		1861	1958	076	MOONEY, William H.	
George T. MOONEY		09-17-1851	04-04-1890	076	MOONEY, George T.	
				076		
James MOONEY		1809	1886	076	BREAKEY, Mary	
Mary BREAKEY Mooney		1816	1904	076	MOONEY, James	

Name	Birth	Death	Code	Index	Notes
James MOONEY	1848	1934	076	MOONEY, James	
Henry J. WATSON	1835	1904	076	MOONEY, Sarah A.	
Sarah A. MOONEY Watson	1841	1904	076	WATSON, Henry J.	
			076		
Sarah Ann WATSON	12-23-1841	04-08-1904	076	WATSON, Sarah Ann	(Duplicated marker. She was Sarah Mooney, wife of Henry Watson)
			076		
			076		
			076		
John MCALLISTER	08-28-1850	07-16-1909	076	MCALLISTER, John	
			076		
Esther DENT Norwich	07-01-1819	02-07-1905	076	NORWICH, William S.	Born In Sheffield, England
			076	DENT, Esther	
			076		
William ROBSON	1794	1888	076	SMITH, Ann	
Ann SMITH Robson			076	ROBSON, William	(DOB-DOD buried and could not read)
			076		
			076		
John T. ROBSON	1834	1920	076	APPLETON, Frances	
Frances APPLETON Robson	1838	1916	076	ROBSON, John T.	
			076		
Charles H. MCCARROLL	1838	1914	076	GREEN, Sarah A.	(GAR) Co. L., 1st VT Cav
Sarah A. GREEN MCCarroll	1851	1912	076	MCCARROLL, Charles H.	
			076		
Charles H. MORRISON	1838	1914	076	_____, Sarah	
Sarah _____ MORRISON	1832	1901	076	MORRISON, Charles H.	
			076		
Mary E. DOWNEY	54Y 19D	02-19-1904	076	DOWNEY, Mary E.	
			076		
Ellen NEAL McIver	1843	1925	076	MCIVER, James	(NOI James McIver)
			076	NEAL, Ellen	
			076		
Richard CAWLEY	1853	1923	076	CAWLEY, Richard	
			076		
Arthur J. TENNY	1849	1917	076	TENNY, Arthur J.	
			076		
John B. SWEENEY	1848	1925	076	KILEY, Ada	
Ada KILEY Sweeney	1874	1943	076	SWEENEY, John B.	
			076		
Lydia MCCLUSKEY	10-28-1852	12-16-1944	076	MCCLUSKEY, Lydia	
			076		
William W. MOFFATT	1858	1918	076	WARD, Anna	
Anna WARD Moffatt	1858	1926	076	MOFFATT, William W.	(Dau Of Hugh Ward who is buried at St. Andre's,Sutton, Quebec)
			076		
			076		
John DONOVAN	1849	1917	076	HALE, Jennie A.	

NAME	POB	DOB/AGE	DOD	CEM	SPOUSE/INDEX	INSCRIPTION
Jennie A. HALE Donovan		1853	1922	076	DONOVAN, John	
				076		
Rose A. MCKENZIE		1855		076	MCKENZIE, Rose A.	(NOI DOD)
				076		
James KEENAN		1850	1923	076	KEENAN, James	
				076		
Dewitt B. SEXTON		70 Years	04-08-1911	076	SEXTON, Dewitt B.	(GAR) Co. I 10th VT Inf
				076		
Thomas COLEMAN		1841	1911	076	COLEMAN, Thomas	
				076		
Harry CANHAM		71 Years	02-26-1911	076	CANHAM, Harry	
				076		
Eliza Ann KELLEY Kimball		03-24-1848	05-22-1910	076	KIMBALL, Seldon	(NOI Seldon Kimball)
				076	KELLEY, Eliza Ann	
				076		
William R. SIMPSON		1855	1932	076	MCINTYRE, Martha	
Martha MCINTYRE Simpson		1858	1934	076	SIMPSON, William R.	
				076		
William W. WATSON		67 Years	08-06-1890	076	O'DONNELL, Catherine	
Catherine O'DONNELL Watson		38 Years	01-18-1880	076	WATSON, William W.	
				076		
O. R. KIRK		1846	1893	076	_____, Aceneth K.	
Aceneith K. _____ KIRK		1845	1901	076	KIRK, O. R.	

Greenwood Cemetery, (Old Catholic Burial Ground) Opposite 165 South Main St., St. Albans, VT

NAME	POB	DOB/AGE	DOD	CEM	SPOUSE/INDEX	INSCRIPTION
W.R. ROBSON		60 Years	05-10-1890	100	HOGAN, Margaret L.	
Margaret L. HOGAN Robson		47 Years	09-06-1892	100	ROBSON, W.R.	
				100		
Matty _____ O'HEER		60 Years	03-29-1850	100	O'HEER, Michael	(NOI Michael O'Heer)
				100	_____, Matty	
				100		
Joseph DOYLE	Co. Wexford	42 Years	08-04-1885	100	DOYLE, Joseph	Born In Wexford County, Ire.
				100		
J. O'LAUGHLIN		77 Years	11-15-1900	100	O'LAUGHLIN, J.	
				100		
Patrick CARROLL		25Y 10D	01-01-1866	100	CARROLL, Patrick	Son Of John & Ellen Carroll
				100	CARROLL, John	
				100		

Name	Age	Date		Relations	Notes
James MCNALLY	51 Years	09-02-1847	100	_____, Mary	After A Long And Painful Ill-
			100		ness endured With Resignation
			100		To The Will Of God And Having
			100		Received With Abiding Faith
			100		The Holy Sacraments Of The
			100		Church.
			100		
Mary _____ MCNALLY	56 Years	05-07-1852	100	MCNALLY, James	(NOI James McNally)
Henry MCNALLY	24 Years	12-24-1847	100	MCNALLY, Henry	Son Of James and Mary McNally
			100		
Mary KANE	19Y 2M	03-02-1850	100	KANE, Mary	Dau Of _____ & Catherine Kane
			100		(Father probably Charles)
			100		
Melchor DEPATIE	23 Years	1855	100	DEPATIE, Melchor	
			100		
William Alexander DRISCOLL	*5 Months	1855	100	DRISCOLL, William A.	Son Of Daniel DRISCOLL and
			100	DRISCOLL, Daniel	Marguerite
			100		
John FALLON	*50 Years	1867	100	FALLON, John	
			100		
Francis D. GALLIN	*2 Years	1859	100	GALLIN, Francis D.	
			100		
Ellen CROWLEY Hickey	*61 Years	1868	100	HICKEY, Patrick	(NOI Patrick Hickey)
			100	CROWLEY, Ellen	
Bridget _____ INGRAM	*		100	INGRAM, William E.	(NOI William Ingram)
			100		
Joseph JERROR	*5 Years	1853	100	JERROR, Joseph	S/O Mitchel JERROR and Ester
			100	JERROR, Mitchel	
			100		
Ellen KANE	*11 Months	1853	100	KANE, Ellen	D/O Dennis KANE and Mary
			100		
J. D. LAUGHLIN	*77 Years	1900	100	LAUGHLIN, J.D.	
			100		
W. M. MCCOLLIFF	*		100	MCCOLLIFF, W.M.	(GAR) Co. E. 12th VT (NOI)
			100		
William O'NEIL	*41 Years	1864	100	O'NEIL, William	
			100		
Bridget _____ SCELE	*		100	SCELE, Hugh	(NOI Hugh Scele. This surname
			100	_____, Bridget	possibly SEELEY)(NOI DOB/DOD)
*Entries with DOB/AGE preceeded with an * have been extracted from*			100		
Records of the St. Albans Free Library and in about 50% of the			100		
cases, the stone is either down or completely missing.			100		

Mt. Calvary Cemetery of Holy Angels Parish, St. Albans, VT. Off North Elm Street

NAME	POB	DOB/AGE	DOD	CEM	SPOUSE/INDEX	INSCRIPTION
Daniel BIRD		67 Years	04-0-8-1898	077	_____, Kathleen M.	(NOI Kathleen M.)
				077	BIRD, Daniel	
				077		
Joseph H. SMITH		1813	1895	077	SMITH Joseph H.	
				077		
Moses CARLEY		12-13-1844	04-06-1909	077	CROGAN, Eliza	(GAR)Co. A.17th Reg VT Inf Vol
Eliza CROGAN Carley		10-06-1844	02-08-1898	077	CARLEY, Moses	
				077		
William P. NOLAN		1855	1926	077	CROSS, Ada B.	
Ada B. CROSS Nolan		1864	1926	077	NOLAN, William P.	
				077		
				077		

St. Albans Bay Cemetery, St. Albans Bay, Vermont - Route 36 East of Bay.

NAME	POB	DOB/AGE	DOD	CEM	SPOUSE/INDEX	INSCRIPTION
John MURPHY		8Y 3M	05-27-1847	112	MURPHY, John	Son Of Thomas & Anne Murphy
				112	MURPHY, Thomas	
				112	MURPHY, Anne	
				112		
Sophia M. KENNEDY		83 Years	03-07-1882	112	KENNEDY, Sophia	
				112		
Joseph CROSBY		1826	1898	112	_____, Sarah M.	
Sarah M. _____ CROSBY		1825	1889	112	CROSBY, Joseph	
				112		
Joseph SHILVOCK		1852	1926	112	MCCREA, Eliza	
Eliza MCCREA Shilvock		1851	1940	112	SHILVOCK, Joseph	
				112		
John F. MCINTOSH		69Y 10M	01-12-1890	112	MITCHELL, Jane	
Jane MITCHELL McIntosh		64Y 7M	09-07-1876	112	MCINTOSH, John F.	
				112		
Alex CAVANAGH		58 Years	04-25-1895	112	CAVANAGH, Alex	
				112		
George F. BRADY		1856	1931	112	THAYER, Eva	
Eva THAYER Brady		1865	1941	112	BRADY, George F.	
				112		
John F. RYAN		1854	1926	112	_____, Abbie H.	
Abbie H. _____ RYAN		1873	1916	112	RYAN, John F.	

				112		
Richard WARD		1848	1924	112	CALLAN, Elizabeth	
Elizabeth CALLAN Ward		1846	1906	112	WARD, Richard	
				112		
Warren W. CONGER		1842	1930	112	MCINTOSH, Alice C.	(GAR) Co. B 1ST VT CAV
Alice C. MCINTOSH Conger		1844	1910	112	CONGER, Warren W.	
				112		
Caroline HADLEY McKillop		1849	1920	112	HADLEY, Caroline	(NOI Mr. McKillop)
				112		
Barney H. STICKNEY		1826	1905	112	WEBBER, Mary L.	
Mary L. WEBBER Stickney		04-29-1844	02-05-1900	112	STICKNEY, Barney H.	
				112		

112

St. Albans Point Cemetery, St. Albans Bay, Vermont - Route 36 West of Bay.

NAME	POB	DOB/AGE	DOD	CEM	SPOUSE/INDEX	INSCRIPTION
Thomas A. GALLAGHER		1853	1926	119	LASELLE, Emma W.	
Emma W. LASELLE Gallagher		1854	1926	119	GALLAGHER, Thomas A.	
				119		
Joseph GALLAGHER		76 Years	09-11-18__	119	MCCLURE, Adelia	(Stone is down and broken)
Adelia MCCLURE Gallagher		17 Years	01-22-1863	119	GALLAGHER, Joseph	
				119		
Stephen S. COLLINS		1812	1885	119	CONNOR, Thankful	
Thankful W. CONNOR Collins		1817	1860	119	COLLINS, Stephen S.	
				119		
David G. BROOKS		02-27-1808	11-21-1880	119	CONNER, Euseba	
Euseba CONNER Brooks		79Y8M6D	07-10-1887	119	BROOKS, David G.	
				119		
John P. CONNER		1828	19091-1880	119	BOOMHOWER, Sarah	
Sarah BOOMHOWER Conner				119	CONNER, John P.	(NOI DOB-DOD Sarah Boomhower)
				119		
Thankful WEEKS Conner		1793	1876	119	CONNER, Benjamin	(NOI Benjamin Conner)
				119	WEEKS, Thankful	
				119		
Mary ASELTYNE McClure		69Y4M22D	10-03-1874	119	MCLURE, John	(NOI John McClure)
				119	ASELTYNE, Mary	
				119		
Harris SKINNER		1824	1899	119	CONNER, Arvesta J.	
Arvesta J. CONNER Skinner		1829	1899	119	SKINNER, Harris	

Mt. Calvary Cemetery, St. Johnsbury, Vermont. St. John Street from Route 5, North of City

NAME	POB	DOB/AGE	DOD	CEM	SPOUSE/INDEX	INSCRIPTION
James MURRIHY	Co. Clare	25 Years	06-15-1861	078	MURRIHY, James	Born In Ireland, County Clare.
				078		Died at Barnet, VT. Age 25 Yrs
				078		
Edmond BALEY	Co. Cork	66 Years	09-26-1871	078	BALEY, Edmond	A Native of Kildoree (Kildor-
				078		rery), Co. Cork, Ireland
				078		
Mary MALONEY Pinard	Co. Limerick	57 Years	12-03-1881	078	PINARD, Cleophas	Born In Limerick, Ireland (NOI
				078	MALONEY, Mary	Cleophas Pinard)
				078		
John Henry FITZPATRICK	Newfoundland	17Y 8M	06-22-1880	078	FITZPATRICK, John Henry	Native of Newfoundland.Son of
				078		Michael & Anna Fitzpatrick.
				078		
Mary _____ FOLEY	Co. Tyrone	42 Years	04-28-1870	078	FOLEY, Michael	Native of County Tyrone. (NOI
				078	_____, Mary	Michael Foley)
				078		
Patrick SAVAGE	Co. Cork	65 Years	09-26-1865	078	SAVAGE, Patrick	Born In Mallow, Co.of Cork,
				078		Ireland. Died in St. Johnsbury
				078		
John TODD	Co. Tyrone	1799	02-17-1881	078	SKELLY, Mary	Born In Fymore, County Tyrone,
				078		Ireland.(Fymore Todd or Fymore
				078		Mourtray-same place - sheet 59
				078		Ordnance Survey)
Margaret SKELLY Todd		80Y 9M	12-03-1884	078	TODD, John	
				078		
Anna _____ MCGOWAN	Co. Sligo	64 Years	04-17-1867	078	MCGOWAN, Martin	Born In Parish Kilglass, Co.
				078	_____, Anna	Sligo, Ireland (NOI Martin
				078		McGowan)
				078		
John MCGOWAN	Co. Sligo	33 Years	01-28-1870	078	MCGOWAN, John	Native of Parish Kilglass, Co.
				078		Sligo, Ireland (Same plot as
				078		Anna McGowan)
				078		
Eliza C. LOANE Hoye	Co. Tyrone	53 Years	03-31-1891	078	HOYE, John	Born In Co. Tyrone, Ireland.
				078	LOANE, Elizabeth C.	(NOI John Hoye)
				078		
J. CASSIDY FAMILY				078	CASSIDY, J.	
Father		1850	1935	078	___, Father	(NOI On Father and Mother - A
Mother		1865	1935	078	___, Mother	Large Granite Marker on Plot
				078		reads "BELFAST")
				078		

Name	Origin	Age/Birth	Death	Code	Relation	Notes
Hanora HALEY Shea	Co. Clare	56 Years	05-06-1868	078	SHEA, Patrick	A Native Of Ballysheena (Bally sheen Beg/Ballysheen Mor), Co. Clare, Ireland
Michael MCCANN	Co. Tyrone	56 Years	02-16-1880	078	O'CONNER, Helen	A Native Of Co. Tyrone, Ire.
Helen O'CONNER McCann	Co. Galway	30 Years	09-16-1863	078	MCCANN, Michael	A Native Of Co. Galway, Ire.
Helen MONAGHAN	Co. Tyrone	72 Years	03-13-1864	078	MONAGHAN, Helen	A Native Of Co. Tyrone, Ire. (Same Stone as Michael McCann)
John HOWARD	Co. Clare	48 Years	06-01-1859	078	HOWARD, John	Erected By John and Patrick Howard In The Memory of Their Father, John Howard, of the Town Of New Market on Fergus, County Clare, Ireland
Thomas HOWARD	Co. Clare	68 Years	05-22-1895	078	HOWARD, Thomas	Born at Inness (Ennis), County Clare, Ireland
Peter P. LONERGAN		53Y 8M	05-23-1880	078	DALY, Julia C.	
Julia C. DALY Lonergan	Co. Tipperary	28 Years	01-08-1861	078	LONERGAN, Peter P.	To The Sacred Memory Of Julia Charlotte, Wife of P.P. Lonergan and Daughter of Jere-miah and Catherine Daly Of The Town Of Cloghreen (Clogheen), Co. Tipperary, Ireland
John MCGOWAN		63 Years	12-05-1894	078	CONAGTON, Bridget A. MCGOWAN, John	(NOI Bridget Conagton)
John REAL		03-07-1822	03-05-1867	078	RYAN, Mary	Born In Ireland. Died at Wells River (Vermont)
Mary RYAN Real		10-01-1828	04-09-1866	078	REAL, John	Born In Ireland. Died at Wells River (Vermont)
James CAMPTON	Co. Kilkenny	08-21-1816	07-02-1879	078	_____, Bridget	Born In Kilkenny,Ireland. Died at East Haven, Vermont
Bridget _____ CAMPTON	Co. Meath	06-24-1827	12-03-1881	078	CAMPTON, James	Born In Meath, Ireland.Died at East Haven, Vermont
Patrick BRADY	Co. Cavan	03-17-1825	04-05-1878	078	O'CONNER, Hannah	Native of County Cavan, Ire.
Hannah O'CONNER Brady	Co. Kerry	05-10-1835	06-06-1877	078	BRADY, Patrick	Native of County Kerry, Ire.
Mary _____ FITZPATRICK	Co. Kilkenny	69 Years	08-15-1864	078	FITZPATRICK, Patrick _____, Mary	Native of County Kilkenny, Ire (NOI Patrick Fitzpatrick)

Name	County	Age/Born	Died	Code	Spouse	Notes
Thomas HOYE	Co. Monaghan	29 Years	01-03-1880	078	HOYE, Thomas	Native of County Monaghan, Ire
Robert LOANE	Co. Tyrone	56 Years	11-20-1892	078	HOYE, Anna	Born In Tyrone County, Ire.
				078		Died In Wheelock,Vermont. (Not
				078		next to Anna but same plot)
Anna HOYE Loane	Co. Monaghan	43 Years	10-24-1880	078	LOANE, Robert	Native of County Monaghan, Ire
				078		
James LOANE	Co. Tyrone	68 Years	03-31-1895	078	LOANE, James	Born In County Tyrone, Ire.
				078		
Peter LOANE	Co. Tyrone	85 Years	07-08-1881	078	RAMSEY, Betty	Born In County Tyrone, Ire.
				078		Died In Wheelock, Vermont.
				078		
Betty RAMSEY Loane	Co. Tyrone	85 Years	07-23-1875	078	LOANE, Peter	Born In Tyrone County, Ire.
				078		Died In Wheelock, Vermont.
				078		
Peter DORAN	Co. Monaghan	68 Years	09-18-1871	078	DORAN, Peter	Native of County Monaghan, Ire
				078		
Michael SHEA	Co. Limerick	69 Years	02-22-1881	078	FARRELL, Mary	Native Of Limerick, Ireland
Mary FARRELL Shea	Co. Limerick	75Y 6M	02-12-1888	078	SHEA, Michael	Native Of Limerick, Ireland
				078		
Patrick TYRRELL	Co. Wicklow	03-17-1798	07-04-1880	078	TYRRELL, Patrick	Born In County Wicklow, Ire.
				078		
William MCCANN	Co. Tyrone	43 Years	11-04-1868	078	FITZGERALD, Mary	Native Of Co. Tyrone, Ireland
Mary FITZGERALD McCann	Co. Kerry	81 Years	09-30-1910	078	MCCANN, William	Native Of Co. Kerry, Ireland
				078		
John JEFFERS	Co. Cork	91 Years	10-27-1910	078	MITCHELL, Margaret	Native Of Co. Cork, Ireland
Margaret MITCHELL Jeffers	Co. Cork	49 Years	01-04-1868	078	JEFFERS, John	Native Of Millstreet, County
				078		Cork, Ireland
				078		
Anthony MCCORMICK		1848	1915	078	SHAY, Ellen	
Ellen SHAY McCormick		1852	1914	078	MCCORMICK, Anthony	
				078		
Matthew J. CALDBECK		07-16-1844	05-09-1912	078	SINNOTT, Mary J.	
Mary J. SINNOTT Caldbeck		02-07-1848	03-29-1926	078	CALDBECK, Matthew	
				078		
James MCLAUGHLIN		1839	1918	078	MAHONEY, Annie	
Annie MAHONEY McLaughlin		1852	1935	078	MCLAUGHLIN, James	
				078		
James KENNEY		1851	1922	078	LONERGAN, Marion	
Marion LONERGAN Kenney		1859	1923	078	KENNEY, James	
				078		
Edward LING		1851	1922	078	HALE, Bridget	
Bridget HALE Ling		1861	1928	078	LING, Edward	
				078		
John KENNEY		71 Years	01-26-1892	078	_____, Catherine	(NOI Catherine)
				078	KENNEY, John	

Name	Born/Age	Died	Code	Relation	Notes
			078		
Charles MCGOVERN	1836	1918	078	FARRELL, Elizabeth	
Elizabeth FARRELL McGovern	1836	1910	078	MCGOVERN, Charles	
			078		
Catherine _____ DALY	58 Years	11-13-1866	078	DALY, Jeremiah	(NOI Jeremiah Daly)
			078	_____, Catherine	
			078		
M. MCCORMICK	10-04-1838	04-08-1913	078	MAGUIRE, Mary	
			078	HOPKINS, Mary	
Mary MAGUIRE McCormick	10-16-1837	12-03-1883	078	MCCORMICK, M.	
Mary HOPKINS McCormick	01-30-1846	08-21-1906	078	MCCORMICK, M.	
			078		
David BROWN	23Y 8M	09-05-1862	078	BROWN, David	Son Of John Brown and Honora
			078		Lane of St. Sylvester, CE
			078		(Canada East-i.e. Quebec)
			078		
Catherine MANLEY Nelson	1830	1913	078	NELSON, Michael	(NOI Michael Nelson)
			078	MANLEY, Catherine	
			078		
Michael ROACH	1809	1900	078	MANEY, Mary	
Mary MANEY Roach	1824	1893	078	ROACH, Michael	
Patrick ROACH	1852	1899	078	GLYNN, Bridget	
Bridget GLYNN Roach	1855	1928	078	ROACH, Patrick	
Margaret ROHAN Maney	1796	1878	078	MANEY, Owen	(NOI Owen Maney)
			078	ROHAN, Margaret	
Thomas A. ROACH	01-04-1856	03-27-1911	078	HURLEY, Mary	
Mary HURLEY Roach	1864	1898	078	ROACH, Thomas A.	
			078		
Patrick QUAIN	1855	1928	078	ELVIDGE, Ellen	
Ellen ELVIDGE Quain	1860	1954	078	QUAIN, Patrick	
			078		
Theresa CASSIDY	1854	1922	078	CASSIDY, Theresa	
			078		
Mary MORRIS Banahan	83 Years	02-16-1903	078	BANAHAN, Patrick	(NOI Patrick BANAHAN)
			078	MORRIS, Mary	
Rose A. BANAHAN	42 Years	09-13-1902	078	BANAHAN, Rose A.	
			078		
Mrs. Mary DOYLE	1817	1896	078	_____, Mary	(NOI Mr. Doyle)
			078	DOYLE, Mr.	
			078		
Jeremiah SULLIVAN	73 Years	11-__-1910	078	_____, M.A.	
M. A. _____ SULLIVAN	80 Years	11-05-1918	078	SULLIVAN, Jeremiah	
			078		
Owen N. TOWER	1854	1925	078	BANAHAN, Maria D.	
Maria D. BANAHAN Tower	1848	1924	078	TOWER, Owen N.	

Julia _____ HAZEL	33Y or 53Y	06-06-1874	078	HAZEL, William	(NOI William Hazel)
			078	_____, Julia	
			078		
Portuas LEITH	1841	1915	078	_____, Mary	
Mary _____ LEITH	1852	1904	078	LEITH, Portuas	
			078		
Katherine PRIOR Gaffney	53 Years	12-24-1890	078	PRIOR, Katherine	
Margaret PRIOR	55 Years	03-20-1899	078	PRIOR, Margaret	
			078		
Thomas FLOOD	03-25-1845	01-29-1902	078	_____, Sarah	
Sarah _____ FLOOD	07-29-1853	02-04-1932	078	FLOOD, Thomas	
			078		
Ann GLEASON Shandly	70 Years	04-20-1881	078	SHANDLY, Edward	(NOI Edward Shandly)
Margaret EARLEY Shandly	1838	1910	078	SHANDLY, Edward	
			078	GLEASON, Ann	
			078	EARLEY, Margaret	
			078		
Margaret KELLEY	1823	1904	078	KELLEY, Margaret	(Rooney/Roderer Marker)
William J. ROONEY	1858	1922	078	COAKLEY, Mary A.	
Mary A. COAKLEY Rooney	1860	1923	078	ROONEY, William J.	
			078		
Patrick BROWN	1851	1929	078	LEONARD, Mary Ann	
Mary Ann LEONARD Brown	1858	1932	078	BROWN, Patrick	
			078		
David BROWN	1846	1907	078	ROONEY, Annie	
Annie ROONEY Brown	1850	1900	078	BROWN, David	
			078		
Michael J. COVENEY	1844	1903	078	NELSON, Margaret	
Margaret NELSON Coveney	1855	1924	078	COVENEY, Michael J.	
			078		
Michael J. TIERNEY	1858	1928	078	LEONARD, Katherine C.	
Katherine LEONARD Tierney	09-05-1861	07-03-1902	078	TIERNEY, Michael J.	
			078		
Terence MCCORMACK	1841	1910	078	COSTELLO, Anna	
Anna COSTELLO McCormack	1853	1928	078	MCCORMACK, Terence	
			078		
Susan RILEY Guyer	37 Years	1881	078	GUYER, John	(NOI John Guyer)
			078	RILEY, Susan	
			078		
Felix ROONEY	52 Years	10-22-1874	078	KELLEY, Mary	
Mary KELLEY Rooney	70 Years	10-27-1896	078	ROONEY, Felix	
Sarah A. ROONEY	1854	1942	078	ROONEY, Sarah A.	
Bridget A. ROONEY	1856	1942	078	ROONEY, Bridget A.	
Patrick J. ROONEY	30 Years	1883	078	ROONEY, Patrick J.	
			078		

Name	Born/Age	Died		Index	Notes
Patrick CUNNINGHAM	03-17-1842	05-21-1899	078	FARRELL, Mary J.	
Mary J. FARRELL Cunningham	11-24-1854	11-26-1919	078	CUNNINGHAM, Patrick	
Owen CUNNINGHAM	1800	02-24-1863	078	_____, Ellen	
Ellen _____ CUNNINGHAM	02-12-1812	10-08-1884	078	CUNNINGHAM, Owen	
Frank M. CUNNINGHAM	01-18-1855	09-08-1885	078	CUNNINGHAM, Frank M.	Their Son (Of Owen & Ellen Cunningham)
			078		
			078		
William LYNCH	05-17-1817	03-01-1873	078	PRIOR, Ellen	
Ellen PRIOR Lynch	08-25-1830	11-18-1905	078	LYNCH, William	
			078		
TIERNEY Family			078	TIERNEY, Family	
Patrick TIERNEY	1814	1878	078	O'MARRAH, Bridget	
Bridget O'MARRAH Tierney	1821	1891	078	TIERNEY, Patrick	
Bridget (TIERNEY)	1861	1873	078	TIERNEY, Bridget	
Edward (TIERNEY)	1861	1875	078	TIERNEY, Edward	
Thomas J. TIERNEY	1854	1925	078	GLEASON, Bridget	
Bridget GLEASON Tierney	1854	1923	078	TIERNEY, Thomas J.	
Katie Agnes (TIERNEY)	1880	1883	078	TIERNEY, Katie Agnes	
Thomas Raymond (TIERNEY)	1892	1893	078	TIERNEY, Thomas Raymond	
			078		
Patrick LEONARD	75 Years	09-10-1910	078	HOGAN, Bridget	
Bridget HOGAN Leonard	76 Years	11-04-1908	078	LEONARD, Patrick	
			078		
Denis O'KEEFE	55 Years	04-14-1896	078	BANAHAN, Catherine	
Catherine BANAHAN O'Keefe	63 Years	07-25-1914	078	O'KEEFE, Denis	
Denis O'KEEFE	79Y 3M	04-03-1871	078	MORISEY, Mary	
Mary MORISEY O'Keefe	74Y 2M	07-20-1868	078	O'KEEFE, Denis	
			078		
Michael BANAHAN	1851	1913	078	MORRIS, Maria	
Maria MORRIS Banahan	54 Years	03-02-1905	078	BANAHAN, Michael	
			078		
Gregory FLOOD	37 Years	09-22-1880	078	FLOOD, Gregory	
			078		
Catherine CONWAY Welch	55Y 9M	03-02-1888	078	WELCH, William	(NOI William Welch)
			078	CONWAY, Catherine	
			078		
John BRENNAN	1827	1914	078	HANLON, Catherine	
Catherine HANLON Brennan	1831	1903	078	BRENNAN, John	
			078		
Wilbur PERSONS	1851	1928	078	_____, Mary E.	
Mary E. _____ PERSONS	1858	1940	078	PERSONS, Wilbur	
			078		
Hannah REAL Brady	75 Years	05-05-1930	078	BRADY, Hannah Real	Daughter of John Real and Mary Ryan
			078		
			078		

Name	Place	Born	Died	Code	Index	Notes
James FLYNN		1850	1921	078	MULLEN, Ellen	
Ellen MULLEN Flynn		1854	1911	078	FLYNN, James	
				078		
James COAKLEY		1835	1911	078	GLYNN, Mary A.	
Mary A. GLYNN Coakley		09-07-1844	07-06-1877	078	COAKLEY, James	
				078		
Patrick T. GLYNN		5Y 6M	09-03-1857	078	GLYNN, Patrick T.	Son Of Patrick & Bridget Glynn
				078		
James GLEASON		60 Years	11-07-1918	078	GLEASON, James	
				078		
Thomas G. RAINEY		1839	1923	078	GOYET, Mary A.	
Mary A. GOYET Rainey		1850	1901	078	RAINEY, Thomas G.	
				078		
Peter DUFFY		01-16-1827	11-12-1903	078	GLYNN, Ann	
Ann GLYNN Duffy		03-17-1830	05-18-1909	078	DUFFY, Peter	
Katie DUFFY		06-18-1851	05-25-1874	078	DUFFY, Katie	
Julia DUFFY		05-27-1856	04-08-1875	078	DUFFY, Julia	
				078		
Michael AHERN		1826	1862	078	GRIFFIN, Catherine	
Catherine GRIFFIN Ahern		1829	1905	078	AHERN, Michael	
				078		
John KENNEDY		71 Years	01-26-1892	078	____, Catherine	(NOI Catherine)
				078	KENNEDY, John	
				078		
James COSGROVE	Co. Armagh	1874	1948	078	____, Maude	Born In County Armagh, Ireland
Maude ____ COSGROVE		1880	1952	078	COSGROVE, James	
				078		
John CROFTON		03-04-1847	10-04-1912	078	CROFTON, John	
Anna WELSH Crofton		04-15-1815	02-19-1887	078	CROFTON, John Sr.	(NOI John Crofton Sr.)
				078	WELSH, Anna	
				078		
Michael BUCKLEY		1832	1896	078	SULLIVAN, Mary	
Mary SULLIVAN Buckley		1840	1916	078	BUCKLEY, Michael	
				078		
Francis BROWNE		09-__-1833	07-17-1924	078	____, Margaret	
Margaret ____ BROWNE		11-__-1830	03-10-1913	078	BROWNE, Francis	
				078		
Patrick A. BROWN		03-13-1822	02-22-1897	078	DEVANEY, Mary	
Mary DEVANEY Brown		11-05-1822	03-07-1900	078	BROWN, Patrick A.	
				078		
John HAUGHEY		73 Years	03-07-1901	078	HAUGHEY, John	
				078		
James GAFFNEY						
Margaret DOUGHERTY Gaffney		80 Years	02-03-1890	078	DOUGHERTY, Margaret	
				078	GAFFNEY, James	(NOI Margaret Dougherty)
Catherine GAFFNEY Moynihan		69 Years	08-15-1899	078	GAFFNEY, Catherine	(NOI Mr. Moynihan)

			078	MOYNIHAN, Mr.	
			078		
Bernard COVENY	1814	1883	078	_____, Mary	
Mary _____ COVENY	1821	1881	078	COVENY, Bernard	
			078		
Jerry REGAN	1819	1869	078	CLEARY, Dora	(These four all found on the same headstone)
Dora CLEARY Regan	1822	1899	078	REGAN, Jerry	
Jerry DENNING	1825	1899	078	LYNCH, Mary	
Mary LYNCH Denning	1831	1870	078	DENNING, Jerry	
			078		
Patrick FITZGERALD	1826	1903	078	_____, Margaret A.	
Margaret A. ____ FITZGERALD	1836	1918	078	FITZGERALD, Patrick	
			078		
John H. RYAN	1844	1916	078	FITZGERALD, Mary A.	(Same plot as Patrick and Margaret Fitzgerald)
Mary A. FITZGERALD Ryan	1855	1884	078	RYAN, John H.	
			078		
Frank CHENEY	1817	1893	078	_____, Rose	
Rose _____ CHENEY	1852	1928	078	CHENEY, Frank	
			078		
John O'KEEFE	06-23-1834	05-01-1888	078	BANAHAN, Ann	
Ann BANAHAN O'Keefe	02-01-1840	07-04-1894	078	O'KEEFE, John	
Patrick BANAHAN	1800	1870	078	BANAHAN, Patrick	
			078		
John AHEARN	67Y10M23D	05-17-1909	078	_____, Mary	
Mary _____ AHEARN	67Y04M02D	03-11-1909	078	AHEARN, John	
			078		
Thomas E. TRAINOR	5 Years	01-17-1868	078	TRAINOR, Thomas E.	Son Of Patrick & Ann Trainor
			078		
Daniel LYNCH	1853	1933	078	_____, Annie M.	
Annie M. _____ LYNCH	1858	1930	078	LYNCH, Daniel	
			078		
John L. CANTY	1820	1917	078	REAGAN, Ellen	
Ellen REAGAN Canty	1825	1897	078	CANTY, John L.	
			078		
Edward FITZPATRICK	64 Years	03-21-1894	078	_____, Mary	
Mary _____ FITZPATRICK	68 Years	11-01-1900	078	FITZPATRICK, Edward	
			078		
Patrick TRAINOR	03-17-1831	11-22-1908	078	FITZPATRICK, Anna	
Anna FITZPATRICK Trainor	10-02-1833	11-22-1901	078	TRAINOR, Patrick	
			078		
Daniel G. HURLEY	1819	1870	078	CHADWICK, Anne	
Anne CHADWICK Hurley	1841	1921	078	HURLEY, Daniel G.	
			078		
Andrew FITZGERALD	1818	1890	078	_____, Mary	
Mary _____ FITZGERALD	1810	1903	078	FITZGERALD, Andrew	

Name	Birth/Age	Death		Related	Notes
			078		
Mary E. BRAY O'Neil	23Y 29D	04-03-1870	078	O'NEIL, James	Dau of Michael & Mary Bray.
			078	BRAY, Mary E.	(NOI James O'Neil)
David BRAY	12 Years	08-12-1863	078	BRAY, David	Children of Michael/Mary Bray
Katie BRAY	8 Years	07-19-1863	078	BRAY, Katie	(NOI Michael & Mary Bray)
Sarah BRAY	6 Years	09-10-1863	078	BRAY, Sarah	
			078		
James FARRELL	52Y02M11D	09-18-1883	078	HART, Rose Ann T.	
Rose Ann T. HART Farrell	32Y06M28D	10-18-1872	078	FARRELL, James	
			078		
Mary MCCAFFREY Judge	1847	1929	078	MCCAFFREY, Mary	
			078		
Charles REAVEY	1832	1918	078	KERRIGAN, Mary	
Mary KERRIGAN Reavey	1833	1900	078	REAVEY, Charles	
			078		
Ellen HOGAN	1831	1902	078	HOGAN, Ellen	
			078		
Edward CUSHING	1848	1889	078	CUMMUSKEY, Margaret	
Margaret CUMMUSKEY Cushing	1857	1888	078	CUSHING, Edward	
			078		
Patrick WHALEN	60 Years	08-01-1884	078	_____, Ellen	
Ellen _____ WHALEN	62 Years	01-22-1887	078	WHALEN, Patrick	
			078		
Frank RASH	65 Years	09-24-1894	078	RASH, Frank	
			078		
Cornelius COLEMAN	1825	1910	078	HARRINGTON, Sarah	
Sarah HARRINGTON Coleman	1826	1904	078	COLEMAN, Cornelius	
			078		
Elizabeth MCKAIGE Courtney	01-__-1852	06-__-1875	078	COURTNEY, T. A.	(NOI T.A. Courtney)
			078	MCKAIGE, Elizabeth	
			078		
Margaret MCNULTY	17 Years	10-31-1866	078	MCNULTY, Margaret	Dau Of Michael & Ellen McNulty
			078		
John CASSIDY	81 Years	03-15-1896	078	_____, Anne C.	
			078	CLOUTIE, Mary	
Anne C. _____ CASSIDY	1838	1897	078	CASSIDY, John	
Mary CLOUTIE Cassidy	49Y 6M	12-16-1870	078	CASSIDY, John	
			078		
James MCKILLOP	1826	1906	078	LESSLIE, Margaret	
Margaret LESSLIE McKillop	1826	1912	078	MCKILLOP, James	
			078		
Patrick F. O'MALLEY	184_	1912	078	CANTY, Julia Ellen	
Julia Ellen CANTY O'Malley	1851	19__	078	O'MALLEY, Patrick F.	
			078		
James BARRY	57 Years	01-16-1908	078	_____, Marry	

Marry _____ BARRY	55 Years	02-02-1901	078	BARRY, James	
			078		
Patrick MCKILLOP	01-30-1841	02-21-1914	078	MCKILLOP, Patrick	
			078		
Nancy MCKILLOP Finley	1836	1901	078	FINLEY, John	(NOI John Finley)
			078	MCKILLOP, Nancy	
			078		
Henry J. GERO	1847	1925	078	MURPHY, Julia A.	
Julia A. MURPHY Gero	1849	1921	078	GERO, Henry J.	
			078		
Nora BRENNAN	1841	1921	078	BRENNAN, Nora	
			078		
John NOLAN	1831		078	CASSIDY, Catharine	(NO Date of Death for Either
Catharine CASSIDY Nolan	1837		078	NOLAN, John	Catharine or John)
			078		
Peter KENNEDY	05-06-1851	09-26-1909	078	HARTLEY, Stasia	
Stasia HARTLEY Kennedy	09-22-1858	12-05-1892	078	KENNEDY, Peter	
			078		
John GADLEY	1828	1917	078	GADLEY, John	Corporal John Gadley, 15th Vt
			078		Infantry (GAR)
			078		
Margaret KELLEY Campbell	1842	1909	078	CAMPBELL, John W.	(NOI John W. Campbell)
			078	KELLEY, Margaret	
			078		
Ann MCGOURTY	30 Years	09-14-1867	078	MCGOURTY, Ann	
			078		
Mary _____ FOLEY	42 Years	04-28-1870	078	FOLEY, John	(NOI John Foley)
			078	_____, Mary	
			078		
Julia _____ PERRY	79 Years	08-06-1903	078	PERRY, Mr.	(NOI Mr. Perry)
			078	_____, Julia	
			078		
Ellen WOOD	38 Years	02-07-1892	078	WOOD, Ellen	
			078		
Matthew WALSH	27 Years	06-17-1877	078	WALSH, Matthew	
			078		
Michael M. CALDBECK	1842	1918	078	MCMANUS, Jane	
			078	BUCKLEY, Bridgett	
Jane MCMANUS Caldbeck	1844	1880	078	CALDBECK, Michael M.	
Bridgett BUCKLEY Caldbeck	1842	1922	078	CALDBECK, Michael M.	
William J. CALDBECK	1793	1874	078	TWOHEY, Bridget	
Bridget TWOHEY Caldbeck	1804	1891	078	CALDBECK, William J.	
			078		
John D. TODD	1844	1920	078	MCKELVEY, Catherine	
Catherine MCKELVEY Todd	1845	1919	078	TODD, John D.	

				078		
John MCDONALD		58 Years	11-02-1892	078	_____, Anna	
Anna _____ MCDONALD		52 Years	09-09-1890	078	MCDONALD, John	
				078		
Mary DOUGHARTY Lynch		52 Years	02-23-1827	078	LYNCH, Charles	(NOI Charles Lynch)
				078	DOUGHARTY, Mary	
				078		
Patrick HOYE		1848	1927	078	BROWN, Susan	
Susan BROWN Hoye		1845	1918	078	HOYE, Patrick	
				078		
Michael FLANAGAN		1810	1892	078	FARELL, Bridget	
Bridget FARELL Flanagan		1821	1889	078	FLANAGAN, Michael	
Michael FLANAGAN		1844	1859	078	FLANAGAN, Michael	
Ellen FLANAGAN		1855	1861	078	FLANAGAN, Ellen	
Mary FLANAGAN		1842	1870	078	FLANAGAN, Mary	
John A. FLANAGAN		1848	1892	078	FLANAGAN, John A.	
William P. FLANAGAN		1859	1878	078	FLANAGAN, William P.	
				078		
John HAFFORD		1821	1870	078	DOLAN, Mary	
Mary DOLAN Hafford		1822	1915	078	HAFFORD, John	
				078		
William KELLEY	Co. Leitrim		02-28-1913	078	TODD, Ellen	Born In Glenade, Co. Leitrim Ireland. (Mitchell's Parish Registers shows Glenade as RC Parish. Index to Towns & Town lands does not show Glenade as Town, townland or parish)
				078		
				078		
				078		
				078		
				078		
Ellen TODD Kelley	Co. Tyrone	02-02-1835	10-22-1914	078	KELLEY, William	Born In Fymore, County Tyrone, Ireland.(Fymore Todd or Fymore Mourtray-same place - sheet 59 Ordnance Survey)
				078		
				078		
				078		
				078		
Joseph REYNOLDS			04-22-1895	078	REYNOLDS, Joseph	(Stone badly deteriorated. Legible names are "Emma", "Mattie","Father")
				078		
				078		
				078		
Charles PATTERSON		1846	1905	078	PATTERSON, Charles	
				078		
Patrick NOONAN		1840	1884	078	_____, Elizabeth	
Elizabeth _____ NOONAN		1836	1899	078	NOONAN, Patrick	
				078		
John MCDONALD		1833	1914	078	FITZGERALD, Mary	
Mary FITZGERALD McDonald		1841	1913	078	MCDONALD, John	
James RIORDAN		1848	1880	078	RIORDAN, James	
				078		

NAME	POB	DOB/AGE	DOD	CEM	SPOUSE/INDEX	INSCRIPTION
Patrick MCGRORAY		52 Years	06-25-1867	078	MCGRORAY, Patrick	
				078		
MCGILL Family				078	MCGILL, Family	
Mother MCGILL		1846	1921	078	MCGILL, Mother	
Father MCGILL		1841	1920	078	MCGILL, Father	
John MCGILL		1876	1958	078	MCGILL, John	
Mary J. MCGILL		1878	1930	078	MCGILL, Mary J.	
				078		
Rose Ann COARR Mullen		1855	1938	078	MULLEN, Frank	(NOI Frank Mullen)
				078	COARR, Rose Ann	
				078		
Sophia MCCULLOUGH Penney		1855	1936	078	MCCULLOUGH, Sophia	
				078		
John TOOMEY		1854	1924	078	TOOMEY, John	

St. Mary's Cemetery, Swanton, VT. Canada Street - Behind Church of the Nativity

NAME	POB	DOB/AGE	DOD	CEM	SPOUSE/INDEX	INSCRIPTION
Margaret KEENAN Stearns		1843	1912	080	STEARNS, Everett	(NOI Everett Stearns)
				080	KEENAN, Margaret	
				080		
Catharine KEENAN Cook		62Y 10M	12-28-1899	080	COOK, George	(NOI George Cook)
				080	KEENAN, Catharine	
				080		
Elizabeth DOON Hebert		1858	1912	080	HEBERT, J.E.	(NOI J.E.Hebert)
				080	DOON, Elizabeth	
				080		
Michael SLAMMON		1837	1907	080	DUGAN, Rachel	
Rachel DUGAN Slammon		1844	1915	080	SLAMMON, Michael	
				080		
Ezekial MULLEN		1842	1911	080	____, Ida A.	PVT, Co. C, 161st REG NY VOLS
Ida A. ____ MULLEN		1853	1913	080	MULLEN, Ezekial	
				080		
Arthur MCNALLY		1836	1919	080	DUNNING, Mary	
Mary DUNNING McNally		1837	1912	080	MCNALLY, Arthur	
				080		
Bridget O'KANE		62 Years	02-28-18__	080	O'KANE, Bridget	
				080		
William SLAMON		80 Years	02-12-1875	080	____, Mary	
Mary ____ SLAMON		72Y 6M	02-08-1875	080	SLAMON, William	
Catharine SLAMON		29Y 3M	01-18-1869	080	SLAMON, Catharine	Dau Of Wm & Mary Slamon
Anna SLAMON		23Y 3M	02-20-1869	080	SLAMON, Anna	Dau Of Wm & Mary Slamon

Name	Place	Born/Age	Died	Code	Index	Notes
Francis SLAMON		28Y	12-10-1871	080	SLAMON, Francis	Son Of Wm & Mary Slamon
James SLAMON		37Y 10M	03-07-1872	080	SLAMON, James	Son Of Wm & Mary Slamon
				080		
Timothy BIRNEY		03-28-1830	07-11-1900	080	BIRNEY, Timothy	
				080		
Louis NOLIN		01-13-1845	02-04-1904	080	CONROY, Ellen	
Ellen CONROY Nolin		02-18-1853	12-29-1925	080	NOLIN, Louis	
				080		
Mary DION Delligan		05-26-1855	12-22-1892	080	DELLIGAN, Joseph	(NOI Joseph Delligan)
				080	DION, Mary	
				080		
James MCCLUSKEY		08-25-1846	03-03-1904	080	____, Mary A.	
Mary A. ___ MCCLUSKEY		02-13-1840	12-20-1903	080	MCCLUSKEY, James	
				080		
Hugh MCCLUSKEY		54 Years	02-20-1870	080	____, Catharine	
Catharine _____ MCCLUSKEY		43 Years	01-19-1869	080	MCCLUSKEY, Hugh	
Ellen MCCLUSKEY		15 Years	08-15-1865	080	MCCLUSKEY, Ellen	Dau Of H & C McCluskey
Barnard MCCLUSKEY		33 Years	05-20-1876	080	MCCLUSKEY, Barnard	Son Of H & C McCluskey
				080		
Katherine A. DELLIGAN Minns		40 Years	07-21-1902	080	MINNS, F.C.	(NOI F.C. Minns)
				080	DELLIGAN, Katherine A.	
				080		
Philip DELLIGAN		1851	1922	080	MOSSEY, Rose	
Rose MOSSEY Delligan		1866	1931	080	DELLIGAN, Philip	
				080		
John MCNALLY		1838	1912	080	DONALDSON, Angeline	(GAR) Co. F. 10TH RGT VT VOLS
Angeline DONALDSON McNally		1845	1914	080	MCNALLY, John	
				080		
Wm BURKE		1848	1915	080	LAFAR, Aurelia	
Aurelia LAFAR Burke		1852	1920	080	BURKE, Wm	
				080		
Patrick DOON		28 Years	07-18-1867	080	DOON, Patrick	
				080		
Mary _____ HAMILL		26 Years	10-26-1860	080	HAMILL, Patrick	(NOI Patrick Hamill)
				080	_____, Mary	
				080		
Morris O'DONNELL	Co. Limerick	59 Years	07-23-1873	080	O'DONNELL, Morris	A Native of Co. Limerick,Ire
				080		
Patrick LENNOX		77 Years	04-23-1869	080	DOON, Rose	
				080		
Rose DOON Lennox	Ireland	1795	1877	080	LENNOX, Patrick	
				080		
Mary DOON	Ireland	1797	1888	080	DOON, Mary	
				080		
Paul KEENEN		71 Years	05-22-1866	080	KEENEN, Paul	

Name	Place	Age/Born	Died	Code	Relative	Notes
				080		
Mary _____ MAHON		61 Years	11-02-1867	080	MAHON, Daniel	(NOI Daniel Mahon)
				080	_____, Mary	
				080		
Catharine MAHON		42 Years	12-03-1874	080	MAHON, Catharine	Dau of Daniel & Mary Mahon
				080		
John FREMORE		84 Years	04-09-1872	080	FREMORE, John	
Mary _____ FREMORE		59 Years	11-24-1876	080	WOOD, Anthony	
				080		
Byron B. BARNEY		1828	1905	080	QUINN, Mary	
Mary QUINN Barney		1859	1924	080	BARNEY, Byron B.	
				080		
James MURPHY		75 Years	09-18-1870	080	MURPHY, James	
				080		
Catharine SHEPARD Jersey		77 Years	01-23-1876	080	JERSEY, Henry	(NOI Henry Jersey)
				080	SHEPARD, Catharine	
				080		
John CANFIELD		1857	1923	080	BOUCHER, Rose	
Rose BOUCHER Canfield		1861	1918	080	CANFIELD, John	
				080		
James O'NEIL		46 Years	11-20-1869	080	O'NEIL, James	
Francis O'NEIL		48 Years	02-28-1874	080	O'NEIL, Francis	
				080		
Margaret _____ O'NEIL		75 Years	----------	080	O'NEIL, John	(Stone is damaged. Cannot read date of death)
				080		
John MCNALLY		05-22-1830	10-02-1914	080	O'KANE, Mary	
Mary O'KANE McNally		05-11-1839	01-31-1919	080	MCNALLY, John	
Henry MCNALLY		03-08-1853	03-12-1906	080	MCNALLY, Henry	
				080		
W. H. MITCHELL		1841	1934	080	MITCHELL, W. H.	(GAR) Co. F, 10 Regt, Vt. VOls
				080		
Peter TELFORD		07-04-1827	03-11-1892	080	MCDORMITT, Bridgett	
Bridgett MCDORMITT Telford		04-18-1826	06-18-1907	080	TELFORD, Peter	
				080		
Mary DONAGHUE Birney	Co. Limerick	65 Years	04-14-1892	080	BIRNEY, John	Native of Pallaskenry, Co. Limerick (NOI John Birney)
				080	DONAGHUE, Mary	
				080		
Mary BIRNEY O'Kane		79 Years	04-02-1890	080	O'KANE, Charles	
				080		
Charles O'KANE		68Y 9M	07-21-1875	080	BIRNEY, Mary	
				080		
Francis MCNALLY		1839	1888	080	O'KANE, Ellen	
Ellen O'KANE McNally		1847	1914	080	MCNALLY, Francis	
				080		
John MULLEN		1802	1875	080	O'KANE, Margaret	

Name	Place	Birth/Age	Death	Code	Index Name	Notes
Margaret O'KANE Mullen		1807	1889	080	MULLEN, John	
John Mullen JR.		1836	1910	080	MULLEN, John Jr.	
James MULLEN		1833	1898	080	MULLEN, James	
				080		
Michael CRONIN		09-__1854	10-18-1922	080	PENELL, Rosa E.	
Rosa E. PENELL Cronin		07-06-1866	07-02-1906	080	CRONIN, Michael	
				080		
John PENELL		12-13-1829	07-15-1910	080	DOOLING, Mary Ann	
Mary Ann DOOLING Penell		09-28-1837	11-14-1897	080	PENELL, John	
				080		
Michael O'DAY		1851	1917	080	O'DAY, Michael	
Anna O'DAY		1858	1908	080	O'DAY, Anna	
Frank O'DAY		1864	1920	080	O'DAY, Frank	
				080		
John O'DAY		1847	1918	080	_______, Delia	
Delia ____ O'DAY		1865	1930	080	O'DAY, John	
				080		
Patrick O'DAY		1849	1877	080	O'DAY, Patrick	
Mary _____ O'DAY		1857	1860	080	_____, Mary	
				080		
Patrick QUINN		1843	1932	080	______, Catherine	
Catherine ___ QUINN		45 Years	07-03-1883	080	QUINN, Patrick	
John C. QUINN		1872	1947	080	QUINN, John C.	
Theresa QUINN		13 Years	01-30-__	080	QUINN, Theresa	
				080		
John O'NEILL		1789	1834	080	O'HARRA, Margaret	
Margaret O'HARRA O'Neill		1795	1871	080	O'NEILL, John	
James O'NEILL		1820	1849	080	O'NEILL, James	
Francis O'NEILL		1832	1854	080	O'NEILL, Francis	
Michael O'NEILL		1848	1878	080	O'NEILL, Michael	
William O'NEILL		1852	1935	080	O'NEILL, William	
				080		
Mary FOLEY Fitzgerald		76 Years	12-15-1886	080	FITZGERALD, Martin	(NOI Martin Fitzgerald)
				080	FOLEY, Mary	
				080		
Mathew QUINN	Co. Down	90 Years	08-01-1898	080	______, Mary	Town Of Kilkeel, County Down,
				080		Parish Of Moren (Mourne)
Mary _____ QUINN	Co. Down	71 Years	07-24-1893	080	QUINN, Mathew	Town Of Lairen, County Down,
				080		Parish Of Moren (Mourne) (No
				080		such town as Lairen)
				080		
Martin O'CONNOR		62 Years	03-17-1907	080	O'CONNOR,Martin	
Rose DOON O'Connor		40Y 6M	09-26-1831	080	DOON, Rose	
				080		
Neal DOON		1816	1886	080	MCIVER, Margaret	

Margaret MCIVER Doon		1817	1900	080	DOON, Neal	
John DOON		1841	1908	080	DOON, John	Their Son
				080		
Patrick KIDWELL		34 Years	09-13-1832	080	KIDWELL, Patrick	
				080		
Sarah E. ____ GREEN		29 Years	06-26-1868	080	GREEN, Rufus L.	(NOI Rufus Green)
				080	_____, Sarah E.	
				080		
James MCNALLY		32Y 4M	01-06-1865	080	MCNALLY, James	Son Of Henry & Ellen McNally
Catherine MCNALLY		21Y 3M	03-05-1865	080	MCNALLY, Catherine	Dau Of Henry & Ellen McNally
				080		
James E. FARRELL		06-25-1850	02-15-1898	080	COOK, Mary	
Mary COOK Farrell		1852	1936	080	FARRELL, James E.	
				080		
Annie FARRELL Farley		53 Years	10-12-1909	080	FARLEY, James	(NOI James Farley)
				080	FARRELL, Annie	
				080		
Julia MCLEOD Watson		01-27-1845	07-19-1899	080	WATSON, Amos A.	(NOI Amos A. Watson)
				080	MCLEOD, Julia	
				080		
John MCIVER	Co. Armagh	75 Years	11-22-1874	080	MCIVER, John	Cty Of Armagh (County)
				080		
Henry DUGAN	Ireland		09-04-1878	080	DUGAN, Henry	Native Of Ireland
				080		
Catherine ____ KEENEN			11-16-1876	080	KEENEN, Paul	(NOI Paul Keenen)
				080	_____, Catherine	
				080		
Thomas COLEMAN		35 Years	04-22-1861	080	COLEMAN, Thomas	
				080		
Mary CRONIN		87 Years	12-19-1910	080	CRONIN, Mary	
				080		
Rosa KEENAN Keenan		74 Years	1877	080	KEENAN, Alexander	(NOI Alexander KeenAn)
				080	KEENAN, Rosa	
				080		
Thomas F. KELLEY		1856	1926	080	KELLEY, Thomas F.	
Catherine A. KELLEY		1856	1925	080	KELLEY, Catherine A.	
				080		
Catherine ____ YOUNG	Co. Dublin	28 Years	08-15-1867	080	YOUNG, James	A Native Of Dublin City, Ire
				080	_____, Catherine	(NOI James Young)

NAME	POB	DOB/AGE	DOD	CEM	SPOUSE/INDEX	INSCRIPTION
Sylvester DONALDSON		1837	1911	113	DONALDSON, Sylvester	
Phebe Anna _____ DONALDSON		1837	1906	113	_____, Phebe Anna	
Mary P. DONALDSON		1844	1937	113	DONALDSON, Mary P.	
				113		
Gilbert H. CHAPPEL		76 Years	09-21-1919	113	PATTON, Maggie	
Maggie PATTON Chappel		54 Years	02-28-1901	113	CHAPPEL, Gilbert H.	
				113		
Harry A. O'KANE		08-30-1855	03-29-1901	113	O'KANE, Harry A.	
				113		
Aaron KEENAN		02-17-1852	07-27-1908	113	_____, Annie M.	
Annie M. _____ KEENAN		12-23-1852	01-20-1938	113	KEENAN, Aaron	
				113		
Francis A. SMITH		06-30-1826	06-13-1902	113	MCKINNEY, Jane	
Jane MCKINNEY Smith		11-21-1833	05-17-1905	113	SMITH, Francis A.	
				113		
Horatio J. SCHOOLCRAFT		1858	1928	113	DONALDSON, Mary	
Mary DONALDSON Schoolcraft		1850	1943	113	SCHOOLCRAFT, Horatio J.	
Emily DONALDSON Fitzpatrick		1845	1929	113	DONALDSON, Emily	(NOI Mr. Fitzpatrick)
				113		
Frank H. FOSTER		1852	1907	113	DONALDSON, Amanda	
Amanda DONALDSON Foster		1852	1937	113	FOSTER, Frank H.	
				113		
Martin KEENAN		1829	1861	113	_____, Catherine	
Catherine _____ KEENAN		1831	1893	113	KEENAN, Martin	
				113		
Theabold M. TOBIN		1847	1918	113	CHASE, Sarah J.	
Sarah J. CHASE Tobin		1852	1936	113	TOBIN, Theabold M.	
				113		
William TOBIN		70 Years	12-01-1889	113	O'FLANEGAN, Mary A.	
Mary A. O'FLANEGAN Tobin		88 Years	11-04-1914	113	TOBIN, William	
				113		
Barney MULLEN		1845	1915	113	DONALDSON, Lillie	
Lillie DONALDSON Mullen		1863	1930	113	MULLEN, Barney	
				113		
Albert M. DONALDSON		07-09-1842	08-03-1939	113	HAZEN, Cornelia M.	(GAR) Co. K. 11th VT Vol
Cornelia M. HAZEN Donaldson		05-25-1845	07-23-1932	113	DONALDSON, Albert M.	
				113		
Sabins W. DONALDSON		1845	1932	113	BOOMHOWER, Nancy M.	
Nancy M. BOOMHOWER Donaldson		1848	1943	113	DONALDSON, Sabins W.	
				113		

Chester R. BURNS		10-04-1835		113	POOLER, Sarah	
Sarah POOLER Burns		04-09-1833	02-12-1909	113	BURNS, Chester R.	
				113		
Charles KEENAN		1827	1910	113	PEGGS, Anna	(GAR) Corp Co. D. 74th Ohio
				113		Regt Sergt Co. L 1st Reg,U.S.
				113		Engineers.
Anna PEGGS Keenan		1856	1935	113	KEENAN, Charles	
				113		
Jane DONALDSON Wood		1843	1921	113	DONALDSON, Jane	(NOI Mr. Wood)
				113		
Archibald MACDONALD		01-11-1841	03-26-1908	113	LIVINGSTON, Lydia	Lodge No. 134, B Of LF&E
				113	LIVINGSTON, Hezekiah	(Brotherhood of Locomotive
Lydia LIVINGSTON MacDonald		08-09-1841	01-10-1915	113	MACDONALD, Archibald	Firemen and Engineers)
Hezekia LIVINGSTON MacDonald		03-04-1837	11-15-1923	113		
				113		
Judson JANES		1847	1908	113	MCCUMMINGS, Alice	
Alice MCCUMMINGS Janes		1855	1911	113	JANES, Judson	
				113		
Andrew J. CARMAN		1830	1907	113	DONALDSON, Mary R.	
Mary R. DONALDSON Carman		1840	1917	113	CARMAN, Andrew J.	
				113		
Henry C. MCGREGOR		1845	1914	113	LAMPMAN, Celia E.	
Celia E. LAMPMAN McGregor		1847	1918	113	MCGREGOR, Henry C.	

Church Street Cemetery, Swanton, Vermont. Just East of the Village Green.

NAME	POB	DOB/AGE	DOD	CEM	SPOUSE/INDEX	INSCRIPTION
Sally B. DUNBAR Murphy		41 Years	--_--_1839	120	MURPHY, James	Sally B. Consort of James
				120	DUNBAR, Sally B.	Murphy & Dau Of John & Lucinda
				120		Dunbar.(James Murphy is buried
				120		St. Mary's Cemetery, Swanton)
				120		(Stone badly deteriorated)
				120		
Sally Louisa MURPHY		3 Months	02-13-1831	120	MURPHY, Sally Louisa	Dau Of James & Sally B. Murphy
				120		
Laurance C. MURPHY		31 Years	11-14-1862	120	MURPHY, Laurance	(S/O James & Sally Murphy)
				120		
Thomas COONEY			10-__-1855	120	COONEY, Thomas	(NOI DOB)
				120		
Ammon S. MCGEE		77Y 8M	07-03-1897	120	MCGEE, Ammon	(GAR) Co. D. 5th Rgt VT Vols
				120		

NAME	POB	DOB/AGE	DOD	CEM	SPOUSE/INDEX	INSCRIPTION
Mary A. MANAHAN			08-03-1845	120	MANAHAN, Mary A.	D/O Timothy & Bridget Manahan
				120		(Bottom of stone buried-no DOB
				120		
				120		
Stephen F. BROWN		04-04-1841	09-08-1903	120	MCDONOUGH, Mary	(GAR)Co. K. 13th Rgt and Co. A
				120		17th Rgt (VT Vols)
Mary A. MCDONOUGH Brown		07-19-1851	09-11-1925	120	BROWN, Stephen F.	Born In Chicago, Il.
				120		
Sarah J. WALLACE Barney		09-20-1840	03-22-1883	120	BARNEY, Rufus	(NOI Rufus Barney)
				120	WALLACE, Sarah J.	
				120		
Matthias R. CONROY		32 Years	11-19-1831	120	CONROY, Matthias	In His 32nd Year
				120		
John MELLAN		67Y 9M	05-18-1846	120	MELLAN, John	
				120		
Francis BIRNEY		26 Years	01-21-1842	120	BIRNEY, Francis	S/O Roger & Mary Birney
				120	BIRNEY, Roger	In His 26th Year
				120	BIRNEY, Mary	
				120		
John D. SHERIDAN		74 Years	04-19-1901	120	SHERIDAN, John D.	(GAR)Capt Co. C.5th Rgt VT Vol
				120		
				120		
Sarah G. WILSON McGee		54 Years	01-07-1874	120	MCGEE, Ammon	Wife of Ammon McGee (Not sure
				120		which Ammon. Closest to Ammon
				120		Megee)
				120		
Elisha MEGEE				120	MEGEE, Elisha	(GAR)Co. F 7th VT(NOI DOB-DOD)
				120		
John SKINNER	Glostershire	10-27-1837	03-24-1880	120	SKINNER, John	Born In Glostershire, England.
				120		Died in Swanton, VT
				120		
Ammon MEGEE		73 Years	09-09-1868	120	WILSON, Sarah G.	(GAR) Co. D. 5th Rgt VT Vols
				120		
Oscar MCGREGOR		1848	1927	120	KELLEY, Ella J.	(GAR) Pvt Co. I. 7th VT Vols
Ella J. KELLEY McGregor		1861	1929	120	MCGREGOR, Oscar	
				120		
Mary O. C. MACNAMARA		1Y11M16D	03-16-1805	120	MCNAMARA, Mary O.C.	(Parents Not Indicated)

Greene's Corners Cemetery, VT Route 105, Swanton, Vermont (Sheldon Road)

NAME	POB	DOB/AGE	DOD	CEM	SPOUSE/INDEX	INSCRIPTION
James SHANNON		65Y 6M	03-24-1894	117	AUSTIN, Paulina	

Paulina AUSTIN Shannon		71Y 9M	02-10-1899	117	SHANNON, James	
				117		
Thomas SHANNON		93 Years	02-18-1881	117	SHANNON, Jane	
Jane _____ SHANNON			04-01-1862	117	SHANNON, Thomas	(Stone is buried. Age at death
				117		not readable)
Ada Samantha SHANNON		10Y 9M	04-06-1861	117	SHANNON, Ada Samantha	
				117		
William G. RYE		42 Years	08-08-1880	117	RYE, William G.	
				117		
John FORD		1847	1902	117	WESTOVER, Betsey	
Betsey WESTOVER Ford		1841	1930	117	FORD, John	
				117		
Herbert DWYER		1841	1936	117	ABELL, Martha	
Martha ABELL Dwyer		1845	1910	117	DWYER, Herbert	
				117		
				117		

Little Ireland Road, Starksboro, Vt. (Parishioners St. Ambrose, Bristol , VT)

NAME	POB	DOB/AGE	DOD	CEM	SPOUSE/INDEX	INSCRIPTION
Patrick CONWAY	Co. Limerick	1805	08-18-1865	081	GRIFFIN, Catherine	Born In Limerick, Ireland
Catherine GRIFFIN Conway	Co. Limerick	1805	05-13-1879	081	CONWAY, Patrick	Born In Limerick, Ireland
Bridget CONWAY	Co. Limerick	18 Years	01-01-1855	081	CONWAY, Bridget	Native of Laufmore (Loughmore
				081		Common) Co. Limerick, Ireland
Ann CONWAY	Co. Limerick	23 Years	12-22-1861	081	CONWAY, Ann	Native of Laufmore (Loughmore
				081		Common) Co. Limerick, Ireland
Thomas CONWAY	Co. Limerick	30 Years	08-08-1864	081	CONWAY, Thomas	Native of Laufmore (Loughmore
				081		Common) Co. Limerick, Ireland
James CONWAY		18--	10-15-1905	081	TOBIN, Mary	
Mary TOBIN Conway		04-03-1835	02-08-1921	081	CONWAY, James	
James CONWAY		08-13-1860	10-03-1929	081	CONWAY, James	
				081		
John FITZGERALD	Co. Limerick	70 Years	08-18-1870	081	FITZGERALD, John	Native of 'Valaidade'. County
				081		Limerick, Ireland (Could not
				081		find in references)
				081		
Thomas M. CASEY		11-02-1862	09-01-1907	081	CONWAY, Anna	St. Ambrose Court 753,
				081		Catholic Order of Foresters
Anna CONWAY Casey		05-13-1864	06-06-1930	081	CASEY, Thomas M.	
Maude C. CASEY James		03-30-1890	08-23-1950	081	JAMES, Charles G.	NOI Charles James
				081	CASEY, Maude C.	
				081		
Thomas C. HANNAN		44 Years	04-12-1897	081	STAPLETON, Ellen	

NAME	POB	DOB/AGE	DOD	CEM	SPOUSE/INDEX	INSCRIPTION
Ellen STAPLETON Hannan		41YR 4MO	06-27-1895	081	HANNAN, Thomas C.	
Mary HANNAN		23 Years	07-09-1878	081	HANNAN, Mary	Daughter of T & E Hannan
George HANNAN		18 Years	12-14-1894	081	HANNAN, George	Adopted Son of T.C. Hannan
				081		
Andrew HALPIN		42 Years	11-08-1867	081	______, Johannah	
Johannah ------ HALPIN		28 Years	05-12-1855	081	HALPIN, Andrew	
				081		
Francis HANNAN		67 Years	07-03-1890	081	COONERTY, Ellen	
Ellen COONERTY Hannan		84 Years	11-04-1907	081	HANNAN, Francis	
Hannie HANNAN		8Y 8M	05-02-1878	081	HANNAN, Hannie	
Francis HANNAN		12 Years	07-02-1878	081	HANNAN, Francis	
				081		
Bridget _____ CASEY		56 Years	02-15-1876	081	CASEY, Thomas 2nd	NOI Thomas Casey
				081	_____, Bridget	
				081		
Mary FITZGERALD Hannan		68 Years	12-24-1859	081	HANNAN, Thomas	NOI Thomas Hannan
				081	FITZGERALD, Mary	
				081		
Thomas HANNAN	Co. Limerick	87 Years	05-05-1902	081	HANNAN, Thomas	Born In County Limerick, Ire
				081		
				081		
Margaret ______O'CONNOR		54 Years	03-26-1887	081	O'CONNOR, John	NOI John O'Connor
				081	Margaret _____	
				081		
Maurice O'CONNELL		10Y 4MO	06-08-1878	081	O'CONNELL, Maurice	
				081		
Thomas CASEY	Co. Clare	82 Years	10-20-1874	081	PIERCE, Annory	Born In The Parish of Rogan,
				081		(Roughan) Co. Clare, Ireland
Annory PIERCE Casey		56 Years	05-27-1860	081	CASEY, Thomas	

St. Thomas Cemetery (Old) Lower Valley Road, Underhill, VT

NAME	POB	DOB/AGE	DOD	CEM	SPOUSE/INDEX	INSCRIPTION
Bridget _____ GILL		45 Years	07-27-1854	082	GILL, James	(NOI James Gill)
				082	GILL, Bridget	
Mary WALL		18 Years	07-31-1860	082	WALL, Mary	Dau of D. & B. Wall
Annie WALL			11-01-1859	082	WALL, Annie	Dau of D. & B. Wall
James WALL			01-30-1853	082	WALL, James	Son of D. & B. Wall
				082		
John MCNULTY		2 Years	11-08-1852	082	MCNULTY, John	Son of B. & A. McNulty
				082		

Maria MARLOW	_ Months	06-21-1852	082	MARLOW, Maria	Dau of C. & B. Marlow
			082		
John CARNEY	2Y 5M 2D	01-09-1852	082	CARNEY, John	Son of James & Jane Carney
			082	CARNEY, James	
			082		
Susannah MCMANUS	3 Years	04-01-1866	082	MCMANUS, Susannah	Dau of Bernard & Mary McManus
			082	MCMANUS, Bernard	
			082		
Margaret KELLEY	4 Years	07-28-1847	082	KELLEY, Margaret	Dau of G. & M. Kelley
			082		
Mary ____ MCGLYNN	26 Years	12-02-1856	082	MCGLYNN, Patrick	(NOI Patrick McGlynn)
			082	_____, Mary	
			082		
Peter DUFFY	65 Years	06-05-1851	082	DUFFY, Peter	
			082		
Catharine ____ WAUGH	35 Years	01-24-1851	082	WAUGH, Thomas	(NOI Thomas Waugh)
			082	_____, Catherine	
			082		
Thomas DORAN	45Y 8M	12-06-1871	082	ELLSWORTH, Emily A.	
Emily A. ELLSWORTH Doran	40Y 1M	12-30-1873	082	DORAN, Thomas	
			082		
Patrick DORAN	78 Years	03-15-1862	082	NUGANT, Mary	(Stone toppled, deteriorated)
Mary NUGANT Doran	95Y 9M	01-26-1872	082	DORAN, Patrick	(Stone toppled, deteriorated)
			082		
Susan DORAN	5Y 3M	02-12-1866	082	DORAN, Susan	Son of T. & E.A. Doran
			082		
James A. DORAN	2 Months	09-23-1858	082	DORAN, James A.	Son of T. & E.A. Doran
			082		
Thomas DORAN	5 Months	09-25-1847	082	DORAN, Thomas	Son of J. & M. Doran
			082		
Edward L. DORAN	9Y 3M	02-22-1866	082	DORAN, Edward L.	Son of T. & E.A. Doran
			082		
Eliza J. DORAN	3Y 8M	03-11-1866	082	DORAN, Eliza	Dau of T. & E.A. Doran
			082		
Emily A. DORAN	2Y 8M	11-20-1862	082	DORAN, Emily	Dau of T. & E.A. Doran
			082		
			082		
Michael BEIRNE/BURNS	44 Years	12-15-1851	082	BEIRNE, Michael	
			082	BURNS, Michael	
			082		
Thomas BURNS	17Y 2M	06-24-1865	082	BURNS, Thomas	S/O Michael & Elizabeth Burns

Irish Settlement Cemetery   Irish Settlement Road, Underhill, VT

NAME	POB	DOB/AGE	DOD	CEM	SPOUSE/INDEX	INSCRIPTION
Edward BREEN		11-16-182_		083	CAVANAUGH, Mary	(Could not read date of death)
Mary CAVANAUGH Breen		52 Years	01-22-1889	083	BREEN, Edward	
Katie BREEN		13 Years	09-28-1886	083	BREEN, Katie	Dau of E. & M. Breen
Rosannah ____ BREEN		75 Years	04-23-1863	083	BREEN, John	(NOI John Breen)
				083		
Edward L. BARRETT		23Y 3M		083	BARRETT, Edward L.	(Could not read date of death)
				083		
Margaret TUNNEY Barrett		40 Years	02-09-1876	083	BARRETT, John	
				083	TUNNEY, Margaret	
Ellen E. BARRETT		13Y 7M	07-06-1875	083	BARRETT, Ellen E.	Dau of J. & M. Barrett
Charles BARRETT				083	BARRETT, Charles	Son of John & Margaret Barrett
Frederick BARRETT		1869	1888	083	BARRETT, Frederick	
Mary MCTIERNEY Barrett		38 Years	06-04-1884	083	BARRETT, John	Wife of John Barrett
John BARRETT		79 Years	07-25-1871	083	BARRETT, John	
Mary E. BARRETT				083	BARRETT, Mary E.	(NOI DOB/DOD)
Patrick BARRETT		28 Years	05-25-1865	083	BARRETT, Patrick	
Elizabeth CONNERS Barrett		70 Years	12-21-1868	083	CONNERS, Elizabeth	Wife of John Barrett
Luke BARRETT		28Y 8M	09-08-1855	083	BARRETT, Luke	(This family plot was copied
Anna BREEN BARRETT		72 Years	11-17-1868	083	BARRETT, Michael	in order of the markers. Not
Michael BARRETT		75 Years	01-20-1870	083	BREEN, Anna	easy to figure out if wives
				083		of John Barrett were all wed
				083		to the same John)
				083		
Patrick BARRETT		1829	1887	083	____, Celia	
Celia ____ BARRETT		1830	1895	083	BARRETT, Patrick	
Michael BARRETT		1859	1878	083	BARRETT, Michael	
John H.BARRETT		1866	1869	083	BARRETT, John H.	
Francis BARRETT		1855	1856	083	BARRETT, Francis	
				083		
Catherine FLANNIGAN Barrett		28Y 2M 10D	01-09-1851	083	BARRETT, John	(No marker for John Barrett)
				083	FLANNIGAN, Catherine	
Frank BARRETT		1 Year	12-08-1853	083		Son of J. & C. Barrett
Thomas BARRETT			1853	083		Son of J. & C. Barrett
				083		
Michael BARRETT		1828	1888	083	BREEN, Elizabeth	
Elizabeth BREEN Barrett		1827	1912	083	BARRETT, Michael	
John W. BARRETT		1854	1909	083	BARRETT, John W.	
Elizabeth A. BARRETT		1857		083	BARRETT, Elizabeth A.	
Luke F. BARRETT		1859		083	BARRETT, Luke	
Michael BARRETT		1861		083	BARRETT, Michael	

Mary T. BARRETT		1864		083	BARRETT, Mary T.	
Patrick L. BARRETT		1867		083	BARRETT, Patrick L.	
				083	BARRETT, Alice	Native of Co. Wexford, Ire
Alice BARRETT Bulger			01-06-1906	083	BULGER, Moses	Native of Co. Wexford, Ire
Patrick BULGER		7Y 4M	03-04-1853	083	BULGER, Patrick	
Mary BULGER		6 Months	05-06-1849	083	BULGER, Mary	
Moses BULGER	Co. Wexford	84 Years	01-11-1890	083		
				083		
William BREEN		91 Years	05-13-1903	083	BARRETT, Mary	
Mary BARRETT Breen		38Y 9M	02-20-1863	083	BREEN, William	
Rosanna BREEN		2Y 5M	04-26-1853	083	BULGER, Rosana	Dau of W. & M. Breen
Elizabeth BREEN		4Y 6M	08-26-1863	083	BULGER, Elizabeth	Dau of W. & M. Breen
				083		
Thomas TUNNEY		83 Years	08-11-1883	083	TUNNEY, Thomas	
				083		
Edward W. ENOUS		1858	1911	083	HANLEY, Margaret A.	
Margaret A. HANLEY Enous		1856	1938	083	ENOUS, Edward W.	
				083		
John DOON	Co. Armagh	10-20-1806	01-10-1898	083	BARRETT, Catharine	B/I County Armaugh (Armagh),
				083		Ireland
				083	COX, Ellen	
Catharine BARRETT Doon		35Y 6M	07-17-1857	083	DOON, John	
Ellen COX Doon		11-09-1826	03-30-1896	083	DOON, John	
Henery DOON		13 Years	04-16-1853	083	DOON, Henery	Son of John & Catharine Doon
				083		
Edward M. HANLEY		64Y 15D	03-01-1875	083	HANLEY, Edward M.	
				083		
Mary FAY Patterson		47 Years	03-30-1861	083	PATTERSON, A.	(NOI A. Patterson)
				083	FAY, Mary	
Edward PATTERSON		6 Months	02-23-1854	083	PATTERSON, Edward	Son of A. & M. Patterson
Alexander PATTERSON		2 Years	09-17-1851	083	PATTERSON, Alexander	Son of A. & M. Patterson
				083		
Ann BREEN Kavanagh		51 Years	11-13-1850	083	KAVANAGH, Charles	(NOI Charles Kavanagh)
				083	BREEN, Ann	
				083		
Arthur CAVANAGH		1833	1914	083	MCELROY, Ann	
Ann MCELROY Cavanagh		1834	1921	083	CAVANAGH, Arthur	
Sarah CAVANAGH			10-11-1932	083	CAVANAGH, Sarah	
				083		
Barnaby SHANLY		18 Years	08-02-1844	083	SHANLEY, Barnaby	S/O Barnabus & Rosann Shanly
Mary SHANLY		33 Years	04-01-1845	083	SHANLEY, Mary	
				083		
Patrick CALE		69 Years	04-05-1883	083	SHANLEY, Catherine	(Could be surname GALE.Hard to
Catherine SHANLEY Cale		38Y 10M	05-27-1854	083	CALE, Patrick	read inscriptions)
James CALE		36Y 7M	11-10-1883	083	CALE, James	Died In Socoro, New Mexico

Name	Place	Age	Date	Code	Related	Notes
				083		
Barnabus SHANLEY	Co. Leitrim	88 Years	03-09-1872	083	____, Rose Anna	B/I County of Latrim
				083		(Leitrim),Ireland. Died in
				083		Underhill
Rose Anna ____ SHANLEY		85 Years	03-20-1870	083	SHANLEY, Barnabus	
				083		
Ellen ____ KANE		20& 9M	03-25-1872	083	KANE, Owen M.	(NOI Owen M. Kane)
				083	_____, Ellen	
				083		
Thomas SHANLEY		68 Years	09-15-1888	083	BARRETT, Alice	
Alice BARRETT Shanley		52Y2M16D	07-08-1880	083	SHANLEY, Thomas	
				083		
Frederick SHANLEY		3Y10M11D	01-19-1853	083	SHANLEY, Frederick	Son of T & A Shanley
				083		
Mary JOICE Gill	Co. Mayo	63 Years	05-28-1863	083	GILL, Patrick	Native of Clonborough(Clonbur)
				083	JOICE, Mary	Parish of Burriscarra, County
				083		of Mayo (NOI Patrick Gill)
				083		
John GILL		15 Years	02-04-1853	083	GILL, John	Son of Patrick & Mary Gill
				083		
Ann GILL		8 Months	02-13-1853	083	GILL, Mary	Dau of Mary Gill
				083		
James DOON		1850	1919	083	DOON, James	
Mary J. HANLEY Doon		1852		083	HANLEY, Mary J.	
Michael J. DOON		1881	1940	083	DOON, Michael A.	
Frances M. DOON		1889	1902	083	DOON, Frances M.	
				083		
John DOON				083	FAY, Mary	(Stone damaged. Cannot read)
Mary FAY Doon		81 Years	09-05-1868	083	DOON, John	
				083		
Felix DOON		84 Years	01-12-1890	083	MALONE, Margrett	
Margrett MALONE Doon		76 Years	02-16-1883	083	DOON, Felix	
Ellen DOON		25 Years	01-15-1871	083	DOON, Ellen	Dau of Felix & Margaret Doon
				083		
Francis DUFFEY		46 Years	02-02-1880	083	____, Mary	
Mary ____ DUFFEY		32 Years	02-09-1873	083	DUFFEY, Francis	
				083		
James GARVILL		35 Years	05-28-1885	083	DUFFEY, Mary	
Mary DUFFEY Garvill		18__	1918	083	GARVILL, James	
				083		
James REYNOLDS		20Y7M27D	04-18-1862	083	REYNOLDS, James	S/O Michael & Allice Reynolds
William H. REYNOLDS		11Y11M12D	08-13-1861	083	REYNOLDS, William H.	S/O Michael & Allice Reynolds
				083	REYNOLDS, Michael	
				083	REYNOLDS, Allice	
				083		

Name	Age/Born	Death	Code	Index Name	Notes
James REYNOLDS	19Y 7M	04-30-1871	083	REYNOLDS, James	
			083		
James SHANLEY	1823	1904	083	HANLEY, Maria	
Maria HANLEY Shanley	1825	1902	083	SHANLEY, James	
William SHANLEY	1850		083	SHANLEY, William	
Frederick SHANLEY	1853		083	SHANLEY, Frederick	
Julia SHANLEY	1856		083	SHANLEY, Julia	
James C. SHANLEY	1858		083	SHANLEY, James C.	
Lewis J. SHANLEY	1861	1901	083	SHANLEY, Lewis J.	
Maria SHANLEY	1865	1866	083	SHANLEY, Maria	
			083		
Richard HINES	78 Years	07-23-1872	083	____, Mary	
Mary ____ HINES	65 Years	06-12-1870	083	HINES, Richard	
			083		
Elizabeth MORRIS Stinson	54 Years	07-22-1897	083	STINSON, Edward	(NOI Edward Stinson)
			083	MORRIS, Elizabeth	
			083		
Mary ____ SWENEY	60 Years	02-12-1859	083	SWENEY, Edward	(NOI Edward Sweney)
			083	_____, Mary	
			083		
Mary M. JORDAN	1861	1939	083	JORDAN, Mary	
			083		
Martin MCGRATH	95 Years	04-11-1882	083	____, Mary	
Mary ____ MCGRATH	90 Years	03-19-1891	083	MCGRATH, Martin	
Catherine MCGRATH	23 Years	06-24-1869	083	MCGRATH, Catherine	Dau of Martin & Mary McGrath
Margaret MCGRATH	27 Years	03-07-1865	083	MCGRATH, Margaret	Dau of Martin & Mary McGrath
Mary MCGRATH	22 Years	03-17-1866	083	MCGRATH, Mary	Dau of Martin & Mary McGrath
			083		
Michael LEDDY	85 Years	12-03-1865	083	LEDDY, Michael	
			083		
John LEDDY	23Y10M7D	06-29-1873	083	LEDDY, John	
			083		
Margaret LEDDY Gill	25Y5M4D	07-26-1881	083	GILL, John	(NOI John Gill)
			083	GILL, Margaret	
			083		
Mary A. Gill Leddy	32 Years	06-11-1884	083	LEDDY, Michael	(NOI Michael Leddy)
			083	GILL, Mary A.	
			083		
James CASEY	97Y 5M	09-30-1890	083	WADICK, Jane	
Jane WADICK Casey	78Y5M22D	08-29-1878	083	CASEY, James	
James M. Casey Jr	11Y 5M	05-28-1886	083	CASEY, James M. Jr.	
			083		
Moses LEARY	40 Years	10-15-1852	083	LEARY, Moses	(Stone deteriorated. YOD C/B 1882)
			083		
			083		

Name	Birth/Age	Death	Code	Index Name	Notes
Mathew CASEY	1815		083	BREEN, Ellen	
Ellen BREEN Casey	1824	1893	083	CASEY, Mathew	
Julia CASEY	1852		083	CASEY, Julia	
Mary CASEY	1854	1873	083	CASEY, Mary	
James CASEY	1861	1892	083	CASEY, James	
			083		
Catharine MCVEY		06-19-1873	083	MCVEY, Catherine	Dau of D & R McVey
			083		
Robert FARRELL	1800	1888	083	GOLDEN, Catherine	
Catherine GOLDEN Farrell	1813	1888	083	FARRELL, Robert	
			083		
Barney GRAY	58 Years	12-21-1876	083	____, Ellen	
Ellen ____ GRAY	56 Years	09-18-1875	083	GRAY, Barney	
Ann GRAY	1849	1918	083	GRAY, Ann	Born In Ireland
			083		
Michael GRAY	5 Years	07-25-1861	083	GRAY, Michael	Son of J & F Gray
			083		
James GRAY	45 Years	05-02-1862	083	GRAY, James	
			083		
Michael MCHUGH	1829	1913	083	MCGETTRICK, Mary	
Mary MCGETTRICK McHugh	1838	1921	083	MCHUGH, Michael	
Charles Peter MCHUGH	1870	1872	083	MCHUGH, Charles Peter	
Catherine Ann MCHUGH Levins	1862	1916	083	MCHUGH, Catherine Ann	(NOI Mr. Levins)
Francis (McHugh or Levins?)	1865	1932	083	_____, Francis	(Surname not given. Is he Mr. Levins or McHugh?)
			083		
			083		
Jane FITZGERALD	5Y 9M	10-11-1862	083	FITZGERALD, Jane	Dau of P & G Fitzgerald
Sarah FITZGERALD	1Y 2M	10-18-1862	083	FITZGERALD, Sarah	Dau of P & G Fitzgerald
Michael FITZGERALD	4Y 8M	10-07-1862	083	FITZGERALD, Michael	Son of P & G Fitzgerald
			083		
Mary MCMANNIS Gale	57 Years	12-25-1878	083	GALE, Patrick	(NOI Patrick Gale)
			083	MCMANNIS, Mary	
			083		
Rosa MCMANUS Patterson	68 Years	02-16-1887	083	PATTERSON, Alexander	(NOI Alexander Patterson)
			083	MCMANUS, Rose	
			083		
Mary E. BURN	22 Years	09-28-1872	083	BURN, Mary E.	Dau of M & Elizabeth Burn
			083		
Alexander NEVINS	1847	1917	083	NEVINS, Alexander	
			083		
Patrick CORBETT	55 Years	07-01-1872	083	CORBETT, Patrick	
			083		
Thomas HENNESSEY	1841	1913	083	FOLEY, Margaret	
Margaret FOLEY Hennessey	1834	1910	083	HENNESSEY, Thomas	
			083		

Barney MCNULTY	62 Years	09-05-1880	083	CASEY, Ellen	
Ellen CASEY McNulty	53 Years	01-18-1870	083	MCNULTY, Barney	
			083		
Edmond CORBETT	1851	1929	083	CAVANAGH, Ann Eliza	
Ann Eliza CAVANAGH Corbett	38 Years	03-16-1893	083	CORBETT, Edmond	
			083		
Patrick CORBETT	1810	1872	083	CAREY, Margaret	
Margaret CAREY Corbett	1827	1901	083	CORBETT, Patrick	
			083		
John MCMANNIS	37 Years	12-19-1874	083	MCMANNIS, John	
			083		
Patrick MCMANNIS	73 Years	02-12-1872	083	NICHOLS, Aurilla	
Aurilla NICHOLS MxMannis	62Y9M8D	03-26-1870	083	MCMANNIS, Patrick	
			083		
William CORBETT	08-08-1855	04-13-1918	083	BARRETT, Sarah	
Sarah BARRETT Corbett	10-23-1856	09-30-1936	083	CORBETT, William	
			083		
Elizabeth ____ REYNOLDS		12- -1871	083	REYNOLDS, Patrick	(NOI Patrick Reynolds. Stone deteriorated)
			083		
			083		
Barney CAHILL	1807	1885	083	CASTLE, Susan	
Susan CASTLE Cahill	1808	1892	083	CAHILL, Barney	
Mary CAHILL			083	CAHILL, Mary	(Dau of Barney & Susan Cahill)
Francis CAHILL			083	CAHILL, Francis	(Son of Barney & Susan Cahill)
Rose CAHILL			083	CAHILL, Rose	(Dau of Barney & Susan Cahill)
			083		
J. ADDRIAN	57 Years	03-13-1870	083	MALANIFF, Mary	
Mary MALANIFF Addrian	57 Years	01-01-1879	083	ADDRIAN, J.	Former Wife Of J. Addrian
			083		
James MORRIS	03-07-1831		083	DUFFEY, Elizabeth	
Elizabeth DUFFEY Morris	05-25-1837		083	MORRIS, James	
			083		
James SHANLEY	1840	1904	083	REYNOLDS, Ellen	
Ellen REYNOLDS Shanley	32Y10M	04-29-1877	083	SHANLEY, James	
			083		
Peter REYNOLDS	75 Years	07-22-1887	083	____, Ellen	
Ellen ____ REYNOLDS	75 Years	12-22-1883	083	REYNOLDS, Peter	
			083		
Jane REYNOLDS	5Y 13D	12-05-1870	083	REYNOLDS, Jane	Dau of P & R Reynolds
			083		
James REYNOLDS	03- -1833	04- -1891	083	REYNOLDS, James	
			083		
John FLYNN	1821	1887	083	____, Ann	
Ann ___ FLYNN	1838	1901	083	FLYNN, John	
			083		

Name	Age/Born	Date	Code	Index Name	Notes
James CULLEN	8 Years	08-21-1861	083	CULLEN, James	Son of Patrick & Honora Cullen
			083		
Patrick CULLEN	83 Years	09-12-1904	083	____, Katherine	
Katherine ____ CULLEN			083	CULLEN, Patrick	
			083		
Owen MARLOW	73 Years	11-06-1859	083	____, Ellen	
Ellen ____ MARLOW	72 Years	02-17-1856	083	MARLOW, Owen	
			083		
____ ____ MARLOW	65 Years	04-03-1864	083	MARLOW, Darbey	Wife of Darbey Marlow. (NOI Darbey and name of spouse is unreadable)
			083		
			083		
Patrick MCGOWEN		06-13-1858	083	MCGOWEN, Patrick	
			083		
Hugh MCGOWAN	26 Years	10-10-1873	083	MCGOWEN, Hugh	
			083		
James HARVEY	17 Years	10-31-1862	083	HARVEY, James	
			083		
Ann ____ STINSON	26 Years	09-03-1867	083	STINSON, E.	(NOI E. Stinson)
			083	_____, Ann	
			083		
John Edward HOGAN	10 Years	03-22-1843	083	HOGAN, John Edward	Son of Michael & Annie Hogan
			083	HOGAN, Michael	
			083		
Martha F. FLYNN Shanley	01-31-1863	04-05-1911	083	SHANLEY, Fred	(NOI Fred Shanley)
			083		
Peter GLEASON	56 Years	08-26-1866	083	GLEASON, Peter	
			083		
Julia M. ____ MOORE	45Y 7M	02-16-1884	083	MOORE, Thomas	(NOI Thomas Moore)
			083	_____, Julia M.	
			083		
Joseph FLYNN	15Y 8M	03-08-1897	083	FLYNN, Joseph	
			083		
James FLYNN	31 Years	12-15-1875	083	FLYNN, James	
			083		
Mathew BRUEN	1814	1864	083	BARREY, Ann	
Ann BARREY Bruen	1818	1894	083	BRUEN, Mathew	
Bernard BRUEN	1850	1851	083	BRUEN, Bernard	
Elizabeth (BRUEN?)	1863	1874	083	_____, Elizabeth	(Does not say she is a Bruen or spouse of Bernard Bruen)
			083		
			083		
John DORAN	1797	1870	083	BARRETT, Mary A.	
Mary A. BARRETT Doran	1818	1903	083	DORAN, John	
			083		
Mary A. HAGGERTY Tyler	31 Years	12-17-1881	083	TYLER, Frank G.	(NOI Frank G. Tyler)
			083	HAGGERTY, Mary A.	

				083		
Manric HAGGERTY		70 Years	09-06-1875	083	HAGGERTY, Manric	(Maurice?)
				083		
Martin LYNCH		17 Years	02-04-1873	083	LYNCH, Martin	Son Of Thomas & Ellen Lynch
				083	LYNCH, Thomas	
				083		
William H. FAY		22Y7M16D	02-08-1855	083	FAY, William H.	
				083		
James RAVEY		42Y7M26D	01-08-1865	083	RAVEY, James	
				083		
Terrence REAVEY				083	____, Catherine	(Stone damaged/deteriorated)
Catherine ____ REAVEY		61 Years	04-11-1861	083	REAVEY, Terrence	
				083		
Martin FLYNN		1816	1898	083	BARTLEY, Ellen	
Ellen BARTLEY Flynn		1821	1897	083	FLYNN, Martin	
Mattie E. FLYNN		1858	1879	083	FLYNN, Mattie E.	
Martha J. FLYNN		1853	1856	083	FLYNN, Martha J.	
James BARTLEY		1816	1898	083	BARTLEY, James	
				083		
Francis CAMPBELL		26 Years	03-28-1866	083	CAMPBELL, Francis	
				083		
John SHANLEY		1832	1862	083	ROWLEY, Mary	
Mary ROWLEY Shanley		1831	1909	083	SHANLEY, John	
Thomas SHANLEY		1861	1901	083	SHANLEY, Thomas	
				083		
Martha BEIRNE		1861	1880	083	BEIRNE, Martha	
				083		
Patrick DUFFEY	Co. Monaghan	68Y5M19D	12-06-1864	083	MOAN, Mary	A Native Of Lawbrallic (or)
				083		Lawbralhic, Co. Monoghan, Ire
				083		(or Laisbraihic)
Mary MOAN Duffey		72 Years	11-09-1877	083	DUFFEY, Patrick	
				083		
Paul KELLEY		18 Years	04-30-1872	083	KELLEY, Paul	Son Of C. & C. Kelley
				083		
Call KELLEY		70 Years	04-12-1883	083	KELLEY, Call	
				083		
Patrick CAMPBELL		1834	1918	083	CAMPBELL, Honora	
Honora CANNON Campbell		66 Years	08-09-1893	083	CAMPBELL, Patrick	
				083		
Lizzie GALE Farrell		30Y 11M	05-11-1873	083	FARRELL, F. G.	(NOI F.G. Farrell)
				083	GALE, Lizzie	
				083		
Edward FARRELL		73 Years	06-15-1887	083	CARROLL, Rose	
Rose CARROLL Farrell		49 Years	08-26-1867	083	FARRELL, Edward	
				083		

NAME	POB	DOB/AGE	DOD	CEM	SPOUSE/INDEX	INSCRIPTION
John FARRELL		82 Years	04-14-1898	083	FARRELL, John	
				083		
James MURPHY		1813	1897	083	____, Alice	
Alice ____ MURPHY		1829	1912	083	MURPHY, James	
John MURPHY		1855	1872	083	MURPHY, John	
Rose MURPHY		1858	1939	083	MURPHY, Rose	
Elizabeth MURPHY		1866	1873	083	MURPHY, Elizabeth	
Margaret MURPHY		1868	1949	083	MURPHY, Margaret	

St. Thomas Cemetery, Underhill Center, Vermont

NAME	POB	DOB/AGE	DOD	CEM	SPOUSE/INDEX	INSCRIPTION
Peter REYNOLDS		71 Years	05-13-1913	084	REYNOLDS, Peter	(Does Not state if Peter/Rose Ann Were husband and wife)
Rose Ann _____ REYNOLDS		67 Years	12-01-1906	084	REYNOLDS, Rose Ann	
				084		
James CASEY		1831	1924	084	____, Ellen	
Ellen ___ CASEY		1834	1921	084	CASEY, James	
Thomas CASEY		1867	1919	084	DOON, Ella	
Ella DOON Casey		10-16-1870	04-20-1913	084	CASEY, Thomas	
				084		
William FLYNN		1849	1922	084	SHANLEY, Joan	
Joan SHANLEY Flynn		1853	1931	084	FLYNN, William	
				084		
Michael LEDDY		1849	1916	084	CALE, Maria	
Maria CALE Leddy		1847	1925	084	LEDDY, Michael	
				084		
Mary Ann REYNOLDS		1853	1919	084	REYNOLDS, Mary Ann	(On ALGER stone-NOI Alger's)
				084		
Felix DOON		1853	1937	084	DUFFEY, Laura	
Laura DUFFEY Doon		1863	1950	084	DOON, Felix	
				084		
James W. MCLANE		1852	1909	084	TORPEY, Margaret	
Nancy DUFFY McLane		1846	1921	084	CORBITT, Michael	
				084		
Thomas ADRIEN		1844	1927	084	REDDY, Ellen	
Ellen REDDY Adrien		1850	1924	084	ADRIEN, Thomas	
				084		
George W. FITZSIMONS		1854	1937	084	CAVANAGH, Mary	
Mary CAVANAGH Fitzsimmons		1857	1946	084	FITZSIMONS, George W.	
				084		
James H. CARROLL		1844	1914	084	REDDY, Margaret	
Margaret REDDY Carroll		1852	1935	084	CARROLL, James H.	

Name	Born	Died	No.	Index	Notes
			084		
Michael DIXON	1855	1926	084	MCLAINE, Julia A.	
Julia A. MCLAINE Dixon	1853	1918	084	DIXON, Michael	
			084		
Wm J. HANLEY	1844	1921	084	REYNOLDS, Joanna	
Joanna REYNOLDS Hanley	1847	1923	084	HANLEY, Wm J.	
			084		
Eugene P. MUDGETT	08-29-1854	NOI	084	O'NEILL, Ellen	
Ellen O'NEILL Mudgett	10-11-1855	01-26-1912	084	MUDGETT, Eugene P.	
			084		
George H. WHITE	1853	1929	084	___, Elizabeth A.	
Elizabeth A. __ WHITE	1868	1953	084	WHITE, George A.	
			084		
Francis MARLOW	1835	1920	084	MARLOW, Francis	(Does Not state if Francis &
Mary MARLOW	1839	1908	084	MARLOW, Mary	Mary were husband and wife)
			084		
John HARMON	1831	1905	084	HARMON, John	(GAR) Co. D. 13 Regt Vt Inf
			084		
Francis BARRETT	1839	1905	084	DORAN, Nancy	
Nancy DORAN Barrett	1843	1926	084	BARRETT, Francis	
			084		
Henry MCNULTY	1824	1908	084	SAULTRY, Mary	
Mary SAULTRY McNulty	1817	1902	084	MCNULTY, Henry	
			084		
Louis DOREY	06-13-1845	--	084	PHALEN, Ellen	
Ellen PHALEN Dorey	08-23-1851	05-22-1905	084	DOREY, Louis	
			084		
John DUFFEY	10-12-1835	09-30-1900	084	HANLEY, Ellen J.	
Ellen D. HANLEY Duffey	02-29-1836	--	084	DUFFEY, John	
James FITZSIMONS	82 Years	10-09-1912	084	________, Bridget	
Bridget ____ FITZSIMONS	74 Years	08-02-1900	084	FITZSIMONS, James	
Rose FITZSIMONS	1855	1918	084	FITZSIMONS, Rose	
			084		
William MCELROY	1819	1903	084	_______, Clarissa	
Clarissa ____ MCELROY	1831	1894	084	MCELROY, William	
			084		
John MCELROY	1762	1851	084	________, Bridget	
Bridget ____ MCELROY	1793	1876	084	MCELROY, John	
			084		
John FITZSIMONDS	48 Years	12-06-1882	084	NCNULTY, Margaret	
Margaret MCNULTY Fitzsimonds	73 Years	07-12-1908	084	FITZSIMONDS, John	
			084		
John SMITH	1822	1898	084	MCELROY, Mary	
Mary MCELROY Smith	1821	1911	084	SMITH, John	
Jane SMITH	1849	1939	084	SMITH, Jane	

John SMITH	1851	1929	084	SMITH, John	
Mary SMITH	1853	1884	084	SMITH, Mary	
Annie SMITH	1855	1934	084	SMITH, Annie	
Sarah SMITH	1857	1934	084	SMITH, Sarah	
Ellen SMITH	1859	1937	084	SMITH, Ellen	
Nicholas SMITH	1861	1962	084	SMITH, Nicholas	
Bridget SMITH	1862	1954	084	SMITH, Bridget	
James SMITH	1864	1888	084	SMITH, James	
Elizabeth SMITH	1866	1878	084	SMITH, Elizabeth	
Agnes SMITH	1868	1962	084	SMITH, Agnes	
Catherine SMITH	1871	1943	084	SMITH, Catherine	
			084		
John HARVEY	1843	1934	084	____, Bridget	
Bridget ____ HARVEY	1849	19--	084	HARVEY, John	
			084		
James HURSON	--	09-01-1909	084	____, Bridget	(GAR Marker - NOI Bridget)
Bridget ____ HURSON			084	HURSON, James	(Try Co. E, 2nd Rgt, VtVols)
Mary E. HURSON	01-14-1871	12-09-1887	084	HURSON, Mary E.	Dau of James & Bridget Hurson
			084		
John CARROLL	1850	1933	084	BULGER, Anna M.	
Anna M. BULGER Carroll	1858	1911	084	CARROLL, John	
			084		
Catherine ____ STINSON	62 Years	01-15-1897	084	STINSON, Samuel	NOI Samuel Stinson
			084	____, Catherine	
			084		
Helen SPEARS Meglynn	62 Years	04-17-1890	084	MEGLYNN, Patrick	NOI Patrick Meglynn
			084	SPEARS, Helen	
			084		
Philip CARROLL	79 Years	04-05-1877	084	CAVANAGH, Mary	
Mary CAVANAGH Carroll	80 Years	03-12-1885	084	CARROLL, Philip	
			084		
Frank LADEAU	1838	1922	084	SEYMOUR, Caroline	
Caroline SEYMOUR Ladeau	1840	1921	084	LADEAU, Frank	
			084		
Peter J. LEDDY	1853	1928	084	LYNCH, Elizabeth	
Elizabeth LYNCH Leddy	1858	1923	084	LEDDY, Peter J.	
			084		
Daniel WALL	76 Years	08-25-1881	084	____, Bridget	
Bridget ____ WALL	63 Years	10-03-1885	084	WALL, Daniel	
			084		
Daniel WALL	11-16-1849	10-08-1929	084	WALL, Daniel	
			084		
Daniel MCGOVERN	1803	1887	084	____, Ann	
Ann ___ MCGOVERN	1811	1895	084	MCGOVERN, Daniel	

Ellen MCGOVERN	1841	1890	084	MCGOVERN, Ellen	
Jane MCGOVERN	1847	1893	084	MCGOVERN, Jane	
			084		
Patrick BURNS	1813	1893	084	HAGGERTY, Ann	
Ann HAGGERTY Burns	1803	1887	084	BURNS, Patrick	
Catherine BURNS	1840	1892	084	BURNS, Catherine	
Patrick BURNS	1841	1918	084	BURNS, Patrick	
Mary A. BURNS	1843	1900	084	BURNS, Mary A.	
			084		
Daniel SPLAIN	75 Years	01-03-1903	084	O'NEIL, Mary	
Mary O'NEIL Splain	52Y5M20D	07-20-1880	084	SPLAIN, Daniel	
			084		
John MCLANE	1821	1898	084	MULLIN, Mary	(GAR-Not in reference)
Mary MULLIN McLane	1828	1882	084	MCLANE, John	
			084		
John QUILLINAN	1835	1912	084	QUILLINAN, John	(Same Marker-does not say if
Christiana QUILLINAN	1838	1894	084	QUILLINAN, Christiana	John/Christiana were spouses)
			084		
Walter E. RUSSELL	84 Years	10-12-1903	084	HANLEY, Nancy	
Nancy HANLEY Russell	1834	1901	084	RUSSELL, Walter E.	Born In Essex, Vt - 1834
			084		Married In Essex, Vt - 1854
			084		Died in Jericho, Vt - 1901
			084		
SPLAIN MEMORIAL			084	MEMORIAL, Splain	(DOES NOT SHOW PARENTS)
Ellen SPLAIN Shanley	26Y10M3D	09-14-1880	084	SHANLEY, William	Died In California
			084	SPLAIN, Ellen	(NOI William Shanley)
Katie SPLAIN	24Y 15D	02-04-1881	084	SPLAIN, Katie	
Anne SPLAIN	20Y1M20D	01-28-1875	084	SPLAIN, Anne	
Eliza SPLAIN	20Y3M9D	01-27-1881	084	SPLAIN, Eliza	
Agnes SPLAIN	16Y2M18d	01-20-1881	084	SPLAIN, Agnes	
Daniel SPLAIN	15Y5M6D	08-31-1881	084	SPLAIN, Daniel	
James SPLAIN	1Y 4M	02-01-1882	084	SPLAIN, James	
Mary SPLAIN	1Y 1M	1885	084	SPLAIN, Mary	
Alice SPLAIN	--	1886	084	SPLAIN, Alice	
			084		
Martin J. FLANNERY	1830	1909	084	TUNNEY, Mary A.	
Mary A. TUNNEY Flannery	1834	1876	084	FLANNERY, Martin J.	
			084		
John B. CHAYER	01-04-1833	03-08-1892	084	RYAN, Margaret	
Margaret RYAN Chayer	12-12-1829	10-25-1915	084	CHAYERN, John B.	
			084		
Bridget BURNS Garland	41 Years	03-05-1881	084	GARLAND, Patrick	(NOI Patrick Garland)
			084	BURNS, Bridget	
			084		
Michael FITZGERALD	1824	1903	084	BROWN, Catherine	

Catherine BROWN Fitzgerald	1835	1908	084	FITZGERALD, Michael	
			084		
John W. MCNICHOLS	65 Years	09-21-1905	084	TUNNEY, Jane L.	Corp Co. C., 5th Rgt VT Vol
			084		Inft (GAR)
Jane L. TUNNEY McNichols	1850	1934	084	MCNICHOLS, John W.	
			084		
Abraham J. MARLOW	12-25-1830	12-25-1917	084	FLYNN, Catherine	
Catherine FLYNN Marlow	04-29-1855	05-21-1883	084	MARLOW, Abraham J.	
			084		
Peter MCNASSAR	--	--	084	HANLEY, Catherine	(No DOB or DOD on Stone)
Catherine HANLEY McNassar	10-26-1829	05-30-1893	084	MCNASSAR, Peter	
Ellen MCNASSOR	1955	1924	084	MCNASSOR, Ellen	
			084		
Frank YOUNG	1833	1901	084	____, Margaret	
Margaret ____ YOUNG	1837	1884	084	YOUNG, Frank	
			084		
Moses LEARY	1852	1892	084	BARRETT, Elizabeth	
Elizabeth BARRETT Leary	1857	1938	084	LEARY, Moses	
			084		
Mary T. MINER	05-16-1858	05-16-1877	084	MINER, Mary T.	Dau of Wm & Hannah Miner (NOI)
Willie L. MINER	5 Years	07-27-1862	084	MINER, Willie L.	Son of Wm & Hannah Miner (NOI)
			084	MINER, William	
Michael REYNOLDS	1825	1889	084	____, Catherine	
Catherine ____ REYNOLDS	1825	1914	084	REYNOLDS, Michael	
			084		
Michael REYNOLDS	--	--	084	WATERS, Alice	(May be same Michael as above-
	--	--	084		stones are in close proximity)
Alice WATERS Reynolds	71 Years	09-07-1886	084	REYNOLDS, Michael	
			084		
Patrick FARRELL	84 Years	09-20-1902	084	BATTELS, Bridget	
Bridget BATTELS Farrell	68 Years	05-06-1890	084	FARRELL, Patrick	
			084		
George W. MABLE	1850	1941	084	FITZGERALD, Ellen	
Ellen FITZGERALD Mable	1851	1898	084	MABLE, George W.	
			084		
Patrick EGAN	1831	1888	084	SHEEHAN, Ellen	
Ellen SHEEHAN Egan	1841	1922	084	EGAN, Patrick	
			084		
Frank BURNS	62 Years	02-26-1900	084	BURNS, Frank	
			084		
James KILPECK	03-12-1847	02-12-1952	084	LEDDY, Ellen	
Ellen LEDDY Kilpeck	07-15-1847	--	084	KILPECK, James	
			084		
Phillip FARRELL	1852	1934	084	CAMPBELL, Bridget	
Bridget CAMPBELL Farrell	1860	1936	084	FARRELL, Phillip	

			084		
Andrew H. MCGEE	1835	1899	084	RYAN, Bridget	(GAR-Try Co.L, 11th Rgt,VtVol)
Bridget RYAN McGee	1832	1911	084	MCGEE, Andrew H.	
			084		
James SHEEHY	1831	1925	084	MARLOW, Mary	
Mary MARLOW Sheehy	60 Years	09-15-1890	084	SHEEHY, James	
			084		
James BREEN	1822	1890	084	BREEN, James	(NOI Spouse)
Elizabeth BREEN	1857	1861	084	BREEN, Elizabeth	
Peter BREEN	1848	1848	084	BREEN, Peter	
Mary BREEN	1852	1893	084	BREEN, Mary	
Moses BREEN	1868	1883	084	BREEN, Moses	
George BREEN	1864	1869	084	BREEN, George	
			084		
John CASEY	33Y10M20D	05-25-1892	084	MAHONEY, Margaret	
Margaret MAHONEY Casey	1855	1926	084	CASEY, John	
			084		
Francis CAHILL	1846	1914	084	CAHILL, Francis	Born In Ireland. Died at
			084		Burlington, Vt.
William REAVEY	1834	05-01-1919	084	CAHILL, Mary	Born In Ireland.
Mary CAHILL Reavey	1841	06-10-1920	084	REAVEY, William	Born In Ireland.
			084		
William O'NEIL	69 Years	05-15-1891	084	O'NEIL, William	
			084		
Michael Gaffney JR.	45 Years	09-13-1880	084	______, Mary	Here Lies The Father & Mother
Mary ___ GAFFNEY	41 Years	06-15-1881	084	GAFFNEY, Michael Jr.	Of Six Orphan Children. Do Not
			084		Forget Them In Your Prayers.
			084		
Patrick MULLEN	1837	1917	084	SMITH, Mary	
			084	LYNCH, Maria	
Mary SMITH Mullen	1847	1875	084	MULLEN, Patrick	
Maria LYNCH Mullen	1847	1875	084	MULLEN, Patrick	
			084		
Patrick DONELLY	1817	1892	084	KANNON, Bridget	
Bridget KANNON Donelly	--	1895	084	DONELLY, Patrick	
			084		
Ellen DONELLY McCabe	43 Years	03-14-1899	084	MCCABE, William	(This was a Donelly Plot - See
			084		Following entry for informa-
			084		tion on William McCabe - ad-
			084		joining plot)
			084		
Wm H. MCCABE	1853	1926	084	DONNELLY, Ellen	
Ellen DONNELLY McCabe	1856	1899	084	MCCABE, Wm. H.	(Apparently a duplicate stone)
			084		
Rosa GREEN	55 Years	08-14-1891	084	GREEN, Rosa	Erected By Her Beloved Sister

				084	LANG, Bridget	Bridget Lang
				084		
Bridget KEOGH Ryan		1840	1897	084	RYAN, Dennis	(NOI Dennis Ryan)
				084	KEOGH, Bridget	
				084		
Dennis EGAN		1810	1883	084	____, Mary	
Mary ____ EGAN		1819	1902	084	EGAN, Dennis	
John EGAN		11-01-1855	06-21-1880	084	EGAN, John	Son Of Dennis & Mary Egan
Hannah EGAN		06-03-1848	07-31-1868	084	EGAN, Hannah	
Jennie EGAN		08- -1859	12-20-1887	084	EGAN, Jennie	
				084		
Matthew ENOS	Ireland	1811	1876	084	CASEY, Bridget	Born In Ireland.
				084		Died In Essex, Vt.
Bridget CASEY Enos	Ireland	1816	1888	084	ENOS, Matthew	Born In Ireland.
				084		Died In Essex, Vt.
Margaret CASEY Hogan	Ireland	1813	1878	084	CASEY, Margaret	Born In Ireland.(NOI Mr. Hogan
				084		
				084		
Kate MURFY Burke		57 Years	05-06-1889	084	BURKE, Felix	(NOI Felix Burke)
				084	MURFY, Kate	
				084		
Peter DONNALLY		--	--	084	____, Catharine	(No DOB DOD recorded)
Catharine ___ Donnally		58 Years	12-26-1885	084	DONNALLY, Peter	
				084		
Sarah ____ LANG		80 Years	09-26-1893	084	LANG, Edward	(NOI Edward Lang)
				084	____, Sarah	
Ellen LANG		25 Years	03-08-1880	084	LANG, Ellen	
Mary Jane LANG		22 Years	09-28-1874	084	LANG, Mary Jane	
Eliza LANG		21 Years	10-24-1876	084	LANG, Eliza	
Ann LANG		26 Years	10-25-1876	084	LANG, Ann	
				084		
Katherine HOGAN Mable		1851	1929	084	HOGAN, Katherine	(NOI Mr. Mable)
				084		
Bernard B. MATTIMORE		1835	1916	084	____, Mary E.	
Mary E. ___ MATTIMORE		1841	19--	084	MATTIMORE, Bernard B.	
				084		
Martin MATTIMORE		1845	1896	084	____, Catherine	
Catherine __ MATTIMORE		1846	1916	084	MATTIMORE, Martin	
				084		
James MATTIMORE		05-12-1842	02-02-1885	084	MATTIMORE, James	
				084		
John MCLAUGHLIN		1842	1918	084	LEDDY, Catherine	
Catherine LEDDY McLaughlin		1845	1925	084	MCLAUGHLIN, John	
Patrick MCLAUGHLIN		27 Years	09-13-1883	084	MCLAUGHLIN, Patrick	
James MCLAUGHLIN		1859	1921	084	MCLAUGHLIN, James	

Thomas KELLEY		1839	1897	084	KELLEY, Thomas	(Does not state if Ellen is
Ellen KELLEY		1839	1882	084	KELLEY, Ellen	the wife of Thomas)
Jane Ann KELLEY		1846	1891	084	KELLEY, Jane Ann	
				084		
Patrick QUINLAN		65Y 4M	12-31-1881	084	HARRINGTON, Bridget	
Bridget HARRINGTON Quinlan		49Y 5M	06-06-1880	084	QUINLAN, Patrick	
				084		
James QUINLAN		77 Years	08-21-1887	084	_____, Bridget	(NOI Bridget)
Michael QUINLAN		22Y4M21D	04-01-1875	084	QUINLAN, Michael	Son Of James & Bridget Quinlan
				084		
James CLEARY		19 Years	04-25-1873	084	CLEARY, James	Children Of John & Jane Cleary
Jennie A. CLEARY		25Y 8M	09-21-1871	084	CLEARY, Jennie A.	(NOI John & Jane Cleary)
Charlie W. CLEARY		20Y 21D	09-21-1874	084	CLEARY, Charlie W.	
				084		
Patrick MCGRATH		1843	1925	084	GREEN, Bridget	
Bridget GREEN McGrath		1846	1929	084	MCGRATH, Patrick	
				084		
William H. ALGER		1853	1915	084	WALL, Ellen	
Ellen WALL ALGER		1851	1915	084	ALGER, William H.	
				084		
Daniel MCVEY		02-12-1830	03-03-1888	084	_____, Bridget	
Bridget ___ MCVEY		02-02-1835	07-10-1910	084	MCVEY, Daniel	
				084		
Francis DOON		1862	1932	084	DOON, Francis	(Does Not Indicate if Anna &
Anna _____ DOON		1873	19--	084	_____, Anna	Francis are spouses)
				084		
John BENJAMIN		1817	1895	084	BENJAMIN, John	(GAR) Co. C. 1 Vt Cav
				084		
Thomas DOYLE		19 Years	11-19-1874	084	DOYLE, Thomas	
				084		
Bridget REYNOLDS Doyle		35 Years	05-22-1874	084	DOYLE, Richard	(NOI Richard Doyle)
				084	REYNOLDS, Bridget	
				084		
Thomas DONELLY		1836	1886	084	CORKIN, Julia	
Julia CORKIN Donelly		1826	1891	084	DONELLY, Thomas	
				084		
John SULLIVAN		1823	1872	084	HURLEY, Sarah	
Sarah HURLEY Sullivan		1826	1911	084	SULLIVAN, John	

St. Peter's Cemetery, Maple Street, Vergennes, VT

NAME	POB	DOB/AGE	DOD	CEM	SPOUSE/INDEX	INSCRIPTION
Thomas BUTLER		74 Years	06-12-1903	085	LAUGHLIN, Catherine	

Name	Born	Died	Code	Spouse/Relation	Notes
Catherine LAUGHLIN Butler	76 Years	11-20-1907	085	BUTLER, Thomas	
			085		
Patrick J. CASEY	06-16-1839	05-30-1928	085	FITZGERALD, Ellen	
Ellen FITZGERALD Caset	06-06-1839	04-22-1937	085	CASEY, Patrick J.	
			085		
Jeremiah J. BARTLEY	1840	1916	085	MONTY, Elizabeth	Co. K, 2nd Vt Batty (GAR)
Elizabeth MONTY Bartley	1850	1938	085	BARTLEY, Jeremiah J.	
			085		
John B. DEMPER	1852	1920	085	LOVERN, Emma L.	
Emma L. LOVERN Demper	1855	1925	085	DEMPER, John B.	
			085		
Patrick RYAN	1820	1886	085		
Michael W. RYAN	01-23-1847	05-03-1889	085	MURPHY, Bridget	
Bridget MURPHY Ryan	02-01-1846	10-30-1885	085	RYAN, Michael W.	
			085		
Eliza A. _____ KELLY	66 Years	03-29-1889	085	KELLY, Patrick	(NOI Patrick Kelly)
Michael D. KELLY	14 Years	11-13-1868	085	KELLY, Michael D.	
Joanna KELLY	14 Years	04-09-1865	085	KELLY, Joanna	
			085		
Dennis HICKEY	66 Years	08-21-1865	085	HICKEY, Dennis	
			085		
Louis C. MORRIS	1837	1913	085	KCKINN, Margaret	
Margaret MCKINN MORRIS	1840	1924	085	MORRIS, Louis C.	
			085		
Edward RYAN	70 Years	__-__-1886	085	HEFFRON, Catherine	(Stone deteriorated)
Catherine HEFFRON Ryan	70 Years	08-18-1907	085	RYAN, Edward	
			085		
James ROCK	06-21-1825	07-19-1904	085	STEBBINS, Mary Addel	
Mary Addel STEBBINS Rock	10-21-1829	03-18-1904	085	ROCK, James	
			085		
Michael FLEMING	28 Years	08-21-1865	085	FLEMING, Michael	
			085		
Timothy HICKEY	1836	1910	085	_____, Ann	
Ann _____ HICKEY	53 Years	06-23-1879	085	HICKEY, Timothy	
			085		
Patrick SINON			085	_____, Margaret	(No DOB/DOD on Patrick Sinon)
Ann _____ HICKEY	53 Years	06-23-1879	085	SINON, Patrick	
			085		
Nicholas J. DOUGLAS	1850	1943	085	_____, Mary Ann	
Mary Ann _____ DOUGLAS	1805	1882	085	DOUGLAS, Nicholas J.	
			085		
William CASSIN	06-16-1802	01-01-1871	085	TRACY, Catherine	
Catherine TRACY Cassin	03-10-1812	06-23-1870	085	CASSIN, William	
			085		
Mary MONAHAN	08-15-1828	10-26-1879	085	MONAHAN, Mary	

Name	Born/Age	Died	Code	Index	Note
Catherine TRACY Cassin	08-11-1857	08-04-1881	085	TRACY, Catherine	(NOI Mr. Cassin)
			085		
Margaret HARVEY	1822	1889	085	HARVEY, Margaret	
			085		
Ann _____ RYAN	50 Years	03-27-1870	085	RYAN, Michael	(NOI Michael Ryan)
			085		
James DONOWAY	1841	1919	085	_____, Ellen	
Ellen _____ DONOWAY	1843	1927	085	DONOWAY, James	
			085		
Timothy BUTLER	55 Years	11-03-1882	085	DILLON, Ellen	
Ellen DILLON Butler	74 Years	02-25-1911	085	BUTLER, Timothy	
			085		
Gary A. ELLIOTT	1852	1908	085	CROAKE, M. Ellen	
M. Ellen CROAKE Elliott	1861	1916	085	ELLIOTT, Gary A.	
			085		
Ellen _____ SULLIVAN	73 Years	06-23-1879	085	SULLIVAN, Patrick	(NOI Patrick Sullivan)
			085		
Daniel DALTON	72 Years	06-15-1877	085	GORMAN, Jane	
Jane GORMAN Dalton	68 Years	05-14-1875	085	DALTON, Daniel	
			085		
Patrick LEONARD	75 Years	06-03-1894	085	DILLON, Catherine	
Catherine DILLON Leonard	73 Years	06-11-1892	085	LEONARD, Patrick	
			085		
Edward DILLON	59 Years	10-25-1877	085	DONNELLY, Catherine	
Catherine DONNELLY Dillon	63 Years	12-08-1898	085	DILLON, Edward	
			085		
Mary _____ O'NEIL	60 Years	04-20-1877	085	O'NEIL, John	(NOI John O'Neil)
			085		
Thomas DILLON	1828	1908	085	HANNAN, Bridget	
Bridget HANNAN Dillon	1832	1906	085	DILLON, Thomas	
			085		
Patrick DILLON	60 Years	07-19-1884	085	HALPIN, Margaret	
Margaret HALPIN Dillon	48 Years	01-26-1875	085	DILLON, Patrick	
			085		
Mrs. Mary MARSHALL	80 Years	04-21-1895	085	MARSHALL, Mrs. Mary	
Bridget COLOPY	63 Years	08-20-1882	085	COLOPY, Bridget	
Richard MARSHALL	20 Years	07-07-1861	085	MARSHALL, Richard	
Michael MARSHALL	19 Years	08-19-1864	085	MARSHALL, Michael	
Margaret MARSHALL Halpin	35 Years	03-03-1879	085	HALPIN, John	(NOI John Halpin)
			085	MARSHALL, Margaret	
			085		
John MURPHY	77 Years	10-09-1894	085	_____, Catherine	
Catherine _____ MURPHY	83 Years	03-27-1910	085	MURPHY, John	
			085		
Bridget _____ COUGHLIN	85 Years	09-24-1886	085	COUGHLIN, Connor	(NOI Connor Coughlin)

Name	Birthplace	Born/Age	Died	Code	Index	Notes
				085		
Michael MURPHY	Co. Wexford	43 Years	03-30-1865	085	_____, Bridget	Died In Vergennes. A Native of
				085		County Wexford, Ireland
Bridget _____ MURPHY			10-10-1898	085	MURPHY, Michael	
				085		
Patrick DALEY		42 Years	09-14-1870	085	DALEY, Patrick	
Catherine DAILY		76 Years	05-07-1873	085	DAILY, Catherine	
				085		
Oliver GORDON		1842	1913	085	_____, Kate	Co. B, 11th Ct Hvy Aty (GAR)
Kate _____ GORDON		1836	1912	085	GORDON, Oliver	
				085		
Oliver GORDON		82 Years	01-08-1893	085	FULLER, Lydia	
Lydia FULLER Gordon		77 Years	08-29-1892	085	GORDON, Oliver	
				085		
James MULLEN		09-05-1856	06-13-1936	085	MONAG, Virginia	
Virginia MONAG Mullen		03-29-1863	01-25-1961	085	MULLEN, James	
				085		
William STANTON		1851	1921	085	CUSACK, Katherine	
Katherine CUSACK Stanton		1854	1924	085	STANTON, William	
				085		
Elizabeth CURRAN		82 Years	04-16-1916	085	CURRAN, Elizabeth	Born In Ireland
				085		
Bridget O'BRIEN Henderson		1842	1917	085	HENDERSON, C.	(NOI C. Henderson)
				085	O'BRIEN, Bridget	
				085		
Henry L. BLANCHARD		1853	1932	085	CUSACK, Katherine	
Mary A. O'DOWD Blanchard		1853	19__	085	STANTON, William	
				085		
John LEAHY		60 Years	10-28-1909	085	GAUL, Joanna	
Joanna GAUL Leahy		82 Years	10-30-1922	085	LEAHY, John	
				085		
John DOUGLAS		89 Years	05-07-1891	085	DOUGLAS, John	
				085		
Charles DOUGLAS		08-25-1854		085	ADAMS, Mary L.	
Mary L. ADAMS Douglas		01-30-1859	09-20-1907	085	DOUGLAS, Charles	
				085		
James DOUGLAS		1836	19__	085	_____, Julia	
Julia _____ DOUGLAS		1851	04-17-1919	085	DOUGLAS, James	
				085		
Michael GRACE		69 Years	10-20-1889	085	DECOURSEY, Margaret	
Margaret DECOURSEY Grace		72 Years	04-12-1904	085	GRACE, Michael	
				085		
Edward DECOURSEY		02-02-1819	10-21-1899	085	SULLIVAN, Mary	
Mary SULLIVAN DeCoursey		90 Years	10-30-1928	085	DECOURSEY, Edward	
				085		

Name	Born	Died		Index	Note
Thomas T. DONNELLY	09-29-1830	05-10-1909	085	MCDONNELL, Mary A.	
Mary A. MCDONNELL Donnelly	08-10-1832	01-09-1905	085	DONNELLY, Thomas T.	
James P. DONNELLY	01-31-1858	05-01-1880	085	DONNELLY, James P.	
William D. DONNELLY	05-03-1872	02-03-1889	085	DONNELLY, William D.	
			085		
John H. DONNELLY	1855	1931	085	_____, K. M.	(NOI on spouse K.M.)
K. M. _____ DONNELLY	1866	1933	085	DONNELLY, John H.	
			085		
Michael MCMAHON	1823	1876	085	FOLEY, Ann	
Ann FOLEY McMahon	1828	1909	085	MCMAHON, Michael	
			085		
John CONNOR	68 Years	04-05-1893	085	CONNOR, John	(NOI on spouse "B")
			085		
John DRISCOLL	1827	1920	085	DALTON, Catherine	
Catherine DALTON Driscoll	1842	1932	085	DRISCOLL, John	
			085		
Garrett DECOURSEY	96 Years	12-22-1868	085	_____, Margaret	
Margaret _____ DECOURSEY		11-11-1884	085	DECOURSEY, Garrett	
			085		
Charles MORAN	1839	1894	085	CLARK, Ann	
Ann CLARK Moran	1839	1887	085	MORAN, Charles	
			085		
Margaret E. MURPHY Tull	10-10-1859	02-08-1917	085	TULL, Charles E.	(NOI Charles E. Tull)
			085	MURPHY, Margaret E.	
			085		
Lillian _____ SULLIVAN	73 Years	07-23-1879	085	SULLIVAN, Patrick	(NOI Patrick Sullivan)
			085	_____, Lillian	
			085		
Edmond GEARY	75 Years	10-14-1865	085	_____, Catherine	
Catherine _____ GEARY	71Y 8M	05-02-1863	085	GEARY, Edmond	
			085		
Daniel GEARY	39 Years	05-01-1874	085	_____, Mary	
Mary _____ GEARY	83Y 12D	04-06-1916	085	GEARY, Daniel	
			085		
Patrick MCDERMOTT	76 Years	06-25-1872	085	_____, Catherine	
Catherine _____ MCDERMOTT	80 Years	04-06-1916	085	MCDERMOTT, Patrick	
Bridget MCDERMOTT	1806	1899	085	MCDERMOTT, Bridget	
Michael MCDERMOTT	1804	1878	085	MCDERMOTT, Michael	
			085		
Catherine DALTON Halmon	65 Years	12-12-1869	085	HALMON, James	(NOI James Halmon--c/b Hannon)
			085	DALTON, Catherine	
			085		
Joanna CONNORS	1842	1866	085	CONNORS, Joanna	
			085		
Jeremiah CROWLEY	06-02-1816	09-02-1887	085	COURSEY, Mary	

Mary COURSEY Crowley	08-24-1814	10-24-1893	085	CROWLEY, Jeremiah	(Possibly DeCoursey)
Jeremiah J. CROWLEY	05-28-1855	04-10-1873	085	CROWLEY, Jeremiah J.	
Mary A. CROWLEY	03-31-1860	12-29-1877	085	CROWLEY, Mary A.	
			085		
Michael DONOVAN	67 Years	07-14-1910	085		
Timothy DONOVAN	74 Years	08-17-1887	085	_____, Bridget	
Bridget _____ DONOVAN		06-20-1877	085	DONOVAN, Timothy	
Simon MCNERY	80 Years	02-18-1888	085	_____, Mary	
Mary _____ MCNERY	79Y 8M	09-15-1882	085	MCNERY, Simon	
			085		
Michael SULLIVAN	03-10-1829	08-04-1923	085	RYAN, Bridget	
Bridget RYAN Sullivan	07-25-1840	07-19-1881	085	SULLIVAN, Michael	
			085		
Hugh RILEY		12-19-1882	085	_____, Margaret	
Margaret _____ RILEY		08-13-1882	085	RILEY, Hugh	
			085		
Edward BRODERICK	88 Years	09-26-1878	085	_____, Honora	
Honora _____ BRODERICK	76 Years	12-06-1866	085	BRODERICK, Edward	
			085		
James COUGHLIN	55 Years	09-07-1890	085	MARSHALL, Alice	
Alice MARSHALL Coughlin	41 Years	10-25-1879	085	COUGHLIN, James	
			085		
George RICHARDS	12-10-1856	04-03-1943	085	TENNIAN, Nellie M.	
Nellie M. TENNIAN Richards	02-08-1858	06-02-1898	085	RICHARDS, George	
			085		
Thomas F. RYAN	24 Years	04-13-1873	085	RYAN, Thomas F.	
			085		
Edward RYAN	12 Years	06-25-1865	085	RYAN, Edward	
			085		
James BARTLEY	1811	1894	085	SULLIVAN, Margaret	
Margaret SULLIVAN Bartley	1818	1846	085	BARTLEY, James	
Annie MCDERMOTT	1816	1884	085	MCDERMOTT, Annie	(Does not say Annie McDermott was wife of James Bartley)
			085		
John BARTLEY	1838	1868	085	BARTLEY, John	
Michael BARTLEY	1848	1865	085	BARTLY, Michael	
			085		
Peter BARROWS	58 Years	10-02-1874	085	BARROWS, Peter	
			085		
Andrew GRADY	1826	1890	085	BULLEY, Adeline	
Adeline BULLEY Grady			085	GRADY, Andrew	
Andrew GRADY	1853	1887	085	GRADY, Andrew	
Nazarus GRADY	1856	1870	085	GRADY, Nazarus	
Adeline GRADY	1858	1889	085	GRADY, Adeline	
Peter GRADY	1860	1885	085	GRADY, Peter	
Stephen GRADY	1862	1865	085	GRADY, Stephen	

Frederick GRADY		1872	1940	085	GRADY, Mrs. Frederick	
Wife (Mrs. Frederick GRADY)		1873	1955	085	GRADY, Frederick	

St. Patrick's Cemetery, Wallingford, VT (Church Street)

NAME	POB	DOB/AGE	DOD	CEM	SPOUSE/INDEX	INSCRIPTION
Philip SMITH		08-17-1823	04-03-1901	086	MCGEE, Susan	
Susan MCGEE Smith		08-15-1824	07-30-1890	086	SMITH, Philip	
Susan SMITH Naven		01-01-1852	03-15-1878	086	NAVEN, Daniel	(NOI Daniel Naven)
				086	SMITH, Susan	
Patrick SMITH		03-28-1868	06-19-1889	086	SMITH, Patrick	
Alice SMITH		04-11-1864	09-26-1879	086	SMITH, Alice	
				086		
Martin DUNN		1847	1896	086	SMITH, Kate	
				086	BUTLER, Mary	
Kate SMITH Dunn		1853	1877	086	DUNN, Martin	
Mary BUTLER Dunn		1857	1900	086	DUNN, Martin	
				086		
Patrick CARNEY		36 Years	01-12-1867	086	HIGGINS, Ann	
Ann HIGGINS Carney		75 Years	10-23-1900	086	CARNEY, Patrick	
				086		
Martin HICKEY	Co. Clare	86 Years	04-16-1900	086	COTTON, Catherine	A Native Of County Clair
Catherine COTTON Hickey	Co. Cork	67 Years	06-28-1891	086	HICKEY, Martin	A Native Of County Cork, Ire
John HICKEY		1858	1908	086	HICKEY, John	(Last names of children were
Bridget HICKEY		20Y9M12D	11-12-1876	086	HICKEY, Bridget	not listed on stone. Assumed
Patrick HICKEY		1854	1917	086	HICKEY, Patrick	that all were Hickeys)
Catherine HICKEY		1862	1921	086	HICKEY, Catherine	
Michael HICKEY		1867	1943	086	HICKEY, Michael	
Mary HICKEY		1860	1926	086	HICKEY, Mary	
				086		
Peter S. BYRNE		1855	1919	086	BYRNE, Delia W.	
Delia W. BYRNE		1860	1932	086	BYRNE, Peter S.	
				086		
Edmund MYLOTT		72 Years	06-26-1873	086	O'BRIEN, Nancy	Native Of Westport,Mayo County
				086		Ireland
Nancy O'BRIEN Mylott		1806	1888	086	MYLOTT, Edmund	
				086		
Thomas WYNNE		27 Years	06-30-1884	086	WYNNE, Thomas	
Michael WYNNE		17 Years	01-24-1879	086	WYNNE, Michael	
Francis WYNNE		71 Years	03-01-1890	086	________, Mary	
Mary ____ WYNNE		65 Years	03.08-1890	086	WYNNE, Francis	
				086		

Name	Birth/Age	Death	Plot	Index	Notes
Mary A. RILEY	24 Years	01-23-1879	086	RILEY, Mary A.	Daughter of John And Hannah
Mother			086		Riley (Also in this plot with
Father			086		NOI-Margaret, Johannah, Mame)
Margaret RILEY			086	RILEY, Margaret	
Johannah RILEY			086	RILEY, Johannah	
Mame RILEY			086	RILEY, Mame	
			086		
Felix MCCONNELL	72 Years	03-02-1871	086	MCCONNELL, Felix	In The 72nd Year Of His Life
Sarah MURPHY McConnell	69 Years	07-11-1872	086	MURPHY, Sarah	
Margaret MCCONNELL	1822	1896	086	MCCONNELL, Margaret	(Surnames not present for
Jane MCCONNELL	1835	1910	086	MCCONNELL, Jane	children.Assumed they were all
Sarah MCCONNELL	1839	1912	086	MCCONNELL, Sarah	McConnells)
Felix MCCONNELL	1841	1923	086	MCCONNELL, Felix	
			086		
John GRIMES	1826	1894	086	______, Rosanna	
Rosanna ____ GRIMES	1828	1896	086	GRIMES, John	
Frank PRENDERGAST	1852	1891	086	PRENDERGAST, Frank	
			086		
Patrick STAPLETON	04-15-1828	12-24-1883	086	SMITH, Margaret A.	
Margaret A. SMITH	08-04-1845	08-29-1918	086	STAPLETON, Patrick	
			086		
John MCCANN	84 Years	03-15-1897	086	_____, Nancy	
Nancy _____ MCCANN	43 Years	05-22-1864	086	MCCANN, John	
John MCCANN	20Y6M	09-02-1868	086	MCINLEAR, Ann	
Ann MCINLEAR McCann	72 Years	- -	086	MCCANN, John	
			086		
William COLEMAN	1841	1927	086	KIMMINS, Annie	
Annie KIMMINS	1838	1904	086	COLEMAN, William	
Margaret COLEMAN	94 Years	10-16-1888	086	COLEMAN, Margaret	
			086		
Anthony WOOD	1853	1882	086	________, Julia	
Julia ____ WOOD	1853	1927	086	WOOD, Anthony	
			086		
Michael MAHER	76 Years	12-13-1891	086	______, Ellen	Co. D, 40th Rgt, NY Vols (GAR)
Ellen _____ MAHER	86 Years	08-13-1902	086	MAHER, Michael	
John MAHER	62 Years	11-24-1905	086	MAHER, John	Co. F, 6th Rgt, VT Vols (GAR)
			086		Son Of M & E Maher
			086		
Edward SHUM	05-30-1826	09-19-1906	086	REYNOLDS, Julia	
Julia REYNOLDS Shum	09-28-1845	08-02-1911	086	SHUM, Edward	
			086		
Matthew MCGINNIS	04-05-1839	04-20-1914	086	MCINLEAR, Katherine	
Katherine MCINLEAR McGinnis	05-08-1850	06-01-1885	086	MCGINNIS, Matthew	
			086		
Julia E. SMITH Brown	10-26-1840	09-24-1889	086	BROWN, Jerome	(NOI Jerome Brown)

				086	SMITH, Julia E.	
				086		
Francis O'BRIEN		1829	1915	086	GUNSHANNON, Mary	
				086	BALLARD, Mary	
Mary GUNSHANNON O'Brien		1849	1877	086	O'BRIEN, Francis	
Mary BALLARD O'Brien		- -	- -	086	O'BRIEN, Francis	(NOI DOB/DOD Mary Ballard)
				086		
Peter BURSEY		08-20-1827	09-18-1899	086	BURSEY, Peter	
				086		
Bridget MANN		16 Years	04-25-1853	086	MANN, Bridget	Daughter Of J & M Mann
John MANN		1803	1855	086	MANN, John	
				086		
Nancy MCLAUGHLIN	Co. Derry	02-02-1832	10-12-1884	086	MCLAUGHLIN, Nancy	Born In County Derry, Ireland
				086		
Michael PICKETT		1834	1903	086	___, Alice M.	
Alice M._____PICKETT		1843	1904	086	PICKETT, Michael	
				086		
Barney A. RILEY		1843	1893	086	___, Margaret A.	
Margaret A. ___ RILEY		1864	1943	086	RILEY, Barney A.	
				086		
John HEALY		37 Years	01-04-1880	086	HEALY, John	
Edward HEALY		1841	1926	086	MCGINNIS, Margaret	
Margaret MCGINNIS Healy		1843	1911	086	HEALY, Edward	
				086		
Lawrence TIERNAN		1807	1884	086	___, Julia	
Julia ___ TIERNAN		1827	1901	086	TIERNAN, Lawrence	
John TIERNAN		12-16-1848	11-10-1914	086	HICKEY, Margaret	
Margaret HICKEY Tiernan		04-10-1852	01-04-1925	086	HICKEY, John	
				086		
Louis CASAVAW		1838	1915	086	O'BRIEN, Margaret	
Margaret O'BRIEN Casavaw		1848	1912	086	CASAVAW, Louis	
				086		
Daniel MCNAMARA	Co. Westmeath	04-05-1822	02-20-1893	086	GANNON, Mary	Born In Rathown (Rathowen), Westmeith (Westmeath), Ireland
				086		
Mary GANNON McNamara	Co Longford	58 Years	12-22-1883	086	MCNAMARA, Daniel	Parish Of Leagan (Possibly Townland of Legan, Parish of Kilglass) County Longford, Ire
				086		
				086		
				086		
James CONNOLLY		04-18-1810	02-21-1886	086	___, Margaret	
Margaret ___ CONNOLLY		04-18-1821	09-04-1880	086	CONNOLLY, James	
John CONNOLLY		04-10-1838	10-01-1849	086	CONNOLLY, John	(Last names of children were note listed on stone. Assumed that they were all Connollys)
Thomas CONNOLLY		05-12-1841	09-02-1891	086	CONNOLLY, Thomas	
Mary CONNOLLY		08-12-1843	10-10-1903	086	CONNOLLY, Mary	
James CONNOLLY		1847	1929	086	CONNOLLY, James	
Catherine CONNOLLY		1851	1935	086	CONNOLLY, Catherine	

Name	Born	Died	Plot	Index	Notes
Elizabeth CONNOLLY	1845	1926	086	CONNOLLY, Elizabeth	
			086		
Martin BRENNAN	1820	1895	086	WELCH, Catherine	
Catherine WELCH Brennan	1832	1912	086	BRENNAN, Martin	
			086		
Daniel MULQUEEN	1826	1914	086	____, Mary F.	
Mary F. ___ MULQUEEN	1838	1916	086	MULQUEEN, Daniel	
			086		
Cornelius V. HOWLEY	1851	1947	086	BRENNAN, Ellen	
Ellen BRENNAN Howley	1855	1919	086	HOWLEY, Cornelius V.	
			086		
James BRENNAN	1820	1883	086	TIMBERS, Mary	
			086	COLE, Bridget	
Mary TIMBERS Brennan	1824	1856	086	BRENNAN, James	
Bridget COLE Brennan	1813	1887	086	BRENNAN, James	
Margaret BRENNAN	1851	1909	086	BRENNAN, Margaret	
Katharine BRENNAN	1853	1936	086	BRENNAN, Katharine	
			086		
Edward O'HEARN	52 Years	11-22-1910	086	O'HEARN, Edward	
			086		
James MOONEY	11-20-1832	08-18-1903	086	O'HERN, Bridget	
Bridget O'HERN Mooney	02-07-1840	01-31-1915	086	MOONEY, James	
			086		
Christopher SMITH	09-15-1834	12-29-1887	086	COMERFORD, Mary A.	
Mary A. COMERFORD	10-09-1837	03-20-1907	086	SMITH, Christopher	
			086		
Ann COMERFORD	47 Years	07-22-1891	086	COMERFORD, Ann	
Thomas COMERFORD	56 Years	11-04-1886	086	COMERFORD, Thomas	
John COMERFORD	83 Years	10-08-1888	086	COMERFORD, John	
Patrick L. COMERFORD	83 Years	03-25-1930	086	COMERFORD, Patrick L.	
Nellie B. COMERFORD	92 Years	11-22-1932	086	COMERFORD, Nellie B.	
			086		
Ellen BUTLER Comerford	65 Years	10-16-1876	086	COMERFORD, John	(This stone adjacent to Comer-
			086		ford Plot - Probably wife of
			086		John Comerford w/d 10-08-1888)
John I. CONGDON	1852	1919	086	MULQUEEN, Mary	
Mary MULQUEEN Congdon	1862	1936	086	CONGDON, John I.	
			086		
Michael MCALEER	18 Years	01-13-1863	086	MCALEER, Michael	Son Of Patrick & Mary Mcleer
			086		
Minnie MCGINNESS	10-17-1848	10-18-1875	086	MCGINNESS, Minnie	Daughter Of P & J McGinness
Kate MCGINNESS	10-17-1848	03-08-1885	086	MCGINNESS, Kate	
			086		
Henry DANVER	33Y 2M	03-07-1876	086	____, Mary	
Mary ___ DANVER	23Y 11M	01-07-1875	086	DANVER, Henry	Common) Co. Limerick, Ireland

St. Andrew's Cemetery, Waterbury, VT. Route 100 South, 1/2 Mile From Route 2. Located in Town of Duxbury.

NAME	POB	DOB/AGE	DOD	CEM	SPOUSE/INDEX	INSCRIPTION
Catherine TRAINER Grace		05-18-1843	05-02-1897	087	GRACE, Edward J.	(NOI Edward J. Grace)
				087	TRAINER, Catherine	
				087		
William H. CLOSSEY		1847	1932	087	____, Christina	
Christina ____ CLOSSEY		1845	1933	087	CLOSSEY, William H.	
				087		
Peter MORIARITY		1827	1923	087	RYAN, Margaret	
Margaret RYAN Moriarity		1829	1902	087	MORIARITY, Peter	
Edward MORIARITY		1860	1932	087	MORIARITY, Edward	
				087		
Patrick KELTY		1836	1950	087	____, Ellen F.	
Ellen F. ____ KELTY		1835	1910	087	KELTY, Patrick	
				087		
Nathaniel F. ENNIS		05-20-1832		087	FRIEL, Bridget	
Bridget FRIEL Ennis		01-01-1833	10-21-1901	087	ENNIS, Nathaniel F.	
Nathan ENNIS		11-19-1865	08-29-1900	087	ENNIS, Nathan	
				087		
William RYAN		05-20-1852	04-06-1894	087	MCCARTHY, Lucy A.	
Lucy A. MCCARTHY Ryan		03-29-1856	11-13-1923	087	RYAN, William	
				087		
Martin HONAN		1824	1902	087	HONAN, Ann	
Ann HONAN		1817	1909	087	HONAN, Martin	
Nora J. HONAN		1866	1947	087	HONAN, Nora J.	
Timothy HARVEY		1815	1892	087	____, Maria L.	
Maria L. ____ HARVEY		1822	1880	087	HARVEY, Timothy	
David T. HARVEY		1857	1938	087	HARVEY, David	
Mary E. HARVEY		1858	1921	087	HARVEY, Mary E.	
				087		
J. W. HARVEY		1856	1936	087	HARVEY, J. W.	
				087		
Matthew CARR		1850	1915	087	____, Sybil	
Sybil ____ CARR		1857	1910	087	CARR, Matthew	
				087		
Mary CARROLL	Ireland	1834	1916	087	CARROLL, Mary	Born In Ireland. Died In Burlington
				087		
				087		
James GOODWIN		08-20-1833	09-17-1901	087	LEARY, Ann	
Ann LEARY Goodwin		05-25-1837	07-16-1897	087	GOODWIN, James	
				087		
Thomas C. O'NEILL			08-04-1943	087	KING, M. Belle	

Name	Birthplace	Born	Died	Code	Related	Notes
M. Belle KING O'Neill			10-14-1929	087	O'NEILL, Thomas C.	
				087		
James FRAHILL			07-28-1868	087	MCCARTY, Ellen	
Ellen MCCARTY Frahill			05-05-1886	087	FRAHILL, James	
Michael J. FRAHILL			05-11-1931	087	FRAHILL, Michael J.	
				087		
Rev. John GALLIGAN	Ireland	06-24-1845	11-05-1907	087	GALLIGAN, Rev. John	Born In Ireland. Died In
				087		
John J. KING		1848	1920	087	____, Ellen	
Ellen ____ KING		1842	1915	087	KING, John J.	
				087		
Bridget KING		81 Years	02-24-1888	087	KING, Bridget	
Michael KING		23 Years	03-13-1870	087	KING, Michael	Son Of Bridget King
				087		
Michael O'DAY		76 Years	08-19-1888	087	O'DAY, Michael	
				087		
Thomas CARR		10-10-1841	12-13-1906	087	DAY, Hannah A.	
Hannah A. DAY Carr		09-13-1843	09-22-1885	087	CARR, Thomas	
				087		
Timothy CAIN		70 Years	07-09-1886	087	____, Mary E.	
Mary E. ____ CAIN		75 Years	01-25-1896	087	CAIN, Timothy	
Ann R. CAIN		23Y 11M	08-28-1879	087	CAIN, Ann R.	
Lawrence CAIN		61 Years	10-28-1913	087	CAIN, Lawrence	Died At Ventura, California
				087		
A. PATTERSON SR.		1824	1888	087	PATTERSON, A. Sr.	
A. J. PATTERSON JR.		1856	1934	087	____, Winifred E.	
Winifred E. ____ PATTERSON		1860	1935	087	PATTERSON, A.J.	
				087		
Thomas CARVER		1837	1919	087	____, Mary E.	
Mary E. ____ CARVER		1847	1910	087	CARVER, Thomas	
Kate WADE		1845	1885	087	WADE, Kate	
				087		
John KALTY		1837	1913	087	MCMULLEN, Nancy	
Nancy MCMULLEN Kalty		1830	1890	087	KALTY, John	
Sarah A. KALTY		1867	1879	087	KALTY, Sarah A.	
				087		
Ella KALTY		09-03-1865	07-18-1900	087	KALTY, Ella	
				087		
James LINNIHAN		1810	1876	087	KIRBY, Catherine	
Catherine KIRBY Linnihan		1808	1888	087	LINNIHAN, James	
Ellen LINNIHAN			09-17-1921	087	LINNIHAN, Ellen	
Alice CARVER Tobin		1835	1885	087	TOBIN, Patrick	(NOI Patrick Tobin)
				087	CARVER, Alice	
Dinnis LINNIHAN		1851	1868	087	LINNIHAN, Dinnis	
James LINNIHAN		1855	1872	087	LINNIHAN, James	

Name	Origin	Born	Died	Code	Index	Notes
				087		
James REYNOLDS		12-24-1837	11-09-1915	087	KELTY, Mary	
Mary KELTY Reynolds		01-12-1846	10-23-1884	087	REYNOLDS, James	
Willie E. REYNOLDS		10-22-1878	02-08-1890	087	REYNOLDS, Willie E.	
				087		
Henry RAVEY		01-06-1820	02-13-1895	087	____, Catherine	
Catherine ____ RAVEY		03-15-1825	03-06-1899	087	RAVEY, Henry	
George BURNHAM		1852	1927	087	____, Catherine	
Catherine ____ BURNHAM		1857	1931	087	BURNHAM, George	
				087		
Thomas RING		1830	1893	087	COOPER, Alice	
Alice COOPER Ring		1827	1901	087	RING, Thomas	
John H. RING		1858	1927	087	MCMAHON, Mary L.	
Mary L. MCMAHON Ring		1862		087	RING, John H.	
				087		
John MCMAHON	Co. Limerick	1827	1904	087	____, Bridget	Native Of County Limerick, Ire
Bridget ____ MCMAHON	Co. Limerick	1831	1891	087	MCMAHON, John	Native Of County Limerick, Ire
John F. MCMAHON		1864	1900	087	MCMAHON, John F.	
Ellen QUINN		07-31-1853	09-22-1918	087	QUINN, Ellen	
Anne C. MCMAHON		05-25-1860	09-09-1920	087	MCMAHON, Anne C.	
James MCMAHON		1856	1923	087	MCMAHON, James	
				087		
Edward F. MCMAHON		1876	1955	087	MCMAHON, Edward F.	
				087		
Thomas HERBERT		01-06-1837	11-22-1917	087	KELTY, Margaret	
Margaret KELTY Herbert		08-05-1833	02-20-1911	087	HERBERT, Thomas	
Katie B. HERBERT		17Y 5M 25D	02-26-1889	087	HERBERT, Katie B.	
Thomas M. HERBERT		09-02-1866	03-14-1936	087	HERBERT, Thomas M.	
				087		
Patrick BURKE	Co. Clare	02-17-1817		087	BLAKE, Ellan	Born In County Clare, Ireland
Ellan BLAKE Burke		70 Years	04-28-1891	087	BURKE, Patrick	
				087		
Will O'NEILL		32Y 6M 2D	01-18-1887	087	____, Mary	Erected By His Wife Mary
				087	O'NEILL, Will	O'Neill (NOI Mary O'Neill)
				087		
Thomas O'NEILL		69 Years	05-25-1888	087	O'NEILL, Thomas	
Mattie O'NEILL		22 Years	04-13-1890	087	O'NEILL, Mary	
Mary O'NEILL			05-17-1923	087	O'NEILL, Mattie	
Patrick H. O'NEILL		1864	1948	087	O'NEILL, Patrick H.	
Robert J. O'NEILL		1860	1951	087	O'NEILL, Robert J.	
				087		
Edward CALLAHAN		01-04-1859	06-05-1891	087	SIMONDS, Nellie	
Nellie SIMONDS Callahan		1868	1945	087	CALLAHAN, Edward	
Timothy CALLAHAN		84 Years	02-04-1894	087	____, Mary	
Mary ____ CALLAHAN		11-15-1812		087	CALLAHAN, Timothy	

				087		
Ellen CORBETT McGrath		64 Years	04-24-1886	087	MCGRATH, Thomas	
				087		
Thomas MCGRATH		1824	1896	087	MCGRATH, Thomas	
Nancy MCGRATH		1834	1887	087	MCGRATH, Nancy	
Anna M. TUNNEY		1862	1937	087	TUNNEY, Anna M.	
				087		
Timothy O'BRIEN			06-14-1823	087	HORIGAN, Catherine	
Catherine HORIGAN O'Brien		70 Years	01-07-1892	087	O'BRIEN, Timothy	
				087		
Michael C. O'BRIEN		1855	1926	087	CALLAHAN, Bridget	
Bridget CALLAHAN O'Brien		1856	1924	087	O'BRIEN, Michael C.	
James CARRIGAN		1858	1931	087	CARRIGAN, James	
Jane CARRIGAN		1857	1917	087	CARRIGAN, Jane	
Jane CARNEY		1828	1910	087	CARNEY, Jane	
James CARNEY		1814	1886	087	CARNEY, James	
John O'CONNOR		1847	1933	087	O'CONNOR, John	
Mary PATTERSON		1880		087	PATTERSON, Mary	
Elizabeth PATTERSON		1853	1900	087	PATTERSON, Elizabeth	
Mary O'CONNOR		1849	1886	087	O'CONNOR, Mary	
Agnes CARNEY		1865	1886	087	CARNEY, Agnes	
Nellie GREVILLE			03-08-1947	087	GREVILLE, Nellie	
				087		
William HAYES	Co. Limerick	1821	1903	087	HEFFERNAN, Julia	
Julia HEFFERNAN Hayes		1822	1912	087	HAYES, William	
Patrick HAYES		1847	1931	087	HAYES, Patrick	
James HAYES		1858	1925	087	HAYES, James	
Annie HAYES		1860	1960	087	HAYES, Annie	
Julia HAYES		1867	1962	087	HAYES, Julia	
Mrs. E.T. HAYES		1865	1938	087	HAYES, Mrs. E. T.	
Mrs. William HAYES		1861	1946	087	HAYES, William	
William HAYES		1856	1923	087	HAYES, Mrs. William	
J. M. HAYES		1862	1915	087	HAYES, J. M.	
				087		
John HEALY		1841	1917	087	HARRINGTON, Mary	
Mary HARRINGTON Healy		1840	1910	087	HEALY, John	
				087		
William CALLAHAN		11-01-1853	11-13-1891	087	CALLAHAN, William	
				087		
Lawrence C. LUCE		12-15-1883	03-17-1952	087	HOLTON, Johanna M.	Born In Rochester, Vt
Johanna M. HOLTON Luce	Ireland	07-02-1877	02-03-1950	087	LUCE, Lawrence C.	Born In Ireland
				087		
John O'CONNOR		56 Years	07-13-1897	087	O'CONNOR, John	
				087		
Patrick HERBERT		04-04-1836	06-25-1897	087	HERBERT, Patrick	

Susan HERBERT	1826	1904	087	HERBERT, Susan	
			087		
Daniel MORIARTY	05-05-1835	12-02-1899	087	KELTY, Winifred S.	
Winifred S. KELTY Moriarty	05-22-1836	11-18-1914	087	MORIARTY, Daniel	
			087		
Thomas E. TIERNEY	1856	1908	087	MORIARTY, Annie T.	
Annie T. MORIARTY Tierney	1867	1920	087	TIERNEY, Thomas E.	
			087		
Robert O'BRIEN	1848	1928	087	____, Mary M.	
Mary M. ____ O'BRIEN	1855	1928	087	O'BRIEN, Robert	
			087		
William THOMPSON	1853	1942	087	RYAN, Nellie E.	
Nellie E. RYAN Thompson	1869	1916	087	THOMPSON, William	
			087		
John J. Ryan JR.	1857	1924	087	RYAN, Nancy	
Nancy RYAN	1854	1921	087	RYAN, John J. Jr.	
			087		
John O'NEIL	1857	1911	087	CULLIGAN, Maria	
Maria CULLIGAN O'Neil	1858	1940	087	O'NEIL, John	
			087		
Julia B. O'CLAIR Doherty	1856	1920	087	DOHERTY, M.	(NOI M. Doherty)
			087	O'CLAIR, Julia B.	
			087		
Michael RAFTER	09-15-1831	06-15-1893	087	RAFTER, Michael	
			087		
Mathew MCCAFFREY	1835	1909	087	MCCAFFREY, Mathew	
			087		
Patrick H. KERIN	1845	1924	087	KERIN, Patrick H.	
Inez M. KERIN	1861	1925	087	KERIN, Inez M.	
			087		
Dennis SHEA	02-26-1833	06-20-1908	087	CONNER, Hannah	
Hannah CONNER Shea	03-21-1839	10-06-1913	087	SHEA, Dennis	
			087		
Edward FORKEY	1840	1911	087	MYOTT, Lizzie	PVT, Co. I, 7th Vt
Lizzie MYOTT Forkey	1843	1938	087	FORKEY, Edward	
			087		
John TRAVERS	1838	1922	087	KINSELLA, Martha	
Martha KINSELLA Travers	1845	1920	087	TRAVERS, John	
			087		
Patrick TOBIN	1833	1908	087	WHALEN, Margaret	
Margaret WHALEN Tobin	1839	1909	087	TOBIN, Patrick	
			087		
Helen C. REYNOLDS	1839	1927	087	REYNOLDS, Helen C.	
			087		
Martin TIERNEY	1844	1902	087	TIERNEY, Martin	

Name	Place	Born	Died	Code	Index	Notes
				087		
Mary KELLEY Paul		1852	1918	087	KELLEY, Mary	(NOI Mr. Paul)
				087		
Michael DEVINE		09-18-1824	01-07-1915	087	MORROW, Bridget	
Bridget MORROW Devine		1839	1923	087	DEVINE, Michael	
William DEVINE		1864	1945	087	DEVINE, William	
Mary C. DEVINE		1865	1943	087	DEVINE, Mary C.	
Thomas M. DEVINE		10-21-1866	05-13-1936	087	MARTIN, Anna	
Anna MARTIN Devine		11-02-1879	03-16-1912	087	DEVINE, Thomas M.	
				087		
Ira MUNN		12-01-1842	03-19-1913	087	____, Ellen	Co. C.,12th U.S. Inf 1861-1865
Ellen ____ MUNN		12-24-1839	05-16-1912	087	MUNN, Ira	
				087		
George HART		1850	1919	087	____, Nora	
Nora ____ HART		1858	1916	087	HART, George	
				087		
Ferdinand COLLINS		1839	1919	087	____, Ellen	
Ellen ____ COLLINS		1856	1942	087	COLLINS, Ferdinand	
				087		
William CAREY		1837	1919	087	KELTY, Nancy	
Nancy KELTY Casey		1841	1922	087	CAREY, William	
				087		
David KEEFE		1834	1919	087	KENNEDY, Margaret T.	
Margaret T. KENNEDY Keefe		1833	1918	087	KEEFE, David	
James E. KEEFE		1857	1930	087	KEEFE, James E.	
Mary E. KEEFE		1867	1936	087	KEEFE, Mary E.	
				087		
John W. RYAN		1847	1923	087	____, Ellen H.	(GAR Marker)
Ellen H. ____ RYAN		1849	1941	087	RYAN, John W.	
James D. RYAN		1866	1937	087	RYAN, James D.	
Lou Jane RYAN		1871	1929	087	RYAN, Lou Jane	
				087		
Eugene GRIFFIN	Co. Kerry	1846	1926	087	GRIFFIN, Eugene	Born In County Kerry, Ireland
				087		
Michael CONWAY		1837	1914	087	____, Ellen M.	Co. D., 2nd VT Regt
Ellen M. ____ CONWAY		1850	1919	087	CONWAY, Michael	
				087		
John HAYES		1853	1919	087	HAYES, John	
				087		
James O'BRIEN		04-28-1846	05-13-1928	087	O'NEILL, Nancy	
Nancy O'NEILL O'Brien		01-06-1852	03-20-1929	087	O'BRIEN, James	
				087		
Barney MCMANIS		1859	1935	087	BREEN, Jennie	
Jennie BREEN McManis		1852	1923	087	MCMANIS, Barney	
				087		

Edward LEE	Co. Sligo	05-08-1862	04-29-1925	087	KELTY, Honora	Born In Silaco Ireland
				087		(Probably Co. Sligo. In nearby
Honora KELTY Lee	Co. Sligo	03-01-1858		087	LEE, Edward	Moretown, Kelty's (Keelty)
				087		were from Co. Sligo)
				087		
J. E. CROSSETT		1854	1916	087	MCMULLEN, Mary J.	
Mary J. MCMULLEN Crossett		1856	1926	087	CROSSETT, J. E.	
				087		
Lucas MORSE		12-02-1833	09-07-1911	087	CROSBY, Mary F.	
Mary F. CROSBY Morse		07-08-1836	02-17-1912	087	MORSE, Lucas	
James W. CROSBY		64 Years	08-22-1894	087	AVERY, Harriet	IOOF Marker
Harriett AVERY Crosby		67 Years	05-14-1896	087	CROSBY, James W.	
				087		
James SMITH		1846	1915	087	COOLEY, Alice	
Alice COOLEY Smith		1858	1893	087	SMITH, James	
				087		
Robert J. MCMULLEN		1846	1904	087	CROSBY, Katie M.	
Katie CROSBY McMullen		1853	1934	087	MCMULLEN, Robert J.	
				087		
Sarah REYNOLDS		1845	1927	087	REYNOLDS, Sarah	
				087		
John MCNAMARA		1820	1898	087	HARVEY, Mary	
Mary HARVEY McNamara		1829	1900	087	MCNAMARA, John	
Michael MCNAMARA		1822	1887	087	MCNAMARA, Michael	
				087		
M. MORIARITY		1834	1915	087	MORIARITY, M.	
H. RYAN		1837	1904	087	RYAN, H.	
				087		
Patrick MANNEY		60 Years	03-08-1887	087	KELTY, Bridget	
Bridget KELTY Manney		1834	1871	087	MANNEY, Patrick	
				087		
William CASEY		1832	1909	087	____, Fanny	
Fanny ____ CASEY		1837	1917	087	CASEY, William	
Michael R. CASEY		1863	1906	087	CASEY, Michael R.	
Anna M. CASEY		1868	1948	087	CASEY, Anna M.	
				087		
David W. PATTERSON		1851	1923	087	PATTERSON, David W.	
				087		
John L. HORAN		1830	1903	087	KING, Bridget	
Bridget KING Horan		1831	1905	087	HORAN, John L.	
Theresa R. HORAN		1866	1925	087	HORAN, Theresa R.	
John F. HORAN		1859	1949	087	HORAN, John F.	
				087		
James FLYNN		03-12-1857	03-21-1925	087	____, Katherine A.	
Katherine A. ____ FLYNN		10-15-1865	11-02-1943	087	FLYNN, James	

				087		
Phillip CASEY			07-03-1897	087	CASEY, Phillip	(NOI DOB)
Jennie CASEY			06-22-1890	087	CASEY, Jennie	(NOI DOB)
				087		
Ellen ____ DONOVAN		74 Years	08-18-1897	087	DONOVAN, John	(NOI John Donovan)
				087		
Frances MCKENNA		10-29-1816	03-17-1880	087	MCKENNA, Frances	
				087		
Mary MCKENNA		05-29-1834	07-07-1859	087	MCKENNA, Mary	
				087		
Dominic MCCOY		10-17-1817		087	CAMPBELL, Mary	
				087	____, Elizabeth	
Mary CAMPBELL McCoy		05-03-1833		087	MCCOY, Dominick	
Elizabeth ____ MCCOY		38 Years	06-29-1852	087	MCCOY, Dominick	
Ellen Jane MCCOY		03-08-1845	03-25-1926	087	MCCOY, Ellen Jane	Dau of Dominic & Elizabeth McCoy
				087		
Arthur O. MCCOY		07-24-1862	06-26-1897	087	MCCOY, Arthur O.	
				087		
Mary MCCOY		1867	1956	087	MCCOY, Mary	
				087		
Willis H. CROSSETT		44 Years	11-21-1892	087	BREEN, Mary	
Mary BREEN Crossett		1855	1943	087	CROSSETT, Willis H.	
				087		
David MANNING		1855	1940	087	____, Mary F.	
Mary F. ____ MANNING		1861	1930	087	MANNING, David	
				087		
Thomas REEVES		1850	1926	087	MCGRATH, Bridget	
Bridget MCGRATH Reeves		1851	1925	087	REEVES, Thomas	
				087		
Jeremiah O'BRIEN		1850	1928	087	____, Lucy J.	
Lucy J. ____ O'BRIEN		1845	1933	087	O'BRIEN, Jeremiah	
				087		
Timothy W. FLANAGAN		1854	1932	087	HUTCHINS, Nancie J.	
Nancie J. HUTCHINS Flanagan		1858	1932	087	FLANAGAN, Timothy W.	

Mountain View Cemetery, Waterville, Vermont

NAME	POB	DOB/AGE	DOD	CEM	SPOUSE/INDEX	INSCRIPTION
G. H. MANN		1845	1916	106	POWERS, Louisa S.	
Louisa S. POWERS Mann		1852	1922	106	MANN, G. H.	
				106		
Simon BURNS		1844	1918	106	PETERS, Evelyn	

Evelyn PETERS Burns		1853	1955	106	BURNS, Simon	
				106		
Moses MCFARLAND		06-25-1821	03-06-1911	106	_____, Livonia A.	
Livonia A. _____ MCFARLAND		05-29-1820	05-22-1889	106	MCFARLAND, Moses	
				106		
Osgood MCFARLAND		83Y11M12D	07-21-1865	106	_____, Mary	
Mary _____ MCFARLAND		75Y2M24D	06-05-1861	106	MCFARLAND, Osgood	
Catherine MCFARLAND		68 Years	06-28-1845	106	MCFARLAND, Catherine	
				106		
William MCMANIMON		91 Years	12-14-1893	106	_____, Jemima	(GAR) Co. H, 9th Vt. Vols
Jemima _____ MCMANIMON		71 Years	12-29-1880	106	MCMANIMON, William	
George H. MCMANIMON		23 Years	03-05-1879	106	MCMANIMON, George H.	
				106		
Cyrus JANES		79 Years	06-01-1889	106	RYAN, Elizabeth	
Elizabeth RYAN Janes		64 Years	09-21-1885	106	JANES, Cyrus	
				106		
John HERREN	Co. Antrim	73 Years	09-07-1854	106	_____, Harriett	A Native Of Carrickfergus,Ire.
Harriett _____ HERREN		67 Years	06-25-1857	106	HERREN, John	A Native Of Wilchire, England
				106		
Robert HERREN	Co. Antrim	43 Years	09-11-1847	106	HERREN, Robert	Carrickfergus,Ireland. Erected
				106		By His Bereaved Widow And
				106		Children, In Memory Of A Kind
				106		Husband And Affectionate
				106		Father. (NOI widow)
				106		
Elizabeth _____ AGNEW	Co. Antrim	49 Years	08-22-1851	106	AGNEW, John R.	Carrickfergus, Ireland. (NOI
				106	_____, Elizabeth	James R. Agnew)
				106		
John MACKINTOSH		72 Years	07-21-1860	106	HERRON, Elizabeth	Interred At Andrew Jackson
				106		County, Illinois
Elizabeth HERRON MacKintosh		88 Years	04-03-1887	106	MACKINTOSH, John	Interred Here
				106		
Patrick TOBIN		03-14-1798	10-14-1873	106	UPTON, Mary	
Mary UPTON Tobin		08-16-1806	11-26-1878	106	TOBIN, Patrick	
Emma Jane TOBIN		18 Years	03-19-1857	106	TOBIN, Emma Jane	
				106		
Robert WALLACE		74 Years	12-30-1856	106	WALLACE, Robert	
				106		
Christopher C. TOBIN		1847	1915	106	MANN, Jane M.	
Jane M. MANN Tobin		1856	1905	106	TOBIN, Christpher C.	
				106		
Nathan MCFARLAND		79Y 1M	03-10-1892	106	WALLACE, Hannah	
Hannah WALLACE McFarland		61Y 4M	12-24-1874	106	MCFARLAND, Nathan	

St. Bridgets Church Cemetery, West Rutland, Vermont

NAME	POB	DOB/AGE	DOD	CEM	SPOUSE/INDEX	INSCRIPTION
James CARROLL		1806	1871	091	FOSTER, Julia	
Julia FOSTER Carroll		1812	1887	091	CARROLL, James	
John CARROLL		1846	1928	091	MUNDAY, Margaret A	(GAR) Co. C 10th Vt Vols
Margaret A. MUNDAY Carroll		1849	1928	091	CARROLL, John	
				091		
John HAYES		07-17-1837	03-23-1911	091	MCGUE, Ann	
Ann MCGUE Hayes		01-04-1838	01-23-1910	091	HAYES, John	
				091		
Johannah QUINLAN Brown		78 Years	02-18-1876	091	BROWN, Thomas	Native of Knockboney, Knockna-
				091	QUINLAN, Johannah	booley), Co. Limerick, Ireland
				091		(NOI Thomas Brown)
				091		
				091		
Martin HINES		1840	1925	091	BRENNAN, Margaret	
Margaret BRENNAN Hines		27 Years	10-12-1877	091	HINES, Martin	
				091		
Thomas BURKE		1841	1916	091	RYAN, Mary	
Mary RYAN Burke		1840	1885	091	BURKE, Thomas	
				091		
Bridget MAUGHAN		1843	1904	091	RYAN, Mary	(Same Plot as Thomas Maughan
				091		of Portarlington, Kings Co)
				091		
Anthony DEACY		1849	1918	091	HOLLERAN, Maria	
Maria HOLLERAN Deacy		1844	1932	091	DEACY, Anthony	
				091		
Mary ____ GALLAGHER		34 Years	01-23-1872	091	GALLAGHER, P.	(NOI P. Gallagher)
				091	_____, Mary	
				091		
Michael MOLONEY		84 Years	09-26-1901	091	RYAN, Mary	
Mary RYAN Moloney		80 Years	03-27-1910	091	MOLONEY, Michael	
				091		
Robert MONAHAN		1827	1904	091	CONLIN, Mary	
Mary CONLIN Monahan		1829	1906	091	MONAHAN, Robert	
John J. MONAHAN		1852	1885	091	MONAHAN, John J.	
Margaret MONAHAN		1853	1856	091	MONAHAN, Margaret	
				091		
Michael HACKETT		1832	1908	091	HANLEY, Margaret A	
Margaret A. HANLEY Hackett		1833	1901	091	HACKETT, Michael	
				091		
Thomas CANFIELD		65 Years	08-02-1884	091	HEYHER, Margaret	

Name		Born/Age	Died		Index	Notes
Margaret HEYHER Canfield		86 Years	08-02-1910	091	CANFIELD, Thomas	
				091		
John HANLEY		75 Years	09-24-1894	091	_____, Margaret	
Margaret _____ HANLEY		54 Years	12-03-1872	091	HANLEY, John	
				091		
Patrick DIFLEY		1815	1858	091	_____, Mary	
Mary _____ DIFLEY		1819	1867	091	DIFLEY, Patrick	
				091		
John CONIFF		58 Years	08-26-1880	091	OWENS, Ann	
Ann OWENS Coniff		65 Years	08-26-1896	091	CONIFF, John	
				091		
Mary CAIN Moylan		1790	1877	091	MOYLAN, Thomas	(NOI Thomas Moylan)
				091	CAIN, Mary	
				091		
John MEEHAN		1839	1915	091	MOYLAN, Ann	
Ann MOYLAN Meehan				091	MEEHAN, John	
				091		
Michael MCMURRAY		84 Years	03-23-1892	091	MCMURRAY, Catherine	
Catherine MCMURRAY		69 Years	02-21-1890	091	MCMURRAY, Michael	(Does not say if spouse)
Bridget Ann MCMURRAY		04-31-1848	01-18-1869	091	MCMURRAY, Bridget Ann	
Mary MCMURRAY		12-15-1851	11-12-1885	091	MCMURRAY, Mary	
Michael E. MCMURRAY		01-12-1858	01-12-1860	091	MCMURRAY, Michael E.	
				091		
Terrance MCCAULEY		1835	1917	091	MCDONOUGH, Mary	
Mary MCDONOUGH McCauley		1837	1906	091	MCCAULEY, Terrance	
				091		
James MORONEY	Co. Clare	29 Years	02-14-1875	091	NAGLE, Kate	
Kate NAGLE Moroney		78 Years	02-21-1924	091	MORONEY, James	Native of County Clare
				091		
Patrick HINES		1847	1905	091	_____, Jane	
Jane _____ HINES		1852	1921	091	HINES, Patrick	
				091		
James MCGUIRE		03-03-1837	1925	091	COX, Ann	
Ann COX McGuire		62 Years	02-06-1900	091	MCGUIRE, James	
				091		
Michael MCLAUGHLIN		1850	1918	091	COLLIGAN, Mary E.	
Mary E. COLLIGAN McLaughlin		1854	1940	091	MCLAUGHLIN, Michael	
John F. COLLIGAN		1845	1912	091	COLLIGAN, John F.	
				091		
Mary _____ CARROLL		71 Years	08-22-1897	091	CARROLL, Thomas	(Next to Catherine Carroll
				091	____, Mary	Colligan of Knockalaghta,
				091		Killglass, Roscommon)
Catherine A. WARD Carroll		8? Years	11-08-1920	091	CARROLL, Thomas	(Same stone as Mary Carroll.
				091	WARD, Catherine A.	(NOI Thomas)
				091		

Name	Age / Born	Died	Code	Index	Notes
John KENNY	89 Years	01-12-1899	091	_____, Sarah	
Sarah _____ KENNY	76 Years	01-16-1912	091	KENNY, John	
			091		
Andrew FARRELL	60 Years	04-08-1898	091	GILFEATHER, Catherine	
Catherine GILFEATHER Farrell	65 Years	02-17-1919	091	FARRELL, Andrew	
John FARRELL	1808	1888	091	FARRELL, John	
			091		
Patrick ROONEY	48 Years	08-09-1888	091	GAFFNEY, Mary J.	
Mary J. GAFFNEY Rooney	34 Years	03-21-1884	091	ROONEY, Patrick	
			091		
Edward WALSH	67 Years	12-31-1893	091	LUNNY, Mary	
Mary LUNNY Walsh	80 Years	02-10-1911	091	WALSH, Edward	
			091		
Michael GOLFIN	1847	1921	091	WALSH, Ann	
Ann WALSH Golfin	1871	1899 1911	091	GOLFIN, Michael	
			091		
Bryan MCTIERNEY	63 Years	09-13-1880	091	MCLAUGHLIN, Alice	
Alice MCLAUGHLIN McTierney	32 Years	03-29-1860	091	MCTIERNEY, Bryan	
			091		
Lizzie A. ROURKE McTierney	32 Years	12-17-1885	091	MCTIERNEY, John	(NOI John McTierney)
			091	ROURKE, Lizzie A.	
			091		
Mathew FOX	63 Years	05-14-1899	091	FARRELL, Elizabeth	
Elizabeth FARRELL Fox	58 Years	03-21-1891	091	FOX, Mathew	
			091		
Thomas BATTLES	75 Years	02-07-1905	091	BROWN, Ann	
Ann BROWN Battles	62 Years	03-14-1899	091	BATTLES, Thomas	
			091		
Daniel MCGUIRE	84 Years	03-28-1884	091	WINTERS, Nancy	
Nancy WINTERS McGuire	63 Years	11-15-1874	091	MCGUIRE, Daniel	
			091		
Lt John F. SINNOTT	25 Years	07-10-1863	091	SINNOTT, Lt John F.	Died of wounds received at
			091		Gettysburg. Co. A. 13th Rgt VT
			091		Vols (GAR)
Mathew QUINLAN	39 Years	01-14-1887	091	HANNAN, Margaret	
Margaret HANNAN Quinlan	1851	1923	091	QUINLAN, Mathew	
			091		
Owen GAFFNEY	65 Years	01-19-1879	091	GAFFNEY, Owen	
			091		
Edward CLIFFORD	1824	1906	091	MCGRATH, Mary	
Mary MCGRATH Clifford	1828	1903	091	CLIFFORD, Edward	
Susan MCGRATH	1851	1858	091	MCGRATH, Susan	
William MCGRATH	1860	1865	091	MCGRATH, William	
Edward MCGRATH	1869	1870	091	MCGRATH, Edward	
			091		

Name	Origin	Birth/Age	Death	Code	Index	Notes
Patrick CASSIDY		50 Years	06-16-1877	091	ROONEY, Bridget	
Bridget ROONEY Cassidy		72 Years	08-22-1916	091	CASSIDY, Patrick	
				091		
Andrew MCDEVITT		41 Years	02-23-1879	091	FITZPATRICK, Margaret	
Margaret FITZPATRICK McDevitt		65 Years	11-25-1898	091	MCDEVITT, Andrew	
				091		
John FARRELL		49 Years	1884	091	_____, Bridget	
Bridget _____ FARRELL		59 Years	1904	091	FARRELL, John	
				091		
John RYAN		1833	1866	091	DWYER, Sarah	
Sarah DWYER Ryan		1834	1906	091	RYAN, John	
				091		
John D. CURRY		1830	1913	091	COLEMAN, Catherine	
Catherine COLEMAN Curry		1834	1864	091	CURRY, John D.	
Julia BOLEN		18	1872	091	BOLEN, Julia	
Mary MCDERMOTT		1844	1910	091	MCDERMOTT, Mary	
Catherine CURRY		1877	1879	091	CURRY, Catherine	
				091		
Bernard CONLIN		1825	1907	091	RADIGAN, Ann	
Ann RADIGAN Conlin		1823	1907	091	CONLIN, Bernard	
Mary _______ MUMFORD		1851	1880	091	MUMFORD, Patrick	(NOI Patrick Mumford)
				091	_____, Mary	
John CONLIN		1853	1901	091	CONLIN, John	
Patrick CONLIN		1859	1865	091	CONLIN, Patrick	
Bernard CONLIN		1857	1911	091	CONLIN, Bernard	
Ellen CONLIN		1861	1932	091	CONLIN, Ellen	
				091		
John J. O'ROURKE		1839	1923	091	CONKLIN, Mary	
Mary CONKLIN O'Rourke		1851	1927	091	O'ROURKE, John J.	
Margaret O'ROURKE		1888	1964	091	O'ROURKE, Margaret	Daughter
William P. HAYES		1888	1948	091	O'ROURKE, Eleanor	
Eleanor O'ROURKE		1886	1949	091	HAYES, William P.	
				091		
Edward MCGOWAN		08-08-1836	10-31-1908	091	MCGOWAN, Edward	
				091		
Robert FORCE		1844	1917	091	O'NEIL, Helen	
Helen O'NEIL Force		1860	1947	091	FORCE, Robert	
				091		
Sarah A. WARD McNeil		54 Years	08-13-1907	091	MCNEIL, James	(NOI James McNeil)
				091	WARD, Sarah A.	
				091		
Patrick MULVEY	Co. Tipperary	26 Years	09-20-1851	091	MULVEY, Patrick	Son & Dau of Thomas Mulvey
Allice MULVEY	Co. Tipperary	24 Years	09-18-1857	091	MULVEY, Allice	of Kildenogue (Kildanoge),
				091	MULVEY, Thomas	Co. Tipperary, Ireland
				091		

Charles QUINLAN				091	DWYER, Bridget	
Bridget DWYER Quinlan		1826	1873	091	QUINLAN, Charles	
				091		
Edward COREY		1804	1879	091	COLTON, Rose	
Rose COLTON Corey		1807	1882	091	COREY, Edward	
John COREY		1849	1879	091	COREY, John	
Sarah COREY		1834	1890	091	COREY, Sarah	
Hugh COREY		1836	1916	091	COREY, Hugh	
				091		
John LONERGAN	Co. Waterford	21 Years	07-29-1860	091	LONERGAN, John	Native of Parish of Rathgor-
				091		mick (Rathgormuck), County
				091		of Waterford, Ireland
				091		
Michael FLANAGAN		80 Years	02-16-1896	091	_____, Jane	
Jane _____ FLANAGAN		40 Years	03-10-1863	091	FLANAGAN, Michael	
Dennis FLANAGAN		35 Years	04-17-1887	091	FLANAGAN, Dennis	(Children of Michael & Jane
Eliza FLANAGAN		42 Years	10-28-1887	091	FLANAGAN, Eliza	Flanagan)
James FLANAGAN		15 Years	01-03-1873	091	FLANAGAN, James	" " " "
				091		
				091		
Mary FLYNN O'Haire		31 Years	67-22-1887	091	O'HAIRE, Patrick	(NOI Patrick O'Haire)
				091	FLYNN, Mary	
				091		
Bridget _____ NORTON		36 Years	04-18-1868	091	NORTON, Thomas	(NOI Thomas Norton)
				091	_____, Bridget	
				091		
Joseph STONE		56 Years	02-12-____	091	STONE, Joseph	
				091		
John COPPS		71 Years	02-09-1892	091	RYANS, Ann	
Ann RYAN Copps		82 Years	08-23-1907	091	COPPS, John	
				091		
Dennis COPPS		71 Years	03-25-1898	091	DARMODY, Hannah	
Hannah DARMODY Copps		74 Years	02-06-1907	091	COPPS, Dennis	
				091		
Susan MADIGAN		35 Years	01-01-1862	091	MADIGAN, Susan	
				091		
Thomas MCGOWEN			06-12-1881	091	MCGOWEN, Thomas	
				091		
Mary A. MOYLAN Meehan		27 Years	07-10-1884	091	MEEHAN, M.	(NOI M.Meehan)
				091	MOYLAN, Mary A.	
				091		
Andrew MCLAUGHLIN		1818	1881	091	KEEGAN, Mary	
Mary KEEGAN McLaughlin		1824	1907	091	MCLAUGHLIN, Andrew	
				091		
John RIORDAN		88 Years	04-04-1906	091	_____, Ellen	

Name	Place	Birth/Age	Death	Code	Relative	Notes
Ellen _____ RIORDAN		61 Years	04-05-1881	091	RIORDAN, John	
				091		
Patrick COSGROVE		28 Years	08-15-1863	091	COSGROVE, Patrick	
				091		
Peter LYNCH		1824	1889	091	_____, Margaret	
Margaret _____ LYNCH		1833	1913	091	LYNCH, Peter	
				091		
Patrick MUMFORD		1848	1922	091	GAFFNEY, Ellen	(GAR) Co. D, 7th Regt, Vt Vols
Ellen GAFFNEY Mumford		1857	1899	091	MUMFORD, Patrick	
				091		
Lizzie MCDONOUGH		19 Years	03-27-1879	091	MCDONOUGH, James	(NOI James McDonough)
				091	_____, Lizzie	
				091		
Patrick HALEY	Co. Sligo	05-17-1800	02-25-1888	091	HALEY, Patrick	Born In County Sligo, Ireland.
				091		
Margaret HALEY Logan		06-05-182?	01-02-1863	091	LOGAN, James	(NOI James Logan)
				091	HALEY, Margaret	
				091		
Edward O'BRIEN		1833	1909	091	CRAHAN, Mary	
Mary CRAHAN O'Brien		1842	1884	091	O'BRIEN, Edward	
				091		
Bernard MCLAUGHLIN		1855	1925	091	MCGINLEY, Katherine	
Katherine MCGINLEY McLaughlin		1859	1916	091	MCLAUGHLIN, Bernard	
				091		
Mary E. CARMODY Clifford		37 Years	12-02-1896	091	CLIFFORD, Patrick	(NOI Patrick Clifford)
				091	CARMODY, Mary E.	
				091		
Edward MCCORMICK		1836	1906	091	LLOYD, Anne	
Anne LLOYD McCormick		1846	1926	091	MCCORMICK, Edward	
				091		
Mary MOORE McGinley		42 Years	12-28-1908	091	MCGINLEY, Charles	(NOI Charles McGinley)
				091	MOORE, Mary	
				091		
David GORMAN		1848	1905	091	_____, Ellen	
Ellen _____ GORMAN		1858	1939	091	GORMAN, David	
				091		
John MCDEVITT		90 Years	03-17-1916	091	GALLAGHER, Susan	
Susan GALLAGHER McDevitt		72 Years	09-14-1905	091	MCDEVITT, John	
				091		
Michael MELEADY		1848	1932	091	BATTLES, Catherine	
Catherine BATTLES Meleady		45 Years	01-17-1899	091	MELEADY, Michael	
				091		
John MORONEY		52 Years	10-20-1892	091	SAMMON, Margaret	
Margaret SAMMON Moroney		1844	1914	091	MORONEY, John	
				091		

Name	Origin	Born/Age	Died	Code	Index	Notes
Michael MORAN		1814	1896	091	ELLIOT, Phoebe	
Phoebe ELLIOT Moran		1832	1898	091	MORAN, Michael	
				091		
Patrick BARTLEY		82 Years	04-02-1913	091	MURPHY, Winifred	
Winifred MURPHY Bartley		60 Years	01-10-1897	091	BARTLEY, Patrick	
				091		
Thomas LYNCH		1839	1903	091	DONEGAN, Mary A.	
Mary A. DONEGAN Lynch		1848	1920	091	LYNCH, Thomas	
				091		
Florence MCCARTHY		45 Years	06-09-1896	091	SULLIVAN, Mary E.	
Mary E. SULLIVAN McCarthy		48 Years	04-15-1909	091	MCCARTHY, Florence	
				091		
Owen MCCARTHY		05-25-1840	19-02-1913	091	POWERS, Bridget	
Bridget POWERS McCarthy		10-09-1841	11-24-1903	091	MCCARTHY, Owen	
				091		
Rev. Michael Joseph CARMODY		1853	1934	091	CARMODY, Rev. Michael J.	
				091		
Eugene SWEENEY	Co. Cork	21 Years	05-27-1871	091	SWEENEY, Eugene	Native(s) of Thaunadromin
				091		Co Cork Ire (No such place)
				091		(Son of Patrick & Julia)
				091		(Think this is a corruption
				091		of the Town Of Dromin, aka
				091		Dromin, Co. Cork)
				091		
Jeremiah SWEENEY	Co. Cork	2 Years	02-26-1856	091	SWEENEY, Jeremiah	Native(s) of Thaunadromin
				091		Co Cork Ire (No such place)
				091		(Son of Patrick & Julia)
				091		(See note above on town)
Michael BURKE		1848	1895	091	FOLEY, Mary	
Mary FOLEY Burke		1846	1874	091	BURKE, Michael	
Dennis FOLEY		1846	1872	091	FOLEY, Dennis	
				091		
John GAVIN		1829	1879	091	FLYNN, Ann	
Ann FLYNN Gavin		1836	1928	091	GAVIN, John	
				091		
Martin MOLONEY		1823	1896	091	DAVINE, Margaret	
Margaret DAVINE Moloney		1830	1893	091	MOLONEY, Martin	
				091		
Michael C. MURPHY		1857	1888	091	FLYNN, Catherine H.	
Catherine H. FLYNN Murphy		1854	1917	091	MURPHY, Michael C.	
				091		
John DAVINE		1839	1902	091	SMITH, Margaret	
Margaret SMITH Davine		1849	1921	091	DAVINE, John	
				091		
James DAVINE		60 Years	08-28-1888	091	______, Bridget	

Bridget __ DAVINE	62 Years	07-28-1896	091	DAVINE, James	
			091		
Timothy O'BRIEN	69 Years	01-27-1909	091	SMITH, Bridget	
			091	FOLEY, Charlotte	
Bridget SMITH O'Brien	30 Years	01-18-1874	091	O'BRIEN, Timothy	
Charlotte FOLEY O'Brien	73 Years	05-06-1913	091	O'BRIEN, Timothy	
			091		
Patrick MCCORMICK	1832	1927	091	BRENNAN, Bridget	
Bridget BRENNAN McCormick	34 Years	09-04-1880	091	MCCORMICK, Patrick	
			091		
Roger CARMODY	1836	1875	091	DAVINE, Ann	
Ann DAVINE Carmody	1840	1911	091	CARMODY, Roger	
			091		
Mary CAIN	65 Years	05-16-1885	091	CAIN, Mary	
			091		
John MCGARRY	1818	1904	091	CANNON, Bridget	
Bridget CANNON McGarry	1830	1906	091	MCGARRY, John	
Margaret MCGARRY	1782	1863	091	MCGARRY, Margaret	Grandmother
			091		
Bridget CARMODY Gilrane	19 Years	04-29-1869	091	GILRANE, James	(NOI James Gilrane)
			091	CARMODY, Bridget	
			091		
Edward QUINN	80 Years	09-03-1918	091	COLLINS, Bridget	
Bridget COLLINS Quinn	87 Years	02-01-1917	091	QUINN, Edward	
			091		
Patrick DAVINE	1820	1886	091	MOYLAN, Mary	
Mary MOYLAN Davine	1837	1871	091	DAVINE, Patrick	
			091		
James SHERIDAN	74 Years	12-22-1902	091	______, Eliza	
Eliza ___ SHERIDAN	62 Years	06-24-1896	091	SHERIDAN, James	
			091		
Catherine HAYDEN Ceasy	62 Years	08-25-1890	091	CEASY, James	(NOI James Ceasy)
			091	HAYDEN, Catherine	
			091		
Mary FOSTER Farrell	33 Years	07- -1878	091	FARRELL, James	(NOI James Farrell)
			091	FOSTER, Mary	
			091		
William GAFFNEY	01-01-1834	03-13-1899	091	LYONS, Catherine	
Catherine LYONS Gaffney	03-25-1833	11-25-1901	091	GAFFNEY, William	
			091		
Thomas E. KELLEY	79 Years	06-01-1906	091	FOLEY, Ann	
Ann FOLEY Kelley	62 Years	07-05-1892	091	KELLEY, Thomas E.	
			091		
Rose CLARK Martin	1854	1928	091	MARTIN, Rose Clark	
			091		

Patrick MCGINLEY		80 Years	03-13-1897	091	MUMFORD, Catherine	
Catherine MUMFORD McGinley				091	PHILOMY, Jane	
Jane PHILOMY McGinley				091	MCGINLEY, Patrick	(NOI Jane Philomy)
Margaret ___ MUMFORD		54 Years	03-29-1863	091	MUMFORD, James	(NOI James Mumford)
				091	_____, Margaret	
Edward MCGINLEY		22 Years	08-01-1874	091	MCGINLEY, Edward	
				091		
Patrick TIGHE		1831	1914	091	MCGOWAN, Margaret	
Margaret MCGOWAN Tighe		1836	1903	091	TIGHE, Patrick	
Michael TIGHE		1851	1870	091	TIGHE, Michael	
Ellen TIGHE		1800	1875	091	TIGHE, Ellen	
Darby TIGHE		1833	1908	091	TIGHE, Darby	
Darby TIGHE		75 Years	09-21-1908	091	TIGHE, Darby	
				091		(Small Stone In Tighe Plot
Dennis J. LENIHAN		1842	1905	091	CROWLEY, Mary	
Mary CROWLEY Lenihan		1840	1906	091	LENIHAN, Dennis J.	
				091		
Peter EVERIN		11-20-1835	10-02-1862	091	TRAINOR, Cathrine	
Cathrine TRAINOR Everin		06-05-1832	12-08-1858	091	EVERIN, Peter	
				091		
James MCQUADE		1829	1906	091	MUNDAY, Mary	
Mary MUNDAY McQuade		1834	1916	091	MCQUADE, James	
				091		
Ann MCGUIRE Holton		78 Years	10-19-1897	091	HOLTON, Garret	(NOI Garret Holton)
				091	MCGUIRE, Ann	
				091		
Thomas MUNDAY		1798	1892	091	LEONARD, Alice	
Alice LEONARD Munday		1810	1894	091	MUNDAY, Thomas	
John F. MUNDAY		1852	1904	091	MUNDAY, John F.	Their Son
				091		
Edward MCCORMACK	Co. Roscommon	88 Years	08-18-1880	091	_____, Margaret	Native Of Co. Roscommon, Ire.
Margaret D. _____ MCCORMACK		68 Years	05-31-1862	091	MCCORMACK, Edward	Native Of Little Rock, Canada
				091		
John CROONELL		73 Years	05-13-1906	091	_____, Catherine	
Catherine M. _____ CROONELL		71 Years	05-16-1907	091	CROONELL, John	
				091		
Thomas MELADY		84 Years	12-04-1916	091	_____, Bridget	
Bridget ___ MELADY		75 Years	08-31-1912	091	MELADY, Thomas	
				091		
Patrick HANSON		45 Years	08-29-1863	091	HANSON, Patrick	
				091		
Timothy COLLINS	Co. Cork	65 Years	04-30-1897	091	SLATTERY, Ann	A Native Of the City Of Cork
				091		
Ann SLATTERY Collins		59 Years	11-09-1891	091	COLLINS, Timothy	
				091		

Michael CROWLEY		1829	1889	091	MCCARTHY, Mary	(NOI Mary MCCarthy)
				091	CROWLEY, Michael	
				091		
Peter FLANNIGAN			01- -1904	091	_____, Elizabeth	Dearly Beloved Husband Of
				091		Elizabeth Died January 1904.
				091		Brothers Patrick, Thomas,Peter
Elizabeth ___ FLANNIGAN			03- -1869	091	FLANNIGAN, Peter	Dearly Beloved Wife Of Peter
				091		Died March 1869.Sisters Maria,
				091		Elizabeth, Rose, Bridget
				091		
Patrick CARROLL	Co. Tipperary	47 Years	01-10-1874	091	_____, Elizabeth	(NOI Elizabeth).Native of
				091	CARROLL, Patrick	Casheltown Parish, County
				091		Tipperary. Erected by His
				091		Wife, Elizabeth.
John CARROLL		12 Years	12-18-1862	091	CARROLL, John	Son Of P. & E. Carroll
				091		
Patrick STAPLETON	Co. Tipperary	24 Years	03-20-1873	091	STAPLETON, Patrick	Son Of James and Mary Staple-
				091	STAPLETON, James	ton. Native of Co. Tipperary
				091		
Maurice RALEIGH		60 Years	03-10-1873	091	_____, Ellen	(NOI Ellen)
				091	RALEIGH, Maurice	
				091		
Thomas COONEY		1833	1913	091	_____, Alice	
Alice ___ COONEY		1835	1864	091	COONEY, Thomas	
				091		
Mary ____ FORD			04-19-1857	091	FORD, Patrick	In Memory Of Mary, Wife of
				091	_____, Mary	Patrick Ford. (NOI Patrick)
				091		
Patrick LYNCH		1830	1903	091	_____, Margaret	
Margaret ___ LYNCH		1833	1907	091	LYNCH, Patrick	
				091		
John KINNEALY			04- -1865	091	KINNEALY, John	
James KINNEALY			1866	091	KINNEALY, James	
Michael KINNEALY			06-11-1860	091	KINNEALY, Michael	
				091		
John RALEIGH		56 Years	05-03-1895	091	_____, Catherine	
Catherine __ RALEIGH		44 Years	05-01-1889	091	RALEIGH, John	
				091		
Edward E. POWERS		40 Years	02-11-1893	091	POWERS, Edward E.	
				091		
Mark MADDEN		19 Years	11-19-1864	091	MADDEN, Mark	Erected By Hannah Madden, In
				091	MADDEN, Hannah	Memory of Her Brother
				091		
Mary ___ LLOYD		40 Years	03-05-1867	091	LLOYD, Edmond	(NOI Edmond Lloyd)
				091	_____, Mary	

			091		
Bridget __ DOOLEY	26 Years	08-09-1860	091	DOOLEY, David	(NOI David Dooley)
			091	_____, Bridget	
			091		
James HANLEY	69 Years	01-06-1893	091	______, Ellen	
Ellen ____ HANLEY	67 Years	03-20-1896	091	HANLEY, James	
			091		
Patrick COFFEY	95 Years	10-13-1896	091	________, Ann	
Ann ____ COFFEY	75 Years	04-04-1886	091	COFFEY, Patrick	
Ann COFFEY	5 Years	04-18-1853	091	COFFEY, Ann	
Bridget COFFEY	2Y 5M	06-02-1855	091	COFFEY, Bridget	
			091		
Matthew CAIN	49 Years	11-10-1887	091	BOLAN, Mary	
Mary BOLAN Cain	06-10-1828		091	CAIN, Matthew	(No DOD on Mary Bolan)
			091		
John HAMILTON	92Y 10M	04-11-1911	091	CLARK, Margaret	
Margaret CLARK Hamilton	88 Years	06-28-1906	091	HAMILTON, John	
			091		
Bridget GAFFNEY Campbell	25Y 9M	09-19-1875	091	CAMPBELL, Thomas	(NOI Thomas Campbell)
			091	GAFFNEY, Bridget	
			091		
Ellen M. HANLEY Brown	28Y9M17D	09-19-1873	091	BROWN, William	(NOI William Brown)
			091	HANLEY, Ellen M.	
			091		
Peter GAFFNEY	1820	1885	091	FLYNN, Bridget	
Bridget FLYNN Gaffney	1822	1885	091	GAFFNEY, Peter	
Reverend Peter GAFFNEY	1855	1916	091	GAFFNEY, Reverend Peter	
Edward GAFFNEY	1863	1903	091	GAFFNEY, Edward	
James GAFFNEY	1845	1899	091	GAFFNEY, James	
Charles GAFFNEY	1859	1861	091	GAFFNEY, Charles	
Jane GAFFNEY	1851	1896	091	GAFFNEY, Jane	
Margaret GAFFNEY	1860	1897	091	GAFFNEY, Margaret	
Mary GAFFNEY Mathiey	1843	1922	091	GAFFNEY, Mary	(NOI Mr. Mathieu)
Bridget GAFFNEY Campbell	1849	1875	091	GAFFNEY, Bridget	(NOI Mr. Campbell)
Ellen GAFFNEY Copps	1852	1881	091	GAFFNEY, Ellen	(NOI Mr. Copps)
			091		
Gilbert HANLEY	47 Years	12-03-1884	091	______, Margaret	Erected by His Son, John B. Hanley
			091		
Margaret ___ HANLEY	41 Years	12-02-1880	091	HANLEY, Gilbert	
			091		
James J. GILLIGAN	1847	1929	091	CAREY, Mary	
Mary CAREY Gilligan	1847	1924	091	GILLIGAN, James J.	
			091		
John QUINN	1825	1884	091	NERNEY, Ann	
Ann NERNEY Quinn	1840	1890	091	QUINN, John	

Name	Origin	Birth	Death	Code	Relation	Notes
				091		
Andrew HANLEY		1854	1925	091	CASEY, Hanora M.	
Hanora M. CASEY Hanley		1860	1929	091	HANLEY, Andrew	
				091		
Michael MULLIN		1834	1912	091	MCGUE, Margaret	
Margaret MCGUE Mullin		1844	1890	091	MULLIN, Michael	
				091		
Patrick MULLIN		1829	1897	091	____, Ann	
Ann ___ MULLIN		1826	1900	091	MULLIN, Patrick	
				091		
Edward GALVIN		47 Years		091	HENRY, Martha	
Martha HENRY Galvin				091	GALVIN, Edward	
Edward GALVIN		46 Years	05-23-1901	091	GALVIN, Edward	
				091		
John MCHUGH		1814	1903	091	____, Jane	
Jane __ MCHUGH		1824	1907	091	MCHUGH, John	
				091		
John RYAN		62 Years	07-07-1905	091	WINTERS, Sarah J.	
Sarah J. WINTERS Ryan		58 Years	07-11-1908	091	RYAN, John	
Patrick T. GILLIGAN		40 Years	12-06-1890	091	MCNEIL, Mary J.	
Mary J. MCNEIL Gilligan		71 Years	08-29-1928	091	GILLIGAN, Patrick T.	
				091		
James K. MCDEVITT		1854	1932	091	HANLEY, Margaret	
Margaret HANLEY McDevitt		1862	1919	091	MCDEVITT, James K.	
				091		
Ann ___ STEELE		72Y6M5D	12-19-1906	091	STEELE, Samuel	(NOI Samuel Steele)
				091	_____, Ann	
				091		
William BURKE		1847	1920	091	_______, Bridget	
Bridget ____ BURKE		1856	1918	091	BURKE, William	
				091		
Patrick MCMAHON		03-17-1843	01-25-1915	091	MCMAHON, Patrick	(GAR) Co. A, 13th Vt. Vols
				091		
Catherine CARROLL Colligan	Co. Roscommon	62 Years	04-10-1880	091	COLLIGAN, Patrick	Native of Knockall (Knocka-
				091		laghta), Parish of Killglass
				091		(Kilglass), Co. Roscommon
				091		(NOI Patrick Colligan)
				091		
Bridget FLANNIGAN McGuire	Co. Roscommon	34 Years	06-29-1872	091	MCGUIRE, Terrins	Born In Parish of Kelltrusten
				091	FLANNIGAN, Bridget	(Kiltrustan), Co. Roscommon,
				091		Ireland. (NOI Terrins McGuire
Daniel A. MCGUIRE	Co. Roscommon	84 Years	05-28-1884	091	WINTERS, Nancy	Both Natives of Parish of
				091		Kilglass, Co. Roscommon
Nancy WINTERS McGuire	Co. Roscommon	63 Years	11-15-1874	091	MCGUIRE, Daniel A.	Both Natives of Parish of
				091		Kilglass, Co. Roscommon

Name	County	Born/Age	Died	Code	Related	Notes
Thomas MAUGHAN	Co. Kings	1801	1868	091	BRENAN, Ann	Natives of Portarlington, King Co., Ireland
Ann BRENAN Maughan	Co. Kings	1811	1893	091	MAUGHAN, Thomas	Natives of Portarlington, King Co., Ireland
Michael RODDY	Co. Roscommon	46 Years	10-16-1882	091	NORTON, Margaret	A Native of Parish Kilglass, Co. Roscommon, Ireland
Margaret NORTON Roddy	Co. Roscommon	56 Years	09-18-1890	091	RODDY, Michael	
Mary RODDY Green		27Y4M27D	03-26-1886	091	GREEN, Michael RODDY, Mary	(NOI Michael Green)
Thomas MONAHAN	Co. Donegal	60 Years	06-26-1862	091	MCCARTHY, Mary	Both Born In Ballyshannon, County Of Donegal, Ireland
Mary MCCARTHY Monahan	Co. Donegal	83 Years	05-30-1890	091	MONAHAN, Thomas	Both Born In Ballyshannon, County Of Donegal, Ireland
Martin HINES		1840	1925	091	BRENNAN, Margaret	
Margaret BRENNAN Hines	Co. Galway	27 Years	10-12-1877	091	HINES, Martin	A Native of The Parish Of Oranmore, Co. Galway, Ire.
Bridget CARROLL Carmody	Co. Clare	30 Years	11-09-1869	091	CARMODY, Simon CARROLL, Bridget	A Native Of the Parish Of Kilmealy (Kilmaley), Co. Clare, Ireland (NOI Simon Carmody)
John CARMODY	Co. Clare	16 Years	01-29-1869	091	CARMODY, John	A Native of the Parish Of Killfin (Killofin),Co. Clare, Ireland (Same Plot as Bridget Carroll Carmody
John MORONEY	Co. Clare	29 Years	02-14-1875	091	MORONEY, John	In Memory Of John Moroney (Same plot as Bridget Carroll Carmody)
Margaret KEEFE Carmody	Co. Clare	35 Years	11-14-1878	091	CARMODY, Michael KEEFE, Margaret	A Native of Co. Clare (NOI Michael Carmody)
John C. DERVEN		1829	1901	091	CONNIFF, Bridget	Roberts Post 14, Rutland
Bridget CONNIFF Derven		1838	1926	091	DERVEN, John	
James CONLON		69 Years	08-08-1898	091	____, Ann CONLON, James	(NOI Ann)
Michael CONLON	Co. Clare	72Y 8M	06-10-1871	091	CONLON, Michael	Born in the Parish Kilmaely (Kilmaley) County Clare,Ire
Bridget CONLON	Co. Clare	1839	08-09-1883	091	CONLON, Bridget	Born in the Parish Kilmaely (Kilmaley) County Clare,Ire

Mary CONLON		70 Years	04-21-1901	091	CONLON, Mary	
				091		
Patrick CONLON		07-10-1824	06-26-1886	091	GAVIN, Margaret	
Margaret GAVIN Conlon		03-06-1836	12-30-1900	091	CONLON, Patrick	
				091		
William J. O'ROURKE		11-11-1844	09-26-1913	091	O'LEARY, Joanna,	
				091		
Joanna O'LEARY O'Rourke	Co. Cork	1843	12-06-1916	091	O'ROURKE, William J.	Native Of The Parish Of Bantry
				091		County Cork, Ireland
				091		
				091		
Catherine FOLEY Cawley		72 Years	11-02-1914	091	FOLEY, Catherine	Wife Of Patrick Cawley (NOI)
				091	CAWLEY, Patrick	
				091		
Mary CARMODY Foley		28 Years	06-07-1877	091	CARMODY, Mary	Wife Of John H. Foley (NOI)
				091	FOLEY, John H.	
				091		
Michael FOLEY	Co. Roscommon	88 Years	10-20-1886	091	MCGUIRE, Margaret	Both Natives Of Parish Kil-
Margaret MCQUIRE Foley	Co. Roscommon	77 Years	03-20-1886	091	FOLEY, Michael	glass, Co. Roscommon, Ire.
				091		
Ellen M. Foley BURKE		28 Years	04-24-1874	091	FOLEY, Ellen M.	Wife Of Thomas Burke (NOI)
				091	BURKE, Thomas	
				091		
Michael CLARK	Co. Leitrim	59 Years	12-10-1873	091	_____, Rose Ann	Native of Parish of Kilu-
				091		mery (Killanummery), Co.
				091		Leitrim, Ireland
Rose Ann _____ CLARK		59 Years	03-26-1887	091	CLARK, Michael	
				091		
Martin MULHEARN	Co. Roscommon	63 Years	03-22-1885	091	MCKEONE, Ann	Native of Parish of Boyle
				091		Co. Roscommon, Ireland
Ann MCKEONE Mulhearn	Co. Leitrim	59 Years	03-26-1887	091	MULHEARN, Martin	Native of Parish of Kill-
				091		argue (Killarga), County
				091		Leitrim, Ireland
				091		
Patrick DALEY	Co. Donegal	60 Years	10-25-1888	091	MCPHILMY, Sarah	Native of County Donegal
Sarah MCPHILMY Daley	Co. Tyrone	62 Years	07-01-1901	091	DALEY, Patrick	Native of County Tyrone
				091		
David MCDEVITT	Co. Tyrone	06-13-1831	01-28-1897	091	CORY, Mary	Native of Parish Ardstra
				091		(Ardstraw), Co. Tyrone.
				091		2nd LT, Co. A., 13th Rgt,
				091		Vt. Vol Inf.
Mary COREY McDevitt	Co. Tyrone	08-06-1818	05-01-1906	091	MCDEVITT, David	Native of Parish Dromore
				091		Co. Tyrone, Ireland
				091		
Thomas BATTLES	Co. Roscommon	40 Years	03-31-1874	091	BATTLES, Thomas	Parish of Boyle, County

Name	County	Age/Born	Died	Plot	Spouse	Notes
				091		Roscommon
William EVERIN	Co. Tipperary	78 Years	03-21-1918	091	KENNEDY, Bridget	Both Natives of County Tipperary, Ireland
Bridget KENNEDY Everin	Co. Tipperary	67 Years	10-01-1909	091	EVERIN, William	
Thomas MULHERN	Co. Roscommon	03-30-1828	02-11-1896	091	MCGOWAN, Jane	Both Natives of Boyle, Co. Roscommon, Ireland
Jane MCGOWAN Mulhern	Co. Roscommon	1839	19051-1909	091	MULHERN, Thomas	
John LONERGAN	Co. Tipperary	75 Years	11-07-1891	091	DWYER, Margaret	A Native of the Parish Kil-fackle (Kilfeakle) County Tipperary, Ireland
Margaret DWYER Lonergan	Co. Tipperary	48 Years	08-15-1877	091	LONERGAN, John	A Native of the Parish Kill-carty (No town/Parish by this name (Kilcarra?), Co. Tipperary, Ireland
Bridget _____ MCMAHON	Co. Clare	45 Years	06-02-1863	091	MCMAHON, Thomas	Native of County Clare, Ire
Jeffrey POWERS	Co. Cork	43 Years	06-20-1884	091	MOONEY, Mary	Native of Parish of Mitchells-town, County Cork, Ireland (No such parish - probably Town Of)
Mary MOONEY Powers	Co. Kings	34 Years	02-14-1872	091	POWERS, Jeffrey	Native of Parish of 'Lether__' or 'Leither___' (possibly Letterluna), Kings County. (Stone has deteriorated badly)
Captain Jeremiah NUNAN	Co. Cork	31 Years	12-27-1864	091	NUNAN, Capt. Jeremiah	Born In The Parish Of Mallow County Cork, Ireland. Captain, Co. I, Pennsylvania Reserve Cavalry (Believe his name was Noonan as there are Noonans in this plot).
Thomas MULVEY	Co. Tipperary	65 Years	02-07-1866	091	MEEHAN, Mary	A Native of Kildenogue(Kil-danoge), Co. Tipperary, Ire.
Mary MEEHAN Mulvey		60 Years	10-25-1864	091	MULVEY, Thomas	
Mary NOONAN O'Connell	Co. Cork	63 Years	03-26-1888	091	O'CONNELL, Patrick	Natives of Mallow, County Cork Ireland. No Info on Patrick except word "Natives"
Patrick MCDEVITT	Co. Tyrone	---	---	091	MCDEVITT, Patrick	Native Of Parish of Astra (Probably Ardstraw) County

Name	County	Birth/Age	Death	Cem.	Related	Notes
				091		Tyrone. Stone broken. Date of death appears to be 1860's.
Mary MCLAUGHLIN Gaphney	Co. Leitrim	48 Years	10-12-1863	091	GAPHNEY, Owen MCLAUGHLIN, Mary	Erected By Owen Gaphney IMO his wife of Altevera (Altavra) Parish Of Kilaragy (Killarga) Co. Leitrim, Ireland. (NOI Owen Gaphney)
Daniel DUNIGAN	Co. Cork	49 Years	04-20-1862	091	HART, Katherine	Sacred To The Memory Of Dan'l Born in Dunowen, Ardfield Parish, Cork County, Ireland
Katherine HART Dunigan	Co. Cork	75 Years	09-03-1894	091	DUNIGAN, Daniel	Born In Raebarry, Cork County Ireland (Ross Carberry?)
Patrick DEMPSEY	Co. Roscommon	08-03-1841	10-26-1889	091	MCLOUGHLIN, Margaret	Native of The Parish Of Croughin, County Roscommon, Ireland. (Did not find this Parish - Possibly it is the Town of Croghan)
Margaret MCLOUGHLIN Dempsey	Co. Roscommon	11-20-1840	07-10-1924	091	DEMPSEY, Patrick	Native of The Parish Of Boyle, Co. Roscommon, Ireland
Ellen BATTLES	Co. Roscommon	31Y1M7D	05-27-1887	091	BATTLES, Ellen	Native of The Parish Of Boyle, Co. Roscommon, Ireland
Anna _____ BATTLES		05-17-1824	07-06-1909	091	BATTLES, B.	(NOI B. Battles)
James BATTLES		01-04-1847	04-11-1915	091	BATTLES, James	
Patrick KEAVNEY		1844	1919	091	BATTLES, Bridget	
Bridget BATTLES Keavney		1849	1937	091	KEAVNEY, Patrick	
William DEVER	Co. Donegal	01-02-1826	07-04-1889	091	MCMAHAN, Ann	Born In Donegal, Ireland Boyle, Co. Roscommon, Ireland
Ann MCMAHAN Dever	Co. Clare	87 Years	02-06-1896	091	DEVER, William	A Native Of The Parish Of Faikle (Feakle), County Clare, Ireland.Stone reads: "Mrs. Ann McMahan,wife of William Dever"
Mary O'HALLORAN Burns	Co. Clare	05-04-1842	11-21-1894	091	BURNS, John	Native of The Parish Of Ennistymon, County Clare, Ire

John BURNS		08-03-1847	07-07-1938	091	O'HALLORAN, Mary	NOI
William GLEASON	Co. Tipperary	95 Years	12-29-1879	091	______, Johanna	Native Of The Parish Of Kille____, County Tipperary. (Possibly Killaloan) (NOI Johanna)
Anna SLOWAY Gallagher	Co. Fermanagh	35Y2M15D	05-25-1879	091	GALLAGHER, Patrick	Native Of Parish Rosslay (Rossory), Co. Fermanagh, Ire. NOI Patrick Gallagher.
Ellen TOUHY McEllicott	Co. Kerry	60 Years	11-13-1882	091	MCELLICOTT, James	Native Of Listry, County Kerry, Ireland. NOI James McEllicott
David MORRISON	Co. Limerick	64 Years	07-08-1883	091	TULLEY, Ann	Native of The Parish Of Rockhill, County Limerick, Ire (No Such Parish - Could be Parish of Rathkeale orRock -hill Town)
Ann TULLEY Morrison		54 Years	04-08-1889	091	MORRISON, David	
Thomas MULLANEY		83 Years	03-19-1920	091	MCLAUGHLIN, Mary	
Mary MCLAUGHLIN Mullaney	Co. Roscommon	67 Years	03-02-1896	091	MULLANEY, Thomas	Native Of Boyle, Co. Roscommon
Daniel CARMODY	Co. Clare	49 Years	04-11-1864	091	LILLIS, Margaret	Native(s) Of County Clare, Ire
Margaret LILLIS Carmody	Co. Clare	72 Years	04-13-1889	091	CARMODY, Daniel	Native(s) Of County Clare, Ire
John BARRETT	Co. Tipperary	83 Years	08-16-1902	091	DURICK, Margaret	Native Of Castletown, County Tipperary, Ireland
Margaret DURICK Barrett	Co. Tipperary	40 Years	02-15-1874	091	BARRETT, John	Native Of Castletown, County Tipperary, Ireland
John MURPHY	Co. Kerry	73 Years	03-09-1900	091	CAIN, Catherine	Native Of County Kerry, Ire
Catherine CAIN Murphy	Co. Clare	45 Years	11-15-1870	091	MURPHY, John	Native Of The Parish of Dunaha Co. Clare, Ireland (No Such Parish)
Daniel HANLY	Co. Roscommon	26 Years	12-18-1870	091	________, Eliza	Born In County Of Roscommon, Parish Of Kilglass (Erected by his wife) (NOI Eliza)

				091		
Donald MCCARTHY	Co. Cork	65 Years	01-03-1877	091	______, Catherine	Native(s) Of The Parish Of
				091		Thaunadromin, Co. Cork, Ire.
				091		(No such parish)
Catherine ____ MCCARTHY	Co. Cork	70 Years	08-31-1875	091	MCCARTHY, Donald	Native(s) Of The Parish Of
				091		Thaunadromin, Co. Cork, Ire.
				091		(No such parish)
				091		
John SWEENEY	Co. Cork	70 Years	03-31-1884	091	______, Julia	A Native Of The Parish Of
				091		Kilmurry, County Cork, Ire.
Julia _____ SWEENEY	Co. Cork	75 Years	12-07-1897	091	SWEENEY, John	Native Of The Parish Of
				091		Thaunadromin, Co. Cork, Ire.
				091		(No such parish - Possibly
				091		Phonetics - 'Town Of Dromin'
				091		
James MCKEON		65 Years	08-24-1901	091	_______, Mary	
				091		
Mary _____ MCKEON	Co. Leitrim	46 Years	01-21-1888	091	MCKEON, James	Native Of County Leitrim
				091		
Patrick CARMODY	Co. Clare	70 Years	12-27-1887	091	DAVINE, Maria	A Native Of The Parish Of
				091		Kilmaley, County Clare, Ire
Maria DAVINE Carmody		1820	1893	091	CARMODY, Patrick	NOI
				091		
Patrick EVERIN		83 Years	07-20-1914	091	FLOOD, Catherine	
				091	FARRELL, Margaret	
Catherine FLOOD Everin		38 Years	12-21-1865	091	EVERIN, Patrick	
Margaret FARRELL Everin	Co. Kilkenny	68 Years	06-06-1893	091	EVERIN, Patrick	Native of County Kilkenny
John COLLINS		1855	1923	091	HOLLERAN, Margaret	
Margaret HOLLERAN Collins		1854	1893	091	COLLINS, John	
				091		
Thomas COLLINS	Co. Limerick	90 Years	01-19-1883	091	______, Johanna	Born In Corkmore (Corcamore)
				091		Parish Of Ballyburn (No Such
				091		Parish) County Limerick, Ire
Johanna ____ COLLINS	Co. Limerick	86 Years	09-15-1887	091	COLLINS, Thomas	Born In Corkmore (Corcamore)
				091		Parish Of Ballyburn (No Such
				091		Parish) County Limerick, Ire
				091		
Catherine ____ LLOYD	Co. Tipperary	56 Years	01-15-1862	091	LLOYD, Richard	A Native Of Tipperary, Ireland
				091	_____, Catherine	Erected By Her Son, John Lloyd
				091		NOI Richard Lloyd
				091		
Maurice RALEIGH	Co. Limerick	56 Years	03-15-1873	091	______, Ellen	Natives Of The Parish of Bally
				091	RALEIGH, Maurice	bricken, Co. Limerick, Ire (No
				091		Such Parish-Probably Bally-
				091		bricken town (E,N,S,W) NOI

				091		Ellen.
John BATTLES	Co. Roscommon		03-21-1906	091	PENDERGAST, Mary	Born In The Town Of Garrow, Parish Of Boyle, County Roscommon, Ireland
Mary Pendergast BATTLES		11-16-1830	04-22-1914	091	BATTLES, John	
Mary Carney CARTER	Co. Tipperary	38 Years	09-27-1874	091	CARTER, James	A Native Of The Parish Of New Port, County Tipperary, Ire.
John MURPHY	Co. Clare	55 Years	10-27-1860	091	MURPHY, John	A Native Of The Parish Of 'Killuren' (Killuran) (Erected BY His Wife - No Name Given)
James HOPKINS	Co. Clare	77 Years	01-26-1875	091	____, Catherine	A Native Of The Parish Of Temple Port, County Clare,Ire (No such parish or town in Co. Clare - There is a parish Templeport in County Cavan) Erected BY His Wife. (NOI wife Caatherine)
Margaret KEARNEY Rearden	Co. Tipperary	19 Years	05-18-1858	091	REARDEN, Michael KEARNEY, Margaret	Native of Newport Parish County Tipperary, Ireland. Erected By Her Brothers. NOI Michael Rearden
Catherine GRADEY Cearney	Co. Limerick	42 Years	04-06-1876	091	CEARNEY, John	A Native Of The Parish Of Quinn, County Limerick, Ire. (NOI John Cearney) (This stone immediately adjacent to Margaret Kearney Rearden) (No such parish or town in Co. Limerick. There is a Parish of Quin in Co. Clare & Par. Of Glin in Co. Limerick)
Thomas DAVIN	Co. Clare	32Y 7M	07-03-1866	091	DAVIN, Thomas	Parish Of Kilmaley, County Clare, Ireland. Erected By His Wife. (NOI his wife). This stone in plot with DAVINE surnames.
Mary SULLIVAN Crowley	Co. Kerry	42 Years	04-07-1871	091	CROWLEY, Daniel	Native of The Parish Of Dingle

Name	County	Age / Born	Died	Code	Index	Notes
				091	SULLIVAN, Mary	County Kerry, Ireland. NOI Daniel Crowley.
Mary HOGAN Martin HOGAN Catherine HOGAN		1Y 2M 1Y 8M 6D 1Y 6M17D	10-12-1862 10-22-1869 04-26-1879	091	HOGAN, Mary HOGAN, Martin HOGAN, Catherine	Children of Patrick and Ellen Hogan, Natives of the Parish of Kilraghtis, County Clare Ireland
James O'NEILL	Co. Tipperary	80 Years	05-13-1904	091	_____, Julia	Born In County Tipperary, Ire
Julia ____ O'NEILL		82 Years	01-25-1908	091	O'NEILL, James	
John RIORDAN	Co. Cork	88Y 28D	04-04-1906	091	_____, Ellen	Native Of The Parish Of Kilnamartery, County Cork
Ellen ____ RIORDAN		61 Years	04-05-1881	091	RIORDAN, John	
James GRIFFIN	Co. Limerick	63Y 28D	04-04-1888	091	MCNAMARA, Mary	Born In County Limerick, Ire Kilnamartyra,(Kilnamartery) Co. Cork, Ireland
Mary MCNAMARA Griffin		1834	1914	091	GRIFFIN, James	
Patrick MCLAUGHLIN	Co. Leitrim	1841	1904	091	GALLAGHER, Matilda	Born In County Leitrim, Ire,
Matilda GALLAGHER McLaughlin		1849	1919	091	MCLAUGHLIN, Patrick	
Hannah LEE Gooley	Co. Tipperary	27 Years	02-24-1861	091	GOOLEY, Phillip LEE, Hannah	Erected By Phillip Gooley in Memory of his beloved wife who Departed This Life---She was a Native Of The Parish Of Kil-cummin, County Tipperary, Ire. (Did not find Parish. Possibly Kilcommon Town). (NOI Phillip)
Thomas COONEY Alice ____ COONEY	Co. Tipperary	1833 1835	1914 1864	091	____, Alice COONEY, Thomas	Erected By Thomas Cooney in Memory of his beloved wife Alice who died 3-18-1864, age 29. A Native Of The Parish Of Donohill, County Tipperary, Ireland. In the same plot a second stone reads: Thomas 1833-1913 Alice 1835-1864

Name	County	Born/Age	Died	Code	Related	Notes
Hanora LAWTON Haley	Co. Sligo	50 Years	07-31-1866	091	HALEY, Thomas LAWTON, Hanora	Native of the County Of Sligo Parish Of Ahamlish, Ireland NOI Thomas Haley
Bartholomew MATTIMORE	Co. Sligo	03- -1819	1912	091	FLYNN, Catherine	Native of Knockmore, Parish of Kilmactranny, County Sligo
Catherine FLYNN Mattimore	Co. Leitrim	68 Years	08-11-1894	091	MATTIMORE, Bartholomew	Native of County Leitrim
John HANLEY	Co. Roscommon	06-23-1830	04-24-1920	091	_____, Mary	Native(s) Of The Parish Of Kilglass, Co. Roscommon, Ire
Mary ____ HANLEY	Co. Roscommon	06-20-1830	07-09-1910	091	HANLEY, John	Native(s) Of The Parish Of Kilglass, Co. Roscommon, Ire
Mary FLYNN O'Hara	Co. Leitrim	34 Years	07-22-1883	091	O'HARA, Patrick FLYNN, Mary	Native of Kilaragy(Killarga) Co. Leitrim, Ireland. (In same Plot as Catherine Flynn Matti-more). NOI Patrick O'Hara
Daniel DONOVAN	Co. Cork	53 Years	04-26-1880	091	DONOVAN, Daniel	A Native Of The Parish Of Ballymartin (Ballymartle) Co. Cork, Ireland
William O'BRIEN	Co. Tipperary	68 Years	03-08-1898	091	O'BRIEN, William	A Native Of The Parish Of Donohill, Co. Tipperary, Ire
Thomas O'BRIEN	Co. Tipperary	26 Years	02-21-1864	091	O'BRIEN, Thomas	A Native Of The Parish Of Donohill, Co. Tipperary, Ire
John O'BRIEN		76 Years	09-25-1878	091	____, Catherine	(No Identification but in same Plot as William and Thomas O'Brien)
Catherine ___ O'BRIEN		77 Years	10-18-1875	091	O'BRIEN, John	
John F. MULCAHEY	Co. Waterford	05-11-1836	06-30-1901	091	MULCAHEY, John F.	Born In Waterford, Ireland
Margaret HOGAN Halloran	Co. Clare	38 Years	10-31-1857	091	HALLORAN, George	Erected By George Halloran In Memory Of His Beloved Wife. A Native of Parish of Killrock-dish (Kilraghtis) Co. Clare. NOI George Halloran.

Name	Origin	Birth/Age	Death	Code	Relation	Notes
Patrick MCNEAL	Co. Roscommon	50 or 60 Y	07-18-1862	091	_______, Ann	Natives Of The Parish Of ____
				091		County Roscommon, Ireland
				091		Stone Badly Deteriorated
Ann ___ MCNEAL	Co. Roscommon	40 Years	01-09-1864	091	MCNEAL, Patrick	
				091		
Bridget MCNEAL Carmody		31 Years	04-29-1887	091	CARMODY, T. A.	(NOI T. A. Carmody)
				091	MCNEAL, Bridget	
				091		
James KELLEY		09-22-1842	04-28-1903	091	MCPHILOMY, Margaret	
Margaret MCPHILOMY Kelley		12-24-1843	12-13-1897	091	KELLEY, James	
				091		
Patrick BUSHELL		91 Years	11-12-1915	091	______, Catherine	
Catherine _____ BUSHELL		64 Years	12-11-1890	091	BUSHELL, Patrick	
				091		
John HARTE		1841	1906	091	_____, Mary	
Mary _____ HARTE		1849	1889	091	HARTE, John	
Anna HARTE		1886	1960	091	HARTE, Anna	
				091		
Michael FITZPATRICK	Co. Cavan	52 Years	07-04-1877	091	FITZPATRICK, Michael	Killi____, Co. Cavan. (This
				091		stone badly deteriorated.)
				091		
Patrick KENNEDY		1830	1900	091	HAHAR, Ellen	
Ellen HAHAR Kennedy		1815	1898	091	KENNEDY, Patrick	
Edward R. THORNTON		1858	1926	091	THORNTON, Edward R.	
				091		
John LYONS		03-17-1835	10-11-1917	091	O'ROURKE, Mary	
Mary O'ROURKE Lyons		03-26-1842	01-02-1903	091	LYONS, John	
				091		
Patrick RYAN		03-25-1845	09-03-1903	091	_____, Johanna	
Johanna ____ RYAN		06-29-1852	03-21-1913	091	RYAN, Patrick	
Mary A. RYAN		1880	1953	091	RYAN, Mary A.	
				091		
James GOULD		1842	1906	091	GOULD, James	
Annie _____ GOULD		1842	1925	091	_____, Annie	
				091		
Andrew THORNTON		1855	1929	091	HOLLERAN, Bridget	
Bridget HOLLERAN Thornton		1859	1943	091	THORNTON, Andrew	
Bessie B. THORNTON		1884	1950	091	THORNTON, Bessie B.	
				091		
Mathew PARKER		1838	1912	091	____, Ann	
Ann _____ PARKER		1848	1917	091	PARKER, Mathew	
				091		
John MCGINLEY		38 Years	10-01-1899	091	FLANAGAN, Catherine	
Catherine FLANAGAN McGinley		61 Years	12-23-1920	091	MCGINLEY, John	
				091		

Name	Origin	Birth/Age	Death	Code	Spouse/Related	Notes
Michael CALLAHAN		-- -- --	01-10-1898	091	BURKE, Nancy	(NOI DOB-DOD)
Nancy BURKE Callahan		-- -- --	02-15-1901	091	CALLAHAN, Michael	
				091		
Nellie MANLEY Enfield		44 Years	11-15-1899	091	ENFIELD, G.C.	(NOI G.C. Enfield)
				091	MANLEY, Nellie	
				091		
George TAYLOR		1837	1892	091	HAMILTON, Sara	
Sara HAMILTON Taylor		1848	1918	091	TAYLOR, George	
				091		
Timothy LUNDRAGAN		1817	1901	091	MCMAHON, Bridget	
Bridget MCMAHON Lundragan		1830	1914	091	LUNDRAGAN, Timothy	
				091		
Ann COREY	Co. Tyrone	1836	1886	091	COREY, Ann	Natives of Co. Tyrone
Mary COREY	Co. Tyrone	1840	1905	091	COREY, Mary	
Sarah COREY	Co. Tyrone	1827	1907	091	COREY, Sarah	
				091		
Mary E. DIFLEY White		1849	1904	091	DIFLEY, Mary E.	
				091		
Thomas J. MUMFORD		1841	1912	091	MCNEIL, Ann	(GAR) 2nd VT REG Co. G
Ann MCNEIL Mumford		1845	1906	091	MUMFORD, Thomas J.	
				091		
Michael MOYLAN	Co. Clare	1831	1906	091	MOYLAN, Michael	Born In _____, Co. Clare
Margaret MOYLAN	Co. Clare	1846	1914	091	MOYLAN, Margaret	(Brother & Sister)
				091		
Mary A. PHALEN		1857	1940	091	PHALEN, Mary A.	
Mathew PHALEN		1891	1963	091	PHALEN, Mathew	
Catherine PHALEN		1870	1873	091	PHALEN, Catherine	
				091		
Michael POWERS		1845	1925	091	HAHER, Mary	
Mary HAHER Powers		1841	1924	091	POWERS, Michael	
				091		
Roger RYAN		72 Years	06-18-1929	091	RYAN, Roger	(Does Not Say if husband/wife)
Ann RYAN		62 Years	10-20-1924	091	RYAN, Ann	
				091		
Philip BRENNAN		1845	1915	091	DOOLEY, Margaret	
Margaret DOOLEY Brennan		1846	1917	091	BRENNAN, Philip	
James DOOLEY		1847	1916	091	DOOLEY, James	
				091		
Richard FOLEY		1850	1917	091	RICE, Mary	
Mary RICE Foley		1861	1920	091	FOLEY, Richard	
				091		
Michael O'NEILL		1822	1893	091	SHORTELL, Ellen	
Ellen SHORTELL O'Neill		1820	1899	091	O'NEILL, Michael	
Margaret O'NEILL		1848	1890	091	O'NEILL, Margaret	
Thomas O'NEILL		1857	1888	091	O'NEILL, Thomas	

Nellie O`NEILL	1861	1872	091	O'NEILL, Nellie	
			091		
Margaret MCKEON McCloughlinCo. Leitrim	37 Years	06-05-1885	091	MCKEON, Margaret	Born In County of Leitrim
			091		
Dennis LEONARD	64 Years	02-27-1880	091	______, Mary	
Mary ____ LEONARD	78 Years	01-05-1892	091	LEONARD, Dennis	
			091		
Peter BURNS	42 Years	11-30-1881	091	FLOOD, Mary	
Mary FLOOD Burns	30 Years	08-18-1877	091	BURNS, Peter	
			091		
James BURNS	42 Years	11-11-1871	091	BURNS, James	
			091		
Michael SHANAHAN	59 Years	01-08-1906	091	MCLAUGHLIN, Mary	
Mary MCLAUGHLIN Shanahan	43 Years	11-17-1895	091	SHANAHAN, Michael	
			091		
Patrick DURICK	63 Years	06-13-1889	091	KAIN, Margaret	
Margaret KAIN Durick	60 Years	10-04-1907	091	DURICK, Patrick	
			091		
John RICE	06-29-1832	02-01-1899	091	_____, Bridget	67 Years
Bridget ____ RICE	01-01-1836	03-29-1914	091	RICE, John	
			091		
Bartholomew SMITH	29 Years	10-17-1872	091	SMITH, Bartholomew	Son Of M&C Smith. Native of
			091		Province of PO(sp)
Elizabeth KELLY Duffy	65 Years	04-16-1882	091	DUFFY, James	(NOI James Duffy)
			091		
Michael C. DUFFY	18 Years	11-02-1869	091	DUFFY, Michael C.	Son Of James & Eliz Duffy
			091		
William FAGAN	56 Years	02-28-1899	091	FAGAN, William	
			091		
Patrick RODDY	03-27-1842	08-24-1894	091	O'RIELLY, Anne	
Anne O'RIELLY Roddy	10-11-1846	02-13-1892	091	RODDY, Patrick	
			091		
Thomas MONAGHAN		1911	091	MUNDAY, Ann	
Ann MUNDY Monaghan		1915	091	MONAGHAN, Thomas	
			091		
Michael DUFFY	84 Years	02-10-1899	091	PADGIN, Ann	
Ann PADGIN Duffy	62 Years	01-19-1892	091	DUFFY, Michael	
			091		
Michael DUFFY	16Y 8M	10-03-1877	091	DUFFY, Michael	
			091		
Sarah GAYERS Milon	84 Years	04-06-1878	091	MILON, T.	(NOI T.Milon)
			091	GAYERS, Sarah	
			091		
William GALLAGHER	56 Years	06-13-1890	091	COREY, Mary	
Mary COREY Gallagher	70 Years	11-15-1904	091	GALLAGHER, William	

				091		
Charles MUMFORD		1840	1906	091	MCGUIRE, Ann	
Ann MCGUIRE Mumford		1848	1875	091	MUMFORD, Charles	
Anna MUMFORD		1848	1848	091	MUMFORD, Anna	
				091		
Ann ___ MCMAHON	Co. Clare	87 Years	02-06-1896	091	MCMAHON, William	Born In Parish of Faikle
				091		(Feakle) Co. Clare, Ire
Patrick DWYER	Co. Tipperary	03-15-1838	08-18-1896	091		Born In Tipperary, Ire.
				091		Died at Castleton, VT
Mrs. Patrick DWYER		07-01-1840	01-05-1913	091	PATRICK, Dwyer	
				091		
John PATTEN		1831	1906	091	DEVLIN, Margaret	
Margaret DEVLIN Patten		68 Years	02-14-1898	091	PATTEN, John	
				091		
Hannah ____ MOONEY		28 Years	12-31-1868	091	MOONEY, Kearan	(NOI Kearan (Kieren?) Mooney
				091		
James COREY	Co. Tyrone	49 Years	12-22-1885	091	CARROLL, Julia	Native Of Co. Tyrone, Ireland
				091		(GAR) Co. A. 13th Vt Vols
Julia CARROLL Corey	Co. Mayo	68 Years	06-22-1914	091	COREY, James	Native Of Co. Mayo, Ireland
				091		
Martin O'BRIEN		1839	1907	091	MEAGHER, Bridget	
Bridget MEAGHER O'Brien	Co. Mayo	1837	1910	091	O'BRIEN, Martin	
				091		
John MCGUE		76 Years	03-13-1908	091	_____, Margaret	
Margaret ______ MCGUE		68 Years	10-09-1908	091	MCGUE, John	
				091		
Daniel DUFFY		1836	1883	091	BRIDGET, Carroll	
Bridget CARROLL Duffy		1834	1937	091	DANIEL, Duffy	
				091		
Thomas MCGARRY		1828	1902	091	GIBNEY, Mary	
Mary GIBNEY McGarry		1829	1890	091	MCGARRY, Thomas	
James MCGARRY		1859	1881	091	MCGARRY, James	
John MCGARRY		1864	1892	091	MCGARRY, John	
Bernard T. MCGARRY		1855	1908	091	MCGARRY, Bernard T.	
Patrick G. MCGARRY		1862	1911	091	MCGARRY, Patrick G.	
				091		
Bridget A. CLARK Donnelly		38 Years	06-14-1896	091	CLARK, Bridget A.	(NOI Patrick Donnelly)
				091	DONNELLY, Patrick	
				091		
Patrick KENNY		78 Years	09-27-1896	091	HOWARD, Mary	
Mary HOWARD Kenny		82 Years	06-06-1903	091	KENNY, Patrick	
				091		
William RYAN		1834	1908	091	TODD, Johanna	
Johanna TODD Ryan		1837	1890	091	RYAN, William	
				091		

Margaret DWYER		39 Years	10-08-1887	091	DWYER, Margaret	Native Of Parish of Anacarty,
				091		County Tipperary, Ireland
Bridget DWYER		87 Years	08-05-1894	091	DWYER, Bridget	Native Of Parish Of Anacarty,
				091		County Tipperary, Ireland
				091		
Dennis RYAN		1848	1914	091	MAHAR, Johanna	
Johanna MAHAR Ryan		1856	-- -- --	091	RYAN, Dennis	
				091		
Neil MCBRIDE	Ireland	35 Years	11-06-1876	091	MCBRIDE, Neil	Native Of _____ Ireland (Badly
				091		Deteriorated Stone)
				091		
Dennis LYONS		82 Years	11-28-1923	091	_____, Catherine	
				091	MCKEON, Bridget	
Catherine _____ LYONS		34 Years	03-15-1876	091	LYONS, Dennis	
Bridget MCKEON Lyons		70 Years	05-07-1911	091	LYONS, Dennis	
				091		
James BURKE		1839	1915	091	GLEASON, Mary	
Mary GLEASON Burke		1834	1923	091	BURKE, James	
				091		
James RYAN		47 Years	01-20-1899	091	DWYER, Johannah	
Johannah DWYER Ryan		55 Years	04-30-1911	091	RYAN, James	
				091		
Michael WALSH		1819	1877	091	RUANE, Mary	
Mary RUANE Walsh		1828	1898	091	WALSH, Michael	
				091		
Mary HAYES Cooney		1837	1894	091	HAYES, Mary	
				091		
James FOLEY		87 Years	05-30-1896	091	_____, Eliza	
Eliza ____ FOLEY	Co. Clare	66 Years	10-19-1870	091	FOLEY, James	She Was A Native Of The Parish
				091		of Ruan, Co. Clare, Ireland
Bridget FOLEY Quest		29 Years	05-24-1871	091	FOLEY, Bridget	Daughter of J & E Foley
				091		
Bernard MCCUE		27 Years	08-21-1876	091	_____, Maria	
Maria _____ MCCUE		41 Years	08-18-1889	091	MCCUE, Bernard	
Patrick HANLEY		25 Years	10-29-1876	091	HANLEY, Patrick	(Same plot as Bernard McCue)
				091		
John YOUNG		1852	1921	091	MONOHAN, Mary	
Mary MONAHAN Young		1858	1944	091	YOUNG, John	
				091		
Edward A. SHELDON	England	32 Years	12-01-1869	091	_____, Mary	Born In Manchester, England.
Mary _____ SHELDON		1831	1917	091	SHELDON, Edward A.	Erected by His Wife Mary
				091		
James GALLAGHER	Co. Fermanagh	1836	1902	091	O'DONNELL, Margaret	Born In County Fermanagh, Ire
Margaret O'DONNELL Gallagher	Co. Fermanagh	1835	1899	091	GALLAGHER, James	Born In County Fermanagh, Ire
				091		

				091		
Patrick KENNEDY		1812	1854	091	_____, Margaret	
Margaret KENNEDY		1813	1871	091	KENNEDY, Patrick	
Father (KENNEDY)		1839	1920	091	KENNEDY, Father	
Mother (KENNEDY)		1838	1923	091	KENNEDY, Mother	
				091		
John HACKETT		1854	1921	091	GALLAGHER, Mary A.	
Mary A. GALLAGHER Hackett		1858	1922	091	HACKETT, John	
				091		
James GILLESPIE		1854	1939	091	DALEY, Elizabeth	
Elizabeth DALEY Gillespie		1862	1929	091	GILLESPIE, James	
				091		
John J. BATTLES		1851	1933	091	WALSH, Catherine	
Catherine WALSH Battles		1864	1937	091	BATTLES, John J.	
				091		
James HORNIDGE		1840	1901	091	_____, Catherine	
Catherine _____ HORNIDGE		1840	1891	091	HORNIDGE, James	
				091		
James GALLAGHER		1832	1920	091	_____, Elizabeth	
Elizabeth _____ GALLAGHER				091	GALLAGHER, Elizabeth	
Fanny MONAHAN		1795	1876	091	MONAHAN, Fanny	
Katherine MONAHAN		1831	1904	091	MONOHAN, Katherine	
				091		
Patrick MCGARRY		1854	1902	091	_____, Mary	
Mary ____ MCGARRY		1860	1916	091	MCGARRY, Patrick	
				091		
Michael HERBERT	Co. Clare	11-20-1841	04-02-1909	091	DONAHUE, Margaret	Native Of Co. Clare, Ireland
Margaret DONAHUE Herbert	Co. Clare	11-12-1851	06-24-1914	091	HERBERT, Michael	Native Of Co. Clare, Ireland
				091		
Michael CLIFFORD		1833	1905	091	LEE, Julia	
Julia LEE Clifford		1830	1927	091	CLIFFORD, Michael	
				091		
George MUMFORD		1834	1899	091	DIFLEY, Bridget	Erected By His Wife, Katherin
				091	MULHERN, Katherine	Mulhern (NOI Katherin Mulhern)
Bridget DIFLEY Mumford		1844	1875	091	GEORGE, Mumford,	
				091		
Rose MCCORMICK	Ireland	74 Years	12-12-1881	091	MCCORMICK, Rose	A Native Of Ireland
				091		
Edward R. COPPS		32 Years	02-10-1886	091	MOLONEY, B. J.	
B. J. MOLONEY Copps		46 Years	01-18-1902	091	COPPS, Edward R.	
				091		
Helen DOWNEY		78 Years	08-07-1897	091	DOWNEY, Helen	
				091		
Owen MCCORMICK		1845	1915	091	_____, Ann	
Ann _____ MCCORMICK		1853	1923	091	MCCORMICK, Owen	

				091		
Edward O'NEIL		78 Years	10-10-1895	091	GLEESON, Mary	
Mary GLEESON O'Neil	Co. Clare	67 Years	11-15-1893	091	O'NEIL, Edward	Native of County Clare
Mary O'NEIL Mullin		28 Years	07-18-1886	091	O'NEIL, Mary	Wife Of James Mullin (NOI
				091	MULLIN, James	
James O'NEIL		39 Years	03-08-1895	091	O'NEIL, James	
Bridget O'NEIL				091	O'NEIL, Bridget	
				091		
John MORAN		85 Years	11-24-1915	091	_____, Ann	
Ann _____ MORAN		83 Years	06-02-1913	091	MORAN, John	
				091		
Margaret RADIGAN Moran		1798	1890	091	RADIGAN, Margaret	Wife Of James Moran(NOI James)
				091	MORAN, James	
				091		
Mary STAPLETON Walsh		32Y 2MO	02-04-1880	091	STAPLETON, Mary	Erected by John Walsh IMO His
				091		Wife (NOI John Walsh)
Ellen CASSIDY Rinn		35 Years	01-15-1875	091	CASSIDY, Ellen	(NOI Patrick Rinn)
				091	RINN, Patrick	
				091		
Michael FINNELLY		30 Years	03-27-1873	091	MULHERN, Catherine	
Catherine MULHERN Finnelly		1840	19252-1913	091	FINNELLY, Michael	
Mary MULHERN		101 Years	03-10-1904	091	MULHERN, Mary	
				091		
Catherine COLLINS SMITH		03-04-1851	03-23-1885	091	COLLINS, Catherine	Wife Of Patrick Smith Dau of
				091	SMITH, Patrick	Elizabeth & James Collins
				091		
James FOLEY		1824	1873	091	HANLY, Bridget	(On A MCNEIL Memorial but no
Bridget HANLY Foley		1829	1899	091	FOLEY, James	inscriptions for McNeil)
				091		
Bryan MOLONEY		1835	1919	091	TEELON, Catherine	
Catherine TEELON Moloney		1839	1899	091	MOLONEY, Bryan	
				091		
Patrick MCDERMOTT		1854	1935	091	DAVIN, Katherine	
				091	GENTY, Annie M.	
Katherine DAVIN McDermott		04-08-1860	12-28-1890	091	MCDERMOTT, Patrick	
Annie M. GENTY McDermott		05-10-1861	10-10-1920	091	MCDERMOTT, Patrick	
Ann COLLINS		1851	1926	091	COLLINS, Ann	
				091		
Richard RALEIGH		86 Years	02-09-1910	091	LANAN, Bridget	
Bridget LANAN Raleigh		84 Years	02-10-1920	091	RALEIGH, Richard	
				091		
John J. PATTEN		1838	1918	091	MADIGAN, Ellen	
Ellen MADIGAN Patten		1847	1917	091	PATTEN, John J.	
				091		
Patrick RALEIGH		31Y 10M	06-22-1885	091	CLIFFORD, Catherine	

NAME	POB	DOB/AGE	DOD	CEM	SPOUSE/INDEX	INSCRIPTION
Catherine CLIFFORD Raleigh		60 Years	09-17-1917	091	RALEIGH, Patrick	
				091		
John DORSEY		02-06-1847	09-25-1918	091	LYONS, Mary	
				091	O'DONNELL, Bessie	
Mary LYONS Dorsey		05-08-1848	12-24-1876	091	DORSEY, John	
Bessie O'DONNELL Dorsey		1837	1929	091	DORSEY, John	
				091		

St. Anthony's Cemetery, Nutt Street, White River Junction, Vt

NAME	POB	DOB/AGE	DOD	CEM	SPOUSE/INDEX	INSCRIPTION
Martin CALLAHAN		49 Years	10-29-1889	092	CALLAHAN, Martin	
				092		
Joseph M. HODET		63 Years	11-04-1902	092	HODET, Joseph M.	Co. M, 7th Mass VOl Inf (GAR)
				092		
Patrick GILMORE		1822	1891	092	CLANCY, Ellen	
				092	MCNAMARA, Ann	
Ellen CLANCY Gilmore		1824	1859	092	GILMORE, Patrick	
Ann MCNAMARA Gilmore		1826	1917	092	GILMORE, Patrick	
				092		
Frank MCCARTHY		1847	1908	092	CORBETT, Mary	
Mary CORBETT McCarthy		1852	1920	092	MCCARTHY, Frank	
				092		
Bridget Ellen WOOD		1848	1885	092	WOOD, Bridget Ellen	
				092		
Anthony HAGARTY		1823	1884	092	_____, Catherine	
Catherine _____ HAGARTY		1837	1897	092	HAGARTY, Anthony	
				092		
Hugh MARTIN		79 Years	09-02-1881	092	_____, Elizabeth	
Elizabeth _____ MARTIN		67 Years	10-08-1889	092	MARTIN, Hugh	
				092		
Michael GLEASON		1829	1899	092	DRISCOLL, Kate	
Kate DRISCOLL Gleason		1842	1922	092	GLEASON, Michael	
				092		
Mary DUFFY Banagan		75 Years	08-06-1883	092	BANAGAN, Philip	(NOI Philip Banagan)
				092	DUFFY, Mary	
				092		
Mary CROWLEY McCarthy		95Y10M14D	02-14-1879	092	MCCARTHY, Patrick	(NOI Patrick McCarthy)
				092	CROWLEY, Mary	
				092		
Cornelius O'LEARY		63 Years	03-21-1884	092	_____, Julia	
Julia _____ O'LEARY		97Y08M11D	04-28-1905	092	O'LEARY, Cornelius	
				092		

Name	Birth/Age	Death		Index	Notes
John O'NEIL	63 Years	11-01-1873	092	_____, Katie E.	
Katie E. _____ O'NEIL	__Y 10M	1876	092	O'NEIL, John	(Cannot read age at death)
			092		
Thomas MANION	68 Years	11-01-1897	092	_____, Ellen	
Ellen _____ MANION	50 Years	10-04-1879	092	MANION, Thomas	
			092		
Jeremiah SCANNELL	12-21-1816	07-14-1884	092	BARRY, Hanora	
Hanora BARRY Scannell	06-23-1816	04-08-1905	092	SCANNELL, Jeremiah	
			092		
John MCCARTHY	84 Years	04-29-1886	092	_____, Ellen	
Ellen _____ MCCARTHY	73 Years	08-04-1891	092	MCCARTHY, John	
			092		
William AGAN	1808	1883	092	ENRIGHT, Ellen	
Ellen ENRIGHT Agan	1835	1900	092	AGAN, William	
Ellen BOIL Enright	1798	1875	092	ENRIGHT, James	(NOI James Enright)
			092	BOIL, Ellen	
			092		
Edward ENRIGHT	50 Years	09-24-1875	092	KESSANE, Mary	Son of Timothy & Mary Enright
Mary KESSANE Enright	53 Years	05-15-1874	092	ENRIGHT, Edward	D/O James & Margaret Kessane
			092		
Dennis M. O'SULLIVAN	1841	1912	092	MURPHY, Hannah	
Hannah MURPHY O'Sullivan	1842	1926	092	O'SULLIVAN, Dennis M.	
John MURPHY	1845	19__	092		
			092		
Jeremiah O'DONOHUE	45 Years	03-28-1885	092	O'DONOHUE, Jeremiah	Son of Dennis & Catherine
			092		Dougherty O'Donohue
			092		
William RENEHAN	69 Years	07-24-1892	092	RYAN, Mary	
Mary RYAN Renehan	70 Years	08-05-1895	092	RENEHAN, William	
			092		
Patrick DUNLEY	1834	1914	092	STARR, Bridget	
Bridget STARR Dunley	1835	1912	092	DUNLEY, Patrick	
			092		
Patrick WELSH	61Y 5M	12-16-1877	092	_____, Bertha	
Bertha _____ WELSH	52Y 8M	10-30-1876	092	WELSH, Patrick	
			092		
Margaret _____ WHELAN	76 Years	09-13-1879	092	WHELAN, Thomas	(NOI Thomas Whelan)
			092	_____, Margaret	
			092		
John STARR	1828	1897	092	O'DONNELL, Catherine	
Catherine O'DONNELL Starr	1837	1913	092	STARR, John	
			092		
Ellen MCCARTHY	03-17-1836	12-19-1906	092	MCCARTHY, Ellen	
			092		
John KAVENY	66Y 11M	05-19-1895	092	_____, Margaret	

Margaret _____ KAVENY		66 Years	03-17-1893	092	KAVENY, John	
				092		
Patrick DEGNAN		1828	1904	092	GLEASON, Johanna	
Johanna GLEASON Degnan		1834	1907	092	DEGNAN, Patrick	
				092		
John MAHER		74 Years	10-18-1922	092	_____, Ellen	
Ellen _____ MAHER		26 Years	12-07-1877	092	MAHER, John	
Nancy STARR Maher		97 Years	09-14-1914	092	STARR, Nancy	
				092		
Mathew CARRIGAN		65Y 3M	08-25-1893	092	ELLIOTT, Catherine	
Catherine ELLIOTT Carrigan		70 Years	04-27-1894	092	CARRIGAN, Mathew	
				092		
Arthur GODSILL		73 Years	12-07-1881	092	_____, Margaret	
Margaret _____ GODSILL		74 Years	06-26-1897	092	GODSILL, Arthur	
				092		
Daniel CLANCY		62 Years	09-06-1891	092	CLANCY, Daniel	
Mary CLANCY O'Gara		68 Years	09-28-1899	092	O'GARA, John	(NOI John O'Gara)
				092	CLANCY, Mary	
				092		
John GRIFFIN		60 Years	12-02-1889	092	GRIFFIN, John	
				092		
James CAUFIELD		1835	1918	092	O'DONNEL, Mary	
Mary O'DONNEL Caufield		1837	1880	092	CAUFIELD, James	
				092		
James BUTLER		23 Years	01-__-1871	092	BUTLER, James	
				092		
John O'DONNELL		1841	1931	092	O'DONNELL, John	
				092		
Catherine MCGOUGH McStay		1842	1932	092	MCSTAY, James J.	(NOI James J. McStay)
				092	MCGOUGH, Catherine	
				092		
Francis SHIRLOCK	Co. Kildare	04-16-1811	03-03-1880	092	MCDONOUGH, Mary	Born in County Kildare, Ire.
				092		Died at Sharon, Vermont
Mary MCDONOUGH Shirlock	Co. Fermanagh	09-25-1826	11-25-1917	092	SHIRLOCK, Francis	Born County Fermanagh, Ire.
				092		Died at Sharon, Vermont
				092		
William T. MURPHY	Co. Tipperary	66 Years	05-27-1892	092	O'BRINE, Margaret	A Native of Co. Tipperary, Ire
Margaret O'BRINE Murphy	Co. Limerick	77Y 9M	04-25-1915	092	MURPHY, William T.	A Native of Co. Limerick, Ire.
				092		
Owen MCCABE		1794	1873	092	MOONEY, Mary	(Also have headstone in Mount
Mary MOONEY McCabe		1799	1891	092	MCCABE, Owen	Olivet Cemetery(New Catholic))
Bernard MCCABE		1839	1910	092	CONNELLY, Kate	" " " "
Kate CONNELLY McCabe		1840	1885	092	MCCABE, Bernard	" " " "
				092		
Owen MCCABE	Co. Monaghan	11-__-1847	06-26-1902	092	BANNAGAN, Mary	

NAME	POB	DOB/AGE	DOD	CEM	SPOUSE/INDEX	INSCRIPTION
Mary BANNAGAN McCabe		80 Years	06-29-1910	092	MCCABE, Owen	
				092		
Tobias BURKE		1849	1925	092	QUALTERS, Mary	
Mary QUALTERS Burke		1854	1924	092	BURKE, Tobias	
				092		
Eugene BOUDETTE		1855	1923	092	FITZGERALD, Isabelle	
Isabelle FITZGERALD Boudette		1856	1938	092	BOUDETTE, Eugene	
				092		
John HANRAHAN Sr.		1804	1901	092	HANRAHAN, John Sr.	
John Francis HANRAHAN		1848	1931	092	SLATTERY, Bridget	
Bridget SLATTERY Hanrahan		1847	1923	092	HANRAHAN, John Francis	
				092		
John W. BRALEY		05-16-1841	05-01-1922	092	WELSH, Elizabeth	(Also have headstone in Mount
Elizabeth WELSH Braley		06-15-1839	12-23-1909	092	BRALEY, John W.	Olivet Cemetery(New Catholic))
				092		
Patrick HEALY		1857	1940	092	MANION, Annie	
Annie MANION Healy		1861	1910	092	HEALY, Patrick	
				092		
Mary CROWLEY		1834	1896	092	CROWLEY, Mary	
Thomas O'NEILL		1855	1921	092	CROWLEY, Ellen	
Ellen CROWLEY O'Neill		1853	1941	092	O'NEILL, Thomas	
				092		
Patrick CALLAHAN		1845	1912	092	LANE, Katherine	
Katherine LANE Callahan		1855	1923	092	CALLAHAN, Patrick	

Mt. Olivet Cemetery, St. Anthony's Parish, White River Junction, Vermont

NAME	POB	DOB/AGE	DOD	CEM	SPOUSE/INDEX	INSCRIPTION
Michael J. ARMSTRONG		1869	1944	093	KIRK, Julia J.	
Julia KIRK Armstrong		1868	1935	093	ARMSTRONG, Michael J.	
				093		
Patrick DALY		1828	1908	093	LEONARD, Ann	
Ann LEONARD Daly		1829	1904	093	DALY, Patrick	
				093		
Michael R. STARR		1825	1892	093	_____, Catherine K.	
Catherine K. _____ STARR		1830	1886	093	STARR, Michael R.	
				093		
Maria BURKE		1856	1900	093	BURKE, Maria	
				093		
James A. GILBERT		1858	1926	093	STARR, Annie	
Annie STARR Gilbert		1863	1954	093	GILBERT, James A.	
				093		

Name	Birth/Age	Death	Ref	Index	Notes
Dennis A. DRISCOLL	08-22-1857	01-03-1935	093	MCNAMARA, Margaret	
Margaret MCNAMARA Driscoll	10-06-1845	11-19-1909	093	DRISCOLL, Dennis A.	
			093		
Jeremiah RELIHAN	07-01-1854	05-20-1938	093	SHEEHAN, Margaret	
Margaret SHEEHAN Relihan	06-01-1854	03-04-1904	093	RELIHAN, Jeremiah	
			093		
James B. FITZGERALD	12-04-1822	10-11-1898	093	_____, Catherine J.	
Catherine J. ____FITZGERALD	08-15-1832	06-17-1895	093	FITZGERALD, James B.	
			093		
Ann _____ MORAN	09-25-1859	01-09-1893	093	MORAN, Martin	(NOI Martin Moran)
			093	_____, Ann	
			093		
Thomas CARROLL	84Y 9M	09-23-1925	093	GRACE, Mary	
Mary GRACE Carroll	53Y 8M	02-17-1897	093	CARROLL, Thomas	
			093		
James E. DEVINS	1848	1916	093	LYNCH, Ellen	
Ellen LYNCH Devins	48Y 9M	05-22-1889	093	DEVINS, James E.	
			093		
James AHEARN	67 Years	06-17-1908	093	MURPHY, Mary	
Mary MURPHY Ahearn	60 Years	04-17-1901	093	AHEARN, James	
			093		
Jane YOUNG Fitzmorris	55 Years	05-23-1895	093	FITZMORRIS, Michael	(NOI Michael Fitzmorris)
			093	YOUNG, Jane	
			093		
Patrick EVERETT	80 Years	09-22-1915	093	EVERETT, Patrick	
			093		
Hugh MARTIN	72 Years	09-02-1881	093	_____, Elizabeth	
Elizabeth _____ MARTIN	67 Years	10-08-1889	093	MARTIN, Hugh	
			093		
Henry CARROLL	12-19-1845	01-06-1923	093	O'NEILL, Mary A.	
Mary O'NEILL Carroll	09-17-1846	03-23-1910	093	CARROLL, Henry	
			093		
Margaret MAGUIRE O'Neill	79Y10M22D	11-17-1887	093	O'NEILL, Francis	(NOI Francis O'Neill)
			093	MAGUIRE, Margaret	
			093		
Bridget HYNDS	70 Years	10-31-1903	093	HYNDS, Bridget	
			093		
William John O'CONNOR	88 Years	05-03-1935	093	O'CONNOR, William John	Son Of Hugh & Mary O'Connor
Mary Ann KOAN O'Connor	77 Years	10-08-1891	093	O'CONNOR, Hugh	(NOI Hugh O'Connor)
			093	KOAN, Mary Ann	
			093		
James BANAGAN	59Y 11M	05-02-1900	093	GODSILL, Mary	
Mary GODSILL Banagan	39 Years	05-23-1891	093	BANAGAN, James	
			093		
Peter HARRIGAN	77 Years	07-21-1896	093	_____, Mary	

Name	Born/Age	Died	Code	Index	Notes
Mary _____ HARRIGAN	70 Years	02-15-1894	093	HARRIGAN, Peter	
			093		
Martin CALNAN	64 Years	12-28-1903	093	_____, Margaret	
Margaret _____ CALNAN	50 Years	05-23-1901	093	CALNAN, Martin	
Michael CALNAN	54 Years	08-05-1900	093	CALNAN, Michael	
Nora CALNAN	83 Years	09-23-1892	093	CALNAN, Nora	
			093		
Roger J. DONAHUE	09-29-1848	07-23-1909	093	FITZPATRICK, Mary	
Mary FITZPATRICK Donahue	09-15-1857	08-28-1937	093	DONAHUE, Roger J.	
			093		
Thomas CARLIN	76 Years	04-22-1892	093	HINCKEY, Annie	
Annie HINCKEY Carlin	62 Years	12-18-1888	093	CARLIN, Thomas	
			093		
Annie CUNNINGHAM Flanders	06-05-1835	02-10-1906	093	FLANDERS, John B.	(NOI John B. Flanders)
			093	CUNNINGHAM, Annie	
			093		
James O'GRADY	72Y 9M	02-15-1901	093	_____, Margaret	
Margaret _____ O'GRADY	05-10-1832	03-02-1905	093	O'GRADY, James	
			093		
Thomas MCNAMARA	89 Years	01-11-1900	093	FAHEY, Margaret	
Margaret FAHEY McNamara	87 Years	09-02-1901	093	MCNAMARA, Thomas	
			093		
Sarah M. _____ KELLY	75 Years	03-11-1888	093	KELLY, John	(NOI John Kelly)
			093	_____, Sarah M.	
Katie S. KELLY	25/28 Yrs	10-02-1882	093	KELLY, Katie S.	Dau Of John & Sarah Kelly
			093		
James FITZPATRICK	06-21-1837	09-22-1906	093	HANRAHAN, Margaret	
Margaret HANRAHAN Fitzpatrick	10-20-1841	01-19-1896	093	FITZPATRICK, James	
			093		
John MURPHY	71 Years	03-01-1886	093	MURPHY, John	
John MURPHY	82 Years	09-19-1924	093	CASHMAN, Hanora	
Hanora CASHMAN Murphy	05-13-1828	07-18-1908	093	MURPHY, John	
			093		
Mary A. DWYER O'Brien	68 Years	11-01-1898	093	O'BRIEN, James F.	(NOI James O'Brien)
			093	DWYER, Mary A.	
Julia DWYER	60 Years	04-09-1873	093	DWYER, Julia	
Daniel DWYER	1830	1910	093	DONOVAN, Margaret	
Margaret DONOVAN Dwyer	1849	1919	093	DWYER, Daniel	
			093		
John B. ASHEY	43 Years	09-24-1886	093	_____, Lucy	Co. A, 13th Rgt, Vt Vols and
			093		Co. I, 14th Rgt, NH Vols (GAR)
Lucy _____ ASHEY	46Y 9M	04-09-1885	093	ASHEY, John B.	
			093		
Michael MCDONNELL	02-01-1823	01-01-1902	093	MCNAMARA, Catherine	
Catherine MCNAMARA McDonnell	05-25-1832	04-21-1919	093	MCDONNELL, Michael	

			093		
Timothy MCNAMARA	63 Years	08-23-1897	093	COYNE, Ann	
Ann COYNE McNamara	89 Years	04-26-1922	093	MCNAMARA, Timothy	
Hanora EGAN McNamara	99 Years	04-02-1881	093	MCNAMARA, Timothy Sr.	
			093		
Thomas HINCHEY	03-22-1828		093	_____, Nora	
Nora _____ HINCHEY	75 Years	03-02-1905	093	HINCHEY, Thomas	
			093		
John FARRELL Jr.	37 Years	08-20-1876	093	FITZMORRIS, Mary	
Mary FITZMORRIS Farrell			093	FARRELL, John Jr.	(NO DOB-DOD Mary Fitzmorris)
			093		
Bridget KENNEDY Farrell	70 Years	07-18-1873	093	FARRELL, John Sr.	(NOI John Farrell Sr.)
			093	KENNEDY, Bridget	
			093		
Patrick DAILEY	66 Years	08-17-1876	093	DAILEY, Patrick	
			093		
Bridget MCCANNA Hughes	64 Years	09-27-1898	093	HUGHES, James	(NOI James Hughes)
			093	MCCANNA, Bridget	
			093		
Michael O'NEILL	10-04-1850	09-15-1931	093	HUGHES, Ellen	
Ellen HUGHES O'Neill	12-17-1857	01-28-1930	093	O'NEILL, Michael	
			093		
John FLOOD	76 Years	05-13-1899	093	MORGAN, Catherine	
Catherine MORGAN Flood	53 Years	06-08-1879	093	FLOOD, John	
			093		
Patrick MCNAMARA		08-32-189_	093	MCNAMARA, Patrick	(Stone badly deteriorated)
			093		
Dennis O'DAY	1847	1881	093	O'DAY, Dennis	
			093		
John O'CONNOR	01-01-1809	02-13-1901	093	CUMMINGS, Annie	
Annie CUMMINGS O'Connor	11-25-1837	03-26-1910	093	O'CONNOR, John	
			093		
Cathrine GOFF	34 Years	05-29-1872	093	GOFF, Cathrine	Dau Of Michael & Mary Goff
			093		
Catharine SCULLY Lawrence	60 Years	07-22-1871	093	LAWRENCE, Richard	(NOI Richard Lawrence)
			093	SCULLY, Catharine	
			093		
Richard LYNCH	45 Years	1881	093	_____, Bridget	
Bridget _____ LYNCH	57 Years	12-19-1892	093	LYNCH, Richard	
			093		
William GARRITY	1857	1932	093	SPRY, Lydia Ann	
Lydia Ann SPRY Garrity	1855	1921	093	GARRITY, William	
			093		
Catherine CAWLEY Carver	78 Years	05-07-1902	093	CARVER, George	(NOI George Carver)
			093	CAWLEY, Catherine	

Name	Born	Died		Related	Notes
			093		
John P. RYAN	02-14-1846	02-19-1924	093	WARD, Mary	
Mary WARD Ryan	02-14-1857	02-01-1929	093	RYAN, John P.	
			093		
Thomas MCDONNELL	1808	1881	093	COLLINS, Margaret	
Margaret COLLINS McDonnell	1810	1883	093	MCDONNELL, Thomas	
Anna MCDONNELL	1845	1918	093		
Sarah COLLINS McNamara	1822	1895	093	MCNAMARA, Michael	(NOI Michael NcNamara)
			093	COLLINS, Sarah	
			093		
Patrick WARD	1832	1920	093	SULLIVAN, Johanna	
Johanna SULLIVAN Ward	1848	1916	093	WARD, Patrick	
			093		
Daniel AHEARN	1838	1908	093	MURPHY, Hanora	
Hanora MURPHY Ahearn	1841	1892	093	AHEARN, Daniel	
			093		
Michael MCNAMARA	1853	1929	093	MCCUE, Elizabeth	
Elizabeth MCCUE McNamara	1865	1931	093	MCNAMARA, Michael	
			093		
Daniel KINGSLEY	1853	1920	093	MCDONNELL, Elizabeth	
Elizabeth MCDONNELL Kingsley	1853	1931	093	KINGSLEY, Daniel	
			093		
John KEATING	1860	1929	093	HICKEY, Mary	
Mary HICKEY Keating	1866	1912	093	KEATING, John	
			093		
Thomas O'BRIEN	06-16-1857	03-13-1930	093	MCNAMARA, Hannah	
Hannah MCNAMARA O'Brien	09-05-1856	05-08-1929	093	O'BRIEN, Thomas	
			093		
Alexander WHITE	1847	1902	093	GRIBBON, Jane	
Jane GRIBBON White	1842	1906	093	WHITE, Alexander	
			093		
John W. BRALEY	05-16-1841	05-01-1922	093	WELSH, Elizabeth	(Also have headstone in Nutt
Elizabeth WELSH Braley	06-15-1839	12-23-1909	093	BRALEY, John W.	St. Cemetery (Old Catholic))
			093		
Rose A. BOYLE Welch	05-05-1836	01-02-1913	093	WELCH, Richard	(NOI Richard Welch)
			093	BOYLE, Rose A.	
			093		
John MCCUE	1837	1926	093	MCDONNELL, Mary	
Mary MCDONNELL McCue	39 Years	08-21-1878	093	MCCUE, John	
			093		
Peter MCCABE	1837	1909	093	MCCABE, Peter	
Owen MCCABE	1794	1873	093	MOONEY, Mary	(Also have headstone in Nutt
Mary MOONEY McCabe	1799	1891	093	MCCABE, Owen	St. Cemetery (Old Catholic))
Bernard MCCABE	1839	1910	093	CONNOLLY, Katie	" " " "
Katie CONNOLLY McCabe	1840	1885	093	MCCABE, Bernard	" " " "

NAME	POB	DOB/AGE	DOD	CEM	SPOUSE/INDEX	INSCRIPTION
				093		
Martin TEWEY		1836	1915	093	MOONEY, Mary	
Mary MOONEY Tewey		1845	1912	093	TEWEY, Martin	
				093		
Mary E. RYAN		1851	1926	093	RYAN, Mary E.	
				093		
John HALEY		49 Years	01-10-1876	093	HARRINGTON, Mary	
Mary HARRINGTON Haley		1827	1916	093	HALEY, John	
				093		
Bernard DAMIEN		1843	1910	093	ROY, Mary	
Mary ROY Damien		1853	1929	093	DAMIEN, Bernard	
				093		
Patrick MANN		69 Years	08-22-1896	093	MANN, Patrick	
				093		
Timothy MURPHY		75 Years	11-06-1888	093	RIORDAN, Nellie	
Nellie RIORDAN Murphy		73 Years	08-16-1882	093	MURPHY, Timothy	
				093		
William MERCHANT		1849	1909	093	O'BRIEN, Annie	
Annie O'BRIEN Merchant		1849	1916	093	MERCHANT, William	
				093		
Hugh J. BANAGAN		01-01-1847	09-17-1908	093	MORSE, Minnie C.	
Minnie MORSE Banagan		11-11-1858	01-31-1943	093	BANAGAN, Hugh J.	
				093		
Mathew J. GODSILL		08-31-1855	01-20-1918	093	MORSE, Mary	
Mary MORSE Godsill		02-18-1857	02-16-1911	093	GODSILL, Mathew D.	
				093		
Joseph ASHEY		07-15-1839	11-19-1912	093	TYE, Mary	
Mary TYE Ashey		08-17-1846	05-06-1909	093	ASHEY, Joseph	
				093		
Patrick O'BRIEN		07-25-1842	03-15-1920	093	CUSHING, Mary	
Mary CUSHING O'Brien		05-04-1852	08-08-19_9	093	O'BRIEN, Patrick	
				093		
Hugh QUINN	Co. Fermanagh	90 Years	05-10-1901	093	QUINN, Hugh	Born In Co. Fermanagh, Ireland
Annie QUINN O'Connor		80 Years	10-01-1933	093	O'CONNOR, William J.	(NOI William J. O'Connor)
				093	QUINN, Annie	

St. Francis of Assisi Cemetery, Windsor, Vermont - On Vermont 44, West End Of Village

NAME	POB	DOB/AGE	DOD	CEM	SPOUSE/INDEX	INSCRIPTION
Lucy SORRELL		1850	1931	094	SORRELL, Lucy	
				094		
Elizabeth COLBURN Darling			09-17-1920	094	COLBURN, Elizabeth	(NOI Mr. Darling or Her DOB)

Name	Born	Died	Sec.	Index	Notes
			094		
Mary MEYERS	12-25-1830	06-11-1916	094	MEYERS, Mary	
			094		
John W. GALLAGHER	06-29-1852	11-29-1908	094	SLADE, Alice L.	
Alice L. SLADE Gallagher	02-11-1862	04-14-1927	094	GALLAGHER, John W.	
			094		
Micheal F. COYLE	1855	1934	094	COYLE, Aurelia	
Aurelia _____ COYLE	1861	1942	094	COYLE, Micheal F.	
			094		
Patrick BRAINEY	1837	1913	094	CONNOLLY, Mary Ann	
Mary Ann CONNOLLY Brainey	1837	1900	094	BRAINEY, Patrick	
			094		
Fredrick PETTES	1831	1907	094	PETTES, Catherine	
Catherine _____ PETTES	1831	1910	094	PETTES, Fredrick	
John CONNOLLY	65 Years	04-06-1898	094	CONNOLLY, John	
			094		
Thomas SEARS	1837	1917	094	LARKIN, Catherine L.	
Catherine L. LARKIN Sears	1835	1915	094	SEARS, Thomas	
Ann LARKIN			094	LARKIN, Ann	Grandmother (NOI DOB/DOD)
			094		
William E. MCCARTY	1852	1939	094	MCCARTY, Ellen	
Ellen _____ MCCARTY	1854	1923	094	MCCARTY, William E.	
			094		
John MCCARTY	04-24-1853	05-13-1909	094	KENNEDY, Mary A.	
Mary A. KENNEDY McCarty	03-12-1854	03-11-1919	094	MCCARTY, John	
			094		
William CONLIN	04-14-1858	04-10-1906	094	CONLIN, William	S/O John-Mary Conlin. Brother
Mary A. CONLIN	05-25-1856	12-18-1943	094	CONLIN, Mary A.	Sister
Ellen E. CONLIN	04-20-1862	10-14-1931	094	CONLIN, Ellen E.	
Martin CONLIN	12-23-1866	03-02-1934	094	CONLIN, Martin	S/O John-Mary Conlin. Brother
			094	CONLIN, John	(NOI John Conlin)
			094	CONLIN, Mary	(NOI Mary Conlin)
			094		
Rose A. PLUNCKETT	31 Years	03-02-1875	094	PLUNCKETT, Rose A.	(This stone badly eroded)
			094		
Mary E. DUFF	64Y 1M	01-30-1896	094	DUFF, Mary E.	(This stone badly eroded)
			094		
Catherine MCGUE Keenan	59 Years	12-06-1893	094	KEENAN, James	(NOI James Keenan)
			094	MCGUE, Catherine	
			094		
Margaret MANN	66 Years	04-11-1898	094	MANN, Margaret	Mother
			094		
Joseph BEAN	1817	1881	094	BARNEY, Adelaide	
Adelaide BARNEY Bean	1827	1910	094	BEAN, Joseph	
			094		

Name	Origin	Born	Died	Code	Spouse / Index	Notes
Frank MCCUE		1850	1911	094	MARLARKEY, Mary	
Mary MARLARKEY McCue		1856	1927	094	MCCUE, Frank	
				094		
Thomas S. BURKE	Co. Galway	1888	1935	094	DUFFY, Bessie A.	Born Galway County, Ireland
Bessie DUFFY Burke	Co. Mayo	1889	1971	094	BURKE, Thomas S.	Born In Mayo County, Ireland
John BURKE	Co. Galway	1894	1947	094	BURKE, John	Brother Of Thomas S. Burke,
				094		Born Galway County, Ireland
				094		
Michael QUIRK		1834	1905	094	QUIRK, Michael	Born In Ireland. Died In West
				094		Windsor, Vermont
				094		
Ellen E. MCCUE		09-25-1840	11-29-1910	094	MCCUE, Ellen	
				094		
Alice MCCUE Paulding		57Y 11M	03-26-1904	094	MCCUE, Alice	(NOI Mr. Paulding)
				094		
Maurice HARRINGTON		1847	1925	094	GALLAGHER, Katherine	
Katherine GALLAGHER Harrington		1858	1909	094	HARRINGTON, Maurice	
				094		
John GALLAGHER		1810	1865	094	MCCLINTON, Jane	
Jane MCCLINTON Gallagher		1818	1905	094	GALLAGHER, John	
Jennie GALLAGHER		1854	1912	094	GALLAGHER, Jennie	Daughter
				094		
Edward MORAN		76 Years	01-01-1868	094	MORAN, Ann	
Ann _____ MORAN		85 Years	04-29-1887	094	MORAN, Edward	
Lizzie MORAN Casavant		26 Years	06-08-1868	094	CASAVANT, Augustin	(NOI Augustin Casavant)
Thomas B. COONERTY		12-03-1859	04-07-1906	094	MORAN, Mary A.	
Mary A. MORAN Coonerty		04-15-1853	01-30-1916	094	COONERTY, Thomas B.	
				094		
Patrick GALLAGHER		1837	1896	094	MCKERN, Nora	
Nora MCKERN Gallagher		1834	1896	094	GALLAGHER, Patrick	
				094		
Joseph MCCLINTON		1831	1913	094	TRACY, Jane	
Jane TRACY McClinton		1837	1895	094	MCCLINTON, Joseph	
				094		
Richard C. HICKSON		11-04-1809	11-21-1883	094	MACLEASE, Margaret	
Margaret MACLEASE Hickson		02-15-1819	03-09-1901	094	HICKSON, Richard C.	
				094		
Michael HANLON		55 Years	02-17-1889	094	O'DAY, Mary	
Mary O'DAY Hanlon		91 Years	11-08-1924	094	HANLON, Michael	
				094		
Michael MCCARTY		1830	1914	094	SEARS, Katherine	
Katherine SEARS McCarty		67Y10M3D	08-05-1894	094	MCCARTY, Michael	
Elizabeth MCCARTY		79 Years	09-29-1893	094	MCCARTY, Elizabeth	Mother Of Michael McCarty
				094		
John M. CONLIN		1854	1927	094	CONLIN, Catherine H.	

Catherine H. _____ CONLIN		1864	1962	094	CONLIN, John M.	
				094		
Felix MCCUE		45 Years	03-13-1852	094	MCCUE, Bridget	(Stone is worn.YOD for Bridget possibly 1874)
Bridget _____ MCCUE		58 Years	09-04-1871	094	MCCUE, Felix	
				094		
Ann _____ DRURY		24 Years	10-02-1865	094	DRURY, Ann	Wife Of James Drury.(NOIJames)
				094	DRURY, James	
				094		
William R. MCCUE		52Y 6M	11-02-1897	094	MCCUE, William R.	(GAR) Co. C. 4th Vt Vols
				094		
James CONLIN		63 Years	06-04-1915	094	MANN, Mary	
				094	MCMANUS, Rose	
Mary MANN Conlin		31 Years	03-18-1892	094	CONLIN, James	
Rose MCMANUS Conlin		1849	1927	094	CONLIN, James	
John CONLIN		73 Years	01-15-1892	094	SEARS, Mary	
Mary SEARS Conlin		63 Years	08-03-1891	094	CONLIN, John	
Delia JELLETT Conlin		28 Years	04-30-1883	094	CONLIN, James	(Not sure if 3d wife of James)
				094	JELLETT, Delia	

St. Stephen's Cemetery, Winooski, Vermont   Route 15, East of Village

NAME	POB	DOB/AGE	DOD	CEM	SPOUSE/INDEX	INSCRIPTION
John J. NIXON		1823	1908	096	_____, Sarah Ann	
Sarah Ann _____ NIXON		1832		096	NIXON, John J.	
				096		
James BRODERICK		1833	1919	096	WELCH, Ellen	
Ellen WELCH Broderick		1839	1913	096	BRODERICK, James	
				096		
Edward CRUSE		67 Years	04-13-1913	096	RILEY, Margaret	
Margaret RILEY B. Cruse		82 Years	09-01-1932	096	CRUSE, Edward	(Full name of this person is Margaret Riley Broderick Cruse. NOI on possible Mr. Broderick)
				096		
				096		
				096		
				096		
Patrick FRIEL		08-13-1838	11-29-1911	096	FRIEL, Patrick	
				096		
John E. DILLON		1850	1922	096	_____, Agnes M.	
Agnes M. _____ DILLON		1867	1937	096	DILLON, John E.	
				096		
James T. MCGEE		1858	1916	096	HORAN, Elizabeth	
Elizabeth HORAN McGee		1867	1918	096	MCGEE, James T.	
				096		
Bridget MAGUIRE	Co. Louth	1831	1909	096	MAGUIRE, Bridget	Iniskeen Parish, County Louth

Riverside Cemetery, Woodstock, Vermont - On River Street, Route 4, West of Village

NAME	POB	DOB/AGE	DOD	CEM	SPOUSE/INDEX	INSCRIPTION
Gustavus MCCLAY		1826	1912	097	SHAW, Rosina	
Rosina SHAW McClay		1828	1914	097	MCCLAY, Gustavus	
Eva B. MCCLAY		1853	1914	097	MCCLAY, Eva B.	
Emma M. MCCLAY		1856	1929	097	MCCLAY, Emma M.	
				097		
Frank E. MCGLINCHY		08-30-1858	01-02-1914	097	MCGLINCHY, Frank E.	
				097		
Daniel L. BAKER		1836	1914	097	MCCAULY, Elizabeth H.	
Elizabeth H. MCCAULY Baker		1852		097	BAKER, Daniel L.	
				097		
Patrick MCCARTHY		07-29-1840	04-25-1914	097	WALKER, Susan	
Susan WALKER McCarthy		10-31-1840	09-05-1915	097	MCCARTHY, Patrick	
				097		
Samuel R. KELLY		1849	1933	097	KELLY, Susie M.	
Susie M. _____ KELLY		1863	1943	097	KELLY, Samuel R.	
				097		
William MCCOLLOM, MD		1831	1909	097	DEERING, Marion	
Marion DEERING McCollom		1841	1915	097	MCCOLLOM, William	
				097		
John WARD		72 Years	08-01-1897	097	_____, Catherine	
Catherine _____ WARD		75 Years	07-14-1914	097	WARD, John	
				097		
Susan T. G. CUMMINGS		28 Years	10-12-1884	097	CUMMINGS, Susan T. G.	In Memory Of His Beloved Wife.
				097	CUMMINGS, John	Erected By John Cummings (NOI)
				097		
Henry WARD		77 Years	06-19-1903	097	_____, Bridget	
Bridget _____ WARD		78 Years	10-24-1902	097	WARD, Henry	
				097		
John MOORE		77 Years	02-20-1897	097	_____, Catherine	
Catherine _____ MOORE		69 Years	04-01-1897	097	MOORE, John	
John A. MOORE		1857	1943	097	MOORE, John A.	
				097		
CASSIDY				097	CASSIDY, Family	
Mother				097	CASSIDY, Mother	
Father				097	CASSIDY, Father	
Mary CASSIDY				097	CASSIDY, Mary	
Bernard CASSIDY				097	CASSIDY, Bernard	
Michael CASSIDY				097	CASSIDY, Michael	
				097		
Michael SHAW		87Y 5M	05-12-1882	097	SHAW, Sarah	

Name	Born/Age	Died	No.	Index	Notes
Sarah _____ SHAW	72 Years	12-04-1866	097	SHAW, Michael	
Sarah Eliza SHAW	57Y 11M	01-16-1900	097	SHAW, Sarah Eliza	Dau Of Michael and Sarah Shaw
			097		
			097		
Norman W. SMITH	1822	1899	097	SHAW, Susan D.	
Susan D. SHAW Smith	1830	1909	097	SMITH, Norman W.	
			097		
John WARD	1854	1920	097	COLLINS, Henrietta E.	
Henrietta E. COLLINS Ward	1857	1935	097	WARD, John	
			097		
Thomas MACCARTY	08-26-1844	08-16-1899	097	METCALF, Inez O.	(GAR) Co. G. 44th Mass. Rgt
Inez O. METCALF Maccarty	08-17-1848	12-07-1919	097	MACCARTY, Thomas	
			097		
Joseph A. GALLUP	1848	1921	097	SHAW, Sarah A.	
Sarah A. SHAW Gallup	1856	1933	097	GALLUP, Joseph A.	
			097		
Franklin B. SHAW	1824	1898	097	PALMER, Joanna M.	
Joanna M. PALMER Shaw	1829	1901	097	SHAW, Franklin B.	
			097		
William LUDLAM	12-29-1843	04-02-1910	097	LUDLAM, Harriet L.	Born In Leeds, England
Harriet L. _____ LUDLAM	03-11-1849	05-04-1916	097	LUDLAM, William	
			097		
Harriet HEALEY	38 Years	09-22-1859	097	HEALEY, Harriet	
			097		
MACKENZIE			097	MACKENZIE, Family	
C.J.M.	1846	1900	097		
L.J.M.	1848	1902	097		
M.D.M.	1815	1898	097		
L.J.M.	1816	1889	097		
			097		
Murty J. RILEY	1834	1911	097	HYNES, Catherine E.	
Catherine E. HYNES Riley	1858	1935	097	RILEY, Murty J.	
Catherine ROACH Riley	79Y 8M	03-06-1889	097	RILEY, William	(NOI William Riley)
			097	ROACH, Catherine	
Katie M. RILEY	47 Years	12-14-1888	097	RILEY, Katie M.	
			097		
Henry C. PHILLIPS	03-11-1838	12-30-1891	097	MCBRIDGE, Cornelia	
Cornelia MCBRIDGE Phillips	11-17-1836	01-02-1917	097	PHILLIPS, Henry C.	
Evelyn W. BRIDGE	08-16-1850	03-06-1905	097	BRIDGE, Evelyn W.	Born & Died at Pomfret, VT
			097		
Michael KENEFICK	1843	1922	097	CONNOR, Catherine	
Catherine CONNOR Kenefick	1852	1904	097	KENEFICK, Michael	
			097		
Daniel COUGHLIN	72 Years	12-20-1900	097	BRANNAN, Mary Ann	
Mary Ann BRANNAN Coughlin	74 Years	05-17-1911	097	COUGHLIN, Daniel	

			097	
James S. WARD	03-13-1857	04-03-1913	097	WARD, Mary A.
Mary A. _____ WARD	05-31-1859	02-24-1911	097	WARD, James S.
Edward LEONARD	08-19-1857	05-21-1935	097	LEONARD, Edward
			097	
John H. WARD	1854	1920	097	COLLINS, Henrietta E.
Henrietta E. COLLINS Ward	1857	1935	097	WARD, John H.

Pleasant Valley Cemetery, Abercorn, PQ

NAME	POB	DOB/AGE	DOD	CEM	SPOUSE	INSCRIPTION
Bridget COWAN Westover		04-26-1846	05-08-1920	700	COWAN, Bridget	(NOI Lewis Westover)
				700	WESTOVER, Lewis	
				700		
John L. SHEPARD		1847	1923	700	O'BRIEN, Jeanette	
Jeanette O'BRIEN Shepard		1851	1920	700	SHEPARD, John L.	

St.Andre's Cemetery, Rue Principale Nord, Sutton, PQ. Adjacent to St. Andre's Church - Old Cemetery

NAME	POB	DOB/AGE	DOD	CEM	SPOUSE	INSCRIPTION
John M. DUBE		77 Years	07-26-1897	701	QUEEN, Jane	
Jane QUEEN Dube		74 Years	05-17-1898	701	DUBE, John M.	
				701		
Patrick O'BRIEN		63 Years	04-03-1887	701	DOLAN, Bridget	
Bridget DOLAN O'Brien		66 Years	12-01-1899	701	O'BRIEN, Patrick	
Thomas O'BRIEN		8 Years	05-26-1867	701		
Mamie H. BLACKBURN O'Brien		26 Years	01-26-1898	701	BLACKBURN, Mamie H.	(NOI Frank O'Brien)
				701	O'BRIEN, Frank	
				701		
John O'BRIEN		65 Years	12-13-1876	701	O'BRIEN, Mary	
Mary _____ O'BRIEN		92 Years	05-06-1898	701	O'BRIEN, John	
				701		
Jane COWAN		59 Years	04-24-1904	701	COWAN, Jane	(Jane and Frank Cowan stones are side by side but relationship not indicated)
				701		
Frank COWAN		04-27-1869	04-22-1893	701	COWAN, Frank	
				701		
Thomas COWAN		01-15-1832	03-22-1912	701	KIRK, Sarah	
Sarah KIRK Cowan		09-25-1842	04-03-1930	701	COWAN, Thomas	
				701		
Owen COWAN		72 Years	04-26-1881	701	COWAN, Owen	
				701		
Mary QUINN McWilliams		51 Years	10-16-1871	701	QUINN, Mary	(NOI James McWIlliams)
				701	MCWILLIAMS, James	
				701		
Thomas MCGRATH		65 Years	08-26-1886	701	MONAN, Bedelia	
Bedelia MONAN McGrath		72 Years	06-13-1904	701	MCGRATH, Thomas	
				701		
Thomas KIRK		80 Years	08-20-1891	701	FLANAGAN, Mary	

Mary FLANAGAN Kirk		57 Years	02-08-1876	701	KIRK, Thomas	
				701		
Ellen O'MALLEY		34Y 2M	04-07-1875	701	O'MALLEY, Ellen	
				701		
Mary O'BRIEN Donlon		67 Years	07-18-1887	701	O'BRIEN, Mary	(NOI Patrick Donlon)
Susan DONLON		1 Year	08-03-1857	701	DONLON, Susan	D/O P & M Donlon
				701	DONLON, Patrick	
				701		
Patrick O'BRINE		76 Years	12-12-1846	701	O'BRINE, Bridget	
Bridget _____ O'BRION		69 Years	04-12-1855	701	O'BRINE, Patrick	
Catharine O'BRINE		19 Years	09-13-1846	701	O'BRINE, Catharine	D/O Patrick & Bridget O'Brine
				701		
Elizabeth O'BRIEN Cluskey		80 Years	03-05-1843	701	O'BRIEN, Elizabeth	(NOI William Cluskey)
				701	CLUSKEY, William	
				701		
Thomas G. CARROLL		77Y_M10D	05-02-1868	701	CARROLL, Thomas G.	
				701		
Hugh WARD		81 Years	10-26-1889	701	MURPHY, Susan	
Susan MURPHY Ward		90 Years	03-30-1894	701	WARD, Hugh	
Kattie WARD Boneau		31 Years	11-11-1887	701	WARD, Kattie	(NOI Siprien Boneau)
Thomas Frances BONEAU		11 Days	11-20-1887	701	BONEAU, Thomas Francis	S/O Siprien & Kattie Boneau
Willie MOFFATT		2 Days	07-05-1888	701	MOFFATT, Willie	
				701	BONEAU, Siprien	
				701		
Jane TAYLOR Knuckey		77 Years	12-16-1891	701	TAYLOR, Jane	(NOI William Knuckey)
				701	KNUCKEY, William	
				701		
Ellen M. KNUCKEY		36 Years	01-05-1890	701	KNUCKEY, Ellen M.	D/O William & J. Knuckey

St Andre's Cemetery, Rue Academie, Sutton, PQ - Rue Acadamie, Off Rue Principale Nord, Top Of Hill - New Cemetery

NAME	POB	DOB/AGE	DOD	CEM	SPOUSE	INSCRIPTION
Pierre BOUCHER		1859	1918	702	HEARE, Mary	
Mary HEARE Boucher		1853	1929	702	BOUCHER, Pierre	
				702		
Margaret MCCORMICK Gauthier		1849	1920	702	MCCORMICK, Margaret	(NOI Monsieur Gauthier)
				702		
Elizabeth MCCAFFREY Blackburn		1835	1920	702	MCCAFFREY, Elizabeth	(NOI Lowen Blackburn)
				702	BLACKBURN, Lowen	
				702		
Thomas O'BRIEN		1810	1888	702	LALLY, Catherine	
Catherine LALLY O'Brien		1814	1899	702	O'BRIEN, Thomas	

NAME	POB	DOB/AGE	DOD	CEM	SPOUSE	INSCRIPTION
Amelia A. O'BRIEN		1852	1912	702	O'BRIEN, Amelia A.	Their Daughter
				702		
Peter STURGEON		1854	1948	702	EAGLETON, Bridgett	
Bridgett EAGLETON Sturgeon		1844	1940	702	STURGEON, Peter	

Catholic Cemetery, Dunham, PQ - North of Village

NAME	POB	DOB/AGE	DOD	CEM	SPOUSE	INSCRIPTION
Bernard HARVEY		04-08-1809	03-10-1888	703	SHANNON, Catherine	
Catherine SHANNON Harvey		07-15-1814	12-23-1895	703	HARVEY, Bernard	
				703		
Margaret HARVEY Palmer		25Y1M23D	03-19-1865	703	HARVEY, Margaret	(NOI Solomon Palmer)
				703	PALMER, Solomon	
				703		
Bernerd HARVEY Jr.		19Y10M16D	11-19-1861	703	HARVEY, Bernerd Jr.	S/O Bernerd & Catharine Harvey
				703	HARVEY, Bernerd	(NOI-Bernerd/Catherine Harvey
				703	HARVEY, Catherine	
				703		
John DURACK		57Y 10M	04-15-1866	703	DURACK, Sarah	
Sarah _____ DURACK		45 Years	01-12-1854	703	DURACK, John	
				703		
Charles MONAGHAN		31 Years	06-08-1865	703	MONAGHAN, Charles	S/O Francis & Sarah MONAGHAN
				703	MONAGHAN, Francis	(NOI Francis & Sarah Monaghan)
				703	MONAGHAN, Sarah	
				703		
William RAVIN		52 Years	08-04-1880	703	MURPHY, Julia	
Julia MURPHY Ravin		89 Years	11-09-1905	703	RAVIN, William	
				703		
Joseph O'HALLORAN				703	MCGLYNN, Margaret	Erected In Memory Of By Their
Margaret MCGLYNN O'Halloran				703	O'HALLORAN, Joseph	Son James O'Halloran - 1873.
				703		(No dates of birth or death)
William MCSORLEY		60 Years	01-17-1876	703	MCSORLEY, William	
				703		
William LAVERY		96 Years	10-04-1878	703	AYERS, Mary	Native Of Ireland
Mary AYERS Lavery		51 Years	05-16-1854	703	LAVERY, William	
				703		
Joseph LAVERY		67 Years	11-09-1911	703	JUBERY, Mary J.	
Mary J. JUBERY Lavery		37 Years	10-11-1887	703	LAVERY, Joseph	
				703		
C. Edwin LAVERY		03-22-1856	10-22-1945	703	DOHERTY, Hannah J.	
Hannah J. DOHERTY Lavery		03-23-1859	09-14-1943	703	LAVERY, C. Edwin	
				703		

Peter MCCULLOUGH	31 Years	02-16-1878	703	MCCULLOUGH, Peter	
			703		
William J. LAVERY	05-10-1828	03-12-1915	703	HARVEY, Mary Ann	
Mary Ann HARVEY Lavery	06-16-1834	05-08-1921	703	LAVERY, William J.	
			703		
Peter J. LAVERY	02-02-1831	12-30-1902	703	SNIDER, Ann Jane	
Ann Jane SNIDER Lavery	12-06-1830	04-06-1910	703	LAVERY, Peter J.	
			703		
Catherine BARNES Clair		08-03-1883	703	BARNES, Catherine	(NOI Robert Clair, DOB)
			703	CLAIR, Robert	
			703		
William ROYSTON	04-10-1842	04-02-1927	703	ROYSTON, William	
			703		
			703		
Ellen J. GARRY		04-02-1881	703	GARRY, Ellen J.	D/O Patrick & Fanny GARRY
			703	GARRY, Patrick	(NOI Patrick & Fanny Garry)
			703	GARRY, Fanny	
			703		
Michael MCCULLOUGH	1797	1873	703	MCALEER, Theresa	
Theresa MCALEER McCullough	1809	1865	703	MCCULLOUGH, Michael	
James MCCULLOUGH	1833	1895	703	LAVERY, Lucretia	
Lucretia LAVERY McCullough	1833	1895	703	MCCULLOUGH, James	
John MCCULLOUGH	1842	1861	703	MCCULLOUGH, John	
Martha J. MCCULLOUGH	1869	1914	703	MCCULLOUGH, Martha J.	
Michael MCCULLOUGH	1870	1952	703	DUNLAVAY, Mary J.	
Mary J. DUNLAVAY McCullough	1880	1950	703	MCCULLOUGH, Michael	
John MCCULLOUGH	1866	1878	703	MCCULLOUGH, John	
Patrick MCCULLOUGH	1864	1928	703	MCCULLOUGH, Patrick	
			703		
Michael SWEENEY		March	703	SWEENEY, Michael	S/O James & Mary SWEENEY.
			703	SWEENEY, James	(Stone broken, unreadable
			703	SWEENEY, Mary	NOI James & Mary Sweeney)
			703		
Patrick BARRY	71 Years	12-20-1891	703	BARRY, Patrick	
			703		
Andrew DOWD	30 Years	06-11-1884	703	MCGINNIS, Mary	
Mary MCGINNIS Dowd			703	DOWD, Andrew	(NOI DOB-DOD Mary McGinnis)
Francis DOWD	20 Years	04-03-1868	703	DOWD, Francis	(GAR) Co. A 12th Rgt Conn Vol
			703		
Michael MCGOVERN		05-01-1858	703	MCGOVERN, Michael	(NOI DOB)
			703		
Michael CUNNINGHAM	21Y 6M	04-01-1855	703	CUNNINGHAM, Michael	
William CUNNINGHAM	__Y 9M	__-__-1855	703	CUNNINGHAM, William	S/O O. & J. Cunningham
			703		
Michael ROYSTAN	1847	1921	703	O'HEAR, Rose	

Rose O'HEAR Roystan	1862	1949	703	ROYSTAN, Michael	
			703		
Michael KERLEY	65 Years	01-27-1848	703	KERLEY, Michael	Erected By His Son Wm Kerley
			703		
John MCGRATH	86 Years	03-23-1901	703	MCGARRY, Ann	
Ann MCGARRY McGrath	56 Years	04-10-1878	703	MCGRATH, John	
Catharine MCGRATH	21 Years	04-29-1878	703	MCGRATH, Catherine	D/O John & Ann McGrath
Sarah Emily MCGRATH			703	MCGRATH, Sarah Emily	Infant Daughters of John & Ann McGrath
Bridget E. MCGRATH			703	MCGRATH, Bridget E.	
Julia A. MCGRATH	29 Years	08-24-1892	703	MCGRATH, Julia A.	D/O John & Ann McGrath
John B. MCGRATH	77 Years	05-27-1929	703	BURNS, Julia	
Julia BURNS McGrath	35 Years	01-06-1883	703	MCGRATH, John B.	
			703		
Patrick RAVEN	60 Years	12-26-1890	703	WHITE, Mary Ann	
Mary Ann WHITE Raven	62 Years	09-21-1893	703	RAVEN, Patrick	
Eliza WHITE Lawrence	55 Years	12-09-1892	703	WHITE, Eliza	(NOI David S. Lawrence)
			703	LAWRENCE, Davis S.	
			703		
Patrick DOYLE	1843	1911	703	MCGRATH, Mary	
Mary MCGRATH Doyle	1850	1895	703	DOYLE, Patrick	
			703		
John MCGARRY	87 Years	09-26-1889	703	MCGARRY, John	(Two stones in this plot are missing but bases seem to be identical indicating other family members were present)
			703		
			703		
			703		
			703		
Elizabeth SLOAN O'Hear	70 Years	07-06-1901	703	SLOAN, Elizabeth	(NOI William O'Hear)
			703	O'HEAR, William	
			703		
Mary L. O'HEAR Roystan		01-01-1887	703	O'HEAR, Mary L.	(NOI William Roystan)
			703	ROYSTAN, William	
			703		
George ROYSTAN	05-06-1808		703	CURLEY, Cathrine	(NOI DOD George Roystan)
Cathrine CURLEY Roystan	12-25-1819	05-22-1883	703	ROYSTAN, George	
Cathrine ROYSTAN	01-28-1854	05-02-1857	703	ROYSTAN, Cathrine	
George ROYSTAN	06-16-1856	11-03-1857	703	ROYSTAN, George	
George P. ROYSTAN	10-22-1858	11-15-1858	703	ROYSTAN, George P.	
Eliza ROYSTAN	47 Years	05-19-1891	703	ROYSTAN, Eliza	
James E. ROYSTAN	43 Years	05-20-1893	703	ROYSTAN, James E.	Died At Sacramento, Calif
			703		
James MCGRATH	73 Years	03-05-1883	703	RAVEN, Catherine	
Catherine RAVEN McGrath			703	MCGRATH, James	(NOI DOB-DOD - 1/2 stone gone)
Ellen MCGRATH	28Y 11M	03-26-1882	703	MCGRATH, Ellen	D/O James & Catherine McGrath
			703		
Catherine MCNALLEY Failey	93 Years	02-11-1866	703	MCNALLEY, Catherine	(NOI Patrick Failey)

Name	Born / Age	Died	Code	Index	Notes
			703	FAILEY, Patrick	
			703		
Terrance MCLAUGHLIN	1847	1927	703	MCLAUGHLIN, Terrance	
			703		
Patrick CALVEY	05-10-1802	03-21-1874	703	ROYSTON, Catharine	
Catharine ROYSTON Calvey	06-09-1808	03-20-1880	703	CALVEY, Patrick	
William CALVEY	06-15-1837	07-18-1865	703		
Daniel J. CALVEY	07-02-1840	02-16-1898	703	MCGRATH, Ellen	
Ellen MCGRATH Calvey	10-13-1847	01-05-1929	703	CALVEY, Daniel J.	His Beloved Wife
Elizabeth CALVEY	10-14-1838	09-16-1879	703	CALVEY, Elizabeth	
			703		
Margaret MCGRATH McLaughlin	45 Years	05-11-1875	703	MCGRATH, Margaret	(NOI Patrick McLaughlin)
			703	MCLAUGHLIN, Patrick	
Mary E. MCLAUGHLIN	25Y 10M	11-01-1882	703	MCLAUGHLIN, Mary	D/O Pat'k-Margaret McLaughlin
Louise Kate MCLAUGHLIN	24Y3M27D	03-05-1885	703	MCLAUGHLIN, Louise Kate	D/O Pat'k-Margaret McLaughlin
			703		
James MCLAUGHLIN	03-20-1828	02-23-1914	703	BUTLER, Elizabeth	
Elizabeth BUTLER McLaughlin	03-18-1839	02-05-1913	703	MCLAUGHLIN, James	
			703		
Ellen _____ MCGRATH	33 Years	01-29-1865	703	_____, Ellen	(NOI Thomas McGrath. Stone
			703	MCGRATH, Thomas	repaired-last name cemented
			703		over)
Catharine O'NIEL	24 Years	10-03-1857	703	O'NIEL, Catharine	D/O Peter & Anette O'Niel
Elizabeth O'NIEL	26 Years	01-15-1862	703	O'NIEL, Elizabeth	Also Her Sister (Stone down)
			703		
Joseph EVENS	22 Years	11-04-1850	703	EVENS, Joseph	IMO Joseph Evens Who DIed in
			703		The 22nd Year of His Age
			703		
Stephen JOHNSON	75 Years	06-18-1910	703	LAVERY, Ellen	(NOI Ellen Lavery)
			703	JOHNSON, Stephen	
			703		
Michael HEARNE	78 Years	11-12-1876	703	FOLLIARD, Bridget	
Bridget FOLLIARD Hearne	72 Years	01-20-1909	703	HEARNE, Michael	
Thomas HEARNE	42 Years	03-20-1862	703	HORAN, Dolly	
Dolly HORAN Hearne	80 Years	11-17-1869	703	HEARNE, Thomas	
John HEARNE	36 Years	05-28-1855	703	HEARNE, John	
			703		
Terrience KIRK	08-12-1812	01-14-1898	703	MURPHY, Rosie	
Rosie MURPHY Kirk	06-24-1826	12-01-1899	703	KIRK, Terrience	
Mary Jane KIRK	6M 4D	01-11-1860	703	KIRK, Mary Jane	
Elizabeth CONNELL	08-11-1824	06-10-1910	703	CONNELL, Elizabeth	
Elizabeth KIRK Clossey	07-23-1854	10-01-1940	703	KIRK, Elizabeth	
George CLOSSEY	1895	1986	703	CLOSSEY, George	(NOI Mr. Clossey)
Peter KIRK	05-22-1853	03-09-1915	703	KIRK, Peter	
John KIRK	11-25-1862	03-15-1945	703	KIRK, John	

NAME	POB	DOB/AGE	DOD	CEM	SPOUSE/INDEX	INSCRIPTION
				703		
John MURPHY		1756	1841	703	MURPHY, John	
William MURPHY		1794	1874	703	O'CONNOR, Margaret	
Margaret O'CONNOR Murphy		1817	1849	703	MURPHY, William	
				703		
Honor MCGARRY Fay		27 Years	03-10-1852	703	MCGARRY, Honor	(NOI Michael Fay)
				703	FAY, Michael	
John FAY		74 Years	01-28-1926	703	FAY, John	
				703		
James HENSY		21 Years	01-29-1855	703	HENSY, James	Who Died In The 21st Year of His Age (C/B HENNESY,HENNESSY)
				703		
				703		
John MULLEN		63 Years	10-26-1865	703	MCCULLAH, Mary	
Mary MCCULLAH Mullen		86 Years	10-08-1892	703	MULLEN, John	(Probably Mary MCCULLOUGH)
Mary MULLEN O'Brion		21 Years	02-02-1851	703	MULLEN, Mary	(NOI Thomas O'Brion)
				703	O'BRION, Thomas	
James H. MULLEN		26 Years	08-08-1858	703	MULLEN, James	S/O John & Mary Mullen
Catherine MULLEN		17 Years	12-04-1858	703	MULLEN, Catherine	D/O John & Mary Mullen
Anna A. MULLEN		25 Years	08-19-1870	703	MULLEN, Anna A.	D/O John & Mary Mullen
				703		
George W. JOHNSON		1852	1945	703	LAVERY, Eliza J.	
Eliza J. LAVERY Johnson		1849	1910	703	JOHNSON, George W.	
				703		
T. M. BAKER		1868	1943	703	MCDERMOTT, Margaret	Born In Bristol, England
Margaret MCDERMOTT Baker		1884	1978	703	BAKER, T. M.	Born in Omagh (Co. Tyrone),Ire

St. James (or St. John's) Cemetery, Philipsburg, PQ

This burial ground was originally Anglican in origin. Today it is a cemetery shared with the United Church.

NAME	POB	DOB/AGE	DOD	CEM	SPOUSE/INDEX	INSCRIPTION
Mary KIRK		4M 11D	06-11-1823	704	KIRK, Mary	Dau Of Peter & Catherine Kirk. Who Departed This Life (NOI parents)
				704	KIRK, Peter	
				704	KIRK, Catherine	
				704		
Caroline M. HARRIGAN		71Y 9M	12-08-1899	704	O'BRIEN, Jeanette	
				704		
				704		
John MCCARTY		37 Years	12-15-1813	704	HILLIHER, Elizabeth	
Elizabeth HILLIHER McCarty		32 Years	03-__-1815	704	MCCARTY, John	
				704		
Maxwell MCCULLOUGH		81 Years	07-25-1886	704	TAYLOR, Ann	

NAME	POB	DOB/AGE	DOD	CEM	SPOUSE/INDEX	INSCRIPTION
Ann TAYLOR McCullough		59 Years	03-02-1866	704	MCCULLOUGH, Maxwell	
				704		
Reverend Hugh MONTGOMERY	Co. Antrim	07-26-1812	08-02-1893	704	MEGARRY, Annie	Formerly Rector Of This Parish
				704	SLACK, Eliza Mary	Born In Belfast, Ireland
				704	SAWTELL, Edelia M.	
Annie MEGARRY Montgomery		22 Years	02-26-1834	704	MONTGOMERY, Hugh	Wife Of Now Rector of This Par
Eliza Mary SLACK Montgomery		11-29-1839	09-02-1928	704	MONTGOMERY, Maxwell	Wife Of Rev. H. Montgomery.
Edelia M. SAWTELL Montgomery		01-17-1822	03-04-1864	704	MONTGOMERY, Maxwell	Wife Of H. Montgomery, Rector Of This Parish
				704		
John L. SOLOMON		1830	1908	704	DRISCOLL, Hannah	
Hannah DRISCOLL Solomon		1832	1924	704	SOLOMON, John L.	
				704		
Christopher BEATTY		45 Years	11-10-1894	704	BEATTY, Christopher	IMO Christopher Beatty . Died at Kanapaho, Florida
				704		
				704		
Tabor E. MCKENNY		11-13-1835	03-05-1914	704	OLDS, Cyrena A.	
Cyrena A. OLDS McKenny		06-20-1850	01-02-1938	704	MCKENNY, Tabor E.	
				704		
James White AITKEN		1860	1945	704	HILL, Mary	Native Of Scotland
Mary HILL Aitken		1869	1945	704	AITKEN, James White	
				704		
John Jay FALLON		1840	1913	704	SOLOMON, Catherine E.	
Catherine E. SOLOMON Fallon		1868	1944	704	FALLON, John Jay	
				704		
E. C. BURKE		76 Years	10-14-1907	704	SIXBY, M. E.	
M. E. SIXBY Burke		09-15-1836	05-22-1919	704	BURKE, E. C.	
				704		
William SHIRLEY		1841	1924	704	CRONIN, Hannah	
Hannah CRONIN Shirley		1847	1923	704	SHIRLEY, William	

St. Francis Of Assisi, Freleighsburg, PQ. Opposite church.

This burial ground is 99% French-Canadian. Only two Irish families found. One did not qaulify for inclusion.

NAME	POB	DOB/AGE	DOD	CEM	SPOUSE/INDEX	INSCRIPTION
Hugh MONAGHAN		75 Years	08-22-1916	705	______, Mary	
Mary ______ MONAGHAN		74 Years	06-04-1919	705	MONAGHAN, Hugh	
Amy MONAGHAN		1850	1934	705	MONAGHAN, Amy	
Bridget MONAGHAN		63 Years	09-24-1919	705	MONAGHAN, Bridget	

St. Joseph's Cemetery, Route 133, St. Sebastien, PQ

NAME	POB	DOB/AGE	DOD	CEM	SPOUSE/INDEX	INSCRIPTION
John SHERIDAN		01-04-1842	12-06-1903	706	MCNERNY, Mary	
Mary MCNERNY Sheridan		09-19-1843	06-27-1905	706	SHERIDAN, John	
				706		
Thomas SHERIDAN		71 Years	10-20-1915	706	MCGEE, Maggie	
Maggie MCGEE Sheridan		42 Years	05-02-1902	706	SHERIDAN, Thomas	
Francis KIRK		05-12-1833	12-06-1907	706	DOUD, Emelie	
Emelie DOUD Kirk		06-29-1837	10-15-1915	706	KIRK, Francis	
				706		
John O. HAGEN		80 Years	11-30-1881	706	HAGEN, John O.	
				706		
Mary HAGAN Roy		64Y 6M	08-05-1900	706	ROY, Joseph	(NOI Joseph Roy)
				706	HAGAN, Mary	
				706		
Farrell DOWD		75 Years	02-26-1873	706	DOWD, Farrell	
				706		
Catharine _____ MAHONEY				706	MAHONEY, James	(NOI James Mahoney)
				706	_____, Catharine	

Sacred Heart Cemetery, Crown Point, New York - Route 22 - Opposite Church

NAME	POB	DOB/AGE	DOD	CEM	SPOUSE/INDEX	INSCRIPTION
Margaret BURGEY North		10-12-1835	02-10-1911	800	NORTH, George	(NOI George North)
				800	BURGEY, Margaret	
				800		
Samuel SMITH		1846	1930	800	BRESNEHAN, Mary	
Mary BRESNEHAN Smith		1845	1923	800	SMITH, Samuel	
				800		
Michael MULLEN		81 Years	11-08-1898	800	MOONEY, Margaret	
Margaret MOONEY Mullen		79 Years	05-27-1901	800	MULLEN, Michael	
				800		
Thomas KELLY		1842	1919	800	HOLLEY, Ann	
Ann HOLLEY Kelly		1848	1922	800	KELLY, Thomas	
				800		
Patrick MCNAMARA		73 Years	01-27-1902	800	_____, Ann	
Ann _____ MCNAMARA		01-01-1836	06-15-1910	800	MCNAMARA, Patrick	
				800		
Edward JORDAN		70 Years	11-15-1898	800	JORDAN, Edward	
				800		
Mary MURPHY Bradshaw		03-08-1846	04-16-1904	800	BRADSHAW, Patrick	(NOI Patrick Bradshaw)
				800	MURPHY, Mary	
				800		
John M. HOWE		1849	1947	800	KIEFE, Anna L.	
Anna L. KIEFE Howe		1869	1937	800	HOWE, John M.	
				800		
Alexander MCNULTY		08-01-1857	09-17-1901	800	_____, Catherine J.	
Catherine J. _____ MCNULTY		02-11-1866	04-25-1954	800	MCNULTY, Alexander	
				800		
Simon HALLORAN		60 Yers	11-24-1887	800	_____, Ellen	
Ellen _____ HALLORAN		79 Years	12-22-1916	800	HALLORAN, Simon	
				800		
Nicholas J. HOLLAND		1864	1905	800	HALLORAN, Nellie M.	
Nellie M. HALLORAN Holland		1862	1917	800	HOLLAND, Nicholas J.	
				800		
Michael O'BRIEN		12-23-1844	04-19-1924	800	O'BRIEN, Michael	
				800		
Thomas SMITH		74 Years	1905	800	_____, Annie	
Annie _____ SMITH		66 Years	1917	800	SMITH, Thomas	

Immaculate Conception Cemetery, Keeseville, NY

This a partial collection of inscriptions as we extracted only those indicating a place of origin or birth.

NAME	POB	DOB/AGE	DOD	CEM	SPOUSE/INDEX	INSCRIPTION
James GRACE	Co. Limerick	35 Years	02-24-1844	802	GRACE, James GRACE, Philip DALTON, Ellen (?)	A Native Of The County Of Limerick, Parish Of Grain (Grean).Erected by his brother Philip Grace (Stone not in close proximity to Ellen Dalton but he is only James Grace in cemetery)
Mary _____ MURPHY	Co. Tyrone	32 Years	08-08-1847	802	MURPHY, James _____, Mary	A Native Of "Feniner", County of Tyrone. (Could be Fintona. Stone is badly eroded) (NOI James Murphy)
Mary _____ DOYLE	Co. Dublin	43 Years	02-06-1847	802	DOYLE, Thomas _____, Mary	From The County of Doublin (Dublin), Parish of Rafarnum (Rathfarnham), Kilmardan (Kilmartin), Ireland (NOI Thomas Doyle)
James MALONAY	Co. Tipperary	75 Years	10-19-1887	802	MALONAY, James	A Native Of County Tipperary, Parish Of Antecasteen. (Could not find in references. This stone is in good condition and letters are bold.Closest found is Parish Annacarty)
Timothy RYAN	Co. Limerick	11-24-1824	11-23-1897	802	_____, Mary	Born In County Limerick, Parish Of Ola (Oola), Ireland
Mary _____ RYAN		1828	1912	802	RYAN, Timothy	Born In Kilkenny, Ireland
John GAINEY	Co. Clare	05-05-1803	09-27-1887	802	GAINEY, John	County Clare, Ireland
Thomas FITZPATRICK	Co. Cavan	69 Years	10-12-1875	802	FITZPATRICK, Thomas	Native Of Parish of Kildallon, (Kildallan), Co. Cavan, Ire.
John CUNNINGHAM	Co. Cork	18Y 5M	03-08-1837	802	CUNNINGHAM, John	Son Of Thomas and Catherine Cunningham. Parish Of Timoleague, County Cork, Ireland

Mrs. Mary MCCORMICK	Co. Tipperary	80 Years	04-14-1899	802 802	MCCORMICK, Mary	Native of County Tipperary
William O'BRINE	Co. Limerick	37 Years	08-05-1850	802 802	_____, Judy	Native of County Limerick, Parish of Capamore (Cappamore)
Judy _____ O'BRIEN	Co. Limerick	69 Years	11-19-1880	802 802 802	O'BRIEN, William	Native of County Limerick, Parish of Capamore (Cappamore)
Mary FROKEY O'Neil	Co. Tipperary	51 Years	03-20-1878	802 802 802 802 802 802	O'NEIL, Daniel FROKEY, Mary	Native of The Parish Of Raugh County Tipperary, Ireland . Stone is badly eroded. Appears to be Raugh but could not find anything close in references.)
Philip LACY	Co. Tipperary	21 Years	04-29-1846	802 802 802 802	LACY, Philip	County Tipperary, Parish of Killaan(Killenaule, Killanave) (Old stone and badly eroded)
James LACY	Co. Tipperary	30 Years	08-09-1847	802 802 802 802	LACY, James	County Tipperary, Parish of Killaan(Killenaule, Killanave) (Old stone and badly eroded)
Patrick MULVEY	Co. Kilkenny	38 Years	04-23-1844	802 802 802	MULVEY, Patrick	A Native Of Ireland, Parish Of Kilkenny
Catherine COYNE Curran	Co. Longford	55 Years	09-23-1876	802 802 802 802 802 802	CURRAN, Michael COYNE, Catherine	Beloved Wife of Michael Curran. Born in The Town Of Newpark, Parish Of Cashel, Co. Longford, Ire. (NOI Michael Curran)
Patrick MCAULIFF	Co. Cork	55 Years	08-08-1853	802 802 802	MCAULIFF, Patrick	A Native Of The Parish Of Kil-brin, Co. Cork, Ireland
Thomas KINNEY Margaret BOWE Kinney	Co. Longford Co. Kilkenny	1815 1830	1880 1915	802 802 802	BOWE, Margaret KINNEY, Thomas	Born In Longford, Ireland Born In Kilkenny, Ireland
John KENNEY	Co. Longford	26 Years	05-06-1857	802 802 802 802	KENNEY, John	A Native of County Of Longford, Parish Of Cashel, Town of Claris (Claras)
Ellen DOHARTY Kennedy	Co. Tipperary	42 Years	08-24-1863	802 802 802 802	KENNEDY, Michael DOHARTY, Ellen	Born In The Parish Of Cu_____, Co. Tipperary (NOI Michael Kennedy)

Name	County	Birth/Age	Death	Ref.	Relatives	Notes
Michael JAMES	Co. Sligo	65 Years	08-28-1850	802	JAMES, Michael	Born In The Parish Of Balan-vaugh (Ballinvally), County Sligo, Ireland
Bridget DOYLE O'Brine	Co. Kildare	31 Years	06-19-1849	802	O'BRINE, Patrick DOYLE, Bridget	From The Townland of Kilboggon (Kilboggan) and County Of Kildare. (NOI Patrick O'Brine)
Ellen DALTON Grace	Co. Westmeath	90 Years	04-26-1885	802	GRACE, James DALTON, Ellen	A Native Of Co. Westmeath, Ire (NOI James Grace)
Nella _____ MCARTHA	Co. Down	71 Years	10-01-1849	802	MCARTHA, Hugh _____, Nella	A Native Of County Down, Town And Parish Of Dromara, Ireland (NOI High McArtha)
Simon PAINE	Co. Sligo	67 Years	05-16-1849	802	PAINE, Simon	Born In The Town and County Of Sligo, Ireland (Hard to read 67 Years at death may be in question)
Margaret LANG Foy		1769	1878	802	FOY, Mr. LANG, Margaret	Our Great Grandmother, A Widow Came Here From Ireland In 1813 With Her Eight Young Children Who Have Given Her Generations Of Great Grandchildren.
Thomas BARRY	Co. Cork	1828	1919	802	_____, Margaret	Cork, Ireland
Margaret _____ BARRY	Co. Tipperary	56 Years	07-16-1898	802	BARRY, Thomas	Born In Tipperary, Ireland
James FINNIGAN	Co. Kerry	84 Years	01-06-1906	802	BAIRD, Maria	Born In County Kerry, Ireland
Maria BAIRD Finnigan	Co. Mayo	84 Years	01-25-1916	802	FINNIGAN, James	Born In County Mayo, Ireland
Michael COGGINS	Co. Sligo	43 Years	06-03-1856	802	COGGINS, Michael	A Native Of The Parish Of Easky, County Sligo, Ireland
Ellen CROW Dwan	Co. Limerick	29 Years	12-11-1845	802	DWAN, John CROW, Ellen CROW, Timothy	County Of Limerick, Parish Of Doone (Doon), Ireland. Erected by Timothy Crow(NOI John Dwan)
Mary _____ KATEN	Co. Limerick	50 Years	01-13-1842	802	KATEN, Patrick _____, Mary	Parish Of Cappamore (County Limerick, Ireland (YOD hard to read. Looked like 1812 which is unlikely,1842 or 1872. 1842 seems most likely-NOI Patrick)

Name	County	Born/Age	Died		Related	Notes
Bernard CARROLL	Co. Louth	77 Years	01-25-1889	802	CARROLL, Bernard	A Native Of County Louth, Parish Of Ardee
David BENNETT	Co. Limerick	60 Years	09-09-1855	802	BENNETT, David	Born In The Parish Of Fedamore, Co. Limerick, Ire.
Dennis CONNELL Catherine RYAN	Co. Tipperary	1840 1842	1902 1906	802	CONNELL, Dennis RYAN, Mary	Native Of Co. Limerick, Ire. (Does not say if these two are husband and wife. Same plot.)
Bridget REILLY Fitzpatrick	Co. Cavan	75 Years	05-01-1878	802	FITZPATRICK, Edward REILLY, Bridget	Native Of Ireland,County Cavan Parish of Kildallen (Kildal-lan)(YOD hard to read)
Catherine GRIFFIN Ryan	Co. Kilkenny	41 Years	03-15-1872	802	RYAN, Thomas GRIFFIN, Catherine	Wife Of The Deceased Thomas Ryan. A Native of Kilmachque (No County listed. Could be Parish Kilmacow,Co. Tipperary)
Ward O'HEREN	Co. Cork	85 Years	11-08-1881	802	O'HEREN, Ward	Son Of Daniel O'Heren & Betsy Morrison. A Native Of Parish Fermoy, County Cork, Ireland (Buried in O'HEARN plot)
William KANE	Co. Derry	54 Years	02-24-1855	802	KANE, William	Native Of Kilrea, County Derry
Catherine _____ RYAN	Co. Tipperary	65 Years	07-15-1883	802	RYAN, Robert	Native of Parish of Cappa___, Co. Tipperary, Ireland.(This could be Parish Cappawhite. Stone worn,only Cappa readable See Mary Ryan Geary)
Thomas MCGUIRE	Co. Fermanagh	11-12-1804	07-02-1889	802	MCGUIRE, Thomas	Born In The Co. Fermanagh, Ire
Michael CONNAL	Co. Tipperary	10 Years	1851	802	CONNAL, Michael	Native Of County Tipperary, Parish Of (not readable), Ire.
James SHEEHAN	Co. Cork	77 Years	11-15-1896	802	COLLINS, Jane	A Native Of Co. Cork, Ireland
Jane COLLINS Sheehan	Co. Limerick	47 Years	02-25-1876	802	SHEEHAN, James	A Native of the Parish Of Ulah (Oola), Co. Limerick, Ireland.
Dennis FOX		1814	1863	802	DWYER, Bridget	

Bridget DWYER Fox	Co. Limerick	58 Years	12-18-1881	802	FOX, Dennis	A Native of the Parish Of Doon
				802		County Of Limerick, Ireland
				802		
Mary RYAN Geary	Co. Tipperary	63 Years	10-19-1891	802	GEARY, John	A Native of Tipperary, Parish
				802	RYAN, Mary	of Cappawhite, Ireland (NOI
				802		John Geary)
Richard MCAHAN	Co. Derry	11-15-1815	02-14-1885	802	MCAHAN, Richard	A Native Of County Derry, Ire.
				802		
Daniel O'NEIL	Co. Tipperary	02-11-1822	02-16-1899	802	O'NEIL, Daniel	Born In County Tipperary, Ire.
				802		
Catherine SULLIVAN Baxter	Co. Tipperary	48 Years	07-09-1876	802	BAXTER, David	County Of Tipperary
				802	SULLIVAN, Catherine	(NOI David Baxter)
				802		
Mary MALLOY Sullivan	Co. Tipperary	75 Years	11-02-1873	802	SULLIVAN, Patrick	County Tipperary
				802	MALLOY, Mary	(NOI Patrick Sullivan)
				802		
Michael O'LOUGHLIN	Co. Clare	71 Years	02-26-1872	802	LADON, Mary	A Native Of County Clare, Ire.
Mary LADON O'Loughlin	Co. Clare	67 Years	02-24-1877	802	O'LOUGHLIN, Michael	A Native Of County Clare, Ire.
Anne O'LOUGHLIN	Co. Clare	18Y 2M	01-03-1865	802	LADON, Mary	D/O Mary & Michael O'Loughlin
				802		A Native Of County Clare, Ire.
				802		
James MCCARTHY	Co. Clare	55 Years	01-03-1899	802	BROWN, Alice	A Native Of County Clare, Ire.
Alice BROWN McCarthy		06-29-1845		802	MCCARTHY, James	(NOI DOD Alice Brown)
				802		
Timothy MCCARTY	Co. Cork	73 Years	03-29-1876	802	CAIN, Catherine	A Native Of County Cork,
				802		Parish Of Cloyne, Ireland
Catherine CAIN McCarty	Co. Longford	80 Years	01-02-1894	802	MCCARTY, Timothy	A Native Of Co. Longford, Ire.
				802		
Francis GANEY	Co. Clare	22 Years	04-01-1871	802	GANEY, Francis	Son Of Patrick & Ellen Ganey.
				802		Native of Horse Island, Parish
				802		of Kildysart, Co. Clare, Ire.
				802		
Dennis RYAN	Co. Limerick	87 Years	11-25-1876	802	_____, Mary	A Native Of Co. Limerick, Ire.
Mary _____ RYAN	Co. Tipperary	67 Years	11-03-1876	802	RYAN, Dennis	A Native Of Co.Tipperary, Ire.
				802		
Jeremiah DAVRAN	Co. Tipperary	75 Years	12-17-1875	802	COUGHLIN, Anna	A Native Of The Parish Anna-
				802		carty, Co. Tipperary, Ireland
Anna COUGHLIN Davran	Co. Limerick	1809	1906	802	DAVRAN, Jeremiah	A Native Of Co. Limerick, Ire.
				802		
John CONNORS		43 Years	01-18-1852	802	COSGRIFF, Bridget	
Bridget COSGRIFF Connors		59 Years	11-02-1882	802	CONNORS, John	
Patrick CONNORS	Co. Tipperary	39 Years	11-01-1884	802	CONNORS, Patrick	Son Of John & Bridget Connors.
				802		A Native of the Parish Emly,
				802		Co. Tipperary, Ireland

St. John The Baptist, Plattsburgh, New York - U. S. Route 9, South Of Village

This a partial collection of inscriptions as we extracted only those indicating a place of origin or birth.

NAME	POB	DOB/AGE	DOD	CEM	SPOUSE/INDEX	INSCRIPTION
Michael HAGERTY	Co. Mayo	84 Years	11-23-1876	803	ADAMS, Margaret	A Native of Ballenagh
				803		(Ballina),Co. Mayo, Ireland
Margaret ADAMS Hagerty		82 Years	07-25-1882	803	HAGERTY, Michael	
Andrew N. HAGERTY		19 Years	11-23-1853	803	HAGERTY, Andrew N.	
William H. HAGERTY		16 Years	07-20-1854	803	HAGERTY, William H.	
Edward K. HAGERTY		21 Years	07-21-1862	803	HAGERTY, Edward K.	Member of Co.H, 16th Regt,NYSV
				803		
John LOUGHAN		83 Years	04-11-1895	803	_____, Sarah	(NOI Sarah)
				803	LOUGHAN, John	
James H. LOUGHAN		31Y 6M	03-28-1887	803	LOUGHAN, James H.	Son Of John & Sarah Loughan
				803		
John NOONAN		83 Years	04-17-1897	803	SPELLMAN, Katherine	
Katherine SPELLMAN Noonan		76 Years	11-27-1890	803	NOONAN, John	
				803		
Patrick FINNEGAN		71 Years	12-22-1889	803	MCANANEY, Catherine	
Catherine MCANANEY Finnegan		86 Years	11-16-1907	803	FINNEGAN, Patrick	
Patrick FINNEGAN Jr.		29 Years	10-23-1879	803	FINNEGAN, Patrick Jr.	
				803		
Mary _____ RYAN	Co. Limerick	09-29-1798	02-06-1877	803	RYAN, Mr.	Born In Parish Of Doone (Doon)
				803	_____, Mary	Co. Limerick, Ireland (NOI Mr.
				803		Ryan)
James B. RYAN	Co. Limerick	06-17-1820	03-24-1889	803	CARROLL, Margaret	Born In Parish Of Doone (Doon)
				803		Co. Limerick, Ireland
Margaret CARROLL Ryan		07-09-1826	05-26-1890	803	RYAN, James B.	
Peter J. RYAN		07-31-1849	08-01-1877	803	RYAN, Peter J.	
James B. RYAN Jr.		08-08-1857	03-01-1878	803	RYAN, James B. Jr.	
Mary R. RYAN		06-14-1851	06-29-1873	803	RYAN, Mary R.	
Thomas W. RYAN		12-21-1855	02-03-1876	803	RYAN, Thomas W.	
John F. RYAN		01-28-1853	04-01-1885	803	RYAN, John F.	
William C. RYAN		03-22-1859	11-04-1881	803	RYAN, William C.	
				803		
Sally REILLY	Co. Kildare	11-28-1818	11-28-1897	803	REILLY, Sally	Born In Kildare, Ireland
				803		
Edward KELLEY		79 Years	08-12-1876	803	SKEANE, Bridget	
Bridget SKEANE Kelley		70 Years	04-21-1875	803	KELLEY, Edward	
				803		
John BYRNS	Co. Limerick	56 Years	09-08-1869	803	MCGUIRE, Ann	Native Of Co. Limerick, Ire.

Ann MCGUIRE Byrns	Co. Limerick	56 Years	06-18-1873	803	BYRNS, John	Native Of Co. Limerick, Ire.
				803		
Margaret KENNY		80 Years	11-14-1890	803	KENNY, Margaret	
				803		
Matilda _____ BOYCE		69 Years	12-03-1897	803	BOYCE, James	
				803	_____, Matilda	
				803		
John F. HEATH		1839	1888	803	HEATH, John F.	
				803		
Stephen HAZELTINE		11-07-1829	04-15-1888	803	HAZELTINE, Stephen	Born In England
				803		
J. W. GARLICK		40 Years	08-18-1881	803	GARLICK, J. W.	(No indication of relationship
Bridget HANNAGAN		63 Years	03-17-1871	803	HANNAGAN, Bridget	but same plot.Bridget Hannagan
				803		stone is deteriorated. Can see
				803		---nard as possible last name
				803		but do not know who it is.)
				803		
Margaret _____ CARROLL		57 Years	10-07-1880	803	CARROLL, Paul	(NOI Paul Carroll)
				803	_____, Margaret	
				803		
James CLARK		08-24-1820	01-28-1900	803	CARROLL, Matilda	
Matilda CARROLL Clark		08-08-1823	09-03-1901	803	CLARK, James	
				803		
Charles GOOD		1843	1927	803	CARROLL, Mary E.	(GAR) Co. L., 1st NY Eng
Mary E. CARROLL Good		1851	1903	803	GOOD, Charles	
				803		
Ann FARRELL Callinan		—	10-1874	803	FARRELL, Ann	(Stone badly deteriorated. It
				803		could be Callahan - NOI Mr.)
				803		
M. John HOWARD		1822	1903	803	SULLIVAN, Catharine	
Catharine SULLIVAN Howard		1840	1871	803	HOWARD, M. John	
				803		
Jerome B. FISK		1832	1901	803	MCDONNELL, Jennette	
Jennette MCDONNELL Fisk		1836	1890	803	FISK, Jerome B.	
				803		
F. X. RITCHIE		79 Years	08-15-1913	803	LANDRY, Edith	
Edith LANDRY Ritchie		63 Years	10-10-1899	803	RITCHIE, F. X.	
				803		
Martin MORRISSON		83 Years	01-29-1881	803	_____, Mary C.	
Mary C. _____ MORRISSON		82 Years	09-22-1889	803	MORRISSON, Martin	
				803		
Michael LYNCH		53 Years	03-24-1900	803	_____, Hannah	
Hannah _____ LYNCH		50 Years	06-15-1891	803	LYNCH, Michael	
				803		
Edward MORRISSON		1822	1900	803	_____, Catherine	

NAME	POB	DOB/AGE	DOD	CEM	SPOUSE/INDEX	INSCRIPTION
Catherine _____ MORRISSON		1826	____	803	MORRISSON, Edward	(NOI YOD for Catherine)
				803		
Mary _____ O'BRIEN		1837	1897	803	O'BRIEN, William	(NOI William O'Brien)
				803	_____, Mary	

MEMORIALS IN STAINED GLASS - ST. JOHN THE BAPTIST CHURCH, PLATTSBURGH, NY - Commemerated in 1875:

	CEM	INDEX
In Memory Of Annie KEIRNAN	803	KEIRNAN, Annie
In Memory Of Mr. & Mrs. James RYAN	803	RYAN, James
In Memory Of Mr. & Mrs. Charles LYNDON	803	LYNDON, Charles
In Memory Of Edmund WALSH	803	WALSH, Edmund
In Memory Of Martin MORRISON	803	MORRISON, Martin
Gift of Mr. & Mrs. Michael WARD	803	WARD, Michael
Gift of Mr. & Mrs. John HANNAN	803	HANNAN, John
In Memory Of Mr. & Mrs. John RYAN	803	RYAN, John
In Memory Of Mr. & Mrs. William FARRELL	803	FARRELL, William
In Memory Of Mr. & Mrs. George FITZPATRICK and Four Children	803	FITZPATRICK, George
In Memory Of Mr. & Mrs. Edward KELLY	803	KELLY, Edward
In Memory Of James FITZPATRICK	803	FITZPATRICK, James
In Memory Of Mr. & Mrs. Patrick FOY	803	FOY, Patrick
In Memory Of Mr. & Mrs. Patrick MOFFITT	803	MOFFITT, Patrick
In Memoriam Lawrence and Hanah SPELLMAN	803	SPELLMAN, Lawrence
In Memory of Michael Byrnes and Wife and their son Patrick	803	BYRNES, Michael
	803	BYRNES, Patrick

Moriah Catholic Cemetery, St. Patricks Church, Porty Henry, NY

This a partial collection of inscriptions as we extracted only thoseindicating a place of origin or birth. Cemetery is quite large. Early burials are Irish followed later in the century with Eastern Europeans.

NAME	POB	DOB/AGE	DOD	CEM	SPOUSE/INDEX	INSCRIPTION
Francis GOLLIGLEY	Co. Armagh	72 Years	02-10-1872	804	GOLLIGLEY, Francis	A Native Of County Armagh, Ire
				804		
Bridget _____ ANGLEY	Co. Clare	80 Years	10-16-1880	804	ANGLEY, James	A Native Of Ross,County Clare, Ireland (NOI James Angley)
				804	_____, Bridget	
				804		
Thomas MCARDLE	Co. Louth	02-08-1816	05-18-1881	804	_____, Catherine	Born In Parish Lordship, County Louth, Ireland
				804		
Catherine _____ MCARDLE	Co. Monaghan	10-31-1829	05-06-1890	804	MCARDLE, Thomas	Born In Parish _______, County Monaghan, Ireland (Stone is badly deteriorated)
				804		
				804		

Name	County	Age	Date		Relations	Notes
James FANT	Co. Cork	68 Years	12-08-1878	804	_____, Ann	Native Of Cork, Ireland,
Ann _____ FANT		59 Years	07-22-1880	804	FANT, James	
				804		
Hanora _____ NAVIN	Co. Tipperary	30 Years	08-05-1866	804	NAVIN, John	A Native Of Tipperary, Ire,
				804	_____, Hanora	(NOI John Navin)
				804		
_____ LEARY	Co. Cork	23 Years	12-19-1871	804	LEARY, _____	A Native Of Bandon,County Cork
				804	LEARY, Timothy	Ireland. Dau Of Timothy/Ellen
				804		Leary
				804		
Cornelius COOK	Co. Meath	85 Years	03-19-1877	804	_____, Anne	A Native Of County Meath, Ire.
Anne _____ COOK		77 Years	12-11-1877	804	COOK, Cornelius	
				804		
John BURNS	Co. Wicklow	36 Years	12-19-1877	804	BURNS, John	A Native Of County Wicklow,Ire
				804		
Bridget CLEARY Starr	Co. Tipperary	81 Years	06-27-1879	804	STARR, Thomas	Born In Parish Kilmore, County
				804	CLEARY, Bridget	Tipperary, Ireland (NOI Thomas
				804		Starr)
				804		
Frank KERNAN	Co. Longford	80 Years	11-10-1894	804	_____, Jane	A Native Of County Longford,
				804		Ire
Jane _____ KERNAN	Co. Cavan	55 Years	03-02-1888	804	KERNAN, Frank	A Native Of The Co. Cavan, Ire
				804		
Cornelius KELLY	Co. Antrim	30 Years	02-22-1865	804	KELLY, Cornelius	Native Of Lisburn, Antrim
				804		County, Ireland
				804		
Mary KENNEDY	Co. Roscommon	72 Years	02-09-1867	804	KENNEDY, Mary	A Native Of Parish _____, Co.
				804		Roscommon, Ireland
				804		
Mary _____ FITZPATRICK	Co. Cork	32 Years	01-03-1860	804	FITZPATRICK, Jeremiah	Native Of Kanturk,County Cork,
				804	_____, Mary	Ire.(NOI Jeremiah Fitzpatrick)
				804		
Mary MAGUIRE Malone	Co. Monaghan	62Y 5M	01-27-1877	804	MALONE, John	Native Of Co. Monaghan, Ire.
				804	MCGUIRE, Mary	(NOI John Malone)
				804		
Ann MAGUIRE Flynn	Co. Monaghan	07-03-1833	04-17-1889	804	FLYNN, Timothy	Native Of Co. Monaghan, Ire.
				804	MCGUIRE, Ann	(NOI Timothy Flynn)
				804		
Patrick CUNNINGHAM	Co. Galway	54 Years	02-24-1871	804	CUNNINGHAM, Patrick	A Native OF Ahascragh, County
				804		Galway, Ireland
				804		
Martin SINNOTT	Co. Waterford	61 Years	10-24-1886	804	_____, Margaret	Born In Waterford County, Ire.
Margaret _____ SINNOTT	Co. Kildare	67 Years	01-26-1888	804	SINNOTT, Martin	Born In Kildare County, Ire.
				804		

NAME	POB	DOB/AGE	DOD	CEM	SPOUSE/INDEX	INSCRIPTION
James WALL	Co. Tipperary	29 Years	03-13-1879	804	WALL, James	Son Of Martin & Bridget Wall.
				804	WALL, Martin	Born In County Tiprarey,
				804		(Tipperary),Parish Of
				804		Kilashuley (Killoscully,
				804		Kilsheelan), Ireland.
				804		
John WALL		22 Years	11-25-1865	804	WALL, John	(NOI but stone immediately
				804		adjacent to James Wall)
				804		
John KELLY	Co. Armagh	85 Years	1866	804	KELLY, John	A Native Of Armagh County,
				804		Parish Of Creggan, Ireland
				804		
Thomas KELLEY		83 Years	02-14-1907	804	KELLEY, Thomas	Born In Ireland
				804		
Bernard MCNAMEE	Co. Armagh	78 Years	08-07-1896	804	_____, Alice	Born In Armagh County, Ireland
Alice _____ MCNAMEE		68 Years	01-25-1890	804	MCNAMEE, Bernard	
				804		
Margaret _____ DUNDASS	Co. Fermanagh	08-27-1824	02-24-1890	804	DUNDASS, James	Native Of County Fermanagh,Ire
				804	_____, Margaret	(NOI James Dundass)
James MURPHY	Co. Armagh	68 Years	11-07-1885	804	CALLAGHAN, Margaret	Born In Armagh County, Ireland
Margaret CALLAGHAN Murphy	Co. Armagh	62 Years	06-03-1887	804	MURPHY, James	
Francis H. MURPHY		1856	02-07-1877	804	MURPHY, Francis	
						(NOI James Dundass)

St. Philip Neri Cemetery, Westport, NY

NAME	POB	DOB/AGE	DOD	CEM	SPOUSE/INDEX	INSCRIPTION

This a partial collection of inscriptions as we extracted only those indicating a place of origin or birth. A Very small burial ground.

NAME	POB	DOB/AGE	DOD	CEM	SPOUSE/INDEX	INSCRIPTION
Cornelius MURPHY	Co. Cork	07-12-1817	11-16-1897	805	VAUGHN, Mary	Born County Cork, Ireland
Mary VAUGHN Murphy		1819	02-11-1913	805	MURPHY, Cornelius	
				805		
Felix MCMANUS	Co. Cavan	77 Years	10-09-1884	805	MCMANUS, Felix	Born In County Cavan, Ireland

South Cemetery (Ancient Burial Ground), Gilsum, NH (Near Keene, NH)

NAME	POB	DOB/AGE	DOD	CEM	SPOUSE/INDEX	INSCRIPTION
Mr. John MARK	Co. Antrim	1746	12-29-1832	900 900 900	_____, Ann	Native of Parish Ahughill, County Antrim. Lived In New Hampshire 61 Years
Ann _____ MARK	Co. Antrim	1748	01-24-1824	900 900 900 900	MARK, John	Native of Parish Ahughill, County Antrim. Lived In New Hampshire 52 Years

KEY TO CEMETERIES

Key To Cemeteries Visited

Cem Nbr	Town	Cemetery Name	RC	Year Church Dedicated	Year Cemetery Dedicated	Year Of 1st Irish Burial	Ethnic Composition Of Cemetery	Comments
001	Alburg	St. Amadeus	x	1858/1876	YES	1886	F	
002	Arlington	St. Columban	x	1874	YES	1851	I	
004	Barre	St. Monica	x	1888	1894	1894	I/F	
005	Barton	St. Thomas	x	????	YES	1903	F/I	
006	Bakersfield	St. George	x	1872	1869	1854	I/F	
007	Bellows Falls	Restland Cemetery	x	1855	OLD	1846	I/F	
008	Bellows Falls	St. Charles	x	1884	1894	1883	I/F	
105	Belvedere	Belvedere Center Cemetery				1859	ALL	
010	Bennington	St. Francis DeSales Old	x	1854	YES	1842	I	
009	Bennington	St. Francis DeSales New	x	1854		1854	I	
110	Bennington	Sacred Heart Of Jesus	x	1892	NONE	----	F	
011	Bennington	Park Lawn Cemetery				1884	ALL	
012	Bloomfield	St. Stanislaus	x	1879	1881	1885	F/I	Mission of Island Pond
013	Brandon	St. Mary's	x	1852/1876	1852	1860	I/F	
121	Brandon	Catholic - Maple Street	x			1855	I/F	
014	Brattleboro	St. Michael's	x	1856	1866	1855	I/F	
015	Bristol	Mt. St. Joseph	x	1877	Yes	1860	F/I	
016	Burlington	St. Joseph's	x	1838	Yes	1833	I	
017	Burlington	Mt. Calvary	x	1850/1887	1878	1885	F	

Key To Cemeteries Visited

Cem Nbr	Town	Cemetery Name	RC	Year Church Dedicated	Year Cemetery Dedicated	Year Of 1st Irish Burial	Ethnic Composition Of Cemetery	Comments
018	Castleton	St. John The Baptist	x	1844	None	----	I	
108	Castleton	Hillside Cemetery				1840	ALL	
109	Cavendish	Village Cemetery				1849	ALL	
019	Charlotte	Our Lady of Mt. Carmel	x	1864	1886	1850	F/I	
003	E. Berkshire	Congregational				1874	A	
022	East Dorset	St. Jerome	x	1868	1860-61	1860	I/F	
102	East Dorset	St. Jerome	x		1868/1887	1861	I/F	
023	Ely Mines	St. Lawrence	x	1880	1880	1880	I	Mission for Groton Pond, South Ryegate, Westmore, Burke Hollow. (AKA Copperfield, Vershire.)
024	Enosburgh	St. John Baptiste (Old)	x	1865	Yes	1872	F/I	
025	Enosburgh	St. John Baptiste (New)	x		1897	1898	F/I	
026	Essex Jct.	Holy Family	x	1893	Yes	1896	F/I	
027	Fairfield	St. Patricks	x	1847/1872	1844	1832	I/F	
028	Fairfield	Barlow				1830	ALL	
029	Fairfax	St. Magdalen/St. Lukes	x	1876/1943	YES	1943	F/I	
030	Fairfax	Sanderson Corners Cemetery				1853	ALL	
031	Fairhaven	St. Louis	x	1870	NONE	----	F	
032	Fairhaven	St. Mary's Cemetery	x	1855/1876	YES	1847	I/F	
033	Franklin	Village Burial Ground				1871	ALL	
034	Franklin	St. Mary's Cemetery	x	1874	YES	1904	F/I	
035	Graniteville	St. Sylvester's	x	1895	YES	1916	I/F	

Key To Cemeteries Visited

Cem Nbr	Town	Cemetery Name	RC	Year Church Dedicated	Year Cemetery Dedicated	Year Of 1st Irish Burial	Ethnic Composition Of Cemetery	Comments
036	Highgate Ctr	St. Louis	x	1849	1853	1849	F/I	
103	Highgate Ctr	Village				1845	ALL	
118	Highgate Falls	Episcopal				1835	ALL	
037	Hyde Park	St. Theresa	x	1898(1872)	1866	1863	F/I	
038	Isle LaMotte	St. Josephs	x	1871	YES	1883	F/I	
039	Isle LaMotte	North or Methodist Cemetery				1862	ALL	
040	Island Pond	St. James The Greater	x	1859/1862/1899	YES	1868	I/F	
104	Island Pond	Lakeview Cemetery	x		YES	1904	I/F	
124	Johnson	St. John's Cemetery	x			1851	I/F	
125	Johnson	Whiting Hill Cemetery				1830	ALL	
041	Leicester Jct	St. Agnes	x	1883	NONE	----	F/I	Mission. Some parishioners buried in Brandon & Middlebury.
128	Lemington	O'Neill Cemetery	x		NONE	1856	I	
042	Lowell	St. Ignatius (Old)	x	1867/1875	1867	1862	F/I	
098	Lowell	St. Ignatius (New)	x			1858	F/I	
043	Ludlow	Ch. Of The Annunciation	x	1876	NONE	----	I/F	
043	Ludlow	Hillside-Loveland Cemetery				1804	ALL	
044	Lyndonville	St. Elizabeth	x	1876/1893	1892	1893	F/I	
045	Manchester	Church of St. Paul	x	1896	NONE	----	---	Some parishioners buried in E.Dorset and Arlington
046	Middlebury	St. Mary's Cemetery	x	1840	1881/6	1841	I/F	
047	Middlebury	Middlebury West Cemetery				1802	ALL	

Key To Cemeteries Visited

Cem Nbr	Town	Cemetery Name	RC	Year Church Dedicated	Year Cemetery Dedicated	Year Of 1st Irish Burial	Ethnic Composition Of Cemetery	Comments
048	Middletown Sp	St. Ann's	x	1885	NONE	----	I/F	
048	Middletown Sp	Pleasant View				1854	ALL	
049	Milton	St. Ann's	x	1859	1859/66	1842	I/F	
050	Montgomery Ct	Church of St. Isadore	x	1882	1891	1891	F/I	
051	Montpelier	St. Augustine's	x	1854	1857	1843	I/F	
111	Montpelier	City Cemetery					ALL	
052	Moretown	St. Patricks	x	1857/1882	1857	1845	I/F	Mission in 1899.
053	Mount Holly	Our Mother Of Mercy	x	1876	NONE	----	I	Mt. Holly is near Ludlow
054	Newport	St. Mary's Cemetery	x	1875	1875	1838	F/I	
055	N. Bennington	St. John The Baptist	x	1871	YES	1886	I/F	
056	Northfield	Calvary Cemetery	x			1857	I/F	
057	Northfield	St. John The Evangelist	x	1856	1854	1852	I/F	
058	North Hero	St. Benedicts(Mission)	x	1887	NONE	----	F	
058	North Hero/Grand Isle - All Cemeteries					1811	ALL	All North Hero and Grand Isle North End, Jerusalem, Graveyard Point, Hyde, W. Shore, South End, Grand Isle,Grand Isle Sta
059	Norton Mills	St. Bernard	x	1886	1888	1929	F/I	
127	Norton Mills	Old Catholic Cemetery	x	1886		1904	F/I	
060	Orwell	St. Pauls	x	1867	YES	1872	I/F	
061	Pittsford	St. Alphonsus	x	1859	YES	1843	I/F	
062	Poultney	St. Raphaels	x	1864	YES	1862	I/F	

Key To Cemeteries Visited

Cem Nbr	Town	Cemetery Name	RC	Year Church Dedicated	Year Cemetery Dedicated	Year Of 1st Irish Burial	Ethnic Composition Of Cemetery	Comments
063	Proctor	St. Dominic	x	1880	1881	1875	I	
107	Proctor	Riverside Cemetery				1894	ALL	
099	Proctorsville	Hillcrest Cemetery				1869	ALL	Some Ludlow Catholics buried here.
064	Randolph	Sts Donatian & Rogatian	x	1863	YES	1868	F/I	
065	Readsboro	St. Joachim	x	1892	NONE	----	F	
066	Richford	All Saints	x	1873	1891	1877	F/I	
067	Richmond	St. Mary's Cemetery	x			1905	I/F	
068	Richmond	Our Lady Of The Rosary	x	1858	1868	1868	I/F	
069	Rutland	St. Joseph's	x	1870	1882	1890	F	
070	Rutland	Calvary	x	1855	1887	1853	I	
123	Rutland	West Street (Old Catholic)	x			1833	I	
071	Shelburne	St. Catherine	x	1895	1895	1882	F/I	
114	Sheldon	St. Anthony's Catholic	x	1907	YES	1920	F/I	
115	Sheldon	Sheldon Cemetery				1833	ALL	
116	Sheldon	Sheldon Union Cemetery				1845	ALL	Also known as Rice Hill Cemetery
129	Sheldon	Poor Farm Cemetery				1890	ALL	
072	Shoreham	St. Genevieve	x	1856	1883	1858	F/I	Prior to 1883 some parishioners were buried in Ticonderoga, NY and Orwell, VT
073	South Hero	St. Rose Of Lima	x	1854/1898	NONE	----	F	
073	South Hero	Village Cemetery				1831	ALL	

Key To Cemeteries Visited

Cem Nbr	Town	Cemetery Name	RC	Year Church Dedicated	Year Cemetery Dedicated	Year Of 1st Irish Burial	Ethnic Composition Of Cemetery	Comments
074	Springfield	St. Mary's Cemetery	x	1871	YES	1903	I	
901	Charleston,NH	St. Catherine's	x			1865	I	Some Springfield, VT Catholics are buried here.
075	St. Albans	Holy Cross Cemetery	x	1864	1873	1840	I	
076	St. Albans	Greenwood				1810	ALL	
100	St. Albans	Old Catholic (Greenwood)	x		1845	1847	I	
077	St. Albans	Mount Calvary Cemetery	x	1872	1894	1895	F	
112	St. Albans Bay	Village Burial Ground				1847	ALL	
119	St. Albans	Point Cemetery				1860	ALL	
078	St. Johnsbury	Our Lady Of Victories	x	1858/1889	1876	1861	F/I	These two parishes combined and renamed St. John's after Notre Dame burned in 1966. Only one Catholic cemetery - Mt. Calvary.
079	St. Johnsbury	St. Aloysius	x	1897	1876	1861	I/F	
080	Swanton	Church of The Nativity	x	1842	1892	1832	I/F	
113	Swanton	Riverside Cemetery				1861	ALL	
120	Swanton	Church Street Cemetery				1805	ALL	
117	Swanton	Greene's Corners Cemetery				1861	ALL	
081	Starksboro	Little Ireland Road	x			1855	I	Origin of St, Ambrose, Bristol
082	Underhill	Pleasant Valley Cemetery	x	1856	1846	1847	I	
083	Underhill	Irish Settlement Road Cemetery				1843	I	
084	Underhill	St. Thomas @ Underhill Ctr	x		1873	1848	I	

Key To Cemeteries Visited

Cem Nbr	Town	Cemetery Name	RC	Year Church Dedicated	Year Cemetery Dedicated	Year Of 1st Irish Burial	Ethnic Composition Of Cemetery	Comments
085	Vergennes	St. Peter	x	1871	1862	1861	F/I	
086	Wallingford	St. Patricks	x	1866	1873	1849	I/F	Mission in 1899.
087	Waterbury	St. Andrews	x	1857	YES	1852	I/F	
106	Waterville	Mountain View Cemetery				1845	ALL	
088	Wells River	Our Lady Of Lourdes	x	1877	NONE	----	F	
088	Wells River	Village Cemetery				----	ALL	Found no Irish surnames here.
089	W. Castleton	St. Josephs	x	1879	NONE	----	I	
090	W. Rutland	Sacred Heart of Jesus	x	1869	1889	1860	F	
091	W. Rutland	St. Bridgets	x	1855	1864	1848	I/F/E	All three Catholic cemeteries in W. Rutland are in same geographic location on Main Street, known as St. Bridget's
092	White River	St. Anthonys (Old)	x	1871	1868	1859	I/F	
093	White River	Mt. Olivet (New)	x			1872	I/F	
094	Windsor	St. Francis D'Assisium	x	1881	1876	1852	F/I	
095	Winooski	St. Francis Xavier	x	1870	1870	1860	F/I	
096	Winooski	St. Stephens	x	1872	YES	1908	I/F	Burial ground is just over the Colchester Town Line on Rte. 15
097	Woodstock	Our Lady Of The Snow	x	1870/1894	NONE	----	F/I	In 1899 was mission for South Royalton, Randolph,Quechee. Barnard, Bethel, S.

Key To Cemeteries Visited

Cem Nbr	Town	Cemetery Name	RC	Year Church Dedicated	Year Cemetery Dedicated	Year Of 1st Irish Burial	Ethnic Composition Of Cemetery	Comments
QUEBEC:								
700	Abercorn - Pleasant Valley Cemetery							
701	Sutton - St. Andre's Church (Old Cem)		x					
702	Sutton - St. Andre's Church (New Cem)		x					
703	Dunham - Old Catholic Cemetery		x					
704	Philipsburg - Anglican Burial Ground							
705	Freleighsburg - St. Frances of Assisi		x					
706	St. Sebastian - St. Josephs Cemetery		x					
NEW YORK:								
800	Crown Point	Sacred Heart	x					
802	Keeseville	Immaculate Conception	x					
803	Plattsburg	St. John The Baptist	x					
804	Moriah	St. Patricks	x					
805	Westport	St. Philip Neri	x					
NEW HAMPSHIRE:								
900	Gilsum	Village Burial Ground						

Key To Cemeteries Visited

Cem Nbr	Town	Cemetery Name	RC	Year Church Dedicated	Year Cemetery Dedicated	Year Of 1st Irish Burial	Ethnic Composition Of Cemetery	Comments

KEY:

CEM NBR .... Cemetery number assigned for data base identification.

TOWN .... City, village or town where cemetery is located.

CEMETERY NAME .... Self explanatory.

RC .... Indicates if Roman Catholic burial ground.

YEAR CHURCH DEDICATED .... Date extracted from History Of Catholic Church In New England (1899). If no date is entered, history did not indicate same.

YEAR CEMETERY DEDICATED .... Date extracted from History Of Catholic Church In New England (1899). If no date is entered, history did not indicate same.

YEAR OF 1ST IRISH BURIAL .... Date extracted from cemetery inscription text files in this work.

ETHNIC COMPOSITION OF CEMETERY.. F = French-Canadian/Franco-American
I = Irish/Irish-American
E = European
ALL = Nondenominational or other religious burial ground where all are interred, Irish, French-Canadian, Others.

Note: I/F indicates cemetery is predominantly Irish in composition while F/I indicates the reverse situation.

COMMENTS .... Self explanatory.

BIBLIOGRAPHY

Byrne, Very Rev. William, and Rt. Rev. John S. Michaud. *History Of The Catholic Church In The New England States.* Boston: The Hurd & Everts Co., 1899.

General Alphabetical Index to the Townlands and Towns, Parishes and Baronies of Ireland, Based on the Census of Ireland for 1851. Dublin, Ireland: 1861. Reprint. Baltimore, Maryland: Genealogical Publishing Company, Inc., 1984.

Hemenway, Abby Maria. *Vermont Historical Gazetteer: Volume I.* Burlington, Vermont: Abby Maria Hemenway, 1867.

Hemenway, Abby Maria. *Vermont Historical Gazetteer: Volume II.* Burlington, Vermont: Abby Maria Hemenway, 1871.

Hemenway, Abby Maria. *Vermont Historical Gazetteer: Volume III.* Claremont, New Hampshire: The Claremont Manufacturing Co., 1877.

Hemenway, Abby Maria. *Vermont Historical Gazetteer: Volume IV.* Burlington, Vermont: Abby Maria Hemenway, 1882.

Hemenway, Abby Maria. *Vermont Historical Gazetteer: Volume V.* Brandon, Vermont: Carrie E. H. Page, 1891.

Hyde, Arthur L. *Burial Grounds of Vermont.* Bradford, Vermont: The Vermont Old Cemetery Association, 1991.

Kennedy, John Fitzgerald. *A Nation Of Immigrants.* New York: Harper & Row, 1963.

Lewis, Samuel. *A Topographical Dictionary of Ireland.* London: 1837. Reprint. Baltimore, Maryland: Genealogical Publishing Company, Inc., 1984.

MacLysaght, Edward, *The Surnames of Ireland.* Dublin, Ireland: Irish Academic Press, 1978.

Maginnis, Thomas Hobbs. *The Irish Contribution to America's Independence.* Philadelphia: The Doire Publishing Company, 1913.

Mitchell, Brian. *A Guide to Irish Churches and Graveyards,* Baltimore, Maryland: Genealogical Publishing Company, Inc., 1990.

Mitchell, Brian. *A Guide to Irish Parish Registers.* Baltimore, Maryland: Genealogical Publishing Company, Inc., 1988.

Ordnance Survey Road Atlas of Ireland. Goldenbridge, Dublin, Ireland: Gill & Macmillan, 1985.

Peck, Theodore S. *Revised Roster of Vermont Volunteers and Lists of Vermonters Who Served in the Army and the Navy of the United States During the War of the Rebellion, 1861-1866.* Montpelier, Vermont: Press Of The Watchman Publishing Company, 1892.

U.S. Bureau of the Census. *Heads of Families at the First Census of the United States Taken in the Year 1790: Vermont.* Washington, D.C.: Government Printing Office, 1907. Reprint: Baltimore, Maryland: Genealogical Publishing Company, Inc., 1975.

Walker, Francis A., Superintendent of Census. *A Compendium of the Ninth Census: June 1, 1870.* Washington, D.C.: Government Printing Office, 1872.

PARISH SKETCH INDEX

B

C

D

E

F

G

H

PARISH SKETCH INDEX

INSCRIPTION INDEX

A

INSCRIPTION INDEX

INSCRIPTION INDEX

E

F

H

I

J

K

N

O

P

CPSIA information can be obtained at www.ICGtesting.com
Printed in the USA
LVOW05s0630190214

374263LV00006B/80/P